Footprint Argentina

Christabelle Dilks
Third edition

The air was crisp, a few gilt-edged, feathery clouds broke the monotony of the pale green sky, and the beech forest that clothed the lake's steep banks to the water's edge had not yet completely lost its brilliant autumn colours. The evening light gave the remote ranges a purple tint impossible to describe or paint.

Lucas Bridges *Uttermost Part of the Earth*

Argentina Highlights

See colour maps at back of book

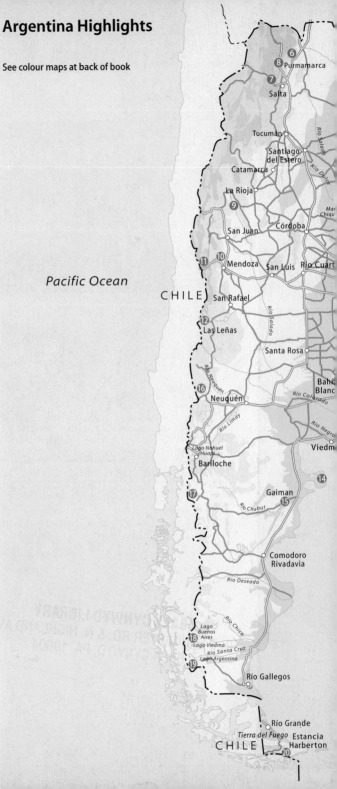

1 Palermo Viejo
Fine food and smart bars in the charming, fashionable district of Buenos Aires

2 San Antonio de Areco, the Pampas
A gaucho town with *asado*, live music and atmospheric estancias

3 Esteros del Iberá
Bird watchers' heaven; floating islands in paradise

4 Iguazú Falls
Get right under the gushing water in rainforest abundant in wildlife

5 San Ignacio Mini Evocative Jesuit ruins reclaimed from the jungle

6 Calilegua National Park
Lose yourself in jungly cloud forest

7 Santa Rosa de Tastil
Ruins of a pre-Inca city in the breathtaking Quebrada de Toro

8 Purmamarca
An idyllic oasis village perched by the mountain of seven colours in a vast gorge of vivid terracotta rock

9 Ischigualasto
See 200 million years of strata and dinosaur fossils in a weird lunar landscape

10 Bodegas, Mendoza
Superb wines grown in the foothills of the Andes

PARAGUAY

Rio Pilcomayo

Rio Bermejo

BRAZIL

Formosa

Rio Alto Paraná

Resistencia
Corrientes

Posadas

③

④

⑤

Rio Paraguay

Rio Uruguay

Santa Fe

URUGUAY

Rosario

San Antonio
de Areco

② ①

BUENOS
AIRES

Rio de
la Plata

Tandil

⑬ Pinamar

Mar del Plata

Atlantic Ocean

N

0 km 100

0 miles 100

*Falkland Islands/
Islas Malvinas*

○ Darwin

⑪ **Acongagua,
Mendoza Province**
The highest peak in
the Americas, with
stunning trekking

⑫ **Las Leñas,
Mendoza**
Spectacular views at
the country's most
famous ski resort

⑬ **Pinamar**
Perfect beaches and
great nightlife

⑭ **Península
Valdés**
Basking whales,
penguin colonies,
and harems of sea
lions on glorious
beaches

⑮ **Gaiman,
Patagonia**
Huge quantities of
cake in the original
Welsh pioneer village

⑯ **Pehuenia,
Lake District**
Find perfect
peace among
undiscovered
monkey puzzle
forests

⑰ **Los Alerces
National Park**
Glacial lakes, green
rivers and 2,600 year
old alerce trees

⑱ **Mount Fitz Roy**
Trekking heaven
around this striking
granite peak

⑲ **Perito Moreno
and Upsala Glaciers**
Boat trips and
walks across endless
ice fields

⑳ **Estancia
Harberton, Tierra
del Fuego**
The house of
Argentina's bravest
pioneer: utter
tranquillity at the
end of the world

Contents

The West

The Northwest

The Northeast

The Lake District

Patagonia

Chilean Patagonia

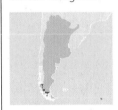

Tierra del Fuego

Head in the clouds
The snow-capped peaks of the extinct Volcan Lanín, one of the youngest volcanoes in the Andes.

Cold front
The turquoise folds and mystical chasms of Perito Moreno, until recently one of the world's few advancing glaciers.

A foot in the door

Argentina's contrasts never cease to amaze. One day you're on a boat rushing through subtropical rainforest towards spectacular waterfalls as electric blue butterflies and dusky swifts flit and dive through the spray where rainbows hover, next thing you know, you're walking across the sculpted surface of an immense and silent glacier, which suddenly ruptures with a roar into a milky turquoise lake.

Argentina's many natural wonders are breathtaking and untouched, perfect for adventure. Trek the length of the Andes, from the giddy heights of Salta to the jagged peaks of Tierra del Fuego, land turned to fire with scarlet beech trees in autumn. Ski down the foothills of mighty Aconcagua, or hike up the peaks in the Lake District, where navy, pea green and prussian blue lagoons are surrounded by virgin rainforest. Escape from it all in the vastness of Patagonia: just sheep, armadillos and wind-whipped clouds, where Mount Fitz Roy's granite turrets rise up from the steppe, rose pink at sunset. Just you and a thousand penguins on a beautiful wild beach, a colony of seals, and whales basking in the bay right next to your boat.

Be dazzled by salt flats in the deserted puna, where llamas roam under a flawless blue sky. Then hike down to lush green cloudforest jungle, along roads built by Incas and ruined ancient cities. Steep yourself in luxury at a grand estancia, or pitch your tent by a limpid river and fish a giant trout. Allow longer than you think. You won't want to leave.

The road less travelled

As you stand gasping in awe at the Iguazú Falls, a wry Argentine might tell you their favourite joke. 'God created Argentina full of natural wonders: waterfalls, glaciers, lakes and forest. He put in all kinds of wildlife, from exotic birds to whales and penguins. He put in gold, silver and precious stones, and the finest cattle, fruit and wine, so that the people would never go hungry. It was a paradise. And then he put in the Argentines.'

Once the breadbasket of the world, Argentina reached financial ruin in 2002, when the peso was devalued, and unemployment and widespread poverty followed. But how could a rich country lose its wealth? Everyone has a theory, but most blame the corrupt politicians. President Menem in the 90s sold the nationalized industries to Spanish companies, and pegged the peso to the dollar, but Argentine goods became uncompetitive and production slumped. Middle class Argentines had been happy with their mobiles, 4WDs, and holidays in Miami; the recent crisis has come as a

Rock and rolling bands
The striped mountain and deep gorges of the Cerro de las Siete Colores, Purmamarca, Quebrada de Humahuaca.

shock. Certainly the IMF saddled the country with impossible debts, but everyone admits that corruption is endemic, from politicians getting their friends jobs, to the police conspiring with criminal gangs, and everyone evading taxes. While Argentines mourn a loss of identity, 20-somethings have fled back to the European countries from which their great-grandparents emigrated. President Kirchner is battling with insecurity and corruption, but an even greater challenge is to unite the diverse races and cultures of this immense land.

But one benefit of economic collapse is that Argentina is suddenly affordable for visitors. Travellers not daunted by sensationalist reports have found a safe, unspoilt paradise here, one of the world's last true wildernesses, where luxury comes cheap. Tourism is raising income and boosting national pride. It's the Argentines themselves who make their country so appealing. Incredibly hospitable, they'll invite you to *asados* or to drink a mate and you'll make new friends wherever you go.

Class oars
Puerto Madero, Buenos Aires' 19th-century dockland, has been reincarnated as stylish office blocks, high class restaurants and tasteful apartments.

1 *The end of the world. Estancia Harberton is a haven in the vast wilderness of Tierra del Fuego.* ▸▸ *See page 527.*

2 *Península Valdés. One of the best places in the world to see the majestic southern right whales who come to breed between June and December each year.* ▸▸ *See page 438.*

3 *Football is Argentina's unofficial religion, played here with world cup fervour at a café in the Pampas.* ▸▸ *See page 108.*

4 *The rare arrayán tree with its twisting cinnamon trunk creates a fairy woodland near Villa La Angostura, in the Lake District.* ▸▸ *See page 387.*

5 *Mate, the pre-Columbian, stimulating herbal brew is the essential Argentine beverage.* ▸▸ *See page 37.*

6 *The thrusting granite towers of Mount Fitz Roy, Patagonia.* ▸▸ *See page 476.*

7 *Idyllic Molinos with its fine church and charming hostería is the perfect place to relax in Los Valles Calchaquíes.* ▸▸ *See page 240.*

8 *The vibrant blooms of the heliconia flower; few countries offer such rich and varied vegetation as Argentina.* ▸▸ *See page 568.*

9 *Alluring tango demonstations in the capital's arty district of San Telmo.* ▸▸ *See page 76.*

10 *The rolling countryside of the Sierras de Córdoba.* ▸▸ *See page 157.*

11 *The plummy façade of the Iglesia San Francisco in the romantic and vibrant city of Salta.* ▸▸ *See page 228.*

12 *Charming Iruya, a simple hamlet situated in breathtaking landscapes, perfect for hiking and relaxing.* ▸▸ *See page 256.*

Bright lights, open plains

The capital Buenos Aires is another Argentina, with its swift pace, chic restaurants and Parisian architecture. Its fashion-conscious residents know how to have fun: they eat late, dance all night and still don't stop for a siesta. Trendy *milongas* are the place to tango: marvel at the intricate tangling of limbs or let a handsome stranger sweep you off your feet. Escape from the city to the wide open pampas, saddle your horse and go galloping over the plains. There are cowboy towns and colonial estancias, where gauchos roam, and an *asado* means half a cow barbecued to perfection over an open fire.

Remains of the day

Far beyond tango and gauchos, Argentina's history stretches back to pre-Inca cultures, whose ruined cities are perched on hillsides in immense cactus-strewn valleys throughout the northwest. Quiet adobe villages are green oases in the Quebrada de Humahuaca, a vast gorge of vermilion rock, with simple churches but riotous carnivals. Wander through palm-filled plazas on balmy evenings in the colonial city of Salta to a vibrant *peña*, where crowds of locals clap and sing to passionate folklore music. Peace and solitude on the high desert puna give way to exuberant wildlife in the cloudforest parks below. Across the sweltering flatlands of the Chaco, in the marshy Esteros del Iberá, storks and alligators perch on islands of vegetation, a birdwatcher's heaven. More exotic creatures fill the Parque Nacional Iguazú, whose mighty waterfalls exceed all expectation. Follow red earth roads through emerald jungle to find evocative Jesuit ruins at San Ignacio.

The mighty Iguazú Falls, where dancing butterflies, perpetual rainbows and emerald green vegetation form one of Argentina's most spectacular natural wonders.

60 million year old araucaria trees in the Bosque Petrificado Ormachea, Patagonia.

River deep, mountain high

Majestic snow-capped peaks are the backdrop to sophisticated Mendoza, whose vineyards produce such superb wines. From here, climb Aconcagua, or ski down its foothills. Steep yourself in hot springs, or 200 million years of history: find dinosaur fossils in the strange lunar landscape of Ischigualasto park, or their footprints near Neuquén further south. The many lakes and rivers nestling in the mountains offer breathtaking rafting and trekking, and magical places to unwind. Taste wild boar and chocolate in chalet-style Bariloche, home-made beer in laid-back El Bolsón, and traditional Mapuche bread in the shadow of Volcano Lanín. Find lively nightlife at Villa la Angostura and San Martín de los Andes, charming towns on sparkling lakes, or perfect solitude in the mystical monkey puzzle forests of Pehuenia, and in the magnificent Los Alerces park, with its emerald river and barley sugar arrayanes trees.

To the end of the world

There is no experience like Patagonia. Whether escaping like Butch and Sundance or seeking freedom like the Welsh pioneers, you'll find liberating expanses of nothing. From remote estancias on the iconic Ruta 40 to the quaint Welsh village of Gaiman where tea is an epic meal, the welcome is warm and the wind relentless. Tierra del Fuego is the ultimate wilderness, with the upbeat city of Ushuaia, backed by mountains, looking out to the Beagle Channel. Sail to the estancia of the first pioneer, and contemplate the end of the world in utter tranquillity.

Seasoned landscape
The shimmering salt flats of the Salinas Grandes in the puna, Jujuy province.

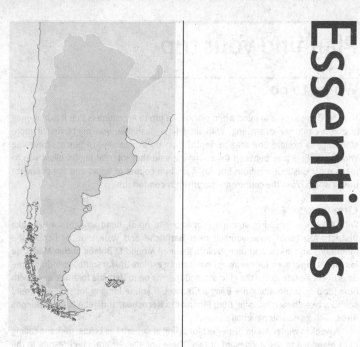

Planning your trip

Where to go

The first thing to bear in mind when planning a trip to Argentina is that it is immense and you can't see everything. With little time available, you might find it more satisfying to explore one area in depth, than try to see several places, travelling enormous distances between them. Having said that internal flights allow you to reach most destinations from Buenos Aires in a couple of hours and the overnight buses which cross the country are surprisingly comfortable.

One week

With a week to spend in summer (November to April), head straight for the **Lake District**. You could base yourself near **Bariloche** and walk, ride or fish in the mountains and lakes, and then explore the area around **El Bolsón** or **San Martín de los Andes** to get even further away from it all. Or explore the far south, spending three days in **El Calafate** to see the glaciers, and then fly on to **Ushuaia** for three days, with time for a boat trip along the **Beagle Channel**. If you're longing for sun, you could spend a week beach-hopping from **Pinamar** to **Necochea**, and get a taste of **Buenos Aires**, with its non-stop nightlife.

A week in winter would be perfect for skiing at superb **Las Leñas**, perhaps calling in at **Mendoza** to see a vineyard or two. There are also several good resorts in the lakes, near **Villa La Angostura**, **Bariloche** or **Esquel**, or **Ushuaia** where the cross-country skiing is superb.

At any time of year, a visit to the **Iguazú Falls** is a must. In three days, you could enjoy the national park and visit the ruined missions at **San Ignacio**. For a contrast, combine this with a day in Buenos Aires and then escape to the **Pampas** spending a night or two on an estancia to get a feel for the gaucho culture and life on the land, the essence of Argentina.

Two weeks

With two weeks, you could combine any of the highlights above, or get to the heart of some of Argentina's treasures. Head for the colonial city of **Salta** for its culture and nightlife, and then travel to the villages along the **Quebrada de Humahuaca** and even more remote **Iruya**, before relaxing in **Cachi** or the wine-growing centre of **Cafayate**. This area is sunny at any time of year, but best for long hikes in spring or autumn.

Mendoza is a great base for a couple of weeks' stay in summer to visit the surrounding vineyards and mountains to the west. You'd need two weeks to climb **Aconcagua** but there are many more peaks to the north near quiet villages in lush valleys. There are the intriguing **Ishigualasto** and **Talampaya** parks, and fantastic horseriding in the south.

Two weeks in **Patagonia** would give you time to see the wildlife along the coast and the whales (spring) in **Península Valdés**, and then get into the wilds with a longer trip for hiking, cycling or horseriding. Two weeks in summer would be perfect for the Lake District where there are unspoilt places to retreat to, and plenty of treks from two days to a week or more. You won't want to rush around this area of astounding beauty, and it's worth taking time to get off the few beaten tracks. There's spectacular trekking at **Fitz Roy** near **El Chaltén**, a short hop from the glaciers, and while you're in the south, plan to visit at least a couple of estancias, where you can enjoy the wilderness from the comfort of Patagonian hospitality.

A month

A month is the ideal time to spend in Argentina; it allows you to get a feel for its extraordinary contrasts. Start with a couple of days in **Buenos Aires** for steak, art and tango, and then head off for an adventure and leave civilization behind. Arrive in summer, and you could travel through the south: reach some of the remoter extremes of the **Lake District**, continue south to see the glaciers and go walking in **El Chaltén** and land up at the end of the world in **Ushuaia**. Alternatively, spend a month in the west and northwest. From **Mendoza**, travel through the wilds of **San Juan** and **Catamarca**, and then get lost in the puna, the cloudforests, or the past, with lots to discover in the **Valles Calchaquíes** and **Quilmes** staying in timeless villages where you can completely relax. Whatever you do, try to keep three days at the end of your trip to see the **Iguazú Falls**, a marvellous finale for any trip.

When to go

In Argentina, summer is from late December to March, spring from mid-September to November, autumn from March to May and winter from June to August. Being in the southern hemisphere makes Argentina an appealing destination for warm, sunny holidays in the middle of the northern hemisphere winter, though since the country covers such a vast area, there is somewhere to visit at any time of year.

The north of Argentina can be searingly hot in summer, when even the most energetic might take to the shade in the afternoon for a siesta, or escape to the cooler mountains. However, the northeast, around Iguazú Falls can be enjoyed in winter, when it's cooler and drier, and in spring an autumn when it's pleasantly warm. Winter is also a good time to visit the northwest, when many high altitude places remain warm and sunny, though routes to Chile across the Andes might be closed because of snow. Spring and autumn are lovely here, and the Quebrada de Humahuaca is wonderful at Easter where there are lively festivities. For trekking west of Mendoza, summer between December and March is the best time, although the city and surrounding vineyards can be enjoyed at any time of year. The ski season all along the Andes runs from mid-June to early September, often with sunny days, and even in Ushuaia winters can be mild and windless. Avoid the whole of July, since everywhere is booked solid for school holidays and prices rise.

Buenos Aires is definitely best in spring and autumn. With oppressively hot and humid summers the coastal resorts are packed in January and unless you're longing to mingle, it's better to come in December or late February with a good balance of heat without crowds. Many resorts close down completely in winter but Mar del Plata, Pinamar and Villa Gesell remain pleasantly quiet and mild. The Lake District is at its best in the summer, but the more touristy centres are very busy in January, and Bariloche is inundated with teenagers in November and December, as it's the traditional destination for school groups. The end of the summer season is ideal, throughout December and from February to April. Many bus services closing down outside these months. The same goes for Patagonia where the touristy areas such as El Chaltén and El Calafate are fully booked in January, but ideal in late summer, and closed (and inhospitably cold) throughout winter. Ushuaia too can become overwhelmed with visitors in mid-summer, and is much more pleasant in December, or February and March. Tierra del Fuego is particularly ravishing in autumn, when the forested mountains turn yellow and scarlet.

Tourist information

There are tourist information offices in provincial capitals and in major tourist destinations and many bus terminals in popular destinations also have a tourist desk. It's usually worth calling in at a tourist office when you arrive at a new place, to get a map and a full list of accommodation, as well as the tours, sights and festivals in the area. Staff in more popular tourist areas usually speak at least some English (and sometimes French, German, Italian) and are usually helpful. Opening hours are long – typically 0800-2000 in summer but may close at weekends. All bus terminals have an office (often signed *Informes*) which provides bus information. Argentina is just beginning to exploit its enormous tourist potential, and some areas are more prepared than others with the information and services required by demanding international tourists used to high standards at home. You might have to be patient in some parts of the country, even when requesting the most basic information on buses and accommodation. Take comfort from the fact that you're exploring a part of the world that's little visited!

Most provinces in Argentina have their own website and it's useful to have a look before you come for inspiration and information, particularly on hotels and *cabañas* (see Sleeping page 43) often with photos. All these provincial sites, and many hotels and tour operators, can be accessed through the main Argentine government tourist website: www.turismo.gov.ar a fast, excellent site, which is in English.

Tours and tour operators

If the choices available in Argentina are overwhelming, and you have little time to spend, or if you're not keen on travelling alone, it's worth considering booking a package with a specialist tour operator. These range from the conventional to the adventurous, and the advantage is that it's all done for you.

Austral Tours, *20 Upper Tachbrook St, London SW1V 1SH, T0207-2335384, F2335385, www.latinamerica.co.uk* Interesting and imaginative tours of Argentina, such as 5 nights trekking or horseriding across the mountains from Chile to Bariloche.

Condor Journeys and Adventures, *2 Ferry Bank, Colintraive, Argyll, PA22 3AR, UK, T 01700 841318, F 01700 841398, www.condorjourneys-adventures.com* Adventure and ecological tour specialist including expeditions, Magellan Strait cruises and estancia visits.

Encounter Overland, *267 Old Brompton Rd, London, SW5 9JA, T0207-3706845,* *wwwencounteroverland.co.uk* Adventurous expeditions in groups across wild terrain. Slide shows in London to give you an idea.

Exodus, *Grange Mills, Weir Rd, London SW12 ONE, T020 8675 5550, www.exodus.co.uk* Excellent, well-run tours of Patagonia, and Chile, with trekking and climbing included.

Journey Latin America, *12-13 Healthfield Terr, Chiswick, London, W4 4JE, T0208-7478315, and 28-30 Barton Arcade, Deansgate, Manchester, M3 2BH, T0161-8321441, www.journeylatin america.co.uk* Deservedly well-regarded, this long-established company running adventure tours, escorted groups and tailor made tours to Argentina and other destinations in South America. Also cheap flights and expert advice.

Ladatco, *3006 Aviation Av, 4C, Coconut Grove, FL 33133, T800-327 6162, www.ladatco.com*

Last Frontiers, *Fleet Marston Farm, Aylesbury, Buckinghamshire, HP18 0QT, T01296-658650, www.lastfrontiers.co.uk* Wide range of tours

in Argentina including great estancias, and some remote adventurous expeditions. Also fishing, skiing, birdwatching holidays.

Latin America Travel, *103 Gainsborough Rd, Richmond TW9 2ET, T0870-4424241, www.latinamericatravel.co.uk* Offers a tour taking Península Valdés and the glaciers.

Trailfinders, *194 Kensington High St, London, W8 7RG, T0207-9383939,* www.trailfinders .co.uk Reliable for cheap flights and tours.

Trips Worldwide, *14 Frederick Pl, Clifton, Bristol, BS8 1AS, T0117-311 4400, www.tripsworldwide.co.uk* Tailormade trips to Latin America and the Caribbean.

Travelbag, *15 Turk St, Alton, Hampshire, GU34 1AG, T01420-541007, www.travelbag -adventures.com* For trips exploring Patagonia.

Cox & Kings Travel, *St James Court, 45 Buckingham Gate, London, T0207-8735001, F6306038, cox.kings.sprint.com*

Adventures Abroad, *www.adventures -abroad.com* Impressive company running superb tours for small groups to Patagonia, Iguazú and Puerto Madryn, among others.

Southtrip, *Sarmiento 347, 4th floor of 19, Buenos Aires, Argentina, T5411-43287075, www.southtrip.com* Excellent company offering estancia stays throughout Argentina.

South American Explorers, *T0800-274-0568, T607 277 0488, www.SAexplorers.org* Volunteer programmes, languages courses and guided tours.

STA Travel, *offices worldwide.* Cheap flights and sell Dragoman's trip which includes Argentina. www.statravel.co.uk

Steppes Latin America, *T01285-885333, www.steppeslatinamerica.co.uk* Tailor made holidays including Patagonia escorted tours, riding trips and bird watching.

4StarSouthAmerica.com *T1-800-887-5686 (US) T0871-711-5370 (UK) T49 700 4444-7827 (rest of the world).* Tour operator and flight consolidator based in Washington DC, Stuttgart, Germany and Rio de Janeiro, offering escorted tours in Argentina and South America. For flights, www.4starflights.com

din
whe
no s
are
Airli
and
will
trav

indi
www
to ti
Soci
by /
jourr

Ga

Sad
hom
cities
and
enco
publ
Aires
webs
trave
for th
bars

Stu

If you
Card
whic
conc
can t
trave
for th
Arger
Aires
occu
resta

Tra

Trave
the c
extre
socie
partie

Language

Your experience in Argentina will be completely transformed if you can learn even a little of the language before you arrive. Spanish is the first language, with a few variations and a distinctive pronunciation, definitely Italian-influenced. In areas popular with tourists, you'll find some people speak English, and perhaps French or Italian, but since much of the pleasure of Argentina is in getting off the beaten track, you'll often find yourself in situations where only Spanish is spoken. Argentines are welcoming and curious, and they're very likely to strike up conversation on a bus, shop or in a queue for the cinema. They're also incredibly hospitable (even more so away from Buenos Aires), and are quite inclined to invite you for dinner, to stay or to travel with them, and your attempts to speak Spanish will be enormously appreciated. If you have a few weeks before you arrive, try and learn a few basic verbs and numbers. If you're reading this on the plane, it's not too late to get a grasp of basic introductions, food and directions. See page 574 for a useful list of words and phrases, and page 580 for the food and drink glossary.

Argentina's distinctive pronunciation varies chiefly in the replacement of the 'll' and 'y' sounds by a soft 'j' sound, as in 'beige ', though not in Mendoza and several other northern provinces. The 'd' sound is usually omitted in words ending in 'd' or '-ado', and 's' sounds are often omitted altogether at the ends of words. Another peculiarity is that when 's' comes before a consonant, it's usually pronounced as a Scottish or German 'ch', so that *mosca* becomes a kind of moch-ka. And in the north and west of the country, you'll hear the normal rolled 'r' sound replaced by a hybrid 'rj'. The big change, grammatically, is that the Spanish 'tú' is replaced by 'vos' used almost universally

luego (see you later). Strangers are generally treated with great kindness and generosity and your warmth in return will be greatly appreciated.

If you're introduced to new people or friends alike, you'll be kissed, once, on the right cheek as you say hello and goodbye. This goes for men to men too, if their friends, as well as all the other combinations. It's more of a touching of cheeks than a kiss, but you should respond enthusiastically. In a business context, Argentines tend to be formal, and very polite, and this goes for officials too. It's wise not to show impatience, and to avoid criticizing in public. Always, always ask permission before taking photographs of people.

The mate ritual Wherever you go in Argentina, you'll see groups of people sharing a *mate* (pronounced *mattay*). Whatever their class, or job, everyone, from students and upwards, drinks several *mates* a day. Dried *yerba* leaves, similar to tea, are placed in a hollowed out gourd into which hot water (not boiling) is poured, and the resulting infusion is drunk through a metal straw with a filter at the bottom. The cup is filled with water for each person in the group, who then drinks in turn. If offered, you should definitely give it a go, though prepare for it to taste bitter at first. Usually drunk *amargo* (bitter), you can add a little sugar to make it more palatable. Even if you find it revolting, persevere, since the experience of sharing it somehow includes you in the social group and your new Argentine friends will be enormously impressed.

Appearance Argentines of whatever class tend to dress neatly, and take care to be clean and tidy so it's much appreciated if you do the same. In the *'interior'*, outside Buenos Aires particularly, people are more conservative, and the way you dress is mostly how people will judge you. Buying clothing locally can help you to look less like a tourist, and clothes are cheap in Argentina in comparison with western Europe. Shorts are worn in Buenos Aires and residential suburbs in spring, summer and autumn, but they're not usually worn outside the capital, except on the beach.

Begging There's little begging in Argentina but you might be asked for *una moneda* (some change) outside big city supermarkets.

Safety

Argentina was one of the safest countries in South America, until the economic breakdown of 2001/2. Suddenly, petty crime increased dramatically, in Buenos Aires particularly, along with rather less petty crimes such kidnapping, which was reported in the media to be a daily occurrence for a while. With increased stability, crime is less prevalent, but security remains a concern in certain areas of Buenos Aires, and in places that can be risky in any large city such as bus stations and crowded markets. The following tips are meant to forewarn but not alarm you. They apply to Buenos Aires and major cities. Everywhere else in Argentina is still extremely safe.

Protecting documents and valuables Keep all documents secure in a pouch worn under your clothes. Hide your main cash supply in different places or under your clothes: extra pockets sewn inside shirts and trousers, pockets closed with a zip or safety pin, or a moneybelt. Keep your camera in a bag, preferably with a chain or wire in the strap to defeat the slasher. Don't wear wrist-watches or jewellery. If you carry a shoulder-bag in a market, carry it in front of you. Backpacks are vulnerable to slashers – try not to stand still for too long. Use a pack which is lockable at its base. It is best, if you can trust your hotel, to leave any valuables you don't need in a safe-deposit there, when sightseeing locally. Always keep an inventory of what you have deposited. If you don't trust the hotel, lock everything in your pack and secure it in your room. Bring a padlock for your case or backpack, which you can also use for lockers in hostels. If you lose valuables, or if you're mugged, always report to the police and get a copy of

Yerba Mate

Mate (pronounced *mattay*) has been drunk in Argentina since pre-Columbian times, and remains the essential Argentine drink, consumed all over the country by people at all social levels. It's a stimulating herbal tea made from the leaves of the yerba mate plant, *ilex paraguaiensis*, which have been allowed to mature for one to two years after picking. The Jesuits encouraged it as an alternative to alcohol, and produced some of the best quality yerba in their plantations in the northeast of Argentina, where it's still the most important crop today.

Much more than just a hot beverage, it's the ritual involved in drinking mate that makes it so special. Whenever groups of friends, family or acquaintances get together, they share a mate. The dried yerba leaves, are placed in the mate (the word for the container as well as the drink) to just over half full, and hot water is added to create the infusion, which is then sipped through a *bombilla*, a perforated metal straw. One person in the group acts as *cebador*, trickling fresh hot water into the mate and passing it to each person in turn to sip. The water must be at 80-82°c (just as the kettle starts to 'sing') and generally mate is drunk *amargo* – without sugar. But you can add a little if it's your first time, as the drink is slightly bitter. The container itself can also be made from wood or tin, and you'll see very ornate varieties made to traditional gaucho patterns by the best silversmiths. The drink is mildly stimulating, less so than caffeine, and effective at ridding the body of toxins as well as being mildly laxative and diuretic. When you've had enough, simply say *gracias* as you hand the mate back to the *cebador*, and you'll be missed out on the next round.

If you're invited to drink mate on your visit to Argentina, always accept, since refusing can seem rude, and keep trying it, as it might take a few attempts before you actually like the stuff. And don't worry – you won't catch any diseases from the bombilla! To share a mate is to be part of a very special Argentine custom, and you'll delight your hosts by accepting.

the report – for insurance purposes.

When you have all your luggage with you at a bus or railway station, be especially careful: don't get into arguments with any locals if you can help it, and lock all the items together with a chain or cable if you are waiting for some time. Take a taxi between airport/bus station/railway station and hotel, if you can afford it. Keep your bags with you in the taxi and pay only when you and your luggage are safely out of the vehicle. Make sure the taxi has inner door handles, in case a quick exit is needed. Travelling on night buses is generally extremely safe in Argentina and they arrive in the early morning, which is much safer than late at night. Watch your belongings being stowed in the boot of the bus, and keep the ticket you'll be given since you'll need it to claim your luggage on arrival (a small tip, 25 centavos, is appreciated when you collect your luggage.

Tricksters In Buenos Aires and other major cities beware of the common trick of spraying mustard, ketchup or some other substance on you and then getting an accomplice to clean you off (and remove your wallet). If you are sprayed, walk straight on. Ignore also strangers' remarks like 'what's that on your shoulder?' or 'have you seen that dirt on your shoe?'. Furthermore, don't bend over to pick up money or other items in the street. These are all ruses intended to distract your attention and make

⁞ Eco travelling

1 Preserve the beauty of Argentina's environment. Never leave rubbish or any sign of your visit, and carry a spare plastic bag so that you can take your rubbish away with you.

2 Use water and electricity carefully. In most of Argentina, the water pressure is weak, and toilets can't cope with anything other than organic waste. Throw all toilet paper and tampons in the bin provided.

3 Respect local culture. Find out about, and be aware of, local customs, and never take photographs of people you don't know. It causes great offence. If you really want to take a photo, always ask permission first, and respect a negative reply.

4 Don't give money or sweets to children. It encourages begging, and undermines the attempts of others making handicrafts to sell. Give money to local projects, charities or schools instead.

5 Stay in locally owned hotels, rather than international or foreign enterprises.

6 Spend money on locally produced, rather than imported, goods and services, and use common sense when bargaining. Your few dollars saved may be a week's salary to others.

you easy for an accomplice to steal from. While you should take local advice about being out at night, do not assume that daytime is safer than night-time. If walking after dark in dangerous parts of big cities, walk in the road, not on the pavement.

Be wary of 'plainclothes policemen'; insist on seeing identification and on going to the police station by main roads. Do not hand over your identification (or money – which he should not need to see anyway) until you are at the station. On no account take them directly back to your lodgings. Be even more suspicious if he seeks confirmation of his status from a passer-by. If someone tries to bribe you, insist on a receipt. If attacked, remember your assailants may well be armed, try not to resist.

Rape If you are the victim of a sexual assault, you are advised in the first instance to contact a doctor (this can be your home doctor if you prefer). You will need tests to determine whether you have contracted any sexually transmitted diseases; you may also need advice on post-coital contraception. You should also contact your embassy, where consular staff are very willing to help in cases of assault.

Drugs Users of drugs, even of soft ones, without medical prescription should be particularly careful, as some countries impose heavy penalties – up to 10 years' imprisonment – for even possession of such substances. In this connection, the planting of drugs on travellers, by traffickers or the police, is not unknown. If offered drugs on the street, make no response at all and keep walking. Note that people who roll their own cigarettes are often suspected of carrying drugs and can be subjected to intensive searches. It is advisable to stick to commercial brands of cigarettes.

Police Whereas in Europe and North America we are accustomed to law enforcement on a systematic basis, enforcement in Argentina is more of a sporadic affair. Many people feel that the police are corrupt and not reliable. In fact, they are usually courteous, and will be helpful to tourists.

Getting around

Air

Internal air services are run by **Aerolíneas Argentinas, Austral, Southern Winds, American Falcon** (for Bariloche and Puerto Madryn) **Dinar** (for the central and northwest areas), **LAER** (Entre Ríos, Mesopotamia), and the army airline **LADE**, which provides a weekly service connecting towns in Patagonia, useful to avoid going via Buenos Aires.

After the devaluation of the peso in 2002, two price categories were introduced: for Argentines, who are eligible for discounted tickets booked in advance, and foreigners, who have to pay the standard fare. See below for information about the **Aerolíneas Argentinas** Airpass (several internal flights prebooked.)

Even though sometimes offices in various towns may tell you the flights are full, it is usually worth trying at the airport. All local flights are fully booked way in advance for travel in December and January, and internal flights at Easter and in July too. Flights to El Calafate, Ushuaia, Bariloche and Puerto Iguazú are particularly heavily booked. It's wise to leave some flexibility in your schedule to allow for bad weather, which may delay flights in the south, at El Calafate and Ushuaia. Internal flights are subject to a US$14 tax, payable at the airport on departure. Meals are rarely served on internal flights, though you'll get a hot drink and a cake. Don't lose your baggage ticket; you won't be able to collect your bags without it.

Airpasses Airpasses are no longer the most cheapest way of getting around, and can be very restricting since you have to book all dates when you book your international ticket. Instead, just book internal flights separately. It's cheapest to do this once you arrive in Argentina, though you risk not being able to get the dates you want, and all flights fill up fast in the main holiday seasons: December, January, July and August. The most reliable option is to book them before you go to Argentina, and prices for the most popular destinations are listed below, through **Aerolíneas Argentinas**; (call 0845 6011915). The following are the cheapest available fares, one way, from Buenos Aires. To: Bariloche (2 hrs) US$140, Salta (2 hrs) US$125, El Calafate (3 hrs 15') US$141, Iguazú (2 hrs) US$120, Ushuaia (4 hrs) US$155, Trelew (2 hrs) US$94, Chapelco ski resort, San Martín de los Andes, (2 hrs) US$140. Other useful routes for connecting popular destinations without having to return to Buenos Aires: Trelew to El Calafate US$167, Ushuaia to El Calafate US$159, El Calafate to Bariloche US$202. **American Falcon** also connects Trelew and Puerto Madryn with Bariloche and El Calafate. **Aerolíneas Argentinas** www.aerolineas.com.ar **American Falcon** www.americanfalcon.com.ar **Southern Winds** www.sw.com.ar

Bus

This enormous country is connected by a network of efficient long-distance buses, which are by far the cheapest way of getting around. They are safe and comfortable, and long journeys are travelled overnight, which saves time, as long as you can sleep. There are three levels of service: *commún*, which offers little comfort for overnight buses, and with lots of stops (*intermedios*), *semi-cama*, with a slightly reclining seat, and *coche-cama*, where seats recline (some almost completely flat) and there are few stops. On *semi-cama* and *coche-cama* services videos will be shown (usually action movies, very loud, just as you're about to go to sleep), and meals will be provided. This might be anything from a *sandwich de miga* (very soft white bread with a slice of cheese and ham) to a full meal, with wine and a pudding. There will also be a toilet on board (of dubious cleanliness), and the bus will usually stop somewhere en route for toilets and food. The difference in price between the services is often small, and *coche-cama* is most definitely worth the extra for a good night's sleep. It's a good idea to bring with you on long bus journeys: water, both to drink and for brushing your teeth, as the water in the toilet usually runs out; tissues or toilet roll, fruit or snacks, and a sandwich if you'd vegetarian, since the food provided will inevitably be meaty.

Local buses are to be recommended too: often travelling to small villages and places in mountains, steppe or puna. Services are less frequent, but worth waiting for, to get off the beaten track, and completely away from other tourists. Information on frequency and prices is given in the text, where possible, but services may change, so it's worth ringing the bus terminal to check.

Bus companies may give a 20% student discount if you show an international student card, and to teachers and university professors, with proof of employment, though discounts aren't usually available December to March. You can usually request the seat you want from the computer screen; on old busesseats at the back can be intolerably noisy with air conditioning (take a sweater in summer, since the air conditioning can be fierce). Make sure your seat number is on your ticket. Luggage is safely stored in a large hold at the back of the bus, and you'll be given a numbered ticket to reclaim it on arrival. *Maleteros* take the bags off the bus, and expect a small tip – 50 centavos or a peso is fine (many Argentines refuse to pay).

Bus company websites: www.andesmar.com.ar www.viabariloche.com.ar useful for route planning across Argentina. The website www.plataforma10.com has useful routes, timetables and prices near Buenos Aires.

Car

You'll undoubtedly have more freedom if you have your own transport, especially if you're keen to explore the remoter areas of Argentina, where buses and tours haven't yet been established. Distances are long, and road surfaces in rural places often earth (*tierra*) or gravel (*ripio*), so allow plenty of time – 60km an hour is the maximum speed for cars on *ripio*. Some main roads now have private tolls, charging around US$1-2 every 100 km, and generally main road are in good condition. With the exception of roads around Buenos Aires, there's little traffic and roads are single lane in each direction. Service stations for fuel, toilets, water and food are much further apart than in Europe and the States; carry water always and keep the tank full if you're driving.

Car hire You're most likely to rent a car to get around, since buying a car in Argentina is impractical in the current economic climate (cheap to buy, but you can't sell it). Renting a small car costs from US$40 to US$100 a day, depending much mileage (*kilometrage*) is included. Busy tourist places are more expensive than quieter towns, but small towns have fewer cars for hire. For most roads, even *ripio*, a conventional car will be fine, but if you're planning to head off into the puna, jungle, or remoter Patagonia, consider hiring a four wheel drive vehicle (referred to in the text as 4WD). These may be *camionetas* in Argentina – small trucks, high off the ground, and with space at the back, useful for storing luggage and bicycles. Diesel (*gasoil*) cars are much cheaper to run than petrol (*nafta*), and the fuel is easily available.

Make sure that **insurance** is included, and note that the insurance excess (what you'll have to pay if there's an accident) is extremely expensive in Argentina. This is because tourists have a history of turning cars over on *ripio* roads. Take all roads at a reasonable speed, and never try to rush on *ripio*. Apart from the unreliability of the gravel surface, there are unpredictable potholes and rocks in the road, and swerving at speed is inevitably dangerous. Check the vehicle carefully with the hire company for scratches and cracks in the windscreen before you set off, so that you won't be blamed for them on your return.

Discounts are available for several days', or weekly rental, and you'll need a credit card. Hire companies take a print of the card as their guarantee instead of a deposit, but are honourable about not using it for extra charges. You'll be required to show a drivers' renting is 25 (private arrangements may be possible). You must ensure that the renting agency gives you ownership papers of the vehicle, which have to be shown at police and military checks, and if you plan to take the car over a border into Chile or Bolivia, for example, you must let the hire company know. They need to arrange special papers for you to show, which may take 24 hours to arrange, and the car must have the numberplate etched on its windows. The multinational car hire companies (**Hertz, Avis**) are represented all over Argentina, along with Brazilian company *Localiza*, who are very reliable. Local companies may be cheaper, but check the vehicles carefully.

Regulations All motorists are required to carry two warning triangles, a fire-extinguisher, a rigid tow bar, a first aid kit, full car documentation together with driving licence and the handbrake must be fully operative. Safety belts are supposed to be worn if fitted, though in practice Argentines don't bother, apart form in Buenos Aires. Always wear a safety belt on the open road, even if you don't bother in town. Always fill up with fuel when you can in less developed areas like Chaco and Formosa, in the Northwest, and in parts of Patagonia, as filling stations are infrequent. Diesel fuel 'gas-oil' prices are US$0.50 per litre. *Nafta* comes in normal and super, almost always unleaded now: *Super* is US$0.65 per litre, and *Normal* US$0.60 per litre.

Fuel Fuel prices are a third lower in Patagonia than in the rest of the country as no tax is levied. Cars in Argentina are increasingly converting to gas GNC, *gas natural comprimido*, which costs about 25% of using *nafta*. However, if you're taking a gas-run vehicle from a neighbouring country, check that it will run on Argentine gas: there is a difference. All Argentine gas-run cars should have an authorised sticker displayed in the windscreen. GNC stations are further apart than petrol stations and there can be long queues, but it's incredibly economical.

Security Car theft has become common in Buenos Aires, much less so in the rest of the country, but park the car in busy well-lit places, where possible throughout the country. Always remove all belongings and leave the empty glove compartment open when the car is unattended to reduce temptation. In tourist areas, street children will offer to guard your car, worth 50 centavos, or outside restaurant areas in cities, there may be a man guarding cars for a peso.

Automóvil Club Argentino This motoring association has fuel stations, hotels and hosterías, as well as offering a useful route service from offices in major cities. The office in Buenos Aires can be found at Av Libertador Gen San Martín 1850, 1st floor, touring department on 3rd floor, 1425 Buenos Aires, T011-48026061/9, www.aca.org.ar open 1000 to 1800. Members of other recognized motor associations (like the **AA** in UK) should check if they have reciprocity with **ACA**, thus allowing use of **ACA** facilities and benefit from discounts. The **Touring Club Argentino**, office at Esmeralda 605 and Tucumán 781, third floor, T392-6742, has similar travel services but no service stations.

Cycle

If you have the time, cycling offers you one of the best ways to explore Argentina. You can get to all the out of the way places, and enjoy some exhilarating rides, especially in the Andes – anywhere between Salta to El Calafate, with some breathtaking and hair-raising rides in the lakes in between. Travelling by bike gives you the chance to travel at your own pace and meet people who are not normally in contact with tourists. There's little traffic on the roads in much of the country, which are wide enough to let trucks past with ease in most places. The challenges are the enormous distances, that there are few places for food and drink stops in much of the country, and there's almost no shade.

Main roads are paved, apart from the famous Route 40 in its southern half, and many roads into rural areas, which are *ripio,* gravel. For these, a mountain bike is advisable.

Equipment A small but comprehensive tool kit (to include chain rivet and crank removers, a spoke key and possibly a block remover), a spare tyre and inner tubes, a puncture repair kit with plenty of extra patches and glue, a set of brake blocks, brake and gear cables and all types of nuts and bolts, at least 12 spokes (best taped to the chain stay), a light oil for the chain (for example Finish-Line Teflon Dry-Lube), tube of waterproof grease, a pump secured by a pump lock, a Blackburn parking block (a most invaluable accessory, cheap and virtually weightless), a cyclometer, a loud bell, and a secure lock and chain.

Strong and waterproof front and back panniers are a must. When packed these are likely to be heavy and should be carried on the strongest racks available. Poor quality racks have ruined many a journey for they take incredible strain on unpaved roads. A top bag cum rucksack (for example Carradice) makes a good addition for use on and off the bike. A Cannondale front bag is good for maps, camera, compass, altimeter, notebook and small tape-recorder. (Other recommended panniers are Ortlieb – front and back – which is waterpoof and almost 'sandproof', Mac-Pac, Madden and Karimoor). 'Gaffa' tape is excellent for protecting vulnerable parts of panniers and for carrying out all manner of repairs.

All equipment and clothes should be packed in plastic bags to give extra protection against dust and rain. Also protect all documents, et cetera carried close to the body from sweat. Always take the minimum clothing. It's better to buy extra items en route when you find you need them. Naturally the choice will depend on whether you are planning a journey through tropical lowlands, deserts, high mountains or a combination, and whether rain is to be expected. Generally, it is best to carry several layers of thin light clothes than fewer heavy, bulky ones. Always keep one set of dry clothes, including long trousers, to put on at the end of the day. The incredibly light, strong, waterproof and wind resistant goretex jacket and overtrousers are invaluable. Training shoes can be used for both cycling and walking.

Useful tips Wind, not hills, is the enemy of the cyclist. Try to make the best use of the times of day when there is little; mornings tend to be best but there is no steadfast rule. In parts of Patagonia there can be gusting winds of 80 kph around the clock at some times of year, whereas in other areas there can be none. Take care to avoid dehydration by drinking regularly. In hot, dry areas with limited supplies of water, be sure to carry an ample supply. For food, carry the staples (sugar, salt, dried milk, tea, coffee, porridge oats, raisins, dried soups, etc) and supplement these with whatever local foods can be found in the markets.

Give your bicycle a thorough daily check for loose nuts or bolts or bearings. See that all parts run smoothly. A good chain should last 2,000 miles, 3,200km, or more but be sure to keep it as clean as possible – an old toothbrush is good for this – and oil it lightly from time to time. Always camp out of sight of a road. Remember that thieves are attracted to towns and cities, so when sight-seeing, try to leave your bicycle with someone such as a café owner. However, don't take unnecessary risks; always see that your bicycle is secure (most hotels will allow bikes to be kept in rooms). In more remote regions dogs can be vicious; carry a stick or some small stones to frighten them off. Most towns have a bicycle shop of some description, but it is best to do your own repairs and adjustments whenever possible. In an emergency it is amazing how one can improvise with wire, string, dental floss, nuts and bolts, odd pieces of tin or 'Gaffa' tape!

Most cyclists agree that the main danger comes from other traffic, especially on major roads. A rearview mirror has been frequently recommended to forewarn you of vehicles which are too close behind. You also need to watch out for oncoming, overtaking vehicles, unstable loads on trucks, protruding loads etc. Make yourself conspicuous by wearing bright clothing and for protection wear a helmet.

Cycling tours are organized by **MTB Tours**, 3 de Febrero 945, Buenos Aires, T00 54 11 4776 3727, www.gordonsguide.com They offer fabulous trips in the Andes and in Salta's Valles Calchaquíes.

Hitchhiking

Argentina is increasingly difficult for hitching, and long waits are inevitable since there's so little traffic on the roads.

Train

The British built a fine network of railways all over the country, which gradually fell into decline through the second half of the 20th century, and were dealt the final blow by handing over control to the provinces in 1994. Few provinces had the resources to run trains and now the few tracks operating run freight trains only.

The only passenger services are within the area of Gran Buenos Aires, to Tigre with **Tren a la Costa** T011-4732 6343, and an efficient service from Buenos Aires Constitución station south through the Pampas to the coast: via Chascomús to Mar del Plata, Necochea and Tandil, run by **Ferrobaires** T011-4304 0038. There are only two long-distance train lines: from Buenos Aires to Tucúman with **TUFESA**. The other is from Viedma (on the east coast, south of Bahía Blanca) to Bariloche in the Lake District, a comfortable overnight service which also takes cars. In Viedma T02920 422130, in Bariloche, T02944 423172, www.trenpatagonico.com.ar.

The only other train services are the tourist **Tren a las Nubes** which runs from Salta up to San Antonio de los Cobres in the puna, www.laveloztur ismo.com.ar and the narrow gauge railway from Esquel in Patagonia, La Trochita (made famous by Paul Theroux as the Old Patagonian Express), www.latrochita.com.ar

---

Sleeping

Hotels, hosterías, residenciales and hospedajes

The standard of accommodation in Argentina is generally good, and excellent value for visitors from western countries. In cities, and reasonably large tourist destinations, there's usually a good choice of hotels and *hosterías*. Almost all of these have rooms with private bathrooms, but with showers rather than bath tubs, which you'll find only in the more expensive establishments. *Hosterías* have less than 20 rooms, and the name is no reflection on quality. Often more personal attention, and a warmer welcome is offered in a smaller, family-run places. In cities you'll also find *residenciales* and *hospedajes* which are much humbler but usually safe and clean. Prices often rise in high season (*temporada alta)* which means high summer (January/February) and at Easter (*semana santa)* and in some places, for the winter school holidays in July too. During public holidays or high season you should always book ahead. A few of the more expensive hotels in Buenos Aires and major tourist centres started to charge foreigners different prices after the devaluation of the peso. There's not much you can do to get around this since a passport is required as proof of Argentine residency. If you're given a price in US$, ask if there's a reduction if you pay cash in pesos. Few places accept credit cards.

Many hotels, restaurants and bars have inadequate water supplies. In most places toilet paper should not be flushed down the pan, but placed in the receptacle provided. This applies even in quite expensive hotels. Failing to observe this custom will block the pan or drain, a considerable health risk. Women should note that tampons can't be flushed.

A bed for the night

LL (+ **US$151**) and L (**US$101 -150**) Usually top quality hotels in tourist centres, or business hotels in big cities (often more international style places). They should offer well-equipped rooms with everything you're likely to need, and a pool, sauna, gym, jacuzzi, business facilities (often internet in the rooms for laptop users), restaurants and bars. And excellent service. The more luxurious estancias fall into this category.

AL **US$81-100** and A **US$61-80** These should all be very comfortable, with more than the standard facilities, and the rooms should all have TV, minibar and safe deposit box, a/c and often a pool too. They'll often provide pick ups from the airport, tours and tourist information, and good service. Breakfasts are usually '*Ámerican buffet*': a good spread of fruit and pastries, ham and cheese. Lots of estancias are in this category; incomparable with ordinary hotels, because although the accommodation may be simpler, activities are usually included, and they're in extraordinary places.

A **US$46-60**, B **US$31-45** and C **US$21-30**) Hotels and *hosterías* in these categories vary widely, but are generally very good and reliable. All rooms have bathrooms and a/c (if in a hot area), and breakfast is included. Very often you'll be amazed by the value for money in places of C category in a rural area, where prices are low because there are few tourists, but rooms are comfortable, and the attention is personal and friendly.

D **US$12-20**, E **US$7-11** F **US$4-6** and G **under US$4** These are simpler *residenciales* and *hospedajes*, sometimes very basic, with shared bathrooms, but usually supplying a towel and toilet paper. D category establishments can often be very pleasant indeed, especially in rural areas, where a lovely setting makes up for the lack of facilities. Youth hostels, to be found in most cities and tourist areas, are generally E, F or G per person, offering a bunk bed in a room shared between 4 to 8 people, sometimes with bathroom, more often with large communal men's/women's bathrooms. Rooms for more than 4 are likely to be noisy, and you should check if they're divided men/women (many aren't). Breakfast might be included, but sheets might be extra. There are often cooking facilities, internet access, lockers, laundry, tours offered and barbecue nights, good for making friends. There are 2 useful chains of hostels: Argentina Hostels Club, www.argentina hostels.com, in Buenos Aires and all over the country, and Hostelling International Argentina, www.hostels.org.ar

Most websites for the provinces of Argentina (given in the text for each place) show hotels, usually with links to the hotel's own site, if they have one. Other useful websites for finding hotels: www.patagonia-chile.com www.interpatagonia.com

Estancias

Estancias are the large farms and cattle ranches found all over the country. Broadly speaking they're extremely comfortable places to stay, offer the best horseriding and other activities such as birdwatching and walking, quite apart from the authentic experience of life on the land. They can be pricey; varying between US$50 for two in the most humble places, to US$150 per person, with all meals drinks, transfers and activities included, for the most luxurious. See Sport and activities below for more information.

Cabañas

Cabañas are a great option if you have transport and there are at least two of you. These are self-catering cottages, cabins, or apartments, usually in rural areas, and often in superb locations. They're tremendously popular among Argentine holiday makers, who tend to travel in large groups of friends, or of several families together, and as a result, the best cabañas are well-equipped and comfortable. They can be very economical, too, especially for groups of four or more, but are feasible even for two, with considerable reductions off season. If you're travelling by public transport, cabañas are generally more difficult to get to, but ask the tourist office if there are any within walking or taxi distance.

Camping

Organized campsites are referred to in the text immediately below hotel lists, under each town. Camping is very popular in Argentina (except in Buenos Aires) and there are many superbly situated sites, most have good services, whether municipal, or private. There are many quieter, family orientated places, but if you want a livelier time, look for a campsite (often by the beaches) with younger people, where there's likely to be partying until the small hours. Camping is allowed at the side of major highways and in all national parks (except at Iguazú Falls), but in Patagonia strong winds can make camping very difficult. Wherever you camp, pack out your rubbish, and put out fires with earth and water. Fires are not allowed in many national parks because of the serious risk of forest fires. It's a good idea to carry insect repellent.

Equipment If taking a cooker, the most frequent recommendation is a multifuel stove which will burn unleaded petrol or, if that is not available, kerosene, *benzina blanca*, etc. Alcohol-burning stoves are simple reliable, but slow and you have to carry a lot of fuel. Fuel can usually be found in chemists/pharmacies. Gas cylinders and bottles are usually exchangeable, but if not can be recharged; specify whether you use butane or propane. Gas canisters are not always available. White gas (*bencina blanca*) is readily available in hardware shops (*ferreterías*).

Eating and drinking

Asado and parrilla → *See also language glossary page 574.*

Argentina may not have a particularly sophisticated cuisine, but it doesn't really need one. The Argentine steaks are legendary: huge, juicy and lean. The great classic meal throughout the country is the *asado* – beef or lamb cooked expertly over an open fire. This ritual is far more than a barbecue, and with luck you'll be invited to sample an *asado* at a friend's home or estancia, to see how it's done traditionally. *Al asador* is the way meat is cooked in the country, with a whole cow splayed out on a cross shaped stick, stuck into the ground at an angle over the fire beneath. And in the *parrilla* restaurants, found all over Argentina, cuts of meat are grilled over an open fire in much the same way. You can order any cuts from the range as individual meals, but if you order *parrillada* (usually for two or more people), you'll be brought a selection from the following cuts: *achuras* – offal, *chorizos* – sausages including *morcilla* – British black pudding or blood sausage, *tira de asado* – ribs, *vacío* – flank, *bife ancho* – entrecote, *lomito* – sirloin, *bife de chorizo* – rump steak, *bife de lomo* – fillet steak. You can ask for *cocido* to have your meat well-done, *a punto* for medium, and *jugoso* for rare. Typical accompaniments are chips (*papas fritas*), salad, and the spicy *chimichurri* sauce made from oil, chilli pepper, salt, garlic and vinegar. Other Argentine dishes to try include the *puchero*, a meat stew, very good indeed; *bife a caballo*, steak topped with a fried egg; *carbonada*, onions, tomatoes and minced beef. A *choripán* is a roll with a *chorizo* inside (hot dog). and *arroz con pollo* is a delicious combination of rice, chicken, eggs, vegetables and strong sauce. *Puchero de gallina* is chicken, sausage, maize, potatoes and squash cooked together. *Milanesas* (breaded, boneless chicken or veal) are found everywhere and good value. Good snacks are *lomitos*, a juicy slice of steak in a sandwich, and *tostados*, delicate toasted cheese and tomato sandwiches (often made from the soft crustless *pan de miga*).

Italian influences

It might seem that when Argentines aren't eating meat, they're eating pizza. Italian immigration has left a fine legacy in thin crispy pizzas available from even the humblest pizza joint, adapted to the Argentine palate with some unusual toppings. *Palmitos* are tasty, slightly crunchy hearts of palm, usually tinned, and a popular Argentine delicacy, and they're often accompanied on a pizza with the truly unspeakable *salsa golf*, a lurid mixture of tomoato ketchup and mayonaise. You'll probably prefer excellent provolone or roquefort on your pizza – both Argentine and delicious. Fresh pasta is widely available, bought ready to cook from dedicated shops. Raviolis are filled with ricotta, spinach (*verduras*), or *cuatro quesos* (four cheeses), and with a variety of sauces. These are a good option for vegetarians, who need not go hungry in this land of meat. Most restaurants have *pasta casero* – home made pasta – and sauces without meat, such as *fileto* (tomato sauce) or pesto. *Ñoquis* (gnocchi), potato dumplings normally served with tomato sauce, are cheap and delicious (traditionally eaten on the 29th of the month). But vegetarians must specify: *'No como carne, ni jamón, ni pollo'*, (I don't eat meat, or ham, or chicken) since many Argentines think that vegetarians will eat chicken or ham, and will certainly not take it seriously that you want to avoid all meat products.

Vegetables in Argentina are cheap, of excellent quality, mostly organic, and available fresh in *verdulerías* (vegetable shops) all over towns. Look out for *acelga*, a large leafed chard with a strong flavour, often used to fill pasta, or *tarta de verduras*, vegetable pies, which you can buy everywhere, fresh and very good. Butternut squash, *zapallo*, is used to good effect in *tartas* and in filled pasta. Salads are quite safe to eat in restaurants, and fresh, although not wildly imaginative. The basic salad is *ensalada mixta*, which can involve nothing more exotic than lettuce, tomato, carrot and onion, but often there will be *remolacha* (fresh beetroot), *choclo* (sweet corn) and boiled egg too. Only in remote areas in the north west of the country should you be wary of salads, since the water here is not reliable.

Regional variations

The Argentine speciality *empanadas* are tasty small semicircular pies traditionally filled with meat, but now widely available filled with cheese, *acelga* (chard) or corn. They originate in Salta and Tucumán, where you'll still find the best examples, but can be found all over the country as a starter in a *parrilla*, or ordered by the dozen to be delivered at home with drinks among friends. Around Salta and Jujuy you'll find *humitas*, parcels of sweet corn and onions, steamed in the corn husk, superb, and *tamales* : balls of corn flour filled with beef and onion, and similarly wrapped in corn husk leaves to be steamed. The other speciality of the region is *locro* – a thick stew made of maize, white beans, beef, sausages, pumpkin and herbs. Good fish is serves in many areas of the country. Along the east coast, you'll always be offered *merluza* (hake), *lenguado*, (sole), and often salmon too. If you go to Puerto Madryn or the Atlantic coast near Mar del Plata, the seafood is a must: *arroz con mariscos* is similar to *paella* and absolutely delicious. There will often be *ostras* (oysters) and *centolla* (king crab) on the menu too. In the lakes, trout are very good, best served grilled, but like all Argentine fish, you'll be offered a bewildering range of sauces, such as roquefort, which drowns the flavour rather. Also in the Lake District, try smoked trout and the wild boar. Berries are very good here in summer, with raspberries and strawberries abundant and flavoursome. In the northeast, there are some superb river fish to try: *Pacú* is a large,

firm fleshed fish with lots of bones, but very tasty. The other great speciallity is *surubí*,
a kind of catfish, particularly good cooked delicately in banana leaves.

Puddings

Argentines have a sweet tooth, and are passionate about *dulce de leche* – milk and
sugar evaporated to a pale, soft fudge, and found on all cakes, pastries, and even for
breakfast. If you like this, you'll be delighted by *facturas,* sweet *media lunas*
(croissants) and other pastries, stuffed with *dulce de leche*, jams of various kinds,
and sweet cream fillings. Look out for the more sophisticated variations, and buy
them by the dozen for around US$1.30.

Helados – ice cream – is really excellent in Argentina, and for US$0.80 in any
Heladeria, you'll get 2 flavours, from a huge range, piled up high on a tiny cone; an
unmissable treat. Other popular desserts are *almendrado* (ice cream rolled in
crushed almonds), *dulce de batata* (sweet potato preserve), *dulce de membrillo*
(quince preserve), *dulce de zapallo* (pumpkin in syrup); these *dulces* are like very
solid jam, and (unbelievably) often eaten with cheese. If both elements are good, this
can be a pleasing combination, though not immediately appealing. *Postre balcarce*, a
cream and meringue cake, is popular, but the most loved of all is flan, not a flan at all,
but crème caramel, often served on a pool of caramelized sugar, and pretty good.
Everyone loves *alfajores*, soft maize-flour biscuits filled with *dulce de leche* or apricot
jam, and then coated with chocolate, especially the brand *Havanna*. Croissants
(*media lunas*) come in two varieties: *de grasa* (savoury, made with beef fat) and *dulce*
(sweet and fluffy). These will often be your only breakfast since Argentines are not
keen on eating first thing in the morning, and only supply the huge buffet style
'American breakfast' in international hotels to please tourists. The reason they're not
hungry at 8 in the morning is because they have only just had dinner.

Eating out

Restaurants rarely open before 2100 and most people turn up at around 2230, often
later. If you're invited to someone's house for dinner, don't expect to eat before 2300,
and have a few *facturas* at 1700, the Argentine *medienda*, to keep you going.

The *siesta* (afternoon nap) is strictly observed everywhere but Buenos Aires city.
Offices usually close between 1300 and 1630. At around 1700, many people go to a
confitería for *merienda* – tea, sandwiches and cakes. Dinner usually begins at 2200
or 2230; Argentines are very sociable, like to eat out, and usually bring babies and
children along, however late it is.

Cheap meals: Ask for the *menu fixo* – set price menu, usually good value, also
try *tenedor libre* (free fork) restaurants – eat all you want for a fixed price. Markets
too usually have cheap food. If self-catering, you'll find supermarkets cheap and
good quality.

Drink

The great Argentine drink, which you must try if invited, is *mate* (pronounced mattay).
A kind of tea made from dried *yerba* leaves, drunk from a cup or seasoned gourd
through a silver perforated straw, it is shared by a group of friends or work colleagues
as a daily social ritual. Argentine wines are excellent and drinkable throughout the
price range. Red grape varieties of merlot, syrah, cabernet sauvignon, and the white
torrontes are particularly recommended; try brands Lurton, Norton, Bianchi, Trapiche
or Etchart in any restaurant. Good champagnes include the brut nature of Navarro
Correas, whose Los Arboles cabernet sauvignon is an excellent red wine, and
Norton's Cosecha Especial. The local beers, mainly lager-type, are fine: Quilmes is the
best seller, but look out for home-made beers in the lakes, especially around El
Bolsón. Spirits are relatively cheap, other than those that are imported; there are
cheap drinkable Argentine gins and whiskeys. *Clericó* is a white-wine *sangría* drunk

in summer. It is best not to drink the tap water; in the main cities it's safe, but often heavily chlorinated. Never drink tap water in the northwest, where it is notoriously poor. Many Argentines mix soda water with their wine (even in red wine) as a refreshing drink in summer.

Entertainment and nightlife

Argentines, of whatever age, are extremely sociable and love to party. This means that even small towns have a selection of bars catering for varied tastes, plenty of live music and somewhere to dance, even if they are not the chic clubs you might be used to in western urban cities. The point of going out here is to meet and chat rather than drink yourself under the table, and alcohol is consumed in moderation. If invited to an Argentine house party, a cake or *masitas* (a box of little pastries) will be just as much appreciated as a bottle of wine. Argentine women generally stick to soft drinks with meals, and while women travellers needn't miss out on all that fine wine, you'll certainly feel foolish (afterwards, at least) if you actually get drunk.

Dancing

Argentines eat dinner at 2200, and then go for a drink at around midnight, so the dancing usually starts at around 0200, and goes on til 0600 or 0700. *Boliches* can mean anything from a bar with dancing, found in most country towns, to a disco on the outskirts, a taxi ride away from the centre. In Buenos Aires, there's a good range of clubs, playing the whole range from tango, salsa, and other Latin American dance music, to electronic music (see Buenos Aires Entertainment, page 90). In the interior (everywhere else in Argentina), nightclubs play a more conventional mixture of North American and Latin American pop with the odd bit of Argentine Rock Nacional thrown in, though you'll find a more varied scene in the bigger cities like Córdoba, Rosario and Mendoza. Tango classes are hugely popular all over the country, and especially in Buenos Aires, where *milongas* are incredibly trendy now: a class followed by a few hours of dancing. Even if you're a complete novice, it's worth trying at least one class to get a feel for the steps, and being whisked around the floor by an experienced dancer is quite a thrill even if you haven't a clue what to do with your legs. (See box on tango, page 76.)

Music

Live music is everywhere in Argentina, with bands playing Latin American pop or jazz in bars even in small cities. The indigenous music is *folclore* (pronounced *foke-LAW-ray*) which varies widely over the country. Traditional gaucho music around the pampas includes *payadores*: witty duels with guitars for two singers, much loved by Argentines, but bewildering if your Spanish is limited to menus and directions. The northwest has the country's most stirring *folclore*, where you should seek out *peñas* to see live bands playing fabulous *zambas* and *chacareras*. The rhythms are infectious, the singing passionate, and Argentine audiences can't resist joining in. Even tourist oriented *peñas* can be atmospheric, but try to find out where the locals go, like **La Casona del Molino** in Salta. Most cities have *peñas*, and you'll often see some great bands at the gaucho *Day of Tradition* festivals (mid-November) throughout Argentina and at local town fiestas (dates given in the relevant town's sections).

Festivals and events

The main holiday period is January to March when all Argentine schoolchildren are on tourist destinations become extremely busy at this time, with foreign visitors adding to the crowds, particularly in Bariloche, El Calafate and Ushuaia. You should book transport and accommodation ahead at these times. During Easter week, and the winter school holidays throughout July, hotels may also fill fast, particularly in ski resorts. No one works on the national holidays, and these are often long weekends, with a resulting surge of people to popular holiday places: 1 January, Good Friday, 2 April, 1 May, 25 May, 10 June, 20 June, 9 July, 17 August, 12 October and 25 December. Banks are closed and there are limited bus services on 25 and 31 December.

There are gaucho parades throughout Argentina on the days leading up to the *Día de la Tradición,* 10 November, with fabulous displays of horsemanship, gaucho games, enormous *asados* and traditional music. It's well worth seeing the festivities in any small town. On 30 December (not 31 because so many offices in centre are closed) there is a ticker-tape tradition in downtown Buenos Aires: it snows paper and the crowds stuff passing cars and buses with long streamers. The northwest particularly, has a rich culture, and many colourful festivals; see page 267.

Shopping

Best buys
Shopping in Argentina has suddenly become relatively cheap for visitors from western Europe and USA since the devaluation of the peso in 2002. Argentine fashion and leather goods are particularly good value; shoes, sunspecs and outdoor gear too, are very reasonably priced, and if you have a free afternoon in Buenos Aires, it might be worth considering buying them here when you arrive.

Argentine specialities
In Buenos Aires, leather is the best buy, with many shops selling fine leather jackets, coats and trousers, as well as beautifully made bags and shoes. With a mixture of Italian influenced design, and a flavour of the old gaucho leatherworking traditions, there's a strong emerging Argentine style.

Handicrafts, *artesanía,* are available all over the country, and are distinctly region to region. Traditional gaucho handicrafts, available across most of the country, include woven or plaited leather belts of excellent quality, as well as key rings and other pieces made of silver. These are small and distinctive and make excellent gifts. Look out, too, for the traditional baggy gaucho trousers, *bombachas*, comfortable for days in the saddle, and ranging from cheap sturdy cotton to smart versions with elaborate tucks.

Take home a *mate* , the hollowed gourd, often decorated, and the silver *bombilla* that goes with it, for drinking the national drink (or decorating your mantlepiece). In the northwest there are beautifully made woven items: brightly coloured rugs, or saddle mats, and the country's best *ponchos*. Look out for the hand-dyed and woven *ponchos*, instead of the mass-produced variety, available in smaller rural areas, or in the fine handicrafts market at Salta or Catamarca. There are the deep red *Güemes* versions or soft fine *ponchos* made of *vicuña* (a local cousin of the llama), usually in natural colours. In markets all over the northwest, you'll find llama wool jumpers, hats and socks, and brightly coloured woven bags, Bolivian influenced, but typical of the puna region. There are also fine carved wooden pieces. In the lakes too, there's lots of woodwork, and weavings of a different kind, from the Mapuche peoples, with distinctive black and white patterns. Smoked fish and meat, and delicious home made jams from *sauco* (elderberry) or *frambuesa* (raspberry) are among the local delicacies to be tried. In the northeast, there are Guaraní handicrafts, wooden toucans, and bows and arrows; definitely touristy, but appealing. The local produce, whether tea or *mate* is very good. Argentina's national stone, the fleshy pink and marbled rhodochrosite, is mined in the northwest, but available all over Buenos Aires too, worked into fine jewellery, and less subtle paperweights and ashtrays.

Sport and activities

Argentina's spectacular geography offers a huge range of adventure tourism from white water rafting to skiing, and some of the finest trekking and horseriding anywhere in the world. The variety of climates and terrain means that there's enormously varied wildlife and birdlife, particularly in the extensive network of national parks, and some of the finest fishing on the planet in many places. Spectator sports are heavily biased towards football, but there's polo and basketball too.

If you're looking for culture and history, there are good museums of Buenos Aires, but perhaps even more fascinating are the ancient cultures of the northwest. And you can delve further into the past at several pre-historic sites and along the dinosaur belt. You could base a whole trip around the picturesque wine producing areas of Argentina, and to get to the heart of the country's great rural tradition, seek out the estancias.

Estancia tourism

An estancia refers to an extensive area of farmed land with a substantial house at its centre, and includes cattle ranches, sheep farms, polo pony stables, tobacco plantations and country houses. These great homes belonging to some of the country's wealthiest landowners are now opening their doors to paying guests offering wonderful places to stay. There's a whole spectrum of estancias from a simple dwelling on the edge of a pristine lake in the Patagonian wilderness to a Loire-style chateau in the Pampas. They might offer incredible luxury and the chance to be completely pampered, or, more typically, a rare opportunity to spend a few days in the middle of otherwise inaccessible natural beauty and enjoy activities such as walking, horseriding, birdwatching and fishing. Often there's the chance to learn about how the farm is run, watching sheep shearing, or even to join in with cattle mustering. You'll certainly be treated to the traditional *asado*, meat cooked over an open fire, and most impressively, *asado al palo*, where the animal is speared on a cross-shaped stick and roasted to perfection.

Gauchos still work the land on horseback in their traditional outfit of *bombachas* (baggy trousers, comfortable for spending hours on horseback), *trensa* (a wide leather belt with silver clasps), a poncho (in the northwest), a *pañuelo* (neckerchief), a *boyna* (beret) and on the feet *alpargatas* (simple cotton shoes). The best part about an estancia visit is the chance to get to know the *dueños* (owners) and gain an insight into the history and traditions of estancia life, which is so essential to understanding the country. Some estancia owners have turned to tourism as a means of earning extra income as farming fails to be profitable, and on some estancias it is fast becoming their main activity, with added facilities like a pool or tennis courts. Perhaps the most charming places simply offer the splendour of their land, and the genuine hospitality of the owners. Many speak English and are fascinating hosts.

Price Estancias can be pricier than hotels, but since devaluation, are now accessible even to travellers on a budget, at least for a day visit. *Dia de campo* (day on the farm) is offered by lots of estancias, a full day of horseriding, or a ride in a horse-drawn carriage, an *asado* lunch, and then often other farm activities, or time to relax in the peaceful grounds. Costs for staying overnight vary between US$50 for two in the most humble places, to US$150 per person with all meals drinks, transfers and activities included for the most luxurious.

Location Though estancias are found throughout rural Argentina, they vary enormously in style and activities. In the province of Buenos Aires you will find estancias covering thousands of hectares of flat grassland with large herds of cattle and windpumps to extract water; horseriding will certainly be offered and perhaps cattle-mustering, at *La Luisa* and *Palantelén* for example. Some of the finest buildings are in this area, such as *Dos Talas* and *La Porteña*. In Patagonia there are giant sheep estancias overlooking glaciers, mountains and lakes, such as *Estancias Maipú, Helsingfors*, or *Alma Gaucha*. There are estancias on Tierra del Fuego, full of the history of the early pioneers who built them: *Viamonte* and *Harberton*, while on the mainland nearby, *Estancia Monte Dinero*, has a colony of Magellanic penguins on its doorstep. There's more wildlife close at hand in the estancias on Península Valdés. And in Salta, there are colonial-style *fincas* whose land includes jungly cloudforest with marvellous horseriding.

Further information The most distinctive or representative estancias are mentioned in the text, but for more information see the national tourist website: www.turismo.gov.ar in English, with all estancias listed, www.vivalaspampas.com.ar for estancias in the province of Buenos Aires, and www.caminodelgaucho.com.ar an excellent organisation which can arrange stays in the Pampas estancias. www.estanciasdesantacruz.com is a helpful agency which arranges estancia stays Santa Cruz and the south, including transport, and www.raturstancias.com.ar which covers estancias over the whole country. A useful book *Tursimo en Estancias y Hosterías* is produced by **Tierra Buena**, www.tierrabuena.com.ar who arranges visits through www.southtrip.com You can of course contact estancias directly, and reserve, ideally with a couple of weeks warning.

Fishing

Argentina offers some of the world's finest fishing, in incomparably beautiful surroundings of virgin landscape, and with good accommodation. In the Lake District, there's world renowned fly fishing for trout (rainbow, brown and brook); and for Chinook or landlocked salmon. The epicentre is around Junín de los Andes and Bariloche, in rivers Quilquihue, Chimehuín, Collón-Curá, Meliquina and Caleufú, and Lagos Traful, Gutiérrez, Mascardi, Cholila, Futalaufquen (in Los Alerces National Park), Falkner, Villarino; Huechulafquen, Paimún, Epulafquen, Tromen (all in Lanín National Park), and, in the far north, Quillén. Throughout the lakes the season lasts usually from November to Easter.

In Tierra del Fuego, huge brown trout can be fished from Río Grande, and Lago Fagnano, while over the border in Chilean Tierra del Fuego, Lago Blanco is fast becoming popular. In the northeast, *sorubim* and giant *pacu* can be fished at the confluence of rivers Paraná and Paraguay, as well as *dorado*, known for its challenging fight. The closed season in this area is November to January. On the Atlantic Coast, San Blas is famous for shark fishing, for bacota shark and bull shark weighing up to 130kg, while all along the coast, there's good sea fishing. Fishing can also be found in other parts of the country and is offered by many estancias. Pejerrey, corvina and pescadilla can be found in large quantities along the coast of Buenos Aires province, and many of the reservoirs of the Central Sierras, the West and Northwest are well stocked.

All rivers are 'catch and release', and to fish anywhere in Argentina you need a permit costing US$5 per day, US$15 per week, US$50 per year. It certainly makes sense to do some research before you arrive, to find the right area for the kind of fishing you want to do. The national tourism website has a helpful section: **www.turismo.gov.ar/pesca**; fishing queries to **fishing@turismo.gov.ar** will be answered in 48 hrs, and they produce a helpful booklet *Pesca Deportiva en la Patagonia Argentina*, which you can request. **www.flyfishingtravel.com** is a good site in English with descriptions of places you can fish and where to stay, and if you're looking for fishing guides, contact the following in Chubut, **rsm@teletel.com.ar** in Neuquén, **patout@smandes.com.ar** and **www.guiaspatagonicos.com.ar** for northern Patagonia. For fishing licences, contact the **Fly Fishing Association** of Argentina, T011-4773 0821, and for Patagonia, there's assistance from the **National Parks Administration**, 011-4311 8853/0303. More information and accommodation is given in the travelling text for the appropriate area.

Birdwatching

It's no surprise in a country so rich in untouched natural habitats that the bird life is extraordinary, and extremely varied. From the wealth of seabirds at **Península Valdés** to the colourful species in the subtropical rainforest near the **Iguazú Falls** from the marshlands of **Esteros del Iberá** or the **Chaco savannah** to the **Lake District** and the mountainous interior of **Tierra del Fuego** there marvellous opportunities to spot birds. At least 980 of the 2,926 species of birds registered in South America exist in Argentina, and in many places, with easy access. There are specialist tours led by expert guides in most areas: see the travelling text for details.

All Patagonia, **www.allpatagonia.com/Eng** runs birdwatching trips in Patagonia and Tierra del Fuego. In the northeast, contact the excellent Daniel Samay, **Explorador Expediciones**, www.rainforestevt.com.ar And in the Lake District, **Angel Fernandez**, T02944-524609, 15609799, is warmly recommended, along with **Daniel Feinstein**, T/F02944-442259, both extremely knowledgeable.

Adventure tourism

The skiing season runs from mid-June to mid-October, but dates vary between resorts. The country's best, and deservedly famous is **Las Leñas**, south of Mendoza, due to its long, varied and challenging pistes, its spectacular setting, superb accommodation, and also for being a dedicated snowboarding area. It's also the most expensive resort, and if you're looking for a cheaper option in the same area, consider **Los Penitentes**, a more modest but friendly resort. There's good skiing all along the Lake District, with the biggest centre at **Cerro Catedral**, near Bariloche. This is a huge resort with scope for cross country skiing and snowboarding, and the advantages of major town with excellent hotels and services. Nearby, the smaller but upmarket resorts of **Cerro Bayo** at Villa la Angostura and **Cerro Chapelco** at San Martín de los Andes have even more beautiful settings and cater for families. **La Hoya**, near Esquel, is much cheaper with a laid-back family feel. And at the end of the world, in Ushuaia, there's great cross-country skiing at **Cerro Castor**, as well as down-hill. Details of all of these resorts are given in the text, together with their websites.

Trekking

The whole of the west of the country, along the mountains of the Andes, offers superb opportunities for trekking. The **Lake District** in summer is the most rewarding because there are so many spectacular landscapes to explore within easy reach of the centres of Bariloche, El Bolsón and San Martín de los Andes. The national parks here are well set-up for walkers, with good information and basic maps available, and *refugios* and campsites convenient for accommodation in longer hikes. However, it's worth exploring the lesser known extremes of the lakes, at **Pehuenia** in the north, with wonderful walks among the araucaria trees, and at **Los Alerces National Park** with trekking into the virgin forest. All these walks are described in detail in the relevant areas. The season for walking is December to April.

The mountainous region to the west of Mendoza, around **Aconcagua**, offers good and challenging trekking, as well as further north in the **Cordon del Plata** in San Juan, where oasis villages in the valley are good bases for several peaks around Mercedario. Altitude sickness can be a problem in these areas, and you should allow time in your of landscape. The puna to the west is dramatic desert, dropping to the arid and rocky mountainous landscape in the **Quebrada de Humahuaca**, and continuing east, there are cloudforests. It's possible to walk through all three zones in a single extended expedition, though you'd need to go with a guide. Throughout the area there are attractive villages to use as bases for day walks. In the northeast, there are a few good walks in the national park of the **Iguazú Falls**, and many more good places to walk in the provinces to the south. The centre of the country, in the sierras around **Córdoba** are good for day walks, especially in the Traslasierra. In Patagonia, there are petrified forests and caves with pre-historic handprints to walk to, as well as the remoter reaches of **Parque Nacional Perito Moreno**. The most dramatic trekking is in the south of Patagonia, whether in the mountains around **Mount Fitz Roy** or ice trekking on the glaciers themselves in **Parque Nacional los Galciares**. And near Ushuaia, there are unforgettable views from peaks in the **Parque Nacional Tierra del Fuego**, along the shores of the Beagle Channel and from wilder peaks in mountains behind the town.

These are the highlights, but wherever you go in Argentina, you can find somewhere to trek . The spaces are wide open and there really are no limits. Try checking out **www.parquesnacionales.gov.ar** for more detailed information.

What to take You could consider taking the following equipment: Many of the clothes and camping supplies are available in large towns. **Clothing**: a warm hat (wool or man-made fibre), thermal underwear, T-shirts/shirts, trousers (quick-drying and preferably windproof, never jeans), warm (wool or fleece) jumper/jacket (preferably two), gloves, waterproof jacket and over trousers (preferably Gore-Tex), shorts, walking boots and socks, change of footwear or flip-flops. **Camping gear**: tent (capable of withstanding high winds), sleeping mat (closed cell – Karrimat – or inflatable – Thermarest), sleeping bag (three-season minimum rating), sleeping bag liner, stove and spare parts, fuel, matches and lighter, cooking and eating utensils, pan scrubber, survival bag. Food: very much personal preference but at least two days more supplies than you plan to use; tea, coffee, sugar, dried milk; porridge, dried fruit, honey; soup, pasta, rice, soya (TVP); fresh fruit and vegetables; bread, cheese, crackers; biscuits, chocolate; salt, pepper, other herbs and spices, cooking oil. **Miscellaneous**: map and compass, torch and spare batteries, pen and notebook, Swiss army knife, sunglasses, sun cream, lip salve and insect repellent, first aid kit, water bottle, toiletries and towel.

Safety Hikers have little to fear from the animal kingdom apart from insects (although it's best to avoid actually stepping on a snake), and robbery and assault are very rare. You are much more of a threat to the environment than vice versa. Leave no evidence of your passing; don't litter and don't give gratuitous presents of sweets or money to rural people. Respect their system of reciprocity; if they give you hospitality or food, then is the time to reciprocate with presents.

Off-roading

Large areas of Argentina are ideal for off-roading. Across wide expanses of flat land or gently rolling hills there are no woods to obstruct you, nor snow or ice; the vegetation is sparse and there are few animals and hardly any people. Patagonia in particular, with its endless steppes interrupted only by rivers, gorges and gullies, is recommended but some of the Andean valleys of the west and northwest are also worth exploring in this way. Three of the rougher roads in the Andes are especially recommended: the route from **San Antonio de los Andes to Catamarca** via Antofagasta de la Sierra; the route from **Catamarca to Chile** via Paso San Francisco and the **Laguna Brava area** in La Rioja.

Though four-wheel drive vehicles are difficult to hire in Buenos Aires, try hire companies such as **Localiza** and **Hertz** in some major cities of the interior, notably Mendoza, Tucumán, Bariloche and Ushuaia, as well as from **Marina Servicios** in Salta. Prices are high, from US$1,500 for 10 days. Buy road maps in advance from the **Automóvil Club Argentino** (ACA) in Buenos Aires. Before setting out you should obtain as much information as possible; employees in the provincial tourist information offices are unlikely to be able to answer your questions, so it is more important to ask them for names of local guides (*baqueanos*). It is important to avoid the coldest and the wettest months of the year; spring (October and November) and autumn (April and May) are the best seasons.

Health

A good standard of education means that there are some excellent doctors and medical facilities. As with all medical care, first impressions count. If a facility is grubby, and the staff are wearing grey coats instead of white ones, then be wary of the general standard of medicine and hygiene. A good tip is to contact the embassy or consulate on arrival and ask where the recommended clinics (those used by diplomats) are. This information can also be useful if a friend/relative gets ill at home and there is a desperate search for you around the globe. Diseases you may be exposed to are caused by viruses, bacteria and parasites. Altitude sickness may affect you along the entire length of the Andes.

The greatest disease risk in Tropical Argentina is caused by the greater volume of insect disease carriers in the shape of mosquitoes and sandflies. The parasitic diseases are many but the two key ones are malaria and American trypanosomiasis (known as Chagas Disease). The key viral disease is Dengue fever which is transmitted by a mosquito that bites in the day. Bacterial diseases include tuberculosis (TB) and some types of travellers' diarrhoea. Malaria in Argentina is restricted to the rural areas of Salta and Jujuy Provinces (along the Bolivian border) and Misiones and Corrientes Provinces (along the border of Paraguay).

Ideally see your GP or travel clinic at least six weeks before departure for general advice on travel risks, malaria and vaccinations. Make sure you have travel insurance, get a dental check, know your own blood group and if you suffer a long-term condition such as diabetes or epilepsy make sure someone knows or that you have a Medic Alert bracelet/necklace with this information.

Vaccinations

Polio Recommended if nil in last 10 years.

Tetanus Recommended if nil in last 10 years (but after five doses you have had enough for life).

Typhoid Recommended if nil in last three years.

Yellow Fever Not obligatory for Argentina. However, if you are travelling around South America it is best to get this vaccine since you will need it for the northern areas.

Rabies Recommended if going to jungle and/or remote areas.

Hepatitis A Recommended as the disease can be caught easily from food/water.

An A-Z of health risks

Altitude sickness

Symptoms This can creep up on you as just a mild headache with nausea or lethargy. The more serious disease is caused by fluid collecting in the brain in the enclosed space of the skull and can lead to coma and death. A lung disease with

Cures The best cure is to descend as soon as possible.

Prevention Get acclimatised. Do not try to reach the highest levels on your first few days of arrival. Try to avoid flying directly into the cities of highest altitude such as La Paz. Climbers like to take treatment drugs as protective measures but this can lead to macho idiocy and death. The peaks are still there and so are the trails, whether it takes you a bit longer than someone else does not matter as long as you come back down alive.

Chagas Disease

Symptoms The disease affects locals more than travellers, but travellers can be exposed by sleeping in mud-constructed huts where the bug that carries the parasite bites and defaecates on an exposed part of skin. You may notice nothing at all or a local swelling, with fever, tiredness and enlargement of lymph glands, spleen and liver. The seriousness of the parasite infection is caused by the long-term effects which include gross enlargement of the heart and/or guts.

Cures Early treatment is required with toxic drugs. Sleep under a permethrin treated bed net and use insect repellents.

Dengue Fever

Symptoms Present throughout Argentina. In travellers this can cause a severe flu like illness with fever, lethargy, enlarged lymph glands and muscle pains. It starts suddenly, lasts for two- three days, seems to get better for two to three days and then kicks in again for another two to three days. It is usually all over in an unpleasant week. The disease is self limiting and forces rest and recuperation on the sufferer.

Prevention The mosquitoes that carry the Dengue virus bite during the day unlike the malaria mosquitoes. Sadly this means that repellent and covered limbs are a 24-hr issue. Check your accommodation for flower pots and shallow pools of water since these are where the Dengue-carrying mosquitoes breed.

Diarrhoea/intestinal upset

This is almost inevitable. One study showed that up to 70% of all travellers may suffer during their trip.

Symptoms Persistence beyond two weeks, with blood or pain, require specialist medical attention.

Cures Ciproxin will cure many of the bacterial causes but none of the viral ones. Immodium and Pepto-Bismol provide symptomatic relief. Dehydration can be a key problem especially in hot climates and is best avoided by the early start of Oral Rehydration Salts (at least one large cup of drink for each loose stool).

Prevention Be careful with water and ice for drinking. If you have any doubts then boil it or filter and treat it. Be wary of salads, re-heated foods or food that has been left out in the sun having been cooked earlier in the day. There is a simple adage that says 'wash it, peel it, boil it or forget it'. Also be wary of unpasteurized dairy products. These can transmit a range of diseases from brucellosis (fevers and constipation), to listeria (meningitis) and tuberculosis of the gut (obstruction, constipation, fevers and weight loss).

Hanta virus

Some forest and riverine rodents carry hanta virus, epidemics of which have occurred in Argentina and Chile, but do occur worldwide. Symptoms are a flu-like illness which can lead to complications. Try as far as possible to avoid rodent-infested areas, especially close contact with rodent droppings. Campers and parents with small children should be especially careful.

Hepatitis

Symptoms Hepatitis means inflammation of the liver. Viral causes of Hepatitis can be acquired anywhere in Argentina. The most obvious sign is if your skin or the whites of your eyes become yellow. However, prior to this all that you may notice is itching and tiredness.

Cures Early on, depending on the type of hepatitis, a vaccine or immunoglobulin may reduce the duration of the illness.

Prevention Pre-travel Hepatitis A vaccine is the best bet. Hepatitis B is spread by a different route by blood and unprotected sexual intercourse, both of which can be avoided. Unfortunately there is no vaccine for Hepatitis C or the increasing alphabetical list of other Hepatitis viruses.

Leishmaniasis

Symptoms A skin form of this disease occurs in all countries of South America except Chile and Uruguay. The main disease areas are in Bolivia, Brazil and Peru. If infected, you may notice a raised lump, which leads to a purplish discoloration on white skin and any possible ulcer. The parasite is transmitted by the bite of a sandfly. Sandflies do not fly very far and the greatest risk is at ground levels, so if you can avoid sleeping on the jungle floor do so. Seek advice for any persistent skin lesion or nasal symptom.

Cures Several weeks treatment is required under specialist supervision. The drugs themselves are toxic but not if taken in sufficient amounts recurrence of the disease is more likely.

Prevention Sleep above ground, under a permethrin treated net, use insect repellent and get a specialist opinion on any unusual skin lesions soon after your return.

Malaria

Symptoms Malaria can cause death within 24 hours. It can start as something resembling an attack of flu. You may feel tired, lethargic, headachy or worse, develop fits, coma and then death. You should have a low index of suspicion because it is very easy to write off vague symptoms, which may actually be malaria. Whilst abroad and on return get tested as soon as possible, the test could save your life.

Cures Treatment is with drugs and may be oral or into a vein depending on the seriousness of the infection.

Prevention This is best summarized by the B and C of the ABCD: Bite avoidance and Chemoprophylaxis. Some would prefer to take test kits for malaria with them and have standby treatment available. However, the field test of the blood kits has had poor results. When you have malaria you do not perform well enough to do the tests correctly to make the right diagnosis.

Rabies

Remember that rabies is endemic throughout Latin America so avoid dogs that are behaving strangely and cover your toes at night from the vampire bats, which also carry the disease. If you are bitten by a domestic or wild animal, do not leave things to chance: scrub the wound with soap and water and/or disinfectant, and seek medical assistance at once.

Sexual health

Unprotected sex can spread HIV, Hepatitis B and C, Gonorrhea (green discharge), chlamydia (nothing to see but may cause painful urination and later female infertility), painful recurrent herpes, syphilis and warts, just to name a few. You can cut down on the risks by using condoms, a femidom or if you want to be completely safe, by avoiding sex altogether.

Ticks

Ticks usually attach themselves to the lower parts of the body often after walking in areas where cattle have grazed. They take a while to attach themselves strongly, but the area will swell up as they start to suck blood. The important thing is to remove them gently, so that they do not leave their head parts in your skin – this can cause a nasty allergic reaction some days later. Do not use petrol, vaseline, lighted cigarettes etc to remove the tick, but, with a pair of tweezers remove the beast gently by gripping it at the attached (head) end and rock it out in very much the same way that a tooth is extracted. Certain tropical flies which lay their eggs under the skin of sheep and cattle also occasionally do the same thing to humans with the unpleasant result that a maggot grows under the skin and pops up as a boil or pimple. The best way to remove these is to cover the boil with oil, vaseline or nail varnish so as to stop the maggot breathing, then to squeeze it out gently the next day.

Water
There are a number of ways to purify water in order to make it safe to drink. Dirty water should first be strained through a filter bag (available in camping shops) and then boiled or treated. Bringing water to a rolling boil at sea level is sufficient to make the water safe for drinking, but at higher altitudes you have to boil the water for a few minutes longer to ensure that all the microbes are killed. There are sterilizing methods that can be used and there are proprietary preparations containing chlorine (eg Puritabs) or iodine (eg Pota Aqua) compounds. Chlorine compounds generally do not kill protozoa (eg Giardia). There are a number of water filters now on the market available in personal and expedition size. They work either on mechanical or chemical principles, or may do both. Make sure you take the spare parts or spare chemicals with you and do not believe everything the manufacturers say.

Further infomation

Organizations and websites
Foreign and Commonwealth Office (FCO) This is a key travel advice site with useful information on the country, people, climate and lists the UK embassies/consulates. The site also promotes the concept of 'Know Before You Go', and encourages travel insurance and appropriate travel health advice. It has links to the Department of Health travel advice site, listed below. www.fco.gov.uk

Department of Health Travel Advice This excellent site is also available as a free booklet, the T6, from Post offices. It lists the vaccine advice requirements for each country. www.doh.gov.uk/traveladvice

Medic Alert This is the website of the foundation that produces bracelets and necklaces for those with existing medical problems. Once you have ordered your bracelet/necklace you write your key medical details on paper inside it, so that if you collapse, a medical person can identify you as someone with epilepsy or allergy to peanuts etc. www.medicalalert.co.uk

Blood Care Foundation The Blood Care Foundation is a Kent based charity 'dedicated to the provision of screened blood and resuscitation fluids in countries where these are not readily available.' It will dispatch certified non-infected blood of the right type to your hospital/clinic. The blood is flown in from various centres around the world. www.bloodcare.org.uk

Public Health Laboratory Service This site has the malaria advice guidelines for travel around the world. It gives specific advice about the right drugs for each location. It also has useful information for those who are pregnant, suffering from epilepsy or planning to travel with children. www.phls.org.uk

Centers for Disease Control and Prevention (USA) This site from the US Government gives excellent advice on travel health, has useful disease maps and has details of disease outbreaks. www.cdc.gov

World Health Organization The WHO site has links to the WHO Blue Book on travel advice. This lists the diseases in different regions of the world. It describes vaccination schedules and makes clear which countries have Yellow Fever Vaccination certificate requirements. www.who.int

Tropical Medicine Bureau This Irish based site has a good collection of general travel health information and disease risks. www.tmb.ie

Fit for Travel This site from Scotland provides a quick A-Z of vaccine and travel health advice requirements for each country. www.fitfortravel.scot.nhs.uk

British Travel Health Association This is the official website of an organization of travel health professionals. www.btha.org

NetDoctor This general health advice site has a useful section on travel and has an ask the expert, interactive chat forum. www.Netdoctor.co.uk

Travel Screening Services This is the author's website. A private clinic dedicated to integrated travel health. The clinic gives vaccine, travel health advice, email and SMS text vaccine reminders and screens returned travellers for tropical diseases. www.travelscreening.co.uk

Books and leaflets
Advice for travellers on avoiding the risks of HIV and AIDS (Travel Safe) available from Department of Health, PO Box 777, London SE1 6XH. The Blood Care Foundation. Order from PO Box 7, Sevenoaks, Kent, TN13 2SZ, T 01732 742 427.
The Travellers Good Health Guide, Dr Ted Lankester, (ISBN 0-85969-827-0).
Expedition Medicine, (The Royal Geographic Society), Editors David Warrell and Sarah Anderson. (ISBN 1 86197 040-4).
International Travel and Health, World Health Organisation, Geneva (ISBN 92 4 158026 7).
The World's Most Dangerous Places, by Robert Young Pelton, Coskun Aral and Wink Dulles (ISBN 1-566952-140-9).
The Travellers Guide to Health, (T6) can be obtained by calling the Health Literature Line on T0800 555 777

What to take
Travel With Care Homeway, Amesbury, Wiltshire, SP4 7BH, T0870 7459261, www.travelwithcare.co.uk Provides a large range of products for sale.
Mosquito repellents DEET (Di-ethyltoluamide) is the gold standard. Apply every four to six hours but more often if you are sweating heavily. If a non-DEET product is used check who tested it. Validated products (tested at the London School of Hygiene and Tropical Medicine) include *Mosiguard*, Non-DEET *Jungle formula* and non-DEET *Autan*. If you want to use citronella remember that it must be applied very frequently (ie hourly to be effective).
Anti-malarials Remember that these are only required for a few areas of Argentina. Specialist advice is required as to which type to take. It is risky to buy medicinal tablets abroad because doses may differ and there may be a trade in false drugs.
Insect bite relief If you are prone to insects' bites or develop lumps quite soon after being bitten, carry an Aspivenin kit. This syringe suction device is available from *Boots*

Chemists and draws out some of the allergic materials and provides quick relief.

Painkillers Paracetomol or a suitable painkiller can have multiple uses for symptoms but remember that more than eight paracetemol a day can lead to liver failure.

Antibiotics Ciproxin (Ciprofloxacin) A useful antibiotic for travellers' diarrhoea (which can affect up to 70% of travellers). It can be obtained by private prescription in the UK which is expensive or bought over the counter in Argentina pharmacies, but if you do this check that the pills are in date. You take one 500 mg tablet when the diarrhoea starts and if you do not feel better in 24 hours the diarrhoea is likely to have a non-bacterial cause and may be viral. Viral causes of diarrhoea will settle on their own. However, with all diarrhoeas try to keep hydrated by taking the right mixture of salt and water. This is available as Oral Rehydration Salts in ready made sachets or can be made up by adding a teaspoon of sugar and a half teaspoon of salt to a litre of clean water. Flat carbonated drinks can also be used.

Diarrhoea treatment Immodium is a great standby for those diarrhoeas that occur at awkward times ie before a long coach/train journey or on a trek. In the author's view it is of more benefit than harm, as it is believed that letting the bacteria or viruses flow out had to be more beneficial. However, with Immodium they still come out but in a more solid form. Pepto-Bismol is used a lot by the Americans for diarrhoea. It certainly relieves symptoms but like Immodium it is not a cure for underlying disease. Be aware that it turns the stool black as well as making it more solid.

Sun block The Australian's have a great campaign, that has reduced skin cancer. It is called Slip, Slap, Slop. Slip on a shirt, Slap on a hat, slop on sun screen. Do not just use higher factors to stay out in the sun longer. 'Flash frying' (desperate bursts of excessive exposure), as it is called, is known to increase the risks of skin cancer.

MedicAlert These simple bracelets, or an equivalent, should be carried or worn by anyone with a significant medical condition.

Emergency supplies For longer trips involving jungle treks taking a clean needle pack, clean dental pack and water filtration device.

Keeping in touch

Internet

The best way to keep in touch is undoubtedly by email. Telephone is disproportionately expensive in Argentina, and so all Argentines have adapted rapidly to Internet, with broad band and speedy services widely available even in small towns. There are dedicated centres on almost every block in towns and cities, since few people have internet in their homes; some serving drinks, but usually a room full of computers with a counter selling sweets and drinks. There are Internet places dedicated to games too, which often have the fastest machines, if not the most relaxing environment. Most *locutorios* (phone centres) have an Internet connection, or can tell you where to find the nearest place. Prices vary, the more expensive in more remote towns from around US$0.30 to US$1 per hour.

Post

Letters from Argentina take 10-14 days to get to Europe and the USA. Rates for letters up to 20 g to Europe and USA: US$1.40, up to 150g, US$8. Post can be sent from the *Correo* (post office) or form private postal service *Oca,* through any shop displaying the purple sign. The post service is reliable, but for assured delivery, register everything.

Small parcels of up to 2kg can be sent from all post offices. Larger parcels must be sent from the town's main post office, where your parcel will be examined by customs to make sure that the contents are as stated on your customs form, and taken to *Encomiendas Internacionales* for posting. Any local *correo* (post office) can tell you where to go. Customs usually open in the morning only. Having parcels sent to Argentina incurs a customs tax, which depends on the value of the package, and all incoming packages are opened by customs. *Poste restante* is available in every town's main post office, fee US$1.

Telephone

Phoning in Argentina is made very easy by the abundance of *locutorios* – phone centres with private booths where you can talk for as long as you like, and pay afterwards, the price appearing on a small screen in your booth. There's no need for change or phone cards, and *locutorios* often have Internet, photocopying and fax services. The system works as follows: walk in and ask *'Una cabina, por favor'* and you'll be given a number corresponding to one of the booths in the shop. Simply dial from the comfort of the booth, as many calls as you like. They're added up and you pay at the counter at the end. All *locutorios* have phone directories, and staff are usually helpful sources of information. For local calls, if you can't find a *locutorio*, use a public payphone with coins, often next to *kioskos*, minimum 25 centavos.

Using the phone is relatively expensive in Argentina, and it's remarkable that even the friendly and helpful Argentines will rarely offer you their phone to make a call. One solution is to carry a ready supply of plastic phone cards, which are much cheaper for long-distance national and international calls. Two good brands are **Argentina Global** and **Hable Mas**, available from *kioskos* and *locutorios* for 5 or 10 pesos. Dial the free, 0800, number on the card, and a code (which you scratch the card to reveal), and you can phone anywhere in the world. These can usually be used in *locutorios* too, though the rates are more expensive.

Media

Newspapers

The national daily papers are *La Nación,* a broadsheet, intelligent and well-written (www.lanacion.com.ar), *Clarín* more accessible, also a broadsheet (www.clarin.com.ar). Both these papers have good websites and excellent Sunday papers with informative travel sections. Other daily national papers are *La Prensa, La Razón,* and the left wing *Página-Doce,* always refreshing for a different perspective. There's a daily paper in English, the *Buenos Aires Herald,* www.buenosairesherald.com which gives a brief digest of world news, as well as Argentine news. Magazines you might like to look at include: *Noticias* news and culture, *Gente* a kind of Hello! for Argentina, *El Gráfico*, a good sports magazine, and particularly *Lugares.* This glossy monthly travel magazine has superb photography and is a very useful resource for travel tips and ideas of where to go, often with English translation at the back. Issues are themed; the Northwest, the lakes, etc, and previous issues are often available from *kioskos* too.

Few foreign language newspapers are available outside Buenos Aires, but to keep in touch with news around the world, websites of your own favourite newspaper are invaluable. Many hotels have cable TV in the rooms, but rarely have any English news channels.

Radio

English language radio broadcasts can be heard daily on short wave: 0100-0130 on 6060 KHz 49m, 0230-0300 on 11710 KHz 25m, 0430-0500 and 2230-2300 on 15345 KHz 19m; **BBC World Service** in Buenos Aires: 97.1Mhz from 1200 noon to 0500. **Radiodifusión Argentina al Exterior**, Casilla de Correo 555, 1000, Buenos Aires. This is a government station and broadcasts also in Japanese, Arabic, German, French, Italian and Portuguese. Broadcasts by foreign radio stations (including the BBC) are receivable on short wave.

Buenos Aires

Introducing Buenos Aires

The magnificent city of Buenos Aires is the most European of South America's cities, yet its passions are entirely Argentine: the nostalgic **tango** danced in the *milongas*, the euphoria of football matches at La Boca stadium, and the steaks you smell grilling on *parrillas* all over the city. Buenos Aires' inhabitants are known as Porteños. Sharp witted, fast moving, fashion conscious, and energetic – their legendary nightlife is only just starting in the early hours, and they don't stop for a siesta! The city's streets are filled with cafés and restaurants. Whether drinking coffee in **Café Tortoni**, the traditional home of poets and intellectuals, or sipping cocktails in the newly fashionable **Palermo Hollywood** or **Las Cañitas**, or tasting fine wine from Mendoza with your huge steak grilled to perfection in **Puerto Madero**, you'll have a great evening out.

Buenos Aires owes its superb architecture to its wealthy heyday in the early 20th century. Baroque buildings line **Plaza de Mayo** and **Avenida de Mayo**, and Italianate Renaissance-style palaces flank leafy **Plaza San Martín** and the broad green parks of **Palermo**. Near the elaborate cemetery of **Recoleta**, where Eva Perón is buried, wealthy Porteños live life to the full in cafés, restaurants, museums and chic shops. Atmospheric **San Telmo** is home to many artists, and its narrow streets of crumbling old buildings make it a great place to stroll on Sundays, when tango dancers entwine in **Plaza Dorrego**'s vibrant cafés and bars. If the pace of urban life becomes too much you can escape to a network of jungly rivers in the **Tigre Delta**. On the eastern bank of **Río de la Plata** is the Uruguayan city of **Colonia del Sacramento**, with its charming Portuguese colonial architecture.

★ Don't miss...

❶ San Telmo Wander around the Sunday market, looking for antique bargains, and then stroll along Defensa, listening to street musicians and watching street tango, to find an atmospheric bar for lunch, page 79.

❷ Museo Isaac Fernández Blanco Gaze at exquisite colonial art, and relax in the Spanish-style garden, page 73.

❸ Teatro Colón Pay two pesos for a Monday night concert and appreciate the dazzling opulence of the 1900s opera house, page 73.

❹ A football match Brace yourself for a stirring game at the home of one of the country's big rivals: Boca Juniors or River Plate, page 94.

❺ A polo match Watch the world's finest players thunder with style across the hallowed field of the Hurlingham Club (November), page 94.

❻ Tigre delta Take a boat along overgrown rivers and stay the night at El Tropezón, Hemingway's former haunt, page 105.

❼ Tango milonga Dance with the new wave of young tango aficionados, or see the experts on show at El Viejo Almacén, page 76.

❽ Palermo Stroll by the chic shops of Palermo Viejo before settling down to a steak and a superb bottle of Argentine malbec in one of the smart new restaurants overlooking the plaza, page 76.

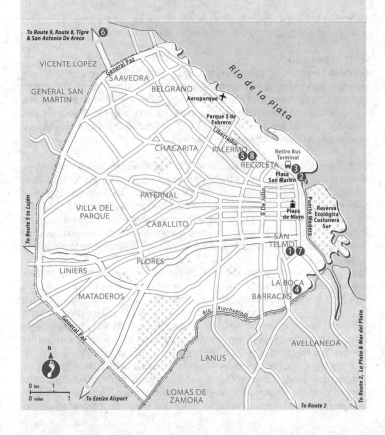

Buenos Aires

Ins and outs → *Phone code: 011 Population: 2,988,006, Gran Buenos Aires 13,333,670*

Getting there → *Ezeiza airport information, T5480 6111, Aeroparque information T4576 5111*

Air Buenos Aires has two airports: **Ezeiza** for international flights, 35 km southwest of the centre, and **Aeroparque** for domestic flights, just to the north of Palermo. An efficient bus service run by *Manuel Tienda León* links Ezeiza with the centre, (every 30 minutes, charging US$4 for the 40-minute journey). Ordinary taxis, charging US$9, are less reliable than *remise* taxis which have a fixed fare, and booked in advance from a desk at the airport, and charge US$8-10, for example, *La Terminal* T4312 0711. Aeroparque is 4 km north of the city centre on the riverside; *Manuel Tienda León* buses charge US$2, for the 20-minute journey to the centre, *remises* US$3 and ordinary taxis US$2.50. *Transfer Express* operates *remise* taxis, vans and minibuses from both airports to any point in town; convenient for large groups.

Bus Buses arrive from all over Argentina and from neighbouring countries at Retiro bus terminal at Ramos Mejía y Antártida Argentina, about five blocks north of Plaza San Martín, T4310 0700. However close, it's best to take a remise taxi into town, since the area is insalubrious, and ordinary taxis here are not reliable: *La Terminal* T4312 0711, booked from the main platform.

Ferry A ferry port receives fast catamarans and slower boats from Uruguay. For more detailed information, see Transport, page 95.

Train Next to the bus terminal is Retiro railway station, serving the suburbs and a few provincial stations, with only one long-distance train to Tucumán.

Getting around

Colectivo There is a good network of buses – *colectivos* – covering a very wide radius; frequent, efficient and very fast (hang on tight). The basic fare is US$0.30, or US$0.40 to the suburbs, paid with coins into a machine behind the driver. Check that your destination appears on the bus stop, and in the little card in the driver's window, since each number has several routes. Useful guides *Guía T* and *Lumi*, available at news stands and *kioskos*, give routes of all buses.

Subte (Metro) There are five lines, labelled 'A' to 'E' which run under major avenues – 4 of which link the outer parts of the city to the centre. The fifth line 'C' links Plaza Constitución with the Retiro railway station and provides connections with all the other lines. In the centre 3 stations, 9 de Julio (Line 'D'), Diagonal Norte (Line 'C') and Carlos Pellegrini (Line 'B') are linked by pedestrian tunnels. A single fare is US$ 0.25, payable in pesos only at the ticket booth, and trains run Monday to Saturday 0500-2250 and Sunday 0800-2200. Free maps are available from Metro stations and the tourist office.

Taxi Taxis are painted yellow and black, and carry "Taxi" flags, but for security they should never be hailed on the street. Taxis are the notorious weak link in the city's security, and you should always phone a *Radio Taxi*, since you're guaranteed that they're with a registered company; some 'Radio Taxis' you see on the street are false. Call one of these numbers; *Radio Taxi Sur*, T4638 2000, *Radio Taxi 5 Minutos*, T4523 1200, *Radio Taxi Diez*, T4585 5007, give your address and a taxi will pick you up in five minutes. You may need to give a name or phone number for reference, or describe what you're wearing. Fares are shown in pesos. The meter starts at US$0.35 when the flag goes down; make sure it isn't running when you get in. A fixed rate of US$0.04 for every 200m or one-minute wait is charged thereafter. A charge is sometimes made for each piece of hand baggage (ask first). Alternatively, *remise* taxis charge a fixed rate to anywhere in town, and are very reliable, though can work out more expensive for short journeys. *La Terminal*, T4312 0711 is recommended, particularly from Retiro bus station. *Remise* taxis operate all over the city; they are run from an office, have no meter but charge fixed prices, which can be cheaper than regular taxis. About 10% tip is expected. For more detailed Transport information, see page 95.

Orientation

The city of Buenos Aires is situated just inland from the docks on the south bank of the Río de la Plata. The formal centre is around the Plaza de Mayo, where the historical Cabildo faces the florid pink presidential palace **Casa Rosada**, from whose balcony presidents have appealed to their people, and people have come to protest. From here the broad Parisian-style boulevard of the **Avenida de Mayo** leads to the seat of government at the Congreso de la Nacion, lined with marvellous buildings from the city's own belle époque, including the *Café Tortoni* which was frequented by Borges. Halfway, it crosses the 22 lanes of roaring **Avenida 9 de Julio**, with its mighty central obelisk and the splendid Teatro Colón, which heads north to **Avenida del Libertador**, the main road leading out of the city to the north and west.

The main shopping streets are to be found north of Plaza de Mayo, and you can buy everything from chic leather bags to cheap CDs along the popular pedestrianized **Calle Florida**, which leads to the elegant and leafy Plaza San Martín. This central area is easy to walk around.

Metro (Subte)

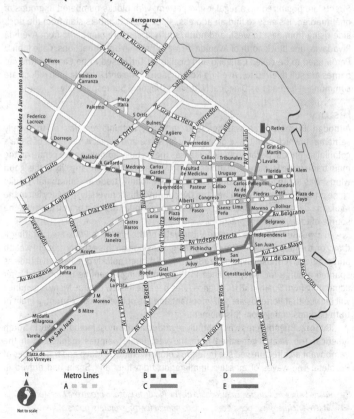

In **Recoleta** there are the smart apartments of wealthy Porteños, whose barrio boasts most of the city's finest museums, and the famous Recoleta Cemetery. In this miniature city of stone angels, you'll find Evita Perón buried in illustrious company, while just outside there's a busy craft market, and inumerable cafés and bars. From here, you could museum hop to the green parks of **Palermo**, with animals, planets and the trees of Argentina represented in the zoo, the planetarium, and the botanical garden. Nearby, **Palermo Viejo** has become *the* place to hang out, its old cobbled streets and genteel 1920s buildings buzzing with good restaurants and shops laden with style.

Buenos Aires makes the most of its waterfront with a successfully renovated docks area at **Puerto Madero**, where busy restaurants fill the handsome brick warehouses; a good place to stroll, past old sailing ships and painted cranes. Further south, the green spaces of the **Costanera Sur** are busy in summer with Porteños relaxing, groups of friends sipping *mate* or barbecuing steak. Here there's a Reserva Ecológica where you could retreat for some inner city wildlife, and walk or cycle for a couple of hours. Just inland, the city's most atmospheric barrio is irresistable **San Telmo**, once the city's centre, with narrow streets where cafés and antique markets are tucked away in the attractively crumbling 1900's buildings. Now the area is a lively and bohemian artistic centre with a popular market in the quaint Plaza Dorego on Sundays, where tango is danced for tourists, among the silver, plates and bric-a-brac. Nightlife is lively here, but the best restaurants can be found in Recoleta or the Las Caritas area of Palermo.

Street layout

Streets are organized on a regular grid pattern, with blocks numbered in groups of one hundred. It's easy to find an address, since street numbers start from the dock side rising from east to west, and north/south streets are numbered from Avenida Rivadavia, one block north of Avenida de Mayo rising in both directions. Calle Juan D Perón used to be called Cangallo and Scalabrini Ortiz used to be Canning (the old names are still referred to). Avenida Roque Sáenz Peña and Avenida Julio A Roca are commonly referred to as Diagonal Norte and Diagonal Sur respectively.

History

Although Buenos Aires was founded in 1580, nothing remains of this early settlement, which didn't take off as a city for some 200 years. It has none of Salta's colonial splendour because while Salta was then a busy administrative centre on the main trade route for silver and mules, Santa María del Buen Aire, the city of the 'good winds' was left to fester, her port used only for a roaring trade in contraband. Jesuits came and built schools, churches and the country's first university, a legacy left in the Manzana de las Luces, which you can still explore today and, according to some, the source of today's corrupt practices.

In 1776 Buenos Aires became Viceroyalty of the Río de la Plata area, putting it firmly on the map for trade. The city's strategic position on this estuary brought wealth and progress. A British invasion in 1806, which though quickly quelled, nevertheless sparked a surge for independence in the burgeoning Argentine nation, and after separating from Spain in 1816, Buenos Aires became its new capital. Many Argentines will tell you that Porteños are self important and the politicians are corrupt; a grain of truth perhaps dating from this moment.

By 1914, Buenos Aires was rightfully regarded as the most important city in South America. The wealth generated from the vast fertile pampas manifested in the flamboyant architecture you see in Teatro Colón, Avenida de Mayo and the palaces of Recoleta. The waves of massive immigration from Italy and Spain had arrived in

● *Buenos Aires was strategically located on the Río de la Plata, a broad brown estuary*
● *which is neither silver nor a river, but was named for the explorers' hopes of treasure.*

24 hours in the city

Start with a traditional Buenos Aires breakfast of strong coffee and *medialunas* at **Café Tortoni**, lapping up the atmosphere of leather chairs and art nouveau loved by poets and intellectuals. Then wander down Avenida de Mayo with its splendid buildings to **Plaza de Mayo** where you can admire the bright pink **Casa Rosada**, and pop into the **Cabildo** for a taste of history. Take a taxi to **MALBA**, the stunning new museum of Latin American art, and have tea at its chic café before strolling through the airy galleries of colourful paintings. From here take a taxi to **Palermo Viejo** for French, Vietnamese, Armenian or Italian food at any of a crop of great new restaurants. Choose *Azafran* perhaps, for its views of the leafy Plaza.

If it's a sunny day, take a stroll around the **botanical gardens** in Palermo's parks, and cool off with an ice cream at *Volta*, watching fashionable porteños wander by with their beautifully-dressed children. If you'd rather shop for stylish clothes instead (now that they're so cheap) jump into a taxi and head to **Patio Bullrich** or **Palermo Alto**. By now it's around five-ish, and time for tea. The Argentines call it *merienda* but it's a very English affair of sandwiches and fancy cakes at *Café Victoria* in **Recoleta**. While you're here, you'll want to see the colonial church **El Pilar**, and the cemetery next door, a maze of impressive mausoleums,

where Eva Perón is buried. Just outside, there's a huge **craft market**, selling cheap chic jewellery and handcarved *mate* pots, or you could pop into the **Buenos Aires Design Centre** for some traditional Argentine handicrafts.

By now you'll be ready to relax in your hotel for an hour, and get ready for the night out. Put on your dancing shoes! At nine-ish, take a taxi to **Las Cañitas** and choose a restaurant that appeals from a huge range along Calle Baez: *Campo Bravo* or *Baez*, or *Novecento*, for one of those legendary steaks. Hold back from eating too much though, because your **tango** class at the **milonga** starts at 2230. Head for *Confitería Ideal* or *La Virutia*, and let the experts take you in hand. Once you've mastered the basic steps, the band strikes up and you'll be swept off your feet. And if that's too daunting, sit back and watch the city's best dancers' breathtaking display at *El Viejo Almacén*'s superb show. By now you might be ready for bed, but if you've caught the infectious porteño rhythm, have a cosy cocktail at a **Palermo Viejo** bar, such as *Omm*, until the nightclubs open at 0200, perhaps *El Divino* or *El Living*. You won't emerge before dawn, when you can appreciate Buenos Aires' beautiful architecture in the crisp early light before staggering to *Clasico y Moderno* for a laid-back breakfast.

Buenos Aires first, creating the characteristic Argentine identity, and the language described most accurately as Spanish spoken by Italians. The tango was born, music filled with nostalgia for the places left behind, and currently enjoying a revival among 20-somethings, filling the *milongas* and breathing new passion into old steps. Now, nearly a third of the country's 36 million inhabitants live in Gran Buenos Aires, in the sprawling conurbation which stretches west from the smart areas of Palermo, San Isidro and Martinez, to the poorer Avellanda and La Matanza.

Sights

City centre

Plaza de Mayo

This broad open plaza is the historic heart of the city, surrounded by some of the major public buildings including the famous pink Casa de Gobierno or **Casa Rosada**, which lies on the east side, looking out towards the Río Plata,ⓘ *tours: Mon-Fri 1500, 1700, free (from Hipólito Yrigoyen 219; passport is required), T4344 3804, changing of the guards every 2 hours from 0700-1900.*

The decision to paint the seat of government pink resulted from President Sarmiento's desire to symbolize national unity by blending the colours of the rival factions which had fought each other for much of the 19th century: the Federalists (red) and the Unitarians (white). The colour itself was originally derived from a mixture of whitewash and cows' blood to render the surface impermeable. The Plaza has been the site of many historic events: from its balcony, Perón appeared before the masses gathered in the plaza, and when the economy crumbled in December 2001, angry crowds of *cacerolazas* (middle-class ladies banging their *cazerolas*, or saucepans) rioted outside, together with angry mobs. Since 1970, the Mothers of the Plaza de Mayo (*Madres de los Desaparecidos*) have marched in silent remembrance of their children who disappeared during the 'dirty war'. Every Thursday at 1530, they march anti-clockwise around the central monument with photos of their disappeared loved-ones pinned to their chests.

In the plaza, there are statues of General Belgrano in front of the Casa Rosada and of Columbus, behind the Casa Rosada in the Parque Colón. The guided tours of the Casa de Gobierno allow you to see its statuary and the rich furnishing of its halls and its libraries.

Opposite the Casa Rosada, on the west side of the plaza is the white-columned **Cabildo**, which has been rebuilt several times since the original structure was put up in the 18th century, most recently in 1940. Inside is the **Museo del Cabildo y la Revolución**. ⓘ *T4334 1782, Wed-Fri 1130-1800, Sat-Sun 1300-1800, US$0.30.* Paintings, documents, furniture, arms, medals and maps record the May 1810 revolution and the 1806 British attack. In the patio is a café and stalls which sell handicrafts on Thursdays and Fridays from 1100-1800.

The **Cathedral Metropolitana**, on the north side of the plaza, lies on the site of the first church in Buenos Aires, built in 1580.ⓘ *Masses Mon-Fri 0900, 1100, 1230, 1800, Sat 1100, 1800, Sun 1100, 1200, 1300, 1800, visiting hours Mon-Fri 0800-1900, Sat-Sun 0900-1930. For guided tours, T4331 2845.* The current structure was built in classical style between 1758 and 1807, and inside, in the right-hand aisle, is the imposing tomb of General José de San Martín (1880) Argentina's greatest hero who liberated the country from the Spanish, guarded by soldiers in fancy uniforms.

Just east of the cathedral, the **Banco de la Nación** is regarded as one of the great works of the famous architect Alejandro Bustillo (who designed the *Hotel Llao Llao* in Bariloche). Built between 1940 and 1955, its central hall is topped by a marble dome 50 m in diameter. ▸▸ *For Sleeping, Eating and other listings, see pages 83-102.*

La City

Just north of the Plaza de Mayo, between 25 de Mayo and the pedestrianized Calle Florida, lies the main banking district known as La City, with some handsome buildings to admire. The **Banco de Boston**, Florida 99 and Avenida R S Pena, dates from 1924, and while there are no guided visits, you can walk inside during banking hours to appreciate its lavish ceiling and marble interior. There's the marvellous art deco **Banco de la Provincia de Buenos Aires**, San Martín 137, built in 1940, and the **The Bolsa de Comercio**,

66 99 Buenos Aires looks like Paris, tastes like Italy, and moves with the pace of New York...

25 de Mayo y Sarmiento, which dates from 1916 and houses the stock exchange, though visits aren't permitted. The **Banco Hipotecario** (formerly the Bank of London and South America), Reconquista y B Mitre, was designed by SEPRA (Santiago Sánchez Elia, Federico Peralta Ramos, and Alfredo Agostini). It was completed in 1963, in bold 'brutalist' design. You can visit during banking hours.

The **Basílica Nuesta Señora de La Merced**, ① *J D Perón y Reconquista 207, weekdays 0800-1800, with a craft fair Thu and Fri 1100-1900*, founded in 1604 and rebuilt 1760-1769, was used as a command post in 1807 by Argentine troops resisting the British invasion. Its highly decorated interior has an altar with an 18th-century wooden figure of Christ, the work of indigenous carvers from Misiones, and it has one of the few fine carillons of bells in Buenos Aires. Next door, at Reconquista 269, is the **Convento de la Merced** originally built in 1601, but reconstructed in the 18th and 19th centuries with a peaceful courtyard in its cloisters.

There are a few museums here for historians: **Museo Numismático Dr José Evaristo Uriburu** , in the Banco Central library, tells the history of the country through its currency. The **Museo y Biblioteca Mitre**, ① *San Martín 336, T4394 8240, Mon-Fri 1300-1830, US$0.30*, preserves intact the colonial-style home of President Bartolomé Mitre. More accessible is the bizarre **Museo de la Policía Federal**, ① *San Martín 353, piso 8 y 9, T4394 6857, Tue-Fri 1400-1800*, which portrays the fascinating history of crime in the city, and includes an absolutely gruesome forensic section, definitely not for the squeamish. ▶ *For Sleeping, Eating and other listings, see pages 83-102.*

South of Plaza de Mayo

To the south west of the Plaza de Mayo is an entire block of buildings built by the Jesuits between 1622 and 1767, called the **Manzana de las Luces** (Enlightenment Square) – bounded by streets Moreno, Alsina, Perú and Bolívar. The former Jesuit church of **San Ignacio de Loyola**, ① *guided tours Sat and Sun 1700 but open at other hours*, begun in 1664, is the oldest colonial building in Buenos Aires and the best example of the baroque architecture introduced by the Jesuits (renovated in the 18th and 19th centuries), with splendid golden naves dating from 1710-1734. Also in this block are the **Colegio Nacional de Buenos Aires**, ① *Bolívar 263, guided tours Mon-Fri 1000 and 1400, T4331 0734 phone to book in advance*, formerly the Jesuits' Colegio Máximo in the 18th century, and now the city's most prestigious secondary school. Below these buildings are **18th-century tunnels**, ① *guided tours, from Perú 272, with a glimpse of the tunnels. Mon-Fri 1500, Sat and Sun 1500, 1630, 1800, (Mon 1300 free tour from Alsina y Perú;) in Spanish (in English by prior arrangement), arrive 15 mins before tour, US$1.30, T4342 4655/9930*. These are thought to have been used by the Jesuits for escape or for smuggling contraband from the port. For centuries the whole block was the centre of intellectual activity, and although little remains to see today, the history is fascinating.

Museo de la Ciudad, ① *Alsina 412, Mon-Fri, 1100-1900, Sun, 1500-1900, US$ 0.30, free on Wed, T4343 2123*, is worth visiting for an insight into 19th-century Buenos Aires life, a historical house including a 1900s chemist's shop Farmacia La Estrella, and has a permanent exhibition covering social history and popular culture, with special exhibitions on daily life in Buenos Aires. The **church of San Francisco**, ① *Alsina y Defensa, Mon-Fri 0700-1300, 1500-1900, guided visits Tue 1530 and 1630, Sat 1630 and 1730*, was built by the Franciscan Order 1730-1754 and given a new façade in 1911 in German baroque style. There's a fine baroque pulpit and the chapel of San Roque.

To Palermo Parks & Aeroparque

To Recoleta

Related maps
A Recoleta, page 74
B San Telmo, page 80

Av del Libertador

Basavilbaso

Quintana

Guido

Juncal

Arroyo

Palacio
San Martín

Gral
San Martín

Montevideo

Arenales

British
Airways Iberia

Manuel Tienda
León Office

General San Martín

Av Callao

Av Santa Fe

MT de Alvear

Plaza
Libertad

Esmeralda

Maipú

Paraguay

Pizzurno

Callao

Av Córdoba

Cerrito

Viamonte

Dellepiane

Paraná

Uruguay

Talcahuano

Libertad

Plaza
Lavalle

Teatro
Colón

Tucumán

Tribunales

Lavalle

To La Chacarita Cemetery

Rodríguez Peña

Montevideo

Uruguay

Av Corrientes

Plaza de la
República &
Obelisco

Carlos
Pellegrini

Av Corrientes

Callao

Sarmiento

9 de Julio

Diagonal
Norte

Carabelas

Av R S Peña

Juan D Perón

Bartolomé Mitre

Rivadavia

Av de
Mayo

Palacio
Vera

Congreso

Plaza del
Congreso

Saenz
Peña

Lima

Piedras

Edificio
Drabble

Palacio del
Congreso

H Yrigoyen

Av de Mayo

Piedras

Alsina

Av de Julio

Moreno

Av Entre Ríos

Solís

Virrey Ceballos

L Saenz Peña

San José

Santiago del Estero

Moreno

Bernado de Irigoyen

Belgrano

Roca

Chacabuco

Venezuela

México

Tacuarí

Chile

Salta

Independencia

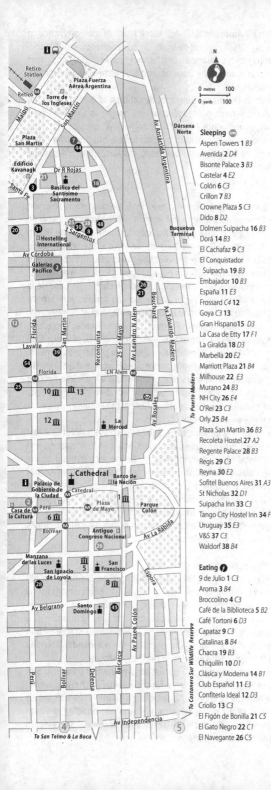

Sleeping 🛏
Aspen Towers **1** *B3*
Avenida **2** *D4*
Bisonte Palace **3** *B3*
Castelar **4** *E2*
Colón **6** *C3*
Crillon **7** *B3*
Crowne Plaza **5** *C3*
Dido **8** *D2*
Dolmen Suipacha **16** *B3*
Dorá **14** *B3*
El Cachafaz **9** *C3*
El Conquistador
  Suipacha **19** *B3*
Embajador **10** *B3*
España **11** *E3*
Frossard *C4* **12**
Goya *C3* **13**
Gran Hispano **15** *D3*
La Casa de Etty **17** *F1*
La Giralda **18** *D3*
Marbella **20** *E2*
Marriott Plaza **21** *B4*
Milhouse **22** *E3*
Murano **24** *B3*
NH City **26** *E4*
O'Rei **23** *C3*
Orly **25** *B4*
Plaza San Martín **36** *B3*
Recoleta Hostel **27** *A2*
Regente Palace **28** *B3*
Regis **29** *C3*
Reyna **30** *E2*
Sofitel Buenos Aires **31** *A3*
St Nicholas **32** *D1*
Suipacha Inn **33** *C3*
Tango City Hostel Inn **34** *F3*
Uruguay **35** *E3*
V&S **37** *C3*
Waldorf **38** *B4*

Eating 🍴
9 de Julio **1** *C3*
Aroma **3** *B4*
Broccolino **4** *C3*
Café de la Biblioteca **5** *B2*
Café Tortoni **6** *D3*
Capataz **9** *C3*
Catalinas **8** *B4*
Chacra **19** *B3*
Chiquilín **10** *D1*
Clásica y Moderna **14** *B1*
Club Español **11** *E3*
Confitería Ideal **12** *D3*
Criollo **13** *C3*
El Figón de Bonilla **21** *C5*
El Gato Negro **22** *C1*
El Navegante **26** *C5*

El Palacio de la Papa
  Frita **27** *C3/D1*
El Querandí **28** *E4*
Empire **30** *B4*
Exedra **15** *B3*
Florida Garden **31** *B4*
Fratello **16** *C3*
Gran Victoria **17** *C3*
Güerrín **33** *D2*
La Casona del
  Nonno **35** *C3*
La Estancia **36** *C3*
La Pipeta **39** *C4*
Las Nazarenas **44** *A4*
La Taska **20** *B4*
La Ventana **45** *E4*
Los Inmortales **46** *C2/C3*
Madeleine Express **23** *B3*
Morizono **48** *B4*
Natura **24** *D2*
Richmond **54** *C4*
Sorrento Corrientes **25** *C4*
Tomo Uno **57** *C3*

Bars & clubs 🎵
Alexandra **2** *B4*
Druid Inn **7** *A4*
Kilkenny **18** *B4*

Museums 🏛
Casa de Gobierno
  (Casa Rosada) &
  Museo de los
  Presidentes **1** *D5*
Museo de Armas **2** *B3*
Museo de Arte
  Hispanoamericano
  Isaac Fernández
  Blanco **3** *A3*
Museo de Arte
  Moderno & Teatro
  General San
  Martín **4** *D1*
Museo de la
  Ciudad **5** *E4*
Museo del Cabildo
  y la Revolución
  de Mayo **6** *E4*
Museo del Teatro
  Nacional Cervantes **7** *B2*
Museo Etnográfico
  JB Ambrosetti **8** *E4*
Museo Judío **9** *C2*
Museo y Biblioteca
  Mitre **10** *D4*
Museo Nacional
  Ferroviario at Retiro
  Station **11** *A3*
Museo Numismático Dr
  José Evaristo
  Uriburu **12** *D4*
Museo de la Policía
  Federal **13** *D4*

The **Museo Etnográfico J B Ambrosetti**,ⓘ *one block south of the San Francisco church at Moreno 350, T4345 8196, daily 1400-1900 (in summer 1600-2000), US$ 0.30, T4345 8196,* contains anthropological and ethnographic collections from Argentina and around the world, including Bolivian and Mapuche silverwork, in an attractive building dating form 1880.

One block further south at Defensa y Belgrano, the **church of Santo Domingo**, ⓘ *Mon-Fri 0900-1300, Sun 1000-1200, guided visits on Thu 0900-1500,* was founded in 1751. During the British attack on Buenos Aires in 1806 some of Whitelocke's soldiers took refuge in the church and it was bombarded by local forces; but the bullet holes seen on the left hand tower are fake. General Belgrano, a major figure in Argentine independence, is buried here.

Avenida de Mayo

From the Plaza de Mayo, take a stroll down this broad leafy avenue which links the Presidential Palace to the Congress building to the west. It was constructed between 1889 and 1894, inspired by the grand design of Paris, and filled with elaborate French Baroque and art nouveau buildings. At Perú and Avenida de Mayo is the **subte station Perú**, furnished by the Museo de la Ciudad to resemble its original state, with posters and furniture of the time. You'll need to buy a US$0.25 ticket to have a look, or take a train.

Along the avenue west from here, you'll see the splendid French-style **Casa de la Cultura** at number 575, home of the newspaper *La Prensa* and topped with bronze statues. At number 702 is the fine Parisian-style **Edificio Drabble**, and at number 769, the elegant **Palacio Vera**, from 1910. Argentina's most celebrated writer, Jorge Luis Borges, was fond of the many cafés which once filled Avenida de Mayo, of which **Café Tortoni**, at no 825, is the most famous in Buenos Aires, the haunt of illustrious writers, artists and poets since 1858. Its high ceilings with ornate plaster work and art nouveau stained glass, tall columns and elegant mirrors plunge you straight back into another era. It's an atmospheric place for coffee, but particularly wonderful for the poetry recitals, tango and live music, which are still performed here in the evenings. There are also plenty of places for a quick lunch, and lots of hotels.

Continuing west over Avenida 9 de Julio, there's the superb 1928 **Hotel Castelar** at number 1152, still open (see Sleeping page 83), and retaining its former glory, and the beautiful art nouveau **Hotel Chile** at number 1297. At the western end of the avenue, is the astounding **Palacio Barola**, at number 1370,ⓘ *Mon-Fri 0700-2200, Sat 0700-1200,* built by a textile magnate in 1923, and taking its inspiration from the Italian poet Dante. Avenida de Mayo culminates in the Plaza del Congreso, with the **congress building**,ⓘ *guided visits can be arranged by calling T4953 3081, ext 3885, Mon, Tue Thu, Fri 1100, 1700, 1900,* in Italian academic style, housing the country's government. ▶▶ *For Sleeping, Eating and other listings, see pages 83-102.*

Plaza San Martín and around

Ten blocks north of the Plaza de Mayo is the splendid Plaza San Martín, on a hill originally marking the northern limit of the city. It has since been designed by Argentina's famous landscape architect Charles Thays, and is filled with luxuriant mature palms and plane trees, and popular with runners in the early morning and office workers at lunchtimes. At the western corner is an equestrian **statue of San Martín**, 1862, and at the northern end of the plaza is the **Falklands/Malvinas memorial** with an eternal flame to those who fell in the War, 1982.

Around the plaza are several elegant mansions, among them the **Palacio San Martín**, designed in 1909 in French academic style for the wealthy Anchorena family, and now occupied by the Ministry of Foreign Affairs. Most striking is the elegant art deco **Edificio Kavanagh**, east of the plaza, which was the tallest building in South America when completed in 1936. Behind it is the **Basilica del Santísimo Sacramento** (1916), the church favoured by wealthy porteños.

The **Plaza de la Fuerza Aérea**, northeast of Plaza San Martín was until 1982 called the Plaza Británica; in the centre is a clock tower presented by British and Anglo-Argentine residents in 1916, still known as the Torre de los Ingleses.

Three blocks northwest of Plaza San Martín is one of the city's most delightful museums, the **Museo de Arte Hispanoamericano Isaac Fernández Blanco**, ⓘ *Suipacha 1422, Tue-Sun, 1400-1900, US$0.30; Thu free, closed Jan. For guided visits in English or French T4327 0228; guided tours in Spanish Sat, Sun 1600*. Housed in a beautiful 1920s neo-colonial mansion with tiled Spanish-style gardens, it contains a fascinating collection of colonial art, with fine Cuzqueno school paintings, and dazzling ornate silverware from Alto Peru and Río de la Plata. There are also temporary exhibitions of Latin American art. Highly recommended.

The road linking Retiro with Plaza San Martín is filled with market stalls, and a notorious place for petty crime: be alert, don't carry valuables.

North of Plaza San Martín is **Retiro railway station**, really three separate termini. The oldest and finest is the westernmost of these, the Mitre, dating from 1908, a classical construction with a crumbling but atmospheric interior, and a *confitería*. Behind the station is the **Museo Nacional Ferroviario**, ⓘ *accessed from Avenida del Libertador 405, Mon-Fri 1000-1600*, for railway fans. It contains locomotives, machinery and documents on the history of Argentine railways.

Avenida 9 de Julio is one of the world's widest thoroughfares, with eleven lanes of traffic in each direction, leading south to Plaza de la Constitución and routes south of the city. It's crossed by the major streets of Avenida de Mayo and Córdoba, and at the junction with Corrientes is the city's famous landmark, a 67m-tall **obelisk** commemorating the 400th anniversary of the city's founding, where football fans traditionally congregate in crowds to celebrate a victory. From Plaza San Martín, the city's main shopping street, Avenida Santa Fe crosses Av 9 de Julio, and heads through Retiro and Recoleta to Palermo, with most well known shops to be found betweenTalcahuano and Av Pueyrredon.

Just a block north of the obelisk on 9 de Julio is **Teatro Colón**, ⓘ *A guided tour is highly recommended; tickets from the entrance at Toscanini 1168 (on C Viamonte side) or from Tucumán 1171, Mon-Sat 1100, 1200, 1300, 1430, 1500, 1600, Sun 1100, 1300, 1500; (Jan-Feb: Tue-Sat hourly 1000-1700, Sun hourly 1100-1500), in Spanish, French (on request) and English, T4378 7132/33, visitas@teatrocolon.org.ar, US$3 (children or ISIC card US$1.50). Opera and ballet tickets sold two days before performance, from the Calle Tucumán side of the theatre, ticket office open Tue-Sat 1000-2000, Sun 1000-1700. Good opera tickets are around US$35, with the cheapest seat at US$1.30 (available even on the same day) and 'El Paraíso' tickets are available for standing room in The Gods – queue for a good spot*. One of the world's greatest opera houses, opened in 1908, and an extraordinary testimony to the country's former wealth. Behind the classical façade, the foyer is decorated with three kinds of marble brought from Europe, a Parisian stained glass dome in the roof, and Venetian tiled mosaic floor. The auditorium is French Baroque style, perfectly preserved, from the handelier in the ceiling (where singers or musicians can be hidden to produce music from the heavens) to the French gilded lights and red velvet curtains. It has an almost perfect acoustic, due to the horseshoe shape and the mix of marble and soft fabrics, and an immense stage 35m deep. Workshops and rehearsal spaces lie underneath the Avenida 9 de Julio itself, and there are stores of costumes, including 22,000 pairs of shoes. The theatre is home to three orchestras, as well as the city's ballet and opera companies; world class performances can be seen in their season from April to early December.

Four blocks west of Plaza de la República, **Centro Cultural San Martín**, ⓘ *Avenida Corrientes 1530, Museum entrance US$0.30, Wed free, www.CCGSH.gov.ar www.tangodata.com.ar* is an austere 70s concrete building which houses good photography exhibitions, the Teatro Municipal San Martín and a salon of the Museo Municipal de Arte Moderno. There's also a tango information desk at the entrance. ➠ *For Sleeping, Eating and other listings, see pages 83-102.*

North of the centre

Recoleta

The areas of Recoleta and Retiro are known as Barrio Norte, the chic places to live in the centre of the capital. Situated north of Plaza San Martín, beyond Avenida 9 de Julio, Recoleta became a fashionable residential area when wealthy families started to move here from the crowded city centre after the yellow fever outbreak of 1871. Many of its French-style mansions date from the turn of the 20th century, and there are smart apartment blocks with marble entrances, making for a pleasant stroll around its streets filled with cafés, art galleries and museums. At its heart is the **Plaza de la Recoleta**, and running down its southeastern side is Calle Ortiz, lined with *confiterías* ranging from the refined and traditional to touristy eateries, most with tables outside. Overhead are the branches of the **gran gomero**, a rubber tree, whose limbs are supported on crutches. At weekends, the **Plaza Francia** is filled with an art and craft market from 1100 until 1800, when the whole place is lively, with street artists and performers.

Recoleta is famous for its cemetery, where Eva Perón is buried, among other illustrious figures from Argentina's history. **Cementerio de la Recoleta**, ⓘ *0700-1745, tours on the last Sun of month (not in summer), 1430, T4803 1594, also tour guide Luz La Rocca T4799 5103, a 45-min tour for US$2*, is like a miniature city, narrow streets weaving between imposing family mausoleums built in every imaginable achitectural style, a vast congregation of stone angels on their roofs. To negotiate this enormous labyrinth, a guided tour is recommended, but at the very least, you'll want to see Evita Perón's tomb, lying in the Duarte family mausoleum. To find it from the entrance, walk straight ahead to the first tree-filled plaza; turn left, and where this avenue meets a main avenue (go just beyond the Turriata tomb), turn right and then take the third passage on the left.

Recoleta

Related maps
A Buenos Aires centre, page 70
B Palermo, page 77

Sleeping	Eating	Bars & clubs	La Madelaine 11
Alvear Palace 1	El Mirasol 1	Buller Brewing	Lola 12
Etoile 2	Ice Cream Freddo 5	Company 6	Rodi Bar 13
Four Seasons 3	Las Nazarenas 3	Café Victoria 7	Sirop 14
Milonga Hostel 4	La Tasca de Plaza	El Sanjaunino 8	
Recoleta Hostel 5	Mayor 2	Grants 9	
	Winery 4	Juana M 10	

The former Jesuit church of **El Pilar**, next to the cemetery, is a jewel of colonial architecture dating from 1732, restored in 1930. There are stunning 18th-century gold alterpieces made in Alto Peru, and a fine wooden image of San Pedro de Alcántara, attributed to the famous 17th-century Spanish sculptor Alonso Cano, preserved in a side chapel on the left. Downstairs is an interesting small museum of religious art, from whose windows you have a broad view of the cemetery next door.

The **Centro Cultural Recoleta**, *Tue-Fri 1400-2100, Sat, Sun, holidays 1000-2100, T4803 0358*, alongside the Recoleta cemetery, occupying the cloisters of a former monastery, has constantly-changing exhibitions of contemporary local art by young artists. A passage leads from this centre to the **Buenos Aires Design Centre**, where you can buy stylish contemporary designs for the home and well made handicrafts from all over Argentina. There are also lots of good restaurants here, some with views over the nearby plazas from their open terraces, recommended for an evening drink at sunset. In **Plaza San Martín de Tours** next door, there are more huge gomera trees with their extraordinary sinuous roots, and here you're likely to spot one of Buenos Aires' legendary dog walkers, managing an unfeasible 20 or so dogs without tangling their leads! There's a tourist information booth at Ayacuco 1958, T4804 5667. **Village Recoleta**, on Vicente López y Junín, T4805 2220, houses a multiplex cinema, with bookshops and cafés at its entrance.

For a taste of superb Argentine art, the **Museo de Bellas Artes**, is highly recommended. ⓘ *Avenida del Libertador 1473, just north of La Recoleta cemetery, T4801 3390, www.mnba.org.ar Film shows on Fri 1830; classical music concerts on Sun 1730. Tue-Fri 1230-1930, Sat-Sun 0930-1930. Guided tours Tue-Sun 1700 for Argentine art, 1800 for European art, tours for children Sat 1500, free, T4801 3390. Tue-Sun, 1400-1900, US$0.30; Thu free, closed Jan. For guided visits in English or French T43270228; guided tours in Spanish Sat, Sun 1600.* There is a varied collection of Argentine 19th- and 20th-century paintings, sculpture and wooden carvings, in addition to some fine examples of European works, particularly post-Impressionist paintings and Rodin sculptures. ▸▸ *For Sleeping, Eating and other listings, see pages 83-102.*

North of Recoleta

The wide and fast avenue **Avenida del Libertador** runs north from Recoleta towards Palermo past further parks and squares as well as several major museums.

The **Biblioteca Nacional**, or National Library, ⓘ *Avenida del Libertador 1600 y Agüero 2502, T4806 6155, www.bibnal.edu.ar, Mon-Fri 0900-2100, Sat and Sun 1200-1900, closed Jan, excellent guided tours (Spanish) daily 1600 from main entrance, for tours in other languages contact in advance*, is a huge cube standing on four sturdy legs in an attractive garden with a bust of Eva Perón. Only a fraction of its stock of about 1.8 million volumes and 10,000 manuscripts is available, and it's worth a look to enjoy some of its frequent exhibitions and recitals.

The **Museo Nacional de Arte Decorativo**, ⓘ *Avenida del Libertador 1902, daily 1400-1900, T4802 6606, US$0.60, half-price to ISIC holders. Guided visits Wed, Thu, Fri 1630*, contains collections of painting, furniture, porcelain, crystal, sculpture. It also hosts classical music concerts on Wednesdays and Thursdays. In the same building, but temporarily closed, is the **Museo Nacional de Arte Oriental**, containing a permanent exhibition of Chinese, Japanese, Hindu and Islamic art.

The **Museo de Motivos Populares Argentinos José Hernández**, ⓘ *Avenida Libertador 2373, T4802 7294, www.malba.org.ar for current exhibitions, www.malbacine.org for cinema screenings, Wed-Sun 1300-1900, US$0.30, free Sun, closed in Feb*, is named after the writer of Argentina's famous epic poem *Martín Fierro*, and contains one of the most complete collections of folkloric art in the country. There are plenty of gaucho artefacts: ornate silver *mates*, wonderful plaited leather *talebartería* and decorated silver stirrups, together with pre-Hispanic artefacts, and paintings from the Cusco school. There is also a handicrafts shop and library.

⦙ Tango

Argentina's tango revival continues amongst 20- and 30-somethings, flocking to classes and filling the city's trendy *milongas* – lively informal dance venues where anyone can dance tango or *milonga*, (a more upbeat style of music with less formal dance steps).

Tango shows may be tourist-oriented but the dancing is superb: **El Viejo Almacén** has the city's finest, Balcarce and Independencia, T4307 7388, www.vie joalmacen.com Also recommended: **Esquina Carlos Gardel**, Carlos Gardel 3200, T4867 6363, and **La Ventana**, Balcarce 431, T4331 8689, US$45 for dinner and a 2 hour show. There are demonstrations at **Café Tortoni**, Av de Mayo 829, T4342 4328, and free shows at San Telmo's Sunday market in Plaza Dorrego.

Tango classes at *Milongas* start at around 2000, followed by dancing from 2200 onwards, sometimes with a live orchestra. Even with a few basic steps, it's a pleasure being whisked around the floor. Try the **Confitería Ideal**, Suipacha 384, T1550064102, or the fashionable **LaViruta** in Palermo Viejo, Armenia 1366, T4774 6357; also **Porteño y Bailarín**, Riobamba 345, T4372 6080. English is spoken in many places, and at **Centro Cultural Torquato Tasso**, Defensa 1575, T4307 6506. There's free dancing downstairs at **Galerías Pacíficos** every Friday evening.

Buenos Aires' fabulous tango week is in early March, with free classes and lots of performances. Visit the tango information desk in the cultural centre at Sarmiento 1551, T4373 2823, www.tangodata .com.ar Free guided tours themed around tango singer Carlos Gardel are offered weekly by the city tourist office, T4373 2823. Tour operators *Tangol*, Florida 971, www.tangol.com organize accommodation, tango outings and classes, and tango guide Ani Acorta will introduce you to the circuit, T4326 4908, tangoingto @hotmail.com

For all tango related information, www.elfueyetango.com.ar

· The museum not to be missed is the **Museo de Arte Latinoamericano (MALBA)**, ⓘ *Av Figueroa Alcorta 3415, daily 1200-2000 (Wed free till 2100; Tue closed), US$1.30 (free for ISIC holders, cinema tickets US$1.30, book in advance, T4808 6500*, opened in 2001 to house a permanent collection of Latin American art, and temporary exhibitions. The minimalist building may strike you as rather stark, but the works inside are full of passion – powerful, humorous and moving pieces, very accessible and highly recommended. There's also an elegant café serving delicious food and cakes, and a cinema showing well-chosen art house films as well as Argentine classics.

Palermo

Northwest of Recoleta is the attractive sprawling barrio of Palermo, named after Giovanni Domenico Palermo who transformed these lands into productive orchards and vineyards in the 17th century. De Rosas built a sumptuous mansion, **La Quinta**, here in the early 19th century, and it has a series of great parks which were established by Sarmiento and designed by Charles Thays in the early 20th century. It remains a sought-after residential area for middle-class Porteños, and the wondeful parks are the most popular inner-city green space at weekends.

Of this series of parks, the **Parque Tres de Febrero**, ⓘ *Winter: Mon-Fri 0800-1800, Sat/Sun 0800-2000; Summer 0800-2000 daily*, is the largest, with lakes, tennis courts and a rose garden. Also in the park is the **Museo de Arte Moderno Eduardo Sivori**, ⓘ *Tue-Fri 1200-2000 (winter 1800), US$0.70, Sat and Sun 1000-2000 (winter 1800), US$0.30, Wed free, T4774 9452*, where you can immerse yourself in a fine collection of

Argentine art, with 19th- and 20th-century paintings, engravings, tapestries and sculptures. South of here is the beautifully harmonious **Japanese garden**, ① *1000-1800, US$0.70, T4804 4922, guided visits Sat 1500, 1600,* with koi carp to feed, and little bridges over ornate streams, a charming place to walk, and delightful for children. There's also a good café with Japanese dishes available among the usual menu. To the east of both of these is the **Planetarium**, ① *museum open Mon-Fri 1000-1500, free. Planetarium shows Sat and Sun at 1500, 1630, 1800, US$1.30,* with

Palermo

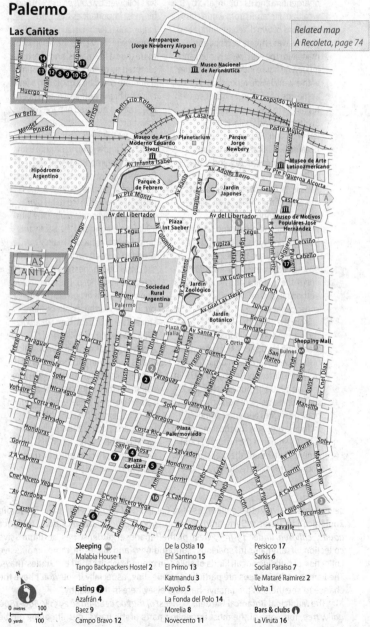

Las Cañitas

Related map
A Recoleta, page 74

Sleeping 🛏	De la Ostia 10	Persicco 17
Malabia House 1	Eh! Santino 15	Sarkis 6
Tango Backpackers Hostel 2	El Primo 13	Social Paraíso 7
	Katmandu 3	Te Mataré Ramirez 2
Eating 🍴	Kayoko 5	Volta 1
Azafrán 4	La Fonda del Polo 14	
Baez 9	Morelia 8	Bars & clubs 🍸
Campo Bravo 12	Novecento 11	La Víruta 16

0 metres 100
0 yards 100

⁝ Jorge Luis Borges 1899-1986

More than any writer, it is Borges who has drawn most vividly the city of Buenos Aires. Born in the city, he was obsessed with the myths and realities of Argentina and its culture,and by the wealth of literature from world classics. His blend of two different worlds and sources was entirely original, and made him the most widely cited and influential figure in Argentine culture with a world-wide reputation. In 1914, at the age of 15, Borges travelled with his family to Europe, where he lived in Switzerland and Spain. Here he learned Latin, French and German, became acquainted with various modernist movements, and started to write. When he returned to Buenos Aires in 1921, he became an active member of the literary avant garde. Borges contributed to small magazines, and publishing seven books of poetry and essays. This early works established his lifelong obsessions, a view of life from '*las orillas*' the margins, and an appraisal of authorship and individual consciousness.

From the 1930's he worked as a librarian and literary journalist, producing his first book of short stories, *Historia Universal de la Infamia* (A Universal History of Infamy) in 1935. In the late 1930's he published in quick succession a series of significant essays, book prologues and short stories, including arguably the most important series of stories in the history of Latin American literature, the great *Ficciones* (Fictions, 1944). Here, Borges overturned conventions of literary nationalism and realism, exploring the nature of literature itself, together with philosophy and metaphysics. *Ficciones* was followed by *El Aleph* in 1949 and his most important essays, *Otras Inquisiciones* (Other Inquisitions, 1952). A masterful story teller, he never wrote more than a few pages, and was never tempted by the novel form, insisting that more could be explored in a few elliptical highly suggestive and poetic lines than in hundred of pages of dull realist prose.

The late forties brought almost total blindness and a running dispute with the Perón regime; Borges considered Perón's populist nationalism the worst aspect of Argentine identity. Borges' opposition to Perón led to his own work being overlooked until the late 1960's, in Europe and the US. By this time, Borges' work was mainly confined to poetry, a form, which with the onset of blindness, he could compose in his head. The world-wide popularity of his fiction led him to publish two further books of short stories later in life, *El Informe de Brodie* (Dr Brodie's Report, 1970), and *El Libro de Arena* (The Book of Sand, 1975), which makes a good introduction to his work. Borges claimed that these stories were realist, but they're just as ironic and subversive as his earlier work. In his final years, he kept up the publishing of essays, and poems, and travelled the world with his companion María Kodama, whom he married. He died in Geneva in June 1986.

several impressively large meteorites from Campo del Cielo at its entrance. The **Jardín Zoológico Las Heras y Sarmiento**, ① *1000-1900, guided visits available, US$2 for adults, children under 13 free*, west of the Japanese gardens, has an impressive collection of animals, in spacious surroundings, and an even more impressive collection of buildings of all kinds of styles, in grounds landscaped by Charles Thays. The llamas and guanacos are particularly appealing, especially if you won't have the chance to see them in their native habitats elsewhere in the country.

The **Municipal Botanical Gardens**, ① *west of the zoo at Santa Fe 2951, 0800-1800 daily, free*, form one of the most appealing parts of the parks, despite being a little unkempt. Thays designed the gardens in 1902, and its different areas represent various regions of Argentina with characteristic specimens; particularly interesting are the trees native to the different provinces.

North of the zoo are the showgrounds of the **Sociedad Rural Argentina**, ① *entrance is from Plaza Italia (take Subte, line D)*, where the Annual Livestock Exhibition, known as Exposición Rural, is staged in July, providing interesting insights into Argentine society.

Further north is the 45,000 seater Palermo race track, **Hipódromo Argentino**, ① *races 10 day per month, US$ 0.30-3, T4777 9001*, well worth a visit even for non-racegoers. Nearby are the **Municipal Golf Club**, **Buenos Aires Lawn Tennis Club**, **riding clubs** and **polo field**, and the **Club de Gimnasia y Esgrima** (Athletic and Fencing Club). The parks are bordered to the north by Aeroparque (Jorge Newbery Airport), the city's domestic airport.

Palermo Viejo

The oldest and most atmospheric part of Palermo can be found in the area between the avenidas Córdoba and Santa Fe, south of Juan B Justo and north of Av Scalabrini Ortiz. It's a very seductive place, with cobbled streets of tall bohemian houses bedecked with flowers and plants, and leafy plazas and gardens. It's become a very fashionable place to live, and many bars, cafés and chic boutiques have opened up along Calle Honduras, making it a relaxing area for an afternoon stroll. The focus is **Plaza Serrano**, recently renamed Plaza Cortázar, after the Argentine writer, whose novel *Rayuela* (Hopscotch) is set around here. This is a great place for meeting in the evenings, with trendy bars and eclectic restaurants, also around **Plaza Palermo Viejo** with a children's playground in the middle. ▸▸ *For Sleeping, Eating and other listings, see pages 83-102.*

South of the centre

San Telmo

The city's most atmospheric barrio is also its oldest. San Telmo starts south of the Plaza de Mayo, and is built along the slope which marks the old beach of the Río de la Plata. Formerly one of the wealthiest areas of the city, it was abandoned by the rich during the great outbreak of yellow fever in 1871, and so was never modernised or destroyed for rebuilding. It's one of the few areas where buildings remain from the mid-19th century, crumbling and largely unchanged. San Telmo is a delightful place to stroll and explore artists' studios and small museums hidden away in its narrow streets, with plenty of cafés and shops selling antiques, records, handmade shoes, second-hand books, and crafts of all kinds.

A quiet place to meander during the week, the barrio comes alive on Sundays when there's an antiques and bric-a-brac market held in the central **Plaza Dorrego**, a small square enclosed by charming old houses. This is a good place to start meandering, after enjoying the free tango demonstrations which take place in the plaza on Sundays 1000-1800. Behind the plaza, on Carlos Calvo, there's a wonderful indoor market – **Mercado de San Telmo** built in 1897, whose elaborate wrought-iron structure you'll have to appreciate from the outside, since it's closed. Walk south along Calle Defensa, filled with street musicians on Sundays, many of them excellent, and pop into the artists' studios, antique shops and cafés which line the street. Just a block from the plaza is the white stuccoed church of **San Pedro González Telmo**, ① *Humerto 1, T4361 1168, guided tours Sun at 1500, 1600, free.* Begun by the Jesuits in 1734, but only finished in 1931, it's a wonderful confection of styles with ornate baroque columns and Spanish-style tiles.

One block further south, in an old tobacco warehouse, the **Museo de Arte Moderno de Buenos Aires**, ① *San Juan 350, Tue-Fri 1000-2000, Sat, Sun and*

📍 *If visiting San Telmo alone at night, it's best to take a Radio Taxi, such as Radio Taxi Sur T4638 2000.*

holidays 1100-2000. Guided tours Tue-Sun 1700, US$0.30, Wed free, T4361 1121, houses good visiting exhibitions of contemporary international and Argentine art. There is also a small fine art bookshop.

At the end of Defensa, is the **Parque Lezama**, ① *Defensa y Brasil, Sat and Sun 1000-2000,* originally one of the most beautiful parks in the city, but now a little run down, and not recommended for a picnic, though at the weekends there is a craft fair. According to tradition, Pedro de Mendoza founded the city on this spot in 1535, and there's an imposing statue to him in the centre of the park. This is not a safe place to wander at night. On the west side of the park is the **Museo Historico Nacional,** ① *Defensa 1600, T4307 1182, Tue-Sun 1300-1800, US$0.30, guided tours Sat and Sun 1530, T4307 1182,* which presents the history of the city and of Argentina through the key historical figures and events, with some impressive artefacts, portraits and war paintings, particularly of San Martín. Sadly, there's currently little information available in English.

There is an ever-growing number of restaurants along Defensa, many of them cheap and lively places to eat, and several venues offering tango shows. The best is the historical **El Viejo Almacén,** ① *reservations T4307 7388, www.viejoalmacen.com, US$45 for dinner and a 2-hour show,* at Balcarce y Independencia, started by celebrated tango singer Edmundo Riviero in the late 1960's. Here the city's finest tango dancers demonstrate their extraordinary skills in a small atmospheric theatre, with excellent live music and singing from some the great names of tango. Highly recommended. ▸▸ *For Sleeping, Eating and other listings, see pages 83-102.*

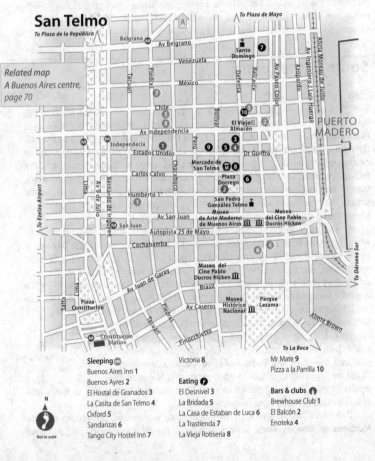

San Telmo

Related map
A Buenos Aires centre,
page 70

Not to scale

Sleeping
Buenos Aires Inn 1
Buenos Ayres 2
El Hostal de Granados 3
La Casita de San Telmo 4
Oxford 5
Sandanzas 6
Tango City Hostel Inn 7

Victoria 8

Eating
El Desnivel 3
La Bridada 5
La Casa de Esteban de Luca 6
La Trastienda 7
La Vieja Rotiseria 8

Mr Mate 9
Pizza a la Parrilla 10

Bars & clubs
Brewhouse Club 1
El Balcón 2
Enoteka 4

La Boca

East of the Plaza de Mayo, behind the Casa Rosada, a broad avenue, Paseo Colón, runs south towards the old port district of La Boca, where the Riachuelo flows into the Plata. An area of heavy Italian immigration in the early 1900s, La Boca was known for the brightly-painted blue, yellow and lime green zinc façades of its houses, a tradition brought over by Genoese immigrants who painted their homes with the leftover paint from ships. It's a much-touted tourist destination, although there is really only one block of reconstructed houses to see on the pedstrianised street **El Caminito**, leading from the little triangular plaza **La Vuelta de Rocha**. On the first block of Calle Magallanes next door, there's a small arcade of artists' workshops and a couple of cafés in the **Centro Cultural de los Artistas**, with street entertainers and touristy souvenir shops. Do not stray from this busy area, since the surrounding streets are notorious for petty crime, and in any case, the Riachuelo river is far from picturesque, with its distinctive rotting smell. The real attractions here are two

❧ *It's best to visit La Boca as part of a tour, or in a group, and certainly not alone: this is Buenos Aires' worst area for street crime.*

fine museums: La Boca really owes its fame to the artist Benito Quinquela Martín (1890-1977) who painted its ships, docks and workers all his life, and whose vivid and colourful paintings can be seen in the **Museo de Bellas Artes 'Benito Quinquela'**, ① *Pedro de Mendoza 1835. Tue-Fri 1000-1730, Sat-Sun 1100-1730, closed Jan, US$0.35, T4301 1080.* This is where the artist lived for many years, and you can also see his own extensive collection of paintings by Argentine artists, figureheads rescued from ships, temporary exhibitions of Latin American artists, and sculpture on a roof terrace with wonderful views. Superb. From the roof there are panoramic views over the whole port, revealing the marginalised poverty behind the coloured zinc façades.

There's more art a block away in the **Fundación Proa**, ① *Av Pedro de Mendoza 1929, Tue to Sun, 1100-1900. US$1, T4303 0909,* a modern space behind the ornate Italianate façade of a 1908 warehouse, showing temporary exhibitions of Argentine, Latin American and international contemporary art. Check the press for details. The roof terrace here is also great, and a nightclub venue for electronic music at times.

La Boca is home to one of the country's great football teams, Boca Juniors, and the area is especially rowdy when they're playing at home: do not attend a match alone. Tours can arrange a ticket as part of a group, and fans will be entertained by the **Museo de la Pasión Boquense**, ① *Brandsen 805, T4362 1100, Tue-Sun 1000-1800 (tickets available for a museum visit together with a stadium seat for a match on the same day), US$2.50.* To reach La Boca from the centre take a Radio taxi, US$3 (Radio Taxi Sur T4638 2000, Radio Taxi Diez T4585 5007, and call from the locutorio in Centro Cultural on Magallanes for the return journey). If there's a group of you, take bus 152 which runs along Santa Fe and Alem, or bus 29 from Plaza de Mayo, US$0.25. Police are on hand in the Vuelta de Rocha to help and advise tourists. ▸ *For Sleeping, Eating and other listings, see pages 83-102.*

Along the Costanera Sur

Puerto Madero

East of the city centre at Puerto Madero, the 19th-century docks have been successfully transformed into attractive buildings housing modern developments of offices, shops, housing and even a university campus. It's a good place for a walk, among the tall brick buildings, with their cranes and winches now smartly painted, and lots of smart restaurants catering for office workers and tourists alike. These are mostly along the waterside of the old warehouses lining Avenida Alicia M de Justo from the northern end of Dique No 4, where you'll find a helpful tourist information kiosk in a glass construction under one of the cranes.

Walking south, by Dique no 3, is the **Fragata Presidente Sarmiento**, ① *Avenida*

⁞ Carlos Gardel

Gardel, the legendary singer whose name is virtually synonymous with tango, was born in 1890 in Tolouse, France, to Berthe Gardés and an unknown father. To avoid social stigma, his mother emigrated to the Abasto market area of Buenos Aires when her son was just two years old, and it was partly these humble beginnings that helped him to become an icon for poor *porteños*.

Just as the exact origin of tango itself is something of a mystery, Gardel's formative years around the city are obscure, until around 1912 when he began his artistic career in earnest, performing as one half of the duo Gardel-Razzano. He began his recording career with Columbia with a recording of 15 traditional songs, but with it was with his rendition of *Mi Noche Triste* (My Sorrowful Night) in 1917, that his mellifluous voice became known. As *tango-canción* became popular – the song rather than just a musical accompaniment to the dance –

Gardel's career took off, and by the early 1920s he was singing entirely within this new genre, and achieving success as far afield as Madrid.

Gardel became a solo artist in 1925, and with his charm and natural machismo, was the very epitome of tango both in Argentina and, following his tours to Europe, around the world. Between 1933 and 1935, he was based in New York, starring in numerous Spanish speaking films, and the English language *The Tango* on Broadway in 1934. On 24 June 1935, while on a tour of South America, his plane from Bogota to Cali crashed into another on the ground while taking off. Gardel was killed instantly, to the immense grief of his public. Gardel had recorded some 900 songs during his career, and the brilliance of his voice, the way he represented the spirit of the Río de la Plata to his fans at home, and the untimely nature of his dramatic death ensured the endurance of his popularity.

Dávila y Perón, T4334 9386, Mon-Fri 0900-2000, Sat/Sun 0900-2200, US$0.70, free for children under 5, which was the Argentine flagship from 1899 to 1938, and now an interesting museum. Also over Dique 3 is the striking harp-like construction of the **Puente de la Mujer** (Bridge of Women), ① T4314 1090, daily 0800-2100 all year, suspended by cables from a single arm. Walking further south, in Dique 1, Puerto Madero Av Garay, is the **Corbeta Uruguay**, the sailing ship which rescued Otto Nordenskjold's Antarctic expedition in 1903.

The Costanera Sur

At the southernmost end of Dique No 1, cross the pivoting bridge (level with Calle Brazil) to the broad avenue of the Costanera Sur. This pleasant wide avenue used to run east of the docks, a fashionable promenade by the waterside in the early 20th century. Now it's separated from the River Plata by the wide splay of land created in a 1970s landfill project, but it's enjoying a revival, and there are many restaurants with twinkling lights along the boulevard at night, and it's a pleasant place to walk by day. There's a wonderfully sensuous marble fountain designed by by famous Tucumán sculptress Lola Mora, **Las Nereidas**, at the entrance to the **Reserva Ecológica**, ① daily 0800-1900 (in winter, closes at 1800), entrance is at Av Tristán Achával Rodríguez 1550, T4315 1320/4129; for pedestrians and cyclists only. Take buses 4, 29, 33, 54, 74, 86. This stretch of marshland reclaimed from the river now forms an interesting wildlife reserve, where you might be lucky enough to spot one of more than 200 species of birds, including the curve-billed reed hunter. There are free guided tours available at weekends 1030-1530, and on one Friday a month there's a guided walk is on offer at 2030. It is 30-minute walk from the entrance to the river shore, and it takes about two hours to walk the whole perimeter. Take a hat in the summer, when it is very hot with little shade. For details (birdwatching, in particular) contact **Aves Argentinas/AOP** (see Directory, below). You could also cycle to the reserve as part of a tour run by **Bike Tours**, T4311 5199, www.biketours.com.ar ▸▸ *For Sleeping, Eating and other listings, see pages 83-102.*

Mataderos

On the western edge of the city in an area where historically cattle were slaughtered, there is now a popular market, the **Feria de Mataderos**, ① *Lisandro de la Torre y Av de los Corrales, every Sun and holidays from 1100 (Sat 1800-2400 in summer), subte E to end of line then taxi (US$ 2.50), or if there's a group of you, take buses 36, 92, 97, 126, 141.* A Radio Taxi all the way will cost US$7. It's a long way out of the centre, (some two hours by bus) but worth it to see this fair of Argentine handicrafts and traditional artwork, with music and dance festivals, demonstrations of gaucho horsemanship skills, typical regional food, and games such as *pato*, a game played on horseback, originally with a duck, and *carrera de sortijas* where players on horseback have to spear a ring on a string with their lance. Nearby is the **Museo de los Corrales**, ① *Av de los Corrales 6436, T4687 1949, Mon-Fri 1030-1930, Sat 1400-2000, Sun 1200-1800.* ▸▸ *For Sleeping, Eating and other listings, see pages 83-102.*

Excursions

There are several popular places for excursions from the city, either for the day, or an overnight trip. Highly recommended are trips to the historical town of **San Antonio de Areco**, with its many estancias all around, and boat trips to the historical Uruguayan town of **Colonia de Sacramento**. You could take the coastal train to the **Tigre Delta**, where there are houses on the water front and islands, and there are also many estancias within easy reach south and west of Buenos Aires; highly recommended for a taste of Argentine rural life.

🛏 Sleeping

Hotels in the upper ranges can often be booked more cheaply through Buenos Aires travel agencies. The tourist offices at Ezeiza and Jorge Newbery airports book rooms.

Hotels and guest houses may display a star rating, but this does not match up to international standards. The **Dirección de Turismo** fixes maximum and minimum rates for 1, 2 and 3-star hotels, but 4 and 5-star places can apply any rate they wish. Many more expensive hotels charge different prices for *extranjeros* (non-Argentines), in US dollars, and there's not much you can do to get around this, since a passport is required as proof of residency. Make it clear that you'll pay in pesos in cash and you may get a reduction.

Room tax (VAT) is 21% and is not always included in the price. Air conditioning is a must in high summer. Many of the cheaper hotels in the central area give large reductions on the daily rate for long stays. Hotels with red-green lights or marked *Albergue Transitorio* are hotels for homeless lovers (for stays of 1½-2 hrs). All hotels will store luggage for a day, and most have English-speaking staff.

Centre *p68, map p70*

LL **Alvear Palace**, *Alvear 1891, T/F4808 2100, reservations 4808 7777, www.alvear palace.com* The height of elegance, an impeccably preserved 1930s Recoleta palace, taking you back in time to Buenos Aires' wealthy heyday. A sumptuous marble foyer, with Louis XV-style chairs, and a charming orangerie where you can take tea with superb patisseries (US$10). Antique-filled bedrooms. Unique. Recommended.

LL **Crowne Plaza Panamericano**, *Carlos Pellegrini 551, T4348 5250, www.panameri cano-bue.com.ar* Extremely smart and modern city hotel, with luxurious and tasteful rooms, a lovely covered rooftop pool, and superb restaurant, Tomo 1. Excellent service too.

LL Four Seasons, *Posadas 1086, T4321 1200, www.fourseasons.com/buenosaires* An entirely modern palace in traditional style, offering sumptuous luxury in an exclusive atmosphere. Spacious public areas, adorned with paintings and flowers, chic lavishly decorated rooms, and 7 suites in *La Mansión* residence, pool and health club.

LL Marriott Plaza, *Florida 1005, T4318 3000, www.marriott.com* With a superb location overlooking Plaza San Martín, this is the city's most historic hotel, built in Parisian style in 1909, and retaining period elegance in the public rooms and bedrooms, which are charming and luxurious. A pool and fitness centre, excellent restaurant, the *Plaza Grill*, and very good service throughout.

LL NH City Hotel, *Bolívar 160, T4121 6464, www.nh-hoteles.com* Very chic indeed, with perfect minimalist design for an exclusive younger set, this is one of three in the Spanish-owned chain in central Buenos Aires, with beautifully designed modern interiors in a 1930's building off Plaza de Mayo, and luxurious rooms. Small rooftop pool, good restaurant.

L Aspen Towers, *Paraguay 857, T4313 1919, www.aspentowers.com.ar* A modern minimalist foyer in this small hotel belies the traditional 1900 French-style bedrooms, all with jacuzzi baths, and all facilites including a good breakfast and a pool.

L Hilton, *Av Macacha Güemes 351, Puerto Madero, T4891 0000, reservationsba @hilton.com* A modern business hotel built on the revamped docks area with views of the Costanera Sur, and with plenty of restaurants nearby, this has neat functional rooms, the *El Faro* restaurant, a health club and pool.

L Murano Hotel, *Carlos Pellegrini 877, T5239 1000, www.muranohotel.com* A smart modern hotel overlooking Av 9 de Julio, a light entrance lounge and spacious comfortable bedrooms, sauna and gym. Not luxurious, but welcoming, with good service.

AL Dolmen, *Suipacha 1079, T4315 7117, www.hoteldolmen.com.ar* In a good location, this has a smart spacious entrance lobby, with a calm relaxing atmosphere, good professional service, comfortable modern well-designed rooms, and a little pool.

AL Etoile, *R Ortiz 1835 in Recoleta, T4805 2626,*

www.etoile.com.ar Outstanding location, rooftop pool, rooms with kitchenette.

AL Plaza San Martín Suites, *Suipacha 1092, www.plazasanmartin.com.ar* Neat modern self-contained apartments, comfortable and attractively decorated, with lounge and little kitchen, so that you can relax in privacy, right in the city centre, with all the services of an hotel. Sauna, gym, room service. Good value.

A Colón, *Carlos Pellegrini 507, T4320 3500, www.colon-hotel.com.ar* With a splendid location overlooking Av 9 de Julio and Teatro Colón, in the heart of the city, extremely good value. Charming bedrooms, comfortable, pool, gym, great breakfasts, and perfect service. Highly recommended.

A-B Crillon, *Santa Fe 796, T4310 2000, www.hotelcrillon.com.ar* Centrally located on Plaza San Martín, this is a comfortable, if slightly old-fashioned place with attractive floral décor in the lovely light rooms (ask for Plaza view) and professional, welcoming staff. Very good value. Recommended.

A-B El Conquistador, *Suipacha 948, T4328 3012, www.elconquistador.com.ar* A stylishly modernized '70s boutique hotel, which retains the wood and chrome foyer, but has bright modern rooms, and a lovely light restaurant on the 10th floor with great views. Well situated and good value.

B Bisonte Palace, *MT de Alvear 910, T4328 4751, www.hotelbisonte.com* A rather charming place, with calm entrance foyer, which remains gracious thanks to charming courteous staff. The rooms are plain, but spacious, breakfast is ample, and this is in a good location. Very good value.

B Castelar, *Av de Mayo 1152, T4383 5000, F4383 8388, www.castelarhotel.com.ar* A wonderfully elegant 1920s hotel which retains all the original features in the grand entrance and bar. Cosy warmly-decorated bedrooms, charming staff, and excellent value. Also a spa with turkish baths and massage. Highly recommended.

B Dorá, *Maipú 963, T4312 7391, www.dorahotel.com.ar* Charming old-fashioned place with comfortable rooms, good service, an attractive lounge decorated with paintings. Warmly recommended.

B Embajador, *Carlos Pellegrini 1181, T4326 5302, www.embajadorhote.com.ar* Nothing fancy, but good value for such a central location, this has comfortable plain rooms,

some overlooking Av 9 de Julio, good service, and a small breakfast is included.
C Frossard, *Tucumán 686, T4322 1811, www.hotelfrossard.com.ar* A lovely old 1940s building with high ceilings and the original doors, attractively modernized, and though the rooms are small, the staff are welcoming, and this is good value, near C Florida.
C Orly, *Paraguay 474, T/F4312 5344, www.orly.com.ar* Good location, and smartened-up comfortable rooms in an old hotel, with helpful service.
C Regis, *Lavalle 813, T4327 2605, www.orho-hoteles.com.ar* Good value in this old-fashioned but modernized place, with good breakfast and friendly staff. Good beds and spacious bathrooms. Full breakfast.
C Waldorf, *Paraguay 450, T4312 2071, www.waldorf-hotel.com.ar* Welcoming staff and a comfortable mixture of traditional and modern in this centrally-located hotel. Good value, with a buffet breakfast, English spoken. Recommended.
D Goya, *Suipacha 748, T4322 9269, www.goyahotel.com.ar* A range of rooms offered in this friendly welcoming and central place, worth paying C for the superior rooms, though all are comfortable and well maintained. Good breakfast, English spoken.
D Marbella, *Av de Mayo 1261, T/F4383 3573, info@hotelmarbella.com.ar* Modernized, and central, though quiet, breakfast included, English, French, Italian, Portuguese and German spoken. Highly recommended.
D Suipacha Inn, *Suipacha 515, T4322 0099, www.fullmen.com.ar* Good value, neat small rooms with a/c, basic breakfast.
E España, *Tacuarí 80, T4343 5541.* Delightful, old-fashioned and full of character, run by a charming eccentric old couple. Recommended.
E La Giralda, *Tacuarí 17, T4345 3917, F4342 2142.* Nicely maintained and good value. Popular with budget travellers, with discounts for students and for long stays.
E O'Rei, *Lavalle 733, T4393 7186,* F without bath, central, simple but comfortable, spotless, laundry facilities, helpful staff.
E Uruguay, *Tacuarí 83, T4334 3456.* A central and traditional old hotel, very clean and welcoming, good value.

Youth hostels

Most youth hostels are in San Telmo, (see below) but there are a few in Recoleta and Palermo. Price codes are per person:
E St Nicholas, *B Mitre 1691 (y Rodríguez Peña), T4373 5920/8841, www.stnicholas hostal.com.ar* Beautifully restored old house, spotless rooms, cooking facilities, large roof terrace, luggage store; also D double rooms. Discounts for HI members. Recommended.
F Che Lagarto, *Av San Juan 1836, T4304 7618 (subte line E to Entre Ríos; buses 37, 53, 126), www.chelagarto.com.ar* A long way from the centre, but this backpackers' hostel offers special events to involve guests in local culture, including tango classes, lively atmosphere, breakfast (D double rooms), pool, internet access, self-catering, free airport pick up. Highly recommended.
F El Cachafaz, *Viamonte 982, T4328 1445, www.elcachafaz.com.ar* Shared rooms, with breakfast, internet access, laundry facilities.
E V&S, *Viamonte 887, T4322 0994, www.hostelclub.com* C in attractive double room with bath. A central and popular hostel, with welcoming café and place to sit, tiny kitchen, internet access, tours arranged.

Palermo *p76, map p77*

A Malabia House, *Malabia 1555, Palermo Viejo, T4831 2102, www.mala biahouse .com.ar* An elegant bed and breakast with individually designed bedrooms and lovely calm sitting rooms. Highly recommended.
F Tango Backpackers Hostel, *Thames 2212, T4776 6871, www.tangobp.com* Well situated to enjoy Palermo's nightlife, this is a friendly hostel with shared rooms, and all the usual facilities.

San Telmo *p79, map p80*

D La Casita de San Telmo, *Cochabamba 286 T/F4307 5073/8796, guimbo@pinos.com* 6 rooms in restored colonial house, rooms rented by day, week or month.
E Victoria, *Chacabuco 726, T/F4361 2135.* Rooms with bath, fan, kitchen and laundry facilities, good meeting place.
F Oxford, *Chacabuco 719, T4361 8581.* With breakfast, spacious rooms with bath and fan.

For an explanation of the sleeping and eating price codes used in this guide, see the inside front cover. Other relevant information is provided in the Essentials chapter, page 44.

Worldwide chain Hostel-Inn has opened hostels in Buenos Aires, www.hostel-inn .com **Buenos Aires Inn**, *Humberto 1 No. 820, T4300 7992*, **E** pp in double room. Also **E The Tango City Hostel Inn**, *Piedras 680, T4300 5764*. Both are well organized, lively, and offer lots of activities, and the usual facilities. **E Buenos Ayres**, *Pasaje San Lorenzo 320, San Telmo, T4361 0694, www.buenosayres hostel.com* A new hostel also has double rooms with bath, kitchen, laundry, internet access with breakfast included.
E/F El Hostal de Granados, *Chile 374, T43625600, www.hostaldegranados.com.ar* Small well-equipped rooms in an interesting building, lots of light, for 2 to 4, with bath, breakfast included, kitchen, free internet, laundry service, reductions for longer stays.
F/E Sandanzas, *Balcarce 1351, T4300 7375, www.sandanzas.com.ar* Arty hostel run by a group of friends who've created an original and welcoming space, small but with a nice light airy feel, lounge and patio, internet, kitchen, breakfast included.

Student residences

Accommodation for students and tourists with host families is arranged by **Argentina B&B**, run by Silvia Demetilla, with reliable and cheap accommodation in Buenos Aires and in other towns; recommended. Many hosts speak English, others will give you a chance to practice your Spanish; www.argentinabandb.com.ar
F pp **Dido**, *Sarmiento 1343 T4373 5349, hosteldido@bigfoot.com www.residencia suniversitarias.8m.com* With kitchen, TV, single or shared rooms. ISIC discounts.
La Casa de Etty, *Luis Sáenz Peña 617, T4384 6378*. Run by Esther Corcias, who also runs **Organización Coret** (host families), coret@ciudad.com.ar
B&T Argentina, *T4804 1783, www.bytarg entina.com* Accommodation in residences and host families; also furnished flats.

Apartments/self catering

Buenos Aires Flat Rental, *Luis Sáenz Peña 277 p 5, T4372 5422, T155 183 5367, www.rioflatrental.com*

🍴 Eating

Eating out in Buenos Aires is one of the city's great pleasures, with a huge variety of restaurants from the chic to the cheap. To try some of Argentina's excellent steak, choose from one of the many *parrillas*, where your huge slab of lean meat will be expertly cooked over a wood fire.

Argentines are very sociable and love to eat out, so if a restaurant is full, it's usually a sign that it's a good place. Remember, though, that they'll usually start eating between 2130 and 2230. In doubt, head for Puerto Madero, where there are lots of good mid-range places serving international as well as local cuisine. In many mid- to upper-range restaurants, lunch is far cheaper than dinner. A portion at a *comidas para llevar* (take away) place costs US$1.50-2.50. Many cheaper restaurants are *tenedor libre*: eat as much as you like for a fixed price. The following list, for reasons of space, gives only those restaurants easily accessible for people staying in the city centre.

Retiro, and the area between Plaza de Mayo and Plaza San Martín *p72*

$$ Chiquilín, *Sarmiento 1599*. Parrilla and pasta, good value.
$$ Club Español, *B de Irigoyen 180 (on Av 9 de Julio, near Av de Mayo)*. Luxurious ambience in a fine building, recommended for a quiet dinner, with very good food.
$$ Criollo, *Maipú 442*. Serves good *parrilla*.
$$ El Figón de Bonilla, *Alem 673*. Rustic-style atmosphere and good Spanish style cuisine.
$$ El Navegante, *Viamonte 154*. Seafood.
$$ El Palacio de la Papa Frita, *Lavalle 735 and 954, Corrientes 1620*. Great place for a filling feed, with a large menu, and quite atmospheric, despite the bright lighting.
$$ El Querandí, *Perú 302 y Moreno*. Good food in an intimate atmosphere in this historical place that was opened in the 1920's.
$$ La Casona del Nonno, *Lavalle 827*. Popular with tourists for its cheap set price menu, Italian-style food, cheap pastas and *parrilla*.

$$La Chacra, *Av Córdoba 941 (just off 9 de Julio)*. A superb traditional *parrilla* with excellent steaks brought sizzling to your table (US$13 for complete parrilla and salads for 2), impeccable old-fashioned service, and a lively buzzing atmosphere.

$$La Estancia, *Lavalle 941*. A slightly touristy but reliable *parrilla* with frieze of estancia life on the wall, popular with business people at lunchtime, and serving good grills, US$13 for two.

$$La Pipeta, *San Martín 498*. Downstairs, a traditional place, established 40 years, for good food in a noisy atmosphere, closed Sun.

$$9 de Julio, *Carlos Pellegrini 587*. A smart traditional *parrilla*, no frills, but good steaks, and very popular.

$$La Taska, *Paraguay between Maipú and Florida*. Really authentic Basque food, delicious dishes: recommended.

$$Sorrento *Corrientes 668, (just off Florida)*. Intimate, elegant atmosphere, with dark wood, nicely lit tables, serving traditional menu with good fish dishes and steak.

$Broccolino, *Esmeralda 776*. Good Italian food, very popular, try *pechuguitas*.

$Capataz, *Maipú 529, T4326 6068*. Argentine food, *empanadas* and steak and vegetables on the *parrilla*, in a bright trendy atmosphere. Very good value. Also delivery to your home or hostel. Recommended.

$Catalinas, *Reconquista 850*. Recommended for fish and seafood.

$Exedra, *Carlos Pellegrini and Córdoba*. A welcoming traditional-style café right on Av 9 de Julio, serving cheap set-price menu for US$4, including a glass of wine.

$Fratello, *Tucumán 688*. Cheap pastas and other Italian dishes in attractive Italian-style surroundings.

$Gran Victoria, *Suipacha 783*. Good value *tenedor libre*, including parrilla, in a cheery though not elegant atmosphere, also cheap set price meals.

$Los Inmortales, *Lavalle 746*. Specializes in pizza, all tasty and good value to share.

$Tomo 1, *Crowne Plaza Hotel, Carlos Pellegrini 521, T4326 6695*. Argentine regional dishes and international cuisine of a high standard in a sophisticated modern atmosphere.

La Recova *map p74*

Three blocks west of Plaza San Martín, under the flyover at the northern end of Av 9 de Julio, between C Arroyo and Alvear, are several recommended restaurants.

$$$El Mirasol, *Posadas 1032*. Serves top quality parrilla in an elegant atmosphere.

$$$La Tasca de Plaza Mayor, *Posadas 1052*. Good Spanish food.

$$$Piegari, *Posadas 1042*. Great for good Italian food.

$$Juana, *Carlos Pellegrini 1535*. Popular for a good range of dishes, and salads in a spacious basement.

$$Las Nazarenas, *Reconquista 1132*. Good for beef and international food.

$$Winery, *Paseo La Recova, off Libertador 500*. A great place to sample the best of Argentina's fine wines, in a chic wine bar with light dishes such as salads and gourmet sandwiches. Also at *Av Alem 880*.

Recoleta *p74, map p74*

$$$Lola, *Roberto M Ortiz 1805*. Well known for superb pasta dishes, lamb and fish. Recommended.

$$El Sanjuanino, *Posadas 1515*. Atmospheric place offering the best of Argentina's typical dishes from the northwest: *humitas, tamale*, and *empanadas*, as well as unusual game dishes.

$$Empire Bar, *Tres Sargentos 427*. Serves Thai food in a tasteful atmosphere.

$$Morizono, *Reconquista 899*. Japanese sushi and sashami, as well as other dishes. Also delivery, T4314 4443.

$$Rodi Bar, *Vicente López 1900*. Excellent *bife* and other dishes in this typical *bodega* (wine cellar), a welcoming unpretentious place.

$$Sirop, *Pasaje del Correo, Vte Lopez 1661, T4813 5900*. Delightful chic design, delicious French-inspired food, superb patisserie too. Highly recommended.

$Grants, *Junín 1155*. Tenedor libre, which serves mainly Chinese but also parrilla, pasta, seafood, very good value.

$La Madeleine, *Av Santa Fe 1726*. Great for cheap and delicious pastas in a bright cheerful place, open 24 hrs. Recommended.

$Güerrín, *Corrientes 1368*. A Buenos Aires institution, serving incredibly cheap and filling slabs of pizza and *faina* (chick pea polenta) which you eat standing up at a zinc bar, or at tables, though you miss out on the colourful local life that way. Wonderful.

San Telmo *p79, map p80*

There are plenty of restaurants along C Defensa, and in the surrounding streets, and new places are opening all the time. This is a selection:

$$$ La Brigada, *Estados Unidos 465, T4361 5557*. The best choice in San Telmo, this is a really superb and atmospheric *parrilla*, serving excellent Argentine cuisine and wines in a cosy buzzing atmosphere. Very popular, and not cheap, but highly recommended. Always reserve.

$ El Desnivel, *Defensa 855*. Popular for cheap and basic food, jam packed at weekends, good atmosphere.

$ La Casa de Esteban de Luca, *Defensa 1000*. Parrilla and pastas in a lively café atmosphere, though service is slow.

$ La Trastienda, *Balcarce 460*. Theatre café with lots of live events, also serving meals and drinks from breakfast to dinner, great music. A relaxed and cool place hang out, with an arty crowd. Recommended.

$ La Vieja Rotiseria, *Defensa 963*. Cheap café for bargain *parrilla*, US$4 for two, packed at weekends, so come early.

$ Sumo, *Independencia y Piedras*. Good ice cream.

Puerto Madero *p81*

The revamped docks area is an attractive place to eat, and to stroll along the waterfront before dinner. There are many good places here, generally in stylish interiors and with good service: along Av Alicia Moreau de Justo (from north to south), these are recommended.

$$$ Katrine, *No 138*. Delicious fish and pasta.

$$$ Bice, *No 192*. Italian-influenced food.

$$$ La Parolaccia, *Nos 1052 and 1160*. Pasta and seafood, does bargain executive lunch for US$4 Mon-Fri only.

$$$ Las Lilas, *No 516*. Excellent *parrilla*, popular with Porteños.

$$ El Mirasol del Puerto, *No 202*. Well known and loved for a broad menu. The cheapest places are next to the boat, Fragata Sarmiento on *Dique 3*.

Palermo *p76, map p77*

This area of Buenos Aires is becoming very popular, with many chic restaurants and bars in Palermo Viejo and the Las Cañitas district, (see below). It's a sprawling district, so you could take a taxi to one of these restaurants, and walk around once you're in the area, before deciding where to eat. It's also a great place to stop for lunch, with cobbled streets, and 1900's buildings, now housing chic clothes shops. There are lots of restaurants around the *Plaza Cortázar*, and along *Honduras*.

$$$ Te Mataré Ramirez, *Paraguay 4062, T4831 9156*, (also at San Isidro). A wonderful place for an intimate dinner, Buenos Aires' only aphrodisiac restaurant. Red velvet, cupids on the walls, mellow live jazz, and excellent cuisine. Try the marinaded prawns, or fillet steak in oyster sauce. Highly recommended.

$$ Azafrán. *On the plaza at Honduras 5143*. A lovely relaxed place with a hip warm atmosphere for modern mediterranean-style cooking. Recommended.

$$ Katmandu, *Córdoba 3547*. Serves tasty Indian dishes in an exotic atmosphere.

$$ Kayoko, *Gurruchaga 1650*. Serves sushi and other Japanese dishes.

$$ Luciana, *Amenabar 1202, T4788 4999*. Excellent Italian food in a trattoria atmosphere.

$$ Sarkis, *Thames 1101*. Serves delicious Arabic cuisine, superb couscous and meat dishes, with belly dancers later on at weekends. Recommended.

$$ Social Paraiso, *Honduras 5182*. Simple delicious dishes in a relaxed chic atmosphere. Good fish and tasty salads.

Las Cañitas *p76, map p77*

This area of Palermo is fashionable for a wide range interesting restaurants mostly along C Baez, and most opening at around 2000, though only open for lunch at weekends:

$$ Baez, *next door to Morelia*. Very trendy, with lots of orange neon, serving sophisticated Italian-style food, delicious goat's cheese ravioli.

$$ Campo Bravo, *Baez y Arevalo*. A stylish minimalist place serving superb steaks and vegetables on the *parrilla*, in a friendly atmosphere. Popular and recommended.

$$ De la Ostia, *Baez 212*. A small and chic bistro for tapas and Spanish-style food, with a good atmosphere.

$$ Eh! Santino, *Baez 194*. A trendy small restaurant for Italian style food and drinks, dark and cosy with lots of mirrors.

$$ Morelia, *Baez 260*. Cooks superb pizzas on the *parilla* or in wood ovens, and has a lovely roof terrace for summer.

$$ Novecento. Across the road from *De la Ostia* is a lively French-style bistro, stylish but unpretentious and cosy, serving good fish dishes among a broad menu.

$ El Primo, *on the opposite corner from Campo Bravo*. A popular and buzzing *parrilla* for slightly older crowd. Cheap set menus in a relaxed atmosphere with fairy lights.

$ La Fonda del Polo, *on the opposite side of Baez*. Serves standard meat dishes in an intimate environment with lots of polo bric-a-brac on the walls, great value set menus, wine included.

Cheap eats

For quick cheap snacks the markets are recommended.

Also huge choice in basement of **Galerías Pacífico**, *Florida y Viamonte* .

Some supermarkets have good, cheap restaurants: **Coto supermarket**, Viamonte y Paraná, upstairs. Many supermarkets have very good deli counters and other shops sell *fiambres* (smoked, cured meats) and cheeses and other prepared foods for quick, cheap eating. Good snacks all day and night at Retiro and Constitución railway termini. The snack bars in underground stations are also cheap. **Güerrin**, *Corrientes 1368*, is a fabulous atmospheric place for cheap tasty pizzas and *faina*, standing at the zinc bar. A Buenos Aires institution. **Delicity bakeries**, several branches, have very fresh *facturas* (pastries), cakes, breads, and authentic American donuts. Another good bakery for breakfasts and salads is **Bonpler**, *Florida 481, 0730-2300*, with the daily papers, classical music. Other branches throughout the city.

Tea rooms, café-bars and ice cream parlours

Retiro, and the area between Plaza San Martín and Plaza de Mayo *p72*

Aroma, *Florida y Alvear*. A great place to relax in the centre, with a huge space upstairs, comfortable chairs by big windows onto C Florida, so you can read the papers, and watch the world go by.

Café Tortoni, *Av de Mayo 825-9*. This most famous Buenos Aires café has been the elegant haunt of artists and writers for over 100 years, with marble columns, stained glass ceilings, old leather chairs, and photographs of its famous clientele on the walls. Excellent coffee and cakes, and good tea, all rather pricey, but worth a visit for the interesting *peña* evenings of poetry and music, see also Jazz and Tango, below.

Café de la Biblioteca, *M T de Alvear 1155* (Asociación Biblioteca de Mujeres). Coffee and light snacks, and lots of books.

Confitería Ideal, *Suipacha 384*. One of the most atmospheric cafes in the city. Wonderfully old-fashioned 1930's interior, almost untouched, serving good coffee and excellent cakes with good service. Upstairs, tango is taught: Mon-Thu 1200-1500, and Tue, Wed, Sat, 1500-2100, and there's tango dancing at a *milonga* here, Mon, Wed, Thu, Sun 15-2200, and Fri at 1400-2030. Highly recommended.

El Querandí, *Perú 302 y Moreno*. Popular with intellectuals and students, good atmosphere, well known for its Gin Fizz.

El Gato Negro, *Corrientes 1669*. An old pharmacy, serving a choice of coffees and teas, and good cakes. Now a popular tango venue.

Florida Garden, *Florida y Paraguay*. Another well-known café, popular for lunch, and tea.

Richmond, *Florida 468, between Lavalle and Corrientes*. Genteel, old fashioned and charming place for tea with cakes, and a basement where chess is played between 1200-2400 daily.

Clásica y Moderna, *Callao 892*. One of the city's most welcoming cafés, with a bookshop at back, lots of brick and wood, this has a great atmosphere, good for breakfast through to drinks at night, with live music Thu to Sat. Highly recommended.

Recoleta *p74, map p74*

Café Victoria, *Roberto M Ortiz 1865*. A wonderful old-fashioned café, popular with marvellous perfectly-coiffed ladies sipping tea in a refined atmosphere, great cakes.

Ice Cream Freddo, *Pacheco de Melo y Callao, Ayacucho y Quintana, Santa Fe y Callao and at shopping malls*. Known for the best ice cream.

Persicco, *Salguero y Cabello, Maure y Migueletes and Av Rivadavia on 4900 block*. The grandsons of Freddo´s founders also offer excellent ice creams.

Palermo has lots of good cafés opposite the

park, including the fabulous ice creams at **Volta**, *Av del Libertador 3060, T4805 1818*.

🌑 Bars and pubs

Retiro and between Plaza San Martín and Plaza de Mayo *p72*
British: **The Alexandra**, *San Martín 774.*
Curries, fish and seafood, attractive bar, closed in evening.
Irish: **The Kilkenny**, *MT de Alvear 399 esq Reconquista. Open 1730-0600 (Sat opens at 2000), happy hour 1730-2100.* Very popular. **The Shamrock**, *Rodríguez Peña 1220.* Irish-run, popular, expensive Guinness, happy hour for ISIC card holders. Also **Druid In**, *Reconquista 1040.* Live music weekly, English spoken. Next door is **Porto Pirata. Celta Bar**, *Rodríguez Peña y Sarmiento.* **The Temple Bar**, *MT de Alvear 945.*

San Telmo *p79, map p80*
Good bars in San Telmo around *Plaza Dorrego*, for example **El Balcón**, and on *Humberto I.*
Enoteka, *Defensa 891 (Tue-Sun 1100-2300).*
Good wine bar charging from US$1.30 a glass from a wide selection.
Brewhouse Club, *Estados Unidos 745* .

Recoleta *p74, map p74*
Buller Brewing Company, *Roberto M Ortiz 1827.* Happy hour till 2100.

See also **live music** listings, below.

🌑 Entertainment

Details of most events are given in the Espectáculos section of newspapers, *La Nación* and *Clarín*, and the Buenos Aires Herald (English) on Fri, and also in www.laguia .clarin.com

Cinemas

The selection of films is excellent, ranging from new Hollywood releases to Argentine and world cinema; details are listed daily in all main newspapers. Films are shown uncensored and most foreign films are subtitled in Spanish, though children's films are often dubbed. Tickets are best booked in the early afternoon to ensure good seats (average price US$2; there are discounts on Wed and for first show daily; other discounts depend on cinema).

Shopping malls
There are many cinemas in shopping malls, in Puerto Madero (dock 1) and in Belgrano (Av Cabildo and environs). On Fri and Sat nights many central cinemas have *trasnoches*, late shows starting at 0100. At **Village Recoleta**, *Vicente López y Junín*, there is a cinema complex with **trasnoche** programme on Wed, Fri and Sat. Independent foreign and national films are

shown during the *Festival de Cine Independiente*, held every Apr.

Ticket agencies
Tickets obtainable, sometimes cheaper, from ticket agencies (*carteleras*), such as **Vea Más**, *Paseo La Plaza, Corrientes 1660, local 2, T6320 5319* (the cheapest), **Cartelera**, *Lavalle 742, T4322 1559*, **Cartelera Baires**, *Corrientes 1382, local 24* and **Entradas con Descuento**, *Lavalle 835, local 27, T4322 9263.* Seats can also be booked by phone with credit card in shopping centres for US$ 0.30 each ticket.

Cultural events and activities

Luna Park stadium, *Bouchard 465, near Correo Central, T4312 2135, www.lunapark.com.ar* Pop/jazz concerts, sports events, ballet and musicals.
Tango Week. Events culminate in *National Tango Day* (11 Dec), and there are free events all over the city, details posted around the city and at tourist offices.
Teatro Gen San Martín, *Corrientes 1530, T4371 0111/8 or 0800-333 5254, www.teatrosanmartin.com.ar* Organizes many cultural activities, many free, including concerts, 50% ISIC discount for Thu, Fri and Sun events (only in advance at 4th floor, Mon-Fri). The

theatre's **Sala Leopoldo Lugones** shows international classic films, daily, US$1.
Centro Cultural Borges, *Galerías Pacífico, Viamonte y San Martín, T5555 5450/5449.* Music and dance concerts, special exhibitions, some shows with students discounts.
Centro Cultural Recoleta, *Junín 1930, next to the Recoleta cemetery.* Many free activities.
Palais de Glace, *Posadas 1725, T4804 1163/4805 4354.* Temporary art exhibitions and other cultural events.
Fundación Proa, *Av Pedro de Mendoza 1929, T4303 0909.* Contemporary art in La Boca.

Live music

There are lots of bars and restaurants in San Telmo, Palermo Viejo and Las Cañitas districts, with live music (usually beginning 2330-2400). Good and popular are:
Club del Vino, *Cabrera 4737, T4833 8300.* Live music, various styles including tango.
Niceto, *Niceto Vega 5510 (Palermo Hollywood district) and La Cigale, 25 de Mayo 722, T4312 8275.*

Bailanta ('tropical' music)
El Reventón and **Fantástico Bailable**, *Plaza Once, near Av Rivadavia y Av Pueyrredón.*
Maluco Beleza, *Sarmiento 1728.* Live Brazilian dance music.

Jazz
Café Tortoni, *Av de Mayo 825, T4342 4328 www.cafetortoni.com.ar* Classic tango spot, features the *Creole Jazz Band* (dixieland), Fri 2100, also tango (see below).
La Revuelta, *Alvarez Thomas 1368, T4553 5530.* Live jazz and tango.
Notorious, *Av Callao 966, T4813 6888, Mon-Sat 2100.* Live jazz at a music shop.
Thelonious, *Salguero 1884, T4829 1562.*

Salsa
La Salsera, *Yatay 961.* Highly regarded.
Kiko Salsa, *Alvarez Thomas 1166, T4551 6551.* Popular Fri and Sat late night.
Azúcar, *Av Corrientes 3330, T4865 3103.*
La Trastienda, *Balcarce 460, Wed 2030, US$ 0.50.* Salsa classes and also some jazz shows.

Tango
There are basically two ways to enjoy Buenos Aires' wonderfully complicated and passionate dance: watch superb tango at a

show, or learn to dance at a *milonga*. There is tango information desk at the **Centro Cultural San Martín**, *Sarmiento 1551, T4373 2823, 1000-2000, www.tango data.com.ar* For a guide to tango spots in town, contact teacher Any Acosta, T4326 4908 tangoingto@hotmail.com

Tango shows Best of all is **El Viejo Almacén**, *Independencia y Balcarce, T4307 7388.* Daily, with dinner from 2030, show at 2200, US$40 with all included. Very impressive dancing from the city's best dancers, excellent live band, and great singing from some of tango's great names. Highly recommended.
La Ventana, *Balcarce 431, T4331 0217.* Daily dinner from 2000 (dinner and show US$40) or show with 2 drinks, 2200, US$25, touristy but very good, and the only show to include some of Argentina's traditional folklore music.
La Esquina de Carlos Gardel, *Carlos Gardel 3200, T4867 6363.* Dinner at 2030, and show at 22.15, US$50 for both. Recommended.
El Querandí, *Perú 302, T5199 1770.* Tango show restaurant, daily, dinner 2030, show at 2215, US$50 for both.
La Cumparsita, *Chile 302, T4302 3387, 2230-0400.* Authentic, US$10 including drink and some food.
Bar Sur, *Estados Unidos 299, T4362 6086.* 2030-0300, US$15 including all-you-can-eat pizza, drinks extra.
Café Tortoni, see cafés above. Daily evening tango shows, US$ 4 (a US$2 min expenditure at the bar is requested).

Milongas
Milongas are increasingly popular among young dancers, since tango is experiencing a revival, and you can take a class at these relaxed places, before the dancing starts a couple of hours later. Both traditional tango and milonga are played, and venues occasionally have live orchestras. Cost is usually around US$2, and even complete beginners are welcome.
Most popular among a young trendy crowd is **La Viruta**, *Armenia 1366, Palermo Viejo, T4774 6357, www.laviruta tango.com* Wed, Sun 2300, Fri and Sat 2400.
Dandi, *Piedras 936, T4361 3537.* Wed/Fri 2200.
Central Cultural Torquato Tasso, *Defensa 1575, T4307 6506, www.tango tasso.com* Classes at 2000 Fri and Sat, dancing at 2230. English spoken.
Confitería Ideal, *Suipacha 384, T4605 8234.*

Dancing Mon 1500-2300, Fri 2100-0300,
Classes Wed, Thu and Sun 1500-2100..
La Catedral, *Sarmiento 4006, T15-5325 1630*.
Dancing Fri 2300.
Porteno y Bailarin, *Riobamba 345, T4372 6080*. Tue class 2000, dancing 2100.

Clubs

Generally it is not worth going to discos
before 0230 at weekends. Dress is usually
smart. The latest, highly recommended trend
is the supper club, a fashionable restaurant
serving dinner around 2200, which clears the
table at 0100 for all-night dancing.

Supper clubs

El Living, *M T de Alvear 1540, T4811 4730*.
La Diosa, *Av Costanera Rafael Obligado 3731
(Costa Salguero), T4806 1079*. Very popular
with young people.
Moliere, *Balcarce y Chile, T4343 2623*. Very
popular, cheap beer.

Discos

Cemento, *Estados Unidos 1234*. Disco with
live shows.
New York City, *Alvarez Thomas 1391, T4552
4141*. Chic.
Mitos Argentinos, *Humberto I 489, near Plaza
Dorrego, T4362 7810*. Dancing to 'rock
nacional' music, in the daytime, and has tango

and lunch with live music.
El Dorado, *H Yrigoyen y 9 de Julio*. Different.
Pacha, *Av Costanera Rafael Obligado y
Pampa, T4788 4280*. Electronic music.
El Divino, *Cecilia Grierson 225 (Puerto
Madero, on dock 4), T4316 8400*.
Buenos Aires News, *Paseo de la Infanta
Isabel s/n, T4778 1500*.
Luna Morena, *Av Chiclana 4118, T4925 7478*.

Gay discos

Most gay discos charge US$2-3 entry on door.
Amerika, *Gascón 1040, www.ameri-k.com.ar*
Sitges, *Av Córdoba 4119*. Gay and lesbian bar,
near Amerika.
Pride Travel, *Paraguay 523, T5218 6556,
www.pride-travel.com* Organizes nights out
in Buenos Aires.

Theatre

About 20 commercial theatres play all year, and
there are many amateur theatres, with a
theatre festival at the end of May. You are
advised to book early for a seat at a concert,
ballet, or opera. Tickets for most popular shows
(including rock and pop concerts) are sold also
through **Ticketek**, *T5237 7200*, **Entrada Plus**,
T4324 1010 or **Ticketmaster**, *T4321 9700,
www.tm.com.ar* For other ticket agencies, see
Cinemas, above. Listings are in the daily press.

○ Shopping

Clothes

The main shopping streets are the
pedestrianized C Florida, stretching south
from Plaza San Martín, and Santa Fe,
especially going west from Av 9 de Julio to
Av Pueyrredon. Here you'll find all the major
Argentine names: for women look out for
Chocolate, Wanama, 47th Street, *María
Vazquez, Kill*. For children's clothes, *Mimo*
and *Cheeky*. For men, the international
names are all represented, and there are
good *Levis* and *Wrangler* stores selling cheap,
good quality Argentine-made clothes.
   Shopping malls (known as Shoppings) are a
convenient way of seeing all the main brands.
Along Florida, **Galerias Pacificos** is

recommended: a good range and cheap food
court. Designer clothes shops can be found in
exclusive shopping mall **Patio Bullrich** (see
below) and along Arenales and Santa Fe,
between 9 de Julio and Callao. Cheaper clothes
can be found in the **Abasto** shopping mall.

Handicrafts

Business Design Centre, *Recoleta*. High
quality handicrafts from the north of
Argentina are for sale.
El Boyero, *Galería Larreta, Florida 953, T4312
3564*. High quality silver, leather, wood work
and other typical Argentine handicrafts.
Art Petrus, *Florida 969*, and **Hotel
Panamericano** at *Carlos Pellegrini 551*. For

objects made of rhodochrosite, the beautiful, pink-grained national stone.

Kelly's, *Paraguay 431*. A very large selection of reasonably-priced Argentine handicrafts in wool, leather, wood, etc.

Regionales La Rueda, *Paraguay 728*. Gaucho artefacts, woollen goods, silver, leather, good prices.

Plata Nativa, *Galería del Sol, Florida 860, local 41*. For Latin American folk handicrafts.

Martín Fierro, *Santa Fe 992*. Good handicrafts, stonework etc. Recommended.

Arte y Esperanza, *Balcarce 234, Alhué, Juncal 1625 and Artesanías Argentinas, Montevideo 1386*. Very good aboriginal-style crafts.

Leather

As you'd expect from all the cattle Argentina produces, leather is cheap and of very high quality here. **Campanera Dalla Fontana**, *Reconquista 735*, is a leather factory producing fast, efficient and reasonably-priced made-to-measure clothes. Quality inexpensive leather goods are available at **All Horses**, *Suipacha 1350*. **Aida**, *Galería de la Flor, shop 30, Florida 670*. Here you can have a leather jacket made to measure in the same day.

Galería del Caminante, *Florida 844*. A variety of good shops with leather goods, arts and crafts, souvenirs, etc.

Antiques

There are many high quality antiques for sale around Recoleta: a stroll along the streets around Callao and Quintana will yield some great buys. For cheaper antiques, and second hand bric-a-brac, San Telmo is the place. The market on Sun is a good place to start, but on other days all the shops along Defensa are still open, and it's worth searching around for bargains. China, glass, rugs, old silver *mates*, clothes and jewellery are among the goodies you can pick up. **Pasaje de la Defensa**, *Defensa 1179*. A beautifully-restored colonial house containing small shops.

Bookshops

Foreign books are hard to find, and prices are very high. Foreign newspapers are available from news stands on Florida, in Recoleta and

the kiosk at Corrientes y Maipú.

French bookshop, *Oficina del Libro Francés, Esmeralda 861*.

Distal, *Corrientes 913* (sells Footprint), with branches at *Florida 528 and 738*.

Librería Rodríguez, *Sarmiento 835*. Good selection of English books and magazines upstairs, has another branch at *Florida 377*.

Librería Ensayo, *Lavalle 528*. Good selection of English and German books.

Asociación Dante Alighieri, *Tucumán 1646*. Italian books.

Kel Ediciones, *MT de Alvear 1369 and Conde 1990 (Belgrano)*. Good stock of English books.

Acme Agency, *Suipacha 245, p 1 and also Arenales 885*. Imported English books.

El Viajero, *Carlos Pellegrini 1233, T4394 7941, www.elviajero.com* Large stock of travel books, library, information service, good place to research travel plans.

Lola, *Viamonte 976, 2 p, T4322 3920. Mon-Fri 1200- 1830*. The only specialist in Latin American natural history, birdwatching, most books in English.

Camping equipment

Imperio Deportes, *Ecuador 696*. Also repairs. Recommended.

Buenos Aires Sports, *Panamericana y Paraná, Martínez (Shopping Unicenter, 2nd level)*.

Cacique Camping, *Esteban Echeverría 3360, Munro, T4762 4475*. Manufactures clothing and equipment.

Ecrin, *Mendoza 1679, T4784 4799, info@ escalada.com* Imported climbing equipment. *Guatemala 5451*. Good camping stores. *Callao 373, T4375 1018*. Every kind of battery (including for Petzl climbing lamps).

Camping gas Britam, *B Mitre 1111*, **Todo Gas**, *Sarmiento 1540*, and **El Pescador**, *Paraguay y Libertad*.

Markets

Every April a huge book fair, Feria del Libro, is held at the Rural Society grounds, on Plaza Italia; exhibitions, shows and books for sale in all languages.

Plaza Dorrego, *San Telmo*. A wonderfully atmospheric market for souvenirs, antiques, and all kinds of curious bric-a-brac. With free tango performances and live music, Sun 1000-1700.

Feria de Las Artes, *further along Defensa, around Alsina*. Sat and Sun 1200-1700.
Plaza Italia, *Santa Fe y Uriarte (Palermo)*. Second-hand textbooks and magazines are sold daily, and handicrafts market on Sat 1200-2000, Sun 1000-2000.
Parque Rivadavia, *Rivadavia 4900*. Books and magazines (daily), records, toys, stamps and coins, Sun 0900-1300.

Parque Centenario, *Díaz Vélez y L Marechal*. Sat market, with local crafts, good, cheap hand-made clothes.
Museo de los Corrales, *Av de los Corrales 6436, T4687 1949, Mon-Fri 1030-1930, Sat 1400-2000, Sun 1200-1800*.
Mercado de las Luces, *in the Manzana de las Luces, Perú y Alsina, Mon-Fri 1100-1900, Sun 1400-1900*. Handicrafts.

● Sport and activities

Cricket

Cricket is played at four clubs in Greater Buenos Aires between Nov and Mar. More information at **Asociación de Cricket Argentino**, *T4806 7306*.

Golf

Visitors wishing to play at the private golf clubs should bring handicap certificate and make telephone booking. There are about a dozen clubs. Weekend play possible with a member. Good hotels may be able to make arrangements. **Campo de Golf de la Ciudad in Palermo**, open to anyone, US$7. For information, **Asociación Argentina de Golf**, *T4325 1113*.

Horse racing

At **Hipódromo Argentino de Palermo**, a large, modern racecourse, popular throughout the year, and at **San Isidro**. Riding schools at both courses.

Motor racing

There are stock racing and Formula 3 competitions, mostly from Mar to mid-Dec and drag racing all year round, Fri evenings, from US$1 at the **Oscar Alfredo Gálvez Autodrome**, *Av Coronel Roca y Av General Paz, T4605 3333*.

Polo

Argentina has the top polo players in the world. The high handicap season is Sep to Dec, but it is played all year round (low season Mar-May). A visit to the national finals at Palermo in Nov and Dec is recommended. For information, **Asociación Argentina de Polo**, *T4342 8321*.

Rugby and football

Association and rugby football are played to a high standard. Soccer fans should see Boca Juniors, matches Sun 1500-1900; also sometimes on Fri or Sat (depending on time of year), cheapest entry US$3-5, (stadium La Bomb- onera, Brandsen 700, La Boca, open weekdays for visits – buses 29, 33, 53, 64, 86, 152), or their arch-rivals, River Plate. The soccer season Mar-Jun, Aug-Dec. Rugby season Apr-Oct/Nov.

Swimming

Public baths near **Aeroparque**, *Punta Carrasco* (best, most expensive, also tennis courts), *Costa Salguero and Parque Norte*, both popular. At **Club de Amigos**, *Av Figueroa Alcorta y Av Sarmiento, T4801 1213*, US$ 6.50 (including entrance), open all year round.

⟲ Tours operators

An excellent way of seeing Buenos Aires and its surroundings is by a three-hour tour, especially for those travelling alone, or concerned about security. Longer tours include dinner and a

tango show, or a gaucho fiesta at an estancia (farm or ranch), with excellent food. Bookable through most travel agents.
Buenos Aires Tur (BAT), *Lavalle 1444, T4371*

2304. City tours (US$6) twice daily; Tigre and Delta, daily, 5hrs (US$13).

Buenos Aires Vision, *Esmeralda 356 p 8, T4394 4682*. City tours, Tigre and Delta, Tango (US$ 33, cheaper without dinner) and Fiesta Gaucha (US$27).

Eternautas, *Arcos 2514, T4781 8868, www.eternautas.com* Historical, cultural and artistic tours of the city and Pampas, guided by university historians in English, French or Spanish, flexible, also Tue and Sat walking tours from steps of **Banco de la Nación**, *Rivadavia y 25 de Mayo*, 1000 and 1700, 2 hrs.

Urban biking, *Sarmiento 212 p 12, T4371 1338, www.urbanbiking.com* Four-hour cycle tours, south or north of the city, (US$18, meal included); also by night and day tours to Tigre.

Bike Tours, *Florida 868, T4311 5199, www.biketours.com* Organizes good, bilingual, three-hour tours of the city and the nature reserve on Costanera Sur, daily at 0930, and 1430, US$25. Friendly, helpful, bikes, helmets and water provided.

Tangol, *www.tangol.com* Organize accommodation, Spanish course, tango outings, football tickets and shows in town.

Tripping, *Marcos Dartiguelongue and Leonardo Kawakami, T4791 6769, T15-4993 3848 (mob), trippingbsas@hotmail.com* Tours to dance clubs, football matches, parachute jumps, horseback trips and city bike tours.

Travel agents
Among those recommended are:
ATI, *Esmeralda 567, T4329 9000*. Mainly group travel, very efficient, many branches.
Eves Turismo, *Tucumán 702, T4393 6151*. Helpful and efficient, recommended for flights.
Exprinter, *San Martín 170, T4341 6600*, Galería Güemes, info@exprinter-viajes.com.ar (especially their 5-day, 4-night tour to Iguazú and San Ignacio Miní).
Turismo Feeling, *San Martín 969 p 9, T4313 5533*. Excellent and reliable horseback trips and adventure tourism.
Flyer, *Reconquista 621, p 8, T4312 9194/95*. English, Dutch, German spoken, repeatedly recommended, especially for estancias, fishing, polo, motorhome rental.
Southdoors Group, *MT de Alvear 776 4 floor, office 41, T4313 9093, www.southdoors.com* Very helpful for estancia visits.

● Transport

Air
Airports
Buenos Aires has two airports, Ezeiza for international flights and Aeroparque for domestic flights.

Ezeiza (officially Ministro Pistarini), is 35 km southwest of the centre by a good dual carriageway, which links with the General Paz circular highway round the city. There are two terminals: B for **Aerolineas Argentinas**, and the larger A for all other airlines, with *Casas de cambio*, and *Banco de la Nación*, open 24 hrs; ATMs; pharmacy; left luggage office, attended 24 hrs, US$1 per piece; *locutorio*, no post office. There's a tourist office immediately as you enter the Arrivals hall, open 0700-2000, offering maps, guides, and a free hotel booking service. The duty-free shop is also open to arriving passengers. You can apply for the return of tax paid on expensive goods, (with all the receipts) at a desk marked *Devolución IVA*.

Aeroparque is 4 km north of the centre on the river, smart and modern, with bars and restaurants on the 1st floor, several shops and the airport tax counter. Also tourist information, car rental, bank, ATMs, exchange facilities, post office, *locutorio* and luggage deposit (between sections A-B at the information point), US$ 1.30 per piece a day.

Transport to and from the centre
Airport bus The safest way to get between airports, or to get to town, is by an airport bus service run by **Manuel Tienda León**, whose convenient desk in Ezeiza is as you exit customs into the Arrivals hall. Buses run 0600-0100 every half hour to Av Santa Fe 790 on Plaza San Martín right in the centre of town, (US$4, 40 mins) and then onto the domestic airport Aeroparque (US$5, another 25mins); buses leave from outside terminal B.

Their helpful office on Plaza San Martín has free luggage storage, and offers free transfer/pick up to your hotel, T43143636, 0800 7770078. Manuel Tienda León bus to Aeroparque from the centre run every 30 mins, US$2, 20mins.

Local bus From Ezeiza, No 86 bus (white and

blue, marked Empresa Duvi, T4302 6067) runs to the centre from outside the airport terminal to the left as you leave the building, 2 hrs, US$ 0.45, takes coins only and no change given, runs every 14 mins during the day. To travel·to Ezeiza, catch the bus at Av de Mayo y Perú, one block from Plaza de Mayo (many other stops, but this is central) – make sure it has the red 'Aeropuerto' sign in the window as many 86s stop short of Ezeiza. There are no direct bus services between Ezeiza and the Retiro bus and train stations. From Aeroparque, No 45 runs from outside the airport to the Retiro railway station, then follows Av Alem and Paseo Colón to La Boca. No 37C goes from Plaza del Congreso to Aeroparque but make sure it has 'Aeroparque' sign, US$0.70.

Taxi Taxis from Ezeiza to the centre charge US$ 8 (plus US$ 1 toll), but do not have a good reputation for security, and you'll have to bargain. Far better to take a Remise taxi: these charge a fixed fare and can be booked from the **Manuel Tienda León** counter at Ezeiza, US$ 14 (plus US$ 1 toll) payable in advance. Taxis from Aeroparque to Congreso US$7, Plaza de Mayo US$6, Retiro US$5. *Remise* are operated by *Universal* fleet (office in *Austral* section, T47722950), Manuel Tienda León charge US$11-13 to centre, US$35 to Ezeiza. *Transfer Express* operates on-request *remise* taxis, vans and minibuses from both airports to any point in town and between them; convenient for large groups.

Road

Bus

Boats and buses heavily booked Dec-Mar, especially at weekends.

All long-distance buses arrive at the **Retiro** bus terminal at *Ramos Mejía y Antártida Argentina*. The terminal is on 3 floors. Arrivals and departures are on the middle floor where food and gifts are sold and departures are displayed on screens. Ticket offices are on the upper floor, but there are hundreds of them so you'll need to consult a list of companies and their office numbers at the top of the escalator. They're organized by regions of the country, and each region is colour-coded. There are left-luggage lockers, requiring tokens from kiosks, US$2.50. Large baggage should be left at *guarda equipage* on the lower floor. The service of

luggage porters is supposed to be free. Buenos Aires city tourist information is at desk 83 on the upper floor. Bus information at the Ramos Mejía entrance on the middle floor. Taxis leave from the official rank on the lower floor, one level below arrivals, but these are not reliable. For security, phone for a Radio Taxi, eg **Radio Taxi Sur**, T4638 2000, telling the company to pick you up at *Puente 3, arriba* (bridge 3 upper level) for example (there are 5 such bridges leading from the arrivals level). Otherwise, take a *remise* taxi, **Remis La Terminal** T4312 0711, booked from 1 of 2 booths on the bus platform itself, a little more expensive but very secure. There are no direct bus services to either airport. It's not advisable to walk into town from the bus terminal, since the road is lined with stalls, where thieves act.

Car hire

Hiring a car is best done on the spot and less expensive than if done from home. Driving in Buenos Aires is no problem if you have eyes in the back of your head and nerves of steel.
Avis, *Cerrito 1527*, T43265542, F3266992.
AL International, *San Luis 3138*, T43129475.
Budget, *Santa Fe 869*, T43119870. ISIC and GO 25 discount.
Hertz, *Ricardo Rojas 451*, T43121317.
There are several national rental agencies, eg **AVL**, *Alvear 1883*, T48054403.
Ricciard Libertador, *Av del Libertador 2337/45*, T47998514.
Localiza, *Paraguay 1122*, T43143999.
Unidas, *Paraguay 864*, T43150777.

Sea

The *Buenos Aires Herald* (English language daily) notes all shipping movements. **Flota Fluvial del Estado** (*Corrientes 489*, T43110728) organizes cruises from **Buenos Aires**, Dársena Sur (*T43614161/0346 dock*), up the **Paraná River**. **South Coast**, down to **Punta Arenas** and intermediate **Patagonian** ports, served by the **Imp & Exp de la Patagonia**. Very irregular sailings.

Boat connections

1 Direct to **Montevideo**, Buquebus, *Terminal de Aliscafos, Av Córdoba y Madero and in Patio Bullrich shopping centre, p 1, loc 231*, T4316 6500/ 4316 6550, *www.buque bus.com*, twice a day, 2½-3 hrs, US$52 tourist class, US$63 1st class one way, vehicles US$ 57-70, motorcycles US$ 44, bus connection to **Punta del Este**, US$ 8.50.

2 To **Colonia de Sacramento**, services by 2 companies: *Buquebus*: 2 ferry services a day, 2 hrs 40 mins, US$16 tourist class, US$22 1st class one way, with bus connection to **Montevideo** (US$ 6 extra) and to **Punta del Este** (US$12). Motorcycles US$15, cars, US$ 23-30. *Ferrylíneas Sea Cat*, operates a fast service to Colonia from same terminal, 2 to 3 daily, 50 mins, US$28 tourist class, US$34 1st class one way, vehicles US$39-44, motorcycles US$21.

3 To **Piriápolis**, Buquebus, weekly, 3 hrs 15 mins, tourist class US$60, 1st class US$75, vehicles US$84-102, motorcycles US$54.

4 From **Tigre** to **Carmelo**, boats are operated by **Cacciola** at 0830, 1630, 3 hrs, US$9 (18 return) to Carmelo, and US$14 to **Montevideo**. Cacciola office: *Florida 520, p 1 oficina 113, T4393 6100 and international terminal, Lavalle 520, Tigre, T4749 0329, www.cacciolaviajes.com* Credit cards accepted. It is advisable to book in advance; connecting bus from offices to port and from Carmelo to Montevideo.

5 From **Tigre** to **Nueva Palmira**, Líneas Delta Argentina, from Tigre 0745, also 1700 Fri 3 hrs, US$ 16 round trip, bus connections to **Colonia** (US$17 round trip from Tigre), *T4749 0537*, information *T4731 1236*. NB No money changing facilities in Tigre, and poor elsewhere.

Train

Retiro train information T4311 8704. There are 4 main terminals: **Retiro** (3 lines: Mitre, Belgrano, San Martín in separate buildings), **Constitución**, **Once**, **Federico Lacroze**.

Retiro
Mitre line (run by TBA, *T4317 4407 or T0800-333 3822, www.tbanet.com.ar* Urban and suburban services: to **Belgrano**, **Mitre** (connection to Tren de la Costa, see below), **Olivos**, **San Isidro**, **Tigre** (see below), **Capilla del Señor** (connection at Victoria, US$ 0.90), **Escobar** and **Zárate** (connection at Villa Ballester, US$ 0.90); long-distance services: to

Rosario Norte, one weekly on Fri evening, 6 hrs, US$3.50, to **Tucumán** via Rosario, Mon and Fri, 2100, returning Mon and Thu 1000, 26 hrs, US$ 20 sleeper, US$16 pullman, US$ 13 1st (service run by NOA Ferrocarriles, *T4893 2244*).

Belgrano line run by Ferrovías, *T4511 8833*.

San Martín line run by Metropolitano, *T4018 0700, www.tms.com.ar* Urban and suburban services: to **Palermo**, **Chacarita**, **Devoto**, **Hurlingham** and **Pilar**. Long distance services: to **Junín**, daily, 5hrs, US$4.

Constitución
Train information T4304 0028
Roca line (run by Metropolitano, see above). Urban and suburban services to **La Plata** (US$0.50), **Ezeiza** (US$0.35), **Ranelagh** (US$ 0.27) and **Quilmes** (US$0.20). Long-distance services (run by Ferrobaires, *T4304 0028/3165*): **Bahía Blanca**, 5 weekly, 12½ hrs, US$7-13; to **Mar del Plata** daily in summer, US$ 7-13, 5 hrs; to **Pinamar**, 2 weekly, US$7-13, 6 hrs; to **Miramar**, in summer only, daily, 7 hrs, US$7-13; to **Tandil**, US$7-13, weekly, 7½ hrs; to **Quequén**, 2 weekly, 12 hrs, US$7-13.

Federico Lacroze Urquiza
Train line information, and **Metro headquarters** (run by Metrovías, *T0800-555 1616* or *T4555 1616, www.metrovias.com.ar*). Suburban services: to General Lemos.

Once
Train information T4861 0043.
Once Sarmiento line (run by TBA, see above). Urban and suburban services: to **Caballito**, **Flores**, **Merlo**, **Luján** (connection at Moreno, US$0.60), **Mercedes** (US$1) and **Lobos**. Long distance services to **Santa Rosa** and **General Pico** can be seasonally interrupted by floods. A fast service runs daily between **Puerto Madero** (station at *Av Alicia Moreau de Justo y Perón*) and **Castelar**. Tickets checked before boarding and on train and collected at the end of the journey; urban and suburban fares are charged according to different sections of each line; cheapest fare is around US$0.15 (depending on the company).

● *For an explanation of the sleeping and eating price codes used in this guide, see the inside*
● *front cover. Other relevant information is provided in the Essentials chapter, page 44.*

● Directory

Airline offices

Aerolíneas Argentinas and Austral, *Perú y Rivadavia, Av LN Alem 1134 and Av Cabildo 2900, T0810-2228 6527, www.aerolineas.com.ar* Extremely helpful and efficient staff. Aerovip, *Cerrito 1318, T0810-444 2376.* Air Canada, *Av Córdoba 656, T4327 3640.* Air France, *San Martín 344 p 23, T4317 4700 or T0800-222 2600.* Alitalia, *Av Santa Fe 887, T4310 9910.* American, *Av Santa Fe 881, T4318 1000, Av Pueyrredón 1889* and branches in Belgrano and Acassuso. Avianca, *Carlos Pellegrini 1163 4thfl, T4394 5990.* British Airways, *T4320 6600, Carlos Pellegrini 1163 10th fl.* Dinar, *Carlos Pellegrini 675 10th fl, T5371 1100.* Cubana, *Sarmiento 552 p 11, T4326 5291.* Iberia, *Carlos Pellegrini 1161 1st fl, T4131 1000.* KLM, *Suipacha 268, 9th fl, T4326 8422.* LAB, *Carlos Pellegrini 141, T4323 1900.* LAER, *Suipacha 844, T4311 5237.* Lan Chile, *Cerrito y Paraguay, T4378 2200, www.lanchile.com* Líneas Aéreas del Estado (LADE), *Perú 714, T4311 5334, Aeroparque T4514 1524, reservas@ lade.com.ar* Erratic schedules, uninformed office. Lufthansa, *M T Alvear 636, T4319 0600, www.lufthansa-argentina.com* Mexicana, *Av Córdoba 755 1st fl, T4312 6152* Pluna and Varig, *Florida 1, T4342 4420 or T4329 9211, www.pluna argentina.com.ar, www.varig.com.br* Quantas, *Av Córdoba 673 13th fl, T4514 4726, www.qantas argentina.com.ar* Southern Winds, *Av Santa Fe 784, T0810-777 7979, www.sw.com.ar* Swiss International Airlines, *Santa Fe 846 1st fl, T4319 0000,* Taca. *Carlos Pellegrini 1275, T4325 8222.* TAM, *Cerrito 1030, T4819 4800 or T0810 333 3333.* United, *Av Madero 900, T0810-777 8648.*

Banks

ATMs are widespread, and it's easiest and safest to use credit cards for withdrawing cash. Since the economic collapse of 2001/2, credit cards are no longer widely accepted in shops and restaurants, except for more expensive items in big establishments. Travellers' cheques can be hard to change, most banks charge a hefty commission (as much as US$10) and you may be asked for proof of purchase. American Express TCs are less of a problem than Thomas Cook. US

dollars aren't reliable either, and bills are often scanned electronically for forgeries, only new notes are accepted in many places. The best solution is to use credit cards for withdrawing cash from ATMs (*cajeros automáticos*) since these are widely available all over the city, and commission is cheaper than on TCs. Note that in Argentine ATMs you'll be given your money and receipt BEFORE your card is returned. Banks open Mon-Fri 1000-1500, be prepared for long delays. For lost or stolen cards: Mastercard *T4340 5700,* Visa *T4379 3333.*

   Lloyds TSB Bank, *Florida 999, T0810-555 6937.* Visa cash advances. It has 14 other branches in the city, and others in Greater Buenos Aires. Bank Boston, *Florida y B Mitre, T4820 2000.* Citibank, *B Mitre 502, T0810-444 2484,* changes only *Citicorp's* TCs cheques, no commission, also Visa, MasterCard; branch at *Florida 199.* Bank of America, *25 de Mayo 537, T4319 2600.* HSBC, 25 de Mayo 258, also at Florida 229, changes Thomas Cook TCs with US$10 commission. American Express offices are at *Arenales 707 y Maipú, by Plaza San Martín, T4311 1906,* where you can apply for a card, get financial services and change Amex TCs (1000-1500 only, no commission into US$ or pesos). Visa and MasterCard ATMs at branches of Banco de la Nación Argentina, ABN Amro Bank, BNP, Itaú and others. MasterCard/Cirrus also at Argencard offices.

   Several casas de cambio found at *San Martín* and *Corrientes.* Also Forex, *MT de Alvear 540,* opposite *Marriott Plaza Hotel,* and Eves, *Tucumán 702,* open 1000-1500. Major credit cards usually accepted but check for surcharges. General MasterCard office at *Perú 151, T4348 7070,* open 0930-1800. Visa, *Corrientes 1437, p 2, T4379 3333.* Other South American currencies can only be exchanged in *casas de cambio.* Western Union, branches in several Correo Argentino post offices and at *Av Córdoba 975;* check for other branches, *T0800-800 3030.*

Communications

Internet

Broadband Speedy is widely available, and prices range from US$0.30 to US$0.65 per hr, so shop around. Many *locutorios* (phone centres) have internet access. There are many all along Florida and Lavalle. **De la City**, Lavalle 491. **Cybercafé**, *Maipú 486 (basement)*. Several PCs, good 24-hr service, **Comunicar**, *Lavalle y Cerrito*, US$ 0.26 per hr at weekends.

Post office

Correo Central – now privatized, **Correos Argentinos**, *Sarmiento y Alem, Mon-Fri, 0800-2000, Sat 0900-1300. Poste restante* on ground floor (US$0.50 per letter). Philatelic section open Mon-Fri 0900-1900. **Centro Postal Internacional**, for all parcels over 2kg for mailing abroad, at *Av Comodoro Py y Antártida Argentina*, near Retiro station, many languages spoken, packaging materials available, *open Mon-Fri 1000 to 1700* Check both Correo Central and Centro Postal Internacional for *poste restante*. Post office without queues at *Montevideo 1408 near Plaza V López*, friendly staff, speaking Spanish only. Also at *Santa Fe 945*. **UPS**, *Bernardo de Irigoyen 974, T4339 2877*.

Telephone

Locutorios are available on almost every block, making phoning easy (see Essentials, page 60). Public telephone boxes operate with coins: 25 centavos (US$0.08) is the minimum charge for local calls. Cards can be used (available at *kioskos*), don't accept cards without a wrapper or with a broken seal. International telephone calls from hotels may incur a 40-50% commission in addition to government tax of about the same amount.

Cultural associations

British Council, *M T de Alvear 590, p 4, T4311 9814, F4311 7747 (Mon-Thu 1100-1500), www.britishcouncil.org* Organizes British cultural events, film festivals, arts, English language courses. **Goethe Institut**, *Corrientes 319, T4311 5338/8964*. German library (Mon,Tue,Thu 1230-1930, Fri 1230-1600) and newspapers, free German films shown, cultural programmes, German language courses. In the same building, upstairs, is the **German Club**, Corrientes 327. **Alliance Française**, *Córdoba 946, T4322 0068*. French library, temporary film and art exhibitions.

Clubs

American Club, *Viamonte 1133, T4373 8801*,

facing Teatro Colón, temporary membership available. **English Club**, *25 de Mayo 586, T4312 0689*, open for lunch only, temporary membership available to British business visitors. The American and English Clubs have reciprocal arrangements with many clubs in USA and UK. **Swedish Club**, *Tacuarí 147, T4334 7813*. **Organización Hebrea Argentina Macabi**, *Tucumán 3135, T4963 9161*, social and sporting club for conservative Jews.

Embassies and consulates

All open Mon-Fri unless stated otherwise. **Australia**, *Villanueva 1400 y Zabala, T4777 6580, www.argentina.embassy.gov.au 0830-1100*. Ticket queuing system; take bus 29 along Av Luis María Campos to Zabala. **Austria**, *French 3671, T4802 1400, www.austria.org.ar, Mon-Thu 0900-1200*. **Bolivian Consulate**, *Belgrano 1670, 1st fl, T4381 0539*, or *Corrientes 545, T4394 6042, 0900-1400*, visa while you wait or a month's wait (depending on the country of origin), tourist bureau. **Brazilian Consulate**, *C Pellegrini 1363, 5th fl, T4515 6500, www.conbrasil.org.ar, 1000-1300*, tourist visa takes at least 48 hrs, US$ 25-120. **Canada**, *Tagle 2828, T4808 1000, www.dfait-maeci .gc.ca/bairs, Mon-Thu 1400-1600*, tourist visa *Mon-Thu 0845-1130*. **Chilean Consulate**, *Tagle 2762, T4801 2761, 0900-1300*. **Denmark**, *Alem 1074, 9th fl, T4312 6901/6935, ambadane@ ambadane.org.ar Mon-Thu 0930-1200*. **Israel**, *Av de Mayo 701, p 10, T4338 2500, Mon-Thu 0900-1200, Fri 0900-1100*. **Italy**, consulate at *M T de Alvear 1125, T4816 6133/36*, or *Billinghurst 2577, T4802 0071, 0900-1300*. **Japanese Consulate**, *Bouchard 547 15th fl, T4318 8200, 0915-1230, 1430-1630*. **Netherlands**, *Olga Cossentini 831 p 3, on dock 3 (across the bridge), Puerto Madero, T4338 0050*, or *Av de Mayo 701, p 19, T4338 0050, bue@min buza.nl 0830-1230*. **New Zealand**, *C Pellegrini 1427 5th fl, T4328 0301, T4328 0747, kiwiargentina@datamarket.com.ar Mon-Thu 0900-1300, 1400-1730, Fri 0900-1300*. **Norway**, *Esmeralda 909, 3rd fl B, T4312 1904, T4312 2204, 0900-1400*. **Paraguayan Consulate**, *Viamonte 1851, T4814 4803, T4802 3432, 0800- 1400*. **Portugal**, *Maipú 942 17th fl, T4515 0520, 0900-1230*. **Spain**, *Guido 1760, T4811 0070, 0830-1400*. **Sweden**, *Tacuarí 147 p 6, T4342 1422, 1000-1200*. **Uruguay**, *Av Las Heras 1915, consulate T4807 3040, www.embajadauruguay. com.ar, open 0930-1530*, visa takes up to 72 hrs.

US Embassy and Consulate General, *Colombia 4300, T5777 4533/34 or T4514 1830, 0900-1800.*

Spanish language schools

Encuentros, *Scalabrini Ortiz 2395 p 6 M, T/F4832 7794.* **Argentina I.L.E.E,** *Av Callao 339, p 3, T4372 0223, www.argentinailee.com* Recommended by individuals and organizations alike. *Programa Tango* adds tango lessons to Spanish. Accommodation arranged. **PLS,** *Carabelas 241 p 1, T4394 0543, F4394 0635, www.pls.com.ar* Recommended for travellers and executives and their families; also translation and interpreting services. Spanish classes at **Instituto del Sur,** *Bernardo de Irigoyen 668, p 1, T4334 1487, www.delsur. com.ar* Individual and groups, cheap. **Universidad de Buenos Aires,** *25 de Mayo 221, T4334 7512 or T4343 1196, idlab@filo.uba.ar* Offers cheap, coherent courses, including summer intensive courses. **Cedic,** *Reconquista 715, p 11 E, T/F4315 1156.* Recommended. For other schools teaching Spanish, and for private tutors look in *Buenos Aires Herald* in the classified advertisements. Enquire also at **Asatej** (see Useful addresses).

Teaching English in Argentina

Before being allowed to teach, you must officially have a work permit (difficult to obtain) but schools may offer casual employment without one, particularly to people searching for longer-term employment. If unsure of your papers, ask at Migraciones (address below). A degree in education or TEFL/TESL is often required. 'Coordinadoras', who do not have an institute but run English 'schools' from their homes, hire native English-speakers and send them out on jobs. Pay varies between US\$3-7 per hr. Adverts appear in the Buenos Aires Herald, but most contacts are by word of mouth. Schools which teach English to Argentines include: **International House,** *Pacheco de Melo 2555, T4805 6393, www.inter national-house.com.ar* British- owned and run. **Berlitz,** *Av de Mayo 847, T4342 0202,* several branches. There are many others. Vacancies are advertised in the *Buenos Aires Herald* or search on www.inglesnet.com

Medical services

Urgent medical service: for free municipal ambulance service to an emergency hospital department (day and night) Casualty ward,

Sala de guardia, *T107* or *T4923 1051/58*.

Public Hospitals Hospital Argerich, *Almte Brown esq Pi y Margall 750, T4362 5555/5811*. Hospital Juan A Fernández, *Cerviño y Bulnes, T4808 2600*. Good medical attention. Asthma sufferers can receive excellent treatment at the Hospital de Clínicas José de San Martín, *Av Córdoba 2351, T5950 8000*. Eye Hospital, *Av San Juan 2021, T4941 5555*.

Safety

If robbed or attacked, call the tourist police, Comisaría del Turista, *Av Corrientes 436, T4346 5748 (24 hrs)*. English spoken. Keep this number in your pocket. Street crime is on the rise, especially in the tourist areas of La Boca, San Telmo and Recoleta, and individuals walking alone are more at risk than couples or groups. Be careful when boarding buses, and near the Retiro train and bus stations. La Boca is a dangerous area and you should not leave the tourist spot, or go to La Boca alone. Do not change money on the street. If your passport is stolen, call your embassy for emergency help.

Tourist information

See www.turismo.gov.ar also in English, and buenosaires.gov.ar

Tourist offices The national office is at *Santa Fe 883. Open Mon-Fri 0900-1700, T4312 2232/5550, info@turismo.gov.ar www.turismo.gov.ar* For tourism in the city, there are kiosks at Aeroparque (Aerolíneas Argentinas section), and at Ezeiza Airport, daily 0900-2000. There are city-run tourist kiosks open 1200-2000 on Florida, junction with Roque Sáenz Peña, at Abasto Shopping Mall (*Av Corrientes 3200*), in Recoleta (*on Av Quintana, junction with Ortiz*), in Puerto Madero, Dock 4, and at Retiro Bus Station (*ground floor*). For free tourist information anywhere in the country *T0800-555 0016 (0800-2000)*. Those overcharged or cheated can go to any tourist office or to Casa del Consumidor, *Esmeralda 340, T4326 4540 (Mon-Fri 0900-1700)*.

Guides and information resources Good guides to bus and subte routes are *Guía T, Lumi, Peuser* and *Filcar* (covering the city and Greater Buenos Aires in two editions), US\$1-4 available at news stands. Also handy is *Auto Mapa*'s pocket-size *Plano guía* of the Federal Capital, available at news stands, US\$2.70. *Buenos Aires Day & Night* is a free bimonthly magazine with a downtown map available together with other publications at tourist kiosks and some hotels. *La Nación* and *Clarín* newspapers both have Sun tourism section (very informative), and an entertainments section on Fri. *Clarín* runs an up-to-date website on entertainment, www.laguia. clarin.com; Página 12 has a youth supplement on Thu called *NO*. The *Buenos Aires Herald* publishes *Get Out* on Fri, listing entertainments. Information on what's on at www.buenosairesherald.com

Useful addresses

Migraciones: (Immigration), *Antártida Argentina 1335/55, edificios 3 y 4, T4317 0200, F4317 0282, 0800-1300*. Visas extended mornings. Central Police Station: *Moreno 1550, Virrey Cevallos 362, T4370 5911/5800 (emergency, T101 from any phone, free)*. Comisión Nacional de Museos y Monumentos y Lugares Históricos: *Av de Mayo 556, T4343 5835.* Heritage preservation official agency.

Administración de Parques Nacionales, *Santa Fé 690, opposite Plaza San Martín, T4311 0303.* Mon-Fri 1000-1700, has leaflets on national parks. Also library (Biblioteca Perito Moreno), open to public Tue-Fri 1000-1300, 1400-1700. **Aves Argentinas/AOP** (a Birdlife International partner), *25 de Mayo 749 p 2, T4312 8958.* Information on birdwatching and specialist tours, good library open Wed and Fri 1400-2000 (closed Jan).

Student organizations

Asatej: Argentine Youth and Student Travel Organization, runs a Student Flight Centre, *Florida 835, p 3, oficina 320, T4114 7500, F4311 6158, www.asatej.com* Student discounts including cheap one-way flights (waiting lists), hotels and travel; information for all South America, noticeboard for travellers, ISIC cards sold (giving discounts; Argentine ISIC guide available here), English and French spoken; also runs: **Red Argentino de Alojamiento Para Jovenes** (affiliated to HI), **Asatej Travel Store,** at the same office, selling travel goods. **Oviajes,** *Uruguay 385, p 6, T4371 6137,* also at *Echeverría 2498 p 1, T4785 7840/7884,* and at *Sarmiento 667, p 3, T5199 0830, www.oviajes.com.ar* Offers facilities, ticket sales, information, and issues HI and Hostels of Europe, ISIC, ITIC and G0 25 cards, aimed at students, teachers and independent travellers. Cheap fares also at **TIJE,** *San Martín 674 p 3, T4326 2036,* or branches at *Paraguay 1178, T5218 2800* and *Zabala 1736, p 1, www.tije.com* **YMCA:** (Central), *Reconquista 439, T4311 4785.* **YWCA:** *Tucumán 844, T4322 1550.*

Around Buenos Aires

There's a huge variety of places to visit within an hour or two of Buenos Aires, to give you a taste of the rest of the country's landscape and culture. Most highly recommended are the estancias – large traditional farms, often with imposing main houses. You can visit for the day, or for several nights, for a complete rest in beautiful surroundings, and a chance to sample gaucho life with superb open air asados (so much more than a barbecue), and horseriding. Northwest of the city along the Río de la Plata estuary lie several attractive suburbs, easily reached by train or bus, on the way to the Tigre delta, a popular weekend spot. East of the city, the perfectly preserved 19th-century town of San Antonio de Areco is a charming place for a few days' escape, where gaucho culture is celebrated on the Day of Tradition, and with several important estancias close by. South of the city are more fine estancias, near Chascomús, and Dolores (see The Pampas, page 119). Along the Uruguayan coast of the Río de la Plata are several attractive little towns, which are growing in popularity as a tourist centre.

The northern suburbs

The northern suberbs can be reached by trains from Retiro station; particularly recommend is the Tren a la Costa, which goes through the suburbs, and allows you to get off and on again on the same ticket.

Olivos → *Population: 160,000*

Olivos is the site of the presidential home, in a smart upmarket residential district. From the station, walk up Calle Corrientes with its neocolonial architecture and mature, shady trees until you reach the river and the Puerto de Olivos, with a private yacht club and several popular *parrillas*. On Saturday and Sunday a catamaran sails from here to Tigre taking two hours, a pleasant trip, giving you the chance to see lavish riverside mansions. **Martínez,** nearby, is a very swanky and attractive residential area, with a good shopping area. You can also go sailing and windsurfing

San Isidro → *Colour map 4, B5*

Just beyond Olivos, this is one of the most attractive suburbs on the coast and a fashionable nightlife spot, especially along the river bank. There are a number of fine colonial buildings including several *quintas* (country houses). **Quinta Pueyrredón**, which houses the Museo Pueyrredón, contains artefacts from the life of General Juan Martín Pueyrredón. The church, built in 1895, is in French neogothic style. Also French-inspired is the **Villa Ocampo**, built in 1890 and inhabited by the famous writer Victoria Ocampo. San Isidro is a resort for golf, yachting, swimming and athletics but is most famous for the **Hipodromo San Isidro**, its magnificent turf racecourse. There's also a smart shopping mall. ▶▶ *For Sleeping, Eating and other listings, see pages 105-106*

Tigre → *Colour map 4, B5*

The city's most popular weekend destination lies on the lush, jungly banks of the magnificent river delta of the Río Paraná, some 29 km northwest. It has a fun fair and an excellent fruit and handicrafts market at nearby **Canal San Fernando**, on C Sarmiento, daily 1100-2000. North of the town are innumerable canals and rivulets, with holiday homes and restaurants on the banks and a fruit growing centre. The fishing is excellent and this is a peaceful place to escape to. Regattas are held in November and March. Take a trip on one of the regular launch services (*lanchas colectivas*) which run to all parts of the delta, including taxi launches – watch prices for these – from the wharf (Estación Fluvial), see page 106.

There is a tourist office at Estación Fluvial, T4512 4497, 0900-1700, www.tigre.gov.ar The *Centro de Guías de Tigre y Delta*, T4749 0543, www.guiasdelta .com.ar offers guided walks and launch trips.

Worth a visit, the **Museo Naval**, ① *Paseo Victoria 602, T4749 0608, Mon-Thu 0830-1230, Fri 0800-1730, Sat/Sun 1000-1830 US$0.60*, covers the origins and development of Argentine navy, with lots of model ships. There are also relics of the Falklands/Malvinas War on display outside. Situated near the location of Liniers' landing in 1806, the **Museo de la Reconquista**, ① *Padre Castañeda 470, T4512 4496, Wed-Sun 1000-1800, free to ISIC card holders, closed Jan*, celebrates the reconquest of Buenos Aires from the British in 1806-07. Several stations on **Tren de la costa line**, see page 106 have shopping centres (eg San Isidro), and the terminus, Estación Delta has the huge fun fair El Parque de la Costa and a casino. You can get off and on the train as many times as you want on the same ticket. ▶▶ *For Sleeping, Eating and other listings, see pages 105-106.*

Isla Martín García → *Colour map 4, B5 Population: 200*

Situated in the Río de la Plata just off the Uruguayan town of Carmelo and some 45 km north of Buenos Aires, Martín García is now a provincial nature reserve and one of the best excursions from Buenos Aires, with many trails through the cane brakes, trees and rocky outcrops – interesting birds and flowers.

The site of Juan Díaz de Solís' landfall in 1516, the strategic position of the island has given it a chequered history, used for quarantining immigrants from Europe and then as a prison: four 20th-century Argentine presidents have been detained here, including Juan Perón. In 1914 British sailors were interned here, as were survivors from the Graf Spee in the Second World War. Evidence ranges from stone-quarries used for building the older churches of Buenos Aires, to four gun batteries, and a *faro* (lighthouse) dating from 1890. The **Museo Histórico** in the former *pulpería*, houses a display of artefacts, documents and photos. **Wildlife** is varied, particularly around the edges of the island and includes laurels, ceibo and several species of orchid. Over 200 species of birds visit the island. Take insect repellent.

There are four weekly boat trips, which run from Tigre at 0900, returning 2030, taking three hours. Prices are around US$16 including a light lunch, *asado* and guide (US$33 pp including weekend overnight at inn, full board). Reservations can be made through *Cacciola* (address, Ferries to Uruguay, page 106), who also handle bookings for the inn and restaurant on the island. ▸▸ *For Sleeping, Eating and other listings, see pages 105-106.*

Estancias near Buenos Aires

Many of the province's finest estancias can be visited relatively easily from Buenos Aires, either to spend a day (*dia de campo*) or longer. *Dia de Campo* usually includes horseriding, or riding in a horse-drawn carriage over the estancia's lands, followed by lunch. This is usually a traditional *asado*, often cooked outside with half a cow speared over an open fire: quite a spectacle and absolutely delicious. In the afternoon, you may be treated to demonstrations of farm life, music and dancing from the region, or you might just choose to walk in the beautiful grounds of the estancia, read under a tree, or swim in the pool. To really appreciate the luxury or peace of an estancia, an overnight stay is recommended. Most places are still run as working farms by their owners, who will welcome you personally, and staying with them gives you a unique insight into Argentine rural life and history. ⓘ *Several good websites gives details of estancias: www.turismo.gov.ar, caminodelgaucho.com, www.raturestancias.com.ar*

There are many *estancias* grouped around the attractive towns of **San Antonio de Areco** (see page 113), **Chascomús** (see page 117) and **Dolores** (see page 119), all listed under The Pampas.

Colonia del Sacramento ➔ *Phone code: +598-(0)52 Colour map 4 B6*

A Portuguese colonial town on the east bank of the Río de la Plata, Colonia del Sacramento is a very popular destination for excursions from Buenos Aires. The modern town with a population of 22,000, which extends along a bay, is charming and lively with neat, leafy streets. The small historic section is particularly interesting because there is so little colonial architecture in this part of South America.

There is a pleasant Plaza 25 de Agosto and a grand Intendencia Municipal (Méndez y Av Gen Flores, the main street). The best beach is Playa Ferrando, 2km to the east (buses from Gen Flores every two hours). There are regular sea and air connections with Buenos Aires and a free port.

Sights With its narrow streets (wander around Calle de los Suspiros), colonial buildings and reconstructed city walls, the Barrio Histórico has been declared *Patrimonio Cultural de la Humanidad* by UNESCO. ⓘ *Entry to the museums in this historic quarter is by combined ticket bought from* **Museo Municipal**, *US$1. The opening hours tend to be 1100-1730 every day.* The **Plaza Mayor** (Plaza 25 de Mayo) is especially picturesque. At its eastern end is the **Puerta del Campo**, the restored city gate and drawbridge. On the south side is the **Museo Portugués**; see also the narrow Calle de los Suspiros, nearby. At the western end of the Plaza are the **Museo Municipal** in the former house of Almirante Brown (with indigenous archaeology, historical items, paleontology, natural history), the **Casa Nacarello** next door, the **Casa del Virrey**, and the ruins of the **Convento de San Francisco** (1695), to which is attached the *faro* or lighthouse built in 1857. Free – tip or donation appreciated.

Just north of the Plaza Mayor a narrow street, the Calle Misiones de los Tapes, leads east to the river. At its further end is the tiny **Museo del Azulejo** housed in the

❖ *Colonia del Sacromento is in Uruguay. Remember to take your passport with you. There are no transport taxes although you will be subject to immigration formalities if you travel further into Uruguay.*

Casa Portuguesa. Two blocks north of here is the Calle Playa which runs east to the Plaza Manuel Lobo/Plaza de Armas, on the northern side of which is the **Iglesia Matriz**, on Vasconcellos, the oldest church in Uruguay. Though destroyed and rebuilt several times the altar dates from the 16th century. Two blocks north of the church on the northern edge of the old city are the fortifications of the **Bastión del Carmen;** just east of it is the **Teatro Bastión del Carmen.** One block south of the Bastión, at San José y España, is the **Museo Español,** formerly the house of General Mitre.

Listings: around Buenos Aires

Sleeping

Tigre *p103*

There are no good hotels in Tigre itself. On the islands of the Delta:

A **Los Pecanes**, *90 mins by launch from Tigre*, *T4728 1932*. Price is for a weekend for 2, rooms have fan, mosquito nets (20% discount on weekdays); Anglo-Argentine owners, meals extra, home-grown vegetables, good *asados*. Day visits for US$8 pp including meals.

C **Delta Youth Hostel**, *Río Luján y Abra Vieja*, *T4728 0396/4717 4648*. Clean, 3-ha park, hot showers, double rooms with bath, including breakfast, table tennis, volleyball, canoes, restaurant, basic cooking facilities.

Restaurants on the waterfront in Tigre across the Río Tigre from railway line; cheaper places on Italia and Cazón on the near side. There are also restaurants on islands in the delta to which excursions run.

C pp **El Tropezón**, *T4728 1012*. An old inn on the Río Paraná de las Palmas island, including meals, formerly a haunt of Hemingway, now frequented by affluent porteños. Highly recommended despite the mosquitoes.

D pp **l'Marangatú**, *Río San Antonio, T4728 0752*. Includes breakfast and dinner, pool, sports facilities.

Martín García *p103*

Hostería Martín García, owned by *Cacciola*. For bungalow rental *T(0315) 24546*.
Camping Martín García. Also has hostel accommodation.

Colonia del Sacramento *p104*
Barrio Histórico

L-AL **Plaza Mayor**, *Del Comercio 111*, *T/F3193*. Lovely, English spoken.

L-AL **Posada del Virrey**, *España 217*, *T/F2223*. Suites and rooms.

AL **Posada del Gobernador**, *18 de Julio 205*,

T3018. Breakfast included, charming. Recommended.

A **Hostal del Sol**, *Solís 31, T23179, F23349, in Buenos Aires 011 15441 5 2605*. A beautiful small hotel, with luxurious rooms in a lovely 300 year old building, in a quiet position on the coast. Highly recommended.

Centre

A **Posada Los Linajes**, *Washington Barbot 191, T24181*. Central, a/c, TV, cafeteria, warmly recommended.

A **Royal**, *General Flores 340, T22169*. Breakfast included, gloomy, poor restaurant, pool, avoid rooms on street (noisy), noisy a/c.

A-B **Italiano**, *Lobo 341, T22103*,B Without bath, good restaurant, hot water but no heating. Recommended.

A-B **Leoncia**, *Rivera 214, T22369, F22049*. A/c, modern, good.

A **Posada San Antonio**, *Ituzaingó 240*, *T25344*. Breakfast included,B during week.

B **Hostal de los Poetas**, *Mangarelli 675*, *T/F25457*. With bath, quiet, pleasant. Recommended.

B **Los Angeles**, *Roosevelt 213, T22335*. Small rooms, no restaurant, English spoken.

C-D **Hospedaje Colonial**, *Flores 436, T22906*. Recommended but noisy, restaurant below.

D **Hospedaje Las Tejas**, *Rosenthal y Fray Bentos, T24096* Breakfast included, shower.

D **Señora Raquel Suárez**, *T22916*. Spacious rooms to rent, good value.

Youth hostel
Hotel del Prado, *C Nueva Helvecia, T0554 4169*. Open all year, 15 beds, family rooms, no cooking facilities.

Camping
Municipal site, *Real de San Carlos, T24444*, US$3.50 per person,C in mini-cabañas, electric hook-ups, 100 m from beach, hot

showers, open all year, safe, excellent.
Recommended.

● Eating

Colonia de Sacramento *p104*
$ **El Aljibe**, *Flores 248 e Ituzaingó*. Good fish
dishes.
$ **El Asador**, *Ituzaingó 168*. Good *parrilla* and
pasta, nice atmosphere, value for money.
$ **El Frijol Mágico**, *Galería Americana at
Rivadavia y Méndez*, open 1130-1400. Good
vegetarian food.
$ **La Torre**, *Av Gral Flores y Santa Rita*. In old
town, bar and restaurant, loud disco music,
but fine panoramic views especially at sunset.
$ **Mercado del Túnel**, *Flores 227*. Good meat
dishes, fresh vegetables.
$ **Pulpería Los Faroles**, *just off Plaza Mayor,
old town*. Recommended, friendly.

⊃ Tour operators

Tigre *p103*
Interisleña, *Río Tigre, T4731 0261/63* and **Río
Tur**, *Puerto de Frutos, T4731 0280*. Tourist
catamarans, 5 services daily, 1 to 2-hr trips,
US$ 2.50-3.50.
Catamarán Libertad, *Puerto de Olivos*. At the
weekends, longer trips (4½ hrs) to the open
Río de la Plata estuary.

⊖ Transport

Tigre *p103*
Bus
Take No 60 from Constitución: the 60 'bajo'
takes a little longer than the 60 'alto' but is
more interesting for sightseeing.

Ferry
To **Carmelo**, Uruguay (3 hrs, twice a day,
US$18 return plus port tax) leaves from
Cacciola dock. Overnight trips to **Carmelo**
(from US$35 including accommodation) and
bus connections to **Montevideo** (6 hrs from
Tigre, US$28 return plus port tax) are also
available from Cacciola.

Train
Take train from Retiro station, Buenos Aires,
(FC Mitre section) to Tigre or to Bartolomé
Mitre and change to the Maipú station (the
stations are linked) for the **Tren de la Costa**,

T4002 6000, US$0.60 one way (US$0.50
Mon-Fri, non-stop ticket), every 10 mins
Mon-Thu 0710-2300, Fri 0710-2400, Sat-Sun
0830-0010, 25 mins journey. (Buses to Tren
de la Costa are 60 from Constitución, 19 or
71 from Once, 152 from centre.)

Colonia de Sacramento *p104*
Book in advance for all sailings and flights in
summer, especially at weekends.
Air
Flights to Aeroparque, **Buenos Aires**, most
days, generally quicker than hydrofoil. The
airport is 17 km out of town along Route 1;
for taxi to Colonia, buy ticket in building next
to arrivals, US$2.

Road
Bus Bus company offices: COT, *Flores 432,
T23121*; **Tauril**, *Flores y Suárez*; **Tauriño**, *Flores
436*. To **Montevideo**, 2½ hrs, COT and Tauril,
½ hrly service, US$7; to **Carmelo**, 1½ hrs,
Tauriño), 4 per day (not Sun), US$2.50
Chadre/Agencia Central.
Car hire Budget, *Flores 472*; Punta, *Paseo
de la Estación L, on Méndez near Flores*; also
car hire at airport.
Motorcycle and bicycle hire *Flores y
Rivera* and *outside ferry dock*, US$5per hr,
US$15 per day, recommended as a good
way of seeing the town, traffic is slow.

Sea
Ferries to **Buenos Aires** are operated by
Buquebus (*T22975*) and **Ferryturismo**
(*T42919*). See under Buenos Aires for details.

● Directory

Colonia de Sacramento *p104*
Banks Open pm only. **Banco Comercial**, on
plaza, gives cash against Visa. **Cambio
Viaggio**, *Flores 350 y Suárez, T22070*, Mon-Sat
0900-1200, 1300-1800, Sun 1000-1800 (also
outside the ferry dock, with car hire). **Cambio
Colonia** and **Banco de la República Oriental
del Uruguay** at the ferry port (dollars and
South American currencies). **Tourist
offices** *Flores y Rivera, T23700/26140/27000*,
open Mon-Fri 0800-1830, Sat and Sun
0900-2200, good maps of the Barrio
Histórico. Also at passenger terminal at the
dock, T4897.

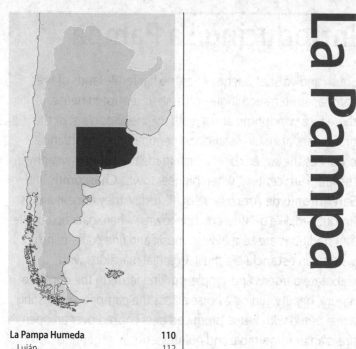

Introducing La Pampa

South and west of Buenos Aires the flat fertile lands of the Pampas stretch seemingly endlessly, interrupted here and there by a windpump and a feathery line of poplars, or the grand park of an old estancia. Argentina's rural heartland produces the superb beef which made the country wealthy in the late 19th century, when pioneer towns **Chascomús** and **San Antonio de Areco** were built. Today, they remain almost untouched, like genteel cowboy towns, where gaucho culture and traditions are kept alive in music and fine craftsmanship. Visiting an **estancia** is a must. Colonial mansions with elaborate gardens and simple working farms in the depths of natural beauty. Riding a horse across the pampas, and tasting a real *asado* with home produced beef cooked over an open fire is an unforgettable and quintessentially Argentine experience.

The great curve of Atlantic coast boasts 500 km of beaches with chic resorts and unspoilt retreats. There are casinos and nightlife at **Mar del Plata**, and a laid back atmosphere for a younger crowd at **Villa Gesell**. Upmarket **Pinamar** buzzes with life, while **Cariló** chic and exclusive, is for the Argentine jet-set. To have the beach to yourself, seek out tranquil **Mar de las Pampas**, or the long stretch of dunes of **Necochea**, where you can walk for miles without seeing a soul.

Two of the oldest mountain ranges in the world pop up from the pampas at **Tandil** and **Sierra de la Ventana**, both offering great walking and marvellous views. The university city of **La Plata** has expansive parks and a superb natural history museum, while quieter **Bahía Blanca** boasts splendid architecture. This is the ideal base for exploring Sierra de la Ventana or the family beach resorts of **Pehuén Có** and **Monte Hermoso**.

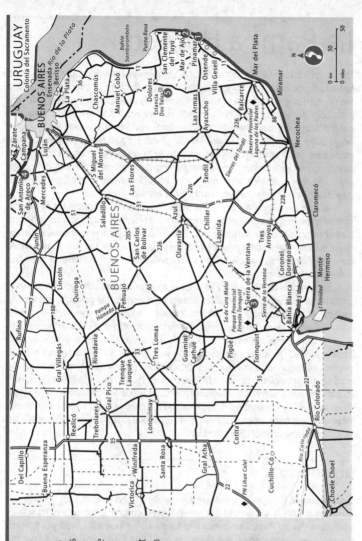

★ Don't miss...

① **Pinamar** Lie on the beach and sip a *cerveza* at a chic café as the sun goes down. Dine to the sound of the waves and live local music, page 126.

② **Gaucho style** Ride a horse along the beach at Mar de Ajó from Palantelén estancia, page 125.

③ **Cerro de la Ventana** Hike up and get an aerial view of the pampas through the natural window in the world's oldest mountains, page 143.

④ **Day of Tradition** Watch the finest gaucho horsemanship in a *jineteada* at San Antonio de Areco in mid-November. Any other time of year, watch a game of *pato* and the silver being worked the traditional way, page 113.

⑤ **Estancia Dos Talas** Sleep in luxury, walk in superb grounds, and dine in style with the descendents of the pioneer who built it, page 119.

La Pampa Humeda

The pampas is home to one of the most enduring images of Argentina: the gaucho on horseback, roaming the plains. Gauchos still work the land all over Argentina, and their culture is very much a part of rural life. In many towns on the pampas which are practically unchanged since the late 19th century you'll find the old pulpería, the general store and bar where peones (workers) and patrónes (their bosses) alike would come to drink strong spirits caña or ginebra. You'll hear traditional gaucho payadores: two singers with guitars, each trying to outdo the other with challenging questions and witty answers while maintaining the rhythms of the music. Visit the quiet old towns of Mercedes and Luján, (also known as a place of Christian pilgrimage) where these pulperías or boliches are well-preserved.

All over the region, the Day of Tradition (November) is celebrated in boisterous style, with impressive displays of horsemanship at rodeos, gaucho games of pato (a kind of early polo, originally using a duck as the ball), live music and a display of the finest gaucho handicrafts. Inevitably, lunch is gaucho-style too: the asado criollo consists of an entire cow speared on a stick poised at an angle above an open fire: indescribably delicious.

San Antonio de Areco finds any excuse to have a party, and is home to expert craftsmen, working silver and leather into the belts worn by the gauchos, trensas and rastras. It's an amazingly unspoilt small town, with many of the finest and most historical estancias within easy reach; El Ombú, La Bamba and La Porteña.

Further southeast, Chascomús is similarly charming, a traditional cowboy town come to life, with pristine examples of 1870's architecture, and a good museum of the pampas and gauchos, and a lake for water sports in summer. But its real appeal is the profusion of estancias in the area: La Horqueta, La Fe, and best of all, Dos Talas, with its extraordinary history and beautiful grounds. At Lobos, where there are three more fine estancias, La Concepción, Santa Rita, and the Loire chateau-style La Candelaria. Whether you stay the night or just visit for an afternoon to eat lunch and ride, you'll get an unforgettable taste of life on the land.

Ins and outs

Getting around The province is Argentina's easiest to get around, with a **bus** to and from Buenos Aires, and a good bus network between towns. A couple of **train** lines operate to Mar del Plata, Chascomús and Tandil. Hiring a **car** will enable you to reach the more remote estancias, and there are good fast roads radiating out from the capital (with tolls: be prepared) to Mar del Plata, via Chascomús and Dolores, San Antonio de Areco, Junín, and Lobos. The are is well equipped for tourism, without being commercialized and there's plenty of reasonably priced accommodation.

Tourist information Each if the above towns has its own **tourist information** centre, and website – worth checking for extra information, and for dates of local festivals. Most of them have good **camping** facilities too, since they're popular with visitors from Buenos Aires in the summer. They are listed here starting to the due west of the capital, and then from La Plata south.

Useful **websites** www.chascomus.com.ar www.lujanargentina.com.ar www.san antoniodeareco.com www.turismo.gov.ar also has links to all these small towns.

Estancias

Argentina's ranches vary enormously from exquisitely-decorated luxurious mansions to simple colonial-style ranches which still work as cattle farms. Usually, you'll be welcomed as a guest of the family; as you dine with the owners, they'll tell you their family's history, and give a rare insight into Argentine rural life, turning a tourist experience into a genuine encounter, with people who will become firm friends. In some, you'll sleep in splendid rooms filled with the family antiques. Others are simpler affairs, with an old farm house where you can enjoy the peace and quiet of their extensive lands; perfect places to retreat and unwind for a few days.

Almost all estancias offer horse riding, and galloping across the plains on a criollo horse has to be one of the biggest thrills of visiting the country. If you're not experienced, let your hosts know beforehand so that they can arrange for you to ride an especially docile creature and find you a riding hat: the gaucho style is a beret-like boyna but never a riding hat! The horse-shy might be offered a ride in a *sulky*, the traditional open horse-drawn carriage, more relaxing but just as exhilarating. These pleasures can usually be enjoyed in a day visit, and many establishments will pick you up from the nearest town if you don't have a car.

The colour maps at the back of the guide show the most appealing estancias in the province, but for further information on estancias, with photographs and descriptions, visit websites: www.caminodel gaucho.com.ar an excellent organisation which views estancias as friendly eco-museums; see also www.vivalaspampas.com the website for tourism in the Province of Buenos Aires, and www.south trip.com (English), the website of helpful company Tierra Buena, which organizes estancia stays. Prices range from US$150 per person for the most luxurious to US$30 for the simpler places, or US$20 for a day visit.

La Pampa La Pampa Humeda

Background

Travelling through these calm lands, field after field of sunflowers, you wouldn't think they'd had such a violent past. But these are the rich fertile plains that justified conquering the indigenous peoples in the bloody 19th-century Campaign of the Desert. Their produce made Argentina the 'breadbasket of the world', and the sixth richest nation, exporting beef, lamb, wheat and wool when a growing Europe demanded cheap food and clothing. When you see these perfect wheat fields, and superbly healthy Aberdeen Angus cattle roaming vast plains, you might wonder how a country with such rich land can possibly be suffering an economic crisis. It's one of the great enigmas of Argentina. Visit an estancia with history, like Dos Talas, to get some idea of Argentina's former wealth, and ask their owners what went wrong. Some blame Perón for encouraging passivity in the lazy populace, or Menem's desperate measures to keep up with the United States selling the nationalized industries. Farmers complain that successive governments impose impossible taxes for those who produce from the land. The fields of Buenos Aires province provide more than half of Argentina's cereal production, and over a third of her livestock, but many estancias' owners have had to turn to tourism in order to maintain the homes built by their ancestors in more affluent times. It's a rare privilege, to be wholeheartedly enjoyed.

The pampas is rich in wildlife and on lakes and lagunas, you'll spot Chilean flamingos and herons, maguari storks, white-faced Ibis and black-necked swans, and there are ostrich-like greater rheas in many parts. Migratory birds from the northern hemisphere can be seen in vast numbers at the reserve at Bahía Samborombón, at the south of the bay on the Atlantic coast. However, this is also the country's richest hunting ground, attracting keen hunters from all over the world to chase deer, wild boar, partridges and hares.

Over the whole of the pampas the summers are hot, reaching 40 degrees during January and February in the interior, but on the coasts it is a pleasant 30-35 degrees maximum. The winters are mild, though temperatures can fall to five below zero in the south of the region, and the coast is wetter and milder than the interior.

Luján → Phone code: 02323 Colour map 4, B5 Population: 56,500. .

Luján, 66 km west of the capital, is the country's most important place of pilgrimage in Latin America, and its attractive riverside location makes it a very popular spot for weekend trips from Buenos Aires. The town's centre is dominated by the **Basílica Nacional** (1887-1932), a massive, striking construction in bold neo-Gothic style, with stained glass windows and twin towers rising to 107 m, standing on **Plaza Belgrano**. The **tourist office** is a block west of the plaza, on the river between San Martín and Lavalle, in the Casa de Cúpula, T420453. www.lujanargentina.com

The basilica is approached from Avenida Nuestra Senora de Luján, along which five million faithful come to worship the tiny figure of the Virgin of Luján who sits inside. The story goes that in 1630, an image of the Virgin brought by ship from Brazil, was being transported to its new owner in Santiago del Estero by ox cart, when the cart got stuck, despite strenuous efforts by men and oxen to move it. This was taken as a sign that the Virgin had decided she should stay there, a chapel was built for the image, and around it grew Luján. The chapel has long since been superseded by the mighty basilica and the Virgin now stands on the High Altar. Each arch of the church is dedicated to an Argentine province, and the transepts to Uruguay, Paraguay and Ireland. For guided tours of the basilica, T435101.

Next to the basilica is a huge musuem complex, including the fine 18th-century **Cabildo**, built in traditional style with two floors of galleries with regular arches, which has been an administrative centre, a school and also a prison, where General Beresford was briefly held after Britain's failed invasion attempt in 1806. Inside the Cabildo, the **Museo Histórico Colonial** ① *Wed-Sat 1200-1730, US$1*, traces the

❧ Behind the Cabildo, the river bank is an attractive place to stroll, with plenty of restaurants, and the departure point for cruises along the river.

historical and political development of Argentina and includes some rather dry sections on Argentine presidents, and more interesting displays on gauchos, and the region's indigenous peoples. Next to it, is the **Casa del Virrey**, an 18th-century mansion which was occupied by the Viceroy escaping the British invasion of 1806. Also worth visiting is the **Salon de Arte Hispanoamericano** with paintings from the Cuzco school, and other Spanish and indigenous art. In the same complex is **Museo del Transporte**, Argentina's largest transport museum, containing some impressive horse-drawn carriages, *La Porteña* – the first railway engine to operate in the country – and several early bicycles as well as a fine collection of veteran cars. Quite unexpectedly, there are also two stuffed horses, *Gato* and *Mancha*, used by the Swiss explorer Tschiffely, who rode from Buenos Aires to New York in the 1930's. Highly recommended. ① *Wed-Sun 1200-1800.* ▸▸ *For Sleeping, Eating and other listings, see pages 119-123.*

Around Luján

Some 30 km west of Luján is the tranquil town of **Mercedes**, founded in 1752, and with a beautifully preserved **Pulpería**, the last bar and general store of its kind, a feature of gaucho and Borges' folklore. The **tourist office** is at Avenida 29 and Calle 26, T02324-426738. Nearby, there's wonderful horse riding at **Las Patronas stables**

• Steaks on high

Though Argentina is famous for its excellent beef, cattle were not indigenous to the Pampas. After Juan de Garay's expedition in 1580 brought cattle from Paraguay, the animals roamed wild on the fertile plains, reproducing so quickly that by the time the Spanish returned to the Pampas in 1780, there were 40 million cattle. By then, the local indigenous groups were driving herds of cattle through the Andean passes to trade with Mapuche in southern Chile. Gauchos, meanwhile, were hunting cattle with the use of *boleadoras* (a lasso with three stone balls), and slaughtering them by the thousand for their hides alone, leaving the meat to rot. Salting plants – *saladeros* – changed such wasteful practices after 1810, and hides were transported to Europe, together with tallow for candles. The meat was turned into *charqui*, strips of beef dried and salted, sold to feed slaves in Brazil and Cuba. Access to the salt flats of southern Buenos

Aires province was essential for the process, and incursions into dangerous territory became a key consideration in relations with the indigenous tribes.

With the invention of refrigerated ships, Argentina's produce was able to meet the growing demand for beef in an expanding Europe. Cattle-farmers introduced new breeds to replace the scrawny pampas cattle, and sowed alfalfa as richer fodder than pampas grasses. Today Herefords and Aberdeen Angus are still bred for meat.

Argentine beef is so succulent, they say, because with such vast expanses of land to roam, the cattle are well-toned and lean, producing meat high in Omega 3. Certainly, unless you're vegetarian, you should try a few different cuts at a *parrilla* (steak restaurant) or at a friend's *asado* where meat is expertly cooked the traditional way over an open wood fire or grill. See page 580 for an explanation of the cuts on offer.

La Pampa San Antonio de Areco

ⓘ *To2324-430421 or 15581903, laspatronas@yahoo.com.ar* run by enthusiastic experts Adriana and Alejandra, whose knowledge of the region, of traditional Argentine horses and riding, and of the local area will give you a wonderful day out. Prices around US$35 for a complete day at the ranch with horse riding and lunch, accommodation can also be arranged. ▸▸ *For Sleeping, Eating and other listings, see pages 119-123.*

San Antonio de Areco → *Phone code: 02326 Colour map 4, B5 Population: 15,000*

San Antonio de Areco, 113 km northwest of Buenos Aires, is a charming, completely authentic late 19th-century town, with crumbling atmospheric single-storey buildings around a plaza filled with palms and plane trees, streets lined with orange trees, and an attractive *costanera* along the river bank: a great place to swim and picnic. There are several estancias nearby, and the town itself has historical *boliches* (combined bar and provisions stores), where you can lap up the atmosphere, hear live music and meet locals. The gaucho traditions are maintained in frequent weekend activities, and the town's craftsmen produce wonderful silver craftsmanship, textiles and leather handicrafts of the highest quality. There are *pato* games in January, a poncho parade in February, a *Fiesta Criolla* in March, and most important of all, the *Day of Tradition* in the second week of November (book accommodation ahead) with traditional parades, gaucho games, events on horseback, music and dance. A perfect escape from Buenos Aires.

El Gaucho

The gaucho is the cowboy of the Pampas, found too in other parts of Argentina, and an important cultural and political symbol in Argentina. Gauchos emerged as a distinct social group in the early 18th century, hunting wild cattle on the pampas and adopting aspects of the indigenous peoples' lifestyle. The classic gaucho lived on horseback, dressing in a poncho, *bombachas* (baggy trousers) held up by a *tirador* (broad leather belt) and homemade boots with leather spurs. He was armed with a *facón* or large knife, and *boleadoras*, a lasso made from three stones tied with leather thongs which when expertly thrown, wrapped around the legs of animals and brought them to the ground. He roamed the pampas hunting the seemingly inexhaustible herds of wild cattle and horses in the long period before fencing protected private property. The gaucho's wild reputation derived from his resistance to government officials who tried to exert their control over gauchos and the pampas lands by the use of anti-vagrancy laws and military conscription. And the urban population regarded the gaucho as a savage, on a par with the 'indians'.

The gaucho's lifestyle, was doomed, of course, in the advent of railways, fencing, and by the campaigns against the indigenous peoples and the redistribution of land which followed. Increasingly the term gaucho came to mean an estancia (ranch) worker who made a living on horseback tending cattle. As the real gaucho disappeared from the pampas, he became a major subject of Argentine folklore and literature, most famously in José Hernández' epic poem of 1872, *Martín Fierro* and in Güiraldes' later novel *Don Segundo Sombra*. You can still see gauchos in their traditional dress at work today. Visit any estancia, or visit San Antonio de Areco, just west of Buenos Aires, for displays of traditional gaucho horsemanship and music, silversmithing and leatherwork.

Museo Gauchesco Ricardo Güiraldes ① *Camino Güiraldes, daily except Tue, 1100-1700, US$0.70*, is a replica of a typical estancia of the late 19th century, with impressive gaucho artefacts and displays on the life of Güiraldes, a sophisticated member of Parisian literary circles, and an Argentine nationalist who romanticized gaucho life. He spent much of his early life on the **Estancia La Porteña**, 8 km from San Antonio, and settled on the estancia to write his best-known book, *Don Segundo Sombra* (1926), which was set in San Antonio. The estancia and sites in the town such as the old bridge and the Pulpería La Blanqueada (at the entrance to the museum), became famous through its pages.

Superb gaucho silverwork is for sale at the workshop and **Museo de Juan José Draghi** ① *Alvear 345, T454219, open daily 0900-2000*. Excellent chocolates are made at **La Olla de Cobre**, Matheu 433, T453105, with a charming little café for drinking chocolate and trying the most amazing homemade *alfajores*. There is a large park, **Parque San Martín**, spanning the river to the north of the town near the tourist information centre ① *at Zerboni and Arellano, T453165, www.sanantonio deareco.com* Two blocks west of here, there's a small zoo **Parque de Flora y Fauna Carlos Merti** opposite the old bridge Puente Viejo ① *1000-1300, 1700-1900 summer, 1000-1700 winter, US$ 0.70*. Also on Alsina 66 is the city museum, **Centro Cultural y Museo Usina Vieja** ① *Tue-Fri 0800-1400, Sat, Sun, holidays 1100-1700, free*. There are ATMs on the plaza, but nowhere to change travellers cheques. At the **country club** you can play golf (green fees US$7), or watch a polo match, in restful surroundings, ask tourist office for directions. ⇥ *For Sleeping, Eating and transport, see pages 119-123.*

Junín → *Phone code: 02362 Colour map 4, B4 Population: 63,700*

Junín, 256 km west of Buenos Aires, was founded as a fort in 1827, and it's not a spectacularly interesting place. Its main claim to fame is that Eva Perón lived here between age 11 and 15, before moving to Buenos Aires. You can visit the house where she lived, and the place where she married Perón. The **tourist information office** is at Av R Sáenz Pena 145 ① *T444856, www.junin.mun.gba.gov.ar, open Mon-Fri 0800-1900, Sat 0900-1300.*

If you find yourself here on a sunny day, you could head for one of three lakes nearby, of which the most developed for tourism is **Laguna de Gómez**, 12 km west of Junín, with lots of weekend homes, a few campsites, and lots of sports on offer, both in and out of the water. **Club Náutico** here runs all the water sports, has bikes and boats for hire, and a campsite, US$3 for 2, together with a *parador* where you can eat. A boat for 4 costs US$10 a day. **Laguna el Carpincho**, 4 km west, is a wilder place, popular with anglers, and another lake, **Laguna Mar Chiquita** is in a totally natural state, and is also popular with fisherman, see page 122 for clubs and fishing guides.

▸▸ *For Sleeping, Eating and other listings, see pages 119-123.*

La Plata → *Phone code: 0221 Colour map 4, B6 Population: 642,000*

The capital of Buenos Aires province is La Plata, situated near the Río de la Plata 56 km southeast of Buenos Aires. It's one of the country's most important university cities, with a lively student population, and consequently a good nightlife, with lots of good restaurants and bars. La Plata was built according to late 19th-century European ideas on urban planning, a perfect grid with broad avenues, many leafy plazas, and elaborate public buildings. But it feels decidedly young and vibrant: football and rugby are both major passions here, to the extent that the city has a huge new high-tech stadium, and no less than five rugby clubs. At the east of the city there's a beautiful park, **Paseo del Bosque**, popular at weekends with families for asados, with its famous science museum, the magnificent Museo de Ciencias Naturales.

Ins and outs

Getting there La Plata is just 56 km southeast of Buenos Aires, 45 minutes by **car**, easily reached by **bus** from Buenos Aires, leaving every 30 minutes, taking about 1½ hours (from Retiro all day and night and from Plaza Constitución day only). There are also frequent **trains**, taking 1 hour 10 minutes. Long distance buses arrive here from all major cities. The terminal is at Calle 4 and Diagonal 74, and a taxi into the central area costs US$2.

Getting around The city is easy to get around, since the streets have numbers, rather than names, and the layout is a perfect grid. It does have one peculiarity, however; diagonal streets cross the entire city, which can be very confusing if you have a poor sense of direction. When you approach one of these crossroads with six choices, hold your nerve and remember the number of the street you're on! There's an efficient network of buses all over the city, and taxis are safe, cheap and plentiful.

Tourist information www.laplata.gov.ar www.cultura.laplata.gov.ar There are two tourist offices: a small **municipal tourist office** at Pasaje Dardo Rocha, Calle 50 between 6 and 7, (also an art gallery) T427 1535, 427 1210. Mon-Fri 1000-1700, and on long weekends and Easter too. The other office is at Palacio Campodónico, Diagonal 79, between 5 and 6, T422 9764. Another helpful office for exploring all kinds of estancias, stables, and for visiting artists and craftsmen in the pampas is **Camino del**

Gaucho, Calle 57 No 393, T425 7482. This imaginative enterprise is extremely informative, will help you arrange your own itinerary, and the staff speak perfect English, www.caminodelgaucho.com.ar (in English).

Sights

The major public buildings are centred around two parallel streets, Calles 51 and 53, the **eje monumental**, which run east from the Plaza Moreno to the Plaza San Martín and from there to the Paseo del Bosque at the east of the city centre. On the west side of Plaza Moreno is the enormous brick neo-gothic **cathedral** ⓘ *visits daily 0900-1300, 1500-1800*, designed by Benoit, built between 1885 and 1936, and inspired by Cologne and Amiens, but a little lacking in elegance. It does, however, have splendid views from a viewpoint at the top, 60m above the ground, looking over Río de la Plata. Opposite is the

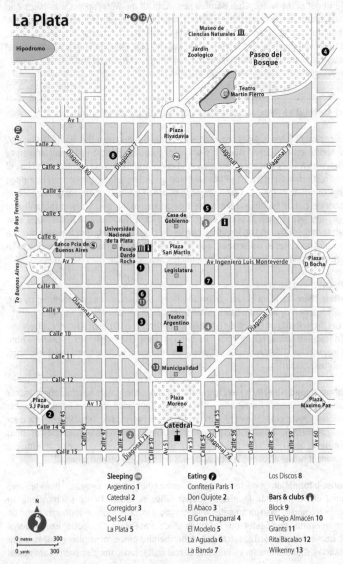

La Plata

Hipodromo

Museo de Ciencias Naturales

Jardín Zoológico

Paseo del Bosque

Teatro Martín Fierro

Av 1

Plaza Rivadavia

Casa de Gobierno

Universidad Nacional de la Plata

Banco Pcia de Buenos Aires

Pasaje Dardo Rocha

Plaza San Martín

Av 7

Av Ingeniero Luis Monteverde

Legislatura

Plaza D Bocha

Teatro Argentino

Municipalidad

Plaza J J Paso

Av 13

Plaza Moreno

Plaza Maximo Paz

Catedral

To Bus Terminal

To Buenos Aires

Calle 2, Calle 3, Calle 4, Calle 5, Calle 6, Calle 8, Calle 9, Calle 10, Calle 11, Calle 12, Calle 14, Calle 15

Diagonal 80, Diagonal 77, Diagonal 78, Diagonal 79, Diagonal 74, Diagonal 73

Calle 45, Calle 46, Calle 47, Calle 48, Diagonal 73, Calle 50, Av 51, Av 53, Calle 54, Diagonal 74, Calle 55, Calle 56, Calle 57, Calle 58, Calle 59, Av 60

N

0 metres 300
0 yards 300

Sleeping	Eating	Los Discos 8
Argentino 1	Confitería París 1	
Catedral 2	Don Quijote 2	**Bars & clubs**
Corregidor 3	El Abaco 3	Block 9
Del Sol 4	El Gran Chaparral 4	El Viejo Almacén 10
La Plata 5	El Modelo 5	Grants 11
	La Aguada 6	Rita Bacalao 12
	La Banda 7	Wilkenny 13

large white building of the **Muncipalidad**, in German renaissance style, with a striking clock tower. Plaza San Martín, six blocks east, is bounded by the **Legislature**, designed by the German architects Heine and Hageman with its huge neoclassical façade, and, opposite, the **Casa de Gobierno** is a mixture of French and Flemish Renaissance styles. On the north side of the plaza is the lovely **Pasaje Dardo Rocha**, designed in Italian Renaissance style by the Italian Francisco Pinaroli as the main railway station. It now houses the **Centro Cultural**, with a gallery of contemporary Latin American art, a café and two theatres. ① *Calle 50 between 6 and 7, T427 1843, gallery open 1000-1300, 1500-1800, weekends 1500-1800, free. www.cultura.laplata. gov.ar/ for what's on.* East of the Municipalidad, **Teatro Argentino** has its own orchestra and ballet company. Nearby on Calles 6 and 7 are the imposing **Universidad Nacional** and the **Banco Provincial**. The main shopping streets are on Calles 8 and 12. A good market selling handicrafts and local *artesania* is in Plaza Italia at weekends.

Among the attractions of the **Paseo del Bosque** are woodlands and an artificial lake, much enjoyed at weekends for *asados* and picnics, as well as the **Zoological Gardens**, astronomical observatory and the Hipodromo, dating from the 1930s and one of the most important racecourses in the country. However, the park is most famous for the **Museo de Ciencias Naturales** ① *www.fcnym.unlp.edu.ar, daily 1000-1800, closed 1 Jan, 1 May, 25 Dec,US$1.50, free guided tours, weekdays 1400, 1600, Sat-Sun hourly, in Spanish and in English (phone first to request T425 7744, F425 7527)*, one of the most famous museums in Latin America. Founded by Francisco Perito Moreno, it houses an outstanding collection, particularly the sections on dinosaurs, anthropology and archaeology. A huge collection of pre-Columbian artefacts includes pre-Incan ceramics from Peru, and beautiful ceramics from the northwest of Argentina. Highly recommended.

Around La Plata

The **República de los Niños** ① *Col Gral Belgrano y Calle 501, T484 1409, 1000-2200, US$0.30, children free, parking US$1, train to Gonnet station, 8 km northwest of the city*, is Eva Peron's legacy, built under the first Perón administration. A delightful children's village, with scaled down castles, oriental palaces, boating lake, cafés and even a little train, it's a fun place for families to picnic. The **Parque Ecológico** ① *Camino Centenario y San Luis, at Villa Elisa, T473 2449 open 0900-1930, free, 8 km north off main road to Buenos Aires, take bus 273 D or E*, is another good place for families, a large expanse of countryside with native forest, and llamas, armadillos and ñandú roaming around.

The **Islas del Río Santiago** are east of the city. At **Punta Lara**, a holiday resort 7 km east, there is a **nature reserve** ① *entry is strictly controlled: guided tours on Sun only 1000-1300 and 1400-1800, T0221-660396 first*, protecting the southernmost remaining stretch of riverine forest in South America, with diverse plants and wildlife.

Parque Costero Sur is a large nature reserve 110 km south, a UNESCO biosphere site, along 70 km of coastline, protecting a wide range of birds. It includes several estancias, including at Punta Indio, 165 km, the 1920's Tudor-style **Estancia Juan Gerónimo**, set on the coast, where you can walk and horse ride in the 4,000-ha estate, enjoying total peace. Swimming and birdwatching also offered. Closer to hand, **Casa de Campo La China** is a charming 1930´s adobe house set in eucalyptus woods, with beautifully furnished accommodation and far-reaching views. At both you can stay or visit for the day, ride horses and enjoy carriage rides. ▶ *For Sleeping, Eating and other listings, see pages 119-123.*

Chascomús → *Phone code: 02241 Colour map 4, B6 Population: 40,000*

This quaint historical town, 126 km south of Buenos Aires, is worth a visit just to enjoy its Wild West feel, or to take a boat out on its huge laguna, but it's also the base for a

La Pampa Chascomús

⁝ The Conquest of the Wilderness

Until the 1870's, the indigenous tribes of the Pampas controlled large parts of Argentina. After independence, Rosas launched the first attempt to claim territory from the natives in Buenos Aires province in his 1883 Campaign of the Desert. In the 1870's pressure grew for a campaign to defeat the 'indians' and force them to submit to Buenos Aires. The withdrawal of Argentine troops from the borders to fight in the War of Triple Alliance led to a series of increasingly audacious raids by indigenous armies, *malones*, such as the attack led by *Calfucurá* with 2,000 warriors on Córdoba, which made off with 2,000 head of cattle and 200 prisoners.

In the 1870's, war minister Alsina planned a series of forts, connected by a moat and ramparts to defend the territory he'd won from the indigenous peoples, his Zanja de Alsina. But his successor, Roca, who had criticised these plans as too defensive, called for a war of extermination. Roca's Conquest of the Desert was launched in 1879, with 8,000 troops in five divisions, one of them led by Roca himself. Five important indigenous chiefs were captured, along with 1,300 warriors. 2,300 more were killed or wounded. Roca's view was that 'it is a law of human nature that the Indian succumb to the impact of civilized man' and destroyed villages and forced the inhabitants to choose between exile in Chile, or life in a reservation. After the campaign, mountain passes to Chile were closed, and any remaining indigenous groups were forced onto reservations.

Although Roca claimed victory in the Conquest of the Desert as a personal triumph, he was helped by technological advances such as the spread of the telegraph, which gave commanders intelligence reports to offset the indigenous peoples' knowledge of the terrain and enabled them to co-ordinate their efforts. Railways moved troops around swiftly, and Remington repeating rifles enabled one soldier to take on five indigenous people and kill them all.

Roca was hailed as a hero, elected president in 1880, and dominated Argentine politics until his death in 1904. The land he conquered was handed out mainly to Roca's friends, since the campaign had been funded by mortgaging plots in advance, with bonds worth 25,000 acres being bought by only 500 people. Argentina has yet to come to terms with this shameful part of its history.

couple of fine estancias. Chascomús was founded in 1779, when a fort was built as protection against the indigenous tribes. In 1839 it was the site of the Battle of the Libres del Sur (the Free of the South), and all its streets are full of well-preserved buildings dating from the mid-1800s, and lined with mature trees. Despite the presence of history here, the town has a lively feel, and its position along the eastern edge of the huge Laguna Chascomús gives it an attractive costanera which comes to life in the summer. The main tourist office is 4 blocks from the main avenue, Las Astras ① *Libres del Sur 242, 1st floor, T430405, 0900-1900 daily, www.chascomus.com.ar www.chascomus.net* There is also an office on the *costanera* and Espana 12.

Sights

Around the quiet Plaza Independencia are the fudge-coloured colonial-style **Palacio Municipal** and **Iglesia Catedral** opposite. Southeast of the plaza is the extraordinary **Capilla de los Negros** (1862) ① *daily 1000-1200, 1700-1900*, a small brick chapel with earth floor, built as a place for worship for black slaves who were bought by wealthy families here in the early 1800s, an atmospheric place which still holds their offerings. There's a highly recommended museum, the *Museo Pampeano Av Lastra y Munoz i T 425110, Tue-Fri 0800-1400, Sat-Sun 0900-1300, 1730-1930, free, with lots on gaucho culture, fabulous maps of the Spanish conquest, furniture, and all the evident wealth of the early pioneers. Well worth visiting.*

To the south of the town lies the **Laguna Chascomús**, one of a chain of seven connected lakes; the **costanera** is a pleasant place to stroll, you can sail and windsurf in the summer, and there are frequent regattas. It's also an important breeding place for *pejerrey* fish, with amateur fishing competitions held from November to March.

▶▶ *For Sleeping, Eating and other listings, see pages 119-123.*

Dolores → *Phone code: 02245 Colour map 4, C6 Population: 30,000*

Dolores, 204 km south of Buenos Aires, was founded in 1818, the first town in independent Argentina, a lovely quiet place filled with attractive old buildings. In the Parque Libres del Sur, **Museo Libres del Sur** ⓘ *Daily 1000-1700*, has interesting and well displayed local history particularly about the conquest of the desert and revolt against Rosas. Lots of gaucho silver, plaited leather *tableros*, branding irons, and a huge cart from 1868 among its old buildings. There's a charming plaza at the heart of the town, with its central obelisk and impressive classical-style church, the **Iglesia Nuestra Senora de Dolores**, to the side. In mid- to late-February, there's the *Fiesta de la Guitarra*, with performances from internationally famous musicians, dancing and processions. Book ahead; this is a good time to visit. For further information, contact the tourist office, T442432, www.dolores.mun.gba.gov.ar

‡ *Look at estancias online: www.vivalaspampas.com.ar www.turismo.gov.ar/active tourism*

Estancia Dos Talas

The most beautiful estancia in the pampas, and one of the oldest, is **Dos Talas** ⓘ *10 km away from Dolores, T443020, 15513282, www.dostalas.com.ar* A fabulously elegant house in grand parkland designed by Charles Thays, with a lovely chapel copied from Notre Dame de Passy and fascinating history, evident in all the family photos, artefacts and the vast library, in this beautifully decorated home. Come for the day or even better stay. See Estancias pages 43 and 111.

Listings: La Pampa Humeda

⬤ Sleeping

Luján *p112*
C **Hoxon**, *9 de Julio 760, T429970*. The best on offer, this 4-star hotel has well-decorated rooms, breakfast included.
C **Los Monques** *Francia 981, T420606*. The second best option, a new hotel with comfortable rooms.
D **Catedral**, *9 de Julio 1074, T430670*. Modern comfortable rooms with bath, breakfast included.
D **Centro**, *Francia 1062, T420667*. The same owners as the *Catedral*, but cheaper, a simple place with decent enough rooms, all with bathrooms, and welcoming staff, breakfast included.

San Antonio de Areco *p113*
C **Hostal Draghi**, *San Martín 477, T454515, draghi@arecoonline.com.ar* Most charming, traditional-style rooms, very comfortable, with kitchen and bathroom.
D **Hostal de Areco**, *Zapiola 25, T456118*,
D **Posada del Ceibo**, *Irigoye y Smith, T454614*, and
D **Los Abuelos**, *Zerboni y Zapiola T456390*, all have comfortable rooms in renovated 1900's

houses retaining the original features, in traditional style. Rooms have bathrooms and breakfast is included. All three can be recommended.

E Res San Cayetano (and **San Antonio** next door), *Segundo Sombra 515, T456393*. The cheapest in town, this is basic, but the rooms are pleasant and breakfast is included.

Camping

There are three sites in the park by the river, the best of which is **Club River Plate**, *Av del Valle y Alvear, T452744*, an attractive sports club, offering shady sites with all facilities, a pool and sports of all kinds, US$3 per tent. Also **Auto-camping La Porteña**, a beautiful spot 12 km from town on the Güiraldes Estancia, good earth access roads. There are many *parrilladas* at picnic spots along the bank of the Río Areco.

Estancias

Some of the province's finest estancias are within easy reach of San Antonio for day visits, offering horse riding, an *asado* lunch, and other activities. Better still, stay overnight to really appreciate the peace and beauty of these historical places. These are recommended:

L La Bamba, *T456293, T011-4732 1269, www.la-bamba.com.ar* A plum-coloured colonial-style building dating from 1830, in grand parkland, with charming rooms and welcoming English-speaking owners who have lived here for generations, utterly relaxing and highly recommended. Also serves superb meals.

AL El Ombú, *T492080, T011-4710 2795, www.estanciaelombu.com* A fine house with magnificent terrace, dating from 1890, comfortable rooms, horse riding, English-speaking owners.

AL La Porteña, *T453770, www.estancial aportenia.com.ar* Atmospheric house dating from 1823, where Güiraldes lived and wrote, simple spacious rooms with original features, a terrace with views of the polo pitch.

La Cinacina, *T452054 or T452773, www.lacinacina.com.ar* A day estancia, US$10pp for a visit, with traditional music and *asado*.

Junín *p115*

There are plenty of places to stay, but recommended is **C La Barca**, *Route 7, km 274, T02362-1551 1216, 445088*. Well-equipped cabins for 4 people, with TV and maid service.

Laguna el Carpincho and Laguna Gómez *p115*

C Hotel Copahue, *Saavedra 80, T423390*. The best accommodation on offer is at this 4 star, with smart modern rooms decorated with a homely touch. It's worth paying extra for the superior rooms, all with TV, bathroom, breakfast and parking included.

C Embajador, *Sáenz Peña y Pellegrini, T421437*. More economical, and also comfortable, and there are a slew of more basic 1-star places.

La Plata *p115, map p116*

The tourist office has a list of **casas de familia**, if ever the town fills up. There's no youth hostel. There are a few reasonable mid-price hotels, but little for the budget traveller.

B Hotel Corregidor, *Calle 6 No 1026 (between 53 and 54), T425 6800, www.hotelcorregidor.com* An upmarket modern business hotel, with well furnished rooms with bath, pleasant leafy public rooms. Good value.

C Hotel Argentino, *Calle 46 No. 536 (between 5 and 6), T423 4111, www.hotel argentino.com* Comfortable, very central, with bright modern rooms, all with bath.

D Catedral, *Calle 49 No.965 (between 14 and 15), T483 0091*. Modest but very welcoming. Small modern rooms with fan and bathroom, breakfast included.

D La Plata Hotel, *Av 51 No 783 (between 10 and 11), T/F422 9090*. Slightly more comfortable than the *Catedral* with more spacious rooms, and better bathrooms.

D Del Sol, *Calle 54 No 754 and 10, T421 6185, www.hotel-delsol.com.ar* Another modest place, but useful for the centre.

Estancias

L Estancia Juan Gerónimo, *T011-4937 4326, juange@datamarkets.com.ar,*

For an explanation of the sleeping and eating price codes used in this guide, see the inside front cover. Other relevant information is provided in the Essentials chapter, page 44.

www.tierrabuena.com.ar/juangeronimo
set Simple and elegant accommodation,
and exquisite food. Full board, all activities
included. English and French spoken. Guided
tours arranged. US$15pp for day visits.
A Casa de Campo La China, *60 km from La
Plata on Route 11, T0221-421 2931,
casadecampolachina@yahoo.com.ar*
Beautifully decorated spacious rooms off an
open gallery, with great views. Day rates
(US$25). Charming hosts Cecilia and Marcelo
speak perfect English. Delicious food. Highly
recommended.

Chascomús *p117*
There are a few, very reasonably priced
places to stay:
D Laguna, *Libres del Sur y Maipú, T422808.*
The town's most comfortable hotel, with its
70's style lounge, and spacious rooms with
old fashioned but clean bathrooms – the
renovated rooms are by far the best, but all
are acceptable. Breakfast is included and the
staff are friendly.
D El Mirador, *Belgrano 485, T422273.* An
attractively-renovated old building.
E pp Colón, *Libres del Sur 70 T422977.* Decent
rooms with TV and bath.
More classy accommodation is to be found
in the apart hotels and *cabañas* near the lake
shore:
A La Posada, *Costanera Espana, T423503.* On
the laguna, is delightful, very comfortable.
A Torre Azul, *Mercedes y Tandil, TT422984,
torre_azul@topmail.com.ar* Pool and spa.

Estancias
AL La Horqueta, *3 km from Chascomús on
Route 20, T011-4813 1910, www.lahorqueta
.com* An 1898 Tudor-style mansion in lovely
grounds with a laguna for fishing,
horseriding, bikes to borrow, English
speaking hosts, especially good for children,
with safe gardens to explore. Comfortable
rooms, though the food is nothing special.
LL Haras La Viviana, *45 km from Chascomús,
T011-4791 2406, www.laviviana.com* Perfect
for horse riding, since fine polo ponies are
bred here. Tiny cabins in gardens by a huge
laguna where you can kayak or fish, very
peaceful, good service, and a welcome from

the lady novelist owner, quite a character,
who speaks fluent English. Both estancias
will collect you from Chascomús.

Camping
7 sites all with good facilities. *Monte Corti is
closest, 2.2 km away, T430767,* but there are 5
on far side of the laguna, including **La
Alameda**, *12.6 km away, T15684076,* and
Mutual 6 de Septiembre, *8 km away,
T011-1551 823836,* which has a pool.

Dolores *p119*
The best accommodation is in the estancias.
D Hotel Plaza, *Castelli 75, T442362.* The only
recommendable place to stay in town.
Comfortable and welcoming old place on
the plaza, all rooms with bath and TV,
breakfast extra, good *confiteria* downstairs.
There's another good café next door.

Estancias
L Dos Talas, *T443020, 15513282,
www.dostalas.com.ar* One of the oldest
estancias, you are truly the owners' guests
here. The rooms and the service are
impeccable, the food exquisite; stay for days,
and completely relax. Pool, riding, English
spoken. See page 119 for further details.

Cabañas
There are *cabañas* at the aerodrome,
Cabañas Aero Golf Club, *T446681.*

Camping
Camping del Náutico at Lago Parque
Náutico.

❼ Eating

Luján *p112*
There are numerous restaurants along the
river bank and just off the plaza.
L'Eau Vive, *15 blocks from the centre on the
road to Buenos Aires at Constitución 2112.* This
excellent (and famous) restaurant is in lovely
surroundings. Take a taxi.

San Antonio de Areco *p113*
La Filomena, *Vieytes 395.* An elegant
modern restaurant serving delicious food,

with live music at weekends. Recommended.
El Almacén, *Bolívar 66*. Popular with locals, serving good food in a characterful original 1900's store.
La Costa Reyes, *Zerboni y Belgrano, on the costanera near the park*. Delicious *parrilla*.
Ramos Generales, *signposted from the plaza*. Historical and very atmospheric; the perfect place to try regional dishes such as *locro*.
La Vuelta de Gato, *opposite the park*. Serves good pizzas, and local salami to taste with traditional *patero* wine.

Junín *p115*

There are lots of *parrillas* along the shores of Laguna Gomez. You could also try **Paraje del Sauce**, *Km 258 on Route 7*, which is picturesque and serves tasty food, and **El Quincho de Martín**, *B de Miguel y Ruta 7*.

La Plata *p115, map p116*

Don Quijote, *Plaza Paso*. A very good restaurant, delicious food in welcoming surroundings. Well known and loved.
La Aguada, *C 50 entre 7 y 8*. The oldest restaurant in town is more for *minutas* (light meals) than big dinners, but famous for its *papas fritas* (chips); the chip soufflé is amazing.
Los Discos, *Calle 48, No 441, T424 9160*. The best *parrilla* in town, with superb steaks.
El Gran Chaparral, *C 60 y 117 (Paseo del Bosque)*. Another, more basic *parrillada* situated in the lovely park.
El Modelo, *C 54 y 5*. A traditional *cervecería*, with a good range on its menu, and great beer in slightly German-style surroundings.
La Banda, *C 8 and 54, T425 9521*, and **El Abaco** *C 49 between 9 and 10*. Two more fashionable places to eat, with a younger crowd. Both serve superb food and are highly recommended.

Cafés
Confitería Paris, *C 7 y 49*. The best croissants, and a great place for coffee.

Chascomús *p117*
El Colonial, *Lastra y Belgrano*. Great food, and very cheap, at the traditional old parilla.
El Viejo Lobo, *Mitre y Dolores*. Good for fish.

Dolores *p119*
The following selection can all be recommended:

Parilla Don Pedro, *A del Valle y Crámer*.
Restaurant La Farola, *C Buenos Aires 140*.
Pizzeria Cristal, *C Buenos Aires 226*.

♠ Bars and clubs

San Antonio de Areco *p113*
Pulpería La Ganas, *Vieytes y Pellegrini*. An atmospheric place for an evening drink, in an authentic traditional old bar, full of ancient bottles, with live music at weekends, from 2200 onwards.

La Plata *p115, map p116*
These are popular with students, and have a lively atmosphere: **Block**, *Calles 122 and 50*, and **Rita Bacalao**, in Gonnet, a pleasant residential area to the north of the city. The Irish-style pub, **Wilkenny**, *Calles 50 and 11*, is also hugely popular. **The Grants**, *Calles 49 and 9*, lively bar with cheap *tenedor libre* food.

❷ Entertainment

La Plata *p115, map p116*
Tango and tropical music at **El Viejo Almacén**, on *Diagonal 74, Calle 2*. There are free concerts during the summer in the **Teatro Martín Fierro** in the *Paseo del Bosque*.

☉ Sport

San Antonio de Areco *p113*
At the **country club**, you can play golf (green fees US$7), or watch a polo match, in restful surroundings. Good food is also served. Ask tourist office for directions.

Junín *p115*
Angling
Club de Cazadores de Junín, *Sr Roberto Greco, T422961*. Entry is US$0.35, boat hire US$5 per day, free camping.
Club de Pescadores de Junín, *contact Sr Amadeo Salim, T423556*. Entry US$0.35, boat hire US$7.30, camping US$3.40 per tent, including full services.
Fishing guides *Osvaldo Pagani, T428325*, **Oscar Burgos** *T424429*. **Pepe Perrone**, *Laguna Mar Chiquita, T433632, 15675530, pepeperrone@ciudad.com.ar* Fly-fishing guide.

⊕ Transport

San Antonio de Areco *p113*
Bus From **Buenos Aires** (Retiro bus terminal): 2 hrs, US$3.60, leaving every hour with **Chevallier** or **Pullman General Belgrano.**

Lujan *p112*
Bus From **Buenos Aires** (Plaza Once), bus 52, frequent, 2 hrs, and (Plaza Italia at Palermo) bus 57, frequent, 1 hr 50 mins with direct service, US$ 1.50. To **San Antonio de Areco**, 3 a day, US$ 1.20, **Empresa Argentina**, 1 hr. Train to Once station, 2 hrs, US$ 0.60 (change at Moreno).

Junín *p115*
Train To Buenos Aires (Retiro), Fri, Sun 1813, 5 hrs, First US$4, Tourist US$3.

La Plata *p115, map p116*
Bus The terminal is at Calle 4 and Diagonal 74. To **Buenos Aires**, 1½ hrs, US$2, about every 30 mins. From **Buenos Aires**, from Retiro day and night, and from Plaza Constitución, daytime only. If you arrive on an overnight bus at 0600, the *confitería*

opposite the bus terminal is safe and will be open. *T427 3186, 427 3198.*
Train To/from **Buenos Aires** (Constitución) run by TMR, frequent, 1 hr, 10 mins, US$1.50. (At Constitución ticket office hidden behind shops opposite plat 6).

Chascomús *p117*
Bus terminal information, T422595. Frequent services, several per day, to **Buenos Aires**, US$3, **La Plata**, **Mar del Plata**, and daily to **Bahía Blanca**, **Tandil** and **Villa Gesell**, with companies: El Cóndor, El Rápido, **Río de la Plata**, La Estrella.
Train Station, T422220. To **Buenos Aires** (Constitución), 2 daily, US$5 1st class. Also 1 a week to **Tandil** and daily to **Mar del Plata**.

Dolores *p119*
Bus Terminal T440351, El Rápido T02245-441109. To **Buenos Aires**, 3 hrs, US$4.50, and to **La Plata**, US$4.
Taxi There is a stand at *Belgrano y Rico, 1 block from plaza, T443507*.
Train Station 15 mins from centre; daily service to **Buenos Aires**, US$6 .

The Atlantic Coast

Argentina has 500 km of beautiful beaches and almost uninterrupted resorts spread out along the great sweeping curve of the Atlantic coastline between La Plata and Bahía Blanca. Closest to Buenos Aires, there's a string of sleepy seaside towns from San Clemente de Tuyú to Mar de Ajó, known as the Partido de la Costa, and better for sea-fishing than beach combing, since they're old resorts popular with young families and older Argentines. Continuing southwest, the jewel of the whole coast is attractive upmarket Pinamar, with its excellent hotels and fine restaurants. Its neighbour, smarter still, is chic Cariló, where the balnearios are exclusive and the cabañas luxurious. Nearby Villa Gesell was created as an ecological resort in the 1930's, and although it's now overwhelmed with students in January when the nightlife is wild, it retains a relaxed and friendly village feel for the rest of the year. The glorious beaches here continue southwest to two quiet places to enjoy the natural beauty in complete peace: In Mar Azul and Mar de las Pampas, you can rent a cabaña set in idyllic woodland right next to the sea.

Argentina's first and most famous resort is Mar del Plata, with a grand golf course and exclusive hotels, packed beaches and casinos, perfect for those want to party. To the west are two charming old-fashioned resorts: Miramar is quiet and low-key, great for young families; and larger Necochea has an appealing woodland park along its coastline, with a vast stretch area of unspoilt dunes to explore on horseback or in 4WDs. The great curve of coastline ends at Bahía Blanca, an attractive town inland from its port; a good place to stop on the way south.

Ins and outs

Getting there and around All resorts on the coast are linked to each other and to Buenos Aires by frequent bus services. Some are connected by train too, making it easy to get there, and then to hop between resorts if you feel like exploring more than one. Having your own transport helps to get to estancias and remoter parts of the pampas. A fast privatised road the RN 2 (with US$1 tolls every 100 km), leads directly south from Buenos Aires to Mar del Plata, via Chascomús and Dolores, with a good road branching off to Pinamar. Another fast road, the RN 11, (also with tolls), runs from Buenos Aires to San Clemente de Tuyú and then parallel to the coast, changing names at Necochea to RN 88. Mar del Plata also has a domestic airport.

Best time to visit Avoid January, if you can, when the whole coast is packed out. December and late February are ideal for hot weather with fewer crowds, and many resorts are really pleasant in spring and autumn.

Tourist information There are well-organized tourist information offices in all resorts with complete lists of accommodation, which is plentiful all along the coast; therefore only a small selection is listed here. See www.lacostaturismo.com.ar There's at least one bank with ATM in each town, though travellers' cheques cannot easily be changed.

Partido de la Costa

The nearest coastal resort to Buenos Aires, San Clemente de Tuyú is the first of a string of 14 small seaside towns, known as Partido de la Costa, stretching down to Mar de Ajó. First built in the 1930s, they lost popularity when the more glamorous resorts were built further south, where the water is warmer and clearer. Today they are slightly run-down places, with peeling 1950's seafront hotels and tacky attractions, though they're also rather cheaper than the more upmarket resorts further south. The beaches are crowded in January and absolutely deserted at other times; these are particularly forlorn in winter. However, there are lovely areas of natural beauty to explore, excellent sea fishing, for shark, pejerrey and brotola from piers or from boats, and fish can often be bought on the beach from local fishermen. ▸▸ *For Sleeping, Eating and other listings, see pages 134-142.*

San Clemete del Tuyú → *Phone code: 02252 Colour map 4, C6*

Just 320 km from Buenos Aires, San Clemente has an extraordinary nature reserve on its doorstep, but boasts as its main attraction **Mundo Marino** ① *Av Décima No 157, clearly signposted from the main road into town, T430300, www.mundomarino .com.ar, open daily 0800-2000, adults US$7, children US$5*. This is the biggest sea life centre in South America, where you can watch performing seals and dolphins, whales and penguins go through the familiar and completely unnatural routines, fun for children. There's also a smaller, far less spectacular theme park, **Bahía Aventura**, ① *T423000, open daily 0800-2000, US$1.20, take the road to Faro San Antonio, at the far south of the Bahía Samborombón,* where children can identify birds, and ascend in a lift to the top of a historical lighthouse, giving impressive views.

Far more appealing is the unspoilt wildness of **Reserva Natural Punta Rasa,** ① *5 km from San Clemente, take the road to Faro San Antonio, free, owned by the Fundación Vida Silvestre, www.vidasilvestre.com.ar,* a long tongue of sand stretching into the Bahía Samborombón where the Río de la Plata meets the sea. Vast numbers of migrating birds, and a resident population of crabs and shellfish make this an interesting place to spend an afternoon, and a great place for a walk; there's also a short self-guided stroll, and a lighthouse to visit. The peninsula is 5 km long, and vehicles can be driven along its length. Information from *guardaparques* at the entrance and at the tip of the peninsula.

San Clemente has a busy fishing port, with the characteristic yolk-yellow boats of the area, and the **Club Nautico** offers all kinds of water sports. South of the centre, there's an attractive area of woodland, **Vivero Cosme Argerich** ① *T421103, daily 1000-1200, 1300-1700, free, guided visits offered,* a 37-ha park, with woodlands, plant nursery and sports centre. For further information on activities in the area, visit the **tourist office** in San Clemente ① *Calle 2 y 63 Sur, T430718, also at the bus terminal, T422525. www.lacostaturismo.com.ar* ▸▸ *For Sleeping, Eating and other listings, see pages 134-142.*

Santa Teresita → *Phone code: 02246 Population: 9,000*

From San Clemente, drive through Toninas and Costa Chica to reach Santa Teresita, whose biggest attraction is **fishing**, though there's also a good golf course, tennis and horseriding on offer. The **pier**, entrance US$1.30, is one of the largest on the coast, and is lit for night fishing. There are plenty of fishermen offering boat trips for fishing off the coast, costing around US$18 pp for a three- to four-hour trip. **Cristian**, *Calle 38 No 751, T430461*, **Omar Morelli**, *Calle 37 No 1089, T15669179*, and **Lugaro**, *Diag.20, between 42 and 43, T525344.*

There's a **motor museum** ① *Av 32 No 1550 between 15 and 16, T525786, 0930-2000, adults US$2, children US$0.30,* which is fun for enthusiasts, with some stylish 1920's models. The **tourist office** ① *Calle 3 y 42, T420542, www.santater esita.com.ar,* can advise on accommodation.

Mar del Tuyú → *Phone code: 02246 Population: 38,000.*

The administrative centre of the Partido, 20 km south of Buenos Aires, is a tranquil place to visit in February, with a little more life than the other resorts nearby in winter. Boat trips are organized along the coast in summer, all the way to **Faro San Antonio**, where you can see whales basking at close proximity in August and September. Fishing is also the main attraction, see page 140. The dynamic, helpful **tourist office** Av 79 y Calle 13, T434431, is in the town hall building. ▸▸ *For Sleeping, Eating and and other listings, see pages 134-142.*

Mar de Ajó → *Phone code: 02257 Colour map 4, C6 Population: 13,000*

Another quiet old fashioned resort, 40 km south of Buenos Aires, Mar de Ajó has couple of real natural pleaures, besides its **motor racing**, **casino** and **shipwreck**. **Autodromo Regional** ① *Rotonda de acceso a Mar de Ajó, T420074*, holds important motor racing championships every summer. Dive or swim at the **Naufrago Margarita**, a large German ship, wrecked off the coast here in 1880, is one of the oldest in the region. Mar de Ajó has one of the largest fleets of small fishing boats in the region, as well as the largest pier. Boat trips to fish for *corvina pescadilla, casones,* and shark are offered by the best guide to the area, **Lopecito**, Av Costanera No 870, T15638093. Half-day trip including all equipment US$15pp. There's also an excellent small shop selling fishing equipment on the seafront at Costanera 910, T429487.

The most spectacular part of this area of coastline is **Altos Medanos** a long stretch of high sand dunes that are, apparently, constantly changing shape. It's one of the wildest and most unspoilt areas of the coast, bordered along the shore by wide flat beach, perfect for walking, horseriding or 4WD.

The best way to enjoy this area is by visiting one of the province's few estancias. **Palantelén** ① *T420983, www.palant elen.com.ar, 15 km south of Mar de Ajó,* is owned by descendants of a pioneering Pampas family, whose charming house is beautifully furnished and lined with mahogany panels salvaged from a shipwreck. Walk onto the sands, birdwatch or gallop across the miles of beaches, either on horseback or in a *sulky* (open horsedrawn carriage). Spend a few days here and absorb the complete peace – you could even have private tango lessons on the terrace under the stars – also full or half days to go riding, and picnic on the dunes. All highly recommended. Owner María Laura Viñales de Ramos Mejía, speaks perfect English. ▸▸ *For Sleeping, Eating and other listings, see pages 134-142.*

Pinamar and Cariló → *Phone code: 02254 Colour map 4, C6 Population: 10,000*

89 km south of San Clemente, the two most desirable resorts on the coast are next to each other, with the quieter old fashioned **Ostende** in between, built by Belgian pioneers in the early 1900's. Now there are just the remains of a wooden *rambla*, though this is a wilder part of the coast where there are plenty of campsites, and the only youth hostel.

Pinamar is great for young people and families. There are far more smart hotels here than elsewhere on the coast, and the town has a modern upmarket feel with sophisticated places to eat, and good nightlife. It's also one of the most attractive resorts, stylish and well maintained with mature trees lining its avenues.

If this is your first experience of the *balneario* – a beach facility – then it helps to know that for a fee of between US$3 and $7 per group per day, you can use of all the *balneario's* facilities, and rent a *carpa* – not tents, but in fact little wooden beach huts, built in tightly packed rows perpendicular to the sea, and furnished with tables and chairs to use when you retreat from the hot sun. Alternatively, you can rent a big beach umbrella, and stake a claim on an area closer to the sea. Renting either will allow you to use the showers, toilets, restaurants, and beach games, even, belonging to the *balneario*. Pinamar's *balnearios* range from chic, quiet places with superb restaurants, to very trendy spots with loud music, beach parties and live bands at night. There is public access to the beach between the *balnearios*, but it's worth visiting one for a day to enjoy beach life, and restaurants are open to those not renting *carpas* too.

The town also has fine **golf courses** and **tennis courts**, and there are fine hotels and smart restaurants along the main street, Avenida Bunge, running perpendicular to the sea. Explore the dunes at **Reserva Dunicola**, 13 km north, by horse or 4WD. The **tourist office** ① *Avenida Bunge 654, T491680, www.pinamar.gov.ar www.pinam arturismo.com.ar*, is helpful and arranges accommodation. English spoken.

Cariló is the most exclusive resort of all, a huge area of mature woodland, where its luxury apart-hotels and *cabañas* are all tastefully concealed. The *balnearios* are neat and exclusive – of which **Hemingway** is *the* place, full of wealthy Porteños – and there are good restaurants and chi-chi arcades of shops around the tiny centre, on Cerezo and Carpintero.

In **Ostende**, located between Pinamar and Cariló, little remains of the small town founded by Belgian entrepreneurs in 1908, since it was abandoned when the settlers returned to Belgium on the outbreak of the First World War. The only building surviving from that period is the **Viejo Hotel Ostende**, formerly the **Hotel Termas**, which was a favourite of Antoine de Saint-Exupéry. Another hotel, **Atlantic City**, unfinished in 1914, now functions as a youth hostel. There's an old wooden walkway on the beach, much photographed.

Around Pinamar and Cariló

General Madariaga is a quaint 1900s town 28 km inland, definitely worth visiting for the *Fiesta Nacional del Gaucho*, on the second weekend in December, with processions, singing and dancing. From General Madariaga, fishing fans could visit the **Laguna Salada Grande**, the largest lake in the province, where there is a nature reserve, and a paradise for fishing *pejerrey*. The **tourist office**, municipalidad Guerrero 2039, T02267-421058, www.madariaga.gov.ar, can also advise on places to stay. ▸▸ *For Sleeping, Eating and other listings, see pages 134-142.*

The ideal alternative to Mar del Plata, 106 km west and 22 km south of Pinamar, Villa Gesell was planned by a brilliant German inventor Carlos Gesell, who came to live here in 1931, determined to grow trees for wood on its barren sand dunes. The project then emerged into an ecological holiday retreat when he invited the first guests here in the 1930's, and he planned and built the town along environmentally friendly lines filled with shady trees that would draw water to the surface, and constructing roads around the dunes, rather than on the traditional grid.

Villa Gesell has retained its relaxed feel, and it's a completely unsnobby place, but Gesell would probably be aghast at the seaside town feel of the main street, Avenida 3, filled with arcades, street performers and noisy cafes at night. Look out for the main **tourist office** on the right hand side of the road as you enter the town ① *Av de los Pioneros, 1921, T458118, 458596, open 0800-2200 daily in summer*. The office is helpful, with accommodation advice, and English spoken. Accommodation information: www.villagessell.gov.ar and www. guiagessell.com

The beach itself is great, with good sand and far more room than in Mar del Plata. And just 5 km south, two quieter resorts are growing – **Mar de las Pampas**, and **Mar Azul**, where there are lots of *cabañas* for rent, rather than hotels. The beach here is broad and practically empty. Best avoided in January, when thousands of students descend on the town, Villa Gesell is best in December and late February, when it's particularly popular with families.

The **Reserva Forestal y Parque Gesell**, at the eastern end of Avenida 3, is where Carlos Gesell built his first house, now a museum in the woods, **Casa Histórica**. ① *Daily summer 1400- 2100, guided visit of area 1730, T468424. (ring to check winter opening times)*. There is inspiring biographical information (in English) and an interesting tour. Gesell's second house **Chalet Don Carlos Gesell** is now a cultural centre for exhibitions and concerts. ➤ *For Sleeping, Eating and other listings, see pages 134-142.*

Villa Gesell

Reserva Forstal y Parque Gesell

Chalet Don Carlos Gesell

Casa Histórica y Museo

Paseo 101
Paseo 102
Av Buenos Aires
Paseo 103
Paseo 104
Paseo 105
Paseo 106
Paseo 107
Paseo 107
Paseo 108
Paseo 108
Paseo 109
Paseo 110
Paseo 111
Paseo 112
Paseo 113
Paseo 114
Paseo 114
Paseo 115
Paseo 116

Disco

Handicrafts

To Bus Terminal

N
Not to scale

Sleeping 🛏
Atlantico **1**

Delfin Azul **2**
Hospedaje Aguas Verdes **3**
Hostería Gran Chalet **4**
Inti Huasi **5**
Playa **6**
Terrazas Club **7**

Mar del Plata → *Phone code: 0223*
Colour map 4, C6 Population: 502,000

The oldest and most famous Argentine resort has lost much of its charm since it was built in 1874. It's now a big city, with plenty of entertainment, but unless you're a lover of crowds or casinos, there are

La Pampa Mar del Plata

better beaches elsewhere. There are good new bars and cafés, however, along Calle Guëmes, and Alem, near the cemetery, and superb fish restaurants by the port. There are hundreds of hotels, all busy (and double the price) in January and February but it's a good place to visit in winter, when it's much quieter and can be pleasantly warm.

Ins and outs

Getting there There are daily flights from Buenos Aires (several in summer) to the airport 10 km north of town, and flights to towns in Patagonia too. Minibuses runs into town, or US$4 in a taxi. The bus terminal is very central and slightly squalid. Trains run from Buenos Aires and along the coast to Miramar in summer.

Tourist information The city's tourist office is at Belgrano 2740, T495 1777, 0800-1500, or, more conveniently, next to ex-Hotel Provincial, 0800-2000, www.mardelplata.gov.ar, English spoken, good leaflets on daily events with bus routes. Also lists of hotels and apartment/chalet letting agents. The province's office, in the ground floor of the *Hotel Provincial*, Blvd Maritimo 2500 y Peralta Rammos, T495 5340, www.vivalaspampas.com.ar For what's on: www.todomardelplata.com

Best time to visit There are lively **festivals** on *17 November*, **Day of Tradition**, with gaucho-related events, and the **national fishing festival** in late January. The **international film festival** is over two weeks, mid March, showing Argentine and world cinema. January is best avoided however, because of overcrowding, and the beaches are far more pleasant in December, or late February, when it's still hot.

Mar del Plata

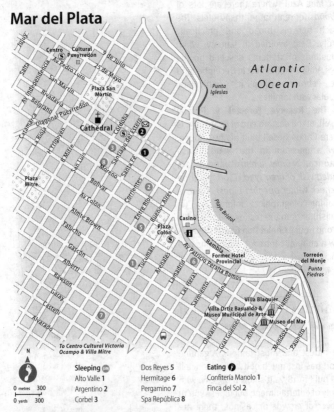

Sleeping
Alto Valle **1**
Argentino **2**
Corbel **3**
Dos Reyes **5**
Hermitage **6**
Pergamino **7**
Spa República **8**

Eating
Confitería Manolo **1**
Finca del Sol **2**

0 metres 300
0 yards 300

N

Sights

The city centre is around **Playa Bristol**, where a broad promenade, the Rambla, runs past the fine casino (upper floor open to the public) and the abandoned **Gran Hotel Provincial**, both of which were designed by Bustillo and date from the late 1930s. Six blocks north along Avenida San Martín is the Plaza San Martín, flanked by the attractive **cathedral**, and where pedestrian streets Rivadavia and San Martín head north, full of shops and restaurants. Ten blocks southwest, the area of **Los Troncos** contains some remarkable mansions dating from Mar del Plata's heyday, from mock Tudor **Villa Blaquier** to **Villa Ortiz Basualdo** (1909), inspired by a Loire chateaux, now the **Museo Municipal de Arte** ① *Av Colón 1189, daily in summer 1700-2200, US$1, including guided tour*, with rooms furnished in period style. Nearby is the splendid **Museo del Mar** ① *Av Colón 1114, T451 3553, www.museodelmar.org, 0800-2000, 2400 on Sat, US$1.50*, an imaginatively designed place on several levels, with a vast collection of 30,000 sea shells, small aquarium, café and roof terrace. The **Centro Cultural Victoria Ocampo** ① *Matheu 1851, T492 0569, daily in summer; ring to check current opening times. US$1*, is set in a beautiful 1900's wooden house in lovely gardens, where the famous author entertained illustrious literary figures. In summer concerts are held in the grounds. Nearby is the **Villa Mitre** ① *Lamadrid 3870, Mon-Fri 0900-2000 Sat/Sun 1600-2000, in summer, US$0.70*, owned by a son of Bartolomé Mitre; with an eclectic collection of artefacts including old photos of the city.

Beaches include fashionable **Playa Grande**, where the best hotels and shops are, as well as the famous golf course, with private *balnearios* for wealthy Porteños, and a small area open to the public. **Playa La Perla** is packed in summer, far from relaxing, and **Playa Punta Mogotes** further west, is by far the most appealing beach. The **port area**, south of Playa Grande, is interesting when the old orange fishing boats come in, and at night, for its wonderful seafood restaurants. A sealion colony basks on rusting wrecks by the **Escollera Sur**, the southern breakwater, and fishing is good all along the coast, where *pejerrey*, *corvina* and *pescadilla* abound. Beyond the port are the **Punta Mogotes** lighthouse, ① *Thu 1330-1700*, built in 1891, and the **Bosque Peralta Ramos**, a 400-ha forest of eucalyptus and conifers. There's no shortage of entertainment, with lots of theatres and cinemas, live music and the Casino (see below).

Around Mar del Plata

Santa Clara del Mar is a low-key family resort 18 km north, with *balnearios*, and a relaxed feel. Though it's far from chic, it's a welcoming place. For further information, contact the tourist office, T460 2433, www.marchiquitadigital.com.ar Beyond, some 34 km northeast, is the **Mar Chiquita**, a lagoon joined to the sea by a narrow channel, with huge dunes in between, offering good beaches, sailing, fishing and boating, and rich bird life. For excursions to the Laguna de los Padres and to Balcarce, see page 140. ▸▸ *For Sleeping, Eating and listings, see pages 134-142.*

Balcarce, 68 km northwest and inland from Mar del Plata, is an attractive small town, with some splendid art deco buildings, and a leafy central plaza. You're most likely to visit, though, to see the **Museo Juan Manuel Fangio** ① *Calle 18 y 17 No 639, T02266-425540, daily summer 0900-1900, winter 1000-1700, US$2.30, children US$1*. Argentina's most loved racing driver was born here, and the municipalidad on the plaza has been turned into a great museum, housing all his trophies, and many of the racing cars he drove. Recommended. For further information, contact the **tourist office**, Calle 17 No 671, T02266-425758, www.balcarce.mun.gba.gov.ar

The **Laguna Brava**, 38 km away, at the foot of the Balcarce hills, offers *pejerrey* fishing, and plentiful birdlife in lovely wooded surroundings. Visit **Estancia Laguna Brava** ① *RN 226 km 37.5, T460 8002*, for horse riding, trekking, mountain biking and water sports on the lake with fine views of Sierra Brava. For fishing, **Club de Pesca Balcarce**, Villa Laguna Brava, T460 8029.

Miramar, 53 km southwest of Mar del Plata along the coast road, is a charming small resort, known as the 'city of bicycles', and oriented towards families with small children. It has a big leafy plaza at its centre, a good stretch of beach with soft sand, and a very pleasant relaxed atmosphere; a quieter, low-key alternative to Mar del Plata. The most attractive area of the town is away from the high rise buildings on the sea front, at the **Vivero Dunicola Florentino Ameghino**, a 502-ha forest park on the beach, with lots of walks, restaurants and picnic places for *asado* among the mature trees. There's also a small **Museo Municipal**, with displays of animal fossils and indigenous Querandí artefacts. Further east is the dense wood of the **Bosque Energético** where the allegedly magical magnetic energy attracts large twigs to hang from tree trunks, and groups of silent meditators. Golfers will enjoy the fine course at **Club de Golf Miramar Links**, 4.5 km away from the centre on RN11, T433001, 420833, the only links-style course in South America, and now a smart apart-hotel too. There are plenty of banks with ATMs around the plaza. The **tourist office** ① *on the northern corner of the plaza at Calle 28 No 1086, T02291-420190, www.miramar-digital.com, 0700-2100 Mon-Fri, and weekends 0900-2100,* has helpful accommodation lists and maps.

From here, you can easily visit **Mar del Sur**, 14 km south, a peaceful resort with good fishing in a lagoon and bathing on the beach among dunes and black rocks.

Necochea → *Phone code: 02262 Colour map 4, C5 Population: 70,000*

Necochea, 110 km from Miramar, is well-established resort, famous for its enormously long (74 km!) stretch of beach, and while the central area is built up and busy in summer months, further west there are beautiful empty gorgeous expanses of sand and high dunes, perfect for exploring on foot, horseback or 4WD. There's also a huge forest park, a fine golf club and rafting nearby on the river Quequén.

Ins and outs There are several **buses** daily from Mar del Plata, Buenos Aires and Bahía Blanca to Necochea's bus terminal, rather inconveniently northwest of the administrative centre at Av 47 y Av 58, T422470 (take local bus 513 or 502 to the beach area).There are **trains** from Buenos Aires, via Tandil to the station in Quequén, C563 y 580 (take bus 512 from the bus terminal). There's a good bus network all over the city.

Orientation The town lies on the west bank of the Río Quequén, and is in two parts, with its administrative centre 2 km inland from the seafront area. On the opposite bank of the river, Quequén (population 14,000), is mostly a residential area, with one of the most important grain exporting ports in the country. The two towns are linked by three bridges, one of them, Puente Colgante, a 270 km hanging bridge built in Cherbourg in 1929.

Tourist information There are two helpful centres: on the seafront opposite main Av 79 which runs down to the sea, T425983, 430158, www.necochea natural.com Also upstairs at the municipalidad, C56 No 2956, T422631. There are plentiful banks with ATMs and *locutorios* along the main pedestrianised shopping street C83.

Sights The **Parque Miguel Lillo** (named after the Argentine botanist) starts three blocks west of Plaza San Martín, and stretches along the seafront, a wonderful dense forest of over 600 ha with more than a million species of tree. There are lovely walks along paths, many campsites and picnic spots, a swan lake with paddle boats, an amphitheatre, lots of restaurants, and places to practise various sports. There are a few museums, **Museo Histórico Regional**, small and rather dull, and the **Museo de Ciencias Naturales** ① *open summer daily and winter weekends* with stuffed animals.

West of Necochea, there's a natural arch of rock at the **Cueva del Tigre**, and beyond it stretches vast empty beach, separated from the land by sand dunes up to and the dunes are popular for 4WD riding. Vehicles and buses stop where the road ends at **Parador Médano Blanco** (a good place for lunch) where you can rent 4WDs, T15568931, US$30, jeep for 4.

East of Quequén harbour there are equally tranquil beaches, particularly **Balneario La Villazón**, and a lighthouse built in 1921, with a good 18-hole golf course.

Around Necochea
Rafting on the **Río Quequén**, and excursion to the **Cascadas de Quequén**, small waterfalls just 13 km north. Nearby is the forested **Parque Cura-Meucó**. 70 km north, on the river, is the splendid **Balneario Puente Blanco**. There's also diving off the coast to a submerged diving park at **Parque Subacuático Kabryl**, just 1500m from the coast. ▸▸ *For Sleeping, Eating and transport, see pages 134-142.*

Bahía Blanca → *Phone code: 0291 Colour map 4, C4 Population: 260,000*

With the province's most important port and a big naval base, Bahía Blanca is a busy city, and yet it's a relaxed and attractive place with superb early 20th-century architecture around its large plaza. It's a good stopping point on the route south, or a base for exploring the beautiful mountains 100 km north at Sierra de la Ventana.

Ins and outs
Getting there There are several flights daily from Buenos Aires to the airport 11 km north of town, and weekly flights with *LADE* to many places in Patagonia. There are buses from all over the country to the terminal, 2 km east of the centre, US$2 in a taxi. There are also trains to the station 6 blocks east of the plaza from Buenos Aires.

Getting around The city is pleasant to walk around, with a small centre, and most things you'll need on streets Alsina or San Martín north/east of the plaza. There's a good network of local buses, taking *tarjebus* cards rather than cash, which you'll need to take if you want to get to the to the shopping mall 20 blocks north. Taxis are cheap, plentiful and safe.

Tourist information The tourist office is in the Municipalidad on the main plaza, Alsina 65, through a small door on the outside of the building to the right, T459 4007, www.bahiablanca.gov.ar, Mon-Fri 0730-1900, Sat 1000-1300. Very helpful.

Background
Bahía Blanca was founded in 1828 as a fort, the Fortaleza Protectora Argentina, both to control cattle rustling by the indigenous population, and to protect the coast from Brazil whose navy had landed in the area in 1827. Though the native population of the area was defeated in the campaigns of Rosas, the fortress was attacked several times, notably by 3,000 Calfucurá warriors in 1859. An important centre of European immigration, it became a major port with the building of railways connecting it with grain-producing areas of the pampas. The biggest industry now is a huge petrochemicals plant 8 km from town at the port. Despite the recent economic crisis, the city remains reasonably well off, with poverty limited to the *villas* on its outskirts. It's a friendly city with the rhythm of a town, where everyone knows everyone else, and strangers are warmly welcomed.

Sights
Bahía Blanca is a pleasant walk around, with well-preserved architecture from the early 20th century. At the city's heart is the large **Plaza Rivadavia**, a broad, well kept

leafy space, lively with men playing chess or cards in the afternoons, planted with a wide variety of trees, and edged with palms, with a striking sculpture at its centre. On the west side is the Italianate **Municipalidad** (1904), and to the south the impressive French-style **Banco de la Nación** (1927); it's well worth popping in to see its perfectly preserved interior. Three blocks north there's the classical **Teatro Colón** (1922), which hosts regular theatre, live music and dance, T456 3973. At the side of the theatre, at Dorrego 116, the **Museo Histórico** ① *T456 3117, Tue-Sun 1500-2000*, has interesting displays on the city's history; interesting on the pre-Hispanic period and early immigration with interesting photos of early Bahía Blanca. Outside is a statue of Garibaldi, erected by the Italian community in 1928. There's a small collection of fine art at the **Museo de Bellas Artes**, in the basement of the Municipalidad ① *Alsina 65, Tue-Sat 0930-1300, Thu-Sun 1600-2000, free*. More inspiring, is the **Museo de Arte Contemporánea** ① *Sarmiento 450, Tue-Fri 1000-1300, 1600-2000*, with changing exhibitions.

To the northwest of the centre, along the attractive Avenida Além, the **Parque de Mayo**, is filled with eucalyptus trees, with children's play areas, bars, and a fine golf course and sports centre nearby. The **Parque Independencia**, at Ruta 3 y Av Pringles, is less charming, and has a rather run-down **Jardín Zoológico**.

Not to be missed is the **Museo del Puerto**, Torres y Carrega, 7 km away at the port area, known as *Ingeniero White*, ① *open weekends, summer 1700-2030, winter 1500-2000, and weekdays for schools, and public by arrangement, free, take bus 500A or 504 from the plaza, running hourly at weekends, or a taxi; US$3*. Set in a former customs building, this has entertaining and imaginative displays on immigrant life in the early 20th century, with witty phographs, evocative music and sound. And there's a great café in one of the exhibition spaces on Sundays. Highly recommended.The port also has a couple of fine fish restaurants amidst its red light district. ›› *For Sleeping, Eating and other listings, see pages 134-142.*

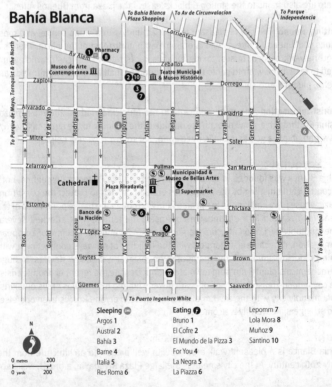

Bahía Blanca

To Bahía Blanca Plaza Shopping / To Av de Circunvalacion / To Parque Independencia

To Parque de Mayo, Tornquist & the North

To Bus Terminal

To Puerto Ingeniero White

N

0 metres 200
0 yards 200

Sleeping 😴
Argos **1**
Austral **2**
Bahía **3**
Barne **4**
Italia **5**
Res Roma **6**

Eating 🍴
Bruno **1**
El Cofre **2**
El Mundo de la Pizza **3**
For You **4**
La Negra **5**
La Piazza **6**

Lepomm **7**
Lola Mora **8**
Muñoz **9**
Santino **10**

Bahía Blanca is fortunate in having either mountains or beach less than an hour away. At **Pehuén-Có,** 84 km east, there's a long stretch of sandy beaches, with dunes, all relatively empty and unspoilt (beware of jellyfish when wind is in the south), signposted from the main road 24 km from Bahía Blanca. It has a wild and untouristy feel, with a single hotel, several campsites well shaded by pine trees, and a couple of places to eat.

There's a more established resort at **Monte Hermoso,** 106 km east, with good hotels and better organized campsites, but still a quiet, family feel, and wonderful beaches for bathing, famous for being one of the few places where the sun rises and sets over the sea (here too, don't swim when wind is in the south, because of jellyfish). To get there, **Combis Ariber,** T456 5523, runs a door-to-door minibus service; they will collect you from anywhere in town, US$3.50.

> 2.5 km from Pehuén Có, there are some astoundingly large fossilised dinosaur footprints. Ask at the Bahía Blanca tourist office for a guide.

At the entrance to Monte, turn 10 km northeast to **Laguna Sauce Grande,** a large lake where there is windsurfing, *pejerrey* fishing and boats can be hired.

For **hunting** red deer, puma and wild boar on the pampas nearby, there are expert guides and comfortable accommodation in beautiful landscape at **Estancia Parque San Bernardo,** Cuchillo Có. Contact Joaquin Palavecino, T486 1163, 156499181, sanbernardo10@hotmail.com

Santa Rosa de Pampa → *Phone code: 02954 Colour map 4, C2 Population: 70,000*

Santa Rosa is the capital of La Pampa province, founded in 1892, an important adminstrative centre 663 km from Buenos Aires, and not a wildly exciting destination, though it's a friendly place. There aren't really any tourist sights, though the **Teatro Español,** Lagos 44, dates from 1908, and ten blocks west of the Plaza San Martín is Laguna Don Tomás and a park with sports facilities. The **tourist office** is on San Martín y Luro, opposite the bus terminal, www.santarosa.gov.ar

The main reason to stop over here is to visit the **Parque Nacional Lihué Calel,** (see below). But closer still, there's **Parque Luro,** 32 km south of Santa Rosa, which covers over 6,500 ha (two buses a day from Santa Rosa). This provincial park occupies the former estate of Pedro Luro, see page 111, who created his own hunting grounds for visiting aristocratic friends from Europe, introducing red deer and wild boar, running wild in the park, with many species of birds. Luro's mansion, a French-style chateau, has been turned into a museum, and opposite is a **Centro de Interpretación Ecológico,** with displays on the flora and fauna of the Pampas. ▸▸ *For Sleeping, Eating and other listings, see pages 134-142.*

Parque Nacional Lihue Calel → *Further information: www.parquesnacionales.gov.ar*

The Lihue Calel National Park is situated 240 km southeast of Santa Rosa and 120 km from General Acha and reached by paved Route 152. The name derives from the Mapuche for 'place of life', and you can understand why when you see its low vegetated hills rising out of rather arid desert. It's microclimate allows it to support a wide variety of plant species, including a number of unique species of cactus in its rocky terrain. Wildlife includes pumas, but you're more likely to spot *maras*, the patagonian hare, vizcachas, guanacos and rheas as well as a wide variety of birds. The area was home to various indigenous groups 2,000 years ago; there are geometric cave paintings in the **Valle de los Pinturas** and the **Valle de Namencurá,** seen on one of two self-guided trails through the park. The other trail **El Huitru,** climbs the highest hill in the park and introduces some of its flora. The park is best visited in Spring. At the administrative centre for the park, there's a camping area and toilets. T02952-436595, 432639, apnlc@gralacha.com.ar ▸▸ *For Sleeping, Eating and transport, see pages 134-142.*

Listings: the Atlantic Coast

🛏 Sleeping

San Clemente del Tuyú p124
C **Fontainebleau**, *Calle 3, No 2294*, *T421187*, *www.fontainebleau.com.ar* Comfortable 4-star hotel on the coast, good value, with an elegant entrance and light airy rooms.
D **Morales**, *Calle 1 No 1856, T430357, www.hotelmorales.com.ar* A very welcoming budget option.
D **Solmar**, *Av Costanera y 50, T421438, www.hotelguia.com/hoteles/solmar* 3-star hotel with attractive rooms in a modern block.
E **Sun Shine**, *Talas deTuyú No 3025, T430316, www.rpm-net.com.ar/sunshine* The most recommendable of the cheaper places to stay.
E **Sur**, *Calle 3 No 2194, T521137, www.serviciosdelacosta.com.ar/hotelsur*

Campsites
ACA, *Av II No 96, T421124*, and **Cetan**, *Av IX y Calle 45, T421487*.

Santa Teresita p125
C **San Remo Resort**, *Calle 35 No 344, T420215, www.sanremohoteles.com* The best of the 3-stars, this is a huge holiday hotel catering largely for families.
C **Sorrento**, *Calle 37 No 235 between 2 and 3, T420 0298, hotelsorrento@telpin.com.ar* Another 3 star, with a smart entrance and pleasant rooms.
D **Hostería Santa Teresita**, *Av Costanera No 747, T420202, www.go.to/hosteria* A nicely maintained simple family hotel.
E **Turista**, *Av 32 No 464, T430334, www.santateresita.com.ar/turista* Rather basic, but clean and friendly.

Campsites
Estancia El Carmen, *Calle 23 y Playa, T420220, www.estanciaelcarmen.com.ar* A really excellent site on the beach, but with grassy shaded areas, and all facilities, including D *cabañas* for rent. Recommended.

Mar del Tuyú p125
There's little on offer in Mar del Tuyú itself, but Costa del Este next door has a couple of places, both comfortable;
C **Terrazas al Mar**, *Av Costanera between 1 and 2, T434662, www.vacationpoints.com.ar*
C **Sea Forest Inn**, *Av Costanera No 335, T434173, www.costadeleste550.com*

Campsites
El Refugio, *Calle 94 between 2 and 3, T435195, gen@sinectis.com.ar*

Mar de Ajó p125
This town has a couple of recommendable places to stay, but there is better accommodation offered at the next resort along, San Bernado, see below.
C **Gran Playa Hotel**, *Costanera 190, T420001, www.hotelgranplaya.com* The best choice in town and also the oldest; a comfortable beachfront place owned by the original family who have recently modernised it. All rooms have bathrooms and sea views, some have jacuzzis too: good buffet breakfast.
C **Hostería Mar de Ajó**, *Av Costanera Norte 205, T420023, www.hosteriamardeajo.com* Next best option in the area, a modest but comfortable beach front *hostería*.

Camping
ACA, *Avellaneda y Melón Gil, T420230.*

San Bernardo p133
B **Bel Sur**, *Mitre y Esquiú, T460368*. A huge busy holiday hotel in season, with pool, www.hotelbelsur.com.ar
B **Neptuno Plaza**, *Hernández 313, T461789, www.neptunoplaza.com.ar* A well-equipped 4-star place with good service.

Pinamar p126
There are 120 hotels in Pinamar, of a high standard, all 4-stars have a pool. Book ahead in Jan and Feb.
AB **Del Bosque**, *Av Bunge 1550, T482480, elbosque@telpin.com.ar* Very attractive, though not on the beach. Smart 4-star with

---

🔴 *For an explanation of the sleeping and eating price codes used in this guide, see the inside*
🔴 *front cover. Other relevant information is provided in the Essentials chapter, page 44.*

pool, tennis courts, good restaurant.

AB Ramada Resort, *Av Del mar y de las Gaviotas, T480900, www.ramada pinamar.com.ar* Everything you'd expect from the international chain: luxurious rooms, pool and spa, pricey but excellent food, professional staff. Very comfortable, and a prime position on the beach.

AB Reviens, *Burriquetas 79, T497010, www.hotelreviens.com* Another modern, international-style hotel with luxurious roms and with beach access. Recommended.

B Hotel Las Araucarias, *Av Bunge 1411, T480812, www.pinamarturismo.com.ar* Attractive rather cottagey rooms in this smaller hotel with pretty gardens.

B Playas, *Av Bunge 140, T482236, www.pinamarsa.com.ar* A lovely setting with stylishly-decorated rooms, and comfortable lounge, a small pool, and really good service. Recommended.

C Soleado Hotel, *Sarmiento y Nuestras Malvinas, T490304, www.pinamar turismo.com.ar* A lovely bright welcoming beachfront hotel with elegant entrance and cosy spacious rooms. Recommended.

D La Posada, *Del Odiseo 324, T482267, www.oinamar.com.ar/laposada* Good value, a rather more old fashioned style. Comfortable, vividly-painted rooms.

D Hotel Trinidad, *Del Cangrejo 1370, T488993, hoteltrinidad@telpin.com.ar* A lively welcoming little hotel with good *asado* in its *parrilla* restaurant.

Youth hostel, *Mitre 149, T482908*. This hostel is the best budget option in town.

Camping

There are several well-equipped sites (US$5-8 per day for a 4-people tent) near the beach at Ostende.

Villa Gesell *p127, map p127*

There are many hotels scattered over the town, many between Av 3 and the beach.

AL Hotel Terrazas Club, *Av 2 between 104 105, TT462181, www.terrazasclubhotel .com.ar* Quite the smartest in town, great service, huge breakfasts, pool, and access to the marvellous Azulmarina Spa, *T450545, www.spaazulmarina.com.ar*

A Delfin Azul, *Paseos 104 No 459, T462521, www.ghoteldelfinazul.com.ar* Very cosy with attractive rooms and sauna.

C Atlantico, *Av Costanera y Paseo 105, T462561, www.villagesell.net.com.ar /atlantico* A rather charming and old-fashioned seafront hotel that's been nicely modernized, with comfortable rooms, some with sea views, and all with bathrooms. A relaxing welcoming place.

C Hotel Playa, *Alameda 205 y calle 303, T458027.* The first ever hotel, situated in the wooded old part of town, now renovated and very comfortable.

D Hostería Gran Chalet, *Paseo 105 No 447 y Av 4-5, T462913.* You couldn't wish for a warmer welcome here: spacious comfortable rooms, a good breakfast, and the charming owner Mariana knows all about the area. Good value. Highly recommended.

D Inti Huasi, *Alameda 202 e Av Buenos Aires y Bosque, T462537.* A friendly little *hospedaje* in an attractive chalet-style building, in woodlands right on the edge of Parque Gesell, near the museum. With bath, breakfast included, and a bar for drinks on the terrace.

E pp Hospedaje Aguas Verdes, *Av 5, between 104 and 105, T462040, clo@terra.com.ar* A nice airy place with a little garden for drinking beer or barbecuing fish. Rooms for 2 to 6, very welcoming owners speak some English.

Mar de las Pampas *p127*

A Posada Piñen, *Juan de Garay al 600 y R Payró, T479974, www.posadapinen.rtu. com.ar* A very comfortable cottagey *hostería*, close to the sea.

Cabañas and campsites

There are many attractive well-equipped *cabañas*, including: **Arco Iris**, *Victoria Ocampo s/n, T011-4775 8536, www.arcoiris .com.ar* There are many sites, clustered between Villa Gesell and Mar de las Pampas.

La Pampa Listings: the Atlantic Coast

● **Phone codes** *San Clemente del Tuyú: 02252; Santa Teresita, Mar del Tuyú: 02246; Mar de Ajó: 02257; Pinamar & Cariló: 02254; Villa Gesell: 02255; Mar del Plata: 0223; Balcarce: 02266; Miramar: 02291; Necochea: 02262; Bahía Blanca, Monte Hermoso, San Bernardo: 0291; Santa Rosa de Pampa, Parque Nacional Lihue Calel: 02954.*

There are few hotels, these 2 apart hotels are luxurious, and have swimming pools:

AL Marcin, *Laurel y el Mar, T570888, www.hotelmarcin .com.ar* Modern very swish, right on the beach.

AL Cariló Village, *Carpintero y Divisadero, T470244, www.carilovillage.com.ar* Well-designed, cottagey, and has a spa.

Mar del Plata *p127, map p128*
Busy traffic makes it impossible to drive along the coast in summer: choose a hotel near the beach you want. There are over 700 hotels and all other categories of accommodation. During summer months it is essential to book in advance. Many hotels open in season only. Out of season, bargain everywhere.

L Costa Galana, *Bv. Marítimo 5725, T486 0000, reservas@hotelcostagalana.com.ar* The best by far, a stylish 5-star at Playa Grande with everything you could possibly want. Gorgeous.

A Hermitage, *Bv Marítimo 2657, T451 9081, www.lacapital.net.com.ar/hermitage* Charming old-fashioned 4-star located on the seafront.

B Dos Reyes, *Av Colón 2129, T491 0383, www.dosreyes.com.ar* Long-established but newly modernized town-centre hotel with smart, well-equipped rooms and its own *balneario*, big breakfast, good service, and lots of cheap deals.

B Hotel Spa República, *Córdoba 1968, T492 1142, hosparep@statics.com.ar* Friendly modern hotel with attractive rooms, swimming pool and spa, good restaurant, attentive service. Recommended.

C Argentino, *Belgrano 2225 y Entre Ríos, T493 2223, www.argentinohotel -mdp.com.ar* Modernized rooms in this traditional 4-star in the city, also apartments. Good value. Recommended.

C Corbel, *Córdoba 1870, T493 4424, www.hotellasrocas.com.ar/hotelcorbel* A modernized 60s building with very pleasant rooms, good service, and a good location in the centre. Recommended.

C Sasso, *Av Martínez de Hoz 3545, T484 2500.* Welcoming older place, with comfortable rooms and pool, near Playa Punta Mogotes.

D Alto Valle, *Buenos Aires 2338, T495 8743.* Beyond the 80s entrance foyer, with its mirrors and cream vinyl, there are simple but decent rooms in this modest but well-maintained central hotel.

D Selent, *Arenales 2347, T494 0878, www.hotelselent.com.ar* This small and central family owned hotel is great value, with warm and welcoming staff and owners on hand, and quiet, very neat rooms, with good bathrooms. Highly recommended.

D Los Troncos, *Rodríguez Peña 156, T451 8882.* A small chalet-style place, handy for the restaurants and bars along Güemes, with a garden.

D Apart Hotel Family, *Av Martínez de Hoz 1837, T485 0253.* In the same area, a good place for groups or families in well maintained little apartments facing the sea. Nothing fancy, but good value and comfortable.

E Costa Mogotes, *Martínez de Hoz 2401, T484 3446.* A neat and modern hotel, with airy *confitería*, on the main drag, but in the quiet area of Playa Punta Mogotes.

E pp Pergamino, *Tucumán 2728, T495 7927.* This youth hostel near the terminal is friendly and clean.

Camping
Many on the road south of the city, but far better sites at Villa Gesell.

Apartment rental
Monthly rent for flats US$100-180, chalets (sleeping 4-6) US$170-400. The tourist office has a list of agents, and a helpful section in English on their website, www.mardel plata.gov.ar Try **Gonnet**, *Corrientes 1987 (y Moreno), T495 2171, www.gonnet .com.ar* Very cheap off season: US$15 per night for a flat for 4.

Balcarce *p129*
D Balcarce, *C17 y 16, T422055.* Next to the museum, this is the most comfortable option, with friendly service.

Campsites
Campsites are plentiful: **Complejo Polideportivo**, *Route 55, Km 63.5, T420251.* Pools and good facilities, all kinds of sports too. **Club de Pesca de Villa**, *Laguna Brava RN 226, km 38.5.* Well-organized site, with all facilities, and good fishing.

Miramar *p130*

There are dozens of hotels and apartments between Av 26 and the sea.

C Gran Rex Hotel, *Av Mitre 805, T420783*. A rather austere modern block, but with comfortable rooms, and good bathrooms.
C Hotel América, *Diag Rosende Mitre 1114, T420847*. One of the most attractive places to stay. Located in a Spanish colonial-style building, surrounded by trees, with lots of games for children, bikes for hire, and lovely gardens. Recommended.
D Hotel Brisas del Mar, *C29 No 557, T420334*. Sea front family-run hotel with plain very neat rooms, a cheery restaurant, welcoming attention, good value.

Camping

Lots of sites including **F** per person **El Durazno**, 2 km from town, with good facilities, shops, restaurant and *cabañas*. Take bus 501 marked 'Playas'.

Necochea *p130*

Many hotels close off-season, when it's worth bargaining with those remaining open. Most hotels are in the seafront area just north of Av 2, at least 100 within 700m of the beach. There are many apartments for rent; ask the tourist office for a list.
B Asturias, *San Martín 842, T424524*.
B Doramar, *C83, No 329, T425815*. Family run, helpful.
C Hotel Bahía, *Diagonal San Martín No 731, T42353*. A really welcoming place with kind service from the friendly owners, comfortable rooms. Recommended.
C Hotel España, *C89 No 215, T422896, (ACA affiliated)*. Less luxurious, but a more modern option, well suited to families, with warm attentive staff.
C Hotel León, *Av 79 No 229, T431123*. There are lots of reasonably priced 3-star hotels, this smart hotel, with business facilites and a suite is thê best option.
C Ñikén, *C87 No 335, T432323*. The best and newest hotel in the seafront area, just two blocks from the sea, a very comfortable 4-star with pool, good facilities, a good restaurant and excellent service.
C Presidente, *C4 No 4040, T423800*. Another 4-star hotel, recommended for excellent service, comfortable rooms and pool.
C San Miguel, *C85 No 301, T/F425155,*

affiliated to ACA. 2 blocks from the sea, both open all year: good service, and comfortable rooms are good value.
D Hostería del Bosque, *C89 No 350, T/F420002*. 5 blocks from beach, a quiet comfortable place with a lovely atmosphere, rustic rooms individually designed with old furniture, and a great restaurant.
D Hotel Marino, *Av 79 No 253, T524140*. Open summer only, this is a historic choice, one of the first hotels, with a wonderful staircase and patios, faded grandeur and a bit run down, but full of character.

Camping

Recommended sites are **Camping UATRE**, *Av 10 y 187, T438278*. The best site, a few km west of town towards Médano Blanco, with great facilities, and beautifully situated *cabañas* too; US$1pp per day. **Río Quequén**, *Calle 22 y Ribera Río Quequén, T428068*. Sports facilities, pool, bar, cycle hire, well-maintained. US$5 for 2 people per day. Also **Camping Villa del Parque**, *Av 10 y Pino de Japon, T421032*. A very natural site in beautiful surroundings, but with few services.

Bahía Blanca *p131, map p132*

B Argos, *España 149, T455 0404, www.hotelargos.com.ar* Three blocks from the plaza, the city's finest is a smart 4 star business hotel with comfortable rooms, and good breakfast. Also a restaurant.
B Austral, *Colón 159, T456 1700, F455 3737, www.hoteles-austral.com.ar* A friendlier 4-star with plain spacious rooms, good bathrooms, and good views over the city, very attentive service, and very decent restaurant.
C Bahía Hotel, *Chiclana 251, T455 0601, www.bahia-hotel.com.ar* A new modern business hotel, this is good value for well-equipped rooms, though they're comfortable rather than luxurious, with a bright airy bar and *confitería* on street level. Recommended.
C Italia *Brown 181, T456 2700*. Set in a lovely 1920s Italianate building, this is one of the town's oldest, full of character, but some rooms are badly in need of a face lift. But it has a good *confiteria*, and is central.
D Barne, *H Yrigoyen 270, T453 0294*. A friendly low-key family-run place, good value, and welcoming.

D **Res Roma**, *Cerri 759, T453 8500*. Near the railway station, this budget option has clean rooms, though some are without windows, in this quiet area – take care here at nights.

Camping
Far better to head for Pehuen Có or Monte Hermoso – both lovely beach places an hour away by bus, with plentiful campsites. But if desperate, there's **Balneario Maldonado**, *4 km from centre, in a grim area near petro-chemical plant, bus 514 along Avenida Colón every hour*; US$3 per tent, US$0.50 pp, summer only. In the Tiro Federal area by the slightly run down Parque de Independencia, there's free camping with services, for a couple of days, open all year.

Monte Hermoso *p133*
B **La Goleta**, *Av Pte Perón y Calle 10, T481142*. In the town, this is a modern upmarket place. Lovely rooms with seaviews and balconies, in a central part of the beach.
D **Hotel Cumelcan**, *Av San Martín y Gonzalez Martines, T497048*. A simple 2-star, but in a great position overlooking the beach, with a restaurant providing simple meals, price given is for half board.
D **Petit Hotel**, *Av Argentina 244, T491818*. Simple rooms with bath, modernized 1940s style in this friendly family-run place right on the beach, with relaxed atmosphere, and cheap restaurant, *El Faro*, on the beach (breakfast extra). Recommended.

Camping
There are many sites with good facilities.
Camping Americano, *T481149 signposted from main road 5 km before town (bus or taxi from town)*. A lovely sprawling shady site by a quiet stretch of beach, with excellent facilities, hot showers, pool, electricity, restaurant, fireplaces, food shop, *locutorio*. Recommended. US$11 for 4 per day.

Santa Rosa de Pampa *p133*
B **Calfucura**, *San Martín 695, T433303, www.calfucurah.com.ar* A smart modern 4-star, business-oriented place with well-decorated comfortable rooms, pool and restaurants, and a few apartments to rent.
B **Club de Campiña**, *Route 5 km 604, T456800, www.lacampina.com* A rather more appealing option if you have transport,

attractive gardens, with a pool, gym and spa.
C **Lihuel Calel**, *Av Santiago Marzo 2535, T423001, www.cpenet.como.ar* Back in town, this is a good value option with attractive rooms, and a restaurant.

Camping
There is a municipal site near the Laguna Don Tomás.

Parque Nacional Lihue Calel *p133*
ACA Hostería, *Ruta Nacional 152, Km 152, T/F436101*. 8 decent rooms with TV, and a restaurant, on the road in an attractive setting in open landscape, 2 km south of park entrance. There is a camping site near the park entrance, good facilities.

❷ Eating

Pinamar *p126*
The restaurants listed here are the best options in town.
$ **Tante**, *De las Artes 35, T482735*.
$ **La Carreta**, *De las Artes 153, T484950*.
$ **Viejo Lobo**, *Av Del mar y Av Bunge, T483218*. Good seafood and international menu on the beach.

Mar de las Pampas *p127*
There are two wonderful tea rooms in the woods: **Lupita!**, *Cruz del Sur y Los Incas, T479699*, and **Viejos Tiempos**, *Leonicio Paiva e Cruz del Sur, T479524*.

Mar del Plata *p127*
There are *tenedor libre* restaurants of all kinds along the pedestrianized street **San Martín**. Three blocks from the fishing port, the modern **Centro Comercial Puerto** has many seafood restaurants, and there are cheap pasta and *parrilla* restaurants along **Rivadavia**. Two areas have become popular for attractive smaller shops, trendy bars, pubs and restaurants; Calle C Güemes and the western end of Alem, next to cemetery:
$ **El Condal**, *opposite La Bodeguita*, popular with a young crowd for *picadas* and drinks.
$ **La Bodeguita**, *Castelli 1252*. A Cuban bar with food, a good place for a drink.
$ **Tisiano**, *San Lorenzo 1332*. Good pasta.

Centre of town
$ **Confitería Manolo**, *Rivadavia 2371*, and on

the coast at *Castelli 15*. Famous for *churros* (the sausage-shaped doughnuts), with hot chocolate for party-goers in the early hours. Lively atmosphere, packed in high summer, tasty pizzas with a sea view.
$ **Parilla Trenelauken**, *Mitre 2807*.

Centro Comercia Puerto
Good for seafood restaurants, although many are brightly lit and not very atmospheric.
$ **El Viejo Pop**, *T480 1632*. Candle-lit and designed like a ship, this is the best option here, and serves superb paella.
$ **Taberna Baska**, *12 de Octubre 3301*. Serves good seafood.

Vegetarian
$ **Finca del Sol**, *San Martin 2459*. Good.

Miramar *p130*
Lots of restaurants along C21, and at the *balnearios* on the sea front.
$ **Cantina Italiana**, *C19 No 1461, T15510072*. More pasta and seafood, also delivery.
$ **Pavarotti**, *Av 9 No 1485, T432819*. Good Italian food, pastas and seafood.
$ **Restaurant El Mundo**, *C18 No 1144*. Cheap *tenedor libre*, US$2.30 for dinner, including parilla and pudding.

Mar de Ajó *p125*
$ **El Quincho** and **Parrilla San Rafael** can both be recommended. If self-catering, do buy fresh fish on beach front when fishermen come back 1000.

Necochea *p130*
$ **Cantina Venezia**, *Av 59 No 259, T424014*. This is the most famous of the excellent seafood restaurants, near the port.
$ **Chimichurri**, *C83 No 345, T421014*. Recommended for parrilla.
$ **El Rincón de Lopez**, *Av 10 No 3288, T521076*. Good local fish dishes.
$ **La Cascada**, *C85 y 6, T433434*. The town's smartest place to eat, serving a wide range of excellent food.
$ **Parrilla EL Loco**, *Av 10 y 65, T437094*. Classic *parrilla*, deservedly popular for superb steaks.
$ **Pizzería Tempo**, *C83 No 310, T435141*.
$ **Río Piedra**, *C22 T15464873*. A superb little campsite restaurant, serving really

spectacular food in a tiny riverside cabin in gorgeous surroundings.

Monte Hermoso *p133*
$ **Marfil**, *Valle Encantado 91*. The smartest option, serving delicious fish and pastas, US$6 for 2 courses.
$ **Pizza Jet**, *Valle Encantado y Int. Majluf*. Hugely popular for all kinds of food, arrive before 2130.

Bahía Blanca *p131, map p132*
$ **El Mundo de la Pizza**, *Dorrego 53*. Fabulous pizzas, thin bases loaded with toppings, lots of choice in this big atmospheric place, the city's favourite. Unbeatable.
$ **For You**, *Belgrano 69*. Cheap *tenedor libre parrilla* and Chinese food, as much as you can eat for US$3.
$ **La Negra**, *Av Alem 59*. Recommended for great Italian food, delicious pastas and fish, in a lively atmosphere, deservedly popular: arrive early (2100).
$ **Lola Mora**, *Av Alem and Sarmiento*. The city's most sophisticated restaurant serves delicious Mediterranean-style food, in an elegant colonial-style house. US$8 for 3 courses and wine. Excellent.
$ **Micho**, *Guillermo Torres 3875, Ingeniero White, T457 0346*. There are several good fish restaurants in the port area, but this elegant restaurant is the best. Be sure to take a taxi at night, as it's in an insalubrious area.
$ **Santino**, *Dorrego 38*. Italian-influenced, with a relaxed but sophisticated atmosphere, and a welcoming glass of champagne, very good value. Recommended. US$6 for 2 courses and wine.

Cafes and ice cream parlours
La Piazza, *on the corner of the plaza at O'Higgins and Chiclana*. Great coffee in a buzzing atmosphere, good salads and cakes.
Lepomm, *Alsina 390*. The best place for ice cream, especially their *chocolate amargo* and *flan de dulce de leche*.
Muñoz, *O'Higgins and Drago*. Sophisticated café for reading the papers.

◑ Bars and clubs

Mar del Plata *p127, map p128*
Most **nightclubs** are on Av Constitución, and start at around 0200:

Chocolate, *Av Constitución 4471*. Big and chic, under 25s.

Sobremonte, *Av Constitución 6690*. Huge complex of bars and dancefloors (fine to be over 25 here).

Bahía Blanca *p131, map p132*
Lots of **discos** on *Fuerte Argentino* (along the stream leading to the park) mainly catering for under 25s: **Chocolate**, **Bonito**. Best decent places for anyone over 25: **La Barraca**. **El Cofre**, *Dorrego 2 and Yrigoyen*. A welcoming, laid-back bar, good for a coffee during the day with internet access, and drink and live music at weekends with a young crowd.

🎭 Entertainment

Mar del Plata *p127*
On Wed 50% discount at all cinemas. Lots more listed in the free leaflet *Guia de actividades* from the city tourist office. Reduced price theatre tickets are often available for theatre performances etc from **Cartelera Baires**, *Santa Fe 1844, local 33* or from **Galería de los Teatros**, *Santa Fe 1751*. Many shows, comedy especially, in summer. See *Guia de actividades*.
Casino central, open Dec to end Apr, 1600-0330; 1600-0400 on Sat. Winter opening, May-Dec, Mon-Fri 1500-0230; weekends 1500-0300, free; minimum bet US$0.50. Three other casinos operate nearby in summer.
Cinema Cine Arte, *Centro Cultural Pueyrredón, 25 de Mayo y La Rioja*. Every Mon, US$1.50, followed by discussion.

🎫 Sports and activities

Mar del Plata *p127, map p128*
Cycling Bici Aventura – cicloturismo, *T481 0082*. Bikes are brought to your hotel, US$2 per hr.
Bicicleteria Madrid Yrigoyen, *2249 Plaza Mitre, T494 1932, (take buses 573, 551 or 553)*. US$6 per day, also bikes for 2.
Fishing There is good fishing all year along the coast from the shore, and off shore in hired boats: *pejerrey*, and *corvina* abound; you can charter a private launch for shark fishing. Offshore fishing is best in Nov and Dec, when *pescadilla* are plentiful: winter is ideal for *pejerrey*. Deep sea fishing yields high salmon and sea bass. Contact tourist office for advice:

T495 1777, www.turismo.mardel plata.gov.ar Fishing licences are available from **Dirección de Fiscalización Pesquera**, *Mitre 2853*, and fishing gear shops.
Golf Mar del Plata Golf Club, *T486 2221*.
Horse riding **Acción Directa Cabalgatas**, *Campo del Mar, T475 4520*. Full day's riding on beach, 11 km away by bus, T460 5448.

Mar del Tuyó *p125*
Fishing Excellent fishing either from the pier, and or on a boat trip. **Tiburon II**, *Av 1 BIS No 7503 y C75, T434698, eltiburon@infovia.com.ar* Organizes three-hour boat trips, leaving daily at 0700.
Whale watching Timonel Juan Angel Lorenzo, *Calle 58 No 332, T15527626*, **Gabriel Carral**, *Calle 66 No 152, Dto 6, T15638156*.

Villa Gesell *p127*
Horseriding **Tante Puppi**, *Blvd y Paseo 102*.

Necochea *p130*
Bike hire Rodados Villa, *Diag. San Martín 786, T438054*. **Fishing** For boats contact: **Fernando Espar**, *T425229*, **Antonio Dato** *T428601, C57 No 935*. Fishing shops: **Punta Florida Fishing Shop**, *Av 10 No 3616, T527831*. Also splendid fishing on beautiful lagunas at **Estancia La Pandorga**, *T15504413*, and at **Laguna Loma Danesa**, *T15506504*.
Golf Golf club Armada, *Argentina y 575, Quequén, T450684*. **Horseriding Caballo's**, *Villa Marítima Zabala y Av 10, T423138*. **ACA**, *Av 59, No 2073, T422106*.

🛍 Shopping

Bahía Blanca *p131*
There's a smart modern shopping mall **Bahía Blanca Plaza Shopping**, *2 km north of town on Sarmiento*. Cheap food hall, cinema (*T453 5844*) and supermarket. Also supermarket **Cooperativa** on Donado.

🧭 Tour operators

Mar del la Plata *p127*
City tours leave from Plaza San Martín and Plaza Colón. Tours also to Miramar and the sierras. Boat trips visiting Isla de los Lobos, Playa Grande, Cabo Corrientes and Playa Bristol leave from the harbour, US$2, 40 mins, summer and weekends in winter.

Longer cruises on the *Anamora*, 1130, 1400, 1600, 1800, from *Dársena B, Muelle de Guardacostas* in the port, US$5, *T489 0310*.

⊖ Transport

Mar del Plata *p127*
Air
Camet airport 10 km north of town. Daily flights in summer to **Buenos Aires**, Lapa (T4922112) and **Aerolíneas Argentinas/ Austral** (T4960101). LADE flies to towns in **Patagonia** once a week. Remise taxi from airport to town, also combi (minibus) service US$3.50.

Bus
The bus terminal, T451 5406, is located in a former railway station, is central at Alberti y Las Heras, but fairly squalid, and short on facilities, though well-connected for bus servives. Not a place to hang around at night.
Local El Rápido *T451 0600, 451 2843*, Flecha bus *T486 0512*, TAC, *T451 0014*, Chevalier *T451 8447*. La Estrella *T486 0915*.
Long distance To **Buenos Aires**, 6 hrs, US$13 , many companies; Chevalier, and Costera Criolla, also have *coche cama*. To **La Plata**, 6 hrs, US$12. El Cóndor and Rápido Argentino. To **San Clemente del Tuyú**, Empresa Costamar, frequent, 5 hrs, US$8. To **Miramar** hrly, 45 mins, US$1.30. To **Bahía Blanca**, only Pampa, 6 daily, US$11, 5½ hrs. Change here for buses to **Bariloche**.

Car hire
Primer Mundo, *Jujuy 967, T473 9817*; Rent A Car Internacional, *Hotel Dora, Buenos Aires 1841, T491 0033*; Dollar, *Córdoba 2270, T493 3461*; Avis, *at airport, T470 2100*; Budget, *Bolívar 2628, T495 6579*.

Train
Long distance Buenos Aires (Constitución) from Estación Norte, *Luro 4599, T475 6076*, about 13 blocks from the centre. Buses to/from centre 511, 512, 512B, 541. Daily services at 0745 and 2845, 5 1/2 hrs, US$10 Pullman to US$6 for Tourist. Also services to **Miramar**.

San Clemente del Tuyó *p124*
Bus To **Mar del Plata** (and to resorts in between) services are frequent, **Rápido del Sud**, El Rápido Argentino, US$5, 5 hrs. To **Buenos Aires**, several companies, US$4-7

Pinamar *p126*
Bus The terminal is 4 blocks north of the main plaza, at Av Bunge y Intermédanos, T403500. To **Buenos Aires**, US$12, 4-5hrs, several companies. For trains, see under Buenos Aires. **Train** To **Buenos Aires** (Constitución), US$13 First, US$9 Tourist.

Villa Gesell *p127*
Air
From **Buenos Aires**, Airport, 5 km away, taxi US$3, usually minibuses meet each flight. Ask tourist office which companies are flying this year. 5hrs to BA, $30.

Bus
Terminal at Av 3 y Paseo 140, information, T477253. Direct to **Mendoza**, **Cordoba** as well as **Buenos Aires**, with Plusmar, Alberino, Rápido Argentina 5hrs, US$12.

Balcarce *p129*
Bus Frequent services from **Mar del Plata**, El Rápido, *T451 0600 (in Mar del Plata)*.

Miramar *p130*
Bus
To **Buenos Aires**, 8 per day, US$10. To **Mar del Plata**, US$1.40. Rápido del Sur, *from C23 y 24, T423359*.

Train
Ferrobus daily except Sun to **Mar del Plata**. Station at *Calles 40 and 13, T420657*.

Necochea *p130*
Bus
The terminal at Av 58 y 47, 3 km from the beach; take bus 513, 517 from outside the terminal. Taxi to beach area US$1. To **Buenos Aires**, US$15, La Estrella, Plus-Mar and Costera Criolla; to **Mar del Plata**, Pampa, US$3; to **Bahía Blanca**, El Rápido US$10.

Train
The train station is in Quequén, east of Necochea over the bridge. To **Buenos Aires** (Constitución) daily, 7 hrs, **Pullman** US$8, First US$6, Tourist US$5.

Boat
Trips with **Nova Ví Tour**, *Av 59 No 1722, T436009*. 2-hr trip US$5pp. Fishing and pleasure boat trips, **La Ciudad de Napoles**,

Calle 57 No 935, T428601. Wonderful fishing on huge lagunas just inland at La Pandorga, with accommodation in rustic lakeside cabins, set in beautiful countryside, T15504413.

Bahía Blanca *p131*
Air
Airport Comandante Espora, lies 11 km northeast of centre, US$3 in a taxi. Airport information T486 1456. Daily flights to **Buenos Aires** with AR/Austral (*T456 0561/0810-2228 6527*), LADE (*T4521063*). LADE has weekly flights to **Bariloche**, **Mar del Plata**, **Neuquén**, **Puerto Madryn**, **San Antonio Oeste**, **San Martín de los Andes** (may involve changes).

Bus
Local US$0.40, not cash, you need to buy *tarjetas* (Tarjebus cards) from kiosks for 1, 2, 4 or 10 journeys.
Long distance Terminal in old railway station 2 km from centre, at *Estados Unidos y Brown, T481 9615,* connected by buses 512, 514, or taxi US$2, no hotels nearby. To **Buenos Aires** frequent, several companies, 8½ hrs, US$10-15, shop around. Most comfortable by far is **Plusmar** suite bus US$20 (*T456 0616*). To **Mar del Plata**, El Rápido, US$10, 7hrs. To **Córdoba**, US$18, 12 hrs. To **Neuquén**, 6 a day, 8 hrs, US$10. To **Necochea**, El Rápido, 5 hrs, US$ 8. To **Viedma** Ceferino, Plusmar and Río Paraná (to **Carmen de Patagones**), 4 hrs, US$5-6. To **Trelew**, Don Otto and others, US$28, 10 ½ hrs. To **Río Gallegos**, Don Otto US$34. To **Tornquist**, US$2, Río Paraná and La Estrella/El Cóndor, 1 hr 20 min; to **Sierra de la Ventana** (town) La Estrella/El Cóndor and Expreso Cabildo, US$4. Also *combi* (Minibus service like a shared taxi) with **Geotur** *T450 1190, terminal at San Martín 455*. Companies: Andesmar *T481 5462,* Ceferino *T481 9566,* Don Otto *T481 8585,* Rápido del Sur *T481 3118*.

Taxi
Taxi Universitario, *T452 0000, 453 0000*.

Trains
Long distance The station is at *Av Gral Cerri 750, T452 9196.* To **Buenos Aires** 3 weekly, 12½ hrs, Pullman US$10, own room, First US$8, Tourist US$6.

Santa Rosa de Pampa *p133*
Bus The terminal at *San Martín y Luro,* 7 blocks east of Plaza San Martín. To **Buenos Aires** US$17, 8 hrs. To **Neuquén**, 8 hrs, US$15. Andesmar *T432841,* El Valle (Via **Bariloche**) *T423554.*

⊕ Directory

Mar del Plata *p127*
Airline offices Aerolineas Argentinas, Austral, *Moreno 2442, T496 0101;* LADE, *Rambla Casino Loc 5, T493 8220.* **Banks** Many ATMs all around the central area, along *Peatonal San Martín,* at *Santa Fe y Rivadavia* and 3 close together around the casino. **Casas de Cambio Jonestur**, *San Martín 2574, and Av Luro 3101,* gives the best rates for TCs and all cash exchange. **Cultural centres** Centro Cultural Pueyrredón, *25 de Mayo y La Rioja.* A cinema, theatre and lots of cultural activities. **La Cultura** (formerly Sociedad de Cultura Inglesa) *San Luis 2498,* friendly, extensive library. **Communications** Post office *Luro 2460,* also international parcels office (open till 1200). **Telephone** There are many *locutorios* around the town, and broadband **internet** everywhere. **Laundry** Laverap, *Buenos Aires 2680, Colón 1716, Entre Ríos y Rivadavia* and *Moreno y Corrientes.*

Necochea *p130*
Post office In the centre, on *Avenida 58, No 3086, near beach, C6, No 4099.*
Telephone Telecommunications Telefónica, *C61, No 2432.*

Bahía Blanca *p131*
Airline offices Aerolineas Argentinas, *San Martín 198, T426934.* LADE, *Darregueira 21, T437697.* **Banks** Many ATMs on plaza (all major cards). Lloyds TSB Bank, *Chiclana 299, T455 3263.* Citibank, *Chiclana 232.* Pullman, *San Martín 171,* changes TCs. **Communications** Post Office *Moreno 34.* Telephone Big *locutorio* at *Alsina 108,* also internet. Internet Try places along Estomba and Zelarrayand near plaza. **Consulates** Chile, *Güemes 102, T455 0110, F258803;* Italy, *Colón 446, T454 5140.* Spain, *Drago 70, T422549.* Migraciones, *Brown 963.* **Laundry** Laverap, *Av Colón 197;* Las Heras, *Las Heras 86.* **Tour operators** ASATEJ, *Zelarrayán 267, T456 0666, bblanca@ asatej.com.ar*

The Southern Sierras

The Sierra de Tandil is a range of mountains 340 km long, and 2,000 million years old, among the oldest in the world. These beautiful long curved hills of granite and basalt, offer wonderful walking and riding, with the pleasant airy town of Tandil as a base. There are plenty of small hotels, though nearby estancias offer the best way to explore the hill. Easily accessible from Buenos Aires, it's a good place for a weekend break.

The magnificent Sierra de la Ventana is the highest range of hills in the pampas, and so called because craggy Cerro de la Ventana has a natural hole near its summit. Within the Parque Provincial Ernesto Tornquist, in easy reach of Bahía for a day or weekend visit, the attractive villages of Villa la Ventana and Sierra de la Ventana are appealing places to stay. They're as old as those in Tandil, but much more accessible for long hikes, with stunning views from their craggy peaks. There are daily buses and combis from Bahía Blanca, but you could break the journey at quaint sleepy Tornquist.

Tornquist → *Phone code: 0291 Colour map 4, C4 Population: 5,672*

Tornquist is a pretty, sleepy little rural town, which you pass through on the way to Sierra de la Ventana and is 70 km north of Bahía Blanca by Route 33. It has an attractive church on the large central plaza, which is more like a tidy park, with a strangely green artificial lake, and big children's play area. It's not a touristy place, but that's precisely its appeal, and it's a good starting point for excursions into the sierra, 25 km to the east. Nearby is the Tornquist family mansion, built in a mixture of French styles. The town is named after Ernesto Tornquist (1842-1908) the son of a Buenos Aires merchant of Swedish origin. Under his leadership the family established the industrial investment bank which still bears his name, and Tornquist helped to establish the country's first sugar refinery, meat-packing plant and several chemical firms. There's **tourist information** at Plaza Ernesto Tornquist, 9 de Julio y Alem, T494 0081. ▸▸ *For Sleeping, Eating and other listings, see pages 145-146.*

Parque Provincial Ernesto Tornquist → *Phone code: 0291*

The sierras are accessed from the Parque Provincial Ernesto Tornquist which is 25 km northeast of Tornquist on Route 76. The entrance is signposted from the road, turn left AFTER the massive ornate gates from the Tornquist family home. Nearby is Campamento Base, camping in attractive shady site, also basic dormitory accommodation, T491 0067, hot showers, very hospitable. At the entrance to the park itself, there's a car park and interpretation centre with *guardaparques* who can advise on walks.

Walks From the park entrance, it's a three-hour walk, clearly marked, but with no shade, up **Cerro de la Ventana** (1,136m), which has fantastic views from the 'window' in the summit ridge. You have to register with *guardaparques* and set off by midday. Alternative hikes from here are a gentle hour's stroll to **Garganta Olvidada**, (one hour each way) where you can set off up to 1700, to the Piletones, small pools (two hours each way), and Garganta del Diablo (six hours return) a wonderful narrow gorge with waterfalls. It's US$1 to enter the park, and guides are available to take you on walks, US$20 per group.

The other entrance to the park is 4 km further along Route 76, with a visitors' centre, T491 0039, from where you can go on a guided visit to Cueva del Toro (only with own vehicle, 4-5 hours), natural caves, and the Cueva de las Pinturas Rupestres which contains petroglyphs. US$1.20pp. Good walks from here too, including up Cerro Bahía Blanca (2hrs return), a gentle climb, rewarded with panoramic views, highly recommended. There's lots of wildlife to spot, but you're most likely to see grey foxes, guanacos, wild horses and red deer.

Some 10 km further from the park's second entrance is an attractive laid-back wooded settlement of weekend homes, many *cabañas* for rent, and a municipal campsite by river with all facilities. There's an excellent teashop, *Casa de Heidi*, and good food at rustic *Las Golondrinas*. The pretty village is the base for climbing Cerro Tres Picos (1,239 m), to the south of the park, which is the highest peak in Buenos Aires province. The ruins of the Hotel Club Casino, which when built in 1911 was the most luxurious hotel in Argentina, can be seen; it burned down in 1983. There's a helpful tourist office at entrance to village, T491 0095, www.sierradelaventana.org.ar ▸▸ *For Sleeping, Eating and other listings, see pages 145-146.*

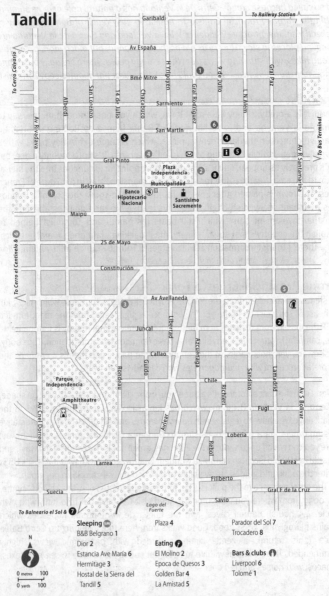

Tandil

Sleeping 🛏
B&B Belgrano 1
Dior 2
Estancia Ave María 6
Hermitage 3
Hostal de la Sierra del Tandil 5

Plaza 4

Eating 🍴
El Molino 2
Epoca de Quesos 3
Golden Bar 4
La Amistad 5

Parador del Sol 7
Trocadero 8

Bars & clubs 🍸
Liverpool 6
Tolomé 1

The town of Sierra de la Ventana, further east, is a good centre for exploring the hills, with a greater choice of hotels than Villa Ventana, and wonderful open landscapes all around. There is a 18-hole golf course, and good trout fishing in the Río Sauce Grande. There's a wonderful tea shop, *La Angelita*, in the leafy lanes of Villa Arcadia, and several places to bathe. Helpful tourist information at office on Av Roca, just before railway track, T491 5303 (website above). The tourist offices both have a complete list of all hotels, *cabañas* and campsites with numbers and prices.

Tandil → *Phone code: 02293 Colour map 4, C5 Population: 125,000*

Tandil is an attractive town, with a light breezy feel, a good base for exploring the sierras, with a couple of marvellous estancias close by and a clutch of restaurants, cafés and bars within the town. On the south side of the main Plaza Independencia are the neoclassical **Municipalidad** (1923) and **Banco Hipotecario Nacional** (1924) and the **Iglesia del Santisimo Sacramento**, inspired by the Sacre Coeur in Paris. Six blocks south of the plaza, on a hill and offering fine views, is the **Parque Independencia**, with a granite entrance in Moorish style, built by the local Italian community to celebrate the town's centenary. Inside the park, the road winds up to a vantage point, where there's a Moorish style **castle**, built by the Spanish community to mark the same event, with marvellous views over the sourrounding sierras. At the base of the hill is an amphitheatre, where there's a famous community theatre event throughout Easter week (book accommodation ahead). South of the park is the **Lago del Fuerte**, where watersports are practised, and at the Balneario del Sol you can bathe in a complex of several swimming pools. West of the plaza on the outskirts of town is **Cerro Calvario** with the stations of the cross leading to the **Capilla Santa Gemma**, on top. The nearest peak, 5 km away, **Cerro El Centinela** offers wild countryside for riding, climbing, walking, ascent by cable car, and regional delicacies at the restaurants. There is a very helpful office at 9 de Julio 555, T432073, open 0900-2000, or at the bus terminal. www.tandil.gov.ar www.tandilturismo.com

At the **Reserva Natural Sierra del Tigre**, 6 km south, 140 ha, which protects the **Cerro Venado**, from which there are good views over Tandil. Foxes and guanacos can be seen and there is a small zoo.

Listings: the Southern Sierras

🛏 Sleeping

Tandil *p145, map p144*

B Cabañas Brisas Serranas, *Scaviniy Los Corales, T423111*. Very comfortable and well-furnished *cabañas*, pool, lovely views and welcoming owners.

B Las Acacias, *Av Brasil 642, T423373, www.posadalasacacias.com.ar* Attractive modern *hostería* in traditional-style house, good service, Italian and English spoken.

B Plaza, *Gral Pinto 438, T427160*. Central modernized hotel with a cramped foyer, decent rooms (noisy at the front, as this is on the plaza) with bath and breakfast. Over priced, but useful if everywhere else is full.

C Dior, *Rodriguez 471, T431190, hoteldior@infovia.com.ar* Much more appealing, this modernized 1970's place has a light airy foyer and lounge with views over the pretty plaza, is much quieter, and has the town's most attractive comfortable rooms with modern bathrooms, breakfast included. Friendly staff, and good value.

C Hermitage, *Av Avellaneda y Rondeau, T423987*. Good value in this quiet hotel in a good position next to the park, some smart modernized rooms, all very simple, but the service is welcoming.

C Hostal de la Sierra del Tandil, *Av Avellaneda 931/41, T422330*. Attractive, vaguely Spanish-style building, and a modern hotel, with boldly-designed rooms with bath, and appealing areas to sit, a good restaurant, and a covered pool.

D **Bed and Breakfast Belgrano 39**, *Belgrano 39, T426989, www.cybertandi.com .ar/byb* Quite the most welcoming place in town, owned by a charming British couple, this has 2 comfortable secluded rooms for couples or families in an idyllic walled garden with small pool. Recommended.

Estancias
The real experience of Tandil lies in the beauty of its surroundings, best explored by staying in an estancia.

L **Siempre Verde**, *T02292-498555, lasiempreverde@dilhard.com.ar* 45 km southwest of Tandil, with the most magnificent setting amongst the sierras, is this 1900's house with a long history. Traditional-style rooms have good views over the grounds, and the owners, descendants of one of Argentina's most important families, are very hospitable and helpful. Wonderful extensive horse riding and walking among the magical sierras in the estate, fishing, *asados* on the hill side. Also camping. Highly recommended.

A **Ave Maria**, *16 km from Tandil, past Cerro El Centinela, T422843, www.avemariatandil.com.ar* While it may call itself a *hostería*, this is a splendid Norman-style building set in beautiful gardens overlooking the rocky summits of the sierras. You're encouraged to feel at home, and ramble around the place as you please. The rooms are exquisite and impeccably designed and discreet staff speak perfect English. A great place to relax and swim in the pool or walk in the grounds, hills and woodland. Highly recommended.

Eating

Tandil *p145, map p144*
Some of the cheapest options in town are the ubiquitous cheap pizzerias.
$ **El Molino**, *Juncal 936*. Serves a broad menu of good food.
$ **Epoca de Quesos**, *San Martín y 14 de Julio, T448750*. An atmospheric place for delicious local produce, wines and *picadas*. Recommended.
$ **La Amistad** *Pinto 736*. Cheap *tenedor libre*.

$ **La Tranquera**, *Falucho y Nicaragua*. Great for *parrilla*, popular with locals.
$ **Parador del Sol**, *Zarini s/n, T435697*. Located in the attractive *balneario* by Lago del Fuerte, serving great pastas and salads in a smart beach-style trattoria.
$ **Un Lugar**, *Av San Gabriel 2380, T15507895, a couple of km from the centre, call for directions*. Recommended for excellent food in lovely surroundings. Closed Mon.

Cafés
There are many cafés along *9 de Julio*, but **Golden Bar** serves good coffee and sandwiches, and **Trocadero** is a lively meeting place.

Bars and clubs

Tandil *p145, map p144*
Bar Tolomé, *Rodríguez y Mitre*. Trendy crowd.
Liverpool, *9 de Julio y San Martín*. Beatles-style, very relaxed and friendly.

Sport and activities

Tandil *p145, map p144*
Flying Gliders' club, *Ayacucho, 15 km from Tandil on Route 74, T421201*.
Golf Tandil golf club, *Av Fleming s/n, T440976*. **Hiking** Contact an approved guide who will take you to otherwise inaccessible privately-owned land for trekking. **Eco de las Sierras**, *T442741, 15621083*. **Lucrecia Ballesteros**. Highly recommended guide, young, friendly and knowleadgable. **Horizonte Vertical**, *T432762*. Mountain climbing and walking. Tandil Aventuro, *T421836*. Trekking and mountain biking.
Horseriding Cabalgatas Autóctono *T427725*.

Transport

Tandil *p145, map p144*
Bus Terminal at *Av Buzón 650*, travel information *T432092*. To **Buenos Aires**, 6 hrs, US$12, 1 daily to **Bahía Blanca**, 6 hrs.
Train The train station is at *Av Machado y Colón*, 12 blocks north of the plaza, *T423002*. To **Buenos Aires** and **Bahía Blanca**, several a week.

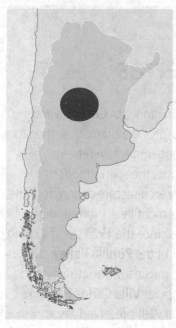

The Central Sierras

Introducing the Central Sierras

Like islands in a sea, the mountain ranges of **Córdoba** and **San Luis** rise from the low plains, giving a dramatic setting to popular holiday villages and remote mountain retreats. Córdoba is the region's main centre, the sparky modern capital with elegant 17th-century architecture dating from the Jesuits' occupation, and fabulous nightlife. Its surrounding hills have been weekend escapes since the 1920's, and a string of towns lie tucked into the folds of the **Punilla Valley**, such as **Cosquín** with its famous folklore music festival, attracting the country's best musicians, and popular **Villa Carlos Paz**. Take the **Camino de la Historia** to find well-preserved Jesuit estancias, and the astounding rock art of **Cerro Colorado** with indigenous paintings of the Spanish invasions in a beguiling rocky landscape.

For the most stunning scenery, head west into **Traslasierra**, high along the **Camino de las Altas Cumbres**, to **San Javier** and **Yacanto**. Hidden away in the mountains, these villages are the perfect starting points for long hikes, adventurous biking, and for the **Parque Nacional Quebrada del Condorito**, where majestic birds wheel above the dramatic peaks. The sleepy provincial capital of **San Luis** lies at the foot of its own magnificent sierra, and the nearby **Parque Nacional Sierra de las Quijadas**, with its dramatic red sandstone canyon. **Merlo**, with its microclimate and spectacular mountain setting, is much loved by Argentines, but seek out quieter **El Trapiche** and **Carolina**, pretty villages where you can even mine for gold.

The Central Sierras

★ Don't miss...

1 **Jesús María** Stroll around the fascinating Jesuit estancia, page 158.

2 **Laguna Mar Chiquita** Float in the salty lagoon, page 159.

3 **Sierra de Comechingones** Paraglide down from Merlo, page 178.

4 **Parque Nacional Quebrada del Condorito** Watch baby condors taking flight, page 165.

5 **Cerro Champaquí** Climb from the pretty village of San Javier, page 167.

6 **Alta Gracia** Visit Che Guevara's house, page 169.

7 **Villa General Belgrano** Eat sausages with chucrut followed by Apfelstrudel, page 169.

Córdoba Province

At the centre of an area of great natural beauty lies a modern city with a fascinating past. Córdoba is Argentina's second largest city, capital of one of the country's most densely populated provinces, and proud of its architectural heritage. To the west lie the Sierras de Córdoba, easily visited in a day. The holiday towns in the Punilla Valley were charming in the 1930's, but Villa Carlos Paz and Cosquín are now very busy. Head instead for sedate and traditional La Cumbre or La Falda. The Jesuit estancias at Jesús María and Santa Catalina are certainly worth exploring, on your way to Cerro Colorado, to the north of the city. The most interesting area for independent travellers, though, is the Translasierra area, accessed by the breathtaking Ruta de las Altas Cumbres where small towns Nono, and Villa Yacanto make good bases for walking. And the national park Quebrada de los Condoritos is a dramatic setting for spotting the majestic flight of condors.

Córdoba City → *Phone code: 0351 Colour map 4, A2 Population: 1,370,000.*

Córdoba is the buzzing capital of a wealthy province, modern and industrial, with a lively university population. It lies on the Río Suquía, extending over a wide valley, with the Sierras visible in the west. The city has been an important trade centre since the area was colonised in the 16th century, and retains an unusually fine set of colonial buildings at its heart, the astonishing Manzana de los Jesuitas, complete with its temple still in tact. Cordobéses are renowned throughout the country for their sharp sense of humour, defiant attitude and a lilting accent that other regions delight in imitating. However their strong sense of civic and sartorial pride makes Córdoba one of the most hospitable areas in the country. ▶▶ *For Sleeping, Eating and other listings, see pages 154-157.*

Ins and outs

Getting there Long-distance buses connect the city with almost everywhere in the country arrive at the central bus terminal, eight blocks east of the main plaza (a taxi to Plaza San Martín costs US$0.65). There are frequent flights from Buenos Aires, Santiago de Chile and major northern Argentine cities to Córdoba's airport, 12km northwest of centre, best reached by taxi (US$3-5), since the bus service is unreliable.

Getting around Most of the city's sights can easily be visited on foot within a day or so. There's a leafy pedestrian shopping area to the north of the Plaza San Martín, and the historical Manzana de los Jesuitas is two blocks southwest of here. Buses share the main roads with trolleybuses, which (for some reason) are driven only by women. Both charge a fixed fee of US$0.30, and don't accept cash; buy tokens (*cospeles*) or cards from kiosks. Ordinary yellow taxis are usually more convenient for short distances than green *remise* taxis, (green) which are better value for longer journeys. Tourists are allowed to park free in the centre, but must display a sticker, free from hotels and tourist offices, valid for a week and easily renewable.

Best time to visit Avoid the hot and stormy summer months from December to February, when daytime temperatures are around 30°c. The dry season is April to September, with clear skies, cooler temperatures, but still pleasantly warm.

Tourist information There are tourist offices at several points in the city: at Cabildo, Deán Funes 15, T428 5856, with a small gallery, restaurant and bookshop. 0900-2100 (Mon 1400-2100). Also at Centro Obispo Mercadillo (on Plaza San Martín), Rosario de

⦂ Jesuits in Córdoba

Each of the Spanish military campaigns were accompanied by a religious mission, intended to convert the natives as their lands were being taken from them. The most well known Jesuits missions were those of Paraguay and the Argentine province of Misiones, but the first Jesuits arrived in Córdoba in 1587, and soon it became the headquarters for the Order's activities in the whole of South America. Córdoba owes its university – one of the first in the continent – to the fact that the Jesuits needed to train their priests, and founded a Jesuit College in the city, which became in 1621 the university of San Carlos. The Novices studied Latin, theology and the arts, and tuition was free. The university became the focus of cultural life, and by the 18th century Córdoba Docta (learned Córdoba) was recognised as the cultural capital of the Vice regency of La Plata.

The cost of maintaining the university with its 40 Jesuit teaching staff was met by selling the produce from efficiently farmed orchards and estancias which can still be seen today at Alta Gracia, Jesús María, Santa Catalina and La Candelaria.

Santa Fe 39, T428 5600, or at Patio Olmos Shopping Mall, Av San Juan y Vélez Sarsfield, T420 4100, as well as at the bus terminal and at the airport. All open early morning to late at night, with useful city maps and information on guided walks and cycle tours. Take the City Tour, leaving daily from the Centro Obispo Mercadillo (Rosario de Santa Fe 39); ask at tourist information. For information on the province, head 8 km northwest of centre to Complejo Ferial, on Av Cárcano, Chateau Carreras, T434 8260, dacyt.turismo@cba.gov.ar See websites www.cordobatrip.com and www.cordoba.net in Spanish, with information on the whole province.

History

Founded in 1573 by an expedition from Santiago del Estero led by Jerónimo Luis de Cabrera, Córdoba was the most important city in the country in colonial times. During the late 16th and 17th centuries, the Jesuit Order set their headquarters here for the southern part of the continent and founded the first university in the country, giving the city its nickname 'La Docta' (the Learned). In 1810 when Buenos Aires backed independence, the leading figures of Córdoba voted to remain loyal to Spain, and after independence the city was a stronghold of opposition to Buenos Aires. It's remained fiercely independent ever since, supporting many Radical party governments, and in May 1969, disturbances in the city ignited opposition to military rule throughout the country. Since the 1940s Córdoba has grown from a cultural, administrative and communications centre into a large industrial city, though in the last 4 years, recession has resulted in growing unemployment. However, the city has an upbeat feel and a fabulous nightlife.

Sights

The Old City Córdoba's centre comes as a pleasant surprise. Its most interesting buildings are grouped around a pedestrianized area, enabling you to gaze up at the magnificent architecture without being mown down by traffic. Most of the older buildings lie within a few blocks of the Plaza San Martín, which dates from 1577 when it was the site for the odd bullfight. Now it's a wide open space, with lots of cafés, a fine statue of San Martín and Jacaranda trees: a mass of purple in late spring. On the west side, the former **Cabildo**, built in 1610, with characteristic arches and two interior paties, has a colourful history. It has served as a prison, courthouse, and clandestine detention centre during the last military dictatorship. Next to it, the **cathedral** ① *0800-1200, 1630-2000*, is the oldest in Argentina, an extraordinary confection of 17th and 18th styles from successive renovations. The marvellous neo-baroque interior has wooden doors from a Jesuit temple and statues of angels resembling the indigenous peoples, with an 1800 silver tabernacle and lavishly decorated ceiling. Don't miss one of the most remarkable collections of religious art in the country, just

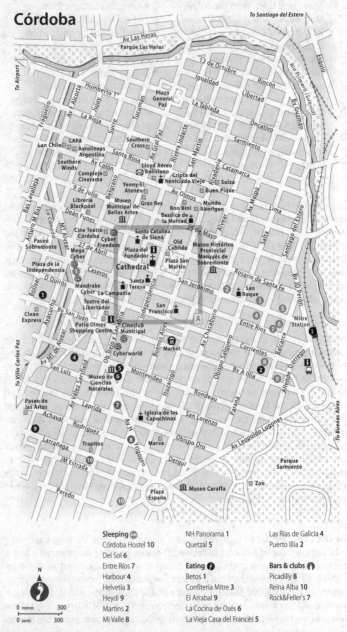

Córdoba

To Santiago del Estero

N

| 0 metres | 300 |
| 0 yards | 300 |

Sleeping	NH Panorama 1	Las Rías de Galicia 4
Córdoba Hostel 10	Quetzal 5	Puerto Illia 2
Del Sol 6		
Entre Ríos 7	**Eating**	**Bars & clubs**
Harbour 4	Betos 1	Picadilly 8
Helvetia 3	Confitería Mitre 3	Reina Alba 10
Heydi 9	El Arrabal 9	Rock&Feller's 7
Martins 2	La Cocina de Osés 6	
Mi Valle 8	La Vieja Casa del Francés 5	

Teresa ① *Independencia 122, Wed-Sat 0930-1230, US$0.35. Guided visits also in English and French.* A beautiful building; highly recommended.

On the west side of the pleasant Plaza del Fundador, one block west, the convent and church of **Santa Catalina de Siena**, founded in 1613, but rebuilt in the late 19th century, contains a splendid collection of paintings from Peru as well as colonial Spanish tapestries and carpets. For more contemporary art, the **Museo Municipal de Bellas Artes** ① *Av General Paz 33, Tue-Sun 0900-2100, US$0.35, T433 1512*, has a permanent collection by celebrated Argentine artists in an early 20th French-style mansion.

The **Manzana Jesuítica**, contained within the streets Av Vélez Sarsfield, Caseros, Duarte Quirós and Obispo Trejo, has been declared a world heritage site by UNESCO. The **Iglesia de la Compañía**, at the corner of Obispo Trejo and Caseros, was originally built between 1640 and 1676, and its curious vaulted ceiling is a ship's hull, created by a Jesuit trained in the Dutch shipyards. Behind the church, on C Caseros, is the smaller, most beautiful **Capilla Doméstica**, a private 17th-century Jesuit chapel, accessible only with a guided tour, but worth seeing for the indigenous painting on the altar. The main building of the **Universidad Nacional de Córdoba** ① *T4332075, Tue-Sun 0900-1300, 1600-2000, US$1*, originally the Jesuit Colegio Máximo, now houses one of the most valuable libraries in the country, as well as the Colegio Nacional de Montserrat, the most traditional high school of the province. ① *All guided visits (in English) to the church, chapel, university (called Museo Histórico) and school leave from Obispo Trejo 242, Tue-Sun 1000, 1100, 1700 and 1800.*

Other fine examples of religious architecture are the **Iglesia de San Francisco**, Buenos Aires y Entre Ríos, on a leafy plaza, and the **Iglesia de San Roque**, Obispo Salguero 84. One block east of plaza San Martín is the **Museo Histórico Provincial**, ① *Marqués de Sobremonte, Rosario de Santa Fe 218, T433 1661, Tue-Sat 1000-1600 (in summer Mon-Fri 0900-1500), US$0.35, texts are in English and German*, the only surviving colonial family residence in the city, dating from 1760, and a labyrinth of patios and simply decorated rooms. The **Basílica de La Merced**, at 25 de Mayo 83, has a fine gilt wooden pulpit dating from the colonial period and beautifully carved wooden doors, with fine ceramic murals revealing Córdoba's history on the outside by the local artist Armando Sica.

Other sights

Attractive areas for a stroll are along **La Cañada**, a stream running a few blocks west of the plaza, and the **Nueva Córdoba** district, south of the plaza San Martín, with cafés and an eclectic mix of building styles along Av Hipólito Yrigoyen. The neo-gothic **Iglesia de los Capuchinos** ① *T4333412, Tue-Sun 1100-1900*, displays the night skies for every month of the year. **Parque Sarmiento** is the largest green area of the city, laid out by French architect Charles Thays in 1889 with small lakes, a neat rose garden and a zoo, among steep hills, ① *Zoo: 0900-1800, US$1.20*. The magnificent **Mitre railway station**, near the bus terminal, has a beautiful tiled *confitería*, still in use for Sunday evening tango

Córdoba centre

Iglesia de Santa Catalina de Siena
Unión de Artesanos
Barujel
Exprinter
Cabildo
Rosario de Santa Fe
25 de Mayo
Av Gral Paz
Plaza del Fundador
Tienda de la Ciudad
Plaza San Martín
Bank Boston
Banco de Galicia
Lloyds
Western Union
Cathedral
Museo San Alberto
Iglesia de Santa Teresa
Museo de Arte Religioso Juan de Tejeda
Capilla Doméstica
Iglesia de la Compañía
Teatro Real
Manzana Jesuítica
Universidad Nacional de Córdoba
Centro Cultural España-Córdoba
Buenos Aires
27 de Abril
Iglesia de San Francisco
Citibank
Ituzaingó
Caseros
Alvear
Corrientes
Ob Trejo y Sanabria
Independencia

N

0 metres 200
0 yards 200

shows (see Entertainment and nightlife below). The lively crowded market, **Mercado de la Ciudad**, provides a taste of local urban culture.

Listings: Córdoba *Phone code: 0351 map p152*

● Sleeping

Good value accommodation is hard to find. There are several small places next to the bus terminal, but they're unreliable.

A **NH Panorama**, *Marcelo T de Alvear 251, T410 3900, F410 3950, www.nh-hoteles.com* Situated on La Cañada stream, this 4-star has comfortable business-style rooms and excellent views of the sierras from its upper floors. Small pool, gym and a restaurant.

A **Windsor**, *Buenos Aires 214, T422 4012, www.windsortower.com* A small, smart 4-star, and warm atmosphere, large breakfast, sauna, gym and pool, but is a bit overpriced.

C **Cristal**, *Entre Ríos 58, T424 5000, www.hotelcristal.com.ar* Comfortable rooms with a/c and a large breakfast.

C **Sussex**, *San Jerónimo 125, T422 9070, F421 8563, hotelsussex@arnet.com.ar* Though it looks a bit run down, rooms are well kept, have a/c, and some have lovely views of Plaza San Martín. Pool; breakfast included.

D **Del Sol**, *Balcarce 144, T423 3961*. Decent option with recently renovated rooms, a/c and breakfast.

D **Heydi**, *Bv Illia 615, T421 8906, www.hotelheydi.com.ar* By far the best value accommodation in town, this spotless, quiet 3-star has pleasant rooms, breakfast included.

E **Entre Ríos**, *Entre Ríos 567, T/F 423 0311*. Clean, basic place with welcoming staff. Some rooms have a/c and all include breakfast. One room adapted for wheelchair users. 10% discount for ISIC members.

E **Martins**, *San Jerónimo 339, T421 2319, martinshotel@yahoo.com.ar* Lobby and corridors are an eclectic mix of 70s and sumptuous early 20th-century décor. The plain rooms are decent and clean, though bathrooms are cramped.

E **Quetzal**, *San Jerónimo 579, T/F422 9106*. Recently refurbished with dubious taste, this is good value, spotless rooms with bath;

breakfast extra.

F pp **Córdoba Hostel**, *Ituzaingo 1070, T468 7359, www.cordobahostel.com.ar* The only hostel accommodation of the city is located in the Nueva Córdoba district. Small and not beautiful, it does have decent facilities and large breakfasts. Small discount for HI members.

● Eating

$$ **Betos**, *Bv San Juan 450*. Large, popular *parrilla* serving the best *lomitos* in town.

$$ **L' América**, *Caseros 67, T427 1734*. A small but imaginative menu with modern twists on traditional dishes from sushi to French food, all beautifully cooked. Large selection of wines, homemade bread and excellent service, in minimalist surroundings, with cheap set menus.

$$ **La Cocina de Osés**, *Independencia 512*. Formal and well decorated, this is a good place for fish, meat dishes and homemade pastas.

$$ **La Vieja Casa del Francés**, *Independencia 508*. Delicious grills in an inviting atmosphere, where you can have a chat with the French expat owners.

$$ **Las Rías de Galicia**, *Montevideo 271*. Superb seafood.

$$ **Novecento**, *at the Cabildo*. A lively smart place, with a lovely light patio, appealing décor with dark wooden tables and immaculate tablecloths. Superb fresh Mediterranean-style cooking, lots of fish and pasta, and excellent service. Recommended. Lunch only, bar open 0800-2000.

$$ **Upacanejo**, *San Jerónimo 171*. Theme restaurant based on a popular Argentine comic character, with friendly staff dressed accordingly, this is actually an unpretentious *parrilla* serving excellent beef and chicken.

$ **Alfonsina**, *Duarte Quirós 66, T427 2847*. Mixing rural décor and food (including *mate*) with young urban crowds and music, in an

---

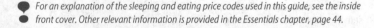

For an explanation of the sleeping and eating price codes used in this guide, see the inside front cover. Other relevant information is provided in the Essentials chapter, page 44.

inviting old house, this is perfect for simple meals, pizza, *empanadas árabes*, *milanesas* or breakfasts with homemade bread.

Cafés

El Ruedo, *Obispo Trejo y 27 de Abril*. Lively *confitería*, also serving light meals.
Ignatius, *Buenos Aires y Entre Ríos*. Tasty *facturas* and good music.
Puerto Illia, *Bv Illia 555*. Next to the bus terminal, and open 24 hours, serving breakfasts and simple meals – great if you arrive at night or have a long wait.
Sorocabana, *Buenos Aires y San Jerónimo*. Great cheap breakfasts for US$1, in this popular place on plaza San Martín.

Bars and nightclubs

Córdoba has a rich and varied nightlife, with young crowds gathering in different areas of the city mainly on Fri and Sat, but on weekdays too during holidays. Northwest of town Cerro Las Rosas, locally referred to as *Cerro*, has a lively area of bars and clubs (US$3.50 pp) along Av Rafael Núñez:
Arcimboldo, *Av Rafael Núñez 4567*.
Factory, *Av Rafael Núñez 3964*. A club for all ages mixing electronic with latin dance music.
Villa Agur, *José Roque Funes y Tristán Malbrán*. Rock and roll with food and live music.
Another popular nightlife area lies further northwest in Chateau Carreras:
Carreras, *Av Ramón J Cárcano*. The most popular club, frequented by trendy crowds in their 20's.
For lower budgets, El Abasto district, on the river (about 8 blocks north of plaza San Martín) has several good places:
Casa Babylon, *Bv Las Heras 48*. A disco night on Fri and rock music on Sat.
Divino, *Pasaje Agustín Pérez 32 (behind Puente Alvear)*. Before 1900 you can enjoy wine tasting.
There are plenty of affordable options around Bv San Juan and Av Vélez Sarsfield, along La Cañada or south of Bv Illia at Nueva Córdoba district:
Reina Alba, *Obispo Trejo y Fructuoso Rivera*. A redesigned old house open after sunset, with a happy mix of trendy clothes and books were the chic people drink.

Rita, *Independencia 1162*. Another refurbished old house with a trendy clientele.
Studenty bars along Rondeau between Av Hipólito Yrigoyen and Chacabuco. The less noisy places are:
Rock&Feller's, *Av Hipólito Yrigoyen 320*. Bar and restaurant.
Picadilly, *Av Hipólito Yrigoyen 464*. Live jazz, blues and bossa nova after midnight.
Alfonsina, *Duarte Quirós 66*. If you need to express yourself on piano or guitar.

Entertainment

See free listings magazines *La Cova* and *Ocio en Córdoba*, local newspaper *La Voz del Interior*, and www.cordoba.net for events.
Cinema Mainstream films also at **Complejo Cinerama**, *Av Colón 345* and **Gran Rex**, *Av General Paz 174*. Independent, old and foreign language films at **Cineclub Municipal**, *Bv San Juan 49* and at **Cine Teatro Córdoba**, *27 de Abril 275*.
Theatre The *Festival of Latinamerican Theatre* is held every October.
Teatro del Libertador, *Av Vélez Sarsfield 367*, *T433 2312*, is traditional and sumptuous with a rich history. On Plaza San Martín is **Real**, *San Jerónimo 66*, *T433 1669*. Smaller places are next to Puente Alvear, **Espacio Cirulaxia**, *Pasaje Agustín Pérez 12*, and **Quinto Deva**, *Pasaje Agustín Pérez 10*.
Cuarteto Very definitively a Cordobés invention, this tropically inspired music has given fame to 'La Mona' Giménez, and many impersonators, whose gigs are attended by hysterical crowds. (Also described as 'worse than *cumbia*' – the other Colombian-inspired Cordobés musical tradition).
The most popular venues are **Asociación Deportiva Atenas**, *Aguado 775*, **Estadio del Centro**, *Santa Fe 480*, and **La Vieja Usina**, *Av Costanera y Coronel Olmedo*.
Tango This Buenos Aires tradition also has a home in Córdoba, every Sunday from 2000 at **Confitería Mitre**, *Bv Perón 101* (in the railway station), tango class before *milonga* (public place to dance) begins, US$1.30. The patio at the Cabildo on Fridays is a picturesque venue for tango lessons and dance. **El Arrabal**, *Belgrano y Fructuoso Rivera*, restaurant with a tango show after midnight, Fri and Sat, US$1.70 extra.

O Shopping

The main shopping area is along the pedestrian streets north of the plaza. On Belgrano, 700 and 800 blocks, there are several antique shops.

Shopping malls **Córdoba Shopping**, *José de Goyechea 2851 (at Villa Cabrera), T420 5001*. **Nuevocentro**, *Av Duarte Quirós 1400, T482 8193*. **Patio Olmos**, *Av Vélez Sarsfield y Bv San Juan, T420 4100*.

Handicrafts **Paseo de las Artes**, *Achával Rodríguez y La Cañada, Sat-Sun 1600-2200 (in summer 1800-2300)* Market selling ceramics, leather, woodcrafts and metalware. **Unión de Artesanos**, *San Martín 42 (Galería San Martín, local 22)*. **Mundo Aborigen**, *Rivadavia 155*.

Bookshops **Librería Blackpool**, *Deán Funes 395*. Imported English books. **Tienda de la Ciudad**, *on a patio at the Cabildo*. Specializes in local and regional interest books. **Yenny-El Ateneo**, *Av General Paz 180*. English language titles.

Outdoor equipment **Buen Pique**, *Rivadavia 255*. **Suiza**, *Rivadavia y Lima*.

ʔ Tour operators

On average, tours are charged around US$10 pp for half-day excursions and US$17 pp for a full day trip. Main destinations are in the Punilla, Calamuchita and Traslasierra valleys and all Jesuit related places. The city tourist office offers city tours on foot or bike, and also cheap guided visits to the Jesuit estancias in Jesús María and Alta Gracia. Red double-decker buses leave once or twice a day from Plaza San Martín for a 1½ hr city tour with bilingual guides, US$3.
Tincunaco, *T468 2888, jorge_raul_lima@hotmail.com* Run by experienced traveller Monchi Lima, who offers flexible itineraries, including remote villages in the province and almost any destination in the country.
Bon Bini, *San Martín 180, p 1, T428 1857*.
Nativo, *Av Rafael Núñez 4624, T481 6525*. Conventional tours.
Southern Cross, *Av General Paz 389, p 3,*

T424 1614, www.terraargentea.com. Off the beaten track.

⊖ Transport

Air
Pajas Blancas airport, T475 0392 or T475 0871. 12 km northwest of centre, reached by taxi or (less reliable) bus. There are several flights to **Buenos Aires** daily, about 1 hr, Aerolíneas Argentinas, Southern Winds. Aerolíneas Argentinas also flies daily to **Mendoza**, **Tucumán** and **Ezeiza airport**, and 3 times weekly to **Jujuy** and **Salta**. Lan Chile has daily flights to **Santiago de Chile**, 1½ hr. Lloyd Aéreo Boliviano flies weekly to **Santa Cruz de la Sierra**, via Salta.

Bus
Buses and trolleybuses charge US$0.30, only payable in tokens (*cospeles*) or cards from kiosks: Terminal is at Bv Perón 250, T434 1700 or T434 1692, with restaurants, internet facilities, a supermarket, left luggage lockers, US$0.65 per day (2 coins of $1); *remise* taxi desk, ATM and a tourist office at the lower level, where the ticket offices are. To leave the terminal go upstairs and cross bridges towards city centre. A taxi charges US$0.65 to plaza San Martín. Minibuses, *diferenciales*, have better services to the Sierras and depart from nearby platform; tickets on bus or from offices at Terminal, 1st floor.
To **Buenos Aires**, Chevallier, General Urquiza, TAC, 9-11 hrs, US$12-17 (*coche cama*). To **Catamarca**, General Urquiza, TAC, 5-7 hrs, US$7. **Jujuy**, Balut, TAC, 12 hrs, US$15. To **La Rioja**, Chevallier, General Urquiza, Socasa, 6-7 hrs, US$7. To **Mendoza**, Andesmar, Autotransportes San Juan-Mar del Plata, CATA, Expreso Uspallata, TAC, 10-12 hrs, US$10-12. To **Puerto Iguazú**, Expreso Singer, 20 hrs, US$27-30. To **Rosario**, General Urquiza, TAC, 5-6 hrs, US$7-8. To **Salta**, Chevallier, La Veloz del Norte, 12 hrs, US$18. To **San Luis**, Andesmar, Autotransportes San Juan-Mar del Plata, TAC, 7 hrs, US$6-8. TAC and **Andesmar** have connecting services to several destinations in Patagonia.
To provincial destinations To **Alta Gracia**, SATAG and Sarmiento (stop in centre), **Sierras de Calamuchita** (stops at El

Crucero on route, half an hour walk from centre), 1 hr, US$0.70. To **Cerro Colorado**, Ciudad de Córdoba, 3 weekly, 4½ hrs, US$5. To **Jesús María**, Ciudad de Córdoba, Colonia Tirolesa, 1 hr, US$1. To **Laguna Mar Chiquita**, Expreso Ciudad de San Francisco goes to Miramar, 3½ hrs, US$3.50. Transportes Morteros goes to **Balnearia**, 3 hrs, US$3.80. To **Punilla valley**, Ciudad de Córdoba, TAC, (La Falda, US$1.70; La Cumbre, US$2) and La Calera, El Serra, Transierras, Lumasa. To **Río Ceballos**, La Quebrada, 1 hr, US$0.70; Ciudad de Córdoba goes also to **Río Ceballos** and continues north to **Ascochinga** and then, **Jesús María**. To **Río Cuarto**, TUS, 3-3½ hrs, US$5. To **Traslasierra valley**, Ciudad de Córdoba, TAC, (**Mina Clavero**, 3 hrs, US$4) and Sierra Bus and Panaholma minibus services. To **Villa Carlos Paz**, Ciudad de Córdoba, also Car-Cor and El Serra minibus services, 45 mins, US$0.80. To **Villa General Belgrano**, TUS, Sierras de Calamuchita (runs also minibus services, like Lep, La Villa and Pájaro Blanco), 1½-2 hrs, US$3.
International services To **Santiago** (Chile), US$20, 17-19 hrs, **CATA**, **TAC**. To **Tacna** (Peru), US$75, with change at Mendoza and Santiago de Chile. To **Bolivia** take **Balut** or **Andesmar** services to the border at **La Quiaca** (19 hrs, US$20) or **Pocitos** (17 hrs, US$20-23).

Car hire
Europcar, *Entre Ríos 70, T481 7683, www.europcar.com.ar* Four Way, *T499 8436, fourway@arnet.com.ar*

Remise taxis
Alta Córdoba Remis, *T4710441.* Auto Remis, *T472 7777.*

Train
There are weekly trains from the Mitre station, Bv Perón 101 (next to bus terminal) to **Villa María**, Thu, Fri, Sun 1800, 3½ hrs, US$1.30-1.70.

❻ Directory

Airline offices Aerolíneas Argentinas/Austral, *Av Colón 520, T410 7676,* Lan Chile, *Figueroa Alcorta 206, T475 9555.* Lloyd Aéreo Boliviano, *Av Colón 166, T421 6458.* Southern Winds, *Figueroa Alcorta 192, T0810-7777979.* **Banks** Open in the morning. LECOP bonds are in circulation together with pesos, but a discount is applied when changing into pesos. Lloyds Bank, Banco de Galicia, Boston Bank and Banco de la Nacion, all on *Plaza San Martín,* all have ATMs. Exchange and TCs at Exprinter, *Rivadavia 47,* only Amex TCs (low commission) or at Barujel, *Rivadavia y 25 de Mayo,* Amex TCs (15% commission), VISA TCs; also **Western Union** branch.
Communications Post office: *Av Colón 210,* parcel service on the ground floor beside the customs office. Internet: Many places charging US$0.35/hr including: Cyber freedom, *27 de Abril 261,* Cyber world. *Obispo Trejo 443.* Mandrake Cyber, *Marcelo T de Alvear 255.* Mega Cyber, *Marcelo T de Alvear 229.* Open until 0500.
Consulates Dirección Nacional de Migraciones, *Caseros 676, T422 2740.* Bolivia, *Av Rafael Núñez 3788, T481 7381.* Chile, *Crisol 280, T469 0432.* **Useful addresses** Hospital Córdoba, Av Patria 656, T434 9000. Hospital de Clínicas, Santa Rosa 1564, T4337010. Nuevo Hospital de Niños Santísima Trinidad, Bajada Pucará 1900, T434 8800, (children's Hospital).

Sierras de Córdoba

The Sierras de Córdoba offer spectacular mountainous landscapes riven with rivers and streams, with the advantage of a developed infrastructure and good accessibility. Popular for tourism among the upper classes in the late 19th century, the area was opened up for mass tourism in the 1940's with the building of lots of hotels. More recently, adventure tourism has taken off, and so there's something for everyone among the beautiful mountains, quiet valleys, tranquil towns and busy resorts. The most visited sights in the sierras lie along the valleys of Punilla, Traslasierra and

Calamuchita, and on the east side of the sierra Chica, north of Córdoba, all forming itineraries of about 70 km long each. There's a useful network of dirt roads (usually used for rally competitions!) which enable you to get right into the mountains, and it's probably best to explore just a few places in detail than try to do too many. ACA publishes an excellent map of Zona Serrana de Córdoba.

North of Córdoba → *Visit www.sierraschicas.net and www.delnortecordobes.com.ar*

The oldest settlements in Córdoba lie in the north of the province, along the Camino Real, the route used by the Spanish to link the city with Lima and the Alto Perú mines. The Jesuit missionaries established fine estancias here to finance their educational and artistic work, elegant buildings which you can explore at **Jesús María** and **Santa Catalina**. Just north of Córdoba, head along the east side of the **Sierra Chica**, with its chain of small resort towns to the attractive countryside north of **Ascochinga**, or follow the picturesque mountain roads going west into the **Punilla valley**. Further north is **Cerro Colorado**, an important archaeological site with the most numerous and varied petroglyphs in the country, while in the northeast corner of the province **Laguna Mar Chiquita** is a paradise for migratory birds. ⇒ *For Sleeping, Eating and other listings, see pages 162-164.*

Sierra Chica → *Phone code: 03525*

All the roads across the Sierra Chica are unpaved and winding, with no public transport, but offer splendid views. **La Calera**, one of the first summer resorts of the local aristocracy, is situated on the Río Primero. From here you could take the more picturesque route to the Punilla valley along the narrow Quebrada del Río Primero (avoiding Villa Carlos Paz). **Saldán** and **Villa Allende**, were the exclusive resorts of the early 20th century, but have rather lost their charm: 1950's workers union hotels and languishing old villas share the hilly landscape with small shops, handicrafts stalls and packed *balnearios* (bathing places).

From Villa Allende, route E 54 goes to Cosquín, while route E 57 connects Río Ceballos and La Falda via the 35 km long camino de El Cuadrado. **Candonga**, on the road to la Cumbre, has a beautifully situated 18th-century chapel, and **Ascochinga**, lies in pleasant forested surroundings. Heading west, there are waterfalls at **Tres Cascadas**, and the **Estancia San Miguel** and **Estancia La Paz**, T492073, www.estancialapaz.com a summer retreat of the former president Roca, now offering exclusive accommodation. A handful of minor roads spread north from Ascochinga across a picturesque landscape of hills, pampas and villages, which can be explored if you have a map and a good vehicle. One of these goes to the **Jesuit Estancia Santa Catalina**, 14 km northeast of Ascochinga (described under Jesús María) ① *Bus company Ciudad de Córdoba runs regular services from the capital to Ascochinga (2 hrs, US$1.60), with frequent stops at every village. Fewer daily services link Ascochinga and Jesús María (30 mins, US$0.50).*

❧ Summer rainstorms on the mountains may cause sudden floods along riversides. Beware when choosing a campsite.

Jesús María → *Phone code: 03525 Colour map 4, A3 Population: 27,000*

This sleepy town (533 m) is the best base to visit the **Jesuit estancias** and the nearby **Colonia Caroya**. The town livens up during the first half of January for the *Festival de Doma y Folklore*, a popular folk music and gaucho event whose profits benefit local schools (entry US$2-2.50). Two tourist offices hand out useful information, at the bus station and on the way into town on route 9, T465700.

The **Estancia de Jesús María** is a well-conserved example of Jesuit-built estancias whose production supported the schools opened in Córdoba. Argentina's first vineyards were created here, and wine from Jesús María was reputed to have been the first American wine served to the Spanish royal family. The residence and church, built mainly in the 17th century, form a u-shaped building enclosing a neat garden. In the **Museo Jesuítico**, Cusco-style paintings, religious objects and a curious collection of plates are on display. The whole place, with its lovely pond underneath mature trees and a small graveyard to the left of the church, is very attractive and peaceful, highly recommended for a few hours' visit ⓘ *Mon-Fri 0800-1900, Sat-Sun 1000-1200, 1400-1800 (1500-1900 in summer and spring), US$0.65, Mon free, T420126. Easy 15 min-walk from bus station: take Av Juan B Justo, north, turn left at Av Cleto Peña, cross bridge on river and follow a dirt road right about 300 m.*

The other Jesuit **Estancia de Caroya** ⓘ *daily 0900-1300, 1400-1800 (1500-1900 in summer and spring), US$0.35, T426701. It is a 20 min-walk from bus station: take Av Juan B Justo, south, and turn right at Av 28 de Julio. After 500 m, gates of the estancia are on the left side of the road.* A rather more humble place, it lies in the southern suburbs. Dating from the 17th century, all its rooms surround a lovely central patio, with a quaint stone chapel beside it, and the fascinating history is well presented. Ruins of a dam and a mill can be seen in the surrounding gardens .

The **Estancia de Santa Catalina** ⓘ *Tue-Sun 1000-1800 (1100-1900 in summer), free, T421600. The access to the estancia is by a 13 km-long dirt road branching off route E 66 to Ascochinga, 6 km west of Jesús María (signposted). From the bus station, remise taxis charge US$8-10 return including 2 hours at the estancia.* It remains in private hands and only its church is accessible to the public, but it's beautifully located in the countryside northwest of Jesús María, though there's no public transport. This is the largest of the estancias and cattle grazing was the main activity. This is a splendid building and its magnificent church is a fine example of the baroque style.

Next to Jesús María, **Colonia Caroya** was the heart of the Italian immigration where you can taste delicious salami at any of the local restaurants. The long access road is beautifully flanked by an uninterrupted avenue of mature sycamore trees, where you'll find **Bodegas La Caroyense** ⓘ *Av San Martín 2281, T466270, Mon-Fri 0800-1200, 1500-1900, Sat-Sun 1000-1800, free*, a winery with guided visits. Set picturesquely among hills, 22 km west of route 9, the attractive old village of Villa Tulumba has hardly changed since colonial times. It's worth visiting for the beautiful 17th-century baroque tabernacle in its church, crafted in the Jesuit missions. ▸▸ *For Sleeping, Eating and other listings, see pages 162-164.*

Parque Arqueológico y Natural Cerro Colorado

This provincial park covering 3,000 ha of rocky hills and woodlands protects about 35,000 rock paintings scattered among some 200 sites, some of them underground. Painted by the indigenous Comechingones sometime between the 10th century and the arrival of the Spanish, the paintings, in red, black and white, portray animals, hunting scenes and even battles against the Spanish. There's a small **archaeological museum**, and a rare *mato* forest in the park, where you can also spot small armadillos. ⓘ *0800-1800, US$0.35, the park can only be visited with a guide, available from the administration building, whose tours, lasting 1 to 1½ hours are included in the entry fee.* The park is reached by an unpaved road, 12 km, which branches off Route 9 at Santa Elena, 104km north of Jesús María. Buses *Ciudad de Córdoba* goes to/from Córdoba 3 times weekly, 4½ hrs, US$5. ▸▸ *For Sleeping, Eating and other listings, see pages 162-164.*

Laguna Mar Chiquita → *Phone code: 03563 Colour map 4, A3*

Though an obvious attraction for birdwatchers, this sea-size lake, 192 km northeast of Córdoba, set in the borders of the pampas and the chaco has wider appeal. As the lake is shallow (maximum depth 12 m) and has no outlet, its size varies – 65 to 80 km by 30 to 40 km – according to rainfall patterns. At times the water is so salty you can float in. The lake and its coastline form the Reserva Natural Bañados del Río Dulce y Laguna Mar Chiquita, an important nature reserve popular in summer for migratory birds from the northern hemisphere, and a large resident population of flamingos. There is fishing for *pejerrey* all year round and during the summer visitors flock here too; its salt waters are used in the treatment of rheumatic ailments and skin diseases. Park administration is situated in Miramar on the southern shore, where there are a few hotels and campsites. The **tourist office** is at Libertad 351, T493003. *For Sleeping, Eating and other listings, see pages 162-164.*

The Punilla Valley → *Tourist information at www.sierrascordobesas.com.ar*

Situated between the Sierra Chica to the east and the Sierra Grande and undulating pampas to the west, the Punilla valley is the most popular tourist area of the Sierras de Córdoba. From Villa Carlos Paz Route 38 runs north along the valley for 75 km through a string of resorts, Cosquín, La Falda and La Cumbre where there are many hotels and campsites.The northern resorts are more interesting than the southernmost ones, and quieter too, particularly in Argentina holiday periods. Try the delicious *cabritos* or *chivitos* (kid), the local speciality. ▶▶ *For Sleeping, Eating and other listings, see pages 162-164.*

Villa Carlos Paz and around
→ *Phone code: 03541 Colour map 4, A2 Population: 56,000*

Villa Carlos Paz (640 m), situated on Lago San Roque 35 km west of Córdoba, is a large and overpopulated resort, bristling with hotels and brimming with Argentine tourists in summer. There are lots of activities on offer and a chair-lift runs from the Complejo Aerosilla, to the summit of the Cerro de la Cruz, which offers splendid views (US$3.30). Villa Carlos Paz is a transport hub and there are frequent buses to Buenos Aires and other main national destinations, as well as to the towns in the Punilla and Traslasierra valleys, and the town is well stocked with hotels in all price categories. There is a **tourist information** office at Avenida San Martín 400 (behind the bus station), and at Avenida San Martín 1000, T0810-8882729, 0700-2100.

To getaway from the crowds, head for quieter *balnearios* along Río San Antonio, like the one at **Villa Las Jarillas**, 15km south of town. **Cerro Los Gigantes**, (2,374 m), west of Villa Carlos Paz, is a paradise for climbers. It is reached by an unpaved road which runs through **Tanti** over the Pampa de San Luis to **Salsacate**. At Km 30, west of Tanti, a road branches west to Los Gigantes, which is the base for climbing the granite massif.ⓘ *Tanti can be reached by local bus from Villa Carlos Paz, and from there to Los Gigantes. Daily buses with TAC to Salsacate stop at Los Gigantes. Remise taxi charges about US$11.*

Cosquín → *Phone code: 03541 Colour map 4, A2 Population: 18,800*

On the banks of the wide Río Cosquín, Cosquín (708 m) is perhaps not the prettiest (but probably the cheapest) town in the valley, and still offers attractive riverbanks with several *balnearios*, of which **Pan de Azúcar** is the quietest option. Cosquín is also known as the National Folklore Capital, the site of Argentina's most important folklore festival, beginning in the last two weeks in January, during which bands and singers play every night on **Plaza Próspero Molina**, with plentiful food and handicrafts stalls. An increasingly popular rock festival is held in early February so that accommodation is almost impossible to find between 10 January and 10 February. The **tourist office** is at Avenida San Martín 560 (on Plaza Próspero Molina), T453701. There are good views over the Punilla Valley from **Cerro Pan de Azúcar** (1,260 m), situated 7 km east of town in the **Sierra Chica**.ⓘ *Chairlift to top (all year round); remise taxis charge US$5 from centre, including a 30 min wait.* **Museo Camín Cosquín**ⓘ *on Route 38, 3 km north of*

a large collection of minerals, fossils and comechingon pottery; worth a visit. ▸▸ *For*
Sleeping, Eating and other listings, see pages 162-164.

La Falda → *Phone code: 03548 Colour map 4, A2 Population: 15,000*

La Falda (934 m) is a popular resort, and is a good base for walking in the surrounding
hills and pampas. The tourist office, Avenida España 50 (at the former railway
station), T423007, infolafalda@arnet.com.ar has good town maps.

The busy town centre has little appeal today, built in the town's heydays of the
1920's when Argentina's wealthy and influencial all holidayed at the magnificent
Hotel Edén. Now sadly in ruins, but the bar gives you a flavour of its former grandeur,
with an exhibition of old photographs. ① *Visits only allowed through guided tours,*
available at the hotel's entrance, US$0.65. There are horses for hire close to the hotel
during high season.

Around La Falda

To the **sierras** on the east: Cerro La Banderita (1,350 m) is a 1½ hr walk, or less on
horseback, from the left side of Hotel Edén, taking Calle Austria, for panoramic views
of the valley, also popular with paragliders. Camino de El Cuadrado crosses the
sierras to Río Ceballos, passing an excellent vantage point at Balcón de las Nubes
and the 18th-century Estancia El Silencio, 11 km from La Falda, with outdoor activities.

To the **pampas** on the west: an 80 km long rough winding road goes to La
Higuera, on the west side of the Cumbres de Gaspar. On its way, the road crosses the
vast pampa de Olaén, a 1,100 m high grass-covered plateau with the tiny Capilla de
Santa Bárbara, an 18th-century chapel (20 km of La Falda) and the Cascadas de
Olaén, with three waterfalls, 2 km south of the chapel. More beautiful rivers and
waterfalls are at Río Pintos (26 km of La Falda) and Characato (36 km of La Falda).
Jesuit Estancia La Candelaria lies on this road, 53 km west of La Falda. No public
transport goes either east or west of La Falda. Tour operators run guided trips to
nearby sights in the sierras or to all the main sights in the western pampas. *Remise*
taxis can be an option, but pricey unless you're a group of three or four people,
charging US$10 for return trips to Estancia El Silencio or to Capilla Santa Bárbara.
Walking is only recommended to nearby points as in areas such as the pampa de
Olaén, as there are no facilities at all. Cycling is probably a much better option; take
water. *For Sleeping, Eating and other listings, see pages 162-164.*

La Cumbre and around → *Phone code: 03548 Colour map 4, A2 Population: 7,200*

La Cumbre lies at the highest point (1,141 m) in the Punilla valley, the favourite spot for
the most affluent holiday makers, with an abundance of good quality accommodation.
The former train station houses the **tourist office**, Avenida Caraffa 300, T452966, open
daily from early morning until late in the evening. The town centre is quiet and has some
smart shops. South of town, at the foot of the sierras, there's a leafy residential area
with a nicely situated golf course. For a pleasant stroll, walk along Calle Posadas,
Avenida Argentina and Calle Monseñor Cabrera, and along here up to the next village
Cruz Chica. Among lush vegetation in a wealthy residential area is **El Paraíso**, La Casa
de Manuel Mujica Lainez, ① *Jan-Feb: 1030-1330, 1630-1930 (rest of the year: Sat-Sun*
1430-1800), US$1, T491596, there are no guided visits in English, recommended, home
of the late Argentine writer, a fascinating character and socialite.

Estancia El Rosario, 6 km southeast, is the home of the famous brand of *alfajores*,
soft maize flour biscuits covered in chocolate and sandwiched with *dulce de leche*
which Argentines adore. There are free guided visits to the small factory where fruit
preserves and other sweet delicacies are also made.

A few kilometres further east, unpaved route E 66 begins the 32 km mountain
crossing to Ascochinga. A road branches southeast to the historical chapel of

Candonga. North of La Cumbre, there's a short picturesque diversion which passes closer to the hills, via Cruz Chica, Cruz Grande and Los Cocos. On the road are two popular places for families with children: **El Descanso** with its well-designed garden with a maze, and **Complejo Aerosilla**, with a chairlift to the nearby hills, (US$2). West of La Cumbre, just 9 km away on a dirt road, is the impressive paragliding site of Cuchi Corral, a natural balcony overlooking río Pintos valley a few hundred metres below. ⓘ *Buses La Calera runs several daily services to Capilla del Monte via Los Cocos. As no public transport goes east or west of route 38, only remise taxis can take you to Estancia El Rosario (US$2) or Cuchi Corral (US$5). Tour operators run trips to Cuchi Corral as a part of a circuit to the northwest area of La Cumbre.* ▸▸ *For Sleeping, Eating and other listings, see pages 162-164.*

Capilla del Monte and around
→ *Phone code: 03548 Colour map 4, A2 Population: 8,940*

Capilla del Monte (797 m) is a quiet town, and not wildly appealing, apart for some old villas and a view of the imposing peak Uritorco, however it does offer a base for good trekking and paragliding and for exploring nearby rock formations. The well-organized tourist office, T481903, turismocapilla@arnet.com.ar, is at the end of the diagonal Calle Buenos Aires. To reach **Cerro Uritorco**, 1,979 m, start walking 3 km east of town; it's another 5 km to the summit. A four-hour climb with no shade (US$1.30 entry). Along route 17 are the curious rock formations and amazing landscape of **Quebrada de la Luna**, **Los Terrones** and **Parque Natural Ongamira** from where are short trails, lying all northeast of town. Take Calle Vélez Sarsfield, opposite the chapel, and then Avenida Sabattini to cerro Uritorco and Dique Los Alazanes. Buses go as far as San Marcos Sierras. Buses going north can drop you off next to Los Paredones or at route 17 (7.5 km north of town). From there, it's 17 km up to Ongamira, the farthest of all the mentioned sights. Remise taxis charge US$13 to Ongamira including return, and a one-hour wait or US$9 to San Marcos Sierras. ▸▸ *For Sleeping, Eating and other listings, see pages 154-157.*

Listings: Sierras de Córdoba

● Sleeping

Jesús María *p158*
D **Napoleón**, *España 675, T423020*. The best option, only 2 blocks from bus station, with a/c and a pool.
D **La Gringa**, *Tucumán 658, T425249*, One block across the railway lines from bus station, with a/c and breakfast included.

Cosquín *p160*
C **La Puerta del Sol**, *Perón 820, T452045, lapuertadelsol@hotmail.com* This hotel undeservedly has the best reputation in town. Still, it's a decent choice if you want to use the pool or take advantage of the half board deals or car hire.
E **Siempreverde**, *Santa Fe 525 (behind Plaza Molina), T450093, siempreverdehosteria@ hotmail.com* Spotless place (breakfast included) run by welcoming and informative

owner María Cristina. Some rooms are small, but still comfortable and there's a gorgeous garden with a huge tree.

Camping
There are several campsites but **San Buenaventura**, *8 km west on Río Yuspe*, has in the nicest location with shady trees, beaches and places for a good swim, US$2.30 per group (*remise taxis charge US$7 for an open return trip from Cosquín*).

La Falda *p161*
About 80 hotels in all categories, all full in holiday season.
Two fine former villas with welcoming owners sharing the same block are:
D **La Asturiana**, *Av Edén 835, T422923, hotellaasturiana@yahoo.com.ar* Simple and comfortable rooms, a pool and a superb breakfast including rice pudding.

D **L'Hirondelle**, *Av Edén 861, T422825*. Some rooms retaining their original parquet floor, a large garden with a pool, and a restaurant.
E **El Colonial**, *9 de Julio 491, T421831*. Though lacking comfort, there's well-preserved early 50s décor in the reception and dining room with magnificent wooden-framed windows. And the cheap rate includes the use of a large pool at the back.

Camping

Balneario 7 Cascadas, *next to the dam and the seven falls (west of town), T425808*. Nicely located site with hot showers, electricity and a food shop, US$1.30 a day pp. *Remise* taxi charges US$1.70.

La Cumbre *p161*

C **Gran Hotel La Cumbre**, *Posadas 680, T451550, www.granhotellacumbre.com.ar* Alpine style on top of a hill, and rather impressive, this hotel has wonderful views from its comfortable (though not luxurious) rooms. Larger rooms with balcony are 20% extra and include breakfast. Pool and restaurant.
E **El Cóndor**, *Bartolomé Jaime 204, T452870, el_condor_2001@yahoo.com.ar* This hostel-like accommodation has rooms for 4 to 7 people for US$3 pp, doubles with bath and a beautiful apartment for US$4 pp (min 2 people). Breakfast, includes fruit costs an extra US$1.20, and a lovely kitchen can be used for an extra US$0.35. English spoken. They also run a rustic *rancho* restaurant on the corner **La Cabaña de El Cóndor**, recommended for its good grilled meats, especially delicious *cabrito*, and for its laid-back atmosphere.

Cruz Chica *p161*

C **Hostal de la Luna**, *Monseñor Pablo Cabrera s/n, T/F451877, laluna@punillanet.com.ar* A cosy place ideal for couples, remarkable for its splendid location on a steep slope with panoramic views, and privacy in its 6 attractively decorated rooms. It has a pool and a moderately priced restaurant.

Capilla del Monte *p162*

D **La Casona**, *Pueyrredón 774, T482679, silviadon48@hotmail.com* This 19th-century villa has a distinctly haunted house look. At the top of a hill, surrounded by palm trees,

there is a pool and the best views of the sierras. The interior retains some magnificent examples of former opulence and the welcoming owners also offer homemade meals, including smoked hams and cheeses; English spoken. Recommended.
D **Petit Sierras**, *Pueyrredón y Salta, T481667, petitsierras@capilladelmonte.com.ar* A renovated hotel with clean and comfortable rooms. The owners run the restaurant *A Fuego Lento*, at the access of town, where trout is offered as well as discounts and free transport for guests.

Camping

G pp **Calabalumba**, *600 m north of the centre, T481903*. Municipal shady site with pool, hot water, *cabañas* for 4 to 6 people.

🍴 Eating

Jesús María *p158*

Viejo Comedor, *Tucumán 312*. Popular for cheap meals, including local specialities.
Fertilia, *signposted from Av San Martín 5200, Colonia Caroya, T467031, buses stop on the main road, from here it's a 15 min-walk along a dirt road to the farm*. An unmissable treat. Welcoming farmers serve excellent quality salamis and ham accompanied by delicious local red wine.

Cosquín *p160*

$ **Wissen**, *Av Juan B Justo y Ruta 38 (100 m north of bridge), T454097*. Open for lunch and dinner, this former German family residence with sumptuous décor and a pleasant terrace offers an unpretentious menu, with excellent home made pastas, and several meat-based dishes at moderate prices with a wide selection of wines.
$ **La Encrucijada del Supaj-Ñuñú**, *on the way to the Cerro Pan de Azúcar, T15532267*. Pleasant restaurant, teahouse and brewery, where varied meals such as fondue, cakes or sandwiches are offered at moderate prices.

La Falda *p161*

$$ **Hotel L'Hirondelle**. This hotel, see above, has a moderately-priced restaurant open to non-residents, offering good set menus.
$ **El Cristal**, *San Lorenzo 39*. Very good

cooking where the locals eat.

$**Pachamama**, *Av Edén 127*. If you're tired of eating beef, there is a health food shop with a few neat tables at the back, where you can have cheap organic vegetable pies, or wholemeal pizzas and *empanadas*.

La Cumbre *p161*

$$ **Señora de Tal**, *25 de Mayo 498*. A lively atmosphere, recommended for homemade pastas, salads or *parrilla* dishes.

O Sport and activities

La Cumbre *p161*

Paragliding Fechu, *T15574566*, **Toti López**, *T494017*, or **El Comechingón**, *T15566645*, who also specializes in climbing and fishing. Jorge González runs **Escuela de Montaña y Escalada**, *T492271*, for climbing and mountain trekking courses and excursions.

ᕀ Tour operators

La Falda *p161*

Turismo Talampaya, *T470412 or T15630384*, *turismotalampaya@yahoo.com.ar* Run by Teresa Pagni who guides 4WD full-day trips to the pampa de Olaen and Jesuit estancia La Candelaria for US$15 pp.

VH, *T424831 or T15562740*, *vhcabalgatas@ hotmail.com* Horse riding to nearby hills from US$5/hr pp.

La Cumbre *p161*

These three operators all go to Cuchi Corral and Río Pintos:

Cerro Uritorco, *Corrientes 96, T451470*.

Gonzalo Gili, *T492201*. **4x4 Turismo Aventura**, *T15566664*.

Aventura Family Club, *T423809*, *www.estanciapuestoviejo.com* Covers the area, as part of a day trip to a remote estancia, northwest of La Cumbre.

Chachito Silva, *T451703 or T15635673*. Hires horses and offers half-day, 1 and 2-day guided horseriding trips to the sierras and Candonga.

ᕀ Transport

Jesús María *p158*

Bus Direct to **Córdoba**, Ciudad de Córdoba, Colonia Tirolesa, 1 hr, US$1 or minibus Fono Bus, US$1.10. To **Córdoba** via Ascochinga, Ciudad de Córdoba, 2½ hrs, US$1.90. To **Colonia Caroya**, Ciudad de Córdoba, Colonia Tirolesa, US$0.30.

Cosquín *p160*

Bus Terminal at Perón y Salta. La Calera, TAC and Ciudad de Córdoba run frequent buses along the **Punilla Valley** and to **Córdoba**: to **La Falda**, US$0.70, to **La Cumbre** US$1, to **Capilla del Monte** US$1.40. Several minibuses do same route. To **Córdoba**, 1-1½ hrs, US$1.50. **Mountain bike hire** Centro, *Perón 937, T15622983*. **Remise taxis** El Cerro, *Av San Martín 1036, T450444*.

Laguna Mar Chiquita *p159*

To/from **Córdoba**, Expreso Ciudad de San Francisco (from **Miramar**), 3½ hrs, US$3.50 and Transportes Morteros (from **Balnearia**), 3 hrs, US$3.80.

La Falda *p161*

Bus Terminal at Av Buenos Aires (route 38), 5 min-walk north of Av Edén. Chevallier, General Urquiza and Sierras de Córdoba go daily to **Buenos Aires** and to several other national destinations. La Calera and Ciudad de Córdoba run frequent buses along the **Punilla valley** and to **Córdoba**: to **Cosquín**, US$0.70, to **La Cumbre** US$0.60, to **Capilla del Monte** US$1. Several minibuses do same route as well. To **Córdoba**, US$1.70-2. **Mountain bike hire** Club Edén 201, *Av Edén 201*, US$3.50 per day. **Remise** taxis Casa Blanca, *9 de Julio 541, T426323*.

La Cumbre *p161*

Bus Daily services to **Buenos Aires**. Ciudad de Córdoba and La Calera run frequent buses along the Punilla valley and to Córdoba, as well as minibuses run by El Serra and Transierras. Mountain bike hire **Jorge**, *Rivadavia 377*, *US$3.50 per day*. **Rent a bike**, *T451575*. **Remise taxis Millennium**, *25 de Mayo 422, T452452*.

Capilla del Monte *p162*

Bus Daily buses to **Buenos Aires** and to **Córdoba** (US$3). Ciudad de Córdoba and La Calera and minibuses El Serra run services along the **Punilla valley**. Twice a day, Ciudad de Córdoba goes to **Traslasierra valley** via Cruz del Eje. **Mountain bike hire** Claudio, *Deán Funes 567*. **Remise taxis** El Cerro, *Pueyrredón 426, T482300*.

The Traslasierra Valley

Situated west of the Sierra Grande, (literally across the mountains) Traslasierra is far less developed for tourism than neighbouring valleys, but ideal for those looking for a more adventurous experience. With its drier climate and generally slower pace of life, it's also a perfect place to relax for a few days. It can either be accessed from Córdoba by the camino de las Altas Cumbres from the north, via the long but not uninteresting route 15 across the pampa de Pocho, or from the south, via Villa Dolores into San Luis province. → *For further information, try www.traslasierramix.com.ar*

Camino de las Altas Cumbres → *Phone code: 03544*

The main road to the valley from Córdoba is the most spectacular route in the Sierras. Running southwest from Villa Carlos Paz, the road passes Villa Icho Cruz before climbing into the Sierra Grande and crossing the Pampa de Achala, a huge granite plateau at 2,000 m, and descending into the Traslasierra valley near Mina Clavero.

At **La Pampilla**, 55 km of Villa Carlos Paz, is the entrance to the **Parque Nacional Quebrada del Condorito**. Covering 40,000 ha of the Pampa de Achala and the surrounding slopes, the park was created in 1995 to protect the spectacular Quebrada del Condorito, an 800 m deep gorge which is the easternmost habitat of the condor and a flying school for fledgling birds. Though condors are elusive and sightings are not guaranteed, you may lucky enough to see them take a bath under the waterfalls. There's also great trekking on the *pastizal de altura* (sierran grassland) with some rare *tabaquillo* trees. The only accessible section of the park is its northeast corner, reached by a short walk from La Pampilla (no signs there). It takes about three hours to get to the first vantage point or *balcón norte* and two more hours to the *balcón sur*, with the crossing of the Río de los Condoritos. There are three camping areas with no facilities, along the path. Take a warm jacket and beware of the slippery ground next to the Quebrada. Tours are available from Villa Carlos Paz. If you go with your own vehicle, park it at the NGO Fundación Cóndor (9 km before La Pampilla), beside a handicraft shop (1 km before La Pampilla) or at El Cóndor (7 km after La Pampilla). Buses Ciudad de Córdoba and TAC, will both stop at La Pampilla on their way to Mina Clavero, (from Villa Carlos Paz: 1 hr, US$1.90). National Park administration at Sabattini 33, T433371, Villa Carlos Paz, www.carlospaz.gov.ar/pncondorito

Mina Clavero → *Phone code: 03544 Colour map 4, A2 Population: 6,800*

Mina Clavero (915 m) has the best nightlife, or most raucous atmosphere in the entire valley, depending on your point of view, with nightclubs, theatres, a casino and dozens of hotels, restaurants and small shops. Though not the most appealing place in high season, it's a good base for trips into the surrounding natural beauty. It lies at the foot of the **Camino de las Altas Cumbres** and at the confluence of the Ríos Panaholma and Mina Clavero, which form many small falls among impressive rocks right in the town centre, and there are attractive views along the riverside. The large **tourist office** with an ATM is next to the intersection of Av San Martín and Av Mitre, T470171, 0900 until very late, mclavero.turismo@traslasierra.com

On the other side of the rivers Panaholma and Los Sauces is the quieter **Villa Cura Brochero**, named after Father Brochero who built schools, roads and aqueducts, leading the local social development at the end of the 19th century. Every March, around the 20th, he is remembered with the *Cabalgatas brocherianas*, a gaucho procession on horses and mules that follows a section of the former road across the mountains he helped to build. ➤➤ *For Sleeping, Eating and other listings, see pages 167-168.*

Nearby rivers offer several attractive places for swimming among huge rocks and waterfalls, all busy in high season. About 5 km north of Villa Cura Brochero, a dirt road passing San Lorenzo branches east to the **Cascada de Toro Muerto**, where icy water falls into a 7 m deep pool. The *balneario*, (bathing area) serves very good meals. From San Lorenzo, 4 km north is **Las Maravillas**, a *balneario* set in a deep ravine, and another 7 km to the hamlet of Panaholma with its old chapel. The **Camino de los Artesanos** is an 18 km long road from Mina Clavero to Villa Benegas along which a dozen families offer handicrafts: hand-woven pieces and distinctive black ceramics. North of Villa Cura Brochero, route 15 crosses the vast **Pampa de Pocho**, covered by palm trees, a strange landscape with small inactive volcanoes on the background. At Taninga, route 28 branches off east across the Sierra Grande to Villa Carlos Paz via Los Gigantes (see above) and to the west off towards Chepes via the **Camino de los Túneles**, a spectacular road passing through five tunnels, and then descending the steep **Cuesta de Chancaní**, with marvellous views of the *llanos riojanos* lying 700 m below, and an impressive waterfall to the east. A turning beyond leads off to the Parque Natural Chancaní, 4,920 ha, which protects one of the last remnants of Chaqueño forests in this area. ① *TAC buses go to Panaholma and some villages in the pampa de Pocho. Other nearby places are only accessible with own vehicle or with a remise taxi (eg to Toro Muerto: US$10; to Villa Benegas: US$9). No buses go along the camino de los Túneles, only tour operators.* ⇉ *For Sleeping, Eating and other listings, see pages 167-168.*

Nono and around → *Phone code: 03544 Colour map 4, A2*

Nono (900 m) is an attractive little town, so far unspoilt by increased tourism. On the plaza, with its handicraft market in summer, is the lovely little church, and among other well conserved houses, historic **Casa Uez**, a shop, cafe and basic hotel which has been the lively meeting point for locals since 1931. Traslasierra Tur runs a very good **tourist office**, T498310, www.traslasierra-info.com.ar at a wood cabin next to the petrol station on the road, open 0900-1500, 1600-2200, with internet facilities. The most visited sight is the absolutely extraordinary **Museo Rocsen**① *5 km east, following Av Los Porteños, 0900 till sunset, US$1, T498218, www.museorocsen.org, US$1.30 by taxi.* This eclectic selection of fabulously bizzare objects spanning archaeology, anthropology and human history is the personal vision of Frenchman Juan Santiago Bouchon. Don't miss it.

A network of minor roads east and southeast link the town with the foot of the mountains across a pretty landscape of rivers and hamlets, such as **Paso de las Tropas** and **El Huayco**. To the west, a dusty road leads from the church to the sandy beaches of **Río Los Sauces** and 11 km beyond to the village of **Piedras Blancas**. The Cerro Champaquí is also accessible from Nono (via San Javier) but you need to take a guide. ⇉ *For Sleeping, Eating and other listings, see pages 167-168.*

Los Hornillos and around→ *Phone code: 03544*

South of Nono route 14 gets closer to the foot of the imposing mountains amid lush vegetation and scattered villages offering some accommodation. At Los Hornillos (15 km from Nono) there are good walks 500m east of the route (left of camp site), along Río Los Hornillos. From there, footpaths lead to the nearby summits, such as the five-hour trek to La Ventana (2,300 m) passing a 50m fall halfway. A 1½ hr walk upstream along the riverbed takes you to Piedra Encajada, a huge rock supported by other two blocks with waterfalls. At Los Hornillos, the Von Ledebur family has run the lovely hotel Alta Montaña, since 1947, see page 167. Ten kilometres northwest is Dique La Viña with a large reservoir and an impressive 106 m high dam, not recommended for vertigo sufferers.

West of the sierras the main town is **Villa Dolores**, a useful transport hub, with a couple of banks and a few hotels, though there's no reason to stop here, unless

San Javier and Yacanto → *Phone code: 03544*

These two neighbouring villages lie at the foot of the **Cerro Champaquí** (2,790 m) the highest peak in the sierras. They are both very pleasant, peaceful place to stay, with old houses under mature trees, and even if not keen to climb the peak itself, you could relax by the streams or stroll around the picturesque area. The ascent up the Champaquí takes about seven hours from San Javier along the quebrada del Tigre, but take a guide, since many people get lost. For more information, contact the Municipalidad, T482041. Further south there are more small resort towns where tourist is developing, such as La Población, Luyaba, La Paz and nearby Loma Bola, which lie along the road to Merlo, 42 km of San Javier. All these towns are linked by regular TAC buses services, which run between Villa Dolores and Merlo (via San Javier). ▸▸ *For Sleeping, Eating and other listings, see pages 167-168.*

Listings: the Traslasierra Valley

⬤ Sleeping

La Pampilla *p165*
La Posta del Qenti, *19 km west of La Pampilla, T426450, www.lapostadelqenti.com.ar* A pricey but comfortable resort at 2,300 m offering rooms and dormitory accommodation together with outdoor activities. Book in advance, and ask about full board promotional offers.

Mina Clavero *p165*
There are over 70 hotels in Mina Clavero and Villa Cura Brochero, though many are closed in the off season.
D **Abuelo Juan**, *Los Pinos 1919 (take C Bolívar to the west from Av Mitre), T470562*. In a leafy residential area south of town, next to the amphitheatre. Run by artists, there is a large garden with a pool and eight spotless, cosy rooms with a large breakfast. It is oriented to guests with no kids. Recommended.
Remnants from better days, 2 central hotels have retained their distinctive character and decent rooms with bath and breakfast:
D **Porteño**, *Av San Martín 1441, T470235*, and E **Oviedo**, *Av San Martín 1500, T15571719*.

Camping
Several sites in Mina Clavero, but better to go to the less crowded Villa Cura Brochero.

Nono and around *p166*
Several family houses next to the plaza have signs offering rooms for rent by the day.

A **Gran Hotel Nono**, *Vicente Castro 289, T498022, www.granhotelnono.com.ar* On the riverside with views of the sierras and surrounded by a large and leafy park with a pool and tennis courts, this is a very comfortable and welcoming place, with attractive rustic décor. It has a restaurant and breakfast is included with lots of fruit. Rates are for half board accommodation.
B **La Gloria**, *on the way to Museo Rocsen, 800 m from C Sarmiento, T498231, www.hostal-lagloria.com.ar* On the rural outskirts among 5 ha of park, this old house has comfortable though not luxurious rooms in a relaxed atmosphere. It has a pool and access to the river, and a delicious breakfast is included.
E **Lo de Teresita López**, *Sarmiento 216 (no sign, just knock), T498030*. A welcoming former head teacher offers several comfortable rooms and kitchen in her home, whose garden has a beautiful view of the sierras. Recommended.

Camping
A road to the left of the church goes west to the river where are 3 sites, of which **Los Canadienses**, *T498259*, is the best choice. A well-kept shady place with clean bathrooms and electricity supply; no pets or large groups allowed. Open high season only. From US$5 a day per tent.

Los Hornillos *p166*
D pp **Alta Montaña**, *300m east of route*

(signposted), T499009 (in Bs As, T011-4768 5075), www.hosteriaaltamon tania.com Neat, comfortable rooms and splendid views from the grounds to the sierras. It also has a pool, a restaurant and 8 ha of virgin land by the river. Rates are for half board accommodation; kids under 7 pay half rate. Recommended.

San Javier and Yacanto p167

B Yacanto, T482002, www.hotelya canto.com.ar A traditional 1920's hotel, the Yacanto offers comfortable accommodation beside its beautifully situated 9-hole golf course. Rates are for high season standard rooms with breakfast. In low season there is only half board accommodation.

B San Javier, T482006, www.hosteria sanjavier.com.ar Lovely gardens, a pool and good rooms with a large breakfast. Several excursions can be arranged.

🍴 Eating

Mina Clavero p165

$$ **Rincón Suizo**, *down by the river, on C Recalde, one block of Av San Martín*. This house owned by Françoise Harster is an unmissable treat. While it's basically a cosy tea room serving rich strudel or chocolate cakes, if you book half a day in advance, you can be served delicious French meals such as coq au vin.

Nono and around p166

$$ **La Casona de Nono**, *Sarmiento 302*. Less attractive, but offers *pollo al disco* (grilled chicken) and *humita* as its specialities.
$$ **La Pulpería de Gonzalo**, *on the plaza, opposite the church*. Alfresco dining in the wonderful romantically lit patio. *Parrilla* dishes are the speciality, but fish is also recommended.

🧭 Tour operators

Mina Clavero p165

Short half-day trips to the surroundings are about US$4-5 pp and the longer Camino de los Túneles costs US$7 pp. **Andar**, T471426, andar@arnet.com.ar **Conocer**, *behind bus station*, T472539.

Nono and around p166

Traslahuella, *Vicente Castro 210*, T498084, T15610621, traslahuella@yahoo.com.ar Local guide Martín Zalazar runs half-day guided treks and mountain bike tours along rivers and to the nearby mountains for about US$5-8 pp. Also a day walk to the summit of cerro Champaquí for US$20 pp with a meal included.
Camp Aventura, T0351-156535014. An old lorry is used for weekend short trips to the surroundings of Dique La Viña, leaving from 1 block east of plaza.

🚍 Transport

Mina Clavero p165

Bus Terminal in centre at Av Mitre 1191. To **Córdoba**, Ciudad de Córdoba (via Altas Cumbres), 3 hrs, US$4, (via Cruz del Eje), 6 hrs, US$6 and **TAC** (stopping at villages in **pampa de Pocho**), 6 hrs, US$5; to **Buenos Aires**, Chevallier, Expreso del Oeste, TAC, 12 hrs, US$17; to **Mendoza**, Andesmar, 9 hrs, US$11; to **Merlo**, Expreso del Oeste, Monticas, 2 hrs, US$3. Minibuses Expreso Mina Clavero goes to **Villa Cura Brochero** and south to **Nono** and **Villa Dolores**, calling at villages in between. Panaholma and Sierra Bus go direct to **Villa Dolores** (45 mins, US$1) and **Córdoba** (3 hrs, US$4).
Mountain bike hire at *Urquiza 1318*, US$4 per day. **Remise taxis** Servicar, T471738. Valle, T472145.

Nono and around p166

Bus Expreso Mina Clavero going to **Villa Dolores** (50 mins, US$0.90) or up to **Villa Cura Brochero** (15 mins, US$0.45) runs the only bus and minibus services that stops hourly at Nono centre (stop on C Sarmiento next to tcol for both directions). Other companies stop on route. **Mountain bike hire** at Traslahuella (see above), US$4.50 per day. **Remise taxis** Tele Taxi, Sarmiento 94, T498115.

Los Hornillos p166

Expreso Mina Clavero stops at Los Hornillos on its way between **Villa Dolores** and **Villa Cura Brochero**.

📞 *Phone codes* All towns and villages in this area: 03544

The Calamuchita Valley

South of Córdoba, this prosperous agricultural area is dotted with large reservoirs and small towns at the foot of the Sierra Chica. The villages to the west are picturesque, in a hilly area between the high peaks of the Sierra Grande and Sierra de Comechingones. There's superb walking in wooded countryside, with excellent bases at Villa General Belgrano and La Cumbrecita, while Alta Gracia's fine Jesuit buildings have been declared a world heritage site by UNESCO.

Alta Gracia and around → *Phone code: 03547 Colour map 4, A2 Population: 42,600*

Alta Gracia is built on the site of a 17th-century Jesuit estancia, whose beautiful buildings are grouped around a central pond, attractively lit at night. Steer clear of the unlovely commercial area, and seek out instead the fine examples of aristocratic summer villas in the nearby residential area. With the arrival of the railway and the building of the Hotel Sierras (1908), the town became a popular resort among the upper classes, and sufferers of respiratory diseases, among them the young Che Guevara, whose former home can be visited (see below).

The major buildings of the **estancia** are situated around the plaza. The church, completed in 1762, with a baroque façade but no tower, is open only for mass. The clock tower, on its corner, dates from 1938 and now houses the **tourist office**, T428128.

The **Museo Manuel de Falla** ⓘ *Carlos Pellegrini 1100, 0900-1900, free*, is the attractive Spanish-style house where the composer spent his final years, with great views from its elaborate garden. There are monthly concerts from April to November and on November 14 the *Festival de Falla* takes place. Don't miss the **Museo Casa de Ernesto Che Guevara** ⓘ *Villa Nydia, Avellaneda 501, T428579, 0900-1850, US$0.65*, from the Sierras Hotel, go north along C Vélez Sarsfield-Quintana and turn left on C Avellaneda, where Che lived in his childhood, with his personal possessions, and some moving letters from people close to him in his early years. There is also the letter addressed to Fidel Castro in which Che resigns from his position as Minister of Interior in Cuba (in Spanish, but staff will translate into English if asked).

There are a couple of easy walks: to **Los Paredones** (5 km) with the remains of a Jesuit mill in a rocky section of the river ⓘ *follow Av Sarmiento to the west and cross the river, leaving the bus station on your left*. On the way is the **gruta de Lourdes** where every February 11 hundreds of pilgrims arrive by foot from as far away as Córdoba. Nearby lies the **Laguna Azul**, a small lake surrounded by impressive cliffs. Take Avenida Sarmiento, turn right at Vélez Sarsfield and left at Carlos Pellegrini until the end of the road where you have to turn right and follow the road passing Parque García Lorca on your left.

Some 21 km northwest is the **Observatorio Bosque Alegre** ⓘ *visits are guided by astronomers, Fri-Sun 1000-1300, 1500-1800 (Tue-Sun, same times, in summer), there is no public transport, remise taxis charge about US$5, plus waiting time*, built in 1942 for astrophysics research, and at 1,250 m offering good views over Alta Gracia, Córdoba and the Sierra Grande. South of Alta Gracia on the way to Villa General Belgrano, route 5 passes the large reservoir of embalse **Los Molinos** offering good views and fishing for trout and pejerrey. Regular buses and minibuses go along embalse Los Molinos. ⇥ *For Sleeping, Eating and other listings, see pages 171-173.*

Villa General Belgrano → *Phone code: 03546 Colour map 4, A2 Population: 5,900*

This small leafy resort town (840 m) has a distinctly German feel and a splendid mountainous setting. You can eat genuine German smoked sausages with a wide variety of breads, delicious Viennese cakes, drink locally brewed beer and celebrate

Graf Spee

The famous *Graf Spee* was a German 'pocket' battleship, launched in 1934, and successful because she was more heavily gunned than any cruiser afloat, and was faster than any vessel which could outgun her. In 1939, the *Graf Spee* sank nine merchant ships in the Atlantic before being cornered outside Uruguay on 13 December by three British cruisers. After a 14-hour battle in which one British ship was badly damaged, the *Graf Spee's* commander Captain Hans Langsdorff retreated into the neutral port of Montevideo, where the 36 dead German crewmen were buried. Langsdorff asked to stay in Montevideo for two weeks to repair his ship; the Uruguayan government, under British pressure, gave him 2 days. On 17 December, the *Graf Spee* sailed out to sea. Crowds lined the shore in the fading light, expecting to see a battle, but saw the vessel sink within minutes. All the remaining crew and 50 captured British seamen on board were rescued. Hitler had given the order to scuttle the vessel rather than allow it to be captured. Two days later in Buenos Aires, Langsdorff wrapped himself in the flag of the Imperial German Navy and committed suicide.

Most of the crew were interned in Argentina where they were warmly welcomed by the German community of Buenos Aires, but received a more mixed reception in cities of the interior when British pressure forced the Argentine government to disperse them. In Córdoba they were welcomed by the governor, while in Mendoza they were stoned by the locals and beaten up by the police. Many of the officers escaped and returned to serve with the German navy. The German embassy, meanwhile, tried to enforce military discipline and to prevent the men from getting too friendly with local women.

In 1954 the US and British governments demanded the repatriation of all the men to Germany. Nearly 200 managed to avoid this by marrying Argentine women, and another 75 escaped, but in 1946 the British navy deported over 800 men to Germany. Many, after six years in Argentina, had no wish to return to a country shattered by defeat, and within two years all those who wished to return to Argentina were allowed to do so. The strong German feel of pretty Villa General Belgrano in Córdoba, with its German architecture, beer festival and superb chocolate and pasties, derives from the members of the *Graf Spee* crew who made their homes here.

the *Oktoberfest* in the first half of every October, when the town is packed with tourists. The *Fiesta de la Masa Vienesa*, in Easter week and the *Fiesta del Chocolate Alpino* during July holidays, are also very popular with lovers of pastries and chocolates.

The town was founded in the 1930s, its German character boosted by the arrival of interned seamen from the *Graf Spee*, some of whom later settled here. German is still spoken by older inhabitants, and the architecture along the main street, Av Julio Roca, is dominated by Swiss chalet-style and German beer-houses. The **tourist office** is at Avenida Roca 168, T461215, (or free T125) www.elsitiodelavilla.com daily 0800-2000. A good area for a stroll is along the two streams **La Toma** and **El Sauce**, with access from Calle Ojo de Agua, 200 m east of Avenida Roca. ▸▸ *For Sleeping, Eating and other listings, see pages 171-173.*

A paved road heads north for 7 km to tiny **Los Reartes** with its old chapel, and from here it's another 18 km west, on *ripio* roads, to Villa Berna, a hamlet set at 1,350 m among mature trees. Some 8 km further is **La Cumbrecita**, a charming, if pricey, Alpine-style village hidden away in forested hills, and very crowded in summer. There are short walks to **La Cascada** and **La Olla**, a natural pool which is good for swimming. Longer walks or horse rides follow footpaths or 4WD vehicle tracks to the **Cerro Cristal**, the pools along **Río del Medio**, or an hour's walk to the curiously named **Cerro Wank** (1,715 m). A footpath leads south to Villa Alpina, a four hour-walk. For more information, contact the local **tourist office**, T481088, www.lacumbrecita.info

South of La Cumbrecita is **Villa Alpina**, a small remote resort set in the forested upper valley of **Río de los Reartes**, 38 km west, along a poor gravel road. This is the best base for a two-day trek to the **Cerro Champaquí** (2,790 m), 19 km away from the village, a rewarding hike not only for the superb mountainous scenery, but also for the chance to meet local inhabitants as you stop at the several *puestos* on the way to the summit. Expect to meet many other trekkers too in high season, but hire a local guide to avoid getting lost: information at Villa General Belgrano tourist office.

There are more picturesque hilly landscapes with streams and falls close to **Yacanto de Calamuchita**, a village 32 km by paved road from Santa Rosa de Calamuchita on route 5, 10 km south of Villa General Belgrano. Santa Rosa is the largest town in this part of the valley, a very popular, but drab resort. From Yacanto de Calamuchita you can drive almost to the summit of Cerro Champaquí thanks to a dirt road climbing up to Cerro de los Linderos, leaving you only a 40-minute walk. Regular minibuses go to Los Reartes, Villa Berna, La Cumbrecita, Villa Alpina, Santa Rosa and Yacanto de Calamuchita. Remise taxis to La Cumbrecita, US$20 return, two hrs wait, up to four people. Buses going south to Río Cuarto pass Embalse de Río Tercero. Tour operators from Villa General Belgrano and Santa Rosa de Calamuchita guide excursions to almost all these areas.

The Southern Sierras

The southern end of the Sierras de Comechingones has a lovely area on its eastern slopes with a multitude of rivers descending among woodlands. A few resort villages offer the only facilities; all can be reached from the nearby town of Río Cuarto; a large, sprawling, unattractive place. From Río de los Sauces to Achiras, all the villages are accessible from roads branching off the main routes, but there is one dirt road, 72 km long, linking the northern resorts of Río de los Sauces, Alpa Corral and Villa El Chacay, also giving access to Achiras. These villages have attractive riverbanks with waterfalls, offering easy walks in the surroundings. ▸▸ *For Sleeping, Eating and other listings, see pages 171-173.*

Listings: the Calamuchita Valley

 Sleeping

Alta Gracia *p169*

D **Hispania**, *Vélez Sarsfield 57, T426555*. Run by a Spanish family, this old residence with neat garden offers very comfortable and spotless rooms with breakfast. Indulge yourself by sitting at the verandah enjoying a fine panoramic view of the sierras while trying some excellent *tapas*. Recommended.

D **Savoy**, *Av Sarmiento 418, T421125*. This 1970s hotel has seen better days, but still has decent rooms, though rather noisy if on the street; breakfast extra.

E **Asturias**, *Vélez Sarsfield 127, T423668*. Welcoming owners have clean but cramped rooms on a small building at the back of the old house; breakfast extra.

Camping

Los Sauces, *in the Parque Federico Garcia Lorca, northwest corner of town, T420349.*

D **Kuhstall**, *T481025, kuhstall@lacumbrecita.info* Rooms with cooking facilities cost 10% more; breakfast extra in all cases.

D **La Campana**, *T481062, lacampana@lacumbrecita.info* All rooms with cooking facilities.

Villa General Belgrano *p169*
In high season, summer, July and Easter, accommodation is usually pricey and fully booked.

D **Baviera**, *El Quebracho 21, T461476, baviera@elsitiodelavilla.com* On Av San Martín, with a leafy garden and a large pool, this tidy family oriented motel-like place has cosy rooms; though you need your own vehicle. Breakfast includes homemade cakes.

D **Berna**, *Vélez Sarsfield 86, T/F461097, berna@tecomnet.com.ar* Next to the bus station is Swiss owners run this large hotel with good rooms with breakfast and a large garden with a pool. Rates are 50% higher in high season.

D **La Posada de Akasha**, *Los Manantiales 60, T462440.* A comfortable house with pool and welcoming owners. Prices rise in high season.

G pp **El Rincón**, *T461323, rincon@calamuchitanet.com.ar* The only hostel in town is beautifully set in 20 hilly hectares with dense forests and green clearings. Welcoming owners offer dormitories, very good double or single rooms with bath (US$4 pp) and camping (US$1.30 pp). US$1 extra either for bedlinen or superb breakfasts. Meals for US$2.30 on request. 20% ISIC and HI discounts available, half price for children under 16. In high season rates are 25% higher and is the hostel is usually full. 10 min-walk from terminal. Recommended.

Eating

Alta Gracia *p169*
$$ **Hispania**, *Urquiza 90.* The owners of Hostal Asturias run this excellent restaurant serving fish and seafood, including *paella* and *fidebua*, with *sangría* and occasionally *gazpacho*. Desserts, such as *crema catalana* are fabulous.

$$ **Morena**, *Av Sarmiento 413.* Adds a wider selection of dishes to the usual beef, pizza or pastas, including trout and Spanish dishes in the welcoming atmosphere of an old house.

Villa General Belgrano *p169*
$ **Brunnen**, *Av Roca 73.* Refreshing locally brewed lagers, German dishes and a visit to the brewery in the backyard. Over 30 different pizzas are on the menu.

$ **Ottilia**, *Av San Martín y Strauss.* A traditional cosy Austrian run place. Try sausages with tasty chucrut or delicious cakes such as Apfelstrudel or Kirschtorte.

Tour operators

Villa General Belgrano *p169*
Aero Club, *on Av Jorge Newbery, T462502.* Short flights over the valley, US$20 for 2 people.

DAPA, *Av Roca 76, T463417, dapaturismo@calamuchitanet.com.ar* One-day trips to La Cumbrecita and guided walks in the surroundings for US$7 pp, to Cerro Champaquí in 4WD and an hour's walk to the summit for US$13 pp, to El Durazno or San Miguel de los Ríos for US$7 pp.

Friedrich, *Av Roca 224, T461372, friedrich@calamuchitanet.com.ar* One-day trips to La Cumbrecita including 4 hours there for US$7 pp or to Yacanto de Calamuchita. Also a 10 hour-walk to the east across sierras Chicas along Camino de los Chilenos.

Transport

Alta Gracia *p169*
Bus Terminal on the riverside, at C Paravachasca y Nieto, a 10 min walk from centre, for some national destinations and for **SATAG** buses which also pick up passengers along Av Libertador to El Crucero roundabout. Sarmiento buses to **Córdoba** depart from Belgrano 71 and to **Villa Carlos Paz** stop at C Paravachasca y Nieto. For **Villa General Belgrano** and other towns in Calamuchita valley, buses stop at El Crucero roundabout, a 30 min-walk from centre. To **Córdoba**, SATAG, Sarmiento, Sierras de Calamuchita (from El Crucero), 1 hr, US$0.70. To **Villa Carlos Paz**, Sarmiento, 1 hr,

US$0.85. To **Villa General Belgrano**, Sierras de Calamuchita, 1 hr, US$2.

Villa General Belgrano p169
Bus To/from **Córdoba**, TUS, Pájaro Blanco, La Villa, Lep, Sierras de Calamuchita, 1½-2hrs, US$3. To **Buenos Aires**, Chevallier, Valle de Calamuchita, Sierras Cordobesas, TUS, 11-12 hrs, US$16. To **La Cumbrecita**, Pájaro Blanco, every 2 to 4 hours,

1 hr 20 mins, US$5.50 return. Pájaro Blanco, (*office at Av San Martín 105, T461709*) goes also to the nearby villages of **Los Reartes**, **Villa Berna**, **Villa Alpina** and **Yacanto de Calamuchita**.
Car and mountain bike hire DAPA and **Friedrich**, see under tour operators.
Fly Machine, *Av Roca 50, T462425*.
Remise taxi Central de Remises, *Av Roca 95, T462000*.

San Luis Province

San Luis province used to be considered Córdoba's poorer sister, lying further from Buenos Aires, in more arid land and with a more basic infrastructure. However, in recent decades, the development of the resort town Merlo and the creation of a national park at the spectacular Sierra de las Quijadas have definitively put the province on the map. Increased tourism may change the quiet charm of the more remote places, but San Luis is still a very appealing place to explore, both for families and for lone travellers wanting to lose themselves in the vast and untouched splendour of the landscape.

San Luis City → *Phone code: 02652 Colour map 4, B2 Population: 162,000*

San Luis is a lively and easy going provincial capital. Founded by Martín de Loyola, the governor of Chile, in 1596, it wasn't until the late 19th century that it really took off. The result is a modern city with few remarkable buildings, but it's a friendly place, and a great centre for exploring the Sierra de San Luis and the Parque Nacional Sierra de las Quijadas, offering decent accommodation and good food.

Sights
The centre lies around **Plaza Pringles**, filed with beautiful jacarandas, aguaribay, eucalyptus and palm trees and thronging with young crowds after sunset. In the **Cathedral** ① *1000-1300, 1830-2000, US$0.20*, with its slender towers and sumptuous interior, there are replicas of famous Murillo paintings and the extraordinary pesebre electrónico, a very personal vision of the birth of Christ, with figures moving figures to the accompaniment of Beethoven's 9th symphony mixed with Scottish pipes. Kitsch and marvellous. Northwest of the plaza, Av Illia strikes out diagonally six blocks towards the magnificent and decaying former railway station. At the corner of Av Illia and Junín the large **tourist office** has little information.

Along Av Illia are the top hotels and bars which become lively at night. If you're keen on geology and read Spanish, visit the tiny **Museo de Historia Natural** ① *Behind the bus terminal at the back of the main University buildings, Tue-Sun 1000-1300, US$0.35*, which traces the evolution of San Luis, including the fossil of an alarming giant spider and a dinosaur footprint. The main commercial heart of the city is on Rivadavia, and three blocks away lies the quieter Plaza Independencia, with its extraordinary Moorish Dominican temple, with a Mozarabic façade. The 18th-century **Convento de Santo Domingo** is the oldest building in the city, but sadly cannot be visited. Next to the church, in the **Centro Artesanal San Martín de Porres** ① *25 de Mayo 955, T424222, Mon-Fri 0800-1300*, woollen rugs are woven and sold.

The main attraction here is undoubtedly in the sierras, plus two artificial lakes just outside the city, **Embalse Potrero de los Funes**, 15 km northeast (via the picturesque Quebrada de los Cóndores), and **Embalse Cruz de Piedra**, 10 km east, which offers good fishing. In **Potrero de los Funes**, north of the lake, is a wooded residential area with family-oriented places to stay and eat. From the bus terminal there it's an easy walk to **Salto de la Moneda**, a 14 m waterfall with a deep section of the river for good swimming. In summer, contact Toni at terminal, T495130, who can guide you to this and other nearby sights in the sierras. Even if you're on a tight budget, it is worth at least having a drink at the bar of the 4 star-hotel on the lake. Just north of the latter is **El Volcán**, a leafy small town on a river with a *balneario* with camping and picnic. To Potrero de los Funes and El Volcán take C Junín to the east, which leads to Av del Fundador, later route 20. About 12 km from centre, one road goes to Potrero de los Funes (4 km), the other, to El Volcán (6 km). There are frequent minibuses to both sites from San Luis terminal.

Provincial Route 3 N goes north from San Luis along the foot of the western slopes of the sierras and after 17 km reaches the 3 km access road to **Suyuque Nuevo**. This beautifully situated Benedictine convent has opened a small shop where you can buy honey and fruit preserves produced by nuns. **Villa de la Quebrada**, 14 km north, is another sleepy village, famous for its religious procession on May 3rd and its Via Crucis with marble statues. For Suyuque and Villa de la Quebrada take Colón north, and then route 3n. Two daily buses heading for Nogolí, pass 3 km from Suyuque Nuevo and go to Villa de la Quebrada. **Balde** (35 km west) has a splendid new thermal spa complex, **Los Tamarindos**, with two pools open also to non-residents (see Sleeping below), and 20 km south are the saltflats **Salinas del Bebedero**. For Balde and Salinas del Bebedero, take Av Lafinur south and route 7 to the west. There are two daily buses via Balde, carrying salt plant workers. Though the saltflat is visible from the bus stop, a return walk to the shore takes the 20 minutes that the bus stops: make sure the driver knows your intention before getting on in San Luis. ▶ *For Sleeping, Eating and other listings, see pages 176-180.*

Parque Nacional Sierra de Las Quijadas

→ *Phone code: 02652*

Situated 125 km northwest of San Luis in the northwestern corner of the province, the park covers 150,000 ha of wonderful scenery. ⓘ *Entry: US$2 (Argentines), US$4 (foreigners). Open from dawn till dusk. T490182, visit early in the morning or late in the afternoon for better views and to avoid the heat.* Its only accessible area, Potrero de la Aguada, is an immense natural amphitheatre of nearly 4,000 ha surrounded by steep red sandstone walls, eroded into strange shapes. There's a small **archaeological site** next to the access road, and the fossil-rich field of Loma del Pterodaustro shows intriguing evidence of dinosaurs and pterosaurs (winged reptiles). The vegetation is largely scrub, and *jarillas* are very common though there are trees such as the *quebracho blanco*. Wildlife includes guanaco, collared peccaries, *pumas*, tortoises, crowned eagles, peregrine falcons and condors. A hundred metres from park warden's place is the only site for camping (free) next to a basic canteen. From nearby *Mirador de Elda*, the first of the two vantage points on the Potrero, two optional footpaths go to **Mirador Superior** (an easy 45 min return walk) or down to the *huella* (a more demanding two hours return walk to a dinosaur footprint). This path also leads to the impressive cliffs of **Farallones**, reached by a five-hour return walk and only advisable well after midday, ⓘ *an unpaved 6 km road which turns off from Route 147 (San Luis to San Juan) at Hualtarán.* Tour operators in San Luis and Merlo run half or full day tours to the park. ▶ *For Sleeping, Eating and other listings, see pages 176-180.*

Sierra de San Luis

Situated northeast of the city of San Luis, this range of hills is little known to travellers, but has become more easily accessible with the recent paving of several secondary roads. There are just two frequently visited resorts, the small town of El Trapiche and the reservoir in La Florida. The rest of this vast hilly region is only sparsely inhabited, with quiet villages which maintain old rural traditions and a simple way of life. The eastern edge of the sierras and the upper valleys and high pampas around Carolina, can be visited by taking Route 9 north from San Luis. Regular buses go up to Carolina and Intihuasi. ▸▸ *For Sleeping, Eating and other listings, see pages 176-180.*

El Trapiche → *Phone code: 02651*
An attractive village (Km 40, 1,050 m) set on the Río Trapiche in wooded hills; there are summer homes, hotels and picnic sites. There are good easy walks to **Los Siete Cajones** on the sparkling waters of Río Grande and 6 km west, to pleasant surroundings of rivers **Virorco** and **De las Aguilas**.

Carolina → *Phone code: 02651 Colour map 4, A2*
Carolina is a former gold-mining town founded in 1792 at the foot of Tomolasta (2,018 m) which offers great views from its summit. It's a picturesque village with stone houses and a goldmine, which can be visited through tour operators. The local *Huellas* agency, T490224, huellashuellas@hotmail.com, dresses you up as a miner and guides you along 300 m tunnel for about 1½ hr (English spoken), and provides tools in case you suddenly feel the desire to dig. From Carolina a rough track leads north over the Cuesta Larga to San Francisco del Monte de Oro, on route 146. Two other roads in better condition cross attractive scenery of undulating pampas and volcanic peaks to Libertador General San Martín or to La Toma.

Eastern San Luis

Villa Mercedes → *Phone code: 02657 Colour map 4, B2 Population: 90,000*
Founded in 1856 as a fortress, Villa Mercedes is an important route centre and an alternative transport hub, though of little of interest to the tourist. It lies on route 7, 100 km southeast of San Luis. Accommodation is mainly found along Avenida Mitre (6 blocks east of bus terminal) towards centre (20 blocks south). Bus terminal, T428035 and tourist office, both at Avenida 25 de Mayo 1500. Villa Mercedes is also the gate to the southern plains with dozens of small lakes, attractive for anglers. *Pejerrey* is the main catch and the fishing season runs from November to August. Accommodation is only offered at local estancias (ask at tourist office).

The Conlara Valley → *Phone code: 02656 Population: 90,000*
Lying east of the Sierra de San Luis and west of the Sierra de Comechingones, this broad valley runs into the Traslasierra Valley to the north, with a number of attractive places to visit and stay. **San José del Morro**, has an 18th-century chapel in its blissful unchanged village. Nearby, the **Sierra del Morro** (1,639 m), is the remains of a collapsed volcano; inside its crater are small volcanic cones, and lots of rose-quartz can be found here (access through Estancia La Morena). At tiny **Renca**, every May 3 one of the most popular religious festivities in the region, *El Señor de Renca*, is celebrated. **Santa Rosa del Conlara** is a pleasant small town by a river, a good alternative for accommodation when Merlo is packed (reached by bus or *combi* from San Luis). A more scenic journey is via Provincial Route 1, which runs parallel to the east of route 148 along the base of the Sierra de Comechingones through a string of

pretty villages: Papagayos, surrounded by natural palm tree groves of '*Trithrinax campestris*', Villa Larca, where the waterfall chorro de San Ignacio and upper natural pools offer lovely walks, Cortaderas, Carpintería and up to the well-promoted Merlo.

Merlo → *Phone code: 02656 Colour map 4, A2 Population: 11,000*

Situated almost at the San Luis-Córdoba border, Merlo (895 m) is a popular holiday centre on the steep western slopes of the Sierra de Comechingones. It's lost much of its charm in recent years, due to mass tourism which has made it busy and overpriced. It claims to have a special microclimate, and sunny days can certainly be enjoyed throughout the year. The town was founded in 1797, but the **church** on the plaza, said to be of Jesuit origin, dates from the early 18th-century, and is soon to be replaced by the huge new redbrick church behind. There's a brand new airport and bus terminal and two **tourist offices** at the busy roundabout on route 5 and route 1 and next to the plaza, at Coronel Mercau 605, ① *0800-2000 (closing at 2200 in summer), T476079, sectur@merlo-sl.com.ar, www.merlo-online.com.ar*

Merlo's surroundings are still pleasant for good walks along the foot of the mountains or to their summits (for example the **Circuito de Damiana Vega**, three to four hours). The slopes are covered with woods and scrub and there are numerous refreshing streams with falls; nearby heights are excellent sites for paragliding; an experienced pilot recently reached heights of 5,000 m here. A paved road (15 km long) leads to the top of the sierras at **Mirador del Sol**, where there are great panoramic views (better at sunrise or sunset; accessible by bus), also the starting point for a rough track leading across 82 km of pampas and sierras de Córdoba to Embalse del Río Tercero. Quieter places to stay are spread in the neighbouring small settlements of Piedra Blanca (4 km north) or Rincón del Este (4 km east), but book ahead everywhere in high season. ▸▸ *For Sleeping, Eating and other listings, see pages 176-180.*

Listings: San Luis Province

● Sleeping

San Luis *p173*
C Gran Hotel San Luis, *Av Illia 470, T425049, F430148, hotelsanluis@hotmail.com* Pricey 3 star-place with traditional décor. A good pool, breakfast included.
D Aiello, *Av Illia 431, T425609, F425694, www.hotelaiello.com* Best value in town: good rooms with a/c, welcoming staff, breakfast included and a very nice pool; internet access available.
D Grand Palace, *Rivadavia 657, T422059*. The lively atmosphere and friendly staff make this a good choice. Rooms are not spectacular but have attractive parquet floors and some have a/c. Breakfast included, and there is a good restaurant at the back.
E Belgrano, *Belgrano 1440, T435923*. This is probably the best budget option with welcoming staff, renovated rooms with fan

and bath and breakfast included.

Around San Luis *p174*
C Campo La Sierra, *19 km east of San Luis (access via route 20), T494171, www.campolasierra.com.ar* Swiss owners warmly welcome guests to their 70-ha farm with native flora (Austrian cacti experts visit annually) and offer German style cooking. Pool and breakfast included, and you can also practice archery.
C Hotel Potrero de los Funes, on route 18, Km 16, T440038, 423898, hpfreser@ sanluis.gov.ar Set in a mountainous area, this lakeside resort offers affordable rooms, some with splendid views (slightly pricier). A pool and sport facilities are included (also ATM), as well as a large breakfast. Ask for a discount if staying over 3 nights.
C Los Tamarindos, *Balde, T442220*. Rates at this attractive spa resort include breakfast

---

● *For an explanation of the sleeping and eating price codes used in this guide, see the inside front cover. Other relevant information is provided in the Essentials chapter, page 44.*

and rooms with a/c in small flats for up to 6 people; there are both indoor and outdoor pools accessible to non-guests for US$3 pp. Also cabins with a/c where you can rest after the baths for US$4/hr.

Camping
A few sites in El Volcán on the river bank (20 km from San Luis).

El Trapiche *p175*
F pp **El Parqu**, *T493176*. A family oriented hotel where also full and half board accommodation are also offered very cheaply; kids under 5 free.
F pp **La Adolfina**, *next to the school, T493009.* A decent place to stay with leafy gardens, a pool and clean rooms, breakfast included. Open only in summer.
D (for 4) **Villa Alinor**, *T493038.* A group of small houses at the most attractive location on a natural rocky balcony next to the river. Each house sleeps 4 or 6 with kitchen, fridge and phone; bed linen and towels extra. Delightful. Recommended.

Camping
At the north end of town, to the right side of the bridge. Nearby is the La Florida reservoir which offers good fishing, accessible via a paved road encircling the lake. On its northern shore there is a small natural reserve, intended to preserve the original flora and wildlife.

Carolina *p175*
D pp **Hostería Las Verbenas**, *T02652-15669797, www.lasverbenas.com.ar* Situated in the beautiful Pancanta valley (10 km south of Carolina), this is an ideal base for walking and horseriding or for enjoying a relaxing stay. Price is for full board accommodation.
D **La Posta del Caminante**, *T490223, www.lapostadelcaminante.com.ar* Housed in a former residence for mining engineers at Carolina, it offers comfortable rooms with bath and breakfast (cheaper with shared bath) and has a small restaurant next door; walks to the mines and horseriding excursions are also organized.

E **Cerro Blanco**, *T492012.* Next to a nicely-maintained *balneario*, where the river was dammed, this place has clean and comfortable rooms; with breakfast.

Merlo *p176*
Book well in advance for high season: Jan-Feb, Easter, July-Aug, and long weekends throughout the year. Dozens of recently opened places follow the same format: house, garden and pool, differentiated only in size and quality of service. Prices rise 10-20% in high season.
B **Villa de Merlo**, *Pedernera y Av del Sol, T475335, F475019.* Comfortable rooms have splendid views of the sierras and the large garden with pool. There are sport facilities, though the quiet atmosphere of this rather exclusive 3-star hotel is more appealing for a relaxing holiday. There's also a moderately priced restaurant.
D **Colonial**, *Av Dos Venados y P Tisera, T475388, hotelcolonial@hotmail.com* Probably the best value, in a quiet residential area not far from the centre. An attractive neo-colonial building has simple rooms on a patio with an incredibly small pool. Breakfast is included, internet access (not free).

Camping
Las Violetas, *Chumamaya y Av Dos Venados, T475730, lasvioletas@merlo-sl.com.ar* The closest site to centre has a small shady area for tents, pool, canteen, grocery and clean but not spotless bathrooms. US$4 per campsite plus US$0.35 per day.

🍴 Eating

San Luis *p173*
Chivito (kid) is the main local dish, though not always on offer on menus. Its usual accompaniment is *chanfaina* (a stew whose main ingredients are the goat's entrails).
$$ **La Porteña**, *Junín y General Paz, T431722.* Go for simple meals such as the *plato del día* and prepare for enormous portions in the enjoyable atmosphere of this popular place.
$ **Crocantes**, *San Martín 630.* A bakery where cheap and superb sandwiches are prepared at your request and with your chosen bread.

$ **Grand Palace**, *Rivadavia 657*. At the hotel of the same name, the experienced chef Pedro Pardo offers a selection of very good dishes based on grilled meats, fish or pork with scrumptious homemade desserts.

$ **La Pulpería del Arriero**, *9 de Julio 753, T432446*. Combining tasty regional specialities with live folk music in the evenings, this is the place for trying *empanadas* or *asado* cooked in the most traditional ways during a lively night out. Set menus are good value.

$ **Los Robles**, *Colón 684, T436767*. The atmosphere is formal, the food is very good and though some dishes on offer are pricey, you can eat very well at moderate prices at this smart *parrilla*. There is a wide choice of meat dishes (*bife de chorizo* is great), including *chivito* and trout, and a varied wine list. Recommended.

Cafés and bars

There's a cluster spread along Av Illia and C Rivadavia between 800 and 1000 blocks: **Liberato**, *Av Illia 378*. Popular with young crowds by night. More formality during daytime can be found at the two cafés on the plaza: **Aranjuez** and **Ocean**. **Macedonio**, *San Martín 848*. A laid back cafe-bookshop.

Conlara Valley *p175*

Manía, *San Martín 199*. Very good pizza and simple and cheap meals.

Merlo *p176*

$$ **El Establo**, *Av del Sol 450*. A handsome *parrilla* place, where the grill or asador is strangely trapped in a glass enclosure. Try *chivito* here.

$$ **El Ciprés**, Av del Ciprés 114. Popular with locals, so good filling meals are guaranteed though the menu is pretty standard.

$$ **La Vieja Posada**, Av del Sol 2. A simple place for enjoying any of the more than 30 different pizzas with a folk music show on Saturday evenings.

$ **La Estrella de Merlo**, *Becerra y Av del Sol*. Locals come here for tasty homemade pastas.

✹ Festivals

San Luis *p173*

Every *August 25* a religious procession

commemorates the day of **King Saint Louis** and it is a national holiday across the whole province. The popular religious festival of **Cristo de la Quebrada** takes place on *May 3* at nearby Villa de la Quebrada.

✹ Sport and activities

Merlo *p176*

El Nido, *San Martín 370, T475994, elnidoparapente@yahoo.com.ar* This paragliding school offers courses all year round (accommodation provided) and jumps for beginners (with instructor) from a platform at 2,020 m (1,100 m above Merlo). Usually lasting 15-20 minutes, each flight costs US$23.

⟲ Tour operators

San Luis *p173*

All agencies offer similar tours at standard rates (note that rates in leaflets usually do not include access fee to National parks). If a tour isn't running on your chosen day, try the next tour operator. A half-day tour to Sierra de las Quijadas is the most popular (US$12 pp plus entry) and includes a walk to Los Miradores (1-1 ½ hr) and to La Huella (2-2 ½ hrs). Weather permitting (usually not in summer), a more demanding walk to Los Farallones (4-5 hrs) is organized (US$13 pp plus entry). The Circuito Serrano Chico (US$7 pp) is a short walk around El Volcán, Potrero de los Funes and the town itself, while the Circuito Serrano Grande (US$10 pp) adds El Trapiche and La Florida. Circuito de Oro (US$12 pp) goes up to Carolina and Intihuasi and may include the Circuitos Serranos. Two other tours are to religious sites in Suyuque and Villa de la Quebrada and to the hot springs of Balde and the saltflats in Salinas del Bebedero. A day trip to Merlo via onyx town La Toma is also available (US$17 pp). **Bruno Aliberti**, *T426021, T15502971*. Guides only with your own vehicle.
Dasso, *Rivadavia 540, T421017, T15645410*.
Gimatur, *Av Illia y Caseros, T435751, gimatursl@hotmail.com* English spoken.
Luciano Franchi, *Chile 1430, T420345, T15657441*.
Remises Sur, *T455000*. Good value trips if there are 3 or 4 of you.

Merlo *p176*

Agencies run excursions not only to local sights but to the main provincial attractions, including full day tours to Sierra de las Quijadas (US$13 pp plus entry fee). Closer destinations include half-day trips to Mina Los Cóndores (US$8 pp plus entry fee) and to Bajo de Véliz, an over promoted palaeontological site, where giant spiders used to live million of yeas ago (US$6.50 pp). Surrounding villages may also be explored for a few hours (US$5-7 pp). These more conventional tours are organized by: **La Plaza**, *Becerra y Av del Ciprés, T476853* and **Sol**, *Av del Sol 171, T475346*.

More physically demanding activities like climbing hills, visiting a remote ghost mining town, sleeping in caves or crossing rivers are also on offer; a good ways to enjoy the mountains. These activities are run by **Cimarrón incursiones**, *Av del Sol 300, T478934*, T02652-15664251, **Juan Carlos Sciamarella**, *02652-15548536* or **Los Tabaquillos**, *Av de los Césares 2100, T474010*.

⊖ Transport

San Luis *173*
Air
Airport, T422427, 3 km northwest (access via Colón, Av Justo Daract and Sargento Baigorria); ordinary and *remise* taxis charge about US$1-1.20 from centre. To **Buenos Aires**, 1¼ hr, **CATA** (from Merlo).

Bus
Terminal at Av España 990, T424021. Triangular shaped building with offices in and outside and bus stops on all sides (check at office where your bus leaves). To reach the centre (10 min walk from plaza), take C Rivadavia. Left luggage at Kiosko Portos (facing University), open 24 hrs, US$0.65 per item half day. To **Buenos Aires**, several companies, 10-11 hrs, US$13-18. To **Lima** (Perú), **El Rápido Internacional** (direct), 2½ days, US$100. To **Santiago** (Chile), Tur Bus, Tas Choapa, Cata, 9-10 hrs, US$12-15. To **La Rioja**, Socasa, 7½ hrs, US$9. To **Mendoza**, several companies, 3-4 hrs, US$6. To **Córdoba**, several companies, 6-7 hrs, US$6-8. To **San Juan**, Andesmar, Autotransportes San Juan, Autotransportes San Juan-Mar del Plata, TAC, Del Sur y

Media Agua, 4 hrs, US$7. To **Santa Rosa** (La Pampa), **Dumas**, 10 hrs, US$8.50; also to destinations in southern San Luis. To **Merlo**, **Expreso Uspallata**, **TAC**, **SENA**, **Automotores Merlo** (usually packed minibuses), 3 hrs, US$3. To **Balde** and **Salinas del Bebedero**, Dasso, 2 daily Mon-Fri, 45 mins (US$0.45) and 1 hr (US$0.75), respectively. To **El Trapiche**, María del Rosario, San José, US$0.65; same services go to La Florida and Río Grande. To **Carolina** and **Intihuasi**, Polos, 3 daily (unreliable timetable), US$1.70 and US$2.10, respectively.

Car hire
Avis, *Belgrano 1440, T440288 or T15506897*. **Localiza**, *Chacabuco 649, T438500, localizasanluis@ciudad.com.ar*

Remise taxis
Cosmos, *Chacabuco 1151, T440000*. **Zoo**, *Bolívar y Falucho, T421000*.

Parque Nacional Sierra de las Quijadas *p174*
Only 2 bus companies with very few daily services link San Luis and San Juan (**Autotransportes San Juan** and **Del Sur y Media Agua**) and stop at **Hualtarán** (US$3 and US$2, respectively).

Merlo *p176*
For frequent services to destinations in Córdoba province, go to Villa Dolores.
Air Airport, on route 148, T492840, 23 km west of Merlo T422427. To/from **Buenos Aires**, 1 hr 50 mins, **CATA** (stops at San Luis), desk at tourist office (at Merlo roundabout), T478460. *Remise* taxis charge US$5. Bus Terminal on route 1, next to roundabout, 10 mins walk from plaza. Frequent services to **San Luis**, Expreso Uspallata, TAC, SENA, Automotores Merlo, 3 hrs, US$3. To **Buenos Aires**, TAC, Expreso del Oeste, Autotransportes San Juan-Mar del Plata, Sierras Cordobesas and Chevallier, US$15-18, 10-12 hrs. To **Córdoba**, TAC, Expreso Uspallata, Andesmar, Monticas, 5 hrs, US$6. To **Mina Clavero**, Monticas, Expreso del Oeste, 2 hrs, US$3. To **Villa Dolores**, TAC, 2 hrs, US$1.70 (via San Javier) or Sierras Cordobesas and TAC, 1 hr, US$1.30-2 (via route 148). Urban bus station, on *C Pringles y Av Los Almendros (2 blocks*

south of plaza). **La Costa** goes daily along route 1 to Cortaderas, Villa Larca and Papagayos. **STU** runs frequent services to **Mirador del Sol**, stopping there for 10 mins, US$1.20 return.

Cycle hire **Sis**, *Coronel Mercau y Los Huarpes (2 blocks north of plaza)*, US$2.70 per day. **Remise taxis** **Avenida**, *Becerra 575, T476031*. **Unión**, *Videla 114, T478444*.

ⓘ Directory

San Luis *p173*
Airline offices **CATA**, *Av España 950, T439156*. **Banks** **Banex**, *Rivadavia y Pringles,* T440004. Changes US$ and all TC's but these take at least 3 days, with a 1.5% commission for Amex TC's. Exchange facilities also at **Banco de Galicia**, *Colón y Pringles*, and at **Montemar**, *Belgrano 980*.
Communications **Internet**: Cyberclub **Buskar**, *Pedernera 1305*, US$0.35/hr (US$0.25/hr after midnight). **Ego!**, *Av Illia 320*. US$0.65/hr (US$0.35/hr after 2200). Telecentro, *Av Illia 127*, US$0.65/hr. **Post office** *San Martín y Av Illia*; Western Union branch.
Telecommunications *Telecentros* are mainly on C San Martín and on Av Illia.

The West

Introducing the West

Stretching east from the Andes to hot dry plains, with lush oases in the valleys between, the provinces of Mendoza, San Juan and La Rioja offer some of Argentina's most spectacular natural beauty, and its best kept secrets.

Mendoza is the dynamic heart of the region, a stylish modern city of wide leafy avenues, fine restaurants and cafés, set against a purple veil of mountains beyond. Its surrounding vineyards are miraculous expanses of green, irrigated since pre-Inca times by mountain snowmelt, where a perfectly sunny climate produces superb wines. Head west through a gorge of red stratified rock to the giants of the Andes, **Aconcagua** and **Tupungato**, both feasible climbs with stunning landscape in their foothills. Or head north to **San Juan** province, where magnificent **Mount Mercedario** is the backdrop to idyllic oasis villages **Barreal** and **Calingasta**, peaceful places to walk under deep blue skies. Feel dwarfed by time and space in the extraordinary landscapes of two national parks. The 'moon valley' of **Ischigualasto** is a lake-bed 225 million years old, strewn with fossils from first life forms to dinosaurs. And **Talampaya**'s vast canyons of terracotta rock, eroded by wind into gigantic sculptures, are magnificent at sunset when they turn a vivid red.

Further south, peaceful **San Rafael**, steeped in vineyards and olive groves, makes a good base for white water rafting in the eerie ravine of **Cañon del Atuel**. You can ski down great heights at chic **Las Leñas** or explore deep underground caves from sleepy **Malargüe**. And here too are secret places waiting to be discovered: the tranquil lagoons of **Llancanelo** with thousands of flamingos on its Prussian blue waters, and the starkly beautiful volcanic landscape of **La Payunia**, where guanacos roam.

★ **Don't miss...**

❶ **Mendoza** Sip vintage malbec from the terrace at Bodega Norton, page190.

❷ **Las Leñas ski resort** Ski downhill for an uninterrupted 7 km, page 204.

❸ **Ischigualasto** Wander through 250 million years of strata, solving the mystery of the dinosaur eggs, page 212.

❹ **La Payunia** Ride horses across virgin plains amidst a hundred roaming wild guanaco, page 205.

❺ **Cerro Mercedario** Sleep beneath the clearest starry skies on the planet, page 211.

❻ **Cacheuta** Lie in thermal waters and do absolutely nothing, page 190.

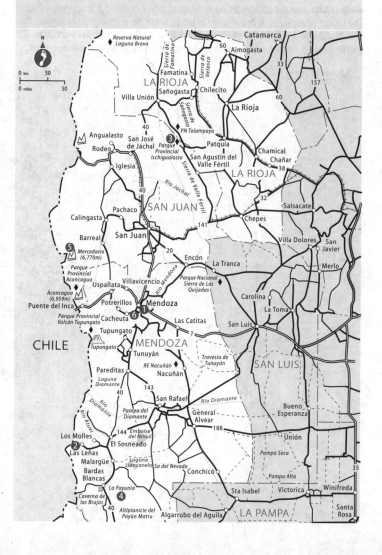

The West

Mendoza Province

The southernmost of the three western provinces, Mendoza is the most developed for tourism. Quite apart from the appeal of Mendoza City itself, the surrounding area is covered by vineyards and to the west are the peaks of the Andes. Here, in Alta Montaña, you can climb Aconcagua from one of the hamlets strung out on the mountain road to Chile, visit the Puente del Inca, or ski at the family resort of Los Penitentes in winter. The upland valley village of Uspallata is a good stopping point, reached either by a dramatic road through Villavicencio, or via the thermal spa at Cacheuta and the laid-back summer village of Potrerillos with its rafting and horse riding.

South of Mendoza City, the town of Tupungato is a good base for fishing and for riding into the wild mountains around its volcano. In Southern Mendoza, the biggest centre is the town of San Rafael, known for its vineyards, and from here you can go white water rafting near the canyon at Cañon de Atuel, which is also a popular holiday spot. The region's best skiing is at the resort of Las Leñas to the northwest of Malargüe. This area is still little developed for tourism but includes two natural reserves – at Llancanelo and La Payunia – and the caves at Caverna de las Brujas, all well worth the expedition.

Mendoza

Sleeping
Aconcagua **4** *C4*
Carollo & Gran
  Princess **2** *B3*
Churrasqueras del
  Parque **3** *B1*
Damajuana **5** *D2*
Dam-sire **6** *B6*
Gran Balbi **8** *B4*

Gran Mendoza **9** *B4*
Gran Ritz **10** *C3*
Hostel Campo Base **1** *C4*
Hostel Internacional
  11 *D4*
Imperial **12** *B4*
Monterrey **14** *B4*
Necochea **15** *B4*
Nutibara **16** *C4*

Palace **17** *B4*
Park Hyatt **18** *C4*

Eating
3 90 (Tres con Noventa)
  18 *C2*
Azafrán **1** *C2*
Boccadoro **2** *A4*
Don Otto **4** *B4*

Mendoza City

→ *Phone code: 0261 Colour map 3, A2 Population: 121,000.*

Mendoza is one of the country's most attractive cities, with its wide tree-lined avenues and five leafy plazas, and an almost perfectly sunny climate. It's surrounded by picturesque vineyards, and at nearby Maipú and Lujan de Cujo you can visit both enormous commercial bodegas and smaller family concerns to see the process from start to finish and sample of the country's most excellent wine. The city has some small interesting musems, a good zoo, and lively nightlife with sophisticated bars and restaurants serving all kinds of fine food. It's a good place to plan a trip into the mountains, hire ski gear, or merely to gaze at the snow-capped peaks which form the centre of its splendid park, Parque San Martín, which is the venue for a spectacular festival to celebrate the wine harvest every March.

Ins and outs

Getting there 1,060 km from Buenos Aires. Daily flights connect Mendoza's El Plumerillo airport, 8 km north, with Buenos Aires (1 hr 50 mins), and Santiago de Chile. Long distance buses arrive at Mendoza from almost everywhere in the country, with several services daily to Buenos Aires and to cities of San Rafael and San Juan. Mendoza is a good stopping point for routes in and out of Chile with frequent services to Santiago, many of which stop at Uspallata and at various points through the mountains, for those wanting to trek or ski.

Getting around Mendoza's city centre is easy to find your way around on foot, with the large leafy Plaza Independencia occupying four blocks at its centre. Pedestrianized Peatonal Sarmiento runs between the plaza and the main shopping street San Martín which runs north/south. It's worth making the most of the *bodegas* (vineyards) around the nearby towns of Luján de Cuyo and Maipú, reached by bus. Each bus has two numbers – a big number painted onto the bus at the top front corners (the bus company), and a smaller number – subnumero – on a card propped in a window (the route). So if you're going to the *bodega* La Rural in Maipu for example, you'll need 170, subnumero 173, and don't be tempted to get on all the other 170's that go past. Buses are cheap, US$0.40 to get to Maipu, and drivers will tell you when to get off if you ask. You're unlikely to need transport in the centre, but if you do, taxis are plentiful and safe.

Best time to visit The biggest festival of the year *Fiesta de Vendimia* is held in early March to celebrate the start of the wine harvest, with a carnival queen, a procession of floats, wine tastings and outdoor extravaganzas in the park. Bodegas can be visited all year round but at harvest time in March and April you'll see the machinery working. Trekking in the mountains is only viable from November to April, when the snow has melted, and is most pleasant in December to February, which is the only feasible season for the higher altitudes. Skiing at Los Penitentes is from July to October, though Las Leñas is open from mid-June.

Tourist information Mendoza is one of the country's best-prepared provinces for tourism with helpful staff in tourist offices sprinkled over the city. The biggest is at San Martin 1143, opposite Peatonal Sarmiento, T420 1333, 420 2800, with an additional booth on the street outside They'll give you a city map, direct you to bodegas and explain the buses. English, French and German are spoken. Smaller offices are in the civic centre near the university at 9 de Julio 500, T449 5185, and at Las Heras 342, T429 6298. All open 0900-2100. There's another extremely helpful office at the entrance to Parque San Martin, open Monday to Friday 0800-1300, 1600-2000 and Saturday 0900-1300. Visit www.turismo.mendoza.gov.ar (a well-designed but very slow site), www.mendoza. com.ar and www.vendimia.mendoza.gov.ar

History

Mendoza was founded by Pedro de Castillo in 1561 when he was sent from the Spanish colony in Chile by Captain General García Hurtado de Mendoza to cross the 4,000 m pass over the Andes, and found a new city. Mediterranean fruits were introduced to the region soon afterwards, and thrived in its sunny climate, aided by pre-Hispanic irrigation channels which still water the dry lands with abundant snowmelt. The city's wealth grew, although it remained largely isolated throughout the colonial period, being governed from Chile and having little contact with modern-day Argentina. The city's greatest blow came on Easter Saturday in 1861 when it was completely destroyed in a devastating earthquake which killed some 4,000 of its 12,000 inhabitants. Very quickly, a new centre was built by the French architect Ballofet, several blocks to the southwest of the original. This modern city was designed with low, quake-proof buildings and broad avenues with many attractive plazas to aid evacuation in case of further tremors. Plane trees were planted on all the streets, watered by a network of irrigation channels which still gush with water every spring. Now Mendoza's main industry is wine, though a busy university and, increasingly, tourism help to sustain its wealth and lively character.

Sights

The large **Plaza Independencia** is a popular meeting place for mendocinos with its shady acacia and plane trees and pretty fountains. In the middle is the small **Museo de Arte Moderno** ① *Mon-Sat 0900-1300, 1700-2100, Sun 1700-2100, free,* originally designed to be an emergency bunker for victims of future earthquakes, now showing temporary exhibitions. On the western side is the new and luxurious **Hyatt Plaza Hotel,** once a splendid 1920's palace where Juan Perón and Evita stayed. The eastern side is filled with a handicrafts market at weekends, where Peatonal Sarmiento runs to San Martín. Around the four corners of this central plaza are four smaller plazas. The most attractive is the **Plaza España**, to the southeast. Its floor and benches are beautifully tiled and it's a lovely place to sit beneath its richly varied trees, gazing at the rather sentimental mural displaying historical episodes and scenes from *Don Quijote* and the famous gaucho poem, *Martín Fierro*. Four blocks due west along Montevideo, with its pretty Italianate and colonial-style buildings, is Plaza Italia. You could pop into the small **Museo del Pasado Cuyano** ① *Montevideo 544, T423 6031, Mon-Fri 0900-1230, US$0.50,* housed in a beautiful 1873 mansion owned the Civit family, celebrated governors of Mendoza. There's lots of San Martín memorabilia,

San Martín El Libertador

On any visit to Argentina, you'll see San Martín frequently, his equestrian statues are at the centre of almost every plaza in the country. One of the greatest independence heroes of South America, José Francisco de San Martín hoped to unite Spanish America after independence. Though he failed to achieve this aim, his military genius played a major role in securing independence, since he possessed a tremendous organizational ability, even when leading troops scattered over large distances and mountainous terrain. His epic crossing of the Andes in 1817 was a turning point in the Wars of Independence, and the campaigns that followed in Chile and Peru ended Spanish rule in South America.

Born in Yapeyú, Corrientes, in 1778 and educated in Spain, San Martín served in the Spanish army in North Africa, Spain and France, gaining his first combat experience at the age of 15. In 1811 he resigned from the army and made contact with Francisco de Miranda and other supporters of South American independence, returning to Buenos Aires in 1812 to train the new cavalry regiment. The following year, he replaced Belgrano as commander of the northern armies but he soon resigned, disagreeing that the way to defeat the Spanish stronghold of Peru was by an attack through Bolivia. He requested to be appointed governor of Cuyo province, and from his base in Mendoza, spent the next two years preparing to capture Peru by means of a giant flanking movement through Chile and up through the coast to Lima. San Martín's 'Army of the Andes' was drawn from regular troops sent

by Buenos Aires, but he personally reconnoitred the mountain passes to plan the crossing to Chile himself. He also planned a brilliant deception, calling a meeting of Pehuenche chiefs to ask their permission to cross their territory to invade Chile via mountain passes south of Mendoza. As he'd expected, spies carried this news across the Andes, leaving San Martín free to use a more northerly route, with the main force crossing by Los Patos and Uspallata passes. Some 3,778 men set out on 18-19 January 1817 with equipment, support services and 10,791 horses and mules, and crossed the Andes in 21 days, arriving on time at their intended destinations. Within days the army defeated the Spanish at Chacabuco and entered Santiago, Chile, in triumph, though the conclusive victory was at the Battle of Maipú in April 1818.

With Chilean independence secure, San Martín led his forces by sea to Peru in 1820. Avoiding battle against the larger Spanish forces, he negotiated a truce, and encouraged army desertions. Finally entering Lima in triumph in July 1821, he assumed political and military command of the new republic of Peru. Afterwards, San Martín resigned his post and returned to his small farm in Mendoza, before travelling to Europe in 1824 to settle in Brussels and then Grand Bourg, France. He died in Boulogne-sur-Mer in 1850, and his remains lie now in Buenos Aires cathedral. Symbolizing to many Argentines the virtues of sacrifice, bravery and the lack of personal gain, he's remembered by street names in even the smallest towns.

and an exquisite Spanish 15th-century carved altarpiece. The knowledgeable director will give you an excellent tour and insights into the city's history.

The original city centre, destroyed by the earthquake in 1861, was 12 blocks northeast of today's Plaza Independencia, and now known as the **Area Fundacional**. Here there is a broad tranquil plaza and a beautifully designed museum whose glass floor reveals continuing excavations of foundations from the old Cabildo and the buildings that followed, with an array of objects salvaged from the rubble. The informative free tour is highly recommended to give you a picture of Mendoza's history. Under the plaza you can see the first fountain to bring running water to the city, and nearby are the ruins of the Jesuit **Iglesia de San Francisco** ① *Alberdi and Videla Castillo, T425 6927, Tue-Sat 0800-2000, Sun 1500-2000 US$0.50, kids under 6 free. Buses 10, 110, 80, 60.* Plaza Pellegrini is another attractive little plaza, at Avenida Alem y Avenida San Juan, where wedding photos are taken on Friday and Saturday nights, and there's a small antiques market on Friday lunchtimes.

Ten blocks west of Plaza Independencia are the wrought iron entrance gates to the great **Parque General San Martín**, 350 ha of lavishly planted parkland designed by Charles Thays, with sports facilities, a big lake where regattas are held, a sports stadium, and an amphitheatre. On a hill in the park is the **Cerro de la Gloria**, popular with paragliders, and giving splendid views of the Andes to the west with a monument to San Martín, showing various episodes of his leading his army across the Andes to liberate Argentina and Chile from the Spanish. From the east end of the park, on Avenida Libertad, an hourly bus ('Oro Negro') runs to the top of the Cerro de la Gloria – otherwise it's a long walk (45 mins). On the side of the Cerro is the **Jardín Zoológico**, one of the country's best zoos. ① *T4250130, Tue-Sun 0900-1700, US$1.* There's a helpful information office next to the main gates and around the lake. The restaurant **Terrazas del Lago** is open from breakfast to the early hours of the morning. At the south end of the lake is the **Museo de Ciencias Naturales y Antropologicas** ①*T428 7666, Tue-Fri 0830-1300*, with an ancient female mummy amongst its fossils and stuffed animals. In the city centre, kids might enjoy the small aquarium **Acuario Municipal** ① *daily 0900-1230, 1500-2030, US$0.50*, underground at Buenos Aires e Ituzaingó.

In the nearby suburb of **Luján de Cuyo**, there's a small, charming collection of Argentine paintings in the house where Fernando Fader painted his beautiful murals, at the **Museo Provincial de Bellas Artes** in the Casa de Fader ① *Carril San Martín 3671, Mayor Drumond. T496 0224, 0900-1800, Sat/Sun 1400-1830, US$0.50, Tue-Fri . Reached by bus 200, 40 mins*. There are also sculptures in the lovely gardens. For the Museo Nacional del Vino, see below. ▸▸ *For Sleeping, Eating and other listings, see pages 191-195.*

Wine region → *The tourist office has a list of Mendoza's vineyards – phone first to check tour times*

Wine is at the heart of Mendoza's landscape and industry, and you really can't visit the province without seeing at least one of its many bodegas, and tasting their excellent produce. Lying between 750 and 1,100 m above sea level, and irrigated by snowmelt from the Andes, these vineyards benefit from the perfect climate – cool nights and warm dry days – for growing a wide variety of grapes. Many of the wines are exported to England and the United States, since within Argentina, wine-dwindled in popularity in the last 20 years. Argentines are less accustomed to the habit of drinking wine with meals from early childhood than their Spanish and Italian forebears; lager being cheaper, and most women particularly preferring soft drinks. However, fine wine consumption is now growing, and most of the bodegas are happy to open their doors to visitors with free informative tours and worthwhile tastings, hoping both to educate the public and to boost sales. You can visit a couple of bodegas in any excursion through a tour operator, and without your own transport this is really the only viable option, since the bodegas are some way out of town, and you may wait a while for the buses. Try to see both the big modern wineries and the smaller and more intimate places.

The closest winery to the city is the historical **Bodegas Escorihuela** ① *Belgrano 1188, Godoy Cruz, T424 2744, tours Mon-Fri 0930, 1030, 1130, 1230, 1430, 1530. Easily reached by Bus T from 9 de Julio or bus 170, subnumero 174, 200 (204) from Rioja, or 40 from the Plaza*, which also has an excellent and expensive restaurant run by the famous chef Francis Mallman, and a stunning centrepiece in the cellars, an ornately carved barrel from Nancy. If your Spanish isn't strong, you might like to visit this bodega before

Argentine wine

Wine was made in Argentina long before the Spanish planted their first vines here in 1554. In the early 20th century, it was among the five biggest wine producers of the world, though Argentine wine was little known abroad, since almost all the wine produced was for home consumption. However, in the 1970s, with the market glutted with cheap wine which was not of the best quality, Argentines stopped drinking wine in such quantity, preferring beer (*cerveza*) and soft drinks, which were cheaper, although far inferior as accompaniment for their superb steak. Then the wine industry failed to export fine Argentine wines as successfully as Chile, whose confident marketing style has secured them a place on every European supermarket shelf. But in recent years, Argentine wines have become more popular again within the country, and the rest of the world is also realizing what excellent quality they are.

Argentina's wine growing country extends along the length of the Andean foothills, from Cafayate in southern Salta to the Río Negro valley south of Neuquén. However, the centre of wine is undoubtedly Mendoza province, which produces 70% of the country's output. Surrounded by semi-arid lands with little vegetation, the rich green vineyards stretch out miraculously in perfectly ordered rows, against a dramatic backdrop of mauve snow-dusted mountains. This area benefits from the ideal climate for wine growing, with almost consistently sunny weather all year round, hot dry days and cold nights. The intense climate ensures the rich

flavour of the grapes. The other magical ingredient is the snowmelt from the Andes which provides some of the purest and most mineral rich water available anywhere, fed to the vines via an elaborate series of irrigation canals, laid before the Incas came. This system compensates for the low rainfall, less than 200m a year.

The main grapes grown are of French origin: Cabernet Sauvignon, Merlot, Malbec and Syrrah for red wines, and Chardonnay, Chenin and Sauvignon Blanc for whites. The white Torrontés grape is almost uniquely grown in Argentina, most successfully in the south of Salta around El Cafayate, a delicious dry, fruity wine with a sweet bouquet. Etchart's Torrontés is particularly recommended and if you're in doubt what to order with dinner, try Seneteiner's Malbec and any wine by Norton, particularly their Cabernet Sauvignon. Argentine champagne is cheap and very drinkable, most popularly produced by San Rafael-based Chandon, whose *champagnerie* you can visit. There are many bodegas in the Mendoza area, opening their doors to visitors with a tour and a tasting. Check the text for details, and if you're short of time, make it Bodega La Rural (San Felipe) at Montecaseros 2625, Coquimbito, which has a fascinating wine museum.

Wines can be bought in supermarkets for between US$1.50-3 a bottle, but there's little choice in the upper price range. It is better by far to go to a *Vinotequa*, or specialist wine shop, where you can buy really excellent wines for around US$5.

the others for its helpful brochure explaining the process in pictures!.

There are many bodegas in the satellite town of **Maipú**, 15 km, southeast of the city, and if you've only time for one, make it **Bodega La Rural** (San Felipe)

ⓘ *Montecaseros 2625, Coquimbito, T497 2013. Tours Mon-Sat 1000-1630, Sun 1000-1300, US$0.30. Bus 170 (subnumero 173) from La Rioja y Garibaldi.* This is a small traditional bodega, renowned for its marvellous **Museo del Vino** where you can see the history of winemaking through an amazing display of implements dating back to the pre-Colombian skin of an entire cow where grapes were trodden in the belly so that juice flowed out of its neck. Wonderful.

Also in Maipú is the smaller **Bodega Cavas del Conde** ⓘ *Dorrego s/n, Coquimbito, T497 2624, tours Mon-Sat 0930-1230, 1500-1700,* and **Finca Flichman** ⓘ *Munives 800, Barrancas, T497 2039, tours Wed-Sun 1000-1300, 1400-1700,* which produces deservedly famous and delicious fine wines. **Vina el Cerno** is small and has a lovely country house, ⓘ *Moreno 631, Coquimbito, tours Mon-Fri 0900-1700,* while **Bodega Gioil** is beautifully old fashioned ⓘ *Ozamiz 1040, T497 6777/4398447, tours Mon-Sat 0900-1900, Sun 1100-1400.*

There's nowhere to stay in Maipú itself but the historic bodega of **Inti Huaco** ⓘ *Carril Gómez 3602, Coquimbito, T420 1079, bodegaintihuac@infovia.com.ar,* has elegant mid priced rooms in beautiful surroundings. Contact Juan Morales.

Just south of the city, **Luján del Cuyo** is another wine producing town in whose leafy suburb, Chacras de Coria, you'll also find restaurants and nightclubs. Highly recommended is the splendid **Bodega Norton** ⓘ *Perdriel, Km 23.5, Ruta Provincial 15, T488 0480, tours on the hour from 0900-1200, 1400-1700. Bus 380 from the terminal,* with a very informative tour, and a generous tasting including their delicious premium wines.

Other bodegas worth visiting include **Pequeña Bodega** ⓘ *Ugarte 978, La Puntilla, T439 2094, tours Mon-Fri 0900-1300, 1600-2000, bus 10 (Ugarte) from 25 de Mayoa,* a small winery with a museum. Further south on RN40, Km29 is **Chandon** ⓘ *T490 9966, call for information on tour times, bus Mitre (no 380) from the terminal, platform 53 /54,* an impressive modern bodega, whose wines are well known in Argentina. Finally, **Nieto Senetiner** ⓘ *Guardia Vieja s/n, Vistalaba, T498 0315, tours Mon-Fri 1000-1600, Sat 0930-1100,* has really excellent wines, provides lunch if you book ahead and has some accommodation.

Around Mendoza

Various day trips are offered by tour companies, both of the sedentary kind and the more adventurous. There are thermal springs and a good place for lunch at the pretty village of **Cacheuta**, 29 km west, which also has a good hotel; You could do a day's rafting, walking or horseriding at **Potrerillos**. 6 km beyond. If you're driving, note that since the river was dammed there is no road between the two.

At **Villavicencio**, 47 km north, there are gentle walks and a charming rustic restaurant in spectacular mountain scenery, though the famous hotel you see on all the bottles of Villavicencio water is still being renovated. (See page 196 for more details). For watersports, **Embalse El Carrizal**, an artificial lake 60 km south of Mendoza, has yachting and fishing, campsites and picnic areas. If you're here to hike into the mountains, you'll need more than the day trip to Alta Montaña offered by agencies, though these will introduce you to the magnificent scenery on this road to Chile, allow you to visit the strange natural bridge of Puenta del Inca. For skiing in the winter, it's possible to make a day trip to **Los Penintentes**, 174 km away, but since there's plenty of accommodation there, it's better to go for a couple of days. Vallecitos is closer, at 80 km, but the resort is very basic and the *ripio* roads can be tricky.

● *For an explanation of the sleeping and eating price codes used in this guide, see the inside front cover. Other relevant information is provided in the Essentials chapter, page 44.*

Listings: Mendoza

● Sleeping

Like all tourist areas in Argentina, hotels fill up quickly in the holiday periods of January, July and Easter, and the spring festival 21 September.

AL Park Hyatt, *Chile 1124, on main plaza, T441 1234, F441 1235, www.mendoza.park .hyatt.com* Extremely swish and very comfortable with an excellent and affordable restaurant, pool, spa and casino.

B Gran Hotel Balbi, *Las Heras 340, T423 3500 F4380626.* Splendid entrance and spacious rooms, small pool and terrace.

B Gran Hotel Mendoza, *Espana 1210 y Espejo, T425 2000, www.hotelmendoza.com* Spacious rooms, and stylish decor make this an appealing though slightly pricey option. However, it's very central and there are larger rooms for families.

B Hotel Nutibara, *Av Mitre 867, T/F4295428.* Welcoming, slightly old fashioned place, with eclectic decor but a lovely pool, a leafy patio, comfortable rooms, and a quiet but central location.

C Gran Hotel Ritz, *Peru 1008, T423 5115, aristo@infovia.com.ar* Highly recommended for its excellent service, comfortable rooms and great location, within quick reach of the centre and the restuarants on Aristides Villanueva.

C Hotel Carollo, *25 de Mayo 1184, T423 5666.* Comfortable, slightly old fashioned and welcoming, this hotel shares its pool and facilities with **Gran Hotel Princess** next door.

D Monterrey Hotel, *Patricias Mendocinas 1532, T438 0901, hoteles@ciudad.com.ar* Great value at this stylish and spacious place, with nice modern rooms.

D Hotel Necochea, *Necochea 541, T425 3501.* Pleasant and friendly place, very reasonable and central, with some family rooms.

D Palace Hotel, *Las Heras 70, T423 4200, F429 5930.* A lovely quiet place, with clean modern rooms. Good value.

D Hotel Provincial, *Belgrano 1259, T425 8284, www.hotelprovincialmza.com* Reasonably priced place with good beds and a great view of the cordillera at breakfast.

E Hotel Imperial, *Las Heras 88, T15 414 4680.* Old fashioned, with plain but comfortable and quiet rooms in this hotel surrounded by restaurants, and excellent value.

F pp Dam-sire, *Viamonte 410, San José Guaymallén, T431 5142, 5 mins from terminal.* A new family run place with spotless rooms, breakfast included.

Youth hostels

F Hostel Internacional, *Espana 343, T424 0018, www.hostelmendoza.net* By far the most comfortable of the 2 hostels, located a short walk south of the plaza, this has rooms for 2 to 6, a warm and friendly atmosphere, great food in the evenings and a huge range of excursions from rafting to bodegas to horse riding at night. Warmly recommended.

F Hostel Campo Base, *Mitre 946, T429 0707 www.hostelcampobase.com.ar* A livelier and sometimes rowdier option, with slightly cramped rooms, but lots of parties and barbecues. Particularly ideal if you're planning to climb Aconcagua, as friendly and expert guide Roger Cangiani leads expeditions, providing all you need, as well as treks in the Alta Montaña for all levels. Highly recommended.
www.cerroaconcagua.com

F/D Damajuana, *Aristides Villanueva, 282, T425 5858, www.damajuanahostel.com.ar* A recommended new hostel with stylish comfortable rooms and shared dorms in a great location, with pool in lovely garden.

Camping

Churrasqueras del Parque, *T4526016, 155123124.* Right in the centre of the beautiful Parque General San Martin, at Bajada del Cerro.
There are 2 cheaper sites at El Challao, 6 km west of the city centre, reached by Bus 110 (El Challao) leaving every hr from Calle San Rioja:
Camping Suizo, *Av Champagnat, 9 km from city, T444 1991.* Modern with pool, barbecues, hot showers, friendly, recommended.
Saucelandia, *on Tirasso s/n, 9 km east at Guaymallén, T451 1409.* Take insect repellent.

❷ Eating

There are 2 main areas to eat in the centre of the city: around the main Plaza Independencia with restaurants along Peatonal Sarmiento and around Las Heras; and for a more exciting range of places, head for the street Aristides Villanueva, just 10-mins walk southwest of the main plaza. There are several cheap *tenedor libres* along Las Heras, which will fill you up for very little.

Around Plaza Independencia

$$$ **Bistro M**, *Park Hyatt Hotel, Chile 1124*. Recommended for its impeccably stylish setting, imaginative menu, and offering cheaper choices too.

$$$ **1884 Frances Mallman**, *Bodega Escorihuela, Belgrano 1188, T424 2282*. Further afield in Godoy Cruz, this is the place to go for a really special dinner. Mallman is one of the country's great chefs and the menu is exotic and imaginative. Lunch or dinner, but reservation advisable.

$$ **Boccadoro**, *Av Mitre 1976*. Renowned locally for its *parrilla*.

$$ **El Meson Espanol**, *Montevideo 244*. Authentic Spanish food, great paella and live music at weekends. Cheap lunch menus.

$$ **Facundo**, *Sarmiento 641*. A welcoming and friendly *parrilla* with lots of other choices and a good salad bar.

$$ **Ferruccio Soppelsa**, *Sarmiento 55, or Espana y Las Heras*. For the best ice cream with a great range of flavours.

$$ **Il Dolce**, *Sarmiento 81*. A friendly place for inexpensive set lunches and dinners, and good vegetarian options.

$$ **La Chacra**, *Sarmiento 55*. Resist the first café along Peatonal Sarmiento and head here for good set menu lunches and a vast range from pastas caseras to great traditional Mendocino steaks. Recommended. Groups are welcome.

$$ **Marchigiani**, *Av Espana 1619, T423 0751*. One of Mendoza's best restaurants is also great value. Wonderful Italian food in traditional style, swirly plaster and wrought iron lamps, and charming service. Families and glamorous couples alike. Fantastic *parrillas, pastas caseros* and delicious puddings. Recommended.

$$ **Montecatini**, *General Paz 370*. Good Italian food and *parrilla* in smartened decor, but is slightly lacking in atmosphere.

$$ **Sr. Cheff**, *Primitivo de la Reta 1071*. One of the city's longest established restaurants with a good reputation for *parrilla* and fish.

$$ **Terrazas del Lago**, *Av Las Palmeras s/n, T428 3438*. This really splendid café is located in the park.

$$ **Via Civit**, *Emilio Civit 277*. Wandering back to town from the park, try the wonderful smoked trout sandwiches, tasty tarts and exquisite pastries in a relaxed but refined atmosphere.

$ **Don Otto**, *Las Heras 242*. Cheap and cheerful deals.

$ **Mambru**, *Las Heras 554*. Huge, busy and popular for its great range and good value *tenedor libre*. Recommended.

$ **Mr Dog**, *Las Heras y Patricias Mendocinas*. This local chain is better than average for fast food. Also try the atmospheric indoor market on Las Heras at nights for cheap and delicious pizza, *parrilla* and pasta. Also heaps of cured meats, dried fruits, pastries, wines and herbs and a cheap snack bar.

Aristides Villaneueva

This area is the place to stroll in the evenings for more exciting bars and restaurants with a younger crowd, 10 mins walk southwest of the main plaza. (Note that this street changes its name to Colón at Belgrano).

$$ **Azafrán**, *Aristides Villanueva 287*. A fine-wine lover's heaven, with an extensive range from all the best bodegas, expert advice and also a fabulous delicatessen where you can enjoy superb *picadas*.

$$ **Mal de Amores**, *Aristides Villanueva 303 (Wed -Sun only, dinner)*. Highly recommended for its delicious and imaginative Mediterranean food at good prices in a warm and stylish atmosphere.

$$ **Por Acá**, *Aristides Villanueva 557*. Most original, comfy and stylish, pizzas and drinks til late with a cosy living room feel.

$ **3 90 (Tres con Noventa)** *Aristides Villanueva 451*. Unbeatable for a delicious bargain. Highly recommended for all the pasta possibilities imaginable with any combination of sauce, all excellent, and a warm studenty atmosphere.

$ **Guevar**, *Aristides Villanueva y Huarpes*. Great for eggs with everything, a fun atmosphere and a young crowd.

$ **Nativa**, *Aristides Villanueva 650*. A light airy place. Huge sandwiches on excellent home-made bread, popular with families and students.

O Shopping

The best shopping centre for clothes is Av San Martín and Av Las Heras, where there are good souvenir, leather and handicraft shops, and vast sports emporia. Further north on San Martín are cheap fabric shops and old department stores – C&A with an Argentine slant! Las Heras has 2 indoor markets – one for good food, and the other for cheap necessities.

Books
Centro Internacional del Libro, *Lavalle 14*. Small selection of classics and paperbacks in English. English language magazines and *Buenos Aires Herald* usually available from kiosks on San Martín.

Camping equipment
Casa Orviz, *Juan B Justo 532, T/F4251281 www.orviz.com* Sales and rental, transport, guides, information.

Handicrafts
There's a market on the eastern side of Plaza Independencia at weekends. **Mercado Artesanal**, *San Martín 1143*. For traditional leather, baskets, weaving. **El Turista**, *Las Heras 351*. Most of the traditional local souvenirs, piled high and pretty cheap. **Raices**, *España 1092, just off Peatonal Sarmiento*. Higher quality than **El Turista**. **Las Vinas**, *Las Heras 399*. A good range of T shirts, *ponchos* and ornate *mates*.

Shopping centres
Centro Comercial Plaza Mendoza, *about 5 km east, T449 0100, 1000 to 2200*. Known as **Mendoza Plaza Shopping**. The best indoor shopping mall with supermarkets, shops, fast food and cinemas, and a play area for kids; take bus T or 100. **Palmares**, *7 km south*. Much smaller than the **Mendoza Plaza**, includes supermarket, shops, cinema, restaurants; take bus T on 9 de Julio.

Wine
All the bodegas sell their produce 10% cheaper than in shops, and stock many wines you can't find elsewhere. **Vinoteca**, *Alem 97, T420 3924*. A great range from the local wineries is available. **Azafrán**, *Aristides Villanueva 287*. Expert advice.

☉ Sport and activities

Buy and rent equipment here for skiing and all other kinds of adventure sports.

Ballooning
Known as *globonautica*, this is popular, T421 7993 for information.

Swimming pools
Marina Natación, indoor swimming pool, *San Lorenzo 765, T423 6065*. **Gimnasia y Esgrima**, *Gutierrez 62, T425 0315*.

Mountain climbing
Club Andinista, *F L Beltrán 357, Gillén, T431 9870*. See also p198 for more information on climbing Aconcagua.

River rafting
Popular at Potrerillos and more widely available at Valle Grande from San Rafael. **Argentina Rafting**, *T02624 482037, www.argentinarafting.com*

Skiing
There are 2 resorts within reach. The most satisfying is **Los Penitentes**, *T423 9328, www.penitentes.com*, 174 km west on the road to Chile, with a good range of pistes, plus hotels and restaurants and affordable equipment hire – though rather too far for a day trip, there is good accommodation here. **Vallecitos**, *T4236569, www.skivallecitos.com*, is a very basic place with simple accommodation but can be reached in a day, at 80 km from the city, on the winding road from Portrerillos. The best skiing is at the world-class resort of Las Leñas, *T02627 4293200 www.laslenas.com*, 440 km away, south west of San Rafael. See page 204below. **Equipment hire Ski2002**, *Peatonal Sarmiento 133, T445 6978*, **Piré**, *Las Heras 615, T425 7699*, and other agencies.

↻ Tour operators

There are lots of operators, especially on Peatonal Sarmiento. Most go to the same places but shop around for the best deals. As a rough guide, Mendoza city tour, US$5,

Wine tour, US$6, Alta Montana and Puente del Inca, US$10. There are also longer excursions including a long trip to the Valle de la Luna, US$25 (more comfortable from San Juan) and to Cañon del Atuel, US$20 (easier from San Rafael). These companies are recommended:

Asatej, *San Martín 1360 (at back of shopping arcade), T/F429 0029, mendoza@asatej.com.ar* Enormously helpful offering lots of trips and cheap travel deals.

Aymara Turismo, *9 de Julio 1023, T420 5304, www.aymara.com.ar* email *info@aymara.com.ar* for the bilingual brochure. Excellent professional company offering a huge range from adventure tourism, horseriding and climbing Aconcagua to more conventional excursions to bodegas and Alta Montaña.

El Cristo, *Espejo 228, T/F4291911*. A good range and some cheap deals.

Huentata, *Las Heras 680, T425 7444*. The usual plus Villavicencio, Cañon del Atuel.

Mendoza Viajes, *Peatonal Sarmiento 129, T438 0480*. Comfortable coaches, professional service, also offer cheap deals.

Inca Expedicion, *Juan B Justo 343, Ciudad 5500, T429 8494, www.aconcagua.org.ar* Private and programmed climbing expeditions, including Aconcagua.

Casa Orviz, *Juan B Justo 536, T4251281, www.orviz.com* Guides, mules, transportation and hire of mountain trekking equipment for Aconcagua.

Campo Base youth hostel (see above) runs good expeditions up Aconcagua and elsewhere, and has a helpful website in English: www.cerroaconcagua.com

---

◎ Transport

Bus

Local Each bus has 2 numbers – a big number painted onto the bus at the top front corners (to signify the bus company), and a smaller number – subnumero – on a card propped in the window (the route). So if you're going to bodega La Rural in Maipú for example, you'll need 170, *subnummero 173*, and don't be tempted to get on all the other 170's that go past. Ask drivers for the bodega you want, and they'll tell you when to get off. Buses are US$0.20 per trip, cheaper with prepaid *Mendobus* card which you put into a

machine on the bus, sold in shops, the bus terminal and ticket offices everywhere. US$0.30 for 2 trips, US$1.75 for 10. There are 2 trolley bus routes, red and blue, US$0.25.

Car hire

Shop around and barter for cheap car hire since 'international tourists' are charged double the Argentines' rate.

Avis, *De la Reta 914, T420 3178*, or at airport, *T447 0150*. Reliable and efficient. **Dollar**, *De la Reta 936, T429 9939*. **Herbst**, *at the airport, T448 2327*. **Localiza**, *San Juan 913, T429 0876*.

Cycle hire

Cycles El Túnel, *at exit from bus terminal*, buys and sells cycles, also repairs, friendly. **Piré**, *Las Heras 615, T425 7699*. Also at **Campo Base**, *Mitre 946, T429 0707*. **Motorcycle repairs** César Armitrano, *Rubén Zarate 138, 1600-2100*. Highly recommended for assistance or a chat; he will let you work in his workshop.

Air

El Plumerillo airport, *8 km north of centre*, T430 7837, has a bank, tourist information, a few shops, restaurant and *locutorio* but no left luggage. Reached from the centre by bus No 60 (subnumero 68) from Alem y Salta, every hr at 35 mins past the hr, 40 mins journey; make sure there is an 'Aeropuerto' sign on the driver's window. Taxi to/from centre US$5. To **Buenos Aires**: 1 hr 50 mins, **Aerolíneas/Austral**, To **Santiago** (Chile) **Lan Chile**, daily.

Bus

Beware of thieves at all times in the bus station. The big, modern terminal is on the east side of the major road Av Videla, 15 mins walk from centre, via an underpass which leads from corner between platforms 38 and 39 to Calle Alem. Call the helpful information centre for all companies and times, *T431 5000/431 3001, mterminal@rcc.com.ar*

Andesmar, *Espejo 189, T/F4380654*, and at the bus terminal.

Provincial services To **San Rafael**, many daily, Empresa Uspallata, TAC, Andesmar, El Rapido, 3½ hrs, US$4. To **Malargüe**, Empresa Uspallata, TAC, 5½ hrs, US$7, also combi service, Transportes Viento Sur, 2 a day, 4 hrs, US$8. To **Potrerillos**, Empresa Uspallata, TAC, 5 a day, 1 hr, US$4 . To

Uspallata, Empresa Uspallata, 5 a day, 2 hrs, US$4. To **Puente del Inca**, Uspallata, 2 a day. **Long distance** To **Buenos Aires**, 15 hrs, US$18-27, companies include Chevallier, TAC, Jocoli, El Rápido, Andesmar, Expreso Uspallata, La Estrella. To **Bariloche**, Andesmar daily, US$17, 22 hrs, book ahead (alternative is TAC to Neuquén and change).

To **Córdoba**, TAC, 11 hrs, US$10. To **San Luis**, TAC frequent, several other companies including Jocoli, US$5, 3 hrs. To **San Juan**, TAC, frequent, San Juan Mar del Plata, Andesmar, US$4, 2 hrs.

To **Tucumán**, US$14, Andesmar, Autotransportes Mendoza, TAC, all via **San Juan**, **La Rioja** (US$10, 10 hrs) and **Catamarca** (12 hrs, US$12). To **Salta**, Andesmar, America (via San Juan, La Rioja and Catamarca), 20 hrs, US$14.

To **Mar del Plata**, TAC daily, 8 hrs. To **Neuquén**, Andesmar, 3 daily, Alto Valle coche-cama service, 12hrs. To **San Martín de los Andes**, TAC, daily with change at Neuquén, 20 hrs. To **Comodoro Rivadavia**, Andesmar, 2 a day, TAC, 1 a day, US$30, 32 hrs. To **Río Gallegos**, Andesmar and TAC daily 1900. To **Santa Fe**, TAC, Villa María, 13 hrs. To **Rosario**, US$12, 12 hrs. No services to **Puerto Iguazú**, TAC direct, daily, 24 hrs, US$27.
International services To **Santiago**, Chile: US$10, 7-8 hrs depending on border crossing, TAC and El Rápido, 5 daily, Tur Bus, CATA and Chile Bus, 2 daily, also Ahumada coche-cama service, Chile Bus. Highly recommended; some adverse reports on El Rápido. Passport required when booking, tourist cards given on bus. Children under 8 pay 60% of adult fare, but no seat. Book at least 1 day ahead, shop around.

The journey over the Andes is spectacular (see p199 for a description). If you want to return, buy an undated return ticket Santiago-Mendoza; it is cheaper. There are also minibus services, US$12, 5½-6 hrs, run by Chiar, 4 a day, and Nevada, 2 a day, minimum of 10 passengers, ensure that they will pick you up and drop you at your hotel. Taxi to Santiago costs about US$40 for 4-5 people. To **Viña del Mar**, 7 hrs, US$12, Tur Bus, 2 daily, Tas-Choapa, 3 daily, TAC, CATA and El Rápido daily; to **La Serena**, 12-14 hrs, US$18, El Rápido, CATA, Corvalle.

To **Lima**, 56 hrs, El Rápido, US$35, Mon, Wed, Sat 0830, Ormeño, US$40, Wed, Thu,

Sun 0700. To **Montevideo**, 10 hrs, US$27, **El Rápido**, Tue 2000, also **EGA**, Sun 1600.

---

① Directory

Airline offices Most open till 2000 Mon-Fri, and some open Sat morning. **Aerolíneas Argentinas/Austral**, *Paseo Sarmiento 82,T4204185*. **Lapa**, *España 1002, T423 1000, airport T448 7961*. **Dinar**, *Paseo Sarmiento 119, T/F4204520*. **Ecuatoriana/VASP/TAN**, *España 1008, T434 0240*. **Iberia**, *Rivadavia 180, T429 6248*. **Lan Chile**, *Rivadavia 135, T425 7900*. **Lufthansa**, *9 de Julio 928, T429 6287*. **Quantas**, *España 943, 1 Piso, of 65. T429 6077*. **Southern Winds**, *España 943, T429 3200*. **Varig/Pluma**, *Rivadavia 209, T429 3706*. **Banks** There are many ATMs along San Martin taking all cards: **Banelco**, *San Martin 831, 1056, also at Espana 1168, Peatonal Sarmiento 29*. **Link**, *San Martin y Gutierrez, 9 de Julio 1228, Espana y Pedro Molina*. Many *casas de cambio* along San Martín, including **Exprinter**, *Espejo 74, T438 0333*, Santiago, *San Martin 1199, T420 0277*, **Maguitur**, *San Martin 1203, T423 3202*.
Communications Internet Cyber Cafe at the huge *locutorio* on *San Martin y Garibaldi*, **Arlink**, *San Martin 928*. **Spacenet**, *Rivadavia 424*, **Telecentro Rediphone**, *San Martin 940*.
Post office *San Martín y Colón, T429 0848. Mon-Fri 0800-2000, Sat 0900-1300*. **United Parcel Service**, *9 de Julio 803, T423 7861*.
Telephone **Telefónica de Argentina**, *San Martin 723*. There are many *locutorios* around the centre: a huge one on *San Martin y Garibaldi*, also at *San Martin y Rivadavia, Alem y P. de la Reta, Mitre y Gutierrez*.
Consulates Spain, *Agustín Alvarez 455, T425 3947*; Italy, *Peru 1396, T423 1640*; France, *Houssay 790, T429 8339*; Germany, *Montevideo 127, 2nd floor, D1, T429 6539*; England, Holland and Finland, *Emilio Civit 778, T423 8514*; Israel, *Lamadrid 738, T428 2140*.
Medical services
Emergencies *T4280000*. Central hospital near bus terminal, *Alem y Salta, T420 0600, 4490500*. **Lagomaggiore**, public general hospital at *Timoteo Gordillo s/n, T425 9700*. **Hospital Materno y Infantil Humberto Notti**, *Bandera de los Andes 2683, T445 0045*.
24-hour pharmacies Del Aguila, *San Martín 996, T424 8444*. Del Puente, *Las Heras 201, T425 9209*. Mitre, *San Martin 701, T423 7123*.

Alta Montaña

West of Mendoza City, Route Nacional 7 leads to Chile and the nearby capital Santiago, threading through the world's highest mountains outside the Himalayas, and some of the country's most amazing scenery. This is an essential part of any trip to the province, even if you're not crossing the border, or planning to climb Aconcagua. From the pretty oasis town of Uspallata, the road climbs up between the jagged snow-capped mountains, with staggering views of Volcano Tupungato in the distance to the south and Aconcagua closer at hand to the north. In winter, you'll quickly reach the snowline, the charming small ski resort of Los Penitentes and beyond it, the natural wonder of the bridge at Puente del Inca, also the base for climbing Aconcagua. The road climbs finally to the border crossing at Tunel Cristo Redentor, and if you continue to Chile, the steep descent on the other side offers yet more superb views. In winter, this road is sometimes blocked by snow, so check conditions from Mendoza or Uspallata.

Closer to Mendoza, there are two ways to reach Uspallata, both offering great views. Most dramatic is the climb north via many hairpin bends to the spa resort of Villavicencio, or you can also head south from Mendoza to pleasant Portrerillos and via the thermal springs at Cacheuta.

Villavicencio → *Phone code: 0261 Colour map 3, A2*

Famous to all Argentines from the image of its Alpine-style 1930's hotel found on all bottles of the ubiquitous mineral water, Villavicencio (1,700 m, Km 47) is reached by a wonderful drive. From Mendoza, head north along Route 52, across flat plains growing nothing but scrubby *jarilla* bushes, and following the *pre-cordillera* on your left. The road suddenly rises steeply to climb through thickly forested mountains to the beautiful old spa resort, closed for many years, but now the centre of a nature reserve – a good place for a picnic and a stroll. The hotel has been taken over by French company Danone who plan to turn it into a luxury resort and who, meanwhile, run a smart information centre on the local wildlife, and employ helpful *guardaparques*, who can direct you to nearby walks. You can also stroll around the splendid grounds of the hotel, visit its chapel and eat at the Hostería Villavicencio, T4246482, run by a friendly local family who offer good value lunches and teas with fine local produce such as *jamon crudo* (prosciutto) and *chivo* (goat), which you can enjoy in the Alpine setting at tables outside.

Beyond Villavicencio the *ripio* road climbs up over the spectacular **Cruz del Paramillo**, via Caracoles de Villavicencio, the many (allegedly 365) hairpin bends which give the road its name *La Ruta del Año* (Route of the Year). At an altitude of 3,050 m there are breathtaking views all around, a marvellous introduction to the vast peaks of Aconcagua, Tupungato and Mercedario. Descending to the fertile valley of Uspallata, there are fantastic jagged teeth of rocks popping up through the earth in extraordinary colours from aubergine through to oxidized copper green, orange and creamy white with pinky flesh colours in between. There are no bus services but many tour operators include this trip. With your own transport, this makes for a great route to Uspallata. Cyclists should carry plenty of water and be warned that there's no shade.

Potrerillos → *Phone code: 02624 Colour map 3, B1*

Potrerillos (1,354 m, Km 58) is a charming laid-back village sprawling among the foothills of the Cordón del Plata mountains. In the summer it's a popular retreat among mendocinos, but it's excellent for a weekend's walking or riding at any time of year, though particularly lovely in spring, or in autumn, when the avenues of alamo trees are a rich yellow against the mauvey haze of mountains beyond. From December to February, you can practise watersports – rafting and kayaking – on Río Mendoza

than a hotel, campsite and YPF station on a crossroads – you could take the road
south up to Vallecitos via the little hamlets of El Salta, Las Vegas and San Jorge, where
there's a small *cervezaria* (beer makers). There are *parrillas*, tea rooms and lots of
cabañas for hire around these areas, and the views are wonderful.

Rodolfo Navio organizes good trips kayaking, trekking, climbing, kayacking,
mountain biking, with **Argentina Rafting** T155691700, www.argentina rafting.com
Prices are around US$13-17 for two hours, all equipment and transport included.
There's a lovely walk to Cascada del Salto, but the path isn't marked, so ask Rodolfo
for a guide. In summer you can hike from Potrerillos to Vallecitos over two days. ▸ *For
Sleeping, Eating and other listings, see pages 200-201.*

Vallecitos → *Phone code 02622*

This tiny hamlet (2900 m) is 21 km southwest along a madly winding *ripio* road,
certainly not to be attempted in poor weather conditions. There's little here apart from
a good hostel for walkers, and a rather basic family ski resort, popular as a day trip
from Mendoza. There's more accommodation and a snack bar at the unsalubrious
ski-lodge. ⓘ *Valles del Plata Centro de Esqui: T488810, www.skivallecitos.com: 4.7
km of pistes, mostly intermediate standard, 4 ski lifts and a ski school, pass US$9 pp
per day, equipment hire US$8.*

Uspallata → *Phone code: 02624 Colour map 3, A2 Population: 3,000*

The picturesque village of Uspallata (1,751 m, 100 km from Mendoza and 52 km from
Potrerillos) has become a popular stopping point on the road to Chile, since all routes
pass through it, and yet it's retained a rather charming unspoilt atmosphere – out of
peak season at least. With distant mountains glimpsed through a frame of *alamo*
(poplar) trees, it suggested the Himalayas to the makers of *Seven Years in Tibet*, part
of which was filmed here. Stay for a day at least, to explore the mysterious white
egg-shaped domes of **Las Bóvedas** ⓘ *5 km on RN39 north, US$0.30*, built by the
indigenous Huarpes, under instruction by the Jesuits, to melt silver, where there is a
small, interesting museum. From Uspallata, the RN39 leads north to **Barreal** and
Calingasta (see page 210), unpaved for its first part and tricky when the snowmelt
floods it in summer. Here you'll find the remains of the Inca road, one of the most
important archaeological sites in the region, with foundations of a pre-Columbian
dairy too. There are two food shops, bakeries, a post office and a YPF station with
motel, restaurant, shop and *locutorio*, open 0900-2200. ▸ *For Sleeping, Eating and other
listings, see pages 200-201.*

Los Penitentes → *Phone code: 02624*

From Uspallata, a good paved road to Chile crosses a broad plain, in which maroon
and chalk-white rocks stick up from the rolling land, then winds alongside a ravine
with a surprising thread of turquoise water meandering through it. The road then
climbs up into the mountain pass, where amazing rock formations in vivid terracotta
come into view, and there is a heart-stopping glimpse of Volcan Tupungato beyond,
one of the giants of the Andes, rising to 6,800 m. The first tiny village of Punta de
Vacas has a large *gendarmería* but no accommodation. Continue on, climbing
quickly beyond the snowline in winter, to the charming small resort of Los Penitentes
(2,580 m, Km 165). Named after the majestic mass of pinnacled rocks on its
mountainside, suggesting a group of cowled monks climbing upwards, this is a
low-key family resort right by the road, though it's surprisingly quiet. There is good
skiing on the 28 pistes (total length of 24 km, with eight lifts); most of them are
graded difficult but there are a couple of long descents of medium difficulty and two
beginners' slopes. It's good value and uncrowded. ⓘ *May-Sep. Daily ski hire US$9,
lift pass US$15.*

Puente del Inca (2,718 m, km 172), 6 km further on, is set among breathtaking mountains and is a great base for exploring them on foot or on horseback, with access to the Parque Nacional Aconcagua. The naturally formed bridge, after which the village is named, is one of the wonders of South America. Crossing Río Mendoza at a height of 19 m, with a span of 21 m, and 27 m wide, the bridge, an eerie orangey colour seems to have been formed by sulphur-bearing hot springs below which have stained the whole ravine an incredible ochre yellow. Marvel at the ruins underneath the bridge of a 1940's spa hotel, now mostly washed away by the river, but from whose walls a torrent of hot sulphurous water still gushes. (Watch your footing on the steps as they are extremely slippery). The old baths, to the side of the river, between the bridge and the small church, have basic facilities, but are still good for a soak amidst magnificent scenery. They're usually free, or a *guardaparque* might charge you US$0.50 or so. West of the village there is a fine view of Aconcagua, sharply silhouetted against the sky. **Los Horcones**, the Argentine customs post, is 1 km west. To visit the Laguna Horcones in the Parque Nacional Aconcagua, see below. ▸▸ *For Sleeping, Eating and other listings, see pages 200-201.*

Parque Provincial Aconcagua

→ *75,000 ha. www.cerroaconcagua.com for information in English*

Apart from Aconcagua itself, the Parque Provincial Aconcagua includes 30 other peaks over 4,000 m, nine of them over 5,000 m. Entry is 2 km west of Puente del Inca, via the Valle de los Horcones. There is a *guardería (*ranger station) and free camping, open in the climbing season. You'll see excellent views of Aconcagua here, especially in the morning.

Aconcagua → *The highest peak in the world outside Asia, altitude: 6,959 m*

The mountain gets its name from the Quechua for 'stone sentry', and it is indeed a majestic peak with five great glaciers hanging from its slopes. While its north face is relatively easy to climb (the list of successful ascents includes two Italians on bicycles in 1987 and four blind climbers in 1994) the south face is almost impossible. The north face was first climbed by Zurbriggen of the Fitzgerald Expedition in 1897, and in 1985, a complete Inca mummy was discovered at 5,300 m. The best time for climbing is from the end of December to the end of February. At Plaza de Mulas you will also find the highest hotel in the world. ▸▸ *For Sleeping, Eating and other listings, see pages 200-201.*

Permits For trekking or climbing in the park at any time of year, it is necessary to obtain a permit. These vary in price for high, mid or low season and depending on the number of days. In high season (15 December to 31 January), a permit to climb Aconcagua (lasting 21 days) costs US$200, for short trekking US$20. Permits must be bought in person only at Edificio Cuba, Av Los Robles y rotonda del Rosedal, just by the entrance to Parque San Martín, Mendoza, 0800-1800 Monday-Friday, 0900-1300, Saturday/Sunday. This applies in the summer only, from 15 November to 15 March. Outside this period, permits can be bought only at the *Jefatura* (rangers station) in Refugio de Horcones, at the entrance to Parque Provincial Aconcagua.

In Mendoza you can book *refugio* reservations and programmes which include trekking, or climbing to the summit, with all equipment and accommodation or camping included (see Tour operators, above). Treks and climbs are also organized by Sr Fernando Grajales, the famous climber, at Moreno 898, 5500 Mendoza, T493830, expediciones@grajales.net (or T421 4330 and ask for Eduardo Ibarra at **Hotel Plaza de Mulas** for further information), and by Roger Cangiani at **Campo Base** in Mendoza, T429 0707, www.campo-base.com.ar Near the Cementerio is **Los**

Access It's best to allow two weeks for the complete trip. Climbing Aconcagua is not technically difficult: the problem lies in taking time to adjust to the sudden high altitude, and many fail because they take it too fast. All climbers should allow at least one week for acclimatization at lower altitudes before attempting the summit, and patience may also be required for the weather. There are two access routes: Río Horcones and Río Vacas, which lead to the two main base camps, Plaza de Mulas and Plaza Argentina respectively. Río Horcones starts a few kilometres from Puente del Inca, at the Horcones ranger station. About 80% of climbers use this route. From here you can go to Plaza de Mulas (4,370 m) for the north face, or Plaza Francia (4,200 m) for the south face. At Plaza de Mulas there is a rescue patrol and the area is very crowded in summer. Plaza de Francia is less crowded. The intermediate camp for either is Confluencia (3,300 m), four hours from Horcones. No drinking water is available after this point: take your own. Río Vacas is the access for those wishing to climb the Polish Glacier. The Plaza Argentina base camp is three hours from Horcones and the intermediate camps are Pampa de Leñas and Casa de Piedra. From Puente del Inca mules are available (list at the **Dirección de Recursos Naturales Renovables,** about US$200 for 60 kg of gear one way; arrange return before setting out for a reduced two-way price. At Plaza de Mulas the highest hotel in the world and an accident prevention and medical assistance service (climbing season only) are situated; crowded in summer. The same service is offered at Plaza Argentina in high season only. Climbers are advised to make use of this service to check for early symptoms of mountain sickness and oedema.

Equipment Take a tent able to withstand 100 miles per hour (160kph) winds, and clothing and sleeping gear for temperatures below -40°C.

The Chilean border
The road to the Chilean border, fully paved, goes through the 3.2km **Cristo Redentor** toll road tunnel to Chile (open 24 hours; US$1 for cars, cyclists are not allowed to ride through). The last settlement before the tunnel is tiny forlorn Las Cuevas, 16 km from Puente del Inca, offering a kiosko and café but no accommodation. In summer you can take the old road over La Cumbre pass to the statue of **El Cristo Redentor** (Christ the Redeemer), an 8 m statue erected jointly by Chile and Argentina in 1904 to celebrate the settlement of their boundary dispute. Take an all day excursion from Mendoza, drive in a 4WD, after snow has melted, or walk from Las Cuevas, (4½ hrs up, 2 hrs down – only to be attempted by the fit, in good weather). Expreso Uspallata runs buses to Mendoza.

The Chilean border is beyond Las Cuevas, but customs is near Los Horcones, 2 km west of Puente del Inca. No fresh food is to be brought into Chile. Hire cars need special papers.

Cacheuta
For the alternative route to Uspallata, head south out of the city by Avenida J Vicente Zapata, Access Route 7, leading to Route 40. Follow signs to Potrerillos, Uspallata and Chile, passing the area's biggest petrochemical plant, before you climb up into the hills. Since the river has been dammed to create a huge reservoir, Cacheuta (1,245 m) is no longer on the road to Potrerillos, but its pretty setting merits the detour. There's a fine hotel where you can visit the thermal waters as a non-resident but a stay is recommended to really enjoy the mountain scenery. ▸▸ *For Sleeping, Eating and other listings, see pages 200-201.*

Listings: Alta Montaña

😴 Sleeping

Cacheuta *p199*
B **Hotel Termas**, *Route 82, Km 38, T431 6085, www.termascacheuta.com* A warm and inviting place with very comfortable rustic style rooms, access to the lovely spa included, but non-residents can visit. Recommended.

Potrerillos *p196*
C **Gran Hotel Potrerillos**, *Ruta Nacional 7, Km 50, T482010*. Breakfast, faded resort hotel, nice location, pool, and many *cabañas*, of which B (for 4 in peak season) **Cabañas Andinas**, *T483120, www.cumbresandinas.com* Recommended, very comfortable with fabulous views.

Camping
ACA campsite, *T482013*. Excellent nicely maintained well-shaded site, with a pool, and hot water after 1800. US$4 per tent and car. Public phone on the road outside.

Vallecitos *p197*
D pp **Refugio San Bernado**, *T154183857, www.alpes-andes-location.fr* Down the hill from the ski centre is this cosy *refugio* and hostel run by friendly, French-speaking mountain guides with bunks and hot showers. They will also take you paragliding, on guided treks and mountain climbing. There's no public transport to the resort.

Uspallata *p197*
A **Valle Andino**, *Ruta 7, T420033*. The town's best. A modern airy place with good rooms, pool and restaurant.
C **Hotel Uspallata**, *on RN 7 towards Chile, T420066*. This is one of several hotels built in Perón's post-war era, now modernized and spacious, in a lovely location with big gardens and a pool a couple of kilometres away from the centre. The rooms are comfortable and good value, and there's a cheap restaurant.
D **Los Cóndores**, *T420002, www.hostallos condores.com.ar* Great value, bright neat

rooms, good restaurant with tasty pasta and cheap set menu. Highly recommended.
E pp **Viena**, *Las Heras 240, T420046*. Small family run place with good little rooms, breakfast included.

Camping
Very basic municipal site, US$2 per tent, hot water but dirty showers and toilets, poor.

Los Penitentes *p197*
Hotels on the same side of the road as the ski resort offer a 20% reduction in ski passes.
B **Ayelén**, *on the opposite side of the road to the ski resort, T420299*. A huge, old fashioned, and shabby place, usually filled with large groups of students. Convenient but overpriced, poor restaurant, terrible service. Last resort.
C **Apart Hotel Las Lomas Blancas**. Modern, functional units, handy for the ski lifts, and there's lively laid-on nightlife. Prices are for an apartment for 4 people.
C **Hostería Penitentes**, *Villa Los Penitentes T155090432, penitentehostería@ hotmail.com* This is a cheery place near the slopes with a good café and offering cheap deals for several nights. The friendly owner speaks perfect English. Recommended.
E pp **Hostel Refugio Penitentes**, *T429 0707, www.cerroaconcagua.com* A warm, welcoming and popular place, also offering Aconcagua services in the summer.

Puente del Inca *p198*
C **Hostería Puente del Inca**, *RN7, Km 175, T420266, www.aymara.com.ar* Doubles and rooms for 4-8, huge cosy dining room, helpful advice on Aconcagua, good atmosphere. Warmly recommended. It's more expensive if booked in Mendoza.
F pp **Hostel La Vieja Estacion**, *100 m off the road next to the bridge, T0261-155631664*. Basic but cheery hostel, cheap meals, use of kitchen.
F **Refugio de Montaña**. Small dormitories in the army barracks, helpful.

● Phone codes *Villavicencio: 0261; Vallecitos: 02622; all other areas: 02624*

Camping

Possible next to the church, if your equipment can withstand the winds, also at Lago Horcones inside the park.

Aconcagua *p198*

AL **Hotel Plaza de Mulas**. Full-board or Cwithout meals, good food, information, medical treatment, recommended, also camping area, open high season only.

🍴 Eating

Potrerillos *p196*

$ **El Futre**, *opposite the ACA campsite*. Serves typical Cuyo food, vegetarian dishes and home-made pizzas. Open all day every day.
$ **Los Pinos**, *Av Los Cóndores, on the left hand side as you go up the hill*. Recommended.

Uspallata *p197*

There are several reliable *parrillas* in town; the cheapest is **La Estancia de Elias**, opposite the YPF station. Right on the crossroads, **Pub Tibet** is a welcoming bar with photos from the filming here of *Seven years in Tibet*, and a warm atmosphere. **Bodega del Gato**, in the centre, is a good *parrilla*, offering local *chivito* (kid) too.

🎯 Tour operators

Uspallata *p197*

Desnivel Turismo Aventura, *Galería Comercial local 7, T420275, desnivelturismo aventura@yahoo.com.ar* Rafting, riding,

mountain biking, trekking, climbing and skiing.

⊖ Transport

Cacheuta *p199*

Daily **bus** service in summer from **Mendoza**'s terminal.

Uspallata *p197*

Empresa Uspallata, to and from **Mendoza**, 5 a day, 2 hrs, US$4. Buses to **Chile** can pick you up here, if ticket booked in advance.

Los Penitentes *p197*

Bus Expreso Uspallata from Mendoza for **Uspallata** and **Puente del Inca**, stop at Los Penitentes, US$4, 3 hrs, 2 a day in the morning, returning in the afternoon. Local buses also go on to **Las Cuevas**, Expreso Uspallata, US$4.50 return (NB take passport). You can go to **Chile** from Puente del Inca with **Tur Bus** at 1000 and 1400, US$10, but be sure to ask for an international ticket.

Puente del Inca *p198*

Bus Expreso Uspallata from **Mendoza** for **Uspallata** and **Puente del Inca**, US$4, 3½ hrs, 2 a day in the morning, returning from Puente del Inca in the afternoon. Uspallata-Puente del Inca US$1.50. Local buses also go on from Puente del Inca to **Las Cuevas**, Expreso Uspallata, US$4 return (NB take passport). You can go to Chile from Puente del Inca with **Tur Bus** at 1000 and 1400, US$10, but be sure to ask for an international ticket.

Southern Mendoza

The southern half of the province is wilder and less visited than the area around Mendoza, probably because public transport has only recently made it accessible, but it's well worth taking a few days to explore. There are two main centres, the closest of which is the town of San Rafael with its tree lined streets, and excellent bodegas, with the extraordinary Cañon del Atuel within reach for a day's rafting. Further south is the fledgling tourist centre of Malargüe, a base for skiing at Las Leñas, or for visiting two areas of natural beauty at La Payunia and Llancanelo. There are two possible routes to the south of the province: you can take the fast Route 40 directly to San Rafael, or the picturesque route from Potrerillos along the Cordon del Plata to Tupungato, a sleepy place with a superb vineyard and starting point for long excursions into Parque Nacional Tupungato. An appealing detour here is to scenic Manzano Historico, right in the foothills of the Andes.

The road from Potrerillos (Route 89) is picturesque, descending along the Córdon del Plata, with splendid views of the mountains, and through the fertile fruit-growing valley Valle de Uco to the quiet little town of Tupungato (1,050 m). Otherwise, take Route 86 from the RN40, south of Mendoza. Nearby are the stunningly wild mountain landscapes of Parque Nacional Tupungato, named after the imposing peak of its volcano, 6,800 m, and inaccesible to the public unless you go with an approved guide, see page 207.

For more relaxing pleasures, there are many vineyards around; recommended is **Bodega Salentein**, 15 km south, *T0261-423 8514, www.bodegasalentein.com, tours of the bodega Tue to Sat 1000-1800,* beautifully set against the foothills of the Andes, the bodega produces some of the country's finest wine (the Malbec is exquisite) and you can stay in Posada Salentein, (L) which has comfortable rooms, extremely hospitable hosts, and perfect peace in which to walk, ride, and relax. Recommended.

Continue south from Salentein to **Manzano Historico**, a tiny hamlet in fabulous scenery, where a statue of San Martín marks his victorious return via this route from Chile. A *hostería* and campsite make this a good base for trekking, and there's a little shop and bar for provisions. For tourist information in Tupungato, head to the foyer in the **Hotel Turismo**, also the Municipalidad, Belgrano 348, T488007. Ask them about estancia visits for horseriding.

San Rafael → *Phone code: 02627 Colour map 3, B2 Population: 107,000*

San Rafael (688 m, 236 km south of Mendoza) is a quiet, airy town in the heart of fertile land producing wine, fruit and olives in abundance. It's a relaxed, friendly place, smaller and less sophisticated than Mendoza but with a good range of accommodation, and makes an ideal base for exploring the vineyards and participating in adventure sports at nearby Cañon de Atuel. There are lovely, leafy boulevards of French influenced buildings, thanks to a significant French community in the early 1900s, and it's a trim and well-maintained place, where there are more bicycles than cars on the streets. The main street is Hipolito Yrigoyen, changing names at the central north/south street Avenida San Martín. ▸▸ *For Sleeping, Eating and other listings, see pages 205-208.*

Sights

Río Diamante runs just south of the town, with a park, **Parque Mariano Moreno**, 2 km from the centre, on Isla del Río Diamante. The **botanical gardens** and a small **Museo Municipal de Historia Natural** ① *Tue-Sun 0800-2000, free, take Iselin bus along Av JA Balloffet*, with displays on natural history, are among its attractions.

Wines produced here are at least as excellent as those of Mendoza, and one of the country's most important bodegas, **Bianchi** ① *Informes@vbianchi.com, T422046, tours at 1015, 1115, 1315, 1415, 1550 and 1615,* has vineyards you can visit. The *champagnerie* ① *5 km west of town, take a taxi as buses are infrequent, T435353, tours hourly from 0900-1200, 1500-1800,* is worth seeing for the fascinating process and rather excessive building. Their bodega in town at Cte Torrres y O De Rosas, also gives an excellent and detailed tour, and sells the top wines at reduced prices after a generous tasting. More intimate, the small bodega **Jean Rivier** ① *H Yrigoyen 2385, T432675, bodega@jrivier.com,* produces excellent wine, and can be visited.

There are ATMs and *locutorios* all along Yrigoyen, and a friendly and helpful **tourist office** is seven blocks west of San Martín at Yrigoyen and Ballofet, T437860, 0800-2222555, www.msanrafael.com.ar and www.sanrafael-tour.com

San Rafael is a great centre for all kinds of activities: rafting, horseriding, trekking, climbing and fishing. Most spectacular is the **Cañon de Atuel**, 35 km southwest. It's an atmospheric drive along the *ripio* road through this 20 km long ravine of extraordinary rock formations, metalic sulphurous greens next to vivid terracotta, pinks and cream. There are constantly changing views and an eerie feel in places, with birds of prey wheeling overhead. The gorge lies between two lakes 46 km apart, **El Nihuil** (9,600 ha), and **Valle Grande** (508 ha) ① *From San Rafael 3 buses (Iselin and others) a day go to the Valle Grande at the near end of the gorge, and return in the evening, 35 km, US$3. There is no public transport through the gorge to the El Nihuel dam.* There is plenty of accommodation and campsites here along the pretty river banks, and river rafting and horse riding are on offer.

Lago Reyunos is another popular excursion, 35 km west of San Rafael, a lake in barren rocky landscape. No buses, only tours. But far more spectacular is the **Laguna Diamante**, northwest of San Rafael, an ultramarine blue expanse of water, whipped by perpetual winds, against the craggy backdrop of the Andes and the perfectly conical Volcan Maipo. Only 4WD vehicles will make it over the last 60 km or so of track, and it's best to go on an excursion with **Taiel Viajes** (see page 208). Horse riding excursions are also offered from El Sosneado (see below) to see the place where the Uruguyan plane crashed in the mountains, subject of the film *Alive!* (see box), in amazing stark landscapes. Laguna del Atuel, 200 km west of San Rafael, has incredible turquoise water lapping against ochre mountains, another fabulous five day horseriding trip.

West of San Rafael

A good paved road (the 144 and then the 40) leads west across the vast plain of the Río Atuel passing saltflats and marshland heading towards stark snow dusted mountains rising steeply out of the ochre coloured land. The only settlement is **El Sosneado**, Km 138, with a service station, *hostería* and a small shop for fine home cured hams and olives, where you can also take away delicious sandwiches. The YPF station sells snacks and hot drinks.

A *ripio* side road leads off and follows the valley of the Río Atuel northwest to **Laguna El Sosneado**, 42 km away, in whose crystalline waters you can fish for rainbow trout. Some 13 km or so further on, there are natural thermal pools, the **Termas el Sosneado**, where you can bathe in sulphurous waters for free, since there's no organization here, and the **Hotel Termas El Sosneado** is in ruins. Ahead, you'll see the Overo volcano (4,619 m). El Sosneado is the starting point for treks into the mountains, but there is no infrastructure in the village itself, and tours should be arranged from San Rafael or Malargüe. ▸▸ *For Sleeping, Eating and other listings, see pages 205-208.*

Los Molles → *Phone code: 02627 Colour map 3, B1*

Some 28 km southwest of El Sosneado and 166 km southwest of San Rafael, a *ripio* road follows the Río Salado west into the Andes towards Las Leñas. After 30 km, it passes the tiny hamlet of Los Molles, little more than a cluster of hotels, the oldest of which has access to thermal springs. None of these establishments is luxurious but they do make Los Malles a feasbile alternative to staying in Las Leñas if you're going there to ski. Opposite Los Molles, a *ripio* road leads to the *refugio* of the **Club Andino Pehuenche** and 8 km further on, to the **Laguna de la Niña Encantada**, a beautiful little lake and shrine to the Virgin. Continuing towards Las Leñas, there are the strange **Pozo de las Animas**, two natural circular pits, filled with water (the larger is 80 m deep); when the wind blows across the holes, a ghostly wail results, hence the name (Well of the Spirits). They're a curious sight, but don't quite merit a special excursion. ▸▸ *For Sleeping, Eating and other listings, see pages 205-208.*

⦂ Alive

Some 8 km from **Hotel Termas El Sosneado** a plaque marks the site of a crash of an Uruguayan airforce plane in October 1972. The plane, a Fairchild F-27 en route from Montivideo to Santiago, carried 45 passengers and crew, including the members of a rugby team. The pilot, co-pilot and several passengers died on impact and despite the efforts of the Chilean and Argentine airforces, the wreckage was not found. Two of the survivors crossed the mountains to Chile, by an enormously long journey of many days, and finally found a local man who told them that they'd been within 17 km of a settlement to the east in Argentina.

They brought help to the remaining passengers and crew who had spent 70 days on the Las Lágrimas glacier, substantially extending all known capacity for the human body to survive, by eating the flesh of their dead companions. The incident inspired the best-selling book *Alive!* by Piers Paul Read, and the films *Survive* (1976) and *Alive!* (1992). Today, you can go on a spectacular three-day horseriding expedition from Malargüe to visit the crash site, a rather morbid form of tourism perhaps, but it will give you an appreciation of a struggle for survival, and the landscape is outstandingly beautiful.

Las Leñas → *Phone code: 02627 Colour map 3, B1*

Las Leñas (2,250 m), 49 km off the San Rafael-Malargüe road, is deservedly internationallly renowned for its excellent skiing, and also earns its reputation as Argentina's most chic resort. Set at the end of a spectacular valley, in the middle of five snow-capped peaks, it has powder snow throughout the season on 41 pistes with a total length of 75 km, with 11 ski-lifts. It's the only place in Argentina where you can ski uninterrupted down 7.5 km of slopes and a drop of 1200 m, and has the advantage that you can walk straight out of your hotel and onto the pistes. A constantly circulating free bus service picks up guests from further flung hotels in the resort. The season runs mid June to early October but the busiest and most expensive time is throughout July and August, when prices are at least 50% higher. Ski passes in high season are US$30 per day, equipment hire is US$18 daily. (There is a 50% reduction on ski pass if you stay in a Malargue hotel). The resort also has a ski school, a special snowboard park, many cafés, bars and restaurants, several right on the pistes, a useful information point where there are lockers, banks, doctors, and many ski patrol units all over the pistes. For further information, T471100, www.laslenas.com Las Leñas also operates as a summer resort for adventure sports, such as trekking and climbing. Beyond Las Leñas the road continues into **Valle Hermoso**, a beautiful valley accessible December-March only. ▸▸ *For Sleeping, Eating and other listings, see pages 205-208.*

Malargüe → *Phone code: 02627 Colour map 3, B2 Population: 15,000*

Situated 96 km southwest of San Rafael in reach of splendid, unspoilt landscapes, Malargüe (1,426 m) is a good centre for hiking and horseriding. It promotes itself rather grandly as the national centre for adventure tourism but the standard of accommodation and service is disappointing. It's certainly a cheap alternative to Las Leñas in the ski season when there are frequent minibus services between the two. However the best time to come is from spring to autumn, when you can make the most of the landscape for walking and riding. The *Fiesta Nacional del Chivo* (locally produced goat, to eat rather than admire) is held in the first fortnight of January and attracts national folklore stars, as well as Chilean performers and public from across the Andes.

The town is little more than a broad main street, San Martín, with an assortment of small shops, *locutorios*, cafés and the odd hotel. On the way into town from the north, there's an impressive modern conference centre on the right, built for conventions of the nearby Philip Auger Observatory of Cosmic Rays but mostly used for showing films. It has a smart bar. Next to it is the helpful **tourist office** where the director Graciela is extremely knowledgeable and helpful, and can arrange for you to visit the national parks (see below), T471659, open 0800-2300. www.malargue.net and www.malargue.gov.ar ▶ *For Sleeping, Eating and other listings, see pages 205-208.*

Around Malargüe

Four protected sites nearby provide the main tourist attractions, and unless you have your own transport, they can only be visited through an excursion. The most remarkable is the **La Payunia** reserve 208 km south, dominated by the majestic peaks of several snow-capped volcanoes. A vast expanse of seductive altiplanic grasslands, riven with volcanic peaks, deep red and black crags of extraordinary sculpted lava, made even more magical by the sudden appearance of hundreds of guanaco running wild across your path. Best enjoyed on horseback, on a three-day expedition. The entrance is 100 km south of Malargüe on sandy *ripio* roads – get directions from tourist office, who will also radio the *guardaparques* to expect you. They take you on a tour in their 4WD, though it's better to take an excursion from Malargüe with Karen Travel, see page 208.

The **Laguna Llancanelo** (pronounced *shancannELLO*), 65 km southeast, is filled with hugely varied birdlife in spring, when 150 species come to nest on its lakes. At any time of year you'll see Chilean flamingoes, rising in a pink cloud from pale turquoise waters where volcanic peaks are perfectly reflected. You may also see tern, curlews, grebes, teal and black-necked swans, among others. ① *Contact* guardaparque *Miguel Espolin via the tourist office, or go on a trip from Malargüe wth Karen Travel.*

At **Caverna de las Brujas** ① *Guided tours usually take 2-3 hrs, and lights and helmets are provided. Children over 7 are welcome.* There are 5 km of underground caves to explore, taking you through different eras off the earth's development from the Jurassic period onwards, and a fantastic variety of elaborate stalagtites and stalagmites.

Border with Chile

Paso Pehuenche (2,553 m) is reached by a *ripio* road which branches off Route 40, 66 km south of Malargüe. On the Chilean side the road continues down the valley of the Río Maule to Talca. The border is open from December to March 0800-2100 and April to November 0800-1900.

Listings: Southern Mendoza

⊜ Sleeping

Tupungato and around *p202*
Hostería Don Romulo, *in the hamlet of Manzano Historico, www.donromulo.com.ar*
This *hostería* is owned by Rómulo Nieto, simple rooms with TV and bath for 2 to 4 with a cosy lounge to relax in and decent, very inexpensive, food from pasta to *parrilla*

in the restaurant. Recommended.
D **Hotel Turismo**, *Belgrano 1060, T488007.*
A slightly modernized 1940's place, basic but comfortable rooms with wonderful kingfisher blue tiles in the bathrooms, some family rooms, a pool and a good restaurant.

Camping
Patios de Correa, *T15673299, 4.3 km northeast*

● For an explanation of the sleeping and eating price codes used in this guide, see the inside
● front cover. Other relevant information is provided in the Essentials chapter, page 44.

66 99 Seductive altiplanic grasslands, riven with volcanic peaks, deep red and black crags of extraordinary sculpted lava, made even more magical by the sudden appearance of hundreds of guanaco running wild across your path...

of Tupungato. A good site in woods of willow and walnut trees, on the river bank, also a good picnic spot.

Camping is possible at various attractive spots in the Manzana Historico, but the *Camping ACA* is recommended, with good facilities.

C Samay Huasi, *T492004, or in Mendoza, T0261-423 4545*.

San Rafael *p202*

There are lots of appealing small hotels.

B Tower, *Av Yrigoyen 774, T427190, www.towersanrafael.com* The smartest option is this international-style hotel easily spotted in the main street, an 8 storey peachy yellow building. It's slightly soulless, but has luxurious rooms, great bathrooms, very professional service, a small pool and spa.

C Kalton, *Yrigoyen 120, T430047, www.kaltonhotel.com.ar* The oldest, and still the most welcoming with charming comfortable rooms, a bright small bar and excellent service. Highly recommended.

C Regine, *Independencia 623, T430274, www.reginehotel.com.ar* A delightful rustic place, slightly eccentric, with its pool in the garden, popular with older guests, and a relaxing atmosphere. Rooms with pastel decor have TV and bath and there's a *quincho* for *parrillas*. Good value.

C San Rafael, *Day 30 T/F428251 www.sanrafaelhotel.com.ar* Smart choice with comfortable modern rooms and welcoming bar area. Good value.

D Jardin, *Yrigoyen 283, T434621*. Welcoming modern place with stylish rooms off a lovely patio. Great value, with breakfast.

D Tonin, *Pellegrini 330, T422499, www.sanrafael-tour.com/tonin* A lovely quiet family run place, with modern spacious rooms, TV and bath. Good location next to the plaza.

Youth hostels

E pp Puesta del Sol, *Deán Funes 998, 3 km, T434881, www.hostels.org.ar* 20 blocks from the centre, a popular place with gardens, doubles and dorms, and good facilities. Don't be put off by the unwelcoming staff.

Camping

El Parador, *at the park on Isla Río Diamante, 5 km southeast, T420492, complejoparador@ infovia.com.ar*

There are also many sites at Valle Grande.

Around San Rafael *p203*

B-C Valle Grande Hotel & Resort, *T15580660, www.hotelvallegrande.com* Nicely situated on the banks of the river, with a big terrace and good views from its restaurant, this has smart rooms, and a pool, friendly service, and lots of activities laid on for guests. Also cabañas, popular with families and very lively in summer.

West of San Rafael *p203*

E Hostería Hostal El Sosneado, *T421551, www.sanrafael-tour.com /elsosneado* Half board, simple clean rooms with rustic furniture, and 5 cabañas, sleeping 4-6, with breakfast included, and welcoming owners, who also organize horseriding excursions US$150 for 5 days.

Los Molles *p203*

Far cheaper accommodation than Las Leñas, but all basic.

B-D Lahuen-Co, *T499700*. The most welcoming hotel, built in 1938. Its special feature is its sulphurous thermal baths, in which you can fully immerse yourself in private cabins in a decaying extension at the back.

Las Leñas p204

Budget travellers should consider staying in Malargüe or Los Molles. The options are all L – A and have restaurants: **Piscis**, 5-star with exceptional facilities and pools – 1 outdoor heated pool, fine restaurants. **Aries**, 4-star, with a sauna, gym and pool. **Escorpioski**, great views. **Acuario** right in the thick of the action. **Geminis**, an apart hotel, also with pool and sauna. For further information on all these hotels, *T471100*. There are also cheaper apart-hotels and dorm houses.

Malargüe p204

Hotels issue guests with a voucher for 50% discount on Las Leñas ski pass.
B **Río Grande**, *Ruta 40 Norte, T471589, hotelriogrande@slatinos.com.ar* The best of a poor range. Book in advance for the smart very comfortable 'VIP' rooms, others, D, are old and a bit dark, with cramped bathrooms.
C-E **La Posta**, *Av Roca 374, T471306.*
A welcoming place with wood panelled entrance hall and rooms, very reasonable for groups of 6 in the larger rooms. Also has a *parrilla*, serving good goat and trout.
D **Hotel del Turismo**, *San Martín 224, T/F471042*. On the main street, with drab rooms but a good cheap restaurant, **Puli Huen**. There are several cabañas for rent, none of which can be recommended.

Camping

Castillos de Pincheiras, *Rufino Ortega 186 Sur s/n, T471283, pincheira@slatinos.com.ar*

Around Malargüe p205

Puesto La Agüita, *T011-4299 2577, kine-turismo-rural@sinectis.com.ar* Lovely accommodation, and guided treks on horseback by **Ariel Sagal**, US$20 per day. Call in advance.

⊘ Eating

Tupungato p202

Apart from the hotels' restaurants, there are a few pizzerias to choose from on the main street, Belgrano.

San Rafael p202

San Rafael lacks exciting places to eat but most are clustered along the western end of Yrigoyen, and you won't have to walk far for a steak. All are mid-range to cheap.
$$ **La Fusta**, *Yrigoyen 538*. A smart traditional restaurant with really delicious Italian style food, superb *parrilla* and good home-made pastas. Warmly recommended.
$$ **Tienda del Sol**, *Yrigoyen 1669*. The town's busiest place serves everything in a cheery family atmosphere, recommended for pizzas and pastas.
$ **Ouvina**, *Olascoaga 177 (closed Mon) and at Yrigoyen 1268 (closed Tue)*. This is a great take away pizzeria, cheap and delicious.
$ **Pagoda**, *Av Mitre 216*. This Chinese *tenedor libre* is a potless bright place with a huge variety, US$2.30 for as much as you can eat.

Cafés

There are lots of cafés but most appealing for a drink or coffee is **Gath & Chavez** at *Chile and San Martín*, with tables outside and a cosy woody interior. Fantastic *lomitos* too.

Malargüe p204

The town's best restaurant is to the side of the Río Grande, where the set menu is around US$4, the trout is recommended.
$ **Dona Maria**, *San Martín 156*. A cosy simple place for home cooked food, pizzas and pastas, lunch and dinner. Very welcoming. Recommended. The impressive conference centre, next to the tourist information office, has an attractive bar for an evening drink.

⊛ Sport and activities

Around Malargüe p205

For **horseriding**, contact **Kiñe tourism**, and stay at their delightful *hostería*, **Puesto La Agüita**, see Sleeping above for details.

⌕ Tour operators

Tupungato p202

A highly recommended guide is **Rómulo Nieto**, *donromulo@slatinos.com.ar*; he runs trekking, horseriding and fishing excursions into the national park, from 6 hrs (US$20, lunch included) to 6 days (US$300 with all food, horses and camping equipment provided). Summer only, call or email in

The West Listings: Southern Mendoza

advance for longer trips. There are also 2-day fishing trips into the park from Nov to Mar, (US$100, all included), and trekking along the old path to Chile from Manzano Historico to Portezuelo de los Pinquenes, incredibly stirring landscapes. Also contactable through his *hostería* in the town, see Sleeping above.

San Rafael and around *p202*
Travel agencies run all-day excursions to Cañon del Atuel and there are several rafting companies at Valle Grande.
Raffeish, *T436996, www.raffeish.com.ar* Recommended for being very professional, offering a range from very secure family trips to more adventurous expeditions for the experienced, US$8 for 2 hrs. A great trekking excursion too, returning by boat.
Sport Star, *T15581068, www.sportstar.com.ar* US$8 for 3-hr trip over 12 km. Also good, on the far side of the river.
Portal de Atuel for horseriding, catamaran and rafting trips across Lago Grande.
Taiel Viajes, *Yrigoyen 707, T427840, www.taiel.com.ar* Run both conventional and adventure tours of all kinds. Wonderful 5-day horseriding trip to Laguna del Atuel, 4WD trips to Laguna el Diamante and Volcan Maipo, and rafting of all grades. Very helpful and professional.
Cañon del Atuel, *Day 45, T424871.* Conventional tours to the local bodegas, Los Reyunos, and through the Cañon itself.
Joker Vajes, *San Martín 236, T436982, info@jokerviajes.com.ar* Some good variations on the usual tours, combining a bodega with lunch at Los Reyunos, for example.

Malargüe *p204*
Karen Travel, *San Martín 1056, T470342, www.karentravelcom.ar* Highly recommended for excursions to all the nature reserves Above (US$10-20 for full day)

and also horseriding trips, such as the one to the crashed Uruguyan plane known as *Homenaje al Avión de los Uruguayos*.

⊖ Transport

Tupungato *p202*
There are daily **buses** from **Mendoza** to the bus terminal at Las Heras and D. Chaca.

San Rafael *p202*
Air 3 flights a week with **Aerolíneas Argentinas** from **Buenos Aires**, 2 hrs, US$70 each way. **Bus** Central terminal at Coronel Saurez y Avellaneda. To **Mendoza**, frequent, US$9; to **Neuquén**, US$20. **Buenos Aires** US$23 *coche cama*, Malargüe, US$4.50. TAC *T422209*, Iselín *T424618, www.isebess.com*, Expreso Uspallata, *www.turismous pallata.com T423169*, Andesmar *T427720*, La Union *T433233*.

West of San Rafael *p203*
Several buses daily to **Malargüe** from **San Rafael** stop here, and you can pick up buses from either places passing through to **Los Molles** and **Las Leñas**.

Las Leñas *p204*
Bus from **San Rafael**, daily 1000, US$4; from Malargüe. There are several minibuses season. **Buenos Aires**, 15 hrs, in skiing season only.

Malargüe *p204*
Air The airport is on southern edge of town, *T471265*. There are weekly scheduled flights from **Buenos Aires**, and many charter flights in the skiing season. **Bus** The terminal is at Aldao and Beltrán. Daily buses from **Mendoza** with TAC and Expreso Uspallata, minibuses with **Transporte Viento Sur**, both 4 hrs, U$7.

San Juan Province

The province of San Juan extends north and west from its capital, which lies in the broad valley of the Río San Juan, an important wine-producing area. Its real pleasures lie in the little-visited west of the province, where the foothills of the Andes rise in ranges separated by beautiful, lush valleys. There is great climbing and trekking here, with several Andean peaks to explore, including the mighty Mercedario, 6,770m. The area northeast of the San Juan Valley, on the provincial border with La Rioja, is almost inhospitably hot and dry almost all year round and the landscape starkly beautiful but empty. In the middle of this arid land are two of the most popular attractions in this region: the Parque Provincial Ischigualasto – often known as the Valle de la Luna and the Parque Nacional Talampaya, which is over the border in La Rioja.

San Juan → *Phone code: 02646 Colour map 3, A2 Population: 122,000*

The provincial city (650 m and 177 km north of Mendoza) is much less inviting than the marvellous landscapes all around and you're most likely to arrive here on the way to the Cailngasta Valley or the national parks further north. However, it's a good place to plan those trips and there are several good places to stay and eat. Although the city was founded on its present site in 1593, little of the original settlement remains since the most powerful earthquake in Argentine history struck in 1944 killing over 10,000 inhabitants. Though it's been rebuilt in modern style, San Juan has not yet recovered as Mendoza did. At a fund-raising event at Luna Park in Buenos Aires for the victims of the tragedy, Juan Perón met Eva Duarte, the radio actress who became his second wife. ▸▸ *For Sleeping, Eating and other listings, see pages 213-214.*

Sights

Wine is a major industry here and it's worth a visit to a bodega if you haven't seen those in Mendoza. One of the country's largest producers, **Bodegas Bragagnolo**, is on the outskirts of town at Route 40 y Avenida Benavídez, Chimbas. ① *Bus 20 from terminal; guided tours daily 0830-1330, 1530-1930, not Sun.*

Bodegas offering tours include: **Antigua Bodega**, *Salta 782 (N), T421 4327*, **Bodega Viñas de Seguisa**, *Aberastein y calle 11 Pocito, T492 1807*. The **Mercado Artesanal Tradicional**, *España y San Luis, T421 8530*, sells the woven handicrafts, such as blankets and saddlebags, for which the province is famous. And if you haven't time for a bodega tour, sample the local wine at **Vinoteca San Juan**, *Av San Martín 2154(oeste)*, with a good selection of wines, champagnes and olives.

San Juan's museums are mostly rather dry, but it's worth visiting **Museo Casa Natal de Sarmiento** ① *Sarmiento 21 Sur, daily 0830-1330, also 1500-2000 Tue-Fri and Sun. US$1, free on Sun*, the birthplace of Domingo Sarmiento, the important Argentine President and educator, (see box). The **Museo de Ciencias Naturales** ① *Predio Ferial, España y Maipú, Tue-Fri, 0800-1300. Mon and Sat 0830-1330, US$1, free Sun*, has some of the fossils from Ischigualasto Provincial Park, which you won't see at the site itself (see below). The **tourist office** is at Sarmiento Sur 24 y San Martín, ① *T422 2431, F422 5778, www.ischigualasto.com Open (in theory) Mon-Fri, 0730-2030, Sat-Sun 0900-2000; also at bus terminal.* Note that the main street, Av San Martín, is often called Libertador.

Around San Juan → *See page 212 for Parque Provincial Ichigualasto*

There's a wonderful collection of pre-Hispanic indigenous artefacts including several well-preserved mummies at the **Museo Arqueológico** of the University of San Juan at La Laja, 26 km north. Fascinating insights into the culture of the indigenous Huarpe peoples and into the Incan sacrifice practices. There are also inexpensive open-air thermal baths nearby at **Baños Termales** La Laja① *daily 0930-1700, US$2, bus No 20 from San Juan, 2 daily, but you need to take the first (at 0830) to give time to return*, with very smelly but healing sulphurous water.

● *Those piles of bottles at roadside shrines you see throughout Argentina are offerings made to Argentina's favourite pagan saint, La Difunta Correa, to bring safe journeys on the road. Miraculously, La Difunta's baby boy survived at her breast even after she had died of thirst: millions of pilgrims leave amazing tributes at her gaudy shrine in Vallecito.*

Vallecito, 64 km east, has a famous shrine to **La Difunta Correa**, Argentina's most loved pagan saint ① *buses from San Juan to la Rioja stop here for 5 mins, or Vallecitos runs frequent services.* During Holy Week, 100,000 pilgrims visit the series of shrines at Vallecito, where there are splendidly florid effigies of Difunta and her child. Testimony to their faith is a remarkable collection of personal items left in tribute, including number plates from all over the world, cars, photographs, stuffed animals, tea sets, hair (in plaits), plastic flowers, trophies, tennis rackets and guitars – and vast numbers of bottles of water (used for the plants, and the plastic recycled). There are cafés, toilets, a hotel and souvenir stalls. Bizarre and fascinating. ▶▶ *For Sleeping, Eating and other listings, see pages 213-214.*

Calingasta Valley

The most beautiful part of the province, this long fertile valley lies 100 km west of San Juan between the jagged peaks of the snow-capped Andes *cordillera* and the stark crinkled range of the Sierra del Tontal, west of San Juan city. Inhabited since at least 10,000 BC, the Calingasta Valley was once the route of the Camino del Inca and though little of this history remains today, it still carries a compelling attraction. Its few oasis villages are charming places to stay in to explore the hills.

The valley is usually reached from San Juan by the scenic Provincial Route 12, though this has been disrupted by work on two dams and is currently only open between Pachaco and Calingasta. To reach Pachaco, take RN40 north of San Juan, and at Talacasto, a new *ripio* road branches west to Pachaco. It's worth phoning the tourist office (T422 2431) or ACA (T4223781) for advice on which roads are open. About half way between Calingasta and Barreal, this passes, to the east, the Cerros Pintados, a range of red, white and grey stratified hills, striped like toothpaste. There are beautiful views of the whole valley here with its meandering river, a ribbon of green running through the dusty plain between cordillera and Sierra del Tigre. ▶▶ *For Sleeping, Eating and other listings, see pages 213-214.*

Calingasta → *Phone code: 02648 Population: 2,000*

The road from Pachaco to Calingasta follows the winding course of the Río San Juan, through a steep sided gorge of astonishingly coloured and stratified rock. After Pachaco, the landscape opens out, and Calingasta lies at the confluence of the Ríos de los Patos and Calingasta, a vivid green splash on the otherwise arid landscape. This idyllic, secluded little village (1,430 m. 135 km west of San Juan) is a delightful place to rest for a few days or plan a trek into the mountains. The Jesuit chapel, **Capilla de Nuestra Señora del Carmen**, is worth seeing, a simple adobe building dating from the early 1600s, with the ancient original bells. Tourist information at the Municipalidad, Lavalle y Sarmiento, T421066.

Barreal → *Phone code: 02648 Colour map 3, A2 Population: 1,800*

Another peaceful oasis, Barreal (1,650 m) offers more accommodation and services than Calingasta, and is the best base if you plan to trek into the Andes. However, it's still small and quiet enough to feel like a village and offers spectacular views of the Andes. From here you can explore the mountains of **Sierra de Tontal**, which rise to 4,000 m and give superb views over San Juan, Mercedario and Aconcagua, or climb the mighty **Cerro Mercedaria** (6,769 m) itself, one of the Andes' greatest peaks. For all mountain expeditions, contact Sr Ramón Luis Ossa at Cabañas Doña Pipa (see page 213, T441004, www.ossaexpedicion.com, www.fortunaviajes.com.ar). He runs trips to **Mercedario**, with mules and all equipment included, fantastic treks into the Andes from 1 to 15 days, and can organise horseriding, 4WD trips and wind cars too.

Barreal is famous for *caravelismo* (wind-car racing) thanks to its vast expanse of

Sarmiento 1811-88

Argentina owes its high literacy level and (until recent years) excellent education system to Domingo Faustino Sarmiento, San Juan's most famous son, born in 1811. In a career which extended over some 60 years as a writer, educator, journalist, historian, diplomat and politician, he consistently advocated education as the solution to Argentina's problems. He taught in local schools while still a teenager and started a girls' secondary school. In 1840, as a result of his opposition to Rosas (see box, page 118) he was again forced into exile in Chile but on friendly terms with prominent politicians and writers, he ran a teacher training college and promoted his educational theories, having significant influence on the Chilean educational system.

Sarmiento's fame as a writer is based on his work *Facundo: Civilisation and Barbarism*, published 1845, an allegorical biography of a Federalist caudillo (local strong man) and a passionate attack on Rosas, whose barbarism is identified with the backward interior and the introverted nationalism of provincial caudillos. Civilization, according to Sarmiento, lay in adopting European patterns in the political cultural and social spheres. Argentina had to open up its trade to the rest of the world, attract European immigrants, and acquire sociability and respectability to lead the country out of fragmentation caused by excessive individualism.

Rosas responded by having Sarmiento extradited, but the Chilean government sent him to study educational methods in Europe and the United States. Having participated in the overthrow of Rosas, Sarmiento fell out with his successor, Urquiza, and as head of education for Buenos Aires province, his support for universal public education with an emphasis on science and gymnastics for both boys and girls met with fierce opposition.

However, as President of Argentina, 1868-1874, he encouraged European immigration and achieved greater trade, improvements in public health and the building of schools, libraries, roads and railways.

Until his death in 1888, he worked tirelessly in a succession of public posts, and still managed to found a newspaper and an educational journal, get married, leave his wife for another woman, and father a son who was killed fighting in the War of Triple Alliance.

flat land known as Barreal del Leoncito, parallel to the road, south of town. The climate here is so perfectly sunny, with 320 clear nights a year, that at **El Leoncito** (2,348 m) nearby there are two space observatories ⓘ *you can visit daily 1000-1100, 1600-1800, US$3, but there's no public transport; Ossa Expediciones runs informative tours, www.ossaexpedicion.com, as detailed above. An unpaved road (17 km) which turns off the Route 412, 22 km south of Barreal. Ranger post at entrance; no facilities, take all supplies*. There's also an immense nature reserve, covering 76,000 ha of the eastern slopes of the Sierra de Tontal and rising to over 4,000 m. To the west there are fine views of Mercedario and other peaks in the *cordillera* with the flat plain and lush valley between. Fauna includes guanacos, red and grey foxes and peregrine falcons.

Cerro Mercedario

Known in Chile as El Ligua and rising to 6,770 m, Mercedario lies southwest of Calingasta and is thought by many mountaineers to be a more interesting climb than

Aconcagua. It was first climbed in 1934 by a Polish expedition which went on to climb the nearby peaks of Pico Polaco (6,050 m), La Mesa (6,200 m), Alma Negra (6,120 m) and Ramada (6,410 m). A guide (*baqueano*) should always be hired, who can provide mules if necessary, since there are no facilities and no rescue service. The best time to climb is mid-December to the end of February. Contact Ramón Ossa, as above. No authorization is required to climb but it is advisable to inform the *Gendarmería Nacional* at Barreal. Note that it is illegal to cross the border to/from Chile in this region. ▶▶ *For Sleeping, Eating and other listings, see pages 213-214.*

San Agustín del Valle Fértil → *Phone code: 02646 Population: 3,000*

San Agustín is a rather charming little town, the best base for exploring Ichigualasto, with several good places to stay and eat. You could also fish in the Dique San Agustín, and buy ponchos and blankets from the local weavers. There's a very helpful tourist information office at the municipalidad on the plaza, Gral Acha s/n, T420104, who can give you a map and advise on accommodation, open until 2100.

Parque Provincial Ischigualasto → *Colour map 3, A2*

Popularly known as the Valle de la Luna (Valley of the Moon), this protected area covers 62,000 ha of spectacular desert landforms, and is the site of important archaeological discoveries. Named after a Huarpe Indian chief, the site occupies a large basin, formerly filled by a lake, lying, at an average altitude of 1,200 m, between the scarlet red Cerros Los Colorados to the east and the green, black and grey rocks of Los Rastros to the west. The vegetation is arid scrub and bushes; you may be lucky enough to see guanacos, vizcachas, patagonian hares or red foxes and rheas. For many visitors, the attraction lies in the bizarre shapes of massive lumps of rock which are dotted around the park's other worldly terrain. With the Argentines' charming penchant for naming all natural structures after things that they resemble, these are signposted accordingly: 'The Submarine', 'The Kiosk', 'Gusanos' (Worms), and 'La Cancha de Bochas' (the Bowling Green) – extraordinary spheres of fine compacted sand. Sadly, 'El Hongo' (the Mushroom) has fallen over. However, the park's real fascination lies in the 250 mn years of strata that you can see in the eroded cliffs of the rocks where fossils from all the geological periods have been found, among them fossils of the oldest dinosaurs known, including *Eoraptor*, 225 mn years old and discovered in 1993. Sadly, there's no evidence of these finds here: you'll have to go to the **Museo de Ciencias Naturales** in San Juan. The views throughout the park are impressive, and the span of time you can witness here is mind-blowing. It's a highly recommended excursion.

Tours and access Entrance US$2.00. There is one tour route, lasting 2½ hours, visiting only a part of the park but encompassing the most interesting sites. If you're in your own vehicle, you'll be accompanied by one of the rangers, whose knowledge and interest vary greatly. There's no fee but a tip is appreciated. It can be crowded at holiday times, January, Easter and July. Tours in a bus from San Juan cost US$20 (including breakfast and lunch) and take 14 hour. You can also find guides in San Agustín, charging US$10 (in both towns, ask at tourist office). A taxi to the park costs US$7 from San Agustín (recommended if there are four to five people), more expensive out of season. If you are travelling in your own transport plan to overnight at San Agustín or the less lovely Villa Unión. From San Juan both parks can be reached by taking Route 20 east through Caucete and joining Route 141, via Difunta Correa to Marayes, then turning north onto Route 510 (paved but poor in parts) for 135km northwest. You can camp opposite the ranger station, which has a small museum, but bring all food and water as there's only an expensive *confitería* here, and nothing else for miles. Visit www.ischigualasto.org (in English), a really excellent website full of interesting research and articles about the park, well worth a look before you come.

⬤ Sleeping

San Juan *p209*
Hotels in A to C range all include breakfast
and parking.
B Hotel America, *9 de Julio 1052 (oeste), T421
4514, www.hotel-america.com.ar*
A smart, modern hotel, nicely designed and
very comfortable with good service, tours
arranged. Recommended.
B Alkázar, *Laprida 82 Este, T421 4965,
www.alkazarhotel.com.ar* A well-run central
4-star hotel with very comfortable rooms,
pool and gym. Also an excellent restaurant,
where you can eat well for US$11 including
wine.
C Alkristal, *Av de Circunvalacíon 1055 (sur),
T425 4145*. One of the city's best bargains can
only really be enjoyed if you have your own
transport. Very comfortable well-equipped
rooms in a new high-rise international-style
hotel. Poor breakfast but otherwise
recommended, good value. Also smart
apartments, very cheap for groups.
D Capayan, *Mitre 31 Este, T421 4222,
hcapayan@infovia.com.ar* Next to cinema on
the plaza with a rather sombre foyer
downstairs, but this is a welcoming place with
comfy rooms and good service and a
restaurant too.
E Res Caupolicán, *Av Libertador San Martín
441 Este, T421 1870*. A very friendly family run
bed and breakfast with a lovely garden to sit
in and play area for children, simple rooms
with bath and fan. Recommended.

Calingasta *p210*
D Hotel de Campo Calingasta, *take the left
fork from the gendarmeria, cross the river and
continue 2 km; hotel is up a hill on your right,
T421220*. A restored colonial-style building
with airy rooms coming off a colonnaded
patio, with open views to the mountains, and
a pool in the garden. Very tranquil. Meals also
available. Recommended.
D La Capilla, *T421033*. Includes breakfast,
basic but very clean, family run. Also sells **TAC**
bus tickets and has the only public telephone
in the village.

Barreal *p210*
C Posada San Eduardo, *Av San Martín s/n.*
Charming colonial-style house, whose rooms
open onto a courtyard. Very pleasant and
relaxing. Also has a good restaurant.
D Cabañas Doña Pipa, *Mariano Moreno s/n,
T441004, www.ossaexpedicion.com*
Attractive cabañas sleeping 6-8, well-equipped,
breakfast included, with a swimming pool, and
great views to the mountains, open all year.
Owned by the charming mountain guide
Ramón Luis Ossa. Highly recommended.
D Hotel Turismo Barreal, *San Martín s/n,
T441090, hotelbarreal@yahoo.com.ar* Nicely
refurbished 1940's place with slightly plain
rooms and some hostel space but a good
restaurant and friendly service. Also has a pool,
and can organize riding.

Camping
The municipal site, *T441241*, is shady and well
maintained with a pool, open all year.

San Agustín del Valle Fértil *p212*
During Easter all accommodation is fully
booked. There are a couple of good hotels, and
lots of cabañas, but these are recommended:
C Hostería Valle Fértil, *Rivadavia s/n, T420015,
www.alkazarhotel.com.ar* Smart, very
comfortable hotel with fine views from its
elevated position above the town, also has
cabañas and a good restaurant open to non
residents.
F pp Hospedaje Los Olivos, *Santa Fe y
Tucumán, T420115*. Excellent value, with
restaurant.

Camping
There are several campsites, of which the most
highly recommended is **La Majadita** in a lovely
spot on the river to the west of town with hot
showers and great views. There's a municipal
campsite in the town by Dique San Agustin, *Av
Libertador 1176, T421 9726*.

⬤ Eating

San Juan *p209*
$$ Club Sirio Libanés 'El Palito', *Entre Ríos*

33 Sur. Pleasant decor, good tasty food.
$$ Las Leñas, *San Martín 1670 Oeste*. For superb steak head straight to this popular and atmospheric *parrilla* in *quincho* (ranch) style with rustic wooden interior. Arrive at 2100 to avoid queues later in the evening. US$4.40 for the complete *parrilla*.
$$ Remolacha, *Santa Fé 1232 (oeste)*. Stylish, warm and welcoming place with superb Italian inspired menu, delicious steaks and pastas. Recommended.
$$ Soychú, *de la Roza 223 Oeste. T422 1939*. Excellent vegetarian food. Highly recommended, very good value.
$ Amistad, *Rivadavia 47 Oeste*. Chinese, good value, lots of choice.
$ Listo El Pollo, *Av San Martín y Santiago del Estero*. Very good chicken, reasonably cheap.

San Agustín del Valle Fértil *p212*
$ El Astiqueño, *Tucumán next to the Dique*. Good regional specialities.
$ Noche Azul, *Gral Acha s/n. Parrilla*, just off the plaza, offering local *chivito* (kid).

↻ Tour operators

Expediciones Ossa, *T441004*. Ramón Ossa is an expert guide for treks into the mountains northwest of San Juan including up Mercedario and into the Cordón del Plata. Highly recommended.
Fascinatur, *San Martín 1085 Oeste, T155043933*. Recommended for 4WD treks to remote areas, also horseback and mountain bike excursions, English, French German spoken.
Nerja Tours, *Entre Rios 178 (sur), T0264-421 5214, www.nerja-tours.com.ar* Conventional tours, local trips and adventure tourism.
Turismo Vittorio, *Sarmiento 174 sur, T0264-420 4000, www.turismo-vittorio.com.ar* Conventional and adventure tours.

⊖ Transport

San Juan *p209*
Air
Chacritas Airport, 11 km southeast. Bus 19 or 22 (Triunfo) to/from centre, 4 a day, 30 mins, US$1. Remise from city, prices vary, shop around. To **Buenos Aires** Aerolíneas Argentinas/Austral, several daily, US$40 each way.

Bus
Terminal information, *T422 1604, Estados Unidos y Santa Fe, 9 blocks east of centre. Bus 33 and 35 for city centre*. To **La Rioja**, 6 hrs, US$6, 4 companies. **Catamarca**, 4 companies, US$11. **Tucumán**, 5 companies, US$12. **Córdoba**, Socasa, 20 de Julio, Autotransportes San Juan, 9 hrs, US$8 *coche cama*. **Buenos Aires** (Autotransporte San Juan, TAC and others, 11 hrs, US$20 *semi cama*, US$30 *coche cama*). Local destinations: to **San Agustín** with Vallecito, 3 a day, US$5. Hourly departures to and from **Mendoza** with TAC and Media Agua and others, 2 hrs, US$4. Also services to **Barreal** and **Calingasta** with El Triunfo, *T421 4532*. Autotransportes San Juan, *T422 1870*.

Car hire
Parque Automotor, *España y San Martín, T423 3859*. Localiza, *Av Lib San Martín 163, T422 6018*.

Barreal *p210*
There is a **bus** from **San Juan** daily, El Triunfo, at 1900, 5 hrs, US$4. Returning to San Juan at 2100. Also minibus run by José Luis Sosa, *T441095*.

San Agustín del Valle Fértil *p212*
Bus From **Mendoza**, the only service is with **Empresa Mendoza**, 6 hrs, which arrives 0200, better to go from **San Juan**, Vallecito, 0700, 1900, 4 hours, a/c, US$5. To **La Rioja**, daily service, 4 hrs. US$7.

❶ Directory

San Juan *p209*
Banks Open 0700-1200. Many, **Banelco** and **Link**, ATMs accept international credit cards in the centre. **Cambio Santiago**, *Gen Acha 52 Sur, T421 22332*, weekdays until 2100, Sat until 1300. **Communications Internet** Several *locutorios* have internet, those at *Rivadavia y Acha, on the plaza*, and *Mendoza 139 Sur* are open on Sun. Also **Cyber Café**, *Rivadavia 12 Este*, **Interredes**, *Laprida 362 Este*, **IAC**, *Acha 142 Norte, T427 7104*.

La Rioja Province

La Rioja is usually visited for the wonderful Parque Nacional Talampaya, a vast canyon of rock sculpted by wind and water into fantastic shapes, declared a world heritage site by UNESCO. However, there's also stunning scenery beyond the national park and perfect tranquillity, since the area is sparsely populated and little-visited. Between the mountain ranges of the west are the extended Famatina and Vinchina valleys with verdant oasis villages at the foot of colourful eroded hills. In the arid southeast are the extraordinary saltflats, Llanos de los Caudillos, with the beautiful Sierra de los Llanos. The city of La Rioja itself has two fine museums of indigenous art.

La Rioja City → *Phone code: 03822 Colour map 1, C2 Population: 147,000*

Though not obviously touristy, the capital (498 m) does offer decent accommodation and is a good starting point for a trip to the province. Founded in 1591 at the edge of the plains, with views of Sierra de Velasco, a few interesting museums, some neo-colonial houses and the oldest building in the country. Sleepy and oppressively hot from November to March, the town becomes very lively every day after siesta time and during the annual celebrations of the local carnivals 'chaya' and the 'Tinkunaco'.

Sights

The city centre revolves around Plaza 25 de Mayo with shady tipas, sycamores, araucarias and pine trees. Here, in 1637, the head of the native leader of an insurrection was exhibited as a trophy by the Spaniards. On the plaza, is the early 20th-century cathedral with the image of San Nicolás de Bari and a room full of silver offerings.

Other interesting sights on the plaza are the neo-colonial **Casa de Gobierno** and **Poder Judicial**, together with the pink building of the **Club Social**. One block northwest, the **Church of Santo Domingo**, Pelagio B. Luna y Lamadrid, is a quaint

The West La Rioja Province

La Rioja

Sleeping	Vincent's Apart Hotel 4	Café del Paseo 3
King's 3		La Aldea de la Virgen de
Pensión 9 de Julio 2	**Eating**	Luján 6
Plaza 5	Alike 1	La Vieja Casona 5
Savoy 1	Café de la Plaza 2	Los Palotes 4

0 metres 200
0 yards 200

stone temple, sparsely decorated inside but with magnificent wooden-carved doors. Dating from 1623 and renovated in later centuries is said to be the oldest surviving church in Argentina. There is a lovely patio in the adjacent convent.

The corner the **Museo Arqueológico Inca Huasi** ① *Alberdi 650, Tue-Sat 0900-1200, US$0.50*, houses one of the most important collections in the country of pre-Hispanic ceramics made by the ancient cultures who originally inhabited the region including a remarkable funerary urn from the Aguada Culture, dating from 1500 BC. The **tourist office** ① *Pelagio B. Luna 345, Mon-Sat 0800-1300, 1600-2100, Sun 0800-1200, T453982, www.larioja.gov.ar*, is friendly, helpful and hands out a map of the city. Ask here for accommodation, including rooms with families (*casas de familia*). ▶▶ *For Sleeping, Eating and other listings, see pages 219-222.*

Around La Rioja City

The fastest way to escape the heat of the city is to go 10 km west via Route 75 to the **Quebrada del Río Los Sauces**, a shaded river with campsites and a reservoir amidst lovely mountain scenery. From there, a dirt 13-km track (no shade) leads to the summit of the **Cerro de la Cruz** (1,648 m) with great panoramic views and where hang gliding is often practised. Seven kilometres west of La Rioja is **Las Padercitas**, where there is a large stone-built temple protecting the adobe remains of what is supposed to have been a Spanish fortress in the 16th century. The same Route 75 continues north along the 200 km of the Circuito de la Costa. Take Avenida Quiroga to the west, which becomes Route 75 and passes Las Padercitas. After a few kilometres, the road follows the Quebrada for 4 km before heading through a tunnel to the view of the reservoir of Dique Los Sauces. Regular minibuses or 'diferenciales' Transal, to Villa Sanagasta from Lamadrid 116, T460596, take you to Quebrada and **Dique Los Sauces**, US$0.50. *Remise* taxis charge about US$5-7; also some tour operators run short excursions.

Northeastern La Rioja (La Costa)

The long narrow strip of land known as La Costa lies at the edge of the plains, and at the foot of the Sierra de Velasco mountains. There are small villages dotted about, delightful green oases with old chapels, surrounded by vineyards, orchards and olive groves. The whole area can be seen in a couple of days but this is a relaxing place to hang out for longer.

Two roads head north from La Rioja. Route 38 runs northeast to Catamarca and at Km 33 Provincial Route 9 (later 10) branches off north for Villa Mazán, Km 99. Some 7 km north of Villa Mazán is Termas Santa Teresita. Here there is the budget **Hostería Termas Santa Teresita**, *T03827-420445, www.termassantateresita.com.ar*, which has open-air thermal pool, thermal baths in all rooms, breakfast included. The other road, Route 75 to Aimogasta, is more interesting, passing through Villa Sanagasta, Aminga and Anillaco and all the small towns of La Costa.

The first town you'll come across is **Villa Sanagasta**, nicely set among orchards and where, on the last Friday in September, there is a religious procession to La Rioja. **Huaco,** the only estancia, welcomes visitors with its fruit trees, streams, remains of Jesuit buildings and the house where the writer Joaquín V González was born (T03822-426102; access US$3.50 per vehicle). A few kilometres later at **Agua Blanca**, there is a lovely Alpine-style cabin, *El Alpino* where good meals are served.

There are a few curious sights near **Anillaco**: the fairy tale or horror story (depending your mood) castle-like **Castillo de Dionisio** at Santa Vera Cruz; the massive **Señor de la Peña**, a naturally shaped rock and very popular religious sanctuary during Holy Week, lying in a desert plain 30 km east of Anillaco, and the 18th-century **chapel of Udpinango. Aimogasta** is the largest town around, at the heart

The Famatina Valley

One of the richest areas of the province and only a few hours west of the capital, this immense valley is attractively flanked to the west by the magnificent Famatina Mountains, 6,000m high, and to the east by the Sierra de Velasco, rising to 4,000m. Once an important mining area, it's now famous for its tasty wines, olives and walnuts. You can combine the most challenging treks in the region with a relaxing stay in a calm, rural 'finca'.

Chilecito → *Phone code: 03825 Colour map 1, C2 Population: 25,000*

The second biggest town (1,074 m) in the province and certainly the most attractive, lies at the foot of the snow-capped Famatina Mountains in an area of vineyards and olive groves, and is the best base for exploring the hills and nearby villages. Founded in 1715, its name derives from the influx of Chilean miners in the 19th century. The town centre, with many cafés and a modern church, is centred around Plaza de los Caudillos, beautifully shaded with mature pine and red gum trees, and two pergolas covered with grapevines. Each February the plaza is the focus of the *chaya* celebrations (see La Rioja's festivals, page 221) and the anniversary of the town's foundation.

At the **Cooperativa La Riojana** ⓘ *La Plata 646, Mon-Fri 0800, 1000, 1200; shop open 0600-1400, Free guided visits (45 mins) and a smart wine shop*, you can watch local grapes being processed to make a wide variety of wines. An easy five minutes walk from plaza, along C El Maestro, past the pleasant Parque Municipal and up to the **Mirador El Portezuelo** there are splendid panoramic views of the town and the Velasco and Famatina mountains. The **tourist office** is at the bus station (no phone), daily 0800-1230, 1530-2100. For more tourist information and pictures visit www.chilecitotour.com or www.chilecito.net

Finca Samay Huasi ⓘ *San Miguel, 3 km southeast of town, T422629, Mon-Fri 0800-1300, 1330-1930, Sat/Sun 0800-1200, 1500-1900 (closed 22 Dec-6 Jan), US$0.35*, is an attractive place to come and relax for a day. The estate was once the summer residence of Joaquín V González, founder of La Plata University, who designed the gardens with native trees, and strange stone monoliths expressing his love of ancient cultures. There's also a small natural history museum and staying guests also welcome.

Around Chilecito

While the Famatina Mountains are best explored on a guided tour, you can amble to the villages around Chilecito quite easily, with their old adobe houses and historical chapels. In **Famatina**, Good Friday and Christmas Day are celebrated with fabulous processions, and there's also a good site for paragliding. At **Santa Florentina** (8 km northwest of Chilecito), the impressive remains of a huge 20th-century foundry are linked to Chilecito and La Mejicana mine by cable car. A few kilometres west of Sañogasta, Route 40 leads to the eroded red sandstone rocks of **Cuesta de Miranda**, one of the most spectacular routes in the province. Winding its way between Sierra de Famatina and Sierra de Sañogasta, it rises to 2,020 m and drops again, passing through 320 bends in 11,500 m. ▸▸ *For Sleeping, Eating and other listings, see pages 219-222.*

Parque Nacional Talampaya → *Phone code: 03825*

Extending over 215,000 ha at an altitude of 1,200 m, Talampaya is a remarkable natural area for its impressive rock formations, of which the 4-km-long gorge or canyon of the River Talampaya is the main feature. A stroll through this vast chasm gives you an unforgettable experience of being entirely dwarfed by the landscape. Though some sections of the park are only accessible by vehicle, guided walks and cycles are available.

The park itself occupies a basin between the Sierra Morada to the west and the Sierras de Sañogasta to the east. This is the site of an ancient lake, where sediments piled up have been eroded by water and wind for the last 200 mn years, forming a dramatic landscape of pale red hills named **Sierra de los Tarjados**. Numerous fossils have been found, and some 600 year-old petroglyphs can be seen not far from the access to the gorge. Along the canyon extraordinarily shaped structures have been given names such as 'the balconies', 'the lift', 'the crib' or 'the owl'. At one point, the gorge narrows to 80 m wide and rises to 143 m. A refreshing leafy spot in the centre of the gorge has been named 'the botanical garden' due to the amazing diversity of plants and tree specimens living here. The end of the *canyon* is marked by the imposing cliffs of 'the Cathedral' and the curious 'King on a camel'. 'The chessboard' and 'the monk', 53 m high, lie not far beyond the gorge, marking the end of the so-called circuito El Monje. Only accessible with 4WD vehicles, circuito Los Cajones continues in the same direction up to 'los pizarrones', an enormous wall of rock covered with petroglyphs, and then to '*los cajones*', a narrow pass between rock walls. Circuito Ciudad Perdida is another possible excursion in the park, southeast of the gorge, accessible only with 4WD vehicles, leading to an area of high cliffs and a large number of breathtaking rock formations. ▸▸ *For Sleeping, Eating and other listings, see pages 219-222.*

Access and information The park is reached by a paved side road, 14 km long, which turns off Route 76 at Km 144 (217 km far from La Rioja), 61 km north of the police checkpoint at Los Baldecitos and 55 km south of Villa Unión. Tour operators from La Rioja and Chilecito, sometimes combine a visit with nearby Valle de la Luna, otherwise difficult to access. (Check that the entrance and guide's fee are included). Independent access is possible, since buses or combis linking La Rioja and Villa Unión stop at the park entrance (a long walk to the administración) or better, at Pagancillo (a village 30 km north), since most of the park wardens live there and will offer free transfer to the park early in the following morning (contact Adolfo Páez). A basic campsite is in the park next to the office (US$1 pp)

Excursions Trips can be arranged at the administración office. Guided walks (five hours, US$5) include Quebrada Don Eduardo and the whole canyon. Guided bike rides (2½ hrs, US$4, cycle and helmet provided) follow the whole length of the cañón up to 'la catedral'. A shorter journey is also on offer up to 'the botanical garden'. Vehicle guided visits (prices are for the whole group of up to eight people) for circuito El Monje (1½ hours, US$20), circuito Los Cajones (3 hours, US$40) and circuito Ciudad Perdida (6 hours, US$50). Access with own 4WD vehicle is allowed with a guide (US$5, US$10 or US$13 per vehicle for same described itineraries). Entry US$ 2 (for Argentines), US$4 (for foreigners). 0800-1700 (summer), 0900-1700 (rest of year), T470397. Best time to visit is in the morning, with the best natural light and avoiding strong winds in the afternoon. A small restaurant, toilets, public telephones are in the same park administration office.

Western La Rioja

The westernmost inhabited valley in La Rioja is that of the **Río Vinchina** (also known as Valle del Bermejo) which flows along the west side of the Sierra de Famatina. The valley is reached from the provincial capital via Patquía and Route 150, then north along Route 26 via the Parque Nacional Talampaya, or from Chilecito by Route 40,

Villa Unión and around → *Phone code: 03825 Colour map 1, C1 Population: 3,500*

Some 92 km west of Nonogasta, Villa Unión (1,240 m) is the largest settlement in the valley and is another base for visits to the Parque Nacional Talampaya, 67 km south. North of Villa Unión, paved Route 76 heads along the arid valley to **Villa Castelli** and **Vinchina** (70 km north of Villa Unión) offering the last comfortable accommodation option before getting into the high mountains, (D) *Corona del Inca*, T03825-494004, hotelcoronadelinca@ciudad.com.ar

On the west side of Route 76, on the northern outskirts of town, there is the **Estrella de Vinchina,** the only surviving star-shaped stone mosaic made by ancient settlers centuries ago. Immediately north of Vinchina, Route 76 enters the spectacular **Quebrada de la Troya** and 36 km northwest of Vinchina, it reaches **Jagüe** (1,900 m), with food and basic facilities and where you will be approached by park wardens. This is the starting point for a 154 km long road to Chile through the Andean mountain pass of **Pircas Negras** (4,165 m). About every 20 to 30 km and closer to Laguna Brava, stone huts can be sighted; built in the 19th century to shelter wranglers on their way with cattle across the Andes. The road gives also access to a vast and empty territory protected as the **Reserva Natural Laguna Brava.** ▸▸ *For Sleeping, Eating and other listings, see pages 219-222.*

Reserva Natural Laguna Brava → *Colour map 1, C1*

This park covers some 405,000 ha of mountains and a high plateau, rising from 3,800m to 4,360m. Laguna Brava, a salt lake, 4,271 m, 16 km long, 3 km wide, lies further northwest beyond the Portezuelo del Peñón. There are superb views over the lake, with some of the mightiest volcanoes on earth in the background. From the left these are the perfect cone Veladero (6,436 m), Reclus (6,335 m), Los Gemelos (6,130 m), Pissis (6,882 m) the highest volcano in the world, though inactive, and Bonete (6,759 m) which is visible from Villa Unión and Talampaya. The park is home to flamingoes and over 3,000 vicuñas. This is also the destination area of many organized 4WD tours, reaching the high plateau, the Laguna Brava itself and occasionally, the small lagoon Corona del Inca lying at the crater of a volcano at 5,300 m.

Access From Jagüe, 4WD or mountain bike are essential. Summer rainfall and winter snow may limit the access to only a short period in the year; usually April or early May are the best times for a visit. Entry US$5. For tours in this area see under La Rioja and Chilecito tour operators page 221.

Listings: La Rioja Province

☻ Sleeping

La Rioja City *p215, map p215*
Air conditioning or a fan are essential for summer nights. High season is during Jul and winter holidays.

B King's, *Av Quiroga 1070, T422122*. A pricey 4-star hotel with buffet breakfast included, a/c gym, pool and fine rooms, car rental.
C Plaza, *San Nicolás de Bari y 9 de Julio (on Plaza 25 de Mayo), T425215, www.plazahotel-larioja.com.ar* Functional 4-star place with a pool on the top floor and breakfast included; all rooms with a/c. Some have good plaza views but can be noisy.
D Savoy, *San Nicolás de Bari y Roque A Luna, T426894, hotelsavoy@infovia.com.ar* Located in a quiet residential area, this is a tidy and comfortable hotel with breakfast and a/c included, though it has some strangely shaped rooms, and it's worth paying the extra 30% for more spacious rooms with renovated bathrooms on the 2nd floor.
D Vincent Apart Hotel, *Santiago del Estero y San Nicolás de Bari, T432326*. Spotless new flats for up to 4 people with a/c, including a

dining room, a small kitchen and fridge; breakfast is also included. Excellent value for a group of 3 or 4. Recommended.

E **Pensión 9 de Julio**, *Copiapó 197 (on Plaza 9 de Julio)*, *T426955*. The attractive front patio is more inviting than the moody staff, but these cheap rooms with breakfast are comfortable enough and there is plenty of hot water in the spacious bathrooms. Cheaper with shared baths.

Camping

There are several sites along Av Ramírez de Velasco, in the northwest suburbs on the way to Las Padercitas and Dique Los Sauces, but the most appealing with pool, hot water and electricity is the one belonging to Sociedad Sirio-Libanesa at Quebrada de los Sauces, 13 km west of town.

La Costa *p216*

Anillaco has the best place to stay in the area at D **Hostería Anillaco (ACA)**, *T03827-494064*. Breakfast included, a pool and also a decent restaurant.

Chilecito *p217*

D **Mary Pérez**, *Florencio Dávila 280, T423156, hostal_mp@hotmail.com* Best value for its comfortable rooms. Good breakfast. Recommended (though check if the nearby sports club is holding a party).

E **Bellia**, *El Maestro 188, T422181*. All the decent rooms of this small hotel open onto a very nice garden. Breakfast is included and it's a very good place for relaxing.

F pp **Finca del Paimán**, *Mariano Moreno y Santa Rosa (at San Miguel, 3 km southeast of town), T/F425102, www.fincadelpaiman .8m.com* The friendly owner, Alejo Piehl, has opened his own renovated adobe house to welcome guests to share spacious rooms and kitchen, and perhaps a fruit harvest or jam cooking! Includes breakfast and transport to/from Chilecito. The *finca* is a delightful 4½ ha farm where you can just chill out or plan an excursion to the mountains led by Alejo. Warmly recommended, book in advance.

F pp **Finca Samay Huasi** (see above for address). Rooms are basic but decent, with

breakfast and a pool in attractive surroundings. E pp if full board, but discounts are negotiable). Usually full in Jul, 2 days' advance booking is essential all year.

Camping

Three sites at Santa Florentina and Las Talas, 8 km northwest of Chilecito (*remise* taxis charge US$2-2.50).

Villa Unión and around *p219*

D **Pircas Negras**, *on Route 76, T470611*. A brand new hotel, breakfast included.

E **Dayton**, *Nicolás Dávila 115, T470182*. Basic but decent, with breakfast.

E **Noryanepat**, *Joaquín V. González 150, T470372*. Familiar, small modern house with cramped rooms with a/c and breakfast.

Eating

La Rioja City *p215, map p215*

$$ **El Corral**, *Av Quiroga y Rivadavia, T465056*. Try the traditional rustic *comidas de campo*, a rich *locro* or a *puchero*, *asado* or *pollo al disco*; good local wines too.

$$ **La Vieja Casona**, *Rivadavia 427, T425996*. A popular and smart *parrilla*. The *lechón a la parrilla* with apple sauce is superb.

$$ **Los Palotes**, *Hipólito Yrigoyen 128, T15682670*. An eclectic menu of the usual, with added salmon, trout and seafood and a few Mexican dishes too, in a pleasant atmosphere.

$ **Alike**, *Vélez Sarsfield e Hipólito Irigoyen*. Originally a Chinese *tenedor libre*, now offering everything.

$ **La Aldea de la Virgen de Luján**, *Rivadavia 756, T460305*. Fill up cheaply in a lively atmosphere and try the Middle Eastern dishes.

Chilecito *p217*

$$ **Chloé**, *El Maestro y 9 de Julio*. This cafe on plaza serves basic meals.

$ **Club Arabe**, *C 25 de Mayo (between Zelada y Dávila and Famatina)*. Despite its name, Middle Eastern food only available on request, serving the usual dishes on tables outside under dense grapevines.

$ **El Pelado**, *Ocampo 15, T15670238*. If everything is closed try this place for

For an explanation of the sleeping and eating price codes used in this guide, see the inside front cover. Other relevant information is provided in the Essentials chapter, page 44.

takeaway meals.

$ El Rancho de Ferrito, *Pelagio B. Luna 647, T422481*. A very popular *parrilla*, where grilled meats and regional dishes such as *locro* can be enjoyed with local wines.

$ La Rosa, *Ocampo 149, T424693*. Dim lights in this old house create a relaxing atmosphere, where you can eat a huge variety of pizzas. More extensive menu Fri and Sat.

✪ Festivals and events

La Rioja City *p215, map p215*
It's worth planning your visit to coincide with one of La Rioja's 2 lively festivals. At the very popular **chaya** in early Feb, flour and basil are thrown around, while percussion music is played for 4 nights at the Estadio del Centro. Beginning on **New Year's Eve** and lasting 4 days, **Tinkunaco** is a vestige of the peacemaking efforts of San Francisco Solano; a colourful procession accompanies the meeting of the images of San Nicolas de Bari and the Niño Alcalde in front of the Cathedral.

⟳ Tour operators

La Rioja City *p215*
The most common destination, Talampaya, is usually offered together with Valle de la Luna (Ischigualasto Provincial Park) and occasionally Cuesta de Miranda in 1 or 2 days. Check if park entry, IVA (VAT) and meals are included in the price. Trips to the high mountains and plateaux in the west are restricted to good weather conditions, Sep to Apr.
Aguada, *T433695, talampaya_aguada@ciudad.com.ar* A full day excursion to Talampaya is US$40 pp for a minimum of 4 people in a vehicle. Also trips to Laguna Brava for a 3 day trip and charge US$500 for the whole group. Some English and French spoken.
Corona del Inca, *Pelagio B. Luna 914, T450054, www.coronadelinca.com.ar* A wide range of excursions: from a few hours to nearby places, US$15 pp, to 4 day trips all inclusive to the west in 4WD vehicles, US$280 pp; English spoken.
Néstor Pantaleo, *Ecuador 813, T422103*.

Pantaleo is an experienced photographer and runs 4WD trips to La Costa, Talampaya and the mountainous west, up to 6 people US$180 per day to Talampaya and Valle de la Luna. Several languages spoken.
Quebrada de los Cóndores, *T15686555 or office at Hotel de Turismo, reserva@quebradadelcondor.com.ar* Excursions, plus a trip to the south to spot condors in a deep ravine.

Chilecito *p217*
Chilecito is an excellent base not only for amazing treks in the Famatina mMountains, but also for 1 day trips to Talampaya and Valle de la Luna.
Alejo Piehl, *T/F425102, www.talampaya-turismo.8k.com* Experienced guide Alejo offers all inclusive 1 day tours to Talampaya (3-4 hrs walks along Quebrada don Eduardo and Cañón) and Valle de la Luna for US$30 pp and a variety of unforgettable 1 or 2 day treks (US$35) to the colourful slopes of nearby Famatina, visiting abandoned cable car stations on the way to the summit. Occasionally 1 day 4WD trips to El Oro or La Mejicana (4,400 m high) or 4 day 4WD excursions up to La Mejicana and walk down to Chilecito are on offer. Recommended.
Inka Ñan, *T425975*. Organizes excursions to the main attractions in the province.
Asociación Riojana de Turismo Rural, *Av Perón 668, T422828*. Guided visits to local farms, very cheap.

⊖ Transport

La Rioja City *p215, map p215*
Air
Airport VA Almonacid, *T439211*, 5 km northeast (access via San Nicolás de Bari and Route 5); taxi charges US$1.70 from centre, *remise* taxis are US$2-2.30. To/from **Buenos Aires**, Aerolíneas Argentinas, flights usually stop at **Catamarca** or **Córdoba**.

Bus
Terminal 7 blocks south of the Cathedral at Artigas y España, information *T425453*. Left luggage, 0600-2100, US$0.35 a day. To **Buenos Aires**, General Urquiza (*coche cama*), El Práctico, Chevallier, 15-17hrs, US$18-25.

● *Phone codes* La Costa, La Rioja: 03822; Chilecito, Villa Unión: 03825

To **Catamarca**, many companies, 2 hrs, US$3-3.50. To **Córdoba**, General Urquiza, El Práctico, Socasa, Chevallier, 6½ hrs, US$7, also *coche cama*.

To **Mendoza**, many companies, 8 hrs, US$10-12 and **San Juan**, same companies, 5-6 hrs, US$6.50-8. To **San Luis**, Socasa, 7½ hrs, US$9. To **Tinogasta**, **Fiambalá** and **Belén Robledo**, 3 weekly, 5-6 hrs, US$4-5. To **Tucumán**, several companies, 6 hrs, US$5.50-7. Facundo, El Cuyano, Arce or El Riojano go daily to several provincial destinations, mainly **Chilecito** (3 hrs, US$3), **Villa Unión** (4 hrs, US$3.50), **Vinchina** (5 hrs, US$4.50), **San Blas de los Sauces** (referred to as Los Sauces) and **Pagancillo**, close to access to **Talampaya** (3½ hrs, US$3).

Minibus (diferenciales or combis)

Popular alternative to buses, booked in advance, a few extra pesos, but usually faster and more frequent (though less on Sun) than ordinary buses. Arrivals and departures from their offices: El Zonda, *Dorrego 79, T421930*; to **Pagancillo**, **Villa Unión** and **Vinchina**. Interioja, *Rivadavia 519, T421577*; to **La Costa** and **Chilecito**. La Riojana and Family Bus, *Rivadavia 578, T435279*; to **Chilecito** and **Aimogasta**. Maxi Bus, *Rivadavia y Dávila (Esso petrol station), T435979*; to **Chilecito** and **San Blas de los Sauces**. Transal, *Lamadrid 116, T460596*; to **Dique Los Sauces** and **Villa Sanagasta**.

Car hire

Drive, *T15661168*. King's, at the King's Hotel (see address above), *T422122*.

Taxi

Remise taxis La Rioja, *Av Quiroga 1075, T426666, 425473*.

Chilecito *p217*

Bus

Station at La Plata y 19 de Febrero (1 block north of plaza). To **Buenos Aires**, El Práctico, *T425684*, and **General Urquiza**, *T423279*, 17 hrs, US$20. Both go via **Córdoba**, 7 hrs, US$8. To **San Juan**, Vallecito, 7 hrs, US$9. To **Mendoza**, Vallecito, 9½ hrs, US$10. To **La Rioja**, El Cuyano, 3 hrs, US$3. To **Villa Unión**, via Cuesta de Miranda, Ivanlor, 1 daily, 3-4 hrs, US$3.50.

Minibus

Several *combi* services depart at all times from La *Plata y 19 de Febrero*. To **Campanas**, US$2; to **Famatina**, US$0.80; to **Malligasta**, US$0.35; to **Nonogasta**, US$0.50; to **Sañogasta**, US$0.70. To **La Rioja**, US$3.50, also minibuses run by Interioja, from C Castro Barros (on plaza), *T425949*, La Riojana, *El Maestro 61, T424710* and Maxibus, *Mitre 138, T423134*.

Remise taxis

Niño de Gualco, *C La Plata (half block from bus station), T425444*. San Cayetano, *La Plata 162, T425050*.

Around Chilecito *p217*

Daily service with several **minibuses** (*combis*) from **Chilecito** to many of the villages in the valley. **Remise taxis** do a tour for US$6 to Famatina or Sañogasta.

Ivanlor runs the only regular service via **Cuesta de Miranda**, linking **Chilecito** and **Villa Unión**. The **Mogotes Colorados** are on the regular bus route from Chilecito to La Rioja.

⊙ Directory

La Rioja City *p215, map p215*
Airline offices Aerolíneas Argentinas, *Belgrano 63, T426307, F426385*.
Banks LECOP bonds and provincial bonds with the face of Evita are in circulation and changed 1 to 1 into pesos within the province; US$ cash changed at **Banco de Galicia**, *Buenos Aires y San Nicolás de Bari*, and at **Daniel**, exchange facilities at *Rivadavia 525*. Three more national banks on *Plaza 25 de Mayo*. **Communications Internet** Cool.com, *Pelagio B. Luna 684*. US$0.65/hr. Cyber Hall, *Rivadavia 763*. Good service with webcams, US$0.65/hr. Cyber más, *Rivadavia 909*. Open 24 hrs, US$0.35/hr. **Post office** Av. Perón 258; Western Union branch.

Chilecito *p217*
Banks US$ cash only changed at Banco Macro, *Castro Barros 50 (on plaza)*.
Internet Conexión, *San Martín y Castro Barros*. US$0.70/hr. Telecentro Telecom, *La Plata 167*. US$0.95/hr. **Post office** *Joaquín V. González y Pelagio B. Luna*; Western Union branch.

The Northwest

Introducing the Northwest

In a country rich in contrasts, no part has such extreme landscapes as Argentina's northwest. In the space of a day, a trip up the **Quebrada de Toro** takes you from the colonial city of Salta, with its plazas of tall waving palms, through forest-clad valleys, past mighty red mountains and on to the stark beauty of the high altitude puna, dotted with llamas and shimmering saltflats. Indigenous culture still thrives in **Jujuy**, the starting point for the **Quebrada de Humahuaca**. In this vast valley of ochre and terracotta rock, quiet oasis villages add a splash of green. From **Purmamarca** to **Humahuaca**, tiny churches are filled with treasures, Carnival is a riot and Easter is extravagantly celebrated. South of Salta, an exhilarating road snakes up the dramatic **Cuesta del Obispo** to the magical **Valles Calchaquíes**, home to sophisticated cultures before the Incas, whose marvellous ceramics fill every local museum. You'll find calm in the small villages of **Cachi** and **Molinos**, perfect for walking in the mountains or relaxing in lush valleys, with fields of scarlet peppers drying in the sun. **Cafayate**'s picturesque bodegas turn high altitude grapes into delicious wines, while the valley's weavers turn llama wool into the softest ponchos. There are fascinating pre-Incan cities at **Santa Rosa de Tastil** and **Quilmes**, at atmospheric **Las Pailas** and a hilltop fortress at **Tilcara** all commanding breathtaking views of the valleys below.

With three **national parks** protecting rich wildlife in the fabulously dense cloudforest jungle, grand **fincas** offering luxury and the country's finest horseriding, and remote rural hamlets where you can retreat from the modern world, the northwest is the most seductive part of all Argentina.

★ Don't miss...

❶ **Yavi and Uquía** Be dazzled by the stunning gold interior of Yavi's church seen in the lemony light from onyx windows, and angels in armour paintings in Uquía church, pages 255 and 259.

❷ **Maimará** See the stunning array of colours in Quebrada de Humahuaca in the late afternoon light, page 255.

❸ **Horse riding** Ride from the arid cactus-strewn mountains of Tilcara to the lush subtropical forest of cloudforest park Calilegua, page 255.

❹ **Salta** Walk around the romantic city at night, past colonial buildings and through plazas filled with tall palms, to Calle Balcarce, where live folklore music fills the air, page 228.

❺ **Finca El Bordo de las Lanzas** Relax completely in a luxurious and historical farmhouse, page 234.

❻ **Santa Rosa de Tastil** Visit the ancient ruins of the pre-Incan city, page 230.

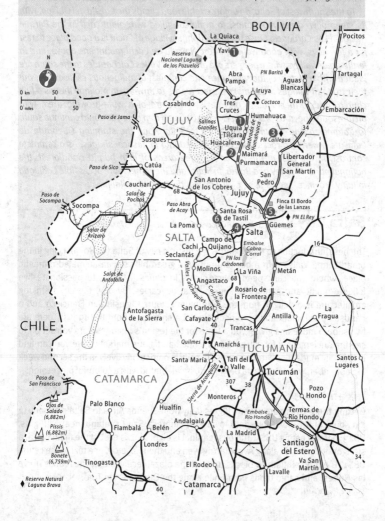

Salta Province

The province of Salta spans an extraordinary range of landscapes, from puna *populated only by llamas to the cloudforest humming with birdlife, and from hillsides of pink rock where cacti thrive, to valleys irrigated by the Incas to produce scarlet fields of red peppers. At the heart of the province the charismatic capital Salta makes the perfect introduction to these wonders. Its fine colonial buildings give the youthful city an air of elegance and a tangible history. And with its dramatic setting amidst the steep velvety mountains of the Valle de Lerma, the city invites you to explore further afield. The* Tren a las Nubes *takes you into the high altitude west, climbing past the secluded village of Campo Quijano through the open gorge Quebrada de Toro with its smattering of neat adobe houses, up into the deserts with shimmering salt flats, via some breathtaking bridges and viaducts. Alternatively, travel by road and stop at Santa Rosa de Tastil, where evidence of a pre-Incan city remains in an elaborate maze of walls and the marvellous ceramics which you can also see in Salta's anthropological museum.*

To the southwest of Salta, an unforgettable road climbs the Cuesta del Obispo, with its steep olive green mountains, to a plateau filled with giant cacti in the Parque Nacional Los Cardones. Close by, the delightful village of Cachi is a good place to rest for a few days, with good walking in the Navada de Cachi mountains above, and in fertile green valleys where peppers are grown. The Valles Calchaquíes to the south are loaded with a history of the resistance and conquest of indigenous civilisations, but their tranquil villages today make perfect places to unwind. In Molinos there's a fine church, and further south, Cafayate is the centre of a wine-growing area, with picturesque vineyards producing excellent wines. From here you could continue south to Catamarca and Tucumán, or return to Salta along the stunning Quebrada de Cafayate, where red rocks have been eroded into fantastical shapes. As a complete contrast, in the east of the region lie three areas of lush humid cloudforest, the national parks of El Rey and Baritú, in Salta, and the rather more accessible Calilegua in Jujuy Province, see page 247, all with wonderfully rich wildlife.

Salta City→ *Phone code: 0387 Colour map 1, B3 Population: 375,000*

The best introduction to this region is the historic city of Salta (1,280 m). Lying in the broad Lerma Valley with a backdrop of dark green hills it's an animated romantic place, where you can spend balmy nights in peñas listening to passionate live folklore music and eating the superb local delicacies. By day, the city's striking architecture is a delight, from the bold plum coloured Iglesia San Francisco and a handsome colonial Cabildo to neo-colonial architecture from the 1930s. There are two superb museums giving you a taste for the region's history before you set off to see the ancient sites for yourself, and a fine handicrafts market where you can find beautifully made blood red ponchos. The city is particularly lively in the second week of September, when the Fiesta del Milagro is celebrated with a colourful procession.

Ins and outs

Getting there There are several flights daily from Buenos Aires to Salta's airport, 12 km south of the city. Buses into town with **Empresa San Cayetano** meet all flights, US$3; or taxi costing US$5. The bus terminal is eight blocks east of the main plaza, a straightforward walk along Avenida Yrigoyen and then Caseros, or a taxi to the centre US$1. The train station, 10 blocks north of the plaza, receives only the tourist Tren a las Nubes, and cargo trains from Chile along the Quebrado de Toro. ▸▸ *See transport, page 238, for further details.*

Getting around The best way to get around Salta is on foot. Most of the famous examples of its splendid architecture lie within four blocks of the plaza, and by walking you can lap up its atmosphere. The main area for nightlife is north and west of the plaza along Balcarce, a delightful 10-block stroll passing attractive Plaza Güemes, or a five minute taxi ride. Frequent buses connect go to the outlying area of San Lorenzo. You'll be keen to explore the many attractions beyond the city, but it's worth allowing yourself a couple of days here to enjoy the nightlife and museums.

Tourist information The provincial tourist office, Buenos Aires 93 (1 block from main plaza), T431 0950, www.turismosalta.com, open weekdays 0800-2100, weekends 0900-2000, is very helpful, gives free maps, and advice, English spoken. Other websites: www.iruya.com and www.redsalta.com ▸▸ *For Sleeping, Eating and other listings, see pages 233-238.*

Salta

Sleeping			
Astur 1	Hostal The Cottage 4	Solar de la Plaza 19	La Casa de Güemes 5
Backpackers 2	Marilian 10	Terra Oculta 20	La Cocina del Pirata 6
Colonial 3	Munay 11	Victoria Plaza 21	La Terraza de la Posta 7
El Correcaminos 5	Petit 12		Plaza Café 10
El Lagar 6	Posada del Sol 14	**Eating**	Sociedad Española 9
Florida 7	Regidor 15	Doña Salta 1	Van Gogh Café 2
General Güemes 9	Res Balcarce 13	El Corredor de	
Gran Presidente 8	Res San Jorge 17	las Empanadas 3	**Bars & clubs**
	Salta 18	El Solar del Convento 4	La Vieja Estación 8

N

0 metres 100
0 yards 100

The first Spanish expedition, led by Diego de Almagro from Cuzco (Peru), entered Argentina in 1536 and soon a busy trade route was established through the Quebrada de Humahuaca, along which the Spanish founded a group of towns: Santiago del Estero, Tucumán, Salta and Jujuy. Throughout the colonial period these were the centres of white settlement and *encomiendas* were established to subdue the indigenous population of the valleys. Jesuit and Franciscan missions were also imposed, but resistance was fierce, especially in the Calchaquí and Humahuaca valleys, and as a result, this is one of the few areas in Argentina which retains a rich indigenous culture. Salta itself was founded in 1582 and became one of the viceroyalty's most important administrative centres, governing a wide area. The city also had an important role in the Wars of Independence between 1810 and 1821, when General Güemes led gaucho anti-Royalist forces to victory, utilising their detailed knowledge of the terrain and inventing the now famous red poncho which his men wore. Through the 19th century, Salta suffered a decline, since trade went direct to the country's new capital, Buenos Aires. Relatively little immigration and expansion here meant that the colonial buildings and layout of the city survived, boosted by neo-colonial architecture in the 1930's when there was a large influx. Today, Salta retains its old aristocratic upper class population, but has a more affluent middle class than its neighbour, Jujuy. The recession has hit hard here, however, and tobacco farming is giving way to tourism as the province's main earner.

Sights

After a couple of hours walking you can get a feel for the city. The heart is the Plaza 9 de Julio, richly planted with wonderful tall palm trees and surrounded by colonial-style constructions. The **Cabildo** of 1783 is one of the few to be found in tact in the country, and behind its pleasingly uneven arches is an impressive museum, the **Museo Historico del Norte** ① *Tue-Sat 0930-1330, Tue-Fri 1530-2030, Sat 1630-2000, Sun 0930-1300, US$0.70*. In a nicely laid out series of rooms around two open courtyards, the collection charts the region's history from pre-Columbian times, with particularly good displays on the Wars of Independence and Güemes leading the gauchos to victory. Upstairs, among some lovely religious art, is a fine golden 18th-century pulpit and Cuzco school paintings, while outside are carriages and an ancient wine press. Wonderful. Opposite, on the north side, is the cathedral, open mornings and evenings, built 1858-78, containing images of the Cristo del Milagro and of the Virgin Mary which are paraded in the also a huge baroque altar of 1807.

Walk east from the plaza, along Caseros, an appealing street full of slightly crumbling buildings. After a block, you'll come to the **Iglesia San Francisco** (1796) ① *Caseros y Córdoba, 0700-1200, 1730-2100*, one of the city's landmarks, with its magnificent plum coloured façade ornately decorated with white and golden stucco scrolls, and its elegant tower rising above the low city skyline. The interior is relatively plain, but there are some remarkable statues to admire such as the rather too realistic San Sebastián. Two blocks further east is the Convent of San Bernardo, Caseros y Santa Fe, built in colonial style in 1846, with an exquisitely carved wooden door dating from 1762. Sadly, you can't enter the convent as it's still the home to nuns, but they'll open up the little shop for you, with a little collection of quaint handicrafts. One block west of the Cabildo are three colonial mansions: the **Casa Leguizamón**, Caseros y Florida the **Casa Arias Rengel**, next door (now housing the Museo de Bellas Artes) and the **Casa Hernández**, Florida y Alvarado. A fourth, the **Casa Uriburu** (see below) lies one block east of the Plaza at Caseros 421.

Continuing along Casesros, you come to the wide open green space of Parque San Martín. It's not an elaborate park particularly, but there's a boating lake, and from here you can take the teleférico (cable car) up to **Cerro San Bernardo** (1,458 m) ① *daily 1000-1930, US$2 return, children US$1*, whose forested ridge looms over the east of the city centre. At it's base, behind the nearby Museo Antropológico, is an impressive statue by Víctor Cariño, 1931, of General Güemes, whose gaucho troops repelled seven powerful Spanish invasions from Bolivia between 1814 and 1821. The top of the hill can be climbed by a steep path (1,136 steps). At the top there is a great café with deck chairs and fabulous views.

Salta has several museums exploring its history but two are particularly recommended. **Museo Histórico del Norte** ① *housed in the splendid colonial Cabildo, at Caseros 549, Tue-Fri 0930-1330, 1530-2030 Sat 0930-1330, 1630-2000, Sun 0930-1300, US$0.60*, offers a well presented survey in rooms around tranquil open courtyards. Diaguitan funerary urns, elegant furniture, evocative portraits of Güemes, and a fine collection of religious art including Cuzqueno paitings and a painted 18th-century Jesuit pulpit.

Better still, the **Museo Antropológico** ① *follow Paseo Güemes behind the statue, and up Avenida Ejercito del Norte Mon-Fri 0800-1830, Sat 0900-1300, 1500-1800, Closed Sun. US$1, www.antropologico.gov.ar*, makes the perfect introduction to the pre-Hispanic cultures of the region, with a superb collection of anthropomorphic ceramics and beautifully painted funerary urns, and an exhibition on high altitude burial grounds complete with mummies, objects found at the ancient ruins of Tastil (see page 230) and most mysteriously, skulls flattened during the owner's life by wearing boards to squash the head (thought to confer higher intelligence). Fascinating. It's all very accessible and well laid out in a modern space with charming expert staff on hand, and there's even a video to watch at the end. Highly recommended.

One of the main pedestrian shopping streets, Florida, has two interesting little museums: **Museo de Bellas Artes** ① *Florida 20, T421 4714, Mon-Sat 0900-1900, Sun 10-1400, US$0.30*, has the city's fine collection of paintings, including superb Cuzqueño school works in a charming 18th-century building, and there are small exhibitions of Salteño painters and sculptors, and further down, **Museo de la Ciudad** 'Casa de Hernández' ① *Florida 97, T437 3352, Mon-Sat 0900-1300, Mon-Fri 1530-2000, closed Sun*, in a fine 18th-century mansion with a collection of old furniture, musical instruments and dull portraits, but a marvellous painting of Güemes. There are also a couple of historical houses worth visiting for a glimpse of wealthy domestic life, of which the best is **Museo Histórico Uriburu** ① *Caseros 421, Tue-Sun 0930-1330, 1500-2000*, situated in the former mansion of the Uriburu family, the most distinguished of salteño families, containing furniture, clothes and paintings. The **Museo de Ciencias Naturales** ① *Parque San Martín, Tue-Sun 1400-1800, US$0.30*, displays a bewildering number of stuffed animals and birds, though the armadillo collection is interesting.

Around Salta

One of the great experiences of staying in this beautiful region is the access to the landscape and its people offered by a stay at its estancias – often called fincas here. Spend the day riding or walking, enjoying delicious home grown meat on the *asado*, and stay, if you can afford it, for at least a night to unwind. Salta's tourist office has a complete list of *fincas*, as well as more simple (and cheaper) *casas de campo* and can advise. ▸▸ *For Sleeping, Eating and other listings, see pages 233-238.*

Northwest Salta and the Tren a las Nubes

The landscape in the northwest of Salta is among the most beautiful in the country. Most frequently seen by passengers in the famous narrow gauge railway *Tren a las Nubes*. Independent travellers can also explore this wonderful route to Chile over the *puna* by car or bicycle (for the adventurous), or with an excursion from Salta along the road that shadows the railway track, RN51. Allow at least a couple of days to get up to the *puna*, and stay a night – either at Santa Rosa de Tastil, to see the ruins, or at the quiet mining town of San Antonio de los Cobres. Beyond San Antonio, the Paso de Sico to Chile is the most used border crossing, however remote. The entire route is unforgettable. If cycling, note that much of the road is *ripio* and that there is no shade. The effects of altitude on the *puna* are not to be underestimated, since you'll be climbing to nearly 4,000m. You must take time for your body to adjust if you're going to exert yourself beyond a quick stroll.

> ▮ There are exciting alternatives to the over-long day on the Tren a las Nubes, such as Movitrack's Safari a las Nubes, or 4WD trips run by local guides. They'll include Argentina's best archaeological site at Santa Rosa de Tastil, and the dazzling salt flats of Salinas Grandes in the beautiful empty puna.

Route to Santa Rosa de Tastil

Leaving Salta's subtropical valleys via the jungly weekend retreat of **Campo de Quijano**, at Km30, which lies in a beautiful valley at the entrance to the gorge. This is an attractive place for a stop, with one *hostería* and several campsites (a municipal site at the entrance to Quebrada del Toro gorge, with hot showers, bungalows, plenty of room for pitching tents. (There is a recommended bus from Salta terminal). The road and track then climb along the floor of the Quebrada del Toro, fording the river repeatedly amidst densely growing *ceibo*, Argentina's national flower, with its striking fringed red blossoms. At Chorrillos, you'll see one of the identical wooden stations along the route with ovens built to heat steel fixings during the building of the track. From here the track zig zags as it climbs past tiny farmsteads lined with alamo trees, and up into the dramatic Quebrada Colorada to Ingeniero Maury at an altitude of 2,350 m, Km 65, where there is a police control point. From Km 96, now paved, the road climbs the Quebrada de Tastil, parting company from the railway which continues through the Quebrada del Toro. The road passes through the tiny hamlet of Santa Rosa de Tastil, where there are marvellous pre-incan ruins, and the only accommodation before San Antonio de los Cobres.

Santa Rosa de Tastil → *Phone code: 0387 Colour map 1, A2*

A picturesque little hamlet (3,200 m, Km 103) near the site of an important pre-Hispanic settlement of over 400 houses and over 2,000 people, believed to have been inhabited from 1336 to 1439 AD. There is a small **museum** ① *at the side of the road, daily 1000-1800, US$0.30*, which is recommended. It has some of the finds from this intriguing culture, among them a well preserved mummy, delicate jewellery

Tren a las Nubes

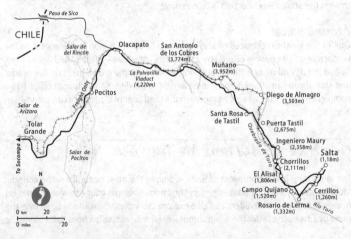

Paso de Sico

CHILE

Salar de del Rincón

Olacapato

San Antonio de los Cobres (3,774m)

Muñano (3,952m)

La Polvorilla Viaduct (4,220m)

Pocitos

Freight Only

Diego de Almagro (3,503m)

Salar de Arizaro

Santa Rosa de Tastil

Puerta Tastil (2,675m)

Tolar Grande

Ingeniero Maury (2,358m)

Salar de Pocitos

Quebrada de Toro

Salta (1,18m)

To Socompa

N

Chorrillos (2,111m)

El Alisal (1,806m)

Campo Quijano (1,520m)

Cerrillos (1,260m)

Rosario de Lerma (1,332m)

Río Toro

0 km   20
0 miles   20

Railway to the clouds

Salta is the starting point for the famous Train to the Clouds, one of Argentina's few running railways, a good way to experience the dramatic landscape of the *puna*.

The building of the track, which runs 570 km from Salta to Socompa on the Chilean border, was the outstanding achievement of Richard Maury, an engineer from Pennsylvania. Work started in 1921, and the first cargo train ran in 1941. Today the tourist train (passengers are not allowed on the cargo trains) runs only as far as La Polvorilla viaduct, just beyond San Antonio de los Cobres (see map), climbing from Salta at 1,200m above sea level, to 4,200m over a journey of 217km. The track took 20 years to build as the diesel engine hauls the 10 carriages up through the dramatic gorge Quebrada del Toro, negotiating several switchbacks ('zig-zags') and stunning 360° loops which allow it to gain height over a short distance and a gentler gradient. The climax is crossing the Polvorilla Viaduct, a delicate bridge across a mighty gorge, spanning 224m long and 63 m high; it feels like you're travelling on air, both scary and exhilarating.

To lay the narrow gauge track 1,000 men, little trained, worked with only the most basic tools, and through impossible conditions, detonating rock, and carving away at steep mountainsides through howling winds and snow.

At 15 hours, it's a long day. Leaving Salta at 0700, when it's cold (and dark in winter) to the cheerful accompaniment of *folclore* singers on the platform, the train edges to the entrance of Quebrada de Toro, steep forested mountains tinged with pink on top as the sun rises, and a light breakfast is served. The landscape changes gradually as you climb through the gorge, dotted with farms and adobe houses, to arid red rock where giant cacti perch, past sculptural mountains, coloured terracotta to chocolate, ochre and pink, to the staggeringly beautiful *puna*. The seven hours of the ascent are kept lively by chats from bilingual guides (English spoken, but French, Portuguese too, on request). Lunch is served, a light three-course meal, designed to be easily absorbed at altitudes, US$5, and the buffet car is open for snacks. You're likely to be affected at least slightly by the *apunamiento*, altitude sickness, and oxygen is on hand. At La Polvorilla viaduct, you can get out briefly to admire the construction, and buy locally made llama wool goods from the people of San Antonio. Don't bother haggling: these shawls and hats, socks and scarves are beautifully made and cheaper than in Salta. At San Antonio, the Argentine flag is raised to commemorate those who worked on the railway, and the national anthem is sung.

Once you've seen the glorious scenery, you may find the return journey tiring. Videos are shown in each carriage, and there's a constant stream of entertainment from folclore singers, a superbly rousing Andean band (Argentine tourists sing along, uninhibited), and a girl singing haunting *bagualas*. Bring a good book as the train chugs through the darkness at 32 km/hr.

The train costs US$70, runs April to November, Saturdays only, with some extra days in Easter and July, when you may need to book 1 month ahead. In summer, Tren Verano goes only as far as Diego Amargo, with trekking / horseriding offered, and lunch at Estancia El Golgota.

and a xylophone of sonorous rocks. The museum's guide will no doubt treat you to a rendition of *Fur Elise*, a wonderful anachronism. The ruins themselves are well worth visiting, with another museum 100 m from the site itself, open daily 1000-1800. Guides will show you around, but are not paid for this, so appreciate a tip.

San Antonio de los Cobres → *Phone code: 0387 Colour map 1, B2*

Beyond Tastil the road climbs through green hanging valleys where cattle roam, and then up over the Abra Blanca pass (4,050 m) where the landscape changes dramatically, suddenly vast and open, eerily empty. At Km 149 there is a turning which runs below the famous La Polvorilla railway viaduct. At the top of the pass, the road drops and runs across the *puna*, offering views of Chañi (5,896 m) to the left, Acay (5,716 m) to the right, and Quewar (6,102 m) in the far distance. San Antonio de los Cobres (3,774 m, 168 km northwest of Salta) is a simple remote mining town of low adobe houses situated in a shallow hollow. There's nothing much to do here but it's a good introduction to the reclusive life of the *puna*, and it does have its subtle charms. People are friendly and the handicrafts you're offered here are of high quality. Altitude sickness can strike heavily here, so avoid eating heavily or drinking alcohol until acclimatized. From here you could head back south along the RN 40 to La Poma and Cachi over the mighty Paso Abra del Acay (4,900 m). See page 239. This road should only be attempted in a 4WD – it is very rough in places. ➤➤ *For Sleeping, Eating and other listings, see pages 233-238.*

From San Antonio to Chile

From San Antonio there are two possible crossings to Chile. Closest, and most used, is the Paso de Sico. Due west on RN51. Alternatively, at Cauchari, take the RN27 following the railway line southwest across the giant Salar de Arizaro to the Chilean border Socompa. (From Cauchari, you could also strike out due south along a very lonely road to Antofagasta de la Sierra). The road runs through very beautiful scenery, salt flats with flamingos and impressive desert dotted with llamas and alpacas, but there are no services whatsoever, so obtain sufficient drinking water and fuel before setting out from San Antonio. Most traffic uses the Paso de Sico crossing and there is virtually no traffic on the other road.

A third crossing, via the Paso de Huaytiquina, shown on many maps, is closed. Because of snowfalls, these routes may be closed two or three times a year, for two or three days each time. Immigration and customs officials in San Antonio can advise about road conditions but truck drivers using it are more reliable. Paso de Sico, open daily 0800-2000, T498 2001. The Argentine immigration offices are in San Antonio de los Cobres at the other end of town from *aduana* (customs house). There is a police checkpoint at Catúa, 26 km east of Paso de Sico. There is a police checkpoint in Toconao but customs and immigration for Chile is in San Pedro de Atacama. No fresh food may be taken into Chile (search 20 km west of Paso de Sico). From Paso de Socompa a poor road runs to Pan de Azúcar, with roads west to the Pan American Highway, north via Salar de Atacama to San Pedro de Atacama. No fuel is available until San Pedro or Calama.

San Antonio to Purmamarca

Another road, the RN 40, leads north from San Antonio to Abra Pampas, or curves around to join a good route to Purmamarca in the Quebrada de Humahuaca (see page 255) which is recommended for a taste of the extraordinary landscapes. The road continues dead flat across the scrubby yellow *puna*, horizons all around edged with pinkish mauve or bronze mountains, with the occasional flock of llamas or cows grazing. It's either wonderfully meditative or unbearably monotonous, depending on your point of view, but the salt flats, which you'll reach in two hours from San Antonio, are certainly worth seeing. The huge expanses of dazzling white salt, crazy paved with crusted lines, are silent and other worldly. There are crossroads some 20 km north of the salt flats, where you could head west to Susques (in Jujuy, see page 247), up to Abra Pampa or follow the spectacular road to Purmamarca down broad slalom bends with breathtaking views of the valley below.

Listings: Salta *Phone code: 0387*

● Sleeping *map p227*

Hotels fill up during Jul and around Sep 10-16 because of the celebrations of *Cristo del Milagro*. Book ahead. Salta has a couple of the finest hotels in the country, plenty of youth hostels, as well as the luxurious estancias within an hour's drive.

L El Lagar, *20 de Febrero 877, T431 9439, ellagar@arnet.com.ar* A wonderful boutique hotel, beautifully decorated rooms filled with fine paintings, an excellent restaurant (guests only), wine tasting cellar, library and gardens with pool. Impeccable service. Complete peace, comfort and privacy. Email or phone to reserve in advance. Closed 20 Dec-10 Jan. Highly recommended.

L Hotel Solar de la Plaza, *Juan M Leguizamon 669, T431 5111, www.solardelaplaza.com.ar* An excellent hotel, and a calm oasis on the lovely palm filled Plaza Güemes, in the traditional house of an old Salteño family, this elegant place has faultless service, a great restaurant and gorgeous spacious rooms.

A Gran Hotel Presidente, *Av Belgrano 353, T/F4312022, reservas@grhotelpresidente .com.ar* Modern and chic, stylish entrance and bar, an excellent restaurant with great value fixed price menu for US$4, all year round pool, gym, and very plush rooms.

A Portezuelo, *Del Turista 1, T431 0104, www.portezuelohotel.com* Great views over Salta from its hill top position, welcoming comfortable modern rooms, a pool and a good restaurant. Also offers cheap deals (check website) and excursions.

B Salta, *Buenos Aires 1, T/F4310740, www.hotelsalta.com* This famous plaza side Salta institution, with its neo-colonial public rooms and splendid mosaics, has disappointingly dull bedrooms and lacks a warm welcome. The suites overlooking the plaza are marvellous.

C Marilian, *Buenos Aires 176, T/F4216700 www.hotelmarilian.com* Of the many C price range options, this is recommended for its excellent service. Modern and central, and though the rooms are simple, the bathrooms are smart and breakfasts are great.

C Regidor, *Buenos Aires 10, T431 1305*. Smart wood panelling everywhere, and though the rooms are small, this is welcoming and has a very decent restaurant.

D Colonial, *Facundo de Zuviria 6, T431 0805*. Basic. Ask for the larger rooms on the plaza.

D General Güemes, *España 446, T431 4800*. Just off the plaza, this is an old 1960s business hotel with surprisingly spacious very clean, dull rooms, all with bath and TV, breakfast included.

D Petit, *H Yrigoyen 225, T421 3012*. Handy for the bus terminal, this hotel has plain, pleasant rooms around a patio, basic breakfast.

D Posada del Sol, *Alvarado 646, T431 7300, www.hotelposadadelsol.com* This is the best in this category, with good service although the rooms are dated.

D Victoria Plaza, *Zuvira 16, T431 8500*. The plaza side location is the best thing about this hotel: which has the edge over the Colonial, with well equipped but unmodernized rooms, and a *confitería*.

E Astur, *Rivadavia 752, T421 2107*. A funny little place on a nice quiet street, friendly owners and good value for couples, with basic but clean rooms, handy for the *Tren a las Nubes*.

E Florida, *Urquiza 716, T421 2133*. Safe but a bit stark, close to the market. Rooms have bath and fan, making this a reasonable budget option.

E Munay, *San Martin 656, T422 4936, munayhotel@hotmail.com* This hotel is by far the best of the budget options. Beautifully decorated with small but smart bathrooms, warmly welcoming and

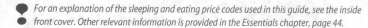

For an explanation of the sleeping and eating price codes used in this guide, see the inside front cover. Other relevant information is provided in the Essentials chapter, page 44.

breakfast included. Highly recommended.
E Res San Jorge, *Esteco 244 y Ruiz de los Llanos 1164, T/F4210443, hotelsanjorge@arnet.com* A homely place with parking, safe deposit, laundry and limited kitchen facilities, and horse and trekking excursions on offer. Bus 3 or 10 from the terminal to San Martín y Malvinas.

E Hostal Las Rejas, *Gral Güemes 569, T421 5971, www.lasrejashostel.galeon.com* Quite the best budget accommodation in Salta, there are lovely doubles **E**, and shared rooms, **G** pp, all with bath and very comfortable, with warm attentive service from the friendly English speaking owners who'll go out of their way to make you feel at home. Also laundry, free internet, and kitchen facilities. Central, peaceful, and highly recommended.

Youth hostels

G pp **Argentina Norte**, *Laprida 456, T430 2716, www.argentinanorte.com/hostel* Another new and comfortable hostel in a restored house, well-equipped kitchen, internet, TV room, English spoken.

G Backpackers, *Buenos Aires 930, T/F423 5910, www.backpackerssalta.com* The official youth hostel is 9 blocks or 30 mins walk from the plaza – or take Bus 12 from the terminal – but it's well run, and affiliated to Hostelling International. Small dormitories, laundry and kitchen and budget travel information. Noisy, crowded and popular.

G El Correcaminos, *Vicente Lopez 353, T422 0731, www.correcamminos.com.ar* A new and neatly kept hostel, 4 blocks from plaza. Modern 8 bed dorms, and 2 small double rooms, all with shared bathrooms, laundry, modern kitchen and a pleasant garden. Safe place to arrive at night.

G pp **Hostal The Cottage**, *Juramento 54, Salta, T421 3668, hostalthecottage@hotmail.com* 5 blocks from terminal, 4 from plaza, (also singles and quadruples), rooms have bath, hot water. Kitchen, internet, library, TV room, cheap excursions. Contact Adrian or Miguel.

G Terra Oculta, *Cordoba 361, T421 8769.* More of a party atmosphere with friendly small dorms of 8 and one double, a homely kitchen, laundry and a lively rooftop bar.

Around Salta *p229*

It's worth considering staying outside Salta if you're in search of more tranquillity.

A-B Hostería Punta Callejas, *Campo Quijano, 30 km west at the entrance to the Quebrada del Toro, T490 4086.* With breakfast, very clean and comfortable, a/c, pool, tennis, horseriding, excursions, meals.

B Hotel del Dique, *Dique Cabra Corral, T490 5112.* Extremely comfortable lakeside position, with a pool and good food.

C Selva Montana, *Alfonsina Storni 2315, T492 1184, www.selvamontana.com* Most highly recommended. Nestling high up in the lush leafy hills of San Lorenzo, just 15 mins by car from Salta. Complete comfort and peace in stylish rooms, with a pool, horses and walking on offer. Attentive service, helpful staff, wonderful. Take a taxi or bus *El Indio interurbanos* from terminal.

C Hostería Punta Callejas, *T0387-490 4086.* Comfortable with bath, a/c, pool, tennis, riding, excursions.

C Las Rias Bajas, *Dique Cabra Corral, T423 2832.* Economical new *hostería* with a lovely position, attractive pool, and trips to Cafayate and Cachi.

D Hostería de Chicoana, *on the way to Cachi, on the plaza in Chicoana at Espana 45, 47 km south, T/F4907009.* A pretty colonial building, with the added advantage of expert guide Martin Pekarek on hand. Www.argentinatravels.com

Estancias

In Salta estancias are known as fincas.

L pp **Finca El Bordo de las Lanzas**, *45km east of Salta, T490 3070, www.estanciaelbordo.com* Formal and luxurious, a taste of aristocratic life, with splendid horseriding and charming hosts. Highly recommended.

A pp **El Golgota**, *T490 4239, leave message.* In the Quebrada de Toro with stunning views and great walking, this colonial place has huge rooms, and a charming owner/guide.

A-B pp **Finca El Manantial**, *La Silleta, 25 km from Salta, T/F439 5506, elmanantial@arnet.com.ar* Beautiful views from the superbly decorated rooms in this historical estancia, offering swimming walking and riding on the estate.

A-B Finca Santa Anita, *Coronel Moldes 60km from Salta, T/F490 5050, clewis@salnet.com.ar*

The whole family makes you welcome on this prize-winning organic farm with superb goats cheese. A complete delight. Highly recommended. Beautiful views, swimming, sports including walks and horseriding. A complete delight. Highly recommended.
B Finca Quisto, *T424 3607, close to PN El Rey*. Offers horseriding amidst sub-tropical vegetation, with English speaking owners.
B Los Los, *just 40 km from Salta at the entrance to the valles Calchaquies, T431 7258, 156, www.redsalta.com/loslos Open Mar to Dec*. Most welcoming and highly recommended, beautifully situated on a hilltop with fabulous views, where you can completely relax. Spacious rooms, prettily decorated with old furniture, beautiful gardens with a pool. Unforgettable horseriding into the forested mountains of the huge *finca*, where you will be cooked lunch in a remote rustic lodge. Handy for the airport and Cachi.

Camping
Municipal Campsite, *Campo Quijano, 30 km west of Salta, at the entrance to Quebrada del Toro gorge*. Hot showers, bungalows, plenty of room for pitching tents. Recommended, bus from Salta bus terminal.

Santa Rosa de Tastila *p230*
Basic accommodation in shared dorms is available in the village for US$2 pp – ask at the museum.

San Antonio de los Cobres *p232*
C Hostería de las Nubes, *on the eastern outskirts, T490 9058, F490 9059*. A smart modern place with lovely comfortable rooms, including breakfast, restaurant. Recommended.
D Hospedaje Belgrano, *T490 9025*. Very friendly, evening meals.
D Hospedaje El Palenque, *Belgrano s/n, T490 9019*. Also café, family run.

⚐ Eating *map 227*

There are lots of great *peñas* serving good regional food at night along the north end of Balcarce. The cheapest *empanadas* and *humitas* are available from stalls in the lively municipal market, at San Martin y Florida,

but there are also lots of good places around the Plaza 9 de Julio for *empanadas*.
$$ El Solar de Convento, *Caseros 444, T421 5124*. One of Salta's finest restaurants and yet reasonably priced. You're greeted with a glass of champagne, the surroundings are elegant, and there's delicious *parrilla* and a fine wine list. Service is excellent.
$$ Hotel Portezuelo, *Del Turista 1, T431 0104*. Eat delicious food in this hotel restaurant with great views over the city.
$ Gauchos de Güemes, *Uruguay 750*. Excellent regional specialities at this *peña*
$ La Casona del Molino, *Caseros 2500*. Another *peña* in a crumbling old colonial house with good food and drink.
$ Doña Salta, *Cordoba 46 (opposite Iglesia San Francisco, with gaudy sign)*. In the house where Güemes lived, serving delicious *carbonada, locro* and other regional delicacies in attractive rustic surroundings, recommended and cheap.
$ El Corredor de las Empanadas, *Caseros 117, T422 0345*. Justifiably renowned, serves fabulous *empanadas* and delicious local dishes in attractive airy surroundings.
$ La Casa de Güemes, *Espana 730*. Atmospheric, serves *empanadas, tamale, humitas*, and *asado*, in the traditional way,
$ La Terraza de la Posta, *España 476*. A huge menu, but is recommended for *parrilla* and pastas, good atmosphere and friendly service, with an excellent value fixed price menu.

Cafés
There are lots of cafés on the plaza:
Plaza Café, *next to Hotel Salta*. This elegant café is more popular with *Salteños*, a nice spot for breakfast.
Van Gogh Café. Bright and popular with tourists. Good for coffee and breakfast.

Around Salta *p229*
Lo de Andres Juan Carlos Davalos and Gorritti, T492 1600. Fabulous restaurant. Great steaks and pasta.

⚑ Entertainment *map p227*

No trip to the northwest is complete without sampling its stirring *folclore* music, and you can eat *empanadas* and watch great musicians playing live in

Salta's *Peñas*. At the north end of Balcarce there are lots of good and lively places including: **La Vieja Estacion**, *Balcarce 885, T421 7727*. Particularly recommended for a great atmosphere.

Casa Güemes, *España 730*. Recommended, and frequented by *Salteños*.

La Casona del Molino, *Caseros 2500, T434 2835, Thu to Sat from 2200*. This is the most authentic place for spontaneous *peña*, where guests help themselves to guitars on the walls and play.

Balderrama, *San Martín 1126, 2200-0200*. Unless you're in a huge coach party and fond of audience participation, avoid this place. The entrance is expensive, US$2, and the food is poor.

⊛ Festivals and events

6-15 Sep, **Cristo del Milagro** (see above). 24 Sep, **Battles of Tucumán and Salta**. 16-17 Jun, **Commemoration of the death of Martín Güemes**: Folk music in afternoon and gaucho parade in mornings around his statue.

Carnival: Salta celebrates Carnival with processions on the 4 weekends before Ash Wednesday at 2200 in Av Belgrano (seats optional at US$2-4); also Mardi Gras (Shrove Tuesday) with a procession of decorated floats and dancers with intricate masks of feathers and mirrors. It is the custom to squirt water at passers-by and *bombas de agua* (small balloons to be filled with water) are on sale for dropping from balconies.

○ Shopping

Salta's main shopping streets are the parallel *peatonales* (pedestrianised streets) of Alberdi coming off the Plaza 9 de Julio, and Florida block to the west.

Disco, *Alberdi*. Big supermarket.

Mercado Municipal, *San Martín y Florida*. Wonderful place for cheap food; great fruit and veg and some handicrafts, is wonderful. Closed 1400-1700, and after 2100.

Mercado Artesanal, *San Martín 2555, on the western outskirts of the city in the Casa El Alto Molino, T421 9195, Mon-Fri 0800-2000, Sat 0900-2000. Take bus 2, 3, or 7 from Av San Martín in centre and get off as bus crosses the railway line*. If you're short of time, head straight for this lovely 18th-century mansion. Highly recommended for beautiful handicrafts made by craftsmen in the surrounding areas. Perhaps a little more expensive than if you buy them from a tiny village, but superb quality, and all under one roof. Look out for soft and warm llama wool socks, wonderful handwoven ponchos, delicate carved wood and weavings.

Librería Rayuela, *Buenos Aires 96*. Foreign-language books and magazines.

○ Tour operators

Unless you have your own transport, there are lots of places you will need to visit in an excursion of some kind. But bear in mind that distances are huge here, and you may end up spending many hours in a bus. All kinds of adventure tourism are on offer. All agencies charge similar prices for tours: Salta City US$9. Quebrada del Toro US$30, Cachi US$23, Humahuaca US$25, 2-day tour to Cafayate, Angastaco, Molinos, Cachi, US$40.

Conventional tours

There are plenty of agencies along C Buenos Aires, first couple of blocks from the main plaza, and advertising in the tourist office.

El Estar del Runa, *www.elestardelruna.com* Wonderful visits to local archaeological sites, great treks and unusual trips to visit rural families. All highly recommended for an insight into indigenous culture.

Tren a las Nubes, *Mitre 101, T432 2600, www.trenalasnubes.com.ar*

Movitren, *Caseros 447, T431 4984, F411264. Tren a las Nubes* excursions, and programme of tours.

MoviTrack, *Buenos Aires 28, T431 6749, www.movitrack.com.ar* A dynamic and well organized company offering many imaginative trips in special 4WD vehicles; highly recommended is their alternative to the *Tren a las Nubes* along the same route, with a fantastic range of landscapes from *selva* to *puna* all in one day, and friendly informative bilingual guides. Also more adventurous options, check website.

Saltur, *Caseros 485, T421 2012, saltursalta@arnet.com.ar* Efficient and recommended for local tours.

TEA, *Buenos Aires 82, T431 1722*. Offers well

organized tours to the usual places, plus Quilmes, Iruya, and some really creative combinations. Recommended.

Yaco, *Buenos Aires 39, T401 0970, toursalta@ yacoturismo.com* A wide range, small groups, English spoken.

Adventure tourism

Bici Tours, *156838067, biker_s_2000@ yahoo.com* Bike trips with range from around the city to the Valles Calchaquíes.

Hernán Uriburu, *Rivadavia 409, T431 0605.* Organizes trekking and horseriding expeditions, expensive but highly professional.

Martín Oliver, *T432 1013, F91052.* Adventure tourism guide.

Norte Rafting, *www.noreterafting.com* Offers fun and professional rafting trips along Rio Juramento to see dinosaur footprints.

Norte Trekking, *T436 1844, www.nortetrekking.com fede@norte trekking.com* Enormously experienced Federico Norte offers great trips to experience the Valles Calchaquíes, *puna*, mountains and *selva* in depth: he's one of the few authorised guides into El Rey cloudforest park, and his trips can combine trekking with 4WD, horse riding and rafting, personally tailored to the group's needs, and not expensive. Highly recommended.

Puna Expediciones, *Braquiquitos 399, T434 1875, punaexp@ciudad.com.ar* Well qualified and experienced guide Luis H Aguilar can also be contacted through the *Res San Jorge* – he organizes treks in remote areas, US$25 a day including transport to trekking region, food, porters. Highly recommended.

Ricardo Clark Expeditions, *Caseros 121, T421 5390.* Specialist tours for bird watchers, English spoken, books on flora and fauna in several languages sold. Highly recommended.

Salta Rafting, *T156856085, T431 6749 www.saltarafting.com* A range of rafting and kayaking excursions and arranges accommodation.

Turismo San Lorenzo, *Dávalos 960, T/F4921757, www.1turismosanlorenzo.com* Horseriding.

Air

The airport is 12 km south, T424 3115, reached by airport bus run by **Empresa San Cayetano**, T423 6629, US$2. Bus 22 to the airport from San Martín, US$0.35; don't be fooled by taxi touts who tell you there is no bus. Taxi from airport to bus station US$4.

LAB to **Santa Cruz** (Bolivia) twice a week, once via Tarija, continuing to Cochabamba. **Austral** and **Dinar** fly to **Buenos Aires**, 2 hrs, minimum. **Dinar**, Lapa, to **Tucumán**, also to **Córdoba** and **Mendoza**. Southern Winds to **Córdoba**, **Tucumán**, **Rosario**, www.turismosalta.com/paginas/datosutilies

Bus

The terminal is 8 blocks east of the main plaza, information T431 5227, is still being rebuilt, so services are limited, but there is a *confiteria*, toilets, *locutorio*, café, *panadería*, kiosks. T401 1143 for information.

Long distance To **Buenos Aires**, several daily, US$30, *semicama*, 20-22 hrs, **TAC**, **Panamericano, Brown, Chevallier, La Internacional** and other companies.

To **Córdoba**, several daily, 12 hrs, US$12-18, **Panamericano**, T401 1118, twice daily, **Veloz del Norte**.

To **Santiago del Estero**, 6 hrs, US$7. To **Tucumán**, 4½ hrs, several companies, including **La Veloz del Norte** recommended, US$6-8.

To **Mendoza** via Tucumán, several companies, daily, 17-20 hrs, US$17-22. To **Jujuy, Balut Hnos, La Veloz del Norte, Atahualpa** and others, hourly between 0600 and 2200, 'directo', US$2-3, 2 hrs.

To **La Rioja**, US$7, 10 hrs. To **Puerto Iguazú**, US$32, 24 hrs, daily. **Local** To **Quijano via Silleta**, hourly. To **Cafayate**, US$6, 3½ hrs, 2-4 daily. To **Santa María**, US$13, daily, to **Angastaco**, daily, except on Thu and Sat, to **Belén**, Wed, El Indio, T431 9389. To **Cachi**, US$5, 4-4½ hrs, 1-2 daily, to **Molinos**, US$7, 6½ hrs, every 2 days (sit on left) and to **La Poma**, US$7, 6½ hrs, 3 weekly (Marcos Rueda, T421 4447). To **Rosario de la Frontera**, US$2.50, 2½ hrs. To **San Antonio de Los Cobres**, 5 hrs, El Quebradeño, Mon-Sat 1500, Sun 1910, US$5.50.

International To **Paraguay** Direct service to **Asunción**, Empresa Sol, US$22 , overnight, 14 hrs. Alternatively travel to **Resistencia**, buses daily 1700, US$25 with La Veloz del Norte, Sáenz Peña or Panamericano, 12 hrs, then change.

To **Chile** To **Bolivia** To **La Quiaca**, on Bolivian border, about 10 buses daily, Atahualpa, US$27, 11 hrs (via Jujuy, prolonged stop), best change to Panamericano in Jujuy. Also **Balut**, 3 a day, US$23, 7 hrs. To **Orán**, 6 hrs, and Aguas Blancas for Bermejo, **Bolivia**.

Car hire

Avis, *at the airport, Route 51, T424 2289, salta@avis.com.ar* Efficient and very helpful, recommended; Europe Rent A Car, *Buenos Aires 186, T422 3609*; Hertz, *Caseros 374, T421 6785, foarentacar@arnet.com.ar* Ruiz Moreno, *Buenos Aires 1, T431 8049, in Hotel Salta*. Helpful.

Train

The station is at 20 de Febrero y Ameghino, 9 blocks north of Plaza de Armas, taxi US$2. Cargo trains no longer take passengers. **Tren a las Nubes** The Train to the Clouds runs between Salta and La Polvorilla viaduct once a week from Apr to Nov, weather permitting, and on additional days in the high season (Jan/Feb and Jul/Aug). It departs promptly at 0705, returning to Salta 2200, costs US$70 (US$50 to Argentine residents), credit cards not accepted. The train is a touristy experience (see box, page 231).

Santa Rosa de Tastila *p230*
El Quebradeño bus for **San Antonio de los Cobres** leaves Salta at 1500, but arrives too late to see the ruins. Taxis cost the same and are more efficient.

Directory

Airline offices Austral, *Caseros 475, T431 0258*. Dinar, *Buenos Aires 46, T/F4310606*. Lloyd Aéreo Boliviano, *Buenos Aires 120, T421 7753*. **Banks** Banks are open 0730-1300, all have ATMs (many on España). Banco de la Nación, *Mitre y Belgrano*, Banco de Salta, *España 550 on main plaza*, cashes TCs. **Communications** There are many fast and cheap **internet** places; Cibercom, *Buenos Aires 97, T422 2514*. There are many *locutorios* including Telecentro Zuviria, *Plaza 9 de Jul*. **Consulates** Bolivia, *Mariano Boedo 32, T421 1040*. Mon-Fri, 0900-1400 (unhelpful, better to go to Jujuy). Chile, *Santiago del Estero, T421 5757*. Paraguay, *Mariano Boedo 38, T/F4321401*. Friendly. Peru, *25 de Mayo 407, T431 0201*. **Cultural centres** Alliance Française, *Santa Fe 20, T421 0827*. **Useful** addresses **Immigration office** *Maipú 35, T422 0438*. **Medical** Hospital San Bernardo, *Tobías 69*. Emergencies T107. Tourist offices **Provincial Tourist Office (Emsatur)**, *Buenos Aires 93 (1 block from main plaza), T431 0950*. Mon-Fri 0800-2100, Sat/Sun 0900-2000. **Municipal Tourist Office**, *San Martín y Buenos Aires, T431 0641*. Open Mon-Fri 0800-2200, Sat/Sun 0900-2000.

Los Valles Calchaquíes

Dramatic, constantly changing and stunningly beautiful, Los Valles Calchaquíes are perhaps the most captivating part of Salta province. Starting to the south of San Antonio de los Cobres, the Río Calchaquí, rises at above 5,000 m on the slopes of the Nevado de Acay and drops from the stark puna through the mountains of the Sierra de Pastos Grandes to the west and the richly vegetated Cumbres del Obsipo to the east. The first village is La Poma, but you're more likely to start exploring at the pretty oasis town of Cachi, reached from Salta by a breathtaking drive. South from Cachi, there are unspoilt oases dotted along the valley, Molinos Seclantás, Angastaco and San Carlos, reached by ripio road RN 40. There are extraordinary rock formations at Quebrada de las Flechas, just north of the more established tourist centre of Cafayate, surrounded by vineyards. South of here, the valley and the R40, continues to Santa María and Amaichá, described in Tucumán, see page 271.

Ins and outs

The valleys can be reached by bus from Salta, with daily departures to Cachi and several daily to Calafate via an alternative route, paved RN 68. Five days a week there are buses from Cachi to Molinos, but from here to Angastaco buses run just once a week, as the road is rough, just passable in an ordinary vehicle, but easier in a 4WD. South from Cafayate, there is a daily service.

History

The valleys of the Río Calchaquí and its tributaries were densely populated in pre-Hispanic times, by a series of sophisticated peoples whose ceramics fill the small museums throughout the region. After the defeat of the indigenous population in the Calchaquí Wars, the Spanish established missions and *haciendas* in the valley. Some of these *haciendas* surivived until the 20th-century, before being seized by the Perón government in the 1940s. During the colonial period the valley prospered, providing pasturage for mules and herds of cattle *en route* over the mountain passes into Chile and Alto Perú (Bolivia). After independence lower parts of the valley became the chief wheat growing and wine-producing area for the provincial capital but the local economy declined in the late 19th-century when the building of railway lines linking Salta with the south brought cheap wheat from the pampas and when local wines were hit by the expansion of wine production in Mendoza.

La Poma to San Antonio de los Cobres

La Poma (3,015 m), with modern adobe houses and a population of 300, below the massive Combre del Libertador General San Martín (6,380 m), is the first village in the valley and 5 km to the west of Route 40. The old village was destroyed by an earthquake in 1930: its ruins lie 2 km north at La Poma Vieja. North of La Poma, Route 40 continues over the Paso Abra del Acay (4,900 m), Km 282, the highest pass in South America negotiable by car. Road conditions vary depending on the weather and whether the bulldozer has passed recently, so a high clearance 4WD vehicle is advised. The critical part is south of the pass at Mal Paso, Km 257, where summer rains can wash the road away. No buses on this road. North of the pass the road runs across the *puna* to San Antonio de los Cobres (see above), Km 324.

Salta to Cachi

Cachi is 170 km west of Salta, along one of the most unforgettable routes in Argentina. Leaving Salta by the RN68 to the south, turn right at El Carril, 37 km, via Chiciana, where you could stay the night in *Hostería de Chicoana* , or in the splendid *Finca Los Los* nearby.

From Chicoana, the road enters the fertile leafy gorge of Quebrada de Escoipe, and a good wide *ripio* road hugs the mountains as it snakes up the breathtaking Cuesta del Obispo. Here you'll pass tiny hamlets of adobe houses, sometimes climbing through low cloud with vast bronze green velvety mountains revealed before you. As you round the head of the valley, with its panoramic views, you might like to take the turning off down to the Valle Encantado, an eerie fascinating place for a picnic amongst bizarre wind-sculpted terracotta rocks. Beyond the arid Piedra del Molino pass (3,347 m), the road runs west along a dead-straight stretch known as **La Recta del Tin-Tin**), through the **Parque Nacional Los Cardones**, at altitudes between 2,700 and 5,000 m, intended to protect the huge candelabra cacti. Walking amongst these giant sentinels is extraordinary experience. To spend some time in the park, take the 0700 Marcos Rueda bus from Salta towards Cachi, get off at La Recta del Tin-Tin and catch returning bus around 1600. There are no *quardeparques* around, and no services. Camping is officially not allowed, 11 km before reaching Cachi, there's the small village of **Payogasta** with Hosteria de Payogasta, T496034. ▸▸ *For Sleeping, Eating and other listings, see pages 243-246.*

⁞ Calchaquí Wars

Though you might find it hard to believe today, the beautiful and peaceful Calchaquí valleys southwest of Salta were the scenes of the strongest resistance to the Spanish rule in the Argentine northwest, and fierce bloody fighting. In 1630, following the failure of Jesuit missionaries to Christianise the local indigenous peoples, the Spanish Governor of Tucumán tried to bring the under the control of the Spanish landowners. The uprising that followed quickly spread beyond the valley, and was only ended with the arrival of reinforcements from Chile. Chamelin, the indigenous leader of the uprising, was hanged and quartered, his head being exhibited in La Rioja, and his right arm in Londres.

A second uprising in 1657 was sparked by the arrival of a Spanish adventurer, Pedro de Bohórquez, who claimed to be a descendent of the last Inca. The Governor of Tucumán responded to his arrival by clearing the valley of its inhabitants: 5,000 people were taken prisoner, and 11,000 more were dispersed throughout the northwest as gifts to Spanish settlers.

Cachi → Phone code: 03868 Colour map 1, B2 Population: 7,200

Cachi (2,280 m, Km 180) is a beautiful tranquil town in a wide green valley at the foot of the majestic Nevado del Cachi (6,380 m). Founded in 1694, it had been a Diaguita settlement long before the Incas arrived in 1450, and the extensive irrigation channels they built to catch the Nevada's snowmelt are still used to water huge fields of peppers. These are an amazing sight when harvested in April and laid out to dry in huge scarlet squares against the arid mountains beyond.

Cachi has a pleasingly simple church, the **Iglesia de San Jose**, whose roof and lecterns are made of cactus wood, and next to it, there's a fascinating survey of pre-colonial Calchaquí culture in the **Museo Arqueológico** ① Mon-Fri 0830-1930, Sat/Sun1000-1300, US$0.30, with painted funerary urns and an intriguing cat/man petroglyph. With its sunny climate, Cachi is the perfect place for a few days rest, but there are satisfying walks in any direction, and panoramic views from its spectacularly sited hill top cemetery, just 20 minutes' walk from the village.

A helpful **tourist office** on the plaza has a useful leaflet and map, open daily 0900-1200, 1500-2000, and also houses an excellent handicrafts shop where you can buy wonderful weavings. There's an ATM on the plaza at Güemes and Ruiz de los Lanos.

Around Cachi There are walks to **La Aguada**, a pretty village 6 km southwest at the head of the lush valley; leave town by Calle Benjamin Zorillo at the southwest of the plaza, and walk along the *ripio* track. There's wonderful accommodation here at *El Molino* and *Samay Huasi* – see Sleeping below. **Cachi Adentro**, on the other side of the valley has more fine views. It's a four-hour walk up into the foothills of Nevada de Cachi to see ancient ruins at **Las Pailas**, 18 km northwest, with more breathtaking views and huge cacti set against snow-topped Andean peaks. Alejandro Jiminez is en experienced mountain guide in the region, who can take you up the surrounding mountains; T0387-439 6035, alejandro@salnet.com.ar ▸▸ For Sleeping, Eating and other listings, see pages 243-246.

Molinos → Phone code: 03868 Colour map 1, B2 Population: 2,419

The road continues from Cachi via the hamlet of Seclantás, with its colonial style houses, and a church dating from 1835. There's just one place to stay here, **La Rueda**, T498041. Some 52 km from Cachi, you come to the village of Molinos (2,000 m), hidden away 1 km off Route 40 at Km 118 in its bowl of craggy mountains. A peaceful place, with a wide plaza and neat adobe houses, this is an idyllic retreat for walking. Founded in 1659, it has a fine church dating from 1692, and a simple gold *retablo*, and contains the mummified body of the last Royalist governor of Salta, Don Nicolás Severo Isasmendi. The house he built, opposite the church, is now an elegant place to stay. For a pleasant two-hour walk, leave the village behind the church, crossing the river bed, and then climbing the hill opposite, from which there are views of Molinos and surrounding country. For advice on who's renting rooms, there's a tourist office in the municipalidad on the plaza at 9 de Julio s/n, open 0900-1300, and 1600-2100 in low season, otherwise 0800-2200. Molinos celebrates *La Virgen de la Candelaria* in February, with processions, music and handicrafts.

Angastago → *Colour map 1, B2 Population: 600*

From Molinos the road is rough *ripio*, manageable in a hired car, as long as it hasn't rained. The landscape is beautiful, tiny settlements with green fields and orchards, against the backdrop of mountains. Angastaco (1,900 m) is a modern village 2 km off Route 40 at Km 77, less picturesque than Cachi, with an archaeological museum in the Centro Cívico. The church is modern, but a much older one, the **Iglesia del Carmen de Angastago** (1800) lies about 8 km further north on the Finca El Carmen. This area is famous for *vino patero*, a sweet wine, red or white, which is supposed to be made by treading the grapes in the traditional manner: sample it at Señor Flore's house close to the bridge in Angastaco. The *Fiesta Patronal Virgen del Valle* is held on the second weekend of December, with processions, music, dancing, gauchos and rodeos. There is tourist information at the Municipalidad on the plaza, Mon-Fri 0900-1300. ▸ *For Sleeping, Eating and other listings, see pages 243-246.*

San Carlos → *Colour map 1, B2 Population: 1,500*

The next stretch of road through the Quebrada de las Flechas (the gorge of arrows) to San Carlos is extraordinary, and you'll want to stop frequently to photograph the strange rock forms in this lunar landscape. Massive rocks eroded into sharp peaks, jutting like giant vertical fish flakes into the blue sky. San Carlos (1,710 m, Km 24) is a pleasant place, and though it took the Spanish three attempts to overcome indigenous resistance to a settlement on this site, it was the most important village in the valley until the growth of Cafayate. The main buildings are on the pretty plaza, including the church, the largest in the valley, which was built between 1801 and 1860, and there's a small **archaeological museum** ① *daily 1000-1400*, nearby which contains a mummified infant, and two (full) funerary urns. Also on the plaza are artisans' shops and workshops and a craft market.

Cafayate → *Phone code: 03868 Colour map 1, B2 Population: 8,432*

Cafayate (1,660 m) sits at the head of a wide valley where the rivers Santa Maria and Calchaquies meet, with mountains on all sides, and it's a good base for exploring the dramatic scenery. It has a well developed tourist infrastructure, and just 186 km south of Salta, on the faster RN68, it's a popular excursion destination. Surrounded by vineyards, it's also an important centre of wine production and home of renowned bodegas such as Etchart and Michel Torino's La Rosa. The torrontes grape, grown uniquely in Argentina, flourishes in the 350 days of sunshine received here each year, and bodegas organize free tours and tastings for you to try their produce, while delicious local food can be eaten at the plaza's many restaurants. ▸ *For Sleeping, Eating and other listings, see pages 243-246.*

Getting there and around There are several buses daily from Salta along the fast RN68, and many excursions, usually including bodega visits. The more scenic route is via Cachi and the Valles Calchaquíes (see above) but the road is rough *ripio* and there's only one bus a week between Molinos and Angastac. Cafayate can also be visited by organized on an excursion from Salta, US$40, including lunch and visit to a bodega. Cafayate is easy to get around on foot, with restaurants and shops located around the main plaza.

Tourist information There's a tiny but informative cente in a hut on the norhwest corner of the central area of the plaza, open daily 0800-2200. They have a good map and accommodation list, and can direct you to bodegas.Tour operators can be found along Calle Gral Güemes – note that this street changes names from Norte to Sur across the plaza, and identical numbers can be found on both sides.

Sights

Museums aren't Cafayate's strong point; it's much more interesting to explore the landscape and the bodegas, but there's the **Museo de la Vid y El Vino** ① *on Güemes Sur, two blocks south of the plaza, daily 0800-2000,* with old old wine-making equipment and a display on the history of wine. The **Museo Arqueológico Rodolfo I Bravo** ① *Calchaquí y Colón, open on request (T421054), US$1,* is tiny but has some beautiful funerary urns, black ceramics from the fifth century, and Inca pieces too, well worth seeing if you haven't come across them elsewhere.

Bodegas

There are several bodegas around Cafayate, all of which can be visited, and all are shown on the tourist office's map. Belonging to Michel Torino, in a stylish setting with superb wines is **Bodega La Rosa** ① *at the junction of Rutas 68 and 40, T421201, www.micheltorino.com.ar,*

Cafayate

To Cachi & Molinos

To Bodega Etchart, Quilmes, Tafidel Valle & Tucumán

with hourly visits Mon-Fri 0900-1200, 1400-1600, Sat/Sun 0900-1300, also accommodation (see below). **Etchart** ①*2 km south on Route 40, tours daily, but ring first to book, T421310* is the other famous name here with excellent wines. Also ask about their boutique *bodega*, the diminutive **San Pedro de Yacochuya**. Also at Yacochuya, **La Finca Domingo** is a good place to visit with handicrafts and ruins as well as the bodega, and views. Smaller, but worth exploring, are: **Vasija Secreta**, (on outskirts, next to *ACA hostería*), T421503, perhaps the most interesting because it is the oldest in the valley, English spoken, and **Domingo Hermanos**, 3 blocks south of the plaza on 25 de Mayo.

Around Cafayate

Apart from exploring the Quebrada de la Flecha or the Quebrada de las Conchas, with their rock formations, there are places to walk, cycle or drive to from the town itself. **Cerro San Isidro**, 5 km west, has cave paintings and views across the Aconquija chain in the south and Nevado de Cachi in the north. And behind it, the waterfalls of **Rio Colorado** are a pretty place for bathing in summer. For a stroll and a good view, take V. Toscano west out of the centre up to **Cerro Santa Teresita**, 2 km each way. ▶▶ *For Sleeping, Eating and other listings, see pages 243-246.*

Quebrada de Cafayate

Heading north from Cafayate, the RN 68 enters the gorge of the Rio Colorado, with its rock formations of eroded clay mountains, red, terracotta and sand. At the start a river winds through the valley, and then the road climbs up through mountains recognizable for the names you see at the side of the road: Los Castillos (The Castles) Km 20, El Obelisco (The Obelisk), Km 23, El Fraile (The Friar) Km 29, El Sapo (The Toad) Km 35, El Anfiteatro (The Amphitheatre) Km 48, and La Garganta del Diablo (The Devil's Throat) Km 49. There's lots of bird life to be spotted, including *ñandúes* (rheas). As you climb, the mountains become more intricate structures, colours change to chocolatey fudge, dark and richly textured. Vegetation becomes denser as you near Salta, with a river winding by your side.

If you haven't got a car but want to experience the Quebrada, take a bus from Cafayate towards Salta, and get off at Los Loros, Km 32, or at the Garganta del Diablo, walk back, and catch a return bus from Salta. Or, hire a bike, take it on the 0545 El Indio bus and cycle back.

Embalse Cabra Corral

North of the Quebrada the road runs along the west side of the Embalse Cabra Corral through Col Moldes and El Carril to Salta. Cabra Corral, 81 km south of Salta, is one of the largest artificial lakes in Argentina; offering water skiing, fishing, camping site and restaurant; the **Hostería Cabra Corral**, T/F4905022, is 4km from the lake, offering half board.

Listings: Los Valles Calchaquíes

🛏 Sleeping

La Poma *p239*
D **Hostería La Poma**, *T491003*. Breakfast included, also serves meals, and welcoming.

Salta to Cachi *p239*
A **Finca Los Los**, *40 km from Salta at the entrance to the Valles Calchaquies, T431 7258,* www.redsalta.com/loslos Open Mar to Dec. Fabulous hilltop views, charming rooms, beautiful gardens, pool. Unforgettable horseriding into the forested mountains to eat *asado*. Handy for the airport and Cachi.
C **Hostería de Chicoana**, *in Chicoana, 47 km south, T490 7009, martinpek@salnet.com.ar* A charming rather bohemian colonial-style place, with simple rooms around a leafy

courtyard, English and German spoken, adventure excursions and horses for hire.

Cachi *p240*

C **ACA Hosteria Cachi** *at the top of Juan Manuel Castilla, T 491904, www.hosteria cachi.com.ar* Comfortable modern rooms, great views from its hilltop position and a pool. Also rooms designed for wheelchair users. The restaurant serves excellent food, recommended for non residents too, who can use the pool if they eat lunch.

C **El Cortijo**, *just opposite the ACA, on Av Automovil Club s/n, T491034, www.hostal elcortijo.com.ar* For something really special El Cortijo is highly recommended. Its charming rooms are full of carefully chosen art, exude a relaxed homely feel, and the owners are warmly welcoming.

C **Hostería Llaq'ta Mawka**, *Cnel. Ruiz de los Llanos s/n, (20 m from the plaza). T491016, hostal_llaqta_mawka@hotmail.com* One of Cachi's oldest buildings, beautifully renovated, a new welcoming *hostería* with very comfortable rooms, pool, huge breakfasts, and helpful local owners who can give tourist information and arrange collection from Salta, trekking and horse riding. Recommended.

E **Hospedaje Don Arturo**, *C Bustamente s/n, T491087.* Homely, and welcoming, with small but very clean rooms on a quiet old street, signposted from the plaza.

G **Hospedaje El Nevado de Cachi**, *Ruiz de los Llanos y Federico Saurez, T491063.* The cheapest option right next to the bus stop. Characterful with impeccable small rooms, all with bathrooms, arranged around a central courtyard. Recommended.

G **Hostal de Turismo**, *10 km south at La Paya, clearly signposted from the road, T491139.* A restored 18th-century house with a pool, all rooms with bathroom.

Camping

Municipal campsite, *Av Travella s/n, T491053*, with pool and sports complex, also *cabañas* and albergue.

Around Cachi *p240*

A **El Molino de Cachi Adentro**, *4 km out of Cachi on the road to La Aguada, T/F491094,*

www.elmolinodecachi.com The most luxurious choice in the area, this is a beautifully restored 300-year-old mill with lovely views from its garden and pool, exquisitely tasteful rooms, and superb food. Nuny and Alberto Durand are charming (and bilingual) hosts, and will happily collect you from Salta airport, arrange personally designed tours on horseback or 4WD.

D **Samay Huasi**, *on the road to La Aguada, just 1 km further on from El Molino, T15639729, samayhuasi@ciudad.com.ar* Fabulous views and lovely simple rooms with nice bathrooms – a laid back friendly place.

Molinos *p240*

B **Hostal Provincial de Molinos**, *T494002, hostaldemolinos@uolsinectis .com.ar* Huge simple rooms with magnificent views arranged around big courtyards in this historic house. Good meals also available, and the guide in residence Raul Goytia also arranges horseriding and fishing nearby. Highly recommended.

F pp **San Pedro Nolasco de Los Molinos**. The local association of handicrafts producers, also has rooms to rent, with shared bath, with visits to see vicunas.

F pp **Hospedaje San Agutín**, *Sarmiento y Abraham Cornejo, T494015.* The nuns here have a dormitory with beds, shared bathroom.

Camping

The **municipal campsite** is in the sports complex, *Alberdi y Mitre, T494003*, which also has *cabañas* for 2. Hot showers, electricity, US$1 per tent, US$7 per *cabaña* per night. There are various simple restaurants around the plaza.

Angastago *p241*

D **Hostería de Angastaco**, *T15639016.* Breakfast, negotiable in low season. Rooms are basic but comfortable and this is especially recommended for its warm welcome. Pool, and meals on request, helpful with information on the region.

E pp **Casa de Alojamiento El Cardón**, *T491123, towards the bridge off the plaza.* Breakfast extra, good, clean and hospitable.

San Carlos *p241*

E **Hostería de San Carlos**, *on the plaza*, *T495071*. With bath, without breakfast.

E pp **Residencial Guemes**, *T495011*.

Camping

The **municipal campsite** is well tended with plenty of shade.

Cafayate and around *p241, map 242*

Cafayate is popular, so book ahead in holiday periods (Jan, Easter and late-Jul). There's lots of accommodation in Cafayate, a lot of it over-priced, though much cheaper off season.

A **Bodega La Rosa**, *Rutas 68 and 40, T421201, www.micheltorino.com.ar* Luxurious, and recommended is this quiet retreat set in gorgeous gardens, with comfortable spacious rooms, fine food and excellent wines.

C **Los Sauces**, *Calchaqui 62, T421158*. Next best is the modern directly behind the cathedral, with small but tasteful rooms, breakfast included.

D **Asembal**, *Güemes Norte y Almagro, T421065*. Attractive rooms all with bath, good restaurant.

D **Asturias**, *Güemes Sur 154, T421328, asturias@infonoa.com.ar* Run down and uncomfortable, popular with coach parties.

D **Briones**, *Toscano 80, on the main plaza, T421270*. A colonial-style place, open in high season only. Good value and welcoming.

D **Hostería Cafayate**, *T421296*. The best accommodation in the town itself is at this *ACA hostería*. Comfortable rooms, nicely decorated, around a colonial-style patio. Reasonably priced restaurant and pool (summer only).

D **Tinkunaku**, *Diego de Almagro 12, 1 block from plaza, T421148*. Very pleasant spacious rooms, with weavings on the walls.

E **Confort**, *Güemes Norte 232, T421091*. Friendly people in this slightly kitsch place with simple rooms, also has cabañas A-B, sleep 6, with kitchen, pool, heating.

E pp **Hostal del Valle**, *San Martín 243, T421039, www.NorteVirtual.com* Highly recommended for comfort and great value, this homely *hostal*, has beautifully maintained spacious rooms, with bath, around lovely plant-filled patio.

F pp **Cafayate Youth Hostel**, *Güemes Norte*

441, on the left as you enter the town, T421440. Small, but welcoming, with hot water, a couple of double rooms (without bath) English and Italian spoken. Organizes trekking. Also well equipped *cabañas* with TV and pool.

F pp **El Hospedaje**, *de Niño y Salta, T421680*. Simple but pleasant rooms, good value.

F **Hostería Docente**, *Güemes Norte 160, T421810*. A great cheap place to stay. Clean rooms, with bath, but not breakfast. Central.

Chalets Seis, *Av Güemes Norte 232, contact Hector Perez, T421091*. Well equipped *cabañas* with TV and pool, contact Hector Perez, Av Guemes Norte 232, T 421091.

Camping

Threre is a well maintained **municipal site**, *on the southern outskirts of RN40, T421051*, with hot water, a pool, and bungalows for rent, E for 4 people. More appealing is the quieter **Camping Luz y Fuerza**, *T421568, also on RN40, south of the town.*

❼ Eating

Cachi *p240*

Hostería ACA is the best choice, see above, but there are a couple of places on the plaza:

Oliver Café. Sandwiches, juices and ice creams in a friendly atmosphere.

Confiteria El Sol, *next door to Olivier*. Serves good cheap regional food.

Cafayate and around *p241, map 242*

Cafayate has lots of choices around the plaza, some huge and prepared for coach parties. In the summer, lots lay on live music while you eat. These are recommended:

$$ **El Rancho**, *Toscano 3, T421256*. The best mid-range option. A traditional restaurant serving *parrilla* and good regional dishes.

$$ **La Carreta de Don Olegario**, *Güemes Norte y Quintana, T421004*. Huge and does good set menus for the usual meat dishes and pastas.

$ **Confitería Bar Las Vinas**, *Güemes Sur 58*. Open all day, serving everything from breakfast to cheap *lomitos*.

$ **El Rincón del Amigo**, *on the plaza at San Martín 25*. Extremely cheap with great set menus and *empanadas*.

$ **El Comedor Criollo**, *Güemes Norte 254*. A small *parrilla*, recommended.

$ Las Dos Marias *next door to El Rincón.* Seriously cheap, small and unimposing, but serves good food.

Ice cream parlours
Helados Miranda, *Güemes Norte 170.* Cafayate's unmissable treat is this fabulous home-made ice cream. The creative owner makes delicious wine-flavoured ice cream.

Shopping

Cachi *p240*
There are some fine handicrafts to be found. There's the **Calchaquí tapestry exhibition** of Miguel Nanni on the main plaza, silver work at **Jorge Barraco**, *Colón 157, T421244.* Oil paintings, woodcarving, metalwork and ceramics by **Calixto Mamani** can be seen in his gallery, *Rivadavia 452,* or contact him at home (*Rivadavia 254*). Ceramics are also made by **Manuel Cruz**, *Güemes Sur 288* (the building itself is worth seeing). Local pottery is sold in the **Mercado Municipal de Artesanía** on the plaza.

Tour operators

Cachi *p240*
Metropolitan tours, *Güemes Norte 128, a block from the plaza, T422130.* A good range of tours, including to Quilmes, with guides and translators, and horse riding treks. Also rents bikes.
Fernando Gamarra, *on the corner at Benjamín Zorrilla y Guemes, T0387-155005471, or T0387-4317305, laspulgas@copaipa.org.ar* Conventional trips in vehicles, with an option on trekking: around Cachi, to Las Pailas, La Poma and Seclantás, including the beautiful Laguna de Brealito. Knowledgeable, reasonably priced, especially if divided amongst a group.
Mountain guides: **Oscar Valenzuela**, *at Artesania Kuyamasi (opposite the ACA hostería), T15639055.* Specializes in trekking to Las Pailas, La Paya, Cerro de la Virgen, using his own vehicle to reach the treks. US$5.30 per person for half a day's trip. Minimum 3 people. Local guide **Walter Tolaba** (known as 'Patacon') is an expert on the mountains, and organizes major treks to the Nevada de Cachi, as well as day walks. Ask at the archaeological museum.

Transport

Cachi *p240*
Bus To **Salta**, Marcos Rueda, T491063, leaves daily at 0900 and 1500, 4 hours, US$5. To **Molinos** 1200 daily; El Indio to **Cafayate** Thu morning, returning afternoon. **Remise taxis** San Jose, *T491907*, Los Calchaquies, *T491071.*

Molinos *p240*
Bus To **Salta** via Cachi, Mon, Tue, Thu, Sat, at 0645, also Sun 1245. **Marcos Rueda**; 2 hrs to **Cachi**, US$4.50, 7 hrs to **Salta**. In Salta T0387-421 1327. From Salta to **Molinos**, Sun, Mon, Wed, Fri, 0700, arriving Molinos 1330. Sat leaving Salta at 1200, arriving 2000. US$7. To **Angastaco**, just 1 bus a week on Thu morning.

Angastago *p241*
Bus To **Cachi** and Salta (US$5.50), Fri, 1100. To **Cafayate** via San Caros, El Indio, 0630 Mon, Wed, Fri, arriving 0900. Taxi to **Molinos** US$20.

San Carlos *p241*
Bus 5 services a day to **Cafayate**, El Indio, 30 mins, US$1.

Cafayate and around *p241, map 242*
Bus There are 2 bus terminals: for **Salta**, go to **El Indio** bus terminal on Belgrano, half a block from the plaza, and for **Tucumán**, to the **Aconquija** terminal at Mitre and Rivadavia. To **Salta**, via the Quebrada de Cafayate, El Indio, 4 a day Mon-Fri, 3 daily Sat/Sun, US$6 (worth travelling in daylight). To **Angastaco**, El Indio, one daily, US$4, 2½ hrs. To **Santa María**, (for **Quilmes**) El Indio, 1 daily. To **Tucumán**, Aconquija, 3 daily, 5 hrs, US$7.
Cycle Cycle hire is popular. Ask at tourist office for list. **Metropolitan Tours**, *Güemes Norte 128, T 422130,* is reliable.

Directory

Cafayate and around *p241, map 242*
Bank Banco de la Nación, *Toscano y NS del Rosario.* ATM, but no Tcs. There is another ATM at **Banco Salta**, *Mitre y San Martin.* Open all year, good service. **Useful addresses Pharmacy** F Pastor, *opposite the bus terminal on Rivadavia.*

Jujuy Province

One of the country's poorest provinces is also one of its richest in terms of natural beauty, and in its culture – with fine churches and ancient settlements, and the vibrant contemporary culture of its indigenous Collas. The small city of Jujuy is all the more interesting for not pandering to tourism with lively street life centred around its excellent market, and a historic plaza.

Stretching north towards the Bolivian border is Quebdrada de Humahuaca, and a series of beautiful villages, some with hilltop forts built in pre-Hispanic times, and all celebrating Easter and Carnival in exuberant style.

Purmamarca is famous for its Cerro de Siete Colores and there are at least seven colours in its vivid stratified rock – a dramatic backdrop.

Tilcara is the best base for exploring the area, with its museum and restored ruined village, and from here the adventurous could trek west into the subtropical cloudforest park of Calilegua, packed with dense vegetation, and the air filled with birdsong.

In all the villages you'll find characteristic squat white adobe churches and in La Quiaca there's an extraordinary collection of Cuzqueño school paintings. Further north, the quiet village of Humahuaca is the departure point for buses to Iruya, and beyond, the road to Bolivia passes the mining village of Abra Pampa and the border town of La Quiaca.

Further west, Jujuy's expanse of puna contains old Jesuit gold mines and the natural reserve of Laguna Pozuelos with a wealth of birdlife. To the east, the church in the village of Yavi is the country's most exquisite colonial gem, its gold decoration seen in the lemony light from onyx windows.

Jujuy City → *Phone code: 0388 Colour map 1, A3 Population: 182,000*

The city of Jujuy (pronounced Choo-Chooey, with ch as in Scottish loch), often referred to by locals as San Salvador, is the capital of Jujuy province, and sits at 1,260 m in a bowl of lushly wooded mountains, at the southeastern end of the Quebrada de Humahuaca 100 km north of Salta. With two fine churches and a rich handicraft tradition, it's a good introduction to the *kolla* culture and a handy base for exploring a variety of landscapes within easy reach.

Originally sited between two rivers, Río Grande and Chico, or Xibi Xibi, it has sprawled south, supporting a growing population on dwindling industry. Wars and earthquakes have ensured that the city has few colonial remains, and architecturally, Jujuy lacks Salta's elegance, but it does have an appealing atmosphere of its own. The Andean culture from its surrounding spectacular landscapes seeps into the city, so that you can sample here the superb food and music for which areas further north are rightly famous. And from the bridge over the Río Xibi Xibi, with its brightly coloured market stalls, you have wonderful views of the dramatic purple mountains contrasting with the thick green vegetation that fills the river bed. ▸▸ *For Sleeping, Eating and other listings, see pages 251-253.*

Ins and outs

Getting there Jujuy's airport, El Cadillal is 32 km southeast, minibuses (US$2.50) to/from **Dinar** office in town; taxi, US$13. The bus terminal is six blocks south of the main street Belgrano, over the river on Dorrego and Iguazú. There are buses to all destinations north of the city, including to Bolivia, also south to Salta and from there to most major destinations. There are direct buses to Buenos Aires taking 22 hrs.

Getting around The city is pleasant to walk around, and is particularly interesting around the market opposite the bus terminal, and on the bridges. The most interesting sites are within six blocks of each other and could comfortably be visited in a day.

Tourist information The tourist office is on the plaza at Gorriti and Belgrano, open Monday-Friday 0700-2100, Saturday/Sunday 0800-1400, 1500-2100; it has a helpful accommodation leaflet and a map, but little information about the rest of the province or transport. Another office at the bus terminal with help for accommodation, 0700-2100 daily. www.jujuy.gov.ar

Background
Jujuy has an extraordinary history. The Spanish attempts to found a city which would join up the chain of cities connecting Alto Peru with Córdoba met extreme resistance from indigenous peoples, first in 1561 and then in 1575. After these attempts were completely destroyed by indigenous groups, the city was finally established in 1593. It prospered through the 18th century, but the province of Jujuy bore the brunt of fighting during the Wars of Independence: between 1810 and 1822 the Spanish launched 11 invasions down the Quebrada de Humahuaca from Bolivia. And in August 1812 General Belgrano, commanding the republican troops, demanded an incredible sacrifice of

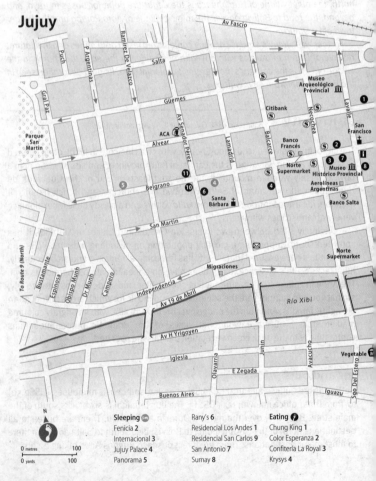

Jujuy

Sleeping		
Fenicia 2	Rany's 6	Eating
Internacional 3	Residencial Los Andes 1	Chung King 1
Jujuy Palace 4	Residencial San Carlos 9	Color Esperanza 2
Panorama 5	San Antonio 7	Confitería La Royal 3
	Sumay 8	Krysys 4

Jujuy's people when he ordered the city to be evacuated and destroyed before the advancing Royalist army. This event is marked on 23-24 August by festivities known as *El Exodo Jujeño* with gaucho processions and military parades. As a tribute to the city for obeying his orders, Belgrano donated a flag which is displayed in the Casa de Gobierno: a painting of this ceremony can be seen inside the cathedral.

Jujuy has suffered growing poverty in recent years, since its industries – traditionally sugar and tobacco – have suffered in the recession with resulting unemployment. It's one of the few Argentine cities whose population has indigenous roots, boosted in the last 20 years by considerable immigration from Bolivia. You may well find your bus journey delayed en route by peaceful demonstrations of *piqueteros* blocking the road, protesting about job and benefit cuts. Tourism is the main growing industry in the area, as the city is slowly waking up to its huge natural asset, the extraordinary beauty on its doorstep.

> ❖ *Jujuy is a quietly bustling place, with calm elegant Plaza Belgrano away from the main shopping streets of Belgrano, Balcarce and Necochea.*

Sights

You may well arrive by bus at Jujuy's more unlovely end, though the bus station is a perfectly typical example of the usual mayhem of 20 different bus companies, huge packages waiting to be carried to remote parts of the *puna*, and people selling refreshments. Walking along Dorrego/Lavalle towards the centre, crossing the bridge across the thickly weeded river bed, the city teems cheerfully with life, and you'll pass the fabulous vegetable market (stock up if you're camping), and stalls selling razors and peaches, tights and herbal cures, pan pipes and plimsols.

To Parque Nacional Calitegua

Former Railway Station
Av Urquiza
Sarmiento
Gorriti
Cabildo
Belgrano
Cathedral
Plaza Belgrano
LAPA
Paseo de las Artesanías
Otero
Casa de Gobierno
Argañaraz
Av H Yrigoyen
J Newberry
Dorrego
M Gorriti
Urdininea
Campero
R De Siria
R Del Libano
Leandro N Alem
L De La Torre
To

Madre Tierra **5**   Tía Bigote **11**
Manos Jujeños **6**
Pingüino **7**   **Bars & clubs** 🎵
Ruta 9 **8**   Savoy **9**
Sociedad Española **10**

In the eastern part of the city is the tranquil **Plaza Belgrano**, a wide square planted with tall palms and lined with orange trees, with a striking equestrian statue of Belgrano at its centre. On the south side stands the **Casa de Gobierno**, a cream French-style neo-classical building built in 1927, where you can see the very flag that Belgrano gave the city in recognition of their great sacrifice, in a sumptuously decorated long hall with pleasing art nouveau statues representing Justice, Liberty, Peace and Progress by the Argentine sculptor, Lola Mora.

On the west side is the **cathedral**, whose neo-classical façade – built in the late 19th century to replace the original, built in the early 1600s and destroyed by an earthquake – does contain an exquisite jewel: a gold plated wooden pulpit, carved by indigenous tribes in the Jesuit missions. Its elegant and naïve biblical illustrations are very moving, and the delicate modelling of the dove overhead and on the angels' faces, many of them painted, is stunning. It's one of Argentina's finest colonial treasures. There are also several fine 18th-century paintings. On the north side of the plaza is the **Cabildo**, built in 1867 and now occupied by the police, with a rather dull police museum inside.

The **Iglesia de San Francisco** ① *Belgrano y Lavalle, two blocks east of the plaza, daily 0900-2100, informed guides*, is modern but has a graceful calm interior, and contains another fine gilded colonial pulpit, with ceramic angels around it, like that at Yavi. The **Iglesia de San Bárbara** (1777), San Martín y Lamadrid is similar in style to the colonial churches in the Quebrada de Humahuaca,

The **Museo Arqueológico Provincial** ① *Lavalle 434, daily 0900-1200, 1500-2100*, has some superb ceramics from the pre-Incan Yavi and Humahuaca cultures, and beautifully painted funerary urns featuring children, some containing tiny bones. It's all under-funded, and poorly displayed, but definitely worth seeing – particularly for a fabulous 2,500 year old sculpture of a goddess giving birth, and the rather gruesomely displayed mummified infant.

The **Museo Histórico Franciscano** ① *in the Iglesia de San Francisco, Belgrano y Lavalle, daily 0900-1300, 1600-2100*, has 17th-century paintings and other artefacts from Cusco. If you like military portraits, you could visit the **Museo Histórico Provincial** ① *Lavalle 252, Mon-Fri 0800-2000, Sat 0800-1200, 1600-2000, US$0.50*, though it's pretty dry, and a whole room is dedicated to the death of Gral Lavalle which occurred in this house, a turning point in the civil war between Federalists and Unitarists. There are a couple of fine Cusco school paintings from 1650, though.

The puna and the Quebrada de Humahuaca can be reached by a full day's excursion from Jujuy, but since distances are it's far better to take a couple of days to explore them properly. The cloudforest park of Calillegua, is reached more easily from Jujuy than Salta, by bus via Libertador Gral San Martín – see details below.

Puna Jujeña and the road to Chile

→ *Phone code: 03882 Colour map 1, A2 Population: 700*

The Puna Jujeña (3,700 m, Km 213) covers all the area to the west of the Quebrada de Humahuaca, and the RN9, and is a spectacularly remote and beautifully bleak place, with few settlements, but extraordinary salt flats, lakes full of bird life, and history to be explored. The road to the crossing to Chile via the Paso de Jama, along (*ripio*) Route 52 from Purmamarca to Susques takes you over the awesome Abra Potrerillos pass (4,170 m) and into the puna. At Km 131-136 the road crosses Salinas Grandes (3,500 m), one of the largest areas of saltflats in the country where there are amazing views especially at sunset. In the winter months, on both sides of the road, you'll see three different ancient types of salt mining by hand can be seen. At Km 180-200 the road winds through the Quebrada de Mal Paso crossing the Tropic of Capricorn several times. From here the road runs northwest, crossing, Route 40, which runs between San Antonio de los Cobres and Abra Pampa, and continues through to Chile. From the crossing to Susques the road is paved.

The only settlement between Purmamarca and the border, **Susques** lies in a hollow at the meeting of the Ríos Susques and Pasto Chicos. The church, dating from 1598, is one of the outstanding examples of colonial architecture in the region, with a roof of cactus-wood and thatch. Inside is an old bellow-organ. There are regular buses from Jujuy, with El Quiaqueño, Monday to Friday, three and a half hours. ⏵ *For Sleeping, Eating and other listings, see pages 251-253.*

Border with Chile

Paso de Jama, (4,750 m) 360 km west of Jujuy, is reached by a 60 km road which branches off Route 70. Argentine customs and immigration are at Susques. On the

Chilean side the road continues (unpaved) to San Pedro de Atacama (Km 514), where fuel and accommodation are available, and Calama. Chilean customs and immigration are at San Pedro de Atacama. *For Sleeping, Eating and other listings, see pages 251-253.*

Listings: Jujuy

Sleeping *map p248*

All hotels are fully booked for the festival of **El Exodo Jujeño**, *23/24 Aug*: book ahead. Near the bus terminal there are a number of cheap places, those listed are safe and comfortable.

B Jujuy Palace, *Belgrano 1060, T/F423 0433, jpalace@imagine.com.ar* Top of Jujuy's range is a popular conference hotel, with cool, plain decor in the well equipped bedrooms, and spacious bathrooms. The restaurant has a good reputation, though it's rather squashed.

C Panorama, *Belgrano 1295, T423 2533, hotelpanorama@mail.com.ar* Appealing, and a couple of blocks further away from the hubub, is this other business hotel. Better value with rather more stylish rooms. No restaurant.

D Fenicia, *19 de Abril 427, T/F423 1800.* Breakfast is included but prices rise to **C** in winter, though there are reductions for longer stays. A nice 1980s modernish place, with lots of marble, swirly chairs and swaggy curtains in the foyer, but the rooms are spacious and very nicely decorated, (ask for the ones with swish bathrooms) some with great views over the city, and this is recommended for its friendly welcome.

D Internacional, *Belgrano 501 (Plaza Belgrano), T423 1599, interjuy@imagine.com.ar* On the northwest corner of the plaza, but it's quiet, and very good value, including breakfast. The comfortably decorated rooms all have bath and TV, and though they're smallish, many have great views over the city, with modern bathrooms. Elegant public rooms, a *confitería*, and very friendly service, recommended.

D Sumay, *Otero 232, T423 5065.* Breakfast is included. Rather dark and pokey, the rooms are nevertheless clean, with bathrooms, and the place is very central, with friendly staff.

E El Balcon, *El Fortin 12, Los Perales district, near* the bus station, T426 0520. Lots of rooms, some for 4 and parking in this comfortable place in a quiet district. 70 cent bus ride each way.

E Huaico, *Av Bolivia 3901, T423 5186, hotelhuaicojujuy@hotmail.com* 1.5 km away from the centre, near the park, this is a great place to sleep if you're heading north. A very pleasant place, breakfast included, and special rates for students.

E Rany's, *Dorrego 327, near the bus station, T423 0042.* Right next door to the *Residencial San Carlos*, below, there are even cheaper rooms without TV, and all rooms have a bath, and although it's pretty basic, the female owner is very kind, and you'd be safe arriving here late at night alone. No breakfast, but loads of cafés around.

E Residencial Los Andes, *República de Siria 456, T422 4315.* Some cheaper rooms are even more economical, without bath or TV, and there's a garage. Reductions for groups. This has a much smarter entrance than most, but you might get a grumpy reception, and the rather dark rooms come off a gloomy patio, but it's clean and safe.

E Residencial San Carlos, *República de Siria 459, T422 2286.* Private bath and TV, this is a nicely maintained, friendly and very comfortable place, with car parking, perfectly safe to arrive at night as it's always attended.

F San Antonio, *Lisandro de la Torre T422 5998, opposite the bus station.* Basic, but recently painted rooms have private bath, looked after by the 3 sisters and the whole family is very kind and welcoming. Recommended.

Around Jujuy *p247*

A-B Hostería Posta de Lozano, *Route 9, Km 18 north, T498 0050, posta@imagine.com.ar* Good restaurant, pools with fresh mountain water, covered parking.

Finca Don Gustavo, *Route 9, km 7 Los Alisos, T424 0784, www.dongustavo.jujuy.com* Rustic accommodation, sampling life on an active ranch, with well equipped rooms around a central gallery, and regional cooking.

A **Hotel Termas de Reyes**, *Termas de Reyes, at an altitude of 1,800 m, 19 km northwest of Jujuy, 6 buses a day from Jujuy bus terminal between 0630 and 1945, returning 0700-2040, US$1 1 hr*. This thermal spa resort with a grand neo-classical hotel is set among magnificent mountains. Prices based on full board. There is also Camping US$5 per person with use of thermal pool, take insect repellent. Non-residents can use the hotel's thermal pool for US$3 (weekends US$5), and there are also municipal baths, daily 0800-1200 and 1400-1700 (Thu 1400-1700 only), US$1.

Cabañas

El Caserio, *Finca Cerro Chico, T156825257, info@caseriojujuy.com* Beautiful *cabañas* and a house available for rent in lovely wild parkland 36 km north of Jujuy on RN9.

Camping

If you keep going north from Jujuy, up in the Quebrada de Humahuaca, there's a campsite in every town.

E pp **El Refugio**, *T/F4909344, elrefugio@ arnet.com.ar* This is the nearest campsite, and is actually at Yala, over the bridge in a pretty spot on the banks of the river, 14 km north of Jujuy city on RN9. There's also a youth hostel, pool, restaurant and trekking and horse riding excursions are on offer. Highly recommended, a great place to relax.

Serranias de Zapala, *T427 7881, www.turismopalpala.com.ar* Another campsite slightly further afield at 24 km in the dull town of Palpala.

Puna Jujeña and the road to Chile *p250*

Residencial La Vicuñita, *San Martín 121, T479 0207, opposite church*. Basic budget accommodation.

🍴 Eating *map p248*

Following Lavalle across the bridge to the bus terminal (where it changes names to Dorrego) there are lots of cheap *empanada* places.

$ **Chung King**, *Alvear 627*. A *jujeño*

institution, (although the accommodation upstairs can't be recommended) this is an atmospheric cheap place for regional food, and its sister restaurant next door serves '50 kinds of pizza.'

$ **Krysys**, *Balcarce 272*. A popular bistro-style *parrilla* restaurant with excellent steaks.

$ **La Candelaria**, *Alvear 1346*. A little further out of town this is welcoming choice for *parrilla*, with good service.

$ **Manos Jujeños**, *Sen Perez 222, T1568 22087*. For delicious regional specialities, and the best *humitas* come straight here. This is an intimate, charming and welcoming place decorated with local weavings. Excellent service, and especially recommended for the folklore music at weekends.

$ **Madre Tierra**, *Belgrano 600*. A great place for vegetarians (or if you want a break from all the meat). Behind the wonderful wholemeal bakery of same name, a cool oasis serves delicious food (closed dinner).

$ **Ruta 9**, *Lavalle 287*. Another great place, slightly cheaper even than *Manos*, above, for *locro* and *tamales*.

Cafés

There are several good cafés on the same busy block of Belgrano between Lavalle and Necochea.

Pingüino is the best *heladería* in the town.

Confitería La Royal, *Belgrano 770*, is a classic café serving good coffee and pastries, slightly pricey lunches, and a great place to watch Jujuy bustle past. Opposite is a new bright café **Color Esperanza** serving cheap *lomitos* and hamburgers.

Tia Bigote, *Perez and Belgrano*, is a hugely popular café and pizzeria, and **Sociedad Espanola**, *opposite on the same corner*, serves good cheap set menus with a Spanish flavour; *mariscos con arroz* and paella.

Puna Jujeña and the road to Chile *p250*

Pastos Chicos, *Route 16, Km 194, T423 5387*. A good eating stop off.

🎭 Entertainment

If you haven't already sampled a *peña* in

💬 *For an explanation of the sleeping and eating price codes used in this guide, see the inside front cover. Other relevant information is provided in the Essentials chapter, page 44.*

Salta, you should hear the region's passionate folklore music played live here. **Manos Jujeños**, *Sen Perez 222, T156822087*, or **Chung King**, *Alvear 627*, and **Savoy**, *Alvear y Urquiza*, all have live music and dancing at weekends, and during the week in busy holiday periods.

○ Shopping *map p248*

Handicrafts are sold from stalls on Plaza Belgrano near the cathedral, from the old train station north of the plaza on Urquiza, and from the rather limited **Paseo de las Artesanías** on the west side of the plaza. **Regionales Lavalle**, *Lavalle 268*. **Centro de Arte y Artesanías**, *Balcarce 427*. **Camping and fishing equipment** at **Tierrita**, *Necochea 508*. For **food**, you can't beat the colourful **Municipal market**, *Dorrego y Alem, near the bus terminal*. Outside it, women sell home baked *empanadas* and *tamales*, and delicious goat's cheese, as well as all kinds of herbal cures. There is a **Norte** supermarket, *Belgrano 825*, and a bigger branch at *19 de Abril y Necochea*.

○ Tour operators *map p248*

Be Dor Turismo, *Lavalle 295, T402 0242, be-dor@imagine.com.ar* Conventional tours offering student reductions.
NASA, *Senador Pérez 154, T422 3938*. Guided tours to Quebrada de Humahuaca (US$30 pp, minimum 4 people); 4WD for rent.
TEA Turismo, *San Martín 128, T423 6270, teajujuy@imagine.com.ar* Recommended for professional trips to the Quebrada over 2 days, with guides and accommodation included.
Horus Turismo, *Belgrano 722, T422 7247, horus@imgine.com.ar* Good for the more predictable trips.
Portal de Piedra, *T(0388)156820564, www.portaldepiedra.8m.com portaldepiedra @yahoo.com* Contact experienced bilingual guides Carlos and Silvia, for horseriding or excursions to the cloudforest, for trekking in Calilegua, bird watching, and archaeology. Recommended.
For visiting Calilegua under your own steam, see Transport, below.

○ Transport *map p248*

Air

Aeropuerto El Cadillal, *32 km southeast, T491505*. Minibuses (US$2.50) to/from **Dinar** and **Lapa** offices in town; taxi, US$13. Flights to **Buenos Aires** and **Salta** with Dinar, *T423 7100*. Dinar also fly to **Tucumán** .

Bus

Local The bus terminal is at Iguazú y Dorrego, 6 blocks south of centre. Information T422 2134.

Via Tucumán to **Córdoba**, Panamericano and La Veloz del Norte, daily; to **Tucumán**, 5 hrs, US$10, and **Córdoba**, 14 hrs, US$18.

To **Salta** hourly, 2 hrs, US$2-3. To the Bolivian border **La Quiaca**, 4-6 hrs, US$7, Panamericano, Balut, El Quiaqueño. Several rigorous luggage checks en route for drugs, including coca leaves. To **Humahuaca**, Evelia and others, US$3, 3 hrs, several daily, via **Tilcara** 2 hrs, US$2.50.

Long distance To **Buenos Aires**, 20-24 hrs, US$36 *semi cama*, several daily with **TAC**, *La Estrella*, Panamericano. To **Orán** and **Aguas Blancas** (border with Bolivia), daily with **Balut** and **Brown**, via San Pedro and Ledesma. To **Purmamarca**, take buses to Susques or Humahuaca (check they call at Purmamarca village, off the main road). To **Susques**, **Purmamarca** andAndes Bus, US$ 5, 4-6½ hrs, daily (except Mon). To **Calilegua**, various companies to Libertador Gral San Martín almost every hour, eg **Balut**, from there take a minibus, or taxi for US$1.50. All **Pocitos** buses pass through **Libertador San Martín** eg Panamericano, Esterella, El Rapido.

Car hire

Avis, *Hotel Jujuy Palace*, T491 1501, F311184 and airport. And also at the airport: **Hertz**, T155801383, *foarentacar@arnet.com.ar* **Localiza**, T156851450, *gilce@jujuytel.com.ar*

○ Directory *map p248*

Airline offices **Aerolíneas Argentinas**, *San Martín 745*. **LAPA**, *Belgrano 616*.
Banks There are ATMs at: Banco de Jujuy, B*alcarce y Belgrano*, changes dollars.

● *Phone codes Jujuy and surrounding areas: 0388*

Citibank, *Güemes y Balcarce*; Bank Boston , *Alvear 802*, Banco Francés, *Alvear y Lamadrid*; Banco Salta, *San Martín 785*. TCs can be changed at travel agencies, Horus, *Belgrano 722*, Be Dor, *Lavalle 295*.
Communications Post office *Independencia y Lamadrid*. In *Galería Impulso, Belgrano 775*, there are *locutorios*, many which have internet. **Cybercafé**, *Belgrano y Balcarce*. **Consulates** Bolivia, *Belgrano 250*, open 0900-1300. Italy, *Av Fascio 660*, *T423199*. Spain, *Ramirez de Velasco 362*, *T428193*. Paraguay, *Tacuarí 430, T428178*.
Useful addresses Pharmacy *Del Pueblo, Alvear 927, T422 2339*.

Quebrada de Humahuaca

The route heading north from Jujuy up to Abra Pampa and the Bolivian border is quite one of the most dramatic areas of natural beauty in the country. The Quebrada is a long gorge of intensely coloured rock, arid mountains of warm terracotta, yellow, orange, pink, cream and malachite green, speckled with giant cacti. In the fertile valley floor of the gorge are several small historic towns, all with neat adobe houses, and with the characteristic simple squat white 18th-century churches of the region. The pretty village of Purmamarca, wth its backdrop of the Cerro de Siete Colores, Tilcara with its handicraft market and restored hillfort town, Maimará with its huge cemetery and La Paleta de Pintor, and the more populous Humahuaca, all have delightful places to stay, to walk and to absorb the ancient history of the area. The indigenous culture is particularly rich here: there area pre-Incan ruins at Tilcara, and throughout the Quebrada there are riotous pre-Lent carnival celebrations. In Tilcara, pictures of the Passion are made of flowers and seeds at Easter and a traditional procession on Holy Thursday at night is joined by thousands of pan pipe musicians.

Ins and outs

Getting around Public transport is easy, since a number of bus companies go up and down the quebrada from Jujuy to Humahuaca, stopping at Purmamarca, Tilcara, Maimará and Uquia. La Quiaquena and Balut go all the way to La Quiaca on the Bolivian border. If driving, fuel is available at Tilcara, Humahuaca, Uquia and Abra Pampa, so you might need to take a spare can if you're heading far into rural areas. It's a good area for cycling, preferably off the RN9, where there can be a lot of traffic through the valley and there's not much shade.

Purmamarca → *Phone code: 0388 Colour map 1, A3 Population: 200*

A tiny, peaceful village with a stunning setting at the foot of the Cerro de las Siete Colores, a mountain striped with at least seven colours, from creamy pink to burgundy, and copper to green, best seen in morning light. Purmamarca retains its own quiet rhythm of life, once the steady trickle of excursion buses has left, with tourists buying souvenirs in the stalls surrounding the plaza. Some 3 km west of Route 9 at Km 61, this is the first stop on the Quebrada, and it's the perfect place to rest and acclimatize yourself to the 2,100 m altitude, with a good choice of places to stay. Its beautiful church, **Iglesia de Santa Rosa** (1648, rebuilt 1778) is typical of those you'll see elsewhere on the quebrada, with its squat tower, whitewashed adobe walls and simple well-balanced construction. Inside there's a splendid time-darkened cactus roof and pulpit, and a series of exquisite paintings depicting the life of Santa Rosa. Next to the church is an *algrarrobo* tree thought to be 500 years old. There's a tiny, helpful tourist office on the plaza, with a map, information on accommodation and bus tickets. ▸▸ *For Sleeping, Eating and other listings, see pages 261-263.*

66 99 A long gorge of intensely coloured rock, arid mountains of warm terracotta, yellow, orange, pink, cream and malachite green, speckled with giant cacti...

Maimará → *Population: 1,600*

About 2 km from Purmamarca at Km 75, Maimará (2,150 m) is a lovely tranquil oasis village. Its green fields of onion and garlic are made more emerald by the backdrop of richly coloured rock, known as La Paleta Del Pintor, to the east of the village. For an enjoyable walk in the low evening light, when the colours of the rock are at their warmest, walk along the old road to the east of Maimará, and take plenty of film: it's a beautiful sight. Just off the road, 3 km south, is La Posta de Hornillos, one of the chain of colonial posting house which used to extend from Buenos Aires to Lima, also the scene of several battles, and where Belgrano stayed. Restored, the building now houses a historical museum with a collection of 18th- and 19th-century furniture as well as weapons and historical documents. North of Maimará, there's a huge cemetery on the hillside, brightly decorated with paper flowers at Easter.

Tilcara → *Phone code: 0388 Colour map 1, A3 Population: 2,900*

Tilcara (2,360 m) lies 22 km north of Purmamarca at Km 84. It's the liveliest Quebrada village, and the best base for exploring the area, with plenty of places to stay and to eat, and with an excellent handcrafts market around its pleasant plaza. It's the site of an important pre-Hispanic settlement too, and you can visit the **Pucará**, a much-restored hilltop fortress, with panoramic views of the gorge from its complex web of low walled dwellings, made more splendid by mighty cacti. Turn right off Belgrano where signposted, and across Río Huasamayo. At the entrance, there's also a small handicrafts shop, where you can get helpful information, and a small botanical garden, with many species of cactus. On the plaza is a superb **Museo Arqueológico** ① *Daily 0900-1230, 1400-1800, US$1. Admission includes entry to Pucará, and vice versa,* with a fine collection of pre-Columbian ceramics, masks and mummies. There are four art museums in town, of which **Museo Regional de Pintura**, Rivadavia 459, is worth a look, with paintings on the customs and traditions of Tilcara. And there are good walks in all directions from the village. **Tourist office** ① *on Belgrano next to Hotel de Turismo, open daily 0900-1200, 1500-2100 (closed Sunday afternoons), no phone, www.tilcarajujuy.com, tiny.*

There are fiestas throughout an extended Carnival period, and at Easter, there's a famous gathering of thousands of pan pipe musicians, who play as they follow the procession of the Virgen de Copacabana down the mountain. Extraordinary and moving. Book accommodation way ahead. ►► *For Sleeping, Eating and other listings, see pages 261-263.*

Huacalera and Uquía

Huacalera lies 2 km north of the Tropic of Capricorn; a sundial 20 m west of the road marks the exact location. The church, several times restored, has a cactus-wood roof and a small museum. Uquía is one of the smaller villages along the Quebrada, and totally untouristy with a tranquil atmosphere, and a narrow street of adobe houses. Close to the road, there's one of the valley's finest churches, its beautifully proportioned white tower very striking against the deep red rock of the mountain behind. Built in 1691, **Iglesia San Francisco de Paula** contains an extraordinary collection of Cuzqueño paintings of angels in 17th-century battle dress, the *ángeles* *arcabuceros*. Painted by local indigenous artists, under the tuition of Jesuits, the combination of tenderness and swagger in these winged figures, brandishing their weapons, is astonishing.

Humahuaca → *Phone code: 03887 Colour map 1, A3 Population 6,000*

Although Humahuaca (2,940 m) was founded in 1591 on the site of a pre-Hispanic settlement, it was almost entirely rebuilt in the mid-19th century. However, it retains a distinctive Andean culture in its narrow streets of low adobe houses, despite being the most popular tourist destination along the Quebrada. It offers more limited accommodation than Tilcara, but once the coach trips have left, it's quiet, and is a useful stopping point for travelling north up to the *puna*, or tolruya.

La Candelaria festival is celebrated on February 2, and the beginning of carnival here is famously lively with *Jueves de Comadres*, and *Festival de las Coplas y de la Chicha*. Book accommodation ahead.

On the tiny plaza is the church, *La Candelaria*, originally constructed in 1631, rebuilt 1873-80, containing wonderfully gaudy gold retablos, and 12 fine Cuzqueño school paintings. Also on the plaza, tourists gather at 1200 daily outside **El Cabildo**, the neo-colonial town hall, to watch a large mechanical figure of San Francisco Solano emerge to bless the town from his alcove high in the wall. You may find this kitsch rather than spiritually uplifting, but in either case, it's quite a sight. Overlooking the town is the massive, and certainly uninspiring, **Monumento a la Independencia Argentina**, commemorating the scene of the heaviest fighting in the country during the Wars of Independence. There is a good *Feria Artesanal* on Avenida San Martín (on the far side of the railway line) and a Fruit Market, Tucumán y Belgrano.

Coctaca, 10 km northeast of Humahuaca, has an impressive and extensive (40 ha) series of pre-colonial agricultural terraces, the largest archaeological site in Jujuy. It's best to go with a guide to find them. Highly recommended is a night at least in the peaceful hamlet of **Iruya** (see below), reached by a wonderful three-hour bus ride. ▸▸ *For Sleeping, Eating and other listings, see pages 261-263.*

Iruya → *Colour map 1, A3 This is one of Argentina's most amazing journeys*

A rough *ripio* road 25 km north of Humahuaca runs northeast from the RN9 8 km to Iturbe (also called Hipólito Irigoyen) where the bus stops for 5 minutes, giving you a chance to glimpse captivating rural life. There are no facilities here. Then the road crosses the river (manageable in an ordinary car if it hasn't rained heavily) and climbs up over the 4,000 m pass, Abra del Cóndor before dropping steeply, around an amazing slalom of many hairpin bends, into the Quebrada de Iruya.

Iruya is an idyllic small hamlet tucked into a steep hillside, remote and hidden away, but full of warm and friendly inhabitants. It has a colourful Rosario festival on first Sunday in October, and lively Easter festivities, when accommodation is booked up in advance. It's worth spending a few days here to lap up the tranquil atmosphere, and to go horseriding or walking in the beautiful valleys nearby. The hike (7 hrs return) to the even more remote hamlet of San Isidro is unforgettable. At **Titiconte** 4 km away, there are unrestored pre-Inca ruins though you'll need to take a guide to find them. Iruya has no ATM or tourist information, but has a public phone, and food shops. ▸▸ *For Sleeping, Eating and other listings, see pages 261-263.*

Casabindo → *Colour map 1, A3*

Around 62 km southwest of Abra Pampa, it's quite a detour over the *puna* to reach Casabindo (3,500 m). Founded in 1602, it is a tiny hamlet with a magnificent church with twin towers, dating from 1772. It's one of the finest in the whole region, beautifully proportioned, and containing a superb series of 16th-century paintings of *angeles arcabuceros* (archangels in military uniforms) like those at Uquía. It's worth trying to visit for 15 August, when there's a lively celebration of the *La Ascensión de la*

⁞ Colonial churches

Some of Argentina's most beautiful churches are to be found in the provinces of Salta and Jujuy, along the Quebrada de Humahuaca and Valles Calchaquíes. The region's church architecture was influenced by the city of Sucre (today in Bolivia), seat of an archbishop, whose architectural style was derived in turn from the medieval churches of Seville. The basic structure, with metre-thick adobe walls, plastered and painted white, and wooden framed roof, has a single nave with side-chapels and a single tower. In the valleys, where the population was entirely indigenous, an atrium or covered area outside was added in front of the church. This was used for teaching the unconverted, and often became the social centre for the village. There are treasures of religious art to be found in Salta's Cabildo Museo Histórico and in the cathedral at Jujuy. To the south, Cachi's church in the Valles Calchaquíes was rebuilt in the 18th century, but has an attractive simple style, with cardon cactus ceiling and lectern. Molinos' striking church of 1692 has twin bell towers, and houses the body of the last Spanish marquis.

As you make your way north up Jujuy's spectacular Quebrada de Humahuaca, try to make time to stop off at its superb churches. The first at Purmamarca, 1778, is one of the most pleasingly proportioned; inside is a series of paintings of the life of Santa Rosa, dating from the early 18th century, and executed in Cusco school style. Tilcara's church has twin bell towers, and a more modern interior with less captivating paintings inside. But one of the most lovely of the valley is that at Uquia, dating from 1691, with a single tower, and housing an extraordinary series of paintings, the *ángeles arcabuceros*, or angels in battledress. These were painted by local indigenous artists under Jesuit tuition, and the combination of tenderness and swagger in these winged figures, brandishing their weapons, is astonishing.

Humahuaca too has a fine church, with smaller but pleasing paintings in the Cusco style. Further northwest, in the puna, there are exquisite churches at Susques, 1598, and Casabindo, dating from 1772, but containing another stunning series of Cusco-style paintings of angels in armour. The crowning glory of the whole area, though, is the church at Yavi, whose golden treasures inside are all lit with the unearthly light from onyx windows, creating the perfect atmosphere for appreciating a gold sculpture of an angel in armour, and an incredibly ornate pulpit. Not to be missed.

Virgen, accompanied by the last and only *corrida de toros* (running with bulls) in Argentina. *El Toreo de la Vincha* takes place in front of the church, where a bull defies onlookers to take the ribbon and medal it carries, a symbolic offering to the virgin rather than a gory spectacle. Basic dorm accommodation is usually possible in the village school, T491129, for the many musicians and any visitors who come. ▶ *For Sleeping, Eating and other listings, see pages 261-263.*

Reserva Nacional Laguna de los Pozuelos → *Phone code: 03887 Map 1, A3*

Reserva Nacional Laguna de los Pozuelos (3,650 m) is a nature reserve 50 km northwest Abra Pampa and centred around a lake visited by huge colonies of flamingos. It's a stunning landscape well worth exploring if you have several days. Be warned though that this is high altitude puna, and temperatures can drop to -25°C at nights in winter; if camping, warm clothing, drinking water and food are essential.

There is a ranger station at the southern end of the Laguna with a campsite nearby. At Lagunillas, further west, there is smaller lagoon, which also has flamingos. There are no visitor services, and no bus transport, and so your only option is to go with a guide. **Park office** in Abra Pampa T491048. Intendencia of park, T154022114, www.parquesnacionales.gov.ar, or go on tour with **Transporte Mendoza** in Humahuaca: Sofia de Mendoza T421016.

La Quiaca and around → *Phone code: 03885 Colour map 1, A2 Population: 11,500*

La Quiaca (3,442 m) lies on the border with Bolivia, linked by a concrete bridge to Villazón on the Bolivian side. Neither town is appealing, but if you have to stay the night, La Quiaca is definitely preferable. Villazón became the more commercial centre when prices were cheaper in Bolivia, before Argentina's devaluation, and it's a depressing hive of *casas de cambio* and stalls selling coca leaves. La Quiaca remains quiet and unexciting, but there are a few decent places to stay, and if you're around here on the third weekend in October, you mustn't miss the three-day *Fiesta de la Olla*. Villagers from the far reaches of the remote *puna* come on donkeys and in pickups to sell their ceramic pots, sheepskins and vegetables here, in colourful festival which involves a lot of dancing and drinking *chiche*. By far the best place to stay around here, though, is the tranquil *puna* village of Yavi, 16 km west, with a good *hostería*, Argentina's most extraordinary church, and beautiful landscape (see below).

If you're keen to explore the wild *puna* further, you could head for the tiny village of **Santa Catalina**, 67 km west along *ripio* Route 5 from La Quiaca. There's a *centro artesanal*, La Negra, and a 19th-century church with a dazzling gold and red interior (ask Doña Pascuala to let you in) and a small museum of artefacts from local history housed in the oldest building in the village. Some four hours east of La Quiaca, the remote town of **Nazareno** offers spectacular landscape, indigenous culture and warm hospitality. ▶▶ *For Sleeping, Eating and other listings, see pages 261-263.*

Border with Bolivia

The border bridge is 10 blocks from La Quiaca bus terminal, 15-minute walk. This crossing is the scene of a lot of illegal (but tolerated) smuggling: searches of locals are thorough. Contrary to popular belief, there is no fee to cross the border either way and any attempts to levy a surcharge or tax are illegal. You should be on your guard at all times at this border crossing; stories of illegal practices are rife.

Immigration and customs Argentine immigration and customs offices open 0700-2400; buses arriving outside these hours have to wait, so check before travelling. Formalities for those entering Argentina are usually very brief but thorough customs searches are made just south of La Quiaca and at Tres Cruces, 102 km south, where documents are also checked. Avoid carrying items such as packets of coca leaves or similar derivatives of the plant. The Bolivian immigration office is in Villazón on Av República de Argentina immediately after the border bridge, open 0700-1900, Mon-Sat. Bolivia is 1 hr behind Argentina from October-April. From May-September Argentina loses an hour and keeps Bolivian time. The Argentine consulate in Villazón is three blocks south of the main plaza at the intersection of Avenida República de Argentina and Calle Río open weekdays 0800-1200 and 1400-1700, closed weekends and holidays. The Bolivian consulate in La Quiaca is on República Arabe Siria y San Juan open from 0830-1100 and 1400-1700 weekdays, Sat 0900-1200 (in theory). Travellers who need a visa to enter Bolivia are advised to get it before arriving in La Quiaca.

Villazón → *Phone code: +591-(0)2 Colour map 1, A2 Population: 13,000*

Villazón (3,442 m) lies on the north bank of the river, 898 km south of the Bolivian capital, La Paz. It's a grim place, little more than the centre of commercial activity in an otherwise remote and uninhabited area, but there is some fascination, if you've been

travelling some time in Argentina, in what's for sale here. The road from the border 259
bridge, Avenida República de Argentina, is lined with shops and stalls selling
sandals, kids toys, underpants and calculators, sunspecs and paper flowers, sacks of
pink puffed corn, and armfulls of coca leaves. Women in the traditional Bolivian
dress, with their enormous skirts, spin wool and weave vivdly coloured textiles on the
pavement, and there's plenty of fresh orange juice and cheap ice cream for sale.
Nowhere decent to stay, however, nor any tourist information. ▸▸ *For Sleeping, Eating
and other listings, see pages 261-263.*

Yavi → *Phone code: 03887 Colour map 1, A3 Population:300*

An intriguing puna village, with its uniformly brown adobe dwellings, and deserted
streets, Yavi (3,300 m) was founded in 1667 and was the crossing point to Bolivia until
rail and road connections were built through La Quiaca. The landscape around it is
wide open with the swooping stratified hills of the Ocho Hermanos to the east,
making the village instantly recognizable as a remarkable place, even before you
stumble across the pre-historic petroglyphs on the rocks at their feet. Ask at *Hostal de
Yavi* for a tour, see below.

Yavi may seem sleepy and unprepossessing, but it has perhaps the finest church
in the northwest, well worth the detour from La Quiaca. The **Iglesia de Nuestra Senora
del Rosario y San Francisco** ⓘ *Tue-Sun 0900-1200 and Tue-Fri 1500-1800*, was built
from 1676 to 1690, a sturdy white construction with buttresses and a single tower.
Inside is the most magnificent gold retablo and pulpit, made by artisans brought, like
the gold, from Peru. The retablo is adorned with a gold sculpture of an angel in
18th-century battle dress (and like the paintings of Uquía, they come to life) and the
tabernacle is lined with mirrors to make candlelight within glow like the sun. Above
the exquisite pulpit, decorated with ceramic cherubs, flies a golden dove. All this
splendour is seen in the yellowy light from windows made of transparent onyx, giving
the beautiful Cuzqueno paintings even more power. It's an impressive and moving
sight. The caretaker Lydia lives opposite the police station and will show you round
the church. Opposite is the 18th-century **Casa del Marqués Campero y Tojo**, the
austere former mansion of the family who were granted large parts of the *puna* by
Philip V of Spain. It's an imposing building around empty courtyards, whose
one-room museum houses a strange and eclectic collection of 18th-century
bedsprings, arrowheads and candelabras. There's a small but excellent selection of
handicrafts for sale inside, and some nicely carved local slate with petroglyphs on a
stall outside, Mon-Sat 0900-1200, 1400-1800. There is a colourful evening
procession during Easter Week. ▸▸ *For Sleeping, Eating and other listings, see pages 261-263.*

Northeast from Jujuy – Las Yungas

The yungas, areas of cloudforest jungle, along the east of this region have been
declared a natural reserve for their many species of wildlife, fragile indigenous
communities and great beauty. Two national parks, El Baritú and Calilegua are very
much worth visiting, though a little planning is required. ▸▸ *For Sleeping, Eating and other
listings, see pages 261-263.*

Parque Nacional Calilegua → *Vegetation varies dramatically according to altitude*

Parque Nacional Calilegua is 125 km northeast of Jujuy and the most accessible of the
three cloudforest parks in the region, and frequent buses (eg Balut T422 2134) leave
from Jujuy's terminal to the nearest town, Libertador General San Martín. From there,
there are minibuses to enter the park, where you'll be met by the *guardaparque*
guides. Park entrance is at Aguas Negras, 12 km northwest of Libertador General San
Martín, reached by Route 83, which runs off Route 34 just north of town. Hitching

possible. The park headquarters are on San Lorenzo s/n, in Calilegua, 4 km northeast of Libertador, To886-22046. There is another *guardaparque* at Mesada de las Colmenas, 13 km further northwest along Route 83. The best time for visiting is outside the rainy season (November-March). Subtropical with a dry season. Average temperatures range from 17°C in winter to 28°C in summer. Mean annual rainfall is 2,000 mm, falling mainly in summer.

The park protects an area of peaks, sub-tropical valleys and cloudforest on the eastern slopes of the Serranía de Calilegua. The highest peaks are Cerro Amarillo (3,720 m), a three-day trek round trip from the entrance, and Cerro Hermoso (3,200 m). Several rivers flow southeast across the park into the Río Ledesma. There are over 300 species of bird including the red-faced guan and the condor. Among the 60 species of mammal are tapirs, pumas, otters and *taruca* (Andean deer). Route 83 unpaved climbs northwest across the park, providing access to the southeast sections and splendid views. There are 22 km of tourist trails, for horse, car or on foot and six walks of different grades of difficulty. A good tourist circuit is to Calilegua and then on to Aguas Calientes, a very rural place, where there are hosterías and a covered pool. At Alto Calilegua near the base of Cerro Amarillo, there is an interesting shepherds' settlement. It is possible to walk west from the park to Humahuaca and Tilcara (allow at least four days). Tony Estrelcof To3886-15650699, runs bilingual excursions, and has a hotel in the Yungas at Aguas Calientes. ▸▸ *For Sleeping, Eating and other listings, see pages 261-263.*

Routes to Bolivia

There are two routes into Bolivia from this area, one via Pocitos and the other via Aguas Blancas. The route via Aguas Blancas is the shorter of the two and provides the opportunity to visit the spectacular cloudforests of the Parque Nacional Baritú, one of the most inaccessible national parks in Argentina. The route **via Pocitos** is longer (though this may shorten your journey in Bolivia) and recommended in wet weather when roads into Bolivia from Aguas Blancas are difficult.

Border with Bolivia

Pocitos lies on the border 56 km north of Tartagal and 362 km northeast of Jujuy. Crossing can take time here, depending on the availability of officials. Argentine customs and immigration at the border. Beware that theft at customs has been reported. Once into Bolivia, the road continues via Yacuiba, 4 km north of the border, to Tarija, 280 km north. From Yacuiba there are regular bus services to Tarija and Santa Cruz de la Sierra, departing mainly 1700-1900. **Aguas Blancas** lies 49 km north of Orán on the west bank of the Río Bermejo, opposite the Bolivian town of Bermejo to which it is linked by a bridge. There is no accommodation, nowhere to change money and Bolivianos are not accepted in Argentina south of here. There are shops and several restaurants including *El Rinconcito de los Amigos*. The Argentine customs and immigration is open from 0700 to 1200 and 1500 to 1900; insist on getting an exit stamp. There is no exit tax.

Parque Nacional Baritú

Situated northwest of Aguas Blancas on the west bank of the Río Bermejo, this is one of the most inaccessible parks in the country, especially difficult during and immediately after wet weather. Covering 72,439 ha of the eastern slopes of the Andean foothills and rising to around 2,000 m, the park is crossed by several streams which feed north into the Río Lipeo (and thence into the Bermejo) and south into the Río Pescado. Most of the park is covered by cloudforest, vegetation varying with increasing altitude. Fauna is also abundant and varied. There are no facilities apart from ranger posts, campsites at the entrances and rustic *cabañas*. Mean temperatures vary from 21°C in winter to 30°C in summer. Mean annual rainfall is 2,000 mm, with the heaviest rainfall in summer.

Listings: Quebrada de Humahuaca

⦿ Sleeping

Purmamarca *p254*

A El Manantial del Silencio, *RN52, km 3.5, T490 8081, elsilencio@cootepal.com.ar signposted from the road into Purmamarca.* The most luxurious option, with comfortable rooms, wonderful views and charming bilingual hosts.

D La Posta, *T/F490 8040.* Highly recommended, with a beautiful elevated setting against the mountain, just 4 blocks up from the plaza. All of its rooms have triple single beds, and they're spacious and comfortable, with modern bathrooms.

E El Viejo Algarrobo, *also known as Hostal Bebo Vilte, T/F490 8038, just behind the church, soshernan@hotmail.com* Modest, but recommended, with small but pleasant rooms, cheaper with shared bath.

Maimará *p255*

C Posta del Sol, *Martín Rodríguez y San Martín, T499 7156, posta_del_sol@ hotmail.com* Lovely comfortable *hostería*, with a good restaurant. The owner is a tourist guide, can take you on a tour of the area, and has helpful information.

Tilcara *p255*

C Hostal Villar del Ala, *Padilla 100, T495 5100, adriantilcara@hotmail.com* Very comfortable 1930's house with grand rooms, a quiet garden with great views, pool, and good food. Recommended.

C Posada con los Angeles, *Gorrito s/n (signposted from plaza), T495 5153, www.tilcarajujuy.com.ar/posadaconlosangels* Charming individually designed rooms, garden with mountain views, relaxed atmosphere, excursions. Recommended.

D Los Establos, *Gorrito s/n (next to Con los Angeles), T495 5379.* Pretty, rustic rooms, decorated in local style, and well-equipped

cabañas for 2-6 people.

D-F pp Malka, *San Martín s/n, 5 blocks from plaza up steep hill, T495 5197, www.tilcara jujuy.com.ar/malka* Quite the most welcoming place to stay in Tilcara is its superb youth hostel, one of the country's best. It has beautifully situated rustic *cabañas* and double rooms, all with kitchen and laundry facilities, Hostelling International affiliated. Owner and guide Juan organizes a great range of trips, including several days' trek to Calilegua, horse riding and bike hire. Highly recommended.

D Quinta La Paceña, *Padilla y Ambosetti, T495 5098, quintalapacena@yahoo.com.ar* A peaceful haven in this architect-designed traditional adobe house, with stylish small rooms for 2 to 4 people, a big gorgeous garden to sit in.

F pp La Morada, *Debenedetti s/n, T/F495 5118.* Good rooms for 2 to 5 people with cooking facilities.

F pp Wiphala, *Jujuy 549, T495 5015, www.wiphala.com.ar* An attractive adobe built *hostería* with a warm atmosphere, use of kitchen, garden and pool. Also organize 4WD trips and horseriding.

Camping

Camping El Jardín, *access on Belgrano, T495 5128.* US$2, per tent, with hot showers, and **F pp** basic hostel accommodation.

Huacalera and Uquía *p255*

C Hosteria de Uquía, *T490523, next door to the Iglesia San Francisco de Paula, elportillo@cootepal.com.ar* Simple rooms around a courtyard, and very good food.

D Hostal La Granja, *Huacalera, T0388-426 1766.* A welcoming and rustic place with pool, outstanding food and service, a good base for exploring the region.

● *Phone codes Purmamarca, Tilcara: 0388; La Quiaca: 03885; Humahuaca, Iruya, Yavi: 03887*

C Camino del Inca, *Calle Ejército del Norte s/n, signposted on the other side of the river, T421136, tito@imagine.com.ar* A smart well-built modern hotel in traditional style with rooms coming off colonnaded galleries, around a pool. Also a good restaurant (set menu US$4), and excursions organized.

D Residencial Humahuaca, *Córdoba y Corrientes, 1 block from bus terminal, T421141.* Good clean *residencial*.

D/E Posada el Sol, *over the bridge, signposted, B Medalla Milagrosa, T421466, posadaelsol@imagine.com.ar* Friendly comfortable hostal, by far the best budget accommodation in town, with some doubles, tours arranged.

F pp Cabaña El Cardón, *T156-29072, www.elcardon.8K.com* Rural *cabaña* for 4-5 people, all facilities, regional meals and excursions offered by charming family.

Iruya *p256*

C Hostería de Iruya, *T156 29152.* Extremely comfortable with beautifully simple rooms, smart bathrooms, and excellent food, this has great views from the top of the village. Highly recommended.

E pp Hostal Federico Tercero, *at Café de Hostal, at the bottom of the steep main street, T15630727.* Owned by delightful singer Jesús, simple rooms, good food from breakfast to dinner, and frequent live music.

F pp Hospedaje Tacacho. A welcoming family owned house, with simple rooms, tremendous views over the valley, and a *comedor* on the plaza.

La Quiaca and around *p258*

D Hostería Munay, *Belgrano 51, T423924, www.munahotel.jujuy.com* Next best place in town, and very pleasant. Comfortable rooms.

D Turismo, *Siria y San Martín, T422243, intenmun@laquiaca.com.ar* The best place to stay. Modern, comfortable rooms with TV, pool, restaurant.

E Cristal, *Sarmiento 539, T422255.* Very basic functional rooms, shared bath.

E pp La Frontera, *Belgrano y Siria, downhill from Atahualpa bus stop, T422269.* This hotel and restaurant has good cheap food, basic but decent rooms. Very hospitable owner.

G pp Hostería Municipal, *ring the village's*

one public phone before you arrive 03887 491140. Huge rooms with several beds, shared bath.

Camping

Camping Municipal. Camping is also possible at the ACA service station about 300 m from the border.

Yavi *p259*

F Hostal de Yavi, *T03887-490523. elportillo@cootepal.com.ar* Simple bedrooms with bath, and some hostel space, with a cosy sitting room, good food cooked by the hospitable Javier and Gino, and a welcoming relaxed atmosphere. Tours also arranged to see cave paintings, moonlight walks, trekking and trips to the Laguna de los Pozuelos. Recommended.

F La Casona 'Jatum Huasi', *Sen Pérez y San Martín, T03885-422316, mccalizaya@laquiaca.com.ar* Homely and welcoming.

Parque Nacional Calilegua *p259*

There is a campsite at Aguas Negras (drinking water from river nearby, and some cooking facilities and tables). To camp at Mesada de las Colmenas ask permission at Aguas Blancas.

🍴 Eating

Purmamarca *p254*

La Posta, *on the plaza.* Excellent local dishes – *humitas* and *tamales* especially recommended.

Ruta 52, *opposite where the bus stops.* Very cheap and delicious food.

Tilcara *p255*

Bar del Centro, *Belgrano 547, T495 5318.* Quite the best in town, delicious inexpensive local dishes, and often live music too, in a beautiful minimalist interior. 3-course dinner US$3. Recommended.

El Patio Comidas, *Lavalle 352.* A welcoming place serving a great range, with a lovely patio at the back.

La Quiaca and around *p258*

Ruta 9, *on Route 9 on the way out of town to the south.* The best place to eat in town.

La Frontera, *in town.* An atmospheric place,

where the set men will cost you around US$2.

🎭 Entertainment

Tilcara *p255*
For a taste of Tilcara's culture, there are a couple of places not to be missed:
El Cafecito, *on the plaza*. Serves good coffee and wonderful locally grown herbal teas during the day, and has superb live folklore and jazz music at weekends from celebrated local musicians.
Lapeña de Carlitos, *on the plaza*. Regional music from the charismatic and delightful Carlitos, also *empanadas*, and drinks.

🧭 Tour operators

Tilcara *p255*
A recommended guide for informative trips to the *puna*, Iruya, Salinas Grandes, and archaeological sites, is historian **Ariel Mosca**, T495 5119, arielpuna@hotmail.com He's very well informed, and speaks English.
Oscar Branchesi, T495 5117, will take you to meet locals and gives you great insight into indigenous culture. Recommended.

Iruya *p256*
Norte Trekking, *T436 1844*, *www.nortetrekking.com* The region's most experienced guide, Federico Norte, runs small tours to Iruya, including other adventurous options, accordgint o the groups needs. Highly recommended.

🚌 Transport

Purmamarca *p254*
Bus Cotta Panamericana and Evelia all run several buses a day to **Jujuy** US$1.50, 1 hr, and up to **Humahuaca**, buses to **Susques**, 5 weekly.

Tilcala *p255*
Bus There are frequent services to all towns on the **Quebrada** and to **Jujuy**, and at least 3 buses a day to and from **La Quiaca** on the Bolivian border. **Cycle** *Malka*, *T495 5197*. Contact Juan for cycling excursions

Iruya *p256*
Bus Daily bus service from **Humahuaca**,

Empresa Mendoza (T421016), 1030 daily, arriving 1330, US$3, US$6.50 return, returning to Humahuaca 1515. Also excursions of several days organized by tour companies. Tickets from the food shop round the corner from the church.

Reserva Nacional Laguna de los Pozuelos *p257*
Diego Bach leads excellent and highly informed excursions, from one day to several days, and may include panning for gold as the Jesuits did. Highly recommended is a 5-day trek on horseback to the cloudforest Parque Nacional El Barritú, punatours@hotmail.com, T03885-422797, 156860691.

Casabindo *p256*
Bus La Quiaqueña bus daily on Route 40 from Jujuy to **La Quiaca** passes through Casabindo. **Burgos Bus** leaves Mon, Wed, Fri, at 0930 to go to **Abras Pamapas**, returning at 1630, cheaper option than tours.

Parque Nacional Calilegua *p259*
Trucks run by **Empresa Valle Grande**, *Libertad 780*, leave Libertador, Tue and Sat, 0730, 6 hrs if road conditions are good, very crowded, returning Sun and Thu 1000. Check with Sr Arcona (the driver, everyone knows him) in Libertador whether the truck is going. Weather unpredictable. Or contact Gustavo Lozano at Los Claveles 358, Barrio Jardín, T421647, who will contact Angel Caradonna to pick you up.

La Quiaca and around *p258*
Bus Terminal at España y Belgrano, luggage storage. Taxi to border US$1.00. There are 6-8 buses a day to **Salta** (US$7-10) with Balut (7½ hrs), **Atahualpa** and **Brown**. Several daily to **Humahuaca**, US$4, 3 hrs, and to **Jujuy**, US$6, 5-6½ hrs. Take your own food, as there are sometimes long delays. Buses may be stopped for routine border police controls and searched for coca leaves; don't carry any drugs. NB overnight buses from Jujuy may arrive in the early morning when no restaurants are open and it's extremely cold outside. To **Buenos Aires**, via Jujuy, US$59 including meals, 28 hrs. From **Jujuy** to **Santa Catalina** via La Quiaca, 19 hrs, twice a week.

Routes to Bolivia *p260*

Bus To **Orán**, 1 hr, US$1.70. To **Pocitos** change at Tartagal, making sure your ticket is stamped with the next bus time or you won't be allowed on it. To **Buenos Aires** US$91. To **Salta** US$14.50, 3 a day. To **Formosa** daily at 1300, 17 hrs, US$40, Atahualpa, but frequently cancelled; alternative is to take bus to **Pichanal**, US$1.25, several companies, change for **J V**

Gonzales, US$10, 1600, and change again for **Resistencia**, 2215, then take a bus to Formosa.

Yavi *p259*
Getting to Yavi is much easier with your own transport, but there are buses from **La Quiaca** 4 times a day, US$0.50. and taxis cost around US$5 each way.

Catamarca Province

Most of the population of this large province is based in the capital, leaving the stunning countryside to the north and west largely empty of people. The city itself is not the region's most lovely, although it's transformed in July by the lively annual poncho festival. The small towns of Belén and Andagalá are animated oases on the way to the puna, where the tiny hamlets of Fiambalá and Tinogasta are possible bases for climbing Mount Psissis in the highlands to the far west. From Belén, a lonely road leads north across the puna to remotest Antofagasta de la Sierra, which is surrounded by a vast expanse of salt flats. From here, you could continue to San Antonio de las Cobres, cross to Chile at the Paso de Socompa or return southeast to Salta. Closer to Catamarca city, the charming town of El Rodeo is a popular weekend retreat for Catamarqueños, with its refreshing microclimate and good walks. And further north, on the border with Tucumán, is the delightful village of Santa María, a lovely place to rest on the way to Salta near the spectacular ruins at Quilmes. The province is not the northwest's most accessible, but you'll be warmly welcomed especially in its remotest reaches; and you'll want to stuff olives, walnuts and superb woven textiles in your bag to bring home.

Catamarca City → *Phone code: 03833 Colour map1, C3 Population: 130,000*

The provincial capital is a rather run down place, Catamarca is most famous for its textiles, and unless you're here for the poncho festival in the second fortnight in July, there's little to draw you to the city, or keep you here. It does have some attractive buildings, designed by the Italian architect Luigi Caravati in the late 19th century, and a wonderful museum, but the accommodation is poor, and the summers are unbearably hot with temperatures up to 45°C. El Rodeo, an hour away by regular minibus, makes a far more appealing alternative if you're on the way to the puna or Chile. ➤➤ For Sleeping, Eating and other listings, see pages 269-271.

Ins and outs
Getting there Catamarca's airport, 20 km south, has a daily flight to and from Buenos Aires. Alternatively, there are four buses from Buenos Aires a day, taking 25 hours. There are several buses a day to Salta, Tucumán, Mendoza and La Rioja, but the route to Santiago del Estero is over high mountains, and only one slow bus a day operates. The bus terminal is seven blocks southeast of the main plaza.

Getting around The city is small enough to walk around, with most hotels situated northwest of the plaza. Buses also link the city to outlying areas of the province and there are many minibuses a day to Villa El Rodeo.

Tourist information Tourist information can be found in a small office on the south side of the plaza right next to the cinema, San Martín 555, T437791, 0900-2100, daily. Extremely helpful staff hand out leaflets on local places of interest, can advise on accommodation and have a rare grasp of bus times and prices. Provincial tourist office, Roca y Virgen del Valle, T/F437594, Mon-Fri 0700-1300, 1400-2000. Also office in airport.

Best time to visit The best time to visit is during the *Poncho* festival in late July, and it's best to avoid the summer, when temperatures exceed 40°. Very sensibly, the siesta is strictly observed here, and everything closes down from 1230 to 1700, www.catamarca.com

> *This area is known for poor water: drink bottled water, don't order salad or ice in the towns and villages*

Sights

The city centres around Plaza 25 de Mayo, designed by Charles Thays, a big leafy central plaza with tall trees of unusual species, providing much needed shade from the scorching summer heat, with a rather striking equestrian sculpture of San Martín. There's a white stuccoed **Casa de Gobierno** (1891), designed by Caravati, and to the west, the faded red bulk of his neo-classical **cathedral** (1878), looking rather forlorn but sporting a pair of fine mosaic tiled cupolas on its towers. The interior is a rather uncelestial peeling *eau de nil*, but the scenes from the life of Christ painted on the ceiling are lovely. In a chapel high above and behind the altar, you can visit the much worshipped Virgen del Valle all dressed up, on a mighty gilded pedestal. Access is up a double staircase system to the *Camarín*, where the walls of the chapel are lined with plaques of offerings and cases crammed with thousands of silver arms, legs hands and eyes offered by her followers over the years. The **Iglesia de San Francisco** (1882), one block north of the plaza, has an impressive colonial-style façade. And five blocks west of the plaza, is the **Paseo General Navarro**, a rather scrappy bit of park surrounded by huge trees, with good views over the town, but not recommended for a quiet picnic.

The Northwest Catamarca City

Catamarca

Sleeping	El Gran **3**	Eating
Ancasti **1**	Pucara **5**	La Tinaja **1**
Arenales **2**	Residencial Rincal **6**	Salsa Criolla **3**
Casino **4**		Sociedad Española **2**

0 metres 200
0 yards 200

There might be local art worth seeing at the **Museo de Bellas Artes** ⓘ *Sarmiento 347, Mon-Sat 0700-1300, 1400-2000, free*, with small temporary exhibitions, and there are handicrafts to buy at the **Feria Artesanal** ⓘ *Mon-Fri, 0800-1200 for the factory but market 0800-1330, 1500-2100*, in the 'Manzana de Turismo' (with no other obvious tourist attractions), which is also a carpet factory.

The must-see of the city is the incredible **Museo Arqueológico** ⓘ *Sarmiento 450, Mon-Fri 0700-1300, 1430-2000, Sat, Sun 1200-1900, US$0.30, T437 413*, containing an enormous collection of artefacts from the sophisticated pre-Hispanic cultures who inhabited the area from around 1000 BC. There are carved stone vessels with animal figures leaping off their sides, beautifully painted funerary urns, deliberately-flattened skulls (compressed by the owners by wearing wooden boards), a comical two headed pot with a smiling llama at one end and an anxious looking man the other, and quite a shocking mummified baby, naturally conserved above 5000 m. Allow at least an hour to discover many more fascinating finds. Highly recommended. ▶▶ *For Sleeping, Eating and other listings, see pages 269-271.*

Excursions

There are two popular escapes from the city. Along the **Valle de Catamarca**, stretching north of the city, are a series of attractive churches, built mostly in the 19th-century, at **San Isidro**, 5 km east, at **Villa Dolores**, 1 km further north, and at **San José**, 4 km further north, whose colonial church dates from 1780. Oldest of all is **La Señora del Rosario**, 2 km east, a simple white building dating from 1715. Some 25 km north of Catamarca, the **Dique Las Pirquitas** lake has good fishing and watersports, as well as trekking and mountain-biking. To get to the lake, bus No 1A from bus terminal, every 30 mins, stops at Hostería de Turismo (with restaurant) at Villa Pirquitas, from where it is about 45-minute walk to the lake.

Some 37 km north of the city is the pretty weekend retreat of El Rodeo in lovely mountain setting with a cool microclimate, with lots of good walks and horseriding. There's a great two-day hike to Cerro el Mancho, 4550 m above sea level, and trout fishing in the Río Ambato. Ask the friendly tourist information T490043. Easy access and charming *hosterias* make this a pleasant alternative to staying in the city. Rodeo runs several combis a day (minibuses) from the car park Estacionamento San Martin, half a block east of the plaza on San Marin. US$5 each way, return buses the same day.

Las Juntas, a further 20 km away on the same road, is another rural retreat from the city, also in attractive mountainous countryside. Los Hermanos Vergara run buses from Catamarca terminal Mon to Sat 0800 and 2000.

For fine panoramic views over the Valle de Catamarca head for the **Cuesta del Portezuelo**, along the road snaking up the Sierra de Ancasti, 20 km northeast of the town. It's the route to Lavalle and Santiago del Estero, but the only bus takes an eternity. The Cuesta rises through 13 hairpin bends to 1,680 m, and from the summit, with a vista over the city and valley below, the road continues via El Alto (950 m). There's a reservoir nearby, Dique Ipizca, good for *pejerrey* fishing. Take a tour, if this appeals. ▶▶ *For Sleeping, Eating and other listings, see pages 269-271.*

Belén → *Phone code: 03835 Colour map 1, B2 Population: 8,800*

Either way you approach Belén (1,240 m) – whether from Andagalá on Route 46, or along the equally poor Route 40, you'll be very relieved to arrive. Route 40 takes you across vast open plains fringed with chocolate-coloured flaking mountains, and through the desolate little village of **Hualfin**, with thermal baths in summer at **Pozo Verde**, to the north. This is a better road than the Route 46, but still should not be attempted in the rainy season (February to March) when the rivers crossing the roads are high. Both roads are easier and safer in a 4WD.

There are good views from the **Cerro de Nuestra Senora de Belén**, a hill above the town, where a newly constructed Virgen (the last one was struck by lightning) watches

Festivals of the northwest

The religious calendar is celebrated in the northwest of Argentina through a series of festivals which mix Christianity with indigenous pagan beliefs such as the worship of La Pachamama. Loosely translated as goddess of the earth, La Pachamama refers to a time and place in the cosmos, the sky and the sea too. She is still worshipped today throughout the Andean region.

On August 1 a month-long celebration of the Pachamama begins when offerings are made to 'feed the earth'. It's supposed that the gods are sleeping under the earth through winter, and that they need to be woken up and fed. This is when the first seeds are planted, so the earth is also fed to thank La Pachamama in advance for a good yield. At this time fires are burned all over the countryside, as the earth is also burned or purified in preparation, and even in Salta there are piles of leaves on fire, with *saumerio* resin or fragrant herbs being added to create smoke. Smoke is important as it's the means of carrying prayers to the gods in the sky realm.

Andean civilizations believe that there are gods in all three realms: in the sky, on the earth's surface and under the earth. The serpent is the symbol of La Pachamama because it can exist in all three levels. Similarly, *apachetas* (piles of rocks), which are also believed to be sacred, are made to reach into the sky from beneath the earth, and on these apachetas offerings are made. On August 1, the traditional offerings are coca leaves, cigarettes, all kinds of liquids including wine and all manner of foods, to encourage the Pachamama to yield such riches again. Often a young animal is slaughtered and laid in the earth as a sacrifice. When the Spanish encountered these piles of stones, they built their churches on them, recognizing them to be significant.

The Christian calendar is maintained, with big celebrations for Carnival for two weeks in November, when the entire Quebrada de Humahuaca is lively, and for Easter, when Tilcara particularly has a special celebration: thousands of pan pipe musicians gather to accompany a religious procession down the mountain. *All Souls Day* is strongly celebrated on November 1, when it's believed the souls of the dead (particularly those in their first year of death) will come back to earth to eat. Elaborate meals are prepared for the loved ones, with figures of sweet bread representing things for them to take back tot the next world. Proof that this is more than a Christian festival comes from the fact that in pre-Hispanic times, the mummies of the dead, and the beautifully decorated funerary urns throughout the region's museums were all disinterred in November to be paraded around the town, and then returned to their burial positions.

On October 4 in remote villages of the *puna*, such as Iruya, there are private festivals which you're unlikely to see, known as *Danza de los Cachis*. A large group of people who have come down to the valley from far-flung parts of the *puna* are gathered together to drink and dance, and at some point a woman may leave to have sex with various members of the group, often as many as five a night. Nothing ill is thought of the woman, and any children born of this time are revered in the village. In small communities, it's one way of avoiding in-breeding.

Bear in mind that these rituals hold great significance for their participants, and are not just tourist attractions.

The Northwest Catamarca City

over the place. There's a small tourist office, **Direccion de Turismo**, at the bus terminal a block from the plaza on Belgrano, T461539, daily 0900-1300, 1600-2000, alpamicuna@cotelbelen.com.ar For excursions in 4WD, go to the friendly and extremely helpful **Ampujaco** just off the plaza on Lavalle, and at Hotel Belén at Gral Roca 190, T461189, who organize interesting tours to historical sites nearby; www.belencat.com.ar ▶▶ *For Sleeping, Eating and other listings, see pages 269-271.*

Londres → *Population: 1,850*

South of Belén, Route 40 is paved to Chilecito via Londres (1,300 m), a pretty and quiet village, with a remote feel. Founded in 1558, it is the second-oldest town in Argentina, though its site was moved several times. It was named in honour of the marriage of Mary Tudor and Philip II: the *municipalidad* displays a glass coat-of-arms of the city of London and a copy of the marriage proposal. There are important Inca ruins, **Las Ruinas Shincal** ① *Mon-Fri 0730-1330, 1700-1900, tours run by the helpful Ampujaco Tur in Belén, T461189*, 5 km northwest, signposted from the second plaza you come to after entering the village from Belén. Londres also celebrates its walnut festival in February. There are no hotels here, but several *hospedajes* and a campsite on the route to Shincal, T491019. Food can be bought from the few shops around the plaza.

North of Belén

There are two routes north to Salta. The most direct is via Route 40 which runs northeast another 176 km, largely unpaved, to Santa María at Tucumán provincial border (see page 275), and on to Cafayate (page 243) and Salta.

The alternative is via Route 43, which branches west off Route 40 at a point 52 km north of Belén and runs across the high *puna* to Antofagasta de la Sierra and San Antonio de los Cobres (see page 232). This route is challenging at the best of times, and impassable for ordinary cars after heavy rains. The stretch just after the junction with Route 40 is very difficult, with 37 km of fords. At Km 87 is Cerro Compo (3,125 m), from which the descent is magnificent; at Km 99 the road turns right to Laguna Blanca, where there is a museum and a small vicuña farm (don't go straight ahead at the junction). There are thermal springs along this road at Villavil, 13 km further north, open from January to April, and a *hostería* too (D). Drivers should note that you'll need enough fuel for 600 km on unmaintained roads, with fuel consumption being double at high altitudes. Fill up at Hualfín and San Antonio de los Cobres.

Antofagasta de la Sierra → *Colour map 1, B2 Population 900*

The main settlement in sparsely populated northwest Catamarca, Antofagasta de la Sierra (3,365 m) is situated on the Río Punilla, 260 km north of Belén and 557 km northwest of the provincial capital. With its low pinkish adobe buildings, surrounded by vast empty lunar landscapes and massive volcanoes, it's a wonderfully remote place. To the west are the salt flats of the **Salar de Antofalla**, though these are inaccessible, and it's easier to reach the **Salar de Hombre Muerte** on Route 43 to San Antonio de los Cobres to the north, going with a guide.

Within reach are several interesting archaeological sites: there are ruins at **Campo Alumbreras**, in the shadow of the volcano of the same name, with a pre-Columbian *pucará* (fort) with nearby petroglyphs. Guides can be found at the small but wonderful museum **Museo del Hombre**, T471001, which contains incredibly well preserved pre-Hispanic textiles, and the mummified baby, 2,000 years old. Fascinating. There's no petrol station, but fuel can be bought from the *intendencia*.

⬤ Sleeping

Catamarca *p264, map p265*

Hotels are pricey here, and all overcharge for single rooms.

C Hotel Casino Catamarca, *Pasaje Cesar Carman s/n, T432928*, Quite the smartest place to stay with its (discretely hidden) casino, large pool (summer only), cheerful bright restaurant, and well-decorated rooms, all with minibar, TV cable, hidden away behind the ACA service station, 4 blocks from the centre. It's peaceful and very welcoming, but beware that in peak summer months of Jan and Feb partying goes on to the early hours, when the hotel is very popular. The best in its range by far.

C Ancasti, *Sarmiento 520, T435952, hotelancasti@cedeconet.com.ar* Next best option in Catamarca, aspiring to be a business hotel. The modernized rooms are comfortable but drab and the bathrooms are tiny. There are sometimes cheaper deals to include dinner in the pleasant airy restaurant.

C Arenales, *Sarmiento 542, T431329/330, www.hotel-arenales.com.ar* Welcoming, but slightly institutional in feel. Pleasant plain rooms with well-equipped bathrooms, minimalist though not stylish exactly, but the most comfy in the range.

D El Gran Hotel Camilo *Melet 41, T426715.* You'll get the friendliest welcome here and it's a real pleasure to walk into such a nicely maintained place, with spacious and comfortable rooms, all with bath TV and A/c, reductions for cash. Recommended.

D Pucara, *Caseros 501, T03833-431569, 430688.* If you've a taste for kitsch, try the *Pucara* with hideously bold decor in the entrance lounge, but the bedrooms are comfortable, if you can cope with pink satin bedspreads and flamenco prints.

E Residencial Rincal, *Vicario Segura 1120, T421083.* There are no youth hostels in the city, so your cheapest option this *residencial*, not recommended for single women. It's the best and newest of the lot, but doesn't include breakfast.

Around Catamarca *p266*

C Hostería El Rodeo, *T490296, Cerro el Mancho www.hotelguia.com/elrodeo* Highly recommended, with lovely spacious rooms, pool, good restaurant, and great views. Can organize climbing, 4WD trips and excursions for children too.

E La Casa de Chicha, *Los Gladiolos s/n, Cerro el Mancho, T490082, la_casa_de_chicha@yahoo.com.ar* With less facilities than **El Rodeo**, but perhaps more idyllic set in a really gorgeous setting right in the mountains, and rooms with antique furniture. Try the excellent restuarant for lunch and dinner, or have tea in the beautiful garden, filled with pear trees.

Belén *p266*

C Belén, *Belgrano y Cubas, T461501, www.belencat.com.ar* The most comfortable place to stay. Recently refurbished with quite stylish plain rooms in a modern block in a little leafy garden, and also a tour operator.

D Samai, *Urquiza 349, T461320.* Old fashioned but very welcoming, and its homely little rooms have bathrooms and fans.

Londres *p268*
Camping

Camping Shincal, at the ruins near Londres, has a good site, but otherwise the **Reserva Natural**, *T461304*, and El Puente, *T461539* are both pleasant.

Antofagasta de la Sierra *p268*

D Albergue Municipal, *T471001.* Without bath, hot water.

E pp Almacén Rodríguez, *Belgrano y Catamarca.* Serves meals, including breakfast.

E pp Pensión Darío, *blue door off main plaza.*

⑦ Eating

Catamarca *p264, map p265*

There are few good restaurants in Catamarca, many cheap ones around the Plaza 25 de Agosto and the bus terminal but this area is not safe at night.

 For an explanation of the sleeping and eating price codes used in this guide, see the inside front cover. Other relevant information is provided in the Essentials chapter, page 44.

$$ **La Tinaja**, *Sarmiento 533. T435853*. The best eating choice by far, this delicious *parrilla* does really excellent pastas. Slightly pricey, but absolutely worth it, and deservedly popular.

$$ **Salsa Criolla**, *Republica 546 on the plaza*. Traditional and popular *parrilla*. Sloppy service, but the beef is recommended. The same owner runs Italian-style **Trattoria Montecarlo** next door, whose speciality is pasta, but you can eat beef from the *parrilla* here too.

$ **Socieded Espanola**, *Virgen del Valle 725, near the Paseo, T431897*. Recommended for its quality and variety, serving paella and other seafood as well as other Spanish specialities, with friendly service, and worth the 5-block walk from the main plaza.

Belén *p266*
The best *parrilla* is **El Unico**, and for a drink or *lomitos*, **Bar El Seminario** is a great meeting point for the whole town, especially at weekends, when its customers spill out onto tables in the plaza.

⊛ Festivals and events

Catamarca *p264, map p265*
The city's major festival is the *Festival Nacional del Poncho* held in the third week in Jul, a huge *feria aretesanal* with the best of the province's handicrafts, as well as those from other parts of the country, and with 4 nights of excellent *folclore* music. There are pilgrimages to the Virgen del Valle Dec 8-16 and the week following Easter, when hotel rooms are hard to find.

Belén *p266*
The town's most important is **Fiesta de Nuestra Señora de Belén**, *20 Dec-6 Jan*; **Carnival** is celebrated in big style in *Feb*. At Easter there are processions for the Virgin.

⊙ Shopping

Catamarca *p264, map p265*
Catamarca specialities are available from **Cuesta del Portezuelo**, *Sarmiento 571, T452675*, and **Fabrica Valdez**, *Sarmiento 578, T425175*. There's a range of handicrafts and

you can see carpets being woven at the **Mercado Artesanal**, *Virgen del Valle 945*, daily 0800-1330, 1500-2100; carpet factory Mon-Fri 0800-1200.

⊘ Tour operators

Catamarca *p264, map p265*
Tours are offered to El Rodeo and there are various opportunities to practice adventure ports:
Club Mountain Bike,
www.mtbcat.com.ar Mountain bike hire.
Agrupacion Calchaqui, *Tourism block, Gral. Roca 1 block, 436368*. Mountaineering organized.
Anibal Vazquez, *T03835-471001*. Walking expeditions in Antofagasta de la Sierra.

⊙ Transport

Catamarca *p264, map p265*
Air
Aeropuerto Felipe Varela, 20 km south, T430080. **Aerolíneas Argentinas, Southern Winds** to **Buenos Aires** and **La Rioja**.

Bus
Modern terminal is 5 blocks southeast of plaza at Güemes y Tucumán T437578, with shops, café, ATM and *locutorio*. The entrance is mysteriously through a car park. Taxi to/from Plaza 25 de Mayo US$0.50. To **Tucumán**, several companies, 3½-4hrs, US$4. To **Buenos Aires**, 4 companies daily, 15 hrs, US$25. To **Córdoba**, 4 companies daily, 6 hrs, US$8. To **Santiago del Estero**, just one service, takes 9 hrs, scenic route, but just as quick to go via **Tucumán**, US$8. To **Mendoza**, several companies, daily, 10 hrs, US$12. To **La Rioja**, several companies, daily, US$4, 2 hrs. To **Tinogasta**, 3 companies, US$6. To **Belén** via Aimogasta and Londres, several companies, 5 hrs, US$6; **Marín** (via Aconquija). To **Andagalá** 2 companies, 4 buses daily, 4½ hrs, US$5.

Belén *p266*
Buses from Belén to **Santa María**, **San Cayetano** and **Parra** (connection there with other companies to Cafayate and Salta), daily, 5 hrs, US$4. To **Tinogasta**, **Robledo**, 3

weekly, 3hrs, US$4. To **Antofagasta de la Sierra**, El Antofagasteño, 3 weekly, 7 hrs, US$12. For more frequent services to **Catamarca** or **La Rioja**, take bus to **Aimogasta**, 1 hour, US$1.50.

Antofagasta de la Sierra *p268*
Buses from **Belén**, Tue, Thu, Sun 0800, or hire a pickup or hitch.

◐ Directory

Catamarca *p264, map p265*
Airline offices Aerolíneas Argentinas,

Sarmiento 589, T424450. Southern Winds, *Prado 357, T431006.* **Banks** Many ATMs for all major cards, along Rivadavia and at bus terminal, and around corner of Esquiu and Republica, and Banco de la Nación, *San Martín 632.* TCs can only be cashed at BBVA Banco Francés, *Rivadavia 520.*
Communications Post office *San Martín 753,* slow, open 0800-1300, 1600-2000. **Telephone** Several *locutorios* including *Rivadavia 758*, open 0700-2400, daily. **Internet** CEDECC, *Esquiu 414.* Telecom, *Sarmiento 741.* Telefónica, *Rivadavia 650.*

Tucumán Province

One of the country's largest cities lies in one its smallest provinces, with a subtropical climate, sugar, tobacco and lemons grown in the province. Outside the modern provincial capital, in the surrounding mountains to the north and west, is the popular weekend retreat of Tafí del Valle, with its cool microclimate. Further northwest still, on the route to Cafayate in Salta, are the delightful small towns of Aimachá and Santa María, over the border in Catamarca, both good bases for exploring Quilmes, one of Argentina's most important archaeological sites. Here you can wander around the extensive remains of a city of 5,000 Calchaquíes, built into the side of a mountain amidst breathtaking scenery.

San Miguel de Tucumán City

→ *Phone code: 0381 Colour map 1, B3 Population: 700,000*

The city of San Miguel de Tucumán, known more simply as Tucumán, lies almost equidistant between Catamarca and Salta on a broad plain just east of the massive Sierra de Aconquija. It is the largest and most important city in the north, made rich on sugar production, but lacking style or architectural splendour. Although it was one of the first cities to be founded by the Spanish, few of its colonial buildings remain, and the city has suffered economically in the recent recession. However, it's a busy centre with plentiful restaurants and a huge park designed by Charles Thays. There are few attractions for visitors, and it's overwhelmingly hot in summer – the siesta here from 1230-1630 is strictly observed – but it does have a couple of good museums and lively nightlife. ▶▶ *For Sleeping, Eating and other listings, see pages 278-282.*

Ins and outs

Getting there The airport, 10 km east of town, is linked to the city by Bus 120 (tokens called *cospeles* required), US$1.50. There are daily flights from Buenos Aires, and from neighbouring cities. This is one of the few places reached by long-distance train from Buenos Aires. There's a huge modern bus terminal, seven blocks from the plaza, where long-distance buses arrive from all parts of the country, as well as Chile and Peru.

Getting around The plaza is the city's heart along with the busy pedestrianized shopping streets north and west of it; it's an easy place to get around on foot, but taxis are cheap and reliable. There are several places to stay worth recommending,

The Northwest San Miguel de Tucumán City

but if this is a strategic stopover for you, you might prefer to retreat to the cooler mountains of Tafí del Valle as the Tucumános do at weekends.

Best time to visit The city's big festivals are the day of Independence, July 9 when Tucumán is capital of the country for the day, and on September 24, celebrating the day Belgrano won the Battle of Tucumán, with a huge procession. Summer is best avoided in the city, because of the heat, January and February especially.

Tourist information There's a very helpful tourist office on the plaza at 24 de Septiembre 484, T430 3644, www.turismoentucuman.com www.tucuman turismo.com, open 0800-2200. Also in the bus terminal and airport.

History
Tucumán was an important city in Spanish colonial times. Founded in 1565 and transferred to its present site in 1685, it was a stragetic stop for mule trains on the routes from Bolivia to Buenos Aires and Mendoza. With a colonial economy based on sugar, citrus fruit and tobacco, it developed a landed aristocracy distinct from those of Buenos Aires and Córdoba. The city was then the site of an important battle during the Wars of Independence: Belgrano's victory here in 1812 over a royalist army ended the Spanish threat to restore colonial rule over the River Plate area. Tucumán's wealth was derived from sugar, and it remains the biggest industry, though tobacco and lemons have also become vital exports in recent decades. The province has suffered badly in the recent recession, with rising unemployment, and – astoundingly – child poverty. The town has consequently a rather neglected air.

Sights
Plaza Independencia in the city's commercial centre, and has many tall palms and mature trees giving welcome shade in the sweltering heat. At night it's full of

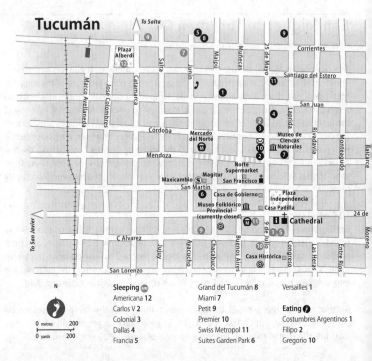

Tucumán

Sleeping
Americana 12
Carlos V 2
Colonial 3
Dallas 4
Francia 5

Grand del Tucumán 8
Miami 7
Petit 9
Premier 10
Swiss Metropol 11
Suites Garden Park 6

Versailles 1

Eating
Costumbres Argentinos 1
Filipo 2
Gregorio 10

tucumanos eating ice cream from the many *heladerías* around. Among its attractive buildings are the ornate Italianate **Casa de Gobierno** (1910), with tall palms outside and art nouveau balconies. Next door is a typical *casa de Chorizo* (sausage house), **Casa Padilla** ① *25 de Mayo 36, Mon-Sat 0900-1230, 1600-1900. closed Sun*, a series of skinny rooms off open patios, whose collection of china and paintings belonging to a wealthy Tucumán family gives you a flavour of 19th-century life. Across the road, the **church of San Francisco** (1891) has a rather gloomy interior, but a picturesque façade and tiled cupola. On the south side of the plaza, the pink and white neoclassical **cathedral** (1852) has a distinctive cupola, but disappointingly bland modern interior, the ceiling painted, uninspiringly, with rainbows and whales.

South of the plaza, on Calle Congreso, is the **Casa Histórica** ① *0900-1300, 1500-1900, US$0.70, son et lumière programme in garden nightly (not Thu, except in Jul) at 2030,adults US$2, children US$1, tickets also from tourist office on Plaza Independencia, no seats*. Here, there are rooms around two attractive patios, filled with old furniture, historical documents and some fine Cuzqueño school paintings. The highlight is the actual room where the Declaration of Independence was drafted, mannequins in 19th-century dress rather bizarrely replacing the important political leaders, whose portraits line the walls. Next to it is a room full of interesting religious artefacts, and there's a *son et lumière* display in the garden. It's also worth visiting the **Museo de Ciencias Naturales** ① *25 de Mayo 265 in University building, T4216024, Mon-Fri, 0800-1330*. The fine collection which includes funerary urns and other artefacts from the pre-Hispanic cultures of the Calchaquí valleys. The **Museo Folklórico Museo Folklórico Provincial** ① *24 de Septiembre 565*, is currently closed, but when open, has an impressive collection of silverwork from Peru and musical instruments in an old colonial house.

Tucumán's enormous park, **Parque Nueve de Julio**, east of the centre, is a much used green space, designed by French landscape architect Charles Thays who designed the *Parque Tres de Febrero* in Buenos Aires. With many subtropical trees, it was once the property of Bishop Colombres who played an important role in the development of the local sugar industry, and whose handsome house is now a museum with a display on sugar-making: **Museo de la Industria Azucarera** ① *0900-1800, US$1*. The park also has a lake and lots of sports facilities.

Il Postino **3**
Klo y Klo **5**
La Leñita **4**
La Mostaza **6**
Los Negros **9**
Maxim **11**

Panadería Villecco **8**
Sir Harris **7**

Northwest Tucumán

Tucumán has stunning mountain scenery to the west and north of the province, along the Nevados de Aconquija, where there are several attractive small towns to visit on the way to Salta. Of the two possible routes, Route 9, via Rosario de la Frontera and Güemes is far quicker, but unless you're rushing, take the road to Cafayate. Travelling through spectacular landscapes all the way, the route also passes the archaeological sites of Tafí del Valle and Quilmes and the charming small towns of Santa María and Aimacha.

Belgrano

The other major name of Argentina's struggle for independence, Belgrano is second only to San Martín, even though his plans to establish a constitutional monarchy failed entirely and his military career was marked by defeat. He did create the Argentine flag, though: first unfurled in a dramatic gesture by the Río Paraná in 1812.

Born into a wealthy merchant family in Buenos Aires in 1770, Belgrano was educated in Spain and on his return became a leading figure in a circle of intellectuals influenced by the European enlightenment. He was an advocate of free trade and breaking away from Spanish colonial rule with its trading restrictions. His first big failure came in 1811, when he commanded a military expedition to Paraguay, convinced that the Paraguayans would support his cause. His 700 men were overwhelmed by 5,000 Paraguayans and defeated. In command of the northern armies, he defeated Royalist forces at Tucumán in September 1812, and Salta in February 1813. But then his attempt to end Spanish control over Alto Peru

(modern Bolivia), by seizing Potosí, failed. He was forced to return to Tucumán where he was replaced by San Martín. However, his saving of the city of Jujuy is fondly remembered by its people each year at the Fiesta of the Exodus, even though their ancestors all lost their homes in the process. In the face of certain attack from battle-hungry Spanish armies descending from the north, Belgrano commanded the people of Jujuy to abandon their homes, burn and raze them to the ground, so that the Spanish would find nothing worth occupying. In an extraordinary sacrifice, this is what they did, and so the site of Jujuy was spared.

In 1815 Belgrano was sent to Europe to persuade Spain to accept Argentine independence if ruled by a king from the Spanish royal family. The mission failed. He then took part in the crucial Congress of Tucumán, arguing successfully for independence, but his schemes for a monarchy, ruled by a descendent of the Incas were again rejected. After a further period with the northern armies, Belgrano died in Buenos Aires in 1820.

Tafí del Valle → *Phone code: 03867 Colour map 1, B3 Population: 2,600*

Quite apart from the relief of leaving the searing heat of the city, the journey from Tucumán to Tafí is very satisfying. Route 307 leads northwest towards Cafayate, climbing through sugar and citrus fruit plantations, and then jungly subtropical forest, before entering the wide Valle de Tafí, surrounded by mountains densely covered in velvety vegetation. At Km 69 there is a statue to 'El Indio', with good views from the picnic area.

Tafí (2,100 m) is a popular weekend retreat from the heat of the city for Tucumános, since it has a cool microclimate, and makes a good base for walking, with several peaks of the Sierra de Aconquija providing challenging day-hikes. Within the sprawling town itself, you can walk by the Ríos El Churqui and Blanquito and to the Parque de los Menhires, where a collection of 129 engraved granite monoliths stand to the south of an attractive reservoir, the **Embalse Angostura**, in the valley below. For hikes into the mountains, it's best to go with a guide: see La Cumbre page 281. There's some excellent accommodation, better at the upper end of the market, makes this an appealing alternative to staying in Tucumán. Most shops are on the main streets Avenida Gobernador Critto (becoming Los Faroles to the west near the plaza) and Av Pte Peron. At the junction you can buy good locally made cheese and delicious bread, while there's a basic **tourist information centre** to the south of the semi circular plaza, 0800-1800 daily, no phone. You'll have to pay for a map, US$1, but they do have lists of accommodation, if you're persistent. Here you will also find Oscar Branchesi, T495 5117, who will take you to rural areas to meet locals and gives great insight into indigenous culture. Recommended.

Sights

Tafi's most historic building is the attractive **Capilla Jesuítica y Museo de La Banda** ① *Mon-Sat 0900-1900, Sun 0900-1600 (closing early off season), US$0.50, includes a guided visit*. This 18th-century chapel and 19th-century estancia has a small museum with interesting finds from the valley, and 18th-century religious art. Cross the bridge over Río Tafí southwest of town, and the museum is on your left after 500m. **Parque de los Menhires** lies in an attractive spot at the south of the Dique la Angostura, 10 km south of the centre of Tafí del Valle. The *menhires* are 129 granite stones, engraved with designs of unknown significance, said by some to symbolize fertility. Though they're undoubtedly intriguing in themselves, this is not quite the mystical site the tourist brochures claim it is, since the stones were put here in 1977, from where they were unearthed in spots all over the valley. There's a decent campsite nearby, and in the summer, windsurfing and sailing are available on the reservoir. 5 km further west, **El Mollar** is another weekend village with campsites and cabañas, and popular with teenage and student crowds. ▶▶ *For Sleeping, Eating and other listings, see pages 278-282.*

Northwest of Tafí del Valle

One of Argentina's most memorable journeys is along Route 307 northwest from Tafí, climbing out of the valley up to the mountain pass **Abra del Infiernillo** (3,042 m) at km 130. There are panoramic views south over the **Cumbres de Mala Mala**, often draped with a layer of cloud, the steeply sided deep green valley below, then breathtaking vistas as you emerge over the pass, looking north over the **Cumbre Calchaquíes** purple veiled in the distance, and finally over the dramatic Valles Calchaquíes. The road (now *ripio*) descends along hairy zigzags to the beautiful rocky landscape of the valley of the **Río del Amaichá**.

Amaichá → *Phone code: 03892 Colour map 1, B2 Population: 400*

Claiming rather grandly to have the best climate in the world, Amaichá (1,997 m) is a lovely tranquil little place which does indeed always seem to be sunny, and is a relaxing place to stay, with a splendid museum, the **Complejo Pachamama**, known also as *Casa de Piedra* ① *T421004, open daily in summer from 0830-1830, rest of year Mon-Sat 0830-1230, 1400-1830, US$1.20, explanations in English too, guided tour in Spanish*. The museum was designed by the well known Argentine sculptor Hector Cruz, who uses the iconography of the region's pre-Colombian art with bold flair in his own ceramics and weavings. It's part archaeological museum, part gallery, and a great place to relax for a couple of hours, with wonderful views from the mosaic cactus gardens. Outside, Cruz's dramatic Pachamama figures frame the surrounding mountains beautifully. Shop selling extensive range of handicrafts and wonderfully bold rugs and hangings, designed by Cruz and made by local weavers. There's an important Pachamama festival at end of Carnival.

The road forks at Amaichá: for Quilmes and Cafayate, take Route 357 north for 14 km to the junction with Route 40 then follow it north; for Santa María and western Catamarca, take Route 337 south to join Route 40 heading south.

Santa María → *Phone code 03838 Colour map 1, B2 Population: 7,500*

With its lively village feel completely untainted by tourist exploitiation, Santa María (1,800 m) makes a very attractive place for a stopover on the road to either Tucumán or western Catamarca. There's a lovely plaza full of mature trees, several friendly places to stay and to eat, and it has a wonderful small museum. **Museo**

⦂ Quilmes

Of all the indigenous peoples of Argentina, perhaps the most tragic was the fate that awaited the inhabitants of Quilmes, the ruined city, just south of the Salta/Tucumán border. In the broad valley beneath the intricate lacework of terraces which climbs high up the mountainside, lived around 5,000 people of the hugely expansive Diaguitan civilisation, from 5,000 years ago until AD 117. Their culture reached its peak at around AD 900, and had a well developed social structure with its own language, kakán, now extinct. The whole Calchaquí valley was the site of frequent warfare between rival clans, and while Quilmes' inhabitants usually lived in the plains below, they built the site as a defensive stronghold to retreat to in times of attack. Its excellent strategic position made it hard for them to be defeated, but they were also hard to dominate thanks to their sophisticated weaponry. They used *boleadoras* made from stones tied with llama hide thongs and slings of plaited lambswool used to hurl egg shaped stones with great accuracy over long distances. Their housing consisted of adjacent dwellings buried some way into the earth, and lined with stone walls, which also served as walkways between houses. Posts of sturdy algarrobo wood were used to support pitched roofs (now vanished), and they lived in clans or family groups. The higher social orders and those who held Shamanic or religious

positions in the community occupy dwellings highest up the mountainside – closest to the gods.

The climate was considerably different in their time, with fruit being grown in the valley, and the successful cultivation of beans, potato, pumpkins and maize, using irrigation canals to trap and redirect snowmelt from the mountain tops. Chicha was the popular mildly alcoholic drink made from ground and fermented algarrobo seeds, and it's thought that their Shamen cured people using local herbs and plants, as they do today.

The Incas were the first to dominate this clan with their powerful cultural colonisation in the late 15th century. The Quilmes people adapted though, and survived. But the arrival of the Spanish in the 17th century proved fatal. The people of Quilmes resisted Spanish attacks for many years, until, frustrated by the indigenous peoples' retreat to their mountainside fortress, the Spanish besieged them and cut off all their supplies. In 1668, the Quilmes surrendered, and the community was broken up, marched off to different parts of the country. The largest group was made to walk to a suburb of Buenos Aires, named Quilmes, after their home. In 1812, the last descendent died, and Argentina's most popular lager brewery was later built in the town, carry the name, though few Argentines are its namesake, this sophisticated civilization.

Arquaeológico Eric Boman ⓘ *Centro Cultural Yokavil, on the plaza, Mon-Sat 0900-2100, Sun 0900-1300, 1600-2100,* houses a fine collection of sophisticated ceramics tracing the development of the various indigenous cultures who lived in the Calchaquí valleys. Ask the well-informed staff to show you around. In the same building is is a handicrafts gallery selling weavings, wooden objects, and the delicious local *patero* wine, and also a helpful tourist office, Belgrano y Sarmiento, T421083, who'll give you a map and a full list of places to stay.

In January the town has handicrafts fairs, and a live music festival, with the crowning of *la reina de Yokavil* (the old indigenous name for Santa María). For the *fiesta* de San Roque on August 16, thousands of pilgrims descend on the town, and accommodation fills up fast. There's a *locutorio* on the plaza, the only ATM for miles around on Mitre and Sarmiento, taking Visa and Mastercard, a post office and several service stations. Buses arrive at Avenida 9 de Julio and Maestro Argentino.

Quilmes → *Colour map 1, B2*

ⓘ *32 km north of Santa María, 5 km along a dirt road off Route 40 (no shade, tiring walk up hill), open 0800-1730, entry US$1, includes guided tour and access to a small museum, café serving good lunches, tasty homemade bread.*

Quilmes is one of the most important archaeological sites in Argentina, sadly little known by most Argentines, who associate the name only with the most popular lager, see box page 276. Situated on the slopes of the Sierra de Quilmes, at an altitude of 1,850 m, in an imposing site with views over the entire valley, this is the ruined city of 5,000 Diaguitan people who lived here peacefully for hundreds of years, until the Incas and then the Spanish arrived. What remains today is an extensive network of thousands of roofless rooms bordered with low walls, mostly heavily reconstructed, but a beautiful and elaborate lacework which continues right up to the top of the mountain. It's a spectacular site, especially early or late in the day, when the silvery walls are picked out against the pale green of the enormous cacti growing throughout the valley. ▸▸ *For Sleeping, Eating and other listings, see pages 278-282.*

Santiago del Estero → *Phone code: 0385 Colour map 1, B3 Population: 201,000*

This quiet, provincial town makes a handy stopping point if you're heading from the flat landscape of the Chaco to explore the northwest. And although little architectural heritage of Argentina's oldest city remains, there are some comfortable places to stay and a couple of museums worth seeing.

Santiago was founded in 1553 and was once an important base for establishing other major cities in the northwest. These left Santiago behind and so the town is now a rather impoverished older neighbour. It's a bit run down, its plaza and bus station shambolic affairs, but it has a warm, laid-back atmosphere and welcoming people.

On the Plaza Libertad stand the **Municipalidad** and **Jefatura de Policia**, built in 1868 in the style of a colonial cabildo. On the west side is the **cathedral**, the fifth on

The Northwest Northwest Tucumán

Santiago del Estero

Sleeping 😴
Carlos 1
Del Centro 2
Libertador 3
Nuevo 4
Savoy 5

Eating 🍴
Cantina China 1
Cerecetto 2
Manjares 3
Mia Mamma 4
Periko's 5

0 metres 100
0 yards 100

the site, dating from 1877. Two blocks southeast of the plaza, at Urquiza y 25 de Mayo, is the **Convento de Santo Domingo**, containing one of two copies of the 'Turin Shroud', but otherwise unremarkable. And six blocks east of the plaza is the welcome greenery of the **Parque Francisco de Aguirre** which stretches to the river, and includes the town's campsite. The **tourist office** is on Plaza Libertad, T421 4243.

The best museum is the **Museo de Cienias Antropologicos y Naturales** ⓘ *Avellaneda 353, Mon-Fri 0730-1330, 1400-2000, Sat/Sun 1000-1200, free*, with the wonderfully eclectic collection of pre-Hispanic artefacts by brothers Emilio and Duncan Wagner, now sadly haphazardly presented and badly conserved. Amongst the stuffed armadillos and bone flutes, delicate spindles and board-flattened skulls, is a quite breathtaking quantity of funerary urns, beautifully decorated, but crammed in dark glass cases with no explanation, some rare bronze ceremonial *hachas*, and anthropomorhic pieces. Mysterious and amazing.

Termas de Río Hondo → *Phone code: 03858 Colour map 1, B3 Population: 25,000*

Argentina's most popular spa town with an altitude of 265 m and 65 km north of Santiago del Estero, is also its most dreary, so you'll be relieved to hear that the warm mineral-laden waters are piped into every hotel in the city, make it unnecessary to leave your accommodation. It's a mecca for older visitors with arthritic or skin conditions in July and August, when you'll need to book in advance. Out of season, it's a desperately depressing place. With the cream bulk of the casino dominating the scruffy triangular plaza, the resort consists of 160 hotels interspersed with *alfajores* shops, mostly in run down and flaking buildings. Even in high season, there's little to make you feel better here, and nibbling another biscuit is hardly likely to help.

Listings: Tucamán Province

● Sleeping

San Miguel de Tucumán *p271, map 272*

B NH Grand Hotel del Tucumán, *Av Soldati 380, T450 2250, www.grandhotel.com.ar* The most comfortable place to stay is this luxurious hotel, overlooking Parque 9 de Julio, with comfortable minimalist decor in the bedrooms, outstanding food and service, and pool (open to non-residents), sauna and gym. Good value, and highly recommended.

B Suites Garden Park, *Av Soldati 330, T431 0700, www.gardenparkhotel.com.ar* The competition next door is this smart and welcoming 4-star, with views over Parque 9 de Julio, pool, gym, sauna, restaurant. Also apartments.

B Swiss Hotel Metropol, *24 de Septiembre 524, T431 1180, www.swisshotelmetropol .com.ar* Central, chic and modern, this is primarily a business hotel, but with its comfortable well-designed rooms, and excellent restaurant, it's a fine place for tourists too. Good service, highly recommended.

C Carlos V, *25 de Mayo 330, T431 1666,*

www.redcarlosv.com.ar Central traditional hotel, with good service, and a civilised restaurant.

C Dallas Hotel, *Corrientes 985, T421 8500.* Very welcoming place with nicely furnished rooms and good bathrooms.

C Premier, *Crisóstomo Alvarez 510, T/F431 0381, info@redcarlosv.com.ar* The rooms are spacious and comfortable, though not all have been refurbished, and those next to the street are noisy next to street, but the bathrooms are modern, and the staff helpful.

D Francia, *Crisóstomo Alvarez 467, T/F431 0781.* A centrally located hotel with plain but comfortable high celinged rooms, and cheap apartments for 5 too. A good budget option.

D Hotel Americana, *on the wide Plaza Alberdi, Santiago del Estero 1064, T430 0810.* A rather dark entrance, but a friendly welcome. The rooms are small, not helped by vinyl wood panelling, but all are cheered up by original paintings, and there's a restaurant offering a very reasonable fixed menu for US$3. If you'd rather be away from the hectic centre, this is a good choice and good value.

D **Versailles**, *Crisóstomo Alvarez 481, T422 9760, F422 9763*. A touch of class in this rather charming older place, a lovely open entrance with reproduction furniture, good service and comfortable beds,. Recommended.
E **Miami**, *Junín 580, T431 0265, F422 2405*. This is the closest Tucumán gets to a youth hostel, a good modern place with discounts for Hostelling International members, pool, a/c, TV.
E **Petit**, *Crisóstomo Alvarez 765, T421 3902*. A rather eccentric hostel, this is a spacious old house with small rooms at the back coming off a modern patio. Pretty basic, but quiet, and cheaper rooms without bath, or fan.

Camping

Avoid the sites in the Parque 9 de Julio. There are 2 roadside campsites 3 km east and northeast of city centre.

Tafí del Valle *p274*

There's lots of comfortable accommodation in Tafí, tending towards the more expensive, with a good range of mid-price hotels. There's a great value estancia, though, right in the centre of town, and a welcoming small hostel.
C **Hosteria Tafí del Valle**, *Av San Martín y Gdor Campero, T421027*. Right at the top of the town, on the apex of the semicircular plaza, with splendid views and an airy restaurant. Its room are luxurious though small, and there's a pool.
C **La Rosada**, *Belgrano 322, T421323/146, miguel_torres@sinectis.com.ar* Huge rooms, good value and just off to the west of the plaza lots of excursions on offer and bikes to borrow.
C **Lunahuana**, *www.lunahuana.com.ar* Also comfy with good views from its stylish rooms. There are spacious 2-floor 'duplex' rooms for 4, and a restaurant.
C **Mirador del Tafí**, *on the RP307 just east of the town, T421219, www. miradordeltafi.com.ar* This is the best option, comfortable and spacious with spectacular views, a fine restuarant, pool, and wonderful service. Recommended.
D **Hostería Los Cuartos**, *Av Juan Calchaquí s/n, T/F421444, or Tucumán T(0381)-15587 4230, www.turismoentucuman.com* Very good value, and full of character, this estancia is right in the middle of town.

Charming hosts, and rooms full of an eclectic collection of antiques. Recommended. They also offer a day at the *estancia*, with lunch, horseriding. Delicious *té criollo*, US\$3, and farm cheese can be bought here or at the cheese shop on Av Miguel Critto.
F pp **La Cumbre**, *Av Perón 120, T421768*. This hostel is a good budget option. Rooms for 2 to 5, a bar, cooking facilities and good atmosphere. The helpful owner is a tour operator – see La Cumbre below.

Amaichá *p275*

F **El Portal de Amaichá**, *on the main road, next to the YPF sation, T421140, www.elportaldeamaicha.8m.com* Quiet and comfortable accommodation with great views either in simple rooms or in *cabañas*.

Quilmes *p277*

C **Parador Ruinas de Quilmes**, *T03892-421075*. Make the most of the site by staying in this peaceful, very comfortable hotel. Its spacious, stylish interior was boldly designed by Hector Cruz (see Amaichá above), filled with his weavings and ceramics, and there's a good restaurant, and free camping. Best of all, there are great views of Quilmes: get up early and have them to yourself. Recommended.

Santa María *p275*

D **Plaza**, *San Martín 285, T420309, on the plaza*. Small and simple but comfy rooms all with bath and TV, breakfast included.
D **Provincial de Turismo**, *San Martín 450, T420240, occupying a block of its own two blocks east of the plaza*. The town's best option. Extremely comfortable well furnished newer rooms (worth asking for these), all with bath, a restaurant, gardens, and a small pool.
E **Caasama**, *9 de Julio s/n, T421627*. A pool and simple adobe building.
E **Res Inti-Huaico**, *Belgrano 146, T432047*. Nice clean rooms with bath, friendly owners, and lovely gardens.

Camping

Municipal campsite at end of Sarmiento, about 6 blocks east of the plaza, with F *albergue* and restaurant too.

Phone codes San Miguel de Tucumán: 0381; Santiago del Estero: 0385; Tafí del Valle: 03867; Santa María: 03838; Amaichá, Quilmes: 03892.

The Northwest Listings: Tucumán Province

C **Carlos V**, *Independencia 110*, *T424 0303*, *hotelcarlosv@arnet.com.ar on the corner of the plaza*. Cheaper and yet more luxurious than the **Libertador**. Good value for a really comfortable international-style hotel with an all year round pool, and a good restaurant, elegant rooms with bathrooms; go for the spacious superior rooms if you can afford it.

C **Hotel Libertador**, *Catamarca 47, T/f4219252, www.hotellibertador.com.ar* The most expensive hotel, this smart place has a spacious light lounge and plain well equipped rooms. There's an attractive leafy patio with pool (summer only) and a very elegant restaurant, also open to non residents. A peaceful place to stay 5 blocks south of the plaza in the better-off part of town.

D **Hotel del Centro** *9 de Julio 131*, *T422 4350*. Light, prettily decorated rooms, all with good bathrooms and minibar and an airy first floor restaurant. Recommended.

E **Nuevo Hotel Santiago**, *Buenos Aires 60, T421 4949*. Modernized and comfortable, this is the better of the remaining decent budget choices. The rooms are small but well equipped and it's quiet for such a central location, a block from the plaza.

E **Savoy**, *Tucumán 39*, *T421 1234*. Cheapest and with most character is the faded grandeur of this central wonderful art nouveau building with swirling stairwell. Rooms are large, simple, and airy, an excellent budget option.

Camping

Las Casuarinas, *Parque Aguirre*, *T421 1390*. Insect repellent essential.

Termas de Río Hondo *p278*

Ask the helpful tourist office for accommodation advice, at Caseros 132, T422143, or www.LasTermasDeRioHondo.com

C **Hotel Termal Rio Hondo**, *T421455, www.hoteltermalriohondo.com.ar* Most comfortable with modern rooms, medical services, pool and a good restaurant too.

C **Hotel de los Pinos**, *T421043*. The next best option, in an attractive Spanish-style building a little removed from the centre at Caseros and Maipu.

ⓞ Eating

San Miguel de Tucumán *p271, map 272*
There are plenty of places to eat along 25 de Mayo, which stretches north from the west side of the Plaza.

$$ **La Leñita**. Highly recommended for excellent *parrilla*, and superb salads, one of the best on the street, also offering live folklore music at weekends.

$$ **Il Postino**. A hugely popular pizza place, stylishly designed, with lots of brick and wood, and a buzzing atmosphere. Generous pizzas, US$3.50 for 2, plus tapas and tortillas too. Recommended.

$$ **Sir Harris**, *Laprida 2005*. A Tucumán institution, serving really good imaginative dishes, some vegetarian choices, pizzas and sandwiches.

$$ **Los Negros**, *Laprida 623*. Good for *parrilla*.

$$ **Klo y Klo**, *Junin 663*. A wide variety of excellent dishes, in a welcoming rather charming environment.

Cafés

Costumbres Argentinos, *San Juan 666, y Maipu*. Good atmosphere in this intimate bar for late drink.

Filipo. A very popular smart café, with a nice atmosphere. Good place for a coffee or a drink.

Gregorio, *2 blocks north of Plaza de Mayo*. Another pleasant place for a coffee, good salads and pasta.

La Mostaza, *San Martín 742*. Lively and trendy café, cheap breakfasts.

Maxim, *Santiago del Estero 502, (25 de Mayo corner)*.

Panadería Villecco, *Corrientes 751*. Superb bread, pastries, and *pan integral* (wholemeal).

Tafí del Valle *p274*

$$ **El Mangrullo**, *opposite Hotel Mirador del Tafí*. A good mid-range family *parrilla* with pastas too, and a play area for kids.

$ **El Paballon**, *on the corner of Critto*. Cheapest of all, recommended for pasta.

$ **El Portal de Tafí**. Very good food, excellent *empanadas*.

$ **Hotel Mirador del Tafí**, *for address, see above*. The good-value food is excellent at this hotel.

$ **Parador Tafinisto**, *at the bottom of Perón*. Frequently recommended for *parrilla* with plenty of regional dishes, and live folklore music at the weekends.
$ **Tequila**, *opposite the YPF station on Peron*. A popular bar serving pizzas.

Santa María *p275*
There are some good and lively places on the plaza:
$ **El Colonial** . Serves *empanadas* and has an attractive *confitería*.
$ **Jandar**, *on the plaza*. Serves excellent and cheap *empanadas* and salads.
$ **J S**, *on 9 de Julio, 5 blocks from the plaza*. The most popular for the best meals.
$ **Tia Selina** *on 1 de Mayo y A Giminez*. For pizzas.

Santiago del Estero *p277, map p277*
The better restaurants at **Libertador** and **Carlos V** hotels.
$$ **Mia Mamma**, *on the main plaza at 24 de Septiembre 15*. Often recommended this is a cheery place for *parrilla* and tasty pastas, with good salad *libre* starters, and friendly service.
$ **Periko's**, *on the plaza*. Lively and popular, for *lomitos* and pizzas, popular with a younger crowd.
$ **Cantina China** Mitre and 24 de Septiembre. Very cheap Chinese *tenedor libre*.

Cafés, bakeries and ice cream parlours
Casa de té. Sells good pastries.
Cerecetto, *a couple of blocks from the plaza at Córdoba y Libertad*. The best ice cream in town.
Manjares, *on the plaza*.

Termas de Río Hondo *p278*
$$ **San Cayetano** or homely **Renacimiento**, *both on the main drag Sarmiento*, and reasonably priced for *parrilla*.
$ **El Chorrizo Loco**, *Alberdi and Sarmiento*. A very cheap lively pizzeria.

◌ Tour operators

San Miguel de Tucumán *p271, map 272*
Turismo de Tucumán, *Crióstomo Alvarez 435 – local 2, T422 7636*. Informative tours to local places, Quilmes, full day, US$22, and Tafí del Valle, full day US$15.

Duport Turismo, *Mendoza 720, Galeria de Rosario, Local 3, T422 0000*. The same tours as above, plus a large circuit of the local valleys, 6 hrs, US$14, Parque Alpa Puyo, half day, US$10, El Cadillal, half day US$12.

Tafí del Valle *p274*
Mi La Cumbre, *Av Peron 120 T421768, www.turismoentucuman.com/lacumbre* Best is this energetic and friendly company who offer 4WD excursions, and full-day walks to all the nearby peaks, to waterfalls Cascada lo Alisos and ruins at Valle de la Ciénaga. Also a recommended trek to Cerro Muñoz, (4,437 m), with an *asado* at the summit.
Oscar Branchesi, *in tourist information office on right at entrance to town, T495 5117*. Trips to rural areas and great insight into indigenous culture. Recommended.

◎ Transport

San Miguel de Tucumán *p271, map 272*
Air
Aeropuerto Benjamín Matienzo, 10 km east of town, reached by bus no 120 from terminal or from Bolívar y Congreso (*cospeles*, US$0.35, required). Taxi US$4. **Cielos del Norte**, T426 5555, minibuses to/from airport to/from any place in town, US$1.50. To **Buenos Aires**, AR/Austral (T431 1030), and **Southern Winds** (T422 5554) also to **Salta** and **Córdoba**.

Bus
Local bus services operate on *cospeles*, US$0.35, which you buy in advance in kiosks. For long-distance services, the modern terminal has 70 ticket offices. There is a helpful information kiosk opposite Disco: T430 4696, 422 2221. The terminal is located 6 blocks east of Plaza Independencia on Av Brigido Teran, with huge shopping complex, left luggage lockers (US$1), tourist information office (by *boleteria* 1), lots of *locutorios*, toilets and banks. Bus 3 goes to the centre from outside terminal, to San Lorenzo y 9 de Julio. Taxi to centre US$0.50-1.

To **Buenos Aires**, many companies, 16 hrs US$20-25. To **Tafí del Valle**, 2½ hrs, US$3. To **Salta** direct (not via Cafayate), 4½ hrs, several companies US$4. To **Cafayate**, 5 hrs US$7. To **Posadas**, La Estrella, Vosa, Almirante Brown, 16 hrs, US$15. To **Mendoza**, 13 hrs, US$12, via

Catamarca, **La Rioja**, and **San Juan**. To **Catamarca**, Aconquija and other companies, 4 hrs, US$4. To **Tinogasta**, via **Andalgalá** and **Belén**, Gutiérrez, 3 a week, daily in high season. To **Córdoba**, 8 hrs, US$7. To **Santiago del Estero**, 2 hrs, US$4. To **La Quiaca** (border with Bolivia), Balut, 10 hrs, US$12. To **Santiago** (Chile) via **Mendoza**, Andesmar and El Rápido Internacional, daily, 24 hrs, US$18-23. To **Lima** (Perú), **El Rápido Internacional**, 3 a week, via **Mendoza**, US$80.

Car hire
Movil Renta, *San Lorenzo 370, T431 0550, info@movilrenta.com and at airport.* Donde Rent a Car, *Gob Gutiérrez 1384, T428 3626.*

Train
To **Buenos Aires** via **Rosario** run by NOA Ferrocarriles, *T422 0861*, more information given under Buenos Aires.

Tafí del Valle *p274*
Bus There's a smart new terminal on Av Critto, which you might mistake for another hotel, with café, toilets, luggage lockers and helpful information, *T421031*. To/from **Tucumán**, Aconquija, T421025, 8 daily, 2½ hrs, US$4. To **Cafayate**, 6 a day, 1½-2½ hrs, US$6 (possible via **Santa María**, US$7). To **Salta**, 6 daily 8 hrs, US$4. To **El Mollar** several daily, US$1. Buses to **Tucumán** stop at El Mollar on request.

Amaicha *p275*
Bus to **Tucumán**, 5 hrs, leaving at 0800 and 1800, US$6, sit on the right for best views.

Santa María *p275*
Bus To **Tucumán**, Aconquija, 4 hrs, US$6, several daily. To **Cafayate**, 1 hr, El Indio, daily US$4. Cayetano to **Belén** 4 hrs, check with tourist office for current times.

Quilmes *p277*
For a day trip take 0600 **Aconquija** bus from **Cafayate** to **Santa María**, get off at stop, 5 km from site, or take 0700 bus from Santa María. Either way you'll have to walk the 5 km up the hill. Take 1130 bus back to Cafayate, US$2.Or take a tour from Cafayate.

Santiago del Estero *p277, map p277*
Air
Mal Paso airport on northwestern outskirts. Aerolíneas Argentinas/Austral to **Buenos Aires** and **Tucumán**.

Bus
Rather shabby terminal at Gallo 480, which does have toilets, a *locutorio*, basic café and *kioskos*, as well as stalls selling food. **Córdoba** 6 hrs US$5-7, **Jujuy**, 7 hrs US$7, **Salta** 6 hrs US$6.50, **Tucumán** 2 hrs US$3, to **Catamarca** (only one daily at 1600, 7 hrs US$5, so you may end up going via Tucumán).

Taxis
Very cheap here, US$0.30 into town, to save you the 8 block walk.

Termas de Río Hondo *p278*
The **bus** terminal Las Heras y España, 8 blocks north of centre near Route 9, but buses will drop you at the plaza, on Alberdi, opposite the casino. To **Santiago del Estero**, 1 hr, US$2 and to **Tucumán**, 2 hrs, US$2; several to **Buenos Aires** US$20.

---

❶ Directory

San Miguel de Tucumán *p271, map 272*
Banks Most banks are along San Martín especially the 700 block between Junín and Maipú. **Magitur**, *San Martín 765, T431 0032.* Accepts TCs. Maxicambio, *San Martín 779, T422 5399.* For currency exchange.
Communications **Post office** *Córdoba y 25 de Mayo.* 0700-1300, 1600-2000 Mon-Fri, 0800-1300 Sat. **Telephone** Lots of *locutorios* all over the cente, many with broad band internet access. Telecom, *Maipú 360.* Open 24 hrs.

Tafí del Valle *p274*
Banks ATM at Banco de Tucumán, *Miguel Critto 311, T421033.* All the major international cards accepted.

Santiago del Estero *p277, map p277*
Airline offices Aerolíneas Argentinas, *Buenos Aires 60, T422 4088;* Austral, *Libertad 766, T4214612.* **Banks** Banco Francés, *9 de Julio y 24 de Septiembre;* Noroeste Cambio, *24 de Septiembre 220,* good rates. Amex, *El Quijote Paladea Turismo, Independencia 342, T421 3207.*

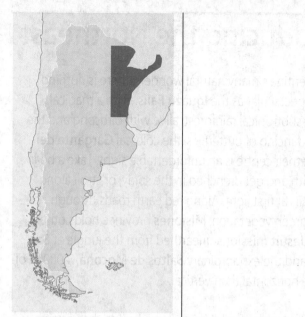

Introducing the Northeast

Of all Argentina's many natural wonders, there is nothing quite as spectacular as the **Iguazú Falls**. With a magical setting in subtropical rainforest, alive with birdsong and the constant dancing of butterflies, the colossal **Garganta del Diablo** at their centre is an unforgettable sight. Take a boat underneath and get drenched in the spray, or stroll along nature trails at first light. Along red earth roads through emerald green vegetation, **Misiones** province holds other delights: **Jesuit missions** unearthed from the jungle at **San Ignacio**, and the extraordinary **Saltos de Moconá**, 3,000 m of falls more horizontal than vertical.

El Litoral's wealth of wildlife is astounding. In the vast wetlands of **Esteros del Iberá**, giant storks and alligators nestle between floating islands and water lilies. In **Mburucuyá** tall palms wave in grasslands and passion flowers thrive in abundance. In the **Chaco**, watch out for pumas, and monkeys, while the palm forests of **Entre Rios** are centuries old.

Weaved along the lazy Paraná river is relaxed, pretty **Colón** with its port and sandy beaches and the faded splendour of **Paraná**. For more stimulation, historical **Corrientes** is a riot at Carnival time, and lively **Rosario**'s hotbed of culture produces the country's finest musicians.

The northeast's rich culture stems from huge **indigenous populations**; the Guaraní and Wichí, which produce beautiful art. The gently meandering rivers set the pace, giving the land its lush vegetation and generating in its people a charming laid-back warmth. *Yerba mate* is grown for the nation's favourite drink, and everywhere you'll encounter friends gathered on riverbanks on balmy afternoons sipping from their *mate* gourd.

★ Don't miss...

1. *Jungle Explorer* Alligators basking above the Iguazú Falls, seen from a gentle punt (at a safe distance!), page 342.

2. **San Ignacio Mini** Wander around the ruins of the Jesuit Mission at sunset, and imagine 4,000 Guaraní living and working there, page 331.

3. **Gualeguaychú** Celebrate carnival dancing to chamamé, page 286.

4. **Refugio de Vida Silvestre La Aurora del Palmar** Drink yatay spirit, while gazing at the view of mature yatay palm forests, page 290.

5. **Alligator *milanesas*** Try the local delicacy at Rosario's best restaurant Rich, page 312.

The Northeast

Along the Río Uruguay

The mighty Río Uruguay is over 1,600 km long, and a staggering 10 km wide in places. It forms Argentina's eastern boundary with Uruguay and Brazil, and along the Argentine side are dotted interesting towns and cities which make good stopping points on a journey north. Gualeguaychú is so keen to party, it celebrates its carnival every weekend for two months, but you can calm down in Concepción del Uruguay, with attractive old buildings or Colón, with its historic port area and sandy beaches. There's a national park protecting splendid palm forests, though the reserve La Aurora del Palmar is more accessible. You can stay on colonial estancias, jungle islands, and with small communities at Irazusta and Arroyo Barú.

Gualeguaychú → *Phone code: 03446 Colour map 4, A5 Population: 74,700*

The first town of any size on the route north, Gualeguaychú is famous for its extended carnival. It's lively thoughout the summer, with an attractive *costanera* on the Río Gualeguaychú, where there are several *balnearios* and restaurants, a pleasant place for a stroll with views of the picturesque port. Carnival is celebrated at the local *corsódromo* (arena), a hugely popular event, lasting well beyond the usual fortnight to fill every weekend for a couple of months. On the eastern bank of the river beautiful Parque Unzué has sports facilities and sailing clubs. The *costanera* is a pleasant place for a stroll, between the bridge and the small picturesque port with its few warehouses, and views of large houses on the islands. The port and *balneario municipal* (town bathing spot) are the departure points for short boat excursions and city tours, T423248 (only in high season). About 200 m south of the port in Plazoleta de los Artesanos, local handicrafts are sold at weekends in summer, and a vast green area, a thatched hut houses the local tourist office, ① *T423668, www.gualeguay chuturismo.com 0800-2000 (closing later in summer).*

On the *costanera* at Gervasio Méndez is **El Patio del Mate** ① *T424371, www.elpatiodelmate.com.ar, daily 0800-2100,* a workshop where dedicated craftsmen make the cups from which *mate* is drunk, varying widely from simple dyed gourds to ornate silver goblets. In a couple of attractive old houses are the **Museo Azotea de la Palma**, San Luis y Jujuy (23 blocks northwest of plaza) with a small collection related to regional history, and the **Casa de Aedo** ① *San José y Rivadavia (on the plaza), Wed-Sat 0900-1145, Fri-Sat also 1600-1845 (in summer afternoon times are 1700-1945),* the oldest house in the city, Garibaldi's headquarters when he sacked the city in 1845. The house, rather than the contents, are the appeal here. ▸▸ *For Sleeping, Eating and other listings, see pages 293-299.*

Around Gualeguaychú

Villa Paranacito, is a village set in the delta islands, 100 km south of Gualeguaychú, where houses are built on tall stilts and boats are the essential means of transport. It's is popular with anglers in the waters of the nearby Río Uruguay (half an hour farther by boat), and anyone looking for a quiet place to stay, immersed in the islander culture. There are campsites, a youth hostel and *cabañas* offering boat excursions. There's delicious local fish at *Annemarie, dorado, pejerrey, surubí* and *boga*.

Estancia La Azotea ① *10 km north of Villarancito, on Route 12 in Ceibas, T03446-492007 (or in Buenos Aires, T011 4393 8057),* is a 19th-century house popular for day visits, with cattle ranching, horseriding, an *asado* lunch, and the use of a pool in summer. At US$10pp it's very good value.

West and northwest of Gualeguaychú, there are a string of small **eco communities** near Larroque and Urdinarrain, newly opened to tourism both to share the tranquillity of these peaceful rural places and to meet their inhabitants. At **Aldea**

San Antonio, 41 km northwest, you can visit a German settlement and tour in a horse drawn carriage. Contact Señora Susana Schaaf, T03446-497045 and Señora Mercedes, T03446-497055 at **Casa Alamana**. At the tiny community of **Irazusta**, 63km west, there's a community of just 350 inhabitants, where Señora Eufemia, T03446-491530 and Señor Abel, T03446-491524 (ask also at local railway station) provide accommodation and meals at family houses, an enriching experience for both guests and hosts. This is a pilot project, intended to stop the depopulation process of small communities: for more information visit www.responde.org.ar So far it's been very successful.

Border with Uruguay

Situated 33 km southeast of Gualeguaychú, the Libertador General San Martin Bridge (5.4 km long) provides the most southerly route across the Río Uruguay, to Fray Bentos. Vehicle toll US$4; pedestrians and cyclists can only cross on motor vehicles, though officials may arrange lifts.

Customs and immigration At opposite ends of the bridge. This is an uncomplicated crossing, formalities taking about 10 mins. No milk and dairy products, meat, fruit and vegetables, flowers, plants and seeds, or animals (pets require a health certificate and a fee payable at SENASA offices; check in advance at tourist office) are allowed to enter into Uruguayan territory. The Argentine consulate is at 18 de Julio 1225, T+598-(0)562 3225, Fray Bentos. Passport details are noted when booking bus tickets and passed to officials at border. Passports inspected on the bus.

Into Uruguay: Fray Bentos
→ *Phone code: +598-(0)562 Colour map 4, A6 Population: 22,000*

Fray Bentos is the main port on the east bank of Río Uruguay, a friendly little town with an attractive *costanera*. The main reason to visit is to see the meat-packing factory. The name Fray Bentos was synonymous with corned beef in Britain throughout the 20th century, and the factory (*frigorífico*) known as El Anglo, which produced *Oxo* for many years has been beautifully restored as the **Museo de La Revolución Industrial** ① *daily except Mon, entry by guided tour only, US$1, 1000, 1430 (1000, 1130 and 1700 in summer), tour 1½ hrs in Spanish, may provide leaflet in English, T3607,* and business park, with a restaurant, *Wolves,* and a disco. The office block in the factory has been preserved with some of the old machinery. See also the *Bovril* estancia, *Vizcacheras,* below. The **tourist office** is at Puente General San Martín, T2369.

There are beaches to the northeast and southwest and also at **Las Cañas**, 8 km south (where there is a tourist complex, entry US$1, including B motel rooms with kitchenette and bath, cheaper without kitchen, all with a/c and fridge; campsite for US$8.50 per day minimum, T2224, including sports facilities and services). ►► *For Sleeping, Eating and other listings, see pages 293-299.*

Concepción del Uruguay
→ *Phone code: 03442 Colour map 2, C1 Population: 64,500*

Concepción del Uruguay lies on the western shore of the Río Uruguay 74 km north of Gualeguaychú, with views of islands in the river opposite. Founded in 1783, it was capital of Entre Ríos province between 1813-21 and 1860-1883, and retains some fine architecture in its public buildings, and has a distinctively lively character, thanks to a

● *You can stay with local people in tiny towns and get a flavour for rural life at many places in the northeast. Go native at Irazusta, or immerse yourself in wildlife at eco friendly Yacutinga Lodge.*

young student population. The **tourist office** is two blocks from the plaza, ① *9 de Julio 844, T425820, open Mon-Fri 0700-1300, 1400-2000, and weekends from 0700-2200 in high season*. There is another information point on the access road at Galarza y Elías, ① *T440812, open daily 0800-2000*.

Sights

The old town is centred on beautiful **Plaza Ramírez**, with the Italian neoclassical-style **Basílica de la Inmaculada Concepción**, containing the remains of General Urquiza on its western side. Next to it is the **Colegio Superior Justo José de Urquiza**, the first secular school in the country, although its 19th-century buildings were largely replaced in 1935. One block northeast of the plaza is **Museo Casa de Delio Panizza** ① *Galarza y Supremo Entrerriano, daily 0900-1200, 1400-1800 (1800-2100 in summer)*, in a mansion dating from 1793 and containing 19th-century furnishings and artefacts.

Around Concepción del Uruguay

Among the interesting places to explore nearby, **Banco Pelay** a long stretch of beach on the Río Uruguay, 6 km north, where there's a campsite and a tourist information point, T424003. **Isla Cambacuá** ① *crossing times at Catamaran Lobopé, T427421, US$0.35*, is a large island close to the town with a beach and a bar. **Estancia Santa Cándida** ① *lies 15 km south, daily 0900-1200,1600-1900 (ring to check times), US$1.70, T422188.*, was founded in 1847 by General Urquiza as a *saladero* (meat-salting plant) by the river. The sumptuous mansion offers accommodation, and can be visited for the day,

    Palacio San José ① *32 km west of the town, Mon-Fri 0830-1230, 1400-1830, Sat-Sun 0900-1745, US$1, info in Spanish, French and English. Free guided visits at 1000, 1100, 1500, 1600, www.palaciosanjose.com* is the former mansion of General Urquiza, which dates from 1848, built in Italian style with 38 rooms and a chapel. It was once the country's most luxurious residence. Now a museum with artefacts from Urquiza's life, the palace stands in a beautiful park with an artificial lake.

    Basavilbaso, 68 km west, is a historical small town which in the early 20th century was an urban centre for Lucienville, inhabited by Jewish immigrants from Russia. There's a **tourist office** ① *Lagocen e Hipólito Yrigoyen, To3445-481015*; information also at *Asociación Israelita*, To3445-481908. There are three well-preserved synagogues, of which the **Tefila L Moises** has a beautifully painted wooden ceiling. It's also worth visiting the **Navibuco synagogue**, 2.5 km of town, dating from 1895, and two Jewish cemetaries nearby. Basavilbaso was a busy transport hub. Though the last passenger train left in 1992, the station houses a museum where the rich history of the local railway history can be explored. ▸▸ *For Sleeping, Eating and other listings, see pages 293-299.*

Colón → *Phone code: 03447 Colour map 2, C1 Population: 19,200*

One of the prettiest towns on the river, Colón was founded in 1863 as a port for the Swiss colony of San José, 9 km west, and it's an excellent base several very interesting places nearby, including the Parque Nacional El Palmar. It is also linked by a bridge to the Uruguayan city of Paysandú, with its interesting old buildings (see below). Colón itself has many well preserved early 19th-century houses, and a beautiful riverbank with long sandy beaches and shady streets.

Sights

The most attractive part of town is the port district, next to the Plaza San Martín, with fine old houses on the plaza and nearby streets leading down to the riverside. The former passenger boat terminal, now houses the **tourist office** ① *Av Costanera Quirós*

At the corner of Avenida 12 de Abril and Paso is **La Casona**, (1868), where there's a handicrafts exhibition and shop. North of the port, Calle Alejo Peyret gives access to the *balnearios* and their sandy beaches on the river and Calle Belgrano leads to the **Complejo Termal** ① *daily 0900-2100, US$1.30, T424717*, where there are 10 thermal pools (ranging from 34° to 40°), in an attractive setting, very popular for treating a variety of ailments. Most shops and banks can be found on Avenida 12 de Abril, with the old **Teatro Centenario**, opened in 1925. ▸▸ *For Sleeping, Eating and other listings, see pages 293-299.*

Excursions

San José, 9 km west, is the site of a Swiss colony founded in 1857. Early settlers with Utopian ideals attempted to create a fair society here, but it didn't last long. There's a **tourist office** at the bus station, Centenario 1430, T470178. San José has a **Museo Histórico Regional** ① *Urquiza 1127, Tue-Fri 1000-1200, 1700-1900, US$0.35, T470088*, which portrays the life of a farming colony through a collection of personal pieces each donated by descendents of the original immigrants. The **Molino Forclaz**, 4 km from Colón, is a mill built in 1888 to process the wheat and corn production of the colony.

Pueblo Liebig ① *12 km northwest, 1000-1900, US$0.65*, is a village created in the early 20th century to accommodate employees of the meat-packing factory operated by the *British Liebig's Extract of Meat Co Ltd*. The buildings are now closed down, but can be visited with guides, Very interesting, there's good accommodation and access to the Río Uruguay at the **Club de Pescadores**. For tourist information, T492042.

Villa Elisa, 30 km west, is popular for its **Complejo Termal**, with six pools (up to 41°; beware of the high salt concentration). The pleasant little town can be explored on bicycles hired at *Biciturismo Villa Elisa*, T480676. Tourist information is available at Urquiza 1790, T480146, www.elisanet.com.ar From the local railway station, an quaint little train departs every Saturday in the morning to the **Palacio San José** and on Sunday mornings to **La Clarita**, where you can spend an afternoon in the countryside. ① *Tickets to Palacio San José, US$5.70, to La Clarita, US$3; T481344*. **Colonia Hocker**, 30 km northwest, is a small rural village with accommodation at *Almacén Don Leandro* ① *T480470, www.almacendonleandro.com.ar*, whose owners organize cheap and interesting tours of the area,

Some 40 km north of Villa Elisa is **Arroyo Barú**, a rural village whose inhabitants have opened their houses to visitors who want to enjoy the tranquility of its small community. This place, together with Irazusta (west of Gualeguaychú), are both study cases for an NGO research. Contact Señora Marta, T03447-496048, turismoenbaru@hotmail.com.

Border with Uruguay

Seven kilometres southeast of Colón, the General José Artigas Bridge gives access to the Uruguayan city of Paysandú. Toll US$4.

Customs and immigration Argentine and Uruguayan formalities are both dealt with at Uruguayan end of the bridge. *Migraciones* officials board the bus, but non-Argentine/Uruguayans should get off bus to have their passports stamped. The Argentine consulate is at Gómez 1034, T22253, Mon-Fri 0800-1300.

Into Uruguay: Paysandú → *Phone code: +598-(0)72 Colour map 2, C1 Population: 100,000*

Situated on the eastern bank of the Río Uruguay, 8 km from the international bridge, Paysandú is the second largest city in Uruguay. It's worth exploring for several fine late 19th- and early 20th-century buildings, particularly the **Teatro Florencio Sánchez** (1876), the **Jefatura de Policía** and the **Basílica de Nuestra Señora del Rosario** dating from 1860. Also worth a look is the **Monumento a la Perpetuidad**, the old cemetery. Museums include the **Museo de la Tradición** ① *north of town at the Balneario Municipal, daily 0900-1800, reached by bus from Zona Industrial*, has *gaucho* artefacts. and the interesting **Museo Salesiano** ① *Florida 1278, Mon-Fri 0830-1130*, attached to cathedral. The **tourist office** is at Plaza de la Constitución ① *18 de Julio 1226, T26221. Open Mon-Fri 0800-1900, Sat-Sun 0800-1800, www.paysandu.com* There is also another office also at Puente Artigas.

Parque Nacional El Palmar → *Colour map 2, C1*

On west bank of the Río Uruguay 51 km north of Colón and 53 km south of Concordia, this park covers 8,500 ha of gently undulating grassland and mature palm forest, including *Yatay* palms hundreds of years old. These graceful trees were once found all over the pampas, until the introduction of cattle, who found the young seedlings irresistible. Growing in *palmares*, or groves, mature trees may reach 12m in height, with fronds some 2m in length. Along the Río Uruguay, and the *arroyos* streams which flow into it, there are gallery forests of subtropical trees and shrubs. You'll find indigenous tombs hidden away on the edge of the Río Uruguay there are **beaches** and the remains of an 18th-century quarry and port. Look out for capybaras, foxes, lizards and vizcachas as well as rheas, monk parakeets and several species of woodpecker.

The entrance gates to the park are on Route 14, where you are given a map and information on walks, and a *ripio* road leads to the administration centre, in the east of the park, near the Río Uruguay, with access to several viewpoints: **Mirador de La Glorieta, Mirador del Arroyo El Palmar, Mirador del Arroyo Los Loros** and to the coast of the Río Uruguay. There are walks between 300 m and 1000 m and you are free to walk around the main roads, though there's little shade. The administration centre is the departure point for guided walks and cycle tours run by *Capybara Aventura* (English spoken). Nearby there's camping (US$2 pp plus US$1.70 per tent in high season, electricity, hot water) with restaurant opposite, and a small shop. Visit at any time of year, but note that the park is very popular at weekends in summer and Easter week, and in summer there are more chances of thunderstorms and very hot *weather.* ▸ *For Sleeping, Eating and other listings, see pages 293-299.*

Refugio de Vida Silvestre La Aurora del Palmar

More accessible that the National Park, the wildlife reserve of La Aurora del Palmar was created to protect a similar environment. Situated 3 km south of Ubajay, on Route 14, km 202, it covers 1,150 hectares of which 200 are covered with a mature palm forest. There are also gallery forests along the streams and patches of *espinal*, or scrub. There's lots of birdlife, but capybaras also can be spotted along the streams. The administration centre is only 500 m from Route 14, and it offers far more organized services for visitors. Since entry is free, you could reach the vantage point of the *quincho panorámico* for a drink (try the *yatay* spirit), while enjoying the view of the palm forest. Guided excursions, include horse riding into the palm forest and the *arroyo de los Pájaros* (2 hrs, US$5 pp, minimum two people), canoe journeys along *arroyo El Palmar* (US$5 pp, minimum two people) and walks to the Mirador del Cerro de Piedra (US$3.35 pp, minimum three people, only at weekends). All recommended.

❧ *Try to stay in El Palmar National Park overnight to see the abundance of wildlife at dawn or at sunset.*

Esteros del Iberá → *Colour map 2, B1*

Long ignored by tourists, this beautiful area at the heart of Corrientes province was until recently a rich territory for hunters and a wasteland for cattle ranchers. This is an immense wetland, where swamps, lakes, streams and floating islands or embalsados are the perfect environment for a rich variety of wildlife. However, the esteros have become more accessible to visitors seeking peace and tranquillity, or keen to spot the abundant wildlife since the creation of a nature reserve here in 1983, and the opening of many local estancias to guests. Due to the particular environmental conditions and the lack of a good road network, access is from the village of Colonia Carlos Pellegrini, reached from Mercedes, which is the base for exploring the Reserva Natural del Iberá. On the western side of the region, in an area of lowlands and higher woodlands, is the Parque Nacional Mburucuyá, where natural conditions are ideal for a close view of the local wildlife. The best time to visit is winter, avoiding the heat of mid-summer, with more chance of rain and thunderstorms.

Mercedes → *Phone code: 03773 Colour map 2, B1 Population: 30,900*

Mercedes is the best starting point for Colonia Carlos Pellegrini and the Esteros del Iberá, with regular transport to Pellegrini, though you may find yourself waiting hours there for the bus or *combi* to depart. It is 250 km southeast of Corrientes. The town is quite attractive with its red stone buildings, and there are a couple of decent places to stay overnight, a few restaurants, internet facilities and ATMs. Both Calle Pujol and Calle San Martín lead from the bus station, where there is a small tourist office, to the plaza. Mercedes' landscape is pretty similar to the grassy pampas region, though you'll see *rheas* emerging from the plains from time to time. And as this is an important cattle grazing area, you're likely to meet local gauchos wearing their distinctive outfits. A few kilometres west, on the road to Corrientes, is a shrine to pagan saint Gauchito Gil at the place where it's said he was killed. Shrines to Gil can be seen all over the country, with their distinctive red flags, see box page 267. ▸ *For Sleeping, Eating and other listings, see pages 293-299.*

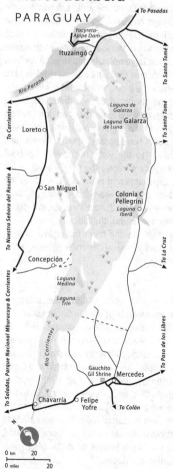

Esteros del Iberá

Colonia Carlos Pellegrini
→ *Colour map 2, B2*

With a remote setting on the beautiful Laguna Iberá 120 km northeast of Mercedes, Pellegini has all the services for the visitors to the **Reserva Natural**. The sprawling village has few inhabitants and the four hotels are a few hundred metres away from each other, all offering very good accommodation as well excursions to the lake and to other nearby sights. A one-night stay allows you to do the usual three-hour boat trip (US$8-12 pp if not included in hotel rates), but some hotels offer more activities if you stay longer, such as horse riding or guided walks. There are also a couple of cheaper places to stay. There are few streetlights in the village so carry a torch at night, and ask anyone for directions to get back to your hotel. A long and lonely dirt road links the village with Mercedes, which is where the only regular transport arrives. Take care when driving by night as there are cows, horses on the road as well as *yacarés* (alligators). Other unpaved roads head north to Route 12 (next to Ituzaingó) and to Route 14 (next to Santo Tomé) but are only suitable for 4WD vehicles and almost impassable after heavy rain.

Reserva Natural del Iberá

This reserve protects nearly 13,000 km sq of wetlands known as the Esteros del Iberá, a vast flat flooded plain which is one of the most important natural areas in Argentina for its wildlife. The area is accessible from Colonia Carlos Pellegrini, from where excursions depart. There's a **visitors centre** ① *by the bridge at the access to Colonia Carlos Pellegrini, open 0730-1800*, where you can see a model of the natural reserve, and a visit to the surrounding area is often included in hotel excursions to see monkey colonies living in the nearby trees.

The Esteros del Iberá are on the old course of the Río Paraná and the marshes extend some 250 km northeast to Ituzaingó on the Alto Paraná, some 70 km wide at their broadest. There are over 60 *lagunas*, or small lakes, of no more than a few metres deep and clear waters cover between 20 to 30% of the protected area, the largest being the *Lagunas Iberá* and *Lagunas de la Luna*. The area is rich in aquatic plants, including the beautiful *irupé* (*Victoriana cruziana*) a kind of floating plate which contains animal and birdlife and when it stretches along the shoreline, it's hard to differentiate the land from the lake. Like islands in the *lagunas*, the *embalsados* are floating vegetation, dense enough to support large animals and trees. A walk on these islands is highly recommended (if you suddenly start sinking, you're advised to spread out your arms before the *embalsado* closes in over you!).

※ Though you might find the lagunas of the Esteros del Iberá inviting for a swim, be aware that palometas (close relatives of piranhas) live in the lakes and become especially hungry in January and February.

Boat excursions along the shores of Laguna Iberá visit those areas where animals are more used to tourists and don't run off even as you get close, though a reduction in sightings has been observed after several boats have passed through in one day. The wildlife is very similar to the wet Chaco, with frequent sightings of the alligator *yacaré negro*, the deer, *ciervo de los pantanos dichotomus*, capybaras and many birds, such as the large and noisy *chajá* or the tiny red-headed *federal*. More difficult to see are the endangered nocturnal *aguará-guazú* (maned wolf), the 3m long *boa curiyú* (yellow anaconda), the alligator *yacaré ñato*. About 300 species of bird have been identified, among them the *yabirú* or *Juan Grande* stork (*Jabiru mycteria*) – the largest stork in the western hemisphere. ▸▸ *For Sleeping, Eating and other listings, see pages 293-299.*

Parque Nacional Mburucuyá

West of the Esteros del Iberá and 180 km southeast of the city of Corrientes, this park, covers 17,660 ha, stretching north from the marshlands of the Río Santa Lucía. The land was donated by Danish botanist Troels Pedersen, whose long research had identified 1,300 different plants, including some newly discovered species. There's a variety of natural environments, ranging from savanna with *yatay* palms and 'islands' of wet Chaco forest, with *lapacho* trees (with purple blossom in late winter) and *timbó* trees to the aquatic vegetation of the *esteros*. You'll also see *mburucuyá* or passionflower that gives its name to the park. Wildlife is easily spotted, including capybaras, the rare *aguará guazu* (maned wolf) and the *aguará pope*, similar to the North American raccoon – though these are both nocturnal animals – deer such as *corzuela parda* (*Mazama gouazoubira*) and *ciervo de los pantanos*, foxes *aguará-í*, monkeys and many bird species, such as the lovely *yetapá de collar* (*Alectrurus risora*) or strange-tailed tyrant, with its beautiful double tail.

Provincial Route 86 (unpaved) crosses the park for 18 km, to the **information centre** and free **campsite** (hot water and electricity) at the centre of the park. From there, two footpaths branch off the access road. The **Sendero Yatay** goes south to a vantage point on Estero Santa Lucía, winding 2.5 km through gallery forests and grassland with mature palms. The Sendero Aguará Popé goes north 1.2 km, through thick vegetation and wet Chaco forests and near the western access to the park, the road crosses the *arroyo Portillo*, where 2m-long *yacarés negros* alligators are often spotted.

Listings: Río Uruguay

Sleeping

Gualeguaychú *p286*

C **Puerto Sol**, *San Lorenzo 477, T/F434017, www.puerto-sol.com.ar* Appealing place to stay with good rooms with a/c, next to the port. The hotel runs a small resort in a nearby island (transfer and access included in room rates) where you can spend the day relaxing.

C **Tykuá**, *Luis N Palma 150, T422625, hoteltykua@arnet.com.ar* Brand-new place with breakfast included, lying 3 blocks from the bridge. Rooms are rather small for 3 people (D in low season).

D **Amalfi**, *25 de Mayo 571, T426818.* A pleasant, centrally located old house with comfortable rooms off a pleasant patio. No breakfast. Helpful owner offers cheaper rates for longer periods (E in low season).

D **Brutti**, *Bolívar 591, T426048.* Kind owners and decent rooms with fans and breakfast included (E in low season).

D **Villa Paranacito Annemarie**, *T495284, www.annemarie .com.ar* Small modern apartments for 2, 3 and 4 people with cooking facilities, heating and some with a/c. They run also a restaurant and own an island 40 minutes away, with basic facilities, where you can spend the day.

D **Bonanza**, *T495199.* These houses by the river are for 6, with cooking facilities and rates are negotiable if there are fewer people. There is also a campsite with hot showers and electricity for US$5 a day per tent up to 4 people.

D **Doña Teresa**, *T495101.* Rooms for 4 or 6 people with cooking facilities and heating. German spoken.

E **Lo de Juan**, *Alem y Bolívar, T433661.* At the back of the shop where Juan sells his

handicrafts. Good rooms with fan and bath, offered all year round; no breakfast is served.

E pp **Rose Marie**, *T495204.* A beautiful house set in a remote position at the mouth of *arroyo* (stream) Martínez (1 km from Río Uruguay and at a 25-min boat journey from the village). Transfer from the village can be arranged in advance or through the local *Guardería Náutica* Los Pinos for an extra US$27. D for full board accommodation, and boat or fishing excursions are on offer.

F pp **Top Maló**, *T495255, topmalo@infovia.com.ar* Affiliated to Hostelling International (discounts for members), this place has E houses, built on stilts 3m above ground, for 2 and 4 people with cooking facilities, shared rooms for up to 5 people, kitchen and bedlinen included, and a **campsite** with hot showers and electricity for US$3.50 a day plus US$0.35 pp payable only for the first day. An attractive rustic style and a warm atmosphere. Short boat excursions from US$2 pp are on offer together with half-day fishing trips. The welcoming owners speak some English, but fluent German and Danish.

Camping

There are several sites along Río Gualeguaychú's banks, next to the bridge and north of it.

Costa Azul, *200 m northeast of bridge, T423984.* A shady willow grove, and a good location on the riverside. Camping (US$4 a day for a 2 man-tent) and also new wooden cabins (US$13 for 4 people) and small flats with cooking facilities (US$20 for 4 people).

Solar del Este, *east end of C Ituzaingó, T433303, www.solardeleste.com.ar* This resort on the Río Gualeguaychú is

The Northeast Listings: Río Uruguay

popular among locals (US$3 a day per tent for up to 2 people).

El Ñandubaysal, *T423298, www.nandu baysal.com.ar* The smartest campsite and the only one on the beautiful Río Uruguay, 15 km southeast, with very good facilities (US$5.50 per tent plus access fee) and a 'VIP' sector (US$7.50 per tent plus access fee).

Fray Bentos *p287*

B **Plaza**, *18 de Julio y 25, T2363*. Comfortable.
E **Colonial**, *25 de Mayo 3293, T2260*. Attractive old building with patio.
E pp **25 de Mayo**, *25 de Mayo y Lavalleja, T2586*. Basic.

Camping

At the **Club Remeros**, near the river and at **Colegio Laureles**, 1 km from centre, T2236.

Concepción de Uruguay *p287*

D **Grand Hotel**, *Eva Perón 114, T422851, www.palaciotexier.com.ar* Originally a French-style mansion with an adjacent theatre built in 1931 for Texier family, it retains some of its former splendour, especially in the hall and casino. Superior rooms (25% more expensive) have a/c and TV but are otherwise similar. Both include a large breakfast.
E **Centro**, *Moreno 130, T427429*. Spotless rooms, comfortable enough. Rooms on shady patio lack the old-fashioned style of the front rooms. Breakfast US$0.80.

Estancias

Founded by Urquiza, these offer excellent accommodation and all meals included:
AL pp **Estancia San Pedro**, *Near Villa Mantero, 39.5 km west of Concepción del Uruguay. T03442-428374 or T03445-482107, esanpedro@ciudad.com.ar* Owned by descendents of Urquiza, this has old rooms full of antiques, very good accommodation.
AL pp **Estancia Santa Cándida**, *T03442-422188*. Offers half-board accommodation at US$90 pp.

Colón *p288*

A **Quirinale**, *Av Costanera Quirós y Noailles, T421133, F421532, www.hquirinale.com.ar* A large, rather overpriced, 5-star overlooking the river. Panoramic views from some of the rooms, spa treatments charged separately.

Restaurant, a casino, open-air and indoor pools, the latter with thermal waters.
D **Holimasú**, *Belgrano 28, T421305, www.hotelholimasu.com.ar* A pleasant patio makes this small place a decent option. Breakfast is included but a/c is extra.
D **Hostería Restaurant del Puerto**, *Alejo Peyret 158, T422698, hosteriadelpuerto@ ciudad.com.ar* By far the nicest and best value place to stay. This old building has been redecorated offering comfort, and retaining the period-style atmosphere. Rooms for 4 people at the front on first floor have balconies overlooking the river, but off-season are also offered as doubles. Breakfast is included.
D **La Chozna**, *Colonia Hocker, T421912*. This posada is open in one of the oldest houses of the colony, retaining its old style with very comfortable rooms. Breakfast is included.
D **La Posada de David**, *Alejo Peyret 97, T423930*. A pleasant family house with a garden. Welcoming owners offer very good double rooms with breakfast and one with cooking facilities.
D **Vieja Calera**, *Bolívar 350, T423761, viejacalera@ar.inter.net* Dark corridors lead to decent rooms here, and breakfast is included.
E **Hostería Liebig**, *Eric Evans 223, Pueblo Liebig, T492049*. Nimia and her husband are very kind hosts at this very pleasant family house with a splendid garden and spacious rooms. Breakfast is included and excellent meals are available. Single ocupants pay double at weekends. Recommended.
E **Rueda de Amigos**, *Eric Evans 125, T15640131, ruedadeamigos @hotmail.com* Adriana, the owner, is an excellent promotor of tourism in the village and welcomes guests to her house/teahouse.
E **Sweet Rose**, *25 de Mayo 10, T15643487*. Rooms are comfortable enough, with small bathrooms. Those at the front overlook a noisy corner. Breakfast is extra.
F pp **Casamate**, *Laprida 128, T422385, www.casamate.com.ar* Affiliated to **Hostelling International** (discounts for members), this is a renovated old house with a nice backyard and a pleasant sitting room with a fireplace. The very welcoming young owners provide excellent information on local sights and on bus connections. Good rooms with shared baths (bedlinen

provided), as well as D doubles with own bath. Breakfasts are superb (US$1.50 if you add scrambled eggs); other meals on request. Cooking and laundry facilities and free use of cycles are also available. German and English spoken. Recommended.

Houses for short term rent

Complejo Las Marías, *25 de Mayo 480, T423589 or in Buenos Aires, T4641 7174, www.complejolasmarias.com.ar* A group of 5 B houses for 5 or 6 people with own kitchen and bed linen provided, surrounded by a garden with a pool.

Boujon Family, *Maipú 430, T421889*. Good breakfast and other meals extra.

Camping

Consult the tourist office for their extensive list, as there are many campsites along the riverside, getting quieter the further you go from the centre, as well as some on nearby rivers. They all charge about US$3 a day per tent for up to 2 people.

Camping Municipal Playa Norte, *T422074*. A few blocks north of the port district.

Piedras Coloradas, *T421451/423548*. Lies on the river a few hundred metres south of Av 12 de Abril.

Paysandú *p289*

C **Plaza**, *Leandro Gómez 1211, T22022, F33545*. A recently renovated place with breakfast, and rooms with a/c.

D **Sarandí**, *Sarandí 931, T23465*. A good option with comfortable rooms.

E pp **Victoria**, *18 de Julio 979, T24320*. Very helpful owners run this decent place; cheaper without bath.

Camping

Club de Pescadores, *Rambla Costanera Norte, T26220*. US$2 per day, includes showers.

Refugio de Vida Silvestre La Aurora del Palmar *p290*

There is a **campsite** (US$1.70-2 pp a day plus US$1.30 per tent) and one of the most extraordinary places to stay; **converted train carriages**: *T03447-421549*,

info@auroradelpalmar.com.ar www.auroradelpalmar.com.ar (G pp, shared room and bath, bed linen extra; D doubles with bath and breakfast provided, also for 3 to 6 people). Book in advance or check availability for the excursions. Surplus charged for tours for 1 person.

Mercedes *p291*

E **Sol**, *San Martín 519, T420283*. An old house with clean rooms and a lovely patio, breakfast included.

F pp **Delicias del Iberá**, *Pujol 1162, T422508*. Located next door to the departure point for *combis* to Pellegrini, this is a relaxing place to stay with breakfast, good meals and a garden. Open early, but closed for the siesta, you can get tourist information here, as well as decent rooms with shared bath for an overnight stay.

Colonia Carlos Pellegrini *p291*

A pp **Hostería Ñandé Retá**, *T/F499411, T011-48112005 (in Buenos Aires), www.nandereta.com* This big wooden house is set under a shady grove and offers full board accommodation with excursions included, as well as a playroom on the upper floor: ideal for long rainy afternoons.

A pp **Posada Aguapé**, *T499412, T/F011-47423015 (in Buenos Aires), www.iberaesteros.com.ar* Situated on the laguna with a garden and a pool, this offers comfortable rooms (some smaller rooms are a bit cheaper) and an attractive dining room in a large *quincho*. Prices are for full board accommodation and include two excursions (B pp for bed and breakfast only).

A pp **Posada de la Laguna**, *T499413, F011-47377274 (in Buenos Aires), www.iberalaguna.8k.com* The local upmarket choice, set on the laguna, run by hospitable painter Elsa Güiraldes. Just a few lovely, very comfortable rooms, a large neat garden and a swimming pool. Full board and excursions are included.

D pp **Posada Ypa Sapukai**, *T420155, www.ypasapukai.com.ar* This is the cosiest and best value place to stay, run by friendly Pedro Noailles and his excellent staff, also offering excellent excursions to the laguna.

● **Phone codes** *Concepción del Uruguay: 03442; Gualeguaychú: 03446; Colón 03447; Mercedes: 03773. In Uruguay Fray Bentos +598-(0)562; Paysandú: +598-(0)72*

(US$8 pp). Rates are for full board (E pp for bed and breakfast). Recommended.

F pp San Cayetano, *T03773-15628763*. A very basic place run by local guide Roque Pera.

Estancias

B pp San Juan Poriahú, *at Loreto, T03781-15608674, T011-47919511 (in Buenos Aires)*. An old estancia with an attractive house run by Marcos García Rams, situated at the northwestern edge of the Esteros del Iberá, next to the village of Loreto, and accessible by a paved road from nearby Route 12. Rates include full board accommodation (half rate for under 12s) and activities such as horse riding and boat trips to appreciate the rich wildlife in an area where there has been no hunting at all. Closed in Jan, Feb and Jul holidays. Recommended.

B pp San Lorenzo, *at Galarza, T03756-481292, www.ibera argentina.com.ar* Set next to two of the biggest lakes of the Iberá (at the northeast edge of the region), this estancia is in a splendid place for wildlife watching, especially rare deer *venado de las pampas*. Welcomingly run by its owners, full board, activities (riding, walking, boat trips to Lagunas de Luna and Galarza) are all included in the rates. Boat excursions by night are charged separately. Access from Gobernador Virasoro (90 km away), via Routes 37 and 41. Transfers can be arranged to/from Gobernador Virasoro or Posadas for an extra charge. Closed in Jan-Feb.

⊘ Eating

Gualeguaychú *p286*

$$ Campo Alto, *San Lorenzo y Concordia*. A large *quincho* (rustic place to eat) at the end of the *costanera*, lots of local fish suchas *surubí*, *boga*, dorado and *patí* are on the menu.
$ Dacal, *Av Costanera y Andrade*. A traditional restaurant, serving good food; the *surubí* is recommended.
$ La Solapa, *3 de Febrero 126*. Serves good home-made pastas in warm family atmosphere, where decoration includes some carnival costumes.

Fray Bentos *p287*

There are several cafés and pizzerias on 18 de Julio near Plaza Constitución.
$ Olla, *18 de Julio near Plaza Constitución*. Seafood and pasta, good value.

Concepción de Uruguay *p287*

$ El Remanso, *Rocamora y Eva Perón*. Good food, popular and moderately priced *parrilla*.

Colón *p288*

$ La Cosquilla de Angel, *Alejo Peyret 180*. The smartest place in town with attractive décor, live piano music in the evenings and tables outside at lunchtime. Varied and moderately priced meals, including fish of the day and also a reasonable set menu.
$ Viejo Almacén, *Urquiza y Paso*. A cosy place offering very good cooking and excellent service at moderate prices. The *surubí* is tasty *al limón* or with a delicate sauce. In the basement, there's a great place for trying wines and *picadas* (nibbles of local cheese and ham).

Paysandú *p289*

$ Artemio, *18 de Julio 1248*. Reputedly the best food in town.

⊛ Festivals

Gualeguaychú *p286*

Local teams or *comparsas* compete in colourful parades, to the powerful drumbeats of the *batucada*, with the spectacularly decorated *carrozas* and dancers dressed in brightly coloured costumes and feathers. **Carnival** is celebrated every weekend throughout **Jan and Feb** at the *corsódromo*, a purpose-built carnival parade ground with grandstand, at the back of the former railway station, *Piccini y Maipú*. It's US$7 for a seat, and while the spectacle is quite amazing, it lacks the spontaneity of a street festival.

Colón *p288*

The **Fiesta Nacional de la Artesanía** is held over 9 evenings **every February** in the Parque Quirós, where 300 craftspeople from Argentina and elsewhere display a wide variety of handicrafts. There are also folklore and pop music concerts.

Tour operators

Concepción del Uruguay p287
Mirst Travel, Colón 301, Villaguay,
T03455-423790, www.mirsttravel.com.ar
Operates tours to the Jewish colonies.

Colón p288
Cambá, Martín Reibel 79, T422114,
T03442-15626033. Offers 3-hr guided
birdwatching walks in small groups of
people to nearby sites in the riverside
(US$6.50 pp).
Ita i Cora, San Martín 97, T423360,
T15576095, www.itaicora.com Very
welcoming and informative people run boat
trips on the Río Uruguay, where you can lie
on the huge beaches or take long walks in
shallow waters, stopping off at islands to
give you a taste of trekking through jungle.
Recommended (45 mins-2½ hrs, US$5-17
pp). Also short 4WD trips, including a visit to
Pueblo Liebig (1½-2½ hrs, US$6.50-10). Boat
departures from Av Costanera Quirós y
Noailles; children under 10 half price.

Parque Nacional El Palmar p290
Capybara Aventura T03442-15580220,
pnpalmar@ciudad.com.ar (at park
administration), T03447-493053, capybara
aventura@ciudad.com.ar Guided walks, day
and night (1-3 hrs, US$1-1.70 pp) and cycle
tours, providing mountain bikes and helmets
(1½-3 hrs, US$1.70-3.35). On weekdays or in
low season, call first. Entry: Argentines: US$2;
foreigners: US$4, T03447-493049,

Transport

Gualeguaychú p286
Bus
Terminal at Bv Artigas y Bv Jurado, T440688
(30-min-walk to centre along Av Artigas and
Av Aristóbulo del Valle to the east; remise taxi
charges US$1.20 to centre). The terminal has
tourist information and a post office, phones,
a small restaurant and 24-hr left luggage
(US$0.35 per day).
To **Buenos Aires**, Flecha Bus, Nuevo
Expreso, Nuevo Rápido Tata, 3-3½ hrs,
US$7-8. To **Paraná**, Nuevo Expreso, Ciudad
de Gualeguay, Jovi Bus, 4½-5 hrs, US$6.
To **Concepción del Uruguay**, Flecha Bus,
Nuevo Expreso, Jovi Bus, 1 hr, US$1.50.

To **Colón**, Flecha Bus, Nuevo Expreso,
Jovi Bus, 1½-2 hrs, US$2-2.50. To **Fray
Bentos**, Ciudad de Gualeguay, 2 daily (1 on
Sun), 1 hr 15 mins, US$2.30 (arrive half an
hour before departure to do the border
paperwork proceedings). To **Villa
Paranacito**, Nuevo Expreso, daily, 2 hrs,
US$3.50. To **El Ñandubaysal**, Expreso
Ñandubaysal, several daily in high season,
US$1.70 open return includes entry fee.

Mountain bike hire
Landaburo, Eva Perón 444 (next to Av
Aristóbulo del Valle), T428668.

Remise taxi
San José, San José y Rivadavia (on plaza),
T431333.

Around Gualeguaychú p286
Villa Paranacito is accessible only via a 22
km dirt road, branching off Route 12, 10 km
south of **Ceibas**. Daily buses **Nuevo Expreso**
to/from **Gualeguaychú**, **Zárate** and **Buenos
Aires**. Buses to **Zárate** or **Buenos Aires** stop
at **Ceibas**, not far from Estancia La Azotea,
and there are regular buses from
Gualeguaychú to **Larroque** and
Urdinarrain, where remise taxis will take you
to **Irazusta** and **Aldea San Antonio**.

Fray Bentos p287
The bus terminal is at 18 de Julio y Blanes.
Buses call here, but do not alight, calling
instead at the company offices around Plaza
Constitución. To/from **Montevideo**, CUT, 4½
hrs, 6 a day, US$7.50, also **Chadre**, US$8.25.
To **Buenos Aires**, Bus de la Carrera, 3½ hrs,
US$12. To **Gualeguaychú**, ETA, 1 hr,
US$3.15, 2 a day.

Concepción del Uruguay p287
The bus terminal is at Rocamora y Los
Constituyentes, T422352, 11 blocks west of
Plaza Ramírez (remise taxi to centre,
US$0.40). Left luggage, free at information
desk. To **Buenos Aires**, Flecha Bus, Nuevo
Rápido Tata, 4 hrs, US$8-9.
   To **Paraná**, Flecha Bus, Nuevo Rápido Tata,
Itapé, 5 hrs, US$7. To **Colón**, several companies,
45 mins, US$1. To **Palacio San José**, Itapé,
Paccot, San José (stopping at El Cruce or at
Caseros), 30 mins, US$0.80. To **Gualeguaychú**,
several companies, 1 hr, US$1.50.

Banco Pelay is accessible by road by taking C 25 de Mayo. *Remise* taxis charge US$1.30 from centre; regular buses depart every half an hour from centre, US$0.35, only in summer. **Estancia Santa Cándida** is accessible via a dirt road branching off Bv Bruno; *remise* taxis charge US$1.30. **Palacio San José** can be reached by taking Route 39 west and turning right after Caseros train station. Buses going to **Paraná** or **Rosario del Tala** will stop at **El Cruce** or **Caseros**, and from here, the *palacios* are 4 and 8 km away, respectively (take *remise* taxi from Caseros). *Remise* taxis charge about US$8 with an hour and a half wait. Tour operators run *combis* (minibuses) only in high season for about US$5 including entrance (check companies at tourist office, since they change every year). A train service arrives on Sat from **Villa Elisa** (see under Colón). **Basavilbaso** has regular buses which link **Concepción del Uruguay** and **Paraná** or **Rosario del Tala**.

Colón *p288*
Bus
Not all long-distance buses enter Colón. Buses going north from Colón will stop at **Ubajay**. Terminal at *Paysandú y Sourigues (10 blocks north of main plaza)*, *T421716*. There is a 24-hr bar where luggage is kept for US$0.35 a day; and the owner provides information on bus timetables. At Ubajay, *Parador Gastiazoro, T0345-4905026*, is a busy bus stop where you can take daily **Expreso Singer** to **Puerto Iguazú** (US$27).
To **Buenos Aires**, Flecha Bus, Nuevo Expreso, Nuevo Rápido Tata, 5-6 hrs, US$8-10. To **Mercedes** (for getting to Iberá), Nuevo Rápido Tata, Flecha Bus, 6-7 hrs, US$6-8. To **Paraná**, Flecha Bus, Paccot, 4-5 hrs, US$7. To **Concepción del Uruguay**, several companies, 45 minutes, US$1. To **Gualeguaychú**, several companies, 1½-2 hrs, US$2-2.50. To **San José**, Paccot, 20 minutes, US$0.50. To **Pueblo Liebig**, Paccot, 45 minutes, US$0.50.
  Access to **Parque Nacional El Palmar**, Flecha Bus, Itapé, Jovi Bus, 1 hr, US$1.50.
  To **Villa Elisa**, Itapé, Mitre Bus, Transporte Ogara, 1 hr, US$1-1.20. To **Paysandú** (Uruguay), Copay, 45 mins, US$2-2.30.

Cycling
Bici Fabián, *on C Sourigues, between Av 12 de Abril and San Martín*. Mountain bike hire.

Remise taxi
Palmar, *Laprida 37, T421278*.

San José *p289*
San José lies almost on main Route 14 and is easily reachable by regular buses from Colón. To get to **Molino Forclaz**, take Av 12 de Abril and at 11 blocks from main plaza turn right at C Las Piedras Norte until there's a left turn, leading to the mill. Pueblo Liebig has regular *combi* (minibus) services from Colón, direct, or via San José, along the unpaved road.
  Villa Elisa is reached by taking Route 130, branching off Route 14, a few kilometres north of San José. There are regular buses.
  Colonia Hocker can be reached from Colón by taking Route 14 northwards. 6 km after its junction with Route 130, a dirt road branches off west, leading after 9 km to the village. From Villa Elisa, a 10 km unpaved road heads north to Colonia Hocker.
  Arroyo Barú is reached via a 35 km long dirt road, branching off Route 130, 5 km west of Villa Elisa, where *remise* taxis, T03447-496010 and *combis*, T03447-496013, will take passengers in good weather.

Paysandú *p289*
The bus terminal is at *Zorrilla y Artigas, T23225*.

Parque Nacional El Palmar *p290*
Buses from **Colón**, 1 hr, US$1.50, or coming from the north will drop you at the entrance, from where you can walk or hitch the last 12 km to the park administration. **Remise taxis** from **Colón** or from **Ubajay** also offer tours (eg from Colón, US$15 for a 4-hr round trip, including a tour or waiting time in the park. Enquire in Ubajay at bus stop Parador Gastiazoro or at petrol station for park wardens who might be going to the park.

Refugio de Vida Silvestre La Aurora del Palmar *p290*
Buses from **Colón** or from the north will drop you at the entrance. Remember to tell the driver you're going to La Aurora del Palmar, to avoid confusion with the National Park. **Remise taxis** from **Ubajay** charge US$1.70.

Mercedes *p291*

To **Colonia Carlos Pellegrini** the *combi* Rayo Bus provides the best service, leaving daily at 1130 from *Pujol 1166, T420184, T15629598*, 3 hrs, US$3.30. Note that it spends an hour picking up passengers from the whole of Mercedes after leaving the office. There is also an unreliable bus Itatí II leaving from the bus station daily, except Sun, at noon, US$3.30 (payable on board).

To **Buenos Aires**, Flecha Bus, Itatí, Nuevo Rápido Tata, Aguila Dorada Bis, San Cristóbal, 9-10 hrs, US$12-14. To **Corrientes**, several companies, 3 hrs, US$3.30-4. To **Puerto Iguazú**, there are two options: via Corrientes; or via any important town along Route 14, where you can take a bus going north. The first takes longer, but there's more chance of a bus. The second option offers the closest connection at Paso de los Libres, 130 km southeast, but this town has become rather unsafe and there are fewer buses.

Colonia Carlos Pellegrini *p291*

To **Mercedes**, *combi* Rayo Bus, 3 hrs, US$3.30, departs daily at 0400. Booking is required before 2200 on the night before at the office in a local grocery (ask for directions). **Buses** Itatí II departs Mon-Sat at 0430. To **Posadas**, occasionally a transfer can be arranged (3 hrs, 5 hrs in bad weather, ask at *Antúnez* grocery on plaza, US$75 for up to 8 people or at *Hostería Ñandé Retá*, US$90). From Posadas see under Posadas tour operators.

Parque Nacional Mburucuyá *p292*

The park lies 12 km east of the small town of Mburucuyá (where there are two places to stay overnight), accessible by a 47 km-long road branching off at Saladas. Unpaved Route 86 (later Route 13) links Mburucuyá with the park and this sandy road leads northeast to Itá Ibaté, on Route 12, 160 km east of the provincial capital. **Buses** San Antonio from Corrientes goes daily to **Mburucuyá**, 2½ hrs, US$2.30. **Remise taxis** from there to the park, US$5. Free entry, *T03782-498022*.

ⓘ Directory

Gualeguaychú *p286*

Banks Banco de la Nación, *25 de Mayo y Alberdi*. Credicoop, *Rivadavia y Perón*. **Uruguayan consulate**, *Rivadavia 810, T426168, Mon-Fri 0800-1400*.

Fray Bentos *p287*

Banks Cambio Fagalde, *Plaza Constitución, open Mon-Fri 0800-1900, Sat 0800-1230*.

Río Paraná

The Río Paraná, formed by the rivers Paranaiba and Grande from Brazil, weaves its lazy course right across the northeast of Argentina, from Misiones to Buenos Aires where it forms a vast delta. Its total length is 3,470 km, and in this part of the country, it divides the provinces of Santa Fe and Chaco, west of the river, from Entre Ríos and Corrientes to the east. There are two main routes north from Buenos Aires. An interesting journey is along the eastern banks of the river, through Paraná via small towns with wildlife spotting and fishing and onwards to Goya and Corrientes; or the more major route north along the western banks, through the cities of Rosario and Santa Fe to Reconquista and Resistencia. This chapter explores the western route first, as far as Santa Fe, and then crosses to the eastern bank to the city of Paraná, and areas north and south.

Rosario → *Phone code 0341 Colour map 4, A5 Population: 1,159,000*

Rosario is Argentina's third largest city, renowned for its rich cultural life, since it's home to many famous artists and pop musicians. Although little visited by travellers, it has some fine buildings in its attractive centre, and a well-kept costanera alongside the Paraná river. The nightlife is lively, with plenty of cafés, restaurants and nightclubs, and there are daily theatre and live music shows at venues all around the

A Revolutionary Life

Che Guevara's *Motorcycle Diaries* makes an entertaining read to accompany your travels to Argentina. The enduring image of youthful revolutionary zeal, Che stands proud , implacable and defiant beneath his black beret on many a student wall. The future revolutionary was born into a middle class family Rosario in 1928, in a house at Entre Ríos and Urquiza. But the city is strangely coy about its links with Guevara, perhaps because his parents soon moved with their asthmatic son to the healthier climate of the Sierras of Córdoba.

Che's eyes were soon opened to the plight of South America's poor during his journey around the continent on a beaten-up old motorcycle. Rather than pursue a career in medicine, which he'd started studying, he decided to dedicate the rest of his life to the flight for the 'liberation of the American continent'.

In 1956 he met Fidel Castro in Mexico, and together they planned to create the ideal Socialist model in Cuba, as well as establish links with other sympathetic nations. But his overriding ambition had always been to spread the revolutionary word, and take the armed struggle to other parts – particularly in his own country. But conditions in Argentina were not right, and so Fidel and Che began their mission to liberate America in Bolivia. Che spent a little time in La Paz, and then travelled to a guerrilla base at Nanchuazú. However the constant movements of the group aroused the suspicion of neighbours and the army were alerted. Fidel and Che fled and spent several months wandering the steep valleys of eastern Bolivia. In August 1967, when Che was just 39, they were ambushed by Bolivian troops. Che was executed and buried in an unmarked grave. In 1997 his body was exhumed and taken to Cuba.

city. To recover from all that entertainment, the nearby islands in the river, just minutes away from the centre, you can relax on sandy beaches. Rosario enjoys a generally sunny climate with hot summer days and although this is not a major tourist destination, it's a good place to break your journey north or west. ▸▸ *For Sleeping, Eating and other listings, see pages 310-318.*

History

Unlike most Spanish American cities, Rosario was never officially founded. Though a fort was established in 1689 by Luis Romero de Pineda, it was just a place to export of mules and tobacco throughout the 18th century. However, it grew rapidly in the late 19th century, with the opening of a railway line to Córdoba in 1870 and the increase of shipping along the Paraná: its port became a major exporter of grain and beef, while new industries were established, including breweries, grain mills, and leather industries. By the 1920s Rosario had earned the nickname of *La Chicago Argentina* after a gang of seven Sicilian immigrants started their criminal careers based on the extortion and kidnapping of local business men. In the late 20th century, Rosario attracted thousands of immigrants from northern provinces of Argentina who settled on the outskirts, later forming one of the largest deprived communities in the country.

The main **tourist office** ① *Av Belgrano y Buenos Aires, on the riverside park next to the Monumento a la Bandera, T480 2230, etur@rosario.gov.ar www.rosario turismo.com* has very efficient staff, and a free tourist card is given for discounts at several hotels, restaurants and other services.

Sights

The old city centre is on the Plaza 25 de Mayo, just a block south of the Parque a la Bandera which lies along the riverside. Around it are the cathedral, in somewhat eclectic style and containing the *Virgen del* Rosario, and the Palacio Municipal. On the north side is the **Museo de Arte Decorativo** ① *Santa Fe 748, T480 2547, Thu-Sun 1600-2000, free,* a sumptuous former family residence housing a valuable private collection of paintings, furniture, tapestries, sculptures, and silver, brought mainly from Europe. To the left of the cathedral, the **Pasaje Juramento** is the the pedestrian access to the imposing **Monumento a la Bandera** ① *T/F480 2238, Mon 1400-1800, Tue-Sun 0900-1800 (in summer till 1900), US$0.35 (tower), free (Salón de las Banderas).* An austere monument built on the site where General Belgrano raised the Argentine flag for the first time in 1812. The tower has a vantage point 70 m high with excellent panoramic views over the city.

From Plaza 25 de Mayo, Calle Córdoba leads west towards Plaza San Martín with the **Paseo del Siglo**, the largest concentration of late 19th- and early 20th-centuries buildings in the city. On Plaza 25 de Mayo, at Córdoba y Laprida, is the **Edificio Bola de Nieve** (1906), appropriately topped with a snowball, and at Córdoba y Maipú, the **Jockey Club** (1908) has a splendid tower. The other commercial street, San Martín, runs southwards, a block west of here with the former store *La Favorita* (1929), at Córdoba y Sarmiento, is a beautiful building now housing the Chilean chain store *Falabella*. At Entre Ríos y Urquiza, three blocks north of Córdoba, there's the **birthplace of Ernesto 'Che' Guevara**, though there's no access inside. At Córdoba y Corrientes is the **Bolsa de Comercio** (1931), the stock exchange, and half a block further, the art deco **Palacio**

Rosario

Minetti (1930), both fine buildings. In the heart of the city, **Plaza Pringles** is an attractive green spot, and three blocks further west, the Plaza San Martín is flanked by two huge buildings, the **Ex Jefatura de Policía** (1916) in a heavy German neoclassic style, now the seat of the provincial government, and on the west side, the **Ex Palacio de Justicia** (1892), now a university building which houses a small **Museo de Ciencias Naturales** ① *Tue-Fri 0900-1200, 1500-1800, Sun 1500-1800, free, T472 1449.*

The palm-lined **Boulevard Oroño** leads north to the riverside parks, the Rosario Norte railway station and south to the **Pichincha district**, popular for nightlife, and to **Parque Independencia** at the south end. This beautiful 126-ha park was designed by the French architect Charles Thays, who designed many of Argentina's finest parks, including those in Palermo, Buenos Aires, and Mendoza. Opened in 1902, it has a large lake and a **tourist information** (Mon-Fri 1500-2100, Sat-Sun 1300-1930). There are gardens with fountains and fine statues, shady avenues, the Newell's Old Boys football club stadium and three museums in the area.

Just outside the park, the **Museo de Bellas Artes** ① *J B Castagnino, Av Pellegrini 2202, T480 2542, Wed-Mon 1400-2000, US$0.35,* is considered one of the best fine arts museums in the country, with a large collection of European paintings, particularly French Impressionist, Italian Baroque and Flemish works, and one of best collections of paintings and sculpture works by renowned Argentine artists.

Next to the stadium is the **Museo Histórico Provincial** ① *T472 1457, Tue-Fri 0900-1700, Sat 1500-1800, Sun 1000-1300 (in summer Thu-Sun 1000-1300), free,* which has a very well displayed collection of Latin American aboriginal artefacts and valuable pieces of religious art including Cusco school paintings and a magnificent altar covered with silver plaques, which was used by Pope John Paul II in 1987. There is also a **Museo de la Ciudad** for local history, opening times unreliable; T480 8665.

The riverside is lined with several parks, making it a very attractive place to walk. Eight blocks south of the Monumento a la Bandera is the **Parque Urquiza** ① *T480 2533, shows on Sun 2000, US$0.65; museum open Sat-Sun 1830-2100, US$0.65,* with sports facilities, an open-air theatre and the **Complejo Astronómico Municipal** with an observatory, a planetarium and a small science museum.

Further north is the **Estación Fluvial** where boats leave for excursions around the islands, containing the **Museo del Paraná y las Islas** ① *T440 0751, Wed-Sun 1600-1930, US$0.35,* which gives an insight into islander culture through local art and artefacts. At the foot of the monument, is the **Parque a la Bandera**, one of the most appealing parks, and the tourist office beyond which is the **Parque de España**, a modern red-brick development which incorporates the old railway arches as an exhibition centre and offers fine views over the Río Paraná.

On the northern outskirts, the riverside between the **Rosario Central** Football Club and the access to the suspension bridge is known as the **Paseo Ribereño Norte** ① *accessible by a seasonal bus service Colectivo de la Costa (only in summer) via Av Belgrano, or by buses No 101, 102, 103, 110 and others from bus terminal; taxis charge US$3 from Monumento a la Bandera.* From south to north, its attractions are the small **Aquarium** with freshwater species in the **Parque Alem** ① *T472 4695, Mon-Fri 0900-1300, 1400-1800, Sat-Sun 1700-2000, US$0.35.* Next is **Barrio Alberdi**, an attractive residential area with traditional yacht clubs; it's worth walking up Avenida Puccio to see the impressive mansion **Villa Hortensia**, Warnes 1917. Further north are the beach resorts **Balnearios Rambla Catalunya I** and **II** and **Balneario La Florida**, the oldest of all (entry US$0.65). From the beach, the **Paseo del Caminante**, a 600 m-long walkway leads to the **Costa Alta** pier, next to the suspension bridge. ▸▸ *For Sleeping, Eating and other listings, see pages 310-318.*

Riverside resorts

The most popular destination for locals as well as visitors are the dozens of riverside resorts on the islands and sandy banks opposite Rosario. These have

stay, with woods, beaches and lagoons. There are campsites and *cabañas* for rent in
some of them. Boats depart daily in summer from *La Fluvial* or from *Costa Alta* to the
island resorts, each with its own transfer service. Weekend services run throughout
the rest of the year.

Santa Fé → *Phone code: 0342 Colour map 4, A5 Population: 451,600*

Santa Fé is capital of its province, one of the oldest cities of the country, though
there's little architectural evidence. It lies near the confluence of the Ríos Santa Fe
and Salado in a low-lying area with lagoons and islands just west of the Río Paraná,
and is connected to the smaller city of Paraná, on the east bank of the river, by road
bridges and a tunnel. It's hot and humid from November to March, but its friendly,
lively atmosphere, makes it a very pleasant place to visit. Take a sunset walk on the
costanera, a few shared 'lisos' of beer downed with some superb fish, and a stirring
classic football match between Colón and Unión for an unforgettable stay. ⏵ *For
Sleeping, Eating and other listings, see pages 310-318.*

History
Founded by settlers from Asunción in 1573 and transferred from nearby Cayastá to its
present site in 1653, it was, in the colonial period, one of the main centres of Jesuit
and Franciscan influence in the country and an important port on the voyage between
Buenos Aires and Asunción. After independence it suffered badly from the struggles
between provincial *caudillos*, but it has remained an important meeting place for
reforms to the country's constitution.

Sights
The city's **commercial centre** lies a few blocks southwest of the bus terminal, along the
partially pedestrianized San Martín. This street leads southwards to the historic centre,
and on San Martín y Juan de Garay is the **Teatro Primero de Mayo**, a quite remarkable
building dating from 1905. The southern part of the city, around the Plaza 25 de Mayo is
the historical centre, with the oldest buildings and a few museums. On the plaza itself
is the cathedral, dating from 1751 but remodelled in 1834, its twin towers capped by
blue tiled cupolas. On the east side is the **Iglesia de Nuestra Señora de los Milagros**, a
rustic little building dating from the end of the 17th century. It has an ornate dome, and
an old painting of the Virgin Mary in an impressive wooden frame. On the southern side
is the majestic French-style **Casa de Gobierno** on the site of the historic Cabildo.

Southeast of the plaza is the **Paseo de las Dos Culturas**, a small park with three
interesting sights. Closer to the plaza is the **Museo Histórico Provincial** ① *3 de
Febrero 2553, T457 3529, all year round: Tue-Fri 0830-1200; Jan-Feb: Tue-Fri
1600-2030, Sat-Sun 1730-2030; Mar-Apr: Tue-Fri 1500-1900, Sat-Sun 1600-1900;
May-Sep: Tue-Fri 1400-1830, Sat-Sun 1500-1800; Oct-Dec:Tue-Fri 1430-1930,
Sat-Sun 1630-1930, free,* in a former family house dating from 1690 (one of the oldest
surviving civil buildings in the country), worth visting for the house itself rather than
the exhibition of two 17th-century Cusco school paintings.

About 100 m south is the **Iglesia y Convento de San Francisco** built between 1673
and 1695. The church has walls nearly 2m thick and fine wooden ceilings, built from
timber floated down the river from Paraguay, carved by indigenous craftsmen and
fitted without the use of nails. The pulpit and altar are 17th-century baroque.

On the opposite side of the park is the superb **Museo Etnográfico y Colonial**
① *all year round: Tue-Fri 0830-1200; Jan-Feb: Tue-Sun 1700-2000; Mar-Apr: Tue-Fri
1530-1900, Sat-Sun 1600-1900; May-Sep: Tue-Fri 1530-1900, Sat-Sun 1530-1830;
Oct-Dec: 1530-1900, Sat-Sun 1600-1900, US$0.20,* with a chronologically ordered

exhibition of artefacts from aboriginal inhabitants from 2,000 BC to the first Spanish settlers who lived in Santa Fe la Vieja, the town's original site. The most remarkable objects are delicate zoomorphic ceramic pots, Spanish amulets and board games, and a model of both Santa Fe towns, showing that the distribution of the main buildings remained unchanged after the moving. Three blocks west of the Plaza 25 de Mayo is the **Museo de Bellas Artes** ① *4 de Enero 1552, T457 3577, Tue-Fri 1000-1200, 1600-1900, Sat-Sun 1600-2000*, showing temporary art exhibitions and a vast permanent collection by local and national artists.

North of the centre are the leafy Boulevards Pellegrini and Gálvez that go east to reach the attractive **Costanera** ① *bus No 16 goes from the historical centre (stop at General López y Primero de Mayo) to the costanera (US$0.30)*, a very popular stroll for locals, and where crowds gather at weekends. Actually there are two *costaneras* on each side of the **Laguna Setúbal**, a large lake which provides limitless views to the northeast. Both sides are linked by a beautiful suspension bridge, rebuilt after being almost completely destroyed in floods during the 1980's. The **Costanera Oeste** (west), Avenida de los 7 Jefes/Avenida Almirante Brown, on the city side has beaches with sports clubs, small parks, an astronomical observatory, open on weekdays, and a few restaurants. This leads to the **Guadalupe** area, with a long beach and a church, site of popular pilgrimage. The newer and much shorter **Costanera Este (east)** has a string of lively bars and nightclubs, some of them with access to small beaches.

The city has three very good **tourist information** points: at the bus terminal, T457 4123, 0700-1300, 1500-2100; at Paseo del Restaurador, Bv Pellegrini y Rivadavia, T457 1881, 0700-1900; and at Boca del Tigre, Av Paso y Zavalía, 0700-1900, www.santafeciudad.gov.ar

Around Santa Fé

Granja la Esmeralda ① *Av Aristóbulo del Valle 8700, T469 6001, on the northern outskirts; reached by buses No 10 and 16, US$0.30, going along Av Aristóbulo del Valle,* is a zoological research station that keeps many specimens from the Chaco region of over 70 different species in 13 ha of attractively set grounds.

Cayastá is a small town on the river San Javier, ① *regular buses from Santa Fe go along Route 1 to Cayastá, with good accommodation options, and beyond.* Cayastá's main attraction is the preserved ruins of **Santa Fe la Vieja**, the original town founded in 1573 by Juan de Garay, 80 km north of its present site. The city was moved after frequent attacks by indigenous groups and floods forced the settlers to move out. The **Parque Arqueológico** ① *open Apr-Sep: Tue-Fri 0900-1300, 1400-1800, Sat-Sun 1000-1300, 1500-1800; Oct-Mar: Tue-Fri 0900-1300, 1500-1900, Sat-Sun 1000-1300, 1600-1900, US$0.20, T03405-493056*, is very well kept, and though the remains of the buildings are unspectacular, archaeological digs have unearthed some adobe walls, and you can see skeletons of the people buried at the church. At the **Museo de Sitio** there's a revealing exhibition with finds from the 16th and 17th centuries.

Paraná → *Phone code: 0343 Colour map 4, A5 Population: 247,600*

Capital of Entre Ríos province, Paraná is situated on the eastern bank of a bend in the Río Paraná, opposite Santa Fe. Its centre lies on a hill offering fine views over the river, and if you're travelling up the Paraná river, it is a good place to stop on a journey north. It was founded in 1649, when Santa Fe was moved from its original spot settlers crossed the river in search of higher ground for cultivation, and a suitable port. In the mid-19th century it gained importance as capital of the Argentine Confederation and a subsequent period of growth left some sumptuous public buildings. The city's faded splendour creates a quiet, rather melancholic atmosphere but there is an appealing calm pace of life here.

Ins and outs

Getting there and around The city can easily be visited on foot, since the most interesting sights lie around the two main plazas, Plaza 1 de Mayo and three blocks north, Plaza Alvear.

Tourist information Paraná has four city tourist offices (all open daily 0800-2000): in the centre at Buenos Aires 132, at the bus terminal, at Parque Urquiza (on the east side), T420 1837, and at the Hernandarias tunnel, www.turismoenparana.com

Sights

Three blocks north of Plaza Alvear, Av Rivadavia leads to the beautiful **Parque Urquiza** and the riverside. Though nothing remains from the colonial period, the city retains many fine 19th- and 20th-century public buildings, centered around the Plaza Primero de Mayo. On the east side is the impressive **Cathedral**, built in 1883 in Italianate neoclassical style, with a fine dome and colonaded portico, though the interior is plain. Next door, at the corner of Monte Caseros and Urquiza is the **Colegio del Huerto**, seat of the Senate of the Argentine Confederation between 1854 and 1861 (no visits allowed). Also on the plaza are the **Municipalidad** (1890) with its distinctive tower, and the **Club Social** (1906), for years the elite social centre of the city. Take pedestrianized San Martín half a block west of the corner with 25 de Junio, to see the fine **Teatro 3 de Febrero** (1908). Two blocks north is the **Plaza Alvear**, and opposite one of its corners, the provincial **tourist office** ① *Laprida 5, T420 7989, turismoer@infovia.com.ar www.vivientrerios.com, Mon-Fri 0700-1230*. On the same block is the mildly engaging **Museo Histórico Martiniano Leguizamón** ① *Laprida y Buenos Aires, T420 7869, museoleguizamon@ciudad.com.ar, Tue-Fri 0800-1200, 1530-1930, Sat 0900-1200, 1600-1900 (Jan-Feb, Mon-Fri 0800-1200), US$0.35*.

On the west side of the plaza is the **Museo de Bellas Artes** ① *Buenos Aires 355, T420 7868, Tue-Fri 0900-1200, 1600-2100, Sat-Sun 1700-2130, US$0.35*, housing a vast collection of Argentine artists, with many works by painter Cesáreo Bernaldo de Quirós. On the north side of the plaza is the **Museo de Ciencias Naturales y Antropológicas,** ① *Carlos Gardel 62, T420 8894, Tue-Fri 0800-1200, 1500-1900, Sat 0830-1230, 1500-1900, Sun 0900-1200, US$0.35*, particularly appealing for kids, with an insect collection (see the 25 cm-wide moth!), and lots of stuffed animals. Among fascinating artefacts by Guaraní people are a rare urn, with red geometrical paintings and small utensils made by groups indigenous to the north, and a shocking exhibition of 10 jars containing human foetus, from five weeks to six months old.

From the northwestern corner of the plaza, it's a pleasant stroll along tree-lined Avenida Rivadavia, with the monumental **Escuela del Centenario** (1910), Avenida Rivadavia 168, to reach the city's pride and joy, the **Parque Urquiza**. Extended along the low cliffs of the Paraná river, with wonderful views and many fine statues, the park is well planted with *lapachos*, *palos borrachos* and pines. There's an open-air theatre, and steps to the Avenida Costanera. The cobbled street **Bajada de los Vascos**, which in the 19th century gave access to the port area, is now known as Puerto Viejo and retains some original buildings. The Avenida Costanera is lively, with restaurants, sports clubs and sandy beaches on the river. The **Paraná Rowing Club**, T431 2048, charges US$1.70 per day for beach access, US$3.50 to use its pool. ▶▶ *For Sleeping, Eating and transport, see pages 310-318.*

South of Paraná

Immediately south of Paraná there's picturesque undulating landscape with several neat villages, or *aldeas*, in the heart of farming colonies, surrounded by fields of cereal crops. Route 11 gives access to Diamante and its nearby national park and to the pretty town of Victoria, both reached by public transport from Paraná (one hour and two to three hours respectively).

Parque Nacional Predelta → *Colour map 4, A5*

This park, 48 km south of Paraná and 6 km south of Diamante, covers 2,458 ha of marshland and the riverine forest of the upper section of the Delta del Río Paraná at its northern extreme. It protects a rich wildlife that includes many birds such as the ringed kingfisher, storks, the *caraú* (*Aramus guarauna*) and the *chajá* (*Chauna torquata*). Capybaras are also easily spotted, while the *lobito de río* (*Lontra longicaudis*) or the rare alligator *yacaré ñato* (*Caiman latirostris*) hide in the most remote sites of the park. Snakes are not uncommon, but nothing to worry about, if you're careful where you put your feet

Access A 5 km-long unpaved road goes south from the access road to Diamante to the Paraje La Jaula, the entrance to the park. *Remise* taxis from Diamante charge US$1.50-1.60. The park is open daily 0800-2000, and entrance is free. The park's administration is at Sarmiento 507 (Diamante), T0343-498 3535, predelta@apn .gov.ar At La Jaula there's a free campsite with hot showers and a 200 m footpath leading to a vantage point on the **Laguna de las Piedras**. Most of the park is only accessible by boat and excursions leaving from La Jaula should be arranged in advance with a tour operator in Diamante. There are two itineraries: the shorter is the *vuelta al sombrero*, while the other goes deeper into the forest for over two hours, going to the **Arroyo La Azotea** and including a landing at the **Isla Las Mangas** where is a small lake. *Davimar*, 25 de Mayo 390, T0343-498 4104, turismodte@infoshopdte.com.ar runs boat excursions in the park for about US$8 pp. Accommodation available at Diamante.

Victoria→ *Phone code: 03436 Colour map 4, A5 Population: 27,700*

Victoria is quiet town with an attractive location on high hilly ground overlooking the vast brown and green expanse of islands and canals which separate it from the city of Rosario, about 60 km southwest. Stunning panoramic views can be seen from the **Mirador de la Virgen de Fátima**, west of centre and reached by Calle Laprida. It's worth staying a couple of days to appreciate its architectural richness, with many 19th- and early 20th-century buildings, several of which have preserved wonderful ironworks on their windows. All sights are quite easily visited on foot. A very well run tourist office ① *25 de Mayo y Bv Sarmiento, T421885, daily 0800-1900, www.turismovictoria .com.ar*, is on the northern access road to town.

❖ *Visit now, Victoria is sure to change in the coming years, with the opening of a connecting road to Rosario in 2003 and the arrival of an increasing number of visitors.*

The first Spanish settlers encountered resistence from the resident aboriginal Minuanes/Charrúas, and the town was the site of a bloody massacre in 1750, which eliminated them entirely. The site of the battle, known as **Cerro de la Matanza** and surrounded by a rare *ombú* forest, now can be visited on a hill northwest of town. Not far on Route 11 is the **Abadía del Niño Dios** ① *T423171, www.abadiadelni niodios.com.ar daily 0800-1200, 1500-1830, guided visits to the abbey: daily at 1000 (45 minutes)*, the first Benedictine abbey in Latin America, founded in 1899 by monks from southwestern France. A shop sells their honey and the Benedictine spirit made with 73 different herbs. In the 19th century, many immigrants from the Basque country and from Genova (Italy) settled down in a low area by the marshland now called Barrio Quinto Cuartel. It now extends south of the present town, reached by Bv Moreno, and it's a rather appealing scene with its slowly decaying houses on the coast and grassy and muddy roads.

Around Plaza San Martín are several impressive buildings, such as the **Palacio**

Municipal (1902) with French and Italian influences, such as the central *loggia*, the
neo-Romantic **Iglesia de Aranzazu** (1875) with a richly painted interior and the art
nouveau **Club Social** (1898). There are more fine buildings in surrounding streets,
where the Italian influence can be seen in elaborate wrought iron work on the
windows; the **Societá Italiana** (1863), at Congreso y 9 de Julio, the store **El Sportsman**,
Sarmiento y Alem, and the **Concejo Deliberante**, Laprida 517. At Congreso 593 there is
the **Museo de la Ciudad** ① *T421063, Tue-Sun 1000-1200, 1600-1900*, a small local
history museum in a beautiful house. The port district and the Avenida Costanera,
west of centre, are both popular places to stroll for locals, with a couple of basic
eating places, good for trying the local fish.

North of Paraná

Heading north from Paraná along the Río Paraná, you can take monotonous Route 11
to Resistencia on the western bank, or Route 12 north to Corrientes which closely
follows the eastern banks of the river through varied landscapes, giving access to two
small attractive towns on the coast with good fishing: Santa Elena and La Paz.

Santa Elena → *Phone code: 03437*
Santa Elena lies on the Río Paraná about 150 km north of the capital. It is a small port
whose fishing attracts many anglers and its history has been associated with that of
its meat-packing factory run by British firms from the late 19th century, before it
closed down in 1993. The red brick buildings of the *frigorífico* can still be seen in
town, and the superb estancia built by the *Bovril* company can be visited nearby. At
the end of the *costanera* is the Paseo La Olla, with beautiful views over the river. The
tourist office is at Eva Perón y 9 de Julio, T481223. ▶▶ *For Sleeping, Eating and other listings,
see pages 310-318.*

La Paz → *Phone code: 03437 Colour map 4, A5 Population: 22,700*
La Paz, 68 km north of Paraná, is a small port in an area popular for fishing, where the
fishing festivals *Fiesta Provincial del Surubí* and the *Fiesta Provincial del Dorado* are
held respectively every April and September. The undulating terrain and the cliffs
above the river make a picturesque setting for the old houses still standing in the
town. The **tourist office** is at Vieytes y España, T422389 (ask for information on
accommodation at few nearby estancias).

There is a **Museo Regional**, a small history museum at the Parque Berón de
Astrada, from where there are fine views, while another park, the **Parque de la
Aventura**, has trails along the riverside for walking or cycling ① *access on the way to
La Armonía, reached by Bv 25 de Mayo and then, Yrigoyen.*

Corrientes → *Phone code: 03783 Colour map 1, B6 Population: 316,500*

Capital of Corrientes province, some 30 km southwest of the meeting of the rivers
Paraná and Paraguay, the city is mainly a service centre for its agricultural hinterland
which produces beef, cotton, tobacco, rice and yerba mate. Although Corrientes is
less important transport hub than Resistencia, it is a pleasant place for a stopover.
The city centre, with its peaceful traditional streets and squares, is well preserved and
its costanera is one of the most attractive in the country. The national capital of
Carnival, the city is also famous as the location of Graham Greene's novel The
Honorary Consul. In summer the air can oppressively hot and humid, but in winter the
climate is pleasant. ▶▶ *For Sleeping, Eating and other listings, see pages 310-318.*

History

Founded in 1588 on the Paraná river, next to seven relatively high *puntas*, or promontories, by an expedition from Asunción, led by Juan Torres de Vera y Aragón, Corrientes became important as a port on the Route between Buenos Aires and Asunción. Numerous shipyards led to the development of a naval industry that endured for centuries. The Guaraní population that inhabited the region were mainly absorbed into the Jesuit missions or became workers for the estancias. They progressively mixed with the Spanish newcomers giving the local society a distinctive character, still evident today in the faces of the inhabitants, and also in the daily use of Guaraní words and a particular accent in the spoken Spanish.

Sights

The main Plaza 25 de Mayo, one block inland from the *costanera*, is a beautiful shady space. You could take a pleasant stroll from here around the surrounding blocks, with their fine old houses and river views, and to the Avenida Costanera. On the north side of the plaza is the **Jefatura de Policía**, built in 19th-century French style. The **Museo de Artesanías** ⓘ *Quintana 905, Mon-Fri 0800-1200, 1600-2000, free*, is a large old house with an exhibition of handicrafts made from the most diverse materials imaginable, by indigenous groups, as well as by contemporary urban and rural artisans. Tiny skeleton-shaped images represent San La Muerte, a popular devotion that ensures the bearer a painless death. A large room at the front is a workshop where you can watch the patient work of the local craftspeople. On the east side of the plaza are the Italianate **Casa de Gobierno** (1881-6) and the **Ministerio de Gobierno** (south side is the church **La Merced**, where there are confessionals carved by the

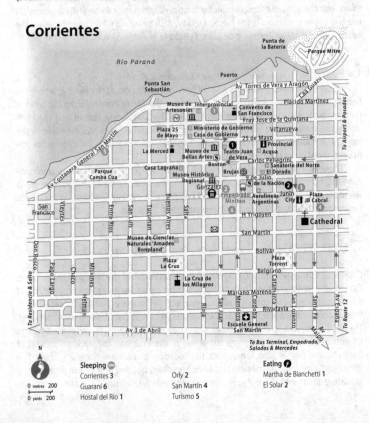

Corrientes

N

0 metres 200
0 yards 200

Sleeping
Corrientes 3
Guaraní 6
Hostal del Río 1

Orly 2
San Martín 4
Turismo 5

Eating
Martha de Bianchetti 1
El Solar 2

indigenous inhabitants of Misiones in the mid-18th century, and a colonial-style altar. The **Casa Lagraña**, a huge building with three interior patios, built in 1860 for the governor, lies one block south. At 9 de Julio 1044 is the **Museo Histórico** ① *Tue-Fri 0800-1200, 1600-2000, free*, displaying among other pieces a collection of religious objects dating from the 18th and 19th centuries. Only two blocks north is the **Teatro Juan de Vera**, San Juan 637, T427743, a lively cultural centre and a beautiful building itself (1913). Across the road is the **Museo de Bellas Artes** ① *San Juan 634, Tue-Fri 0800-1200, 1630-2030, free*, a small arts museum with temporary exhibitions and a permanent collection including valuable works by the painters Petorutti, Fader and Quinquela Martín. The quite impressive **Iglesia y Convento de San Francisco**, Mendoza 450, was rebuilt in 1861 on the site of the original which dated from 1608. Six blocks south of the Plaza 25 de Mayo is the leafy Plaza de la Cruz and opposite, the church of **La Cruz de los Milagros** that houses the Santo Madero, a miraculous cross placed by the founder of the city, the miracle occurring, allegedly, when the indigenous residents who tried to burn it were killed by lightning from a cloudless sky. Near the plaza, the **Museo de Ciencias Naturales 'Amadeo Bonpland'** ① *San Martín 850, Mon-Sat 0900-1200, 1600-2000*, has a large collection of archaeology and plants with a remarkable display of 5,800 insects including a huge wasp nest.

The attractive Avenida Costanera, lined with *lapachos* and *palos borrachos*, leads along the Río Paraná from its southwestern end, next to the bridge, to **Parque Mitre**, from where there are good views of sunsets over the river. On the intersection with Junín, there is a small **zoo** ① *Tue-Sun 0900-1830*, set by the river, with animals of the region.

The city **tourist office** is on the central Plaza Cabral, with another information point at punta Tacuara, on Av Costanera, where you can ask for a good map; daily 0700-2100. The provincial tourist office, 25 de Mayo 1330, also provides information on the city, as well as other Corrientes destinations; Mon-Fri 0700-1300, 1500-2100, T427200, www.planetacorrientes.com.ar

Around Corrientes

All destinations lie on Route 12 or on Routes branching off Route 12; regular buses from Corrientes to each place.

Santa Ana de los Guacarás (referred to just as Santa Ana), 20 km east, is the site of a 17th-century Franciscan mission and now a quiet and pretty village. The chapel, restored in 1889, dates from 1771. The old railway station is a museum to the **Ferrocarril Provincial El Económico**, a narrow-gauge railway line which operated from 1890 to 1960.

Paso de la Patria, 40 km northeast, lies on the Alto Paraná opposite its confluence with the Río Paraguay, and is the most popular resort for the *correntinos*, packed in summer. It was also known as a paradise for fishing *dorado* with the *Fiesta Nacional del Dorado* held every August. However, since the building of the Yaciretá dam, up river, catches are neither as weighty nor numerous as they once were.

Itatí at Km 73, is a tiny port on the Alto Paraná and the site of one of the most massive religious pilgrimages in the country, where every July 16 250,000 people come to witness the crowning of the Virgin of Itatí at the huge **Basílica Santuario Nuestra Senora de Itatí**. According to one version of the story, the Virgin appeared before local indigenous tribes who were attacking the settlers in Itatí and persuaded them to cease fighting. The Basilica, built between 1938 and 1950 has a dome 83 m high, 26 m in diameter and it seats 9,000 people. Nearby there's also an attractive neoclassical building housing the **Museo Sacro** with religious icons and furniture from the colonial period.

Empedrado, 60 km south, is a riverside town on the Paraná with picturesque cliffs above the river. Southwards along Paraná coast are **Bella Vista** (145 km), **Goya** (230 km) and **Esquina** (340 km), attractive towns often visited by anglers, with plentiful accommodation. The weath of fish in the local waters is celebrated every year in the *Fiesta Nacional del Surubí* (in Goya: Apr-May) and the *Fiesta Nacional del Pacú* (Esquina in March). ▸▸ *For Sleeping, Eating and other listings, see pages 310-318.*

Listings: Río Paraná

⊜ Sleeping

Rosario *p299, map p301*

B Riviera, *San Lorenzo 1460, T/F424 2058, www.solans.com* A 4-star hotel, whose A superior rooms are very good, and more business style, while the cheaper standard rooms are smaller but still comfortable, with warmer decor. Both include a large breakfast, and there are sauna, gym and restaurant. The same chain as the *Riviera* owns three more similar upmarket hotels all offering very good accommodation often promotional prices:
B Libertador, *Av Corrientes 752, T/F424 1005.*
B Presidente, *Av Corrientes 919, T/F 424 2789.*
C República, *San Lorenzo 955, T/F424 8580.*
C Garden, *Callao 39, T437 0025, F437 1413, www.hotelgardensa.com* This is a good though pricey option a little way from the centre, in the Pichincha district (next to Bv Oroño) with very good B superior rooms and smaller, but comfortable standard rooms. Also restaurant and children's play area.
C Plaza del Sol, *San Juan 1055, T/F421 9899, plaza@satlink.com.ar* Very comfortable, spacious rooms and a pool on the 11th fl with splendid views. A large breakfast is included.
D La Paz, *Barón de Maua 36 (behind Centro Cultural Bernardino Rivadavia), T/F421 0905.* Family-owned since 1948, this small central hotel, though a bit run down, has decent enough rooms with breakfast.
D Rosario, *Cortada Ricardone 1365 (access from Entre Ríos 900 block), T/F424 2170, hrosario@infovia.com.ar* A central place with good rooms with a/c and breakfast. Larger C rooms in the annexe.
E Savoy, *San Lorenzo 1022, T448 0071.* This early 20th-century mansion is the most appealing place to stay and the best value by far. Once Rosario's best hotel, it now has a charming faded grandeur and welcoming service. Don't miss the sumptuous *fumoir* on the first floor. Breakfast included.

Camping
The nearest site is at **Granadero Baigorria**, *12 km north of centre, at Av Lisandro de la Torre y El Río, T471 4381.* Access to the beach on river with a 7-ha park, hot showers and sport facilities, including a pool for US$0.35 a day pp plus US$0.65 per tent and US$0.65 per vehicle.

Sante Fé *p303*
All listed hotels lie within 10 blocks of the bus terminal.
C Conquistador, *25 de Mayo 2676, T/F400 1195, linverde@gigared.com* Worth the price only if you use the pool, the sauna and the gym, all included in the rate.
C Riogrande, *San Gerónimo 2580, T450 0700, F450 0710, riogrande@santafe.com.ar* Santa Fe's best hotel has very good rooms, with slightly smaller standard ones. A large breakfast is included.
D Castelar, *25 de Mayo y Peatonal Falucho, T/F456 0999.* On a small plaza, this old-style hotel built in the 30s with quality materials is a good value option, offering comfortable accommodation in a formal atmosphere. Breakfast is included. It has a smart but welcoming restaurant on the ground floor.
D Hostal Santa Fe de la Veracruz, *San Martín 2954, T/F455 1740, hostal_santafe @ciudad.com.ar* Traditionally one of the top hotels in town, with 2 types of room categories (C superior rooms), both good value, including a large breakfast and checkout at 1800. It has a restaurant and sauna is for an extra fee.
E Colón, *San Luis 2862, T452 1586.* Welcoming staff contrast with rather gloomy rooms, but still decent enough for a short stay. Breakfast and a/c included.
E Emperatriz, *Irigoyen Freyre 2440, T/F453 0061.* The attractive hispanic style of the building belies plainer decor in the rooms, though they're spacious and comfortable enough. Breakfast and a/c extra.

● *For an explanation of the sleeping and eating price codes used in this guide, see the inside*
● *front cover. Other relevant information is provided in the Essentials chapter, page 44.*

E Niza, *Rivadavia 2755, T/F4522047*. Decent rooms with fan and breakfast, comfortable enough for one night only. A/c extra.

Camping
No campsites in town, better head to **San José del Rincón**, a village on Route 1, 15 km east.

Paraná *p304*
B Mayorazgo, *Av Etchevehere y Miranda, T423 0333, F423 0420, www.mayorazgo hotel.com* A large upmarket hotel on Parque Urquiza with casino, pool, gym, restaurant and four types of room (the standard ones are fine) with good views over the river.
C Gran Hotel Paraná, *Urquiza 976, T422 3900, F4223979, www.hotelesparana.com.ar* Overlooking Plaza Primero de Mayo, this large hotel offers 3 types of room, (all with breakfast included), pricey standard rooms, but very comfortable and spacious B *superior* ones. It has a gym and the smart restaurant *La Fourchette*. Guests get discounts for using the facilities of *Club Atlético Estudiantes*.
C Marán Apart-Hotel, *Buenos Aires y Malvinas, T/F423 5444, www.maran .com.ar* Comfortable small apartments for 1 to 6 people located in a nice residential area next to the park.
D Paraná Plaza Jardín, *9 de Julio 60, T423 1700, F4223205, www.hotelesparana .com.ar* An inviting brightly coloured façade hides an old residence renovated in dubious taste in some places, but still offering good though pricey rooms set around a roofed garden. Breakfast included.
D San Jorge, *Belgrano 368, T/F4221685, www.sanjorgehotel.com.ar* With palm trees growing on the street outside, this is an attractive renovated house, made welcoming by friendly staff and owners. There are cheaper old-style rooms (avoid noisy rooms closer to reception) or modern ones at the back with renovated bathrooms and TV. A light breakfast is included, and there are cooking facilities.

Camping
La Toma, *at the northern end of C Blas Parera (10 km NE of centre), T433 1721*. Entry US$0.35 pp plus US$1.30 per tent up to 2 people. Hot showers, pool, shop. Buses No 5 or 10 go from centre, US$0.35.

Ask at tourist office for information on accommodation at nearby estancias.
C Casablanca, *on Bv Moreno (at access to barrio Quinto Cuartel), T424131, lopezmartin 1676@yahoo.com.ar* A white building in a large attractive garden with a pool, the rooms are decent enough though nothing special, but it's worth paying for the setting and the pool; breakfast included. There's a restaurant for guests only.
D Plaza, *Congreso 455, T421431*. Centrally located, this is an agreeable place to stay with light rooms with a/c, and good value with breakfast included.
E Dennisse, *Congreso 682, T421186*. Spotless comfortable rooms with bath, and breakfast (US$0.65 extra) can be taken on the veranda.
E El Parque, *Alem 222, T421315, opposite bus station*. Decent enough rooms.
E Rizzi, *Hipólito Yrigoyen 700, T421294*. Pleasant enough rooms and a mid-priced restaurant specializing in homemade pastas, as well as *surubí* and *armado* (local fish).

Camping
El Molino de la Abadía, *on Route 11, Km 112.5 (a few km north of town), T421200, www.complejoelmolino.com.ar* Attractively situated in countryside next to an old mill, US$1.20 pp; with hot showers, a food shop, restaurant and for US$3.50 pp it offers basic accommodation with bedlinen included.

Santa Elena *p307*
L Estancia Vizcacheras, *Route 12, km 554,5, T(in Buenos Aires)011 4719 5613, F011 4719 5649, www.vizcacheras.com.ar* South of Santa Elena, the *Bovril* estancia was built in the early 1900's in British colonial-style with Argentine touches. The owners are extremely hospitable, making guests feel at home in luxuriously furnished bedrooms, all with their own bathroom (some with old fashioned bathtubs) and private verandas. Drinks on the terrace with splendid views of the gardens and grasslands beyond, and delicious dinner served under the stars. You'll be invited to see the daily routines of the working cattle ranch, with walking and horse riding, fishing and birdwatching also arranged. Highly recommended.

D **Milton**, *Italia 1029, T422232,
www.miltonhotel.com.ar* A central place
with comfortable enough rooms; a/c and
breakfast extra.
D **Posta Surubí**, *España 224, T421128*. Nicely
located by the river with good rooms with
breakfast and fine views; it has a restaurant.

Camping
El Eucaliptal, *Puerto Márquez, T421108*.
US$1.50 pp, also *cabañas*.

Corrientes *p307, map p308*
Good value accommodation is non-existent
in Corrientes. It is worth while paying extra
pesos to avoid a slew of rather scrappy and
overpriced places. All hotels below have a/c
in their rooms
C **Corrientes Plaza**, *Junín 1549, T/F466 500,
www.hotelplazactes.com.ar* A business
oriented large hotel with comfortable rooms,
gym and a small pool; larger rooms with
bigger beds available for an extra 15%.
C **Gran Hotel Guaraní**, *Mendoza 970,
T433800, F424620, hguarani@gigared.com*
A 4-star business-oriented hotel with
restaurant, pool and gym. Three types of
room, differing in comfort only between the
cheaper standard doubles and the B VIP
ones. Large breakfast included.
D **Hostal del Río**, *Plácido Martínez 1098,
T/F436100, hostal_del_rio@infovia.com.ar*
This apartment block overlooks the port,
offering good views on the river from its
upper floors. Rooms are warmly decorated,
with more comfortable rooms for an extra
30%.
It has a pool and a restaurant and
breakfast is included.
D **Orly**, *San Juan 867, T427248, hotelorly@
arnet.com.ar* The rooms of this central hotel
have been renovated recently, though
standard ones are not as spacious as you'd
expect for the price. Better rooms are 50%
extra. With breakfast.
D **San Martín**, *Santa Fe 955, T/F421061,
hsanmartin@impsat1.com.ar* Another
central hotel, entirely lacking character,
though offering quite comfortable rooms
with breakfast.

D **Turismo**, *Entre Ríos 650, T/F433174*. By far
the most appealing hotel in town, for its
riverside location and its homely style
though the rooms have seen better days,
they're comfortable enough, with ancient
a/c. There is a smart restaurant, a large
swimming pool and an adjacent casino.
Breakfast included.

⊘ Eating

Rosario *p299, map p301*
$$ **Amarra**, *Av Belgrano y Buenos Aires*. Good
food, including fish and seafood, served in a
formal atmosphere. Cheap set menus
Mon-Fri lunchtimes.
$ **Alvear y Nueve**, *Alvear y Nueve de Julio*.
Good for grilled meat.
$ **Bruno**, *Montevideo y Av Ovidio Lagos*. For
homemade pastas.
$ **Club Español**, *Rioja 1052*. Doesn't exactly
serve up Spanish specialities, but the usual
menu is given a vague Spanish flavour, and
it's a nice place to eat.
$ **Escauriza**, *Bajada Escauriza y Av Colombres*,
north of centre at La Florida. The most
traditional fish restaurant in Rosario serving
tasty dorado, *surubí, pacú* or *boga*.
$ **La Estancia**, *Av Pellegrini y Paraguay*.
Another typical *parrilla* a few blocks east of
Parque Independencia.
$ **Pampa**, *Moreno y Mendoza*. A good *parrilla*
with attractive Argentine-style 1940's decor.
$ **Rich**, *San Juan 1031, www.richrestaurante
.com.ar* This is a classic in Rosario, and
indeed, one of the finest restaurants in the
whole country. The food is superb. There's a
widely-varied menu and good set meals
including delicious pastas, excellent meats
and many different salads. Rarities such as
milanesa de yacaré (alligator *milanesas*) are
occasionally served. Recommended.
$ **Gigante**, *San Martín 946*. This large and
popular restaurant offers generous helpings
of good food at incredibly low prices.

Sante Fé *p303*
Many good restaurants, offering excellent
meals with good wine, all moderately priced.
Several in town centre are closed on Sun.
$ **Baviera San Martín**, *San Martín 2941*.

● *Phone codes* Rosario: 0341; Santa Fe: 0342; Paraná: 0343; Victoria: 03436; Santa Elena,
● La Paz: 03437; Corrientes: 03783.

A traditional place in the centre with a varied menu and good food.

$ Club Sirio Libanés, *25 de Mayo 2740*. Very good Middle Eastern dishes, reasonably priced; popular with families on Sun lunchtime.

$ El Brigadier, *San Martín 1670*. This colonial-style place next to the Plaza 25 de Mayo serves superb *surubí al paquete* (stuffed fish) and many *parrilla* dishes.

$ El Quincho de Chiquito, *Av Almirante Brown y Obispo Príncipe, next to boxer Carlos Monzón's statue (on Costanera Oeste)*. A classic fish restaurant, excellent food and good value, with huge helpings.

$ España, *San Martín 2644*. An elegant place in town, serving good food

$ Rivadavia, *Rivadavia 3299*. A traditional *parrilla* for excellent grills.

$ Tasca Real, *25 de Mayo 3228*. A Spanish *bar de tapas* with a good selection of its specialities at a low price.

Paraná *p304*

$$ Giovani, *Urquiza 1047*. A popular place in centre, good for pasta.

$$ La Fourchette, *Urquiza 976 (at Gran Hotel Paraná)*. An upmarket place with some expensive dishes. The menu lists the usual meals, but some more elaborated sauces.

$ Club de Pescadores, *access from Av Estrada at Puerto Viejo*. Another good traditional fish restaurant.

$ Coscoino, *Corrientes 373*. A relaxed family place serving good and very filling homemade pastas, *tenedor libre*, except Sat evenings and Sun lunches.

$ El Viejo Marino, *Av Laurencena 341, on the opposite extreme of the Av Costanera*. Well prepared fish dishes.

$ Playa, *on Av Costanera (at Club Atlético Estudiantes)*. Nicely situated on a sandy beach with fine views of the river, a good place for fish such as *surubí, boga* or *pejerrey* (caught upstream in Corrientes or Misiones).

Cafés

Two appealing cafes are **Viejo Paraná**, *Buenos Aires y Av Rivadavia (on Plaza Alvear)* and **Plaza**, *Urquiza y San Martín (on Plaza Primero de Mayo)*, traditional in style.

Victoria *p306*

$ Bahía, *Alem y Bartoloni*. Small and cheap

pizza place.

$ La Tablita, *Sarmiento 472*. A rustic *quincho* serving good pastas, *surubí* and good quality *milanesas* at moderate prices.

Corrientes *p307, map p308*

The only options lie in the centre and on the Costanera, next to the bridge.

$ El Solar, *San Lorenzo 830*. With an informal atmosphere, and busy at lunchtime, this self-service restaurant serves decent and cheap salads, pastas and *milanesas*.

$ Las Brasas, *Av Costanera y San Martín (near beach)*. A traditional *parrilla*, where you can try the local fish.

Cafés

Martha de Bianchetti, *9 de Julio y Mendoza*. A smart café and bakery.

Bars and cafés

Rosario *p299, map p301*

Albaca, *Italia y Mendoza*. This attractive bar is open during the day, and has live music in the evenings.

Aux Deux Magots, *Av Belgrano y Entre Ríos, at the northern end of Parque de España*. Emulates a Parisian café, overlooking the river, and popular at weekends till the small hours, with cheap set menus.

Café de la Opera, *Mendoza y Laprida (next to the access to the Teatro El Círculo)*. Regular performances of jazz, tango, Russian folk music, poetry and storytelling in this pretty café, open afternoons and evenings.

Kaffa, *Córdoba 1473*. For good coffee served inside the large bookshop *El Ateneo*.

La Favrika, *Tucumán 1816*. A fashionable cafe and restaurant with evening shows, also popular at lunchtimes.

La Sede, *San Lorenzo y Entre Ríos*. An extremely popular cafe, crowded at lunchtimes with office workers having lunch.

La Traición de Rita Hayworth, *Dorrego 1170*. A café/concert venue named after a novel by the Argentine writer Manuel Puig offering live comedy and music shows (usually Wed-Sun evenings, US$1-2) with good food.

Piluso, *Catamarca y Alvear*. A lively meeting point at night, also open during daytime.

Rock & Feller's, *Córdoba 2019*. Expensive theme bar, wth a mix of pop icons and the sumptuous art deco design of an old house. **Victoria**, *Jujuy y Bv Oroño*. One of the oldest cafés in town and most traditional.

Sante Fé *p303*

Santa Fé has a long tradition of brewing, and is one of the few places where local lagers can compete with the big national monopoly, *Quilmes*. Beer is usually sold in a *liso* (not a very large glass). There are lively areas of bars and nightclubs, popular with young crowds, all along the Costanera Este, beyond the bridge on Laguna Setúbal, in the Recoleta district, north of centre, around plaza Los Constituyentes, and next to Bv Pellegrini and to Bv Gálvez.

Don Ernesto, *San Martín y General López*. A traditional café in the civic centre.

Las Delicias, *Hipólito Yrigoyen y San Martín*. A well-preserved early 20th-century café and bakery, with beautiful decor, serving a wide variety of coffees and sweet pastries. Try their speciality, the *alfajorsantafesino*.

Tokio, *Rivadavia y Crespo (on Plaza España)*. Another café with a rich history in Santa Fé.

⚫ Entertainment

Rosario *p299, map p301*

A good listings guide can be found in a section of daily paper *Pagina 12: Rosario 12*, as well as www.viarosario.com

Cinema

In centre are **El Cairo**, *Santa Fe 1120*, **El Patio**, *Sarmiento 778*, **Del Siglo**, *Córdoba y Presidente Roca (at the Shopping Mall Del Siglo)*.

Cultural centres

Centro Cultural Bernardino Rivadavia, *San Martín 1080, T480 2401*. A large centre holding all year round art exhibitions, video screenings, plays, music shows, seminars and a puppet theatre.

Centro Cultural Parque de España, *on Parque de España, T426 0941*. Shows temporary art exhibitions, photography, and plays at the Teatro Príncipe de Asturias.

Centro de Expresiones Contemporáneas, *Sargento Cabral y el río (on the riverside, opposite Ex Aduana building), T480 2245*. A large warehouse with almost daily music, theatre and cinema events.

Nightclubs

Young crowds go for electronic dance music to **New 21** or **Moebius**, both on *Rivadavia 2400 block*. Over 25s looking for a wider variety of music gather at **Madame**, *Av Francia y Brown*, **El Eterno**, *Córdoba y Cafferata*, **Blue Velvet**, *Av Costanera Norte*, or **Satchmo**, *Rivadavia 2100 block*. And over 50s head for the ironically named **Década**, *Santa Fe 3300 block*

Theatre

El Círculo, *Laprida 1235, T424 5349*.
Lavarden, *Mendoza y Sarmiento, T472 1462*.
De la Comedia, *Cortada Ricardone y Mitre, T480 2597*.

⚫ Festivals and events

Rosario *p299, map p301*

Every year during the *first half of November* at the Parque a la Bandera (opposite the monument). **Fiesta de las Colectividades** celebrates the divers origins of the inhabitants, offering food, folk music and dancing from 1800 onwards. The main show is on *Nov 11*, the **Day of Tradition**. On *Jun 20*, **Flag Day**, it is worth going to the Monumento a la Bandera at the swearing-in ceremony made by hundreds of school pupils to the country's flag.

Sante Fé *p303*

A very popular religious pilgrimage to the **Basílica de Guadalupe** is held every in the Guadalupe residential district, near the northern extreme of Av Almirante Brown (Costanera Oeste).

Corrientes *p307, map p308*

Carnival has been one of the most popular celebrations for decades in Argentina and is celebrated on **Fri and Sat evenings thoughout Feb** at the **Corsódromo**. This stadium lies a little distance from the centre reached by bus No 105 along 9 de Julio. The colourful parade opens the competition among the different *comparsas*, passionately supported by the audience as football teams. Tickets are not sold in the stadium, but in many shops in the centre. For more information on Carnival go to Paraguay 598, T427824. The regional music *chamamé* has its own festival in Corrientes every Dec or Jan at **Anfiteatro Tránsito Cocomarola**, *at Barrio 1000 Viviendas, 10 blocks south of Av 3 de Abril*. This cheerful music is danced in couples with the upper body close, legs far apart. Join in!

⊕ Sports

Swimming On Laguna Setúbal, from **El Espigón**, the **Club de Regatas**, next to the bridge or from **Piedras Blancas** on Costanera Este.

⊙ Shopping

Rosario *p299, map p301*
The main shopping street is the pedestrianized Córdoba.

Bookshops
Balcarce, *San Lorenzo 1576*. A massive place for second-hand books and vinyl records.
El Ateneo, *Córdoba 1473*.
Stratford, *Santa Fe 1340*. English books.

Markets
Mercado Retro La Huella, *Av del Valle y Callao (next to Rosario Norte railway station at Pichincha district)*. Every Sun and bank holidays, this is a large flea market where you can find some valuable antiques.
Mercado de Pulgas. Flea market at weekends, next to the tourist office on the riverside.
Feria del Boulevard, *Bv Oroño y Rivadavia*, a weekend handicraft market.

Outdoor gear
El Combatiente, *San Martín 816*.
Central de Pesca, *San Juan 1089*.

Shopping malls
Del Siglo, *Córdoba y Presidente Roca*.
Palace Garden, *Córdoba 1358*.

⌕ Tour operators

Rosario *p299, map p301*
For city tours check agencies at *Asociacion Rosarina de Agencias de Viaje, T421 3554*.
Barco Ciudad de Rosario, *T449 8688*. A large passenger boat leaves from the pier next to Estación Fluvial for 2-hr excursions on the river on weekend afternoons.
Catamarán Victoria Austral, leaving on weekend afternoons from Estación Fluvial.
Transporte Fluvial del Litoral, *T454 4684*. This operator used to run the regular boat

service to Victoria (check if it's still running; recommended) from Estación Fluvial; also has boats for rent at US$17/hr for up to 10 people.

Sante Fé *p303*
Equilibrio, *General López 3697, T459 9663*.
Barbaglia, *La Rioja 3044, T455 2729*. Tours to Cayastá for about US$28 per vehicle of up to 3 people.

Paraná *p304*
Costanera 241, *Buenos Aires 212, T/F 4234385, www.costanera241.com* City tours and boat excursions on the Paraná river.

Victoria *p306*
An excursion to the islands and canals is recommended.
Chulengo Safaris, *T422648, T15610346, www.chulengosafaris.com.ar* Ricardo Núñez is a fishing and tourist guide with boats adapted for shallow waters.
El Gato, *T424108*. Run by el Gato Urreaga, who guides excursions to the marshland.

⊙ Transport

Rosario *p299, map p301*
Air
Fisherton airport is located 15 km west of centre, T451 1226. Daily flights to/from **Buenos Aires** with Aerolíneas Argentinas and **Aerovip**, 45 mins. *Remise* taxis to town charge US$4-5. Transfers also arranged with the airline companies.

Boat
Modern terminal called **Estación Fluvial**, (known as La Fluvial), *Av de los Inmigrantes 410, opposite Monumento a la Bandera, T447 3838*. The main departure point for boat transfer to the island resorts. Cafés and restaurants on an attractive terrace overlooking the river, as well as a museum.
   At **Costa Alta**, *situated between La Florida and the suspension bridge*, is a pier also used for passenger boats going to the island resorts. Tickets US$1-3 return, boat services every 30 min in the summer to some resorts, with a few weekend services during the rest of the year.

Bus
The terminal is at *Santa Fe y Cafferata, about 30 blocks west of the Monumento de la Bandera,*

T437 2384. For local buses a magnetic card must be bought at kiosks in the centre or near bus stops (US$0.25 per trip).

Several bus lines to centre with stops on Córdoba (eg 101, 103, 115), US$0.25; from centre, take buses on Plaza 25 de Mayo, via C Santa Fe, *remise* taxi US$1.50. The terminal has an information point, post office, shops and restaurants; also sells cards for buses, and left luggage, open 24 hrs, (US$0.70 a day per piece). Several companies going to main destinations. To **Buenos Aires**, 4 hrs, US$7. To **Córdoba**, 6 hrs, US$8.50. To **Santa Fe**, 2 hrs 20 mins, US$4-5.

Car rental
Localiza, *T435 1234*, Olé, *T438 6593*, Avis, T435 2299.

Taxi
Radio taxis (painted in black and yellow), T482 2222, T438 1000 or T455 5555. **Remise taxis** Primera Clase, T454 5454. Nuevo Estilo, T454 3000.

Train
Rosario Norte station, *Av del Valle y Av Ovidio Lagos*. The **Buenos Aires-Tucumán** service operated by TBA, *T0800-3333822*, stops weekly in Rosario, though at inconvenient times in the day and tickets are only sold just before departures, at the station. To **Tucumán**, US$12; to **Buenos Aires**, US$3.50. Taxis charge US$0.80.

Sante Fé *p303*
Air
The airport, Sauce Viejo, is located 17 km southwest, *T499 5064*. Daily flights to and from **Buenos Aires** with Aerolíneas Argentinas and Aerovip. Taxis charge US$4 from bus terminal. A bus with a yellow 'L', signed *Aeropuerto*, stops on C San Luis (one block from bus terminal), 20 mins journey, US$0.40.

Bus
The terminal is located near to the centre at Belgrano 2910, *T457 4124*. City tourist information desk with bus information. Taxis charge US$0.65 to centre. Luggage lockers for US$0.65 (insert two $(peso)1 coins).

To **Buenos Aires**, several companies, 6 hrs, US$11-13. To **Córdoba**, several companies, 5 hrs, US$8.50. To **Paraná**,

ETACER, Fluviales, 50 mins, US$1. To **Rosario**, several companies, 2 hrs 20 mins, US$4-5. To **Cayastá** (marked Helvecia), Paraná Medio, 1 hr 40 mins, US$1.70.

Car hire
Localiza, *Av Alem 19098, T453 4300*.

Taxis (Radio and remise)
Cooperativa Radio Taxi Santa Fe, *T0800-5555444*.
Santa Fe, *Moreno 2512, T459 5906*.

Paraná *p304*
Bus
The bus terminal is at Av Ramírez 2598, T422 1282, 10 blocks southeast of Plaza Primero de Mayo; leave the small plaza on your right and take Av Echagüe left to centre, or buses No 1, 4, 5 or 9 to/from centre, US$0.35, *remise* taxis, US$0.50. Left luggage, Mon-Sat 0700-2300, Sun 0800-1200, 1730-2300, US$0.50 a day per piece.

To **Buenos Aires**, several companies, 6-7 hrs, US$11-12. To **Santa Fe**, ETACER, Fluviales, every 20 mins, 50 mins journey, US$1. To **Corrientes**, Flecha Bus, Nuevo Rápido Tata, Chevallier, 8-9 hrs, US$12. To **Puerto Iguazú**, Crucero del Norte, 15 hrs, US$22. To **Colón**, Flecha Bus, Paccot, 4-5 hrs, US$7. To **Diamante**, several companies, 1 hr, US$1.20-1.70. To **La Paz**, ETA, 3 hrs, US$4.50. To **Victoria**, several companies, 2-3 hrs, US$2.50-3.50.

Car hire
Localiza, *25 de Mayo y Arturo Illia, T423 1707*.

Remise taxis
Centro, *3 de Febrero 841, T424 8248*.
Supremo, *Alsina 275, T423 3331*.

Victoria *p306*
Due to the opening of the road to Rosario, boat services will stop when new bus services take over: a 1-hr journey.

Boat
Take the boat to **Rosario**, if it's still running, for a 5-hour journey. Boats run by Transporte Fluvial del Litoral, T0341-4544684.

Bus
The terminal is at *Alem y Junín* (5 blocks north

of the plaza). To **Buenos Aires**, Flecha Bus, Tata, 4½-5 hrs, US$10-11. To **Paraná**, several companies, 2-3 hrs, US$2.50-3.50.

Corrientes *p307, map p308*
Air
Camba Punta airport is10 km east of city reached by Route 12, *T458684*. Minibus pick ups from hotels, *T450072*, US$1.30 (US$2.70 to Resistencia airport). *Remise* taxis charge US$4. Flights to/from **Buenos Aires** only with Aerolíneas Argentinas, 1 hr 20 mins.

Bus
From the town centre, several buses or *combis* go to nearby towns from the centre, with stops around Plaza Cabral or along central streets. To **Santa Ana**, Bus No 11 (Santa Ana), from *9 de Julio y Catamarca*, 30 mins, US$0.35. To **Paso de la Patria**, Mir, office at *La Rioja y 12 de Octubre, T494654*, or Silvitur, *8 de Diciembre 234, T494260*; both charge US$0.50. To **Empedrado**, Empedrado minibus, *Mendoza 837, T15687431*, US$0.80. All these destinations also have regular buses from terminal. The port area around *Av Costanera y La Rioja* is another transport hub with buses Chaco-Corrientes leaving regularly to **Resistencia**, 40 mins, US$0.40 return.

The bus terminal is at *Av Maipú, 5 km southeast of centre*; take bus No 103 (check with the driver, as same line has many different routes) from *Carlos Pellegini y Córdoba* (or any stop along Carlos Pellegrini and Salta), 20 mins, US$0.20. From terminal to centre, take bus No 103 stopping outside, next to the parking area, on Av Maipú. **Left luggage** at Crucero del Norte office, US$0.65 a day, open 0530-0100. Tickets can be bought at same prices at many offices other than the company's own.

To **Empedrado**, López, San Justo, US$1. To **Mburucuyá**, San Antonio, 2½ hrs, US$2.30. To **Mercedes**, several companies, 3 hrs, US$3.30-4. To **Paso de la Patria**, Paso de la Patria, US$0.85 (tickets on bus), 5 daily.

To **Santa Ana**, Bus No 11 (Santa Ana), US$0.35 (tickets on bus), every 2 to 3 hrs. To **Posadas**, several companies, 3½-4 hrs, US$6.50. To **Puerto Iguazú**, Aguila Dorada Bis (change at Posadas), Expreso Singer, Crucero del Norte, Río Uruguay,

Autotransportes Mendoza, 8-9½ hrs, US$8-12. To **Resistencia** bus terminal, Puerto Tirol, 30 mins, US$0.65 (for going to city centre, get off at traffic lights immediately after supermarket *Libertad* and take bus No 9, US$0.23, stopping there; not recommended at night).

To **Buenos Aires**, several companies, 11-12 hrs, US$13-26. To **Salta**, La Nueva Estrella (change at Resistencia), 13 hrs, US$18. To **Tucumán**, La Nueva Estrella, Nuevo Rápido Tata, Vosa, 12-15 hrs, US$16. To **Asunción** (Paraguay), Crucero del Norte, El Pulqui, 5 hrs, US$6-7.

Taxi
Remise taxi Interprovincial, *Av Costanera y La Rioja*.

❻ Directory

Rosario *p299, map p301*
Airline offices Aerolíneas Argentinas, *Santa Fe 1410, T424 9517*. Aerovip, *Mitre 830 local 32, T449 6800*. **Banks** Many banks along *C Córdoba, east of plaza San Martín*. Money **exchange** at Transatlántica, *Mitre y Rioja*. TCs cashed at Banex, *Mitre y Santa Fe*; 2% or US$10 min commission. **Western Union** at *Laprida y San Juan*. **Communications Post Office** *Córdoba y Buenos Aires*. **Internet**: Several places in centre charging US$0.35/hr. **Useful addresses Police**, *T101, T448 6666*. **Medical emergencies**, *T107, T435 1111*. Hospital de Emergencias Clemente Alvarez, *T480 8111*. Hospital de Niños Víctor Vilela (Children's Hospital), *T480 8133*.

Sante Fé *p303*
Airline offices Aerolíneas Argentinas, *Lisandro de la Torre 2635, T459 9461*. Aerovip, *Lisandro de la Torre 2570, T452 2491*.
Banks Banking district around San Martín y Tucumán. Exchange money and TCs at Tourfe, *San Martín 2500*, or at Columbia, *San Martín 2275*. **Communications Internet** El Shuk, *San Martín y Corrientes*, US$0.50/hr. Xiver, *9 de Julio 2344, US$0.40/hr*. **Post office** *Calle San Martín between Tucumán and La Rioja*; Western Union branch. **Laundry** Lavarfe, *25 de Mayo 2879*. San Martín, *San Martín 1786*. Lavamax, *9 de Julio 2138*.

Banks Banco de la Nación, *San Martín 1000.*
Citibank, *25 de Mayo y 9 de Julio.* HSBC,
Pellegrini between 25 de Junio and Urquiza.
Communications Internet Telecentro
Facultad, *Urquiza 713,* US$0.50/hr (US$0.35/hr
before 1500). Conexión.com, *Av Rivadavia 665,*
US$0.35/hr. El Ciber, *Corrientes 253,* US$0.25/hr.
Post office *25 de Mayo y Monte Caseros;*
Western Union branch. **Laundry** Belgrano,
Belgrano 306. **Useful addresses Police,**
T101, T420 9038. **Medical emergencies,**
Hospital San Martín, *Perón 450, T422 6100, T420
9683.* Sanatorio Adventista del Plata, *small
office at Santa Fe 235, T423 6364, T420 0200.*

Corrientes *p307, map p308*

Airline offices Aerolíneas Argentinas, *Junín
1301, T424647.* **Banks** Banco de la Nación, *9
de Julio y Córdoba.* Bank Boston, *San Juan y
Carlos Pellegrini.* El Dorado, *9 de Julio 1343,*
exchanges money and accepts all TCs; **Western**
Union branch. **Communications
Internet** Brujas, *Mendoza 787, US$0.35/hr.*
Post office *San Juan y San Martín.*
Telecommunications Several *locutorios* in
centre. **Useful addresses Police,** T101.
Medical emergencies, T107. Hospital Escuela
General San Martín, *Rivadavia 1250,
T420695/0697.* Sanatorio del Norte, *Carlos
Pellegrini 1358, T421600.*

The Argentine Chaco

*Little visited by travellers, the Argentine Chaco is just part of an immense sprawling
lowland some 900 km wide, covering half of Paraguay and huge areas of Bolivia and
Brazil. Rising gently from east to west, it's crossed by lazy meandering rivers, and filled in
central parts with cattle and cotton fields, soya and sunflowers. Though much of the Chaco
is inaccessible, with little public transport, and rough roads which become almost
impassable after heavy rains, two national parks can easily be reached all year round,
both hosting a rich diversity of wildlife largely uninterrupted by human activity: Parque
Nacional Chaco reached from Resistencia, and Parque Nacional Río Pilcomayo reached
from Formosa. These are the region's two main cities, both close to Río Paraguay, and the
only other settlement is uninspiring Presidencia Roque Sáenz Peña 170 km northwest of
Resistencia, though its thermal waters are among the country's finest.*

*The most fascinating aspect of the Chaco is its pure and extensive indigenous
population. Two of the largest groups are the Toba, mainly settled in towns next to the
Paraná river, and the semi-nomadic Wichí in the west, who maintain their traditions of
fine weaving, woodwork and ancient fishing techniques.*

Ins and outs

Getting there From Resistencia and Formosa, parallel Routes 16 and 81 head dead
straight northwest across the plains, until they encounter the first hills of eastern
Salta, which mark the border of this vast territory. Buses to Salta take Route 16, while
Route 81 has long unpaved sections west of the small town of Las Lomitas, making
the journey tough going after heavy rains.

Background

The Chaco falls into two distinct zones along a line south of the boundary between Chaco
and Formosa provinces: the Wet Chaco and the Dry Chaco. The **Wet Chaco** spreads south
from the Río Pilcomayo (the border with Paraguay) and west of the Río Paraguay, fertile
wetlands supporting rich farming and abundant vegetation, marshlands with savanna
and groves of Caranday palms, hosting many species of birds. Further west, as rainfall
diminishes, the **Dry Chaco** is arid and wild, with little plant life, or indeed human life.
Scrub vegetation, dotted with the algarrobo trees, white quebracho, the spiny bloated
trunks of palo borracho and various types of cacti. This is one of the hottest places in
South America, the western part of the Chaco has been known as 'El Impenetrable'.

Resistencia → *Phone code: 03722 Colour map 1, B6 Population: 359,100*

The hot and energetic capital of the Province of Chaco, Resistencia is the commercial centre for the Chaco region together with the port of Barranqueras, just to the south on the Río Paraná. It's a modern city, not architecturally rich, but boasting an impressive number of sculptures by renowned artists, earning it the title of 'city of statues'. There's also a splendid central plaza, a nature reserve and the lovely **Isla del Cerrito** within easy reach, making it an appealing alternative stopover to neighbouring Corrientes on the journey between Iguazú and Salta. → *For Sleeping, Eating and other listings, see pages 322-326.*

History

Founded in 1878 with the arrival of the first 67 families from Friuli, Italy, Resistencia was born as a farming colony at the edge of a vast plain, then almost unexplored by Europeans, but inhabited by several native communities. This was the first white settlement in the region west of the Paraná, after a few failed attempts made in earlier times by the Spaniards and Jesuits. The capital city of Chaco province together with its adjacent port of Barranqueras, developed rapidly during the first half of the 20th century as a service centre for a booming economy based on cotton and the Chaco forests.

Sights

The large Plaza 25 de Mayo occupies four blocks in the centre of the city, with a variety of indigenous plants and palms turning it into a mini botanical garden. Here, you'll find the city **tourist office** ① *Mon-Fri 0800-2000, T458289*. If they can't give you a map try the **provincial tourist office** ① *Santa Fe 178, Mon-Fri 0630-2000, Sat 0800-1200, T423547, www.chaco.gov.ar/turismo* , where you can get information on other destinations.

Five blocks from here, there's an informal cultural centre, **Fogón de los Arrieros**, (literally, 'the hearth of the muleteers') ① *Brown 350, (between López y Planes and French), open to non-members Mon-Sat 0900-1200, Mon-Fri 2100-2300, US$1.70, T426418*. This rather wonderful institution was formed by artists in the late 1960's, who decided to make the city an open air gallery, with public spaces filled with sculpture and murals. The centre itself still operates as a meeting place and exhibition space. Inspiring, and highly recommended. In the surrounding streets, you'll find more than 175 pieces of art by the country's finest artists.

Take López y Planes (later Sáenz Peña) and turn right at Juan B Justo to reach the **Museo Del Hombre Chaqueño** ① *Juan B Justo 280, Mon-Fri 0800-1200, 1600-2000, free*. This small anthropological museum covers the story of colonialisation in the region, with a fine exhibition of handicrafts by native Wichi, Toba and Mocoví peoples, together with a fascinating mythology section in which small statues represent the Guaraní peoples' beliefs. Many of the rituals detailed are still practised in rural areas today, and are characterized by creatures of the marsh and woodland.

Around Resistencia

The **Isla del Cerrito**, a beautiful island northeast of Resistencia at the confluence of the Ríos Paraná and Paraguay, has a provincial nature reserve of 12,000 ha, covered mainly with grassland and palm trees. At the eastern end of the island (51 km from Resistencia), on the Río Paraná, in Cerrito, there's an attractive tourist complex with white sand beaches, a history museum, accommodation and restaurants, all very busy during the *Fiesta Nacional del Dorado* on the opposite shores in Paso de la Patria. → *For Sleeping, Eating and other listings, see pages 322-326.*

The Chaco National Park, 115 km northwest of Resistencia, extends over 15,000 ha and protects one of the last remaining untouched areas of the Wet Chaco with its exceptional *quebracho colorado* trees, *Caranday* palms and dense riverine forests, with orchids growing along the banks of the Río Negro. It is a very good place for birdwatching, with 340 species having been sighted in the park, including the parrot *loro hablador* (*Amazona aestiva*). You're certain to be woken in the morning by the loud screams of *Carayá* monkeys, though other mammals living in the park may be less obtrusive, like the collared *peccary*, the *corzuela parda* (*Mazama gouazoupira*), the puma and the yaguarundí cat (*Felis jaguamindi*).

At 300 m from the park's entrance there's a visitor centre and a free campsite with hot showers and electricity. There you can hire bicycles or horses for US$1.30/hr and move freely along the park's inner roads. Two short footpaths, *sendero del puente colgante* and *sendero del abuelo*, respectively lead to the banks of the Río Negro, and to an 800-year-old specimen of the *quebracho* tree. A vehicle road goes north 6 km up to two high *mangrullos* or view points, overlooking the two lakes, Laguna Carpincho and Laguna Yacaré, where, with a bit of patience, you'll see *yacarés* (alligators). Another track, suitable only for 4WD vehicles, goes south, through a forest of *quebracho* trees and after 9 km reaches the peaceful Laguna Panza de Cabra. There is a campsite by the lake, without facilities, and where you'll often hear the rare Maned wolf *(aguará guazú)* at night. Tour operators run day-long excursions to the park from Resistencia. Access to the park is free, open 24 hrs, T03725-496166. ▶ *For Sleeping, Eating and other listings, see pages 322-326.*

❢ *The park is best visited between Apr-Oct to avoid intense summer heat and voracious mosquitoes.*

North of Resistencia

Route 11 runs north to Formosa and then onwards to the Paraguayan border near Clorinda, with the city of Asunción just over the border. Crossing low lying pastures with streams and *Caranday* palms, this route offers views of the diverse birdlife of the Wet Chaco, and is beautiful in the evening.

Formosa → *Phone code: 03717 Colour map 2, A1 Population: 198,100*

Formosa is the capital of its province and the only Argentine port of any note on the Río Paraguay. Oppressively hot from November to March, the city is the base for boat trips along the rivers in the eastern part of the province during the winter, when the weather is mild. It's also a possible stopover on the way to the **Parque Nacional Río Pilcomayo** or the **Bañado La Estrella**, and it's close to the Paraguayan capital, Asunción. From the town's small port, boats cross the river to Alberdi, a Paraguayan duty-free spot, (only if you have a multiple entry visa.)

Tourism is not well developed here yet, but increasingly activities are offered: guided excursions and accommodation at estancias; ask at the **tourist office** ① *José M Uriburu 820 (on Plaza San Martín), Mon-Fri 0700-1300, 1600-2000, T420442.*

There's a **Museo Histórico Regional** ① *Av 25 de Mayo y Belgrano, Mon-Fri 0730-1200, 1500-1930, entry free,* in the late 19th-century residence built for the first governor, with a large collection of artefacts but no particular logic to the displays. The **Casa de la Artesanía**, San Martín 830, is a shop selling handicrafts made by the different aboriginal communities of the three ethnic groups of Formosa. ▶ *For Sleeping, Eating and other listings, see pages 322-326.*

Around Formosa

Herradura ① *11 km off a paved road, branching off Route 11, 31 km south of Formosa,* is an attractive place on the horseshoe-shaped **Laguna Herradura**, next to the

Paraguay river, which is very popular with anglers, for good catches of *surubí*, *corvina* or *pacú* with restaurants and campsites. **Bañado La Estrella** lies about 340 km northwest of Formosa and 45 km northeast of Las Lomitas. The dry Chaco woodland was transformed into a wide stretch of wetland during a spate of floods of the Pilcomayo river in the 1940's and 60's. This naturally-created new environment has attracted diverse wildlife, including many bird species, who now inhabit the area. This is marvellous for nature watchers, but will appeal to anyone attracted to the strange and fantastical landscape known locally as *champal*, where ghostly remains of dead trees stand in the water and are completely covered by epiphytes, plants draped over silvery branches. Local tour operators use canoes and horses to cross this area, as well as running guided walks and visits to nearby Pilagá communities. Contact Ricardo Asunción Moreno, Casa 1, Manzana 1, Barrio La Paz, T03715-432436 to make the most of the place, if you haven't hired a guide at Formosa already. There are two hotels in Las Lomitas as well as **Estancia San Carlos**, T03717-432104, T03717-15413237, ninfaviv@yahoo .com.ar which welcomes visitors and arranges excursions to the nearby Bañado.

Parque Nacional Río Pilcomayo → *Best visited in winter*
This park, 162 km north of Formosa, covers 48,000 ha of Wet Chaco environment bordering Paraguay on the southern bank of the Río Pilcomayo. The lower parts may be flooded during the rainy season and the resulting lakes and *esteros*, or marshlands, create the park's most beguiling landscapes. The rest is grassland with *Caranday* palm forests, where rheas can be seen, with some Chaco forest in the upper lands, habitat of three monkey species and several types of woodpecker. Due to its significance as a natural wetland, the park is a Ramsar site with diverse birdlife, including herons and three different species of stork. Anteaters, capybaras, coatis, two species of *yacarés* and *aguará guazu* are on the list of animals protected within the park.

The park has two entrances leading to different areas. The most visited and easier to reach if you are on foot is Laguna Blanca, where there's an **information point** and a free campsite with electricity and cold water. From there, a footpath leads to the **Laguna Blanca**, the biggest lake in the park where you'll spot alligators among the rich aquatic plant life. The lake is not recommended for swimming, since the resident piranhas have a penchant for human toes. The second of the entrances, leads to **Estero Poí**, another information point and a campsite without facilities. Here take the 1,200 m footpath, with informative signs on the botany of the upper areas of the park. A vehicle road goes into the park up the Río Pilcomayo and the international border, but can only be used with special permission.

Border with Paraguay
There are two routes into Paraguay. The easiest crossing is by road via the Puente Loyola, 4 km north of Clorinda. From Puerto Falcón, at the Paraguayan end of the bridge, the road runs 40 km northeast, crossing the Río Paraguay to reach Asunción, (*Empresa Falcón* US$0.50, every hour, last bus to the centre of Asunción 1830).

Immigration Formalities for entering Argentina are dealt with at the Argentine end, at Puerto Pilcomayo, closed at weekends for tourists, and for those for leaving Argentina at the Paraguayan end at Itá Enramada, easy crossing, open 24 hrs. The other route is by ferry from Puerto Pilcomayo, close to Clorinda, to Itá Enramada (Paraguay), US$0.50, five mins, every 30 minutes. Then take bus 9 to Asunción. ➤ *For Sleeping, Eating and other listings, see pages 322-326.*

Asunción → *Phone code: +595-(0)21 Population: over 1,200,000*

The capital and largest city in Paraguay, Asunción is an attractive city with tree-lined avenues and a small centre that can easily be explored on foot. Home to a quarter of Paraguay's population, the city sprawls south and east of its site on the eastern bank of the Río Paraguay. Most of the public buildings date from the Presidencies of Carlos Antonio López and his son, Francisco Solano López, in the late 19th century. In July and August the city is covered in pink when the prolific lapacho trees bloom.

Sights

Most of the public buildings can be seen by following El Paraguayo Independiente southeast from the *Aduana* (customs house). The first is the **Palacio de Gobierno** ⓘ *open Sun*, built 1860-1892 in the style of Versailles. On the northwest side of the Plaza de la Independencia, or Constitución, is the **Antiguo Colegio Militar**, built in 1588 as a Jesuit College, while on the opposite side of the plaza is the cathedral. Two blocks southwest, along Calle Chile, is the large Plaza de los Héroes, with the **Pantéon Nacional de los Héroes**, based on Les Invalides in Paris, which contains the tombs of war heroes and child soldiers who fought in the War of the Triple Alliance. Take Calle Mariscal Estigarribia to get to the **Museo Nacional de Bellas Artes** ⓘ *Iturbe y Mariscal Estigarribia, T447716, Tue-Fri, 0700-1900, Sat 0700-1200*, with Spanish paintings and 20th-century Paraguayan art. Two blocks south is the Plaza Uruguaya and nearby is the railway station, built 1856, and a steam engine, the *Sapucai*, dating from 1861. East of here is the **Museo Dr Andrés Barbero** ⓘ *España y Mompox, T441696, Mon-Fri 0700-1100, and Mon, Wed, Fri 1500-1700, free*, a good anthropological museum with a collection of tools and weapons of the various Guaraní cultures. Recommended. The **tourist office** (Dirección General de Turismo) ⓘ *Palma 468 (esquina Alberdi), open Mon-Fri 0800-1300, T441530, F491230. Information T494110/T440794 open until 1900 Mon-Sat*.

Much further, at Isla de Francia, lies the **Centro de Artes Visuales** ⓘ *access via Avenida General Genes, T607996, www.museodelbarro.com.py, daily except Sun and holidays, 1600-2030, bus 30 or 44A from the centre*; inside is **Museo Paraguayo de Arte Contemporáneo**, with some striking murals, the **Museo de Arte Indígena** and **Museo del Barro**, containing ceramics. Highly recommended. The **Mercado Cuatro** on Petirossi sells cheap food and there's a **handicraft market** on Plaza de los Héroes.

The best of several parks is **Parque Carlos Antonio López**, set high to the west along Colón with grand views, if you can find a gap in the trees with the **Jardín Botánico** on Avenida Artigas y Primer Presidente. The beautiful church of **Santísima Trinidad** (on Santísimo Sacramento, parallel to Avenida Artigas), dating from 1854 with frescoes on the inside walls, is well worth a visit.

Luque, 16 km east (near the airport), was founded in 1636 with some interesting colonial buildings, now famous for the making of Paraguayan harps and fine filigree work in silver and gold. Tours are also offered to the *Circuito Central*, or *Circuito de Oro*, (7 hrs, 200 km long), through a range of picturesque hills with waterfalls and spas. ⓘ *Buses from Asunción terminal leave regularly to individual towns, contact tour operators for a day excursion, US$45*.

Listings: the Argentine Chaco

🛏 Sleeping

Resistencia *p319*

C **Covadonga**, *Güemes 200, T444444, F443444, hotelcovadonga @infovia.com.ar* The city's top hotel offers comfortable rooms with a/c and breakfast included, with pool, sauna and gym.

D **Gran Hotel Royal**, Obligado 211, T443666, F424586, www.granhotelroyal.com Reasonably good value here, with comfortable rooms with a/c and breakfast included.

E **Bariloche**, Obligado 239, T421412, jag@cp sarg.com Definitely the best value place in town, with a welcoming owner and decent rooms with bath and a/c. Unfortunately no breakfast here, but there's a nearby café at *Gran Hotel Royal*.

E El Hotelito, *Av Alberdi 311, T459699*. Acceptable for a night, with shared bathroom and breakfast included.

Camping

Parque Dos de Febrero, *Av Avalos 1000, T458366, 17 blocks northwest of plaza*. A pleasant place to stay in a neat park by the Río Negro, with hot water and electricity, US$0.35 pp plus US$0.65 per tent.

Formosa *p320*

B Turismo, *San Martín 759, T431122, hoteldeturismoformosa@arnet.com.ar* A large, strangely-shaped building by the river offering good views, though the rooms are pricey, all have a/c and breakfast is included.

C Casa Grande Apart-Hotel, *Av González Lelong 185, T431573, www.casagrande apart.com.ar* Situated 8 blocks north of Av 25 de Mayo and next to the river, these are good 1 and 2-room apartments, with kitchen, a/c and breakfast, a gym and pool.

D Colón, *Belgrano 1068, T426547*. Comfortable rooms, a/c, breakfast included.

D Plaza, *José M Uriburu 920, T426767*. On Plaza San Martín, this is a good choice for a swim in the pool. Breakfast included.

F Colonial, *San Martín 879, T426346*. A basic place offering rooms with a/c, set by the river and next to the main road.

F El Extranjero, *Av Gutnisky 2660, T452276*. Opposite bus terminal. Reasonably decent accommodation with a/c.

Camping

Camping Banco Provincial, *Km 4, to the south of Formosa, reached by Route 11*. Good facilities including pool, tennis courts, T429877, US$3 pp.

Las Arianas, 10 km south (turn off Route 11 at El Pucu, Km 6), T427640.

Asunción *p321*

AL Cecilia, *Estados Unidos 341, T210365, cecilhotel@uninet.com.py* A very smart and comfortable hotel with a good restaurant.

AL Gran Hotel del Paraguay, *De la Residenta 902 (y Padre Pucheau), T200051, www.gran hotel.com.py* Full of character, with pool, but

going to seed a little.

A El Lapacho, *República Dominicana 543 (next to Av España)* Family-run, welcoming owners, comfortable rooms and a pool.

B Bavaria, *Choferes del Chaco 1010, T600966, www.bavariaf2s.com* A good-value place with a beautiful garden, pool and comfortable rooms with a/c.

D Plaza, *Eligio Ayala 609, T444772, www.plazahotel.com.py* Spacious rooms with a/c and breakfast. Excellent value.

E Itapúa, *Fulgencio R Moreno 943, T445121*. Breakfast and a/c; transport to airport.

Camping

The pleasant site at the **Jardín Botánico** charges US$1.50 pp plus tent. It has cold showers and electricity, busy at weekends.

🍴 Eating

Resistencia *p319*

There is a lack of choice when it comes to restaurants but these can be recommended:

$$ Kebon, *Don Bosco y Güemes*.

$ San José, *Roca y Av Alberdi, Plaza 25 de Mayo*. A popular café and *confitería* with excellent pastries (try the *medialunas*) and ice creams.

Formosa *p320*

$$ Asador Criollo, *Av Gutnisky*. A popular *parrilla* where *chivito* (kid) is on the menu.

$ El Fortín, *Mitre 602*. A traditional place, good varied local fish dishes.

$ El Tano Marino, *Av 25 de Mayo 55*. An Italian restaurant, serving fine home-made pastas.

$ Yayita, *Belgrano 926*. Regional dishes such as *soyo*, or *sopa paraguaya* are offered in this central restaurant.

Asunción *p321*

$ Bolsi, *Estrella 399*. Excellent food but not cheap, good for breakfast. Under the same ownership is **La Pérgola Jardín**, *Perú 240*.

$ Corea, *Perú y Francia*. Excellent Korean meals.

$ La Molleja, *Av Brasilia 604*. A very good traditional grill.

$ El Molino, *España 382, near Brasil*. Good value, downstairs for sandwiches and homemade pastries and upstairs for full meals in an attractive setting.

$ Le Saint Tropez, *Plaza Uruguaya*. Serves delicious French and Paraguayan food, good prices at lunchtime, closed Sun.

$ Lido, *Palma y Chile*. Good for breakfast and *empanadas*, famous for delicious fish soup.

$ San Roque, *Eligio Ayala y Tacuary*. A traditional and relatively inexpensive place with a turn-of-the- (20th) century atmosphere.

⊛ Festivals

Resistencia *p319*

Fiesta Nacional de Pescado de los Grandes is celebrated every 10-12 October in the Río Antequeros, 14 km away from Resistencia.

Formosa *p320*

The world's longest **Via Crucis** pilgrimage with 14 stops all the way along Route 81 (already registered in the Guinness Book of Records) takes place every **Easter week**, starting in Formosa and ending at the border with the province of Salta, 501 km northwest. On the night of the **last day of July**, the **Festival de la Caña Con Ruda** is held, when a drink of the Paraguayan *caña* flavoured by the *ruda* plant is taken as a protection for the mid-winter blues. The celebration is very popular and organized annually by the local authorities (ask at tourist office about the venue). It's also a good chance to try regional dishes. The **Festival Provincial de Folklore** held every **November** at Pirané (115 km northwest) is the major music festival in the Northeast region, attracting national stars of stirring folklore music.

⊙ Shopping

Resistencia *p319*

Fundación Chaco Artesanal, *Carlos Pellegrini 272*. A charity selling fine handicrafts made by Toba, Wichi and Mocoví native groups in varied materials, whose profits return to those communities.

⊖ Tour operators

Resistencia *p319*

Sudamericana, *San Buenaventura del Monte*

Alto 866, T/F435954, sudevt@ciudad .com.ar One-day tours to nearby sights all for a minimum of 5 people (Isla del Cerrito, US$9 pp, lunch included; Parque Nacional Chaco, US$8 pp).

Formosa *p320*

Domínguez Excursiones, *San Martín 1577, T421264, dominguez_excursiones@ yahoo. com.ar* Excursions to all sights in the province, including the National Parks and Bañado La Estrella.

La Corvina, *Mitre 164, T423702, corvinaderio @hotmail.com* Reinaldo Saporiti is a fishing guide running excursions to Herradura on Paraguay river.

Pedro Iznardo, *Paraguay 520, T420780, iznardo@uol.com.ar* Freddy is a knowledgeable guide specializing in canoeing, who runs very interesting excursions down the nearby rivers lasting several days, such as the Riacho Monte Lindo Grande, north of Formosa. Good for birdwatching. He also runs excursions to Bañado La Estrella.

Asunción *p321*

Circuito de Oro US$45, 3-day trip along the Triangle (Encarnación, Jesuit missions, Itaipú dam and Iguazú falls) for US$185, double room.

Emma Travel, *España 393, T614111, emmatravel@mrholding.com.py* Fluent English, French and German spoken. Tours to Chaco and Iguazú.

Inter Tours, *Perú 436, T211747, www.intertours.com.py* Tours to Chaco, Iguazú and Jesuit missions.

⊖ Transport

Resistencia *p319*

Air

Airport 8 km west of town (no bus), T446009. Flights to/from **Buenos Aires** only with **Aerolíneas Argentinas**, 1 hr 15 mins. Taxis charge US$2.50-3.

Bus

The terminal is on Av Malvinas Argentinas y Av MacLean, on the western outskirts, far from centre, T461098. Buses No 3 and 10 from Oro y Perón, 1 block west of plaza, 20 mins, US$0.23. Taxis charge US$1.70 from centre. Left luggage: on platform, open 24 hrs US$0.35 a day. Tickets can be bought at same prices at several offices.

To **Corrientes**, Chaco-Corrientes buses stop opposite *Norte* supermarket on *Av Alberdi e Illia*, 40 mins, US$0.40 return. To **Capitán Solari** (for going to Parque Nacional Chaco), La Estrella, 3¼ hrs, US$2. To **Corrientes** bus terminal, Puerto Tirol, 30 mins, US$0.65 (drops you off at a small plaza at *Av 3 de Abril y Av España*; Corrientes centre lies six blocks north on Av España).

To **Buenos Aires**, several companies, 12-13 hrs, US$13-26. To **Puerto Iguazú**, Aguila Dorada Bis (change at Posadas), Expreso Singer, Río Uruguay, Autotransportes Mendoza, 8-10½ hrs, US$11-12.

To **Salta**, Flecha Bus, La Nueva Estrella, 12½ hrs, US$17-19. To **Tucumán**, Almirante Brown, Vosa, 12 hrs, US$16. To **Formosa**, several companies, 2-2½ hrs, US$2.70-3.50. To **Laguna Blanca** or **Laguna Naick-Neck** (for Parque Nacional Río Pilcomayo), Godoy, 8 hrs, US$5.70.

To **Asunción** (Paraguay), El Pulqui, Brújula, Godoy, Crucero del Norte, 5-5½ hrs, US$5.50-6.

Taxi
Radio taxi, *T438535, T429443*.

Isla del Cerrito *p319*
Follow Route16 east and turn north 3 km before the bridge to Corrientes: from here a road, the last 20 km of which are dirt (difficult after heavy rain), leads to a bridge, from where it is 17 km unpaved further to Cerrito. **Combi Arco Iris** has 3 daily services (0600, 1100, 1900) to Cerrito, an hour's journey and stopping half an hour there, US$1.20, leaving from bus stop at *Juan B Justo y Av Alberdi* (off *Banco Hipotecario*).

Parque Nacional Chaco *p320*
Paved Route 16 goes northwest from Resistencia and after about 60 km Route 9 branches off it, leading north to Colonia Elisa and beyond to Capitán Solari, which lies 5 km east of the park entrance via a dirt road. If there's a group of you, call the park in advance to be picked up at Capitán Solari. Regular buses La Estrella daily link Resistencia and Capitán Solari, where *remise* taxis should not charge more than US$1 for the short journey to the park, which can also be made on foot.

Formosa *p320*
Air
El Pucu Airport 5 km southwest, T452490; Aerolíneas Argentinas to **Buenos Aires**, direct 1 hr 30 mins (2 hrs 20 mins when calling at Corrientes or Resistencia). *Remise taxi*, US$1.70.

Bus
The terminal is at Av Gutnisky y Av Antártida Argentina (15 blocks west of plaza San Martín), T430817. *Remise* taxis to centre, US$0.65. To **Asunción**, Godoy, El Pulqui, Brújula, 3 hrs, US$5. To **Resistencia**, several companies, 2½ hrs, US$2.70-3.50. To **Buenos Aires**, El Pulqui, Flecha Bus, Puerto Tirol, Godoy, 15-17 hrs, US$16-28. To **Laguna Blanca** or **Laguna Naick-Neck** (for **Parque Nacional Río Pilcomayo**), Godoy, 3 hrs, US$3. To **Las Lomitas** (for Bañado La Estrella), Giroldi Travel, 4 hrs, US$7.

Taxi
Remise taxi Libertad, *José M Uriburu 750, T420700*.

Bañado La Estrella *p321*
Bañado is reached from **Las Lomitas** on Route 81, and from here unpaved Route 28 heads northeast to a handful of villages after crossing the *bañado*, 45km from Las Lomitas. Though occasional transport services go via Route 28, it is better to take a tour. There are regular buses from **Formosa** and **Buenos Aires** to Las Lomitas.

Parque Nacional Río Pilcomayo *p321*
From Formosa, take Route 11 to **Clorinda**, and from there take Route 86 going west. After 47 km, a 5 km dirt road leads north to the entrance to the Laguna Blanca area. Follow Route 86 for a few kilometres further for the 5 km access dirt road to the entrance to the Estero Poí section. Buses **Godoy** run from Formosa or Resistencia to the small towns of Laguna Naick-Neck, 5 km from the park (for going to Laguna Blanca) and from Laguna Blanca, 8 km from the park (for going to Estero Poí). *Remise* taxis from both towns should charge no more than US$3 for these short journeys. Access to the park is free and open 24 hrs, administration centre at town

of Laguna Blanca, Av Pueyrredón y ruta 86, T03718-470045, Mon-Fri 0700-1430.

Asunción *p321*

Air

Silvio Petirossi airport *15 km east of centre, T645600.* Tourist office, bank, restaurant, travel agencies left luggage. Taxis charge US$10-13 to centre. Bus 30 goes every 15 mins from the red bus stop outside the airport to Plaza de los Héroes, US$0.20. Minibus **Tropical**, T424486 (min 2 people).

Bus

Local buses are only recommended outside rush hours; journeys within city US$0.25. The terminal is on República Argentina y Fernando de la Mora (south of centre), T552154, T551737. To the **city centre**, take bus No 8, US$0.20. Taxis, US$2.40. To **Buenos Aires**, 18 hrs, US$30-42. To **Formosa** (US$5.40 plus US$0.50 luggage) and **Resistencia** (6 hrs, US$15), Brújula/ La Internacional; drug searches on this road. To **Salta**, Stel, *T558197*, on Fri 0800, 18 hrs, US$29.

Boat

River boat to **Concepción**, every Mon (return on Sun), 27-30 hrs, US$20 1st class, US$13 2nd, US$7 deck space.

O Directory

Resistencia *p319*
Airline offices Aerolíneas Argentinas, *Juan B Justo 184, T445550.* **Banks** Banco de la Nación, *Güemes y Av 9 de Julio.* Banco de Galicia, *Mitre 153.* El Dorado, *J M Paz 50.*
Money exchange Western Union branch and TCs (bring high denomination US$ cheques, as commission is charged per cheque). **Communications Post office** *Av Sarmiento e Hipólito Yrigoyen on Plaza 25 de Mayo.* **Internet** Klap, *Illia 12.* US$0.40/hr, open 24 hrs. **Useful addresses Police**, *T101, T432002.*
Medical emergencies: Hospital Perrando, *Av 9 de Julio 1101, T425050.* Hospital Pediátrico (Children's Hospital), *Juan B Justo 1136, T441477.*

Formosa *p320*
Airline offices Aerolíneas Argentinas, *Av 25 de Mayo 601, T429314.* **Banks** Banco de la Nación, *Av 25 de Mayo 602.* Banco de Galicia, *Av 25 de Mayo 160.* **Useful addresses Police**, *T101, T429000.*
Medical emergencies, *T110.* Hospital Central, *Fotheringham 550, T426194, T424054.* Hospital de la Madre y el Niño (for children), *Ayacucho 1150, T426097, T429590.*

Misiones

Misiones is the northeasternmost province in Argentina, with stunning landscapes, and a rich culture generated by a heady mix of indigenous Guaraní and European immigrants, particularly from Eastern Europe, together with a constant flow of Paraguayans and Brazilians from over the borders. Oberá's 35 churches represent immigrants from an amazing 15 countries. As part of the Jesuits' extensive empire, Misiones was the site of several religious missions, of which impressive ruins remain at San Ignacio and Santa Ana, with a restored church at Trinidad near Encarnación. The landscape is seductive and picturesque: rich red soil contrasts with rich green subtropical forests, some still primary virgin rainforest where the land has not been cleared for tea or yerba mate fields, or pine forests for paper pulp. It's a fairly wet region: the annual rainfall exceeds 2,000 mm, generating hundreds of rivers and waterfalls, the most magnificent of which are the overwhelming Iguazú Falls, at the province's northernmost tip. The best base for these, and exploring the national park is the atmospheric little town of Puerto Iguazú. And southeast across the province, there are the staggeringly wide Saltos de Moconá, now accessible for visitors. The climate might be uncomfortably hot for much walking in summer, but it's pleasantly warm in winter, while flowers and bird life are most abundant in spring. ▶▶ *For Sleeping, Eating and other listings, see pages 335-338.*

Getting there and around There are two parallel roads running from the southwest to the northeast of the province, but Route 12, the northernmost one, the only one negotiable in an ordinary vehicle, is a fast paved road built for forestry, and used by buses linking the province's main towns. From Corrientes the first town you'll encounter is Posadas, a good place for a stop to arrange buses and tours. The road continues to San Ignacio, with the Jesuit ruins, via a series of small towns such as Eldorado to Wanda (which is famous for its open mines of semi-precious stoneso.) Route 12 ends at Puerto Iguazú, the best base for visiting the Falls. The other road, Route 14, runs parallel and south along the interior of the province, via Oberá to Bernardo de Irigoyen. It's mostly unpaved, although asphalting is in process, and there are no buses along this route. But it does give access to some fascinating little-visited areas of the province, if you have a 4WD vehicle to negotiate the rough terrain.

Best time to visit The climate might be uncomfortably hot for much walking in summer, but it's pleasantly warm in winter, while flowers and bird life are most abundant in spring.

Posadas → *Phone code: 03752 Colour map 2, B2 Population: 280,500*

Posadas is the lively capital of Misiones, set on a bend in the Río Paraná, with excellent views over the river from its attractive costanera. Though there aren't any particularly remarkable sights, Posadas is an appealing place with a constant flow of Paraguayans from over the border, and varied indigenous populations generating an upbeat atmosphere. The tourist office is two blocks south of the Plaza at Colón 1985, T447540, turismo@misiones.gov.ar www.conoz camisiones.com open daily 0800-2000. ▸▸ *For Sleeping, Eating and other listings, see pages 335-338.*

Sights

The centre of the city is the Plaza 9 de Julio with its French-style cathedral and the Gobernación. Nearby there's a peaceful spot at Paseo Bosetti, a quiet plaza with mural paintings, reached from the corner of Bolívar and Buenos Aires. There are a couple of rather uninspiring museums near the Plaza: the cultural centre and arts exhibition hall at **Museo de Arte Juan Yaparí**, Sarmiento 317, with the adjacent **Mercado de Artesanías**, where Guaraní handicrafts are for sale, and the **Museo Arqueológico**, General Paz 1865, T435845.

The riverside districts are the most interesting areas for a stroll, extending east and north of centre. Follow Rivadavia or Buenos Aires north to Avenida **Andrés Guaçurarí** (referred to also as Av Roque Pérez) a pretty boulevard which becomes livelier by night with several popular bars. Immediately north of it is the small and hilly Bajada Vieja or old port district, with some attractive old wooden houses amongst the more modern buildings, remnants of times when *mensú* or temporary workers used to wander around on their way to the *yerba mate* plantations. A few blocks west is the small **Parque Paraguayo** and the **Museo Regional Aníbal Cambas** ① *Alberdi 600, T447539, Mon-Fri 0700-1900*, is Posadas' most intereresting museum with a permanent exhibition of Guaraní artefacts and pieces collected from the nearby Jesuit missions, including the façade of the temple at San Ignacio Mini.

Next to the park and to one side of the amphitheatre, steps go down to the *costanera*, which can also be accessed by Avenida Roca and Calle Arrechea, heading north from centre or via Avenida Andrés Guaçurarí. This is new urban development but the river and the Paraguayan coast make it a very pleasant area for a walk popular with joggers and other locals enjoying their new *paseo*. The **port** lies at the eastern end of the Avenida Costanera and you can still see the two ferries, built in Glasgow in

1911, that operated the river crossing for train coaches until 1990. Nearby, the **Mercado La Placita**, daily 0630-2030, is a colourful market, its inner corridors buzzing with life, and a great selection of intriguing goods for sale.

Around Posadas

Apóstoles 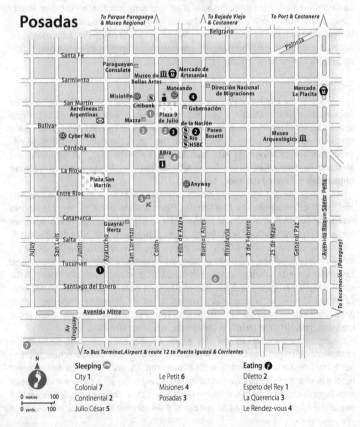 *65 km south of Posadas with regular buses*, is a prosperous town founded in 1897 by Ukrainian and Polish immigrants on the site of a Jesuit mission dating from 1633. Set in the heart of *yerba mate* plantations in a picturesque hilly region, is hosts the *Fiesta Nacional de la Yerba Mate* every July.

The **Museo Histórico Juan Szychowski** ⓘ *13 km further at La Cachuera, follow the 6 km dirt road, branching off Route 1.7 km south of Apóstoles*, is worth a trip from Posadas. It neatly displays tools and machinery invented by a young Polish immigrant, including a cute pram used by all his children, mills for processing rice, corn and *yerba mate*, and his hydraulic works, which can be seen in the grounds still amaze engineers. He was the founder of **La Cachuera** ⓘ *Mar 21-Sep 20: Wed-Fri 0800-1130, 1430-1730, Sat-Sun 1000-1730. Sep 21-Mar 20: Wed-Fri 0700-1130, 1500-1730, Sat-Sun 0800-1200, 1530-1900, 03758-422443, www.yerbamanda .com.ar*, a *yerba mate* processing plant, still operating, now under the brand name of *Amanda*.

Estancia Santa Inés ⓘ *20 km south (Route 105, Km 8.5), T03752-436194, F03752-439998*, a traditional estancia of 2,000 ha, growing lots of *yerba mate*. Activities include walking, horse riding and, between February and October, helping with mate cultivation. Half-day activities US$20, taxi from Posadas, US$15. For

Posadas

Sleeping 🛏
City **1**
Colonial **7**
Continental **2**
Julio César **5**
Le Petit **6**
Misiones **4**
Posadas **3**

Eating 🍴
Diletto **2**
Espeto del Rey **1**
La Querencia **3**
Le Rendez-vous **4**

The Northeast Posadas

arrange transfer to *estancias* or to Colonia Carlos Pellegrini. ▸▸ *For Sleeping, Eating and other listings, see pages 335-338.*

Border with Paraguay

The Puente San Roque links Posadas with Encarnación. Pedestrians and cyclists are not allowed to cross the bridge; cyclists must ask officials for assistance. Pesos are accepted in Encarnación, so there is no need to change them. Paraguay is one hr behind Argentina, except during Paraguayan summer time.

Immigration and customs Formalities are conducted at respective ends of the bridge. The Argentine side has different offices for locals and foreigners, T435329; Paraguay has one for both. Formalities for boat crossing are carried out at both ports. The Argentine consulate is at Mallorquín 788, T3446.

Encarnación (Paraguay) → *Phone code +595-(0)71 Colour map 2, B2 Population: 60,000*

Founded in 1614, Encarnación is the third largest city in Paraguay, exporting the products of a rich agricultural area: timber, soya, *mate*, tobacco, cotton, and hides. Most of the old centre was drowned after the completion of the Yaciretá-Apipé dam, and a modern, but less interesting, centre has been built on higher ground. The **tourist office** is next to Universidad Católica, T203508, open 0800-1200, but a street map can be obtained in the afternoon at the Municipalidad (Oficina de Planificación), Estigarribia y Kreusser.

Around Encarnación → *There are several Jesuit missions nearby worth visiting*

The Jesuit mission of **Trinidad** lies 28 km east of Encarnación on Route 6, which links Encarnación and Ciudad del Este. Regular buses will drop you off at the ruins, US$1. Taxi tours from Encarnación charge US$20. Founded in 1706, the mission was designed by the architect Juan Bautista Prímoli; it is now a UNESCO World Cultural Heritage site. The **Jesuit church** ① *Oct-Apr 0700-1900, May-Sep 0700-1730, US$0.20*, once completely ruined, has been partially restored. Also partially rebuilt is the bell tower which is near the original church (excellent views from the top). You can also see another church, a college, workshops and the Guaraní living quarters. The budget *León* is a good hotel and restaurant next to the entrance.

Parque Manantial, 500 m off Route 6, Km 35, T075-32732, is a nicely located park with two swimming pools, a good restaurant and camping facilities for US$5 per day. Owner Rubén Pretzle, always willing to help visitors, organizes tours to the local countryside and to the nearby ruins.

The Jesuit mission of **Jesús**, is located 10 km northwest of Trinidad; a rough road branches off from Route 6. There are buses every hour from Trinidad (no buses on Sun), 30 mins, US$0.40, and also direct buses to/from Encarnación. Taxis try to overcharge, so ask around. This **Jesuit construction** ① *Oct-Apr 0700-1900, May-Sep 0700-1730, US$0.20*, dating from 1763-1767, includes a church, sacristy, *residencia* and a baptistry, on one side of which is a square tower. The site has been recently cleaned and restored, and there are beautiful views from the top of the main tower.

San Cosmé y Damián, about 90 km west of Encarnación, is located off the highway to Asunción; turn off south about 25 km. There are regular buses from Encarnación, 2½ hrs. This mission was also unfinished in 1767 when the Jesuits were expelled from South America. A huge completion project has recently been carried out following the original plans. ▸▸ *For Sleeping, Eating and other listings, see pages 335-338.*

⁙ On a mission

The Jesuits were the religious force which accompanied the Spanish conquest of much of northern Argentina, and though their impact on indigenous culture was far more positive, their rule remains controversial. Were they pioneers of a primitive socialism or merely exploiting the local Guaraní in the name of religious enlightenment?

Between 1609 when they built their first redacción or mission, in present day Brazil, and 1767 when they were expelled, the Jesuits founded about 50 missions around the upper reaches of the Ríos Paraná, Paraguay and Uruguay. In 1627, they were forced to flee southwards, when their northern missions were attacked by slave-hunting Bandeirantes from São Paul. The priests led some 1,000 converts down the Río Parapanema into the Paraná on 700 rafts, only to find their route blocked by the Guaíra Falls. They pushed on for 8 days through dense virgin forest, built new boats below the falls and continued their journey. Some 725 km from their old homes, they re-established their missions, and trained militias to protect them from further attacks.

The layout of the Jesuit missions was copied from the Franciscans, built around a central square, with the church on the middle of one side. Alongside the church were cloisters, with workshops, priests' quarters and the cemetery. The living quarters of the Guaraní occupied the other three sides of the square, and the mission was run by only two priests. The missions prospered on their agricultural produce, since they chose fertile lands: the Guaraní grew traditional crops such as manioc (the local root vegetable), sweet potatoes and maize, plants imported from Europe, such as wheat and oranges, and they also kept horses and herds

of cattle and sheep. The missions became major producers of *yerba mate* (see page 37) favoured by the Jesuits as an alternative to alcohol. Apart from common lands the Guaraní also farmed their own individual plots.

The decision by Carlos III to expel the Jesuits from South America in 1767 was made under the conditions of highest secrecy: sealed orders were sent out to the colonies with strict instructions that they should not be opened in advance. On the appointed date, over 2,000 members of the order were removed by force and put on ships for Italy. Jesuit property was auctioned, schools and colleges were taken over by the Franciscans and Dominicans, and many missions fell into disuse, or were destroyed in 1817.

The Jesuits had attracted many enemies since founding their first missions. Their wealth and economic power angered landowners and traders, and their control over the Guaraní irritated farmers short of labour: rumours circulated that the missions contained mines and hoards of precious metals. And when in 1750 a border treaty between Spain and Portugal placed seven missions under Portuguese control, the Jesuits resisted with arms, justifying Spanish and Portuguese suspicion of the order. However the Jesuits may have exploited their Guaraní manpower, they certainly defended the Guaraní from enslavement by the Spanish and Portuguese, and many feel their societies were a vanished arcadia.

Only four of the missions reveal their former splendour: San Ignacio Mini in Argentina, Jesús and Trinidad in Paraguay, and São Miguel in Brazil. The first three can be visited with ease from Posadas or Encarnación, along with several others, including Santa Ana and Loreto.

San Ignacio → *Phone code: 03752 Colour map 2, B2 Population: 6,300*

San Ignacio is a small town which is the site of the most impressive remains of a Jesuit mission in the Misiones region, 63 km northeast of Posadas. The site, together with the nearby Jesuit missions of Loreto and Santa Ana, has been declared a World Heritage site by Unesco. The town and its surroundings have other attractive sights, making a nice place to stay for a few days.

History

San Ignacio Mini ('small' in comparison with San Ignacio Guazu – 'large' – on the Paraguayan side of the Río Paraná) was originally founded in 1610 near the river Paranapanema in the present Brazilian state of Paraná, but frequent attacks from the *bandeirantes* forced the Jesuits to lead a massive exodus together with the neighbouring Loreto mission. In 1631 San Ignacio was resettled on the river Yabebiry, not far from its present site, which was definitively settled in 1696.

At the height of its prosperity in 1731, the mission housed 4,356 people. Only two priests conducted the mission; a feat of astounding organization. Latin, Spanish and Guaraní were taught in the school, and nearly 40,000 head of cattle grazed in the surrounding land, along with the cultivation of *yerba mate* and cotton fields. But after the expulsion of the Jesuits in 1767, the mission rapidly declined. By 1784 there were only 176 Guaraní and by 1810 none remained. In 1817, by order of the Paraguayan dictator, Rodriguez de Francia, San Ignacio was set on fire. The ruins, like those of nearby Santa Ana and Loreto, were lost in the jungle until the late 19th century when colonisation policies were implemented and new towns, such as San Ignacio, were founded near the sites of the former missions. It wasn't until the 1980's that there was some attempt to give official protection to the ruins, which were declared a national monument at last in 1943.

The ruins

Like other Jesuit missions, San Ignacio Mini was constructed around a central plaza: to the north, east and west were about 30 parallel one-storey buildings, each with a wide veranda in front and each divided into four to 10 small, one-room dwellings. The roofs have gone, but the massive metre-thick walls are still standing except where they have been destroyed by the *ibapoi* trees. The public buildings, some still 10 m high, are on the south side of the plaza: in the centre are the ruins of the church, 74 m x 24 m, finished about 1724. To the right is the cemetery, to the left the cloisters, the priests' quarters and the workshops; sculpture was of particular significance in San Ignacio. The masonry, a red sandstone, was held together by a sandy mud. There is much bas-relief sculpture, mostly of floral designs, though a couple of faces can be seen carved on the floor of the veranda overlooking the orchard behind the cloisters. The whole area is excellently maintained and is a most impressive sight.

> ‡ At San Ignacio Mini there is a Son-et-lumière show, after sunset daily, which lasts 50 mins, in Spanish only, US$0.80; cancelled in wet weather.

The **Centro de Interpretación Jesuítico-Guaraní**, 200 m inside the entrance to the ruins, is an exhibition which includes representations of the lives of the Guaraní before the arrival of the Spanish, displays on the work of the Jesuits and the consequences of their expulsion, as well as a fine model of the mission in its heyday; well laid out. Next to the exit, to the left, there is also a small **Museo Provincial**, which contains a collection of artefacts from the Jesuit missions, exhibiting a bas-relief of San Ignacio de Loyola, founder of the Jesuit order. ① *The mission is located a few blocks from Av Sarmiento on the northwest side of town, entrance at Calle Alberdi, exit to C Rivadavia; 0700-1900, T470186, US$0.80, US$3.50 with guide (also in English), tip appreciated if the guards look after your luggage.*

Follow Avenida Sarmiento to its very end and turn right for a picturesque view of a row of wooden houses on a reddish road amidst lush vegetation. Next to the Jesuit site entrance is **Galería Bellas Artes** (at La Casa de Inés y Juan), San Martín 1291, where painter Juan Catalano exhibits and sells his works which feature geometrical motifs, or typical local scenes, mounted on wooden boards.

On the opposite side of the town, there's a really delightful stroll to Quiroga's house, a 20-min walk (with little shade) along San Martín, in the opposite direction to the ruins, to the end, where there is the *Gendarmería* headquarters, and two attractive wooden and stone houses. After 200 m the road turns left and 300 m later, a signposted narrow road branches off leading to the **Casa de Horacio Quiroga** ① *0800-1900, T470124, US$0.65 (includes a 40 min-guided visit; ask in advance for an English guide)*, the house of the celebrated Uruguayan writer (1878-1937) who lived there part of his tragic life as a farmer and carpenter between 1910-1916 and again in the 1930s. Many of his excellent short stories, mixing the real with the fantastic, were inspired by the subtropical environment and its inhabitants. The scenery is beautiful, with river views a garden with palms and an amazing bamboo forest planted by him. There is a replica of his first house made for a movie set in the 90's, while his second house is still standing, containing an exhibition of a few of his belongings. Return to the main road, follow it down the slope amongst thick vegetation for a gorgeous riverside (25-min) walk, recommended.

Around San Ignacio

The ruins of the mission of **Loreto**, has much fewer visitors and under thick shady trees, the silence of the still air and the refreshing darkness add an attractive touch of mistery to these ruins. The mission was moved to its present site in 1631, after the exodus from the former Jesuit province of Guayrá; 2,789 people were living there in 1744. It was also the site of the first printing press in the area. Little remains of this once large establishment other than a few walls, though excavations are in progress. Note the number of old trees growing entwined with stone buttresses. ① *0700-1830, US$0.35, reached by a 3 km dirt road (signposted) off Route 12, 10 km south of San Ignacio; no public transport enters Loreto, but buses will drop you off on Route 12, otherwise tours from Posadas or remise taxis from nearby towns.*

Some 16 km south of San Ignacio at **Santa Ana** are the ruins of another Jesuit mission ① *0700-1900, US$0.35, regular buses stop on Route 12.* Moved to its present site in 1660, Santa Ana housed the Jesuit iron foundry. In 1744 the mission was inhabited by 4,331 people. The impressively high walls are still standing and there are beautiful steps leading from the church to the wide open plaza. The ruins are 700 m along a path from Route 12 (signposted).

The **Parque Provincial Teyú Cuaré** ① *11 km south of San Ignacio, follow Av Bolívar, leaving the Gendarmería on your right; there is no regular transport, little shade for a walk, and a rough road for any vehicle,* is a 78-ha reserve which includes the **Peñón Teyú Cuaré**, a 150-m high hill (also known as the *Peñón Reina Victoria* because of its supposed resemblance to the profile of the British queen) and protects a very rare cactus (*Parodia schumanniana*). Steps climb up the steep promontory to a vantage point overlooking the Paraná river and the hilly Paraguayan coast. The only access road is rough, making the journey long and tiresome, but you'll be rewarded by splendid views on the coast. ▸▸ *For Sleeping, Eating and other listings, see pages 335-338.*

San Ignacio to Puerto Iguazú

From San Ignacio Route 12 continues northeast, running parallel to Río Alto Paraná, towards Puerto Iguazú. With its bright red soil and green vegetation, this is an

attractive route which gives an interesting insight into the local economy: plantations
of *yerba mate*, manioc and citrus fruits can be seen as well as timber yards, manioc
mills and *yerba mate* factories. The road passes through several small modern towns
including Jardín America, Puerto Rico, Montecarlo and Eldorado, with
accommodation, campsites, places to eat and regular bus services from Puerto
Iguazú and from Posadas. ▸▸ *For Sleeping, Eating and other listings, see pages 335-338.*

Región de las Flores

Now named by tour operators as the *Region of the Flowers*, this area includes several
towns 150 km along Route 12 with attractive natural sights, worth a brief stop on the
way between San Ignacio and Iguazú, if you have your own transport. Just 100 m from
Route 12 in Capioví, 60 km from San Ignacio, is the **Salto Capioví**, a 7 m-waterfall
immersed in a patch of jungle with a campsite. Nearby, the **Parque Natural Las
Camelias**, a park with camellias, can be visited. Visitors are invited at a few farms and
the Swiss school *Instituto Línea Cuchilla*, T03743-495015, at nearby village Ruíz de
Montoya, where you can buy local produce (for more information, contact the
Municipalidad, T03743-493003).

Puerto Rico, 15 km north, is a small port on the Río Paraná known as the city of
lapachos, with these beautiful trees of pink and yellow flowers lining the local
avenues and blossoming in Jul-Sep. Some 8 km north of Garuhapé, a 6 km dirt road
branches off leading to **Salto 3 de Mayo**, a 5-m waterfall next to a natural cave, with a
campsite (electricity and showers.) Back on Route 12 after 33 km is the access road to
Montecarlo, where every October the *Fiesta Nacional de la Orquídea* is held in the
attractive **Parque Juan Vortisch**. This 6-ha area with trees and orchids, includes a
maze made of bushes. There are about eight orchid nurseries along the main roads in
town, growing over 350 native varieties.

About 2 km north on Route 12, a road gives access to **Zoo Bal Park**, T480103,
whose claim to fame is that it is the only zoo which has a *harpía* (harpy eagle), the
world's strongest bird of prey. Two nearby estancias, **Caraguatay**, T03751-494025
and **La Misionera**, T03751-480006, offer day stays and excursions into the jungle.

At 100 km south of Puerto Iguazú is **Eldorado**, a bustling town with one of the
largest Polish communities in the country and with an interesting archaeological
collection at the **Museo Municipal**ⓘ *T03751-430788, Thu-Sun 1500-1800*.

Wanda, 50 km north, was named after a Polish princess and is famous as the site
of open-cast amethyst and quartz mines which sell gems. There are guided tours to
two of them, Tierra Colorada and Compañía Minera Wanda, daily 0700-1900. Consult
tour operators. ▸▸ *For Sleeping, Eating and other listings, see pages 335-338.*

The interior of Misiones

Away from the main tourist trail, along Route 12, Misiones' hilly interior is dotted with
patches of dense subtropical forests, concealing beautiful waterfalls and, at the
furthest end of the track, the remote **Moconá** falls. A green corridor has been
established along natural reserves and other woodlands in Argentina, Paraguay and
Brazil to protect the subtropical environment and to avoid the isolation of these
'islands'. Tourist services are less well developed here, and with several unpaved
roads the journeys can be rough, but the area is still very appealing to those with time
and ideally, a sturdy 4WD vehicle. There are regular bus services from Posadas to all
main towns, but most of the sights lie on their outskirts, so you will need to walk, hire
a remise or take a tour. Oberá is a good base for exploring Misiones' central sierras,
while for a visit to Moconá, you could stay next to the falls or in San Pedro or El
Soberbio, or take a longer tour from Posadas.

The Northeast The interior of Misiones

Oberá is the second largest town in Misiones, located amongst tea and *yerba mate* plantations, with factories open for visits. It's one of the province's biggest centres of 20th-century European immigration, and there are around 15 different nationalities here, including Japanese, Brazilian, Paraguayan and Middle Eastern communities, represented every September in the annual *Fiesta Nacional del Inmigrante*, held at the Parque de las Naciones. The town has over 35 churches and temples. There is a **zoo** ① *Italia y Alberdi, Tue-Sun 0900-1200*, with the **Jardín de los Pájaros** ① *1500-1900 (in winter until 1800), US$0.35, T427023*, which houses native birds, .

Monte Aventura ① *Tue-Sun 1000-1800, US$0.35, T422430, access from Av José Ingenieros*, is a park with forest trails and entertainment for kids. The tourist office ① *Plazoleta Güemes, Av Libertad 90, T421808, Mon-Fri 0700-1900, Sat-Sun 0800-1200, 1500-1900*, has information on local estancias open to visitors.

Around Oberá

On the outskirts, **Salto Berrondo** ① *6 km west, reached by paved Route 103; buses going to Santa Ana will stop on the road*, is a 12 m waterfall with an adjacent campsite and a pool (entry US$0.35) . More falls at **Salto Krysiuk** ① *14 km southeast, lying on a dirt road, branching off Route 14 to the southeast, a few kilometres south of Oberá,* is a group of several 6 m waterfalls dropping into a 3 m deep pool surrounded by exuberant forest (entry US$0.35) where there is a campsite.

Some 28 km southwest at **Leandro N Alem** ① *Route 14 with regular public transport from Oberá*, there's a dazzling array of orchids at **Blumen Haus** ① *T03754-15660716*, a nursery and an arboretum of 36 hectares with native trees. You could also explore the ruins of the Jesuit mission of **Santa María la Mayor** ① *76 km southwest, on paved Route 2 linking San Javier and Concepción de la Sierra, 9 km west of Itacaruare*, dating from 1637 and never restored. Remains of the church and a jail are still standing, and a printing press operated there in the early 18th century.

Northwards, **Campo Viera** ① *21 km north, on Route 14, with regular bus services from Oberá, as well as the access to Salto Encantado, see below, about 7 km far from the falls*, the 'national capital of tea', has about 8,000 ha of tea fields and 25 processing plants. Its main street is the Avenida del Té and a *Fiesta Nacional del Té* is held at the local amphitheatre every September with the Queen of Tea coronation (for more information, go to the **Casita del Té**, T03755-497090). 72 km northeast is **Salto Encantado**, a magnificent 60 m-high waterfall among lush forest located northeast of Aristóbulo del Valle in a natural reserve; campsite. ▶ *For Sleeping, Eating and other listings, see pages 335-338.*

Gran Salto del Moconá → *These falls are known in Brazil as Yucuma*

For a staggering 3 km, on the Argentine side of the Río Uruguay, water falls over a vast shelf of rock from 18 m up to 120 m, creating one of the most magnificent sights in the region. The rocky edge is quite easily reached on foot from the shores, an area surrounded by dense woodland, protected by the Parque Estadual do Turvo (Brazil) and the Parque Provincial Moconá, the Reserva Provincial Esmeralda and the Reserva de la Biósfera Yabotí (Argentina). The **Parque Provincial Moconá** covers 1,000 ha with vehicle roads and footpaths, and accommodation nearby, where all activities are arranged, including excursions to the falls. In all three natural reserves the hilly forested landscape offers tremendous trekking, kayaking, birdwatching and exploring in 4WD vehicles. Alternative bases for exploring the remains are the small towns of **El Soberbio** (70 km southwest) or **San Pedro** (92 km northwest). Roads from both towns to Moconá are impassable for ordinary vehicles after heavy rains. Regular bus services from Posadas to El Soberbio and San Pedro and from Puerto Iguazú to San Pedro, but no public transport reaches the falls.

❧ *Allow about 1½ hrs for a visit to Gran Salto. Go early to avoid crowds or at sunset for good photography light. There are heavy rains in February. Mosquitoes can be a problem.*

Listings: Misiones

● Sleeping

Posadas *p327, map p328*
B Julio César, *Entre Ríos 1951, T427930,
F420599, www.juliocesarhotel.com.ar* Large
4-star with pool and gym and spacious but
pricey rooms. Breakfast included.
C Continental, *Bolívar 1879 (on plaza 9 de
Julio), T440990, F435302, www.hotel
eramisiones.com.ar* Plain decoration but
comfortable standard rooms and more
spacious B VIP rooms, some with riverviews.
Restaurant on first floor.
C Posadas, *Bolívar 1949, T440888, F430294,
www.hotelposadas.com.ar* Business-oriented
hotel with good standard rooms and bigger
especial rooms. It has a restaurant and guests
have free internet access.
D City, *Colón 1754, T439401,
citytel@arnet.com.ar* Gloomy reception and
corridors give access to very good rooms,
some overlooking the plaza. Breakfast and
a/c included, restaurant on the first floor.
D Colonial, *Barrufaldi 2419, T436149, next to
the intersection of Av Mitre and Av Corrientes,
about 15-min walk from centre.* Run by a
warmly welcoming owner, very good value
with spotless rooms with a/c and breakfast,
situated on a quiet street.
D Le Petit, *Santiago del Estero 1630, T436031,
F441101.* This is another very good value
small hotel a short walk from the centre on a
quiet and shady street. Spotless rooms have
a/c and breakfast is included.
E Residencial Misiones, *Félix de Azara 1960,
T430133.* Very welcoming owners offer
pleasant rooms with fan and bath in a
centrally located old house with a patio. No
breakfast is served, but cooking and laundry
facilities are available. Popular among
travellers.

Encarnación *p329*
A Tirol, *at Capitán Miranda, on Route 6, Km
20, T202388, erik@hoteltirol.com.py* Chalets
with beautiful views, a restaurant and
swimming pools filled with freezing cold
spring water.
B Encarnación Resort Hotel, *at Villa Quiteria
(on outskirts), ruta 1, Km 2, T207264, erhotel@
ita.com.py* A very well-run place with

comfortable rooms.
C Paraná, *Estigarribia 1414, T204440.* Helpful
owners, good breakfasts.
E Germano, *Cabañas y CA López (opposite
bus terminal), T3346.* A small and very
welcoming place with F rooms without bath
or a/c; German and Japanese spoken.
E Liz, *Av Independencia 1746, T202609.*
Comfortable rooms and a restaurant.

San Ignacio *p331*
E El Descanso, *Pellegrini 270, T470207.*
A comfortable place with small detached
houses, five blocks southwest of main Av
Sarmiento.
E San Ignacio, *San Martín 823, T470047.*
Welcoming and very informative owner
Beatriz offers very good rooms with a/c and
apartments for 4 and 5 people. Breakfast
US$1.20. Phone booths and an interesting
aerial view of town at the reception.
G pp El Güembé, *Gendarme Medina 525,
T470910.* German owner Roland runs this
basic place with shared bath, just 100 m
from the Jesuit ruins. He also rents bicycles
for US$3.50 a day next door at Kiosko
Alemán.
G pp La Casa de Inés y Juan, *San Martín
1291 (no sign and no phone).* A warm and
laid-back artist's house (a painter and writer),
very quaint, with two rooms, a small library
and a backyard for pitching tents (US$1.30
pp per day), where there's also a small but
delightful pool and a curious bathroom.
Meals on request. Recommended.
G pp Salpeterer, *Centenario y Av Sarmiento
(follow main Av Sarmiento up to its end and
turn right 50 m), T470362.* A small basic place
but clean and tidy with cooking facilities in a
cosy kitchen. Rooms have fan, but no bath,
but there's one E room for 4 or more with
bath. No breakfast served. Camping facilites
with electricity and a decent bath with hot
water for US$0.65 pp per day.

Camping
Two sites on the river are splendidly situated
and very well-kept on a small sandy bay
among rocky promontories. They are
reached by 45-min walk from town at the
end of the road leading to Quiroga's house:

Playa del Sol, *T470115, on the beach side.*
US$0.35 pp per day plus US$1 per tent.
Club de Pesca y Deportes Náuticos, *on hilly
ground with lush vegetation.* US$0.65 pp per
day plus US$1 per tent.

Oberá *p334*
Ask the tourist office for details of farms run
by host families of different nationalities.
C **Cabañas del Parque**, *Ucrania y Tronador,
T426000, cabanas@arnet.com.ar* Situated
next to the Parque de las Naciones is this
tourist complex of several houses or rooms
for 2 to 8 people with kitchen and a/c,
breakfast included. Large swimming pool
and a restaurant. Also more luxurious
accommodation, B rooms.
D **Premier**, *9 de Julio 1164, T426171.* A good
central option, with a/c, but no breakfast.
E **Cuatro Pinos**, *Sarmiento 853, T425102.*
A well-located hotel, prices without
breakfast.
E **Residencial El Edén**, *Route 14 y Bogotá,
T422875.* Rooms and houses with
kitchenette, garden and a pool. Large
breakfast on request.

Camping
Good sites with showers and small food shops
next to both falls are **Salto Berrondo** and
Krysiuk (also E doubles at old warehouse),
US$0.35 pp plus US$0.65 per tent.

Gran Salto del Mocaná *p334*
Mocaná
E pp **Refugio Mocaná**, *3 km from access to
the reserve, 8 km from the Falls (or contact at
Pasaje Dornelles 450, San Pedro), T03751
-470022, www.mocona.com* Accommodation
in rustic rooms for 4 to 5 people with shared
bath, campsite for US$4.30 a day per tent,
tents for rent (US$8.50 a day), meals for
US$4.30-6 (not including drinks) and many
activities, such as 30-min boat trips to the
Falls (US$63 per group of up to 5), one-hour
walk to the Falls (US$21 per group), and
several other excursions on foot and by 4WD
vehicles. There is also a kayak journey down
the river Yabotí (US$29 pp). Transfer with
sightseeing to/from San Pedro, 2 hrs, US$85
for up to 8 people.

El Soberbio
D **Hostería Puesta del Sol**, *C Suipacha,
T03755-495161 (T43001377 in Buenos Aires),
turismocona@yahoo.com.ar* A splendid
vantage point on the town, with swimming
pool and a restaurant. The rooms are
comfortable with breakfast and a/c . For full
board accommodation add US$6.50 pp. Boat
excursions arranged to the falls, 7 to 8 hours,
landing and meal included, US$20 pp (min 4
people). The journey to the Falls is by an
boat crossing to Brazil, then by vehicle to the
Parque do Turvo, 7 hrs, meal included, US$20
pp. Otherwise, a 4WD journey on the
Argentine side with more chances for
trekking also takes 7 hrs, with a meal
included, US$20 pp.

🍴 Eating

Posadas *p327, map p328*
Most places offer the *espeto corrido* system,
as much *parrilla* as you can eat for a fixed
price: pork, beef, sausages, entrails or
chicken, grilled and brought to the table
speared on a long *brochette* or *al galeto.*
Instead of the usual potato or bread with
meat, in Misiones it's common to eat
mandioca, a potato-like root. The typical
dessert is *mamón en almíbar* (papaya in
syrup). If you haven't already tried *chipá,*
small bread rolls made with manioc flour,
there are lots to try in Posadas. Delicious.
$$$ **El Mensú**, *Fleming y Coronel Reguera (at
Bajada Vieja district).* A very attractive house
in the picturesque old port area offering a
varied menu with fish, pastas and a large
selection of wines included. Closed Mon.
$$ **Diletto**, *Bolívar 1729.* A rather formal
atmosphere, good for fish such as *surubí* and,
curiously, rabbit as the house speciality.
$$ **Espeto del Rey**, *Ayacucho y Tucumán.*
A parrilla with *espeto corrido,* which serves
good food at moderate prices. Try mandioca
frita (fried manioc).
$$$ **Le Rendez-vous**, *San Martín 1786.*
A formal setting for meals with a French
touch, including *moules, foie gras* as starters
and different French sauces for meat.
$$ **La Querencia**, *on Bolívar (on plaza 9 de
Julio).* A large traditional restaurant offering

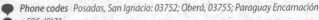
Phone codes Posadas, San Ignacio: 03752; Oberá, 03755; Paraguay Encarnación
+595-(0)71.

parrilla served *al galeto*, *surubí* and pastas at moderate prices.

Encarnación *p329*
Cuarajhy, *Estigarribia y Pereira*. A place where good food is served 24 hrs with terrace seating.
Las Delicias, *Estigarribia 1694*. Good steaks.

San Ignacio *p331*
There are also several large restaurants for tourist crowds (eg **La Carpa Azul**) on the streets bordering the Jesuit site.
La Aldea, *Rivadavia y Lanusse*. An attractive house serving good cheap pizzas, *empanadas* and other simple meals.
Los Hermanos, *San Martín y Av Sarmiento*. Run by a very kind owner, this is the place to go for breakfast, bread or sweet pastries, open from 0700 (when everything else is still closed).
Hotel San Ignacio, *see above*. Simple meals are also offered Tue-Sun after 1700.

Oberá *p334*
$$ **Engüete**, *Cabeza de Vaca 340*. Good food and a varied menu is available.
$$ **El Lapacho**, *Sarmiento 1230 and Juan Alfredo, Av Libertad y Ralf Singer*.

⊛ Festivals

Oberá *p334*
The vibrant **Fiesta Nacional del Inmigrante** lasts a week around **Sep 4** (Immigrant's Day). In the Parque de las Naciones houses built in various national styles are the attractive setting for folk dances, parades, tasting national dishes and the election of a Queen. Very popular, book accommodation ahead.

⊘ Tour operators

Posadas *p326*
Abra, *Colón 1975, T422221, abramisiones @arnet.com.ar* Runs tours to San Ignacio, including Santa Ana Jesuit ruins (US$20 pp), to Jesuit ruins in Paraguay (US$23 pp) and in Brazil (US$48 pp), to Jesuit ruins in Misiones and waterfalls (US$47 pp), to Saltos del Moconá (a 2-day trip, US$136 pp).
Guayrá, *San Lorenzo 2208, T433415, www.guayra.com.ar* Tours to Iberá (US$50-65 pp if 4 people), to Saltos del Moconá (US$80 pp if 4 people), both sites in a 5-day excursion for US$240 pp (if 4

people). Also car rental and transfer to Colonia Carlos Pellegrini (for Iberá).

Oberá *p334*
Transit 21, *Córdoba 17, T402121, www.transit21.com.ar* Ask there for transfer to the nearby Falls, as well as to other sights in central Misiones.

⊖ Transport

Posadas *p327, map p328*
Air
General San Martín Airport is on Route 12, 12 km west, T457413, reached by Bus No 8 or 28 with stops along C Junín in centre, 40 mins, US$0.23, *remise* taxi US$4. To **Buenos Aires**, daily with **Aerolíneas Argentinas**, 1 hr 25 mins (if direct), some flights call at **Corrientes** or **Formosa**, 1 hr 50 mins.

Boat
At Río Paraná, port access from Av Costanera y Av Andrés Guaçurarí, T425044 (**Prefectura**). Boat crossing to Encarnación (Paraguay), 6-8 mins, almost every hour Mon-Fri 0800-1800, US$1. Ticket office at main building.

Bus
The terminal is 5 km out of the city on the road to Corrientes at Av Santa Catalina y Av Luis Quaranta, T456106. Reached by Bus No 4, 8, 15, 21, with stops along C Junín in centre, 20 mins, US$0.23, *remise* taxis charge US$2. Platforms at both levels, so check. Left luggage, Mon-Fri 0730-2100, Sat 0730-2000, US$0.35. To **Buenos Aires**, Crucero del Norte, Expreso Tigre Iguazú, Vía Bariloche, Expreso Singer, Río Uruguay, 12-13 hrs, US$17-25.

To **Mendoza**, Autotransportes Mendoza, 30 hrs, US$32. To **Tucumán**, La Nueva Estrella, Autotransportes Mendoza, 16-18 hrs, US$18-21. To **Salta**, La Nueva Estrella (change at Resistencia), 18 hrs, US$25. To **Puerto Iguazú**, Horiansky, Kruse, Expreso Singer, Aguila Dorada Bis, 5-6 hrs, US$8. Several companies run frequent services to almost all main provincial destinations, including **San Ignacio** (1 hr, US$1.30), **Oberá** (1½ hrs, US$2), **El Soberbio** (3½-4½ hrs, US$5).

To **Encarnación** (Paraguay), **Servicio Internacional**, 50 mins, US$0.65, leaving at least every half an hour from platforms 11 and 12 (lower level), tickets on bus.

If going to **Esteros del Iberá**, there are more frequent services via Corrientes to **Mercedes**. Alternatively, take **Crucero del Norte** to Paso de los Libres (beware, as this town has been reported as unsafe) and from there, any company going to Mercedes.

Car rental
Hertz, *San Lorenzo 2208 (at Guayrá travel agency)*, T433415.

Remise taxi
JC, *Entre Ríos 1945*, T431185. Nivel, *Córdoba 194*, T428500.

Encarnación *p329*
The bus terminal is at *Estigarribia y Memmel*. Buses back to Posadas leave from opposite terminal every 15 mins, *servicio común* US$1.50, *servicio diferencial* (faster service at border) US$3. Buses do not wait for formalities. Alight, keep your ticket and luggage, and catch a later bus. Taxi US$5. Boat crosses to Posadas port every hour 0800-1800, US$1 (in pesos).

San Ignacio *p331*
Buses stop in front of church, leaving every hour to **Posadas** (US$1.30) or to **Puerto Iguazú** (US$5-6) and all towns along Route 12. Don't rely on terminal at end of Av Sarmiento, as only a few stop. More buses stop on Route 12 at the access road (Av Sarmiento). **Remise taxis** stop at Av Sarmiento and San Martín.

Oberá *p334*
Bus
To **Posadas**, Horiansky, Expreso Singer, Capital del Monte, Don Tito, 1½ hrs, US$2. Capital del Monte goes also to **Campo Viera**, **Aristóbulo del Valle**, **Leandro N Alem**. Don Tito goes to **El Soberbio**.

---

❶ Directory

Posadas *p327, map p328*
Airline offices Aerolíneas Argentinas, *Ayacucho 1728*, T432889. **Banks** Banco de La Nación, *Bolívar 1799*. Round the corner on *Félix de Azara* are **Banco Río** and HSBC. Citibank, *San Martín y Colón*. Mazza, *Bolívar 1932*. For money exchange, all TCs accepted. **Communications Post Office** *Bolívar y Ayacucho*. Also **Western Union** branch. **Internet** Anyway, *Félix de Azara 2067*. Cheaper evenings and weekends. **Cyber Nick**, *San Luis 1847*. Mateando, on *Félix de Azara, next to San Martín*. US$0.35/hr. Misiol@n, *San Lorenzo 1681*. Open 24 hrs, US$0.35/hr. **Consulates** Paraguay, *San Lorenzo 179*, T423858. Mon-Fri 0730-1400. All visas in general on the same day. **Immigration** Dirección Nacional de Migraciones, *Buenos Aires 1633*, T427414. **Useful addresses Medical emergencies** Hospital Dr Ramón Madariaga, *Av L Torres 1177*, T447000.

Iguazú Falls

The Iguazú Falls are the most overwhelmingly spectacular waterfalls in South America and are justifiably one of the most popular attractions in Argentina. Situated on the Río Iguazú (in Guaraní guazú means big and I means water), 30 rivers flow into Río Iguazú before reaching the falls. The most spectacular part is the Garganta del Diablo, where the most unimaginably vast quantity of water tumbles 74 m over a horseshoe shaped precipice, and drops with a deafening roar onto basalt rocks below. In all, there are 275 falls stretching over 2.7 km wide; they're 20 m higher than Niagara and about half as wide again, causing Eleanor Rosevelt to comment, 'Poor Niagra'. With reason. These falls are far more impressive, especially since they are approached close up, through the natural splendour of their subtropical setting. The whole chasm is filled constantly with billowing clouds of mist in which great dusky swifts miraculously wheel and dart, and a perpetual rainbow hovers. Viewed from below, the gushing water falling through jungle filled with begonias, orchids, ferns and palms with toucans, flocks of parrots and cacique birds and myriad butterflies, is majestically beautiful.

66 99 The whole chasm is filled constantly with billowing clouds of mist in which great dusky swifts miraculously wheel and dart, and perpetual rainbow hovers...

Argentina shares the Falls with Brazil, and though you can visit them from either side, they are undoubtedly more impressive from the Argentine side, where you can get closer to the falls, walk in the jungle and explore the river banks. The Brazilian side has a smaller, more restricted park, gives a panoramic view but keeps you at a distance. Allow at least two days to see both sides, but if you have to choose one, make it the Argentine side. Accommodation is plentiful in the Brazilian city of Foz do Iguaçu, or the rather more charming Argentine town of Puerto Iguazú, where hotels are cheaper, and the streets are far safer. Whichever side you decide to stay on, most establishments will accept Brazilian reais, Argentine pesos or dollars. Both Argentine and Brazilian sides of the falls are described below, followed by descriptions of Puerto Iguazú, Foz do Iguaçu and the insalubrious city of Ciudad del Este just over the border into Paraguay. For Sleeping, Eating and transport, see pages 348-354.*

Ins and outs

Getting there and around The falls on both sides are contained within national parks, both of which charge entry and have well organized free transport to take you to the falls. In Argentina, park entry costs US$10, and you should allow at least a day, starting early (park opens at 0800), but if you find a brisk pace exhausting in the heat of summer, revisit the park the next day half price. A free train takes you to a flat 1-km long walkway to see the Garganta del Diablo and to two walks taking at least an hour each, with great views of the falls and a possible free boat crossing to Isla San Martín too. On the Brazilian side, park entry costs US$6.50, and a visit takes around 2 hours, with free buses taking you to the start of a walkway with steps down to the falls. On both sides there are optional extra boat trips right up to the falls themselves (Jungle Explorer on the Argentine side is best), and there are cafés and restaurants. Both parks have visitors' centres, though the Argentine Centre is far superior.

When to visit The falls can be visited all year round. There's no rainy season, and even when it rains, it's usually for no more than four days. The average summer temperatures are 25°C and in winter 15°c. The busiest times are the Argentine holiday periods, Easter week and July (book accommodation in advance), and on Sundays when helicopter tours over the falls from the Brazilian side are particularly popular (and noisy). Between October and February Argentina is one hour behind Brazil (daylight saving dates change each year) and, from December to February, one hour behind Paraguay.

History

The first European visitor to the falls was the Spaniard Alvar Núñez Cabeza de Vaca in 1542, on his search for a connection between the Brazilian coast and the Río de la Plata: he named them the *Saltos de Santa María*. Though the falls were well known to the Jesuit missionaries, they were forgotten, except by local inhabitants, until the area was explored by a Brazilian expedition sent out by the Paraguayan president, Solano López in 1863.

Parque Nacional Iguazú (Argentina)

Created in 1934, the park extends over an area of 67,620 hectares of dense sub-tropical rainforest. There is excellent access to the falls themselves from various angles and along two further trails (see below) which wind through the forest to give you an experience of the wildlife. Visits begin at the visitor centre, with free transport by mini train to the start of the walkways and trails.

Getting there

The park lies 20 km east of the town of Puerto Iguazú along Route 12, open 0800-1800 daily in winter, 0800-1900 in summer. *El Práctico* buses run from Puerto Iguazú terminal to the visitor centre every 45 minutes from 0630 to 1910, later in high season, US$1, journey time 30 minutes. You can get on or off the bus at any point in the journey. Park entrance costs US$10 for everyone apart from Argentines, who pay US$4; present your ticket if you return the next day and pay only 50%. For transport between the Argentine and Brazilian sides see under Foz and Puerto Iguazú, below.

Trails

Garganta del Diablo From the visitor centre a small gas-run train (free), the *Tren de la Selva*, whisks visitors on a 25-minute trip through the jungle to the Estacíon del Diablo, where it's a 1-km walk along walkways across the wide Río Iguazu to the

Around the Iguazú Falls

Sleeping
Bourbon 9
Carimá 10
Cataratas 4

Das Cataratas 1
Colonial 7
El Viejo Americano 5
Mabu Termas & Resort 6

Panorama 3
San Martín 8
Sheraton Iguazú 2

Not to scale

However, it's best to see the falls from a distance first, with excellent views from the two well-organized trails along two sets of sturdy catwalks: the **Circuito Superior** and **Circuito Inferior**, both taking around an hour and a half to complete. To reach these, get off the train at the Estación Cataratas (after 10-minutes journey) and walk down the **Sendero Verde** a short distance to where the trails begin.

Start with the **Circuito Superior**, a level path which takes you along the eastern-most line of falls; Saltos Bossetti, Bernabe Mandez, Mbigua (Guarani for cormorant) and San Martín, allowing you to see these falls from above. This path is safe for those with walking difficulties, wheelchairs and pushchairs, though you should wear supportive non-slippery shoes.

The **Circuito Inferior** takes you down to the water's edge via a series of steep stairs and walkways with superb views of both San Martín falls and the Garganta del Diablo from a distance. Wheelchair users, pram pushers, and those who aren't good with steps should go down by the exit route for a smooth and easy descent. You could then return to the **Estación Cataratas** to take the train to Estación Garganta, 10 past, and 40 mins past the hour, and see the falls close up.

An optional extra hour-long circuit is to take the free ferry at the very botom of the Circuito Inferior, which crosses on demand to the small hilly island Isla San Martín where trails lead to *miradores* with good close views of the San Martín Falls. Bathing on the beach here is strictly speaking not allowed.

The park offers two more trails through the forest which allow you to get closer to the wildlife: The **Sendero Macuco**, 7 km return, starting from near the visitor centre and leading to the river via a natural pool (El Pozón) fed by a slender waterfall **Salto Arrechea**, is a good place for bathing (and the only permitted place in the park). The **Sendero Yacaratia**, starts from the same place, but reaches the river by a different route, and ends at **Puerto Macuco**, where you can take the *Jungle Explorer* boat to the see the Falls themselves (see below). This trail is really for vehicles, and less pleasant to walk, best visited with *Safari en la Selva* with *Explorador Expediciones* (see below).

Park information → www.parquesnacionales.gov.ar

The **Guardería** (rangers' station) is next to the Estación Cataratas, on the way to the Circuitos Inferior and Superior. The *guardaparques* are hugely knowledgeable about the park and will give you detailed information on wildlife and where to spot it, and will even accompany you if they're not too busy. They also hand out a helpful leaflet with a clear map of the park. In the rainy season, when water levels are high, waterproof coats or swimming costumes are advisable for some of the lower catwalks and for boat trips. Cameras should be carried in a plastic bag. Wear shoes with good soles, as the walkways can be very slippery in places. At the park entrance there's an excellent **visitors' centre**, with information and photographs of the flora and fauna, as well as books for sale: Recommended are The *Laws of the Jungle* by Santiago G de la Vega, and *Iguazu Life and Colour*, both around US$6, available in English. Near the visitors' centre, there are souvenir and handicrafts shops, also selling film and drinks, toilets, a café, pizzeria and *parrilla*. Further along the Sendero Verde towards the start of the Circuitos Inferior and Superior there's a great open air café (fresh orange juice and fruit salad recommended), *locutorio* and *parrilla*, US$5 for *parrilla tenedor libre*. At the Estación Garganta, there's another little café and shop selling postcards, water and film.

Wildlife

Wildlife in the park is enormously rich, though you'll need to visit the park in the early morning or late afternoon to stand a good chance of seeing the more elusive species: pumas and tapirs, but you are more likely to see brown capuchin and howler monkeys, and coatimundi, along with many of the 400 species of birds. Among the most commonly visible are two kinds of vultures wheeling above the falls themselves, both with fringed wing tips: the red headed turkey vulture, and the black vulture whose wing tips are white. There are also the the blue-winged parrakeet, the red-rumped cacique which builds hanging nests on *pindo* palms, and fruiteaters like the magpie tanager and the colourful purple-throated euphonia. But you can't miss the Toco Toucan, with its huge orange cartoon beak, and the curious plush crested jays, black with pale yellow breasts, who perch inquisitively around the park's restaurants. Over 100 species of butterfly have been identified, among them the electric blue *morpho*, as big as your hand, the poisonous red and black *heliconius* and species of *Papilionidae* and *Pieridae*, some with immaculate black and white designs.

Activities → *For conventional tours to the park, see tour operators below*

The main activity within the park is a series of fabulous boat trips run by *Jungle Explorer*, all highly recommended. *Paseo Ecológico* takes you floating silently 3 km down the river from Estación Garganta to appreciate the wildlife on its banks: basking tortoises, caiman alligators, monkeys and birdlife. A wonderful and gentle introduction to the river; 30 mins, US$5.

Aventura Náutica, is a fast and exhilarating journey by launch along the lower Río Iguazú, from opposite Isla San Martín right up to the San Martín falls and then into the Garganta del Diablo, completely drenching passengers in the mighty spray. Great fun; not for the faint-hearted. 12 mins, US$10.

Gran Aventura combines the Aventura Nautica with a longer boat trip along rapids in the lower Río Iguazú to Puerto Macuco, followed by a jeep trip along the Yacaratiá trail (or in reverse order). 1 hour, US$24. Also recommended. Other combinations at reduced prices, and tailor-made tours. An excellent company. Tickets available at all embarcation points or at Sheraton Hotel. T421696, www.iguazujunglexplorer.com

For a great appreciation of the wildlife in the park, *Explorador Expediciones* offers two good tours in small groups: *Safari a la Cascada* which takes you by jeep to the waterfall Arrechea, stopping along the way to look at plants, bird and animal life, identifying tracks, and involving a short walk to the falls, 2hrs US$12. And *Safari en la Selva*, more in-depth interpretation of the natural life all around, in open jeeps along the longer version of the Yacatariá trail, 2 hrs, US$23. The company is run by expert guide Daniel Somay who leads excellent birdwatching trips, completely accessible for those who have never done it before, and for expert twitchers too. With incredibly rapid identification of bird calls all around, he uses a playback system, sending out

the bird call from a concealed CD and speaker to bring an amazing variety of birds to
the nearby trees. Amazing.

There are also night-time walking tours to the falls when the moon is full. The *Sheraton* also hires mountain bikes, for US$2.50 for a couple of hours. For serious birdwatching and nature walks with English-speaking guides contact, Miguel Castelino, Apartado Postal 22, Puerto Iguazú (3370), Misiones, T420157, FocusTours@aol.com

Parque Nacional Foz do Iguaçu (Brazil)

The Brazilian National Park was founded in 1939 and declared a World Heritage Site in 1986. The park covers 170,086 ha, extending along the north bank of the Rio Iguaçu, then sweeping northwards to Santa Tereza do Oeste on the BR-277. The experience is less impressive than on the Argentine side since you are not immersed in the jungle, and can't get close to the falls. ⟩⟩ *For Sleeping, Eating and transport, see pages 348-354.*

Ins and outs

Getting there It is 17 km from the city of Foz do Iguaçu to the park entrance. Buses leave Foz do Iguaçu, from the Terminal Urbana on Av Juscelino Kubitschek and República Argentina every 40 mins from 0730-1800, and are clearly marked number 400, *Parque Nacional*. You can get on or off at any point on the route past the airport and *Hotel das Cataratas*, 40 mins US$0.80 one way, payable in *reais* only. The driver waits at the Park entrance while passengers purchase entry tickets, which are checked by a park guard on the bus. Taxi US$4, plus US$5.50 per hr for waiting.

Getting around From the entrance, shuttle **buses** leave every 10-15 minutes for the 8 km journey to the falls, stopping first at the start of the Macuco Safari. From there it's another 10 minute drive to the *Hotel Tropical das Cataratas,* and a short walk to the falls.

Park information

Park information Entry is US$6.30, payable in pesos, reais, dollars or euros, and the park is open daily, apart from Monday mornings 0800-1700 in winter, and to 1800 in summer. At the entrance to the park there's a smart modern visitors centre here, with toilets, ATM, a small café and a large souvenir shop, but little information on the park or wildlife. Also a *Banco do Brasil câmbio* (0800-1900). **Best time to visit** If possible, visit on a weekday when the walks are less crowded.

Trails

The 1.2 km paved walk from *Hotel Tropical das Cataratas* to the falls is an easy walk, taking you high above the Río Iguazú, giving splendid views of all the falls on the Argentine side from a series of galleries. At the end of the path, you can walk down to a viewing point almost right under the powerful **Floriano Falls**, a dramatic view, since you're in the middle of the river. A catwalk at the foot of the Floriano Falls goes almost to the middle of the river to give a good view of the **Garganta del Diablo**. From here, there are 150 steps up to the **Porto Canoas complex** (the lift is being renovated May 2003) a quick and easy walk, but for those who find stairs difficult, you can return the way you came, and walk a little further along the road. The Porto Canoas complex consits of a big souvenir shop, toilets, a café, a fast food place (cheeseburger US$1.50) and smart restaurant (full three-course lunch US$7.30, open 1130-1600 Tue to Sun), all recommended, good value, and all with a good view of the falls above the falls. Return to the visitor centre and entrance either by the free shuttle bus, or walk back along the forest path as far as *Hotel das Cataratas*, (where you can also eat a good lunch with a view of the falls for US$13) and take the bus from there. The visit will take you around two hours, plus time for lunch.

Wildlife

Most frequently encountered are the little and red brocket deer, South American coati, white-eared opossum, and a brown capuchin monkey. Much harder to see are the jaguar, ocelot, puma, white-lipped peccary, bush dog and southern river otter. The endangered tegu lizard is common. Over 100 species of butterflies have been identified, among them the electric blue *Morpho* and the poisonous red and black *heliconius*, and the bird life is especially rewarding for the birdwatcher. Five members of the toucan family can be seen including toco and red-breasted toucans.

Tours

The *Macuco Safari Tour*, 1 hr 40 mins, US$33, leaves from the first stop on the free shuttle bus service. Ride down a 3 km-long path through the forest in open electric jeeps, and then a fast motor boat takes you close to the falls themselves, similar to *Jungle Explorer* on the Argentine side, but it's more expensive, and the guides aren't as good. Portuguese, English and Spanish spoken, take insect repellent. Helicopter tours over the falls leave from near the entrance and Parque das Aves, US$20pp, 8 minutes. Apart from disturbing visitors, they disturb bird life, and so the altitude has been increased, making the flight less attractive. Lots of companies on both sides organize conventional tours to the falls, useful more for convenience rather than information, since they collect you from your hotel. Half day, US$10, plus park entrance price.

Puerto Iguazú → *Phone code: 03757 Colour map 2, A3 Population: 19,000*

Puerto Iguazú (210 m) is an atmospheric little place, its low white buildings splashed with the red dust from roads, and bright green vegetation growing abundantly everywhere. Its houses are neat, decorated with flowers, and although the centre is slightly chaotic, the town has an appealing authentic life of its own, not dominated by

Puerto Iguazú

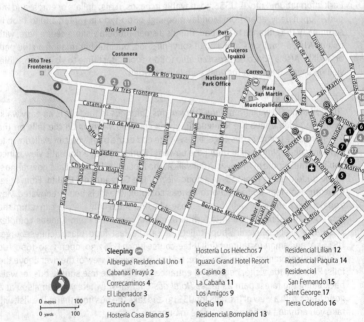

Sleeping
Albergue Residencial Uno **1**
Cabañas Pirayú **2**
Correcaminos **4**
El Libertador **3**
Esturión **6**
Hostería Casa Blanca **5**

Hostería Los Helechos **7**
Iguazú Grand Hotel Resort & Casino **8**
La Cabaña **11**
Los Amigos **9**
Noelia **10**
Residencial Bompland **13**

Residencial Lilian **12**
Residencial Paquita **14**
Residencial
San Fernando **15**
Saint George **17**
Tierra Colorado **16**

N

0 metres   100
0 yards   100

the tourist industry, and very friendly people. It's not sophisticated, but it's a pleasant place to walk around, and with several comfortable and economical places to stay, it's a much more appealing base than Foz on the Brazilian side. ▸▸ *For Sleeping, Eating and transport, see pages 348-354.*

Sights

The town's main street is Avenida Victoria Aguirre where, at No 66, you will find the **park information office**; Parque Nacional Iguazú, ① *T420382, open 0900-2200, wwww.iguazuargentina.com, in park T420180*. This avenue runs northwest from the entrance to the town to the little plaza at its hub, and changes names to Avenida Tres Fronteras as it turns east and heads to the *mirador* high above the meeting of rivers Paraná and Iguazú, the **Hito Tres Fronteras**. You can also reach this point via an attractive *costanera*, running above the Río Iguazú, past the small port where boats leave for cruises along the Paraná and to Paraguay. At the Hito, there's a string of touristy souvenir stands, where children will press you to buy orchid plants, and little rolls the local *chipita* bread. The views over the rivers and neighbouring Paraguay and Brazil are impressive, and you can enjoy them at leisure over a beer at the atmospheric *La Reserva* pub opposite, or from *La Barranca* bar further down the *costanera* (see eating page 348).

There a couple of interesting projects worth visiting for a greater appreciation of the area. **La Aripuca** ① *T423488, www.aripuca.com.ar, US$1.30, turn of Ruta 12 at km 4.5 just after Hotel Cataratas; or get off the bus here and walk 250 m*, is an inspired centre for appreciation of the native trees of the forest. Aripuca is a traditional Guaraní trap for birds, and a giant version of the pyramidic structure has been made from the fallen logs of 30 ancient trees of different species. A 30-minutes guided tour (English, Spanish or German) explains all about the tree life, and then you can clamber up their trunks, or enjoy the sculpture from enormous chairs made from tree roots. In a traditional *choza* (hut) there's excellent produce and high quality handicrafts for sale, made by the nearby Andresito community. Sponsor a living tree in the forest to protect it! Recommended.

Nearby, **Güira Oga** (Casa de los Pájaros) ① *daily 0830-1800, US$1, turn off Ruta 12 at Hotel Orquídeas Palace; T423980, mobile T15670684, and the entrance is 800 m further along the road from Aripuca*, is a sanctuary for birds that have been injured, or rescued from traffickers. Here, they are cured and reintroduced to the wild; exquisite parrots, magnificent birds of prey. A 1 km-long trail from the road winds through forest, and through the large aviaries, with families of monkeys in trees overhead. Endangered species are bred here, and eagles and hawks are taught to hunt, in an entirely self-funded family enterprise. Inspiring and informative. A guided visit in English or Spanish takes 40 mins, after which you can wander around at your leisure, and enjoy the peace of the place.

Eating ⑦
Jardín de Iguazú 1
La Esquina 3
La Rueda 5
Panificadora Real 6
Pizza Color 7
Tía Querido 8

Bars & clubs ⑦
La Barranca 2
La Reserva 4

There are short cruises along the Río Paraná with *Cruceros Iguazú① T421111, or visit the office in the park area of Puerto Iguazú, US$22, including lunch/dinner, www.crucerosiguazu.com*, visiting an indigenous Guaraní group at night, very touristy, and during the day to visit the mines at Wanda. Lunch or dinner and live musical show included. ▶▶ *For Sleeping, Eating and transport, see pages 348-354.*

Border with Brazil

This crossing via the Puente Tancredo Neves is straightforward, and if crossing on a day visit no immigration formalities are required, so you should state clearly if you need your passport stamped on re-entry for another three months in the country. Argentine immigration is at the Brazilian end of the bridge, and if entering Argentina buses stop at immigration. The Brazilian consulate is in Puerto Iguazú, Córdoba 264, T421348.

Border with Paraguay

The ferry service from the port in Puerto Iguazú to Tres Fronteras is for locals only (no immigration facilities). Crossing to Paraguay is via Puente Tancredo Neves to Brazil and then via the Puente de la Amistad to Ciudad del Este. Brazilian entry and exit stamps are not required unless you are stopping in Brazil. There is a US$3 tax to enter Paraguay. The Paraguayan Consulate is at Bompland 355.

Foz do Iguaçu (Brazil)

→ *Phone code: +55-(0)45 Colour map 2, A3 Population: 232,000*

A small modern city, Foz lies 28 km from the falls, with a wide range of accommodation and good communications by air and road with the main cities of southern Brazil and Asunción in Paraguay. It's not a particularly attractive town, and since hotels are no longer cheaper than in Argentina, it's a less appealing alternative as a base. Street crime has increased in Foz in recent years, but the inhabitants are friendly and welcoming, and there are some good places to eat. ▶▶ *For Sleeping, Eating and transport, see pages 348-354.*

Ins and outs

Getting there Buses leave Puerto Iguazú terminal for Foz do Iguaçu every 20 mins, US$2, but do not wait at the border so if you need exit and entry stamps keep your ticket and catch the next bus (bus companies do not recognize each other's tickets). Taxis between the border and Puerto Iguazú, US$15.

Tourist information The main tourist office is at Praça Getúlio Vargas 69, a small plaza at the corner of Avenida JK and Schimmelpfeng. The staff are extremely helpful and well organized, and speak English. There is a freephone tourist helpline number for information, 0700-2300, T0800 451516. There's also a tourist office at the bus terminal at the end of Avenida José María de Brito, and at the airport open for all arriving flights, with map and bus information. A newspaper, *Triplice Fronteira*, carries street plans and other tourist information. Tourists are warned not to stray from the main roads in the town, not to wear jewellery, to leave a copy of your passport in your hotel, and to avoid the river area south of Av JK. Take taxis or tours wherever possible. Av Kubitschek and the streets south of it, towards the river, have a reputation as being unsafe at night as there is a favela nearby. Take care if walking after dark.

Sights

Apart from the Parque Nacional do Iguaçu there are a couple of other attractions. The world's largest hydroelectric dam at **Lago Itaipu** ① *15 km away, T520 6999,* *www.itaipu.gov.br, buses run from outside the Terminal Urbano, Av JK and República Argentina to a village 200 m away from the visitor centre, US$0.50*, is quite a feat of human achievement, an interesting contrast to the natural wonder of the falls. A short film is shown at the visitor centre 10 mins before each guided visit, free, at 0800, 0900, 1000,1400, 1500, 1600, Mon-Sat. Check times with tourist office, and take passport. Night visits are also arranged on Fridays and Saturdays. There are also attractive artificial **beaches** on **Lake Itaipu**, good places for relaxing in the summer. The closest to Foz de Iguaçu are at **Bairro de Três Lagoas**, at Km 723 on BR-277, and in the municipality of **Santa Terezinha do Itaipu**, 34 km from Foz. These leisure parks have grassed areas with kiosks, barbecue sites and offer boat trips and fishing as well as bathing; entry US$2.50. The **Parque das Aves** ① *US$8, next to the visitor centre and park entrance at Rodovia das Cataratas Km 18, just before the falls*, contains some local and Brazilian species, but most of its beautiful caged birds are from Africa and Asia. It's a picturesque setting, particularly the butterfly house, with hummingbirds whirring about your head, but it's far more satisfying to spot birds in the wild, or at Güira Oga on the Argentine side of the falls. There's a café and shop.

Border with Paraguay

The Ponte de Amizade/Puente de Amistad (Friendship Bridge) over the Río Paraná, 12 km north of Foz, leads straight into the heart of Ciudad del Este. Crossing is very informal but keep an eye on your luggage and make sure that you get necessary stamps – so great is the volume of traffic that it can be difficult to stop, especially with

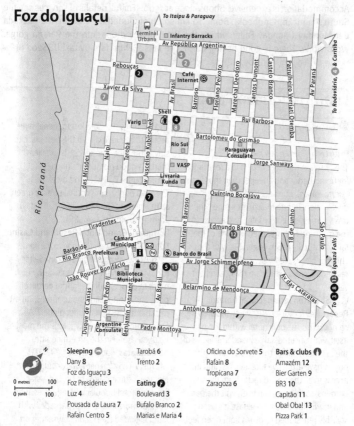

Foz do Iguaçu

the traffic police moving you on. It is particularly busy on Wednesday and Saturday, with long queues of vehicles. Pedestrians from Brazil cross on the north side of the bridge allowing easier passage on the other side for those returning with bulky packages.

Immigration Paraguayan and Brazilian immigration formalities are dealt with at opposite ends of the bridge. There is a US$3 charge to enter Paraguay. Remember to adjust your watch to local time.

Transport Buses (marked Cidade-Ponte) leave from the Terminal Urbana, Av Juscelino Kubitschek, for the Ponte de Amizade (Friendship Bridge), US$0.60. Crossing by private vehicle: if only visiting the national parks, this presents no problems. ▸▸ *For Sleeping, Eating and transport, see pages 348-354.*

Into Paraguay: Ciudad del Este

→ *Phone code: +595-(0)61 Colour map 2, A3 Population: 83,000*

Founded as Ciudad Presidente Stroessner in 1957, the city grew rapidly during the construction of the Itaipú hydroelectric project. Described as the biggest shopping centre in Latin America, it attracts Brazilian and Argentine visitors in search of bargain prices for electrical goods, watches, perfumes etc. Dirty, noisy, unfriendly and brashly commercial, you should be careful with valuables and take particular care after dark. Accommodation is expensive. Shops close at 1500. (For full details of services see the South American Handbook). Some 10 km south of Ciudad del Este are the **Cascada del Monday** (Monday Falls), where the Río Monday drops into the Paraná gorge. Worthwhile. There is good fishing below the falls. Return fare by taxi US$20. ▸▸ *For Sleeping, Eating and transport, see pages 348-354.*

Listings: Iguazú Falls

● Sleeping

Puerto Iguazú *p344, map p344*
The hotels in the city of Foz had a reputation for being better and cheaper than those in Puerto Iguazú, but since Argentina's devaluation, Puerto Iguazú is cheaper, the town is most definitely safer, and access to the more interesting Argentine side of the falls is naturally much easier. Many of the cheaper places are *residenciales* in quiet residential areas, which are really excellent value.

LL-L Sheraton Internacional Iguazú Resort, *T491800, F491810, www.sheraton. com/iguazu.* The only hotel within the park itself, with unsurpassable wonderful views of the falls from half of the stylish rooms (the others have attractive forest views) and open access to all the trails directly from the gardens, so that you can even visit the park and its wildlife before breakfast. It's been stylishly redesigned to give a light open feel,

and while it's standard international style, access to nature makes it the best place to stay in the area. The service is excellent, there's a good restaurant (lunch buffet US$9, dinner buffet US$9.50) and breakfasts. There's a pool, tennis courts, putting green, sauna, bikes for hire (US$2.50, half a day). Transfer to airport, taxi US$12.

LL Iguazú Grand Hotel Resort and Casino, *Ruta 12, km 1640, on the road to the border, T498050, www.casinoiguazu.com* 5-star luxury and elegant style in this newly built modern palace, with delightful gardens, pool, and casino. Sumptuous rooms, superb restaurant (US$17 for buffet dinner). Also a fitness centre and beauty salon. The most luxurious hotel in the Argentine side.

AL Cataratas, *Route 12, Km 4, T421100, F421090, www.fnn.net/hoteis/cataratas-ar* Not the 5 star it claims to be, but a standard modern hotel popular with agencies, who offer far more economical packages with flight included (see *Clarin* newspaper on

Sundays). There's a pool, gym and tennis courts, nightly entertainment on offer, and trips arranged to the falls.

L Esturión, *Av Tres Fronteras 650, T420100, www.hotelesturion.com on the road to Hito Tres Fronteras*. Situated above the river, with panoramic views from its pool, this 70's hotel is being completely renovated to a luxurious standard. Smart modern rooms, and great for families, with nightly entertainment, pool, tennis courts, volley ball and football.

A Saint George, *Córdoba 148, T420633, F420651, www.hotelsaintgeorge.com* The best place to stay in the town itself this is a charming family-run hotel, with very comfortable newly-decorated modern rooms grouped around a leafy pool area, attentive service and a warm relaxing atmosphere. Good restaurant *La Esquina* (see below) too. Tours arranged. Recommended.

C Hostería Casa Blanca, *Guaraní 121, 2 blocks from bus station, T421320* Good value with breakfast included, in this conveniently central, family-run place with pleasant spacious rooms.

C Hostería Los Helechos, *Amarante 76, T420338, www.hosterialoshelechos.om.ar* Another warmly welcoming place, this popular *hostería* has a relaxed easy-going atmosphere and friendly owners, nicely maintained rooms, and a pool. Good value.

D Residencial Lilian, *Beltrán 183, T420968.* One of the most charming *residenciales*, this is impeccably-maintained with bright modern rooms, in a quiet location, just 2 blocks from bus terminal, with breakfast included, and helpful owners.

D Residencial Paquita, *Córdoba 731, opposite the bus terminal, T420434*. An old-fashioned but rather appealing place, some rooms with balcony, all with bathrooms and air conditioning.

D Residencial San Fernando, *Córdoba y Guaraní, near terminal, T421429*. A popular place, and good value, with bathrooms, and breakfast included.

D Tierra Colorada, *Córdoba y El Urú 28, T420572*. One of the most appealing options this is located in a lovely quiet area, with comfortable rooms, and a welcoming atmosphere; breakfast included.

F pp Noelia, *Fray Luis Beltrán 119, T420729.* Also very welcoming, this is a beautifully neat house with pleasant rooms, a lovely garden, and friendly family attention, good value with bathrooms, and breakfast included. Recommended.

F pp Bompland, *Av Bompland 33, T420965.* Conveniently central and family-run place, with decent rooms.

Youth hostels

An ever growing number, most charge US$3.50pp per night in shared dorms. If there are two of you, you might find a *residencial* more comfortable, and only slightly more expensive. Two hostels stand above the rest:

Residencial La Cabaña, *on the costanera at Tres Fronteras 434, T420564, F420393, iguazu@hostels.org.ar* A very well run attractive *residencial* with chalet-style main building and welcoming spaces to sit and eat in, and good rooms. Highly recommended.

Residencial Los Amigos, Fray Luis Beltrán 82, T420756. A lovely quiet spot with well maintained comfortable rooms, very wecoming and well run.

Albergue Residencial Uno, *Beltrán 116, T420529, albergueuno@iguazunet.com* If the best options, above, are full, this slightly institutional, but clean and friendly *hostal* has accommodation in rooms for 2 to 8, areas to cook, and wash (but no machine), and tours and activities arranged.

Correcaminos, *Amarante 48, T420967, www.correcaminos.com.ar* A new place with bright open sitting area, and neat rooms, kitchen, bar and games room, this also has doubles for US$4.20 each. Friendly atmosphere.

Cabañas

C Pirayú, *Av Tres Fronteras 550, on the way to the Hito, T420393, www.pirayu.com.ar* A beautifully built complex of comfortable and well-equipped cabañas, with lovely river views, and sports of all kinds, lots of games for children, attractive pool, and entertainment. Recommended.

 For an explanation of the sleeping and eating price codes used in this guide, see the inside front cover. Other relevant information is provided in the Essentials chapter, page 44.

El Viejo Americano, *Ruta 12, km 3,5,
T420190, www.viejoamericano.com.ar*
The town's best site with 3 pools in pleasant,
nicely tended wooded gardens, 3 km from
town, and *cabañas* and a hostel too,
camping US$1.50 per person, food shop,
electricity, games area, pool, barbecue
places. Recommended.

Parque Nacional Foz do Iguaçu *p343,
map p340*
There is a good selection of hotels and many
also offer excursions to the falls; the excellent
tourist office has a full list.

L-AL Tropical das Cataratas, *directly
overlooking the falls, 28 km from Foz,
T5217000, www.tropicalhotel.com.br* Elegant
pale pink colonial-style building with a pool
in luxuriant gardens, where you might spot
wildlife at night and early morning. The
rooms are disappointingly plain and sombre,
but there's a small terrace with views of the
falls to the front of the hotel, and a
restaurant, also open to non-residents; lunch
and dinner buffet, US$14 also à la carte
dishes and dinner with show.
On the road to the airport and falls (Rodovia
das Cataratas) are:
L Bourbon, *Av.das Cataratas, km 2,5, T529
0123, F529 0000, Toll free: 0800451010,
www.bourbon.com.br* Very smart hotel,
serving excellent buffet dinner, also open to
non-residents (US$12).
L Mabu Termas & Resort, *Av das Cataratas,
KM 3,5-Vila Carimã, T 521-2000, F529-6361,
www.hoteismabu.com.br* An impressive
new resort, a fabulous complex of swimming
pools and spas in attractive gardens.
Recommended.
L San Martin, *Av das Cataratas, km 17, T529
8088, www.hotelsanmartin.com.br*
TV, pool, sports, nightclub, several eating
options, comfortable.
A Carimã, *Av das Cataratas, km 10, Vila
Carimã, T521 3000, www.carima .com.br* A
huge comfortable 4-star, with pool,
restaurant, bars. Very good value.
A Colonial, *Colonial Iguaçu & Spa Hotel, Av
das Cataratas, km 16, T529 7711, F529 7732,
www.colonialhotel.com.br* 1 km from the

airport, pool, fine location, price includes
breakfast and mediocre dinner, packages
including transport and tours can be booked
with a good discount at hotel booking office
at the airport.
A Panorama, *Km 12, T4523 1200, F523 1456.*
Good value, pool.

Foz do Iguaçu centre *p346, map p347*
A Suiça, *Felipe Wandscheer 3580, Jardim São
Paulo, T525 3232, 525 3044, www.hotelsuica
.com.br* It's a little far out of the city, but 2
buses go there, and it's a charming place,
helpful with tourist info, and a pool.
B Foz do Iguaçu, *Av Brasil, 97 T523 4455,
F574 1775, www.hotelfozdoiguacu.com.br*
A smart well-decorated place, with attractive
pool and terrace, well-designed rooms, and
good value.
B Rafain Centro, *Mcal Deodoro 984,
T/F5231213.* Very comfortable and handy for
the airport, with a good restaurant, and pool.
B Recanto Park, *Av Costa e Silva, 3500 Alto
São Francisco T522 3000, F522 3000,
www.recantoparkhotel.com.br* Comfortable
rooms, well decorated, with a decent
restaurant, coffee shop, pool, sauna, popular
with agency groups, but retains a luxurious
feel, with good attention from the staff.
Good value.
C Dany, *Av Brasil, 509, T523 1530.*
Comfortable, a/c, TV, good buffet breakfast.
C Foz Presidente, *Rua Xavier da Silva, 1000,
T572 4450, F572 4450 www.fozpresidente
hoteis.com.br* Slightly old-fashioned now,
but this is still good value, decent rooms, a
restaurant, a small swimming pool, with
breakfast, convenient for buses.
D Luz, *Av Gustavo Dobrandino da Silva, 145.
T522 3535, F522 3535, www.luzhotel.com.br*
Recommended for a good value small hotel.
D San Remo, *Rua Xavier da Silva, 563, T523
1619, F523 5120.* Rooms with a/c, good
breakfast. Recommended.
D Pousada Evelina Navarrete, *Rua Irlan
Kalichewski, 171, Vila Yolanda, T574 3817,
F574 3817.* Lots of tourist information,
English, French, Italian, Polish and Spanish
spoken, helpful, good breakfast and location,
near *Chemin* Supermarket, near Av Cataratas
on the way to the falls. Recommended.

● **Phone codes** Puerto Iguazú+ 03757; Brazil Foz do Iguaçu +55-(0)45; Paraguay Ciudad
● del Este +595-(0)61.

D **Pousada da Laura**, *Rua Naipi, 671, Centro,
T572 3374/574 3628*. An enduringly popular
central place, offering a good breakfast, hot
water, bathroom, kitchen, laundry facilities,
and a friendly atmosphere, a perfect place to
meet other travellers. Times were tough at
the time of writing and Laura is thinking of
selling. Spanish, English, Italian and French
spoken, excellent.

D **Tarobá**, *Rua Tarobá, 1048 T523 9722, F574
2402, www.hoteltaroba.com.br* Highly
recommended, as a good value central
place, with a/c, a small indoor pool, good
breakfast. Recommended.

E **Trento**, *Rua Rebouças, 829, Centro, CEP:
85851-190, T574 5111*. The cheapest option
in town, A/c, with bath, without breakfast,
noisy, but recommended.

Youth hostels

F pp **Paudimar Campestre**, *Av das
Cataratas, km 12,6, Remanso Grande, T529
6061, F529 6061, Ramal 14,
www.paudimar.com.br* From airport or town
take Parque Nacional bus (0530-0100) and
get out at Remanso Grande bus stop, by
Hotel San Juan, then take the free shuttle bus
(0700-1900) to the hostel, or 1.2 km walk
from main road. IYHA, camping as well, pool,
soccer pitch, quiet, kitchen and communal
meals, breakfast, telephone, fax and internet
for use of guests. Very friendly and highly
recommended. For assistance, ask for Gladis.
Tours organized to either side of the falls. In
high season IYHA members only. Note, the
central branch of Paudimar youth hostel has
closed.

Camping

Camping is not permitted by the *Hotel das
Cataratas* and Falls. Sleeping in your car
inside the park is also prohibited. It can be
pretty cold and humid in winter.

Camping Pousada Internacional, *Manêncio
Martins, 600 m from turn off, T523 8183*.
For vehicles and tents, helpful staff, English,
German and Spanish spoken, pool
restaurant, recommended.

Camping Clube do Brasil, *by the National
Park entrance 17 km from Foz, T529 9206
US$10 per person (half with International
Camping Card)*. Clean, pool, no restaurant,
closes at 2300.

● Eating

Puerto Iguazú *p344, map p344*

$ **Jardín de Iguazú**, *Córdoba y Misiones, at
the bus terminal*. A good range of local and
Chinese food, tenedor libre, very good.

$ **La Esquina**, *on the corner of Av Córdoba
148*. Also very good, with a buffet, delicious
beef, and local fish. Warm friendly service.

$ **La Rueda**, *Córdoba 28*. The most appealing
option in town, this has a warm and lively
atmosphere inside a rustic cabin, with
mellow live music, and delicious food
throughout the superb menu, including
well-prepared locally caught *surubí* and *pacú*
fish, steaks and pastas. Great service .

$ **Panificadora Real**, *Córdoba y Guaraní*.
Excellent bread, another branch at *Victoria y
Brasil* in the centre. Try the local *chipita*.

$ **Pizza Color**, *Córdoba y Amarante*. Popular
with locals, this is great for pizzas, and also
parrilla. Reasonably priced.

Foz do Iguaçu *p346, map p347*

Many restaurants stay open till midnight and
accept a variety of currencies. There are lots
of restaurants along Av JK.

$$$ **Bufalo Branco**, *Rebouças 530*.
Sophisticated surroundings and attentive
service, and a superb all-you-can-eat
churrasco for US$15, including filet mignon,
bull's testicles, and a good salad bar.

$$$ **Rafain**, *das Cataratas, Km 6.5, T523 1177*.
A touristy but entertaining affair, extravaganza
with live folklore music from all over South
America, dancing, and buffet. US$12.

$$ **Galletos**, *Av JK and Jorge Sanwais*. Good
food, on a weigh-and-pay basis, tasty and
good value. Recommended.

$$ **Marias e Maria**, *Brasil 50*. Good
confeitaria with warm lively atmosphere.

$$ **Oficina do Sorvete**, *Kubitschek 553*. Very
good ice cream, cakes, and soup in winter.

$$ **Tropicana**, *Juscelino Kubitschek 228*. Pizza
or *churrascaria* with salad bar, good value.

$$ **Zaragoza**, *Quintino Bocaiúva 882, T4574
3084*. Large and upmarket for Spanish dishes
and seafood, recommended.

$ **Boulevard**, *Av das Cataratas 1118*. Bowling
and other entertainments, with a food court
open from 1700, all day Sun.

$ **Barbarela's**, *Av Brasil 1119B*. Excellent juice
and sandwich bar, friendly and popular
place.

🍸 Bars and nightclubs

Puerto Iguazú *p344, map p344*
Around Hito Tres Fronteras, the landmark above the meeting of the rivers,
La Reserva pub is a great place for an evening drink or dinner, in a big wooden building, with a warm atmosphere, good live music. Further down the *costanera*,
La Barranca has great views onto the river Iguazú, for a younger trendier crowd, louder live music, very popular from 2200 onwards. Next to it, there's a great little pizza place, serving *pizzas a piedra* at tables outside with views over the rivers, great in summer when it's warm at nights, and extremely popular.

Foz do Iguaçu *p346, map p347*
There are lots of bars concentrated along the two blocks of Av Jorge Schimmelpfeng from Av Brasil to R Mal Floriano Peixoto. Wed and Sun are the best nights.
Bier Garten, *no 550*. Pizzeria and *choparia*, beer garden in name only, but there are some trees, and a lively rowdy atmosphere in peak season, as this is hugely popular.
Pizza Park, *opposite Bier Garten* on Av Jorge Schimmelpfeng, open from 2000 onwards. Good pizzas in a lively atmosphere, popular with tourists and residents alike.
BR3, *corner with Av Brasil*. Modern barbecue, open 'til 2400.
Oba! Oba!, *das Cataratas 370, T529 6596, (Antigo Castelinho)*. Live samba show Mon-Sat 2315-0015, very popular, US$11 for show and one drink. Also known as *Coopershow*.
Rafain Cataratas, *das Cataratas Km 6.5*. With floor show and *Churrascaria* dinner, see above.
Capitão Bar, *Schimmelpfeng 288 y Almte Barroso*. Large, loud and popular nightspot for drinks, nightclub attached.
Amazém, *R Edmundo de Barros 446*. Intimate and sophisticated, attracts discerning locals, good atmosphere, mellow live music, US$1 cover, recommended.

🔄 Tour operators

Puerto Iguazú *p344, map p344*
Trips to an open mine for semi-precious stones at Wanda, 60 km away, half day,

US$10, to the Jesuit ruins at San Ignacio Miní 250 km away, full day US$20, though these are more easily visited from Posadas. The new Duty-Free Shop is included on some itineraries to the Brazilian side of the falls, though it's hardly a tourist destination, it's a large flash indoor mall between the two customer points, which has yet to fill up with Duty-Free goods and shops. Perfumes and cosmetics, spirits and cigarettes at reduced prices, and a small range of hi hi, but that's about it. Open 1000-2100.
For operators within the park, contact **Jungle Explorer**, *T421696, www.iguazu jungleexplorer.com* and **Explorador Expediciones**, *T421600, T15673318, www.rainforestevt.com.ar www.exploradorexpediciones@bigfoot.com* Both can be booked at the *Sheraton Hotel*, also run 2-day expeditions in 4WDs with expert guides to the otherwise inaccessible Saltos de Moconá on the southern edge of Misiones, 3 km of unending waterfalls up to a height of 20 m. Also superb and expert birdwatchin. Email in advance.
Turismo Cuenca del Plata, *Amarante 76, T421062, cuencadelplata@cuenca delplata.com* Conventional tours to the falls, and a half day trip to a Guaraní village, Fortín M'Bororé, with just-for-tourists display of indigenous Guaraní life, interesting but very touristy, US$9.
Aguas Grandes, *Mariano Moreno 58, T421140, www.aguasgrandes.com.ar* Runs conventional tours to both sides of the falls and Iguazú Forest, a half-day of activities in the forest, including 4WD, some nature explanation, a short trek, – 'flying' through the forest on wires suspended between trees and abseiling down a waterfall, US$15, good fun.
Cabalgatas por la Selva, *Ruta 12, just after the Rotonda for the road to the international bridge, mobile T15542180*. Highly recommended for 3-hour horse riding trips in the forest, US$12.

Foz do Iguaçu *p346, map p347*
Beware of overcharging for tours by touts at the bus terminal. There are many tour operators on Av Brasil.
Caribe Tur at the international airport and **Hotel das Cataratas**, and **Hotel Bourbon**, T523 1612, run tours from the airport to the Argentine side and **Hotel das Cataratas**,

STTC Turismo, **Hotel Bourbon**, *Rodovia das Cataratas, T529 8580*. Cruises on the Río Paraná, with dinner and show, *T03757 421111, ventas@crucerosiguazu.com*

Iguazú Falls *p338, map p340*
4 Star South America T1-800-747-4540 (US), 0871-711-5370 (UK), +49-700-4444-7827 (Rest of world). 4starSouthAmerica.com (tour operator) 4starFlights.com (flight consolidator). Over 400 escorted scheduled tours.

⊖ Transport

Puerto Iguazú *p344, map p344*
Air
The airport is some 20 km southeast of Puerto Iguazú near the falls, T422013. A bus service runs between airport and bus terminal to connect with plane arrivals and departures, US$3. Check times at *Aerolíneas Argentinas* office. Taxis charge US$10 to *Hotel Sheraton*, and around US$15 to **Puerto Iguazú**, US$14 to **Foz do Iguaçu** and US$25 to the **Brazilian airport**. *Aerolíneas*

Argentinas flies direct to **Buenos Aires**, 1hr 40mins, flights fill up fast in summer, Easter and July.

Bus
Terminal *Av Córdoba y Av Misiones*, has a *locutorio*, restaurant, various tour company desks (see below) and bus company offices. Bus terminal information *T423006, T421916 (Crucero del Norte)*. To **Buenos Aires**, 16 hrs, Tigre Iguazú, ViaBariloche, daily, US$28 *semi cama*. To **Posadas**, stopping at San Ignacio Miní, hourly, 5 hrs, US$8. To **San Ignacio Miní**, US$6.50 *servicio común*. Agencia de Pasajes Noelia, *local 3, T422722*, can book tickets beyond Posadas for other destinations in Argentina, ISIC discounts available.

Car hire
Avis at airport. **Localiza**, at airport and *Aguirre 279, T0800-9992999*. Cars may be taken to the Brazilian side for an extra US$5.

Taxi
T420973. Fares: to **airport** US$10, to

Argentine falls US$15, to **Brazilian falls** US$20, to **centre of Foz** US$15, to **Ciudad del Este** US$20, to **Itaipu** US$30 return, to **Wanda gem mines** with wait US$35.

Border with Paraguay *p321*
Direct **buses** (non-stop in Brazil), leave Puerto Iguazú terminal every 30 mins, US$2, 45 mins, liable to delays especially in crossing the bridge to **Ciudad del Este**. **Taxi** from Puerto Iguazú to **Ciudad del Este**, US$70 one way.

Foz do Iguaçu *p346, map p347*
Air
Iguaçu international airport *18 km south of town near the Falls, T521 4200.* In Arrivals is *Banco do Brasil* and *Caribe Tours e Câmbio,* car rental offices, tourist office and an official taxi stand, US$1210 to town. All buses marked Parque Nacional, no 400, pass the airport in each direction, US$0.50 to anywhere around town, allows backpacks but not lots of luggage. Many hotels run minibus services for a small charge. Daily flights to **Rio de Janeiro, São Paulo, Curitiba** and other Brazilian cities.

Bus
For transport to the falls see above under Parque Nacional Foz do Iguaçu.
Long distance terminal (Rodoviária) *Av Costa e Silva, 4 km from centre on road to Curitiba, T522 2590;* bus to centre, any bus that says 'Rodoviária', US$0.65. Book departures as far in advance as possible. As well as the tourist office, open 0630-1800, there is a *Cetreme* desk for tourists who have lost their documents, *Guarda Municipal* (police) and luggage store. To **Curitiba**, Pluma, Sulamericana, 9-11 hrs, paved road, US$15. To **Guaíra** via Cascavel only, 5 hrs, US$10. To **Florianópolis**, Catarinense and Reunidas, US$22, 16 hrs; Reunidas to **Porto Alegre**, US$28. To **São Paulo**, 16 hrs, new buses Kaiowa, and Pluma US$28, *executivo* 6 a day, plus one *leito*. To **Rio** 22 hrs, several daily, US$38. To **Asunción**, Pluma, RYSA (direct at 1430), US$11.

Car hire
Localiza at the *airport, T523 4800, Av Juscelino Kubitschek 2878, T522 1608,* and *Rodovia das Cataratas Km 2.5,* in *Hotel Bourbon,* (see above).

❶ Directory

Puerto Iguazú *p344, map p344*
Airline offices Aerolíneas Argentinas, *Brasil y Aguirre, T420194, 420036.*
Banks ATMs at **Macro Misiones** and **Banco Nación**, both open 0800-1300 and if machine is empty you may have to wait until the next day for cash. TCs can only be changed at **Cambio Libre** in the *Hito Tres Fronteras,* open 0800-2200.
Communications Telecom, *Victoria Aguirre y Los Cedros.* Internet too.
Internet Several places at the town's hub, Aguirre and Brasil, opposite tourist office.
Embassies and consulates Brazilian, *Av Córdoba 264, T421348.*

Foz do Iguaçu *p346, map p347*
Airline offices Rio Sul, and Varig, *J Sanways 779;* TAM, *T574 6080,* (free transport to **Ciudad del Este** for its flights, all border documentation dealt with); Varig, *Kubitschek 463, T523 2111;* Vasp, *Brasil 845, T523 2212 (airport T529 7161).* **Banks** There are plenty of banks and travel agents on Av Brasil. Banco do Brasil, *Brasil 1377.* Has ATM, high commission for TCs. HSBC, *Av Brasil 1151,* MasterCard ATM. Bradesco, *Brasil 1202. Banco 24 Horas* at Oklahoma petrol station. Itaú ATM at *Kubitschek e Bocaiúva* and airport. Exchange at **Vento Sul**, *Av Brasil 1162,* no TCs. Also Corimeira, *Av Brasil 248.*
Communications Post office *Praça Getúlio Vargas 72.* **Telephone** Posto 1, *Edmundo de Barros 281.* **Internet** Net pub @, *Av JK and Rua Rui Barbosa 549,* Zipfoz.com, *R Barão do Rio Branco 412 and Av JK, Smart, a/c,* US$2.50 per hour. Fast but noisy at L@n Zone, *Calçadão y Brasil.*
Embassies and consulates Argentine, *Travessa Eduardo Bianchi 26, T574 2969,* open Mon-Fri 1000-1430.

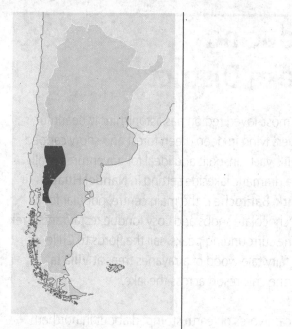

The Lake District

Introducing the Lake District

Argentina's most-loved region has astonishingly beautiful lakes and rivers lying in deep green forest and snow capped mountains. It's vast, unspoilt and ideal for adventures of all kinds. With a dramatic lakeside setting in **Nahuel Huapi National Park**, **Bariloche** is the main centre, popular for its chalet-style chocolate shops and cosy fondue restaurants. Trek for days in the surrounding peaks, sail the fjords to Chile, or wander the fairy tale wood of arrayanes trees at **Villa la Angostura**, the chic resort across the lake.

The largest carnivores on earth stomped about in northern **Neuquén** and you'll be awe-struck by their footprints, perfectly preserved. In tranquil **Pehuenia**, ancient monkey puzzle trees still exert a mysterious force, their silent forests by mirror-calm lakes. **Parque Nacional Lanín's** perfect cone of a volcano turns every snapshot into a Japanese woodcut. Climb to the top for a challenging hike, or admire its reflection in the navy blue waters of **Lago Paimún**. For hiking, biking and lying on beaches, **San Martín de los Andes** is an appealing base, sitting on one end of **Lago Lacar**, and at less touristy **Junín de los Andes**, you could wade into **Río Chimehuin**, and hook a magnificent rainbow trout. **El Bolsón** is so laid back, you need do nothing but sample the local cerveza. But hike up the surrounding mountains and take a dip in turquoise rivers: the views are breathtaking. Follow Butch and Sundance and hide out in sleepy **Cholila** or take the old **Patagonian Express** from pioneer town **Esquel**. Set off into magnificent **Los Alerces** national park, where forested mountains drop steeply into pristine lakes, and as you enjoy the silence of emerald **Lago Verde** you may wonder if you need ever go home.

★ Don't miss...

❶ **Río Manso** Raft down the rushing waters, page 411.

❷ **Bellevue Tea Rooms** Sample the best chocolate cake in the lakes with amazing views, page 403.

❸ **Pampa Linda** Blissful hiking along Paso de los Nubes, page 410.

❹ **Lago Menéndez** Take a boat trip to see 2,600 year old alerce trees and the jade green Lago Cisne, page 418.

❺ **Cerro Otto** Experience the panoramic views over Lago Nahuel Huapi, page 397.

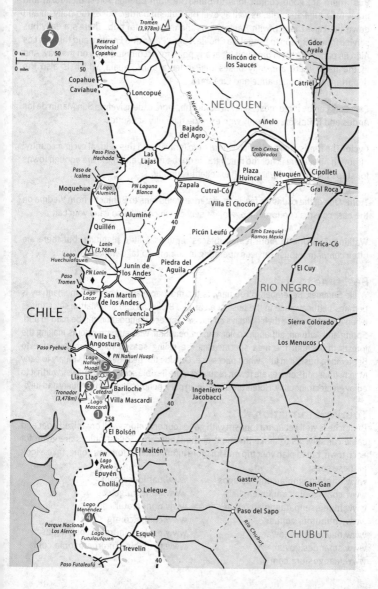

Ins and outs

Getting there

→ *The Lakes are well connected to the rest of the country by many means of transport*

Air There are airports at Bariloche, Esquel and San Martín de los Andes, all receiving daily flights from Buenos Aires. In addition, the army airline *LADE* runs weekly flights connecting Bariloche with other Patagonian towns, and *American Falcon* runs cheap flights in summer to Puerto Madryn and Buenos Aires.

Bus There are good connections to Bariloche from Buenos Aires, Mendoza, and many towns in Patagonia, as well as over the Chilean border. Buses run daily up and down the Lake District, with Bariloche as the most useful hub. There's a daily bus service from El Bolsón to Esquel via Cholila, Lagos Puelo and Epuyen, and through Los Alerces park, which will drop you off at any point for accommodation on the way. And in the north there are daily buses to Pehuenia from Zapala, which is also the departure point for Copahue and Caviahue.

Car Cars can be hired most easily in Bariloche, more expensively in San Martín de los Andes and El Bolsón, and only with extreme difficulty at Esquel.

Cycle The roads are good, even where *ripio* (gravel) and this is ideal cycling country: although hilly, there is not too much traffic on the roads, and there are enough towns for stops for food and water, with excellent camping.

Train One of the country's few long-distance trains runs to Bariloche from Viedma on the east coast, a comfortable overnight service which will also carry your car.

Walking Trekking to more remote places requires a little planning, but there are often *combi* (minibus) services operating in summer to take walkers around.

Best time to visit

While **Summer**, December to February, is the most appealing time to come, January is perhaps better avoided in the busiest areas like Bariloche and San Martín, since this is when Argentines take their holidays *en masse*, and accommodation can be hard to find. **Spring** and **Autumn**, although cooler, can be beautiful, with autumn colours making the forests throughout the area spectacular. The **skiing season** runs from late June to September, busiest in July, when prices rise. Outside the peak season of January to early March, transport services are fewer, requiring more flexible schedules, but well worth it to enjoy greater tranquility. Hotels are all pricier in peak periods, highest in January and July.

Tourist information

Bariloche is well set up for tourism with good tour operators, well organized boat and cable car services to make the most of the landscape. Tourist offices are given for each town, but to plan your trip and for more information before you come, take a look at these sites:

www.interpatagonia.com/loslagos/
www.cpatagonia.com (In English)
www.hotelesenpatagonia.com.ar
www.chubutour.com.ar
www.neuquentur.gov.ar
www.smandes.gov.ar
www.laangostura.com

www.bariloche.com
www.rionegro.gov.ar
www.rionegrotur.com.ar
www.chapelco.org
www.patagonia-travel.com/ingles
www.fly-fishing.interpatagonia.com

Neuquén Province

The province of Neuquén contains the northern part of the Lake District, encompassing an enormous region from just north of Bariloche to beyond Copahue and Caviahue, ending at the border with Mendoza. The warmer eastern region around the city of Neuquén is an important fruit-growing area, providing most of Argentina's apples, pears and grapes. The province is rich in natural beauty and immensely varied, from the arid Copahue in the north, through the araucaria forests of Pehuenia to the dense Valdivian rainforest on the mountains around Huechulafquen and the Bosque de las Arrayanes at Villa La Angustura. Inevitably, such greenery doesn't come without rainfall, and it's wetter the closer you are to the Andes.

Apart from all the opportunities for fishing and adventurous activities in the province, there are thrilling encounters with dinosaurs at several sites easily reached from Neuquén. There are incredibly huge dinosaur footprints at Villa El Chocón, and you'll want to see the skeleton in the museum there as proof that the hugest carnivores ever known actually stomped around these lands 100 million years ago. The area's rich Mapuche culture is starting to be appreciated and even promoted. There are many Mapuche communities around Pehuenia, welcoming visitors to try tasty homecooked food, and around Lagos Paimún and Huechulafquen, you can buy pan casero (home made bread) and tortas fritas from the Mapuches who run the campsites. The Mapuche community at Quila Quina, a short boat trip from San Martín de los Andes, is worth visiting for the lovely setting alone. The gateway to the province is its provincial capital, the pleasant modern city of Neuquén.

Neuquén City and around

→ *Phone code: 0299 Colour map 5, A3 Population: 260,000*

The provincial capital is at its eastern tip, an attractive industrial town, founded in 1904, just after the arrival of the railway. It's on the opposite side of the Río Neuquén from Cipolletti, a prosperous centre of the Río Negro fruit-growing region and while it has no major tourist attractions, it's a useful stopping point for the Lakes, but it's also a good base for exploring the dinosaur finds in the area to the immediate southwest.

Ins and outs

Getting there There are daily flights from Buenos Aires to the airport 7 km west of town, T444 0245. Take a local bus into town for US$0.40 (*tarjeta* bus card needed), or taxi US$4. There are frequent long-distance buses to the central terminal at Mitre 147 from Buenos Aires and towns throughout the lake district as well as north to Mendoza, and west to Chile. No terminal number, but these are useful companies: **Andesmar** T442 2216, **Via Bariloche** T442 7054.

Getting around The town can easily be explored on foot in a few hours, with most hotels and restaurants around the main street Avenida Argentina, which runs north from the disused railway track running east-west across the town, just south of Gral San Martín. Don't get confused with the street Félix San Martín, three blocks further south.

Tourist information ① *Félix San Martín 182, T442 4089, www.neuquentur.gov.ar, turismo@neuquen.gov.ar, daily Mon-Fri 0700-2000, Sat-Sun 0800-2000.* They hand out helpful lists of accomodation and a map.

At the northern end of Av Argentina at the Parque Centenario there is the **Mirador Balcon del Valle** with panoramic views over the city and the confluence of the rivers (be sure not to take the bus to Centenario industrial suburb). In the university buildings at the entrance of the park is the **Museo Paleontológico de Ciencias Naturales**, Argentina 1400, (temporarily closed in 2003) which includes exhibitions of dinosaur fossils found in the region. The former railway station, at Olascoaga y Pasaje Obligado, has been converted into a cultural centre and exhibition centre. The **Museo de la Ciudad Paraje Confluencia**, Independencia y Córdoba, T442 9785, has a small display on the Campaign of the Desert, colonial annihilation of indigenous groups, (see box, page 118). South of the centre there is also a pleasant walk along the Río Limay. Facing Neuquén and connected by bridge is **Cipolletti**, in Río Negro province, a prosperous fruit-growing centre of the region. All the towns in the valley celebrate the *Fiesta Nacional de la Manzana* (apples are the main local crop) in the second half of March. ▶▶ *For Sleeping, Eating and other listings, see pages 363-365.*

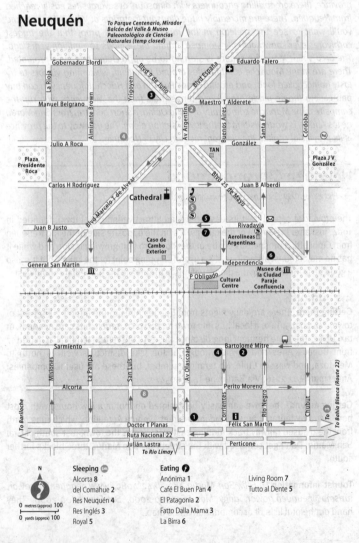

Neuquén

To Parque Centenario, Mirador Balcón del Valle & Museo Paleontológico de Ciencias Naturales (temp closed)

Sleeping 🛏
Alcorta **8**
del Comahue **2**
Res Neuquén **4**
Res Inglés **3**
Royal **5**

Eating 🍴
Anónima **1**
Café El Buen Pan **4**
El Patagonia **2**
Fatto Dalla Mama **3**
La Birra **6**

Living Room **7**
Tutto al Dente **5**

N
0 metres (approx) 100
0 yards (approx) 100

Lago Pellegrini, 36 km north, is an artificial lake, popular in the summer for various watersports, and a good place to spend the day, with restaurants and picnic areas. 40 km northwest, **Embalse Cerro Colorado** is another artificial lake where there are artificial and natural swimming pools (take a tour, or the bus marked 'Banda del Medio' from terminal). North of the lake is **Añelo**, where there is an archaeological museum, and a Mapuche community. There are daily buses to each area from Neuquén's terminal.

West of Neuquén

To the southwest of Neuquén lies the huge **Embalse Ezequiel Ramos Mexía** in an area wihich has become famous in recent years for the wealth of dinosaur fossils found here from the Cretacic period (100 million years ago). There are a number of places where you can see the finds, and even walk in the footsteps of dinosaurs, and although the towns themselves are not appealing, they could make convenient stopping points along the road from Neuquén to the lakes.

Villa El Chocón and around → *Phone code 0299 Colour map 5, A3*

Villa El Chocón lies at the northern end of the lake 72 km from Neuquén, on the most direct road from Neuquén to Bariloche. It's a neat, rather uninspiring town, a strictly functional place built for workers on the hydroelectric dam, but worth a stop for the amazing evidence of **dinosaurs** ① *take Route 237 towards Piedra del Aguila, and turn left at Barrio Llanquén, where indicated, to the lake shore.* Red sedimentary rocks have preserved, in relatively good condition, bones and even footprints of the creatures which lived in this region during the Cretaceous period about 100 million years ago. Some of these can be seen in the **Museo Paleontológico Ernesto Bachmann** ① *in the civic centre of Villa El Chocón, T490 1223, open daily 0900-1900 winter 0800-2100 summer; guides in museum give very good tours. See also www.interpatagonia.com/paseos /ernestobachmann for more information in English.* Exhibits include fossils of the mighty 10-ton, 15-m long *Gigantosaurus Carolinii*, a carnivorous dinosaur larger than the more famous Tyrannosaurus Rex. There's a well laid out and informative display with information on these quite mind-boggling finds. *Aventura Jurásica*, in El Chocón (Alejandro París, T490 1243) offers guided visits to the museum and the surroundings from US$3 pp not including transfers, (two to three hours).

In the **Valle Cretacico**, 18 km south of Villa El Chocón, near the Dique with its pedestals of eroded pink rock, there are two walks beside the lake to see the dinosaur footprints, amazingly well preserved. ►► *For Sleeping, Eating and other listings, see pages 363-365.*

Route to the lakes

From Neuquén, there are various ways to approach the lakes. An attractive route involves continuing due west to Zapala on the RN22, and then south to Junín de los Andes on Rn40. From Zapala, continue west to Villa Pehuenia, or north to Caviahue and Copahue.

For the direct route to Bariloche, continue along the RN237, where you could stop for a break at the next settlement, the one-horse town of **Piedra del Aguila** (clean loos, kiosk and cafeteria). Then 100 km from Bariloche, the road starts to wind through the astounding scenery of the **Valle Encantado**, mountains whipped into jaggy peaks rising surprisingly from rolling scrubby land, and Rio Limay appears, a mysterious milky turquoise as it flows into Embalse Alicura. Entering the valley itself, the road runs close to the water as above you rocks are stacked up high, eroded into fantastical shapes. A beautiful introduction to the lakes. The road continues to Lago Nahuel Huapi where there are fine views over Cerros Catedral and Tronador. ►► *For Sleeping, Eating and other listings, see pages 363-365.*

Dinosaurs

Few countries are as important as Argentina for palaeontologists. The relative abundance of fossils near the surface has made the country one of the most important for the study of dinosaur evolution. The **Ischigualasto** and **Talampaya** parks (of San Juan and La Rioja respectively) have yielded rich evidence of dinosaurs from the Triassic period (225-180 million years ago). Among them is the small *Eoraptor lunensis*, 220 million years old, considered one of the oldest found anywhere in the world. If you're lucky, your Ischigualasto tour guide might rustle up a few fossilised dinosaur bones for you to hold: quite a sensation. Patagonia was home to Jurassic dinosaurs (180-135 million years old) and outstanding examples have been found here. Cerro Cóndor in Chubut is the only site of Middle Jurassic dinosaurs found in the Americas, and has given palaeontologists an important breakthrough in understanding the evolutionary stages of the period. At least five examples of patagosaurus have been found there, indicating that these dinosaurs at least were social creatures, perhaps for purposes of mutual defence. In Santa Cruz traces of dinosaurs from the Upper Jurassic period have been found in rocks which indicate that the climate was arid and desert-like at the time, surprising palaeontologists with the news that dinosaurs could live and breed in such adverse conditions.

The most important discoveries of dinosaurs from the Cretacic period (135-70 million years ago) have been made in Neuquén and Chubut. Dating from the period of separation of the continents of South America and Africa, these provide evidence of the way in which dinosaurs began to evolve in different ways due to geographic isolation. The *Carnotaurus sastrie* has horns and small hands, for example. The Patagonian dinosaurs are relatively huge, the *Argentinosaurus huiculensis* is one of the largest herbivorous dinosaurs found on earth, while the carnivorous *Gigantosaurus carolinii* found near Neuquén city was larger even than the better known *Tyranosaurus Rex*, discovered in North America.

Dinosaur spotting in Argentina: **Villa Chocón**, southwest of Neuquén city, boasts huge and perfectly preserved dinosaur footprints next to the lake. Further finds from the site can be seen in Neuquén's palaeontological museum. **Trelew** on the Atlantic coast, has the country's finest dinosaur museum, and as part of the same foundation, there's an excellent site with 40 million years of history near the Welsh village of **Gaiman**. Many of the most interesting finds are to be seen away from their sites, at the **museums** of **La Plata**, **San Juan** and in **Buenos Aires**. But there are more footprints to be seen at Dique Cabra Corral south of **Salta**, and you shouldn't miss the 200 million years of strata at **Ishigualasto** in San Juan, even if the dinosaur remains are long gone.

Plaza Huincul → Colour map 5, A2 Population: 11,000

There are more dinosaur remains at a quite impressive little museum in the otherwise rather dull town of **Plaza Huincul**. The road to Zapala, Route 22, leaves Neuquén and passes through the fruit-growing region of the Río Limay and the much duller oil-producing zone. Situated 107 km west of Neuquén, Plaza Huincul was the site of the country's first oil find in 1918. The **Museo Municipal Carmen Funes** includes the vertebrae of *argentinossaurus huinclulensis*, believed to have weighed over 100 tons and to have been one of the largest herbivorous dinosaurs ever to have lived on earth as well as a nest of fossilised dinosaur eggs. It's mainly a centre for research, and you can see the results of the fieldwork in fossils, photographs and videos, as well as the skeletons themselves.

Zapala → *Phone code: 02942 Colour map 5, A2 Population: 35,000*

Zapala (1,012 m) lies in a vast dry plain with views of snow-capped mountains to the west. It's modern and unappealing, but a useful place to stop on the RN40, to cross the border into Chile at the Icalma Pass, or to explore the less-visited northern end of the Lake District. There are buses from here to the **thermal baths** at Copahue and the outdoor and **skiing** centre of Caviahue, as well as nearby Pehuenia. Closer still, there's the **Parque Nacional Laguna Blanca** to explore, and an impressive fossil museum. There is **tourist information** ⓘ *at San Martín y Mayor Torres, T421132, open (summer) Mon-Fri 0700-1930, Sat/Sun 0800-1300, 1600-1900, closes earlier off-season.*

The **Museo Mineralógico Dr Juan Olsacher** ⓘ *Etcheluz 52 (next to the bus terminal), neumin@zapala.com.ar, Mon 0900-1500, Sat, Sun 1600-2000, free,* is one of the best museums of its type in South America; it contains over 2,000 types of mineral and has the finest collection of fossils of marine reptiles and marine fauna in the country. On display is the largest turtle shell from the Jurassic period ever found and an ophthalmosaur, as well as photos of an extensive cave system being excavated nearby. ▸▸ *For Sleeping, Eating and other listings, see pages 363-365.*

Parque Nacional Laguna Blanca → *Colour map 5, A2*

Covering 11,250 ha at altitudes between 1,200m and 1,800m, this park is one of only two reserves in the Americas created to protect swans and is 35 km southwest of Zapala. This is, apparently, a rare example of high arid steppe, and its 1,700ha lagoon is one of the most important nesting areas of the black-necked swan in Argentina. Other bird life includes several duck species, plovers, sandpipers, grebes and Chilean flamingos, with birds of prey such as the red-backed hawk and the peregrine falcon nesting on the steep slopes of the laguna. It's best visited in spring, when young can be watched at many sites around the laguna. The landscape is indeed very dry, and rather bleak, with fierce winds, encouraging only the lowest and most tenacious plant life. A rough track runs round the lake, suitable for four-wheel drive vehicles only. Nearby the **Arroyo Ñireco** has eroded the volcanic rock to form a deep gorge, and it's worth seeking out a small cave, inhabited in pre-historic times, with cave paintings. Southwest of the park Route 46 continues through the spectacular Bajada de Rahue, dropping 800m in under 20 km before reaching the town of Rahue, 120 km southwest of Zapala.

Park information The park entrance is 10 km from the junction of Route 46, (which runs across the park) with Route 40. The laguna itself lies lies 5 km beyond this. There's no public transport, so without your own vehicle the only option is a tour from Zapala. There's a *guardería* post near the southeast corner of the laguna, with a visitors' centre and picnic area. Take drinking water and a hat for the heat. There's a hiking trail which takes in 10 lagoons in all Entry US$2. Free camping by the *guardaparque*, otherwise Zapala has the nearest accommodation. www.parquesnacionales.gov.ar   lagunablanca@zapala.com.ar

Listings: Nequén and around

 Sleeping

Neuquén *p359, map p360*
AL **Hotel del Comahue**, *Av Argentina 377, T443 2040, www.hoteldelcomahue.com.ar*

Quite the most comfortable by a long way is this international-style, elegant modern 4-star, with spa and pool, an excellent restaurant, very good service and business facilities.

L-A **Express**, *T449 0100, www.ehotel express.com* Handy for the airport, this is a modern comfortable international-style place, slightly soulless, but well equipped, with pool and golf.

D **Alcorta**, *Alcorta 84, T442 2652.* Also flats for 4, with breakfast, TV in rooms, good value.

D **Royal**, *Av Argentina 145, T448 8902, www.hotelguia.com/hoteles/royal* A smart modern hotel, not grand or luxurious, but with welcoming rooms, car parking and breakfast included, good value.

E **Res Inglés**, *Félix San Martín 534, T442 2252.* Without breakfast, but good value.

E **Res Neuquén**, *Roca 109 y Yrigoyen, T442 2403.* Pleasant, with bath, breakfast and TV.

Camping

There's no site in the town; the nearest is at **Las Araucarios**, 16 km away, where you can also enjoy the activities of the *chacra* (farm), and pool, a great place for kids, before Plottier on RN22.

Villa El Chocón and around *p361*

B **La Posada del Dinosaurio**, *on the lakeshore in Villa El Chocón, Costa del Lago, Barrio 1, T490 1200, www.posada dinosaurio.com.ar* Convenient for dinosaur hunting, this has very plain but comfortable modern rooms, all with views over the lake, and a restaurant.

D **La Villa**, *Club Municipal El Chocón, T490 1252.* The only decent budget choice.

Camping

Club Chocón Lauquen, *T156-318719.*
Las Flores, *T490 1155.*

Plaza Huincul *p362*

C **Hotel Tortorici**, *Cutral-Co, 3 km west, Av Olascoaga y Di Paolo, T496 3730, www.hoteltortorici.com* The most comfortable option is this newly built hotel with neat rooms, a restaurant, which can arrange golf on a nearby course.

Zapala *p363*

A **Hostal del Caminante**, *Outside Neuquén 13 km south towards Zapala,T444 0118.* A popular place in summer, with a pool and garden.

C **Hue Melén**, *Brown 929, T422414.* Good value 3-star hotel, with decent rooms,

and a good restaurant serving the town's best food, including local specialities.

C **Huincul**, *Av Roca 311, T431422.* A spacious place with a cheap restaurant, serving good home-made regional food.

D **Coliqueo**, *Etcheluz 159, T421308.* Conveniently opposite the bus terminal, if the two options above are full (unlikely).

D **Pehuén**, *Elena de Vega y Etcheluz, T423135.* Comfortable, 1 block from bus terminal, with an interesting display of local maps.

Camping

Hostería Primeros Pinos, *Ruta Prov 13, T422637 primerospinos@yahoo.com.ar* Municipal site.

⦿ Eating

Neuquén *p359, map p360*

$$ **1900 Cuatro**, *at the Comahue Hotel, Av Argentina 377.* Posh and a little pricey, but serves superb food.

$ **Anonima** This supermarket has a good *patio de comidas* (food hall), and games to amuse the kids.

$ **El Reencuentro**, *Alaska 6451.* A popular *parrilla* recommended for delicious steaks in a warm atmosphere.

$ **Fatto Dalla Mama**, *9 de Julio 56.* Fabulous filled pasta.

$ **La Birra**, *Santa Fe 23.* Lots of choice, and is very welcoming, with chic modern surroundings.

$ **Rincón de Montaña**, *9 de Julio 435.* Recommended for delicious local specialities and cakes.

$ **Tutto al Dente**, *Alberdi 49.* Recommended for tasty home made pasta.

Cafés

There are lots of cheap cafés opposite the bus terminal on Mitre, recommended are:
Café El Buen Pan, *Mitre y Corrientes, open 0600 to 2300.* A bright modern place for snacks and good bakery too.

El Patagonia. *Lomitos* and sandwiches, with cheap (ish) deals.

Living Room, *Pte Rivadaria.* A lovely comfortable bar-café, with armchairs and table outside, a great place to relax.

Zapala *p363*

See Sleeping, above, for hotel restaurants.

El Chancho Rengo, *Av San Martín y Etcheluz*, *T422795*. This is where all the locals hang out.

Tour operators

Neuquén *p359*
Aventura Jurasica, *Centro Comercial Local 3, T126321863*. Dinosaurs.
Gondwana Tour, *Córdoba 599 T496 3355*, *geoda@copelnet.com.ar* Excursions to dinosaur sites nearby, and accommodation.

Zapala *p363*
Mali Viajes, *Alte Brown 760, T432251*.
Monserrat Viajes y Turismo, *Etcheluz 101, T422497*.

Transport

Neuquén *p359, map p360*
Air
The airport is located 7 km west of centre. *T444 0245*. Regular local buses number 10 and 11 go to the airport, but you must buy a *tarjeta* (bus card); US$0.40 for this journey. Taxi US$4.

To **Buenos Aires**, daily with AR, Austral, and **Aerolíneas Argentinas**.

Bus
The terminal is at *Mitre 147*. Left luggage: US$0.70 a day per item. **Andesmar**, *T442 2216*, **Via Bariloche**, *T442 7054*, **El Valle**, *T443 3293*.

About a dozen companies to **Buenos Aires**, daily, 12-16 hrs, US$25-35. To **Zapala** daily, 3 hrs, US$4.50. To **San Martín de los Andes**, 6 hrs, US$10. To **Bariloche**, 7 companies, 5-6 hrs, US$11, best views if you sit on left. To **Mendoza**, Andesmar, and 3 others, daily, 12 hrs, US$17. To **Junín de los Andes**, 5 hrs, US$8, many companies.

To **Aluminé**, 6 hrs, US$8, many companies. To **Zapala**, 2-3 hrs, US$4.30, Albus, Centenario. To **Plaza Huincul**, 1½ hrs, US$2, same companies. To **Caviahue** (6 hrs, US$10) and **Copahue**, 6½ hrs, US$11, Centenario.

To **Chile** Services to **Temuco** stop for a couple of hours at the border, 12-14 hrs, US$17. Some companies offer discount for return, departures Mon-Thu and Sat; 7

companies, some continuing to destinations en route to **Puerto Montt**.

Taxi
Confluencia, *T443 8880*. Radio Taxi, *T442 2502*.

Zapala *p363*
Bus
The terminal is at Etcheluz y Uriburu, *T423191*. To **Neuquén**, 2-3 hrs, US$4.50, Albus, Centenario, several daily. To San Martín de los Andes, 3-4 hrs, US$8. To **Junín de los Andes**, 3hrs, US$8 with Albus, Centenario, several daily. To **Aluminé**, 2 1/2 hrs, US$4.50, several companies, daily. To **Villa Pehuenia**, 2 1/2 hrs, US$5, 4 a week, go on to **Moquehue** 3 hrs, US$7. To **Caviahue**, (3 hrs, US$7) and **Copahue** (3½-4 hrs, US$7.50) daily with Centenario. To **Bariloche**, Albus, TAC, Vía Bariloche change at San Martín. To **Buenos Aires**, 18 hrs, US$25-30, many companies. To **Temuco** (Chile), US$16, Mon/Wed/Fri, Centenario (buy Chilean currency before leaving).

Directory

Neuquén *p359, map p360*
Airline offices Aerolíneas Argentinas/Austral, *Santa Fe 52, T442 2409*, Lapa, *Argentina 30, T448 8335*. Southern Winds, *Argentina 237, T442 0124*.
Banks Lots of ATMs along Av Argentina.
Casas de Cambio Pullman, *Alcorta 144*, Exterior, *San Martin 23*. **Consulates** Chile, *La Rioja 241, T442 2727*. **Communications Internet** Near the bus terminal at *Mitre 43 T443 6585*, a block from bus station. **Post office** *Rivadavia y Santa Fe*. **Telephone** Many *locutorios* in the centre, often with internet access. Telecom, *25 de Mayo 20*, open daily till 0030, and *Olascoaga 222*, open till 2345. Cheap.

Zapala *p363*
Banks Three banks including Banco de la Nación Argentina, *Etcheluz 465*, but difficult to change TC's, Bansud, *Etcheluz 108*.
Communications Internet Instituto Moreno, Moreno y López y Planes. CPI, *Chaneton y Garayta*.

• *Phone codes Neuquén, Villa El Chocón and surrounding areas: 0299; Zapala: 02942.*

Northern Neuquén

The silent expanses of an unspoilt wilderness to the north of the Lake District are only now opening up to vistors, though there're just as spectacular, with picturesque bases at Villa Pehuenia and Moquehue. The area due west of Zapala, known as Pehuenia is quite different from the southern lakes, thanks to its large forests of ancient pehuén, or araucaria – monkey puzzle trees. And further north, Caviahue is a good base for walking in rugged and unspoilt landscape or skiing in winter, while bleaker Copahue is known for its high-quality thermal waters.

Pehuenia → *Phone code 02942*

The magical and unspoilt area of Pehuenia is named after the country's unique forests of *pehuén* trees, which grow here in vast numbers. Covering a marvellous open mountainous landscape, these ancient, silent trees create a mystical atmosphere, especially around the lakes of Aluminé and Moquehue, where a pair of small villages provide good accommodation.

You could travel the circuit from Zapala, going west on Route 13 to reach Villa Pehuenia, then continuing southwest to Moquehue. From there Route 11 curves around through stunning scenery to the northern shore of Lago Ñorquinco, passing the southern shore of Lago Pulmari, before joining Route 23, while either running north to Copahue and Caviahue, or south to Aluminé and Junín de los Andes. Daily buses from Zapala and Aluminé make this area accessible by public transport, though having your own vehicle is an advantage. The *ripio* is rough for cyclists, but bicycle is perhaps the best way to appreciate the peace and beauty of the area. ▸▸ *For Sleeping, Eating and other listings, see pages 370-373.*

Villa Pehuenia

Reached by *ripio* road, the eastern shores of Lago Aluminé lie 107 km west of Zapala. There's also a service station and *locutorio* as well as two food shops on the main road, and a tourist kiosk is signposted, T(02942) 498027, by the turning for Villa Pehuenia. On the northern shore, picturesquely set in steep wooded hills, is the small isolated village of Villa Pehuenia. This is Mapuche land; this place was chosen for a settlement because there are eight volcanoes in a chain and you can easily see why the area, with its *pehuén* trees, is so sacred to them (see box, above). Infrastructure is slowly building here so that, at the moment, you have the best of both worlds: an unspoilt feel, while a rapidly growing cluster of *cabañas* make it possible to stay here for a few days in comfort. Walk onto the peninsula stretching out into the lake from the village for wonderful walks along the araucaria-fringed shore, and from the **mirador del Cipres** with fabulous views.

▲ **Walks and tours** For lovely walks through the silent, still araucaria forests, continue 4 km further along the road around the lake from Villa Pehuenia, and turn left at the *gendarmeria*, following a dirt road across the bridge over a narrow strip of water, La Angostura. Follow the arrow to a campsite 50m further on, **El Puente** (delightful: recommended). Go past it and when you come to a little hut and a sign to Lago Redonda, take the right fork and follow the track. Park, or leave your bike at the the largest of the three small lagunas, and take the path due south when the track comes to an end at a farmstead by a large lagoon. Climb from here to a ridge with great views, and then take the path which drops and skirts around **Lago Moquehue**. Awe-inspiring. You could walk to Moquehue from here, but you need a map.

Monkey Puzzle Tree

The stunningly beautiful area of Pehuenia is remarkable for its forests of araucaria, or monkey puzzle trees (Araucaria araucana). Growing slowly to a mighty 40m high, the trees exert a powerful presence when seen en masse, perhaps because their forests are silent, moving little in the breeze. A true conifer, the araucaria is a descendent of the petrified pines found in Argentina's Bosques Petrificados. For centuries the *pehuén* or araucaria have been revered by indigenous peoples, and the local Mapuche still eat its pine nuts, rich in vitamins and fats. The custom of collecting their nuts, around which a whole array of foods, and a celebratory harvest festival are based, has been the source of a bitter territory dispute in parts of the northern lake district. The Mapuche feel that they have a natural right to harvest the fruits of their trees, and local landowners, backed by local government, clearly don't agree.

In recent years though, there's a growing respect for the Mapuche in the area, and they are beginning to get involved in the provision of basic tourist services with great success. You'll see *pan casero* (home made bread), *tortas fritas* (fried pastries) and handicrafts for sale on roadsides, as well as the fledgling winter sports centre near Villa Pehuenia, all run by Mapuche. These small enterprises enable them to survive financially, while retaining their traditions and customs, and with luck, access to the magnificent araucarias which they hold so sacred.

Just a few kilometres further along the main road, signposted to the right is the **Batea Mahuida**, a reserve created to protect an area of *pehuén* trees and the majestic volcano, regarded by the Mapuche peoples as sacred. This is a lovely for walking in summer, with tremendous views of all seven volcanoes around, there's a winter sports centre here, Parque de Nieve, administrated by the Mapuche people, offering snowmobile and snowshow walking and husky rides. Delicious homecooked food is served. ▸▸ *For Sleeping, Eating and other listings, see pages 370-373.*

Lago Moquehue

Another 10 km on the Route 13 brings you to the quite sprawling village of Moquehue. It's a wilder more remote place than Villa Pehuenia on the shores of its lake, with a lovely wide river. Famous for fishing, this is a beautiful and utterly peaceful place to relax and walk, and it has a less cultivated feel, inspiring adventurous treks. A short stroll through araucaria forests brings you to a lovely waterfall; a longer hike to the top of Cerro Bandera (four hours return) gives wonderful views over the area, and to Volcán Llaima. There are fine camping spots all around and a couple of comfortable places to stay.

Aluminé → *Population 3800 Colour map 5, A2 Phone code 0294*

In the splendid valley Aluminé, on the Route 23 between Pehuenia and Junín, lies the area's self-proclaimed rafting capital, see Sports and activities page 372. There is indeed superb rafting (grades two-six) nearby on Río Aluminé, and if you have to stop there is somewhere to stay. But despite the lovely setting, it's a drab little place with earth roads: far better to keep going to Villa Pehuenia unless you are here to go rafting. There's a very friendly **tourist office** ① *Calle Christian Joubert 321, T496001, www.alumine.net open 0800-2100 all year.* There's a service station too, the last before Villa Pehuenia. In March, the harvest of the *piñones* is celebrated in the *Fiesta del Pehuén* with horse riding displays and live music.

From Aluminé there is access to Lago Rucachoroi, 23 km west, the biggest Aigo Mapuche community inside the national park, in gentle farmland surrounded by ancient *pehuen* forests. Access is by a rough *ripio* road, best in a 4WD in winter, and spectacular in autumn when the deciduous trees are a splash of orange against the bottle green araucarias. There are two camp sites, offering wonderful Mapuche food, and horse riding, see page 370. Here too, there's a *guardería* where you can ask about a possible trek to Quillén (see below). The landscape here is very beautiful and you will want to linger. ➤ *For Sleeping, Eating and other listings, see pages 370-373.*

Lago Quillén

At the junction by the small town of Rahue, 16 km south of Aluminé, a road leads west to the valley of the Río Quillén and the exquisite Lago Quillén, from where there are fine views of Volcán Lanín peeping above the mountains. The lake itself is one of the region's most lovely, jade green in colour, with beaches along its low-lying northern coast. Further west, where annual rainfall is among the heaviest in the country, the slopes are thickly covered with superb Andean Patagonian forest. There's no transport, and accomm- odation only is at the **Camping Pudu Pudu** (with food shop and hot showers) on the lake's northern shore, just west of the *guardería*. Here you can get advice about walks, and register with *guardaparques* if you plan to hike to Rucachoroi. There's another walk to the remote **Lago Hui Hui** 6 km north from the second campsite, (three and a half hours there and back).

Border crossings with Chile

Paso Pino Hachado (1,864m) lies 115 km west of Zapala via Route 22, which is almost completely paved. On the Chilean side a *ripio* road run northwest to Lonquimáy, 65 km west of the border. Temuco lies 145 km southwest of Lonquimáy. **Argentine immigration and customs** ① *9 km east of the border, open 0700-1300, 1400-1900.* **Chilean immigration and customs** ① *In Liucura, 22 km west of the border, open Dec-Mar 0800-2100, Apr-Nov 0800-1900.* Very thorough searches and two- to three-hour delays reported. Buses from Zapala and Neuquén to Temuco use this crossing.

Paso de Icalma (1,303 m) lies 132 km west of Zapala and is reached by Route 13 (*ripio*). On the Chilean side this road continues to Melipeuco, 30 km west of the border, and thence to Temuco. **Argentine immigration and customs** All paperwork to be carried out at the customs office, clearly signposted ① *9 km east of the border, open 0800-2000 in summer, 0900-1900 approximately in winter.* **Chilean immigration and customs** ① *Open Dec-Mar 0800-2100, Apr-Nov 0800-1900.*

Copahue and Caviahue → *Phone code 02948 Colour map 3, C1*

The extraordinary landscape of Reserva Provincial Copahue at the heart of this region is formed by a giant volcanic crate r, whose walls are the surrounding mountains. An arid, dramatic and other-wordly landscape, the park was created to protect the araucaria trees which grow on its slopes, and there are some wonderful walks that take you to unexpectedly stunning landscapes. 150 km from Zapala, Caviahue is by far the most attractive of the two, with an attractive lakeside setting, and the best base for walking and horse riding, which converts into a skiing and winter sports centre from July to September. It has three ski lifts, excellent areas for cross country skiing, snow-shoeing and snowmobiling, all with tremendous views, and it's one of cheaper resorts in the lake district. Copahue (altitude 1,980 m) is a thermal spa resort enclosed in a gigantic amphitheatre formed by mountain walls and boasting the best thermal waters in South America, though it's decidedly the bleaker of the two towns.

Getting there Both towns are easily reached by public transport from Zapala, 150 km southeast, or by flying to Neuquén, 300 km southeast.

Tourist information The tourist information in Caviahue is on ⓘ *8 de Abril, bungalows 5 and 6, T495036, www.caviahue-copahue.com.ar* For information on the ski centre, Caviahue Base, T495079. There's an ATM at the *municipalidad*, several restaurants and a tea room, as well as some decent accommodation. In Copahue, the tourist information is on the approach road into town, Route 26.

Around Caviahue

The Volcán Copahue last erupted, smokily, in 2000, destroying the bright blue lake in its crater, but it's still a popular destination for horse riding, and the views of the prehistoric landscape are astounding. Most highly recommended, though, is **El Salto del Agrio**, 15 km northeast along RN 27. This is the climax in a series of delightful falls, approached by a road passing between tall, ancient araucaria trees poised on basalt cliffs; a wonderful excursion by horse to see all seven falls. Other fantastic walks in the area are to the extraordinary **Las Máquinas**, 4 km south of Copahue, where sulphurous steam puffs through air holes and against a panoramic backdrop, making the weird-est noises. And at **El Anfiteatro**, there are thermal waters reaching 150°, in a semicircle of rock edged with araucaria trees. Just above Copahue, make the steep climb up to **Cascada Escondida**, a torrent of water falling 15 m over a shelf of basalt into a pool surrounded by a forest of araucaria trees; above it Lago Escondida is a magical spot. ▸▸ *For Sleeping, Eating and other listings, see pages 370-373.*

Chos Malal and around → *Phone code: 02948 Colour map 3, C1 Population: 8,600*

Chos Malal (862 m) is not worth a big detour, but has an interesting history. Now a mining centre, it was founded as a fortress in 1879, when General Uriburu based his soldiers here during the Campaign of the Desert, see box page 118. The restored fortress houses the **Museo Histórico Olascoaga**, which presents a history of the historic battle in this region.

From Chos Malal, you could visit **Parque Provincial Tromen** 37 km northeast, based around Lago Tromen, a nesting site for migratory birds, flamingos, black-necked swans and ducks. East of the lake is the **Tromen volcano** (4,114 m). Another peak, **Cerro Waile** (3,182 m) has a flat summit, where skiing is possible, though there are no services.

Paso Tromen border with Chile → *For climbing Volcán Lanín, see page 373below.*

Paso Tromen, known in Chile as Paso Mamuil Malal, is situated 64 km northwest of Junín de los Andes and reached by *ripio* Route 60 which runs from Tropezón on Route 23, through Parque Nacional Lanín. Some 3 km east of the pass a turning leads north to Lago Tromen, and south of the pass is the graceful cone of the Lanín volcano. This is the normal departure point for climbing to the summit (see page 373below). This crossing is less developed than the Huahum and Puyehue routes further south; it is unsuitable for cycles and definitely not usable during heavy rain or snow (June to mid-November), as parts are narrow and steep. Ring to check: *gendarmería* T02972 491270, or customs 492163. This is a beautiful spot, with a good campsite, and lovely walks: From the *guardaparque* centre, footpaths lead to a *mirador* (one-and-a-half-hours round trip), or across a grassy prairie with magnificent clear views of Lanín and other jagged peaks, through *ñirre* woodland and some great araucaria trees to the point where Lago Tromen drains into Río Malleo (4 km).

Argentine immigration and customs ⓘ *At Puesto Tromen, 3km east of the pass, open 0800-2000 all year.*

Chilean immigration and customsⓘ *At Puesco, 8 km west of the pass, open Dec-Mar 0800-2100, Apr-Nov 0800-1900*. On the Chilean side the road continues through glorious scenery, with views of the volcanoes of Villarrica and Quetrupillán to the south, to Pucón, 6 km west of the pass, on Lago Villarrica. Hire cars will need special documents (ask when you rent), no fruit or veg is to be taken into Chile, and the car's number plate must be etched into all windows.

Listings: Northern Nequén

● Sleeping

Villa Pehuenia *p366*
There's plenty of *cabañas*, many with good views over the lake, and set in idyllic woodland.

C **Cabañas Bahía Radal**, *T498057, bahiaradal@hotmail.com on the peninsula (ask the tourist office for directions, as the tracks are unnamed)*. Luxurious *cabañas*, with clear lake views from its elevated position.

C **Cabañas Caren**. Simple A-frame *cabañas*, but with open views and balconies.

C **Cabañas Puerto Malén**, *Club de Montana, T011 4226 8190 (Buenos Aires), www.puerto malen.com* Well built wooden *cabañas* with clear lake views from their balconies.

C **Las Terrazas**, *T498036, lasterrazasvillapehuenhia@yahoo.com.ar* Warmly recommended: the owner is an architect of Mapuche origin, who has retained Mapuche style in his beautiful design of these comfortable *cabañas* (cheaper than above price for 4), tasteful, warm and with perfect views over the lake, with also D bed and breakfast. Gorgeous. He and his wife know the area intimately, and can direct you to magical places for walking, and to Mapuche communities to visit.

D **Hostería Lago Alumine**. Very welcoming and kind owners who make you feel at home, in this rather old-fashioned but spotless place. Recommended as great value; although rooms are very simple, all have bathrooms. Good home cooking in the restaurant.

D **La Serena**, *T(011)1547940319, www.complejolaserena.com.ar* Beautifullly equipped and designed *cabañas* with great uninterrupted view, gardens going down to beach, sheltered from wind, furnished with rustic-style handmade cypress furniture, and wood stoves, all very attractive.

Camping
There are plenty of sites, but those listed have something special.

Camping Agreste Quechulafquen, *at the end of the steep road across La Angostura*. Situated among lovely steep hills and dense vegetation, run by Mapuche Puels.

Camping El Puente, *at La Angostura*. US$2pp, with hot showers, is a simpler site, in beautiful surroundings.

Las Lagrimitas, *just west of the village, T498063*. A lovely secluded lakeside site on the beach, with food shop, US$2pp, hot showers and fireplaces.

Lago Moquehue *p367*
C **Hostería Moquehue**, *set high above the lake with panoramic views, T02946-156 60301, www.hosteriamoquehue.netfirms.com* Cosy, stylish, rustic rooms, nicely furnished with good views, and excellent food. Try the superb Moquehue trout and local *chivito*. Charming family hosts.
Simpler accommodation is available a short walk from the east of the village on the road to Norquinco, just north of the police checkpoint.

La Bella Durmiente, *T496172*. In a rustic building with no heating, only open in summer, the welcoming owner offers good food and also offers trekking, horse riding, diving in lake, mountain bikes.

Camping
Good camping sites can be found on the lake shores.

Camping Trenel, *in a fabulous site elevavated*

● *Phone codes* Aluminé, Lago Moquehue, Villa Pehuenia and surrounding area: 02942;
● Copahue, Caviahue, Chos Malal and surroundings: 02948.

on the southern shore of Lago Moquehue.
Beautiful shady sites in the thick of little *nirre* trees, with seats and *parrillas* overlooking lake, Recommended, smart, hot showers, restaurant, food shop, information and excursions.
Los Caprichosos, *on Lago Ñorquinco*. Open Nov to April only, with water and food shop.

Cabañas
Along Route 13, 11 km to Lago Ñorquinco, past mighty basalt cliffs with *pehuéns* all around, there's idyllic camping.
Also idyllic, reached by by Route 11 are the smaller campsites of Lagos Pilhué and Ñorquinco camping.
C/D **Cabañas Melipal**, *T432445, 156 61549.* Very attractive, rustic stone-built *cabañas* in secluded sites right on lake side, 1 for 4 the other for 12. Lovely old-fashioned style, well equipped and warm, fabulous views from balcony, use of boats. Highly recommended.
D **Cabañas Huerquen**, *T156 4700, huerquen_patagoni@hotmail.com* Beyond Moquehue on the road to Norquincoare, these lovely secluded stone *cabañas* are in beautifully tranquil surroundings.
Ecocamping Ñorquinco Norquinco, *T496155, ecocamping@hotmail.com* There is one amazing rustic *cabaña* right on the lakeside, with a café by the roadside, $6.50 pp per night $3 for under 12, Dec or March, Apr to Easter. Great fishing, hot showers and a *provedería*. This is a lovely place to sit, eat and drink if it rains.

Aluminé *p367*
D **Aluminé**, *Joubert 336, T496347, hosteriaaluminé@hotmail.com* In the middle of town, opposite tourist information, this is a drab 1960's place, with clean, functional rooms. There's a decent restaurant next door, however, La Posta del Rey.
D **Nid Car**, *Joubert 559, T496131.* Very plain and rather overpriced.
D **Pehuenía**, *just off Route 23 at Crouzeilles 100, T496340, pehuenia2000@yahoo.com.ar* A huge tin chalet-style building, not attractive, but with great views over the hills opposite. The rooms are comfortable and simple, the staff are friendly, and it's good value; by far the town's best choice. Horse riding, bike hire and canoeing at the owner's

campsite, Bahía de los Sueños, 6km from the red bridge north of Aluminé.
There are also *cabañas* (list at tourist office).

Around Aluminé *p367*
There are more inspiring options here.
A **Estancia Quillén**, *Route 46 near Rahue, near the bridge crossing Río Aluminé, T496196, www.interpatagonia.com/quillen panchoyali ciaquillen@alumine.com.ar* A comfortable, traditionally furnished chalet-style house, with spacious rooms, and a restaurant, where you'll be welcomed by the estancia owners. Open Dec to Ap.

Camping
See tourist office map. There are campsites all over the area.
La Vieja Balsa, *T496001, just outside of Aluminé on Route 23 on the Río Aluminé.* A well equipped site, that also offers rafting and fishing, US$1 pp per day to camp, hot showers, food shop, fireplaces, tables, open Dec to Easter.

Rucachoroi *p368*
Camping
There are 2 sites, **Rucachoroi 1** or **2** (as they're called) are respectively before and after the lake; open all year, but really ideal only Dec-Feb. The first has more facilities, with toilets, but no hot water, some food supplies, including wonderful Mapuche home-made bread and sausages, and offers horse riding.

Copahue *p368*
C **Aldea Termal**, *T(0299)442 5605, www;aldeatermal.com* Very attractively decorated. Recommended.
C **Hotel Copahue**, *Olascoaga y Bercovich, T495117.* This lovely old place where you'll be warmly welcomed by Pocho and Moriconi is the most recommended place in Copahue. There are well built wood and stone *cabañas*, at **AB-C** (depending on season).
C **Termas**, *Herrero Doucloux s/n, T495045,* Three-star.
D **Pino Azul**, *Herrero Doucloux y Olascoaga, T495071.* Popular with older visitors.

Caviahue *p368*
B **Nevado Caviahue**, *8 de Abril s/n, T495042, www.caviahue.com* Plain rooms, but

modern, and there's a restaurant, and cosy lounge with wood fire. Also A-B for 6 *cabañas*, well equipped but not luxurious.

C **Lago Caviahue**, *Costanera Quimey-Co, T495110, www.hotellagocaviahue.com* Better value than the Nevado above; comfortable lakeside apartments with kitchen, also a good restaurant, great views, 2km from the ski centre.

La Cabaña de Tito, *Puesta del Sol s/n, T495093*. *Cabañas* near lake, excellent meals.

Farallon, *Caviahue Base, T495085*. Neat apartments, some with kitchens.

Camping
Copahue, *T495111, Hueney Municipal, 495041*.

Chos Malal *p369*
B **Anlu**, *Lavalle 60, T422628, anlu@comsat_ mail.com.ar* A comfortable new hotel, this small place has alpine-style interiors.

Paso Tromen *p369*
Camping
There's a municipal campsite on the Río Curi Leuvú.

CONAF, *Puesco (Chile)*. Free, no facilities.

Puesto Tromen. A superb campsite with shaded areas, hot showers, toilets, *parilladas* and places to wash, well run by friendly people, Dec to Apr US$0.60 per person. Take food.

Eating

Villa Pehuenia *p366*
$ **Costa Azul**, *located on the lakeside, T498035*. The village's best restaurant, where you can taste delicious local dishes and pasta; *chivito* (kid) *al asado* is the speciality of the house.

Aluminé *p367*
Apart from **La Posta del Rey**, the only other decent choice is **Parrilla Aoniken**, near the bus terminal at *Av 4 de Caballería 139*, with pizzas and *milanesas*, and a cheap set menu, US$3 for 3 courses.

Caviahue *p369*
The most recommendable places to eat are mostly in the hotels:
$ **Copahue Club Hotel**, *Valle del Volcán*. Serves good *chivito al asado* and locally caught trout.

$ **Hotel Caviahue**. The hotel restaurant serves kid, along with pastas.

$ **Hotel Lago Caviahue**. The most stylish place to eat with an inspired *chivo a la cerveza* (kid cooked in beer) on the menu, along with more traditional favourites and local specialities.

Chos Malal *p369*
For cheap, light meals you could try the restaurant at **Residencial** Don Daniel, *General Paz 1124, T421707*.

Sport and activities

Río Aluminé *p367*
Aluminé Rafting, *Ricardo Solano, T 02942, 496322*. US$9-15, depending on grade of difficulty, for 3 hrs rafting, grades 2-6. All equipment included. *Circuito Abra Ancha* 2,5 hours, grade 2, 6km very entertaining, suitable for everyone. *Circuito Aluminé Superior*, 12 or 15km run, 5-6 hours, grade 3/4, very technical river leaving Lago Alumine, for those who like a thrill, passing little woods of araucarias and nirres, family trips grades 1 and 2, costs $20pp for Abra Ancha, $60pp for higher level. Trekking $80 per day, trekking in Cordon de Chachil, $120 per day, 2 days minimum, but can be up to a week, also kayaking, and biking.

Tour operators

Villa Pehuenia *p366*
Expedicion Llienan Mapu, *Rute 11 km 17.5, T156 64705*. Horse riding, 4WD excursions, husky rides and cross country skiing in winter. Recommended.

Caviahue *p368*
Caviahue Tours, *San Martín 623, Buenos Aires, T4314 1556*.Good information on the region.

Transport

Villa Pehuenia *p366*
There are 3 buses weekly to Villa Pehuenia and **Moquehue** from **Neuquén** (less predictable in winter, when the roads are covered in snow) and **Aluminé**.

Aluminé p367

There are buses daily to and from Zapala, with either **Aluminé Viajes** (*T496231*), or **Albus** (*T496368*), 3hrs, US$4. Twice a week to **Villa Pehuenia** 1 hr, US$2. Twice a week to San Martín de los Andes, 4 hrs, US$5, with Tilleria *T496048*.

Caviahue p368

Bus

To/from **Neuquén**, El Petroleo and Centenario. Daily, 6 hrs, US$11, via Zapala (US$5). **El Centenario** *T495024*.

Chos Malal p369

To **Neuquén**, 6 hrs, US$4, Cono Sur and El

Petróleo, 1 bus each daily. To **Parque Provincial Tromen**, by *ripio* road which runs north from Chos Malal along the west bank of the lake and then (unpaved) northeast to meet Route 40. For transport from Chos Malal contact **Viajes Wayle**, *Gral Paz 385*, *T/F422003*.

Paso Tromen p369

Officially, Igi-Llaima and Empresa San Martín buses running between **Junín de los Andes** and **Pucón** only pick up passengers at the pass (see Junín transport, page 384). Hitchhiking over the pass is not difficult in summer.

Parque Nacional Lanín

Some of the most beautiful sights in the Lake District are to be found in one of the country's largest national parks, Parque Nacional Lanín, to the west of Junín. Here, Lago Huechulaufquen stretches from smooth lowland hills in the east to steep craggy mountains in the west, heavily clad in native beech trees, and to the base of the magnificent extinct snow-capped Lanín. Lying north, on the Chilean border, this dormant volcano and the view of its sugary peak from the exquisitely pretty crescent-shaped Lake Paimún is worth the trek. All along the northern shores of both lakes, with their grey volcanic sands, are beautiful, if basic, camping grounds, a couple with facilities. Stretching along the border with Chile for some 200km, the park covers 379,000 ha and includes 24 glacial lakes, one of which (Lago Lacar) drains into the Pacific.

Vegetation is very varied throughout the park, due to differences in rainfall and altitude. In the north between Lagos Ñorquinco and Tromen, the araucaria tree dominates, mixed here and there with lenga and ñire. But further south, you'll find a combination of the southern beech species: roble, rauli and the majestic coihue whose elephant grey trunks make a cathedral of the large stretches of woodland. You might be surprised to spot bamboo growing in profusion along Lago Huechulafken – this prehistoric species dies off en masse once every 20 to 30 years, when all the plants simultaneously rot, and new life begins the following year. Wildlife includes wildcats and foxes, the elusive pudu – a pretty small deer – and some red deer introduced for fox hunting. ▶▶ *For Sleeping, Eating and other listings, see pages 379-385.*

Access

Parque Nacional Lanín can be entered at various points. At each point there are *guardaparques* who can advise on hikes.

1 To climb Lanín, access is near **Lago Tromen**, a lovely spot where there is good camping, from Route 60 which leads to the Paso Tromen crossing to Chile. Along this route there are several Mapuche communities which can be visited.

2 The easiest access is at **Lago Huechulaufquen**, past the fishing spot at the mouth of the Chimehuín river, fabulous walks up into the hills and along the shore of this, and along beautiful Lago Paimún further west. There are three *hosterías* and great campsites. Access from Route 61 northwest of Junín, where a bus runs in summer.

3 There are more good walks at **Lago Curruhue** and also natural thermal pools at Termas de Lahuen-Co further west, accessed from Route 62, starting south of Junín.

Park information
Park entry is US$2. The park administration is at San Martín de los Andes, Emilio Frey 749. You're supposed to register here before setting out on any major treks at Huechulafuken, although this is obviously impractical. *Guardaparques* at the Lake should always be notified before you set off, and will advise on routes. Having a good map is essential, however. Wherever you are in the park, fires are a serious hazard here: always put out with lots of water, not just earth. Pack out all rubbish and take it away with you.

▲ Walking in Lago Paimún
There's a range of excellent walks here, with guides only needed for the longer treks where paths are not marked. (For these, ask in the Junín park office or at San Martín de los Andes, address above.) Yellow arrows indicate the paths, allowing plenty of time for return before dark. Ask *guardaparques* for advice on routes before setting off. To cross to other side of Lago Paimún there's a boat operated by Mapuches: just ring the bell. Wherever you are in the park, fires are a serious hazard here: always put out with lots of water, not just earth. Pack out all rubbish and take it away with you.

Routes
1 **El Saltillo Falls**, 2 hrs return, fabulous views, start from campsite at Lago Paimún.
2 **Termas at Lahuen-Co**, 8 hrs to the end of Lago Paimún, then 4 more to reach the Termas, best done over two days. A beautiful walk, and you'll be rewarded by a soak in these simple rustic pools. Start from Puerto Canoa.
3 To the base of **Volcán Lanín** 8 hrs return, a satisfying walk. Start from Puerto Canoa.
4 **Cerro El Chivo** (2,064 m), 7 hrs return, is a more challenging walk through forest. NB heavy snow can lie til January. Set off early, and register in campsite at Bahía Cañicul. Potentially dangerous without a guide.

Horseriding
You can explore much of the area on horseback, including the trek to the base of Volcán Lanín. Five places along the lake hire horses: ask *guardaparques* for advice, or ask at Mapuche comunities.

Lago Curruhue and Termas de Lahuen-Co
It's well worth getting to beautiful Lago Curruhue and the rustic Termas, and if you can't face the two day hike, go west along Route 62 south of Junín de los Andes. Or from via San Martín de los Andes, also along Route 62, passing Lago Lolog, Lago Curruhue, and through ancient pehuén forests along the south shore of the larger Lago Currhue, and Laguna Escorial, where there's an impressive lava field. A path from Lago Verde leads to the base of an inactive volcano Achen Niyeu and Cerro Huanquihue (three hours one way, two hours more to the top of the volcano). ▶▶ *For Lagos Lolog and Lacar see San Martín de los Andes, page 378.*

Climbing Lanín
One of the world's most beautiful mountains, Lanín (3,768 m) is geologically one of the youngest volcanoes of the Andes; it is now extinct. It is three-day challenging climb, with two refugios at 2,400m, free, sleeping 14 to 20 people. The ascent starts from the Argentine customs post at the Tromen pass, where you must register. They will check all climbers' equipment and experience. Crampons and ice-axe are essential, as is protection against strong, cold winds.

The ascent It's vital to get detailed descriptions on the ascent form the *guardaparques*: this is just to give you a rough idea: To climb the north face, follow the path through lenga forest to the base of the volcano, over arroyo Turbio and up the *espina de pescado*. From here there are three paths to the *refugios*: **1** straight ahead, the espina de pescado is the shortest but steepest (four to five hours), **2** to the right, the camino de mulas is the easiest but longest (seven hours) and is marked; and **3** to the left, *canaleta* should be used only for descent. From the refugios, it is six to seven hours over ice fields to the summit.

Equipment Because of its relative accessibility, the risks are often underestimated: crampons and ice-axe are essential. An authorised guide is absolutely necessary for anyone other than the very experienced. Climbing equipment and experience is checked by the *guardaparques* at Tromen pass.

Camping Camping Agreste Lanín. Lovely shaded spots with hot showers, toilets, *parilladas* and places to wash, well run by friendly people, December to April US$0.60 per person. ▸ *For Sleeping, Eating and other listings, see pages 379-385.*

Parque Nacional Lanín

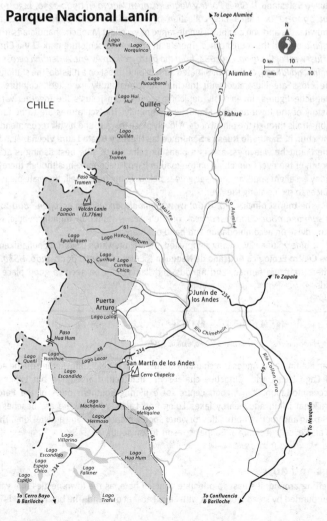

Junín de los Andes → *Phone code: 02972 Colour map 5, A2 Population: 9,000*

Situated on the beautiful Río Chimehuin, the quiet town of Junín de los Andes (773 m) is justifiably known as the trout capital of Argentina. It offers some of the best fishing in the country in world renowned rivers, and the fishing season runs from mid November to the end of April. Junín is also an excellent base for exploring the wonderful virgin countryside of Parque Nacional Lanín and for climbing the extinct volcano itself.

Founded in 1883, Junín is a real town; not as picturesque or tourist-orientated as its neighbour, San Martín – there are definitely no chalet-style buildings, and few chocolate shops here – but it's a quiet neat place with genuinely friendly people.

Sights

Most of what you need can be found within a couple of blocks of the central Plaza San Martín with its fine araucaria trees among mature *alerces* and cedars. The small **Museo Salesiano** ① *Ginés Ponte y Nogueira, open Mon to Fri 0900-1230, 1430-1930, Sat 0900-1230*, has a fine collection of Mapuche weavings, instruments and arrowheads, and you can buy a whole range of excellent Mapuche handicrafts in the *galería* behind the tourist office. There's an impressive sculpture park **El Via Christi** ① *just west of the town, T 491684, from the plaza walk up Av Ant. Argentina across the main road RN 234, to the end*. Situated among pine forest on a hillside, the stations of the cross are illustrated with touching and beautifully executed sculptures of Mapuche figures, ingeniously depicting scenes from Jesus's life together with a history of the town and the Mapuche community. The sculptures are to be found along trails through the pine woods. A lovely place to walk, and highly recommended. The church, **Santuario Nuestra Senora de las Nieves y Beata Laura Vicuña**, also has fine Mapuche weavings, and is a pleasing calm space. The best fishing is at the mouth of the river Chimehuin on the road to Lago Huechulafken, although there are many excellent spots around; see guides below. In the town itself, there are pleasant places to picnic along the river.

The **tourist office** ① *T491160, www.junindelosandes.com.ar, open 0800-2200 in summer, 0800-2100 rest of year,* on the plaza is staffed by friendly people, who can advise on accommodation and hand out maps.

Some 7 km away, clearly signposted, on RN61 towards Lago Huechuflaufken, is the **Centro Ecologico Aplicado de Neuquén** (CEAN) ① *Mon-Fri 0900-1300, US$0.30,* where trout are farmed, and ñandus and llamas can be seen; a good place for kids. ▸▸ *For Sleeping, Eating and other listings, see pages 379-385.*

San Martín de los Andes

→ *Phone code: 02972 Colour map 5, A2 Population: 20,000*

San Martín de los Andes is a charming tourist town in a beautiful setting on the edge of Lago Lacar, with attractive chalet-style architecture and good but expensive accommodation. It's a good centre for exploring southern parts of the Parque Nacional Lanín and nearby lakes Lolog and Lacar, where there are beaches for relaxing and good opportunities for water sports, mountain biking and trekking. There is also excellent skiing at Chapelco resort 10 km south. ▸▸ *For Sport and activities such as watersports, skiing and mountain biking, see page 383.*

Ins and outs

Getting around It's easy to orientate yourself here, as the town nestles in a valley surrounded by steep mountains with Lago Lacar at one end. The bus terminal is just off the *costanera* at Juez del Valle and Villegas. Beware of confusing street names: Perito Moreno runs east-west, crossing Mariano Moreno which runs north-south, and Rudecindo Roca which is two blocks north of General Roca.

Tourist information ① *San Martín y Rosas 790, on the main plaza, T427347. Open*

Junín de los Andes

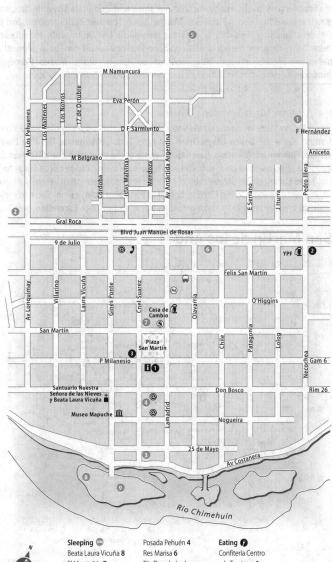

Sleeping 🛏
Beata Laura Vicuña **8**
El Montañés **7**
Hostería Chimehuín **3**
La Isla **9**
Milla Piuke **2**

Posada Pehuén **4**
Res Marisa **6**
Río Dorado Lodge
 & Fly Shop **1**
San Jorge **5**

Eating 🍴
Confitería Centro
 de Tursismo **1**
La Aldea de Pescador **2**
Ruca Hueney **3**

0 metres 100
0 yards 100

0800-2100 all year. They have lists of accommodation, with prices up on a big board, hand out maps and good advice. Staff speak English and French, but are very busy in summer, when it's advisable to go early in the day, before they get stressed. The office for Parque Nacional Lanín is at ⓘ *E. Frey 749, T427233, laninupublico@smandes .com.ar* Also, check out the websites www.chapelco. com.ar www.smandes.gov.ar

Sights

Running perpendicular to the *costanera*, along the lake, is Calle San Martín, where you'll find most shops and plenty of places to eat. There are two plazas, of which Plaza Sarmiento is lovely, woody, nicely maintained and illuminated by little lamps at night. The more functional Plaza San Martin, has a sporadic crafts market, and is more of a public space. It's a pleasant one-and-a-half hour walk to **Mirador Bandurrias** with great views, and a *quincho*-like restaurant run by a Mapuche community. There's a good little museum on local history, **Museo Primeros Pobladores** ⓘ *1000 to 1500, 1800 to 2100 Mon-Fri, Sat and Sun 1300 to 2200.* ⤇ *For Sleeping, Eating and other listings, see pages 379-385.*

Around San Martín de los Andes

Surrounded by lakes and mountains you can explore, the most popular excursions are south along the **Seven Lakes Drive** to **Lagos Traful, Meliquina, Filo Hua Hum, Hermoso, Falkner** and **Villarino**, (see below), north to the thermal baths at **Termas de Lahuen-Co** (also reached on foot from Lago Huechulafquen) and to Lagos Lolog and Lacar. **Lago Lacar** can be explored by car along much of its length, as there's a *ripio* road, Route 48, leading to the Chilean border at **Paso Hua Hum**, 41 km. You can cycle or walk all the way around the lake on rough track, and to **Lago Escondido**, south of

San Martín de los Andes

the lake. At the western end of the lake there are beaches at **Hua Hum**, and rafting on Río Hua Hum nearby. On the southern shore, 18 km away, there is a quieter beach at **Quila Quina**, where you can walk to a lovely waterfall, along a guided nature trail, or a two-hour walk which takes you to a tranquil Mapuche community in the hills above the lake. Both lakeshore villages can be reached by boat from the pier in San Martín, T428427; to Quila Quina hourly, 30 minutes each way, US$5 return. To Hua Hum, US$15 return, three daily in season.

Cerro Chapelco (2,394m), 20 km south, offers superb views over Lanín and many Chilean peaks. The ski resort is well organized, with 22 pistes, many of them challenging, including a lovely long easy piste for beginners. With an overall drop of 730 m, very good slopes and snow conditions, this is a popular resort with wealthier Argentines and, increasingly, foreigners too. There's also a ski school and snowboards for hire. There is a bus from San Martín to the slopes, US$2 return. **Transportes Chapelco**, T(02944) 156 18875, 425808. Details of the resort, passes, equipment hire are available in season from the Chapelco office at San Martín y Elordi, T427845, www.chapelco.com.ar At the foot of the mountain are a restaurant and base lodge, with three more restaurants on the mountain and a small café at the top. In summer this is a good place for cycling (take your bike up on the cable car, and cycle down), trekking, archery, or horse riding.

There are also trips to **Lago Curruhue** and **Termas de Epulafquen** or **Lahuen-Co**, are offered by tour companies, but can also be cycled or driven to along *ripio* roads from Lago Lolog. See PN Lanín, above. There's no public transport to these places at present. ▶ *For Sleeping, Eating and other listings, see pages 379-385.*

Border with Chile

Paso Hua Hum is usually open all year round and is an alternative to the route via the Paso Tromen (see page 369). Paso Hua Hum (659 m) lies 47 km west of San Martín de los Andes along Route 48 (*ripio*) which runs along the north shore of Lago Lacar and crosses the border to Puerto Pirehueico. Buses leave early morning daily, 2 hrs, US$4, check terminal for schedule (T427044); they connect with boat across Lago Pirehueico. Bikes can be taken. The Argentine and Chilean immigration is open summer 0800-2100, winter 0900-2000.

Into Chile

The road (*ripio*, tough going for cyclists) continues on the Chilean side to Puerto Pirehueico at the southern end of Lago Pirehueico, a long, narrow and deep lake, totally unspoilt except for some logging activity. At its northern end lies Puerto Fuy. Accommodation is available in private houses in both Puerto Pirehueico and Puerto Fuy. Ferries cross the lake between the two ports (from January to February, three daily, and from November to December and March to April, two daily, and from May to October they are daily except Sunday). Buses connect Puerto Pirehueico with Panguipulli, from where transport is available to other destinations in the Chilean Lake District.

Listings: Parque Nacional Lanín

Sleeping

Lago Huechulaufquen *p373*
There are superb campsites, but without a tent, your only option is one of three overpriced *hosterías*, all rather taking advantage of their lakeside positions, and the fact that you won't want to leave this

beautiful area at nightfall. Of the three, the most luxurious, though not the most welcoming is **Hostería Paimun**.
LL **Huechulafquen**, *T426075, T02944-156 0973, www.7lagos.com/huechulafken (price for half-board).* The most recommendable, and welcoming of the three options, with comfortable small rooms lined with wood

The Lake District Listings: Parque Nacional Lanín

and well heated, with gardens going down to the lakeside, very peaceful. The owner is a fanatical fisherman, and there's an expert native fishing guide on hand too (extra charge for this). In high season, lunches are served to non-residents here. Other choices for eating are limited, best to take a picnic.
LL Refugio del Pescador, *T491319*. The most basic, and popular, predictably, with fishermen. Full board offered, small golf course.

Camping

Camping Lafquenco, *just after the sign to Bahía Coihues*. This campsite is highly recommended for its friendly welcome and facilities where wild camping is possible in a beautiful spot, but there are no facilities. Lafquenco is run by friendly and helpful Juan Andres, with a good open spot on the lakeside and lots of room, $3pp. There are 3 more campsites beyond *Hostería Paimún*, at **Rincon**, **Mawziche** and finally at **Piedra Mala**, a most beautiful spot on Lago Paimún, where the bus stops. *Piedra Mala* has hot showers, *parrillas* and a *provedería* (food shop). Sites are spread under araucaria and beech trees by 2 beaches, with lovely walks along the water's edge to the end of the lake. $4 adults, $2 children.

Junín de los Andes p376, map p377
L Rio Dorado Lodge and Fly Shop, *Pedro Illera 448, T/F491548, www.ridorado .com.ar* Expensive luxury fishing lodge, designed to lure wealthy North Americans, with comfortable tasteful rooms, lovely gardens and attentive service. Good fly shop.
D Hostería Chimehuín, *tucked away at the end of the road by the river on Suárez y 25 de Mayo, T491132, hosteriachimehuin @jandes.com.ar* A long-established classic fishing *hostería* with beautiful gardens, and friendly owners, quaint cosy decor, and comfortable rooms all with bath and TV. Ask for the spacious rooms with balconies in the block next to the river. Good breakfasts, open all year. Recommended.
D Milla Piuke, *set back from the RN234, at Gral Roca y Av los Pehuenes, T/F492378, millapiuke@jandes.com.ar* Absolutely delightful and welcoming new *hostería*, with tastefully decorated and stylish rooms all with bath and TV, and apartments for

families, very warm hospitality from the radiant owner Vilma. Breakfast included. Highly recommended.
D Posada Pehuén, *Col Suárez 560, T491569, posadapehuen@hotmail.com* A lovely quiet bed and breakfast with pretty, rather old-fashioned rooms, all rooms with TV and bathroom, charming owners, good value.
D San Jorge, *at the very end of Antártida Argentina, T/F491147, www.7lagos.com/ hotelsanjorge open Nov-Apr*. A big, recently modernized 1960's hotel, beautifully located with lovely views and large gardens, homely well furnished rooms, all with bath and TV. Very good value, with good restaurant and internet access. English spoken. Recommended.
E Res Marisa, *Juan Manual de Rosas 360, T491175, www.residencialmarisa.com.ar* A simple place, good value, with plain clean rooms, and cheery family owners. *Confitería* downstairs, but breakfast is US$0.70 extra. It's on the main road, so a little noisy during the day, but handy, the bus terminal and cheap eating places.
E El Montañés, *San Martín 555, T491155*. The cheapest in town, conveniently on the plaza, has simple rooms, all with bath, and also offers fishing tours.

Estancias

L Estancia Huechahue, *southeast of town (reached from the Junín-Bariloche bus), T491303, www.ridingtours.com* A self-sufficent, English-run estancia, with comfortable, farmhouse accommodation, offering horse riding, wonderful 3-5 day trips into Lanín National Park where you camp, with everything included, also fishing, river trips, and farm activities.

Camping

Many sites in the area and two good ones in town.
Beata Laura Vicuña, *Ginés Ponte 861, T491149, campinglv@jandes.com.ar* Located on the river, with hot showers, electricity, small shop, discounts for stays over two days, also very good value *cabañas* for 4 or 7.
La Isla, *T492029*. Also on the river, a quieter spot for skiiing. Prices given are high season.

San Martín de los Andes *p376, map p378*
Single rooms and rates are scarce. There are

2 high seasons, when rates are much higher: Jan/Feb and July.

AL La Cheminée, *Gral Roca y Mariano Moreno, T427617, lacheminee@smandes .com.ar* One of the most luxurious options, with pretty and cosy cottage-style rooms, spacious bathrooms, and a small pool. Breakfast is included, but no restaurant. Overpriced in high season, but reasonable otherwise. English spoken.

L Las Lengas, *Col. Perez 1175, T427659*. You'll get a friendlier reception here than at La Cheminée. A large airy spacious hotel, with plain attractive rooms, all individually designed, and a warm relaxing atmosphere, in a peaceful part of town. Recommended.

A Hotel Del Viejo Esquiador, *San Martin 1242, T427690*. Very comfortable rooms with good beds, in traditional hunting lodge-style, excellent service. English spoken. Recommended.

A La Raclette, *Pérez 1170, T427664*. Delightful characterful rooms in a charming old building, with an excellent restaurant, in a quiet part of town.

B Hostal del Esquiador, *Col. Rhode 975, 427674*. Well decorated rooms, and a sitting room, good service. Great value low season.

B Hostería Walkirias, *Villegas 815, T428307, www.laswalkirias.com* A lovely place, homely but smart, with very spacious and well furnished, tasteful rooms with big bathrooms, breakfast and free transfer from the airport included, sauna and pool room, charming owners. Great value off season.

B La Masia, *Obeid 811, T427879*. Spacious high-ceilinged rooms, chalet style with lots of dark wood, and nice little bathrooms, lots of cosy places to sit in the evenings in bar and lounge.

C Casa Alta, *Obeid 659, T427456*. Deservedly popular, this is a welcoming bed and breakfast, with charming multilingual owners, who will make you feel at home. Comfortable rooms, most with bathrooms, lovely gardens, and delicious breakfast. Closed in low season, book in advance.

C Crismalu, *Rudecindo Roca 975, T427283, crismalu@smandes.com.ar* Simple rooms in attractive chalet-style place, good value with breakfast included.

C Hostería Las Lucarnas, *Pérez 632, T427085*. **381** Really good value, this central and pretty place with simple comfortable rooms, and friendly owner, who speaks English.

D-E pp Hosteria Bärenhaus, *Los Alamos 156, Barrio Chapelco (8370), T/F422775, www.baerenhaus.com* Welcoming English-and German-speaking young owners have thought of everything to make you feel at home here: excellent breakfast, very comfortable cosy rooms with bath and heating, or great value shared dorms. Highly recommended. 5km outside town, free pick-up from bus terminal and airport.

D Hostal del Lago, *Col. Rhode 854, T427598, hostalago@hotmail.com* A relaxed homely place, the rooms have basic bathrooms, but a good breakfast is included.

E pp Hostel Puma, *Fosbery 535 (take Rivadavia to the north, two blocks after crossing the bridge), T422443, F428544, puma@smandes.com.ar* Hostelling International discounts. The cheapest in town is this excellent, really lovely hostel, warm, friendly, and clean, run by an enthusiastic mountain guide who organizes treks to Lanín, rooms for 4 with private bathroom, also double rooms D, kitchen facilities, laundry, information on local trails, internet, cycle hire. Taxi US$0.80 from terminal. Recommended.

Cabañas

Plentiful *cabañas* are available in two main areas: up Perito Moreno on the hill to the north of town, and down by the lakeside. Prices increase in high season, but are good value for families or big groups.

Agua Escondida, *Rhode 1162, T422113, www.aguaescondida.com.ar* Very luxurious aparthotel, very comfortable, nicely designed, spacious apartments, great breakfasts, cosy, wood fires, internet access.

Antuen, *Perito Moreno 1850, T/F428340, www.interpatagonia.com/antuen* Modern well equipped luxurious *cabañas* for 2 to 7, with jacuzzi, pool, games room for kids, with views from elevated position above valley.

Eruizos, *Perez 428, T425856, www.eruizos .com.ar* Plainer *cabañas* in rustic but comfortable style.

● *Phone codes* Junín de los Andes, San Martín de los Andes and surrounding area: 02972.

La Encantada, *Peritor Moreno y Los Enebrs, T/F428364, www.laencantada.com*
In a spectacular position above town in wooded surroundings, large, beautifully furnished cosy *cabañas* for two or more families, with all possible comforts, and pool, games room, fishing guides offered too.

Ojo de Agua, *Perez 1198, T/F427921, www.interpatagonia.com/ojodeagua*
Well equipped *cabañas* for 2 to 7 more like little urban chalet-style houses, crammed next to each other in quiet part of town near the lake.

Cabañas del Lago, *Costanera 850, T/F427898, www.interpatagonia.com/ cabanasdellago* The main attraction is that they're right on the lakeside, simple rustic *cabañas*, not the most luxurious, but great location, and a bit cheaper than most. English and French spoken.

Camping
ACA, *Koessler 2176 (on the access road), T427332*. Hot water, laundry facilities.
Catritre, *Route 234 km 4. On the southern shore of the lake, T428820*. Good facilites in a gorgeous position on the shore.
Quila Quina, *T426919*. A pretty spot and a peaceful place (out of peak season) with beaches and lovely walks.

Lago Curruhue and Termas de Lahuen-Co *p374*
Camping
Camping Agreste Lanín. Lovely shaded spots with hot showers, toilets, *parrilladas* and places to wash, well run by friendly people, Dec to Apr US$0.60 per person.

🍴 Eating

Along Lago Huechulaufquen *p373*
There are lots of pleaces to eat here, with *provedurías*, selling good *pan casero*, home-made bread, at Bahía, Piedra Mala and Rincon, and light meals served at **La Valsa**, at Población Barriga.

Junín de los Andes *p376, map p377*
$$ **Ruca Hueney**, *on the plaza at Col Suárez y Milanesio*. The best place to eat in town, this popular place serves a broad menu: the 'famous' *bife de chorizo Ruca Hueney* and locally caught trout are delicious, US$8 for 2 courses.

$ **Confitería Centro de Tursismo**, *next to the tourist office*. A café-restaurant good for coffee and sandwiches.
$ **La Aldea de Pescador**, *Route 234 y Necochea, on the main road by the YPF station*. This is great place for *parrilla* and trout, very cheap.

San Martín de los Andes *p376, map p378*
Reflecting its status as a posh place for families, San Martín de los Andes has a lot of places to eat, and few of them cheap.
$$$ **Avataras**, *Teniente Ramon 765, T427104, open only Thu Fri Sat from 2030*. The best in town, this pricey, inspired place is absolutely marvellous. The surroundings are elegant, the menu imaginative, with cuisine from all over the world, from fondue to satay, US$13 for three courses and wine, an excellent treat.
$$ **La Chacha**, *Rivadavia y San Martín*. A much-recommended traditional *parrilla* for excellent steaks, and good pasta for vegetarians, with good old-fashioned service to match.
$$ **Pionieri**, *General Roca 1108*. Excellent Italian meals in a cosy house, with good service, English and Italian spoken. Recommended. The same owners run *Los Patos* (next door) for take-away food, *T428459*.
$$ **Pura Vida**, *Villegas 745*. The only vegetarian restaurant in town, small and welcoming, also serving fish and chicken dishes.
$ **Delikatesse**, *opposite El Regional*. Recommended for cheap food in very cheerful surroundings, with great menu deals, egg, goat and pudding for US$3.50.
$ **El Regional**, *Villegas 955*. Hugely popular for regional specialities – smoked trout, patés and hams, and El Bolsón's home-made beer, all in cheerful German-style decor.
$ **Ku**, *San Martín 1053*. An intimate *parrilla*, also serving delicious home-made pastas and superb mountain specialities, with excellent service and wine list.
$ **La Costa del Pueblo**, *on the costanera opposite pier, T429289*. This is one of the best value places overlooking the lake. A big family-orientated place, where kids running around give the place a cheerful atmosphere, offering a huge range of pastas, chicken and trout dishes. Very cheap dish of

the day (US$4 for 2 courses), with good service, recommended.
$ **Tío Pico**, *San Martín y Capitán Drury*. For a drink or lunch on the main street, this is a great bar-café, serving tasty *lomitos* in a warm atmosphere.

Teashops
Casa de Alicia, *Drury 814, T425830*. Delicious cakes and smoked trout.

✪ Shopping

San Martín de los Andes *p376, map p378*
There's a handicraft market in summer in Plaza San Martín. Lots of outdoor shops on San Martín sell clothes for walking and skiing, all pretty pricey, **Mountain Ski Shop**, *San Martín 861*. There are two recommended places for chocolates, among the many on San Martín: **Mamusia** which also sells home-made jams, and **Abuela Goye**, which also serves excellent ice creams.

✪ Sport and activities

Junín de los Andes *p376, map p377*
Fishing
The season runs from second sat in Nov to Easter. For Fly casting and trolling; Lagos Huechulafken, Paimún, Epulaufken, Tromen, Currehue, Rivers Chuimehuin, Malleo, Alumine, Quilquihue. See www.turismo.gov.ar/pesca for more information in English.
Fishing guides Flotadas Chimehuin, *Gines Ponte 143*. Angel Fontanazza offers expert guidance (and tuition for novices) and all inclusive packages with food, transport and accommodation, to all the nearby rivers and lakes. His daughter is also an expert guide. *T491313, fchimehuin@jdandes.com.ar www.todo-patagonia.com/chimehuin*
Río Dorado Lodge, *Pedro Illera 448, T491548, www.riodorado.com.ar* The luxury fishing lodge at the end of town, has a good fly shop, and organizes trips, run by experts and passionate fishermen.
Jorge Trucco, *based in fly shop Patagonia Outfitters in San Martín de los Andes, Perez 662, T427561, www.jorgetrucco.com* Very expert and professional trips, good advice, and many years of experience on the lakes and rivers around.

Alquimia Viajes and Turismo, *Padre Milanesio 840, T491355, www.interpatagonia. com/alquimia* Offers fishing excursions among a range of adventure tourism.
Estancia Quillén, *further north, at Aluminé, T(02942)496196, www.interpatagonia .com/quillen* Offers fishing on the estancia as well as trips to rivers and lakes in the surrounding area.

Trekking guides
There are many listed by the park ofice in San Martín, but also **Eduardo Greco**, *T492191, 491637, treklanin@jandes.com.ar*

San Martín de los Andes *p376, map p378*
Bird watching
Juan Carlos Lizaso, *T421553*. Tours are available in Lanín national park, all year round.

Cycling
Many places rent mountain and normal bikes in the centre, reasonable prices, maps provided.
HG Rodados, *San Martín 1061*. Rents mountain bikes at US$6 per day, also spare parts and expertise.

Fishing
The season runs from mid-Nov to the end of Apr. For guides: contact the tourist office or the National Park office. See www.turismo. gov.ar/pesca for more information (English). The outlets listed sell equipment, and offer fishing excursions.
Jorge Cardillo Pesca Fly shop, *Villegas 1061*.
Orvis Fly shop, *Gral Villegas 835 T425892*.
Patagonian Anglers, *M Moreno 1193, T427376, patagoniananglers@ smandes.com.ar*

Flying
Aeroclub de los Andes, *T426254, aeroclubandes@smandes.com.ar* For flights in light aircraft.

Skiing
Chapelco has 29 km of pistes, many of them challenging, with an overall drop of 730 m. Very good slopes and snow conditions make this a popular resort with foreigners and wealthier Argentines. At the foot of the mountain are a restaurant and base lodge,

with 3 more restaurants on the mountain and a small café at the top. To get to the slopes, take the bus from San Martín, US$2 return, **Transportes Chapelco**, *T02944-156 18875, 425808*. Details, passes, equipment hire from office at *San Martín y Elordi, T427845, www.chapelco.com.ar*

⊛ Festivals and events

Junín de los Andes *p376, map p378*
December 8: Inauguration of the church of **Laura Vicuña**, with a special mass and singing to celebrate the life of Laura Vicuna.
End January: **Agricultural show** and **exhibition of flowers and local crafts**.
mid February: **Fiesta Provincial de Puestero**: Election of the queen, handicrafts, *asados* with local foods, fabulous gaucho riding demonstrations,
the most important country fiesta in the south of Argentina.
March: Carnival.
End of July: **Festival of aboriginal arts**.
Second Sat in Nov: **Opening of the fishing season**.

⊅ Tour operators

Junín de los Andes *p376, map p377*
Alquimia, *Padre Milanesio 840, T491355, alquimia@jandes.com.ar www.volcanlanin. com* Adventure tourism, transport along the lakes, camping and mountain climbing equipment.
Tromen, *Lonquimay 195 (also at Paseo Artesanal, near main plaza in summer), T491498, tromen@jandes.com.ar*

San Martín de los Andes *p376, map p378*
Many are advertised on a helpful board in tourist information. These are the most professional (prices quoted are standard):
El Claro, *Villegas 977, T428876, www.interpatagonia.com/elclaro* Trips to the lakes, and also paragliding, horse riding, and other adventure trips.
Las Taguas, *Perito Moreno 1035, T427483, www.lastaguas.com* For horse riding, this is the best company. Marvellous horse riding trips over the surrounding areas of great beauty. Recommended.
Lucero Viajes, *San Martín 946, T428453, luceroviajes.com.ar* Rafting at Hua Hum

(US$20) horse riding (US$20), both including transfers, 4WD trips, and conventional tours to Hua Hum (US$10), Quila Quina (US$7), and Termas de Lahuen-Co (US$17), as well as selling ski passes in winter.
South Temptations, *San Martín 1254, T425479, www.geocities.com/ southtemptations* This operator runs fishing trips, conventional tours, and also longer 3-10 day trips around the lakes, three times a week, with everything included. To book a tour you need to take your passport. There is an office in the bus terminal, *T457422, or in Chile T56-63311647*.
Tiempo Patagónico, *San Martín 950, T427113, www.tiempopatagonico.com* Both conventional excursions, including the Seven lakes drive, and adventure tourism, including trekking, horse riding, and rafting at Hua Hum.

⊖ Transport

Junín de los Andes *p376, map p377*
Air
Chapelco airport, 19km southwest on the road to San Martín de los Andes (can be reached by taking any bus to San Martín). Taxi US$7. Flights to **Buenos Aires**, Austral, LADE weekly from **Bahía Blanca**, **Esquel**, and **Bariloche**.

Bus
The terminal is at Olavarría y Félix San Martín (do not confuse with Gral San Martín), with public phone, but no other facilites. *Information T492038*. To **San Martín de los Andes**, 45 mins, US$4, several a day, **Centenario, Ko Ko, Airén**. To **Neuquén**, 7 hrs, US$23, several companies. Ask about buses to **Huechulafken**; every year a different company. To **Tromen**, Mon-Sat 1 1/2 hrs, US$5. To **Caviahue** and **Copahue**, change at Zapala. 3 1/2hrs, US$11. To **Bariloche**, 3 hrs US$7, Via Bariloche, Ko Ko. To **Buenos Aires**, 21 hrs, US$30, several companies. To **Chile**: Service Temuco (5 hrs)US$9 via Paso Tromen, daily service with either **Empresa San Martín** 3 a week, **Igi Llaima**, 4 a week.

San Martín de los Andes *p376, map p378*
Air
See Junín de los Andes above. Airport T428388.

Bus *Information, T427044*
The bus terminal is reasonably central, at
Villegas 251, with toilet facilities, kiosk, no
locutorio. Bikes can be carried on most
routes, wheels removed. To **Buenos Aires**,
20hrs, US$40 *coche cama*, daily, 6
companies. To **Bariloche**, 4 hrs, US$7, many
daily, via Bariloche, *T425325*, **Albus**, *T428100*,
via Traful and La Angostura. **Ko Ko**, *T427422*,
daily, fast route via Confluencia, or via the
Seven Lakes in summer only. Over the
border, **Koko** goes to Chile, boat crossings to
Lago Pirehueico, leaving Puerto Fuy at 1230
and leaving Pirehueico at 1600 daily and
takes bikes US$1, car US$5. **Puerto Madryn**
(changing Neuquén) US$30.
   To **Chile**: **Temuco** with Empresa San
Martín, *T427294*, Mon, Wed, Fri, Igi-Llaima,
T427750, Tue, Thu, Sat, US$9 , 6-8 hrs (heavily
booked in summer, via Paso Hua Hum – see
above, sit on the left).

Boat
The boat which crosses the pass to Chile at
Hua Hum also takes cars daily in summer
from Puerto Fuy to Puerto Pirehueico Tourist
office in Panguipuli, *T(63)311311*
www.panguipuli.com

Car hire
Rent a Car La Patagonia, *Villegas 305*,
T421807, 15557669.
Localiza, *El Claro Turismo, Villegas 977, T428876*.

Cycle hire
There are many places where you can rent
bikes along San Martín: **HG Rodados**, *San
Martín 1061*. US$6 per day, also spare parts and
expertise. **Eco Juegos**, *Av Costanera y Villegas*.

❻ Directory

Junín de los Andes *p376, map p377*
Banks Travellers cheques can be cashed
at **Western Union**, *Milanesio 570,
1000-1400, 1600-1930*; and money changed
at **Banco Provincial Neuquén**, *San Martín y
Lamadrid, also has ATM.*
Communications Post office, *Suárez y
Don Bosco*. **Telephone**, *locutorio near
tourist office on plaza at Milanesio 540*.
Internet in the *galería* behind tourist
office. The Parque Nacional Lanín
information office is in same building as
tourist office, *T491160*, and is very helpful.

San Martín de los Andes *p376, map p378*
Airline offices Aerolíneas
Argentinas/Austral, *Drury 876, T427003*.
LADE, *in the bus terminal at Villegas 231,
T427672*. **Southern Winds**, *San Martín 866,
T425815*. **Banks** Many ATMs along San
Martín: Banelco, *at the tourist office, San
Martín y Rosas*. Banco Frances, *San Martín y
Sarmiento*. Casas de Cambio at **Banco de la
Nación**, *San Martín 687*. Banco de la
Provincia de Neuquén, *Obeid y Belgrano*.
Communications Internet Lots of fast
services, **Cybercafe Patagonia**, good place
at back of *galería around San Martín 850*.
Post office *General Roca y Pérez*, Mon-Fri
0800-1300, 1700-2000, Sat 0900-1300.
Telephones Cooperativa Telefónica, *Drury
761*. **Laundry** Laverap, *Drury 880*,
0800-2200 daily.Marva, *Drury y Villegas*, and
Perito Moreno 980. Fast, efficient and cheap.
Medical services Hospital Ramón
Carrillo, *San Martín y Coronel Rodhe*,
T427211.

South to Bariloche

La Ruta de los Siete Lagos

The Seven Lakes Drive is the most famous tourist route in the Argentine Lake District.
It follows Route 234 through the Lanín and Nahuel Huapi National Parks, and passes
seven magnificent lakes, all flanked by southern forests and is particularly attractive
in autumn (April/May) when the forested slopes turn red and yellow. The road is only
partially paved, but decent hard earth, only closed after heavy rain or snowfall.
   The seven lakes are (going form north to south) Lácar, Machónico, Falkner,

Villarino, Correntoso, Espejo and Nahuel Huapi. The road passes Lago Machónico at Km 30 and Lago Hermoso at Km 36. At Km 48 it runs between Lago Villarino and Lago Falkner. As the road emerges to climb up overlooking the shores of Lago Villarino, you're suddenly treated to a welcome open vista of the lake and from here the road is *ripio*. There's a lovely, if exposed, free campsite with no facilites by the deep green Rio Villarino. Popular with fishermen, Lago Falker opposite is wide and open with thickly forested fiord-like mountains descending steeply into it. There's a long narrow sandy beach on the roadside, a good place for a picnic stop, and wild camping, with no facilities. **Camping Lago Falkner** nearby does have facilities. At Pichi Traful, a beautiful spot by the wide green banks of the aquamarine blue river, there's a campsite and even more lovely picnic ground, amidst little beech trees by turquoise water with steeply rising mountains on all sides. The *hostería* may look inviting but it's owned by a religious organization, and is closed to the public.

Before passing the northwestern corner of Lago Traful at Km 58. At Km 77 Route 65 branches off to the east, running along the south shore of Lago Traful through Villa Traful to meet the main Neuquén-Bariloche highway (Route 237) at Confluencia. Camp or stay by Lago Espejo, or stop for a picnic, at least, off the road a few km, with lovely beaches on the lakeshore. There's a car park to admire the falls at Vulcanche. There's a lovely if exposed free campsite with no facilites by the deep green Río Villarino.

Round trip excursions along the Seven Lakes route, taking five hours, are operated by several companies, but it's better in your own transport, as you'll want to stop and explore. Buses will stop at campsites on the route – see under San Martín for companies. It's good for cycling, though more traffic Jan/Feb. ▶▶ *For Sleeping, Eating and other listings, see pages 391-394*

The direct route

There's a quicker route, but also quite attractive, via **Confluencia**. Take Route 63, unpaved, southeast from Route 234, along the tranquil shore of Lago Meliquina and over the Paso de Córdoba, Km 77, (1,300 m) where you enter the Parque Nacional Nahuel Huapi. You could turn off to isolated Lago Filo-Hua-Hum at Km 54 (unpaved track). From Confluencia, take the paved Neuquén-Bariloche highway, running through the astounding **Valle Encantado**, where there are weird rock formations including El Dedo de Dios (The Finger of God) and El Centinela del Valle (The Sentinel of the Valley), before reaching Bariloche, 157 km from San Martín de los Andes.

Villa Traful → *Phone code 02944*

If you want to get off the beaten track, Villa Traful is ideal. Approaching from the west, you'll pass forests of lenga and coihue, their elegant tall trunks creating a woody cathedral, with idyllic spots to camp all along the shore. The quiet pretty village sprawls alongside the narrow deep-blue sliver of Lago Traful, enclosed on both sides by stunning sharp peaked mountains. Popular with fishermen, there are also some wonderful walks and waterfalls to see, and little else to do here but unwind. Best in December or late February/March when the only two restaurants aren't full of tourists. Traful is prone to mercurial winds, so check the forecast if you're coming for a few days. At the heart of the village opposite the main pier, are a payphone, a kiosk selling basic supplies and bus tickets, and the best restaurant. There's a small but very helpful tourist office further along the lakeshore, just past Aiken cabañas, T479020, with information in walks, riding and fishing, www.7lagos.com/traful The *guardería* is opposite the pier, open only in high season, with advice on walks.

Around Villa Traful

A one and a half hour walk from the village centre there are lovely **Cascadas dal Arroyo Coa Có y Blanco**, waterfalls thundering down through beech forest and cañas colihues bamboo. Walk up the hill from the **Ñancu Lahuen** restaurant and take the left

hand path to the mirador over Cascada Coa Có, and from here take the right hand
path through coihue forest to Cascada Blanco. A lovely ride by horse or mountain
bike. Bikes for hire at Del Montanes T479035, *alfajores* makers, along the road
running up the slope behind the centre of the village.

To Villa La Angostura

From Traful, at Km 80, the road runs along the north side of Lago Correntoso before
turning south. Route 234 meets Route 231, the road between Bariloche and the
Chilean border at Paso Puyehue (see below). There is a particularly beautiful view
from the bridge over the Río Correntoso, a few kilometres north of Villa La Angostura.

Villa La Angostura → *Phone code: 02944 Colour map 5, B2 Population: 8,000*

This pretty town with a villagey feel is a popular holiday resort for wealthier
Argentines, and there are countless restaurants, hotels and *cabaña* complexes
around the sprawling town centre, **El Cruce**, and around the picturesque port, known
as **La Villa**, 3 km away at the neck of the Quetrihué Peninsula. There are tourist offices
on the side of Route 231, just above the crossroads north of town, and opposite the
bus terminal, ① *at Avenida Siete Lagos 93, T494124, www.villalaangostura.net.ar
and www.turismoangostura.com, open high season 0800-2100, low season
0800-2000.* This is a busy and helpful office, with good maps with accommodation
and prices marked on a board inside. English spoken.

  Villa La Angostura's great attraction is to be found at the end of the Quetrihué
Peninsula, the **Parque Nacional Los Arrayanes**, accessed from the port area of La Villa
(see below). Also from la Villa, a short walk leads to **Laguna Verde**, an intense
emerald green lagoon surrounded by mixed *coihue* cypress and arrayán forests,
where there's a self-guided trail. A bus runs from El Cruce to La Villa every couple of
hours, taking 15 mins, but it's a pleasant walk. There are no services in La Villa apart
from a *kiosko* and tearoom in high season, and the restaurant at Hotel Angostura.
About halfway between the two centres there is a chapel (1936), designed by Bustillo,
the famous architect who gave this region's buildings their distinctive style and
nearby is **El Messidor** (1942), the luxury summer resort of Argentine presidents, which
has beautiful gardens with lake views. In winter, Villa La Angostura's main attraction
is the popular ski resort **Cerro Bayo**, 9 km north of town, with 24 pistes, many of them
fabulously long, and all with excellent views over the lakes below, 20km in total, and
a great area for snowboarding. T494189, www.cerrobayoweb.com This is one of
Argentina's pricier resorts; here a ski pass costs US$15 for adults for the day, in high
season. There's also a tiny musuem **Museo Regional** ① *on the road to la Villa, Mon
0800-1400, Tue- Fri 0800-1630, Sat 1430-1700,* with interesting photos of the
original indigenous inhabitants. ▸▸ *For Sleeping, Eating and other listings, see pages 391-394.*

Around Villa La Angostura

There are fine views of Lagos Correntoso and Nahuel Huapi from **Mirador Belvedere**, 3
km drive or walk up the old road, northwest of El Cruce; from the *mirador* a path to
your right goes to Cascada Inacayal, a waterfall 50m high, situated in an area rich in
native flora and forest. Another delightful walk leads to beautiful waterfall, **Cascada
Río Bonito**, lying 8 km east of El Cruce off Route 66. The steep path gives tremendous
views, and the falls themselves are impressive, falling 35 m from a chasm in basalt
cliffs to an emerald green pool. Further along the same path, you can reach the
summit of Cerro Bayo 1782 m. Though 1 km further along the road, a ski lift takes you
to the platform at 1,500 m, where there's a restaurant with great views, and from here,
it's a short trek to the summit. The ski lift functions all year and cyclists can take bikes
up in the lift and cycle down.

This park, covering the Quetrihué Peninisula, which dips into the Lago Nahuel Huapi, within the Parque Nacional, was created to protect a rare forest of *arrayán* trees. This is one of the few places where the *arrayán* grows to full size, and some of the specimens are 300 years old. This myrtle-like tree, which grows near water in groves. Their trunks are extraordinary: a smooth powdery or peeling surface and cold to the touch. They have no outer bark to protect them, but the surface layer is rich in tannins which keep the tree free from disease. They have creamy white flowers in January and February, and produce blue-black fruit in March. The sight of so many of these trees together, with their twisting cinnamon-coloured trunks creating a magical light, is wonderful. The most rewarding way to see the wood is to take the boat trip across the sparkling deep blue lake, fringed with spectacular peaks, and take a leisurely walk along the wooden walkways through the trees, once the guided tour has left. Then stroll back to the port through the mixed forest.

Access The park lies 1 2km south of the port area of Villa la Angostura, known as La Villa, and a clear path can be walked or cycled. Three hours one way walking, two hours cycling. There are two boats, each running twice daily in summer (in winter only if there's sufficient demand), US$7 return, with the more attractive boat *Huemul II*, T494233. Tickets from **Hotel Angostura**, US$9.30 return with the catamaran. Boats sometimes run from Bariloche, via Isla Victoria. Bus company **15 de Mayo** runs buses from El Cruce to la Villa every two hours and takes 15 minutes. There's a *confitería* in the park, selling drinks and confectionery.

Border with Chile → *This route is liable to closure after snow*

Officially known as Paso Samore, **Paso Puyehue** (1,280 m) lies 125 km northwest of Bariloche by Route 231, which is unpaved from Villa La Angostura, a spectacular drive. Perhaps less scenic than the ferry journey across Lake Todos Los Santos and Laguna Verde, this crossing is far cheaper, and more reliable. **Argentine customs and immigration** ① *Open winter 0900-2000, summer 0800-2100*. It's another 50 km to Chilean customs over a wonderful mountain pass. Crossing by private vehicle

The **Samoré**, formerly Puyehue Pass. A spectacular six-hour drive. A good broad paved road RN 231, goes around the east end of Lago Nahuel Huapi, then follows the north side of the lake through Villa La Angostura. It passes the junction with 'Ruta de Los Siete Lagos' for San Martín at Km 94, Argentine customs at Km 109, and the spectacular pass itself at Km 125 – an elevation of about 1,280 m. The road is rough *ripio* here, with the odd paved stretch. On the Chilean side the road is paved via Entre Lagos and Lago Puyehue to Osorno. **Chilean immigration** is in the middle of a forest at Anticura, Km 146, 22km west of the border, ① *2nd Sat in Oct to 1 May 0800-2100, winter 0900-2000*, but liable to be closed after snow-falls. For vehicles entering Chile, formalities take about 30 minutes, and include the spraying of tyres and wiping of shoes on a mat, for which you may have to pay US$2 to *Sanidad* and should have Chilean pesos ready. No fresh food is to be taken over the border to Chile, and Argentine hire cars are not permitted to leave the country without necessary documentation, which your car hire company can arrange (takes 24 hrs), and the car's number plate etched on the windows.

Parque Nacional Nahuel Huapi

Covering a spectacular 750,000 ha and stretching along the Chilean border for over 130 km, this is the oldest National Park in Argentina. It was created in 1934, but originated from a donation made to the state in 1903 by Francisco Perito Moreno of 7,500 ha of land around Puerto Blest. Extending across some of Argentina's most dramatic mountains, the park contains lakes, rivers, glaciers, waterfalls, torrents, rapids, valleys, forest, bare mountains and snow-clad peaks. Among those you can climb are Tronador (3,478m), Catedral (2,388m), Falkner (2,350m), Cuyín Manzano (2,220m), López (2,076m), Otto (1,405m) and Campanario (1,049m). The outstanding feature is the splendour of the lakes.

The largest lake is **Lago Nahuel Huapi**, a huge 531 sq km and 460 m deep in places, particularly magnificent to explore by boat since the lake is very irregular in shape and long fjord-like arms of water, or *brazos*, stretch far into the **Parque Nacional Los Arrayanes**, which contains a rare woodland of exquisite *arrayán* trees with their cinnamon-coloured flaky bark. There are many islands: the largest is **Isla Victoria**, with its luxurious hotel. Trout and salmon have been introduced.

North of Villa La Angostura, **Lagos Correntoso** and **Espejo** both offer stunning scenery, and tranquil places to stay and walk. Navy blue **Lago Traful**, a short distance to the northeast, can be reached by a road which follows the Río Limay through the **Valle Encantado**, with its fantastic rock formations, or directly from **Villa La Angostura**. Villa Traful is the perfect place to escape to, with fishing, camping, and walking. Spectacular mountains surround the city of **Bariloche**, where tourism and access are the most developed, offering great trekking and skiing country. The most popular walks are described in Bariloche section, page 395.

West of Bariloche, there are glaciers and waterfalls near **Pampa Linda**, the base for climbing Mt Tronador, and starting point for the trek through Paso de las Nubes to Lago Frias. South of Lago Nahuel Huapi, Lagos Mascardi, Guillelmo, and Gutiérrez have even grander scenery, offering horse riding, trekking, and rafting along the Rio Manso. See South of Bariloche below, page 409, for hotels along their shores. There is skiing at **Cerro Catedral**, and water sports on many of the lakes. Horse riding is available almost everywhere, and is a wonderful way of exploring the area. Swimming in the larger lakes such as Nahuel Huapi and Huechulafquen is not recommended: the water is far too cold. But swimming in smaller lakes can be very pleasant in summer and the water – especially where the bottom shelves to a shingly beach – can be positively warm.

Park essentials

Tourist information Bariloche is the main centre first port of call for entering the park, where you can equip yourself with information on transport, walks and maps. The **Nahuel Huapi National Park** *intendencia*, ① *San Martín 24, T423111, is very helpful, open 0900-1400, www.parquesnacionales.com.ar* Also useful for information on hiking is **Club Andino Bariloche** (CAB) ① *20 de Febrero 30, T422266, 424531 www.clubandino.com.ar, 0900-1300, plus 1600-2100 high season only .*
They sell three hand-drawn maps and one in colour, showing walks, with average walking times, and *refugios*. They can also advise on transport. ▸▸ *For Sleeping, Eating and other listings, see pages 391-394.*

Best time to visit For walking: December to March, though in January many paths are closed because of snow, or fallen trees until conditions have cleared in January. Almost everywhere is packed in January itself, the main Argentine holiday. Secondary school children from all over Argentina come to Bariloche as a rite of passage in December. Skiing is possible late June to August, and July is best avoided, when Argentine schools have holiday. Hotel prices rise in the busiest periods, but be prepared for less transport and infrastructure in low season.

Nahuel Huapi National Park started with a generous donation by explorer and geographer Perito Moreno, who was granted 7,500 ha of land by the Argentine government as thanks for determining the border with Chile. Instead of keeping all this natural beauty to himself, he gave it to the state, an incredibly altruistic act!

Vegetation varies with altitude and climate, but includes large expanses of southern beech forest and near the Chilean border, where rainfall is highest, there are areas of magnificent virgin Valdivian rainforest. Here you will see *coihues* (evergreen beeches) over 450 years old and *alerces* over 1,500 years old, with the ancient species of bamboo cane *caña colihue* growing everywhere, but eastern parts of the park are more steppe-like with shrubs and bushes. Wildlife includes the small *pudú* deer, the

Parque Nacional Nahuel Huapi

The Lake District Parque Nacional Nahuel Huapia

endangered *huemul* and river otter, as well as foxes, cougars and guanacos. Among the birds, Magellan woodpeckers and austral parakeets are easily spotted as well as large flocks of swans, geese and ducks.

Listings: South to Bariloche

⬤ Sleeping

La Ruta de los Siete Lagos *p385*
There are several places to stay, open summer only.
C **Hostería Lago Villarino**, *at Lago Villarino*. A lovely setting, good food, also camping.
C **Lago Espejo Resort**, *at tranquil Lago Espejo, set a little way off the road*. A beautifully situated hotel, rather grandly named, and simple camping area, on the tranquil and secluded shore of the lake, surrounded by *coihue* trees.
D **Hostería Lago Espejo**. Old fashioned and comfortable, with good food in the restaurant, open Jan-Mar only.
D pp **Hostería Los Siete Lagos**, *in a secluded but open spot on the flat shore of lake Correntoso*. A lovely simple *hostería* with just five small, very simple rooms, but some with great views of the lake, a charming place. There is only electricity in the evenings but full board is possible. There is a good restaurant with home-made bread for sale. Also a campsite summer only, no services, free. There's no phone, but the tourist office in Villa la Angostura will radio to reserve.

The direct route from San Martín to Bariloche *p386*
C **Hostería La Gruta de las Virgenes**, *Confluencia, T426138*. Situated on a hill with views over the two rivers, very hospitable.
D **Hostería ACA Confluencia**, *T490800*, at the *ACA* service station, with a *confitería*.
D **Motel El Rancho**, *just before Confluencia*.

Camping
The campsite Lago Espejo Resort is open all year. Facilities include toilets, drinking water, fireplaces, no showers, US$1pp. Further along an earth track is the lovely **Lago Espejo Camping**, a magical spot on quiet shores of the lake and its incredibly blue-grey river. Open all year, mostly visited by fishermen in the season (from Nov to end Apr), US$1pp, no showers, but toilets, drinking water and fireplaces. Also picnic spots, busy Jan, less so in Feb. Recommended.

Villa Traful and around *p386*
There's little choice of accommodation.
B/D **Ruca Lico**, *T479004, 15553960, www.interpatagonia.com/rucalico* Luxurious *cabañas*, in woodland above the lake shore, lavishly furnished in rustic chic style, with jacuzzi and balcony with splendid views. Good value for 6, a fabulous treat for 2. Highly recommended. Horse riding is also organized.
D **Aiken**, *T479048, www.aiken.com.ar* Rustic and compact, but well decorated compact *cabañas* in spacious gardens with old trees, and open views of the lake below. All have *parrilladas* outside and a feeling of privacy. Cheap for 4 or 5. Recommended.
D **Hostería Villa Traful**, *T479005*. A delightful place to stay, elevated above the lakeside, in pretty gardens. Separate little cabins, with comfortable furnishings, and ample bathrooms. There are also pretty *cabañas* for up to 6, US$50. Charming hospitality from the owner, whose son Andres Quelin, *T479005*, also organizes fishing and boat trips.
F/D **Vulcanche**, *T494015, www.vulcanche .com* An attractive chalet-style hostel, F pp, and D 2 *cabañas*, cosy rather than luxurious, set in lovely open gardens with good views. Also simple camping in a pleasant open site, US$2 pp with hot showers, phone, *parrilladas*.

Camping
There are many sites along the lakeshore.
Camping Traful Lauquen, *on the shore, T479030, www.interpatagonia.com*

⬤ *For an explanation of the sleeping and eating price codes used in this guide, see the inside front cover. Other relevant information is provided in the Essentials chapter, page 44.*

/trafullauquen With 600m of beach on the lake, this is among the loveliest of the many sites all along the lake. Facilities include hot showers, light, fireplaces, restaurant, US$2.30 pp, open Nov to Mar. A really calm and beautiful site, much favoured by families wanting a quiet time.

Costa de Traful, *T479023*. If you're under 30 and you've got a guitar, or would like to meet somebody who has, camp at this lively place with 24-hour hot showers, restaurant, fireplaces, *proveduria*, popular with backpackers, US$2.30pp, open Dec to Apr. *Cabañas* for hire, B for 4, rustic basic. Also fishing and horse riding trips as well as trips to see cave paintings on the other side of the lake (3-hr trek each way), US$12, full day, also boat trip to see a submerged cypress forest, diving for those with experience.

Villa La Angostura *p387*

Accommodation is good, but pricey. It's much more pleasant, and cheaper, outside of Jan and Jul peak seasons

L **Las Balsas**, *on Bahía Las Balsas (off Av.Arrayanes), T494308, www.lasbalsas. com.ar* The most famous and exclusive hotel in the area, fabulous rooms and service, in a great lakeside location.

A **Bahía Manzano**, *in a prime position on its own beach at Puerto Manzana, T494341, www.bahiamanzano.com* A smart hotel and aparthotel resort for families, well organised and surprisingly reasonable for larger groups, US$130 for 6, with modern stylish rooms, spa, games rooms, pool, gym, sports and activities organized. And a good restaurant. Perfect for families.

A **Cabañas Aries**, *Los Coihues 141, on the road towards Algo Correntoso, T 494648, www.cabaries.com.ar* Attractive rustic *cabañas*, well equipped, with lake views.

A **Portal de Piedra**, *N231 y Río Bonito, T494278, www.portaldepiedra.com* A welcoming *hostería* and tea room in the woods, with tastefully decorated wood-panelled rooms, and attractive gardens. Guests only restaurant, excursions and activities.

B **Casa del Bosque**, *T595229, www.casadelbosque.com* Luxury and style in these wonderfully designed *cabanas*, lots of glass, with jacuzzis and all possible comforts, in secluded in woodland at Puerto Manzana. Recommended.

B **Hostería Pichi Rincón**, *Route 231, km 64, 2 km northwest of the Cruce, T494186, www.pichirincon.com.ar* Attractive wood and stone chalet in woodland elevated above the lake, with cottagey wood-lined rooms, and comfortable lounge with wood fire. Attentive service, and good restaurant.

B **Hotel Angostura**, *T494224, www.hotel laangostura.com.ar* Open all year, beautifully situated on the lakeside at the port, La Villa, this handsome stone and wood chalet was designed by Bustillo in 1938, and retains a rather charming old-fashioned feel, with lovely gardens, and an excellent restaurant, open to residents in high seaons.

B **La Posada**, *Route 231 km 65, a few km west of town on Route 231 towards Chile, T494450,T494450, www.hosteriala posada.com* In a splendid elevated position off the road and with clear views over the lake, this is a welcoming, beautifully maintained hotel in lovely gardens, with pool and fine restaurant; a perfectly peaceful place to relax.

D **Verena's Haus**, *Los Taiques 268, T494467.* A quaint and welcoming wooden house, with accommodation for adults and non-smokers only, cosy rooms with a pretty garden, delicious breakfasts. German and English spoken. Recommended.

F **Hostel la Angostura**, *T494834, www.hostellaangostura.com.ar* Fortunately, Villa La Angostura does have 2 cheap places to stay: just 300m up the road behind the tourist office is this warm, luxurious and cheap hostel, all small dorms have bathrooms, and the friendly young owners organize trips too. Highly recommended.

F pp **Lo de Francés**, *Lolog 3057, located in a great position on shore of Lago Correntoso, T15564063, www.interpatagonia.com /lodefrances, www.hostels.org.ar* The second of Villa La Angostura's cheaper options, this comfortable chalet-style hostel has great views from all the rooms, with facilities. Hostelling international affiliated. Recommended.

Camping

There are many sites, with good facilites along the Route 231.

Osa Mayor, *signposted off main road close to town, T494304, osamayor@oul. com.ar* Highly recommended is this delightful leafy site on a hillside with good, shaded levelled camping spots, and all facilities and clean bathrooms, run by a friendly family. US$2.30pp. Also rustic, rather basic *cabañas*. Lovely apart from Jan, when the place is packed.

Border with Chile *p388*
AL **Termas Puyehue**, *Route 215 km76, T(56-2)293 6000, www.puyehue.cl* Luxurious accommodation and excellent thermal baths at a huge complex set in beautiful open parkland, framed by mountains, with an impressive spa. Recommended.

🍴 Eating

Villa Traful and around *p386*
$ **Ñancu Lahuen**, *T02944, 479179.*
A delightful tea room and restaurant serving excellent trout and home made pastas, all reasonably priced. Great cakes and delicious home made chocolates, a homely place to hang out if it's raining, with a big open fire.
$ **Parrilla La Terraza**, *T479077.*
Recommended for delicious locally produced lamb and kid on the *asado*, with panoramic lake views.

Villa La Angostura *p387*
Plenty of places are to be found on the main Av Arrayanes, lots of them chalet-style, and open all day from breakfast onwards. Prices reflect the fact that this is a popular tourist town.
$$ **Barba's**, *Av Arrayanes 167.* Unassuming café, with an imaginative menu.
$$ **Hora Cero**, *Av Arrayanes 45.* Hugely popular, a big range of excellent pizzas, and *pizza libre* (as much as you can eat for US$2) on Wed and Sat is a great deal.
$$ **Los Troncos**, *Av Arrayanes 67.*
Offers some of the best local dishes, great trout-filled ravioli, and fabulous cakes and puddings. With a warm atmosphere and live music at weekends.
$$ **Nativa Café**, *Av Arrayanes 198.* This is the most relaxed and welcoming of those on the main drag with a high-ceilinged chalet feel, good music playing, and a menu which manages to be international and individual.

Excellent pizzas – try the smoked goat topping! – and a good place to hang out. Friendly efficient staff and a mixed clientele – couples and families of all ages. Pizza for 2 US$3-8, huge salads. Recommended.
$$ **Rincon Suizo**, *Av Arrayanes 44.* Open only in high season for delicious regional specialities with a Swiss twist, in a rather more authentic chalet-style building.
$ **El Esquiador**, *Las Retames 146 (behind the bus terminal).* Your best bet on a budget is the *parrilla*, with cheap fixed price 3-course menu.
$ **Gran Nevada**, *opposite Nativa café.* Good for cheap *parrilla* US$2, and *noquis* US$1.20 in a cheery friendly atmosphere.
$ **Las Lenas**, *a block south of Gran Nevada.* Takeaway chickens and pastas.

⊕ Sport and activities

Villa Traful and around *p386*
Fishing
Andres Quelin, *T479005.* A fishing guide who organizes boat trips to see a submerged cypress wood. Find him at *Hostería Villa Traful.*
Osvaldo A Brandeman, *Bahía Mansa, T479048, pescaosvaldo@mail.com* Fishing expert and excellent guide. Find him on the lakeshore 200m from Arroyo Cataratas. Horse riding and boat trips are organized by *Camping Costa de Traful* (see below).

Villa La Angostura *p387*
Climbing
Club Andino Villa La Angostura, *Cerro Bayo 295.* Excursions and information.

Fishing
The season runs from mid-Nov to the end of Apr. For permits and a list of fishing guides, ask the tourist office. Fly shops: **Banana Fly Shop**, *Av Arrayanes 282, T494634.* The following fly shops also arrange fishing trips: **Angler's Home Fly Shop**, *Belvedere 22, T495222.* **Class**, *Av Arrayanes 173, T494411.*

Horse riding
Rates are usually about US$5 per hr.

● Phone codes *Villa La Angostura and surrounding area: 02944.*

Los Saucos, *Av Arrayanes 1810, T494853*.
Cabalgatas Correntoso, *T15552950,
cabalgatascorrentoso@cybersnet.com.ar*
Offers horseback excursions in the
surrounding area and to Villa Traful.

Tour operators

Villa La Angostura *p387*
Rucan Turismo, *Av 7 Lagos 90, T495075,
www.rucanturismo.com* Skiing, riding,
mountain biking and conventional tours.
Terpin Turismo, *Los Notros 41, T494551,
terpinturismo@netpatagon.com* Trips to
Chile and surrounding areas, car hire.
Lengas Tour, *Av Arrayanes 173, T494575,
turismo@lengas.com* Horse riding, fishing,
hunting, with bilingual guides.
Turismo Cerros y Lagos, *Av Arrayanes 21,
T495447, www.patagonianadventures
.com* Skiing and adventure sports.

Transport

Ruta de los Siete Lagos *p361*
Round trip excursions along the Seven Lakes
route, 5 hrs, are operated by several
companies, but it's better in your own
transport, as you'll want to stop and explore.
Buses will stop at campsites on the route –
see under San Martín, page 383, for
companies. Good for **cycling**, though there
is more traffic in Jan/Feb.

Villa Traful and around *p386*
In high summer, a daily **bus** between **Villa
la Angostura** and **San Martín** stops here,
but in low season, buses run only 3 times a
week. *Kiosko El Ciervo*, by the *YPF* service
station, sells tickets and has the timetable.

Villa La Angostura *p387*
Bus
The terminal is at the junction of Av 7 Lagos
and Av Arrayanes, opposite the *ACA* service

station. For bus network information,
Andesmar, *T495247*, Via Bariloche/El Valle,
T495415, Albus, *T156 17578*, 15 de Mayo
T495104. To/from **Bariloche**, 1¼ hrs, US$3,
several companies, several daily. If going on
to **Osorno** (Chile), you can arrange for the
bus company to pick you up at **La
Angostura**, US$7 to **Osorno**. Daily buses to
San Martín de los Andes with Ko Ko and
Albus. For other destinations, change at San
Martín de los Andes and Bariloche.

Car hire
Terpin Turismo, *Los Notros 41, T494551,
terpinturismo@netpatagon.com.ar*
Giminez Vidal, *Las Muticias 146, T494336*.

Cycle hire
Expect to pay around US$7 per day.
Free Bikes, *Las Retamas 121, T495047*.
Ian Bikes, *Topa Topa 102 y Las Fucsias, T1555
7294, ianbikes@hotmail.com* Also arranges
spares and repairs.

Taxi
Juan Carlos Pinuen, *T494221*.

Border with Chile
For bus services from Bariloche to **Osorno**,
Puerto Montt and **Valdivia**, see page 400.

Directory

Villa La Angostura *p387*
Banks Andina, *Arrayanes 256, T495197*. For
cash and TC's. Banco de Patagonia, *Av
Arrayanes 275*, and Banco Prov de Neuquén,
Av Arrayanes 172. Both with ATMs.
Communications Internet Punta
Arrayanes, *Av Arrayanes 90, T495288*. **Post
office** *Siete Lagos 26*. **Telephone** Several
locutorios along *Av Arrayanes*. **Medical
services** Hospital Rural Arraiz, *Copello 311
(at barrio Pinar), T494170*.

Bariloche

→ *Phone code: 02944 Colour map 5, B2 Population: 100,000*

Sitting on the steep and wooded southern shore of Lago Nahuel Huapi at an altitude of 770 m, San Carlos de Bariloche, is one of Argentina's most beautifully situated cities, and a good centre for exploring the stunning scenery of Nahual Huapi National Park. The chalet-style civic made of local wood and stone was designed by Bustillo in the 1930s, inspired by the Swiss and German origins of Bariloche's early settlers. Along the tourist-orientated main street, Mitre, the trend for chalet-style continues, in a proliferation of chocolate shops and restaurants serving fondue as well as delicious local trout and wild boar, some of them bordering on kitsch, but appealing nevertheless. Bariloche has long been popular among Argentine holiday makers and is well set up for visitors, with many hotels and restaurants in the town centre, and more extending west along the shore of the lake, towards Llao Llao, where Argentina's most famous hotel enjoys a spectacularly beautiful setting. The area to the south and west of Bariloche offers superb walking, riding and fishing, and in summer there are good bus and boat services to reach these mountains and lakes as well as cable cars up two of the summits, also used in winter, when the ski resort Cerro Catedral is hugely popular.

Ins and outs

Getting there The airport is 15km east of town, taxis charge US$5. A bus service runs by **Del Lago Turismo**, Villegas 222, T430056, and meets each arriving/departing flight. US$1, from Mitre y Villegas outside the door of **Aerolíneas Argentinas** building. Bus and train stations are both 3 km east of town; taxi US$1.50, frequent buses 10, 20, 21. If you are staying in one of the many hotels on the road to Llao-Llao, west of town, expect to pay a little more for transport to your hotel.

Bariloche

N
0 metres 200
0 yards 200

Sleeping
Aire Sur **1** *B2*
Albergue El Gaucho **2** *B1*
Edelweiss **6** *A1*
El Radal **10** *B1*
Güemes **11** *B1*
Hostel 1004 **12** *A1*
La Bolsa **13** *B2*
La Pastorella **14** *B1*
Nevada **16** *A2*
Patagonia Andina **17** *B1*
Periko's **18** *B1*

Piuké **19** *A3*
Premier **20** *A2*
Ruca Hueney **22** *B2*
Tres Reyes **23** *A2*

Eating
El Boliche de Alberto **1** *A1*
El Boliche de Alberto
  Pastas **2** *B2*
Familia Weiss **4** *A2*
Friends **5** *A2*
Jauja **6** *B2*

Kandahar **7** *B1*
La Jirafa **8** *A2*
La Marmite **9** *A2*
Rock Chicken **11** *A2*
Simoca **12** *A2*
Vegetariano **13** *B1*

Bars & clubs
El Viejo Munich **3** *A2*
Pilgrim **10** *A2*

Getting around Bariloche is an easy city to walk around and to orient yourself in, since the lake lies to the north, and the mountains to the south. The main street is Calle Mitre, unmistakeable with its many T-shirt and souvenir shops, running east from the Centro Cívico, where you'll find tourist information. More accommodation and many restaurants are spread out on along Avenida Bustillo, the road running the southern shore of Lago Nahuel Huapi for some 25 km, as far as the famous **Hotel Llao-Llao,** and an area known as Colonial Suiza. Frequent local buses, run by **3 de Mayo,** run along its length. Take number 20 to Llao Llao, for lakeside hotels and restaurants, 10 to Colonia Suiza and Bahia Lopez for trekking, 50 to Lago Gutierrez, and the bus labelled Catedral for Cerro Catedral.

Tourist information www.bariloche.com www.bariloche.org The tourist office is in the **Centro Civico** ① *daily 0900-2100, T423122, T423022.* Helpful staff speak English, French and German, and have maps showing city buses, and can help with accommodation and campsites in the area. **Nahuel Huapi National Park** *intendencia* ① *San Martín 24, T423111, 0900-1400, www.parquesnacionales.com.ar* Also useful for information on hiking **Club Andino Bariloche** (CAB) ① *20 de Febrero 30, T422266, 424531 www.clubandino.com.ar, 0900-1300, also 1600-2100, high season only.*

Best time to visit Argentina's favourite holiday destination is busiest in the school holidays of January and July. It's also the destination for all graduating secondary school students in December and January, though these rarely stray beyond the city's bars and nightclubs. Walking is possible from mid-December to the end of March, and for longer treks it's best to come in January and February when the paths have been cleared of winter snow and fallen trees. Accomodation is cheaper outside of this peak period, and paths are less busy, but beware that bus services slow down when schools restart in early March, and that the weather can be more unpredictable. For skiing, July and August are best, though again, July is busy with families.

Sights

At the heart of the city is the **Centro Cívico,** designed by Bustillo in 'Bariloche Alpine style', on an attractive plaza above the lake, where there's also **Museo de La Patagonia** ① *Tue-Fri 1000-1230, 1400-1900, Mon/Sat 1000-1300, US$1,* which apart from stuffed animals, has indigenous artefacts and material from the lives of the first white settlers. Next to it is **Biblioteca Sarmiento** ① *Mon-Fri, 1000-2000,* a library and cultural centre. The **cathedral,** built in 1946, lies six blocks east of here, with the main commercial area on Mitre in between. Opposite the main entrance to the cathedral there is a huge rock left in this spot by a glacier during the last glacial period. On the lakeshore at 12 de Octubre y Sarmiento is the **Museo Paleontológico,** which has displays of fossils mainly from Patagonia including an ichthyosaur and replicas of a giant spider and shark's jaws. ▸▸ *For Sleeping, Eating and other listings, see pages 400-409.*

Around Bariloche

Avenida Bustillo runs parallel to the lakeshore west of Bariloche, with **Avenida de los Pioneros** running parallel above it. From these roads, with good bus services, there's access to the mountains above. For a summary of some of the many good hikes in the area, see Trekking and climbing below. Lots of companies offer tours to these places, (see Tour operators below); useful if you haven't got transport, or as starting points for longer treks.

Llao Llao

Llao Llao, a charming area 25 km west, for walking or just appreciating the gorgeous views, can be reached by Avenida Bustillo which runs along Lago Nahuel Huapi. Here you'll see the beautiful **Hotel Llao-Llao**, designed by Bustillo, and opened in 1937. It was originally almost entirely a wooden construction, which burned down within a few months and was rebuilt almost immediately, using local stone this time. Superbly situated on a hill with chocolate box views, it overlooks the **Capilla San Eduardo**, also designed by Bustillo, and Puerto Pañuelo, where boats leave for Puerto Blest. It's a good place for tea on the terrace, or at the superb Bellevue tearooms nearby. There are several walks on the Península Llao Llao, to a small *cerro* and to see beautiful virgin forest, rich in wildlife. Take bus No 20, a lovely 45-minute ride, US$0.70. Buses leave from the big bus stop on Moreno y Rolando. or information, T425648. Alternatively, take a half-day tour with an agency to Circuito Chico, see below, or take a full day to cycle. ➤➤ *For Sleeping, Eating and other listings, see pages 400-409.*

Cerro Campanario
At Km 17.7, a chairlift goes up to Cerro Campanario (1049 m) with superb views of the lake edged with mountains, as well as San Pedro Peninsula below and Lago Moreno. This peak of 1049 m is reached by a chairlift from Km 17.7 on the road to Llao-Llao, daily 0900-1200, 1400-1800, US$4, extended opening in summer, T427274.

Circuito Chico
Circuito Chico, one of the 'classic' Bariloche tours, begins on Av Bustillo at km 18.3. The 60-km circular route runs around Lago Moreno Oeste, past Punto Panorámico and through Puerto Pañuelo to Llao Llao. You could also extend this circuit, by returning via Colonia Suiza and Cerro Catedral, (2388 m) the ski resort, both starting points for longer treks (see below). This is a satisying all day cycle ride, see page 409. ⓘ *Take bus 10 to Colonia Suiza, Bus 'Catedral' to Catedral. All buses from the big bus stop on Moreno y Rolando, information T425648.*

Cerro Otto → *For skiing on Cerros Catedral and Otto, see Sports below*
At km 5 on Av de los Pioneros, a cable car (known here as *teleferico*) goes up to Cerro Otto, (1405 m) with its revolving restaurant and really fabulous views over the lakes and mountains all around. Alternatively, 20 minutes walk away on the summit at Refugio Berghof is a *confitería* belonging to Club Andino. Highly recommended. Take hourly bus service from Mitre y Villegas, running from 1030 to 1730, returning hourly 1115 to 1915. A combined ticket for both bus and cable car is US$8 return, T441031. By car, take Avenida de los Pioneros, then the signposted dirt track 1 km out of town. To climb Cerro Otto on foot (two to three hours): turn off Avenida de los Pioneros at Km 4.6, then follow the trail past Refugio Berghof, with splendid views. Not recommended alone, as paths can be confusing.

Cerro Catedral
At Cerro Catedral (2,338 m), 21 km southwest of Bariloche, there is one of the major ski resorts in Argentina. See skiing under Sport and activities below, page 405. As a summer resort, the cable car is useful for starting walks to Refugio Lynch (from where you can walk on to Laguna Jakob) and Refugio Frey, or for cycling down to Lago Gutierriez. To get there, bus "Catedral" from terminal or bus stop on Moreno y Palacios, takes you to the ski station base. Every 90 mins, takes 35 mins, US$1.Cable car for Catedral US$7, T460090.

Tronador
The mighty mountain of Tronador, (3,478 m), overshadows peaceful Pampa Linda, and can be visited in a good day's tour, which takes in beautiful Lagos Gutierrez and Mascardi with plenty of stops to appreciate the tranquility of the place, and lunch at *Hostería Pampa Linda*. Usually included are a trip to the eerie murky glaciar

Ventisquero Negro and the awesome falls at **Garganta del Diablo**, one of the natural amphitheatres in Tronador's slopes, where several waterfalls drop straight from the glacial shelf like sifted sugar. It's well worth the trip to walk up through the *coihue* and *lenga* forests to the falls themselves. A good way to make the most of the area is to take a tour with an agency, and then stay on at Pampa Linda to start trekking (good *hostería* and campsite, see sleeping below), returning with the minibus service run by **Transitando lo Natural** ⓘ *T156 08581, T423918, 3½ hrs, US$8.*

Bosque dos Arrayanes

Two boat trips are deservedly popular: Across to Lago Nahuel Huapi to **Isla Victoria** and Bosque de Arrayanes, where trees with exquisite cinnamon-coloured trunks must be seen. The *bosque* can also be visited by boat from Villa La Angostura. There are half-day excursions (1300-1830) from Puerto Pañuelo, (Bus 10/20/21 to get there) and on to Parque Nacional Los Arrayanes, on the Quetrihué peninsula further north in a full-day excursion (either 0900-1830, or 1300 till 2000 in season) costing US$15; take picnic lunch.

Puerto Blest

The all-day boat trip to Puerto Blest, and **Cascada los Cantaros**, at the western end of Lago Nahuel Huapi, and Lago Frías, visiting native forest and Valdivian rainforest, is highly recommended. This is usually done as a nine-hour excursion, leaving at 0900 from Puerto Pañuelo (km 25,5), and sailing down to fjord-like Puerto Blest, where there's a good *hostería* (see sleeping) and restaurant at the end of the lake. Boats fill up entirely in high season, and are much more pleasant in December and March. *Coihue*-clad mountains drop steeply into prussian blue water, and it's usually raining, but very atmospheric. The tour then continues by short bus ride to **Puerto Alegre** on Lago Frías, and you cross the still, peppermint green lake by launch. From Puerto Blest, the walk through beautiful forest to the **Cascada de los Cántaros** (one hour) is absolutely superb. Set off while the rest of the party stops for lunch, and you'll have time for your picnic by the splendid falls before the crowd arrives by boat. Or walk beyond them up to quiet **Lago de los Cantaros**, enclosed by vertical granite cliffs. This is one of only four places in Argentina where you can see Valdivian rainforest in unspoilt state. US$16 and US$4 for bus transfer, or made slightly cheaper by taking the 0730 bus (US$0.70) to Puerto Pañuelo where boat excursion leaves for Puerto Blest at 0900. Tours are run by *Catedral* and *Turisur*. Boats are comfortable with a good but expensive *cafetería*. Stock up on picnic provisions from the shop next to the Shell garage just before you reach Puerto Pañuelo at km 24.6. Set lunch at *Hostería Blest* is US$6; cheaper sandwiches from the snack bar next door. The *Hotel y Restaurant Puerto Blest* (C) is a small cosy hotel built in 1904, with homely rather than luxurious rooms. It's worth staying a night if you want to try any of the treks from here, or fish trout, and the only other option is camping *libre* with no facilities. The *guardaparques* at Puerto Bleast can advise on the many walks from here, (and their state) but the seven-hour 15 km trek to **Lago Ortiz Basualdo** is recommended (mid-December to March only). There are also boat trips across Lago Mascardi from Del Lago Turismo (see tour operators below). ➤ *For Sleeping, Eating and other listings, see pages 400-409.*

⛰ Walks

Contact **Club Andino Bariloche** to check paths are open before you set off. They also sell a series of hand-drawn maps showing walks and *refugios*. **Club Andino Bariloche**, 20 de Febrero 30, T422266, www.clubandino.com.ar Open Mon-Fri 0900-1300, and also 1600-2100 in high season only. In summer *tábanos* (horseflies) are common on the lake shores and at lower altitudes; their bites are very annoying but not harmful, and the only solution is to climb higher.

Among the many great treks possible here, the following are recommended:

1 There are several easy and very satisfying walks from Llao Llao: a delightful easy circuit in virgin Valdivian rainforest (turn left off the road, just past the golf course, two hours), or the small hill Cerrito Llao Llao, for wonderful views (two hours), or a 3 km trail through to Braza Tristeza (turn right off the road opposite the guardebosque), via tiny Lago Escondido. Bus 20 to Llao Llao, evey 20 mins.

2 Up to **Refugio López** (2076 m) (five hours return), from south-eastern tip of Lago Moreno up Arroyo López, for views. Bus 10 to Colonia Suiza and Arroyo López (check return times), bus 11 in summer only. From Refugio López, extend this to three to four day trek via Refugio Italia to Laguna Jakob and Refugio San Martín (this section is poorly signposted, advisable only for experienced walkers, with compass and well-equipped).

3 From **Cerro Catedral to Refugio Frey** (1700m), with a beautiful setting on small lake, via Rio Piedritas (four hours each way), or via cable car to **Refugio Lynch** and via Punta Nevada (only experienced walkers). Bus 'Catedral' from terminal or bus stop on Moreno y Palacios, takes you to the ski station base. Every 90 mins, takes 35 mins, US$1.

4 To **Lago Gutiérrez**, walk 2 km downhill from Cerro Catedral, along lake shore to the El Bolsón road (route 258) and walk back to Bariloche (six hours), or a bus to Virgen de las Nieves on the way to Cerro Catedral, walking 2 km to arrive at Lago Gutiérrez and then walking along the lake shore to Route 258 which takes you back into Bariloche (about four hours). Bus 50/51 goes via Virgen de las Nieves.

5 From Refugio Neumayer, there are eight paths to walk, and two are particularly recommended, to **Laguna Verde**, and to a mirador through Magellanic forest at Valle de los Perdidos. Office in town 20 de Julio 728, T428995, www.eco-family.com

6 From Pampa Linda, (*hostería*, campsite – see below) there are walks up to **Refugio Otto Meiling** (five hours each way), to tranquil **Laguna Ilon** (five and a half hours each way), or across Paso de las Nubes to **Puerto Frias**, where you can get the boat back to Bariloche (two days, check if open: closed when boggy), all recommended. And up **Mount Tronador itself**. See Pampa Linda below for more details. Bus to Pampa Linda (Bus marked 'Tronador') from outside *Club Andino Bariloche*, 20 de Febrero 28, Jan-Apr, and according to demand in Dec. *Transitando lo Natural*, T156 08581, T423918, 3½ hrs, US$8.

The three lakes crossing to Chile → *No cars carried on the ferries on this route*

This popular route to Puerto Montt, involving ferries across Lago Nahuel Huapi, Lago Frías and Lago Todos Los Santos, is outstandingly beautiful whatever the season, though the mountains are often obscured by rain and heavy cloud. It's a long and tiring journey, however, and is not recommended in heavy rain. Take your passport when booking.

The route is as follows: From Bariloche to Puerto Pañuelo by road, Puerto Pañuelo to Puerto Blest by boat (one and a half hours), Puerto Blest to Puerto Alegre on Lago Frías by bus, cross the lake to Puerto Frías by boat (20 minutes), then 1½ hours by road to Peulla. Leave for Petrohué in the afternoon by boat (two and a half hours), cross Lago Todos Los Santos, passing the Osorno volcano, then by bus to Puerto Montt.

Tickets from various operators; all trips run by *Turismo Catedral*, who own the exclusive rights. *Turismo Catedral Palacios*, Palacios 263, T426444, www.lakecrossing.cl Cost is US$140, plus cost of lunch at Peulla (US$20), credit cards accepted. No student reductions. Book before 1900 the day before, and further in advance during the high season; and beware the hard sell. Take your own lunch, but eat it before you reach Chile, as no fresh food can be taken over the border.

The journey can be done in one or two days: the one-day crossing (operates 1 Sep-30 Apr) does not permit return to Bariloche next day. For the two-day crossing (operates all year round), there is an overnight stop in Peulla. You could also do first section only, from Puerto Panuelo to Puerto Blest and Lago Frías, in a regular day trip: You could also walk the 29km section from Puerto Frías to Peulla, but you will need to do this quickly to catch the boat. To come back, take a regular bus trip from Chile, staying overnight in Puerto Varas. US$10 direct service takes between six and and eight hours, run by several companies: Tas Choapa, Via Bariloche (new service), Río de la Plata, Andesmar, Bus Norte. Cheaper excursion to Puerto Blest and Lago Frias: You can also do the trip as far crossing Lago Frias in a one day trip. You can't take a bike from Puerto Blest to Lago Frias, 'due to the highest level of eco protection'.

Border with Chile

The journey into Chile is via the Paso Perez Rosales Argentine immigration and customs, at Puerto Frías, open all year. Chilean immigration and customs at Peulla, open daily 0800-2100 summer, 0800-2000 winter. The launches (and hence the connecting buses) on the lakes serving the direct route via Puerto Blest to Puerto Montt generally do not operate at weekends; check: T425216. There is an absolute ban in Chile on importing any fresh food – meat, cheese, fruit – from Argentina. Chilean currency can be bought at Peulla customs at a reasonable rate. ▸▸ *For Sleeping, Eating and other listings, see pages 400-409.*

Into Chile: Puerto Montt → *Phone code: +56-(0)65 Population: 110,000.*

Puerto Montt is a popular centre for excursions to the Chilean Lake District, and departure point for boats to Puerto Chacabuco and Puerto Natales. A paved road runs 55 km southwest to Pargua, where there is a ferry service to the island of Chiloé. The little fishing port of **Angelmó**, 2 km west, has become a tourist centre with many seafood restaurants and handicraft shops (reached by Costanera bus along Portales and by collective taxi *Nos* 2,3,20 from the centre, US$0.30 per person). See *Footprint South American Handbook* and *Footprint Chile* for further details. Accommodation is expensive in season, much cheaper off season. Details are available from the **tourist office**, *Sernatur* (Chilean tourist authority) in the Intendencia Regional, ① *Av Décima Región 480 (3rd floor), Casilla 297, T25 4580, open 0830-1300, 1330-1730 Mon-Fri.* There is also a kiosk on Plaza de Armas run by the municipality, open till 1800 on Saturday.

Listings: Bariloche

Sleeping

Bariloche *p395, map p395*
Prices rise in two peak seasons: Jul and Aug for skiing, and mid-Dec to Mar for summer holidays. Prices given are lake-view high-season prices where applicable. If you arrive in the high season without a reservation, consult the listing published by the Tourist Office, *Centro Cívico* T423122. There's also a booking service in Buenos Aires, at *Florida 520 (Galería)*, room 116. In July and October to December. Avoid these hotels, which specialize in schooltrips: *Ayelén, Bariloche Ski, Interlaken, Millaray, Montana, Piedras* and *Pucón*.

Centre
LL Panamericano Bariloche, *San Martín 536/70, T/F425846, reservas@ panameri.com.ar* A huge international-style business hotel with all the facilities you'd expect, including casino, pool and sauna, well equipped rooms, some with lake views, and international cuisine in the restaurant.
L Edelweiss, *San Martín 202, T426165, F425655, www.edelweiss.com.ar* Far more than just a smart international 5-star, with real attention to detail, excellent service, and well furnished, spacious and comfortable rooms. *La Tavola* restaurant serves excellent food, there's a superb indoor pool and beauty salon, and good suites for families. Highly recommended.

● *For an explanation of the sleeping and eating price codes used in this guide, see the inside front cover. Other relevant information is provided in the Essentials chapter, page 44.*

AL **Nevada**, *Rolando 250, T422778, www.nevada.com.ar* A warm and welcoming modern place with nicely furnished cosy rooms. Good restaurant, with traditional dishes.

B **La Pastorella**, *Belgrano 127, T424656, F424212, www.lapastorella.com.ar* A cosy, quaint little *hostería*, whose very welcoming owners speak English. Recommended.

B **Tres Reyes**, *12 de Octubre 135, T426121, F424230, hreyes@bariloche.com.ar* Traditional lakeside hotel with spacious rooms and lounge with splendid views, all recently modernized, and with friendly professional staff who speak English. It's cheaper on the spot than if you reserve by email.

D **El Radal**, *24 de Septiembre 46, T422551.* Small, very clean, comfortable, restaurant.

D **Güemes**, *Güemes 715, T424785.* A lovely quiet bed and breakfast in a residential area, with lots of space, very welcoming, all the simple rooms have bath, breakfast is included, and the owner is a fishing expert.

D **Piuké**, *Beschtedt 136, T423044.* A delightful little bed and breakfast, with simple nicely decorated rooms with bath, breakfast included. Excellent value. German, Italian spoken.

D **Premier**, *Rolando 263, T426168. www.premierhotel.com.ar* Good economical choice in centre of town, with a light spacious entrance and gallery, with neat modern rooms with bath and TV, friendly owners, internet access, English spoken. Recommended.

E **Res No Me Olvides**, *Av Los Pioneros Km 1, T429140, 30 mins' walk or Bus 50/51 to corner of C Videla then follow signs.* Beautiful house in quiet surroundings, use of kitchen, camping. Recommended.

Youth hostels

Bariloche has many good quality hostels. These are the best:

E pp **Aire Sur**, *Elflein 158, T522135, airesur@abari.com.ar* Also well run, light airy peaceful place with dorms sleeping 3-7, and one E double. There is a terrace and garden with climbing-wall. Breakfast extra, internet laundry, cycle hire. Knowledgeable owner also runs mountain bike excursions and kayaking.

E pp **Hostel 1004**, *in the Bariloche Centre building, San Martín y Pagano, 10th floor, T432228, www.lamoradahostel.com* Fantastic views from this penthouse flat, where there are rooms sleeping 3-4, as well as floor space F pp, a central and friendly place, with kitchen facilities, lots of helpful information, English spoken. Recommended.

E pp **La Bolsa**, *Palacios 405 (y Elflein), T423529, www.labolsadeldeporte.com* Recommended for its friendly relaxed atmosphere, and homely rustic rooms – some with great lake views, and a great deck to sit out on.

E pp **Patagonia Andina**, *Morales 564, T421861, www.elpatagoniaandina.com.ar* A quiet place with comfortable dorms, and E double/twin rooms with shared bath. Well equipped small kitchen, TV area, sheets included, breakfast extra, internet, advice on trekking, good atmosphere.

Epp **Periko's**, *Morales 555, T522326, www.perikos.com* A warm and friendly atmosphere, quiet, with an *asado* every Friday, but it's otherwise a calm place, since groups tend to go to the sister hostel, *Alaska* (see below). Towels and sheets included, but breakfast extra. Use of kitchen, and washing machine, nice airy rustic rooms, either all girls or boys, all shared rooms are for 4, and have their own bathroom. Also E double with own bath, garden, free internet access, can also organize horse riding, rent mountain bikes. Highly recommended.

E pp **Ruca Hueney**, *Elflein 396, T433986, rucahueney@bariloche.com.ar* A lovely calm place, with very comfortable beds and duvets! Spotless kitchen, quiet place to sit and eat, and very welcoming owners. Fabulous double room E with extra bunk beds, bathroom and great view. Also Spanish school. Highly recommended.

F pp **Albergue El Gaucho**, *Belgrano 209, T522464, www.hostelgaucho.com.ar* Welcoming modern place in quiet part of town, some doubles with own bath, E pp. English German and Italian spoken.

Outside Bariloche (Road to Llao Llao) *p396*

There are many *hosterías*, *cabañas* and

The Lake District Listings: Bariloche

campsites all along the shore of Lago Nahuel Huapi, on the way to Llao Llao. Buses run every 20-30 mins.

LL **Catedral**, *T460006, F460137, hcatedral@bariloche.com.ar* Large, luxurious, pool, restaurant, sauna, gym, also apartments, discount for one week stay.

LL **Llao Llao**, *Bustillo Km 25, T448530, F445781, www.llaollao.com* Deservedly famous, one of the world's wonderful hotels in a superb location, with panoramic views from its perfect gardens, golf course, gorgeous spa suite, pools, water sports, superb restaurants. Excellent services, worth every peso.

L **La Cascada**, *Bustillo Km 6, T441088, F441076, lacascada@infovia.com.ar* A modern hotel with a really stunning lakeside position, terrace going down to water, and a good, reasonably priced restaurant (3 courses US$7). Not quite luxurious but comfortable.

L **Isla Victoria Resort**, *T011 439499605, www.islavictoria.com* On Isla Victoria just off the coast, recommended for an escape from it all, and amidst its own spectacular island scenery, a resort with pool, sauna, spacious and cosy places to sit and relax, riding and trekking organised all over the beautiful island, good food.

A **Cabañas Villa Huinid**, *km2,5, T523523, www.villahuninid.com.ar* Recommended luxurious *cabanas* for 2-8, beautifully furnished, and well equipped.

A **Tunquelén**, *Bustillo Km 24.5, T448400, F01143949599 www.maresur.com.ar* This is a comfortable 4-star hotel, on the lakeside neary Llao Llao, with really splendid views and a secluded feel, more wild and closer to nature than Llao Llao. Nicely decorated cottage-style rooms, attentive service, superb food, warmly recommended. Much cheaper if you stay 4 days.

B **La Caleta**, *Bustillo Km 1.9, T441837. Cabañas* sleep 4, open fire, excellent value.

C **Katy**, *Bustillo Km 24.3, T448023 adikastelic@yahoo.com* Delightful peaceful place in a garden full of flowers, charming family, breakfast included. Also offers adventure tourism, *www.gringos patagonia.com*

C **Hosteria Santa Rita**, *km7,2, T/F461028, www.santarita.com.ar* Close to the centre, but with peaceful lakeside views,

comfortable rooms, lovely terrace, and great service from the friendly family owners. Warmly recommended. Bus 10, 20, 21, to km 7.5 for this and also:

E PP **Hostel Alaska** *(Hostelling International), Av Bustillo Km 7.5, T461564, www.alaska-hostel.com To get there, take bus 10, 20, 21, to km 7,5).* Well run, cosy chalet-style hostel open all year, doubles and dorms. Kitchen facilites, internet access, rafting and riding.

Camping

Complete list of camp sites is available from the tourist office, with prices and directions, www.bariloche.org/ These are recommended for attractive sites and good facilities: For Avenida Bustillo, towards Llao Llao take buses 10, 11, 20, 21.

El Yeti, *Km 5.6, T442073.* Pretty place, which also has *cabañas.*

Selva Negra, *Km 2.9, T441013.* Very attractive well-equipped site, highly recommended.

Petunia, *Km 13.5, T461969.* Well protected from winds by trees, a lovely shady lakeside site with beach, all facilities and restaurant, and shop, recommended, also *cabañas.*

Goye, *T448627,* and **Huenei Ruca**, *Colonia Suiza, buses 10 and 11 in season.* These two sites both have *cabañas* and lots of facilities.

Around Bariloche *p396*

To get closer to nature, there are many tranquil and beautiful places to stay south of the city, described under the relevant section below. All are within easy reach and accessible by public transport. See El Retorno on the northern shore of Lago Gutierrez, Estancia Peuma Hue, on its southern shore. Along Lago Mascardi there are idyllic hotels and campsites, *Hotel Tronador, Camping Los Rapidos,* and the *hostería* and campsite at Pampa Linda, all described below. For *Hotel y Restaurant Puerto Blest* see above, Tours to Puerto Blest, page 406.

Cerro Catedral *p397*

L **Pire-Hue**, *T011 48078200, www.pire-hue.com.ar* Exclusive 5-star hotel with beautifully decorated rooms and all the facilities.

Peulla (Chile) *p400*

LL **Hotel Peulla**, *PO Box 487, Puerto Montt, T258041.* Includes dinner and breakfast,

cheaper out of season, beautiful setting by the lake, restaurant and bar, good but expensive meals, cold in winter, often full of tour groups (tiny shop at back of hotel).
D pp **Res Palomita**, *50m west of hotel*. Half board, family-run, simple, comfortable but not spacious, separate shower, book ahead in season, lunches.

Camping
There is a site opposite the *Conaf office*, US$1.50, and a good campsite 1¾ hours' walk east of Peulla, take food.

🍴 Eating

Bariloche *p395, map p395*
$$$ Chez Philippe, *Primera Junta 1080, T427291*. Delicious local delicacies, really fine French influenced cuisine.
$$ Kandahar, *20 de Febrero 698, T424702*. Most highly recommended for its excellent food and intimate warm atmosphere. Reserve in high season. Dinner only. Argentine dishes, and other imaginative cuisine served in style, in a cosy place, run by ski champion Marta Peirono de Barber, superb wines and the pisco sour are recommended. US$7 for two courses. Wonderful.
$$ La Marmite, *Mitre 329*. A cosy place with good service, perfect for a huge range of fondues, good wild boar and delicious cakes for tea too. Recommended, US$5.
$$ Vegetariano, *20 de Febrero 730, T421820*. Also serves fish in its excellent set menu, beautifully served in a warm friendly atmosphere. Highly recommended, US$5 for three courses.
$$ Familia Weiss, *also Palacios y V.A.O'Connor*. Excellent local specialities in chalet-style splendour, with live music. The wild boar is particularly recommended. US$6, menu US$4.
$ El Boliche de Alberto, *Villegas 347, T431433*. Very good steak and live folklore music.
$ Friends, *Mitre 302*. A good lively café on the main street, convenient for lunch, open 24 hrs, US$3 for dinner.
$Jauja, *Quaglia 366, T422952*. A quiet welcoming place, recommended for trout, in a friendly atmosphere, and good value. (also take away round the corner at Elflein128).

$ La Jirafa, *Palacios 288*. A cheery family run place for good food, good value, US$3.
$ Simoca, *Palacios 264*. Recommended for delicious and cheap Tucumán specialities, such as *humitas* and *locro*, and huge *empanadas*, US$3.
$ Rock Chicken, *Quaglia y Moreno*. Small, busy, good value fast food (also take away).

Cerro Catedral *p397*
La Raclette, *in the ski resort*. Highly recommended, family place.
El Viejo Lobo. Family owned restaurant, **Refugio Lynch**, up on the slopes. This *refugio* also has a restaurant and *confiteria*.

Café and tea rooms
Bariloche *p395, map p395*
El Viejo Munich, *Mitre 102*. A traditional café serving great coffee and good local dishes, a very comfortable place to hang out for a couple of hours.
Pilgrim, *Palacios 167, between O Connor and Mitre*. One of two Irish pubs in town, serves a good range of beers in a pub atmosphere, also regional dishes, reasonably priced too.

On the road to Llao Llao *p396*
Bellevue, *km24,6, T448389, open 1600-2000, Wed to Sun*. The best tea room is undoubtedly the exquisite Bellevue, it's worth a special trip on the bus to taste Karin's raspberry cheesecake and chocolate cake, in pretty tea room perched high in lovely gardens with incredible views, this is an unmissable treat.
Cerveceria Blest, *Km 11.6, T461026, open 1200-2400*. Wonderful brewery with delicious beers (try their *La Trochita* stout), serving imaginative local and German dishes and, incredibly, steak and kidney pie! in a warm rustic atmosphere. Recommended.
El Patacón, *Km 7, T442898*. Good *parrilla* and game, though pricey.
La Casa del Bosque, *Km 4.6*. A restaurant and Welsh tea room.
Meli Hue, *Km24,7, T448029*. Another tearoom, and bed and breakfast, in a lavender garden and selling fragrant produce, also has lovely views.
Tasca Brava, *km7, T462599*. On the lakeside with an intimate atmosphere, and Patagonian specialities as well as superb Spanish cooking.

⊙ Shopping

Bariloche *p395, map p395*
The main commercial centre is on Mitre between the Centro Cívico and Beschtedt.

Bookshops
Cultura, *Elflein 78*. A good range, some in English and German.
La Barca Libros, *Quaglia 247, T423170, www.patagonialibros.com* For a wonderful range of books on Patagonia, and a good selection in English.

Clothing and outdoor equipment
Arbol, *on Mitre in the 400 block*. Sells good quality outdoor gear, lovely clothes and interesting gifts.
Martin Pescador, *Rolando 257, T422 2275*, Also at Cerro Catedral in winter. Fly shop, for fishing, camping and skiing equipment.
Patagonia Outdoors, *Elflein 27, T426768, www.patagonia-outdoors.com.ar* Maps and equipment, everything you might need, plus adventure tourism organised, trekking and rafting especially.
Scandinavian, *San Martín 130*.

Food and drink
The local chocolate is excellent, and there are many shops along Mitre.
Abuela Goye, *Mitre 258*. Delicious chocs.
El Turista, *Mitre 252*. Very touristy, but you can watch chocolates being made.
Fenoglio, *Mitre 301 y Rolando*. Superb chocolate ice cream.
Jauja, *next door to Trevisan, above*. Ice creams.
Mamushka, *Mitre 216*. Far better chocolate here than at El Turista.
Panaderia Trevisan, *Moreno y Quaglia*. For excellent bread and cakes.
Uno, *Moreno 350* and **Todo**, *Moreno 319*. *Supermarkets which both have a good selection, and are reasonably cheap.*

Handicrafts
Feria Artesanal Municipal, *Moreno y Rolando, daily 0900-2100*. Recommended.
Burton Cerámica, *Av Bustillo 4100*. Makes and sells renowned Patagonian pottery.

⊕ Sport and activities

Bariloche *p395, map p395*
Many activities (eg rafting, horse riding, birdwatching) can be arranged through travel agencies. Excellent trout fishing Nov-Apr; arrange boat hire with tackle shops.

Cycling
This is a great area for mountain biking, with some fabulously challenging descents from the peaks around Bariloche, also easily reached by bus. Even the basic tourist information map shows the main routes, but see *Club Andino* (address above) for more detailed maps and advice on where to go.
Recommended paths
1 Along Avenida Bustillo and around Circuito Chico from Llao Llao, with optional extra ride along the Península de San Pedro. Traffic on this route can be a nuisance in high summer, but the views are great.
2 To Colonia Suiza via a path leading from Av Bustillo km 10,5, and from Colonia Suiza, up to Refugio Lopez via a steep track.
3 Up to Cerro Otto, by a track leading from Av Bustillo, km 2. From the summit, the very hardy could descend to Lago Gutiérrez.
4 Another path leads to Lago Gutiérrez from Calle Campichuelo, southwest end of town.
5 From Cerro Catedral (take your bike on the bus) ride down to the western side of Lago Gutiérrez, a rocky path but with great views. For mountain bike excursions, contact Diego Rodriguez, *www.adventure-tours-south.com*
Bike hire
Dirty Bikes, *V O'Connor 681, T425616, www.dirtybikes.com* Very helpful for repairs too – if pricey.
Bike Way, *VA O'Connor, 867, T424202*.
Aire Sur, *Elflein 158, T522135*. US$5 per day.

Fishing
Excellent trout fishing Nov-Mar (permits required). For guides, consult **Asociacion de Guias Profesionales de Pesca**, *T421515, www.guiaspatagonicos.com/guias*
Martin Pescador, *Rolando 257, T422275, martinpescador@bariloche.com.ar* A great shop for fishing supplies (as well as camping and skiing) and experts there can organize all kinds of fishing expeditions.
Baruzzi Deportes, *Urquiza 250, T424922, F428374*. Offers guided fishing excursions in

the whole area (flycast, trolling, spinning) for experts and newcomers; US$150-300 (Trout Unlimited membership discounts).

Horse riding

Estancia Fortín Chacabuco, *T441766, www.estanciaspatagonicas.com* Superb riding for all levels, with biliingual guides, in a lovely landscape filled with wildlife, east of Bariloche.

Hosteria de Estancia Peuma Hue, *T011-5101 1392, www.peuma-hue.com* Luxury accommodation, see below under Lago Gutiérrez.

Tom Wesley, *in country ranch by the lake at km 15.5, T448193, tomwesley@bariloche .com.ar* A relaxed place with tuition and full day's riding offered, they also have an estancia on the steppe.

Paragliding

Parapente Bariloche, *T462234, 15552403, parapente@bariloche.com.ar* Gliding at Cerro Otto.

Rafting

Río Manso offfers some of the best rafting in Argentina, with sections of river suitable for all levels. The Lower Manso River for grade 2 or 3, the Manso River to Chilean border thorugh lush vegetation, a full day trip, class 3-4, experience needed. Then also 3-day expedition, 35 miles, class 3-4, for the experienced. Superb. Contact **Del Lago Turismo**, see Tour Operators, below.

Skiing

One of South America's most important ski resorts centres is just outside Bariloche, at Cerro Catedral, with 70 km of slopes of all grades, allowing a total drop of 1010 m, and 52 km of cross-country skiing routes. There are also snowboarding areas and a well equipped base with hotels, restaurants and equipment hire, ski schools and nursery care for children.

Information T460125. Open mid-Jun to end Aug, busiest from mid-Jul to mid-Aug for school holidays. Ski lifts open 0900 to 1700. Price of ski lift pass adults US$15 per day, ski school, US$30 per hour individuals. Bus run by 3 de Mayo 'Catedral', leaves Moreno 480 every 90 mins approximately, *T425648*, US$1. Taxi costs US$4. Cable car for Catedral *T460090*. Book ski equipment in advance from: **Robles Catedral**, *T460062, www.roblescatedral.com T460309, www.skipacks.com*

There is also skiing at Cerro Otto. Cable car passengers can take a free bus leaving from hut at Civic centre, hourly 1030 to 1730, returning hourly 1115 to 1915. Ticket for both costs US$8pp, *T441031* there's a revolving *confitería*, craft shop, great views. Also *Club Andino confitería*, 20 mins' walk from main confitería on summit. Ski equipment can also be rented by the day from **Martín Pescador**, *Rolando 257, T422275, martinpescador@bariloche.com.ar* **Cebron** *Mitre 171* or **Milenium**, *Mitre 125*.

Trekking and climbing

There's a good range of peaks around Bariloche, offering walks ranging from 3 hrs to several days. The seaon runs from Dec to Apr, and note that winter storms can begin as early as Apr at higher levels, making climbing dangerous.

The best information is available from **Club Andino Bariloche**, *20 de Febrero 30, T422266, www.clubandino.com.ar (the website lists areas to walk, in Spanish), open Mon-Fri 0900-1300, and also 1600-2100 in high season only.* The club arranges guides; ask them for a list (and see Angel Fernandez and Daniel Feinstein below). Its booklet *Guía de Sendas y Picadas* gives details of climbs and provides 4 maps (1:150,000) and details of *refugios* and paths, though note that these are sometimes out of date, and you should always check with *guardaparques* that paths are open where you're intending to walk. More detailed maps are available from Buenos Aires, at the Instituto Geográfico Militar. There's also a book *Excursiones, Andinismo y Refugios de Montaña en Bariloche*, by Tonchek Arko, available in local shops, US$2, or from the author at *Güemes 691*. There are many *refugios*, run both privately and by *Club Andino Bariloche*, who charge US$3 per night, plus US$1.50 for cooking, or US$2.50 for breakfast, US$4 for dinner. Take a good sleeping bag. See above for a list of good walks. Horseflies (*tábanos*) frequent the lake shores and lower areas in summer: bring insect repellent.

↻ Tour operators

Bariloche *p395, map p395*

There are numerous tours, and most travel agencies charge the same price. It is best to buy tickets the night before, rather than far in advance, although they get very booked up in season, and many trips only run in Jan and Feb or when there is enough demand. Prices are regulated by the tourist office. Many Argentines enjoy seeing their scenery from a bus with commentary and you may find that too much time is spent sitting: check the itinerary before you book. Tours offered include:

Twelve-hour minibus excursions to San Martín de los Andes, US$10, via the Seven Lakes Drive and returning via Paso de Córdoba and the Valle Encantado. There are also tours around the Circuito Chico (60 km), US$5-7, half-day. San Martín and Ruta de los Siete Lagos full day (360 km) US$12, Cerro Tronador and Cascada los Alerces full day (255 km) U$12, El Bolsón full day (300 km, including Lago Puelo) US$12. Whole-day excursions to Lagos Gutiérrez, Mascardi, Hess, the Cascada Los Alerces and Cerro Tronador and the Black Glacier, leaving at 0800, US$10, lots of time spent on the bus. Useful as a way to get to walks at Pampa Linda if the bus from CAB isn't running.

Boat trips Isla Victoria and Bosque de Arrayanes full or half-day US$11/US$16, Puerto Blest and Lago Frias full day, including buses US$20.

Catedral Turismo, *Palacios 263, T425444, www.lakecrossing.cl* This company has the monopoly on the famous Three Lakes Crossing to Puerto Montt in Chile (see below) US$140.

Cumbres Patagonia, *Villegas 222, T423283, cumbres@bariloche.com.ar* Rafting, horse riding, trekking, fishing.

Del Lago Turismo, *Vilegas 222, T430056, cordille@bariloche.com.ar* The best in town, helpful and friendly, and speaking fluent English. Offers all the conventional tours, and lots of more adventurous options, horse riding and kayaking. Also a fabulous boat trip up Lago Mascardi (summer only) to Cascada de los Césares and Hotel Tronador.

San Carlos Travel, *Mitre 213 piso 2, T/F432999, sancartrav@bariloche.com.ar* Birdwatching and other specialist tours.

Tronador Turismo, *Quaglia 283, T421104, tronador@bariloche.com.ar* Tours, trekking and rafting, to Refugio Neumeyer. Expeditions to the Chilean border, and more adventurous great winter sports options.

Turisur, *Mitre 219, T426109, www.bariloche.com/turisur* Boat trips to Bosque de Arrayanes, Isla Victoria and Puerto Blest, and conventional tours.

Adventure tourism

Extremo Sur, *Morales 765, T427301, www.extremosur.com* Professional company offering rafting and kayaking, all levels, full day all-inclusive packages offered, US$30 to US$50, or a three-day trip for US$180 includng accommodaton, check web for more details.

Refugio Neumeyer, *18km from Bariloche.* A good base for lots of activities, a warm, family-run, children-friendly place: office in town *20 de Julio 728, T428995, www.eco-family.com*, trekking, climbing (and tuition), nightwalking with lanterns.

Gringos Patagonia, *T448023, www.gringos patagonia.com, www.gringospatagonia.com* Organized by Adriana and Dirk Gerhards, activities include rafting, mountain biking, paragliding, and cross country skiing, *www.abari.com.ar/airesur.asp*

Aguas Bancas, *Mitre 515, T429940, www.aguasblancas.com.ar* Rafting on the Manso river, all grades, with expert guides, and all equipment provided, also bikes and horse riding, traditional lunches included.

Aire Sur hostel, *Elflein 158, T522135, lionsauma@yahoo.com.ar* Biking, paragliding and canyoning.

Transitando lo Natural, *20 de Febrero 28, T423918, 527926, transita@bariloche.com.ar* Buses to Pampa Linda, and nature trips.

Xtreme Snow Solutions, *T460309, www.skipacks.com* At the Cerro Catedral Ski resort there is a school and equipment hire.

Trekking guides

Angel Fernandez, *T524609, 156 09799.* For trekking, biking, kayaking, natural history expeditions. Speaks English. Recommended.

Daniel Feinstein, *T/F442259.* Speaks fluent English, very experienced in both Argentina and Chile.

Andy Lamuniere, *T428991, 15558423.* (speaks less English).

Andescross.com, *T467502, www.andescross
.com* Trekking to Chile across the Andes, via
Pampa Linda, Lago Frias, Peulla. Expert
guides, all included. Recommended.
Sebastian de la Cruz, *Pampa Linda Hostería,
T490517, in Bailoche 442038, 15557718,
pampalindaa@bariloche.com.ar* Renowned
mountaineer, who lives at the base of
Tronador and owns the Pampa Linda
Hostería. Enormously knowledgeable.

⊜ Transport

Bariloche *p395, map p395*
Air
Airport, 15 km east of town, *T426162.* Bus
service run by **Del Lago Turismo**, *Villegas
222,* leaving 1½ hrs before any flight from
outside **Aerolíneas Argentinas**, *Mitre and
Villegas,* US$1, and meeting all incoming
flights. Bikes can be carried. Taxi to airport,
US$5. Many flights a day to **Buenos Aires**,
with **Aerolineas/Austral, Southern Winds**
and **Lapa. Aerolíneas** also flies twice a week
to **El Calafate** (2 hrs) and **Ushuaia** (2 hrs).
American Falcon flies to **Puerto Madryn**
and **Montevideo. Southern Winds to
Córdoba.** LADE weekly to many
destinations, including **Bahía Blanca,
Comodoro Rivadavia, Mar del Plata,
Puerto Madryn**; book well in advance in
peak seasons.

Bus
Local Frequent buses run by **3 de Mayo**,
Moreno 480, T425648, from terminal into
town and along Av Bustillo: Bus 20 to **Llao
Llao**, for lakeside hotels and restaurants, Bus
10 to **Colonia Suiza** and **Bahia Lopez** for
trekking, Bus 50 to **Lago Gutiérrez**, and the
bus labelled "Catedral" for Cerro Catedral.
   Long distance The bus terminal,
T432860, has toilets, small *confitería, kiosko,*
no *locutorio* but public phones. Left luggage
US$0.50 per day.
   To get there: Buses 10, 20, 21 frequent
service from bus / train station to centre of
town, US$0.60. Taxi US$2.30. Bus company
offices in town: **Vía Bariloche/El Valle**, *Mitre
321, T429012, www.viabariloche.com;*
Andesmar/Albus, *Mitre 385, T430211;*
Chevallier/La Estrella/Ko Ko, *Moreno 105,
T425914;* **TAC**, *Moreno 138, T434727;* **Cruz del
Sur**, *T437699,* **Don Otto/Río de La Plata**, *12*

de Octubre T437699; **Flechabus**, *Moreno 107,
T423090, www.flechabus.com;* **3 de Mayo**, for
local services, *Moreno 480, T425648.*

Taxi
Radio Taxi Bariloche, *T422103, 431717;*
Remises Bariloche, *T430222.* **Remises del
Bosque**, *T429109.* **Puerto Remises**,
T08009-990885 (freephone), 435222, **Melipal
Remises**, *T442300.*

Around Bariloche *p396*
To **Pampa Linda**, (bus says **Tronador**)
minibuses runs by **Transitando lo Natural**
*T156 08581, 423918, from opposite Club
Andino Bariloche, 20 de Febrero 28,* daily
Jan-Apr, according to demand in Dec.
To **Buenos Aires**, 6 companies daily, 22½
hrs, US$50 *coche cama,* **Andesmar**. To **Bahía
Blanca**, 3 companies, US$30. To **Mendoza**,
US$30, **TAC** and **Andesmar**, 19 hrs, via
Piedra de Aguila, Neuquén, Cipolleti and San
Rafael. To **Esquel**, via El Bolson, **Don Otto,
Mar y Valle, Vía Bariloche, Andesmar**, 4hrs,
US$6 . To **Puerto Madryn**, 14 hrs, US$25
with **Mar y Vale** and **Don Otto**. To **San
Martín de los Andes**, **Ko Ko**, 4 hrs, US$8. No
direct bus to **Río Gallegos**; you have to
spend a night in **Comodoro Rivadavia** en
route: **Don Otto** daily, US$38, 14½ hrs. To
Calafate, ask at youth hostel *Alaska,* or
Periko's about **Safari Route 40**, a 4-day trip
down Ruta 40 to **Calafate** via the Perito
Moreno national park, Cueva de Las Manos
and Fitz Roy, staying at Estancia Melike and
Río Mayo en route. US$95 plus
accommodation at US$5 per day.
www.visitbariloche.com/alaska
   To **Chile** To **Osorno** (4-6 hrs) and **Puerto
Montt**, 7-8 hrs US$18-20, daily, **Bus Norte,
Río de la Plata, TAS Choapa, Cruz del Sur,
Andesmar** (sit on left side for best views). For
Santiago or **Valdivia** change at Osorno.

Car hire
Fuel costs about 30% less than national price.
Two companies are recommended: **Hertz**,
*Quaglia 352, T423457, 15581186,
hertz@bariloche.com.ar* Efficient. **Localiza**, *San
Martín 463, T424767, localizabrc@ bariloche
.com.ar* Reliable, English spoken. **Open Rent a
Car**, *Mitre 171, T426325, opencar@bariloche
.com.ar* **Bariloche Rent a Car**, *Moreno 115,
T327638, rentacar@bariloche.com.ar*

Tell your car hire company if you plan to enter Chile; a permit is necessary (no extra charge, but may take 24 hrs), and the number plate must be etched on windows.

Train
Station 3 km east of centre, near bus terminal. Booking office *T423172*. Closed 1200-1500 weekdays, Sat afternoon and all Sun. Information from the tourist office. Tourist service to **Viedma**, also with sleeper section, and carries cars, *T423172*, *www.trenpata gonico.com.ar* See bus section above for transport to the centre. Booking office closed 1200-1500 weekdays, Sat afternoon and all Sun. To **Viedma**, 16 hrs, US$18 *turista*.

Puerto Montt *p400*
Air
El Tepual Airport, 13km northwest of town. ETM bus from terminal 1½ hrs before departure, US$2. To **Santiago** and **Punta Arenas** several daily flights by LanChile, Lan Express and Aero Continente. To **Temuco**, Lan Chile daily. Flights fully booked in advance in summer: worth asking at the airport for cancellations.

Bus
The terminal is on the sea front at *Portales y Lota*. Facilities include, telephones, restaurants, *casa de cambio*, left luggage (US$1.50 per item for 24 hrs). There are services to all parts of the country.

Sea
Shipping offices Cruce de Lagos, www.lakecrossing.cl, includes departures to Puerto Vargas and Bariloche.

❶ Directory

Bariloche *p395, map p395*
Airline offices Aerolíneas Argentinas, *Quaglia 238, y Mitre, T422425*. **American** Falcon, *Mitre 159, T425200*. LADE, *Quaglia 238, T423562*. **Southern Winds**, *Quaglia 262, T423704*. **Banks** ATMs at many banks along Mitre: Bansuf at 424, Citibank at 694, Banco Nación Argentina at 180. Banco Galicia, *Moreno y Quaglia*, Banco Patagonia, *San*

The Lake District Listings: Bariloche

Martin 297, **Banco Frances**, *San Martín 332.*
Exchange and TCs, best rates and service at
Casas de Cambio: **Sudamérica**, *Mitre 63,*
T434555. **Consulates** Austria, *24 de*
Septiembre 230, T424873. Brazil, *Moreno 126*
piso 5, T425328. Chile, *Rosas 180, T422842.*
France, *T441960.* Germany, *Ruiz Moreno 65,*
T425695. Italy, *Beschtedt 141, T422247.*
Lebanon, *Quaglia 242 piso 3, T431471.*
Switzerland, *Quaglia 342, T426111.*
  Customs Bariloche centre *T425216,* Rincon
(Argentina) *T425734,* Pajarito (Chile) *T005664*
236284. **Immigration office** *Libertad 191,*

T423043, Mon-Fri 0900-1300.
Communications Internet Many places
along Mitre, and in the first block of Quaglia.
Post office *Moreno 175, Mon-Fri 0800-2000,*
Sat 0830-1300. **Telephone** Many locutorios
along Mitre, Telecom at Mitre y Rolando is
helpful. **Language schools** La Montana,
Elflein 251, 1st floor, T156 11872,
www.lamontana.com Spanish language
school. **Useful addresses** Medical
services Dial 107 for emergencies, or San
Carlos Emergencias, *T430000,* Clinic: Hospital
Zonal, *Moreno 601, T426100.*

Bariloche to Esquel

South of Bariloche there is more wild and beautiful scenery to explore alongside the
Andes, with a scattering of quieter centres, than the more developed central region.
On the way to El Bolsón, Route 258 passes the picturesque Lagos Gutiérrez and
Mascardi with their backdrop of grand jagged mountains, around which there are
many places to stay and to walk. From Villa Mascardi, just between Lagos Mascardi
and Guillelmo, a road leads west along the southern shore of Lago Mascardi to Pampa
Linda, where there is excellent trekking, or along the Río Manso Medio, famous for
white water rafting, to Lago Hess, where there is a hostería and the lovely Cascasas
Los Alerces. At the pretty and easy-going town of El Bolsón, with its lively craft market
and lots of home-made beer on offer, there are beautiful rivers, waterfalls and
mountains to explore, and a small national park, Lago Puelo, with fishing and walking.
The pioneer town of Esquel is the southernmost centre in the lakes, which can be
reached via Cholila, a wild small settlement where Butch Cassidy hid out. From Esquel,
you can explore the magnificent Parque Nacional Los Alerces, go skiing in winter, take
a ride on La Trochita or visit the appealing Welsh pioneer village, Trevelin.

Lago Gutiérrez → *Phone code: 02944*

Easily accessible by bus from Bariloche, Lago Gutiérrez feels like a fjord, with
mountains dropping steeply into its western side, and spectacular views all around.
There are many ways to access the lake, and it can be explored on foot or bike almost
all the way round. There are many campsites, and fine hotels at both its northern and
southern ends. For an adventurous approach, you could hike down from Refugio Frey
or walk or cycle down the stony track from Cerro Catedral (which can be reached by
bus). Water sports can be practised on the lake in summer. ▸▸ *For Sleeping, Eating and*
other listings, see pages 420-428.

Lago Mascardi → *Phone code: 02944 Colour map 5, B2 Km 35*

At the southern end of Lago Mascardi, Villa Mascardi is a small village from where a
ripio road 81 with a one-way system runs towards Cerro Tronador and Cascada Los
Alerces. Bariloche to El Bolsón buses can be taken to and from here, enabling you to
visit the lake itself. Road access: going west 1000-1400, east 1600-1800, two way
1900-0900. Times may vary: check with the tourist office, *T423022.* Park entry costs
residents US$2 for Argentines, and US$4 for foreigners.
  Along Lago Mascardi, there are several beautifully situated places to stay, all
easily reached by car, or bus when the service is running in summer, including the
luxurious *Mascardi*, with biking, rafting and horse riding. Opposite the lovely straight

beach of Playa Negro, handy for launching boats and fishing, is the peaceful *Camping La Querencia*, at Km 10 on *rute* 258 to Trondador. Shortly afterwards, the road forks, with the left hand branch following the crystalline Río Manso Medio to **Lago Hess**. This is a beautiful spot for a picnic, and there is also good camping at *Camping Los Rapidos*. For further details on accommodation at the lake, see page 391. The **Río Manso** (both inferior, further south, and medio) is popular for rafting (see sports section in Bariloche above). At Lago Hess is *Hostería Lago Hess*, T462249, 490506, piccino@bariloche.com.ar

The right fork follows a narrow arm of Lago Mascardi, with a viewpoint in lovely woodland to see Isla Piuke Huapi in the centre of the lake. A few km further on is the lakeside paradise of Hotel Tronador.

Pampa Linda → *Phone code: 02944*

Pampa Linda lies 40 km west of Villa Mascardi in the most blissfully isolated location, with spectacular views of Cerro Tronador towering above. There's a *guadería* (ranger station) with very helpful *guardaparques* who can advise on walks, and whom you must consult about the state of the paths before setting out, and register your name. From Pampa Linda, a lovely track (*ripio*) continues to **Ventisquero Negro**, a rather filthy-looking glacier, which hangs over a fantastically murky pool in which grey icebergs float. The colour is due to sediment, and while not exactly attractive, the whole scene is very atmospheric. The road ends at the **Garganta del Diablo**, one of the natural amphitheatres formed by the lower slopes of Mount Tronador. A beautiful walk (90 mins walk there and back) from the car park through beach forest takes you to a more pristine glacier, and up to the head of the gorge, where thin torrents of ice melt from the hanging glacier above fall in columns like sifted sugar. Wonderful. ‣ *For Sleeping, Eating and other listings, see pages 420-428.*

Paso de los Nubes

Pampa Linda is also the starting point for a 22 km walk over Paso de los Nubes (1,335 m) to **Laguna Frías** and **Puerto Frías** on the Chilean border. Allow at least two days; start the walk at Pampa Linda, rather than the other way around, as there's a gentler rise to the pass this way. There is camping at *Campamento Alerce* (after four hours) or *Campamento Glacier Frías* (after seven hours); from here it's another five hours to Puerto Frías. You'll see a spectacular glacial landscape, formed relatively recently (11,000 years ago), and the pass lies on the continental divide, with water flowing north to the Atlantic, and south to the Pacific. Views from the Río Frías valley are tremendous, and from Glacier Frías you enter Valdivian rainforest. Boats cross Lago Frías three times a day in summer at roughly 1115, 1315 and 1630, but check this before you leaving Bariloche. You must register with *guardaparques* at Pampa Linda before setting out, and check with them about conditions. The route is not always well marked and should only be attempted if there is no snow on the pass (it's normally passable only between December and February) or if the path is not excessively boggy. Do not cross rivers on fallen bridges or trees. See the excellent leaflet for Paso de las Nubes produced by Parque Nacional Nahuel Huapi. From Puerto Frías a 30-km road leads to Peulla on the shore of Chilean Lago Todos Los Santos. Or, you can take a boat back to Bariloche. Highly recommended. Another pleasant walk is to tranquil **Laguna Ilon** (five-and-a-half hours each way), with bathing on the shore in summer. Also to **Refugio Otto Meiling**, see below. Check with *guardaparques*.

Mount Tronador

From Pampa Linda two other paths lead up **Cerro Tronador** (3,478 m): one, 15 km long, leads to **Refugio Otto Meiling**, (2,000 m), in itself a wonderful walk (five hours each way), situated on the edge of the eastern glacier. Another hour from the *refugio*, a path takes you to a view over Tronador and the lakes and mountains of **Parque**

Nacional Nahuel Huapi; the other path leads to a *refugio* on the south side of the mountain. Otto Meiling is a good base camp for the ascent, with lots of facilities and activities, including trekking and ice climbing; always ask the *guardaparques* in Pampa Linda if there's space (capacity 60) US$3.40 pp per night, dinner US$5, let them know in advance if you're vegetarian.

Río Manso Medio and Lago Hess
Some 9 km west of Villa Mascardi, a road runs 18 km through the beautiful valley of the Río Manso Medio to Lago Hess and on to the nearby **Cascada Los Alerces**. This is the starting point for trekking excursions in a more remote area of small lakes and forested mountains, including Lagos Fonck, Roca, Felipe and Cerros Granito and Fortaleza. Check with *guardaparques* at Lago Hess about conditions on the paths.

Lago Steffen and Lago Martín → *Phone code: 02944*
About 20 km south of Villa Mascardi, another one-way dirt road leads to Lago Steffen, where a footpath runs along both northern and southern shores (of Lago Steffen) to Lago Martín. Both lakes are quite outstandingly lovely, fringed with beech and *álamo* trees, with far-off mountains in the distance, and pretty beaches where you can sit at the waters' edge. There's also great fishing here. Paradise. The *guardería* on Lago Steffen, and further north, wild camping, (no facilities) on the lake shore.

Further south, a road leads west along the Río Manso Inferior towards Chile. There is excellent rafting on the river, and several places where you can buy home-made produce.

El Bolsón → *Phone code: 02944 Colour map 5, B2 Population: 18,000*

El Bolsón is situated in a broad fertile valley 130 km south of Bariloche, surrounded by the mountains of the cordillera on either side, (hence its name: the big bowl), and dominated by the dramatic peak of Cerro Piltriquitrón 2,284m. With a river running close by, and a warm sunny microclimate, it's a magical setting which inspired thousands of hippies to create an ideological community here in the 1970s. They've built a laid-back town with a welcoming, rather nonchalant atmosphere, and produce the handicrafts, beers, fruit and jams for which the town is famous. There are many beautiful mountain walks and waterfalls nearby and swimming and rafting on Río Azul. The small national park of Lago Puelo is within easy reach, with fishing and walking, and if you'd rather just sit and relax, this is a wonderful place to spend a few days. ▶▶ *For Sleeping, Eating and other listings, see pages 420-428.*

Ins and outs
Getting there There are hourly buses from Bariloche and Esquel (and other destinations via these places) to El Bolsón, arriving off the main street at *Via Bariloche*'s offices at San Martín and Gral Roca. Also buses from Parque Nacional Los Alerces, and from destinations in Chile. There are equidistant airports at Bariloche and Esquel.

Getting around El Bolsón sprawls out from the spine of Avenida San Martín which runs through the town, where you'll find places to eat, and a few places to stay. There are buses to Lago Puelo, but buses to other sights are infrequent, and geared to locals rather than tourists. However, El Bolsón is a lovely place to walk around.

Tourist Information ① *on San Martin and Roca opposite Via Bariloche's bus stop, T492604, www.bolsonturistico.com.ar or sec_turismo@elbolson.com. Open 0900-2000 daily, all year, and to 2300 in summer.* The helpful and friendly tourist office, (with plenty of English speakers) is on the side of the semicircular plaza. They'll

66 99 It's a bit hairy, crossing the wood and wire bridges, but worth it for a dip in the sparkling turquoise waters on the way down ...

give you an excellent map of the town and the area and suggest places to stay. *Club Andino Piltriquitrón*, Sarmiento y Roca, T492600, can advise on hikes, and registers all walkers before setting off, (open daily peak season, otherwise only Tuesdays and Fridays, 1730-1930)

Best time to visit A good time to visit El Bolsón is in the summer, when you can take full advantage of the blissful rivers and mountains. It is very busy in January, so it's better to come in February, or March, although it is also lovely in the Spring and Autumn. The Festival Fiesta del Lúpulo (Hop Festival) is at the end of February and the Fiesta de la Fruta Fina (Berry Festival) at the nearby El Hoyo, is in January. May sees the Fiesta de la Cerveza Artesanal. On Tuesdays, Thursdays and Saturdays, there is a craft market in the semi-circular plaza.

Around El Bolsón

There's an impressive long sweep of waterfalls at **Cascada Escondida**, 10 km northwest of town, a good place for a picnic, with a botanical garden and *casa de te* (tea room) *San Jorge* nearby, serving delicious home-made beer in addition to home-made cakes and waffles; all recommended. Also a good *parrilla El Quincho*, which you can find signposted from the road. Rather less exciting falls at **Cataratas Mallín Ahogado**, a little further north, but still a pleasant spot for a stop. *La Golondrina* runs three buses daily Mon-Sat from the plaza to the loop around Mallin Ahogado, but walking is required to reach both falls. See tourist office map.

All along **Río Azul**, there are lovely places to bathe, camp and picnic. For a pleasant hour-long walk, with views over the town, climb **Cerro Amigo.** Follow Gral Roca east until it becomes Islas Malvinas and continue up the hill. Better still are the panoramic views from **Cerro Piltriquitrón**, the jagged peak looming over the town, from where you can paraglide in summer. Drive, or take a taxi 10 km east of the town up winding earth roads. Then it's an hour's walk through the sculpture park of the **Bosque Tallado**, carved from fallen trees by local craftspeople, to the *mirador* with fabulous views over the valley to the Andes beyond, or a six-to seven-hour round trip walking all the way. Food and shelter are available at the *refugio* (1,400 m). There are also good views from **Cabeza del Indio**, so called because the rock's profile resembles a face, a good 6km drive or bike ride from the centre. Take Azcuénaga west to cross the bridge over Río Quemquemtreu, follow signs to Cabeza del Indio. ▸▸ *For Sleeping, Eating and other listings, see pages 420-428.*

▲ **Walks** → *For the Parque Nacional Lago Puelo, see page 413*
There are wonderful treks to the mountains west of the town. Two-day hikes up **Río Motoco**, with *Refugio Motoco* at the top of the path, up Arroyo Lali to **Cerro Lindo** (2,135 m), with *Refugios Cerro Lindo* at the top, and up to **Cerro Hielo Azul** (2,270 m), also with a *refugio*. *Club Andino Piltriquitrón* has details on routes, and transport to start the walk. Another delightful refugio at **Cajón de Azul**, can be reached in a fabulous four-hour walk up **Río Azul**, river which flows from a deep canyon, returning the same day. Set off early to allow for a leisurely lunch at the top, or spend the night in the *refugio*, with its lovely gardens, in the company of Atilio and friends. Take a *traffic*

(minibus) to Wharton, leaving El Bolsón at 0900. There's a well marked path. It's a bit hairy crossing the two wood and wire bridges, but worth it for a dip in the sparkling turquoise water on the way down. You'll be collected by the *traffic* at 2000. Buses and information from Nehuén, Belgrano y Perito Moreno, same office as Andesmar.

South of El Bolsón

Epuyén → *Phone code: 02944 Colour map 5, B2*

Forty kilometres southeast of El Bolsón on Route 258, the little settlement of Epuyén (pronounced epooSHEN) is so far undeveloped for tourists, but is a quiet out of the way place to relax for a day or so, with some pleasant walking around Lago Epuyén, and one attractive *hostería*, which also has rustic *cabañas*, and provides meals on request. A fire destroyed trees all over one hillside two years ago, making the area less attractive for walks, but there's a good trek around the lakeside, and good fishing in the lake.

Cholila → *Phone code 02945 Colour map 5, B2*

A peaceful village spread out in wonderful broad open landscape with superb views of Lago Cholila, crowned by the Matterhorn-like mountains of Cerros Dos and Tres Picos. Cholila lies 76 km south of El Bolsón on Route 71, which branches off Route 258 at Km 179. There's excellent fishing, canoeing and kayaking on rivers nearby, and you can visit the evocative wooden cabins where Butch Cassidy, the Sundance Kid and Etta Place lived between 1901 and 1905. You can understand why they hid out here for so long: Cholila still feels remote and untouched, and the views from their land are breathtaking. The cabins can't be seen from the roadside, but there is a small sign, 13 km north of town along Ruta 71, entry US$3, if there's anyone around. Go out of season and you'll have them to yourself.

There is a good walk around **Lago Mosquito**: continue down the road from El Trébol past the lake then take a path to the left, following the river. Cross the river on the farm bridge and continue to the base of the hills to a second bridge. Follow the path to the lake and walk between the lake and the hills, crossing the river via a suspension bridge just past El Trébol – six hours. ▸▸ *For Sleeping, Eating and other listings, see pages 420-428.*

Leleque → *Colour map 5, B2*

Route 40 (paved) is a faster way to get from El Bolsón to Esquel, and the route the bus takes. You could stop off at Leleque to see the **Museum of Patagonia** ① *off the RN 40, at km 1440, 90 km from Esquel, and 80 km from El Bolsón. US$1. Open 1100-1700, Jan/Feb 1100-1900. Closed Wed and May/Jun, museoleleque@ciudad.com.ar*, in the vast estate owned by *Benetton*, the Italian knitwear company. Though they may be exploiting half of Patagonia, they do look after their work force, and they have created a remarkable museum here, There's a beautifully designed exhibition on the lives of indigenous peoples, with dwellings reconstructed of animal skins, using the original construction techniques, a huge collection of delicate arrowheads and the original *boleadoras* for catching cattle. Other moving exhibits include one on the first pioneers in Patagonia, especially the Welsh. And there's an attractive café in a reconstructed *boliche* (provisions shop and bar).

Parque Nacional Lago Puelo

This lovely green and wooded national park is centred around the deep turquoise-coloured Lago Puelo, 18 km south of El Bolsón on the Chilean border, surrounded by southern beechforest. With relatively low altitude (200 m) and high rainfall, the forest is rich in tree species, particularly the *arrayán* and the *pitra*, *coihues* (evergreen beech) and cypresses. There's lots of wildlife, including the *huemul*, *pudu*

Butch and Sundance

No trip to Cholila, south of El Bolsón, should be complete without a visit to the wooden cabin where Butch Cassidy and the Sundance Kid lived between 1901 and 1905. The tale of the most famous twosome in the American West has become the source of many myths. The 1969 movie showed Butch and Sundance gunned down by the Bolivian army, but rumours have persisted that, having faked their deaths, they returned to the United States. The mystery continues.

There is little mystery about the events which led the two outlaws to move to Cholila along with Etta Place, Sundance's girlfriend. Both Cassidy (real name Robert LeRoy Parker) and the Kid (born Harry Longabaugh) had pursued careers in which periods of legal employment had been mixed with distinctly illegal activity. In the late 1890's the two were part of a loosely-organised gang known variously as the Train Robbers' Syndicate, the Hole in the Wall Gang and the Wild Bunch, which operated out of Brown's Park, a high valley on the borders of Utah, Colorado and Wyoming. Gang members specialised in hold-ups on railway payrolls and banks. In 1900 they celebrated the wedding of one of their colleagues by having their photo taken: a big mistake. The photo was recognised by a Wells Fargo detective, and with their faces decorating Wanted posters across the land, Cassidy, Sundance and Etta left for Argentina in February 1901.

Using the names Santiago Ryan and Harry Place, the outlaws settled on government land near Cholila and applied to buy it, but Pinkerton detectives hot on their trail soon tracked them down and informed the Argentine authorities. They lay low, in the house which you can now visit, still appealingly remote; but by 1905 it was time to move on before the Pinkertons or the locals could make further moves. Needing money to start up elsewhere, the gang raided banks in Villa Mercedes and Río Gallegos, a particularly audacious job. Posing as ranching company agents, they opened a bank account with US$7,000, spent two weeks at the best hotels and socialised with the city's high society, and then entered the bank to close their accounts and empty the safe before escaping to Chile. Shortly afterwards, Etta returned to the United States, and disappeared from the history books.

No longer welcome in Argentina, Butch and Sundance moved to Bolivia, finding work at the Concordia tin mine. Though scrupulously honest in their dealings with the mine, their occasional disappearances for a few days sometimes coincided with hold-ups. Lack of capital to settle as respectable ranchers was, however, their undoing. In 1908 near Tupiza in southern Bolivia, they seized an Aramayo mining company payroll, gaining only a fraction of the loot they expected. With military patrols in pursuit and the Argentine and Chilean forces alerted, they rode into the village of San Vicente and were recognised. Besieged, they did not, as in the film, run into the awaiting gunfire. Curiously, their deaths were not widely reported in the United States until the 1930's. While wild stories of their deaths had circulated long before 1980 they were now reported as having secretly returned to the United States. Butch was said to have become a businessman, a rancher, a trapper and a Hollywood movie extra, while Sundance had run guns in the Mexican Revolution, migrated to Europe, fought for the Arabs against the Turks in the First World War, sold mineral water, founded a religious cult, and still found time to marry Etta. (Adapted from Digging up Butch and Sundance by Ann Meadows, London, 1996). See Cholila for access to their cabin.

and foxes, and the lake is known for its good fishing for trout and salmon. There are gentle walks on marked paths around the northern shore area, boat trips across the lake, and canoes for rent. *Guardaparques* at the park entrance can advise on these, and hand out a basic map. ▶▶ *For Sleeping, Eating and other listings, see pages 420-428.*

Walks **'Bosque de las Sombras'** or Forest of the Shadows, is a delightful overgrown forest which you wander through on wooden walkways, on the way to the shingle beach at 'La Playita'. **Senda a los Hitos**, is a 10-km (three hours each way) walk through marvellous woods, to the rapids at Río Puelo, on the Chilean border, passport required, and there is some wild camping on the way. From the east of the lake, you can hike to **El Turbio** and **Cerro Plataforma**, crossing the lake first by boat to El Desemboque (or taking the bus and walking 14km). It's about seven hours to Río Turbio, where there's a *guardaparque* and then twelve hours to Cerro Plataforma; allow three days for the whole trip. There's a three-day trek through magnificent scenery to **Glaciar y Cerro Aguaja Sur**: get advice and directions from the *guardaparques*.

Access and facilities No entry fee. The main entrance is along a pretty road south from El Bolsón, through *chacras* (small farms) growing walnuts, hops and fruit, to Villa Lago Puelo, 3km north of the park, where there are shops, plenty of accommodation and fuel. From here the road is unpaved. Entrance is also possible at **El Desemboque**, on the eastern side of the park: take the bus from El Bolsón to Esquel, alight at El Hoyo, then walk 14km to El Desemboque. It's best to come between November and April, though the northern shore of the lake can get crowded in January and February. The lake is glorious in April, when the trees turn a vivid yellow. The Administration Centre is 500m north of the lake (all year round Mon-Fri 0800-1500), with a booth at the pier in summer. They have a helpful leaflet and can advise on walks.

   Boat trips across Lago Puelo *Juana de Arco*, T493415, 156 02290, juanadearco@red42.com.ar US$2 for 45mins, US$6 to the Chilean border, including walk through woodland. Recommended. Also run fishing trips. *Zona Sur* run all inclusive fishing trips from November to April, US$100 per day for three people, equipment included. T156 15989, alemaca@yahoo.com.ar

The Lake District Esquel

Esquel→ *Phone code: 02945 Colour map 5, B2 Population: 30,000*

Esquel is a pleasant breezy town in a fertile valley with a dramatic backdrop of mountains. It was originally an offshoot of the Welsh colony at Chubut, 650 km to the east, and still has a pioneer feel to it, in the old fashioned general stores, and many buildings from the early 1900s. It's a busy country town with a life of its own, the streets filled with battered *camionetas* of local farmers. It's not at all touristy and with few sights, but all the more appealing for that. It's the best base for visiting the Parque Nacional Los Alerces, and for skiing at La Hoya in winter, and famous for the railway La Trochita which has a charming old-fashioned station to the northwest of the centre. There are good places to stroll into the hills directly above the town, and you could also take a bus to the village of Trevelin, 40 minutes away, also founded by the Welsh. ▶▶ *For Sleeping, Eating and other listings, see pages 420-428.*

Ins and outs
Getting there and around There's an airport 20 km east, reached by bus or taxi, and a smart modern bus terminal on Avenida Alvear, 6 blocks from the main commercial centre around Av Fontana. Buses arrive here from Comodoro Rivadavia and Bariloche, with connections from those places to all other destinations in Patagonia and to the north. Buses also run daily into Los Alerces National Park.

Tourist infomation ① *Alvear y Sarmiento, T451927, www.esquel.gov.ar, www.esquelonline.com.ar. Open daily 0800-2000, summer 0730-2200. Closed weekends off-season.* This very basic tourist office is friendly but staff have little, or incorrect, information. They do hand out a useful town map, however, with Los Alerces Park on the other side.

Sights

The town is easy to walk around in an hour, with two small musems, mildly interesting. The **Museo Indigenista y de Ciencias Naturales** ① *Belgrano 330 y Chacabuco, open daily except Tue, 1600-2000,* has indigenous artefacts, and the **Museo de Arte Naíf**, Av Fontana y Av Alvear, has a collection of Argentine 'modern primitive' paintings. It's also the departure point for the famous narrow gauge railway, **La Trochita** ① *US$5 adults, under 6 free, in high season (Jan/Feb) there are 5 departures a week, other times Sat only at 1000, tickets from tour operators, or from station office, Estacion Viejo Expreso Patagonico, T451403. www.latrochita.com.ar* Though obviously a tourist experience, this is a thoroughly enjoyable trip, taking in the lovely valley and mountains of the *precordillera* framed through the windows of the quaint old train, with its wood stoves and little tea room. There's Spanish commentary along the way, and home-made cakes and handicrafts for sale at the Mapuche hamlet **Nahuel Pan**, where the train stops, and where you'll hear an interesting explanation of how the engine works. Recommended.

There's good skiing at the low-key family resort of **La Hoya**, 15 km north (see skiing page 426), and some challenging walks in the surrounding mountains. It's an easy climb along a clear path to **Laguna La Zeta**, 5 km from the centre of town, with good views and a lake with bird life. The path is signposted from the end of Av La

Esquel

0 metres 200
0 yards 200

Sleeping 🛏
Albergue El Batxoky 1
Angelina 2
Casa Emma Cleri 3
Cumbres Blancas 4
El Hogar del Mochilero 5

Hostería Los Tulipanes 6
Lago Verde 9
La Posada 7
La Tour D'Argent 8
Millalen 10
Res El Cisne 11

Tehuelche 12

Eating 🍴
Don Chiquino 1
La Española 2
Los Nietos 4

María Castaña 5
Pizzería 6
Shangai 7
Tango Gourmet 8
Vascongada 9

five hours return; walk from the centre of town signposted from the end of the street 25 de Mayo. For longer hikes to **Cerro Veinte Uno**, (five to eight hours return) and the pointy cone of Cerro Nahual Pan, (eight hours return)

Trevelin *Phone code: 02945 Colour map 5, B2 Population: 5,000*

The pretty village of Trevelin, 22 km southwest of Esquel, was once an offshoot of the Welsh colony in Chubut (see box page 440), near Trelew on the east coast. You can still hear Welsh spoken here, and there is plenty of evidence of its rich cultural heritage in several good little museums. With a backdrop of snowcapped mountains, the village is an appealing place to rest for a few days, to go fishing and rafting on nearby Río Futuleufu, or see the beautiful waterfalls at the reserve of Nant-y-fall.

Sights
Trevelin remains a quiet village with a strong sense of community, and its history is manifest in several sights. The Welsh chapel of 1910, **La Capilla Bethel**, is now closed but the building can be seen from the outside, and there is the fine old flour mill of 1918, which houses the **Museo Histórico Regional** ① *daily 1100-1800, US$1*, which has fascinating artefacts from the Welsh colony. **El Tumbo del Caballo** Malacara, 200m from main plaza, is a private garden containing the house of John Evans, one of the first settlers, nicely maintained with all his belongings. Outside is the grave of his horse, Malacara, who once saved his life. Guided tours are available, US$2. Eisteddfods are still held here every year, and you'll be relieved to hear that the other apparently Welsh tradition, *Té Galés*, the Welsh tea (an amazing excess of delicious cakes), is alive and well in *Nain Maggie* tea rooms. There's a very enthusiastic and helpful **tourist office** in Trevelin's central octagonal plaza, T480120, www.trevelin.org offering maps, accommodation, and advice on fishing, English spoken.

Molino Nant Fach, Route 259, 22 km southwest towards the Chilean border, is a beautiful flour mill built by Merfyn Evans, descendant of the town's founder Thomas Dalar Evans, an exact replica of the first mill built in 1899. Merfyn's fascinating tour (in Spanish, but English booklet available to read) recounts a now familiar tale of the Argentine government's persistent mismanagement of natural resources and industry, through the suppression of the Welsh prize-winning wheat industry. It's a beautiful spot, and Merfyn tells the rather tragic story in a wonderfully entertaining way. Highly recommended. Entry US$0.40. The **Nant-y-fall Falls** ① *US$0.25 pp including guide to all seven falls (1½-hr walk).*, lie 17 km southwest on the road to the border, a series of spectacular waterfalls reached through an easy trail through lovely forest. A good picnic spot too.Both Molino Nant Fach and Nant-y-fall Falls are accessible only by car or excursion. ▸▸ *For Sleeping, Eating and other listings, see pages 420-428.*

Fishing is popular in many local rivers and lakes, most commonly in Río Futuleufú, and Corintos, and Lagos Rosario and Greda. The season runs from mid-November to mid-April, and the tourist office can advise on guides and where to go. There's a good day walk to **Refugio Wilson** in idyllic scenery on a mountain side above the town. The *refugio* sleeps 48, and offers food and accommodation. Get directions on the route from the tourist office. It's also a good destination for horse riding or mountain biking.

Parque Nacional Los Alerces → *www.parquesnacionales.gov.ar*

One of the most magnificent and untouched expanses of the whole Andes region, this national park was established to protect the enormously tall and stately *alerce* trees (Fitzroya cupressoides), some specimens over 2,000 years old. They grow deep in the

Valdivian rainforest which carpets these mountains a rich velvety green, beside vivid navy blue Lago Futalaufquen and emerald Lago Verde. There are several good hikes, rafting and fishing in the park, and idyllic lakeside campsites and *hosterías*, making this a great place to spend a few days.

The park, 60 km west of Esquel, is large, though much of it cannot be reached, and contains four large lakes including **Lago Futalaufquen**, with some of the best fishing in the area, **Lago Menéndez** which can be crossed by boat to visit the ancient *alerce* trees, and the exquisite green **Lago Verde**. In order to protect this fragile environment, access is possible only to the eastern side of the park, via *ripio* Route 71 which runs between Cholila and Trevelin alongside Lagos Futalaufquen, Verde and Rivadavia, with many good camping spots and small *hosterías* on their shores. The western side of the park, where rainfall is highest, has areas of Valdivian forest, and can only be accessed by boat or hiking to Lago Krügger. Lago Futalaufquén has some of the best fishing in this part of Argentina (season runs from November 15 to Easter), and local guides offer fishing trips, and boat transport. Ask in the *Intendencia* (park office), or *Hostería Cume Hue* T453639 (am) or T450503 (pm).

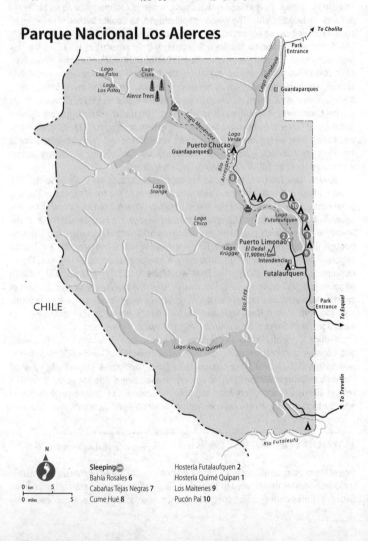

Parque Nacional Los Alerces

Sleeping
Bahía Rosales **6**
Cabañas Tejas Negras **7**
Cume Hué **8**
Hostería Futalaufquen **2**
Hostería Quimé Quipan **1**
Los Maitenes **9**
Pucón Pai **10**

Park information

Entrances to the park are on Route 71, at the northern end of Lago Rivadavia, and 12 km south of Lago Futulaufquen. At the southern tip of this lake is Villa Futulaufquen, a small village there's a visitors' centre with useful information on the park, and the *Intendencia* where helpful *guardaparques* give out maps and advise on walks. There's also a service station, *locutorio*, two food shops, and a restaurant *El Abuelo Monje*. Fishing licences can be obtained either from the food shops, the kiosko or *Hosteria Cume Hue*. For further information, T471020, alerces@ciudad.com.ar Park entrance costs US$2. A daily bus runs along Route 71 in each direction, picking up and dropping off passengers at campsites and *hosterías*. See transport below.

▲ Trekking

Near the park *Intendencia* (km 1) there's a gentle 40-minute trail to see **cave paintings**, a waterfall, and a *mirador* with panoramic views over Lago Futulaufquen. Another lovely stroll to a magical part of the park is across the suspension bridge over Río Arrayanes (km 34,3) to heavenly **Lago Verde**. A self-guided trail leads around a peninsula and to Lago Menéndez, to the pier where boat trips begin. From the road along the west coast of Lago Futalaufquen to Puerto Limonao and Hotel Futalaufquen, there is a longer trek to **Cerro Dedal** (1,900 m), eight hours return, with a steep climb from road to Puerto Limonao, giving wonderful views. Register first with *guardaparques*, and get detailed directions; start before 1000, and carry plenty of water. There is also a two-day (12-14 hour) hike though *coihue* forest to the tip of **Lago Krüger**, a *refugio* open only Jan/Feb, where you can take a boat back to Puerto Limonao.

Boat trips

All boat trips run frequently in high season, and all can be booked through Safari Lacustre, T471008, www.brazosur.com or through Patagonia Verde in Esquel, T454396. Prices US$16-27. US$5 extra for transport from Esquel. There are trips from Puerto Limonao, north of the *Intendencia* across Lago Futulaufquen and along the peagreen Río Arrayanes, lined with the extraordinary cinnamon-barked *arrayán* trees. Even more spectacular, the unforgettable trip from Puerto Chucao, reached after a 30-minute walk across the bridge over Río Arrayanes, across Lago Menéndez (one and a half hours) to see the majestic 2,600 year old *alerce* trees. From 'el abuelo' you walk to the hidden and silent jade-green Lago Cisne, and then back past the rushing white waters of Río Cisne. An unforgettable experience. Boats also go from Puerto Limonao, to Lago Krügger which you can trek to, and take the boat back.

Border with Chile

There are two border crossings just south of Esquel, the spectacularly beautiful Paso Futaleufú and Paso Palena. On the Chilean side roads from these crossings both link up to the route to Chaitén. ▸ *For Sleeping, Eating and other listings, see pages 420-428.*

Paso Futaleufú lies 70 km southwest of Esquel via Trevelin and is reached by Route 259 (*ripio* from Trevelin). The border is crossed by a bridge over the Río Futaleufú, and formalities should take no longer than an hour.

    Argentine immigration and customs On the Argentine side of the bridge. Eat all your fresh food, as no fruit or vegetables may be take into Chile. Cars must have special papers and the numberplate etched into all windows: advise your hire company when booking.

    Chilean immigration and customs In Futaleufú, 9 km west of the border.

Paso Palena lies 120 km southeast of Esquel and is reached by Route 17 from Trevelín which runs to Corcovado, 75 km east of Tecka (reached by ripio road). From Corcovado it is 26 km west to the border.

Argentine immigration and customs, at the border, open daily 0900-1800.

Chilean immigration, at Palena, 11 km west of border. There are *cabañas* in Corcovado and several pensiones in Palena

South of Esquel

The Route 40 continues (paved) south from Esquel across very deserted landscapes that give you a taste for the full experience of Patagonia. It's a tricky section for travel by public transport, since there are few settlements or services along this section of road until you reach. At Tecka (phone code 02945; population 1,000; altitude 710 m), Km 101, Route 62 (paved) branches off east and follows the valley of the Río Chubut to Trelew. Route 40 continues south to Gobernador Costa (population: 1,700; phone code: 02945; altitude: 640 m), a small service centre for the estancias in this area on the Río Genoa at Km 183. ▸▸ *For Sleeping, Eating and other listings, see pages 420-428.*

Río Pico → *Phone code: 02945 Colour map 5, C2 Population: 1,000*
Río Pico lies in a wide green valley close to the Andes and is best visited from December to February. It is the site of an early 20th-century German settlement and some old houses remain from that period. At Estancia Hahn, 4 km east of town, you can see the old store and pioneers' houses, and the grave of Wilson and Evans. Nearby are several lakes, good for fishing and free camping, ask locals for hitching; the northern shore of Lago Tres, 23 km west of town, is a peaceful and remote place, with a rich birdlife and wild strawberries at the end of January. Some 30 km north of Río Pico lies the huge Lago Vintter, reached by Route 44. There are also smaller lakes good for trout fishing. Permits are available from the Municipalidad in Gobernador Costa.

South of Gobernador Costa
At Km 221, Route 40 (poor *ripio*) forks southwest through the town of **Alto Río Senguer** from which visits can be made to the relatively unexplored Lago Fontana and Lago La Plata. Provincial Route 20 (paved) heads almost directly south for 81, before turning east towards Sarmiento and Comodoro Rivadavia. At La Puerta del Diablo, in the valley of the lower Río Senguer, Route 20 intersects provincial Route 22, which joins with Route 40 at the town of Río Mayo (see page 453). This latter route is completely paved and preferable to Route 40 for long-distance motorists.

Listings: Bariloche to Esquel

◉ Sleeping

Lago Gutiérrez *p409*
AL **El Retorno**, *Villa Los Coihues, on the northern shore, T467333, www.hosteria elretorno.com* With a stunning lakeside position, this is a traditional family-run hotel in tasteful hunting lodge style, with lovely gardens running down to the beach, tennis courts, and comfortable rooms. Also a restaurant. Very relaxing.
Estancia Peuma Hue, *on the southern shore of Lago Gutiérrez, 3km off the road, T011-5101 1392, www.peuma-hue.com* Offers accommodation in a beautifully designed

country house, remotely situated on its own stretch of shoreline, with houses in the mountain too, making this a luxury retreat, offering lots of activities: horse riding, fishing and kayaks, rafting in Ríos Mansos. The food is delicious and rooms are individually decorated with great panache, with great views. Jacuzzi under the stars in the huge suite is partcularly recommended.

Camping
Villa los Coihues, *Lago Gutierrez, T467479.* Well equipped and beautifully situated. Take bus 50/51, or take the track down to Gutiérrez from Cerro Catedral (4WD

advisable) or the road to El Bolson, Route 258, and follow signs.

L **Arelauquen Golf and Country Club**, *on the eastern shore of Lago Gutierrez, T467626, www.arelauquen.com* Upmarket golf and country club, with tennis, squash and horse riding too, and swish accommodation in a new chalet-style building. Smallish but luxurious rooms, good restaurant, exclusive atmosphere.

Lago Mascardi *p409*

A pp **Hotel Tronador**, *T441062, hoteltronador@bariloche.com.ar* A lakeside paradise, open mid-Nov to Easter, the lovely rooms have terrific lake views from their balconies, there are beautiful gardens, and the charming owner is truly welcoming. It's a really peaceful place, (especially out of peak season). Can also organize riding, fishing and excursions on the lake. Highly recommended.

B **Mascardi**, *Rute 258 km 36,8, on the route to Tronador, T490518, www.mascardi.com* The first you come to, just a few kilometes from the turning is this luxurious place with a delightful setting in lovely gardens on its own beach by the lake, restaurant and tea room, horse riding, mountains bikes, rafting fly fishing in Río Guillelmo also arranged.

Camping

Camping La Querencia, *T426225, further on, at km 10*. A pretty and peaceful spot on the side of river and on banks of lake, opposite the lovely straight beach of Playa Negro.

Camping Las Carpitas, *also on Lago Mascardi, at km 33, T490527*. Set in a great lakeside position, summer only, with *cabañas* and restaurant.

Camping Los Rapidos, *T/F461861, T422266*. Attractive shaded site going down to the lake, with *confitería*, food store and all facilities, US$2.50pp. Also bunk beds in a basic *albergue* US$3pp (sleeping bag needed). Friendly owners organize trekking, kayaking, fishing and mountain bikes.

Mount Tronador *p410*

D **Hostería Pampa Linda**, *T442038, www.tronador.com* This *hostería* is a luxurious base for climbing Tronador, or a comfortable retreat from which to start other treks. Simple comfortable rooms, all with bath, and all with stunning views. The owners are charming; Sebastian de la Cruz is one of the area's most experienced mountaineers. Horse riding can be organized, as well as trekking and climbing courses. Full board, and packed lunches for hiking available.

Camping

Pampa Linda, *T424531*. Idyllic spacious lakeside site, *confitería* and food shop.

Cascada Los Alerces

C **Hostería Lago Hess**, *T462249, piccino@bariloche.com.ar* Half/full board.

Lago Steffan and Lago Martín

D **Hostería Río Villegas**, pleasant, friendly, restaurant. Rates at refugios are about US$7 per person (details from *Club Andino Bariloche*).

El Bolsón *p411*

There are lots of *cabañas* and *hosterías* up on a hill in the Villa Turismo, 3 km southeast of the centre, a good hour's walk, or a cheap taxi ride. It's difficult to find accommodation in the high season: book ahead.

B **Cordillera**, *San Martín 3210, T492235, cordillerahotel@elbolson.com* A standard modern hotel in the centre of town, 4 blocks north of the plaza, breakfast included, all rooms with bath and TV.

C **La Casona de Odile**, *Barrio Lujan, T492753, odile@red42.com.ar* A really special place to stay, in rustic wooden cabins in this idyllic lavender farm by a stream, with delicious cooking by the charismatic Odile. Reserve ahead. Recommended.

D **Sukal**, *high on a hill in Villa Turismo, T492438, www.sukal/elbolson.com* Gorgeous bed and breakfast, a haven of peace in a flower-filled garden, with glorious views. Also a *cabana*, US$20 for 4. Delightful.

D **La Posada de Hamelin**, *Int Granollers 2179, T492030, gcapece@elbolson.com* One of the most welcoming places, run by charming German-speaking owners, who make a really outstanding breakfast. Lovely chalet-style house with quaint and comfortable rooms all with bathroom, and lovely garden. Highly recommended.

D Amancay, *San Martin y Hernandez, T492222*. Central, old-fashioned but comfortable, if a little institutional, all rooms with small bathrooms, breakfast included.

D Hostería Steiner, *San Martín 670, T492224*. Worth going a little way out of the centre to stay in this peaceful place with huge lovely gardens. Simple plain rooms, wood fires, German spoken. Recommended.

D Valle Nuevo, *25 de Mayo y Belgrano, T156 02325*. Small and basic rooms in this quiet place, breakfast not included, but good value.

Cabañas

There are many *cabañas* in picturesque settings with lovely views, in the Villa Turistica, costing around US$40 for 5 people per night. Call them for directions. Buses to Villa Turismo run by *Comarca Andina*, opposite *Via Bariloche T455400*. The following are recommended:

Cabañas Paraíso, *T492766, www.bolsonturistico.com.ar/paraiso/* Lovely wooden cabins in a gorgeous setting amongst old trees.

Cabañas Piltri Hué, *T492711, www.bolsonturistico.com.ar/piltrihue* Very alpine-style setting for these picturesque little *cabañas*.

La Montana, *T492776, www.montana. com.ar* Very well equipped smart *cabañas* with pool, children's play area.

Lincoln Ranch, *T492073, www.bolson turistico.com.ar/lincolnranch* Big well maintained *cabaña* complex with open views, and pool, great for big groups.

Youth hostels

E pp El Pueblito, *3km north in Luján, 1 km off Route 258, T493560, elpueblito@ elbolson.com* A cosy wooden building in wild open country. Slightly squashed dorms, but a good atmosphere, cooking and laundry facilities, shop, open fire, sheets extra. Cosy double room too. And, there is a great *cabaña* in the middle of a field, US$20 for 3 people per night.

E pp Refugio Patagónico, *Islas Malvinas y Pastorino, T156 35463*. High quality youth hostel, with small dorms all with bathrooms, in a spacious house set in open fields, where

you can also camp, with great views of Piltriquitrón, and just 5 blocks from the plaza. Recommended.

E pp Sol del Valle, *25 de Mayo 2329, T492087*. A bright, more basic, hostel with basic rooms, shared bathrooms, big kitchen and eating space for big groups, sheets/towels extra. Garden with view of Piltriquitrón.

Camping

There are many good sites, fully equipped and lively particularly in Jan.

Arco Iris, *T15558330*. Blissful wooded setting near Rio Azul, helpful owners.

La Chacra, *Belgrano 1128, T492111*. 15 mins walk from town, well shaded, good facilities, lively atmosphere in season.

Quem Quem, *on river bank Rio Quemquemtreu, T493550, quemquem@elbolson.com* Well kept lovely site with hot showers, good walks, free pick-up from town.

Refugio Patagónico, *see hostels above*. A great open site with hot showers and fireplaces, lovely views.

Parque Nacional Lago Puelo *p413*

There are lots of *cabañas*, shops and fuel. Apart from wild camping, there's no accommodation in the park itself, but plenty in Villa Lago Puelo, just outside, with *cabañas*, restaurants and campsites spread out along Route 16 through the little village.

D Hostería Enebros, *T499413*. On the road, is comfortable and can be recommended.

D Posada los Ninos, *T499117*. In a pretty rural setting, is very peaceful.

D Rincón de Azul. Also recommended.

Cabañas

A-D Puelo Ranch, *T499411, www.interpatagonia.com/elbolson/cabanas* or email the caretaker Jorge at *patagoniapuelo @fibertel.com.ar* Hidden from the road is a superb complex of very comfortable *cabanas*

La Granja, *km 13, T499265*. Set in lovely woodland, with a pool.

La Yoica, *Km 3, T492200*. Very attractive.

Villa Antares, *Km 11, T499334*. Well equipped and attractive cabins.

Camping

There are many good sites with all facilities: **La Pasarela**, *km10, T499061*, **Los Quinchos** *km 13*, and **Ailin Co**, *km15, T499078*. All recommended. The two free sites in the park itself, on Lago Puelo, have only basic services, no hot water.

Epuyén p413

D **Refugio del Lago**, 499025. A relaxed place with rustic comfortable rooms in a lovely wooden house, a short walk from the shore, with breakfast included, also good meals. Owners Sophie and Jacques are mountain guides, and can organize trekking and riding. Also camping and *cabañas*. Recommended. Buses between El Bolsón and Esquel stop (briefly) at Epuyén, though some don't enter the village itself. Ask Sophie to check first, and arrive in plenty of time.

Cholila p413

A-B pp **Hostería La Rinconada**, *T498091, larinconada@interlink.com.ar* also **AL** full board, excursions, riding, kayaking.
C pp **El Trébol**, *at Lago Los Mosquistos, T/F498055, eltrebol@teletel.com.ar* Comfortable rooms with stoves, meals and half board also available, popular with fishing expeditions, reservations advised, bus stops in village 4 km away.
D **Hostería El Pedregoso**, *at Lago Cholila, 8 km west, T498319.*
D **Cabanas Cerro La Momia**, *at the foot of the mountain, on Route 71 in Villa Rivadavia, 3 km from the nothern access to Los Alerces park T0297-446 1796, www.cabanascerro lamomia.com.ar* Set in a wonderfully peaceful setting, these are pretty basic *cabañas*, but equipped with everything you need, and with breakfast included.

Camping

F pp **Autocamping Carlos Pelligrini**, *next to El Trébol;* free camping in El Morro park. Camping El Abuelo, *13 km south.*

Esquel p415, map p416

A **Cumbres Blancas**, *Ameghino 1683, T/F455100, www.cpatagonia.com/ esq/cblancas* A little out of the town centre, with great views of surrounding hills, comfortable traditional rooms and an airy restaurant serving a good, slightly pricey

dinner at US$7 **B** low season.
B **Angelina**, *Alvear 758, T452763.* A warm welcoming place, open high season only, serving good food, Italian spoken.
B **Canela**, *C Los Notros, Villa Ayelén, on road to Trevelin, T/F453890, www.canela-patagonia.com* Comfortable bed and breakfast and tearoom. English-speaking owners are knowledgeable about Patagonia.
B **Tehuelche**, *9 de Julio 825, T452420, tehuelche@ar.inter.net* A comfortable redesigned 70's style place with modern rooms, breakfast included, and a good restaurant with cheap set menu.
C **La Tour D'Argent**, *San Martín 1063, T454612, www.cpatagonia.com /esq/latour* With breakfast, the bright plain modern rooms are very good value in this friendly family-run hotel.
D **La Chacra**, *Km 4 on Ruta 259 towards Trevelin, T452471.* Tranquil place with spacious modern rooms and huge breakfast, Welsh/English spoken.
D **La Posada**, *Chacabuco 905, T454095 laposada@art.inter.ar* A real gem, this welcoming tasteful *hostería* in a quiet part of town, with a lovely lounge to relax in, and good spacious rooms, breakfast included. Excellent value. Recommended.
E **Res El Cisne**, *Chacabuco 778, T452256.* With cooking facilities, this quiet and well kept place is good value.
F **Casa Emma Cleri**, *Alvear 1021, T452083, T156 87128 (mob).* Helpful and hospitable.
G pp **Mrs Elvey Rowlands' guesthouse**, *behind Rivadavia 330, T452578.* With a warm welcome, this is a recommended place, though the rooms are simple with shared bath. Breakfast included, Welsh spoken.

Youth hostels

E pp **Albergue El Batxoky**, *San Martin 661, T450581, www.epaadventure.com.ar* A new and welcoming hostel with smallish rooms, kitchen, laundry. Also run-rafting, trekking, climbing and mountain biking.
E **Lago Verde**, *Volta 1081, T454396, patagverde@teletel.com.ar* A modern comfortable place, with rooms for 2, breakfast extra, kitchen, laundry. Handy for

the bus terminal, and 2 blocks from La Trochita. The owners run a travel company and can organize excursions. Recommended.

Camping
El Hogar del Mochilero, *Roca 1028, T452166.* Summer only (Jan-Mar), laundry facilities, 24-hr hot water, friendly owner, internet, free firewood.
La Colina, *Darwin 1400, Laguna Zeta, T454962.* US$1.75 pp, hot showers, kitchen facilities, lounge, log fire, also rooms, **G** pp.
La Rural, *1 km on road to Trevelin, T452580.* Well organized and shady site with facilities.
Millalen, *Ameghino 2063, T456164.* Good services.

Trevelin *p417*
C La Granja, *on the road to Esquel 3km from Trevelin, T480096.* In a lovely open setting, comfortable *cabañas*, and camping facilities, as well as macrobiotic meals and good Italian cooking. Excellent horses for hire.
D Pezzi, *Sarmiento 353, T480146.* Open Jan-Mar only, an attractive small hotel, English spoken, and a garden. Although there are few hotels in Trevelin, there are lots of *cabañas*: the tourist office has a full list.
D-E Casa Verde Hostal, *Los Alerces s/n, T/F48009,casaverdehostel@ciudad.com.ar* 'The best hostel in Argentina' is run by Bibiana and Charley, who'll make you welcome in their log cabin, with gardens. Comfortable dorms for 4-6 people all have bathrooms. Kitchen facilities, laundry, lounge, HI member, meals available. They also run trekking and rafting excursions into Los Alerces national park.
Refugio Wilson, *Cordón Situación, T480427,* can be reached by 4WD.

Camping
There are many sites, especially on the road to Futuleufú and Chile. In town, **La Granja**, *T480096,* can be recommended, and **Aikén Leufú**, on the road to Futaleufú dam, *T451317,* with full facilities and *cabañas* for 2.

Parque Nacional Los Alerces *p417*
On the east side of Lago Futalaufquen:
AL Cume Hué, *T453639.* A rather overpriced fishing lodge with spartan rooms and basic bathrooms, and enclosed in woodland, so

that only some rooms have views, but great for anglers. You can fish directly from the shore here, or in boat trips organized by the owners. Prices are full board.
A Hostería Quimé Quipan, *T471021.* Delightful, comfortable rooms, impeccably clean and attractively decorated, with uninterrupted lake views, and dinner included. Wonderfully peaceful. Paths lead down to a small rocky beach, and there are gardens to sit in. Recommended.
C Bahía Rosales, *T471044.* A welcoming family-run place with spacious *cabañas* to rent, in an elevated position above the lake, also *refugio*-style little *cabañas* to share **F** pp, and camping in open ground with great views, fireplaces and tables and hot showers; restaurant and *quincho*, all recommended.
D Pucón Pai, *T471010, puconpai@ciudad .com.ar* Slightly spartan rooms, but a good restaurant with lovely views, recommended for fishing (holds a fishing festival to open the season); also campsite with hot showers, US$2pp. Gardens go down to the lake.
D Cabañas Tejas Negras, *T471046.* Next door to *Pucón Pai*, these are really comfortable *cabañas* and good facilities for camping. Also recommended tea room.

West side of Lago Futalaufquen
L Hostería Futalaufquen, *just north of Puerto Limonao, T471008, www.brazosur.com* This hotel has an idyllic lakeside setting and architecture, but lacks a warm welcome. The rooms are reasonably comfortable, and some have wonderful views (these are much more expensive). The restaurant is good, but it's over-priced. It's even extortionate for tea.

Camping
There are several campsites on the eastern side of the lake, at Lagos Rivadavia, Verde and Río Arrayanes, ranging from free to US$3 depending on facilities. All have marvellous views, lake access and fireplaces, and can be busy in hugh season. If walking, register with *guardaparques* before you set off, bear in mind that it takes 10 hours to reach the *refugio* at Lago Krügger, and camping is possible (one night only) at Playa Blanca, where fires are not permitted.
Los Maitenes, *Villa Futalaufquen.* Excellent, US$1.50 pp plus US$2 per tent.
Krügger Lodge, Lago Krügger has a *refugio*

and campsite, with hot showers, food shop, meals provided, fishing guides, and boat trips.

❼ Eating

El Bolsón p411

$ **Cerro Lindo**, *next door to La Calabaza*. A slightly more elegant place for dinner, serving delicious pastas.

$ **El Rey de Sandwich**, *Roca 345, T491076*. The cheapest sandwiches in town, next to *Via Bariloche* bus terminal.

$ **Jauja**, *San Martín 2867*. A great meeting place, central and with a welcoming atmosphere and good music, and tasty food. English spoken. The trout-filled pasta is fabulous, there are good salads, delicious local specialities and the country's best hand-made ice creams, including Patagonian *calafate* berry flavour. Divine. Recommended.

$ **La Calabaza**, *San Martín y Hube*. Inexpensive food, with inventive delicious vegetarian dishes, in a warm and relaxed atmosphere.

$ **Parrilla Patagonia**, *on the road 258 2 km out of town*. Superb *parrilla*, recommended for steak, and excellent Patagonian lamb and kid on the *asado* at weekends. Also a cheap set menu and *parrilla libre*.

$ **Acrimbaldo**, *San Martín 2790*. Good value *tenedor libre*, smoked fish and draught beer.

$ **Il Rizzo**, *San Martín 2500*. Good value pizzas and draught beer in a lively café.

$ **La Tosca**, *San Martín y Roca*. Café, restaurant in summer, warm atmosphere.

$ **Martin Sheffield**. Conveniently central and cheap good food, Patagonian specialities, menu of the day, US$2.70.

Tea shops (Casas de té)

Dulcinea, *on the road to El Hoyo*. This delightful tea room is not to be missed. The owner, Debbie (who speaks English) is famous for her cakes and rose hip tea, and there's fondu at nights in season.

San Jorge, *3 km from town towards Cascada Escondida, T491313*. With delicious home-made cakes, beer and *picadas* (cheeses and hams) in pretty gardens.

Martha, *at the and of the Camino de los Nogales, T498105, www.bolsonturistico.com.ar/ martha*. Also has *cabañas* in a lovely wooded setting.

Cholila p413

Las Piedras, *Route 71 outside village*. Welsh tea room, chocolate cake recommended.

Esquel p415, map p416

$ **Don Chiquino**, *behind Av Ameghino 1649*. There's a fun atmosphere here, the walls lined with numberplates, and the owner will entertain you with magic and mind-teasing games while you wait for your pasta and pizzas.

$ **La Española**, *Rivadavia 740*. Serves excellent beef, with salad bar, and tasty pastas. Recommended.

$ **La Tour D'Argent**, *San Martin 1063*. There are delicious local specialities, good value set meals, and a warm atmosphere in this popular and traditional restaurant.

$ **Pizzería Don Pipo**, *Fontana 649*. Pizzas and *empanadas*.

$ **Shangai**, *25 de Mayo 485*. Chinese and everything else *tenedor libre*. Great value.

$ **Tango Gourmet**, *Alvear 949*, A restaurant/bar with tango shows and lessons, open 1100-2400.

$ **Vascongada**, *9 de Julio y Mitre*. Good trout and local specialities.

Cafés and tea rooms

Maria Castaña, *Rivadavia y 25 de Mayo*. A popular place for excellent coffee, reading the papers and watching street life.

Melys, *Miguens 346 (off Ameghino 2000)*. Welsh teas and also a good breakfast.

Trevelin p417

$ **Parrilla Oregon**, *Av San Martín y Laprida*. Large meals (particularly breakfast).

$ **Parrilla Ruca Laufquen**, *Av San Martin y Libertad*. Recommended for *parrilla* and also home-made pasta in a relaxed family atmosphere with the TV on.

$ **Patagonia Celta**, *25 de Mayo s/n*. This is the best place to eat by a long way. Really delicious local specialities, superbly cooked fresh trout, steaks and vegetarian dishes too in elegant stylish surroundings. Very welcoming, and reasonably priced.

Cafés and tea rooms

The best tea room, offering a huge *té galés* and excellent *torta negra* is **Nain Maggie**, *P Moreno 179*. Recommended.

🍸 Bars and clubs

El Bolsón *p411*

La Bandurria. Live music at weekends, and dancing.

Discos: **Bar 442** for rock, **Life** for techno, **Sub Zero** for cumbia.

🛍 Shopping

El Bolsón *p411*

The handicraft and food market is on Tue, Thu, and Sat in season 1000-1600 around the main plaza. Some fine leather and jewellery, carved wood and delicious organic produce.

Centro Artesanal, *Av San Martín 1059, open daily 1100-1900*. If the market's not open, a selection of the best crafts can be bought here.

Cerveza El Bolsón, *on the main road, Route 258, Km 123.9, T492595, info@cervezael bolson.com* Home-made beer.

La Huella, *Sarmiento y Dorrego, T491210*. For tent hire and outdoor equipment.

Laten K'Aike, *T491969*. Also known as Piedras Patagonicas, Mallin Ahogado, for exquisite semi precious stones.

Granja Larix, *Route 258, Km 118.5, T498018, alejandra@bariloche.com.ar* For fabulous smoked trout and home-made jams.

Esquel *p415, map p416*

Casa de Esquel, *25 de Mayo 415*. A range of rare books on Patagonia, also souvenirs.

Librería Patagonica, *25 de Mayo 415, T452544*. Rare books on Patagonia and recent editions, with friendly service.

La Casona de Olgbrun, *San Martín 1137*. A variety of handicrafts and souvenirs.

Benroth, *9 de Julio 1027*. Chocolates.

Braese, *at 9 de Julio 1959*. Home-made chocolates with other regional specialities.

Norte, *9 de Julio y Roca*. Huge supermarket.

Esquel *p415, map p416*

Fishing

There are few opportunites to hire fishing gear; best to take your own. Ask for fishing guides at the tourist office.

Sebastián Ferrer, *T452292*. English spoken, offers a 1-day guided excursion for fly casting and spinning for 2 people in the national park, including boat and meals (licence extra US$50 per person) for US$150.

Skiing

Esquel is a popular resort with Argentines, since it's one of the cheapest, **La Hoya**, 15km north, has 22km of pistes, many of them suitable for kids or beginners, with good challenging pistes too, and 7 ski-lifts. For information ask at **Club Andino Esquel**, *Volta 649, T453248*. There are 3 daily buses to La Hoya from Esquel, US$5 return. A ski pass costs US$7 per day in high season, with reductions for a week or longer, equipment hire US$4 a day. www.esquel online.com.ar

🗺 Tour operators

El Bolsón *p411*

Ernesto Hecker, *O Nelli 3217, T156 37560*. Great walking trips in the mountains and in the national parks, economical trips for small groups, with detailed expertise on vegetation geology and local history. Recommended.

Grado 42, *Av. Belgrano 406 T493124, grado42@elbolson.org* Tours, including La Trochita, helpful information on buses too.

Patagonia Adventures, *P Hube 418, T492513, www.argentinachileflyfishing.com* Rafting, paragliding, fishing, and recommended boat trip on Lago Puelo to remote forest lodge.

Viva Mas Patagonia, *Av San Martín 2526, T156 37665, lamaroma@hotmail.com* Rafting on Río Azul, grade 1 or 3.

Parque Nacional Lago Puelo *p413*

Fishing guides Puel-Co, *Fernando Arroyo, T499486*. Puelo Trout, *Jorge Ruppel, Av los Arrayanes s/n, T499185*. For boat trips across Lago Puelo, *Juana de Arco, T493415, 156 02290, juanadearco@red42.com.ar*

Esquel *p415, map p416*

Esquel Expeditions, *T451763, moranjack@ciudad.com.ar* Knowledgeable and experienced trekking guide Jack Moran leads adventure trips, trekking, mountain biking and canoeing trips tailored to your interests. All the treks in Los Alerces and nearby mountains, as well as up Río Futaleufu into Chile, walking in Valdivian rainforest, and along the Carretera Austral. Recommended.

Patagonia Verde, *9 de Julio 926, T/F454396, patagoniaverde@ciudad.com.ar* Excellent local tours, to Los Alerces, including the wonderful boat trip across Lagos Menéndez and Cisnes, and La Trochita. Also adventure excursions, horse riding (US$12 half day), rafting (US$25 per day, grades 2-4), fishing (US$100 per day, all inclusive), and fabulous 4WD trips to trek in tunnels of ice (US$18 full day). Helpful, professional, English spoken.

Trevelin *p417*
Gales al Sur, *Patagonia s/n, in the same building as the locutorio T/F480427, correo@galesalsur.com.ar* Tours to Chilean border, Los Alerces national park and Futaleufú dam; also La Trochita. Recommended for their rafting, trekking, bike, 4WD and horse riding excursions. Friendly, English spoken. They also run *Refugio Wilson*. Cycle hire (US$5 per day).

Parque Nacional Los Alerces *p417*
Agencies in Esquel or Trevelin run tours including the boat trip across Lago Menéndez to the alerce trees. See Patagonia Verde above, or Gales al Sur in Trevelin. For short guided excursions, ask at the *intendencia* in Villa Futalaufquen.

⊖ Transport

Lago Mascardi *p409*
Bus services from Bariloche to **El Bolsón** pass through **Villa Mascardi**. And buses to **Los Rapidos** run from the terminal in Bariloche at 0900, 1300, 1800 daily in summer.

Pampa Linda *p410*
Transitando lo Natural run minibuses marked 'Tronador' from opposite *Club Andino Bariloche, 20 de Febrero 28, T156 08581, 423918*, daily in Jan-Apr, according to demand in Dec, 3½ hrs, US$8. From Pampa Linda you can often get a lift with an excursion trip returning to **Bariloche**, if there's room, US$7.

El Bolsón *p411*
Air
The nearest airports are Esquel and Bariloche; see respective sections for flights.

Bus
Several daily from **Bariloche** and **Esquel**, with Don Otto, Via Bariloche. Heavily booked in high season. US$5-6.50, 2 hrs.

Other destinations from these two towns. Buses to **Lago Puelo** with **Via Bariloche** every 2 hrs, 4 on Sunday, 45mins, US$1. To **Parque Nacional Los Alerces** (highly recommended route), with **Transportes Esquel** (from *ACA* service station), once a day, 4-5 hrs, via Cholila and Epuyen.

Cycle hire
La Rueda, *Sarmiento 2972, T/F492465*. US$4 per day, open 0830-1330, 1530-2130.

Taxi
Piltri, *T492272*.

Parque Nacional Lago Puelo *p413*
There are regular buses, US$1.40, from Av San Martín y Dorrego in El Bolsón go to the lake via Villa Lago Puelo. *Transportes Esquel* run daily buses connecting Lago Puelo with **Cholila, PN Los Alerces**, and **Esquel**.

Esquel *p415, map p416*
Air
Airport, 20 km east, US$9 by taxi, US$1.50 by bus. To **Buenos Aires** with Aerolíneas Argentinas (agent) *Huala Av Fontana y Av Amedhino, T453614*. LADE, *Alvear 1085, T452124*, to **Bahía Blanca, Bariloche, Comodoro Rivadavia, El Bolsón, Mar del Plata, Neuquén, Puerto Madryn** weekly.

Bus
The modern terminal at *Alvear 1871, T451566*, has toilets, kiosko, *locutorio*, left luggage (US$1 per item per day), and taxis. From **Buenos Aires** travel via Bariloche: **Andesmar** (T450143) can be booked **Esquel-Buenos Aires**, including change in Bariloche, 24 hrs, *semi cama* US$50. To **Comodoro Rivadavia** 9 hrs US$13, **Don Otto** (T453012), 4 times a week (but usually arrives from Bariloche full in season).

To **Bariloche**, 4-5hrs, US$5, Don Otto, Andesmar, Mar y Valle (T453712), **Vía Bariloche** (T453528). To El Bolsón, 2 hrs, US$3, on bus to **Bariloche**, or via **Los Alerces nation- al park**, see below. To **Trelew**, 9 hrs, US$11. Mar y Valle, Emp Chubut, Don Otto, daily. To **Trevelin**, Via Trevelin (T455222), Mon-Fri, hourly 0700-2100, every 2 hrs weekends, US$1.05. To **Los Alerces National Park**, Transportes Esquel (T453529) runs a daily bus through the park from Esquel bus terminal at 0800, arriving at **Futulaufquen** (the entrance and *guardería*) 0900, and onto **Cholila** 1200, **El Bolsón** 1340 and **Lago Puelo** 1400. You can get on or off at any of the campsites or *hosterías* in park. US$3 each way. Returns to Esquel from **Futulaufquen** at 2000, arriving **Esquel** 2115.

To Chile From Esquel to **Paso Futaleufú**, a bus runs at 0800 daily in Jan/Feb, otherwise Mon, Fri, sometimes Wed, with Jacobsen US$3. At the border a bus will be waiting to go to Futuleufu and onto **Chaitén**, with **Transportes Cordillera** T258633, and **Ebenezer**, between them 4 times a week, and daily Jan/Feb. From Chaitén there are services to **Coyhaique**.

Car hire
Localiza, *Rivadavia 1168, T453276*. The only agents who have cars for hire, and even then, you can't rely on them. Book way in advance.

Taxi
Unión, *Roca 477, T0800 333 2806 or 454370*. **Gerardo Parsons**, *T156 87702*. Economical trips to local sights with friendly Gerardo. Gerardoturismo@yahoo.com.ar

Train
La Trochita – the *Viejo Expreso Patagónico*, Old Patagonian Express generally runs from Esquel to **Nahuel Pan** (19 km) 5 times a week, and up to twice a day in high season (much less frequent in winter), taking 2½ hrs, adults US$5, children under 6 free. At wild and remote **Nahuel Pan**, there's just a small terrace of houses, home to a Mapuche community, who sell delicious home baked cakes, and display their knitwear for you to buy, some of it very fine quality. Sometimes there's an extra service from **El Maitén** at the northernmost end of the line on Sat, taking 6 hrs, US$7, with a dining car. Information, in English including schedules in El Maitén, T495190, and in Esquel T451403. www.latrochita.com.ar

Trevelin *p417*
Bus
To **Esquel**, with **Via Trevelin** (T455222), Mon-Fri, hourly 0700-2100, every 2 hrs weekends, US$1.20. To **Chilean border**,

Jacobsen bus from Esquel runs through Trevelin, 0830 daily in Jan/Feb, otherwise Mon, Fri, sometimes Wed, US$3, connecting bus at border to **Futuleufu** and onto **Chaitén**.

Parque Nacional Los Alerces *p417*
From Esquel **Transportes Esquel**, T453529, runs daily buses at 0800 from Esquel (returning at 2115) along the east side of **Lago Futalaufquen**, passing **Villa Futalaufquen** 0915 (return 2000), **Lago Verde** 1030 (return 1845), **Lago Rivadavia** 1120 (return 1830), and continuing on to **Cholila**, **El Bolsón** and **Lago Puelo** (return 1500). The driver will drop you at your accommodation, and you can stop the bus at any point on the road. US$3 each way.

South of Esquel *p420*
Bus From **Esquel** to **Río Pico**, 4½ hrs, Mon/Wed/Sat, Jacobsen, T453528.

South of Gobernador Costa *p420*
Bus From **Esquel** to **Alto Río Senguer**, ETAP, Mon, Thu.

ⓘ Directory

El Bolsón *p411*
Banks Exchange cash and TCs at Banco Patagonia, *San Martín y Roca*, with ATM outside. **Communications** **Internet** Various places open and close. Currently functioning: Ciber Café La Nuez, *Av San Martín 2175, T455182*. **Post** office *San Martín 1940*.

Esquel *p415, map p416*
Airline offices LADE, *Alvear 1085, T452124*. **Banks** Banco de la Nación (am only) *Alvear y Roca*, open 0730-1300. ATM accepts all cards. ATMs also at Banco Patagonia , *25 de Mayo 739*, Bansud, *25 de Mayo 752*. **Communications** **Internet** *Shell station, Alvear y 25 de Mayo*. Two machines open 24 hrs, Cyberplanet, San Martin 994, lots more in the centre. **Post office**, *Alvear 1192 y Fontana*. Mon-Fri 0830-1300 and 1600-1930, Sat 0900-1300. **Telephone** *Locutorios*: many in centre including Unitel *25 de Mayo 528*, Central Sur *Rivadavia 949*, and at bus terminal.

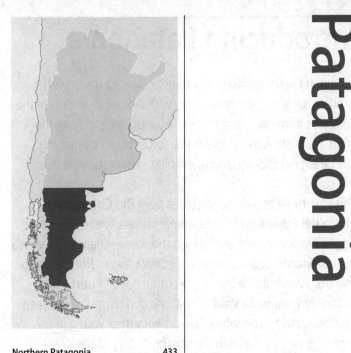

Introducing Patagonia

Everything in Patagonia is on a large scale: vast plains with limitless horizons, enormous skies with whipped-up clouds, the distances from one place to another, your sense of time, the wind, the silence. In Patagonia you forget about everything you've left behind, and roam uninhibited over the wild land.

This vast treeless plateau stretches from **Río Colorado** to **Tierra del Fuego**, with extraordinary diversity at its extreme edges. Marine life abounds along the whole Atlantic Coast: sea lions at **Monte León**, colonies of cormorants in **Ría Deseado**, and dolphins frolicking in the beautiful bay of **Puerto San Julian**. At **Península Valdés**, sealions and penguins gather in their thousands, and whales cavort with their young in the spring. In nearby **Gaiman** the stirring history of the Welsh pioneers is kept alive in traditional Eisteddfods and with sumptuous Welsh teas.

At the northern end of **Parque Nacional Los Glaciares**, the magnificent towers of **Mount Fitz Roy** shoot up from the steppe, offering dramatic hiking country amidst glacial lakes and beech forest. And to the south, **Perito Moreno** and **Upsala Glacier** stretch out infinitely before you: an unforgettable experience, whether you arrive by boat, on horseback, or trek on the glacier's surface.

There are petrified forests and caves full of pre-historic handprints, and along iconic **Ruta 40**, you can travel hundreds of kilometres without seeing a soul. For a little civilization in your wilderness, stay at a luxurious estancia in **Santa Cruz**: commune with nature and still be served an exquisite dinner. The real pleasure of Patagonia is the timeless life on the land. Ride your horse into the Andes and contemplate a perfect blue-green lake until the sky fills with a million stars.

★ **Don't miss...**

❶ **Península Valdés** Watch a mother and baby whale basking off the coast, page 438.

❷ **Mount Fitz Roy** Gaze at granite turrets tinged with scarlet at dawn from your tent by Lago Eléctrico, page 476.

❸ **Gaiman** Tuck into a fabulous Welsh tea at Marta Ree's tea room, page 442.

❹ **Perito Moreno Glacier** Watch a huge slab of glacier breaking off into the milky lake below. Once you hear the roar, it's already gone!, page 473.

❺ **Travel the Ruta 40** Experience the vast emptiness of Patagonia, deserted road for hours and hours from Los Antiguos to El Chaltén, page 453.

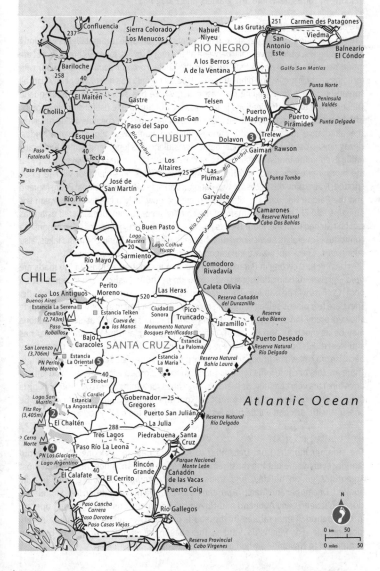

Patagonia

Ins and outs

Getting there and around

Fortunately this vast expanse is served by good public transport. There are daily flights from Buenos Aires to Viedma, Trelew, Comodoro Rivadavia, Río Gallegos and Lago Argentino (the airport at El Calafate), and from three to Ushuaia, all taking less than two hours. However, flying between these towns is more complicated, since there are only weekly fights with the army airline LADE connecting all the towns, and a few flights a week with American Falcon between Puerto Madryn and Bariloche, all heavily booked in summer. From Chile, there are flights from Punta Arenas to Río Gallegos, and buses from Puerto Natales to El Calafate, enabling you to combine trekking in Torres del Paine, the glaciers and Patagonia.

Getting around

The most efficient way to get around is probably to combine internal flights with long distance buses, which travel daily between all the major towns. Journeys are long, but are made bearable if you pay a little extra for the *coche-cama* or *semi-cama* option, with reclining seats, a movie and dinner provided too. Patagonia has few towns of any size, all spread out along Ruta 3 along the east coast, where bus services are most frequent. These are not tourist destinations in themselves, but they make useful stopping points, with transport connections to the more remote inland areas, or coastal wildlife reserves. The alternative road south, the famous Ruta 40, runs west alongside the Andes, zigzagging across the moors. Almost entirely wasteland, it is lonely and carries hardly any traffic even in the tourist season between December and February. However, it is by far the more interesting road, with fine views of the Andes and plenty of wildlife to be spotted; it also provides access to two national parks, the Parque Nacional Perito Moreno and the Parque Nacional Los Glaciares. There are now daily bus services between Los Antiguos and El Chaltén, and many of the country's most beautifully situated estancias can be reached from this road. There's just one long-distance train across this expanse: a comfortable overnight service now runs between Viedma and Bariloche in the lakes, also taking cars. Check out www.trenpatagonico.com.ar for further information.

Driving and cycling in Patagonia require care and patience. Most of the roads are *ripio* – gravel – limiting driving speeds to 60 km per hour, or slower where surfaces are poor. Cyclists will be battling with fierce winds, too, and a complete absence of shade. There are few places selling water and provisions, and a tent is essential, with camping allowed pretty much everywhere. Drivers should carry spare fuel, as service stations may be as much as 300 km apart, carry warm clothing and make sure your car has anti-freeze. Fuel prices are much lower in Patagonia than in the rest of the country because no taxes are imposed (US$0.60 per litre *super*; US$0.50 per litre normal). There are lots of cattle grids (*guardaganados*) to be crossed with care, and you should drive hire cars very carefully, as there are huge fines for turning them over. Hitchhiking is difficult, even on Route 3 in the tourist season, and hitching along the Ruta 40 may be possible with luck and a little help from locals; it helps to speak good Spanish.

Best time to visit

The summer months from December to April are best for trekking: though avoid January everywhere but the most remote places, if you can, since this is when most Argentines go on holiday, and transport and accommodation are both heavily booked. December and March/April can be lovely, and much emptier. Most hotels are closed between early April and mid-November and many bus services don't operate in this period. Temperatures in the south plummet to minus 20, making it very inhospitable. For Península Valdés, the season for spotting whales is between September to November, when all services are open.

There are offices in even the smallest towns that have any tourist potential, and more developed centres in El Calafate and El Chaltén, with exemplary information centres in Puerto Madryn, Trelew and Río Gallegos. Many have good websites, worth a look before you set off, some with links to hotels for booking accommodation.

History

Patagonia was inhabited by various groups of indigenous peoples from thousands of years ago until colonisation by the Europeans. The first European visitor to the coast of Patagonia was the Portuguese explorer Fernão Magalhães in 1519, and the first to traverse Patagonia from south to north was the English sailor, Carder, who survived a shipwreck in 1578 in the Strait of Magellan, walked to the Río de la Plata and arrived in London nine years later.

For several centuries European attempts to settle along the coast were deterred by isolation, lack of food and water and the harsh climate, as well as resistance from the indigenous peoples. However, they were almost wiped out in the bloody war known as the 'Campaign of the Wilderness' in 1879-1883 (see box, page 118). Before this there had been a European colony at Carmen de Patagones, which shipped salt to Buenos Aires, and the Welsh settlement in the Chubut valley from 1865. After the Campaign of the Desert, colonization was rapid. Welsh, Scots and English farmers were among the biggest groups of immigrants including sheep farmers from Las Malvinas/Falkland Islands, as well as Chilean sheep farmers from Punta Arenas moving eastwards into Santa Cruz.

Northern Patagonia

Many visitors to Patagonia head for Península Valdés, a splay of land stretching into the Atlantic which hosts an array of wildlife, most famously the Southern right whales, who come to breed from September to November. Puerto Madryn is the base for this area, a seaside town. Just south, Trelew is worth a visit for its superb palaeontological museum, and also to visit the old Welsh villages of Gaiman and Dolavon to the west, lying in the Chubut valley, made green and fertile thanks to the hard work of those early pioneers. On the way south, you might like to spend a night at historic Carmen de Patagones, facing Viedma across the Río Negro, a lovely spot for bathing, or go shark fishing at Bahía San Blas. Patagonia's fine estancias start here, with riding and sheep mustering at La Luisa.

Carmen de Patagones and Viedma

→ *Phone code 02920 Colour map 5, A5*

These two pleasant towns straddle the broad sweep of the Río Negro, about 27 km from its mouth and 250 km south of Bahía Blanca. Viedma, on the south bank, was founded as Mercedes de Patagonia in 1779, but was destroyed almost immediately by floods, after which Carmen de Patagones was founded on higher ground on the north bank. For many years, this was a European colony which shipped salt to Buenos Aires, and in 1827, it was the site of an extraordinary battle. There are charming streets with quaint adobe houses near the river, where the tiny ferry takes you across to Viedma. Capital of Río Negro province, Viedma was destroyed again by floods in 1899, and it's a quiet place of modern buildings, less pretty than its neighbour, but offering a perfect bathing area along the shaded south bank of the river, a delightful spot in summer, with a good view of Patagones beyond.

Viedma is quite different in character from Carmen de Patagones, since it's the provincial administrative centre, rather than the home of farmers and landowners. An attractive *costanera* runs by the river, with large grassy banks shaded by willow trees, and the river water is pleasantly warm in summer and completely uncontaminated. On a calm summer's evening, when groups gather to sip *mate*, the scene resembles Seurat's painting of bathers. There are two plazas, with the cathedral, built by the Salesians in 1912, on the west of Plaza Alsina. The former convent, next door, the first chapel built by the Salesians in 1887, is now a cultural centre housing the **Museo del Agua y del Suelo** and the **Museo Cardenal Cagliero**, which has ecclesiastical artefacts. Two blocks east, on the Plaza San Martín, are the French-style **Casa de Gobierno** (1926) and, opposite, the **Museo Gobernador Tello** ① *open 0900-1230, 1700-1930 in summer*, with fossils, rocks and indigenous *boleadoras*. Most diverting, though, is the **Museo Gardeliano**, Rivadavi 34, a fabulous collection, amassed by an ardent fan, of all the records of tango singer Carlos Gardel. Four rooms full of biographical artefacts, open Mon Wed Fri 0930-1130. Along the attractive *costanera*, the **Centro Cultural** opposite Calle 7 de Marzo houses a small **Mercado Artesenal** selling beautifully made Mapuche weavings and wood work. The rather impoverished **tourist office** is also on the *costanera*, 3 blocks east of Plaza Alsina, open 0900-2100, T427171, www.rionegrotur.com.ar

Carmen de Patagones Viedma → *Population 16,000.*

The town centre, just east of the river, lies around the Plaza 7 de Mayo, and just west is the **Iglesia del Carmen**, built by the Salesians in 1880. Take a stroll down the pretty streets winding down to the river, to find many early pioneer buildings along the riverside. The **Torre del Fuerte**, tower of the stone fortress built in 1780 against indigenous attacks, the **Casa de la Tahona**, a disused 18th-century flour mill, now housing the **Casa de la Cultura**, with another late colonial building, **La Carlota**, one block east. And nearby there's a fascinating museum, **Museo Historico** ① *Biedma 4, T462729, open daily 0930-1230, 1900-2100, Sun pm only*, giving a great insight into early pioneer life. There are Tehuelche arrowheads, and stone *boleadoras*, silver gaucho stirrups, and great early photos – one of a baptism by Salesians of a 100-year-old Tehuelche man in a field, next to fine furniture and delicate tea cups. Great guided tours too. The **Museo de la Prefectura Naval** ① *Mitre 350, T461742, www.prefecturanaval.edu.ar/museo/* is also worth a look, housed in a building dating from 1886 with a marine history of the area.

Patagones (as it's known) is linked to Viedma by two bridges and a very small ferry which takes 4 mins and leaves every 15 mins, US$0.20. There's a helpful and dynamic tourist office ① *Bynon 186, T462054, www.vivalaspampas.com*

The best time to visit is the *Fiesta de 7 de Marzo* (for a week around the 7th March), for more information, T464360, subcom@patagones.mun.gba.gov.ar

Celebrating the victory at the Battle of Patagones with a week of music and handicrafts, fine food, a huge procession, horse riding displays, and lots of meat on the asados. Great fun. Book accommodation ahead. ▸▸ *For Sleeping, Eating and other listings, see pages 443-451.*

Around Viedma and Carmen de Patagones

At **El Cóndor** ① *30 km south, 3 buses a day in summer*, there is a beautiful beach, with the oldest *faro* (lighthouse) in the country, dating from 1887. Facilities include a hotel, restaurants and shops, open January and February only. There's free camping on beach 2 km south.

This whole stretch of coast is great for shore fishing, with *pejerrey, variada* and even shark among many other species. **Playa Bonita**, 12 km further south is known as a good fishing spot, with more good beaches. Equipment is available in Viedma at *Patagonia Out Doors Life*, 25 de Mayo 340, and *Tiburón* Zatti 250, among others. Ask the tourist office for their leaflet, T427171. **Lobería Punta Bermeja**, 60 km south, is a sealion colony visited by some 2,500 sealions in summer, which you can see at close range. There's also an impressive visitor centre, (with toilets). ① *Daily bus in summer; hitching easy in summer.* There's more lovely coastline, and a well-established little fishing resort at **Bahia San Blas**, 100 km from Patagones, renowned for shark fishing area. There's lots of accommodation here, including the plush *Resort Tiburon* T499202, www.tiburonresort.freeservers.com More information at www.bahiasanblas.com

Estancia La Luisa offers an experience on an old Patagonian estancia, with cattle mustering and riding on polo ponies to another more remote estancia, with home reared lamb roasting on the *asado*. Staying guests are welcome. ① *T463725, eleri@rnonline.com.ar*

Las Grutas → *Phone code: 02934 Colour map 8, C3*

Almost due west of Viedma, 180 km along the coast, on the Gulf of San Matías, is the small town of San Antonio Oeste. It's a nondescript place, its only feature a huge modern fruit-exporting port on its eastern side. It's certainly not a place you'd choose to stop, though you might fancy a swim at Las Grutas, the popular beach resort 17 km south. This 1960s resort fills up in summer, when you can't find a bed, and completely empties in March, when it's quite pleasant, but everything's closed. It has a safe beach with famously warm water (the caves themselves are not really worth visiting), and there's plenty of accommodation, though it's wise to book ahead. The tourist office is at Av Costanera y Catriel, T497468. ▸▸ *For Sleeping, Eating and other listings, see pages 443-451.*

Puerto Madryn and Península Valdés

→ *Phone code: 02965 Colour map 5, B5 Population: 60,000*

Puerto Madryn is a pleasant breezy seaside town with a grand setting on the wide bay of Golfo Nuevo, the perfect base for seeing the extraordinary array of wildlife on Península Valdés, just 70 km east. During breeding seasons you can see whales, penguins and seals at close range, or go diving to explore life underwater. If you want to stay on the peninsula, there's the small popular resort of Puerto Pirámides as well as several estancias to choose from, but Puerto Madryn makes a good place to enjoy the sea for a couple of days. Wherever you stay, try the delicious locally caught seafood in the beachfront restaurants.

Ins and outs

Getting there There are weekly flights with LADE from Buenos Aires and towns in Patagonia to Puerto Madryn's airport, 10 km west. However, there are more frequent flights to Buenos Aires, El Calafate and Bariloche from Trelew's airport, some 60 km south, with buses to Puerto Madryn operated by the airlines. *Mar y Valle* also runs a bus every hour to Puerto Madryn's bus terminal.

Getting around The city centre is easy to get around on foot, with many restaurants and hotels lined up along the seafront at Avenida Roca, and most shops and excursion companies on the streets around 28 de Julio, which runs perpendicular to the sea and past the town's neat little plaza.

Best time to visit Much of Península Valdés' wildlife can be enjoyed throughout the year, with sealions, elephant seals, dolphins and many species of bird permanently resident. The bull elephant seals can be seen fighting for females from September to early November, and at this time, too, killer whales can sometimes be sighted off the coast, staying until April. Penguins can be seen from September to March, and the stars of the show, the southern right whales, come to these waters to breed in spring – September to November.

Tourist information One of the country's best tourist information centres is on the seafront at Av Roca 223, just off 28 de Julio, next to the shopping complex. Its staff are friendly, extremely well organized, and speak English and French. They have leaflets on Península Valdés and accomm-odation, and can advise on tours. T453504, www.madryn.gov.ar Open Mon-Fri 0700- 2100 Sat/Sun 0830-1330, 1530-2030.

Background
Puerto Madryn was the site of the first Welsh landing in 1865 and the town is named after the Welsh home of the colonist, Jones Parry. However, it wasn't officially founded until 1886, when the railway was built from Trelew, to enable the Welsh living in the Chubut valley to export their produce. The town is a modern, relaxed and friendly place, and hasn't been ruined by its popularity as a tourist resort, with a large workforce occupied by its other main industry: a huge aluminium plant (which you can visit by arrangement through the tourist office). Accommodation is generally of a high standard, but can be pricey.

Puerto Madryn
You're most likely to be visiting the town to take an excursion to Península Valdés (see page 438), and it's certainly worth spending at least a day enjoying the wildlife there. You can also spot whales directly from the coast at the long beach of **Playa El Doradillo**, 16 km northeast, along the *ripio* road closest to the coast.

In the town itself, the real pleasure is the sea, and you can stroll along the long

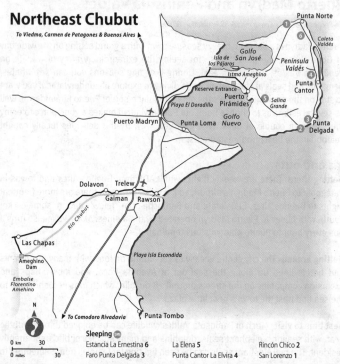

Northeast Chubut

To Viedma, Carmen de Patagones & Buenos Aires ▶

Punta Norte

Caleta Valdés

Isla de los Pájaros

Golfo San José

Península Valdés

Istmo Ameghino

Reserve Entrance

Puerto Pirámides

Playa El Doradillo

Punta Loma

Salina Grande

Punta Cantor

Golfo Nuevo

Punta Delgada

Puerto Madryn

Dolavon   Trelew

Gaiman   Rawson

Río Chubut

Las Chapas

Ameghino Dam

Embalse Florentino Amehino

Playa Isla Escondida

N

0 km   30

0 miles   30

▶ To Comodoro Rivadavia   Punta Tombo

stretch of beach to **El Indio**, a statue on the road at the eastern end, marking the gratitude of the Welsh to the native Tehuelche people whose shared expertise ensured their survival. As the road curves up the cliff here, there's the splendid new **EcoCentro** ① *Julio Verne 784, T457470, www.ecocentro.org.ar 1000-1800 daily (but check with tourist office as times change), US$2.50, reductions for students, children and retired. Take bus linea 2 from 25 de Mayo y Belgrano, and walk 5 minutes from the university*, an inspired interactive sea-life information centre that combines an art gallery, café, and fabulous reading room with comfy sofas at the top of a turret. The whole place has fantastic views of the bay; great for an afternoon's relaxation reading books on wildlife in English or other European languages.

Just a little closer to town, perched on the cliff, is the tiny **Centro Historico** ① *1500-1900 daily except Tue, US$0.50*, of interest if you're tracing the history of the Welsh in Patagonia. It's little more than a couple of rooms of relics, near the caves and basic huts on the cliffs where the settlers first lived, but enthusiastic guides make the visit worthwhile. A more conventional museum, with displays on local flora and wildlife, the **Museo de Ciencias Naturales y Oceanográfico** ① *Domecq García y J Menéndez, Mon-Fri 0900-1200, 1430-1900, Sat 1430-1900 entry US$1*, is informative and worth a visit. ►► *For Sleeping, Eating and other listings, see pages 443-451.*

Excursions → *For Peninsula Valdés, see below*

There are sea lions at the **Punta Loma** reserve, 15 km southeast of Puerto Madryn, open during daylight hours and best visited at low tide in December and January. ① *Information and video, entrance to the reserve is US$3, but free with ticket to Península Valdés. Access is via the coastal road from town, and like the road to the north, makes a great bike ride – allow one a half hours to get there.* To really appreciate the space and natural beauty of the peninsula, staying at an estancia is an appealing (though slightly pricey) option. Ask the tourist office for their leaflet and advice. Day trips are also arranged, with access to some of the most beautiful places. **Estancia Rincón Chico**, T471733, www.rinconchico.com.ar is recommended; Also **La Elvira**, T156 98709, www.laelvira.com.ar ►► *For Sleeping, Eating and other listings, see pages 443-451.*

Puerto Madryn

To Puerto Pirámides

Museo de Ciencias Naturales y Oceanográfico

H Yrigoyen
La Anónima Supermarket
R Sáenz Peña
Portal de Madryn Shopping Centre
Cuyu Co
28 de Julio
Norte Supermarket
Municipalidad
Plaza San Martín
ACA
Belgrano
Banco Nación
9 de Julio
25 de Mayo
Sarmiento
Argentina Visión
Av Gales
España
Storni

El Indio, EcoCentro, Punta Cuevas, Punta Loma Reserv & Playa El Doradillo

N

0 metres 200
0 yards 200

Sleeping
ACA Camping 2
Bahía Nueva & La Posta 1
El Gaulicho 3
El Golfito Camping y Albergue 15
Gran Palace 14
Hostería Torremolinos 4
Marina 5
Muelle Viejo 6
Península Valdés 7
Playa 8
Puerto Madryn Hostelling International 12
Residencial J'Os 13
Santa Rita 9
Tolosa 10
Villa Pirén 11

Eating
Antigua Patagonia 1
Caccaros 3
Centro de Difusión de la Pescada Artesanal 2
Havanna 4
La Casona de Golfo 5
La Vaca y El Pollito 7
Lizard Café 8
Margarita 9
Mitos 10
Placido 11
Shangi Hai 6
Taska Beltza 12
Yoaquina 13

Península Valdés

Whatever time of year you visit Península Valdés ① *entry to the peninsula: US$3, tickets are also valid for Punta Loma, to the south of Trelew*, you'll find a wonderful array of marine life, birds and a profusion of Patagonian wildlife such as guanacos, rheas, patagonian hares and armadillos. But in spring, this treeless splay of land is host to a quite spectacular numbers of whales, penguins and seals, who come to breed in the sheltered waters of the gulf south of the narrow isthmus Ameghino, and on beaches at the foot of the peninsula's chalky cliffs. The land is almost flat, though greener than much of Patagonia, and at the heart of the peninsula are large saltflats, one of which, **Salina Grande**, is 42 m below sea level. The peninsula is privately owned – many of its estancias offering grand places to stay in the middle of the wild beauty, but it is also a nature reserve and was declared a World Heritage Site by UNESCO in 1999. The beach along the entire coast is out of bounds and this is strictly enforced. The main tourist centre for accommodation, and whale trips is Puerto Pirámides, on the southern side of the isthmus.

At the entrance to the reserve on the isthmus, 79 km east of Puerto Madryn, there's an interesting interpretation centre with stuffed examples of the local fauna, many fossils and a wonderful whale skeleton, which makes a great complement to seeing the real thing gracefully soaring through the water. Ask for the informative bilingual leaflet on southern right whales. ▸▸ *For Sleeping, Eating and other listings, see pages 443-451.*

Wildlife → *These are the main marine wildlife colonies*

Isla de los Pájaros, in the Golfo San José, 5 km from the entrance. Its seabirds can only be viewed through fixed telescopes (at 400 m distance). Only recognized ornithologists can get permission to visit. Between September and April you can spot wading birds, herons, cormorants and terns.

Caleta Valdés, 45 km south of Punta Norte in the middle of the eastern shore, has huge colonies of elephant seals which can be seen at close quarters. In the breeding season, from September to October, you'll see the rather unappealing blubbery masses of bull seals hauling themselves up the beach to make advances to one of the many females in their harem. During the first half of August the bull-seals arrive to claim their territory, and can be seen at low tide engaging in bloody battles for their women. At Punta Cantor, just south of here, you'll find a good café and clean toilets. Also three marked walks, from 45 minutss to two hours. A short distance inland is Estancia La Elvira.

Punta Delgada, at the southeastern end of the peninsula, 91 km from the entrance, is where elephant seals and sea lions can be seen from the high cliffs in such large numbers that they seem to stretch out like a velvety bronze tide line on the beautiful beach below. It's mesmerising to watch as the young frolic in the shallow water, and the bulls lever themselves around the females. There's a hotel nearby, Faro Punta Delgada (see below), a good base for exploring this beautiful area further.

Punta Norte, at the northern end of the peninsula, 97 km from the entrance, is not often visited by the excursion companies, but it has colonies of Magellanic penguins and sea lions. Killer whales (orca) have also been seen here, feeding on sea lion pups at low tide in March and April. San Lorenzo estancia is nearby (see below).

Puerto Pirámides → *Colour map 5, B5,*

Puerto Pirámides, 107 km east of Puerto Madryn, is the centre for visits to the peninsula, and whale watching boat trips leave from its broad sandy beach. Every year between June and December 400-500 southern right whales migrate to the Gulfo Nuevo to mate and give birth. It is without doubt one of the best places in the world to watch these beautiful animals. In many places these whales come within just a few metres of the coast. Take a boat trip and with luck you'll be very close to a mother and baby. Sailings are controlled by the Prefectura, according to weather and sea conditions (if you're very prone to sea sickness think twice before setting off on a windy day). There are plenty of places to stay strung out along the road from the beach in this pretty little place, plus a campsite, and a good range of places to eat. All are packed out in January and February. There is a small tourist office on the edge of Puerto Pirámides, offering useful information for hikes and driving tours. T495084, www.piramides ballenas.com.ar ▸▸ *For Sleeping, Eating and other listings, see pages 443-451.*

The Chubut Valley

The Río Chubut is one of the most important rivers in Patagonia, flowing a massive 820 km from the eastern foothills of the Andes into the Atlantic at Bahía Engaño. It's thanks to the Río Chubut that the Welsh pioneers came to this part of the world in 1865, and their irrigation of the arid land around it enabled them to survive and prosper. You can trace their history west along the valley from the pleasant airy town of Trelew to the quiet little village of Gaiman, with a wonderful museum, and oozing casas de té. Further west, past little brick chapels sitting amidst lush green fields is the rather sombre Dolavon, with an old brick chapel. And if you're keen to investigate further into the past, there's a marvellous museum full of dinosaurs at Trelew, and some ancient fossils in the Parque Palaeontológico Bryn-Gwyn near Gaiman. And from Trelew you could visit one of the largest colonies of Magellanic penguins on the coast at Punta Tombo.

Trelew → *Phone code: 02965 Colour map 5, B5 Population: 90,000*

Pronounced *'Trel-Yeah-Oo'*, and some 70 km south of Puerto Madryn, Trelew is the largest town in the Chubut valley. Founded in 1884, it was named in honour of Lewis Jones, an early settler, and the Welsh colonisation is still evident in a few remaining chapels in the town's modern centre. It's a cheerful place with a quietly busy street life, certainly more appealing than the industrial town of Rawson, 20 km east on the coast. Trelew boasts a splendid palaeontological museum, a good tourist office and two fabulous cafés.

Ins and outs
Getting there and around There are flights from Buenos Aires, El Calafate, Ushuaia and Bariloche to Trelew's airport, 5 km north of centre. A taxi costs US$3, and local buses to Puerto Madryn will stop at the airport entrance if asked, and from here it's a 10-minute walk. The bus terminal is north of the centre, 10-minute walk from the main plaza, where you'll fin the very helpful **tourist office** ① *Mitre 387, T420139, open Mon-Fri 0800-1400, 1500-2100, Sat/Sun 0900-1300, 1500-2000. www.turismotrelew.gov.ar* They'll give you an excellent map, directing you to the town's older buildings. Visit mid-October to see the Eisteddfod.

Sights
There's the lovely shady Plaza Independencia in the town centre, packed with mature trees, and hosting a small handicraft market at weekends. Nearby is the **Capilla Tabernacle**, on Belgrano between San Martín and 25 de Mayo, a red-brick Welsh chapel dating from 1889. Heading east, rather more impressive is the **Salon San David**, a Welsh meeting hall first used for the Eisteddfod of 1913, and now sadly, used for bingo. On the road to Rawson, 3 km south, you'll find one of the oldest standing

A Little Wales beyond Wales

Among the stories of early pioneers to Argentina, the story of the Welsh emigration, in search of religious freedom, is courageous. The first 165 settlers arrived in Patagonia in July 1865. Landing on the bay where Puerto Madryn now stands, they were forced by lack of water to walk south across the parched land to the valley of the Chubut river, where they found cultivatable land and settled. The first ten years were harsh indeed, and they were saved by trade from local Tehuelche indigenous peoples, who taught them essential survival skills. The British navy also delivered supplies, and there was also support from the Argentine government, eager to populate its territory.

The settlement was partly inspired by Michael D Jones, a non-conformist minister who provided much of the early finance and recruited settlers through the Welsh language press and through the chapels. Jones, whose aim was to create a 'little Wales beyond Wales', far from the intruding influence of the English restrictions on Welsh religious beliefs, took particular care to recruit people with useful skills such as farmers and craftsmen. Between 1865 and 1915, the colony was reinforced by another 3,000 settlers from Wales and the United States. The early years brought persistent drought, and finding that the land was barren unless irrigated, they created a network of irrigation channels. Early settlers were allocated 100 hectares of land, and when, by 1885 all irrigable land had been allocated, settlement expanded westwards along the valley. The charming town of Trevelin, where Welsh is still spoken, was the result of this westward migration.

The success of the Welsh colony was partly due to the creation of their own successful Cooperative Society, which sold their produce and bought necessities in Buenos Aires. Early settlers were organised into chapel based communities of 200-300 people, which were largely self-governing and organized social and cultural activities. The colony thrived after 1880, growing prize-winning wheat in the valley, and exporting successfully to Buenos Aires and Europe, but was badly weakened by the great depression in the 1930's, and the poor management of the Argentine government. Many of the Welsh survived, however, and most of the owners of Gaiman's extraordinary Welsh tea rooms are indeed descendants of the original settlers. Welsh language is kept alive in both Gaiman and Trevelin, and the musical concerts Eisteddfods are held every October. As you tuck into your seventh slice of Welsh cake, spare a thought for the harsh conditions of those brave early pioneers!

Welsh chapels, **Capilla Moriah**. Built in 1880, it has a simple interior and a cemetery with the graves of many original settlers, including the first white woman born in the Welsh colony.

Back in Trelew itself, not the oldest but quite the most wonderful building is the 1920's **Hotel Touring Club**, Fontana 240. This was the town's grandest hotel in its heyday, and politicians and travellers met in its glorious high-ceilinged mirrored bar, now full of old photographs and relics. You can eat lunch and there's simple accommodation here (see Sleeping and Eating below); you should also ask the friendly owner to see the elegant meeting room at the back.

The town's best museum – and indeed one of the finest in Argentina – is the **Museo Paleontológico Egidio Feruglio** ① *Fontana 140, T432100, www.mef.org.ar, Mon-Fri 1000-2000 spring and summer, 1000-1800 rest of year, Sat/Sun*

1000-2000, US$2.50, reductions for students, the retired and children under 12, full disabled access and guides for the blind. Imaginatively designed and beautifully presented, the museum traces the origins of life through the geological ages, displaying dynamically poised dinosaur skeletons, with plentiful information in Spanish. Tours are free, available in English, German and Italian. There's also a reasonably cheap café and shop. Highly recommended, and great for kids. Also ask about the **Parque Paleontológico Bryn-Gwyn**, 8 km from Gaiman, with fossil remains from over the last 40 million years.

The **Museo Regional Pueblo de Luis** ① *Fontana y 9 de Julio, T424062, Mon-Fri 0800-2000, Sat closed, Sun 1700-2000, US$2,* is appropriately housed in the old railway station, built in 1889, since Lewis Jones founded the town and started the railways that exported Welsh produce so successfully. It has interesting displays on indigenous societies on failed Spanish attempts at settlement and on Welsh colonization. ►► *For Sleeping, Eating and other listings, see pages 443-451.*

Around Trelew

The two most popular excursions are to see the penguin colony at **Punta Tombo**, 107 km south, and the Welsh valley towns of **Gaiman** and (less so) **Dolavon**. The **Embalse Florentino Ameghino**, 120 km west, is less interesting. There is a lovely rock and sand beach with birds and other wildlife at **Playa Isla Escondida**, 70 km south, with secluded camping but no facilities.

Take an excursion from Trelew, or drive if you have a car, to the **Reserva Natural Punta Tombo** ① *Park entrance US$4. Tours from Trelew and Puerto Madryn, US$17; 45 mins at the site, where there's a café and toilets. Access from Route 1, a ripio road between Trelew and Camarones. Closed after March.* This reserve is the largest breeding ground for Magallenic penguins in Patagonia. This nature reserve is 107 km south of Trelew, open from September, when huge numbers of Magallenic penguins

Trelew

0 metres 100
0 yards 100

Sleeping
Centenario 6
Galicia 1
Libertador 2
Rayentray 3
Rivadavia 4
Touring Club 5

Eating
Café Mi Ciudad 5
Delicatesse 1
El Quijote 2
El Viejo Molino 3
La Bodeguita 4

come here to breed. Chicks can be seen from mid-November, and first waddle to the water in January-February. It's fascinating to see these creatures up close, but noisy colonies of tourists dominate the place in the morning; it's quieter in the afternoon. You'll see guanacos, hares and rheas on the way.

Gaiman → *Phone code: 02965 Colour map 5, B4 Population: 3,205*

West of Trelew, the floodplain of the Río Chubut is beautifully green and fertile, thanks to the Welsh irrigation. Gaiman is the first village you come to on Route 25 which heads past Dolavon before continuing through attractive scenery to Esquel and the other Welsh colony of Trevelin. On the way, you'll find old Welsh chapels tucked away amongst the poplars in this green valley. A small pretty place with old brick houses, retaining the Welsh pioneer feel, Gaiman hosts the annual *Eisteddfod* (Welsh festival of arts) in October. Around its pretty plaza are several tearooms, many of them run by descendents of the original pioneers, serving delicious and 'traditional' Welsh teas. Before you fill up on all that cake, though, spare a thought for the spartan lives of those idealistic pioneers. There's a wonderful tiny museum **Museo Histórico Regional Galés** ① *Sarmiento y 28 de Julio, T491007, open Tue-Sun 1500-1900, US$0.50,* with an impressive collection of Welsh artefacts, objects and photographs, all evocative and moving testimony to extraordinary lives in harsh conditions. Curator Mrs Roberts is helpful and hugely knowledgeable, and this is a great resource if you're looking for books on the subject or trying to trace your emigrant relatives.

Many older buildings remain, among them the low stone first house, **Primera Casa** (1874) ① *on the corner of main street Avenida Tello and Evans, open daily 1400-1900*; the old **railway station** (1909), which now houses the regional museum (see above) the **old hotel** (1899), at Tello y 9 de Julio, and the **Ty Nain tea room** (1890), on the Plaza at Yrigoyen 283 (see below). On the south side of the river there are two old chapels: cross the bridge, and then take the first right to find the pretty **Capilla Bethel** (1913) and the **Capilla Vieja** (1888).

A far more recent monument to human energy and inspiration is the extraordinary creation **El Desafío** ① *two blocks west of plaza, daily until 1800, US$1.50,* an imaginative sculptural world, made entirely from rubbish by the eccentric Joaquín Alonso – painted plastic bottles, cans and wire form pergolas and dinosaurs, sprinkled liberally with plaques bearing words of wisdom and witty comments. Beginning to fade now, but still good fun. The **tourist office** ① *T491152, open Mon-Fri 0900-1800, Sat/Sun 1400-1800,* is housed in the Casa de Cultura.

Some 8 km south of town, there are fossil beds dating back 40 million years at the **Parque Paleontológico Bryn Gwyn** ① *T432100, www.mef.org.ar open 1000-1900, end Sept to end March, daily. US$1.80 adults, taxi from Gaiman US$1.70.* A mind-boggling expanse of time brought to life by a good guided tour. It takes one and a half hours to do the circuit, with fossils to see, as well as a visitors' centre where you can experience some fieldwork in palaeonthology. Associated with the Museo Paleontológico Feruglio in Trelew. ►► *For Sleeping, Eating and other listings, see pages 443-451.*

Dolavon → *Phone code: 02965 Colour map 5, B4 Population: 2,700*

Founded in 1919, Dolavon is the most westerly Welsh settlement in the valley, and not as inviting as Gaiman, though if you stroll around its two intersecting streets, you'll find a few buildings reminiscent of the Welsh past. The main street, Avenida Roca, runs parallel to the irrigation canal built by the settlers, where willow trees now trail into the swiftly flowing water, and there's a Welsh chapel, **Capilla Carmel** at its quieter end. The old **flour mill** at Maipú y Roca dates from 1927 and can be visited (ask for the key at the Municipalidad, Roca 188 in office hours). There's Autoserivicio Belgrano at the far end of San Martín for food supplies, but there are no tea rooms, and nowhere to stay, though there's a municipal campsite two blocks north of the river, free, with good facilities.

Welsh chapels

If you're in your own transport, it's worth driving on from Dolavon back towards Gaiman via the neat squared fields in this beautiful irrigated valley, where you'll see more Welsh chapels tucked away among poplar trees and silver birches. Follow the main road that leads south through Dolavon, and then turn left and then the next right, where signposted, to Iglesia Anglicana. The San David chapel (1917) is a beautifully preserved brick construction, with an elegant bell tower, and sturdy oak-studded door, in a quiet spot surrounded by birches. Further on you'll cross the raised irrigation canals the Welsh built, next to them small orchards of apple trees, with tidy fields bordered by alamo trees.

Listings: Northern Patagonia

⊜ Sleeping

See www.argentinahostels.com for youth hostels, and www.tierrabuena.com.ar www.estanciasdesantacruz.com for estancias

Viedma and Carmen de Patagones *p433*

The best places to stay are all in Viedma.
C Austral, *25 de Mayo y Villarino, T422615, viedma@hoteles-austral.com.ar* Along the *costanera*, this modern hotel has well equipped, if slightly old-fashioned, rooms.
C Nijar, *Mitre 490, T422833*. Very comfortable, smart modern rooms, a quiet relaxed atmosphere, and good attentive service. Recommended. The best of the 2 decent, modern mid-range hotels.
D Peumayen, *Buenos Aires 334, T425222*. An old-fashioned friendly place on the plaza.
E Hotel Spa, *25 de Mayo 174, T430459*. A real find, this lovely great value hotel in a quiet complex with steam baths has a very relaxing atmosphere and warm staff.

Camping

There's a good **municipal campsite** near the river, *T421341*, US$2 pp, all facilities including hot showers. Also at the sea lion colony, **La Lobería**, T428883, US$1pp.
Trenitos, *T497098*. US$1pp, good facilities.

Estancias

AL La Luisa, *40 km away, T02920-463725, eleri@rnonline.com.ar* Highly recommended for its beautiful location, this historic 1900's house, in lovely open land, with excellent horse riding on well trained polo ponies through bush and beaches to the even more remote estancia, **San Juan** where you eat *asado* under the stars. Both are traditional Patagonian estancias with young and friendly English-speaking owners. Great hospitality. Highly recommended. All meals, activities and transfers included. Open December to March.

Las Grutas *p435*

There is a huge range of sleeping options.
B Marina Cero, *Bahía Creek Y Nahuel Huapi, T497640, www.marinacero.com* Luxurious, well equipped apartments a block from the beach, good value.
C Golfo Azul, *Chimpay 141, T497109, www.golfo-azul.com.ar* Smart accommodation.
C Patagonia Norte, *Sierra Paileman 8, T497800, www.balneariolas grutas.com.ar* Nicely furnished rooms with air conditioning, pool and restaurant.
E Residencial Las Grutas, *Viedma y Lamarque, T497150*.

Puerto Madryn *p435, map p437*

Accommodation often gets full in spring and summer, when prices rise; book in advance, but watch out for the 'international tourist' price, sometimes double the price Argentines pay.
AL Tolosa, *Roque Sáenz Peña 253, T471850, F451141, tolosa@hoteltolosa.com.ar* An extremely comfortable modern place with faultless personal service and great breakfasts. Note that the superior rooms are

● For an explanation of the sleeping and eating price codes used in this guide, see the inside
● front cover. Other relevant information is provided in Essentials, see page 44.

much more spacious and have full wheelchair access. Bookings made from outside Argentina incur international tourist prices. Free use of bicycles and internet. Highly recommended.

A **Bahía Nueva**, *Av Roca 67, T/F451677, www.bahianueva.com.ar* One of the best seafront hotels, with a welcoming reception area, and high standards in all details. Rooms are on the small side, but comfortable, breakfasts are generous, and staff are helpful and professional. Cheaper in low season, but be aware that this hotel has higher prices for non-Argentines. Recommended.

A **Península Valdés**, *Av Roca 155, T471292, F452584, www.hotel-peninsula-valdes.com* A luxurious place on the sea front, great views from many of its spacious rooms and from the calm minimalist lounge. Spa, sauna and gym. International prices here, plus 30% extra for bookings made from outside Argentina.

B **Patagonia Hotel and Apart Hotel**, *Albarracin 45, T/F452103, www.patagonia aparthotel.com* Modern and spacious rooms and apartments are of a high standard but pricey, since you'll be charged international tourist prices.

B-C **Villa Pirén**, *Av Roca 439, T/F456272, www.piren.com.ar* Excellent modern rooms and apartments in smart seafront building with great facilities. Ask for the junior suite, or rooms with a view.

C **Marina**, *Av Roca 7, T/F454915, teokou@ infovia.com.ar* Great little seafront place with well equipped apartments for up to 5 people. Welcoming owners will also arrange excursions. Worth booking ahead.

C **Playa**, *Av Roca 187, T451446, www.playa hotel.com.ar* Good central sea front location with spacious entrance and airy *confiteria*. All good value and comfortable, there is a range of rooms and it's worth paying extra for the larger, more modern rooms with sea view. Parking costs US$2 per night.

C **Santa Rita**, *Gob Maiz 370, T471050.* Welcoming place and comfy rooms with wash basin – this is good value with dinner included, though you can also use the kitchen facilities. Helpful hosts. Often recommended.

D **Hostería Torremolinos**, *Marcos A Zar 64, T453215.* Nice modern place with simple, well decorated rooms.

D **Gran Palace Hotel**, *28 de Julio 400, T471009.* Attractive entrance to this central and economical place, but rooms are a bit squashed and rather dark, thanks to the mahogany effect wallpaper. But they're clean and have bathroom and TV, making this good value.

D **Muelle Viejo**, *H Yrigoyen 38, T471284.* Ask for the stylish, comfortable modernized rooms in this funny old place. Excellent value large rooms sleep 4 and there are *parrilla* and kitchen facilities if you want to cook.

D-E **La Posta**, *Roca 33, T472422. Residencial laposta@infovia.com.ar* You'll find small but very clean rooms in this welcoming little place on the sea front. Also simple self catering apartments, all popular in high season. Recommended.

E **Residencial J'Os**, *Bolivar 75, T471433.* A friendly small *hostería*, all the rooms have private bathrooms, and breakfast is included.

E **Puerto Madryn Hostelling International**, *25 de Mayo 1136, T/F474426, hi-pm@satlink. com.ar/madryn@hostels.org.ar* 10 blocks from the centre of town, a modern house with garden, laundry and kitchen facilities, rooms for 2 and 4 people, bike rental. Not particularly welcoming, but comfortable enough. English and French spoken.

F **El Gaulicho**, *Marcos A Zar 480, T454163, www.elgaulichohostel.com.ar* By far the best budget place in Puerto Madryn, this new hostel is beautifully designed and run by a friendly and enthusiastic owner. Free pick up from bus terminal, *parrilla*, garden, some attractive double rooms, and bikes for hire – book ahead. Highly recommended.

Camping

ACA, *Boulevard Brown, 3.5 km south of town centre (at Punta Cuevas), T452952.* Open Sep-Apr, hot showers, café, shop, no kitchen facilities, shady trees, close to the sea. Many people camp on the beach, though there is a municipal site **El Golfito Camping y Albergue**, *Ribera Sur, 1 km before ACA site on same road along beach (gives student discount) T454544.* All facilities, very crowded in summer, US$2 per person and US$2 per tent for 1st day. Also room with bunkbeds, F per person. Bus from town stops 100m before entrance.

Península Valdés/Puerto Pirámides *p438*

AL **Patagonia Franca**, *T495006, www.patagoniafranca.com* Right on the beach with splendid views, this comfortable new place is a little soulless. Airport transfers arranged.

B **The Paradise**, *at the far end of the main street, T495030, www.hosteriaparadise.com* Huge very comfortable light rooms, smart bathrooms, and splendid suites with jacuzzis. Also a fine restaurant, serving delicious squid, among other seafood.

C **Cabañas del Mar**, *Av Roca s/n, T495049, cabanas@piramides.net* 5 comfortable 4 bed cabañas, well equipped, but no heating.

C **Motel ACA**, *on beach front, at Av Roca s/n, T495004, 156 61629, curti@satlink. com.ar* Slightly old fashioned, but still modern in feel, this has welcoming rooms, handy for the beach. Also a good seafood restaurant, from whose terrace you might even spot whales!.

Camping

Municipal site, *T495000*. Near the beach, shop, hot showers in evening only, a bit scruffy and very busy, so get there early to secure a place; do not camp on the beach: people have been swept away by the incoming tide.

Estancias

AL **Estancia La Ernestina**, *T471143, www.laernestina.com.ar* A smaller estancia.

AL **Faro Punta Delgada**, *T15406304, www.puntadelagada.com* Comfortable accommodation in a lighthouse, offering half and full board, excellent food, and horse riding, guided walks, recommended.

AL **La Elena**, *near Salina Grande, T421448, alcamar@ciudad.com.ar* An old Spanish settlement, price is for full board, and horse and bike excursions are offered.

AL **Punta Cantor La Elvira**, *T156 68107, www.laelvira.com.ar* Traditional Patagonian dishes, and comfortable accommodation.

AL **Rincón Chico**, *south of Puerto Pirámides.* A working sheep farm, still owned by the original pioneer family who built it. Luxurious, beautifully situated, great for walking. Recommended.

AL **San Lorenzo**, *T456888, www.puntanorte.com* See penguins close up, with wonderful walks to the coast.

Trelew is not a touristy town, and so there's limited choice of accommodation, particularly for low budgets, though there is a good campsite.

B **Rayentray**, *San Martín y Belgrano, T/F434702, rcvcentral@ar.inter.net* Huge modernized 1960s place with comfortable rooms and professional staff – the spacious 'superior' rooms are worth the extra, with sitting area and good bathrooms, and splendid 70s leather panelling. Swimming pool on top floor is free for guests, but gym, sunbed and sauna are extra.

C **Centenario**, *San Martín 150, T420542, hotelcentenario@yahoo.com.ar* This vast 1970's relic is worth seeing for the untouched décor, though it's more amusing than comfortable, and service is poor. Popular with Argentines, but you can always get a room here; not great value.

C **Libertador**, *Rivadavia 31, T/F420220, www.hotellibertador.com.ar* Breakfast is included in this large modern place, highly recommended for its friendly service and comfortable rooms – the newer more spacious rooms are slightly pricier but worth it. Reserve ahead.

E **Galicia**, *9 de Julio 214, T433802, www.sipatagonia.com/hotelgalicia* Breakfast included in this recently refurbished and central hotel, whose smallish rooms don't quite live up to the grand entrance, but are extremely comfortable and well decorated, and the staff are friendly. Excellent value and recommended.

E **Touring Club**, *Fontana 240, T/F425790, htouring@ar.inter.net* After the gorgeous faded style of the bar, the vast staircase and light corridors, the rooms here are on the plain side, but they're quiet and spacious with big bathrooms, and well kept. Breakfast is extra, but this is good value, and the bar is marvellous.

F pp **Rivadavia**, *Rivadavia 55, T434172.* Simple, comfortable rooms with TV and bath, and some even cheaper rather spartan rooms without, in this well-located place. This is the best value in town, if you can ignore the grumpy owner. Breakfast extra.

Patagonia Listings: Northern Patagonia

Camping Patagonia, *Ruta 7 y Rawson*, *T428968*. US$1. Pretty site with *parrilla*, hot showers, football pitch and *proveduría* (food shop). Leave Trelew on RN 7 in the direction of Rawson, pass a roundabout, the road bends sharply to the right, take right fork, a *ripio* road, and the campsite is after 3 blocks on the right.

Gaiman *p442*

B Unelem, *Av Tello y 9 de Julio, T491663, www.unelem.com.ar* Priciest, but very comfortable, is this restored old hotel from 1867, whose restaurant serves Welsh cooking.
C Casa de Té Ty Gwyn, *9 de Julio 111, T491009, tygwyn@cpsarg.com* The next best option in town are the smart new rooms above the tea house.
D pp Gwesty Tywi, *Jones 342, T491292, gwestywi@infovia.com.ar* A pretty and very well kept bed and breakfast.
D Plas Y Coed, *Jones 123, T491133*. Marta Rees' delightful tea room also has double and twin rooms with bath and TV including breakfast.

Camping

Los Doce Nogales is an attractive site south of the river, close to Ty Te Caerdydd tea room, T155-18030, with showers.

⑦ Eating

Viedma and Carmen de Patagones *p433*

$ Camilla's Café, *Saavedra and Buenos Aires*. A smart and relaxing place for coffee, to watch Viedma trundle by on its errands.
$ La Balsa, *on the river at Colon y Villarino*. By far the best restaurant, inexpensive with a pleasant atmosphere. Delicious seafood, and a bottle of superb Río Negro wine, Humberto Canale Merlot, are highly recommended.
$ Parrilla Libre, *Buenos Aires and Colón*. Cheap *tenedor libre* steaks in a cheerful atmosphere, US$2.50 for dinner.

Las Grutas *p435*

$ Aladdin, *Av Río Negro 600*. Recommended for seafood, with shows laid on in summer, and Arabic dancing, would you believe.
$ Limité, *Av Costanera y Cinco Saltos*. On the seafront with tables on the beach, serving delicious seafood, salmon-stuffed ravioli recommended.

Puerto Madryn *p435, map p437*

One of the unmissable pleasures of Puerto Madryn is its great seafood. While you're here, try at least one plate of *arroz con mariscos* (rice with a whole selection of squid, prawns, mussels and clams). Most restaurants are mid-range and charge around the same price, but differ widely in quality. Without doubt, the best place to eat in town is the wonderful **Taska Beltza**, though there's plenty of choice along the coast road.
$$ Antigua Patagonia, *Mitre y RS Pena, T458738*. Large welcoming *parrilla* and seafood restaurant with a warm buzzing atmosphere, array of old objects on the brick walls, and good-value set menu. Popular with families and couples alike. Small play area for kids. Recommended.
$$$ Nativo Sur, *Blvd Brown 2000, T457403*. Smarter than its more popular sister restaurant *Yoaquino*, Nativo Sur is a good place for a quiet dinner on the beach front, with an imaginative menu of local Patagonian produce and seafood.
$$$ Placido, *Av Roca 508, T455991*. For a special dinner or a romantic place to eat. Overlooking the sea, and beautifully designed, with stylish tables and intimate lighting, this has excellent service and a good range of seafood, with cheaper pasta dishes too, lots of options for vegetarians.
$$ Caccaros, *Av Roca 385, T453767*. Stylish simple place on sea front with relaxing atmosphere, good value seafood menu, and cheap lunch menu.
$$ Cantina El Nautico, *Av Roca 790, T471404*. Long-established and now resting on its laurels, this is still popular for its seafood, and family atmosphere. The set menu isn't great value, and you're better off choosing individual dishes.
$$ Centro de Difusion de la Pescada Artesanal, *Brown, 7th roundabout, T15 538085*. Grandly named, but with no sign outside, this is a basic *cantina* on the coast road east, opposite the municipal campsite, where the fishermen's families cook delicious meals with their catch. Hugely popular with locals, so come early. Far more authentic than *El Nautico*.

$$ **La Vaca y el Pollito**, *Av Roca y A Storni*, *T458486*. You can't miss this place as it's partly built into the wooden hull of a boat. A big place but with a cosy atmosphere, the speciality is *parrilla*, very reasonably priced, but there's seafood and pastas too. Great for families, with a big soft play area for kids.

$$ **Taska Beltza**, *9 de Julio 345*, *T156 68085*, *closed Mon*. Chef and owner 'El Negro' cooks superb seafood with great passion and a Basque influence. Even if you're on a budget, his *Arroz con Mariscos* is cheap and superb. Highly recommended. Book ahead.

$$ **Yoaquina**, *Blvd Brown between 1st and 2nd roundabouts*, *T456058*. Great in the summer when you can eat outside, this is a relaxed spacious beachfront place, serving good seafood, if slightly pricey, and open from breakfast to after dinner. Cheap lunch menu, play area for kids, attentive service. Recommended.

$ **La Casona de Golfo**, *Av Roca 349*, *T15 511089*. Good value *tenedor libre* with lots of choices including good *parrilla* and seafood, and 'helados libre' – as much ice cream as you can eat. Great for families – kids pay half price.

$ **Shang Hai**, *28 de Julio y San Martín*, *T457496*. Bright jolly place for cheap *tenedor libre* with a Chinese slant.

Península Valdés/Puerto Pirámides *p435*

There are many restaurants in the main street. There are reasonably priced restaurants at Punta Norte, at Punta Cantor and at the Faro in Punta Delgada. These are recommendations at the beach itself:

$$ **El Salmon**, *T495065*. Closest to the beach on the right hand side, this has great views from its open deck and serves good seafood.

$$ **Paradise**. Just off the beach, good atmosphere and seafood.

$$ **Patagonia Franca**, *T495006*. A good seafood restaurant in the new hotel on the beach front, with perfect sea views.

$$ **Quimey Quipan**, *T156 93100*. By the beach, and next to *Tito Bottazzi*, this family-run place specializes in delicious seafood with rice and has a cheap set menu. Recommended. Always open for lunch, ring to reserve for dinner.

$ **Mc Pato**. Just off the beach, a friendly place with a good atmosphere that serves

huge sandwiches. Recommended.

$ **Mi Sueno**. Close to the beach, good cheap pizzas to share.

Trelew *p441, map p441*

$$ **Delicatesse**, *Belgrano y San Martín*. Serves pizzas in a cheery place, good for families.

$$ **El Quijote**, *Rivadavia 463*, *T15402937*. Traditional *parrilla*, popular with locals.

$$ **El Viejo Molino**, *Gales 250*, *T428019*, *open 1130-0030, closed Mon*. The best restaurant in town, and well worth a visit to see the first flour mill that was built here in 1886, is now beautifully restored with a fine restaurant and cafe in relaxed and stylish surroundings, there's an imaginative menu with Patagonian lamb and homemade pastas, good value set menu with wine included, and Welsh teas. Recommended.

$$ **La Bodequita**, *opposite the cinema on Belgrano*. Serves superb home-made pastas, in a warm and lively atmosphere, with interesting local art on the walls. Recommended.

$ **Hotel Touring Club**, *Fontana 240*. Open from breakfast to the small hours for sandwiches and drinks, worth a visit to see the splendid 1920's bar.

$ **Café Mi Ciudad**, *Belgrano y San Martín*. A smart café serving great coffee; read the papers watching street life.

$ **Norte**, *Soberania y Belgrano*. Cheap takeaway food is available at this supermarket.

Gaiman *p442*

There's a stylish small restaurant **El Angel**, *Jones 850*, serving delicious food in an old-fashioned intimate atmosphere. Also a high quality *panadería* **La Colonia** on the main street, and **Tavern Las**, a small pub, *on the corner of Tello and Miguel Jones*, with a good atmosphere. **Siop Bara** sells cakes and ice creams.

Welsh teas

You're unlikely to be able to resist the scrumptious Welsh teas for which Gaiman has become famous, though quite how the tradition has sprung up remains a mystery. It's hard to imagine their abstemious ancestors tucking into vast plates filled with seven kinds of cake and scones at one sitting, and inevitably, they're not cheap. Tea is served from 1500, all the tea rooms charge about the same – US$4 – and include the most well known of the Welsh cakes *Torta Negra* – a delicious dense fruit cake. The first 3 are all near the Plaza:

Plas Y Coed, *Jones 123*. The first house to start serving tea, has lovely gardens, and the owner Marta Rees is a wonderful raconteur and fabulous cook who can tell you all about her Welsh forebears, married in this very house in 1886. Highly recommended.

Ty Gwyn, *9 de Julio 111*. This large tea house serves a very generous tea in a more modern place with traditional features; the owners are welcoming. Recommended.

Ty Nain, *Yrigoyen 283*. Quite the prettiest house and full of history. Owner Mirna Jones is charming; her grandmother was the first woman to be born in Gaiman.

Ty Cymraeg, *down by the river*. Set in a lovely spot is with room for big groups, and selling good cakes.

Ty Te Caerdydd, *Finca 202, 2 km from the centre, but well sign posted*. A quite staggering theme park of its own, with manicured lawns and dressed-up waitresses; its main claim to fame is that Princess Di took her tea here. The atmosphere is entirely manufactured.

Bars and cafés

Puerto Madryn *p435, map p437*
Havanna, *Av Roca y 28 de Julio*. Smart, buzzing café selling the famous *alfajores* you see all over Argentina, coffees and sandwiches *de miga*. Very central, and open from breakfast to the early hours.

Lizard Café, *Av Roca y Av Gales, T458333*. Lively funky place with friendly people. Good for cheap and plentiful pizzas or for late night drinks on the seafront.

Margarita, *RS Pena, next to Ambigu on RS Pena and Av Roca*. Late night bar for drinks and live music.

Mitos, *28 de Julio 64*. Friendly and welcoming stylish café with good atmosphere, and pictures of tango stars and jazz musicians on the walls. Great for breakfast, or lunch and open until the early hours. Recommended.

Ice cream
Kabom, *Av Roca 530*. Popular ice cream place with big soft play area for kids.

Entertainment

Puerto Madryn *p435, map p437*
Nightclubs
Margarita, *RS Pena y Av Roca*. Live music some nights.
Disco Rancho Cucamonga, *Blvd Brown y Jenkins*. Near beach, young crowd.

Sport

Puerto Madryn *p435, map p437*
Diving La Oveja Negra Safari Submarino, *Blvd Brown 1070, T474110*.
Ocean Divers, *Blvd Brown (between 1st and 2nd roundabout), T472569*. Advanced courses (PADI) and courses on video, photography and underwater communication.
Hydro Sport, *Balneario Rayentray, 5th roundabout, T495065, hysport@ infovia .com.ar* Encounters with dolphins and whale watching.
Na Praia, *Blvd Brown y Perlotti, T473715*, and **Golfo Azul**, *Mitre y H Yrigoyen, T451181*. For windsurf boards, kayaks, jet ski, sailing boats for hire.
Fishing Golfo San José, Jorge Schmid, *T451511*; **Raul Diaz**, *T450812*, **Juan Dominguez** *T156 64772*.
Horse riding El Moro, *T474188*; **El Recuerdo**, *T471126*.

Shopping

Puerto Madryn *p435, map p437*
The sleek new indoor shopping centre **Portal de Madryn**, *28 de Julio y Av Roca*, has all the smart clothes shops, *Café Havanna* on the ground floor, and a kids games area with a fast, but not cheap, food place *Mostaza* on the top floor. **Cardon**, is recommended for regional goods and leather bags. You'll find lots more posh clothes, T shirts with whales and penguins on, high quality Patagonian handicrafts and leather goods, and artesanal *alfajores* and cakes in streets *28 de Julio and Av Roca*. For fishing tackle, guns and camping gear, try **Nayfer**, *25 de Mayo 330*. For diving gear, there's **Nautiflot**, *Av Roca 249*, and **Acquablu**, *Av Roca 536*, and also at **PinoSub**, *Yrigoyen 200*. There are **chemists** all along *28 de Julio*, and a late night **pharmacy** on *Belgrano y 25 de Mayo*.

Península Valdés/Puerto Pirámides *p435*
In summer there are several well-stocked shops, including locally made handicrafts, but take sun and wind protection and drinking water.

Trelew *p439, map p441*
The main shopping area is around San Martín, and from the plaza to Belgrano, though Trelew can't compare with Puerto Madryn for souvenirs, it has a good little handicrafts market on the plaza.
Norte, *Rivadavia y 9 de Julio*. Opposite *Banco Río*. Supermarket.

⟩ Tour operators

Puerto Madryn/Península Valdés *p435*
Lots of agencies in Puerto Madryn do tours to Península Valdés, usually taking in the same places: the interpretation centre and viewing point for the Isla de los Pajaros, (both on the narrow isthmus at the entrance to the peninsula), and then Puerto Pirámides, where the boat trip to see the whales costs US$12 extra. They go on to Punta Delgada and Caleta Valdés, with time to look at wildlife. Trips take 12 hrs, so you should bring water and lunch, though there are places to eat in Puerto Pirámides. All charge US$17, plus US$3 entrance to the Peninsula – but shop around to find out how long you'll spend at each place, how big the group is, and if your guide speaks English. On all excursions take drink, food if you don't want to eat in the expensive restaurants, and binoculars. Most tour companies (addresses above) stay 50-60 mins on location. Usually half price for children under 10, free for under 6s. Tours are also offered to see the penguins at Punta Tombo, or the Welsh village of Gaiman with Ameghino Dam thrown in, but these are both 400 km round trips and better from Trelew.

Excursions to Península Valdés
Alora Viaggio, *Av Roca 27, T/F455106*. A helpful company which also has an office at the bus terminal.
Argentina Visión, *Av Roca 536, T451427, F451108, www.argentinavision.com* Offers 4WD adventure trips and can arrange estancia accommodation at Punta Delgada.

English and French spoken.
Cuyun Co, *Av Roca 165, T451845, www.cuyunco.com.ar* Offers a friendly personal service and a huge range of conventional and more imaginative tours: guided walks with biologists, 4WD expeditions, and also arrange estancia accommodation. Bilingual guides. Recommended.
Flamenco Tour, *Av Roca 353, T/F455690, www.flamencotour.com.ar* For slightly more sedate trips and charming staff.
Gray Fox Offers '100% action' trips in 4WDs, kayaks and kite buggies.
Hydrosport, *near the ACA, T495065, hysport@infovia.com.ar* Rents scuba equipment and boats, and organizes land and sea wildlife tours to see whales and dolphins.
Juan Benegas, *T495100*. Offers diving expeditions and provides equipment. Tours do not run after heavy rain in the low season.
Tito Botazzi, *Blvd Brown 1070, T/F474110, www.titobottazzi.com* Particularly recommended for small groups and well informed bilingual guides.

Trelew *p439, map p441*
Agencies run tours to Punta Tombo, US$18, Chubut Valley (half-day), US$10, both together as a full day US$22. Tours to Península Valdés are best done from Puerto Madryn.
Nieve y Mar, *Italia 20, T434114, www.nievmartours.com.ar* Punta Tombo and Valdes, bilingual guides (reserve ahead). Organized and efficient.
Patagonia Grandes Espacios, *Belgrano 338, T435161, www.surturismo.com.ar* Good excursions to Punta Tombo and Gaiman, but also palaeontological trips, staying in *chacras*, whale watching. Recommended.

⊝ Transport

Viedma and Carmen de Patagones *p433*
Air
Aeropuerto Gobernador Castelo, 5 km south. LADE (*Saavedra 403, T/F424420*) fly to **Buenos Aires**, **Mar del Plata**, **Bahía Blanca**, **Neuquén**, **San Martín de Los Andes**, **Trelew** and **Comodoro Rivadavia**.

Terminal in Viedma at *Av Pte Peron y Guido*, 15 blocks from plaza; take a taxi (US$1). To/from **Buenos Aires** 3 daily, 14 hrs, US$20, Don Otto/La Estrella/Cóndor. To **San Antonio Oeste**, several daily, 2½ hrs, US$4, Don Otto. To **Bahia Blanca**, 4 daily, 4 hrs, US$5, **Rio Parana**.

Train

A comfortable sleeper train, which also carries cars, goes from Viedma to **Bariloche** overnight once a week, Friday 1800, and arrives in the morning. On board there's a restaurant and a cinema car showing videos. All reasonably comfortable. US$30 for a bed, US$18 for a *semi-cama* seat. *T02944 431777, www.trenpatagonico.com.ar* Book ahead.

Las Grutas
Air

LADE flies to **San Antonio Oeste**.

Bus

Buses from **San Antonio** hourly US$1. North to **Bahía Blanca** and south to **Río Gallegos** and **Punta Arenas** by Transportes Patagónicos. To **Puerto Madryn** and **Trelew**, Don Otto, 0200 and 1530, 4 hrs, US$8. To **Buenos Aires**, US$21 via Bahía Blanca, frequent. Bus terminal information T497001.

Puerto Madryn *p435, map p437*
Air

Puerto Madryn Airport, 10 km west of centre, reached by taxi, US$5. Only LADE operate from here. Flights, once a week to **Neuquén**, **Bariloche**, **Esquel** and **Mar del Plata**, among others. More flights to **Bariloche**, **Buenos Aires**, and **El Calafate** from Trelew airport, 7 km north of Trelew. Buses to Trelew stop at entrance to airport if asked. Taxi US$20. **Mar y Valle** run a bus service to Puerto Madryn's bus terminal.

Bus

Terminal The new terminal is at *Irigoyen y San Martín* (behind the old railway station), with a café, clean toilets, *locutorio*, tourist information, and a kiosko selling drinks and sweets. Walk 3 blocks down R S Pena to get into town. Terminal information T451789. To **Buenos Aires**, 18 hrs US$17-20, several

companies, **Andesmar** recommended. To **Río Gallegos**, 18 hrs; US$18, **El Pingüino** (connecting to El Calafate, Punta Arenas, Puerto Natales), **Andesmar**, **TAC**, **Don Otto**. To **Trelew**, 1 hr, every hr, US$4 with **28 de Julio**, **Mar y Valle**. To **Puerto Pirámide**, 1 hr, US$2, daily, 28 de Julio. To **Bariloche**, 15 hrs, US$46, daily, except Wed, **Mar y Valle**. Companies Andesmar, T473764. Don Otto, T451675. El Pingüino, T456256. TUS, T451962. 28 de Julio/Mar y Valle, T472056.

Car hire

More expensive than other parts of Argentina, and note the large insurance excess for turning the car over. Drive slowly on unpaved *ripio* roads! **Localiza**, *Roca 536, T456300, 0800 9992999*. Recommended for efficient and helpful service. **Puerto Madryn Turismo**, *Roca 624, T452355*.

Mountain bike hire

Future Bike, *Juan B Justo 683, T156 65108*. **Na praia**. *On beach at Blvd Brown and Perlotti, T473715*. **XT Mountain Bike**, *Av Roca 742, T472232*.

Taxi

Outside the bus terminal, T452966/474177.

Península Valdés/Puerto Pirámides *p438*

Península Valdés can most easily be visited by taking one of the many well-organized full day excursions (see Tour operators above for further details) but if you'd rather see the peninsula independently, you can hire a car relatively inexpensively for a group of 4, and then take just the boat trip to see the whales (Sep-Nov) from Puerto Pirámides with **Jorge Schmidt**, T451511/495012. Note that distances are long on the peninsula, and roads beyond Puerto Pirámides are *ripio*, so take your time – car hire companies charge a heavy excess if you turn the car over. A cheaper option is the daily bus to **Puerto Pirámides** with **28 de Julio**, leaving the terminal daily at 1000, returns 1800, 1 hr, US$2 each way.

Carmen de Patagones and Viedma *p433*

Buses link both towns from **Bahía Blanca** and **Puerto Madryn**, as well as the local beach at **Las Grutas**.

Trelew *p439, map p441*

Air

Airport 5 km north of centre; taxis about US$3. Local buses to/from **Puerto Madryn** stop at the airport entrance, turning is 10 mins walk. **Aerolíneas Argentinas** have flights to/from **Buenos Aires**, **Río Gallegos** and **Ushuaia**. **Aerolíneas Argentinas** also to **Río Grande**; Lapa (and TAN) also to **Comodoro Rivadavia**. LADE flies to **Patagonia** airports from **Viedma** to **Comodoro Rivadavia**, and **Bariloche**.

Bus

Terminal On the east side of Plaza Centenario. T420121. **Long distance** To **Buenos Aires**, 20 hrs; US$20, several companies go daily, inc **TAC, El Pingüino, Que Bus, Don Otto, Andesmar, El Cóndor**; to **Comodoro Rivadavia**, 5 hrs, US$8, many companies, to **Río Gallegos**, 17 hrs; US$20, (from here to **El Calafate, Puerto Natales, Punta Arenas**), many companies. To **Esquel**, 10 hrs; US$14, **Mar y Valle, Empresa Chubut, Don Otto**.
Local Mar y Valle and 28 de Julio both go frequently to **Rawson**, 30 mins; US$0.50, to **Gaiman**, 30 mins; US$1, and **Dolavon** 1 hr, US$1.50, to **Puerto Madryn**, 1hr, US$2, to **Puerto Pirámides**, 2½ hrs, US$5, daily, **Mar y Valle**. **Companies** Andesmar, T433535; TUS, T421343; El Pingüino, T427400; Don Otto, T432434; TAC, T431452; El Cóndor, T433748; 28 de Julio/Mar y Valle, T432429; Que Bus, T422760; El Ñandú, T427499.

Car hire

Car hire companies at the airport desks are staffed only at flight arrival times and cars are taken quickly. All have offices in town. AVIS, *Paraguay 105, T/F434634*; Localiza, *Urquiza 310 T435344*; Hertz, *at the airport, T436005*.

Gaiman *p442*
Buses to/from **Trelew**, 1 hr, US$1.50, with company **28 de Julio**, several a day.

Dolavon *p442*
Buses to/from **Trelew**, 1 hr, US$1.50, 28 de Julio, several a day.

● Directory

Travellers' cheques are hard to change throughout Patagonia, and it's easier, and safer, to use credit cards to withdraw cash. There are ATMs in all the main towns, except El Chaltén.

Carmen de Patagones and Viedma *p433*
Banks ATMs at Colon and San Martín in Viedma, and Carmen de Patagones at Bynon and Alsina or Bynon and Paraguay. **Travel agencies** Mona Tour, *San Martín 225, Viedma*. Sells flights and tickets for the train to Bariloche, www.trenpatagonico.com

Puerto Madryn *p435, map p437*
Airline offices LADE, *Roca 117, T451256*. Aerolíneas Argentinas, *Roca 303, T421257/0800-2228 6527*. **Banks** Lots of ATMs at the following: Banco Nación, *9 de Julio 117*. Banco del Chubut, *25 de Mayo 154* and **Río** , *Mitre 102*. **Communications Internet** Internet Centro Madryn, *25 de Mayo y Belgrano*. US$0.60 per hour. Re Creo, *Roque Sáenz Peña 101*. **Post Office**, *Belgrano y Maiz, 0900-1200, 1500-1900*.
Telephone Many *locutorios* in the centre.

Península Valdés/Puerto Pirámides *p435*
Bus

Bus company **28 de Julio** from **Puerto Madryn** to **Puerto Pirámides**, daily at 1000 returns 1800, US$2 each way, 1 hr.

Trelew *p439, map p441*
Airline offices Aerolineas Argentinas, *25 de Mayo 33, T420170*. LADE, *Terminal de Omnibus, offices 12 /13, T435925*. Lapa, *Belgrano 285, T423438*. **Banks** Open Mon-Fri 0830-1300. **Banco de la Nación**, *25 de Mayo y Fontana*. **Banco del Sud**, 9 de Julio 320, cash advance on Visa.
Exchange Currency changed at Turismo Sur (also known as Patagonia Grandes Espacios, Belgrano 338.) **Communications Post Office** *25 de Mayo and Mitre*.
Telephone Telefónica, *Roca y Pje Tucumán*, and several locutorios in the centre.
Internet *25 de Mayo 219*.

Central Patagonia

One of the wildest most uninhabited parts of the planet, there are few places here where tourists are catered for, and you're in for a real adventure. The Ruta 40 hasn't changed much since Che Guevara drove along it, although the bus from Los Antiguos, with a jolly cherry festival in January, takes just 14 hours to reach El Chaltén, the windswept base for hiking around Fitz Roy. Along the way you could linger at rustic estancias, escape from civilization completely, and enjoy horseriding, walking and the warm hospitality of their owners, who will share their experience of life in the middle of nowhere. Estancia La Oriental is the best way to see the stark and beautiful landscape of Perito Moreno National Park (not the one with the glaciers), unless you have a tent, since much of it is inaccessible.

The contrasts here are extreme: there's less than one person per square kilometre in modern Patagonia, but thousands of ancient handprints in the Cueva de las Manos. A short trip from the town of Perito Moreno, the impressive canyon setting is just as striking as this mysterious show of hands. Far from the densely wooded Andes, there are the petrified forests in the desert; huge trunks of monkey puzzle trees turned to stone by volcanic ash 140 million years ago. There are two Bosques Petrificados near Sarmiento, and the Monumento not far from Fitz Roy.

Camarones → *Phone code: 0297 Colour map 5, B5 Population: 800*

Camarones is a quiet fishing port on Bahía Camarones 275 km south of Trelew, whose main industry is harvesting seaweed. This is prime sheep-rearing land, and Camerones wool is world-renowned for its quality. Aside from the salmon festival around 7-9 February, the only real attraction is the penguin colony, which you can walk to from the town. ▶▶ *For Sleeping, Eating and other listings, see pages 457-461.*

Reserva Natural Cabo Dos Bahías → *Colour map 5, B5*

This is a small reserve, 35 km southeast of Camerones at the southern end of the bay and reached by a dirt road. It protects a large penguin colony of some 12,000 couples, which you can see close up, but also lots of other marine life; there are sea lions and and whales too, if you're lucky. The reserve is open all year, and you can see seals and sea lions any time, but there are whales from March to November, and killer whales might be spotted from October to April, US$5.

Comodoro Rivadavia → *Phone code: 02967 Colour map 5, C4 Population: 145,000*

The largest city in the province of Chubut was established primarily as a sheep-exporting port, and early settlers included Boer immigrants fleeing British rule in southern Africa. Its compact centre is at the foot of Cerro Chenque, 212 m high, a dusty bluff overlooking the town unattractively adorned with radar masts, and a shanty town. The city began to flourish suddenly when oil was discovered here in 1907, bringing in many international companies. However, since the petrol industry was privatised by President Menem in the 1990's, there's been consequent unemployment and now the town has a slightly sad, rather unkempt feel, and there's little to make you want to stay.

Situated at the end of the Bioceanic Corridor, a fast road to Chile, Comodoro is the hub for terrestrial transport, and a bus nexus from all areas of Patagonia, though there are some smart hotels and a popular beach nearby. You could visit the **Museo del Petroleo** ① *T4559558, Tue-Fri 0900-1800, Sat/Sun 1500-1800, taxi US$43 km north of the centre at San Lorenzo 250*, for a good history of local oil exploitation. The **Museo Paleontológico** ① *20 km north, open weekends, 1400-1800*, has fossils and reconstructions of dinosaurs. There's a good view of the city from **Cerro Chenque**, a dun-coloured hill whose cliffs give the town its drab backdrop. It's interesting to take a taxi up there if you don't feel like the walk, and see the first pioneers' homes, now dilapidated, but with panoramic views of the bay.

There's good beach at the resort of **Rada Tilly** 12 km south, ① *Buses Expreso Rada Tilly every 30 mins*, packed in summer, where you can walk along the beach at low tide to see sea lions. You could use Comodoro Ravadavia as a base for exploring the Bosques Petrificados (see below), but the little town of **Sarmiento**, some 150 km west, is far more pleasant, ① *There are three buses daily to Sarmiento with Etap, at 0800, 1300, 1900, T447 4841*. The **tourist office** ① *Rivadavia 430, T446 2376, www.comodoro.gov.ar Mon-Fri 0900-1400, or in the bus terminal, daily 0800-2100*, is very helpful, English spoken. ▸▸ *For Sleeping, Eating and other listings, see pages 457-461.*

Comodoro Rivadavia to Chile

Route 26, the Bioceanic Corridor, runs west across the steppe amid oil wells, from Comodoro Rivadavia towards the Chilean border and the Chilean towns of Coyhaique and Puerto Aisén. Mainly used by lorries, it gives access to two unusual sights. There are two petrified araucaria forests, the Bosques Petrificados, within easy reach of Colonia Sarmiento, 156 km west of Comodoro. And from Río Mayo, where Route 26 meets Route 40, you can reach Perito Moreno, the base for seeing the handprint-filled caves, Cueva de los Manos.

Colonia Sarmiento → *Phone code: 0297 Colour map 5, C3 Population: 7,000*

Sarmiento lies on the Río Senguer just south of two great lakes and 156 km west of Comodoro Rivadavia, **Lago Musters** and **Lago Colhué Huapi**, both of which offer good fishing in summer. Founded in 1897 and formally known as Colonia Sarmiento, its early settlers were Welsh, Lithuanians and Boers. It's a quiet and relaxed place, sitting in fertile, well irrigated land, and little visited by tourists, though it's the best base for visiting two areas of petrified forest nearby: Most accessible is the **Bosque Petrificado José Ormachea**, 32 km south along a *ripio* road, entry US$2.50. Less easy to reach is the rather bleaker **Bosque Petrificado Vícor Szlapelis**, some 40 km further southwest along the same road (follow signposts, the road from Sarmiento is in good condition). These forests, 60 million years old, of fallen araucaria trees nearly 3 m in circumference and 15-20 m long, are a remarkable sight, best visited in summer as the winters are very cold. There are *guardaparques* (rangers) at both sites, who can give tours and information. The **tourist office** ① *Avenida San Martín, almost at Alberdi, T489 8220*, helpful, and has a map of the town.

Río Mayo to El Calafate: Ruta 40

If you're travelling Argentina by bus or under your own steam, by bicycle or car, the Ruta 40 through Patagonia is likely to leave a lasting impression. From Río Mayo to El Calafate, the wide stony *ripio* track zigzags its way across windswept desolate land. You might not see a soul all day, and passing a car is a major event. It's one of the most vivid experiences of Argentina. Every few hundred kilometres or so, there will be a small, improbable signpost to an *estancia*, somewhere off the road unseen. Or far off, you'll spot a neat row of alamo trees in the middle of the desert, and know that a house lies behind them, protected from the wind. There are only a few service stations for fuel along the whole stretch, and few places offering accommodation. And when at last you arrive at Mount Fitz Roy, great turrets of granite rising up from the flat steppe, you may well think you've imagined it. It's one of the most magnificent sights in the whole country, made all the more spectacular by hours or days of relentless flat lands under wind-whipped swirly clouds, with only condors for company.

Ins and outs

Getting around Travelling south, the road is paved as far as Perito Moreno, and then good *ripio*, improving greatly after Las Horquetas. If cycling, note that food and water stops are scarce, the wind is fierce, and there is no shade whatsoever. Between them, *Chalten Travel* and *Itinerarios y Travesías* run a daily bus service between Los Antiguos and El Chaltén, and you'd be unlikely to stop en route, except to see the Cueva de las Manos, reached from Perito Moreno. But there are estancias to explore if you have the time, though you'll need transport to get to them. Various companies organize tours along the route, with estancia stays and travel included, see www.tierrabuena.com.ar and www.estanciasdesantacruz.com Hitching along this road is virtually impossible, and can't be recommended, as you could be stranded for days. But you could hit lucky and get a ride to one of the estancias on the route which take guests; it helps to speak Spanish. Super grade fuel is available in most places: it is important to carry extra, especially between Bajo Caracoles and Tres Lagos, since the only source of fuel between them involves a 72 km detour to Gobernador Gregores.

Río Mayo *Phone code: 02903. Colour map 5, C2 Population: 2,600*

Set in beautifully bleak landscape, by the meandering Río Mayo, there's little of tourist interest in this very rural little town, and you're most likely to find yourself here to change for buses or pick up fuel. But every November, it is the site for an extraordinary display of dexterity at the *Fiesta Nacional dela Esquila* (the National Sheep-shearing Competition). Teams of 5 or 6 *esquiladores*, who travel Patagonia from farm to farm in shearing season, compete to shear as many sheep as possible, without cutting the animal or tearing the fleece. A good shearer might get through 20 an hour: quite a sight. ▸▸ *For Sleeping, Eating and other listings, see pages 457-461.*

Border with Chile

There are two roads crossing the border into Chile to take you to Coyhaique from here. The southernmost of the two, via Paso Huemules has better roads. Coyhaique Alto is reached by a 133 km road (87 km *ripio*, then dirt) which branches off Route 40 about 7 km north of Río Mayo. On the Chilean side this road continues to Coyhaique, 50 km west of the border. See below, for bus services.

Chilean immigration At Coyhaique Alto, 6 km west of the border, open May-Aug 0800-2100, Sep-Apr 0700-2300. Paso Huemules is reached by a road which branches off Route 40, some 31 km south of Río Mayo and runs west 105 km via Lago Blanco (fuel), where there is an estancia community, 30 km from the border. There's no hotel but the police are friendly and may permit camping at the police post. This road continues from Balmaceda on the Chilean side of the border to Coyhaique. Chilean immigration is open May-Jul 0800-2100, Sep-Apr 0700-2100.

Perito Moreno → *Phone code: 02963 Colour map 5, C2 Population: 3,000*

Not to be confused with the famous glacier of the same name near El Calafate, nor with Parque Nacional Perito Moreno, this Perito Moreno is a spruce little town, 25 km west of Lago Buenos Aires, and the nearest base for exploring the mysterious cave paintings at the **Cueva de las Manos**, to the south. The town has no sights as such, apart from the pleasure of watching a rural community go about its business. But southwest of the town is **Parque Laguna**, where you can see varied bird life including flamingos and black-necked swans, and go fishing. You could also walk to the crater of **Cerro Volcan**, from a path 12 km outside Perito Moreno: ask at the tourist office for directions. The friendly **tourist office** on main street, San Martín 1222, open and on estancias. You could also visit Santa Cruz's tourist office in Buenos Aires, T0114325 3102, www.estanciasdesantacruz.com There are two ATMs in the main street, at Banco de la Provincia de Santa Cruz and Banco de la Nación, but nowhere to change travellers cheques.

Los Antiguos → *Phone code 02963 Colour map 6, A2*

Though there are two crossings to Chile west of Perito Moreno, the easiest and most commonly used is via the pretty little village of Los Antiguos, which lies just 2 km east of the border. The town lies on the southern shore of Lago Buenos Aires the second largest lake in South America, extending into Chile as Lago General Carrera, where the landscape is very beautiful and unspoilt, and the Río Baker which flows from the lake is world-renowned for excellent trout fishing.

Los Antiguos is a sleepy little place, but has a rather pleasant quiet atmosphere, thanks largely to its warm microclimate, and it's certainly a nicer place to spend the night than Chile Chico. It's a rich fruit-growing area with a popular cherry festival in early January, which attracts national *folclore* stars. While you're here, there are two local *chacras* (small farms) worth visiting. You can walk from the main street to **Chacra Don Neno**, where there are strawberries growing and good jam for sale. You'd have to drive, or take a taxi, though, to the idyllic *Chacra el Paraiso*, which sends its perfect cherries to England, and where the charming owners make really exquisite jams and chutney. Recommended. The **parque municipal** at the east end of the town is a pleasant place to walk, along the bank of the river, with bird life to look at, and two blocks down, there's an superb camp site. The small but willing **tourist office**, on main street, Av 11 de Julio 446, has no phone, open 0800-2200 in summer, am only at other times. www.losantiguos-sc.com.ar ▶▶ *For Sleeping, Eating and other listings, see pages 457-461.*

Border with Chile

Transportes VH buses cross the border by the new bridge to the drab village of **Chile Chico**, 8 km west, US$2, 45 mins. The main reason to enter Chile here is either to explore the largely unvisited and lovely southern shore of **Lago Gral Carrera**, or to take the ferry over the lake north to Puerto Ibáñez with bus connections on to **Coyhaique**, the main town for visiting the Carretera Autral. You can also drive to Puerto Ibáñez, via the paved road which goes around the north side of Lago Buenos Aires.

Bajo Caracoles → *Phone code: 0297 Colour map 6, A2 Population: 100*

After hours of spectacular emptiness, even tiny Bajo Caracoles is a relief. It's nothing more than a few houses, facing into the wind, with an expensive grocery store and very expensive fuel. West of Bajo Caracoles, 72 km along Route 39 are **Lago Posadas** and **Lago Pueyrredón**, two beautiful lakes with contrasting blue and turquoise waters and separated by a narrow isthmus. Guanacos and rheas can be seen and there are sites of archaeological interest.

Cueva de las Manos → *Phone code: 02962 Colour map 6, A2*

Situated 47 km northeast of Bajo Caracoles, the canyon of the **Río Pinturas** contains outstanding examples of handprints and cave paintings, estimated to be around 8,000 years old. In the cave's four galleries, shelves in the rock in a stunning canyon, are over 800 paintings of human hands, all but 31 of which are of left hands, as well as images of guanacos and rheas, and various geometrical designs. Painted by the Toldense peoples in red, orange, black, white and green, the pigments were derived from earth and calafate berries, and fixed with a varnish of guanaco fat and urine. They are mysterious, and rather beautiful, however indecipherable. However, the canyon alone is worth seeing, 270 m deep and 480 m wide, with strata of vivid red and green rock, especially beautiful in the early morning or evening light.

From here Route 41 goes 99 km northwest to the **Paso Roballos** border with Chile, and from there 201 km onwards to Cochrane. 92 km south of Bajo Caracoles is the turning off west to Lago Belgrano and Parque Nacional Perito Moreno (see below). 7 km east, along Route 521 is *Hotel Las Horquetas* (very basic) with a café/bar, and 15 km beyond this is the *Tamel Aike* village (police station, water). 'Super' grade fuel is available in most places, but carry extra, since the nearest fuel before Tres Lagos involves a 72 km detour to Gobernador Gregores. From the Parque Moreno junction to Tres Lagos, Route 40 improves considerably. Paso Roballos is 99 km northwest of Bajo Caracoles via (unpaved) Route 41, which runs past Lago Ghio and Lago Columna. On the Chilean side this road continues to Cochrane, Km 177. Though passable in summer, it is often flooded in spring. No public transport.

Route 40 from Bajo Caracoles to El Calafate

This is a bleak stretch of an already empty road. There is no food between Bajo Caracoles and Tres Lagos though water can be obtained from streams and estancias are about every 25 km, except between Río Chico and Lago Cardiel (90 km). South of Bajo Caracoles Route 40 crosses the Pampa del Asador and then, near Las Horquetas, Km 371, swings southeast to follow the Río Chico. At **Tamel Aike**, Km 393, there is a police station and water but little else. At Km 464 Route 25 branches off to **San Julian** via **Gobernador Gregores**, 72 km southeast, where there is fuel and a good mechanic, while Route 40 continues southwest towards Tres Lagos. At Km 531 a road heads west to Lago Cardiel, a very saline lake with no outlet and good salmon fishing.

From Tres Lagos, Route 40 deteriorates rapidly and remains very rugged until after the turnoff to the Fitz Roy sector of Parque Nacional Los Glaciares. 21 km beyond is the bridge over Río La Leona, with delightful **Hotel La Leona** whose café serves good cakes. **Tres Lagos**, at Km 645, is a solitary village with a supermarket and fuel at the junction with Route 288. A road also turns off northwest to Lago San Martín, which straddles the border (the Chilean part is Lago O'Higgins). ▸▸ *For Sleeping, Eating and other listings, see pages 457-461.*

Parque Nacional Perito Moreno

→ *Phone code: 02962 Colour map 6, A2, accessible only by own transport, Nov-Mar*

Situated southwest of Bajo Caracoles on the Chilean border, this is one of the wildest and most remote parks in Argentina. There is good trekking and abundant wildlife among this large, interconnected system of lakes below glaciated peaks, though much of the park is dedicated to scientific study, and inaccessible. Lago Belgrano, in the park's centre, is the biggest in the chain of lakes, a vivid turquoise, contrasting with surrounding mountains streaked with a mass of differing colours; on its shores, you might find ammonite fossils. The park office is in Gobernador Gregores, Avenida San Martín 409, T491477.

Outside the park, but towering over it to the north is **Cerro San Lorenzo** (3,706 m), the highest peak in southern Patagonia. Between the lakes are other peaks, permanently snow-covered, the highest of which is Cerro Herros (2,770 m). The vivid-hued **Sierra Colorada** runs across the northeast of the park: it's erosion of these coloured rocks which has given the lakes their differing colours. At the foot of **Cerro Casa de Piedra** is a network of caves which contain cave paintings, accessible only with a guide.

Vegetation changes with altitude: dense *coiron* grasses and shrubs cling to the windswept steppe, while there are beech forest on higher slopes, *lenga* and *coihue*. Wildlife includes guanacos, foxes and one of the most important surviving populations of the rare huemul. Birds include flamingos, ñandus, steamer ducks, grebes, black-necked swans, Patagonian woodpeckers, eagles and condors. The lakes and rivers are unusual for Argentina in that only native species of fish are found.

Entrance to the park and camping are free, although much of the park is closed to

Several good hikes are possible from here: to the peninsula of Lago Belgrano, 8 km, where there are fine views of Cerro Herros; to the Río Lacteo, 20 km; to **Lago Burmeister**, via Cerro Casa de Piedra, 16 km. There are also longer walks of up to five days. You should inform *guardaparques* before setting out on a hike. 10 km beyond the park entrance, the *guardaparque*'s office has maps, leaflets on walks and wildlife. ▸ *For Sleeping, Eating and other listings, see pages 457-461.*

Listings: Central Patagonia

Sleeping

Camarones *p452*
B **Kau I Keu Kenk**, *Sarmiento y Roca*. Good food, recommended, owner runs trips to penguin colony. There are 2 others, **C**, the one by the power station is not recommended.

Comodoro Rivadavia *p452*
Hotels are either luxurious or basic, with little in between:
B **Lucania Palazzo Hotel**, *Moreno 676, T449 9338, www.lucania-palazzo.com* A stylish and luxurious business hotel, with a lovely airy spacious reception, and superb rooms, many with sea views, good value. A huge American breakfast, and use of the sauna and gym are included. Recommended.
C **Comodoro**, *9 de Julio 770, T447 2300, info@comodorohotel.com.ar* Buffet breakfast included. Larger rooms are worth paying extra for in this slightly unwelcoming place.
D **Hotel Azul**, *Sarmiento 724, T447 4628*. This is a nice quiet old place, with lovely bright rooms, friendly owners, and great panoramic views from the *confitería*, though breakfast is extra.
D **Hotel Victoria**, *Belgrano 585, T446 0725*. An old fashioned city *hostería*, mostly used by workers in the oil industry, but it's friendly, and clean and comfortable enough. Breakfast US$1.20 extra.
D **Rua Marina**, *Belgrano 738, T446877*. All rooms have TV and bath and breakfast is included; the newer rooms are particularly comfortable. Recommended for the friendly welcome. The best budget choice.
E **Hospedaje Cari Hue**, *Belgrano 563, T472946*. Sweet rooms, with separate bathrooms, coming off a central hallway, but

very nice owners who like backpackers! Breakfast is extra. The best budget choice.

Camping
Municipal site, *Rada Tilly, reached by Expreso Rada Tilly bus from town*. Hot showers.
San Carlos, *37 km north on Route 3, T456 0425*.

Colonia Sarmiento *p453*
B **Hostería Los Lagos**, *Roca y Alberdi, T493046*. Good, heating, restaurant.
C **Chacra Labrador**, *10 km from Sarmiento, T0297-489 3329, agna@coopsar.com.ar* This is an excellent place to stay on a small estancia, breakfast included, other meals extra and available for non-residents. English and Dutch spoken, runs tours to petrified forests at good prices, will collect guests from Sarmiento (same price as taxi).

Camping
Municipal site near Río Senguer, 2 km north of centre on Route 243, basic, no shower, US$3 for tent, US$1 per person.

Río Mayo *p454*
D **Covadonga**, *San Martín 575, T420014*. The oldest hotel in town, established for travelling salesmen in the 1940s, and now restored with comfortable rooms, and a decent restaurant. There is a free camp site on northern outskirts near river.

Perito Moreno *p454*
Outside of Perito Moreno, there are two estancias on RN40: 28 km south.
L **Las Toldos**, *60 km south, 7 km off the road to Bajo Caracoles, T432856, 011-4901 0436*. The closest estancia for visiting the Cueva de

🍴 *Phone codes Camarones, Bajo Caracoles, Colonia Sarmiento: 0297; Cueva de las Manos: 02962; Perito Moreno, Los Antiguos: 02963; Comodoro Rivadavia: 02967.*

las Manos, a modest building, but set in wonderfu landscape, the owners, Alicia and Martín Molina organize trips by horse of 4WD to see the cave paintings, as well as to the lakes and the PN Perito Moreno. They also have an albergue. Open Nov-Easter.
L pp **Telken**, T432079, 432303, in Buenos Aires T011-4797 7216, jarinauta @santacruz.com.ar Formerly a sheep station, now aimed at tourism, and providing comfortable accommodation in the farmhouse, wood-lined rooms, and charming simple bedrooms. All meals shared with the warmly welcoming owners, Joan and Reynaldo Nauta, who also offer horse riding. Highly recommended.
D **Austral**, *San Martín 1327*, T42042. Bath and breakfast, and a decent restaurant. The slightly better of the two hotels in town.
D **Belgrano**, *San Martín 1001*, T42019. Also pleasant, with simple rooms.

Camping

Two campsites: **Municipal site** *2 km at Laguna de los Cisnes, T432072*.

Estancias

If you have your own transport, staying on estancias gives a wonderful experience of Patagonia: www.estancias de santacruz.com www.scruz.gov.ar

Los Antiguos *p455*

A **Hostería La Serena**, *outside Los Antiguos at Km 29*. Very comfortable accommodation, excellent home-grown food, organizes fishing and trips in Chilean and Argentine Lake District, open Oct-Jun; further details from Geraldine des Cressonières, T432340.
B **Antigua Patagonia**, *on the lakeside, signposted from Ruta 43, T491038/491055, www.antiguapatagonia.com.ar* Los Antiguos has one really great hotel, and it's really worth a detour. Luxurious rooms with beautiful views on the shore of the lake, with wide open vistas and big skies reflected in its waters. There's also an excellent restaurant. The charming owner Alejandro also arranges small tours to the Cueva de los Manos and nearby Monte Cevallos. Highly recommended.
D **Argentino**, *11 de Julio 850, T491132*. Comfortable rooms, and a decent restaurant.
F pp **Albergue Padilla**, *San Martín 44 (just off main street) T491140*. The town's cheapest

place to stay. Big shared rooms for 4-8 with bathrooms, cosy quincho and garden to sit in, where you can also camp. Very friendly. Recommended. They sell the El Chaltén travel tickets and receive passengers off the bus from El Chaltén.

Camping

Camping Municipal, *T491308, T156 211855*. An outstanding campsite with hot showers, and every other facility, in lovely grounds 2 km from centre, US$1.25 pp.

Bajo Caracoles *p455*

D **Hostería Lagos del Furioso**, *Lago Posadas, on the peninsula between the lakes, reached along Route 39, T02963-490253, T/FBuenos Aires 011 48120959, www.lagos delfurioso.com* Open Mid Oct-Easter. Comfortable accommodation in cabins by the lake shore, offering superb Patagonian cooking with home produced food, and good wines. Also offers horse-riding, trekking and excursions in 4WD vehicles.
D **Hotel Bajo Caracoles**, *T434963*. Very old fashioned, 1920s building, with plain spacious rooms, but a rather insitutional feel, and not quite welcoming. There are meals, and given the wilderness all around you'll probably be glad of a bed.

Cueva de las Manos *p455*

B **Estancia Turística Casa de Piedra**, *75 km south of Perito Moreno on Ruta 40*.
B **Hostería Cueva de Las Manos**, 20 km from the cave, also known as *Los Toldos*, T02963-432856/839 (Buenos Aires T011-4901 0436, F4903 7161). See sleeping in Perito Moreno above.

Camping

G At this campsite, rooms E pp, are also available. A simple and welcoming place, also running excursions to Cueva de las Manos, 10 km by vehicle then 1½-2 hrs' walk, and to nearby volcanoes by car or horse. Ask for **Senor Sabella**, *Av Perón 941, Perito Moreno, T432199*.

Las Horquetas *p456*

D **Hotel Las Horquetas**. A well-run place offering simple but very decent rooms, and good, very reasonable meals.

Gobernador Gregores *p456*
Estancias
There are some superb estancias in this region: tricky to get to without your own transport, but offering an unforgettable experience of Patagonian life.
A pp **La Angostura**, *T02962-452010, F454318, 55 km from Gobernador Gregores*. Horse riding, trekking, fishing, recommended.
A-B pp **Estancia La Maipú**, *T02966-422613, F011-49034967, Lago San Martín*. The Leyenda family offer accommodation at their working sheep farm, with meals, horse riding, trekking and boat excursions on the lake.

Parque Nacional Perito Moreno *p456*
Camping is possible and there are 4 free sites inside the park: **Lago Burmeister**, **Mirador Lago Belgrano**, **Cerro de Vasco**, **Alberto de Agostini**. All have no facilities, no fires. The only accommodation within the park, apart from camping, is
B **Estancia La Oriental**, *T02962-452196, elada@uvc.com.ar* Open Nov-Mar, full board. In a really splendid setting, rooms are comfortable, and there's superb horse riding organized.

❶ Eating

Comodoro Rivadavia *p452*
$$ **Cayo Coco**, *Rivadavia 102*. A welcoming little bistro, with very cheery staff, and excellent pizzas. Recommended. Good value.
$$ **Dionisius**, *9 de Julio y Rivadavia*. A smart and elegant parrilla, popular wth a more sedate clientele, serving excellent set menus for US$5.
$$ **La Barra**, *San Martín 686*. A pleasant bright café for breakfast, very good coffee or a light lunch.
$$ **La Tradición**, *Mitre 675*. Another popular and recommended *parrilla*, for good *asado*.
$$ **Peperoni**, *Rivadavia 348*. A cheerful modern place with good range of home made pastas, filled with exciting things like king crab, as well as serving seafood and *parrilla*. US$4-7, for main dish.
$ **La Barca**, *Belgrano 935*. Welcoming and cheap: *tenedor libre*.
$ **Superquick**, *La Anónima supermarket, San Martín y Güemes*. Good for quick, cheap food.

Perito Moreno *p456*
There's good food at **Pipach**, *next to Hotel Austral*, **Parador Bajo Caracoles**, or pizzas at **Nono's**, on *9 de Julio y Saavedra*. **Rotiseria Chee's I**, is a cheap and cheery place to eat and does takeaways.

Los Antiguos *p455*
$ **La Perla del Lago**, *Fitzroy y Perito Moreno*. The best *parrilla*.

❷ Tour operators

Comodoro Rivadavia *p452*
Aonikenk Viajes, *Rawson 1190, T446 6768, aonikenk@satlink.com Tours to the petrified forests, with 2 hrs at the site*.
Atlas, *Rivadavia 439, T447 5204*.
Monitur, *Brown 521, T447 1062, monitur@amadeusmail.com.ar*

Cueva de las Manos *p455*
From Perito Moreno, the tourist office can advise: T02963-432222.
Itinerario y Travesias, *Albergue Patagonia, Av. San Martín 495, T493088, alpatagonia@infovia.com.ar This bus from El Chalten to Los Antiguos, stops at the caves for two hours on its journey north*.
Senor Sabella, *Av Perón 941, T432199, Perito Moreno*. Trips organized from Perito Moreno. He'll take you to the edge of the canyon, and it's a spectacular 2-hour walk from here to the caves, alongside the river winding through the green base of the valley.
Transporte Terrestre Guanacondór, *Juan José Nauto 432079* and **Transporte Lago Posados**, *T432431*. All day tour with option of collecting from Bajo Caracoles or **Ea Los Toldos**, US$30-40. Both operators do the Circuito Grande Comarca Noroeste, one of the highlights of Santa Cruz, taking in some of the province's scenery. From Perito Moreno to Bajo Caracoles, Cueva de los Manos, Lago Posada, Paso Roballos, Monte Cevallos, Los Antiguos.

❸ Transport

Camarones *p452*
Don Otto **buses** from **Trelew**, Mon and Fri, 2½ hrs, returns to **Trelew** same day 1600.

Reserva Natural Cabo Dos Bahías *p452*
There are **buses** Mon, Wed, Fri 0800 from
Trelew, El Nañdu, US$4.20, 2½ hrs, returns
same day 1600.

Comodoro Rivadavia *p452*
Air
Airport, 9 km north. Bus No 6 to airport from
bus terminal, hourly (45 mins), US$0.40. Taxi
to airport, US$3. To **Buenos Aires**,
Aerolíneas Argentinas/Austral. LADE flies
once a week to **Puerto Madryn**, **Esquel**,
Bariloche, and **El Calafate**, among other
towns in **Patagonia**.

Bus
Terminal, T3367305, is conveniently located
in the centre at Pellegrini 730; has luggage
store, good *confitería* upstairs, toilets,
excellent tourist information office
0800-2100, and a few kiosks. Services to
Buenos Aires, 2 daily, 28 hrs, US$45. **Chile**:
To **Coyhaique**, **Santiago**, 35 hrs $155. Etap
Angel Giobbi, US$15, 12 hrs, twice a week.
To **Mendoza** 28 hrs, US$42. Andesmar
T420139. To **Bariloche**, 14 hrs, US$19 (Don
Otto). To **Esquel** (paved road) 8 hrs direct
with ETAP and Don Otto, US$18. In summer
buses usually arrive full; book ahead. To **Río
Gallegos**, Don Otto, Pingüino and TAC daily,
11 hrs, US$9. To **Puerto Madryn**, US$8. To
Trelew, Don Otto 3 daily 4 hrs US$6, several
companies. To **Caleta Olivia**, La Unión
hourly, US$1.50. To **Sarmiento**, US$4, 2½ hrs
at 3 daily. TAC *T444 3376*, Don Otto, *T447
0450*.

Car rental
Patagonia Sur Car, *Rawson 1190, T446 6768*.
Avis, *9 de Julio 687, T/F496382*.

Colonia Sarmiento *p453*
Bus
Overnight services to **Esquel** with Etap
(T454756) daily except Sat; take food for
journey as cafés are expensive. Frequent
buses to **Comodoro Rivadavia**. To **Chile** via
Río Mayo, Giobbi, 0200, 3 weekly; seats are
scarce in Río Mayo.

Bosque Petrificado Víctor
Szlapelis *p453*
Dec to Mar, a combi (minibus) service runs
twice daily, contact the tourist office. A taxi

from Sarmiento to the forests costs around
US$16 (three passengers), including 1 hr
wait. Contact **Sr Juan José Valero**, the
guardaparque, Uruguay 43, T097-4898407, for
guided tours, ask him about camping.

Perito Moreno *p456*
Air
Airport 7 km east out of town, and the only
way to get there is by taxi. LADE, *Av San
Martín 1207, T432055*, flies to **Perito Moreno**
from **Río Gallegos**, **Río Grande**, **Ushuaia**, **El
Calafate** and **Gob Gregores**.

Bus
The terminal is on the edge of town next to
the EG3 service station, T432072. To
Comodoro Rivadavia, with La Union 6hrs
US$12. If crossing from Chile at **Los
Antiguos**, there are 2 buses daily in summer,
1hr, US$2, La Union, T432133. Two
companies run to **El Chaltén**, with Chalten
Travel even days 1000, and Itinerarios y
Travesias other days at 1800, US$30. It's a14
hr, 582 km journey over bleak emptiness.
Northbound buses with *Itinerarios y Travesias*
stop at the Cueva de los Manos for a couple
of hours at dawn, and while it's a shame to
miss the ride in daylight, it's a great way to
see the caves.

Río Mayo *p453*
Bus
Giobbi buses from Comodoro Rivadavia to
Coyhaique, **Chile**, pass through Río Mayo 3
times a week.

Los Antiguos *p455*
Bus
To **Comodoro Rivadavia**, US$9, Co-op
Sportman, from near *Hotel Argentino*, daily,
7½ hrs, via Perito Moreno and Caleta Olivia.
To **El Chaltén** and **El Calafate** via Perito
Moreno, Chaltén Travel every even day,
US$40, booked through **Albergue Padilla**,
San Martín 44 Sur, T491140. Itinerarios y
Travesias, run buses along the route every
odd day, tickets in **El Chalten**, *Perito Moreno
152, T493088*, **Albergue Patagonia**, *Av San
Martín 495 T02962-493088, alpatagonia@
infovia.com.ar* To **Chile**, La Union buses to
Chile Chico, 8 km west, US$1, 45 mins.

Cueva de las Manos *p455*
Access is via an unpaved road which branches east off Route 40 3 km north of Bajo Caracoles. US$1.50, under 12 free. A *guardaparque* living at the site gives helpful information. The minibus *Itinerarios y Travesias* from **El Chaltén** to **Los Antiguos** stops here in the early morning for a couple of hours. See El Chaltén transport, page 478, for details.

Parque Nacional Perito Moreno *p456*
There is no transport into the park but it may be possible to get a lift with estancia workers from **Hotel Las Horquetas**, www.parquesnacionales.com also has information.

ⓘ Directory

Comodoro Rivadavia *p452*
Airline offices Aerolineas Argentinas, *9 de Julio 870*, *T444 0050*. LADE, *Rivadavia 360*, *T447 6565*. **Banks** Many ATMs along San Martín: Banco de la Nación, *San Martín 102*, Banco del Chubut, *San Martín 833*. Change money at **Thaler**, *San Martín 270*, Mon-Sat 1000-1300, or at weekends **ETAP** in bus terminal. **Communications** Post office *San Martín y Moreno*. **Locutorio/internet**, *Rivadavia 201*, and along San Martín at Nos 131, 394, 808, 263 and 699. **Consulates** Belgium, *Rivadavia 283*. Chile, *Sarmiento 936*. Italy, *Belgrano 1053*.

Comodoro Rivadavia to Río Gallegos

This southern stretch of the Atlantic coastline is extraordinarily rich in marine life, which you can enjoy in a number of locations with decent services and accommodation. Puerto Deseado, Puerto San Julian, Monte Leon, and on the last spit of land before Tierra del Fuego, Cabo Vírgines. The southernmost town, Río Gallegos, is a pleasant place, with good accommodation, and tours offered.

Caleta Olivia → *Phone code: 0297 Colour map 5, C4 Population: 13,000*
Caleta Olivia lies on the Bahía San Jorge 74 km south of Comodoro Rivadavia. Founded in 1901, it became the centre for exporting wool from the estancias of Santa Cruz. It boomed with the discovery of oil in 1944, but has suffered since the petroleum industy was privatised, and is now a rather sad place. However, there's a lovely 70 km stretch of pebbly beach, popular with locals for bathing, and lots of fishing nearby. There's an ATM at Banco del Chubut, on San Martín, and tourist information at Güemes and San Martín, T485 0988, ask for extension 476.

At Pico Truncado, some 50 km southwest, there's the gas field which feeds the pipeline to Buenos Aires, and an enterprising art project, **Ciudad Sonora** ⓘ *www.ciudadsonora.com.ar* *There's a daily bus service from Caleta Oliva, and nearby Pico Troncado has a few simple hotels, a campsite, and tourist information T499 2202.* In a spectacular open setting, the wind sings through structures made of metal and marble, producing strange and eerie sounds. Quite magical. ▸ *For Sleeping, Eating and other listings, see pages 465-469.*

Monumento Natural Bosques Petrificados
Extending over 10,000 ha in a bizarre, wind-wracked landscape surrounding the **Laguna Grande** ⓘ *open 1000-1800, no charge but donations accepted, access by Route 49 which branches off 86 km south of Fitz Roy*, this park contains much older petrified trees than the forests further north around Sarmiento. The trunks, mainly of giant araucaria trees, are up to 35 m long and 150 cm in diameter, were petrified in the

Jurassic period 140 million years ago by intense volcanic activity in the Andes cordillera which covered the area in ash. The place is more eerie than beautiful, but it does exert a strange fascination, especially when you consider that the fossils of marine animals that you see on the site are a mere 40 million years old, belonging to a sea which covered the land long after the trees had turned to stone. There is a small visitor centre and a well documented 1 km nature walk. Please do not remove souvenirs.

Puerto Deseado → *Phone code: 0297 Colour map 6, A4 Population: 7,100*

Puerto Deseado is a pleasant fishing port on the estuary of the Río Deseado, which drains, strangely, into the Lago Buenos Aires in the west. It's a stunning stretch of coastline, and the estuary has a wonderful nature reserve, Ría Deseado, with Magellanic penguins and several species of cormorants among its inhabitants; as well as being the breeding grounds of Commerson's dolphin. Within reach are more reserves, protecting sea lions and penguins. Outside the former railway station, a rather fine old building, in vaguely English medieval style, is the **Vagón Histórico** ⓘ *San Martín 1525, T487 0220, T156 234351, turismo@pdeseado.com.ar, www.scruz.gov.ar*, an 1898 carriage now used as the tourist office.

The **Reserva Natural Ría Deseado**, the submerged estuary (*ría*) of the Río Deseado, 42 km long, is an important nature reserve, and a stunning area to visit. Among many varieties of seabird, there's a colony of Magellanic penguins, and the crumbling chalky cliffs, mauve and ochre, splattered with guano, are home to four species of cormorants including the unique red-legged cormorant, most appealing with their smart dinner-jacketed appearance. These birds nest from October to April in four islands off the shores. The reserve is also the breeding grounds of Commerson's dolphins, beautiful creatures, who frolic playfully around your boat. Excellent boat tours, run by *Darwin Expediciones*, and *Los Vikingos*, see Tour Operators below, run straight from the town's pier, lasting about 2 hrs, and are best in early morning or late evening. There are several other nature reserves within easy reach, all offering good places to walk, if you have transport to take you closer:

North of Puerto Deseado, some 90 km on the northern shore of the peninsula, is **Cabo Blanco**, the site of the largest fur seal colony in Patagonia. It's another magnificent area, a rocky peninsula bursting out from flat lands, with one of the oldest lighthouses on the coast perched on top, and thousands of seals perched on the rocks below. The breeding season is December to January. A little further west, you should also visit **Reserva Cañadón de Duraznillo** in the estancia of La Madrugada. Here you'll see lots of guanacos, ñandues, foxes and birds, as well as the largest seal colony in the province on spectacular unspoilt beaches. The estancia is a great place to visit or stay, see sleeping below, T431081.

South of Puerto Deseado are two more reserves, at **Isla Pingüino**, an offshore island with a colony of Magellanic penguins, as well as cormorants and steamer ducks, and the **Reserva Natural Bahía Laura**, an uninhabited bay where black-necked cormorants, ducks and other seabirds can be found in abundance. Isla Pingüino is an offshore island, reached by boat, and Bahía Laura, nearby is 155 km south along ripio and dirt roads. *Darwin Expediciones*, and *Los Vikingos*, both run tours.

The **Gruta de Lourdes**, 24 km west, is a cave which attracts pilgrims to see the Virgen de Lourdes. Further south along the same road is the **Cañadon del Puerto**, a mirador offering fine views over the estuary. ▸▸ *For Sleeping, Eating and other listings, see pages 465-469.*

Puerto San Julián → *Phone code: 02962 Colour map 6, A4 Population: 5,300*

The quiet port town of Puerto San Julián, lying on the Bahía San Julian 268 km south of Fitzroy, is the best place for breaking the 834 km run from Comodoro Rivadavia to Río Gallegos. It has a fascinating history, although little of it is in evidence today. The first

Mass in Argentina was held here in 1520 after the Portuguese explorer Magellan had executed a member of his mutinous crew. Then in 1578, Francis Drake also put in here to behead Thomas Doughty, after amiably dining with him. There's plenty of wildlife to be seen in the area, and a paradise of marine life in the coastal Reserva San Julián, all very accessible from the town.

Sights After the 16th-century visitors, there was an attempt to found a colony here in 1780 – Floridablanca, which failed due to scurvy. The current town was founded in 1901 on a peninsula overlooking a fine natural harbour, as a port to serve the sheep estancias of this part of Santa Cruz. There's a little regional museum, **Museo Regional at Rivadavia and Vieytes**, which houses the amazingly well preserved dinosaur footprint found in the town. There are superb tours offered to see the wildlife in the Reserva, which you can ask about at the **tourist office** ① *Av Costanera y 9 de Julio, or San Martín 1126, T454396, centur@uvc.com.ar, www.scruz.gov.ar*

The **Reserva San Julian**, on the shores of Bahía San Julian, includes the islands **Banco Cormorán** and **Banco Justicia**, (thought to be the site of the 16th-century executions, where there is a colony of Magellanic penguins and where there are nesting areas for several species of cormorants and other birds. You're also very likely to spot Commerson's dolphins. It's a lovely location, and the concentration of marine life is stunning. Highly recommended. There are excellent zodiac boat trips, lasting 90 minutes, run by *Excursiones Pinocho*, Almirante Brown 739, T452856, nonois@sanjulian.com.ar Best to visit in December to see dolphins and cormorants, though there's plenty to see from December to April. **Cabo Curiosa**, 15 km north, has fine beaches: there are 30 km of spectacular coastline, and it's a popular bathing place for the whole of the region. You can also visit the ruins of **Florida Blanca**, 10 km west, the site of the failed colony founded in 1870 by Antonio Viedma. It's certainly worth visiting **Estancia La María**, 150 km west, with one of the main archaeological sites in Patagonia. A huge canyon with 87 caves of paintings including human hands and guanacos, 4,000-12,000 years old. The estancia offers transport and accommodation (see below). Highly recommended. Contact Fernando Behm, Saavedra 1168, T452328. ▸▸ *For Sleeping, Eating and other listings, see pages 465-469.*

Piedrabuena → *Phone code: 02962 Colour map 6, B3 Population: 3,300*

Known officially as Comandante Luís Piedrabuena, this quiet town is named after the the famous Argentine explorer and sailor, Piedra Buena, who built his home on Isla Pavón, an island in the river Santa Cruz, in 1859. On this small mound in the deep emerald green fast-flowing river you can visit Casa Histórica Luis Piedra Buena, a reconstruction of the original building where he carried on a peaceful trade with local indigenous groups. However, the island has become most popular as a weekend resort for those fishing steelhead trout. It's a world-renowned fishing spot, and there's a smart 4-star *hostería* as well as an attractive campsite to cater for anglers and their families, on weekend breaks. See sleeping below. In March there's a national trout festival. Piedrabuena is a good base for exploring the (soon to be) **Parque Nacional Monte León**, which protects 40 km of coastline and steppe, 30 km south; see below.

Parque Nacional Monte León
→ *www.parquesnacionales.gov.ar www.vidasilvestre.org.ar*

Soon to gain National Park status, Monte León is a beautiful stretch of steppe and shore, south of Piedrabuena. It includes 40 km of coastline, where there are many species of seabirds, and colonies of penguins and sea lions in its many caves and little bays, as well as the tiny island Monte León, an important breeding area for cormorants and terns. It's owned by North American millionaire Douglas Tompkins, and looked after by the organization *Vida Silvestre*, but so far access is difficult, along 23 km of poor *ripio* road which branches off Route 3, 36 km south of Piedrabuena. But your efforts to get here will be rewarded by wonderful walks along wide isolated beaches with extraordinary rock formations, and cliffs riven with vast caverns, fabulous at low tide. Improved access is one part of the plan for the national park, which will also include turning the old shearing shed into a visitor centre. The old house at the heart of the estancia has been converted to a hostería. The best way to enjoy the park in comfort, is to stay at the beautifully modernized traditional **Estancia Monte León** ① *on RN3, contact info@estancias desantacruz.com for reservations, open Nov-Apr,* which has four impeccably tasteful rooms, all decorated with Tompkins' considerable style.

Río Gallegos → *Phone code: 02966 Colour map 6, B3 Population: 75,000*

The capital of Santa Cruz province lies on the estuary of the Río Gallegos, the river famous for its excellent brown trout fishing. It's a pleasant airy town, founded in 1885 as a centre for the trade in wool and sheepskins, and is by far the most appealing of the main centres on Patagonia's east coast. It receives fewer visitors since the airport opened at El Calafate, but you may well come here to change buses, and could visit the penguin reserve at Cabo Vírgenes some 130 km south, or Monte León 210 km north. The town itself has a couple of museums, and boasts a few smart shops and restaurants.

Ins and outs → *Río Gallegos is pronounced rio ga-shay-gos*
Getting there Flights arrive at the airport from Buenos Aires, 10 km from centre, Ushuaia and Río Grande, as well as the LADE flights connecting all major Patagonian towns. Take a taxi for US$2.50. The bus terminal is inconveniently 3 km from the centre, at the corner of Route 3 and Av Eva Perón. Buses 1 and 12 will take you into town, or take a taxi for US$1.

Río Gallegos

Sleeping 🛏		Eating 🍴	
Apart Hotel Austral 1	Nevada 5	Buena Vista 1	El Horreo 4
Comercio 2	París 6	Confitería Díaz 2	La Vieja Esquina 5
Covadonga 3	Santa Cruz 7	El Club Británico 7	Puesto Molino 6
Croacia 4		El Dragón 3	

open Mon-Fri 0900-2100, Sat 1000-2000, Sun 1000-1500, 1600-2000. An excellent and well-organized office with information for the whole province. The staff are extremely helpful, speak English and have a list of estancias in Santa Cruz. They'll also phone round hotels for you. Also at the airport and a small desk at bus terminal, T442159.

Sights

The tidy, leafy Plaza San Martín, two blocks south of the main street, Avenida Roca, has an interesting collection of trees, many planted by the early pioneers, and a diminutive corrugated iron cathedral, with a wood-panelled ceiling in the chancel and stained glass windows. The best of the town's museums is the small **Museo de los Pioneros** ⓘ *Elcano y Alberdi, open daily 1000-2000, free.* In a house built in England and shipped here in 1890, there are interesting photographs and artefacts telling the story of the first Scottish settlers, who came here in 1884 from the Falklands/Malvinas Islands, by government grants of land. There's an interesting tour given by the English-speaking owner, a descendent of the Scottish pioneers, and great photos of those first sheep-farming settlers. There's art work by local artists at **Museo de Arte Eduardo Minichelli** ⓘ *Maipú 13, Mon-Fri 0800-1900, Sat-Sun and holidays 1500-1900 (closed Jan/Feb).* There's **Museo Regional Provincial Manuel José Molina** ⓘ *Av San Martín y Ramón y Cajal 51, Mon-Fri 1000-1800 1100-1900,* in the Complejo Cultural Santa Cruz, dull rocks and fossils and a couple of dusty dinosaur skeletons. More stimulating, **Museo Malvinas Argentinas** ⓘ *Pasteur 74, open Mon and Thu 1300-1800, Tue, Wed, Fri 1300-1800, third Sun in the month 1530-1830,* aims to inform visitors, with the historical and geographical reasons, why the Malvinas are Argentine. Also a library and video archive.

Around Río Gallegos

Laguna Azul, 62 km south near the Monte Aymond border crossing, is nothing more than a perfect royal blue lagoon in the crater of an extinct volcano. But it does have a certain atmosphere, set in arid lunar landscape, and is a good place for a walk. Take a tour, or get off the bus along Route 3, which stops on the main road.

 Reserva Provincial Cabo Vírgenes, 134 km south, is a nature reserve protecting the second largest colony of Magellanic penguins in Patagonia. There's an informative self guided walk to see their nests amongst the *calafate* and fragrant *mata verde* bushes. It's good to visit from November, when chicks are born, with nests under every bush, to January. Fascinating for anyone; wonderful for children. US$2.30. You can climb the **Cabo Vírgenes lighthouse** (owned by the Argentine Navy) for wonderful views. There's a *confitería* close by for snacks and souvenirs. US$2. Branch off Route 3 onto Route 1 (unpaved), 15 km south of Río Gallegos, and from here it's 119km, 3½ hrs. South of Cabo Vírgenes are the ruins of **Nombre de Jesús**, one of the two settlements founded by Pedro Sarmiento de Gamboa in 1584 and where, tragically, all its settlers died.

 Estancia Monte Dinero, 13 km north of Cabo Vírgenes, is a wonderful base for visiting the reserve, a working sheep farm, where the English-speaking Fenton family offers accommodation, food and excursions; all excellent.

Listings: Comodoro Rivadavia to Río Gallegos

 Sleeping

Caleta Olivia *p461*
C pp **Robert**, *San Martín 2152, T485 1452, hrobert@mcolivia.com.ar* The most comfortable option in town.

D **Grand**, *Mosconi y Chubut, T485 1393.*

Camping
Municipal campsite, *T485 0999, ext 476.*
Hot showers near beach, US$3 pp.

C **Isla Chaffers**, *San Martín y Mariano Moreno, T487 2246, www.islachaffers.wm.com.ar* The town's best, modern and central.
C **Los Acantilados**, *Pueyrredón y España, T487 2167, www.pdeseado.com .ar/acantour* Beautifully-located hotel, popular with anglers, comfortable rooms with bathrooms, good breakfast.

Camping
Camping Municipal, *on the seafront, T156 252890.*
Camping Cañadon Jiminez, 4 km away on RN 281, T487 2135, 156 248602.

Estancias
A **La Madrugada**, *situated on the Atlantic coast, 120 km from Puerto Deseado, reached from the RN 281 to km 79, then RN68, T0297-155 94123, T011-537 155 55, walker@ caminosturismo.com.ar* Splendid views, and plenty of places to spot wildlife from the estancia itself, good Patagonian home cooking, and comfortable accommodation. The owners also arrange excursions to sea lion colony and cormorant nesting area, English spoken, recommended.

Monumento Natural Bosques Petrificados *p461*
There are no services, no water source anywhere close by, and no accommodation in the area, apart from camping at **Estancia la Paloma**, *25 km away*, T02967-443503. No camping is allowed near the park.

Puerto San Julián *p462*
B **Bahía**, *San Martín 1075, T453144, nico@sanjulian.com.ar* Modern and comfortable rooms, good value.
B **Res Sada**, *San Martín 1112, T452013.* Simple accommodation, on a busy road.
C **Municipal**, *25 de Mayo 917, T452300.* Attractive rooms, well-run, good value, no restaurant.

Camping
Municipal campsite, *Magellanes 650 y M Moreno*, T452806. US$2.00 per site plus US$1.00pp, recommended, all facilities.

Estancias
B **Estancia La María**, *150 km west, contact Fernando Behm, Saavedra 1163, T452328.* Simple accommodation in a modern house, with amazing cave paintings. The owers also organize trips to see marine and birdlife.

Piedrabuena *p463*
A-B **ACA Motel**, *T47145.* Simple, functional but good, warm and nice food.
A-B **Hostería El Alamo**, *Lavalle 08, T47249.* Quiet, breakfast extra. Recommended.
A-B **Hostería Municipal Isla Pavon**, Isla Pavón,*T02966 156 38380.* Luxurious 4-star catering to fishermen of steelhead trout.
C **Res Internacional**, *Ibáñez 99, T47197.* Recommended.

Camping
Sites south of town on Route 3; also on Isla Pavón.

Río Gallegos *p464, map p464*
Most hotels are situated within a few blocks of the main street, Av Roca, running north west to south east. Do not confuse the street Comodoro Rivadavia with (nearby) Bernardino Rivadavia.
C **Apart Hotel Austral**, *Roca 1505, T/F434314, www.apartaustral.com.ar* A smart newly built apart hotel, with bright rooms, with attractive sunny décor, and very good value, particularly the superior duplexes. The kitchen facilities are a bit basic, but certainly adequate for a couple of nights. Breakfast US$1.50 extra.
C **Comercio**, *Roca 1302, T422458, F422172, hotelcomercio@informacionrgl.com.ar* Good value, nicely designed comfortable rooms with bathrooms, and breakfast included. There is an attractive cheap *confitería* on the street.
C **Croacia**, *Urquiza 431, T421218.* Cheaper, and one of the best reasonably priced places, with comfortable beds, bright spotless rooms with bath, huge breakfasts, and helpful owners. Recommended.
C **Santa Cruz**, *Roca 701, T420601, www.adv ance.com.ar/usuarios/htlscruz* This modern city-style hotel is excellent value. Go for the slightly pricier, spacious new rooms with

excellent bathrooms and full buffet breakfast included. Highly recommended.

D **Covadonga**, *Roca 1244, T420190.* Attractive old 1930s building, the basic rooms have bath and TV, and come off a long corridor to a courtyard. Breakfast is included, and though rooms are small, it's all clean and well maintained.

D **Nevada**, *Zapiola 480, T435790.* A good budget option, with clean, simple spacious rooms, nice beds and good bathrooms, and welcoming owners.

D **París**, *Roca 1040, T420111.* Fairly simple rooms with bath, set back from the street, a good value choice, though breakfast is extra.

Estancias

A **Hill Station**, *63 km north of Río Gallegos.* An estancia with 120 years of history, run by decendents of the founder, William Halliday. A sheep farm, also breeding criollo horses, this offers wonderful horse riding to see flora and fauna of the coast, and simple accommodation.

A **Monte Dinero**, *near Cabo Vírgines, T428922, www.montedinero.com.ar* On this working sheep farm accommodation is comfortable. The house is lined with wood rescued from ships wrecked off the coast, and the food is delicious and home grown. They'll take you on a tour of the reserve, and give you an impressive demonstration of the incredible prowess of their sheep dogs. Highly recommended.

Camping

Camping ATSA, *Route 3, en route to bus terminal, T420301.* US$2.50 pp plus US$0.50 for tent.

Chacra Daniel, *Paraje Río Chico, 3.5 km from town, T423970.* US$4 pp per day, is also recommended, with parrilla and full facilities.

Club Pescazaike, *Paraje Güer Aike, T421803, some 30 km west of town on Route 3.* Well equipped, and an attractive place US$2 pp per day, also *quincho* and restaurant.

● Eating

Puerto Deseado *p462*
$ **El Pingüino**, *Piedrabuena 958.* Established *parrilla* which serves fabulous rice pudding.
$ **Puerto Cristal**, *Espana 1698.* Panoramic views of the port, a great place for

Patagonian lamb and *parrilla*.

Puerto San Julián *p462*
$ **El Muelle Viejo**, *Mitre 1.* Good seafood on this seafront restaurant. The *pejerrey* is recommended. Also bars and tearooms.
$ **Rural**, *Ameghino y Vieytes.* Good, but not before 2100.
$ **Sportsman**, *Mitre y 25 de Mayo.* Excellent value.

Río Gallegos *p464, map p464*
There are lots of good places to eat here, many serving excellent seafood, and some smart new inexpensive restaurants.
$ **Buena Vista**, *Sarmiento y Gob Lista, T444114.* Most chic, and not expensive. Near the river, with open views across the Plaza de la Republica, this has an imaginative menu, and is reasonably priced.
$ **El Club Britanico**, *Roca 935.* Doing its best to look like a London gentleman's club, though lacking in atmosphere, serves cheap set lunches.
$ **El Dragon**, *9 de Julio 29.* Cheap and varied *tenedor libre*.
$ **El Horreo**, *Roca 863.* Next door to *Puesto Molino.* A more sophisticated option, rather like a bistro in feel, serving delicious lamb dishes and good salads. Recommended.
$ **Puesto Molino**, *Roca 862, opposite the tourist office.* A relaxed airy place, its design inspired by life on estancias, with bold paintings, wooden tables and excellent pizzas (US$5 for two) and *parrilla* (US$10 for two). Recommended.
$ **La Vieja Esquina**, *Sarfield 90.* For pizzas and pastas.

☺ Sport

Río Gallegos *p464, map p464*
Fishing www.scruz.gov.ar/pesca The southern fishing zone includes the Ríos Gallegos, Grande, Fuego, Ewan, San Pablo and Lago Fagnano, near Ushuaia. It is famous for runs of sea trout. Ask the tourist office for fishing guides, and information on permits.

♪ Tour operators

Monumento Natural Bosques Petrificados *p461*
The site can be visited in a day trip with a

tour from San Julián, or from Puerto Deseado with **Los Vikingos**, *Estrada 1275, T0297-4870020, vikingo@puertodeseado.com.ar*

Puerto Deseado *p462*
Darwin Expediciones, *España 2601, T156 247554, www.darwin expediciones. com* and **Los Vikingos**, *Estrada 1275, T156 245141/4870020, vikingo@puertodeseado.com.ar*   Both offer excursions by boat to Río Deseado reserve, and Reserva Provincial Isla Pinguino.

Puerto San Julián *p462*
Tur Aike Turismo, *Av San Martín 446, T452086.*

Río Gallegos *p464*
Macatobiano Turismo, *Roca 908, T/F422466, macatobiano@macatobiano.com* Air tickets and tours to Pingüinero Cabo Vírgenes (see above), all day trip US$15, also to the mystical Laguna Azul, a half-day trip to this beautiful lake in a volcanic crater, and to Estancia Monte León, as well as tickets to El Calafate and Ushuaia.
Tur Aike Turismo, *Zapiola 63, T422436.*
Transpatagonia Expedicion, *at the airport, T422504, 442013, transpatagonia @infovia.com.ar*

Around Río Gallegos *p465*
Day tours to Estancia Monte Dinero and Reserva Provincial Cabo Vírgines, from Río Gallegos are run by: **Tur Aike Turismo**, *Zapiola 63, T422436*, **Macatobiano Turismo**, *Roca 908, T422466, escaltur@ internet.siscotel.com* (recommended), and **Transpatagonia Expedicion**, *Av San Martín 661, Local 10, T422504 transpatagonia@ infovia.com.ar*, US$30 including trip to Estancia Monte Dinero with lunch.

⊙ Transport

Caleta Olivia *p461*
Bus
To **Río Gallegos**, Pingüino, US$8, overnight. Many buses to **Comodoro Rivadavia**, 1 hr, US$1.70 and 3 daily to **Pto Deseado**, US$5. To **El Calafate**, 5 hrs; to **Perito Moreno** and **Los Antiguos**, 5 hrs, US$7, daily. Bus company La Union, terminal: T155 925898/

485 1134. **El Pingüino**, T485 2929, **TAC** T485 3481.

Puerto Deseado *p462*
Sportman, La Unión bus companies, *at terminal T155 928598*, daily to **Caleta Olivia**, US$5.

Puerto San Julián *p462*
Air
Weekly services (Mon) with LADE to **Santa Cruz**, **Río Gallegos**, **El Calafate**, **Puerto Deseado**, **Gob Gregores**, **Comodoro Rivadavia**, and **Río Turbio**. LADE, *San Martín 1552, T452137.*

Bus
To **Buenos Aires**, Transportadora Patagónica, T452072, Pingüino, T452425. To **Río Gallegos**, Pingüino, 6 hrs, US$7. To **Mendoza**, US$50, Andesmar, T454403.

Río Gallegos *p464, map p464*
Air
Airport 10 km from centre. Taxi (*remise*) to/from town US$2.50; Río Gallegos used to be the nearest airport to El Calafate, but there are less flights now that Lago Viedma airport has opened there. However, there are still regular flights to/from **Buenos Aires**, **Ushuaia** and **Río Grande** direct with Aerolíneas Argentinas. LADE to **Río Turbio** and **El Calafate**, twice a week, to **Ushuaia** and **Comodoro Rivadavia** once a week. LADE flights should be booked as far in advance as possible. The Ladeco service from **Punta Arenas** to **Port Stanley** on the **Falkland Islands/Islas Malvinas** stops once a month in either direction. Both Pingüino and Interlagos can arrange packages to **Calafate** including accommodation and trip to Moreno glacier from their offices at the airport.

Bus
Terminal at corner of Route 3 and Av Eva Perón, 3 km from centre (crowded, no left luggage, but a *confitería*, toilets, kiosks); taxi to centre US$1.00 also bus , Nos 1 and 12 from posted stops around town to/from terminal.

   To **El Calafate** 4-5 hrs, US$9, Taqsa and Interlagos, To **Los Antiguos**, Sportman daily at 2100, US$20. To **Comodoro Rivadavia**, Pingüino, Don Otto and TAC, 10 hrs, US$10.

For **Bariloche**, Transportadora Patagonica, daily at 2130. To **Buenos Aires**, 33 hrs, several daily, Pingüino, Don Otto, TAC, US$35.00 . To **Río Grande** and **Ushuaia**, Tecni Austral, Tue, Thu Sat, at 1000, US$18-23, 8-10 hrs. To **Chile**: to **Puerto Natales**, Pingüino, Sat, 7 hrs, US$7. Bus-Sur Tue and Thu 1700. To **Punta Arenas**, Pingüino and others, US$11 daily.

Car
Taking a car to Chile Make sure your car papers are in order (go first to tourist office for necessary documents, then to the customs office at the port, at the end of San Martín, very uncomplicated). Let the hire company know, and allow 24 hrs to get the appropriate papers. The car's windows should be etched with the licence plate number. It is essential to book car rental in advance in high season. **Localiza**, *Sarmiento 237, T424417*; **Cristina**, *Libertad 123, T425709*, **Taxi Centenario**, *Maipú 285, T422320*.

Taxis
Hiring a taxi for group excursions may the same price as a tour bus. Taxi ranks plentiful, rates controlled, *remise* slightly cheaper.

Directory

Puerto San Julián *p462*
Banks Banco de la Nación, *Mitre y Belgrano*, and Banco de la Provincia de Santa Cruz, *San Martín y Moreno*.
Communications Post office *Belgrano y San Martín*.

Río Gallegos *p464, map p464*
Airline offices Aerolíneas Argentinas, *San Martín 545, T422020/0810-222 86527*. LADE, *Fagnano 53, T422326*. **Banks** Change TCs here if going to El Calafate, where it is even more difficult. 24-hr ATMs for all major international credit and debit cards all over the centre. Banco Tierra del Fuego, *Roca 831*, changes TCs. Cambio El Pingüino, *Zapiola 469*. Thaler, *San Martín 484*. Both will change Chilean pesos as well as US$. **Communications Internet** J@va cybercafe (next to British Club on Roca); also various *locutorios* offer internet services US$0.60 per hr. **Post Office** *Roca 893 y San Martín*. **Telephone** *Locutorios* all over town. **Consulates** Chile, *Mariano Moreno 136*, Mon-Fri, 0900-1300; tourist cards issued at border.

Parque Nacional Los Glaciares

Of all Argentina's impressive landscapes, the sight of these immense glaciers may stay with you longest. This is the second-largest national park in Argentina, extending along the Chilean border for over 170 km, almost half of it covered by ice fields from which 13 glaciers descend into two great lakes: Lago Argentino in the southeast, and Lago Viedma to the northeast. Two quite different areas of the park can be visited: the spectacular glaciers themselves can be seen from El Calafate, with bus and boat trips to Glaciares Moreno, Upsala and Spegazzini. From El Chaltén, 230 km northwest, there is superb trekking around the dramatic Fitz Roy massif, and ice climbing on glaciers near its summit. The central section, between Lago Argentino and Lago Viedma, is the Ice Cap national reserve, inaccessible to visitors apart from a couple of estancias. East of the ice fields, there's plentiful southern beech forest, but further east still, the land flattens to the typical wind-blasted Patagonian steppe, with sparse vegetation. Bird life is surprisingly prolific, and you'll spot the scarlet headed magallenic woodpecker, black-necked swans, and perhaps even the torrent duck, diving for food in the streams and rivers. Guanacos, grey foxes, skunks and rheas can be seen on the steppe while the rare huemul inhabits the forest.

Ins and outs

Getting there Access from El Calafate (see below). There are regular flights from Buenos Aires to its airport, 20 km east, and buses from Río Gallegos and Puerto

Natales. Access to the park is very straightforward, with regular bus services as well as many tourist excursions, combining bus access with boat trips, walking and even ice trekking on Glaciar Moreno.

Access from El Chaltén This new tourist town lies on the northeastern edge of the park, reached by several buses daily from El Calafate and Río Gallegos, or from the north along the Route 40 from Los Antiguos. From El Chaltén you can walk directly into the park, with a well established network of trails leading to summits, lakes and

Parque Nacional Los Glaciares

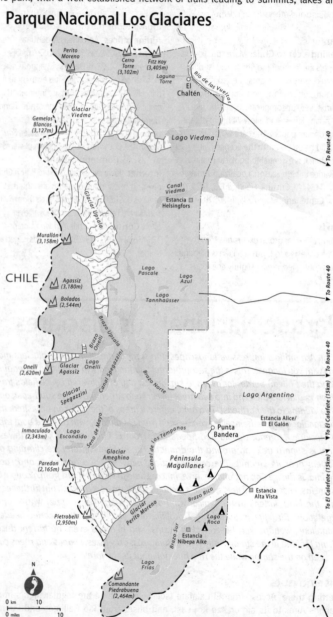

glaciers, with many campsites. The town itself offers a range of expensive accommodation, from hostels to luxury hotels, there are several estancias within reach, and campsites within this southern area of the park, though the tourist infrastructure is less established here.

Best time to visit Although this part of Patagonia is generally cold, there is a milder microclimate around Lago Viedma and Lago Argentina, which means that summers can be reasonably pleasant, with average summer temperatures between 5 and 22°C, though strong winds blow constantly at the foot of the Cordillera. Rainfall on the Hielo Sur, up to 5000 mm anually, falls mainly as snow. In the forested area, around 1500 mm of rain falls annually, mainly between March and late May. In winter, the whole area is inhospitably cold, and most tourist facilities are closed. The best time to visit is between November and April, avoiding January and early February, when Argentines take their holidays, campsites are crowded and accommodation is hard to find.

Tourist information There are helpful tourist offices in both centres: El Calafate's office is in the bus terminal, T491090, www.elcalafate.gov.ar open Oct-Apr daily 0700-2200. At the airport, T491230. The park office (Intendencia) is at Libertador 1302, T491005, open Mon-Fri 0800-1600, www.parquesnacionales.com.ar, apnglaciares@cotecal.com.ar El Chaltén's office is at Güemes 21, T493011, www.elchalten.com An excellent site with accommodation listed, but no email for queries, open 0900-2000 Mon-Fri, Sat/Sun 1300-2000. The park office is across the bridge at the entrance to the town, T493004. Both hand out helpful trekking maps of the area, with paths and campsites marked, giving distances and walking times.

El Calafate → *Phone code: 02902 Colour map 6, B2 Population: 8,000*

El Calafate sits on the south shore of Lago Argentino, a new town existing almost entirely as a tourist centre for visiting the glaciers in the Parque Nacional los Glaciares, 50 km west. From here you can visit Glaciar Perito Moreno by bus and boat, and even go trekking on its surface. Or travel by boat along the western arms of Lago Argentino, between stately floating icebergs, to see Glaciares Spegazzini and Upsala. All are breathtakingly beautiful, an unforgettable part of your trip to Patagonia. The town itself is expensive, and not particularly attractive, and even the growing number of hotels, hostels and *cabañas* can't quite accommodate the hoardes at times in January and February. The town is empty and quiet all winter, but extremely cold, and it's best to come in March or April if you can. ▸▸ *For Sleeping, Eating and other listings, see pages 481-488.*

Ins and outs
Getting there It's easiest to fly to El Calafate, with daily flights from Buenos Aires to its airport, Lago Viedma, 22 km east of town, several daily in summer. You can also fly here from Ushuaia or Puerto Natales in Chile to combine a trip to the glaciers with trekking in Torres del Paine. A minibus service meets all flights, costing US$3, a taxi will cost you US$7. Bus travel is convenient too, with buses from Río Gallegos, and from Ushuaia. There are buses too to Puerto Natales, via Cerro Castillo if you want to get directy to/from Torres del Paine. The bus terminal is centrally located up a steep flight of steps from the main street. More details on services in transport below. There are ATMs and a *locutorio* with internet in the town, and many good hotels and restaurants.

Getting around El Calafate's shops, restaurants and tour operators can mostly be found along its main street, Av del Libertador, running east-west, with hotels lying withing two blocks north and south, with smaller *hosterías* scattered through the newly built residential area sprawling up the hill. There are many estancias nearby, on the way to the national park, and also several campsites. Bus travel and tour trips to the Perito Moreno glaciers are well organized. The cheapest method is with a regular bus service, but tours can be informative, and some include a boat trip. More details in the section on Parque Nacional Los Glaciares, below.

Best time to visit Unbearably busy in January, when you'll have to reserve well ahead for accommodation, marginally better in February, but best of all in December, March and April, when the weather can still be sunny and clear, and there are less crowds. There are couple of festivals worth seeing: people flock to the rural show on 15 Feb, *Lago Argentino* Day, and camp out with live music, dancing and *asados*. There are also displays of horsemanship and *asados* on *Día de la Tradición*, 10 Nov.

Tourist information The tourist office is in the bus terminal, T491090, www.elcalafate.gov.ar It may look disorganized, but the efficient staff speak several languages and have a good map with accommodation shown, as well as helpful information on estancias and tours. Oct-Apr daily 0700-2200. At the airport, T491230. For information on the Parque Nacional Los Glaciares, the park office (*Intendencia*) is at Libertador 1302, T491005. Mon-Fri 0800-1600. www.parquesnacionales.com.ar or email apnglaciares@cotecal.com.ar

Sights

Though El Calafate was founded in 1927, it grew very slowly until the opening of the road to the Perito Moreno glacier in the 1960s, and has expanded rapidly as a tourist

El Calafate

N
0 metres 100
0 yards 100

Sleeping
ACA Hostería El Calafate 1
Albergue Buenos Aires 2
Amado 12
Cabañas Nevis 3

Calafate Hostel 4
Cerro Cristal 6
del Norte 7
El Quijote 8
Hospedaje Alejandra 9
Hospedaje Los
 Dos Pinos 10
Hospedaje Sir Thomas 11
Hostería Ariel 13
Kosten Aike 14
Los Alamos 15

Los Lagos 16
Michelangelo 17
Municipal Campsite 5
Vientos del Sur 18
Youth Hostel
 Albergue del Glaciar 19

Eating
Casablanca 1
El Hornito 3
El Rancho 2

Heladería Aquarela 4
La Cocina 7
La Posta 10
Pura Vida 5
Rick's Café & Mi Viejo 6

Bars & clubs
Shackleton Lounge 8
Tango Sur 9

town since. Many of its hotel owners are new arrivals from Buenos Aires, here to escape the economic stress of the city, and the town is only slowly developing a culture of its own, aside from tourist exploits. Just west of the town centre is Bahía Redonda, a shallow part of Lago Argentino which freezes in winter, when ice-skating and skiing are possible. At the eastern edge of the bay, **Laguna Nimez**, there's a bird reserve where there are flamingos, black-necked swans and ducks, recommended for an hour's stroll either early morning or late afternoon. From the *Intendencia del Parque*, Libertador 1302, follow Calle Bustillo up the new road among cultivated fields and orchards to cross the bridge. Keep heading north: the laguna is signposted. Expert Cecilia Scarafoni, T493196, ecowalks@cotecal.com.ar, leads birdwatching walks, lasting two hours, US$4, Monday to Saturday. There is scope for good hill-walking to the south of the town, while **Cerro Elefante**, west of Calafate on the road to the Moreno glacier is good for rock climbing. ▸▸ *For Sleeping, Eating and other listings, see pages 481-488.*

Around El Calafate

Glaciers For the main excursions to the glaciers, see Parque Nacional Perito Moreno below. El Calafate has a number of other attractions, worth considering if you're here for a few days, and some good places for trekking, horse riding and exploring by 4WD. At **Punta Gualicho**, (or Walichu) on the shores of Lago Argentino, 7 km east of town, there are cave paintings, and though they're rather badly deteriorated, the 30-min walk is worthwhile. There are also excursions by bus or on horseback. 2 hrs, US$16. Walk to the top of the **Cerro Calafate**, behind the town, 2½-3 hrs, for views of the silhouette of the southern end of the Andes, **Bahía Redonda** and Isla Solitaria on Lago Argentino.

Several **estancias** are within reach, offering a day on a working farm, a lunch of superb Patagonian lamb, cooked *asado al palo* (speared on a metal structure over a smouldering open fire), and activities such as trekking, bird watching and horse riding. **Estancia Alice** also known as 'El Galpón', 21 km west, offers walks through a bird sanctuary where 43 species of birds have been identified, displays of sheep shearing and *asado*, in a lovely house with views of Lago Argentino, where you can also stay as a guest (see Sleeping below); English spoken. Horse riding trips to Perito Moreno glacier and Cerro Frias can also be organized. Recommended. Transport arranged, US$40 per person with dinner, US$20 per person without, US$5 per person transport; in Calafate T/F491793; Buenos Aires, T011-4313 0679, elgalpon@estanciaaalice.com.ar

Lago Roca, 40 km southwest, is set in beautiful open landscape, with hills above offering panoramic views, perfect for lots of activities, such as trout and salmon fishing, climbing, walking, and several estancias where you can see farm activities, such as the branding of cattle in summer. There is good camping in a wooded area and a restaurant. At **Estancia Quien Sabe**, strawberries and walnuts are grown, extraordinary so far south, and you can see beehives and sheep shearing, and eat an *asado* lunch, contact Turismo Leutz, leutzturismo.co.ar

Lago Argentino

Glaciar Perito Moreno

The sight of this expanse of ice, like a frozen sea, its waves sculpted by wind and time into beautiful turquoise folds and crevices, is unforgettable. Immense and silent, you'll watch in awe, until suddenly a mighty roar announces the fall of another hunk of ice into the milky turquoise water below. Glaciar Moreno was until recently one of the few in the world that was still advancing. Some 30 km long, it reaches the water at a narrow point in one of the fiords, **Brazo Rico**, opposite Peninsula Magellanes, and here, where it's 5 km across and 60 m high it used to advance across Brazo Rico, blocking the fiord roughly every three years. As the water pressure built up behind it,

66 99 Immense and silent, you'll watch in awe, until suddenly a mighty roar announces the fall of another hunk of ice into the milky turquoise water below...

the ice would break, reopening the channel and sending giant icebergs (*témpanos*) rushing down the appropriately named **Canal de los Témpanos**. This hasn't happened since February 1988, giving concern that global warming may be to blame. Walking on the ice itself is a wonderful way to experience it, climbing up the steep curves of what appear from a distance to be vertical fish flakes, and are in fact huge peaks, with mysterious chasms below, lit by refracted bluish light.

Access There are various ways to approach the glacier. All excursions (and the regular bus service) will take you to the car park where you begin the descent along a series of wooden walkways (*pasarelas*) to see the glacier slightly from above, and then, as you get lower, directly head-on. There are several wide viewing areas, where in summer crowds wait expectantly, cameras poised, for another hunk of ice to fall from the vertical blue walls at the glacier's front into the milky turquoise lake below with a mighty roar. You could also approach the glacier from more of a distance, walking on the tranquil lake shore. From the restaurant, a path leads over big bald rocks carved smooth by ancient glaciers, to see the Perito Moreno glacier through rich *lenga* forest, when it has quite an impact. *Guardaparques* (park rangers) guide an hour-long walk along the lake shore at 1530 and 1730 daily. There are also boat trips which leave constantly during the day to survey the glacier from the water below, giving you a chance to appreciate its magnitude, and its varied sculptural forms. To get closer still, there are guided treks on the ice itself, known as *minitrekking*, where you can walk along those crevices and frozen wave crests in crampons, which are provided. This is possible for anyone with a reasonable level of fitness, and not technically demanding. The glacier is approached by a walk through lovely lenga forest, and there's a place to eat your lunch outside, with wonderful views; but bring your own lunch and water. Tour companies in El Calafate offer all of these, or some in combinations. Details in tour operators below.

Tours From Calafate there are regular buses by *Taqsa* or *Interlagos* to the car park above the walkways. Many agencies in El Calafate also run minibus tours (park entry not included) leaving 0800 and returning 1800, giving you three hours at the glacier, with a return ticket valid if you come back next day, useful for campers (student discount available). *Albergue del Glaciar*'s alternative trips, highly entertaining and informative go out by different route passing the *Estancia Anita* and are highly recommended, full day US$25. Minitrekking is offered by *Hielo y Aventure*, wonderful 2-hour walking trips on the glacier (crampons provided; bring lunch). Taxis, US$45 for four passengers round trip. At the car park facing the glacier is a reasonable restaurant. Out of season, trips to the glacier are difficult to arrange, but you can gather a party and hire a taxi (*remise* taxis T491745/492005).

Boat trips Boat trips on the lake are organized by Fernandez Capbell, Av Libertador 867, T491155, with large boats for up to 60 passengers, known as 'Safari Náutico', US$10 per person, one hour, offering the best views of the glacier.

⁝ Francisco Moreno, El Perito

You can't miss the name of Argentina's favourite as you travel around Patagonia. Francisco Pascasio Moreno (1852-1919) is commemorated by a national park, a town, and a world famous glacier. Moreno, a naturalist and geographer, travelled ceaselessly in Patagonia, exploring areas previously unknown to the authorities in Buenos Aires. At the age of 20, he paid his first visit to Patagonia, travelling up the Río Negro to Lago Nahuel Huapi, along the Río Chubut, and then up the Río Santa Cruz to reach the giant lake which he named Lago Argentino. Expeditions such as these were dangerous: apart form the physical hardships, relations with the indigenous populations were poor. On one expedition, Moreno was seized as a hostage, but escaped on a raft which carried him for 8 days down the Río Limay to safety.

His fame established, Moreno was elected to congress and appointed Director of the Museo de Ciencias Naturales in La Plata. In 1901 he became an expert (*perito*) adviser to the Argentine side in the negotiations to draw the border with Chile. His reward was a grant of lands near Bariloche which he handed over to the state to manage, the initial act in creating the national parks system in Argentina, and an inspiring gesture towards sharing the country's spectacular natural beauty at a time when anyone who could was buying it up as fast as possible. Moreno's remains are buried in a mausoleum on Isla Centinela in Lago Nahuel Huapi.

Upsala Glacier

The fiords at the northwestern end of Lago Argentino are fed by four other glaciers. The largest is the Upsala glacier, named after the Swedish university which commissioned the first survey of this area in 1908, and a stunning expanse of untouched beauty. It's three times the area of the Perito Moreno Glacier, and the longest glacier flowing off the Southern Patagonian icefields. Unusually it ends in two separate frontages, each about 4 km wide and 60 m high, although only the western frontage can be seen from the lake excursion. It can be reached by motor-boat from Punta Bandera on Lago Argentina, 50 km west of Calafate, on a trip that also goes to other, much smaller, glaciers. **Spegazzini**, further south, has a frontage 1½ km wide and 130 m high. In between are **Agassiz** and **Onelli** glaciers, both of which feed into **Lago Onelli**, a quiet and very beautiful lake, full of icebergs of every size and sculpted shape, surrounded by beech forests on one side and ice-covered mountains on the other.

Boat trips The **Upsala Explorer** trip to the Upsala glacier must be recommended, though it's incredibly expensive, ① *US$87-100 (depending on your seat in the boat), including breakfast, snacks, and delicious lunch. The bus leaves from El Calafate at 0700, and takes you to Puerto Bandera, where you take the boat through Brazo Norte to land at Estancia Cristina (also open to paying guests) Bus transfer; extra US$11, and park entry US$2. Book through many agencies.*

The glacier's front is first seen by boat, passing through a lake strewn with icebergs. Then remote Estancia Cristina is visited, on its lonely lakeside, with traditional *asado* lunch and optional horse riding. From here, you're taken in sturdy 4WD vehicles to a point high above the lake, to walk alongside massive rocks polished smooth by the path of glaciers, to see Upsala glacier from above. This is an overwhelmingly beautiful sight, stretching apparently endlessly away from you, with the deep still prussian blue lake below, and all around, rocks the colour of fire. Magnificent. Tour boats usually operate a daily trip to the glaciers; the main company is *Fernández Campbell*, Av

Libertador 867, T491155, US$25. The price includes bus fares and park entry fees, but do take food. The bus departs at 0730 from El Calafate for Punta Bandera, with time allowed for lunch at the restaurant (not included) near the Lago Onelli track. The return bus to El Calafate is at 1930; a long but memorable day.

Around Mount Fitz Roy

The soaring granite towers of Mount Fitz Roy rise up from the smooth baize of the flat steppe, more like a ziggurat than a mountain, surrounded by a consort of jagged snow-clad spires, with a stack of spun cotton cloud hanging constantly above them. **Cerro Fitz Roy** (3,405 m) is one of the most magnificent mountains in the world, towering above the nearby peaks, its polished granite sides too steep for snow to settle. Its Tehuelche name was El Chaltén, ('smoking mountain' or 'volcano'),

The Fitz Roy area

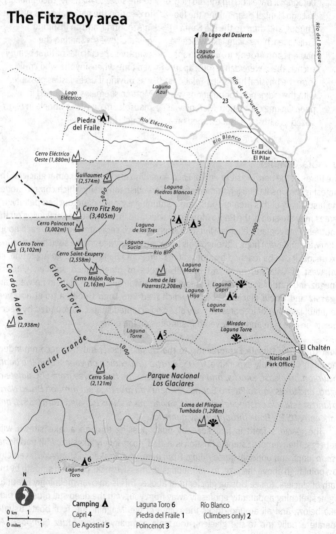

Camping ▲

Capri **4**
De Agostini **5**

Laguna Toro **6**
Piedra del Fraile **1**
Poincenot **3**

Río Blanco
(Climbers only) **2**

perhaps because occasionally at sunrise the pink towers are briefly lit up bright red for a few seconds, the *amanecer de fuego* ('sunrise of fire'). Perito Moreno named the peak after the captain of the Beagle who saw it from afar in 1833, and it was first climbed by a French expedition in 1952. It stands in the northern end of Parque Nacional Los Glaciares, at the western end of Lago Viedma, 230 km north of El Calafate. Around it are **Cerros Torre** (3,128 m), **Poincenot** (3,076 m), and **Saint-Exupery** (2,600 m), in an area of lakes and glaciers that makes marvellous trekking country, every bit as satisfying as Torres del Paine across the border.

Ins and outs

Getting around The base for walking and climbing around Fitz Roy is the modern town of El Chaltén, which has been built right next to the mountains. See below for all details of sleeping and transport in the town. Most paths are very clear and well worn, but a map is essential, even on short walks: the park information centre gives a helpful photocopied maps of treks, but the best is one published by *Zagier and Urruty*, 1992, US$6 (Casilla 94, Sucursal 19, 1419 Buenos Aires, F45725766) and is available in shops in Calafate and Chaltén. For trekking on horseback with guides: *Rodolfo Guerra*, T493020; *El Relincho*, T493007. Do not stray from the paths. Always wear sun screen (factor 30 at least), and be prepared for bad weather.

Park and visitor information The National Park office is across the bridge right at the entrance to the town, T493004. The tourist office is at Güemes 21, T493011, www.el chalten.com Both give trekking maps of the area, with paths and campsites marked, distances and walking times. *guardaparques* can advise on walks, and although you're not required to register, it's a good idea to check with them about the state of the paths and conditions in the mountains. They are friendly, and some speak English.

Best time to visit Walking here is only really viable mid-October to April, with the best months usually March to April when the weather is generally stable and not very cold, and the autumn colours of the beech forest are stunning. Mid-summer, December and January, and spring, September to October, are generally very windy. And in December/January the campsites can be full to bursting, with many walkers on the paths.

▲▲ Hiking

Be warned that the weather changes hourly, so don't wait for a sunny day to go hiking, and be prepared for sudden deterioration in the weather. And don't stray from the paths. These are the most popular walks:

Laguna Torre, (3 hrs each way) After 90 mins you'll come to Mirador Laguna Torre with views of Cerro Torre, and 30mins more along side of lake to busy Camping De Agostini (this used to be called Bridwell), where you have fantastic views of the Cordon Torre.

Laguna de Los Tres (4 hrs each way) Walk up to Camping Capri (2 hrs), with great views of Fitz Roy, then another hour to Camping Poincenot (3 hrs). Just beyond it is Camping Río Blanco, (only for climbers, by arrangement). From Río Blanco you can walk another hour to Laguna de los Tres where you'll get a spectacular view, (not a good walk if it's cloudy). In bad weather, you're better off walking an hour to Piedras Blancas (4 hrs total from El Chalten). You can connect the two views of the two cordons by climbing past Capri (a detour to the side) and taking the signed path to your left, passing two lakes, Laguna Madre and then Laguna Hija, to reach the path that leads to Laguna Torre. From El Chalten to Laguna Torre along this route takes about 7 hrs.

Loma del Pliegue Tumbado (4 hrs each way) Another recommended walk is to this viewpoint where you can see both cordons and Lago Viedma. There's a marked path from the *guardería* (park ranger's office), and this is a good day walk, best in clear weather.

Laguna Toro (6 hrs each way) For more experienced trekkers, a walk to a glacial lake. **Up Río Blanco to Piedra del Fraile** (7 hrs each way) (outside the National Park boundary) This beautiful walk starts at Campamento Río Blanco running north along the Río Blanco and west along the Río Eléctrico via Piedra del Fraile (4 hours) to Lago Eléctrico. At Piedra del Fraile, just outside the park, there are *cabañas* (E per person with hot showers) and campsite, US$5 per person. From here a path leads south, up Cerro Eléctrico Oeste (1,882 m) towards the north face of Fitz Roy, (2 hrs), tough going but with spectacular views. You should take a guide for this last bit. The best day walks are Laguna Capri, and Mirador Laguna Torre, both of which have great views after an hour or so.

Climbing

Base camp for Fitz Roy (3,375 m) is Campamento Río Blanco (see above). Other peaks include Cerro Torre (3,102 m), Torre Egger (2,900 m), Cerro Solo (2,121 m), Poincenot (3,002 m), Guillaumet (2,579 m), Saint-Exupery (2,558 m), Aguja Bífida (2,394 m) and Cordón Adela (2,938 m): most of these are for very experienced climbers. The best time to climb is mid-Feb to end-Mar; Nov-Dec is very windy; Jan is fair; winter is extremely cold. Permits for climbing are available at the national park information office. Guides are available in El Chaltén: ask Sr Guerra about hiring mules to carry equipment. **Fitz Roy Expediciones**, Lionel Terray 212, T02962-493017, www.elchalten.com/fitzroy fitzroyexpediciones@videodata.com.ar, owned by experienced guide Alberto del Castillo, organize trekking and adventure excursions including on the Campo de Hielo Continental, ice climbing schools, horse riding, and fabulous longer trips. You need to be fit, but no technical experience is required; and all equipment is provided. Email with lots of notice to reserve. Highly recommended, English and Italian spoken.

National Park information

Some *guardaparques* speak English, but not all, so this is their general advice to all who go trekking around El Chaltén:

All river water is drinkable. Access is free. Campsites have no services, but all have latrines, apart from Toro. There's no need to register before you leave on walks, and the paths are well marked. But please stick to the centre of the path so as not to make it any bigger and walk in single file (this means at times that you're walking in a rut). The park's *Centro de informes* will give you a good photocopied map which recommends lots of walks, times for walking and tells you where campsites are. Times given on their sheet, and our map, are for walking one way only. And as you leave El Chaltén, please don't let the dogs follow you, as they frighten the *huemules* (rare wild deer, an endangered species). Don't bathe in rivers and lakes, and take water away from source to wash. Don't go to the toilet near water sources, and take all rubbish down the mountain with you. A gas/alcohol stove is essential for camping, as fires are prohibited everywhere in the National Park. Take plenty of warm clothes and a good sleeping bag. It is possible to rent equipment in El Chaltén, ask at park office or *Rancho Grande*. Campsites in National Park: Confluencia, Poincenot, (Note Rio Blanco is only for climbers with prior permission arranged), Capri, Lago Toro.

El Chaltén → *Phone code: 02962 colour map 6, B2*

The small modern town of El Chaltén is set in a wonderful position at the foot of Cerro Fitz Roy and at the mouth of the valley of the Río de las Vueltas. The village was founded very recently, in 1985, in order to settle the area and pre-empt Chilean territorial claims. However, it has grown very rapidly, along with its popularity as a centre for trekking and climbing in summer, and for cross country skiing in winter. It's an expensive and unattractive place, especially when the harsh wind blows, but its visitors create a cheerful atmosphere, and from its concrete and tin you can walk directly into breathtaking landscapes. Tourist infrastructure is still developing in El Chaltén, and so far there are no ATMs (or internet cafés), so take sufficient cash.

Accommodation is available in a range from camping and hostels to not-quite-luxurious hosterías, all hideously overpriced. Food, too, is expensive, though there is increasingly plenty of choice. At the time of writing, credit cards were not accepted, though this may change if the general economic situation in the country improves.

Ins and outs

Getting there The quickest way to reach the town is by flying to El Calafate's airport, 220 km away, (see El Calafate above for flights), and from there it's a four-hour bus journey. There are frequent bus connections from El Calafate, and a daily bus from Route 40 in the north, useful if you've come from the Lake District in either Argentina or Chile.

Tourist information The tourist office is at Güemes 21, T493011, www.elchalten.com This is an excellent website with accommodation listed, but no email for queries. Office open 0900-2000 Mon-Fri, Sat/Sun 1300-2000. National Park office across the bridge at the entrance to the town, T493004. Both hand out trekking maps of the area, with paths and campsites marked, distances and walking times.

Sights

There is a small chapel, the **Capilla Tomás Egger**, named after an Austrian climber killed on Fitz Roy and built entirely from materials brought from Austria. The main attraction here is clearly the trekking around Fitz Roy. But there is also stunning virgin landscape to explore around the **Lago del Desierto**, 37 km north of El Chaltén. The long skinny lake is fjord-like, surrounded by forests, and a short walk to a *mirador* at the end of the road gives fine views. It's reached by unpaved Route 23, which leads along the Río de las Vueltas via Laguna Condor, where flamingos can be seen. A path runs along the east side of the lake to its

El Chaltén

Patagonia El Chaltén

Sleeping
Albergue Patagonia 1
Albergue Rancho Grande 2
Camping El Refugio 6
Cóndor de los Andes 3
Fitz Roy Inn 4
Hospedaje La Base 8
Hostería El Puma 5
Hostería Posada Lunajuim 7
Northofagus 9

Eating
Domo Blanca 2
Fuegia 6
Josh Aike 1
Las Lengas 7
Pangea 4
Patagonicus 5
Ruca Mahuida 3
Zafarancho 8

Not to scale

northern tip, from where a trail leads west along the valley of the Río Diablo to Laguna Diablo. There is a campsite at the southern end of the lake and *refugios* at its northern end and at Laguna Diablo. The estancia **EL Pilar** is quite the best place to stay on the way to the lake (see sleeping) in a stunning position with views of Fitz Roy. Visit for tea, use as an excellent base for trekking up Río Blanco or Río Eléctrico, with a multi-activity adventure circuit. Highly recommended. Lago Viedma to the south of El Chaltén can also be expored by boat. The trips usually pass Glaciar Viedma, with the possibility of ice trekking too, on some excursions. ➤ *For Sleeping, Eating and other listings, see pages 481-488.*

From El Calafate to Chile → *For public transport on this route see under Calafate*

If travelling from El Calafate to Torres del Paine, by car or bike, you'll cross this bleak area of steppe; about 40 km before reaching the border there are small lagoons and salt flats with flamingos. From El Calafate you can take the almost completely paved combination of Route 11, RN 40 and RN 5 to La Esperanza (165 km), where there's fuel, a campsite and a large but expensive *confitería* (accommodation D with bath). From La Esperanza, *ripio* Route 7 heads west along the valley of the Río Coyle. A shorter route (closed in winter) missing Esperanza, goes via El Cerrito and joins Route 7 at Estancia Tapi Aike. Route 7 continues to the border crossing at Cancha Carrera (see below) and then meets the good *ripio* road between Torres del Paine and Puerto Natales (63 km). For bus services along this route see under Calafate.

Border with Chile The Paso Cacha Carrera, 129 km west of La Esperanza and 42 km north of Río Turbio, open all year, is the most convenient crossing for Parque Nacional Torres del Paine. On the Chilean side the road continues to Cerro Castillo, 7 km west of the border, where it meets the road from Puerto Natales, 65 km south, to Parque Nacional Torres del Paine. **Argentine customs and immigration** At Cancha Carrera, 2 km east of the border, fast and friendly. **Chilean customs and immigration** At Cerro Castillo, open 0800-2200.

Río Turbio→ *Phone code: 02902 Colour map 6, B2 Population: 8,000*

A charmless place you're most likely to visit en route to or from Torres del Paine in Chile. The site of Argentina's largest coalfield hasn't recovered from the recent depression hitting the industry. It has a cargo railway connecting it with Punta Loyola, and visitors can see Mina 1, where the first mine was opened. There's a small ski centre nearby, **Valdelén**, which has six pistes and is ideal for beginners, also scope for cross-country skiing between early June and late September. There is tourist information in the municipality on San Martín. ➤ *For Sleeping, Eating and other listings, see pages 481-488.*

Border with Chile

1 Paso Mina Uno/Dorotea is 5 km south of Río Turbio. Open all year, 24 hours 31 November – 31 March, daytime only rest of year. On the Chilean side this runs south to join the main Puerto Natales-Punta Arenas road.

2 Paso Casas Viejas is 33 km south of Río Turbio via 28 de Noviembre. Open all year, daytime only. Runs east on the Chilean side to join the Puerto Natales-Punta Arenas road.

3 Paso Cancha Carrera is 55 km north of Río Turbio this is the most convenient crossing for Parque Nacional Torres del Paine. Open November-April only. Argentine customs are fast and friendly. On the Chilean side the road continues 14 km to the Chilean border post at Cerro Castillo, where it joins the road from Puerto Natales to Torres del Paine. Chilean immigration open 0830-1200, 1400-2000, November-March or April only.

Listings: Parque Nacional Los Glaciares

⊖ Sleeping

El Calafate *p471, map p472*

L **Kosten Aike**, *Gob Moyano 1243, T492424, www.kostenaike.com.ar* A special place, relaxed and yet stylish with large elegant rooms, king sized beds throughout, jacuzzi and gym. The tranquil restaurant is open to non residents (US$10 for 3 courses) and has an excellent chef, there's a cosy bar with a wood fire, and a garden. The staff are extremely attentive and speak English. Recommended.

L **Los Alamos**, *Moyano y Bustillo, T491145, posadalosalamos@cotecal.com.ar* Located in 2 separate buildings, extremely comfortable, with charming rooms, beautifully decorated and equipped, good service, lovely gardens and without doubt the best restaurant in town, La Posta. Recommended.

AL **El Quijote**, *Gob Gregores 1181, T491017, www.hieos.com.ar* This spacious, modern hotel is Italian-owned and designed, and you can tell. An elegant entrance lounge, and very tasteful comfortable rooms with excellent bathrooms, all beautifully decorated with traditional touches, TV, phone and minibar. Great restaurant. Italian and English spoken. Recommended.

AL **Hostería Kau-Yatún**, *25 de Mayo (10 blocks from town centre), T491259, F491260, kauyatun@cotecal.com.ar* A comfortable old estancia house offering many facilities, a restaurant and *asados*, and horse riding tours with guides.

A **Michelangelo**, *Espora y Gob Moyano, T491045, michelangelohotel@ cotecal.com.ar* A lovely, quiet and welcoming place, modern and stylish in design, with a really excellent restaurant, US$10 for 2 courses, such as hare, steak, and ink squid ravioli. All rooms have TV, bath and minibar, breakfast included. Recommended.

B **ACA Hostería El Calafate**, *Av del Libertador 1353, T491004, F491027.* A modern place with good views from a slightly elevated position above the town centre, and open all year. Good value.

C **Amado**, *Libertador 1072, T491134, familiagomez@cotecal.com.ar* Breakfast is included; all rooms have bath TV and phone. The décor is clean and plain; functional but nothing special.

C **Hospedaje Sir Thomas**, *Cte. Espora 257, T492220.* A modern house with comfortable and spacious wood-lined rooms, with private bathrooms, breakfast $5 extra.

C **Vientos del Sur**, *a little way up the hill at Calle 54 2317, T493563.* One of the most welcoming places in town, this traquil retreat is worth the short taxi ride for the views over the lake, comfortable modern rooms with bath and TV, and the kindest attention you could wish for. Recommended.

D **Cabañas Nevis**, *Libertador 1696, T493180.* Well-spaced, A-shaped *cabañas* for 5 and 8, some with lake views. Great value.

C **Cerro Cristal**, *Gob Gregores 979, T491088.* A basic friendly and central place, the simple rooms have modernized bathrooms but no TV, and breakfast is included.

C **del Norte**, *Los Gauchos 813, T491117.* Open all year, kitchen facilities, comfortable, owner organizes tours.

C **Hostería Ariel**, *Casimiro Bigua 35, T493131.* A modern functional place, very clean and well-maintained rooms have bath and TV. Breakfast included. Hardly budget but decent.

C **Los Lagos**, *25 de Mayo 220, T491170, loslagos@cotecal.com.ar* Very comfortable, absolutely spotless cheery rooms with bath, breakfast included in this cosy house: good value. Recommended.

E **Hospedaje Alejandra**, *Cte. Espora 60, T491328.* Great value in this homely place, rooms with shared bath but no breakfast – you can make it yourself, very friendly owner. Also E pp, one flat for 5, equipped with TV. Recommended.

Estancias

LL **Estancia Alta Vista**, *33 km west of El Calafate, T491247, altavista@cotecal.com.ar* The area's most expensive, with a reputation for being exclusive. An attractive place in

● For an explanation of the sleeping and eating price codes used in this guide, see the inside
● front cover. Other relevant information is provided in Essentials, see page 44.

lovely gardens, with excellent cuisine and wines, and good service.

A pp **Estancia Nibepo Aike**, *in the far south of the park on the shores of Brazo Sur of Lago Argentino, T436010, nibepo@ciudad.com.ar* Horse riding, expeditions, fishing, boat tours to glacier, recommended.

E pp **La Leona**, *T491418, 106 km north of Calafate near east end of Lago Viedma, contact info@estancias desantacruz.com* A simple estancia in wide open country, popular with anglers.

Youth hostels

There are some reasonably priced places to stay in El Calafate:

Albergue del Glaciar, *Los Pioneros 255, T/F491243 (reservations in Buenos Aires T/F03488-469416, off season only), www.glaciar.com* The most appealing budget option. Discount for ISIC or IYHA members, open mid-Sep to end May. The original and best hostel in town (often recommended), with a whole range of accommodation for all budgets; shared dorms (F pp), double rooms with shared bath (C double) and more luxurious double rooms with bathrooms (B double). Many languages are spoken by the friendly and helpful staff, there are lots of bathrooms, and also internet access and kitchen facilities. The cosy restaurant *Punto de Encuentro* has a good value fixed menu, and vegetarian options. They also run the much loved *Alternative Glaciar Tour* (see below), and organize a booking service for Navimag and hotels and transport throughout Patagonia, and run free shuttle service from bus terminal. Beautifully run, and highly recommended. Book in advance in summer.

E **Albergue Buenos Aires**, *Buenos Aires 296, 200m from terminal, T491147, hospbuenos aires@cotecal.com.ar* Comfortable, kitchen facilities, helpful, hot showers, luggage store.

E pp **Calafate Hostel**, *Gob Moyano 1226, 300 m from bus terminal, T492450, www.hostels patagonia.com* The other big hostel, this is a huge rangey place, with well-built dorms for 4-6 with shared bath, and C double rooms with private bath. Also has G pp *refugio* space for those with sleeping bags, kitchen facilities, internet access and a huge lively

sitting area. Friendly staff can arrange tours and accommodation in the sister hostal *Albergue Patagonia* In El Chaltén. Book a month ahead for Jan and Feb. They also run the helpful travel agency Chaltén Travel.

E **Hospedaje Los Dos Pinos**, *9 de Julio 358, T491271*. A popular place offering the whole range of accommodation, from dorms, rather cramped (E), cheap cabañas for 7 (C), tiny little studio flats for 2 (B) and a campsite (F), all sharing a nice friendly TV room where you can cook. The helpful owner also arranges tours to glacier.

Parque Nacional Los Glaciares *p469*

LL **Los Notros**, *T/F499510, www.losnotros.com* (in Buenos Aires: *T011-4814 3934*) Luxurious accommodation in spacious, well designed rooms with wonderful views of the Perito Moreno glacier, where you can walk, hike, trek, and ride horses. With breakfast and free transfers to the glacier *passarelas* included, but transport from airport and other meals extra.

L **Estancia Helsingfors**, *T/F02966-420719, www.helsingfors.com* or Buenos Aires *T/F4824 4623/3634, reserva@helsingfors.com.ar* A fabulous place in a splendid position on Lago Viedma, 150 km from El Calafate, with stylish rooms, a welcoming lounge, delicious food, and excursions directly from there to glaciers and to Laguna Azul, by horse or trek, plus boat trips. Recommended.

Camping

Ferretería Chuar, *Libertador 1242*. Gas sold for camping.

Municipal campsite, *behind YPF service station, at Jose Pantin s/n, T492622, campingmuniciapl@cotecal.com.ar* US$2 pp, hot water, security, *parrilladas*, restaurant, open 1 Oct-30 Apr.

There are two campsites in the park en route to the glacier:

Bahía Escondida, *7 km east of the glacier*. The only one with all facilities, fireplaces, hot showers and shop. Crowded in summer, US$ 3pp.

Correntoso, *10 km east of the glacier*. There's an unmarked site here with no facilities but a great location. No fires. US$2pp.

Río Mitre, near the park entrance, is a picnic ground only, no camping, no fires. 50 km from El Calafate, beautifully situated Lago Roca, T499500, US$3 pp, bike hire, restaurant/*confitería*.

El Chaltén *p478, map p479*

The tourist office has a full list, accessible from www.elchalten.com These are the best:

AL Hostería El Puma, *Lionel Terray 212, T542962, www.elchalten.com/elpuma* The most desirable place in town, set a little apart, and with splendid views up the valley, a welcoming lounge with log fire and tasteful stylish furnishings, spacious comfortable rooms with lots of brick, and plush bathrooms. Transfers and a big American breakfast are included. They can also arrange tours through their excellent agency *Fitz Roy Expeditions, www.elchalten. com/fiztroy* Recommended.

AL Hostería Posada Lunajuim, *Trevisán s/n, T/F493047, www.elchalten.com/lunajuim* A stylish yet relaxed and welcoming place, with comfortable rooms (thick duvets on the beds!) with bathrooms, a lovely big lounge with wood fire and art on the walls. Dinner is available to residents, and a full American breakfast is included. Run by a very friendly family, charming hosts. Recommended.

A Fitz Roy Inn, *T493062, caltur@cotecal.com.ar* An overpriced place that seems to have stopped making an effort, this has pleasant but small rooms, often filled with package tour clients. Breakfast included. Also travel agency *Cal Tur* travel.

B El Pilar, *T/F493002, www.hosteriael pilar.com.ar* A special place to stay a little way out of town, this simple country house in a spectacular setting on the confluence of Ríos Blanco and de las Vueltas, with views of Fitz Roy. A chance to sample the simple life with access to the less visited northern part of the national park and beyond. Spacious rooms, great food, recommended. Owner Miguel Pagani is an experienced mountain guide, and takes individuals and groups on individually tailored trekking tours.

C Hospedaje La Base, *Lago de Desierto 97, T493031*. A friendly little place, has basic double rooms with bath rooms. For 3 or 4 (**E**). Tiny kitchen for guests to use, self service

breakfast included, and a great video lounge.
C Northofagus, *Hensen s/n T493087, www.elchalten.com/northofagus/* A small cosy bed and breakfast, with simple double rooms with shared bath, including breakfast. Welcoming and good value.

Youth hostels

E Albergue Patagonia, *T/F493019, www.elchalten.com/alberguepatagonia* The most appealing of several hostels here is IYHA-affiliated, and a small cosy friendly place, with kitchen, video room, bike hire, laundry. Helpful information on Chaltén and also excursions to Lago del Desierto. Next door is their restaurant *Fuegia*, with Patagonian dishes, curries and vegetarian food too.

E Albergue Rancho Grande, *San Martín s/n, T493005*, rancho@cotecal.com.ar HI-affiliated, in a great position at the end of town with good open views, and a welcoming attractive restaurant and lounge. This accommodates huge numbers of trekkers in rooms for 4, with shared bathrooms, and is well run, with friendly staff who speak several languages between them. Breakfast and sheets extra. There are also **C** private double rooms, breakfast extra, and one family room, with private bath. Recommended. Reservations can also be made in the sister businesses in El Calafate: Calafate Hostel and Chaltén Travel.

E Cóndor de los Andes, *Av Río de las Vueltas y Halvorsen, T493101, www.condorde losandes.com* Friendly, small and modern, with nice little rooms for 6 with bathrooms en suite, sheets included, breakfast US$2 extra. Washing service, library, kitchen. Quiet atmosphere, calm place. Recommended.

Camping

Camping Madsen, Several km north, east of Rio de las Vueltas, and **El Refugio**, off San Martín just before Rancho Grande. Neither has facilities. A gas/alcohol stove is essential for camping as fires are prohibited in any campsites of the National Park. Take plenty of warm clothes and a good sleeping bag. It is possible to rent equipment in El Chaltén; ask at park office or Rancho Grande.
Campsites in the National Park:
Confluencia, **Poincenot**, (Note Rio Blanco is only for climbers with prior permission

arranged), **Capri**, **Lago Toro**: None have services, fires are not allowed, all river water is drinkable. Pack out all rubbish, do not wash, or bury waste within 70 m of rivers. **Camping Piedra del Fraile**, on Rio Electrico is beyond park boundary, is privately owned, has facilities.

Lago del Desierto
L **Cabañas Lago del Desierto**. Sleep 5, kitchen, also camping US$6 per person, bookings through *Hotel Lago del Desierto* in Chaltén.

El Calafate to Chile *p480*
Restaurant La Esperanza. Bunk beds, with bath. Also *cabañas* at the YPF service station, A-B, sleep 6.

Río Turbio *p480*
Hotels here are almost always full.
C **De La Frontera**, *4 km from Rio Turbio, Paraje Mina 1, T421979*. The most recommended option.
C **Hostería Capipe**, *Dufour, 9 km from town, T482930, www.hosteriacapipe.com.ar*

🍴 Eating

El Calafate *p471, map p472*
For cheap meals, there are two lively, packed places on the main street, *Libertador*, with good atmosphere and cheapish food: **Rick's Café**, *No 1105*, serving *tenedor libre* for US$5, and **Casablanca**, *Libertador and 25 de Mayo*. A jolly and welcoming place, serving omelettes, hamburgers and vegetarian food too, US$4 for steak and chips.
$$$ **La Posta** The restaurant at *Los Alamos Hotel* is undoubtedly the best in town. With elegant décor, slightly reminiscent of a traditional mountain lodge and a really superb menu, Patagonian lamb and rose hip sauce, king crab-stuffed raviolis, with a refined, but definitely not stuffy, atmosphere, and very friendly staff. Pricey but worth it. US$12 for 2 courses.
$$$ **Hotel Michelangelo** The restaurant *Espora y Gob Moyano* is excellent, US$10 for 2 courses, such as hare, steak and ink squid ravioli.
$$ **El Hornito**, *Buenos Aires 155, just above the bus terminal*. A welcoming intimate place serving excellent pizzas and pastas.

$$ **Pura Vida**. Recommended, for a relaxed place to eat well, with comfortable sofas, homemade Argentine food, lots of vegetarian options, and a lovely warm atmosphere with lake view.
$ **El Rancho**, *9 de Julio y Gob Moyano*. A tiny, cosy and popular place for big cheap pizzas.
$ **La Cocina**, *No 1245*. Pizzería, pancakes, pasta, salads, in cosy warm atmosphere.
$ **Mi Viejo**, *No 1111*. Popular *parrilla*, US$6 for *tenedor libre*.

Ice cream parlours
Heladería Aquarela, *No 1177*. You'll be glad to hear that it does get hot enough for ice cream, and the best is served up here – try the delicious (and beautifully coloured) *calafate*.

El Chaltén *p478, map p479*
$ **Domo Blanca**, *Costanera y D'Agostini*. Makes superb home made ice cream. Several small shops here, but there is a wider selection of goods in El Calafate.
$ **Josh Aike** Excellent *confitería*, delicious homemade food, in a beautiful building. Recommended.
$ **Las Lengas**, *Viedma y Güemes*. There's nowhere cheap to eat in El Chalten, but opposite the tourist office, this place is a little cheaper than most. Plentiful meals, basic pastas and meat dishes. US$3 for 2 courses.
$ **Pangea**, *Lago del Desiero 273 y San Martín*. Open for lunch and dinner, drinks and coffee, in calm comfortable surroundings with good music, a varied menu, from pastas to steak, trout and pizzas US$3 to US$7. Recommended.
$ **Patagonicus**, *Güemes y Madsen*. A lovely warm cosy stylish place with salads, home made pastas and fabulous pizzas for 2, US$4-7. Great family photos of mountain climbers on the walls. Open from midday to midnight. Recommended.
$ **Restaurant Fuegia**, *San Martín*. Also serves good food, with Patagonian dishes and some rather more imaginative options, such as curries and vegetarian food too.
$ **Ruca Mahuida**, *Lionel Terray s/n*. Widely regarded as the best restaurant in El Chaten, for imaginative and carefully prepared food.
$ **Zafarancho**, *behind Rancho Grande*. A great bar-restaurant, serving a good range and reasonably priced. Also equipment rental and tours, see below.

☻ Bars and nightclubs

El Calafate *p471, map p472*
Highly recommended for a drink is
Shackleton Lounge, on the outskirts of
town (US$1 in taxi), a great place to relax,
with lovely views of the lake, old photos of
Shackleton, a great atmosphere good music.
Tango Sur, *9 de julio 265, T491550*. Live
music and amazingly, a long way from
Buenos Aires, a tango show! US$3.350, Tue
and Sun at 2030, 2300, in charming old-style
house.

☺ Shopping

El Calafate *p471, map p472*
All along Libertador there are souvenir shops
selling the inevitable T shirts and postcards,
and useful hats, fleeces and gloves, so that
you can prepare yourself for those chilly boat
rides to see the glacier. There are lots of fine
quality handicrafts, from all over Argentina
and look out for Mapuche weavings and
good woollen items. Also little handicraft
stalls on Libertador at around 1200. All
relatively expensive by Argentine standards.
Supermarkets **Alas**, *9 de Julio 59*.
Wide choice.
Camping supplies **Los Glaciares**,
Libertador y Perito Moreno. **Ferretería Chuar**,
Libertador 1242. The only place selling white
gas for camping.

El Chaltén *p478, map p479*
El Gringuito, *Av Antonio Rojo*. The best
choice, though there are many others
around. All are expensive and have little
fresh food. Fuel is available.
El Super, *Lago del Desierto y Av Güemes,
T493039*. Rent and sell camping and
climbing equipment, maps, postcards and
books, as well as handicrafts.
Zafarancho Restaurant, *Lionel Terray s/n
T493093, www.chaltenoutdoor.com.ar
/elranchito* For renting tents, good sleeping
bags, heaters, cooking set, also general store.
Viento Oeste, *Av San Martín s/n, (at the end
of town on the way to Camping Madsen)
T493021*. Equipment hire; renting tents,
sleeping bags, and everything else you'll
need, and can arrange mountain guides.
Also sell handicrafts.

☺ Sport and activities

El Calafate *p471, map p472*
Ballooning
Hotel Kau Yatun, (details above). Organizes
balloon trips over El Calafate and Lago
Argentino, US$38 for 2½ hrs, US$65 for 5 hrs.

Fishing
Fishing & Adventure, *Roca 2192, T/F493050*.
Offers fishing excursions, from half-day to
three-day expeditions.

Horse riding
Cabalgata en Patagonia, *Libertador 3600,
T493203, 156 20935, cabalgataen
patagonia@cotecal.com.ar* US$12 for 2
hours, US$60 for full day, including lunch.
Treks offered to Bahía Redonda also 5-day
excursion in Parque Nacional Los Glaciares.

Ice trekking
Walking excursions on the Perito Moreno
glacier (known as minitrekking), enormous
fun (and not too physically challenging) for a
close-up experience of the glacier, are run by
Hielo y Aventura, see tour operators below.

Mountain bikes
Bike Way, *Espora 20, T492180*. US$6 per hr,
US$25 per day.

Rafting
Nonthue Aventura, *Libertador 1177,
T491179* Rafting on the Río Santa Cruz, 0800
and 1500, 4-5 hrs, US$30 without transport,
US$40 with transport.

Offroading
Mil Outdoor Adventure, *Av Libertador 1029,
T491437, 491446, gxress@cotecal.
com.ar www.loslgaciares.com/miloutoors*
Offers a variety of excursions in 4WD
vehicles, with excellent opportunities to visit
otherwise inaccessible parts of the
Patagonian steppe, short-trip US$40 per
person, long-trip US$75 per person,
recommended.

El Chaltén *p478, map p479*
Climbing
Base camp for climbing Fitz Roy is
Campamento Río Blanco (see above). Most
of the peaks in the Fitzroy massif are for very
experienced climbers as is the Campo de

Hielo Continental (Ice Field) which mark the border with Chile (no access from Chile). For details on hiring horses to carry equipment see under trekking below.

Tour operators and trekking guides

El Calafate p473, map p472

Most agencies charge the same rates for excursions: To the **Perito Moreno Glacier** US$20; **Minitrekking** (on the glacier itself with crampons included, recommended) US$50; **Upsala Explorer**, (a full day visiting Upsala glacier by boat, then 4WD, and trekking, superb lunch at the remote *Estancia Cristina* and boat trip, unforgettable, recommended) US$65. To **Lago Roca**, a full-day including lunch at *Estancia Anita*, US$30; Horseriding to Gualichó caves, 2 hrs, US$20.

Chaltén Travel, *Libertador 1174, T492212*. The most helpful, with huge range of tours: glaciers, estancias, trekking, and to El Chaltén, also sells tickets along the Ruta 40 to Los Antiguos, offers advice, English spoken. Highly recommended.

Albergue del Glaciar, *Los Pioneros 255*, *T/F491243 www.glaciar.com* This tour operator offers the best glacier trip, the 'Alternative Tour to Moreno Glacier'. Entertaining and informative, it includes lots of information on the landscape and wildlife as you travel along the old road to the glacier, then some light walking to aproach the glacier along the lake shore, followed by the boat trip, to see it up close. US$25. Recommended constantly. They also do a great 2-day trip to El Chaltén, 'Supertrekking en Chaltén', a 2-day hiking trip, featuring the best treks in the Fitzroy massif, including camping and ice trekking. Highly recommended.

Hielo y Aventura, *Av Libertador 935*, *T491053, hieloyaventura@cotecal.com.ar* Run the famous minitrekking, with 90 minutes walking on the glacier with crampons (supplied and fitted by them), after a walk through lovely lakeside *lenga* forests, US$50. Recommended.

Leutz Turismo, *Libertador 1341, T492316, leutzturismo@cotecal.com.ar* Daily excursion to Lago Roca 1000-1800, US$20 pp, plus US$11 for lunch at *Estancia Quien Sabe*, and

an interesting tour of the sheep and fruit estancia.

Mil Outdoor Adventure, *Av Libertador 1029, T491437, www.loslglaciares.com/miloutoors* Exciting excursions in 4WD to see wild places with wonderful views, 4-6 hrs, US$20-40.

Upsala Explorer, *9 de Julio 69, T491133, 491034, www.upsalaexplorer.com.ar* The company that runs this truly spectacular (if pricey) experience, including an excellent lunch at the estancia, but not transfers from El Calafate, which you can book through the same company, US$100 for trip without transfer. Say before if you don't eat meat.

Mundo Austral, *Libertador 1114, T492365, F492116*. Offers all kinds of tours to the park and cheaper trips to the glaciers, with helpful bilingual guide Jorge Mendez, and can also books bus travel.

Hielos, *Gob Gregores 1181, T491017*. The agency in *El Quijote hotel, hielos@cotecal.com.ar* Runs the boat tips in El Chaltén, as well as flights from El Calafate over the glaciers, *www.patagonia adventure.com, www.hielos.com.ar*

El Chaltén p478, map p479

Fitz Roy Expediciones, *Lionel Terray 212, (next to Hostería El Puma) T/F493017, www.elchalten.com/fitzroy* This company is by far the best and most experienced, and are very professional. Owned by mountaineer and guide Alberto del Castillo. They organize trekking, rock climbing courses and ice-climbing courses (one day, US$38), adventure expeditions, including two-day ascents of Cerro Eléctrico and Cerro Solo (US$175pp), and 8-day trekking expeditions on the Campo de Hielo. Also organizes a circuit of the challenging terrain around Estancia El Pilar, ideal for everyone from kids to adults, including kayaking, mountain biking, rappelling, rope bridges, climbing. Great fun, safe, and well organized.

Mermoz, *San Martín 493, T493098*. Boat trips across Laguna del Desierto, including bus transfer, and optional trekking. English spoken, and helpful.

Viedma Discovery, *Av Güemes s/n, T493110, www.elchalten.com/viedmadiscovery* Boat trips along Lago Viedma to see the Glaciar Viedma, including informative chat; transfers US$10 extra. Also a good full day's trip along Lago Viedma, with ice trekking on Glaciar Viedma.

Viviendo Montanas, *De Agostini 141, T/F493068, www.vivmont.com.ar, info@vivmont.com.ar* A young company, organizing climbing schools, and ice climbing expeditions (make sure you take sleeping bag and equipment), guides for trekking too.

Chaltén Travel Excursions from El Chaltén are run daily in summer, and there are daily boat trips to the end of the lake on *La Mariana II*, 1030, 1330, 1630, 2 hrs, US$20 (details and booking, **Hotel El Quijote**, Calafate), which you can combine with trekking. Also a campsite.

NYCA Adventure, *Av Güemes y Río de las Vueltas, T493122, www.nyca.com.ar* Organizes a great adventure circuit in the challenging terrain around Estancia El Pilar, ideal for everyone from kids to adults, including kayaking, mountain biking, rappel, rope bridges, climbing. Great fun, safe, and well-organized.

● Transport

El Calafate *p471, map p472*
Air
Lago Argentino, the international airport, is 22 km east of town, *T491220*. The airport has a tourist information desk *T491230*, and Aerobus runs a minibus service from town to meet all flights, *T492492*, US$3. Taxi *T491655, 492005, US$7*. **Aerolíneas Argentinas** flies daily to/from **Buenos Aires**, with many more flights in summer. **LADE** (*Julio Roca 1004, T491262, ladecalafate@cotecal.com.ar*) flies twice a week to **Río Gallegos** and **Río Grande**, and once a week to **Perito Moreno**. To **Puerto Natales** , Aerovias Dap (finanzas@aeroviasdap.cl) daily, summer only (Oct-Mar). Airport charge for departing passengers US$18.

Bus
Take your passport with you when booking bus ticket to Chile.
Terminal on Roca, 1 block up steep stairs from Libertador. **Taqsa** *T491843*, and **Interlagos** *T492197*, run daily services to Perito Moreno glacier, the cheapest way to get there. To **Ushuaia** take bus to **Río Gallegos**, with **Taqsa** or **Interlagos**, several

daily, US$11. To **El Chaltén**, with Cal-Tur or Chalten Travel, 3 daily, US$14; Taxi *(remise)* To **Río Gallegos**, 4 hrs, US$100 irrespective of number of passengers, up to 5 people.

Along Route 40 To **Perito Moreno** and **Los Antiguos** for Chile, **Chaltén Travel**, *(at terminal and see above) T491833, 492212*. From **El Chaltén** to **Perito Moreno** and **Los Antiguos**, sometimes with a stop at **Cueva de las Manos**, departing daily Dec-Feb (goes north on odd days, comes south on even days), and subject to demand (6 passengers minimum) in Nov and Mar. US$33, book a week in advance. Safari Route 40 to **Bariloche** (see under Bariloche, Buses) can be booked at **Albergue del Glaciar**, *T491243, info@glaciar.com* To **El Chaltén** Daily services in summer, 4 hrs, US$10, one way, are run by **Chaltén Travel**, *Libertador 1174, T492212*.

To Chile To **Puerto Natales**, daily with either **Cootra** *T491444*, or Bus Sur *T491631*, US$16. (Advance booking recommended, tedious border crossing). **Bus Sur** (Tue, Sat 0800) and **Zaahj** (Wed, Fri, Sun 0800) also run to **Puerto Natales** via Cerro Castillo (where you can pick up a bus to **Torres del Paine** in summer). (NB Argentine pesos cannot be exchanged in Torres del Paine).

Car hire
Adventure Rent a Car, *Libertador 290, T492595, adventurerentacar@cotecal.com.ar* **Europcar**, *Libertador 1711, T493606, www.carletti.com.ar* Prices start at US$52 per day for a small car including insurance.

El Chaltén *p478, map p479*
Bus
In summer, buses fill quickly: book ahead. Fewer services off season. Daily buses to **El Calafate**, 4 hrs, US$7 one way: run by Chaltén Travel *T493005*, and **Caltur** *T493062*. To **Los Antiguos** along the Ruta 40, **Itinerarios y Travesías**, *T493088* overnight, even dates (ie 2nd, 4th, 6th), includes trip to Cueva de las Manos in the early morning. **Chaltén Travel** makes trips north odd dates (ie 3rd, 5th, 7th, etc) returning even dates. Prices for both US$40 single, bike US$5, **Overland Patagonia** does trips to **Bariloche**

in 4 days, staying at estancias and visiting Cueva de las Manos, *www.overlandpatagonia.com* Book through **Alaska Youth Hostel Bariloche**, *T02944-461564, info@alaska-hostel.com* or at Periko's *T02944-522326 infor@perikos.com*

Río Turbio *p480*
Bus
To **Puerto Natales**, 1hr, US$2, several daily with: **Cootra**, *Tte.del Castillo 01, T421448 cootra@oyikil.com.ar* **Bus Sur**, *Baquedano 534, Pto. Natales, T+56(0)61–411859, www.turismozaahj.co.cl* **Lagoper**, *Av. de Los Mineros 262, T411831.* To **Calafate**, same companies, **Expreso Pingüino** and **Taqsa** daily. US$7, 4 1/2 hrs. **Río Gallegos**, 4 hrs, US$5.

⊙ Directory

El Calafate *p471, map p472*
Banks Best to take cash as high commission is charged on exchange, but there are ATMs at **Banco de la Provincia de Santa Cruz**, *Libertador 1285*, and at **Banco de Tierra del Fuego**, *25 de Mayo 34*. Change money at **Thaler** *Libertador 1311, T493245, www.cambio-thaler.com* Credit cards are no longer widely accepted in Argentina, apart from at the more expensive hotels.
Communications **Post Office** Libertador 1133. **Telephone** Open Calafate, Libertador 996, is a huge *locutorio* for phones, and also 20 fast internet computers, US$2 per hr. Open 0800-2400.

Chilean Patagonia

Introducing
Chilean Patagonia

A land of fjords, glaciers, lakes and mountains, southern Chilean Patagonia remains a vast unvisited wilderness with areas of staggering beauty. The **Parque Nacional Torres del Paine**'s mighty towers of granite thrust up like fingers from a mass of basalt buttresses, surrounded by minty green and icy blue glacial lakes in which icebergs float. In high summer you'll share this awe inspiring landscape with a steady stream of buses and walkers. Set out for the remoter reaches or come in March if you're looking for solitude and silence.

The remarkable **Parque Nacional Bernardo O'Higgins** is where glaciers descend steeply from **Monte Balmaceda**, a wonderful sight seen from the water. For a taste of adventure, you could go trekking on the glacier itself, or take a boat up the **Río Serrano**, for a different approach to Torres del Paine. The base for visiting both parks is the tranquil and quaint port town of **Puerto Natales**, with its calm vistas over the **Ultima Esperanza Sound**, fringed by lofty far-off peaks.

A complete contrast, Chile's southernmost city **Punta Arenas** has an intriguing history of sheep farming millionaires and valiant, if misguided, missionaries. There are fine stone buildings to explore from its heyday in the 1900s, and if tempted by the views from its port, you could sail from here through the **Magellan Strait** to the Argentine city of **Ushuaia**. For more rugged wilderness on dry land, though, head for **Parque Nacional Pali Aike**, and if you need company, take a boat to **Isla Magdalena**, and its colony of 60,000 penguins.

★ Don't miss...

1. **Torres del Paine** Get up early and trek from the Laguna Amarga *guardería* to the mirador, and see those famous towers up close for yourself, page 508

2. **Sotito** Eat king crab at this traditional seafood restaurant in Punta Arenas, page 497.

3. **Isla Magdalena** Visit the huge Magellanic penguin colony, page 495.

4. **Río Serrano** Zoom up the river and enter Torres del Paine from a different angle, page 503.

5. **Cruce Australis** Wake up and see astonishing glaciers gliding by your porthole on a luxury cruise from Punta Arenas through the Magellan strait and on to Ushuaia, page 500.

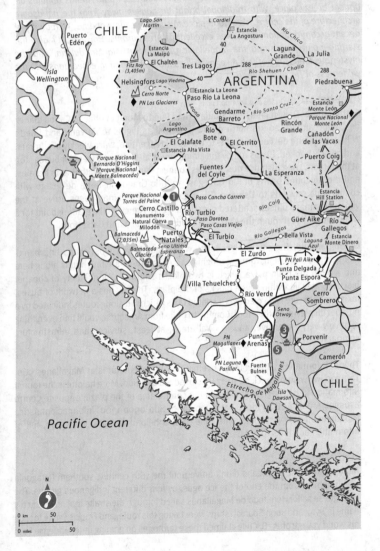

Chilean Patagonia

Punta Arenas → *Phone: +56-(0)61 Colour map 6, C2 Population: 110,000*

After hours of travelling through barren steppe of Patagonia, Punta Arenas comes as a surprise. With a grand plaza surrounded by neo-classical mansions and several fine monuments, Chile's most southerly city has an affluent history. Its strategic position on the eastern shore of the Brunswick Peninsula made it a thriving port of call when trading ships sailed through the Magellan Straits. Landowners Braun and Menéndez made their fortunes from sheep, building a sumptuous palace, filled with treasures: one of the city's two fascinating museums. The other recounts the more sombre history of the ousted indigenous peoples, and their own rich culture. While the cemetery, an oddly beautiful place, also deserves a visit.

Although no longer so wealthy on natural resources, Punta Arenas remains an upbeat breezy place, with traditional bright tin houses away from the handsome architecture of the centre. It's a good place to spend a couple of days, with plenty of decent accommodation, and some excellent fish restaurants. However, it's also the starting point for visiting the Magellanic penguins at Isla Magdalena, and the mysterious landscape of Pali Aike, as well as more challenging expeditions into the wilderness of Tierra del Fuego.

Ins and outs → *See also Transport page 499.*

Getting there Daily flights from Santiago and Puerto Montt in Chile to Carlos Ibáñez de Campo airport, 20 km north of town, as well as flights to Porvenir and Puerto Williams in Tierra del Fuego. Flights to Ushuaia in Argentina, twice weekly in summer, and heavily booked. Buses run by the airlines meet all flights, and regular buses stop at the airport. Long distance bus services connect Punta Arenas with Puerto Natales, and the Argentine towns of Río Gallegos, and Río Grande in Tierra del Fuego with connections onwards to Ushuaia. There's no central terminal, buses arrive at the various company offices scattered over town. Punta Arenas is the starting point for a wonderful cruise through the Magellan Straits to Ushuaia and Cape Horn.

Getting around The city is pleasant to walk around, with most shops and banks along Bories and Colón, running roughly east/west. There are fine hotels along here and around the main plaza which is two blocks south of Colón. Plenty of cheaper places to stay lie within seven blocks of the plaza. The city has a network of buses, taxis and there are *taxi-colectivos* – shared taxis which run along routes indicated by a number displayed on their roof. Coming to Chile from Argentina, you'll find everything relatively very expensive, and in rural areas, at least, services and infrastructure comparatively poor.

Tourist information The Chilean government office Sernatur is at Magallanes 960, T241330, www.sernatur.cl, 0830-1745, closed Sat and Sun. More helpful is the tourist information kiosk, English spoken, in the central area of the plaza, opposite Centro Español. Mon-Fri 0800-1900, Sat 0900-1900, Sun 0900-1300. informacionturstica @puntaarenas.cl, www.patagonia-chile.com, a helpful website, in English, full of information and links to hotels.

History

Although the first Europeans didn't arrive until the 16th century, southern Patagonia was inhabited from the end of the ice ages, by four different indigenous groups. The Portuguese sailor Hernando de Magallanes sailed through the straits that now bear his name in 1519, and soon Spanish ships were taking this route, and Francis Drake too, on his world voyage of 1578. Chile claimed these territories on gaining independence from

Spain, but the area remained uninhabited until 1843, when President Bulnes sent an expedition to establish a fort, detering the French and British who were rumoured to be interested. A replica of the original Fuerte Bulnes can be visited, 56 km south of the present city. Wool fortunes were made by Braun and Menéndez and then, abruptly, with the opening of the Panama Canal, the city lost its strategic advantage, and fell into a decline. Oil production became the major industry in the 1940's, but production has slumped as reserves have become depleted, and natural gas is now the main industry, along with fishing. Sheep farming continues to be important: half of Chile's sheep live here, and as you travel, you'll see vast herds being expertly gathered and moved great distances by shepherds on horseback with their dogs.

Punta Arenas

Sleeping
Finis Terrae **3** *C2*
Hospedaje
  Magallanes **5** *B2*
Hostal al Fin del
  Mundo **6** *C3*
Hostal Calafate 2 **7** *C2*
Hostal Carpa Manzano **8** *B3*
Hostal de la Avenida **9** *C2*
Hostal José
  Menéndez **10** *C2*
Hostal Paradiso **12** *A3*
Hostal Torres del Paine **13** *D2*
José Nogueira (Palacio
  Sara Braun) **14** *C2*
Luna Hostal **15** *B3*
Monte Carlo **17** *C2*
Monterrey **18** *B2*
Residencial Sonia
  Kuscevic **20** *A2*
Tierra del Fuego **22** *C2*

Eating
Centro Español **1** *D2*
Dino's Pizza **2** *B2*
El Puerto Viejo **3** *D3*
El Quijote **4** *C3*
Las Asturias **7** *C3*
Los Patiperros **8** *C2*
Lomit's **9** *C2*
Natta Pizza **10** *B2*
Sotito's **12** *D3*

Bars & clubs
La Taverna **13** *C2*
Pub Olijoe **14** *D3*

Shackleton, 'Yelcho' and the rescue from Elephant Island

Shackleton's 1914-16 expedition to cross the Antarctic is one of the epics of polar exploration. Shackleton's vessel, *Endurance*, which left England in August 1914 with 28 men aboard, became trapped in pack-ice in January 1915. After drifting northwards with the ice for eight months, the ship was crushed by the floes and sank. With three boats, supplies and the dogs, the group set up camp on an ice floe which continued to drift north for eight months. In April 1916, after surviving on a diet largely of seals and penguins, the party took to the boats as the ice broke up. After seven days at sea they reached Elephant Island. From there Shackleton and five other men sailed 1,300 kilometres in one of the boats on a 17-day voyage to South Georgia, where there were whaling stations. On reaching the south shore of South Georgia, Shackleton and two men crossed the island (the first such crossing and achieved without skis or snowshoes) to find help. Shackleton, from whom nothing had been heard by the outside world (*Endurance* had no radio) since leaving the island 18 months before, was not at first recognized.

Though the British government was sending a rescue vessel to Elephant Island, the delays involved led Shackleton to seek help locally. After ice had prevented two rescue attempts, the first from South Georgia and the second from the Falkland Islands/Islas Malvinas, Shackleton went to Punta Arenas, where the British community raised £1,500 to buy *Emma*, a small schooner with a wooden hull (best for the pack-ice) which was towed towards Elephant Island by the tug *Yelcho* but, after continuing alone, *Emma* was threatened by ice and the attempt was abandoned. Shackleton pursuaded the Chilean authorities to permit a fourth attempt using *Yelcho* after meteorological conditions had changed. Leaving Punta Arenas on 25 August 1916, the vessel encountered thick fog, but, unusually for the time of year, little ice and it quickly reached Elephant Island where the men, who had endured an Antarctic winter under upturned boats, were down to four days of supplies.

Though the expedition failed to cross Antarctica, Shackleton's achievement was outstanding: despite the loss of *Endurance*, the party had survived two Antarctic winters in extreme conditions without loss of life. Shackleton himself returned to the region in 1921 to lead another expedition, but in January 1922, though aged only 47, he suffered a fatal heart attack while in South Georgia.

Sights → *Calle Pedro Montt runs, east to west, while Calle Jorge Montt runs north to south*

The city's heart is Plaza Muñoz Gamero, planted with a splendid variety of mature trees, with several neo-classical buildings, the former mansions of the great sheep ranching families of the late 19th century. **Palacio Sara Braun** (1895) now Hotel José Nogueira, has elegant rooms which are open to the public. In the centre of the plaza is a striking statue of the explorer Magellan striding onto new territory, with a mermaid and two indigenous Fuegians at his feet. Around the corner, on Calle Magallanes is the **Teatro Cervantes**, now a cinema, with a beautifully decorated interior, and the fascinating **Museo de Historia Regional Braun Menéndez** ① *Magallanes 949, T244216, guided tours in Spanish, information cards in English Mon-Sat 1030-1700, Sun 1030-1400 summer. (1100-1300 winter), US$1.50. Highly recommended.* This grand mansion was built in 1905 by wealthy landowner Mauricio Braun, and its interiors have been restored so that you can admire the fabulously decorated rooms, filled with ornate furniture, paintings, marble and crystal all imported from Europe, an extreme contrast with the wild Patagonian landscape. Further north is the impressive **cemetery** ⓘ *Avenida Bulnes 929, daily 0800-1800*, where you can trace the town's history of European immigration and shipping disasters, through the huge mausoleums, divided by avenues of tall impeccably domed trees.

The city's best museum, and a perfect compliment to the Brauns' mansions is **Museo Regional Salesiano Mayorino Borgatello** ⓘ *in the Colegio Salesiano, Avenida Bulnes 374 (just as Bories ends and Bulnes begins), entrance next to church. T241096, daily 1000-1230, 1500-1800, (hours change frequently), US$2*. It covers the fascinating history of the indigenous peoples, and their 'education' by the Salesian missions, with many of their original artefacts, intricate weavings and bark canoes, next to the flouncy knitwear the Salesians taught them to make. There's also a fabulous array of stuffed birds, and huge displays on oil drilling and gas extraction, an odd contrast, but this is highly recommended. Ask the staff to see D'Agostini's film. The **Instituto de la Patagonia** ⓘ *Avenida Bulnes Km 4 north (opposite the University), outdoor exhibits open Mon-Fri 0830-1130, 1430-1830, Sat 0830-1230, US$2, T244216*, gives further insights into the tough lives of early pioneers, with an open-air museum, displaying artefacts used by the early settlers, a reconstructed pioneer home, old machinery and botanical gardens. For a view over the town, walk four blocks west of the Plaza along Calle Fagnano to the Mirador Cerro de La Cruz.

Around Punta Arenas

Reserva Forestal Magallanes, 7 km west of town, administration at Conaf in Punta Arenas. Tour operators in Punta Arenas run visits to the park, US$12 per person, is a pleasant place for a stroll, with a 1 km long self-guided nature trail, and several picnic sites in woodland. From the top end of the road running through the reserve, a short path leads to a lookout over the **Garganta del Diablo** (Devil's Throat), a gorge formed by the Río de las Minas, with views over Punta Arenas and Tierra del Fuego. **Fuerte Bulnes**, 56 km south, a replica of the wooden fort erected in 1843 by the crew of the Chilean vessel Ancud to secure these southernmost territories. There's little to see but this is the place where Punta Arenas was founded, and an interesting story. Tours are run by several agencies, US$12.

Parque Nacional Pali Aike, near Punta Delgada. One of the oldest archaeological sites in Patagonia, Pali Aike means 'desolate place of bad spirits' in Tehuelche, and when you reach the eerily coloured volcanic rock you'll see why. There's evidence here of aboriginal life from 10,000-12,000 years ago, making it worth the hike. Tour operators offer a full day trip, US$60, some involving trekking or horseriding.

At **Isla Magdalena**, a small island 30 km northeast of Punta Arenas, the **Monumento Natural Los Pingüinos** is a spectacular colony of 60,000 Magellanic penguins, who come here to breed between November and January. Magdalena is one of a group of three islands (the others are Marta and Isabel), visited by Drake, whose men killed 3,000 penguins for food. Deserted apart from the breeding season, the island is administrated by *Conaf*. Boat trip run by Comapa and by Agencia Broom.

Seno Otway (Otway Sound) ⓘ *entry US$4. Bus Fernández goes daily at 1530, returning 1930, US$12, tours are offered by several agencies, US$17, see below, page 498*, has a long low coastline with a smaller colony of Magellanic penguins, which can be viewed from walkways and bird hides. It's fun for children, as you can get close to the penguins, and ostrich-like Rheas can also be seen. (November-March only). A useful tour with *Patagonia Adventure Leaders*, (see below) goes on to Puerto Natales afterwards, daily departures.

From Punta Arenas a good, mostly flat, paved road runs north to Puerto Natales, 254 km away. Fuel is available in Villa Tehuelches, 100 km from Punta Arenas. See sleeping below for accommodation options en route.

Listings: Punta Arenas

● Sleeping

Prices are substantially lower during the winter months (Apr-Sep). Accommodation can also be found in private houses, usually **E** pp, ask at tourist offices.

LL Finis Terrae, *Colón 766, T228200, www.hotelfinisterrae.com* Modern Great Western owned hotel, international style, with well equipped rooms with bathrooms. American breakfast included, and panoramic views from the restaurant and lounge on the 6th floor, which serves great value dinner for non-residents too. English spoken.

LL José Nogueira, *Plaza de Armas, Bories 959 y P Montt, in the former Palacio Sara Braun, T248840, www.hotelnogueira.com* The best hotel in town with splendid rooms, a warm atmosphere, and excellent service. There's an elegant restaurant in the beautiful loggia, serving imaginatively prepared seafood. US$15 for 2 courses. Ask to see the 'museum', a few of the original rooms with a portrait of Sara Braun, open 1000-1300, 1800-2030, US$2.

L Tierra del Fuego, *Colón 716, T/F226200*. Spacious, tastefully-furnished rooms with calm feel, all with marble bathrooms, TV, phone and minibar. 2nd floor rooms have kitchenette, useful for those with families. The popular *Café 1900* downstairs serves delicious cake, and there's an excellent restaurant with a renowned chef, also open to non residents. Both are recommended.

B Hostal Calafate 2, *Magallanes 926, T/F241281. www.calafate.cl* This hotel has a rough and ready but friendly feel, slightly shambolic, with ropey bathrooms, though the rooms are simple and pleasant. Rooms overlooking the road are noisy, but it's not bad value, and very central. Internet access, travel agency. English spoken. (Also **Hostal Calafate 1**, *Latuaro Navarro 850, T/F248415*, less central, the same price, but quieter).

B Hostal Carpa Manzano, *Lautaro Navarro 336, T/F248864*. This attractive place has comfortable rooms with bath, and is in a quiet area. Recommended.

B Hostal de la Avenida, *Colón 534, T247532*. More of a bed and breakfast, there are attractive rooms with bath and TV here, coming off a pretty courtyard filled with plants. The owner is welcoming and friendly, and breakfast is included.

B Monte Carlo, *Av Colón 605, T/F243438*. In a charming old building, this is a traditional old travellers' hotel, and though a little run down now, it's welcoming, and its restaurant serves cheap basic fillers.

C Hostal José Menéndez, *José Menéndez 882, T/F221279*. Convenient for the Ushuaia bus, this is family-run by helpful people, and there's also a cheaper dormitory.

D Hostal Paradiso, *Angamos 1073, T224212*. A lovely simple welcoming place, bright neat rooms with bath; breakfast, parking, and use of kitchen included. Great value. Recommended.

D Hospedaje Magallanes, *Magallanes 570, T228616*. Nice double rooms with shared bathroom, in a relaxed atmosphere, part of Sebastian's and Marisol's home.

D Hostal Tores del Paine, *Chiloe 1370 y Independencia, T245211*. Rooms with bath, and others **E** to share bath, and lots of space in this friendly family home with 2 kitchens, luggage storage, and a big comfy sitting room where you can relax.

D pp **Luna Hostal**, *O'Higins 424, hostalluna@hotmail.com* A lovely quiet house with delightfully light minimalist rooms, comfy beds with duvets, and breakfast included. Highly recommeded.

E pp **Hostal al Fin del Mundo**, *O'Higgins 1026, T710185, www.alfindelmundo.cl* The best *hostal* in Punta Arenas, a new place in a lovely spacious house just 2 blocks from plaza, run by a young Chilean couple, Carolina and Rodrigo, who are welcoming, helpful, and speak English. Breakfast included, laundry, internet. Highly recommended.

E pp **Monterrey**, *Bories 621, T220636, monterrey@turismoaventura.net* Tiny rooms with private bath and TV, includes breakfast and clothes washing, and there's use of

---

For an explanation of the sleeping and eating price codes used in this guide, see the inside front cover. Other relevant information is provided in Essentials, see page 44.

kitchen. Comfortable, sweet, friendly people, great breakfast.

Fpp **Res Sonia Kuscevic**, *Pasaje Darwin 175, T248543, www.hostalsk.50megs.com* Popular and chaotic, with shoddy bathrooms, this is a friendly and helpful place. HI accepted, sheets provided, lockers, kitchen, tours organized.

North of Punta Arenas *p495*

Along the road from Punta Arenas north to Puerto Natales, (254 km away) are several hotels.

AL **Hostal Río Penitente**, *Km 138, T331694*. Accommodation in an old estancia.

B **Hotel Rubens**, *T226916, Km 183*. In the tiny Morro Chico, roughly halfway between Punta Arenas and Puerto Natales, where there is only a police station, a few shops and the hotel. Comfortable rooms with bath. Popular for fishing.

C **Hostería Llanuras de Diana**, *Km 215, T/F212853/219401 (Punta Arenas), T410661 (Puerto Natales)*. Hidden from road in a lovely open setting. Recommended.

C **Hostería Río Verde**, *Km 90, east off the highway on Seno Skyring, T311122, F241008*. Private bath, heating.

🍴 Eating

The seafood is superb here, and there are a clutch of marvellous traditional restaurants you should try, which are not exorbitantly expensive.

$$$ **El Puerto Viejo**, *O'Higgins 1205, T225103*. Good seafood and pastas in bright chic nautical surroundings, though pricey at US$20 for 2 courses.

$$$ **Las Asturias**, *Navaro 967*. An imaginative Basque inspired menu with meat dishes too, all very reasonably priced (US$10 for 2 courses) in a good atmosphere, popular with locals. Great service. Recommended.

$$$ **Restaurant Panoramico**, *Finis Terrae Hotel*. Serves a good cheap lunch Sun to Fri US$12 for 3 courses and coffee, also recommended their excellent buffet dinner Fri and Sat only, reserve ahead, US$14. On Sundays there's a brunch buffet.

$$$ **Sotito's**, *O'Higgins 1138*. Quite an

institution, and deservedly famous for excellent seafood in elegant surroundings. Try the king crab US$18 and conger eel US$8. Courteous old fashioned service. Book ahead in season.

$$ **Centro Español**, *Plaza Muñoz Gamero 771, above Teatro Cervantes*. Delicious seafood, and large helpings, but a limited selection.

$ **Dino's Pizza**, *Bories 557*. Cheap pizza, US$8 for two people, in a cheerful fast food atmosphere. Lots of choice.

$ **El Quijote**, *Lautaro Navarro 1087*. Good sandwiches, and cheap dinners US$6 for 2 courses, in brightly lit atmosphere, friendly owner. Recommended.

$ **Lomit's**, *Menéndez 722*. There are cheap snacks and drinks here, and it's open when the others are closed.

$ **Los Patiperros**, *Colon 782*. Handy and central, this serves tasty cheap seafood lunches, and their Chilean soup *Cazuela de Pollo* is recommended.

$ **Natta Pizza**, *Bories y Mejicana*. A cheery place with a good range of pizzas, from US$6 to US$14 for 2 people.

Cafés

1900, *Colón 716, next to Tierra del Fuego hotel*. The best in town, this well known and loved café-bar has comfy leather chairs and great home made cake, *torta de alfajor*, layers of fine pancake with *dulce de leche* between.

🍸 Bars and nightclubs

La Taverna, *on the plaza at Magallanes and Roca*. The most popular place in town for evening drinks.

Pub Olijoe, *O'Higgins 1138*. Looking rather like a traditional British pub, just off the costanera, this is a good spot for a beer with a lively atmosphere.

Kamakaze, *Bories 655*. A disco, very popular with tourists, recommended.

☺ Sport and activities

Skiing Cerro Mirador, *9 km west from Punta Arenas in the Reserva Nacional Magallanes*. This is the only place in Chile where you can ski with a sea view. Take

Transtur buses 0900 and 1400 from in front of *Hotel Cabo de Hornos*, US$3, return, taxi US$7. A day ski pass costs US$7; equipment rental, US$6 per adult. Mid-way, there's a lodge selling food and drink and renting equipment. The season runs Jun-Sep, weather permitting. Contact **Club Andino**, *T241479, www.clubandino.tierra.cl* about cross-country skiing facilities.

⊙ Shopping

Many shops close 1230-1500.

Duty Free

Punta Arenas has a duty free shop at Zona Franca, 3½ km north of the centre, opposite Museo Instituto de la Patagonia, though it's hardly cheaper than elsewhere. Closed 1230-1500 and Sunday. (Take bus E or A from Plaza Muñoz Gamero. Many *colectivo taxis*; taxi US$3).

Handicrafts and regional produce

Handicrafts are for for sale at stalls in the plaza. **Artesanias Ñandu**, *O'Higgins 1401*. **Artesanía Ramas**, *Independencia 799*. **Chile Típico**, *Carrera Pinto 1015*. Outdoor stalls at the bottom of Independencia, by the port entrance. **Cava de la Patagonia**, *Magallanes on the Plaza*. Chilean fine wines. **Chocolatta**, *Bories 852*. Delicious hand-made chocolate.

Clothing

Marisol, *Zenteno 0164*. Outdoor Clothing, good quality clothes and wool goods, Fagnano 675.

Supermarkets

Abu-Gosch, *Bories 647*. **Cofrima**, *Lautaro Navarro 1293 y Balmaceda*. **Cofrima 2**, *España 01375*. **Listo**, *21 de Mayo 1133*.

⊃ Tour operators

Most organize tours to Torres del Paine, Fuerte Bulnes and the pingüinera on Otway sound: shop around as prices vary. **Turismo Aonikenk**, *Magallanes 619, T228332. www.aonikenk.com* Excellent tailor-made multi-adventure and trekking tours for all levels of fitness. Exploring mountain wilderness, rainforest and steppe in imaginatively created expeditions. See website for options. Highly recommended. French, German, English spoken. **Turismo Yamana**, *Colon 568, T235773, www.yamana.cl* Conventional tours, plus trekking programmes to Torres del Paine, guides and all camping equipment provided. Plus kayaking in the Magellan straits, and multi adventure trips in Tierra del Fuego, including trekking and riding. Multilingual guides. Recommended. **Turismo Aventour**, *J Nogueira 1255, T241197, aventour@entelchile.net* Specialize in fishing trips, and organize tours to Tierra del Fuego. Helpful, English spoken. **Turismo Comapa**, *Magallanes 990, T200200, www.comapa.com* Offer tours to Torres del Paine, Tierra del Fuego and to see the penguins at Isla Magdalena. Also sell tickets for sailings Pto Montt to Pto Natales. Agents for the highly recommended Cruceros Australis cruise to Ushuaia, Isla Navarino and Cape Horn. US$1600 for 2, summer only, book ahead. www.australis.com **Turismo Laguna Azul**, *Menendez 631, T245331, www.payne.cl* Treking to San Isidro lighthouse, bird watching walks, Pali Aike all day trips, and to Estancia Punta Delgada, including lunch. **LMB Turismo Aventura**, *Colon y Armando Sanhueza, T229706, www.turismo aventuralmb.com* Adventure tours, horseriding and kayaking. **Viento Sur**, *Fagnano 585, T225167, T/F228712, www.vientosur.com* Horseriding, kayaking in the Magellan strait, and hiking at Pale Aike, mountain biking up Mt Fenton, plus conventional tours to Torres del Paine. **Patagonia Adventure Leaders**, *T240104, www.patagoniaaustral.net/pal* They run the useful trip called *Penguin Adventure Line*, to Puerto Natales via the penguin colony at Otway Sound. US$17 compared to US$9for bus alone, daily departures from Punta Arenas at 1500. Lots of chance to stop and take photos, friendly guide, can request English speaker. **Fantastico Sur**, *Magallanes 960, second floor, (next to Sernatur), T/F226054, www.patagonianature.com* Expert birdwatching and nature excursions to see wildlife in Patagonia and Tierra del Fuego, as well as boat trips to the Falkland Islands, and the Patagonian fjords. Recommended.

Isla Magdellena *p495*

Monumento Natural Los Pingüinos Boat trip run by **Comapa**, 3 times a week (Dec-Feb only), 2 hrs each way, with 2 hrs on the island, returns 2100, US$30; take your own refreshments, as they're expensive on board. The trip may be cancelled if windy. Highly recommended. Tours are also run by Melinka of **Agencia Broom** (see Ferries to Tierra del Fuego, below). Boats leave from Terminal Tres Puentes (take colectivo 15 from town). Tue, Thu, Sat 1530 Jan-Feb, returns 2100, US$30.

⊖ Transport

Punta Arenas *p492, map p493*

Airport **NB** Long distance transport is heavily booked from mid Dec to early Feb: advance booking is essential. Carlos Ibáñez de Campo Airport, 20km north of town. There is a bus service run by **Buses Transfer**, *Pedro Montt 966*, between Navarro y O'Higgins. Scheduled to meet flights, US$2.50. Buses to **Puerto Natales** also stop at the airport. **LanChile** and **DAP** have their own bus services from town, US$2.50. Taxi US$12. The airport restaurant is good.

To **Santiago**, LanChile, LanExpress and Aero Continente daily, via **Puerto Montt** (sit on right for views). When no tickets are available, go to the airport and get on the standby waiting list. To **Porvenir**, Aerovías DAP twice daily Mon-Sat, 12 minutes, US$23. To **Puerto Williams**, daily Mon-Sat, 1¼ hrs, US$71. From **Puerto Natales** to **El Calafate**, Mon-Fri, 40mins, US$57. Aerovías DAP also offers Antarctic trips including simple accommodation: Isla Rey Jorge 1 day, 2 days to 4 days US$3,800. Services to Argentina: To **Ushuaia**, Aerovías DAP, twice a week, US$120 (schedules change frequently). Reserve well in advance from mid-Dec to Feb.

Bus

NB Take passport when booking tickets to Argentina. There's no central terminal, so buses leave from company offices. **Pingüino** and **Fernández**, *Sanhueza 745, T242313, www.busesfernandez.com* **Pacheco**, *Colón 900, T242174; Central de Pasajeros, T245811*, useful office for booking all tickets, with **Bus Sur**, at *Colón y Magallanes, T244464*. **Bus Sur 2**, *Menéndez 565, T244464*. **Ghisoni**, *L.Navarro*

975, T222078 www.ghisoni.terra.cl ghisoni@ctcinternet.cl

To **Puerto Natales**, 3½ hrs, Fernández, Bus Sur, and **Buses Transfer** several every day, last departure 2000, US$5, with pick-up at the airport, book in advance. TurBus, **Ghisoni** and **Austral** have services through Argentina to **Osorno** and **Puerto Montt**, US$55 (cheaper off season), 36 hrs. TurBus continues to **Santiago**, US$95 (US$60 in winter), 46 hrs.

Buses to Argentina To Río Gallegos via Punta Delgada, **Pingüino** daily; Ghisoni, Mon Wed, Thu, Sat; **Pacheco**, Fri, Sun, Tue. US$11, officially 5 hrs, but can take up to 8, depending on customs, 15 mins on Chilean side, up to 2 hrs on Argentine side, including 30 mins lunch at Km 160. To Río Grande, via Punta Delgada, **Pacheco**, Mon, Wed, Fri, **Ghisoni** Tue, Thu, Sat, 8-9 hrs, US$20, heavily booked. To **Ushuaia** via Punta Delgada, Ghisoni/Tecni Austral, Tue, Thu, Sat, **Tolkeyen** Mon, Wed, Fri 12-14 hrs, US$30. Book well in advance in Jan-Feb. There are currently no buses Rio Grande via ferry crossing at Porvenir.

Overland to Argentina From Punta Arenas there are 3 routes to **Calafate** and **Río Gallegos**:

1 Northeast via Route 255 and Punta Delgada to the border at Kimiri Aike and then along Argentine Route 3 to Río Gallegos.

2 North along Route 9, turning 9 km before Puerto Natales for Dorotea (good road) and then northeast via La Esperanza (fuel, basic accommodation).

3 Via Puerto Natales and Cerro Castillo on the road to Torres del Paine joining the road to La Esperanza at Paso Cancha Carrera. To get to Ushuaia, take route 255 northeast, cross to Tierra del Fuego at Punta Delgada, and drive south to cross the Argentine border at San Sebastián. Take route 3 to Rio Grande.

Car hire

You need a hire company's authorization to take a car into Argentina, allow 24 hrs to arrange this; mandatory international insurance at US$240. Damage to windscreens in very common, so ask about the company's policy on this before hiring. **Internacional**, *Waldo Seguel 443, T228323*. **Hertz**, *O'Higgins, 987, T229049*.

Ferry Services to **Porvenir** (Tierra del Fuego), daily except Mon, 0900, sunday 0930. Same boat goes on to huge penguin colony at **Isla Magdalena**. US$35, includes guide. Comapa, *Magallanes 990, T200202, www.comapa.cl*

Ship Navimag runs the shipping line from Puerto Montt to **Puerto Natales**, in the same office as **Comapa** (*Compañía Marítima de Punta Arenas*), *Magallanes 990, T200200, www.navimag.com www.comapa.cl* This dramatic 1,460km journey takes 4 days and 3 nights, with full board in a berth, cabin, or reclining seat. Though the scenery is undoubtedly spectacular, the trip has become a 'real gringo experience' with lots of card playing and beer drinking. It's cheaper to fly, or take the bus through Argentina, a very long journey, but a great experience of Patagonia, via the splendours of El Chalten, El Calafate and the Argentine lake district (cheaper and better services than Chile). Fares range from US$250pp economy, with US$297 the cheapest shared cabin, to US$1,513 for a private cabin. Cars and bikes can be carried on the mixed cargo boats, there is video entertainment, and food is poor when boats are busy. See website for sailings.

Highly recommended is the cruise from Punta Arenas through the Magellan Strait and the 'avenue of glaciers' to **Ushuaia**, **Puerto Williams** and **Cape Horn** on **Mare Australis**. Lots of trips to disembark and see wildlife, and talks from experts, accommodation is very comfortable, it is an 'unforgettable experience'. Cruises are for 7-12 days, you can leave the boat at Ushuaia. Details from **Comapa**, and *www.australis.com* US$1600 in summer for 2. Advance booking (advisable) from **Cruceros Australis SA**, *Santiago office T+56-2 442 3110, Buenos Aires office T011-4325 4000.*

To Antarctica Other than asking in agencies for possible spare berths on cruise ships, the only possibility is with the Chilean Navy. The Navy itself does not encourage passengers, so you must approach the captain direct. Spanish is essential. Two vessels, **Galvarino** and **Lautaro**, sail regularly (no schedule); usual rate US$80 pp per day, including 4 meals. Isotop@mitierra.cl

Taxi
Ordinary taxis have yellow roofs. *Colectivos* (all black) run on fixed routes, US$0.50 for anywhere on route. Reliable service from **Radio Taxi Austral**, T247710/244409.

ⓘ Directory

Airline offices LanChile, *Lautaro Navarro 999, T241232, F222366. www.lanchile.cl* Aerovías DAP, *O'Higgins 891, T223340, www.aeroviasdap.cl* Open 0900-1230, 1430-1930. Helpful. **Banks** open Mon-Fri 0830-1400. Most banks and some supermarkets have ATMs; many on the Plaza. *Casas de cambio* open Mon-Fri 0900-1230, 1500-1900, Sat 0900-1230. Scott Cambios, *Magallanes y Colón, T227145*, Sur Cambios, *Lautaro Navarro 1001, T225656*. Outside business hours try Buses Sur, *Colón y Magallanes*, and the major hotels (lower rates). Good rates at Cambio Gasic, *Roca 915, Oficina 8, T242396*, German spoken. La Hermandad, *Lautaro Navarro 1099, T243991*, excellent rates, US$ cash for Amex TCs. Sur Cambios, *Lautaro Navarro 1001, T225656*, accepts Tcs. **Communications** Internet All over the centre (see the tourist office map). Cybercafe del sur, *Croacia 1028*, Hostal Calafate 2, *Magallanes 992*, fast and efficient. **Post Office** *Bories 911 y Menéndez*. Mon-Fri 0830-1930, Sat 0900-1400. Entel, *Lautaro Navarro 957*, Mon-Fri 0830-2200, Sat-Sun 0900-2200, expensive. Many *locutorios*, called *centros de llamadas* here, but shop around, prices vary.

Consulates Argentina, *21 de Mayo 1878, T261912*, open 1000-1530, visas take 24 hrs. Belgium, *Roca 817, Oficina 61, T241472*. Italy, *21 de Mayo 1569, T221596*. Netherlands, *Magallanes 435, T248100*. Spain, *J Menéndez 910, T243566*. UK, *Cataratas de Nicaragua 01325, T211535*. **Library** Biblioteca Patrimonio Austral, *J Menéndez 741*. Specializing in culture and geography of the region. **Medical services** **Hospitals** Hospital Regional Lautaro Navarro, *Angamos 180, T244040*. Public hospital, for emergency room ask for *La Posta*. Clínica Magallanes, *Bulnes 01448, T211527*. Private clinic, medical staff is the same as in the hospital but fancier surroundings and more expensive.

Puerto Natales → *Phone: +56-(0)61 Colour map 6, B2 Population: 20,500*

Beautifully situated on the calm waters of Canal Señoret fjord, an arm of the Ultima Esperanza Sound, edged with spectacular mountains, Puerto Natales is a pretty, quiet town of brightly painted corrugated tin houses. It's the base for exploring the magnificent Balmaceda and Torres del Paine national parks, and although inundated with visitors in the summer, it retains a quiet unhurried feel, a recommended place to relax for a few days.

Ins and outs → *See also Transport page 506.*

Getting there Puerto Natales is conveniently situated for Torres del Paine, 147 km away, and there are several buses daily to and from the park (around 3 hrs). Daily bus services to/from El Calafate in Argentina, (6 hrs) all of which go via the little town of Cerro Castillo, where you can pick up a bus to the park, and avoid Puerto Natales altogether, if short of time. There are hourly buses to Río Turbio to cross the border into Argentina, and from there, buses to Río Gallegos, with a direct service daily too. And several buses a day go to Punta Arenas, 3½ hrs.

Tourist information ⓘ *on the waterfront at Av Pedro Montt y Phillipi, Mon-Sat 0900-1900, T412125, www.chileanpatagonia.com/natales.* No one speaks English in

Chilean Patagonia Puerto Natales

Puerto Natales

0 metres 100
0 yards 100

Sleeping ⊙
Albergue
Path@Gone 1 *B3*
Blanquita 2 *C2*
Bulnes 3 *B2*
Casa Cecilia 4 *B2*
Concepto Indigo 5 *B1*
Costa Australis 6 *C1*
Hospedaje Dos
Lagunas 7 *B1*
Hostal Lady
Florence Dixie 9 *B3*
Hostal Sir Francis
Drake 10 *A2*
Josmar 2 Camping 11 *C2*
Lago Sarmiento 12 *C1*
Martín Gusinde 13 *B2*

Niko's 15 *C3*
Patagonia Adventure
& Sendero Aventura 16 *B2*
Residencial Bernadita 17 *C3*
Residencial Dickson 18 *C2*
Residencial El Mundial 19 *B2*
Saltos del Paine 21 *B1*
Sra Teresa Ruiz 22 *C2*

Eating ⊙
Centro Español 1 *B2*
El Asador

Patagónico 2 *B2*
El Living 3 *B2*
El Marítimo 4 *B1*
La Burbuja 5 *B2*
Los Pioneros 6 *B1*

Bars & clubs ⊙
El Bar de Ruperto 7 *B2*
Kaweshkar 8 *C1*

this (very basic) tourist office, but they have good leaflets on Puerto Natales and Torres del Paine in English, and bus and boat information in the park. The *Conaf* office (though you can get better information elsewhere) is at Carrera Pinto 566. www.patagonia-chile.com is a helpful resource.

Sights

Founded in 1911, Puerto Natales was a sleepy fishing village, which grew thanks to a huge local meatpacking industry, and coal mining, which has since declined. Now tourism is the most lucrative industry, and the town offers a good range of accommodation, and some fine places to eat.

The quiet neat plaza, with its sculptural trees like something form a surrealist painting, lies just northwest of the main streets Eberhard and Bulnes, where you'll find banks and services. Hotels are mostly clustered within a few blocks of here and along the waterfront, a lovely place to walk, with magnificent views. The small **Museo Historico** ① *Bulnes 285, free, open Mon-Fri 0900-1300, 1500-2000, weekends pm only*, has displays and photos of early colonizers. Another good place for a stroll is up to **Cerro Dorotea**, the hill which dominates the town, offering superb views of the Seno Ultima Esperanza and across into Argentina. The base of the Cero can be reached by any bus going east, for Río Turbio or Punta Arenas, and alight at the road for summit (Km 9.5).

Around Puerto Natales → *For access and tours to the Torres del Paine, see page 507.*

The **Monumento Natural Cueva Milodón** ① *25 km north, US$5 to enter park, camping allowed. Regular bus from Prat 517, T412540, leaves 0945 and 1500, returns 1200 and 1700. US$7.50; taxi US$18 return, or ask tour guides if you can get a lift back on their bus. Both Adventur and Fernández tour buses to Torres del Paine stop at the cave.* This is a wide and deep letterbox of a cave (70 m wide, 45 m high and 270 m deep), formed by the lapping of glacial lakes in the ice age, which were then 300 m above the current lake. Remains have been found here of a prehistoric ground-sloth, together with evidence of occupation by early Patagonian humans some 11,000 years ago. The ceiling of the cave is dimpled with mineral deposits, inside it is as silent as a library, and the view of the landscape from its depths is marvellous. There's a small visitor centre, with summaries in English, and toilets.

Border with Argentina

There are three crossing points: **Villa Dorotea**, 16 km east of Puerto Natales. On the Argentine side the road continues to a junction, with alternatives south to Río Turbio and north to La Esperanza and Río Gallegos. Chilean immigration is open all year 0800-2200 (24 hours November-March). **Paso Casas Viejas**, 16 km northeast of Puerto Natales. On the Argentine side this joins the Río Turbio-La Esperanza road. Chilean immigration is open all year 0800-2200. **Cerro Castillo**, 65 km north of Puerto Natales on the road to Torres del Paine. On the Argentine side, Paso Cancha Carrera (14 km), the road leads to La Esperanza and Río Gallegos. All buses from El Calafate now go via Cerro Castillo, making it possible to catch a bus there passing from Pto Natales into Torres del Paine. Chilean immigration is open all year 0800-2200, and the small settlement has several *hospedajes* and *cafeterias*.

Bernardo O'Higgins National Park

Often referred to as the Parque Nacional Monte Balmaceda, this park covers large expanses of the icefields of the Campo de Hielo Sur and the fjords and offshore islands further west, including Isla Wellington. The park is uninhabited; the small community of Puerto Edén on Isla Wellington is outside the park limits. Though the park is inaccessible except by air and sea, the southernmost section of the park, around Monte Balmaceda (2,035 m) lies at the northern end of the Seno Ultima Esperanza and can be reached by boat from Puerto Natales. Two boats *21 de Mayo*

66 99 The ceiling of the cave is dimpled with mineral deposits, and inside it's as quiet as a library. The view of the landscape from its depths through its letterbox mouth is marvellous...

and *Alberto de Agostini* sail daily from Puerto Natales in summer and on Sundays in winter when weather conditions may be better with less cloud and rain.

After a three-hour journey up the Sound, the boat passes the **Balmaceda Glacier** which drops steeply from the eastern slopes of Monte Balmaceda (2,035 m). The glacier is retreating; in 1986 its foot was at sea level. The boat docks one hour further north at Puerto Toro, from where it is a 1 km walk to the base of the Serrano Glacier on the north slope of Monte Balmaceda. On the trip dolphins, sea lions (in season), black-necked swans, flightless steamer ducks and cormorants can be seen. There's an optional extra three-hour boat trip, also recommended, in zodiacs 35 km up the **Río Serrano** into PN Torres del Paine, which you can use to start trekking, or take a bus back to Puerto Natales from the administration centre.

Listings: Puerto Natales

⊜ Sleeping

NB In season cheaper accommodation fills up quickly after the arrival of the 'Puerto Edén' ship from Puerto Montt.

LL Costa Australis, *Pedro Montt 262, T412000, www.australis.com* The smartest hotel in Punta Arenas and with very comfortable traditional-style rooms, all with a relaxing and tranquil atmosphere, and some with lovely views over fjord, equipped with TV minibar, phone. There's a lift and the professional staff speak English. There's a good waterfront restaurant serving international and local seafood specialities. Recommended.

L Martín Gusinde, *Bories 278, T412770, www.chileaustral.com/grey* American-style buffet breakfast is included in this ultra-modern and smart, but slightly soulless place. Rooms have good bathrooms, phone and TV, and parking is included. There's an expensive restaurant.

AL Hostal Lady Florence Dixie, *Bulnes 659, T411158, florence@chileanpatagonia.com* Modern, friendly place. Recommended.

AL Saltos del Paine, *Bulnes 156, T413607,* *www.saltosdelpaine.cl* A modern building with warm and cosy rooms, though the taste is rather odd, with TV and good spacious bathrooms, breakfast included. Comfortable but a bit overpriced.

A Hostal Sir Francis Drake, *Phillipi 383, Eberhard 104, T411553.* A lovely calm and welcoming *hostería* with tastefully decorated rooms with bathrooms, delicious filling breakfasts with home made cakes and good views. Welcoming owner. Recommended.

B Concepto Indigo, *Ladrilleros 105, T413609, www.conceptoindigo.com* An old traditional Chilean house on the water front with great views, this is a relaxed place with a good atmosphere. Simply furnished rooms with bath, some (cheaper) without, and breakfast included. The café restaurant downstairs is a great place to hang out, serving tasty seafood and vegetarian dishes. Internet.

B Lago Sarmiento, *Bulnes 90, T411542, www.hotellagosarmiento.galeon.com* Smart simple modern rooms with dodgy bathrooms, but this is very good value, and has a comfortable living room with a good view.

C Blanquita, *Carrera Pinto 409.* Quiet very friendly place with simple rooms, stores luggage.

Dpp **Casa Cecilia**, *Tomás Rogers 60,
T/F411797, redcecilia@entelchile.net*
Welcoming and hugely popular, this large
house has small simple rooms, some singles,
other doubles B with bath, great breakfast.
English, French and German spoken by the
owners, who also rent camping equipment
and bicycles, and can book tours and
information for Torres del Paine. There are
also E shared rooms with bunk beds.
Recommended.

D **Hostal Patagonia**, *Patagonia 972, T412756.*
Helpful, tea and biscuits at any time, tours
booked, laundry service, use of kitchen.

Dpp **Res Dickson**, *Bulnes 307, T411871,
lodgin@chileaustral.com* Good value, with
breakfast included, helpful, cooking and
laundry facilities.

Epp **Patagonia Adventure**, *Tomás Rogers
179, T411028, patagonia_adventure
@terra.cl* In a lovely house on the plaza,
owned by Karin and Pablo, with a bohemian
feel, homemade bread for breakfast, luggage
store, and equipment hire. Shared
bathrooms but great value. Recommended.
They also run a tour company.

Epp **Albergue Path@Gone**, *Eberhard 595,
T413291, www.chileaustral.com/pathgone*
Comfortable dorm beds, with good
bathrooms, breakfast included. Also a very
helpful agency for Torres del Paine.

Epp **Hosp Dos Lagunas**, *Barros Araña 104,
T415733, doslagunas@hotmail.com*
Welcoming hospitable place with good
breakfast, dinner available, shared bath, use
of kitchen, TV and reading room, excursions
and buses booked, lots of information.

E **Mwono Lodge**, *Eberhard 214, T411018,
www.mwonopatagonia.cjb.net* Nice brightly
decorated place with comfy shared rooms,
and breakfast included. Recommended.

Epp **Res El Mundial**, *Bories 315, T412476,
elmundial@fortalezapatagonia.cl* Large
breakfast, good value meals, luggage stored.

Epp **Sra Teresa Ruiz**, *Esmeralda 463.* Good
value, in this warm and quiet place, breakfast
included, also cheap meals, and tours to
Torres del Paine arranged.

F **Bulnes**, *Bulnes 407, T411307.* With
breakfast, a simple but charming place, clean
with clean comfy rooms, very friendly,
laundry facilities, stores luggage.

F **Niko's**, *E Ramírez 669, F412810.* With
breakfast included, this is a very hospitable
family-run place with kitchen facilities,
luggage store, good meals, information,
travel arrangements made. Recommended.

F **Residencial Bernadita**, *O'Higgins 765.*
Nice clean place, good value.

Camping

Camping Daysee, *Av Espana, Huerto no 70, T
411281*, US$4 per site. All facilities, hot
showers, laundry service, call from bus
terminal for free pickup.

Josmar 2, *Esmeralda 517, in the centre.* Family
run, convenient, with hot showers, parking,
fireplaces, electricity, and café, US$2.50 per
site or F pp in double room.

North of Puerto Natales *p502*
Hotels in the countryside open only in
summer months.

L **Cisne de Cuello Negro**, *Av Colón 782,
Punta Arenas, pehoe1@ctcinternet.cl
T244506, T411498.* In a splendid tranquil
lakeside setting, 5km from town at Km 275
near Puerto Bories. Comfortable rooms with
excellent cooking in the dining room.

L **Hostería y Refugio Monte Balmaceda**,
220174, aventour@entelchile.net Beautifully
situated on the shores of Ultima Esperanza
sound, close to the entry of Río Serrano.
Comfortable rooms with bathrooms, a
restaurant, and also accommodation in a
refugio: well-lit giant tents, with beds and
bathrooms. Also organize tours and rent
equipment rental too. Handy for boat trip up
Río Serrano. Recommended.

A **Cabañas Koten Aike**, *on the costanera at
km 2, T412581.* Modern well maintained
cabañas with a perfect lakeside setting.

A **Hotel 3 Pasos**, *40 km north, T228712,
agencia@vientosur.com* Good value in this
simple, beautiful place.

Border with Argentina *p502*
B **Hostería El Pionero**, *T/F411646 or 691932
extension 722.* Comfortable country house
ambience, good service.

Dpp **Hospedaje Loreto Belén**, *T413063, or
T691932, public phone, ask to speak to Loreto
Belén.* Rooms for 4, all with bath, breakfast
included. Offers meals, good home cooking.

• **Phone codes** Puerto Natales: +56-(0)61.

Eating

There are good mid-range priced restaurants in both *Hotels Costa Australis*, and *Martin Gusinde* (see above).

$$ **Centro Español**, *Magallanes 247. T411181*. Smart surroundings and an impressive menu with local seafood, lamb too every day in summer. *Congrio a la vasca* with cream and pepper and garlic is recommended.

$$ **El Asador Patagonico**, *Prat 158 on the Plaza next to El Living, T413553*. Fabulous lamb on *asado*, salads and good home made puddings, in an attractive bright interior with old furniture. Welcoming owners. US$11 for 2 courses. Recommended.

$ **Concept Indigo**. A laid back restaurant with views over the water, seafood, vegetarian dishes, all in calm atmosphere. US$ 9 for 2 courses.

$ **Don Chicho**, *Luis Martinez 206, T415777*. Also an experience not to be missed, the best and most welcome *parrilla* in town, great fish on *asado* too, great authentic atmosphere with the charismatic Don Chicho himself.

$ **El Living**, Plaza de Armas. Just what you need: comfy sofas where you can relax, drink good tea, read magazines in all languages, listen to mellow music, eat delicious vegetarian food and relax. Absolutely wonderful.

$ **El Maritimo**. This is slightly the better of the two seafront restaurants, the other being *Los Pineros*, below, serving excellent and good value fish, friendly service from the owners, and wonderful views. Try the *congrio* US$6. Recommended.

$ **La Burbuja**, *Bulnes 300*. Recommended for great range of local seafood, eg king crab US$9, filling portions, homely surroundings. Try the fish soup.

$ **Los Pioneros**, *Pedro Montt 166, T410783*. Seafood specialities in smart simple place with family welcome. US$7 for salmon.

Bars and nightclubs

El Bar de Ruperto, *Bulnes 371, T414302*. Friendly lively place with DJs, live music, lots of drinks (try the vodka with chillies) and some food. Open 2100-0500.
Kaweshkar, *Bulnes 43, T415821,*
kaweshkar@yurhouse.com Groovy laid back bar, serving *empanadas*, hamburgers, and vegetarian food. Try the parmesan molluscs tacos. Club at night with lounge music.
Disco Milodon, *Blanco Encalada 854*. Dancing in summer.

Shopping

Camping equipment
Average charges per day: whole set US$12, tent US$6, sleeping bag US$3-5, mat US$1.50, raincoat US$0.60, also cooking gear, US$1-2. (NB Deposits required: tent US$200, sleeping bag US$100.) Camping gas is widely available in hardware stores, eg at *Baquedano y O'Higgins* and at *Baquedano y Esmeralda*. **Patagonia Adventures**, *Tomás Rogers 179*. **Casa Cecilia**, *Tomás Rogers 54*. Recommended. **Las Rosas del Campo**, *Baquedano 383, T410772*. Good, with some equipment for sale including wet weather gear. **Turismo María José**, *Bulnes 386*. Rents good quality equipment, also arranges tours, internet access.

Fishing tackle
Andes Patagónicos, *Blanco Encalada 226, T411594*. Tackle for hire, at US$3.50 per day for rod, reel and spinners; if you prefer fishing with floats, hooks, split shot, etc, take your own.

Handicrafts
Hielo Azul, *Eberhard*. Presents, lovely handmade jumpers.

Supermarkets
El Favorito, *Bulnes 1085*. **Super Dos**, *Bulnes y Balmaceda*. Cheaper in Punta Arenas. 24-hr supermarket.

Tour companies

There are very mixed reports of agencies, especially for their trips to Torres del Paine. It's better to book tours direct with operators in Puerto Natales than through agents in Punta Arenas.
Many companies offer tours into Torres del Paine or O'Higgins national parks, with transport and accommodation included. As you'll see from that section (below) refugios and campsites in Torres del Paine are mostly run by either **Andescape** or **Fantástico Sur**, and boat trips are operated by **Onas**. The

excellent and helpful **Path@gone**, *Eberhard 595 y Blanco Encalada, T/F413290, www.pathagone.com* is the joint office for all of these, which means you can organize transport and all your accommodation in one place, and get good advice on how to plan your trip.

Andescape, *T/F412877, www.chileaustral.com/andescape*
Onas, *T/F414349, www.onaspatag onia.com* *Path@gone* also organize their own all inclusive adventure trips in the park, with expert guides, food and super comfortable camping included, such as the fabulous trip ice trekking in Glacier Grey including the boat trip to Balmaceda glacier and up the Río Serrano. English spoken, highly recommended.

Turismo Paori, *Eberhard 577, T411229, www.turismopaori.com* Conventional day tours into Torres del Paine, cheap, and with English speaking guides.

Bigfoot, *Blanco Encalada 226-B, T414611, explore@bigfootpatagonia.com* Sea kayaking and ice hiking. Recommended.

Sendero Aventura, *Albergue Patagonia Adventure, Tomás Rogers 179, T415636, sendero_aventura@terra.cl* Adventure tours, including trekking to Torres del Paine, boats in Balmaceda park, hiring of camping equipment and bikes. Highly recommended.

Patagonias Last Frontier, *info@avertour aventuras.com* Boat trips from Puerto Natales to Serrano Glacier, trekking, kayakking, ice trekking, and fishing.

Turismo Zalej, *Bulnes 459, T412260, F411355*. Recommended. Several agencies offer tours to the Perito Moreno glacier in Argentina, 1 day, US$40 without food or park entry fee. You can then leave the tour in Calafate to continue into Argentina.

⊖ Transport

Puerto Natales *p501, map p501*
Bicycle hire
Casa Cecilia, (see under sleeping). **Bicycle repairs** **El Rey de la Bicicleta**, Ramírez 540, good, helpful.

Bus
NB In summer buses fill fast: book ahead. Buses leave from company offices: **Bus Sur**, *Baquedano 558, T411325,*

www.bussur.cl **Cootra**, *Baquedano 244, T412785*, Zaahj, *Prat 236, T412260*, **Bus Fernández**, *Eberhard 555, T411111*. **Transfer**, *Baquedano 414, T421616*.

To **Punta Arenas**, several daily, 3½ hrs, US$5, **Fernandez**, **Bus Sur** and **Transfer**. To **Coyhaique**, **Urbina** and **Bus Sur**, twice weekly, Nov-Mar, US$120. To **Argentina**: to **Río Gallegos** direct, **Bus Sur**, US$8.50, Tue and Thu 0630 and **El Pingüino**, Wed and Sun 1200, US8.50. Hourly to **Río Turbio**, Lagoper, *Baquedano y Valdivia*, and other companies, US$2.75, 2 hrs (depending on Customs – change bus at border). To **El Calafate**, **Cootra**, via Río Turbio, daily, US$20, 6 hrs; or **Bus Sur** (2 a week) and **Zaahj** (3 a week) both operating a more direct service via Cerro Castillo, 4½-5 hrs, US$25. Otherwise travel agencies run several times a week depending on demand, 5 hrs, US$30, shop around, reserve 1 day ahead.

Car hire
Car hire agents can arrange permission to drive into Argentina, but it takes 24 hrs and extra insurance is required.
Bien al Sur, *Bulnes 433, T414025*.
Motor Cars, *Blanco Encalada 330, T413593*.
EMSA Avis, *Bulnes 6322, T410775*.

Sea
There are weekly sailings in summer to **Puerto Montt** with Navimag. Their office with *Comapa* is: *Pedro Montt 262 Loc B, Terminal Marítimo, T414300, www.navimag.com www.comapa.cl* This dramatic 1,460km journey takes 4 days and 3 nights, with full board in a berth, cabin, or reclining seat. Though the scenery is undoubtedly spectacular, the trip has become a 'real gringo experience' with lots of card playing and beer drinking. It's cheaper to fly, or take the bus through Argentina, a very long journey, but a great experience of Patagonia, via the splendours of El Chaltén, El Calafate and the Argentine lake district (cheaper and better services than Chile.) Fares range from US$250pp economy, with US$297 the cheapest shared cabin, to US$1,513 for a private cabin. Cars and bikes can be carried on the mixed cargo boats, there is video entertainment, and food is poor when boats are busy. See website for sailings.

Balmaceda Glacier p503

There are sailings to Balmaceda Glacier daily at 0815 in summer, returning 1630, and on Sunday only in winter, (minimum 10 passengers), US$55. Including Rio Serrano, US$85. Bookings direct from *Turismo 21 de Mayo, Eberhard 560, T411978,* Nueva Galicia, *Eberhard 169, T412352,* or Onas Turismo, *Eberhard 599, T412707.* Expensive lunch extra, take picnic, drinks available on board. Heavily booked in high season. Take warm clothes, hat and gloves.

⊙ Directory

Airline offices
LanChile/Ladeco, *Tomás Roger 78.*

Banks NB Poor rates for TCs, which cannot be changed into US$ cash. **Banco de Chile,** *Bulnes 544,* accepts all cards. **Banco Santiago,** ATM. *Casas de cambio* on *Blanco Encalada,* eg *266* (**Enio América**). **Cambio Stop,** Baquedano 380. Cambio Sur, Eberhard 285. Good rates. Others on Bulnes and Prat. Shop around. **Communications Post office** *Eberhard 417.* Open Mon-Fri 0830-1230, 1430-1745, Sat 0900-1230. **Telephone** *CTC, Blanco Encalada 23 y Bulnes.* Phones and fax. **Internet** CTC, *Baquedano 383,* US$5.75 per hr; **Fortaleza,** *Blanco Encalada 226,* also at **Concepto Indigo,** see Sleeping; **Bar de Ruperto,** see Eating above; and **Turismo María José,** see Tour operators above.

Parque Nacional Torres del Paine

→ *Phone code: +56-(0)61 Colour map 6, B2*

Parque Nacional Torres del Paine is spectacular. World-renowned for its challenging trekking, the park contains 15 peaks above 2,000 m. At its centre is the glacier-topped granite massif Macizo Paine from which rise the vertical pink granite Torres (Towers) de Paine and below them the strange Cuernos de Paine (Horns), swooping buttresses of lighter granite under caps of darker sedimentary rock. From the vast Campo de Hielo Sur icecap on its western edge, four main glaciers (ventisqueros), Grey, Dickson, Zapata and Tyndall, drop into vividly coloured lakes formed by their meltwater: turquoise, ultramarine and pistachio expanses, some filled with wind-sculpted royal blue icebergs. Wherever you explore, there are constantly changing views of dramatic peaks and ice fields. Allow 5 to 7 days to see the park properly.

Ins and outs

Park information The park is administered by Conaf: the Administration Centre (T691931) is in the south of the park at the northwest end of Lago del Toro (open 0830-2000 in summer, 0830-1230, 1400-1830 off season). There are park entrances at Laguna Amarga, Lago Sarmiento and Laguna Azul, and you are required to register and show your passport when entering the park, since rangers (*guardaparques*) keep a check on the whereabouts of all visitors. You must also register before setting off on any hike. Phone the administration centre for information (in Spanish) on weather conditions. They also provide a good slide show at 2000 on Sat and Sun, and there are also exhibitions with summaries in English of flora and fauna, but no maps to take away. There are six *guarderías* (ranger stations) staffed by *guardaparques* who give help and advice and will also store luggage (except at Laguna Amarga where they have no room). Entry for foreigners: US$14, less off-season – before 1 Oct (proceeds are shared between all Chilean national parks), climbing fees US$800. The impact of huge numbers of visitors to the park is often visible in litter around the refugios and camping areas. Please take all your rubbish out of the park and remember that toilet paper is also rubbish.

Getting around The park is well set up for tourism, with frequent bus services running from Puerto Natales through the park, to pick up and drop off walkers at various hotels and refugios, to start treks, and to connect with boat trips.

Safety It is vital to be aware of the unpredictability of the weather (which can change in a few minutes), see Climate below, and the arduousness of some of the stretches on the long hikes. Rain and snowfall are heavier the further west you go, and bad weather sweeps off the Campo de Hielo Sur without warning. The only means of rescue are on horseback or by boat; the nearest helicopter is in Punta Arenas and high winds usually prevent its operation in the park.

Equipment and maps Note that mice have become a problem around camping sites and the free refugios; do not leave food in packs on the ground. A strong, streamlined, waterproof tent gives you more freedom than crowded *refugios* and is essential if doing the complete circuit. Also essential at all times of year are protective clothing against cold, wind and rain, strong waterproof footwear, a compass, a good sleeping bag, sleeping mat, camping stove and cooking equipment. Most *refugios* will hire camping equipment for a single night. Sun-screen and sunglasses are also necessary, and you'll want shorts in summer. At the entrance you are asked what equipment you have. Take your own food: the small shops at the Andescape *refugios* and at the Posada Río Serrano are expensive and have a limited selection. Maps (US$3) are obtainable at Conaf offices in Punta Arenas or Puerto Natales. The coloured Torres del Paine Trekking Map, pub. Juan Luis Mattassi, is US$3 from most bookshops, and shows contours and paths with estimated walking times, text in English.

Climate and wildlife

Do not underestimate the severity of the weather here. The park is open all year round, although snow may prevent access in the winter. The warmest time is December to March, but also the most unstable; strong winds often blow off the glaciers, and rainfall can be heavy. It is most crowded in the summer holiday season, January to mid February, less so in December or March. In winter there can be good, stable conditions and well-equipped hikers can do some good walking, but some treks may be closed and boats may not be running.

The park enjoys a micro-climate especially favourable to wildlife and plants: there are 105 species of birds including 18 species of waterfowl and 11 birds of prey. Particularly noteworthy are condors, black-necked swans, rheas, kelp geese, ibis, flamingoes and austral parakeets. There are also 25 species of mammals including *guanaco*, hares, foxes, huemules (a rare species of deer), pumas and skunks. Over 200 species of plants have been identified.

▲ Hikes

There are about 250 km of well-marked trails, and walkers must keep to the paths: cross-country trekking is not permitted. The times indicated should be treated with caution: allow for personal fitness and weather conditions.

El Circuito → *Allow at least 7 days to complete*

The main hike is a circuit round the Torres and Cuernos del Paine: it is usually done anticlockwise starting from the Laguna Amarga *guardaría*. From Laguna Amarga the route is north along the west side of the Río Paine to Lago Paine, before turning west to follow the Río Paine to the south end of Lago Dickson. From here the path runs along the wooded valley of the Río de los Perros before climbing steeply to Paso John Gardner (1,241 m, the highest point on the route), then dropping to follow the Grey Glacier southeast to Lago Grey, continuing to Lago Pehoé and the administration

Camping gear must be carried. The circuit is often closed in winter because of snow. The longest lap is 30 km, between Refugio Laguna Amarga and Refugio Dickson (10 hours in good weather; it has two campsites along it, *Serón* and *Cairón*), but the most difficult section is the very steep slippery slope between Paso John Gadner and *Campamento Paso*, which is exposed to strong westerly winds. The major rivers are crossed by footbridges, but these are occasionally washed away.

The W → *Allow 5 days to complete*

A popular alternative to El Circuito, this route can be completed without camping

Parque Nacional Torres del Paine

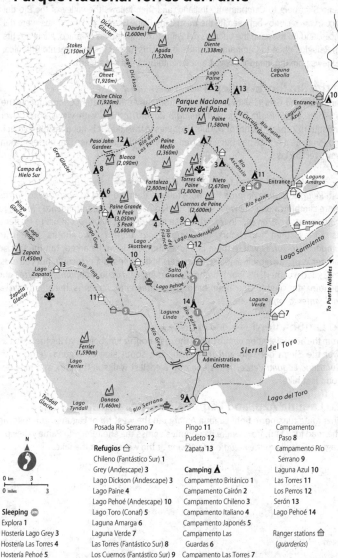

Sleeping ⊜	Refugios ⊟	Camping ▲	Campamento Paso **8**
Explora **1**	Chileno (Fantástico Sur) **1**	Campamento Británico **1**	Campamento Río Serrano **9**
Hostería Lago Grey **3**	Grey (Andescape) **3**	Campamento Cairón **2**	Laguna Azul **10**
Hostería Las Torres **4**	Lago Dickson (Andescape) **3**	Campamento Chileno **3**	Las Torres **11**
Hostería Pehoé **5**	Lago Paine **4**	Campamento Italiano **4**	Los Perros **12**
	Lago Pehoé (Andescape) **10**	Campamento Japonés **5**	Serón **13**
Posada Río Serrano **7**	Lago Toro (Conaf) **5**	Campamento Las Guardas **6**	Lago Pehoé **14**
Pingo **11**	Laguna Amarga **6**	Campamento Las Torres **7**	
Pudeto **12**	Laguna Verde **7**		Ranger stations ⊟
Zapata **13**	Las Torres (Fantástico Sur) **8**	Campamento	*(guarderías)*
	Los Cuernos (Fantástico Sur) **9**		

N

0 km 3
0 miles 3

equipment by staying in *refugios*, and can be done in either direction. It combines several of the hikes described separately below. From *Refugio Laguna Amarga* the first stage runs west via *Hostería Las Torres* and up the valley of the Río Ascensio via *Refugio Chileno* to the base of the Torres del Paine (see below). From here return to the *Hostería Las Torres* and then walk along the northern shore of Lago Nordenskjold via *Refugio Los Cuernos* to Campamento Italiano. From here climb the Valley of the Río del Francés (see below) before continuing to Refugio Pehoé. From here you can complete the third part of the 'W' by walking west along the northern shore of Lago Grey to *Refugio Grey* and Glaciar Grey before returning to *Refugio Pehoé*.

The Valley of the Río del Francés → *Allow 5 hours each way*

From Refugio Pehoé this route leads north across undulating country along the west edge of Lago Skottberg to Campamento Italiano, and then follows the valley of the Río del Francés, which climbs between (to the west) Cerro Paine Grande and the Ventisquero del Francés, and (to the east) the Cuernos del Paine to Campamento Británico. Allow 2½ hrs from Refugio Pehoé to Campamento Italiano, 2½ hrs further to Campamento Británico. The views from the mirador above Campamento Británico are superb.

Up the Río Pingo valley → *Allow 4 hours each way*

From *Guardería Grey* (18 km west by road from the Administration Centre) follow the Río Pingo, via *Refugio Pingo* and *Refugio Zapata* (4 hrs), with views south over Ventisquero Zapata (plenty of wildlife, icebergs in the lake). It is not possible to reach Lago Pingo as a bridge has been washed away. Ventisquero Pingo can be seen 3 km away over the lake.

To the base of the Torres del Paine → *Allow 4-5 hours each way*

From *Refugio Laguna Amarga* the route follows the road west to *Hostería Las Torres* before climbing along the west side of the Río Ascensio via *Campamento Chileno* to *Campamento Las Torres*, close to the base of the Torres. Allow 1½ hours to *Hostería Las Torres*, then two hours to *Campamento Chileno*, two hours further to *Campamento Torres* where there is a lake: the path is well marked, but the last 30 minutes is up the moraine; to see the towers lit by sunrise (spectacular, but you must have good weather), it's worth humping camping gear up to *Campamento Torres* and spending the night. One hour beyond *Campamento Torres* is the good site at *Campamento Japonés*.

To Laguna Verde → *Allow 4 hours each way*

From the administration centre follow the road north 2 km, before taking the path east over the Sierra del Toro and then along the south side of Laguna Verde to the *Guardería Laguna Verde*. This is one of the easiest walks in the park and may be a good first hike.

To Laguna Azul and Lago Paine → *Allow 8½ hours each way*

This route runs north from Laguna Amarga to the west tip of Laguna Azul (following the road for 7 km), from where it continues across the sheltered Río Paine valley past Laguna Cebolla to the *Refugio Lago Paine* at the west end of the lake.

Listings: Parque Nacional Torres del Paine

◉ Sleeping

Accommodation is available on three levels: there are hotels (expensive, at least US$100 per night), 7 well-equipped and staffed refugios, offering meals (US$19 pp per night), 6 free refugios (basic services only), and 14 campsites. All options fill up quickly in peak summer months, Jan and Feb. Book hotels and refugios in advance. All the park's hotels are expensive, and – many feel – overpriced. In Dec or Mar, there are far fewer people.

Hotels

LL **Hostería Pehoé**, *T411390, pehoeuno@ctcinternet.cl* 5 km south of Pehoé ranger station, 11 km north of park administration. Beautifully situated on an island with spectacular view across Lago Pehoe, this is rather run down. Closed Apr-Oct, restaurant Reservations: Antonio Bellet 77, office 605, T235 0252, F236 0917, Santiago.

LL **Hotel Explora**, *T411247. Reservations: Av Américo Vespucci 80, p 7, Santiago, 206-6060 T228 8081, F208 5479, explora@entelchile.net* The park's most expensive and exclusive is nestled into a nook at Salto Chico on the edge of Lago Pehoé, with spectacular views. Everything is included (for US$500 a night, you'd hope so): pool, gym, horse riding, boat trips, tours. They can also arrange packages from Punta Arenas.

LL-L **Hostería Las Torres**, *head office Magallanes 960, Punta Arenas, T710050, F222641 (or Santiago +56-(0)2 960 4804), www.chileaustral.com/lastorres* Superbly comfortable rooms, a beautiful lounge with wood fire and great views of the Cuernos, this has an excellent restaurant with buffet dnner for US$25, arranges horse-riding, spa, and the transport from Laguna Amarga ranger station is included. Recommended. Visitor centre and *confiteria* open to non-residents for sandwiches, but note that prices double after 7pm.

LL **Hostería Lago Grey**, *T/F227528, or Punta Arenas T/F241042/248167, www.chileaustral .com/grey* Great views over Lago Grey, but small rooms, and mediocre food, glacier walks US$50.

AL **Hostería Mirador del Payne**, *T410498, hosteriamiraadordelpayne.com* Beautifully situated on Laguna Verde on the east edge of the park. Comfortable, charming, but inconvenient for park itself. Riding, hiking and birdwatching are offered.

AL **Posada Río Serrano**, *T412911, baqueano@chileaustral.com* An old estancia near the park administration. Some rooms with bath, some without, with an expensive but good restaurant and a shop, may allow use of cooking facilities when quiet. Reservations through **Turismo Río Serrano**, *Prat 258, Puerto Natales, T410684.* The company **Torresdelpaine.org** *T313 3389, hotelschile@terra.cl,* also offers accommodation, transfers and car hire.

Refugios

All **Andescape** and **Fantastico Sur** refugios can be booked through **Path@gone** *Puerto Natales, Eberhard 595, T413291, www.chileaustral.com/pathgone* Book refugios in advance, eg at *Path@gone* in Puerto Natales; *refugios* can only accommodate 20-30 people and may be full when you get there; ask personnel to radio ahead your booking to the next *refugio*, especially if you want an evening meal. There are 3 groups of refugios: one is run by **Conaf**, three by **Andescape** and three by **Fantastico Sur**.

F pp US$5 **Refugio Lago Toro**, *near administration centre, run by Conaf (T691931).* Hot showers, good meeting place, sleeping bag and mattress essential, no camping, open summer only, in the winter months another more basic (free) *refugio* is open near administration centre. All the remaining refugios are open Sep to Apr only. **Andescape refugios** *(T412592)*; all cost US$17pp): **Refugio Lago Pehoé**, on the northeast arm of Lago Pehoé (accepts Visa). **Refugio Grey**, on the eastern shore of Lago Grey. **Refugio Lago Dickson**, at the southern tip of Lago Dickson. **Fantastico Sur** refugios *(T411572)*; all cost US$21pp. **Refugio Chileno**, at Campamento Chileno. Modern, clean, with dorm accommodation (sheets not provided), hot showers (US$2 for non-residents), laundry facilities, meals served (breakfast US$5, dinner US$10), kiosk

with basic food and other supplies, rental of camping equipment, campsite with cold showers (US$3 pp). **D pp Refugio Las Torres**, efficient, good meals served, kitchen.
Refugio Los Cuernos, 6 hrs from *Las Torres* on the way to Campamento Italiano. In addition there are 6 free *refugios*: **Zapata, Pingo, Laguna Verde, Laguna Amarga, Lago Paine** and **Pudeto**. Most have cooking areas but Laguna Verde and Pingo do not. Very crowded in summer (rangers know how many people are on each route and can give you an idea of how busy *refugios* will be).

Camping

Forest fires are a serious hazard. Fires may only be lit at organized *camping* sites, not at *campamentos*. The guardaparques expect people to have a stove if camping. In addition to sites at the **Andescape refugios** there are the following sites:
Camping Serón and **Camping Las Torres** (at *Hostería Las Torres*) both run by *Estancia Cerro Paine*, US$4, hot showers.
Camping Los Perros, run by *Andescape*, US$3 pp, shop and hot showers.
Camping Lago Pehoé and **Camping Serrano**, both run by *Turismo Río Serrano* (address above), US$20 per site at former (maximum 6 persons, hot showers) and US$15 per site at latter (maximum 6 persons, cold showers, more basic).
Free camping is permitted in 7 other locations in the park: these sites are known as *campamentos*. The wind tends to rise in the evening so pitch tent early. Beware of mice, which eat through tents. Equipment hire in Puerto Natales (see above).

☺ Tour operators

There are increasingly mixed reports of tours. Before booking a tour, check carefully on details and get them in writing. After mid-Mar there is little public transport and trucks are irregular.
Several agencies in Puerto Natales. Recommended are:
path@gone, *Eberhard 595, T413291, www.chileaustral.com/pathagone* Organize excursions, manage accommodation and boat trips in Torres del Paine. An umbrella company for: **Andescape**, *T412877, www.chileaustral. com/andescape* (for

camping and *refugios*).
Fantastico Sur (*refugios*) and **Onas**, *T412707, www.onaspatagonia.com* (for boat trips down the Río Serrano in zodiacs to the Serrano glacier and to Puerto Natales, US$85 pp all inclusive). Helpful office English spoken. Recommended.
Turismo Paori, *Eberhard 577, T411229, www.turismopaori.com* Conventional and cheap day tours, English speaking guides.
Sendero Aventura, *at Albergue Patgonia Adventure, Tomás Rogers 179, T415636, sendero_aventura@terra.cl* Adventure tourism, trekking, equipment hire.
Patagonias Last Frontier, *info@avertour aventuras.com* Boat trips from Pto Natales to Serrano Glacier, trekking, kayaking, ice trekking, and fishing.

Boat trips

From Refugio *Lago Pehoé* to *Refugio Pudeto*, US$15 one way with 1 backpack (US$8 for extra backpacks), from Pudeto 0930, 1200, 1800, from Pehoé 1000, 1300, 1900, journey time: 20 mins. In high season reserve in advance at the *refugios* at either end or at *Catamarán Hielos Patagonicos*, Los Arrieros 1517, Puerto Natales, T411380. Off-season, radio for the boat from Refugio Pehoé. Check in advance that boats are running. Along Lago Grey, from *Hostería Lago Grey* at the southern end of the lake to the Grey Glacier: a stunning trip, but often cancelled due to high winds. US$60 including refreshments, 2-3 hrs, minimum 8 passengers, T410172, hgrey@ctcreuna.cl You could also enter the park by 3hr-zodiac boat trip up the Río Serrano from Balmaceda glacier. See Parque Nacional Bernardo O'Higgins for details.

☺ Transport

Bus

From early Nov-mid Apr, there are 4 companies running daily services into the park, listed below. To go the Administration centre, all charge US$9 one way, US$17 return, except Bus Sur US$7.50, return US$14 (return tickets are not interchangeable between different companies). Buses will stop anywhere in the route, but always stop at **Laguna Amarga** entrance, **Salto Grande del Paine** and **Administration centre** near Posada Serrano. JB, *Prat 258, T412824*, leaves 0700, 0800, 1430, returns 1345, 1200, 1830. **Fortaleza**, *Prat 234, T410595*, leaves 0700, 1430, returns 1345, 1815. **María José**, *Bulnes 386, T412312*, leaves 0700, returns 1330. **Bus Sur**, *Baquedano 558, T411325*, leaves 0730 returns 1230.

Buses pass *Guardería Laguna Amarga* at 1030, *Guardería Pehoé* at 1130, arriving at Admin at 1230, leave Admin at 1400 (in high season the buses fill quickly so it is best to board at the Administration). All buses wait at *Refugio Pudeto* until the 1430 boat from *Refugio Lago Pehoé* arrives. Travel between two points within the park (eg Pudeto-Laguna Amarga) US$3. At other times services by travel agencies are dependent on demand: arrange return date with driver to coincide with other groups to keep costs down. **Luis Díaz** is reliable, about US$12 pp, minimum 3 people. In addition, in season there are frequent minibus connections within the park: from Laguna Amarga to *Hostería Las Torres*, US$2.80, and from the administration centre to *Hostería Lago Grey*.

From Torres del Paine to **El Calafate** (Argentina): take services from Puerto Natales (see above); alternatively take a bus from the park to **Cerro Castillo** (106 km south of administration centre) then catch a direct service to El Calafate. 5 buses a week with **Bus Sur** or **Zaahj**. (see Puerto Natales bus info).

Car hire

Budget , *Punta Arenas (at airport and Av O'Higgins 964)*. Hiring a **pick-up** is an economical proposition for a group (up to 9 people): US$415 for 4 days. If driving there yourself, the road from Puerto Natales is being improved and, in the park, the roads are narrow and winding with blind corners: use your horn a lot. It takes about 3½ hrs from Puerto Natales to the administration, 3 hrs to Laguna Amarga. Petrol available at Río Serrano, but fill up in case.

Horse hire

Baquedano Zamora, *Eberhard 565, Puerto Natales, T412911*.
Hostería El Pionero, *Cerro Castillo*.

Check out...

WWW...

515

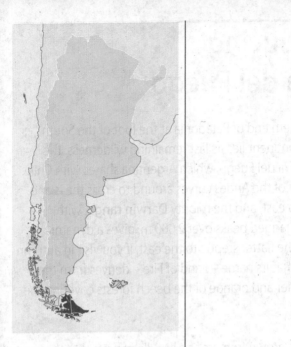

Tierra del Fuego

Introducing
Tierra del Fuego

At the southern end of Patagonia at the foot of the South American continent lies its last remaining wilderness: the island of Tierra del Fuego, which Argentina shares with Chile. Here, the tail of the Andes curves around to cross the island from west to east, and the mighty **Darwin range**, with glaciers and jagged peaks over 2,000 m, gives a dynamic contrast to the flatter steppe to the east. If you visit in autumn you'll think that its name – Land of Fire – derives from the blaze of scarlet and orange of the beech forests covering the mountains.

Ushuaia has grown from its first huddle of houses to the country's best organized tourist town, with the dramatic backdrop of **Cerro Martial**, and a serene natural harbour on the **Beagle Channel**. Sail east to the home of the first settler at Harberton, past islands covered with basking fur seals. It's a good base for exploring the picturesque **Parque Nacional Tierra del Fuego**, where there's a gentle walk around Lago Roca or steep climbs with magnificent views. The only other settlements here are **Río Grande** to the north, and the Chilean village of **Porvenir** northwest. But for the adventurous, the island's real treasure lies away from civilization, with mountains to scale, glaciers to cross, and rivers filled with giant trout in both Chilean and Argentine territory. The lakes and valleys can be explored on foot or on horseback, while on the Chilean island facing Ushuaia, the **Dientes de Navarino** make a serious challenge for any trekker. In winter the valleys are perfect for cross-country skiing, while the slopes at **Cerro Castor** offer good powder snow, with spectacular views of the end of the world.

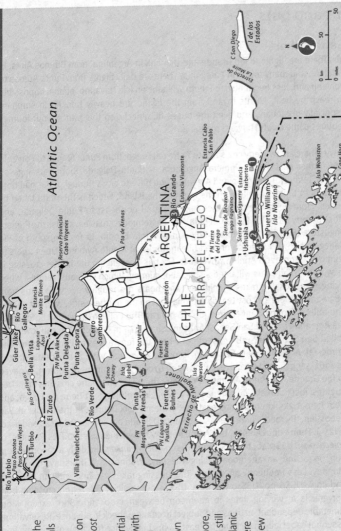

★ Don't miss...

① Beagle Channel Take a boat along the
channel, stop at islands where fur seals
bask, before landing at the historic
Estancia Harberton. Stay at a cottage on
the shore of the bay and read *Uttermost
Part of the Earth*, page 527.

② Ushuaia Take a chairlift to Cerro Martial
and admire the view of the channel with
the mountains of Dientes de Navarin
below you, page 526.

③ Río Grande Fish for enormous brown
trout, page 522.

④ Bahía Ensenada Stroll along the shore,
weaving between beech forests and still
water, spotting scarlet headed magellanic
woodpeckers, to Bahía Lapataia where
you gaze at the perfectly peaceful view
across the sound. Heaven, page 529.

Ins and outs

Getting there

Air There are flights to Río Grande and Ushuaia in Argentina, from Buenos Aires, El Calafate, and many towns in Patagonia. There are daily flights from Punta Arenas to Porvenir and, less frequently, to Puerto Williams on Isla Navarino, almost impossible to reach by boat. Flights to and from the island are heavily booked in summer, especially in January, and even the buses fill quickly, so this part of your journey requires some careful forward planning.

Ferry There are two ferry crossings to Tierra del Fuego: from Punta Arenas to Porvenir, and further east across Primera Angostura at Punta Delgada, both crossings on Chilean territory. From mainland Argentina you have to cross through Chile via Punta Delgada to Chilean territory on the north of the island, which is the route taken by buses. From Punta Arenas, buses take the road northeast to Punta Delgada, and cross by ferry there. **Via Punta Delgada** The easternmost crossing, across the Primera Angostura (First Narrows) to the tiny port of Punta Espora, is 127 km south of Río Gallegos, and 59 km south of the Chilean border at Monte Aymond. Open 24hrs in summer, 0800-2200 April to November. For bus passengers the border crossing is easy, though hire cars will need a special document, which you must request when hiring. The crossing takes 15-minutes, and boats run roughly every 40 mins from 0830-2300. There's a cosy tea room Bahia Azul on the northern side, with hot snacks and toilets. Foot passengers free, US$18 per car. The Chilean/Argentine border is at the Argentine town of San Sebastián, confusingly 14 km east of a Chilean town also called San Sebastián, 128 km south of where the ferry arives at Punta Espora. The border at Argentine San Sebastián is open 24 hours, with a basic ACA motel, T02964-425542; and a service station open 0700-2300. From here Route 3, is paved to Río Grande. **Via Punta Arenas – Porvenir** There is a daily ferry crossing from Tres Puentes, just north of Punta Arenas to Porvenir, in northwestern Tierra del Fuego, and from here a 225 km road runs east to Río Grande (six hours) via the border at San Sebastián. (By road, Punta Arenas and Punta Delgada are connected by a good road, RN255). From Punta Arenas, bus A or E from Av Magallanes goes to Tres Puentes, or *colectivo* 15, US$0.40; taxi US$3. In season, the *Melinka* sails daily at 0900, except Sun 0930 and an afternoon sailing Tuesday, Wednesday, Thursday, no service Monday. Less frequently off season. The crossing takes 2½-hrs, and can be rough and cold, US$6 pp, US$10 per bike, US$34 per vehicle. The return crossing from Porvenir is at varying times in afternoon between 1300 and 1800, except Mon. Timetable dependent on tides and subject to change: check in advance. Reservations essential especially in summer (at least 24 hrs in advance for cars), obtainable from Transboradora Austral Broom, in Punta Arenas, Bulnes 05075, T218100, www.tabsa.com (or T580089 in Porvenir).

Getting around

There are good bus links from Punta Arenas to Río Grande in Argentina, with an option of going via Porvenir, along the decent loop of road on the Chilean side. From Porvenir a *ripio* road leads around Bahía Inútil to near Lago Blanco, though there's no public transport here. The main road running through the Argentine half of the island is Route 3 between Río Grande and Ushuaia, surfaced apart from a 50 km section between 40 km north of Ushuaia and Tolhuin, with several buses a day. A fan of roads spreads out south and west from Río Grande to the estancias in the Argentine side, but these are unpaved, and best attempted in a 4WD vehicle. A good *ripio* road leads from 40 km east of Ushuaia to Harberton and Estancia Moat on the south coast, and part of the way along the north coast to Estancia San Pablo; no public transport here either.

Chilean Tierra del Fuego

Porvenir
Phone code: +56-(0)61 Colour map 6, C3 Population: 5,100

Porvenir is the only town in the main island of Chilean Tierra del Fuego, and the island's capital, founded in 1894 in the gold boom, when many people came seeking fortunes from Croatia and Chiloe. It's a quiet, pleasant place with neat painted houses of zinc and quaint tall domed trees lining the main avenue. There is a small museum, the **Museo Fernando Cordero Rusque**, Samuel Valdivieso 402, with archaeological and photographic displays on the Onas; good displays on natural history and the early gold diggers. **Tourist information** ① *municipalidad, Zavattara 402, T580094, www.patagonia-chile.com*. But there's more helpful information at a tiny kiosk on the waterfront, which also sells fine handicrafts, kuanip@entelchile.net. There's a bank on the Plaza. ▶▶ *See Sleeping, Eating and other listings, page 520-522.*

Around Porvenir

Though small, and not apparently ready for tourism, Porvenir is the base for exploring the wonderfully wild virgin territory of Chilean Tierra del Fuego. The fly fishing here is becoming world renowned, until recently the secret haunt of Hollywood stars such as Stallone, in Río Grande, Lago Escondido and Lago Blanco, where there's a lodge on an island. It's an area rich in brown trout, sea run brook trout and steelheads, weighing 2 to 14 kg. Fishing expeditions are likely to involve camping, and travel by 4WD (or even horseback) over the inhospitable and little travelled ground.

Recommended is horse riding to the forest of the **Darwin cordillera**. Tours can also be arranged to the remote **De Agostini National Park**. These involve sailing from Porvenir to Rio Condor across Bahia Inútil, south of Camerón, with trekking or horseback from Camerón to Seno Almirantazgo, a wild and treeless place, mountains sinking into fjords with icebergs floating in them. Then by boat to Marinelli glacier, where you can also sail, kayak and dive; 6 days in all. A recommended tour along the gold circuit, **Cordon Baquedano**, a 5 hr, 115 km round trip, good on horseback.

Camerón

Camerón lies 149 km southeast of Porvenir on the opposite side of Bahía Inútil, a wonderful windswept bay, with views of distant hills and the snow capped Darwin range all along the horizon. At the eastern end of the bay, at Caleta Josefina, you can visit a handsome ex-estancia built 1833 by Menéndez (see Punta Arenas, page 492), where some old buildings remain. From Camerón a road runs southeast to Lago Blanco, known for its fishing, where there's a *hostería*. From Estancia Vicuña a trail leads southwest to the **Río Azopardo**, which also offers **trout fishing** (sleeping at Estancia Almirantazgo). South of here trails run across the Darwin Range to the **Estancia Yendegaia** near the Beagle Channel. For trips into this country, contact Aonikenk in Punta Arenas, www.aonikenk.com ▶▶ *See Sleeping, Eating and other listings, page 520-522.*

> ✷ *It is impossible to get permission to cross the unmanned border from here to get to Ushuaia or to get a Chilean exit stamp.*

At the border with Argentina

The only legal border crossing between the Chilean and Argentine parts of Tierra del Fuego is at San Sebastián, 142 km east of Porvenir, open 24 hrs. The two settlements called San Sebastián, one on each side of the border, are 14 km apart; taxis are not allowed to cross. On the Argentine side the road continues to Río Grande. Argentine time is one hour ahead of Chilean time, March to October.

Entry When entering Argentina make sure you get an entry stamp for as long as you require. When entering Chile remember that fruit, vegetables, dairy produce or meat are allowed in. Hire cars need special documents you should request when hiring. ▶ *See Sleeping, Eating and other listings, page 520-522.*

Puerto Williams and Isla Navarino

→ *Phone code: +56-(0)61 Colour map 6, C4 Population: 2,500*

Puerto Williams is a Chilean naval base on Isla Navarino, south of the Beagle Channel. Situated about 50 km south east of Ushuaia (Argentina), it is small, friendly and remote. The island is totally unspoilt and beautiful, offering great geographical diversity, thanks to the Dientes de Navarin range of mountains, with peaks over 1000 m, covered with southern beech forest up to 500 m, and south of that, great plains covered with peat bogs, with many lagoons abundant in flora. The island was centre of the indigenous Yaganes culture, and there are 500 archaeological sites, the oldest dated as 3,000 years old. **Museo Martín Gusinde** ⓘ *Mon-Thu 1000-1300, 1500-1800, Sat and Sun1500-1800, Fri closed (subject to change), US$1*, known as the 'Museo del Fin del Mundo' (End of the World Museum) is full of information about vanished Yaganes tribes, local wildlife, and voyages including Charles Darwin and Fitzroy of the Beagle; a must. **Tourist information** ⓘ *Municipalidad de Cabos de Hornos, Pres. Ibañez 130, T621011, isotop@mitierra.cl.* Ask for maps and details on hiking. The town also has a bank, supermarkets and hospital.

Exploring the island

For superb views, climb Cerro Bandera (three to four hours' round trip, very steep, take warm clothes). You can also visit Villa Ukika, 2 km east of town, the place where the last descendants of the Yaganes people live, relocated from their original homes at Caleta Mejillones, which was the last indigenous reservation in the province, inhabited by hundreds of Yagana descendents. There is excellent trekking around the Dientes de Navarin range, the southernmost trail in the world, through impressive mountain landscape, frozen lagoons and snowy peaks, giving superb views over the Beagle Channel. It's a challenging hike, over a distance of 53 km in five days, possible only from December to March, and a good level of fitness is needed. There is no equipment rental on island. Charter flights are available over Cape Horn and to King George Island on northern tip of Antarctic peninsula, where you can see the curvature of the earth on the horizon, with excursions to penguin and sea lion colonies.

Listings: Chilean Tierra del Fuego

🛏 Sleeping

Porvenir *p519*

A Los Flamencos, *Tte Merino, T580049*. The town's best place to stay with good food, and a pleasant place for a drink. Recommended.

C España, *Croacia 698, T580160*. Good restaurant with fixed price lunch.

D Rosas, *Phillippi 296, T580088*. Heating, restaurant and bar. Recommended.

E pp Miramar, *Santos Mardones 366*. D with

full board, heaters in rooms, panoramic views.

At the border with and Argentina *p519*

B pp Hostería de la Frontera, *Chilean San Sebastian, where buses stop for meals and cakes, T61224731, mobile 094995331, www.lafrontera.co.cl* A cosy place, serving good food.

D ACA motel, *Argentine San Sebastián, T02964-425542*. Also has a restaurant and a service station open 0700-2300.

Puerto Williams *p520* ·
A pp **Pensión Temuco**, *Piloto Pardo 224,
T621113*. Price is for full board, comfortable,
hospitable, good food, hot showers.
B pp **Hostería Camblor** Via 2 s/n, T621033.
Heavily booked up, rooms with bath, and
restaurant. You can also stay at private
houses. Camping nearby.
E pp **Coiron**, *owned by Sim Ltd, contact
Jeanette Talavera, T621150,
coiron@simltd.com* A *refugio* with shared
bath and kitchen, 4 beds per room.
Jeanette's husband, **Wolf Kloss**
(www.simltd.com) runs sailing trips, trekking
tours and many other adventure activities.

🍴 Eating

Porvenir *p519*
$ **Croacia Club**, *next to the bus stop on the
waterfront*. A friendly place where you can
get a good lunch for US$5.
$ **El Chispa**, *on Senoret*. Good seafood. There
are many lobster fishing camps where
fishermen will prepare lobster on the spot.
$ **Restaurante Puerto Montt**, *Croacia 1169*.
Seafood. Recommended.

🎫 Tour operators

Porvenir and around *p519*
Karanka Expeditions, *T621127*. Run by
Maurice Van de Maele.
Turismo Aonikenk, *Magallanes 619, in Punta
Arenas, T228332, www.aonikenk.com*
Excellent for multi-adventure and trekking
tours. French, German, English spoken. See
the website.
Turismo Cordillera de Darwin, *Croacia 675,
T(09)6407204, www.explorepatagonia.cl*

🚌 Transport

Porvenir and around *p519*
Air
From **Punta Arenas** – weather and bookings
permitting, **Aerovías DAP**, *Oficina Foretic,
T80089, Porvenir, www.aerovias dap.cl* Fly
twice daily Mon-Sat, taking 12 mins, US$23.
Heavily booked so make sure you have your
return reservation confirmed.

Bus
2 a week between Porvenir and **Río Grande**
(Argentina), Tue and Sat 1400, 5 hrs,
Transportes Gessell, *Duble Almeyda 257,
T580488 (Río Grande 02964-425611)*, US$12,
heavily booked, buy ticket in advance, or
phone to reserve. **Río Grande**-Porvenir, Wed
and Sun 0800. **Car** All roads are *ripio*. Fuel is
available in Porvenir, Cerro Sombrero and
Cullen. **Ferry** Terminal at Bahía Chilota, 5
km west, see above for details. From bus
terminal to ferry, taxi US$6, bus US$1.50.

Camerón *p519*
Bus
To Camerón from **Porvenir**, from Calle
Manuel Señor, twice a week, US$10.

At the border with and Argentina *p519*
Minibus from **Porvenir** to **San Sebastián**,
US$14. For transport between **Porvenir** and
Río Grande, see Porvenir above.

Puerto Williams *p519*
Air
From **Punta Arenas** by air, **Aerovías DAP**
(details under Punta Arenas) daily Mon-Sat,
1¼ hrs, US$71 each way, in 7-seater Cessna,
luggage allowance 10 kg. Book well in
advance; the aircraft seats 20, and there are
long waiting lists (be persistent). The flight
is beautiful, with superb views of Tierra del
Fuego, the Cordillera Darwin, the Beagle
Channel, and the islands stretching south
to Cape Horn. Also army flights available
(they are cheaper), but the ticket has to be
bought through DAP. **Aeropetrel** will
charter a plane to Cape Horn (US$2,600 for
8-10 people).

Boat
No regular sailings from **Ushuaia**
(Argentina). Boats from **Punta Arenas**: Ferry
Patagonia (Austral Broom), once a week,
US$120 for seat, US$150 for bunk, including
food, 36 hrs. www.tabsa.com The Navarino
leaves **Punta Arenas**, the 3rd week of every
month, 12 passengers, US$150 pp one way;
contact the owner, **Carlos Aguilera**, *21 de
Mayo 1460, Punta Arenas, T228066, F248848*
or via Turismo Pehoé. The Beaulieu, a cargo
boat carrying a few passengers, sails from
Punta Arenas once a month, US$300 return,
6 days. Boat trips: Most recommended is the
cruise around Cape Horn and on to Ushuaia,
returning to Punta Arenas, run by **Cruceros**

Australis SA, *Santiago office T56-2442 3110*
www.australis.com Book well in advance.
You may get a lift on a yacht (unlikely); ask at
the yacht club, 1 km west. Navy and port
authorities may deny any knowledge, but
everyone else in Puerto Williams knows
when a boat is due.

❶ Directory

Puerto Williams *p519*
Airline offices Aerovías DAP, LanChile, in
the centre of town. **Communications** Post
office closes 1900. **Telephone:** CTC, Mon-Sat
0930-2230, Sun 1000-1300, 1600-2200).

Argentine Tierra del Fuego

Río Grande → *Phone code: 02964 Colour map 6, C4 Population: 35,000*

Río Grande is a sprawling modern coastal town, the centre for a rural sheep-farming
community which grew rapidly in the oil boom of the 1970's, and with government tax
incentives. The new population was stranded when benefits were withdrawn in recent
years, leading to increasing unemployment and emigration, and leaving a rather sad,
windy dusty town today. The people are friendly but there's little culture, and you're
most likely to visit in order to change buses. There are a couple of good places to stay,
however, and a small museum worth seeing, as well as the splendid historical
Estancia Viamonte nearby. And if keen on fishing, Río Grande's legendary monster
brown trout can be plucked from the water at Estancia María Behety.

Sights

The city's architecture is a chaotic mixture of smart new nouveau riche houses and
much humbler wooden and tin constructions. It seems to have defied municipal
efforts at prettification, and the series of peeling and graffitied concrete 'sculptures'
along some of the avenues do little to cheer it up. But if you do get stuck here, you
could trace the city's history through sheep, missions, pioneers and oil in its
interesting small museum, the **Museo de la Ciudad** ① *Alberdi 555, T430414, open
Tue-Fri 1000-1700.* The city was founded by Fagnano's Salesian mission in 1893, and
you can visit the original building **La Candelaria** ① *11 km north, T421642, open
Mon-Sat 1000- 1230,1500-1900, Sun 1500-1900, US$1.50, afternoon teas, US$3,*
whose museum has displays of natural history and indigenous artefacts, with
strawberry plantations, piglets and an aviary too. **Tourist office** ① *Rosales 350,
T431324, rg-turismo@netcombbs.com.ar, Mon-Fri 0900-2100, Sat 1000-1700.
www.tierradelfuego.org.ar,* small but helpful in the blue-roofed hut on the plaza.

Around Río Grande

Estancia Viamonte, on the coast, 40 km away south, is a working sheep farm with a
fascinating history. Here, Lucas Bridges, son of Tierra del Fuego's first settler, built a
home to protect the large tribe of indigenous Onas, who were fast dying out. The
estancia is still inhabited by his descendents, who can take you riding and to see the
life of the farm. Also a house to rent and superb accommodation. Wonderful. Highly
recommended. **Estancia María Behety**, built by the sheep farming millionaire José
Menéndez, is a heaven for brown trout fishing. ➤➤ *See Sleeping, Eating and other listings
pages 529-536.*

From Río Grande to Ushuaia

From Río Grande, several roads fan out south west to the heart of the island, though
this area is ittle inhabited, with just a few estancias. The paved main road south,

Route 3, continues across wonderfully open land, more forested than the expanses of Patagonian steppe further north, and increasingly hilly as you near Ushuaia. After around 160 km, you could turn left along a track to the coast, to find **Estancia Cabo San Pablo**, 120 km from Río Grande. A simple working estancia in a beautiful position, owned by the charming Apolinaire family, with beautiful native woodland for walking and riding, birdwatching and fishing. Also other trips to places of interest within reach. Open all year, but reserve in advance. Route 3 then climbs high above Lago Fagnano, and Tolhuin. ▸ *See Sleeping, Eating and other listings pages 529-536.*

Tolhuin → *Phone code: 02964*

A friendly small growing settlement close to shore of Lago Fagnano, this is a large expanse of water, right at the heart of Tierra del Fuego, with a stretch of beach close to the village, which remains quiet, and little exploited. There's a YPF service station just off the main road, but it's worth driving into the village itself for the famous bakery **La Union**, where you can buy all kinds of bread, great empanadas and delicious fresh *facturas* (pastries). Also the source of all information in the village. Wonderful. There's a tiny, friendly **tourist office**, open 0900-1500, with very helpful staff, near the YPF station. Handicrafts are available at El Encuentro including fine leather goods, just half a block from tourist information. For **horseriding** in the area, contact **Sendero del Indio**, T15615258 sonia@netcombbs.com.ar From the village a road leads down to the tranquil lake shore, where there are a couple of good places to stay. Further along Route 3, 50 km from Ushuaia, a road to the right swoops down to **Lago Escondido**, a long, fjord like lake with steep deep green mountains descending into the water on all sides. ▸ *See Sleeping, Eating and other listings pages 529-536.*

Ushuaia → *Phone code: 02901 Colour map 6, C4 Population: 30,000*

The most southerly town in the world, Ushuaia's setting is spectacular. Its brightly coloured houses look like toys against the dramatic backdrop of vast jagged mountains. Opposite are the forbidding peaks of Isla de Navarino, and between flows the serene green Beagle Channel. Sailing those waters you can just imagine how it was for Darwin, arriving here in 1832, and for those early settlers, the Bridges in 1871. Though the town has expanded in recent years, sprawling untidily along the coast, Ushuaia still retains the feel of a pioneer town, isolated and expectant. There are lots of places to stay, which fill up entirely in January, a fine museum, and some great fish restaurants. There is spectacular landscape to be explored in all directions, with good treks in the accessible Parque Nacional Tierra del Fuego just to the west of the city, and more adventurous expeditions offered into the wild heart of the island, trekking, climbing or riding. There's splendid cross country skiing nearby in winter, as well as downhill skiing too, at Cerro Castor. And to the east, along a beautiful stretch of coastline is the historic estancia of Harberton, which you can reach by a boat trip along the Beagle Channel. ▸ *See Sleeping, Eating and other listings, page 529-536.*

Ins and outs → *See transport, page 535 for further details.*

Getting there There are daily flights from Buenos Aires, and frequent flights from El Calafate and Punta Arenas, as well as weekly flights from other Patagonian towns to Ushuaia's airport, on a peninsula in the Beagle channel, close to the centre. Airport information T423970. A taxi to the centre costs US$2. Buses arrive at their respective offices around town: Techni Austral and Tolkar at Roca 157, T431408, Líder Gob Paz 921, T430264, Tolkeyen Maipú 237, T437073. tolkeyen@tierradelfuego.org.ar) US$10. To Punta Arenas , Tecni Austral, M'bus terminal from Río Grande, and Punta Arenas, connecting with other destinations in Patagonia.

Tierra del Fuego Ushuaia

Getting around It's easy to walk around the town in a morning, since all its sights are close together, and you'll find banks, restaurants, hotels and shops along San Martín, which runs parallel to the shore, a block north of the coast road, Maipú. Boat trips leave from the Muelle Turistico (tourist pier) by a small plaza, 25 de Mayo on the seafront, Calle Maipú between Calles 25 de Mayo and Laserre. Ushuaia is very well organized for tourism, and there are good local buses to the national park and other sights, as well as many boat trips.

Best time to visit Ushuaia is at its most beautiful in autumn, when the dense forests all around are turned rich red and yellow, and there are many bright clear days. Summer is best for trekking, when maximum temperatures are around 15 degrees, but try to avoid January, when the city is swamped with tourists, both Argentines, and even more foreigners. Late February is much better, and still pleasant enough to go walking. The ski season is from mid-June to October, when temperatures hover around zero, but the wind drops.

Tourist information ⓘ *San Martín 674, corner with Fadul, T/F432000, www.tierradelfuego.org.ar, Mon-Fri 0800-2200, Sat, Sun and holidays 0900-2000.* Quite the best tourist office in Argentina, the friendly and helpful staff here speak several languages between them, and will hand you a map with all accommodation marked and find you somewhere to stay, even in the busiest period. They also have a great series of leaflets in English French, German and Dutch, about all the things to see and do, and bus and boat times. **Tierra del Fuego National Park Office** ⓘ *San Martín 1395, T421315*, has a useful little map of the park.

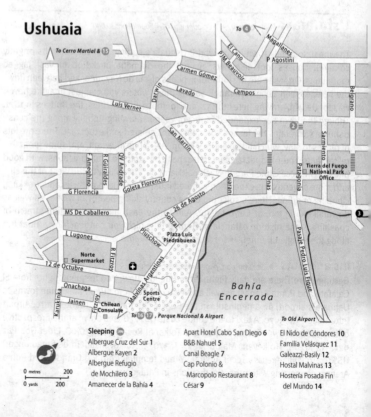

Ushuaia

Sleeping 🛏
Albergue Cruz del Sur **1**
Albergue Kayen **2**
Albergue Refugio
 de Mochilero **3**
Amanecer de la Bahía **4**

Apart Hotel Cabo San Diego **6**
B&B Nahuel **5**
Canal Beagle **7**
Cap Polonio &
 Marcopolo Restaurant **8**
César **9**

El Nido de Cóndores **10**
Familia Velásquez **11**
Galeazzi-Basily **12**
Hostal Malvinas **13**
Hostería Posada Fin
 del Mundo **14**

History

Founded in 1884 after missionary Thomas Bridges had established his mission in these inhospitable lands (see box next page) Ushuaia attracted many pioneers in search of gold. Keen to populate its new territory, the government set up a penal colony on nearby Staten Island, which moved to the town in 1902, and the town developed rapidly. Immigration was largely Croatian and Spanish, together with those shipwrecked on the shores, but the town remained isolated until planes arrived in 1935. As the prison closed a naval base opened, and in the 1970's, a further influx arrived, attracted by reduced income taxes, and cheap car prices. Now the city is capital of Argentina's most southerly province, and though fishing still plays a key role in the local economy, Ushuaia has become an important tourist centre, particularly as the departure point for voyages to Antarctica.

Sights

There are several museums worth looking at, if bad weather forces you indoors. The most fascinating is **Museo del Fin del Mundo** ① *along the seafront at Maipú y Rivadavia, T421863, daily 1000-1300, 1500-1930, US$1.50, students US$1*, in the 1902 bank building, which tells the history of the town through a small collection of carefully chosen exhibits on the indigenous groups, missionaries, pioneeers and shipwrecks, together with nearly all the birds of Tierra del Fuego (stuffed), and you can get an 'end of the world museum' stamp in your passport. There are helpful and informed staff, and also an extensive reference library. Recommended. Further east, the old prison Presidio, at the back of the Naval Base, houses the **Museo Marítimo** ① *Yaganes y Gob Paz, Mon-Sun 0900-2000, US$ 4.00 for foreigners*, with models and artefacts from seafaring days, and, in the cells, the **Museo Penitenciario**, which

Tierra del Fuego Ushuaia

Las Hayas **15**
Los Ñires **17**
Tolkeyen **16**

Eating 🍴
Barcleit 1912 **1**

Café Tante Sarah **2**
El Náutico **3**
El Rancho **4**
Kaupe **5**
La Baguette **6**
La Eatancia **7**

Los Pioneros, Bodegón Fueguino **9**
Moustaccio **10**
Parrilla La Rueda **11**
Tanta Sara Pizzas & Pastas **12**
Tía Elvira **13**
Volver **15**

Bars & clubs 🍸
Café bar de la Esquina **17**
De la Esquina **16**
Lennon Pub **8**
U! Bar **14**

Thomas and Lucas Bridges

The story of the first successful missionary to Tierra del Fuego, Thomas Bridges and his son Lucas, is one of the most stirring in the whole history of pioneers in Argentina, gripping reading for any visit to Ushuaia. An orphan from Bristol, Thomas Bridges was so called because he was found as a child under a bridge with a letter T on his clothing. Adopted by Rev Despard, he was taken as a young man to start a Christian mission in the Tierra del Fuego, and brought his young wife and daughter to establish the mission, after Despard left following the massacre of the Christians by the indigenous inhabitants. Until his death in 1898, Bridges lived near the shores of the Beagle Channel, first creating the new settlement of Ushuaia and then at Harberton, devoting his life to his work with the Yámanas (devoting his life to his work with the Yámanas (Yaghanes) and compiling a dictionary of their language. His son Lucas (1874-1949), one of six children, spent his early life among the Yámanas and Onas, living and hunting as one of them, learning their languages, and even, almost fatally, becoming involved in their blood feuds, and magic rituals. Lucas became both defender and protector of the indigenous peoples whose culture he loved and was fascinated by, creating a haven for them at Harberton and Estancia Viamonte (see next page) when most sheep farmers were more interested in having them shot. His memoirs, Uttermost Part of the Earth (1947) trace the tragic fate of the native population with whom he grew up. A compelling account of 20th-century man colliding with an ancient culture. (Out of print, but try second hand bookshops).

details the history of the prison. **Museo Yámana** ① *Rivadavia 56, T422874, daily 1000-2000 high season, otherwise closed lunchtime, US$1.50,* has interesting scale models showing scenes of everyday life of indigenous peoples, also recommended.

Whatever you do, unless it's absolutely pouring with rain, take the chair lift up to **Cerro Martial**, about 7 km behind the town, for exhilarating views along the Beagle Channel and to Isla Navarino opposite. From the top of the lift, you can walk 90 mins through lenga forest to Glaciar Martial. There are also a splendid tea shop, *refugio* and *cabañas* at the Cerro. ① *The aerosilla (chairlift) runs daily 1000-1800, US$2.20. To reach the chairlift, follow Magallanes out of town, allow 1½ hours walking, or take a bus: several companies, including Lautaro and Kaupen, run minibus services from the corner of Maipu and Roca, hourly in summer, US$ 2-4 return. Last buses return at 1900 and 2100.*

Parque Nacional Tierra del Fuego, (see below) just outside Ushuaia, is easily accessible by bus and offers a superb walks for all levels of fitness. The **Tren del Fin del Mundo** is the world's southernmost steam train, running new locomotives and carriages on track first laid by prisoners to carry wood to Ushuaia. It's a totally touristy experience with relentless commentary in English and Spanish, but it might be fun for children, and is one way of getting into the national park to start a walk. ① *The train runs for 50 mins from the Fin del Mundo station, 8 km west of Ushuaia, into Tierra del Fuego National Park. Four departures daily in summer, one in winter. US$20 (tourist), US$24 (first class) return, plus US$4 park entrance and US$2 for bus to the station. Tickets at station, or from Tranex kiosk in the port, T431600, www.trendelfindelmundo.com.ar Sit on left outbound for the best views. Buses to* reach the train station with companies Ebenezer and Gonzalo, leaving from the corner of Maiú and Roca, departing 0800, 0900, 1400, and returning 1700. US$3 return.

Estancia Harberton

In a land of extremes and superlatives, Harberton still stands out as special. The oldest estancia in Tierra del Fuego, it was built in 1886 on a narrow peninsula overlooking the Beagle Channel. Its founder, the missionary Thomas Bridges (see box, previous page) was granted the land by President Roca for his work amongst the indigenous peoples and for his help in rescuing victims of numerous shipwrecks in the channels. Harberton is named after the Devonshire village where his wife Mary was born, and the farmhouse was pre-fabricated there by her carpenter father and assembled on a spot chosen by the Yámana peoples as the most sheltered. The English connection is evident in the neat garden of lawns shrubs and trees between the jetty and the farmhouse. Behind the buildings is a large vegetable garden, a real rarity on the island, and there's noticeably more wildlife here than in the Tierra del Fuego National Park, probably owing to its remoteness.

Still operating as a working farm, mainly with cattle and sheep, Harberton is run by Thomas Goodall, great-grandson of the founder, whose wife Natalie has created an impressive museum of the area's rich marine life with a thriving research centre. Visitors receive a guided tour either of the museum, or of farm buildings and grounds with reconstructions of the Yámana dwellings. Tea or lunch (if you reserve ahead) are served in the tea room overlooking the bay, and you may well be tempted to rent one of the two simple cottages on the shore. There are wonderful walks along the coast, and nowhere in Argentina has quite the feeling of peace you'll find here.

The **Estancia Harberton**, 85 km from Ushuaia, is the oldest estancia on the island, and still run by descendents of the British missionary Thomas Bridges, whose family protected the indigenous peoples here. It's a beautiful place, with the attractive wood framed house that Thomas built sitting in quiet contemplation on a tranquil bay. You'll get an excellent guided walk (bilingual guides) around the estancia, through protected forest, and delicious teas are served in the Manacatush tearoom overlooking the water. Highly recommended. The impressive **Museo Akatushún** ① *T422742, estanciaharberton@tierradelfuego.org.ar, daily, except Christmas, 1 Jan and Easter. Tour of the estancia US$3, museum entrance US$2,* has skeletons of South American sea mammals, the result of 23 years' scientific investigation in Tierra del Fuego, with excellent tours in English. You can camp free, with permission from the owners, or stay in cottages (see below).Access is from a good unpaved road which branches off Route 3, 40 km east of Ushuaia and runs 25 km through forest before the open country around Harberton; marvellous views, about two hours (no petrol outside of Ushuaia and Tolhuin!). **Boat trips** to Harberton run twice weekly in summer, and allow two hours on the estancia. Regular daily minibus service with Bella Vista and Lautaro, from corner of Maipu and Juana Fadul, US$14 return. Agency tours by land cost US$40 plus entrance. Excursions can also be made to Lagos Fagnano and Escondido: agencies run tours and buses with Ebenezer and Bella Vista run daily, US$10 return for Lago Escondido, US$12 for Lago Fagnano. Buses leave from the corner of Maipú and Juana Fadul. Tour agencies offer many good packages which include trekking, canoeing, bird watching, and horse riding in landscape accessible only by 4WDs. See tour operators below, and the tourist office's list of excursiones, indicating which companies go where.

All these trips are highly recommended, but note that the Beagle Channel can be very rough. Food and drink on all boats is pricey. Excursions can be booked through most agencies, and leave from the Muelle Turístico. If going to Harberton, check that your tour actually visits the estancia and not just the bay, as some do.

These are the main trips: To the sea lion colony at Isla de los Lobos, Isla de los Pájaros, Les Eclaireurs lighthouse, there are three possibilities. Either on a big catamaran, 2½ hrs US$22, the Patagonian Adventure, including 1 hr trekking on Bridges island and hot drink, 4½-5 hrs, US$22, or alternatively on the charming old boat Barracuda, also visiting the with Isla Martillo penguin colony, with excellent commentary. Highly recommended. 4½ hrs, US$18. The third option takes you past the Isla de los Lobos, Isla de los Pájaros, Isla Martillo penguin colony, Les Eclaireurs lighthouse and then visits Estancia Harberton, 8 hrs round trip on catamaran, US$45, includes packed lunch, and entrance. Tuesday, Thursaday, Saturday. In the national park, Bahía Lapataia can be visited by launch in a round trip from Bahía Ensenada. Leaves daily between 1000-1700, 2 hrs, US$15. Reservation essential.

Parque Nacional Tierra del Fuego

Covering 63,000 ha of mountains, lakes, rivers and deep valleys, this small but beautiful park stretches west to the Chilean border and north to Lago Fagnano, though large areas have been closed to tourists to protect the environment. Public access is at the park entrance 12 km west of Ushuaia, where you'll be given a basic map with marked walks. There's good camping in a picturesque spot at Lago Roca, with a *confitería*. All walks are best early morning or afternoon to avoid the tour buses. You'll see lots of geese, the beautiful torrent duck, Magellanic woodpeckers and austral parakeets.

Access and information

The park **entrance** is 12 km west of Ushuaia, on the main road west (a continuation of the coast road) signposted from the town centre. The **park administration** is in Ushuaia, San Martín 1395. Entry for non-Argentines is US$4. In summer, various

Parque Nacional Tierra del Fuego

buses and minibuses run an hourly service, US$3 return to Lago Roca, US$7 return to Bahía Lapataia, leaving from Ushuaia's tourist pier at the corner of Maipú and Roca. Returning from either Bahía Lapataia or Lago Roca, hourly until last bus 2000 or 2100 in summer. Ask at the tourist office for bus details and map of park, with walks. **Topographical maps** are sold at Oficina Antártica, Maipú and Laserre, or consult the Municipal Tourist Office. There are no legal crossing points to Chile. Wear warm, waterproof clothing: in winter the temperature drops to as low as -12°C, and although in summer it can reach 25°C, evenings can be chilly. There's a most helpful *guardaparque* (ranger) at Lago Roca.

For a longer hike, or for a really rich experience of the park, go with **guides** who know the territory well and can tell you about wildlife. Inexpensive trips for all levels with the highly recommended **Compañia de Guias de Patagonia** at hostel El Nido de los Condores, Gob Campos 783, y 9 de Julio, T432642, www.companiadeguias.com.ar, and All Patagonia, Juana Fadul 54, T433622.

🔺 Walks

The leaflets provided at the entrance show various walks, but these are recommended:

1 Senda Costera, 6.5 km, 3 hrs each way. This lovely easy walk along the shore gives you the essence of the park, its rocky costline, edged with a rich forest of beech trees, and glorious views of the low islands with a backdrops of steep mountains. Start at Bahía Ensenada (where the boat trips start, and where the bus can drop you off). Walk along a well-marked path along the shoreline, and then rejoin the road briefly to cross Río Lapataia (ignoring signs to Lago Roca to your right). After crossing the broad green river and a second stretch of water (where there's a small camping spot and the gendarmería), it's a pleasant stroll inland to the beautifully tranquil **Bahía Lapataia**, an idyllic spot, with views across the sound.

2 Sendo Hito XXIV Along Lago Roca, 4 km, 90 mins one way. Another easy walk, beside this peaceful lake, with lovely pebble beaches and through dense forest at times, with lots of bird life. This is especially recommended in the evening, when most visitors have left. Get off the bus at the junction for Lago Roca, turn right along the road to the car park (passing the *guardaparque*'s house) and follow the lake side.

3 Cerro Guanaco, 4 km, 4 hrs one way. Challenging hike up through the very steep forest to a mirador with splendid views over Lago Roca, the Beagle Channel and far-off mountains. The ground is slippery after rain: take care and don't rush. Allow plenty of time to return in light, especially in winter.

Listings: Argentine Tierra del Fuego

⊜ Sleeping

Río Grande *p522*
Book ahead, as there are few decent choices.
B Posada de los Sauces, Elcano 839, T432895, info@posadadelossauces.com.ar By far the best choice. Breakfast included, beautifully decorated and comfortable rooms, good restaurant and cosy bar. Recommended.
C Apart Hotel Keyuk'n, Colón 630, T424435. A good apart hotel, with simple well equipped flats for 2-4.
C Hotel Atlantida, Belgrano 582, T431915,

atlantida@netcombbs.com.ar A modern, rather uninspiring place, with plain comfortable rooms all with bath and cable TV, but good value with breakfast included.
D Hotel Isla del Mar, Güemes 963, T422883, www.hotelguia.com/hotelisladelmar Right on the sea shore, looks very bleak in bad weather and is frankly run down, but cheap, with bathrooms and breakfast included, and the staff are welcoming.
F pp Hotel Argentina , San Martín 64, T422546, hotelargentino@yahoo.com Quite the best cheap place to stay. Much more than the backpackers youth hostel it claims

to be, in a beautifully renovated 1920's building close to the sea front. Kitchen facilities, a bright sunny dining room with space to sit, owned by the welcoming Graciela, who knows all about the local area. Highly recommended.

Camping

Club Naútico Ioshlelk-Oten, *Montilla 1047, 2 km from town on river*. Clean, cooking facilities, camping inside heating building in cold weather. YPF petrol station has hot showers.

Estancias

L **Estancia Viamonte**, *some 40 km southeast on the coast, T430861, www.estanciaviamonte.com* For a really authentic experience of Tierra del Fuego, stay as a guest here. Built in 1902 by pioneer Lucas Bridges, writer of *Uttermost Part of the Earth*, to protect the indigenous Ona peoples, this working estancia is run by his descendants. You'll be warmly welcomed as their guest, in traditional, beautifully furnished rooms, with comfortable bathrooms, and delicious meals (extra cost for these). Also a spacious cottage to let, US$315 for 7. Join in the farm activities, read the famous book by blazing fires, ride horses over the estate, and completely relax. Warmly recommended. Reserve a week ahead.

LL **Estancia María Behety**. Established in 1897, 15 km from Río Grande, on a 40 km stretch of the river that has become legendary for brown trout fishing, with comfortable accommodation for 18 anglers, and good food. At US$5,350 per week, this is one of the country's priciest fishing lodges, apparently deservedly so! Reservations through: **The Fly shop**, www.flyfishingtravel.com guides, equipment and accommodation included.

L **Estancia Rivadvia**, *100 km from Río Grande, on the route H, www.estanciarivadavia.com, myrna@estnciarivadavia.com T02901 492186*. A 10,000 ha sheep farm, owned by descendents of the original Croatian pioneer who built the place. Luxurious accommodation in a splendid house near the mountains and lakes at the heart of Tierra del Fuego, where you can enjoy a trip

around the estancia to see wild horses and guanacos, good food, and trekking to the trout lake of Chepelmut and Yehuin.

Tolhuin *p523*

D **Cabañas Khami**, *T02964 15611243, T/F422296 www.cabaniaskhami.com .ar* Isolated in a lovely open spot at the head of the lake on low lying land, very comfortable and well equipped *cabañas*, nicely decorated, and with great views of the lake. Good value at US$40 per day for 6. Recommended.

D **Terrazas del Lago**, *Route 3, km 2938, T15604851, terrazas@uol.com.ar* A little way from the shore, smart wooden *cabañas*, well decorated, and also a *confitería* and *parrilla*.

D **Parador Kawi Shiken**, *off the main road on the way to Ushuaia, 4 km south of Tolhuin on RN3, km 2940, T15611505, www.hotelguia .com/hoteles/kawi-shiken/* A rustic place with 3 rooms, shared bathrooms, *casa de té* and restaurant. Ring them to arrange for local *cordero al asador* (barbecued lamb). Also horse riding.

Camping Hain del Lago, *T425951, 156-03606, robertoberbel@hotmail.com* Lovely views, fireplaces, hot showers, and a quincho for when it rains.

Camping La Correntina, *T156-05020, 17 km from Tolhuin*. In woodland, with bathrooms, and horses for hire.

Lago Escondido *p523*

There's only one place to stay in this idyllic spot:

A **Hostería Petrel**, *RN 3, km 3186, T(02901)433569, hpetrel@infovia.com.ar* In a secluded position amidst forest on a tranquil beach of the lake, with decent rooms with bath, and a good restaurant overlooking the lake which serves delicious lamb, however pricey, US$7, open to non-residents. There are also tiny basic cabañas right on the water, US$40 for 2-4 people.

F pp**Refugio Solar del Bosque** , *RN3, km 3020, T453276, T156-06176, solardelbosque @tierradelfuego.org.ar* Further along the road 18 km from Ushuaia is a basic hostel for walkers, with shared bathrooms in dorms for 4, breakfast included.

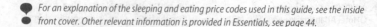

The tourist office has lists of all accommodation, and can help find you somewhere to stay, but in January you must reserve before you come. www.tierradelfuego.org.ar/ushuaia

On the road to the Martial Glaciar overlooking the city are:

LL Las Hayas, *Camino Glaciar Martial, km 3, T430710, www.lashayas.com.ar* Ushuaia's only 5-star hotel, in a spectacular setting, high up on the mountainside with outstanding views over the Beagle channel. Light, tasteful, impeccable rooms. Breakfast included and use of pool, sauna, gym, squash court, 9 hole golf course, shuttle from town, and transfer from airport. A lovely calm atmosphere, friendly staff, recommended.

A Tolkeyen, *Del Tolkeyen 2145, 4 km from town towards national park, T445315, www.tolkeyenhotel.com.ar* A lovely traditional rustic place in a superb setting, with open views from its rooms, which vary between plain and flouncy, but are all spacious and comfortable. Lots of land to walk in, and close to the national park, with free buses into town, and free room service. Also an excellent restaurant, serving king crab and Fuegian lamb. Very relaxing. Recommended.

B Cabaña del Martial, *L F Martial 2109, T430475, cabanasdelmartial @uolsinectis.com.ar* Wonderful views from these comfortable and well-equipped *cabañas*.

A-B Los Ñires, *Av de los Ñires 3040, T443781, www.tierradelfuego.org.ar/losnires* The setting is the feature here, with lovely views, comfortable rooms in simple rustic style, and a good restaurant. Transfers and breakfast included.

B Apart Hotel Cabo San Diego, *25 de Mayo 368, T435600, www.cabosandiego.com.ar* Really comfortable and spacious apartments, very spick and span, well equipped for cooking, good bathrooms and comfortable beds. Great for couples or families.

B Canal Beagle, *Maipú y 25 de Mayo, T421117, hotelcanalb@uolsinectis.com.ar* Good value ACA hotel (discounts for members) recently modernised to luxurious international standards, with clear views over

the channel, and a good, reasonably priced restaurant.

B Cap Polonio, *San Martín 748, T422140, www.hotelcappolonio.com.ar* A smart central modern city hotel with very comfortable minimalist rooms, all with bath, phone, TV, internet; some have views of the canal. There's a chic restaurant cafe downstairs.

B César, *San Martín 753, T421460, F432721, www.hotelcesarhostal.com.ar* Very central, this big tourist place is often booked by groups, but is reasonable value. Simple rooms with bath, breakfast included.

B Hostal Malvinas, *Gob Deloqui 615, T/F422626 hotelmalvinas@arnet.com.ar* Neat, comfortable rooms with excellent bathrooms, and good views, in this central and well run town house hotel. Breakfast is included, and all day tea and coffee. The welcoming owner is a sailing expert. Recommended.

C Hostería Posada Fin del Mundo, *Valdez 281, T437345, posadafindelmundo @infovia.com.ar* A relaxed family atmosphere, homely rooms, and friendly staff. Good value.

D Albergue Kayen, *Gob. Paz 1410, T431497, www.alberguekayen.com.ar* Good value, friendly place with family attention, in an elevated position with fine views over channel. Rooms have shared bath, self service breakfast.

D B&B Nahuel, *25 de Mayo 440, T423068 byb_nahuel@yahoo.com.ar* A delightful house with views over channel, with brightly painted and tastefully decorated rooms, and a lovely welcome from the owner. Great value. Recommended.

D pp El Nido de Cóndores, *Gob. Capos 795 y 9 de Julio, T437753, www.companiadeguias .com.ar* Simple rooms with shared bath, but a really excellent breakfast in this friendly place with a lovely relaxing café below. The owners are Ushuaia's best walking guides, and can arrange superb trekking. Recommended.

E pp Amanecer de la Bahia, *Magallanes 594, T424405, amanecerdelabahia @arnet.com.ar* A light, spacious, impeccably kept hostal, with shared rooms for 4 and 6, also double and triples. Internet, living rooms, breakfast included.

Tierra del Fuego Listings: Argentine Tierra del Fuego

F pp **Albergue Cruz del Sur**, *Deloqui 636, T423110, xdelsur@yahoo.com* There's a very friendly atmosphere in this relaxed small hostal, with cosy dorms, use of kitchen, and a lovely quiet library room for reading. A place to make friends. Recommended.

F pp **Albergue Refugio de Mochilero**, *25 de Mayo 241, T436129, www.refugiodelmochilero .netfirms.com* Nice cosy clean dormitories with shared bathrooms and kitchen facilities. The welcoming owner is expert on Antarctica.

Private homes

Many people offer rooms in private houses: D **Galeazzi-Basily**, *Gdor Valdez 323, T423213, fbasily@quasarlab.com.ar* The best option by far is this cosy and stylish family home, with incredibly welcoming owners Francis and Alejandro, who speak excellent English, in a pleasant residential area just 5 blocks from the centre. Delicious breakfast included. There is also a F 5-bed *cabaña* in the garden. Highly recommended.

F pp **Familia Velasquez**, *Juana Fadul 361, T421719*. Basic rooms in cosy cheerful family home, where the kind owners look after you. Excellent value.

Estancias *www.estanciasdesantacruz.com*

L **Estancia Rolito**, *Route A, km 14, T492007, rolitotdf@hotmail.com* A magical place on the Beagle channel with sweeping views of the coast, cosy accommodation, and friendly hosts Annie and Pepe, booked through Turismo de Campo, 25 de Mayo 50, T432419, www.turismodecampo.com.ar also day visits.

A pp **Harberton**, *T422742, estanciaharberton @tierradelfuego.org.ar* 2 impeccably restored historical buildings on the tranquil lakeside, giving you space and privacy from the main house. Very simple accommodation, but wonderful views, and beautiful walks on the estancia's coastline. 90 km east of Ushuaia, along Route 3 and 33, a spectacular drive.

Camping

Camping Río Pipo, *Ushuaia Rugby Club (Km 4), on the eastern edge of town*. US$2pp, friendly owners, all facilities.

Camping del Solar del Bosque *(Km 18), on Route 3 heading for Río Grande, T421228*. US$2pp. Hot showers.

Camping Haruwen, *in the Haruwen Winter Sports complex (Km 33), T/F424058*. US$2per tent, electricity, shop, bar, restaurant.

Camping Lago Roca, Inside Parque Nacional Tierra del Fuego (entry fee US$4), 21km from Ushuaia. By the forested shore of tranquil Lago Roc, this is a beautiful site with good facilities, reached by bus Jan-Feb, expensive small shop, cafetería.

There are also various sites with no facilities: **Bahía Ensenada Camping** 16 km from Ushuaia; **Camping Las Bandurrias** and **Camping Laguna Verde**, both 20 km from Ushuaia.

🍴 Eating

Río Grande *p522*

$ **La Nueva Colonial**, *Fagnano 669*. Half a block from the plaza, next to Casino Club, where the locals go for delicious pasta in a warm family atmosphere.

$ **La Rueda** , *Islas Malvinas 954, first floor*. Excellent *parrilla* in a welcoming place.

$ **La Nueva Piamontesa** , Belgrano y Mackinlay, T423620, to the side of the charming 24 hr grocery store. Cheap set menus and also delivers food.

$ **Leymi** , 25 de Mayo 1335. Cheap fixed menu.

$ **Pope Pizzas**, *Belgrano 383*.

Tolhuin *p523*

On the same block as the famous **La Union** bakery, open 24 hrs, daily except Monday midnight to Tuesday 0600, there are pizzas at **Pizzería Amistad**, and more of a range at **La Posada de los Ramirez**, a cosy restaurant and *rotisería*, where 3 courses will cost you US$4, open weekends only, lunch and dinner. **Parrilla La Victoria**, *Koshten 324*, is open daily, with beef and lamb on the asado, and also pizzas, call before for delicious Fuegian lamb, *T492297*.

Ushuaia *p523, map p524*

$$$ **Kaupe**, *Roca 470 y Magallanes*. The best restaurant in town with exquisite food. King crab and meat dishes all beautifully served, in a lovely environment – a great treat.

$$ **Los Pioneros, Bodegon Fueguino**, *San Martín 859*. In a stylishly renovated 1896 house in the main street, this stands out from the crowd by serving picadas with

delicious and imaginative dips, and unusual *cazuelas*, *picadas* and dips. A buzzy atmosphere and welcoming staff.

$$$ **Marcopolo**, *San Martín 748*. A chic modern international-style café restaurant for seafood and everything else. Soothing décor, good service. Tango show Fri 2200.

$$ **El Rancho**, *San Martín y Rivadavia*. A *parrilla* with Argentine live music, and rather atmospheric, despite the obvious appeal to tourists. Good steaks too.

$$ **Tante Sara Pizzas and Pastas**, *San Martín 165*. A brightly-lit functional place with tasty filling food.

$$ **Tia Elvira**, *Maipu 349*. Retains its reputation for excellent seafood, with a good choice of fresh fish and good views.

$$ **Volver**, *Maipu 37*. In an atmospheric old 1898 house, with ancient newspaper all over the walls, so that you can read intriguing fragments while you eat. Cosy stoves and an intimate atmosphere. Delicious salmon and *arroz con mariscos*.

$ **Barcleit 1912**, *Fadul 148*. Serves good cheap Italian food, 3 courses for US$2.50, pizzas and pastas.

$ **El Nautico**, *Maipu y Belgrano*. For a good lunch, ask for the US$4 set menu here, seved in a great setting on the waterfront.

$ **La Estancia**, *San Martín in the next block*. Cheery and good value. Both are packed in high season.

$ **Moustaccio**, *San Martín y Gdor Godoy*. Long established, good for cheap fish in a cosy atmosphere.

$ **Parrilla La Rueda**, *San Martín y Rivadavia*. Of the 2 good *tenedor libres* on *San Martín*, this is the best at US$5.20 for great range including lamb *asador al palo*.

Cafés

Café Tante Sarah, *Fadul y San Martín, opposite the tourist office*. The most appealing of the cafés on *San Martín*. Smart and modern with an airy feel, serving good coffee and tasty sandwiches.

La Baguette, *Don Bosco y San Martín*. The best fresh takeaway sandwiches, and also delicious *empanadas* and *facturas* (pastries).

🎵 Bars and clubs

Ushuaia *p523, map p524*
Good places for a late night drink:

Bar de la Esquina, *Fadul y San Martín*. French bistro, delicious sandwiches, cakes and *picadas* with drinks.

Café Bar de la Esquina, *25 de Mayo y San Martín*. Light meals and drinks, in a good atmosphere.

Lennon Pub, *on Maipu*. A lively friendly atmosphere and live music.

U! Bar, *San Martín*. A trendy orange plastic sub aquatic feel.

⚙ Festivals and events

Río Grande *p522*
The **sheep shearing festival** in Jan is definitely worth seeing, if you're in the area. There's a **rural exhibition** with handicrafts, 2nd week of Feb. **Shepherd's day**, with impressive sheepdog display, is the first week in Mar. **Winter solstice**, the longest night with fireworks and ice skating contests takes place **Jun 20/21** , though this is a very inhospitable time of year.

⚙ Sport and activities

Ushuaia *p523, map p524*
Fishing
The lakes and rivers of Tierra del Fuego offer great fishing, for brown and rainbow trout, and stream trout in Lago Fagnano. Both flycasting and spinning are allowed, and permits must be bought. The trout season is 1 Nov-31 Mar, licences US$10 per week, US$5 per day. Contact Asociación de Caza y Pesca at Maipú y 9 de Julio, which has a small museum.

Fly Casting, *Del Michay 667, T435769, fishing@infovia.com.ar* Offer a range of fishing excursions, provide equipment.

Yishka, *Gob Godoy 115, T431535, F431230, yishkatierradelfuego.org.ar* Arranges fishing excursions to Lago Fagnano.

Skiing
For skiing, hiking, climbing contact **Club Andino**, Fadul 5. To get to the remoter areas of the island from Ushuaia, it's worth going on an expedition with an agency. See tour operators below for some excellent packages and day hikes.

Ushuaia is becoming popular as a winter resort with several centres for skiing, snowboarding and husky sledging. There's good powder snow, thanks to the even temperatures (between 5 and -5°C) and the climate isn't as cold as you'd think, despite the latitude, because winter is the least windy season here. The season runs between mid-Jun and mid-Oct, but late Aug to late Sep is recommended, for lighter days, when the snow is still good. The most developed resort is **Cerro Castor complex**, *27 km from town*, *T156 05595 www.cerrocastor.com* With 22 km of pistes of all grades, with plenty for intermediate skiers, and vertical drop of 760 m, it's bettered only by Las Leñas and Bariloche. There's an attractive centre with complete equipment rental for skiing, snowboarding and snowshoeing, ski school, cafés and a hotel, and restaurants on the pistes. Ski pass US$23 per day. 3 regular buses run per day. There's excellent cross country skiing in the area, with various new centres strung along the main road Route 3 at 19-22 km east of Ushuaia, of which **Tierra Mayor** *21 km from town, T437454*, is recommended. In a beautiful wide valley between steep sided mountains, the centre offers half and full day excursions on sledges with huskies for hire, as well as cross country skiing and show shoeing. Equipment hire, and cosy restaurant with wood stoves. In the city itself, **Martial Glacier Winter Sports Centre**, *7 km from the centre*, has a single piste. The **Haruwen Winter Sports** complex is 35 km east on Route 3 also offers winter sports activities.

⌕ Tour operators

Río Grande *p522*
Fiesta Travel, *9 de Julio 663, T431800, fiestatravel@arnet.com.ar*
Mariani Travel Rosales 259, *T426010, mariani@netcombbs.com.ar*
Techni Austral, *Moyano 516, T430610*. Bus tickets to Ushuaia.

Ushuaia *p523, map p524*
Lots of companies now offer imaginative adventure tourism expeditions. All agencies charge the same fees for excursions; ask tourist office for a complete list: Tierra del Fuego National Park, 4 hrs, US$12 (entry fee US$4extra); Lagos Escondido and Fagnano, 8 hrs, US$22 with lunch. With 3 or 4 people it might be worth hiring a remise taxi.

Rumbo Sur, *San Martín 350, T421139, F430699, www.rumbosur.com.ar* Flights, buses and all the conventional tours, Harberton, plus wonderful Antarctic expeditions, mid Nov to mid Mar, 8-20 days (last minute reductions only available from Argentina, around US$2500 pp), friendly, English spoken.
Turismo de Campo, *25 de Mayo 34, T437351, F421233, www.turismodecampo .com.ar* Adventure tourism in small groups with English/French speaking guides. Boat and trekking combinations in the National Park, and trekking for all levels in other remoter places, visiting Estancia Rolito, (full board US$60pp), bird watching tours, horse riding in Monte Susanna, sailing in the Beagle Channel. Also Antarctica. Highly recommended.
Tolkar Viajes y Turismo, *Roca 157, T431412, www.tolkarturismo.com.ar* Flights, bus tickets to Punta Arenas and Río Gallegos, conventional and adventure tourism, mountain biking to Lago Fagnano.
Compañia de Guias de Patagonia, *El Nido de los Condores hostel, Gob Campos 783, y 9 de Julio, T432642, www.companiade guias.com.ar* The best walking guides. Well run expeditions for all levels to the national park, and also to more inaccessible places, for the day, or several days, all equipment and food included. Also ice climbing (training and equipment provided) to Cerro del Medio and Cerro Alvear. Professional, friendly and knowledgeable. Highly recommended.
Travel Lab, *San Martín y 9 de Julio, T436555, travellabush@speedy.com.ar* Tren del fin del Mundo, unconventional tours, mountain biking, trekking, etc. English and French spoken, very helpful.
Canal Fun & Nature, *Rivadavia 82, T437610, www.canalfun.com* Huge range of activities, horse riding, 4WD excursions. Recommended.
All Patagonia, *Juana Fadul 26, T430725, F430707, www.allpatagonia.com/Eng* A wonderful range of tours, sailing, hiking, birdwatching, all making the most of the wild land around Ushuaia. Ask about the birdwatching trip to the centre of the island, and the 6 day trip crossing the Fuegian cordillera. Also Antarctic trips. Well-organized and recommended.

☉ Transport

Río Grande *p522*

Book ahead in summer when buses and planes fill up fast. Take passport when buying ticket.

Air

Airport 4 km west of town, T420600. Taxi US$2. To **Buenos Aires**, Aerolíneas Argentinas daily, 3½ hrs direct. To **Ushuaia**, LADE once a week to **Ushuaia** and **Patagonian towns**.

Bus

Buses leave from terminal at Elcano y Güemes, T420997, or from **Tecni Austral's** office Moyano 516, T430610. To **Porvenir**, Chile, 5 hrs, US$9, **Gesell**, Wed, Sun, 0800, passport and luggage control at San Sebastián. To **Punta Arenas**, Chile, via Punta Delgada, 10 hrs, **Pacheco**, Tue, Thu, Sat 0730, US$15, To **Río Gallegos**, 3 times a week, US$15. To **Ushuaia**, Tecni Austral, 3-4 hrs, 2 daily (heavily booked in sumnmer), US$12, also **Tolkeyen**, US$7.

Car hire

Hertz Annie Millet, *Libertad 714, T426534, hertzriogrande@netcombbs.com.ar.* **Al Rent a Car International**, *Belgrano 423, T430757, ai.rentcar@carletti.com.ar*
Also rents 4WDs and camionettas.

Ushuaia *p523, map p524*

Book ahead in summer, as flights fill up fast. In winter, poor weather often delays flights.

Air

Aeropuerto Internacional Malvinas Argentinas, 4 km from town, taxi, US$2 (no bus). Schedules tend to change from season to season, so call offices for times and prices.

Airport tourist information, T423970. Offices: Aerolíneas Argentinas, *Roca 116, T421218.* LADE, *San Martín 542, Loc 5, T421123.* To **Buenos Aires**, 4 hrs, **El Calafate**, 2 hrs, both with Aerolíneas and LADE. Flights are usually available to **Río Gallegos**, 1 hr, and **Río Grande**, 1 hr, several a week, but check with agents. To **Punta Arenas**, 1 hr, Aerovias DAP, (25 de

Mayo 64, T431110). Note that departure tax must be paid to cities in Argentina, US$15.

Bus

To **Río Grande** 3 hrs, Tecni Austral. Book through **Tolkar**, *Roca 157, 431408,* and **Líder**, *Gob Paz 921, T430264,* both US$8, 2 a day, and **Tolkeyen**, *Maipú 237, T430264, T437073, tolkeyen@tierradelfuego.org.ar* US$10. To **Punta Arenas**, Tecni Austral, Mon, Wed, Fri 0600, US$23, and **Tolkeyen/Pacheco**, Tue, Thu, Sat, 0630, 12 hrs, US$25, via **Punta Delgada** ferry (15 mins' crossing). Both also have less frequent services through **Porvenir** with 2½-hr ferry. No through services to **Río Gallegos**. Go to Río Grande, then change: 8-10 hrs bus journey. Sometimes it's possible to book this whole ticket in Ushuaia at Tolkar. From Río Gallegos, several buses daily to **El Calafate**, 4 hrs.

Car hire

Most companies charge the same, around US$45 per day including insurance and 150 km per day. **Hertz**, *at the airport, T432429.* Localiza, *San Martín 1222, T430739.*

Cycle hire

DDT Cycles Sport , *San Martín 1258.* **Seven Deportes** , *San Martín y 9 de Julio.*

Sea

To **Puerto Williams** (Chile), no regular sailings. Yachts might carry charter passengers in summer, returning the same day, fares likely to be US$25-35 one way, but this is not reliable. Enquire at AIASN agency for the cruise through Beagle Channel. There are spectacular luxury **cruises** around Cape Horn via Puerto Williams operated by the Chilean company, **Crucero Austral**, 7/8 days, US$1,260. Advance booking is advisable, from **Cruceros Australis SA**, *Buenos Aires office (011)4325 4000, www.australis.com*
To **Antarctica** Ushuaia is the starting point for a number of excellent expeditions to Antarctica; informative, adventurous, wonderful experiences.

Antarctic expeditions run mid-Nov to mid Mar, usually 8-11 day trips to the Antarctic peninsula and the Wedell sea, some offering extra activities such as camping and kayaking. It's not a luxury cruise, and there's informal, simple accommodation usually in non-tourist boats used for scientific exploration, so the food is fine but not excessive. The expedition leader organizes lectures during the 3-day journey to reach the Antarctic, with at least 2 disembarkations a day in a zodiac to see icebergs and penguins. There's most ice in Nov and Dec, but more baby penguins in Jan and Feb, and whales in Mar. The landscape is always impressive. A longer trip, 18-19 days, combines the Antarctic with the Malvinas/Falklands and South Georgia islands. It's worth turning up and asking for availability; there's a 30% discount if you book last minute, only available if bought in Ushuaia, when the price is around US$2500pp. Weekly departures in season.

Companies: Rumbo Sur Turismo de Campo, *San Martín 350, T421139, F430699, www.rumbsur.com.ar* helpful, English spoken. **All Patagonia**, *Juana Fadul 54, T433622, www.allpatagonia.com.ar* Handle all companies, give helpful advice, and last minute discounts. **Turismo de Campo**, *25 de Mayo 34, T437351, www.turismodecampo.com.ar*

Taxi
Remise Carlitos, *T422222*. Reliable. Tienda Leon, *San Martín 995, T422222*. Reliable.

Train
For *Tren del Fin del Mundo*, see page 526.

● Directory

Río Grande *p522*
Airline offices   Aerolíneas Argentinas, *San Martín 607, T424467*. **Banks**   ATMs: 4 banks on San Martín between 100 and 300. Banco de la Nación Argentina, San Martín 219. Bansud, *Rosales 241*. Cash advance on Visa. Cash exchange Thaler Rosales 259. **Communications**   Post office *Piedrabuena y Ameghino. Locutorio, San Martín at 170 and 458.*

Ushuaia *p523, map p524*
Airline offices   LADE, *San Martín 542, shop 5, T/F421123.* Aerolíneas Argentinas, *Roca 116, T421218, T0810-222 8652.* Aerovias DAP, *25 de Mayo 64, T431110.* **Banks**   Banks open 1000-1500 (in summer). ATMs are plentiful all along San Martín, using credit cards is by far the easiest, as changing TCs is difficult and expensive. Changing money and TCs: Banco de Tierra del Fuego, *San Martín 396*, Agencia de Cambio Thaler , *San Martín 877*, also open weekends, 1000-1300, 1700-2030, and at Oro Verde , *25 de Mayo 50*, also open Sat 1000-1300.   **Communications**   Post office: *San Martín y Godoy,* Mon-Fri 0900-1300 and 1700-1900, Sat 0830-1200. Telephone: *locutorios* all along San Martín. Internet Many broad-band cyber cafes and *locutorios* along San Martín. **Consulates**   Chile, *Malvinas Argentinas y Jainen, Casilla 21, T421279.* Finland, *Paz y Deloqui.* Germany, *Rosas 516.* Italy, *Yaganes 75.*

History

Much of Argentina's fascinating history is visible on a visit to the country today, not only in colonial architecture and the 19th-century artefacts which fill the museums but in the culture and customs of everyday life. Many towns in the Pampas of Buenos Aires Province are just as they were in the 19th century, such as San Antonio de Areco and Chascomús, where the traditions of a lively gaucho culture are still maintained. The lives of early pioneers can be explored in the Welsh towns of Gaiman and Trevelin in Patagonia and in the remoter estancias throughout the country. Córdoba's history of Jesuit occupation is visible in many buildings in the city and province. But it's in the northwest of Argentina that you'll find the richest evidence of the country's history. This is where the Spanish first arrived in the 16th century, and before them the Incas in the early 15th century, and both have left their mark in colonial architecture and intriguing archaeological evidence. However, long before these invasions, the present day provinces of Salta, Catamarca, Tucumán and Jujuy were inhabited by many sophisticated indigenous cultures whose ruined cities can be visited at Santa Rosa de Tastil, Tilcara and Quilmes, and whose beautiful ceramics fill the area's many museums. This is the most rewarding part of the country to visit if you're interested in exploring Argentina's past.

Archaeology and prehistory

Earliest origins

The first peoples crossed the temporary land bridge spanning Asia and America and the Bering Strait between 50,000 and 60,000 years ago, and began a long migration southwards, reaching South America about 30,000 years ago and Tierra del Fuego around 12,000 years ago. Hunters and foragers, they followed in the path of huge herds of now extinct animals such as mammoths, giant ground sloths, mastodons and wild horses, adapting to fishing along the Chilean coasts. In the northeast of Argentina, these peoples adopted a more sedentary lifestyle, pausing in their semi-nomadic travels long enough to plant and harvest crops of maize and manioc, and domesticating animals.

Northwestern Argentina

Argentina has a rich history of pre-Hispanic indigenous civilisations, with the most important archaeological sites situated in the northwest and west areas of the most highly developed cultures south of the Central Andes. Along a migratory path which followed the Andes, this region became a meeting place for established settlers with peoples and influences from northern Chile, the Central Andes, the Chaco and the hunter-gatherers of the south. Cave paintings and petroglyphs engraved on rocks remain from 13,000 to 10,000 years ago, made by cave dwellers who lived by hunting vizcacha, guanaco, vicuña and birds, some painted with pigments derived from minerals mixed with gesso. Their lines, dots and geometrical forms rather than human figures, belong to a symbolic system impossible to interpret today. The extraordinary quantity of handprints visible in the Cueva de los Manos in Patagonia were made as long ago as 10,000 years, and again, their purpose and origin remains a mystery.

In the northwest, where the richest and earliest remains of human life in Argentina have been found, hunter-gatherers arrived between 13,000 and 11,000 years ago. They hunted using arrowheads honed from stones or hurling sticks to bring down wild camelids (llamas and vicuñas). By around 1000 to 500 BC, the nomadic groups had grown in size and were too large to subsist on hunting alone and so started early attempts at agriculture. They grew potatoes and maize, and a mummy found from this period (displayed in Cachi's museum) with a few artefacts and belongings suggests that these peoples had a developed system of beliefs. By 2,000 years ago, it seems that small communities had started to gather on the alluvial plains, living on agriculture and herding llamas. In many of the area's museums, you'll see large grinding stones made of granite, used to grind maize and other substances against a larger flat stone, as well as fine arrowheads and pipes used for smoking tobacco. Weaving began around this time, with the evidence of delicate spindle whorls, used to weight the sticks on which wool was wound.

Three distinct periods can be identified in the cultural development of the region. The Early period (500 BC to AD 650) witnessed the beginnings of agriculture as well as pottery and metalworking, with the remains of terraces near Humahuaca in Jujuy. The Middle period (AD 650-850) was marked by the influence of the great culture of Tiahuanaco in present-day Bolivia. Fine metal objects, some of them of gold and silver, were made and new plant varieties were introduced. Stone vessels, anthropomorphic clay pieces, and ceramics with ornate detail derive from this period all over the Northwest.

In the Later period (AD 850-1480), known as the period of Regional Development, small groups of settlers formed communities with individual dwellings, usually based on circular stone walls, next to water sources. This period introduced more sophisticated agriculture, and both ritual and functional ceramics were made by peoples known as the Santamariana or Diaguita culture. Although there was no system of writing, their language, Kakán, survived until the Inca invasion. These cultures did leave a remarkable legacy, though, in their large, beautifully painted funerary urns. It's thought that these were used to bury the bones of children, and the infant mortality rate was high. The urns were buried with artefacts and belongings, and the predominant religious beliefs centred around worship of the mother earth goddess, the Pachamama. She's still worshipped in rural communities all over the Northwest today, with lively festivals on 1 August. Wind and percussion instruments were used at this time, as well as pipes for smoking hallucinogenic substances ground from seeds of the high altitude *cebil* tree (see Cachi and Catamarca museums). Textiles were first woven around 1200 AD, fine examples of which can be seen in Salta's archaeological museum from the ruins of Santa Rosa de Tastil.

Crops were grown on terraces, aided by complex irrigation systems, and the indigenous animals such as llamas were domesticated for their wool and meat. Metal working was fully developed and tools made of bones were also used.

The Incas first arrived in the Calchaquíes valleys area between 1410 and 1430, incorporating the area into the part of their empire known as Kollasuyo. Two parallel roads were built along the length of the Andes and along the Pacific shore, linking their communities with the rest of the Inca empire and used as busy trade routes. However, a more complex network of roads further east is being discovered including sites such as Santa Rosa de Tastil in Salta, and the Valles Calchaquíes, where there's evidence that, like any successful empire, the Incas both appropriated and manipulated local customs in clothing, handicrafts and construction in order to retain control of the region. They made Quechua the official language, punished the chiefs of any groups whose members transgressed and absorbed the local cult of the earth goddess Pachamama into their own system of worship of the sun. The Incas also brought with them their own sacrificial burial customs. Three mummies found at the summit of Cerro Llullaillaco on the Salta/Chile border indicate that children were made as offerings. These three, aged between seven and 15, were carried to the summit, dressed in special garments, adorned with feather headdresses and jewellery, and put to sleep using strong local liquor *chicha*. It's thought that they were offered as a sacrifice to the gods in their belief that to gain life, life has also to be sacrificed. Their peaceful faces show no sign of stress so it's likely that they died painlessly within minutes, and Salta's fascinating archaeological museum has photographs and videos of these and other related finds. The Calchaquíes valleys were the site of particularly bloody battles when the Spanish attempted to dominate in the 16th century (see box, page 118) owing to the fierce resistance of these peoples. Many indigenous groups were wiped out, but fortunately, in the northwest of Argentina, there are living descendants from many of the original inhabitants, keeping their customs and beliefs alive.

Central and Southern Argentina

The Comechingones, who inhabited what are now the provinces of Córdoba and San Luis lived in settlements of pit-dwellings and used irrigation to produce a range of crops. In the far northeast on the eastern edge of the Chaco were the Guaraní; organized into loose confederations, they lived in rudimentary villages and practised slash-and-burn agriculture to grow maize, sweet potatoes, manioc and beans. They also produced textiles and ceramics.

Further south, the Pampas and Patagonia were much more sparsely populated than the northwest and most groups were nomadic long after the arrival of the Spanish. One of the most important groups were the Querandí, who eked out a living by hunting guanaco and rheas with *boleadoras*, three balls of stone tied with thong and hurled at the legs of a running animal. Patagonia was inhabited by scattered nomadic groups including the Pampa, the Chonik and the Kaingang, who managed to avoid contact with white settlers until the 19th century. In the steppes of Patagonia, the Tehuelche and Puelche lived as nomadic hunters living off guanaco, foxes and game. In the far south, in southern Patagonia and Tierra del Fuego, there were four indigenous groups, the land-based Ona and Haush, who hunted foxes and guanaco, wearing their hides and constructing temporary dwellings of branches covered loosely with skins. And the sea based Yaghanes and Alacaluf, who made canoes, paddles, bailers and mooring rope, catching fish with spears or by hand, though seals were their main source of food. These peoples survived until the late 19th century and were befriended and protected by the son of Tierra del Fuego's first settler and missionary. Lucas Bridges' account in *The Uttermost Part of the Earth* gives an extraordinary insight into the customs and hunting practices of the Ona and Yaghanes. Within 50 years of the arrival of white sheep-farmers, many had been shot, or coerced into religious missions where they could be controlled, and now no single descendent remains.

European exploration and settlement

At the time of the arrival of the first Europeans the land which is now Argentina was sparsely populated with about two-thirds of the indigenous population living in the northwest. European exploration began in the Plata estuary when in 1516 Juan de Solís, a Portuguese navigator employed by the Spanish crown, landed on the shore of the estuary, though his men were soon killed by indigenous Querandí. Four years later he was followed by Ferdinand Magellan who explored the Plata, before turning south to make his way into the Pacific via the straits north of Tierra del Fuego, now named after him. In 1527 both Sebastian Cabot and his rival Diego García sailed into the estuary and up the Ríos Paraná and the Paraguay. Cabot founded a small fort, Sancti Spiritus, not far from the modern city of Rosario, but it was wiped out by indigenous inhabitants about two years later. Despite these difficulties Cabot took back to Spain stories of a great Indian kingdom beyond the Plata estuary, rich in precious metals, giving the Río de la Plata its misleading name: river of silver. A Portuguese expedition to the estuary, led by Affonso de Souza, returned with similar tales, and this led to a race between the two Iberian powers. In 1535, Pedro de Mendoza set out with 16 ships and a well-equipped force of 1,600 men and founded a settlement at Buenos Aires, which he gave its present name, originally Puerto Nuestra Señora Santa María de Buen Ayre. The natives soon made life too difficult; the settlement was abandoned and Mendoza returned home but not before sending Juan de Ayolas with a small force up the Río Paraná in search of the fabled Indian kingdom. In 1537 this force founded Asunción, in Paraguay, where the natives were friendly.

After 1535 the attention of the Spanish crown switched to Peru, where Pizarro was engaged in the successful conquest of the Inca Empire, where there was instant wealth in gold and silver and a malleable workforce in the enormous indigenous population. The small settlement at Asunción remained an isolated outpost until in 1573, a force from Asunción travelled south to establish Santa Fe. Seven years later Juan de Garay refounded Buenos Aires, but it was only under his successor, Hernando Arias de Saavedra (1592-1614), that the new settlement became secure benefiting both from back up in Asunción and from the many cattle brought over by Mendoza which had increased and multiplied meanwhile.

However, before the time of Mendoza's expedition to the Plata estuary, Spanish expeditions were already exploring northern parts of present-day Argentina. In 1535 Diego de Almagro led a party from Peru which crossed the northwest into Argentina, and in 1543 the Spanish Viceroyalty of Peru was made administrative capital of southern South America. There was greatly increased motivation for exploring the region, however, when silver deposits were found in Potosí (now in Bolivia), and the Governorship of Tucumán was set up as an administrative centre. Explorations set forth from Chile and Peru to find good trade routes and a source of cheap labour to work the mines, and so the oldest towns in Argentina were founded: Santiago del Estero (1553), Mendoza (1561), San Juan (1562), Córdoba (1573), Salta (1582), La Rioja (1591), and Jujuy (1593). A total of 25 cities were founded in present-day Argentina in the 16th century, 15 of which survived, at a time when the total Spanish population was under 2,000.

Colonial rule

Throughout the colonial period the Argentine territories were an outlying part of the Spanish empire and of minor importance since Spanish colonial settlement and government was based in Peru, busy with exploiting the vast mineral wealth of Potosí in Alto Peru (and large supplies of indigenous labour). Argentine lands offered only sparse population and little mineral wealth by comparison. Also, the nomadic nature of many indigenous groups made any attempt at control difficult, whereas in Peru Spanish rule was more readily superimposed on the centralized administration of the defeated Incas.

Buenos Aires failed to become an important port for a couple of centuries because from 1543 all the Spanish territories in South America were governed from Lima, the Vice-Regal capital, and trade with Spain was routed via Lima, Panama and the Caribbean. In fact, Buenos Aires was prohibited from trading directly, though the Paraná delta north of the city near Tigre provided ample opportunities for smuggling British and Portuguese goods into the city, and it rapidly expanded as a centre for contraband. By 1776 the city's population was only 24,000, though this was double the size of any of the cities of the interior. However, the Governorship of Tucumán was more important as a centre, due to the success of the *encomienda* system here, in which lands belonging to indigenous peoples were seized and redistributed to Spanish settlers. The idea was that the *encomenderos* in charge would exchange work done for religious education, but in reality these men were ruthless exploiters of slave labour and offered little in the way of spiritual enlightenment. In the Valles Cachaquiés (see box, page 238) the substantial indigenous population resisted conversion by Jesuit missionaries, and was effectively wiped out when they rose up against the Spanish landowners. So great was the need for workers in Potosí and Tucumán that black slaves were imported in the late 18th century. Settlers in the northeast of the country too had their conflicts with the indigenous population. The Pampas and Buenos Aires province were dangerous areas for white settlement, since in these lands wild cattle had long been hunted for their hides by Tehuelches and Mapuches driving cattle to Chile over the Andes for trade, and their violent armies, or *malones,* clashed regularly with newly arrived settlers. Around the early 18th century, the figure of the gaucho emerged, nomadic men of mixed *criollo* (early Argentine settlers) and indigenous origin, who roamed free on horseback, living off cattle. Once the Argentine state started to control land boundaries, these characters became emblematic of freedom and romanticized in important fictional works, *Martín Fierro* and *Don Segundo de los Sombras.* The gaucho is still a much admired figure today, though less wild and certainly no longer an outcast.

Jesuits came to civilize the native population under the protection of the Spanish crown in the late 16th century. They quickly set up missions which employed the reasonably pliant Guaraní residents of the upper Paraná in highly organized societies, with a militant component equipped to resist the frequent raids by Portuguese in search of slaves. The Guaraní were compelled to comply with their educators since this exempted them from working in the silver mines, and as many as 4,000 Guaraní lived in some missions, also producing *yerba mate* and tobacco as successful Jesuit businesses. The remains of their handsome architecture cn be admired in Córdoba city and northern province, as well as at San Ignacio Mini in Misiones.

Buenos Aires at last gained some considerable power when the new viceroyalty of the River Plate was created in 1776, with the rapidly growing city as head of the large area and now able to trade with Spain and her other ports. However, as the trade of contraband into the city increased, flooding the market with cheaper European-produced goods, conflict increased between those advocating free trade, such as Manuel Belgrano, and those who wanted to retain a monopoly. The population of Buenos Aires increased enormously with the viceroyalty, along with its economy, as estancias sprang up to farm and export cattle, instead of rounding up the wild beasts, and with great success.

The Wars of Independence

As in the rest of Spanish America, independence was partly a response to events in Europe, where Spain was initially allied to Napoleonic France. In 1806 and 1807 the British, at war with Napoleon and attracted by what they thought were revolutionary tensions in Buenos Aires, made two attempts to seize the city but were defeated. In 1808 Napoleon invaded Spain, deposing King Ferdinand VII, and provoking widespread resistance from Spanish guerrilla armies. Throughout Spanish America the colonial elites debated where their loyalties lay: to Napoleon's brother Joseph, now officially King? to Ferdinand, now in a French prison? to the Viceroy? to the Spanish resistance parliament in Cadiz?

On 25 May 1810, the cabildo of Buenos Aires deposed the viceroy and established a *junta* to govern on behalf of King Ferdinand VII, when the city's people gathered in front of the *cabildo* wearing pale blue and white ribbons, soon to become the colours of the Argentine flag. This move provoked resistance in outlying areas of the viceroyalty, Paraguay, Uruguay and Upper Peru (Bolivia) breaking away from the rule of Buenos Aires. Factional rivalry within the *junta* between supporters of independence and their opponents added to the confusion and instability. Six years later, in July 1816, when Buenos Aires was threatened by invasion from Peru and blockaded by a Spanish fleet in the Río de la Plata, a national congress held at Tucumán declared independence. The declaration was given reality by the genius and devotion of José de San Martín, who boldly marched an Argentine army across the Andes to free Chile, and (with the help of Lord Cochrane, commander of the Chilean Navy) embarked his forces for Peru, where he captured Lima, the first step in the liberation of Peru. San Martín was aided by an extraordinary feat from a local *caudillo* in the north, Martín Miguel de Güemes, whose army of gauchos was later to liberate Salta. *Caudillos* were local warlords who governed areas far larger, even, than today's provinces, organizing their own armies of local indigenous groups and gauchos. The *caudillos* did not recognize the Tucumán declaration, but so it was on 9 July 1816 that the United Provinces of the River Plate came into being.

Since independence

The 19th century

Much of the current rift between Buenos Aires and the rest of Argentina has its roots in a long-standing conflict which emerged in the early 19th century. The achievement of independence brought neither stability nor unity, since the new junta was divided between Federalists and Unitarists, a conflict that was to rage for for over 40 years. The Unitarists, found mainly in the city of Buenos Aires, advocated strong central government, free trade, education and white immigration, looking to Europe for their inspiration. The Federalists, backed by the provincial elites and many of the great estancieros of Buenos Aires Province, resisted, defending local autonomy and traditional values. Behind the struggle were also economic interests: Buenos Aires and the coastal areas benefited from trade with Europe; the interior provinces did not. As the conflict raged, the territory, known officially as the United Provinces of the Río de la Plata, had none of the features of a modern state: there was neither central government, army, capital city nor constitution.

Order, of a sort, was established after 1829 by Juan Manuel de Rosas, a powerful *caudillo* (provincial leader) and Governor of Buenos Aires. In 1833, he attempted to gain widespread support from local *caudillos* with a Campaign of the Desert, which claimed vast areas of land from indigenous groups, granted to Rosas' allies. However, his overthrow in 1852 unleashed another round in the battles between Unitarists and Federalists and between Buenos Aires and the provinces. In 1853 a constitution establishing a federal system of government was finally drafted but Buenos Aires province refused to join the new Argentine Confederation, which had its capital at Paraná, and set up its own separate republic. Conflict between the two states erupted over the attempt by Buenos Aires to control and tax commerce on the Río Paraná but the victory of Buenos Aires at Pavón (1861) opened the way to a solution: the city became the seat of the federal government with Bartolomé Mitre, former governor of Buenos Aires became the first president of Argentina. There was another political flare-up of the old quarrel in 1880, ending in the humiliation of the city of Buenos Aires, which was separated from its province and made into a special federal territory.

Although there was resistance to the new constitution from some of the western provinces, the institutions of a modern state were created in the two decades after 1861 by Mitre's important period of government: he set up a national bank, bureaucracy, a postal service and an army. And it was the building of railways across the Pampas which did most to create national unity, breaking the power of the *caudillos* by enabling the federal government to send in troops quickly. The new army was quickly employed to defeat Francisco Solano López of Paraguay in the War of the Triple Alliance (1865-70). They were used again in President Roca's genocidal Conquest of the Wilderness (1879-80) which exterminated the indigenous tribes of the Pampas and the south.

In the last quarter of the 19th century Argentina was transformed: the newly acquired stability encouraged foreign investment; the Pampas were fenced, ploughed up and turned over to commercial export agriculture; and railways and port facilities were built. The presidency of Domingo Sarmiento had been keen on widespread immigration from Europe, which transformed the character of Buenos Aires and other cities around the Plata estuary. He also sought to Europeanize the

From Guerrilla War to 'Dirty War'

The 'Dirty War', unleashed by the armed forces after 1976 in response to the guerrilla attacks of the early 1970s, is one of the most violent incidents in modern South American history. While Argentine society is understandably chastened by the experience, hardly a month goes by without this grim episode provoking further controversy.

Guerrilla groups began operating in most Latin American countries in the 1960s, usually with little success. From 1969 several groups emerged in Argentina, among them the Montoneros and the People's Revolutionary Army (Ejército Revolucionario del Pueblo or ERP). The former, inspired by a curious mixture of Peronism, Catholicism and Marxism, proclaimed allegiance to the exiled Perón. Often middle and upper-middle class by background and wanting to liberate the working classes from the evils of capitalism, they idealized Perón and the 'social justice' of his government of 1946-55, a period which most of them were too young to remember. Since the urban working classes were mainly Peronist, these youthful idealists assumed that Perón was a revolutionary leader and that his return would be the prelude to revolution. The ERP, by contrast drawing their inspiration from Trotsky and Che Guevara, argued that political violence would push the military government towards increased repression which would ignite working-class opposition and lead to civil war and socialist revolution.

If Peronists and non-Peronists disagreed over their aims, their methods were similar: kidnappings and bank robberies raised money and gained publicity; army and police officers were assassinated along with right-wing Peronists. Wealthy Argentine families and multinational companies were forced to distribute food and other goods to the poor to obtain the release of kidnap victims. Perhaps the most spectacular of these episodes was carried out by the Montoneros: in 1970 they kidnapped and later executed General Pedro Aramburu, a former president.

Called upon to denounce the

country and his impressive educational policy included the importing of teachers from North America. Political power, however, remained in the hands of a small group of large landowners, who had been granted territories after the Conquest of the Wilderness, and their urban allies. Few Argentines had the vote, and the opposition Unión Cívica Radical, excluded from power, conspired with dissidents in the army in attempts to overthrow the government.

The 20th century

As the British built railways stretching across the country, the sheep industry flourished, making Argentina's fortune through exporting both wool and meat. Refrigerator ships were invented in the 1870's, enabling meat to be shipped in bulk to the expanding industrial countries of Britain and Europe. One of the landmarks of modern Argentine history was the 1912 Sáenz Peña law which established universal manhood suffrage, since until then, power had been centralized in the hands of the elite, with no votes for the working classes. Sáenz Peña, president between 1910 and 1916, sought to bring the middle and working classes into politics, gambling that the Conservatives could reorganize themselves and attract their votes. The gamble failed: the Conservatives failed to gain a mass following and the Radicals came to power. The Radical Civic Union was created in 1890, but Radical presidents Hipólito guerrillas which operated in his name, Perón from his exile in Madrid, refused. With the return to civilian rule the Montoneros ended their violence and worked to elect their hero. Now operating semi-openly, the movement gained many supporters, especially students and young people. In May 1974, months before his death, Perón, denounced his leftist supporters and after his death they resumed their violence, this time under the slogan "If Evita were alive, she would be a Montonera". In 1974 they kidnapped Jorge and Juan Born, heirs and managers of the giant Bunge y Born grain exporting company, and ransomed them for US$64 million.

Long before Perón's return, right-wing groups linked to the army and police had begun to take action against suspected guerrillas. By 1974 suspected leftists were regularly disappearing at the hands of the Argentine Anticommunist Alliance (known as the 'Triple A') which was linked to José López Rega, Minister of Social Welfare and closest advisor to Isabel Perón who became president after her husband's death. The 'Dirty War', launched by the military government which seized power in 1976 was, in a sense, a continuation of this: all three armed services operated their own death squads and camps in a campaign of indiscriminate violence. By 1978/79 both the ERP and the Montoneros had ceased to function. In the process thousands of people disappeared: although an official report produced after the return to civilian rule put their number at 8,960, some 15,000 cases have now been documented and human rights groups now estimate the total at some 30,000. They are remembered still by the Mothers of the Plaza de Mayo, a human rights group made up of relatives, who march anti-clockwise around the Plaza de Mayo in central Buenos Aires every Thursday at 1530 with photos of their 'disappeared' loved ones pinned to their chests. Their continued protests highlight one of the most controversial aspects of the restoration of civilian rule: the laws passed in 1986/7 which shielded junior officers from prosecution on the grounds that they were obeying orders.

Yrigoyen (1916-22 and 1928-30) and Marcelo T de Alvear (1922-28) found themselves trapped between the demands of an increasingly militant urban labour movement and the opposition of the Conservatives, still powerful in the provinces and with allies in the armed forces. Through the 1920's, Argentina was the 'breadbasket of the world' and its sixth richest nation. Fifty years later, the country had become practically third world, a fall from grace which still haunts the Argentine consciousness. The world depression following the Wall Street Crash of 1929 devastated export markets, but the military coup which overthrew Yrigoyen in 1930 was a significant turning point: the armed forces returned to government for the first time in over 50 years and were to continue to play a major political role until 1983. Through the 1930s a series of military backed governments, dominated by the Conservatives, held power; the Radicals were outlawed and elections were so fraudulent that it frequently happened that more people voted than were on the register. Yet the armed forces themselves were disunited: while most officers supported the Conservatives and the landholding elites, a minority of ultra-nationalist officers, inspired by developments in Europe, supported industrialization and the creation of a one-party dictatorship along fascist lines. The outbreak of war in Europe increased these tensions and a series of military coups in 1943-44 led to the rise of Colonel Juan Domingo Perón. When the military allowed a return to civilian rule in 1946 Perón swept into power winning the

The Anglo-Argentine War of 1982

Though the dispute between Britain and Argentina over the Falkland Islands/Islas Malvinas led to armed conflict in 1982, its historical roots can be traced to before Argentine independence. Records of early European voyages in the area are ambiguous but the Dutch sailor Sebald de Weert made the first generally acknowledged sighting of the islands in 1598. In 1764 France established a small colony on the islands at Port Louis, and the British built an outpost at Saunders Island. In 1766 the French government sold Port Louis to Spain and expelled the British from Saunders Island four years later.

In 1811, following the outbreak of the Wars of Independence in South America, Spain withdrew her forces from the islands. In 1831 a United States warship destroyed a promising colonization project under the auspices of a German-born merchant. After British warships expelled a force from Buenos Aires in 1833, the islands came under British rule.

During his first administration (1946-55) Perón focused on the disputed status of the islands as part of an appeal to Argentine nationalism and linked the issue to his plan to create a 'Greater Argentina'. In 1965 the United Nations called on the two states to resolve their differences peacefully. Talks over the islands took place but were complicated by the hostility of the islanders themselves towards any change in their status.

In 1982, when the British government reduced its military commitment in the area, the Argentine military regime calculated their moment had arrived. Economic problems in Argentina threatened the military's hold on power and the regime calculated that a successful invasion would unite the population behind it. An incident on the island of South Georgia, also claimed by Argentina though not part of the Falklands/Malvinas group, provided the opportunity.

The Argentine force of 5,000 men which landed on 2 April 1982 quickly

Presidential elections. His government is chiefly remembered by many Argentines for improving the living conditions of the workers through the introduction of paid holidays and welfare measures in his *justicialismo:* social justice. Perón was an authoritarian and charismatic leader, and especially in its early years the government was strongly nationalistic, taking control over the British-owned railways in 1948 by buying them back at a staggering £150 million. Opposition parties were harassed and independent newspapers taken over since Perón wasn't at all interested in free press. Although Perón was easily re-elected in 1951, his government soon ran into trouble: economic problems led to the introduction of a wage freeze which upset the labour unions which were the heart of Peronist support; the death of Evita in 1952 was another blow; and a dispute with the church in 1954-55 added to Perón's problems. In September 1955 a military coup unseated Perón who went into exile, in Paraguay, Panama, Venezuela, the Dominican Republic and, from 1961 to 1973, in Spain.

Perón's legacy dominated Argentina for the next two decades. No attempt was made to destroy his social and economic reforms but the armed forces determined to exclude the Peronists from power. Argentine society was bitterly divided between Peronists and anti-Peronists and the economy struggled, partly as a result of Perón's measures against the economic elite and in favour of the workers. Between 1955 and 1966 there was an uneasy alternation of military and civilian regimes. The military officers who seized power in 1966 announced their intention to carry out a Nationalist overwhelmed the small British garrison without loss of life. The British military and civilian authorities were expelled and the 1,700 inhabitants placed under an Argentine military governor. Though most Latin American states sympathized with Buenos Aires over the sovereignty issue, many were unhappy with the use of force. Backed by a United Nations resolution and the crucial logistical support of the United States, the British government launched a naval force to regain the islands. On 25 April, as this fleet approached the area, a British force recaptured South Georgia. Over the following three weeks the war was fought in the air and on the seas around the Falklands/Malvinas: the Argentines lost numerous aircraft, the cruiser *General Belgrano*, and several other vessels. The British lost two destroyers, two frigates and a landing vessel. After the sinking of the *General Belgrano*, the Argentine navy stayed in port or close to shore, leaving the airforce and army to carry on the battle.

The British reoccupation of the islands began with an amphibious landing under heavy fire at San Carlos on 21 May. From here British troops marched across the island and attacked ineffective Argentine defensive positions around the capital. Though some Argentine army and marine units resisted, most of the Argentine troops were poorly trained and equipped conscripts who were no match for British regular forces. On 14 June Argentine forces surrendered.

Casualties in the war outnumbered the small island population. Argentine losses were 746 killed, over 300 on the *General Belgrano*, and 1,336 wounded; the British lost 256 killed and 777 wounded. Three islanders were killed on the final assault on the capital.

The consequences of the war for Argentina were wide-ranging. The military government was, perhaps, discredited less by defeat than by its obvious misjudgement, by its blatant misleading of the public and by the accounts given by returning troops of incompetent leadership and lack of supplies. General Galtieri was replaced as President and preparations were made for a return to civilian rule.

Revolution, with austerity measures to try to gain control of a spiralling economy, but they were quickly discredited by a deteriorating economic situation. The Cordobazo, a left-wing student and workers uprising in Córdoba in 1969, was followed by the emergence of several guerrilla groups such as the Montoneros and the People's Revolutionary Army (ERP), as well as growth of political violence. As Argentina became more ungovernable, Perón, from his exile, refused to denounce those guerrilla groups which called themselves Peronist.

In 1971 General Alejandro Lanusse seized power, promising a return to civilian rule and calculating that the only way to control the situation was to allow Perón to return. When the military bowed out in 1973, elections were won by the Peronist candidate, Hector Campora. Perón returned from exile in Madrid to resume as president in October 1973, but died on 1 July 1974, leaving the presidency to his widow, Vice-President María Estela Martínez de Perón, his third wife, known as 'Isabelita'. Perón's death unleashed chaos: hyper-inflation, resumed guerrilla warfare and the operation of right-wing death squads who abducted people suspected of left-wing sympathies. In March 1976, to nobody's surprise, the military overthrew Isabelita and replaced her with a junta led by General Jorge Videla.

The new government closed Congress, outlawed political parties, placed trade unions and universities under military control and unleashed the so-called 'Dirty War', a brutal assault on the guerrilla groups and anyone else who manifested opposition. The military leaders were not at all interested in trying and convicting those they suspected of being dissidents, and started a campaign of violence against anyone remotely Jewish, Marxist, journalists, intellectuals, psychologists and anyone, according to President General Videla, who was as 'spreading ideas contrary to Western Christian civilisation'. As many as 30,000 people are thought to have 'disappeared' during this period, removed by violent squads who would take them to clandestine detention centres to be raped, tortured or brutally killed. This is one of Argentina's bleakest memories, and that many Argentines maintain that a strong line was needed to deal with guerrillas is a sign of how hidden the reality was at the time. In order that the disappeared should never be forgotten, the Madres de la Plaza de Mayo still parade around the plaza in Buenos Aires with photographs of their lost children pinned to their chests.

Videla's nominated successor, Genereal Roberto Viola took over for three years in March 1981 but was overthrown by General Leopoldo Galtieri in December 1981, who failed to keep a grasp on a plummeting economy, and an increasingly discontent public. Attempting to win the crowds, Galtieri's decision to invade the Falkland/ Malvinas Islands in April 1982 backfired when the British retaliated by sending a fleet to the south Atlantic. After the war was lost in June 1982 Genereal Reynaldo Bignone took over, and promptly created a law giving amnesty to all human rights abusers in the military.

Elections in October 1983 were won by Raúl Alfonsín and his Unión Cívica Radical (UCR) and during 1985 Generals Videla, Viola and Galtieri were sentenced to long terms of imprisonment for their parts in the 'dirty war'. While Alfonsín's government struggled to deal with the legacy of the past, it was overwhelmed by continuing economic problems, the most obvious of which was hyperinflation. Workers rushed to the shops once they'd been paid to spend their earnings before prices rose, and supermarkets announced price increases over the tannoy since they were so unstable. When the Radicals were defeated by Carlos Menem, the Peronist (*Justicialist*) presidential candidate, Alfonsín stepped down early because of economic instability. Strained relations between the Peronist government and the military led to several rebellions, which Menem attempted to appease by pardoning the imprisoned generals. His popularity among civilians declined, but in 1991-92 the economy minister, Domingo Cavallo, succeeded in restoring confidence in the economy and the government as a whole with his *Plan de Convertabilidad*. This, the symbol of his stability, was the introduction of a new currency pegged to the United States dollar, and preventing the central bank from printing money which could not be backed up but the cash in reserve. After triumphing in the October 1993 congressional elections at the expense of the UCR, the Peronists themselves lost some ground in April 1994 elections to a constituent assembly. The party to gain most, especially in Buenos Aires, was Frente Grande, a broad coalition of left-wing groups and disaffected Peronists. Behind the loss of confidence of these dissident Peronists were unrestrained corruption and a pact in December 1993 between Menem and Alfonsín pledging UCR support for constitutional changes which included re-election of the president for a second term of four years.

By the 1995 elections, the majority of the electorate favoured stability over constitutional concerns and returned President Menem. The Peronists also increased their majority in the Chamber of Deputies and gained a majority in the Senate. Menem's renewed popularity was short-lived: joblessness remained high and corruption unrestrained. His decision to privatize the major industries scandalized traditional Peronists in his party, and his legacy remains a cause of despair, since electricity, gas, telephones and YPF, the country's oil industry, all belong to huge Spanish companies. In July 1996, the Radicals won the first direct elections for mayor of Buenos Aires and in mid-term congressional elections in October 1997 the Peronist Party lost its ruling majority. Most votes went to the Alianza Democrática, formed by the Radicals and the Frepaso coalition. The latter's candidate for Buenos Aires province, Graciela Fernández Meijide, defeated Hilda Duhalde of the Peronists, whose husband, Eduardo, was provincial governor. In addition to the Peronists' poor showing, several senior members were embarrassed by alleged involvement with millionaire Alfredo Yabrán. Many suspected Yabrán of criminal activities, not least of ordering the murder of journalist José Luis Cabezas (January 1997). The case fuelled the rivalry between Duhalde and Menem but in May 1998 Yabrán, who was being sought by the police, committed suicide.

In November 1998 Alianza Democrática chose the Radical Fernando de la Rua as its candidate for the October 1999 presidential election. Moves from Menem supporters to put forward Menem for a further (constitutionally dubious) term of office helped delay the Peronist choice of candidate until July 1999 when Eduardo Duhalde received the backing of Menem. Although Alianza Democrática offered little change in economic policy, the Peronists were harmed by the corruption scandals surrounding the Menem administration and the continuing rivalry between Menem and Duhalde, enabling De la Rua to win the presidency and take office in December 1999.

21st Century

Facing recession and impossible debts with the IMF, De la Rua implemented austerity measures, but these were not enough to save the peso, and many jobs which were lost in late 2000. Young people started to leave the country in massive numbers, looking for work elsewhere, many taking their savings with them. In an attempt to keep reserves of cash within the country, De la Rua started the *corralito* (literally meaning 'little pen'), a law determining that individuals could only withdraw 250 pesos from their accounts per week, and converting savings to government bonds. In December 2001, the people of Buenos Aires and other large cities took to the streets in an unprecedented display both of violent rioting and peaceful pot bashing by furious middle-class housewives, the *caserolazas*. The country went through five presidents in a period of a couple of months, but nothing could prevent devaluation, and in January 2002 the peso lost its parity with the dollar. Suddenly Argentina plummeted from being a first world nation on a par (or so the Argentines thought) with the United States, to being a third world state, with a weak currency, and little hope of bolstering the economy. The blow to the Argentine psyche has been severe. Duhalde was the last of the quick succession of presidents, and attempted to impose some order, appeasing the IMF by sacking a large number of public employees who were a considerable drain on public spending. However, corruption remained and street crime increased, with an alarming fashion for express kidnappings among the wealthier Buenos Aires families. Elections held in May 2003 threatened to return Menem to power, in a brief rush of nostalgia for the days of apparent prosperity. But fearing defeat, before a second election could be held Menem stepped down, and ex-governor of Santa Cruz province, Nestor Kirchner, came to power with a meagre 24% of the country's votes. During a short honeymoon period, in mid 2003, Kirchner held the country's support, or at least their hope that there is some way out of this economic disaster through his leadership.

Government and society

Federalism

The country's official name is La República Argentina (RA), the Argentine Republic. The form of government has traditionally been a representative, republican federal system. Of the two legislative houses, the Senate has 72 seats and the Chamber of Deputies 257. Under the 1853 Constitution (amended most recently in 1994) the country is divided into a Federal Capital (the city of Buenos Aires) and 23 Provinces. The Federal government is headed by the President, who is elected by universal suffrage for a four-year term and who may serve two consecutive terms. Each Province has its own Governor, Senate and Chamber of Deputies. The Constitution grants the

Federal Capital self government under a Mayor who is directly elected.

The location of power within this system is complex. Though the Federal government is usually seen as very powerful, this power partly depends on the President's own party having control over Congress. Moreover the Federal Capital and the provinces of Buenos Aires, Santa Fé and Córdoba, which between them contain 70% of the total population, can exercise a powerful counterweight, especially if they are controlled by the opposition.

Population

With an estimated 36,000,000 population, the third largest in South America after Brazil and Colombia, Argentina is one of the least densely populated countries in the continent. Thirty six per cent of the population lives in the urban area of Gran Buenos Aires, leaving most of Patagonia, for example, with 2 km sq per inhabitant. In the province of Buenos Aires, the people are mainly of European origin and the classic Argentine background is of Spanish and Italian immigrants. In Patagonia and the Lake District there's a considerable smattering of Scottish, Welsh, French, German and Swiss inhabitants, with Eastern Europeans to be found in the northeast of the country. In the northwestern provinces, at least half the people are indigenous, or of indigenous descent, mixed in Salta Province, for example, with a long line of *criollo* stock. Although *mestizos* form about 15% of the population of the whole country, the existence of different ethnic groups wasn't recognized until the mid 1990's. There are 13 indigenous groups, totaling about 500,000 people, 3% of the total population, many living in communities in the northwest, and scattered throughout the country. The largest minorities are the *Toba* (20%), the *Wichi* or *Mataco* (10%), the *Mapuche* (10%) and the *Guaraní* (10%). Several of the smaller groups are in danger of extinction: in 1987 the Minority Rights Group reported the death of the last *Ona* in Tierra del Fuego and noted that the 100 remaining *Tehuelches* were living on a reservation in southern Patagonia.

Immigration

The city of Buenos Aires and the surrounding province was transformed through immigration in the 19th century, to a society of predominantly European origin. White immigration was encouraged by the 1853 Constitution and the new political stability after 1862 encouraged a great wave of settlers from Europe. Between 1857 and 1930 total immigration was over 6,000,000, almost all from Europe. About 55% of these were Italians, followed by Spaniards (26%), and then, far behind, groups of other Europeans and Latin Americans. British and North Americans normally came as stockbreeders, technicians and business executives. By 1895, 25% of the population of 4,000,000 were immigrants. Over 1,300,000 Italians settled in Argentina between 1876 and 1914. Their influence can be seen in the country's food, its urban architecture and its language, especially in Buenos Aires where the local vocabulary has incorporated *Lunfardo,* a colourful slang of largely Italian origin, which started out as the language of thieves. Today it is estimated that 12.8% of the population are foreign born.

Culture

Arts and crafts

All over Argentina you'll find fine handicrafts made by local indigenous groups, which vary widely all over the country, or by the continuing tradition of gaucho craftsmen, who make fine pieces associated with rural life.

Gaucho crafts

There's a strong tradition of working precious metals, such as silver, into fine belts and buckles, since the gaucho's way of carrying his wealth with him was originally in the ornate silver *rastras* and buckles which are still used today over leather belts, or to tie *fajas* (woven cloth belts). Silver spurs, stirrups and the fine silver decoration on saddles are all extraordinary examples of traditions dating from the early 18th century. The gaucho *facón* an all purpose knife used especially for cutting his *asado*, is made with elaborately wrought silver handle, and the *mate* (the vessel itself, rather than the drink) which is often just a hollowed out gourd, can also be an exquisitely worked piece of silver which you'd probably rather display than use. Associated objects with the same fine silverwork today include earrings, belt buckles and scarf rings. Leather was always important for making all the items associated with horses, and obviously widely available, and the complexity of the traditional bridles, belts and straps is impressive. Long thin strips of leather are woven into wide plaits, or *trensas* and used still for all parts of horse bridlery, as well as more decorative pieces. The *mate* itself is made most traditionally from the gourd, but also from wood, tin or silver, with attractive examples made by artisans in the Lake District at El Bolsón, for example.

Indigenous crafts

Argentina's many indigenous groups produce fine handicrafts spanning all disciplines from woodwork to weaving, musical instruments to jewellery. In the northeast, the Guaraní produce fine woodwork, much of it inspired by the rich animal and bird life all around them. Delicate fabric for bags is woven from the tough fibrous strands of tree creepers, and there are necklaces made from seeds. Carved wooden animals are widely available, along with replicas for tourists of their traditional weapons, bows and arrows and pea shooters.

Handicrafts are richest in the northwest, particularly the Valles Calchaquíes, near the *puna* and along the Quebrada de Humahuaca, where there is abundant llama wool and vicuña, which is woven into *ponchos*, or knitted into jumpers, socks, scarves and hats. Brightly coloured woven textiles from Bolivia can also be found at many markets. The ubiquitous pan pipes are the most available examples of instruments from the rich Andean musical tradition, and can be found in abundance at Tilcara and Purmamarca markets. *Ponchos* are woven throughout the northwest but particularly fine examples can be found in the Calchaquíes valleys and around Salta, where the red *ponchos* of Güemes are made, and in western Catamarca province, where there are the finest ponchos of woven vicuña are made. You can also fine beautiful woven wall hangings in Los Valle Calchaquíes, often depicting scenes of churches in the valleys, and the local symbol, the ostrich-like *suri* and wood from the giant *cardón* cactus is used for carving distinctive small objects and furniture, with the spines of the cactus leaving attractive slits in the wood. For conservation reasons, only fallen trees are used.

In the Chaco region, bags are made from textile woven from *chaguar* fibre by Wichí, Toba, and other indigenous groups of the area, as they have done for hundreds of years. The Wichí also make fine wooden objects, animals mainly, from *palo santo*, a greenish scented wood, also used extensively in wood carving by communities who live along the Río Pilcomayo which forms the border with Paraguay. In northeastern Salta, painted wooden masks are made by the Chané culture to be used in traditional agricultural ceremonies. They also make charming ceramics in the shape of animals. Isolated indigenous groups of Toba, Chané and Mataco in the lowlands to the east of the province produce exquisite carvings of birds and animals, using a variety of local woods. Cowbones are used to make the beaks and feet, as well as an inlay to decorate spoons and other utilitarian items. And *Palo santo* is also used for *mate* vessels, replacing the traditional gourd. Throughout the south, there are superb Mapuche weavings in natural wool colours with bold geometric designs.

Argentina's cinema is one of its liveliest art forms and has enjoyed a recent renaissance with some brilliant films being made, more in the European or *auteur* tradition, than in Hollywood style, but with a couple of worldwide successes and Oscar nominations. Watching a couple of Argentine films is certainly one of the best ways of tapping into the country's culture before you arrive.

In 1922, Buenos Aires had some 27,000,000 film goers each year and 128 movie theatres, the largest, the Grand Splendid seating 1,350 people. By 1933 there were 1,608 cinemas throughout Argentina, with 199 in the capital. However, the taste of the cinema going public was for Hollywood movies. Hollywood has dominated the screens in Latin America for the first hundred years of film history, averaging some 90% of viewing time in Argentina.

However, in 1950's, New Argentine Cinema started as a movement of independent films which were a far more honest and accurate reflection of life in the country. Film clubs and journals created a climate of awareness of film as an art form and the tenets of Italian neo-realism and the '*politique des auteurs*' of *Cahiers du Cinema* provided alternatives to the studio-based Hollywood system. In Argentina, Leopoldo Torre Nilsson (1924-78) explored aristocratic decadence and his early film *La casa del ángel* (The House of the Angel, 1957) was greeted with praise all over the world. Fernando Birri (1925-) used neo-realist principles to explore the hidden realities of Argentina. His film school in Santa Fé made an important documentary about young shanty town children, *Tire dié* (Throw us a dime, 1957) and helped pioneer a more flexible, socially committed, cinema.

Younger film makers of the 60s like Manuel Antín (1926-), David Kohon (1929-) and Leonardo Favio (1938-) explored middle-class alienation or the sexual rites of passage of the young, set in the cafés and streets of Buenos Aires. Meanwhile, the growing climate of revolutionary sentiment of the late 1960s was reflected in Solanas's *La hora de los hornos* (The Hour of the Furnaces, 1966-68), a key work of populist radicalism.

After a brief spell of radical optimism in the late 1960s and early 1970s, reflected in a number of other nationalist-populist movies, the dream of the second coming of Perón turned into the nightmare that led to the brutal military takeover in March 1976. Strict censorship was imposed on cinema, with only the lightest comedies and thrillers escaping total ban or cuts. Film makers such as Solanas, who went into exile, found it difficult to adapt to the new conditions and remained in a cultural wilderness. Within Argentina, the tight military control began to slacken in the early 1980s and some important films were made, including María Luisa Bemberg's (1922-95) *Señora de nadie* (Nobody's Woman, 1982) which was premiered the day before the invasion of the Falklands/Malvinas.

With the return to civilian rule in 1983, the Radical government abolished censorship and put two well known film makers in charge of the National Film Institute, Manuel Antín and Ricardo Wullicher (1948-). Antín's granting of credits to young and established directors and his internationalist strategy had an immediate effect. For several years there was a great flowering of talent, a development that would only be halted temporarily by the economic difficulties of the late 1980s. The trade paper *Variety* (25 March 1987) commented on this new effervescence: 'Never before has there been such a mass of tangible approval as in the years since democratic rule returned at the end of 1983. In 1986, the Hollywood Academy granted the first Oscar for an Argentine picture, *The Official Version*, directed by Luis Puenzo (1946-), which dealt with the recent traumas of the disappearances of the 'Dirty War', but in rather sentimental Hollywood terms. This followed the massive box office success of Bemberg's *Camila*, which commented by analogy on the same subject. Solanas' two films about exile and the return to democracy, *Tangos, el exilio de* insights in Solanas' idiosyncratic poetic style. Puenzo, Bemberg and Solanas remained the most visible directors in the 1980s and 1990s, but dozens of other directors made movies in a range of different styles. Lita Stantic made perhaps the most complex film about the 'Dirty War' of the military regime, the superb *Un muro de silencio* (A Wall of Silence, 1993). This was a success with the critics, but was ignored by the public who preferred to view politics and repression through a gauze of melodrama and rock music, as in Marcelo Piñeyro's *Tango Feroz* (1993).

After 1989, the Menem government introduced credits and a percentage of box office and video sales to the film industry and Argentine cinema has undergone a revival in the last few years. The hard economic fact is that by far the vast majority of screens in the country show Hollywood product, and home-grown movies have to compete on these very commercial terms. However, the Oscar nomination of Argentine film *El Hijo de la Novia* in 2002 boosted national self confidence, and was a big success within Argentina. Its anti-hero Ricardo Darín also starred in Fabiano Belinski's sophisticated heist movie *Neuve Reinas* (Nine Queens) which through a labyrinth of tricks and scams neatly articulates a Buenos Aires where no one can trust anyone. It was a huge success worldwide as well as in the country, and is now being remade with George Clooney as the lead.

The 2001 London Film Festival celebrated the new Argentine cinema with a clutch of interesting art house movies alongside the accomplished *Nueve Reinas*. A return to cinema with a social conscience, Adrián Gaetano's *Bolivia* addresses the sorry plight of an illegal Bolivian worker in urban Argentina, and his *Un Oso Rojo* (2002) charts the fate of a newly released prisoner trying to reclaim the affection of his daughter from his wife's new boyfriend. Pablo Trapero's *Mundo Grua* is a stark but touching portrayal of the life of a crane driver, while Lisandro Alonso's astonishing *Libertad* shows with utter honesty the life of a peon on an estancia. In Luis Ortega's charming *Caja Negra* a young woman's relationship with her outcast father and eccentric ancient grandmother is explored with great humour and compassion. Two of the most striking films of recent years are *Pizza, Birra, Faso* by Stagnaro and Gaetano, and *No Quiero Volver a Casa* by Albertina Carri. Quite the best of the recent releases, though, is Lucrecia Martel's *La Cienaga,* a vivid portrayal of a divided family's unhappy summer in their country house. Highly allegorical and rich in atmospheric detail, it's a wonderful contemporary portrait of the country.

Most cinemas in the country show Hollywood movies, but the larger cities have an art house cinema, and if you happen to be around during any of the film festivals, you can usually catch a few recent Argentine releases: Mar del Plata Film Festival in mid March, Buenos Aires, film festival in mid April, and Salta's film festival in the first week of December.

Fine art and sculpture

Pre-columbian art

The earliest expressions of indigenous art in Argentina are cave paintings made by hunter-gatherers some 10,000 years ago, the most famous of which is La Cueva de las Manos, in Santa Cruz Province, where the negative images of thousands of hands can be seen, painted on the inside of a huge cave. At many sites all over the country in caves and under rocks, there are petroglyphs, or rock engravings, with geometrical or animal forms made by hunter-gatherers who lived here some 8,000 years ago. At Inca Cueva, near Humahuaca, archaeologists have been able to reconstruct a large pictorial sequence lasting some 10,000 years and stretching from the first geometric paintings to those which record the encounter of the indigenous with the Spanish *conquistadores,* images of strangely dressed armed horsemen which contrast with the simple representations of men with feathers in their hands, bows and arrows in their hands and leading llamas and alpacas. One of the most important collections of cave paintings in the country is Cerro Colorado in the north of the province of Córdoba. There are hundreds of sites with more than 30,000 motifs distributed on the walls and roofs. Among the great variety of figures are battle scenes between indigenous peoples, dressed in feathers and armed with bows and arrows, and Spaniards, represented by horsemen with lances, swords and boots. This is one of the few places in the country where the indigenous peoples' view of the *conquistadores* can be seen. These images, dating from the middle of the 16th century, were made by the ancestors of the Comechingones.

In northwestern Argentina the sedentary agricultural cultures have left numerous archaeological remains of artistic value: stone sculptures, ceramics, metal work, mainly in bronze and gold, and textiles, as well as masks, wood, feathers, and work with *chaquiras* (small pieces of shells) and glass beads.

During the first centuries AD the early planters in the western valleys of the provinces of Salta, Tucumán and Catamarca were experts in working granite. The most complex of these works were made by the Alamito culture and were objects known as 'supplicants', a reference to the position of the figures with their arms and faces looking up and imploring or pleading. These carvings, heavily polished, are schematic representations of humans with some zoomorphological traces. Their originality lies in the high level of abstraction, found both in the lines and the spaces which make them resemble modern sculptures. Very few of these survive. Many can be seen in the Museo de Ciencias Naturales in La Plata as well as in the Museo Adán Quiroga in Catamarca and the Museo Arqueológico Ambato in La Falda. Other important examples of early works in stone include: masks in the form of the human faces, probably used as funeral offerings; and mortars or ceremonial vessels decorated with human and feline motifs, which were used to prepare hallucinogenic substances.

The most common expression of indigenous art in the northwest is, without doubt, ceramic work, which is found in numerous forms, techniques and styles throughout the 2,000 years of cultural development from the origins of the agricultural societies (550BC) right up to the Spanish conquest. In the early or formative period we can find numerous styles, outstanding among which are by La Candelaria and Condorhuasi cultures, both of which produced vessels representing hybrids of humans and animals. Those of La Candelaria are in the form of globes, grey or black in colour, while those of Condorhuasi are red with a complex geometric decoration painted in black and white. Funerary urns are the most strikingly designed creative objects, large ceramic pots, swollen-bellied, with lids, for the burying of bones – often those of children. These were made by the Santa María culture, and it's thought that their bold gestural painting, in black and red, may have been designed for public display as the urns were disinterred and paraded around the community each year. Many of them have human limbs and eyes in relief, made of clay as well as paint, and their designs are sophisticated and impressive. The metal work of this period is also outstanding: discs, axes, bells and other pieces finely decorated with human faces outlined with very simple lines, people with shields and serpents with two heads, all decorated in red.

Southwest, in the province of Neuquén, is the territory of the Mapuche, who crossed the Andes from Chile during the 18th century. Experts in various arts, they are noted particularly for their textiles with its complex and coloured geometric motifs, for their silver-work including breastplates, earrings and brooches worn by women during fiestas and ceremonies, and for the wooden carvings which generally imitate the severe faces which can be found on the *rehues* (trunks which form part of the altars used in shamanic rituals). Contemporary expressions of these artistic traditions can be found in good handicraft shops both in the region and in Buenos Aires.

Colonial art

Argentina (along with neighbouring Uruguay) is arguably the most European of Latin American cultures. Mass immigration and the 19th-century extermination of the few remaining indigenous peoples have created a mainstream culture which defines itself largely in relation to Europe. The exception to this is in the northwest of the country, where the great Andean civilizations struggle to retain their identity against the irresistible tide of westernization and the tourist industry.

As the region, which is now Argentina, was initially of little importance to the Spanish, there is relatively little colonial art or architecture in most of the country. However, in the northern regions of Salta, Jujuy and Misiones, there are some impressive colonial buildings and some good examples of colonial painting, especially the remarkable portraits of archangels in military uniform in the churches at Uquía and Casabindo, as well as some exquisite golden retables and pulpits in the churches of the Quebrada de Humahuaca. Yavi, at the very north, is the most remarkable of all these, with a golden sculpture of an angel in military uniform, and beautiful ceramic cherubs on the golden pulpit. Fine colonial art can be seen at the Museo de Arte Hispanoamericano Isaac Fernández Blanco in Buenos Aires. In Misiones, there are several sites with remains of Jesuits missions, particularly impressive is that at San Ignacio. Córdoba Province too has remains of Jesuit churches and residences at Santa Catalina and Jesús María.

The 19th century

In the 19th century, as Argentina gained Independence and consolidated itself as a modern nation, the ruling elite of the country were determined to make Argentine culture as close to Europe as possible, against what they saw as the 'barbarism' of native customs. The prosperous Buenos Aires bourgeoisie commissioned European architects to build their mansions and collected European fine and decorative arts to decorate them. Rich Argentines travelled to Europe to buy paintings, and gradually began to demand that European painters come to Argentina to depict the wealth and elegance of the ruling class through portraits and landscapes. The most famous foreign artist was Carlos Enrique Pellegrini, whose fine society portraits can be seen in the Museo Nacional de Bellas Artes in Buenos Aires.

By the middle of the century, as Argentina became more politically stable, a new generation of Argentine-trained artists appeared in Buenos Aires. They absorbed some of the techniques and interests of the European artists who were the first to depict their country, but they also discovered a new interest in Romanticism and Realism. Most famous in this period was Prilidiano Pueyrredón (1823-70), whom many Argentines consider to be their first national painter. Of more obvious appeal is the rather eccentric Cándido López (1839-1902) whose work has only recently been re-evaluated. López followed the Argentine army to the north of the country during the wars with Paraguay and Uruguay, where he depicted the great battles in a characteristic naïve style. López left behind a remarkable series of paintings, which are often displayed in their own room in the Museo Nacional de Bellas Artes in Buenos Aires. By the end of the century, many artists were working in Argentina, many of whom had been through the National Art School. Generally speaking, they absorbed European movements several decades after they appeared in their original forms. Benito Quinquela Martin's work celebrated the workers in the dockyards of La Boca, in a colourful naïve style, and his paintings can be seen in the gallery bearing his name in La Boca.

The 20th century

In the 20th century, Argentina really found its artistic expression; the dynamism, size and mix of nationalities in the capital created a complex urban society in which artists and intellectuals have prospered. Some of the bohemian attraction of Buenos Aires can still be felt in its more intellectual cafés and districts. This cultural effervescence has been at the expense of the regions; the capital totally dominates the country, and most artists are forced to move there to have any chance of success.

The first avant-garde artistic movement in Buenos Aires emerged in 1924 with the formation of a groups which called itself 'Martn Fierro', in homage to the national epic poem of the same name. This group brought together a small number of upper-class intellectuals, the most famous of which was the writer Jorge Luis Borges. The most important visual artist was Xul Solar (1887-1963), who illustrated many of Borges's texts. Solar was one of the 20th century's most eccentric and engaging artists. He had a great interest in mysticism and the occult, and tried to create an artistic system to express his complex beliefs, mostly small-scale watercolours in which a sometimes bizarre visionary world is depicted. Many of them are covered in inscriptions in one of the languages he created: Neo-Creole or Pan-Lengua. During the final decades of his life Solar lived in a house on the Paraná Delta near Tigre, where he created a total environment in accordance with his fantastic world, even inventing a new game of chess with rules based on astrology. There is now a Xul Solar Museum in the house where he was born in Buenos Aires and where many of his watercolours and objects are displayed.

Intellectual life in the 1920s was divided into two factions, each named after districts in the city. The elegant Calle Florida gave its name to the Martín Fierro set, who belonged to the elite. Several blocks away, the working-class Boedo district gave its name to a school of working-class socialist artists who rejected the rarefied atmosphere of Florida in favour of socially critical paintings in a grim realistic style. Possibly the most important artist associated with this group was Antonio Berni (1905-81), whose colourful paintings give a vivid impression of Buenos Aires working-class life, and are worth looking for in the Museo de Bellas Artes and MALBA in Buenos Aires.

In the 1940s, with the political crisis provoked by the Second World War, a new avant-garde movement emerged to overtake the Martin Fierro group. In the mid 1940s, a group of young artists founded an abstract art movement called 'Madí' (a nonsense word) which attempted to combine sophisticated abstract art inspired by Russian Constructivism with a more chaotic sense of fun. Madí works are characterized by blocks of bright colours within an irregular frame often incorporating physical movement within the structure of the work. As such, they are somewhere between painting and sculpture. For the first time in Argentina, Madí developed artistic principles (such as the irregular frame, or the use of neon gas) before the rest of the world.

Madí was a short-lived adventure plagued by infighting amongst its members and political divisions. The cultural climate under Perón (1946-55) rejected this type of 'decadent' art in favour of a form of watered-down populism. It was not until the 1960s that cultural life regained its momentum.

The 1960s were a golden age for the arts in Argentina. As in many countries, the decade brought new freedoms and questions to young people, and the art scene responded vigorously. Artistic activity was focused around the centre of Buenos Aires between Plaza San Martin and Avenida Cordoba, an area known as the *'manzana loca'* (crazy block). This area contained a huge number of galleries and cafés, and most importantly the Di Tella Institute, a privately-funded art centre which was at the cutting edge of the visual arts. Artistic movements of the time ranged from a raw expressionism called *'Nueva figuración'* to very sophisticated conceptual art. The most provocative form of art during this period took the form of 'happenings', one of the most famous of which (by Marta Minujin) consisted of a replica of the Buenos Aires obelisk made in sweet bread, which was then eaten by passers-by.

After the military coup of 1966 the authorities began to question the activities of these young artists and even tried to censor some exhibitions. The Di Tella Institute closed, leaving the *'manzana loca'* without a heart, and making it more dangerous for alternative young artists to live without harassment (often for little more than having long hair). During the 'leaden years' of the military government during the 1970s, there was little space for alternative art and many left-wing artists abandoned art in favour of direct political action. However, one space in Buenos Aires continued to show politically challenging art: the Centro de Arte y Comunicación (or CAYC), often through works which were so heavily coded that the authorities would not pick up the message.

Since the restoration of democracy in 1983, Argentina has been coming to terms with the destruction or inefficiency of many of its cultural institutions over recent decades. The last few years have seen a rebirth of activity, with improvements in the National Museum of Fine Arts and the creation of the important Centro Cultural Recoleta and more recently the Centro Cultural Jorge Luis Borges (in the Galerías Pacífico). There are important alternative art centres, especially the Ricardo Rojas Centre and the Klemm Foundation which show some of the most interesting young artists. The art scene in Buenos Aires is now very vibrant, if somewhat confusing, with myriad conflicting and apparently contradictory styles and tendencies.

Literature

Modern Argentina has an extremely high literary rate, around 95%, and good bookshops are to be found even in small country towns, with some really splendid *librerías* in Buenos Aires. Correspondingly, the country has produced some great writers, quite apart from the wonderful Borges, and it's well worth reading some of their work before you come, or seeking out a few novels to bring on your travels.

With an urban culture derived almost entirely from European immigrants, Argentina's literary development was heavily influenced by European writers in the 19th century, the works of Smith, Locke, Voltaire and Rousseau amongst others, being inspiration for the small literate elite of young intellectuals such as Mariano Moreno (1778-1811), one of the architects of the Independence movement. The great theme was how to adapt European forms to American realities, first in the form of political tracts and later in early nationalist poetry. Outside the cities, popular culture thrived on storytelling and the music of the gauchos, whose famous *payadores* are superbly evocative. They recount lively and dramatic stories of love, death and the land in poetic couplets to a musical background, with an ornate and inventive use of words (see Music below). Gaucho poets, like Medieval *troubadours*, would travel from settlement to settlement, to country fairs and cattle round-ups, singing of the events of the day and of the encroaching political constraints that would soon bring restrictions to their traditional way of life.

The theme of Argentine identity has been a constant through the country's development and remains a burning issue today. While many writers looked to Europe for inspiration, others were keen to distance themselves from the lands they had come from and create a new literature, reflecting Argentina's own concerns. The extremes within the country further challenge attempts at creating a single unified identity: the vast stretches of inhospitable and uninhabited land, the vast variety of landscapes and peoples, and the huge concentration of population in a capital which little resembles any other part of the country. These conflicts were clearly expressed in 1845 by politician Domingo Faustino Sarmiento (1811-88): *Facundo: Civilization and Barbarism*. This was the most important tract of the generation, and became one of the key texts of Argentine cultural history. Strongly opposed to the Federalist Rosas, Sarmiento's allegory biography of guacho *Facundo* laments the ungovernably large size of the country which allows *caudillos* like Quiroga and Rosas to dominate. For Sarmiento, the only solution was education and he looked to what he perceived to be the democracy of North America for inspiration.

With the attempt to consolidate the nation state in the aftermath of independence Esteban Echeverría (1805-51) played a leading role in these debates through literary salons, in poetry and in short fiction. Other memorable protest literature against the Rosas regime included Echeverría's *El Matadero* (The Slaughterhouse, published posthumously in 1871) and José Mármol's melodramatic novel of star crossed lovers battling against the cut-throat hordes of Rosas *Amalia* (1855).

The consolidation of Argentina along the lines advocated by Sarmiento and the growth of the export economy in alliance with British capital and technology may have benefited the great landowners of the Littoral provinces. But those who did not fit into this dream of modernity – in particular the gaucho groups turned off the land and forced to work as rural labourers – found their protest articulated by a provincial landowner, José Hernández (1834-86). He wrote the famous gaucho epic poems *El Gaucho Martín Fierro* (1872) and its sequel, *La vuelta de Martín Fierro* (The Return of Martín Fierro, 1879). The first part of *Martín Fierro* is most definitely the most famous Argentine literary work and is a genuine shout of rage against the despotic *caudillos* and corrupt authorities, which disrupt local communities and traditional ways of life. Framed as a gauchesque song, chanted by the appealing hero and dispossessed outlaw, it became one of the most popular works of literature, and *Martín Fierro* came to symbolize the spirit of the Argentine nation.

As a small group of families led the great export boom, the 'gentleman' politicians of the 'Generation of 1880' wrote their memoirs, none better than Sarmiento's *Recuerdos de Provincia* (Memoirs of Provincial Life, 1850.). As Buenos Aires grew into a dynamic modern city, the gentleman memorialist soon gave way to the professional writer. The key poet in this respect was the Nicaraguan Rubén Darío (1867-1916), who lived for an important period of his creative life in Buenos Aires and led a movement called *modernismo* which asserted the separateness of poetry as a craft, removed from the dictates of national panegyric or political necessity. It was Darío who would give inspiration to the poet Leopoldo Lugones (1874-1938), famous also for his prose writings on nationalist, gauchesque themes. Lugones's evocation of the gaucho as a national symbol would be developed in the novel *Don Segundo Sombra* by Ricardo Güiraldes (1886-1927), the story of a boy taught the skills for life by a gaucho mentor.

The early 20th century

The complex urban societies evolving in Argentina by the turn of the century created a rich cultural life. In the 1920s a strong vanguard movement developed which questioned the dominant literary orthodoxies of the day. Little magazines such as *Martín Fierro* (another appropriation of the ubiquitous national symbol) proclaimed novelty in poetry and attacked the dull social realist writings of their rivals the Boedo group. Argentina's most famous writer, Jorge Luis Borges (1899-1986) began his literary life as an avant-garde poet, in the company of writers such as Oliverio Girondo (1891-1967) and Norah Lange (1906-72). Many of these poets were interested in expressing the dynamism and changing shape of their urban landscape, Buenos Aires, this Paris on the periphery. You can explore Borges' haunts in Buenos Aires with a free tour organized by the tourist office: ask in their information centres for dates and times. Roberto Arlt also caught the dreams and nightmares of the urban underclasses in novels such as *El juguete rabioso* (The Rabid Toy, 1926) and *Los siete locos* (The Seven Madmen, 1929).

Much of the most interesting literature of the 1930 and 1940s was first published in the literary journal *Sur*, founded by the aristocratic writer, Victoria Ocampo. By far the most important group to publish in its pages were Borges and his close friends Silvina Ocampo (1903-93), Victoria's sister, and Silvina's husband, Adolfo Bioy Casares (1914) who, from the late 1930s, in a series of short fictions and essays, transformed the literary world. They had recurrent concerns: an indirect style, a rejection of realism and

nationalist symbols, the use of the purified motifs and techniques of detective fiction
and fantastic literature, the quest for knowledge to be found in elusive books, the
acknowledgement of literary criticism as the purest form of detective fiction and the
emphasis on the importance of the reader rather than the writer.

Peronism and Literature
In the 10-year period of Perón's first two presidencies, 1946-55, there was a deliberate
assault on the aristocratic, liberal values which had guided Argentina since 1880.
Claiming to be a new synthesis of democracy, nationalism, anti-imperialism and
industrial development, Peronism attacked the undemocratic, dependent Argentine
elite (personified in such literary figures as Victoria Ocampo or Adolfo Bioy Casares).
This period was seen by most intellectuals and writers as an era of cultural darkness
and some writers such as Julio Cortázar (1914-84) – in the 1940s and 1950s a writer of
elegant fantastic and realist stories – chose voluntary exile rather than remain in
Perón's Argentina. The much-loved novelist, Ernesto Sábato (1911) who later
confronted the *Proceso,* set his best novel *Sobre héroes y tumbas* (On Heroes and
Tombs, 1961) partly in the final moments of the Peronist regime, when the tensions of
the populist alliance were beginning to become manifest. (His novella *El Tunel* (The
Tunnel) is also well worth reading). But Perón was not much interested in the small
circulation of literature and concentrated his attention on mass forms of
communication such as radio and cinema. This period saw further mature work from
the poets Enrique Molina (1910-), Olga Orozco (1922-) and Alberto Girri (1919-91),
whose austere, introspective verse was an antidote to the populist abuse of language
in the public sphere. The literary field was to be further stimulated, after the downfall
of Perón with the development of publishing houses and the 'boom' of Latin
American literature of the 1960s.

The 1960s
In Argentina the 1960s was a decade of great literary and cultural effervescence. The
novel to capture this mood was Cortázar's *Rayuela* (Hopscotch, 1963), which served as
a Baedeker of the new, with its comments on literature, philosophy, new sexual
freedoms and its open, experimental structure. It was promoted in a weekly journal
Primera Plana, which also acted as a guide to expansive modernity. Thousands of
copies of *Rayuela* were sold to an expanded middle-class readership in Argentina and
throughout Latin America. Other novelists and writers benefited from these conditions,
the most significant being the Colombian Gabriel García Márquez who published what
would later become one of the best-selling novels of the 20th century, *Cien años de
soledad* (One Hundred Years of Solitude, 1967) with an Argentine publishing house.
Significant numbers of women writers helped to break the male monopoly of literary
production including the novelists Beatriz Guido and Marta Lynch and the poet
Alejandra Pizarnik (1936-72), with her intense exploration of the inner self.

Literature and dictatorship
The 'swinging' sixties were curtailed by a military coup in 1966. In the years which
followed, Argentine political life descended into anarchy, violence and repression, as a
result virtually all forms of cultural activity were silenced and well known writers, including
Haroldo Conti and Rodolfo Walsh, 'disappeared'. Many more had to seek exile including
the poet Juan Gelman, whose son and daughter-in-law counted among the disappeared.
    Understandably this nightmare world provided the dominant themes of the
literary output of these years. The return in old age of Perón, claimed by all shades of
the political spectrum, was savagely lampooned in Osvaldo Soriano's (1943-98)
novel *No habrá más penas ni olvido* (A Funny, Dirty Little War, published 1982, but
completed in 1975). The world of the sombre designs of the ultra right-wing López
Rega, Isabel Perón's Minister of Social Welfare, is portrayed in Luisa Valenzuela's

(1938-) terrifying, grotesque novel *Cola de lagartija* (The Lizard's Tail, 1983). Of the narrative accounts of those black years, none is more harrowing than Miguel Bonasso's (1940-) fictional documentary of the treatment of the Montoneros guerrilla group in prison and in exile: *Recuerdo de la muerte* (Memory of Death, 1984). Other writers in exile chose more indirect ways of dealing with the terror and dislocation of those years. Daniel Moyano (1928-92), in exile for many years in Spain, wrote elegant allegories such as *El vuelo del tigre* (The Flight of the Tiger, 1981), which tells of the military style takeover of an Andean village by a group of percussionists who bring cacophany.

Within Argentina, critical discussion was kept alive in literary journals such as *Punto de Vista* (1978-) and certain novels alluded to the current political climate within densely structured narratives. Ricardo Piglia's (1941-) *Respiración artificial* (Artificial Respiration, 1980) has disappearance and exile as central themes, alongside bravura discussions of the links between fiction and history and between Argentina and Europe.

The Return to Civilian Rule

Following Alfonsín's election victory in 1983, the whole intellectual and cultural field responded to the new freedoms. Certain narratives depicted in harsh realism the brutalities of the 'Dirty War' waged by the military and it was the novelist, Ernesto Sábato, who headed the Commission set up to investigate the disappearances. He wrote in the prologue to the Commission's report *Nunca más* (Never Again, 1984): "We are convinced that the recent military dictatorship brought about the greatest and most savage tragedy in the history of Argentina".

Current literature echoes the famous lines by Borges in the essay *The Argentine Writer and Tradition*: "I believe that we Argentines ... can handle all European themes, handle them without superstition, with an irreverence which can have, and already does have, fortunate consequences." While many of the writers that first brought modernity to Argentine letters have died – Borges, Victoria and Silvina Ocampo, Girri, Cortázar, Puig – the later generations have assimilated their lessons. Juan Carlos Martini writes stylish thrillers, blending high and low culture. Juan José Saer (1937-), from his self imposed exile in Paris, recreates his fictional world, Colastiné, in the city of Santa Fé, in narratives that are complex, poetic discussions on memory and language. The most successful novel of recent years is Tomás Eloy Martinez's (1934-) *Santa Evita* (1995) which tells/reinvents the macabre story of what happened to Evita's embalmed body between 1952 and the mid 1970s. The narrative skilfully discusses themes that are at the heart of all writing and critical activity. The critic, like the embalmer of Evita's body, "seeks to fix a life or a body in the pose that eternity should remember it by". But what this critic, like the narrator of Eloy Martínez's novel, realizes is that a corpus of literature cannot be fixed in that way, for literature escapes such neat pigeon holes. Instead, glossing Oscar Wilde, the narrator states that "that the only duty that we have to history is to rewrite it". The ending of the novel makes the point about the impossibility of endings: "Since then, I have rowed with words, carrying Santa Evita in my boat, from one shore of the blind world to the other. I don't know where in the story I am. In the middle, I believe. I've been here in the middle for a long time. Now I must write again". (*Santa Evita*, New York and London, 1996, page 369.) See Books, page 572, for recommended reading.

Music

Tango is the country's most prominent and most exported musical form, but by no means its only means of musical expression. The traditional music which binds almost the whole country is folclore (pronounced *folc-LAW-ray*) whose stirring rhythms and passionate singing can be found in varying forms throughout the northern half of the country. Superb music is produced in the north, in the Andean region of Salta and Jujuy. And home-grown Rock Nacional is the country's main strand of pop music, successfully fending off North American and European competition throughout the 1980's and 1990's to form a distinctive sound.

Tango

If your trip to Argentina includes any time in Buenos Aires, you'll undoubtedly see some tango – probably danced on the streets of Florida or San Telmo, though its much more than a tourist attraction. Testimony to the enduring success of the music among Argentines are the radio stations which only play tango, and the *milongas* (dance clubs) filled with young people learning the old steps.

Although also sung and played, the tango was born as a dance just before the turn of the 20th century. The exact moment of birth was not recorded by any contemporary observer and continues to be a matter of debate, though the roots can be traced. The name 'Tango' predates the dance and was given to the carnivals (and dances) of the black inhabitants of the Río de la Plata in the early 19th century, elements of the black tradition being taken over by whites as the black population declined. However, the name 'Tango Americano' was also given to the Habanera (a Cuban descendent of the English Country Dance) which became the rage in Spain and bounced back into the Río de la Plata in the middle of the 19th century, not only as a fashionable dance together with the polka, mazurka, waltz and cuadrille but also as a song form in the very popular '*Zarzuelas*', or Spanish operettas. However, the Habanera led not a double, but a triple life, by also infiltrating the lowest levels of society directly from Cuba via sailors who arrived in the ports of Montevideo and Buenos Aires. Here it encountered the Milonga, originally a gaucho song style, but by 1880 a dance, especially popular with the so-called '*Compadritos*' and '*Orilleros*', who frequented the port area and its brothels, whence the Argentine Tango emerged around the turn of the century to dazzle the populace with its brilliant, personalized footwork, which could not be accomplished without the partners staying glued together.

As a dance tango became the rage and, as the infant recording industry grew by leaps and bounds, it also became popular as a song and an instrumental genre, with the original violins and flutes being eclipsed by the *bandoneón* button accordion, then being imported from Germany. In 1911 the new dance took Paris by storm, thanks to the performance of the dance in a Paris salon by Argentine writer Ricardo Güiraldes, one of a group of aristocrats who enjoyed frequenting the dives where tango was popular. As soon as it was the fashion in Paris, it returned triumphant to Buenos Aires, achieving both respectability and notoriety, and becoming a global phenomenon after the First World War, with the golden voice of Carlos Gardel. Rudolph Valentino helped the image of the dance, when his 1926 movie *The Four Horsemen of the Apocalypse* included a tango scene, and suddenly everyone was doing it, in Paris and London, dressed up like gauchos.

But it was Carlos Gardel (1887-1935), Argentina's most loved tango legend, whose mellifluous voice brought popularity to the music of tango, and whose poor background made him a hero for the working classes too. Tango has always been an expression of the poor and of social and political developments in the country. Gardel recorded 900 songs and was a success in movies too. *The Tango on Broadway* was his big success in 1934. After Gardel's tragic death in 1935, tango slumped a little, frowned upon by the military regime who considered it subversive. Its resurgence in the 1940's was assisted by Perón's decree that 50% of all music played on the radio must be Argentine. Great stars of this era include the brilliant *bandoneón* player Aníbal Troilo, whose passionate and tender playing made him much loved among a wide audience. In the 1950s, tango again declined, replaced in popularity by rock'n'roll. It had become increasingly the preserve of middle class and intellectual circles, with the emphasis on nostalgia in its themes. But its next innovator and star was Astor Piazzolla (1921-), who had played in Troilo's orchestra, and who went on to fuse tango with jazz and create a tango for listening to, as well as dancing. Threatened by the military government in the 1970s Piazzollla escaped to Paris, but his success was already international, and his experimental arrangements opened up the possibilities for other fusions. In the last few years, tango has enjoyed a revival, becoming a popular dance in classes throughout Europe as well as in Argentina. All over Buenos Aires, and all over the province, you can find dance classes where the classic moves are taught, followed by a dance or *milonga* where couples, young and old, breathe life into the old steps. Part of its attraction, perhaps, is that in the world of tango, men are allowed to be macho and seductive, while their women are required to be sensitive to the subtlety of their next move. Unlike salsa, for example, tango is a dance of repressed passion. Try a class, at least once, while you're in Argentina, to get a feel for the dance from the inside. And then, if you can afford it, see the expert dancers' dextrous footwork at a show such as *El Viejo Almácen*.

Folklore

Beyond Buenos Aires, the dominant musical traditions can be broadly described as folklore. This takes various forms over the north of the country, with the finest examples in Salta, but all the northern provinces have a very rich and attractive heritage of folk dances, mainly for couples, with arms held out and fingers clicked or handkerchiefs waved, with the '*Paso Valseado*' as the basic step. The slow and stately Zamba is descended from the Zamacueca, and therefore a cousin of the Chilean Cueca and Peruvian Marinera, where the handkerchief is used to greatest effect. Equally popular throughout most of the country are the faster Gato, Chacarera and Escondido. These were the dances of the gaucho and their rhythm evokes that of a cantering horse with wonderfully stirring syncopation. Guitar and the *bombo* drum provide the accompaniment. Particularly spectacular is the Malambo, where the gaucho shows off his dextrous footwork, creating a complex rhythm using the heels of his boots, alternating with percussion created by whirling the hard balls of the *boleadoras* into the ground, with the spurs of his boots adding a steely note to the rhythm.

Different regions of the country have their own specialities. The music of Cuyo in the west is sentimental and very similar to that of neighbouring Chile, with its Cuecas for dance and Tonadas for song. The northwest on the other hand is Andean, with its musical culture closer to that of Bolivia, particularly on the *Puna*, where the indigenous groups play haunting wind instruments, the *quena* and sound mournful notes on the great long *erke* evocative of huge mountain landscapes. Here the dances are Bailecitos and Carnavalitos, depending on the time of year. Exquisitely beautiful and mournful songs – the extraordinary high pitched *Bagualas* – are sung to the banging of a simple drum. And everyone, from children to grandmothers, can quote you a *copla*: two lines of rhymed verse expressing love or a witty joke. Tomás Lipan's music is worth seeking out, especially his *cautivo de Amor*. Andean bands use the *sikus*, pan pipes and miniature guitar, the *charango*, to create ethereal and festive music which reflects the seasons of the rural calendar. In the northeast provinces of Corrientes and Misiones, the music shares cultural similarities with Paraguay. The *Polca* and *Galopa* are danced and the local *Chamamé* is sung, to the accordion or the harp, in sentimental style. Santiago del Estero has exerted the strongest influence on Argentine folk music as a result of the work of Andres Chazarreta: it is the heartland of the Chacarera and the lyrics are often part Spanish and part Quichua, a local dialect of the Andean Quechua language. Listen, too, to Los Caravajal, and Los Hermanos Abalos. Down in the province of Buenos Aires you are more likely to hear the Gauchos singing their Milongas, Estilos and Cifras and challenging each other to a Payada or rhymed accompaniment. Seek out Atahualpa Yupangui's *El Payador Persguido*. Argentina experienced a great folklore revival in the 1950s and 1960s and some of the most celebrated groups are still drawing enthusiastic audiences today. These groups include Los Chalchaleros and Los Fronterizos, the perennial virtuoso singer and guitarist, Eduardo Falú and, more recently, León Gieco from Santa Fe. Most famous of all, though, is the superb Mercedes Sosa, whose rich voice articulated much of the sorrow and joy of the last 30 years in a brilliant series of albums which also include the most popular folklore songs. Start with *The Best of Mercedes Sosa*. Also listen to Ariel Ramirez, a famous singer and pianist whose moving *Misa Criolla* is among his best known work. The cuartetos of Córdoba, popular since the 1940s with the characteristic dance in a huge circle, can best be sampled in the much loved records of Carlitos 'La Mona' Jiminez.

Rock Nacional

The great stars of Rock Nacional are still much loved and listened to. It started in the 1960s with successful bands *Los Gatos*, and *Almendra*, whose songwriter Luis Alberto Spinetta later became a successful solo artist. But the Rock Nacional found its real strength in expressing unspeakable protests during the military dictatorship from 1976-83. Charly García, who was a member of the enormously successful band *Sui Generis*, captured popular feeling with his song *No te dejes desanimar* (Don't be discouraged) which roused mass opposition amongst young people against the atrocities of the *Proceso*. Inevitably, the military regime cottoned on to this form of subversive behaviour and stopped rock concerts, so that many bands had given up performing by the end of the 1970s. However, the rock movement survived, and the cynical lyrics of Fito Páez in *Tiempos Dificiles* and Charly García in *Dinosaurios* remain as testimonies to that time, and guaranteed them subsequent success. Once democracy had returned, music became more lightweight with likeable output from Los Abuelos de la Nada and Patricio Rey y sus Redonditos de Ricota. Fito Páez has continued to record and his album *El Amor Después del Amor* was a success across Latin America. Los Fabulosis Cadillacs and Andrés Calamaro also made some great records, and Charly García continues, undiminished in popularity.

Sport

It is said that sport came to Argentina through the port of Buenos Aires, brought first by British sailors, who played football on vacant lots near the port watched by curious locals who would later make it their national passion.

Football is out on its own, both in terms of participation and as a spectator sport, with the country being passionately divided between fans of Boca Juniors and River Plate. In second place come two sports which attract far more fans than players: boxing and motor-racing. Although there are now few Argentine boxing champions and world title fights are rarely held here, there is a big TV audience for most title fights abroad. Despite the lack of local world-class drivers, the legend of Juan Manuel Fangio is still very much alive and the Argentine Formula One Grand Prix each April is one of the main events of the year in Buenos Aires, even if there are no Argentine drivers. Tennis is played mostly among the upper-middle classes but the world tournaments attract many TV fans, since Argentines Sabatini and Nalbandian have soared to fame. Basketball and volleyball are both popular participation sports among young people, with strong teams in many sizeable towns, and basketball attracts big TV audiences since Argentine players play for teams in the States.

Though the best polo in the world is played in Argentina, it's only accessible to an elite class, due to its cost. Though it is played throughout the country and all year

The feet of God

Ask anyone with an ounce of sense who was the greatest football player of all time and the answer will be Diego Maradona. Brazilians may disagree and claim Pele earns the title, while the English, perhaps understandably, cannot bring themselves to admit to his genius, but we all know the truth. Diego Armando Maradona was born on 30 October, 1960, in Villa Fiorito, a poor working-class suburb of Buenos Aires. He first burst onto the international scene during the 1982 World Cup where his precocious talents were met with the kind of moves usually only seen inside a Thai kick boxing ring. Not surprisingly, the little Argentine took exception to such treatment and his World Cup ended with a red card against arch-enemies, Brazil. Following a two-year spell at Catalonian über-club, Barcelona, Maradona joined unfashionable Italian side, Naples, whom he led to two Serie A championships and a UEFA Cup title. It was during his seven years at Naples that Maradona had his greatest triumph, leading Argentina to World Cup glory in 1986. On the way to a forgettable final against Germany, Maradona scored one of the all-time great goals when he waltzed past the entire English defence (and midfield) as if they were showroom dummies,

before poking the ball into a grateful net. It was outrageous and it was brilliant, and followed his first goal, an unashamedly brazen punch that fooled no one except the referee. When questioned by the press afterwards, an ebullient Maradona put it down to the 'Hand of God', implying with typical defiance that this was a form of retribution against England for the humiliation of the Falklands War.

In Italia 1990, Maradona managed to guide a fairly average Argentine team to the final, where they lost to Germany, but it would all be downhill from here on in. He fled Italy following a failed dope test in 1991, spent a brief but miserable few months at Seville, before dragging his ravaged body to the USA World Cup finals in 1994 where he faced another doping scandal. It was the end of the road.

Maradona was a flawed genius. He reached for the stars, nutmegged the moon and on the way snorted an entire Milky Way of cocaine. He had the world at his feet and then let money and fame go to his head. In Naples he is still reverred as a god, and in Argentina, the country which produces world-class footballers like others produce rice or potatoes, he will always be 'el pibe de oro' – the Golden Boy.

round, the top Argentine players, who now play all over the world, return only for the high handicap season between September and November. This consists of three main tournaments, played on the outskirts of Buenos Aires, followed by the Argentine Open, which takes place in Palermo's Hurlingham Club, the 'cathedral of polo'.

Golf can be played all year round in the northern half of the country, though it's a purely upper middle class game in Argentina, and half the courses are in Gran Buenos Aires, with famous courses at Mar del Plata and Llao Llao in Bariloche. Argentina's rugby team, the Pumas, remain strong, though the sport is played little outside the expensive private schools.

Argentina's native sports include the squash-like **paleta pilota**, and *pato* (duck), a cross between polo and basketball. Originally played between large bands of gauchos on horseback using a duck in a basket as a ball, it was at one point

prohibited for being dangerous. Today, with proper rules, teams of four horsemen 565
and a football with handles instead of a duck in a basket, it is one sport which is
unique to Argentina.

Religion

Throughout Spanish America the Catholic Church played an important role in the
conquest. From the start of the colonial period Spanish control in South America
was authorized by the Papacy; in return the colonial powers were to support the
conversion of the indigenous population to Catholicism. This close identification of
Church and state helps to explain why the main centres of Church power and
activity were usually (though not always) close to the main centres of Spanish
settlement. While present-day Argentina, a border territory on the outskirts of
empire, was therefore of relatively minor importance to the Church hierarchy, it
became a focus for work by missionary orders, particularly the Jesuits. Jesuit activity
in Argentina was centred in two areas: around Córdoba, where they established a
training college for the priesthood, and in Misiones and adjoining areas of
present-day Paraguay and Brazil, where an extensive network of *reducciones* was
set up to convert and protect the indigenous population.

As in much of Spanish America, the Church lost most of its formal political power at
independence. Although today over 90% of Argentines are officially Roman Catholics,
the Church's political and social influence is much less significant than in neighbouring
Chile or in most other South American countries. One reason for this is the introduction
of a system of non-religious state schools in the 19th century. The great waves of
immigration in the late 19th and early 20th centuries also affected the position of the
Church; while the majority of immigrants were Catholics, significant minorities were
not, including the large numbers of East European Jews and the Arab immigrants from
Lebanon and Syria. Both of these communities have a strong presence especially in
Buenos Aires; the largest mosque in South America was opened in the capital in
September 2000 and there are estimated to be 800,000 Muslims in the country. And
Buenos Aires has the eighth largest Jewish population in the world.

Yet the Catholic Church's power and influence should not be underestimated.
The support of the Church hierarchy was important in bringing Perón to power in 1946
and the rift with the Church played a key role in the overthrow of the latter in 1955. The
strongly conservative nature of the Catholic hierarchy became particularly apparent
during the 1976-83 military dictatorship; unlike its Chilean counterpart, the Argentine
hierarchy was silent on the issue of human rights violations and gave little support to
relatives of the disappeared. According to *Nunca Más*, the official report on the
disappeared, military chaplains attended some torture sessions and even assisted in
the torture! Yet the Church was not untouched by the violence of the dictatorship: at
least 15 priests who were working among the poor were victims of the military regime.

The lingering influence of the Church can be seen in several ways: in the
continuing legal ban on abortion (divorce was finally legalised in 1986) and in the
constitutional provision (removed in the 1994 amendments) which required the
President to be a Catholic (and which necessitated Carlos Menem's conversion). The
extent to which the Church relies on state support was revealed in a 1993 report which
estimated that the Church received annual payments of US$400 million to help it
maintain Catholic schools and universities and to fund the salaries of senior clergy.

As in some other parts of Latin America, this close identification of the Catholic
Church with the state has, in recent years, provided opportunities for evangelical
churches, including the Baptists and Mormons, to recruit followers, particularly
among newcomers to the large cities.

Land and environment

Argentina is the second largest country in South America in area, extending across the continent some 1,580 km from east to west and 3,460 km from north to south. Its northernmost point is at latitude 22°S, that is just within the tropics; at Tierra del Fuego and Isla de los Estados it extends south of 54°S, the latitude of Scotland or Labrador. The coast of this territory, extending over 2,000 km, runs wholly along the Atlantic apart from the north coast of the Beagle Channel which links the Atlantic and the Pacific. The western border with Chile follows the crest of the Andes, but below 46°S, the drainage is complex and border disputes have arisen ever since the Treaty of 1881 between the two countries established the principle that the border should follow the watershed.

Geology and landscape

Together with Brazil, Paraguay and Uruguay, Argentina is the visible part of the South American Plate which has been moving for the past 125 mn years away from its former union with Africa. The submerged part of this plate forms a broad continental shelf under the Atlantic Ocean; in the south this extends over 1,000 km east and includes the Falkland Islands/Islas Malvinas. Since the 'break' between the plates, there have been numerous invasions and withdrawals of the sea over this part of the South American continent, but the Andean mountain building from the end of the Cretaceous (65 mn years ago) to the present day dominates the surface geology. Of the many climatic fluctuations, the Pleistocene Ice Age up to 10000 BC has done most to mould the current landscape. At its maximum, ice covered all the land over 2,000 m and most of Patagonia. In the mountains, ice created virtually all the present day lakes and moraine deposits can be found everywhere. However, the special feature of the heartland of Argentina is the fine soil of the Pampas, the result of ice and water erosion and the unique wind systems of the southern cone of the continent.

The Northwest

Northern and western Argentina are dominated by the satellite ranges of the Andes. Between the mountains of the far northwest is the *puna*, a high plateau rising to 3,400-4,000 m, on which are situated salt flats or *salares*, some of which are of interest for their wildlife. East of this is the *pre-puna*, the gorges and slopes ranging in altitude from 1,700 m to 3,400 m which connect the *puna* with the plains. On the fringe of the Andes are a string of important settlements including Salta, Tucumán and Mendoza. Though the climate of this region is hot and dry, there is sufficient water to support maize and pasture and a thriving wine industry, mostly relying on irrigation. East of the Andes lie several ranges of hills, the most important of which are the Sierras de Córdoba and the Sierras de San Luis. These are mostly of ancient Precambrian rocks.

The Paraná Basin

The vast Paraná Basin stretches from the borders with Brazil and Paraguay to the Atlantic at Buenos Aires. In the northeast it mainly consists of geologically recent deposits. The easternmost part of this basin, between the Ríos Paraná and Uruguay, is the wettest part of the country. Known as Mesopotamia and consisting of the provinces of Entre Ríos, Corrientes and Misiones, it is structurally part of the Brazilian plateau of old crystalline rocks, the 'heart' of the South American Plate. Here there are undulating grassy hills and marshy or forested lowlands, among them the Esteros del

horizontal strata of the rocks in this area is dramatically evident in the river gorges to
the north and the spectacular Iguazú falls shared with Brazil.

The Chaco

Northwest of Mesopotamia and stretching from the Paraná and Paraguay rivers west
to the Andean foothills and north into Paraguay and Bolivia, lies the Gran Chaco, a
vast plain which covers the provinces of Formosa, Chaco and Santiago del Estero, as
well as parts of Santa Fe and Córdoba. It is crossed from west to east by three rivers,
the Teuco-Bermejo, the Salado and the Pilcomayo. Annual rainfall ranges from 400
mm in the western or Dry Chaco, a semi-desert mainly used for cattle ranching, to
800-1,200 mm in the eastern or Wet Chaco, where periodic floods alternate with long
periods of drought.

The Pampas

South of 33°S, the latitude of Mendoza and Rosario, is a great flat plain known as the
Pampas. Extending almost 1,000 km from north to south and a similar distance from east
to west, the Pampas cover some 650,000 sq km, including most of Buenos Aires
Province, southern Córdoba, Santa Fe and Entre Ríos, northeastern La Pampa and a small
part of San Luís. This area is crossed by meandering rivers and streams and there are
many lakes, lagoons and marshes. Geologically the Pampas are similar to the Chaco,
basic crystalline and granite rocks almost completely overlain with recent deposits, often
hundreds of metres thick. Prevailing winds from the southeast and southwest help to
create the fine loess type soils which make this one of the richest farming areas in the
world, ideal for grasslands and cattle ranching. Being comparatively close to the ocean,
extremes of temperature are rare, another favourable feature.

A distinction is often made between the 'wet' Pampa and the 'dry' Pampa. The
former, inland from Rosario and Buenos Aires is the centre of wheat, maize and other
cereal production and the latter, west of 64°W, is where cattle ranching predominates.

The Patagonian Steppe

Patagonia extends from the Río Colorado (39°S) south to the Magellan Straits and
covers some 780,000 sq km. Most of this area consists of a series of tablelands and
terraces which drop in altitude from west to east. The basic rocks are ancient, some
classified as Precambrian, but the surface has been subjected to endless erosion.
Rainfall is lighter and the winds stronger than in the Pampas frequently stripping the
surface of cover and filling the air with dust. Only where rivers have scored deep valleys
in the rock base can soil accumulate, allowing more than extensive sheep farming.

From the Straits of Magellan north to Lago Argentino (46°S) and beyond, a
geological depression separates the edge of the South American Plate from the
Andes. Most of Patagonia was under ice during the Quaternary Ice Age and has been
rising since the ice receded. This area was presumably the last to be uncovered.
However, considerable volcanic activity associated with the uplift of the Andes has
taken place along the depression which is transversely divided into basins by lava
flows. Alluvial and glacial deposits have created relatively fertile soils in some areas,
useful for sheep and producing attractive wooded landscapes in the lake regions in
contrast to the general desolation of Patagonia.

The Andes

Geographically the Isla de los Estados forms the southernmost extent of the Andes,
which then swing north to become the border between Chile and Argentina just north
of the Paine mountains. The 350 km section north of Paine is one of the most dramatic
stretches of the Andes. The crest lies under the Southern Patagonian Ice cap, with
glaciers reaching down to the valleys on both the Argentine and Chilean sides. On the

Argentine side this has created the spectacular range of glaciers found in the Parque Nacional Los Glaciares, the most famous of which, the Perito Moreno Glacier, is one of the highlights for many travellers to Argentina. The northern end of this section is Cerro Fitz Roy, which, along with the Torres del Paine (in Chile) at the southern end, is among the most spectacular hiking and climbing centres in South America.

Further north between 46°S and 47°S there is another ice cap, the North Patagonian Ice cap, centred on Monte San Valentín on the Chilean side of the border. North of this lie 1,500 km of mountain ranges rarely exceeding 4,000 m; on the east side of these are a series of attractive lakes, formed by a mixture of glacial and volcanic activity. The high section of the Andes begins at 35°S and includes Aconcagua, 6,960 m, the highest peak outside the Himalayas. For a further 1,000 km northwards, the ranges continue to the border with Bolivia with many peaks over 6,000 m, the Argentine side becoming progressively drier and more inhospitable.

Climate

Climate ranges from sub-tropical in the northeast to cold temperate in Tierra del Fuego, but is temperate and quite healthy for much of the year in the densely populated central zone. Between December and the end of February, Buenos Aires can be oppressively hot and humid. The Andes have a dramatic effect on the climate of the south: although on the Chilean side of the mountains there is adequate rainfall from Santiago southwards, very little of this moisture reaches the Argentine side. Furthermore, the prevailing winds in Patagonia are southwest to northeast from the Pacific. The result is a temperate climate with some mist and fog near the coast, but not much rain. Further inland, the westerlies, having deposited their moisture on the Andes, add strength to the southerly airstream, creating the strong dry wind (*El Pampero*) characteristic of the Pampas. Only when these systems meet humid maritime air in the northeast of the country does rainfall significantly increase, often through violent thunderstorms, with the heaviest precipitation in Mesopotamia where the summer months are particularly wet.

The highest temperatures are found in the northeast where the distance from the sea and the continuous daytime sunshine produce the only frequently recorded air temperatures over 45°C anywhere in South America. The northwest is cooler due to the effects of altitude, rainfall here occurring largely in the summer months.

Vegetation

Few countries offer as wide a range of natural environments as Argentina; its varied vegetation supports equally diverse wildlife. The main types of vegetation are described below. Details of some of the animals to be seen are given where appropriate in the text; to avoid repetition they are not described here. There are 10 main vegetation types:

Llanura Pampeana

Extensive cattle grazing and arable farming have altered the original vegetation of the Pampas, notably through the introduction of tree species such as the eucalyptus for shelter. The least altered areas of the Pampas are the coastal lowlands, the Paraná delta and the southern sierras. The sandy soils of the coastal lowlands, including marshes and estuaries, are home to pampas-grass or *cortadera*. In the marshy parts of the Paraná delta there are tall grasses with *espinillo* and *ñandubay* (*Prosopis*) woods in the higher areas. Willows and alisos grow along the river banks while the ceibo, the national flower of Argentina, grows in the nearby woodlands.

These are open woodlands and savannahs which extend in an arc around the pampas covering southern Corrientes, northern Entre Ríos, central Santa Fe, large parts of Córdoba and San Luis and the centre-west of La Pampa. In these areas xerophitic and thorny woods of prosopis and acacia predominate. The major prosopis species are the *ñandubay*; the white algarrobo; the black algarrobo and the caldén. The *ñandubay* is found in Entre Ríos and parts of Corrientes, along with the white *quebracho*, *tala*, *espinillo* and, on sandy soils, *yatay* palms. The white algarrobo and black algarrobo are found in areas of Santa Fe, Córdoba and San Luis which have been heavily affected by farming. The caldén appears across large areas of La Pampa, southern San Luis and southern Buenos Aires, along with bushes such as the alpataco and the creosote bush (*Larrea*).

Monte

Monte is a bushy steppe with a few patches of trees, in areas with rainfall from 80 mm to 250 mm. Covering large areas of San Juan, Mendoza, La Pampa and Río Negro, it can be found as far north as Salta and as far south as Chubut. Vegetation includes different species of the creosote bush, which have small resinous leaves and yellow flowers, as well as thorny bushes from the cacti family and bushes such as *brea*, *retamo* and *jume*. In the northern areas of *monte* the white algarrobo and sweet algarrobo can be found, while the native willow grows along the riverbanks as far south as the Río Chubut.

Puna and Prepuna

Low rainfall, intense radiation and poor soils inhibit vegetation in the *puna*, the major species being adapted by having deep root systems and small leaves; many plants have thorny leaves to deter herbivors. These include species of cacti, which store water in their tissue, and the *yareta*, a cushion-shaped plant, which has been overexploited for firewood, as well as the *tolilla*, the *chijua* and the *tola*. The *queñoa*, which grows to over 5 m high in the sheltered gorges and valleys of the *prepuna*, is the highest growing tree in Argentina. These valleys also support bushes from the Leguminosae family such as the *churqui*, and species of cacti, such as the cardoon and the *airampu*, with its colourful blossom.

High Andean Grasslands

Extending from Jujuy to Neuquén, and then in discontinuous fashion south to Tierra del Fuego, these areas range in altitude from over 4,200 m in Jujuy to 500 m in Tierra del Fuego. Main grasses, adapted to the cold and winds include *iros*, *poa* and *stipa* as well as some endemic species.

Subtropical Cloudforest

Often known as *yungas*, this extends into Argentina from Bolivia and covers parts of the sub-Andean sierras. It is found in eastern Jujuy, central Salta and Tucuman and eastern Catamarca. Its eastern sides receive the humidity of the winds which cross the Chaco from the Atlantic. Winters are dry but temperature, rainfall and humidity vary with changes in latitude and altitude. These forests are important regulators of the water cycle, preventing erosion and floods. It is best seen in three national parks: Baritú, Calilegua and El Rey.

Vegetation changes with altitude. Along the edge of the Chaco at the foot of the hills and rising to 500 m, where there is annual rainfall up to 1,000 m, is a transition zone with mainly deciduous trees such as the *palo blanco*, the *lapacho rosado* and *lapacho amarillo* (pink and yellow tabebuia); the *palo borracho* (Chorisia bottle tree), the *tipa blanca* and the huge *timbo colorado* or black eared tree. Higher and reaching from 500 to 800 m in altitude, where there is greater humidity, are montane or laurel forests. Predominant tree species here are the laurel, the jacaranda and the *tipa;* epiphytes (orchids, bromeliads, ferns, lichens, mosses) and climbers are abundant. Above 800 m and rising to 1,300-1,700 m annual rainfall reaches some 3,000 mm, concentrated between November and March. Here myrtle forest predominates, with a great diversity of species, including great trees such as the *horco molle*, a wide range of epiphytes, and, in some areas such as Baritu, tree ferns. Higher still the evergreen trees are replaced by deciduous species including the mountain pine (*Podocarpus*), the only conifer native to the northwest, the walnut and the alder. Above these are clumps of *queñoa* and, higher still, mountain meadow grasslands.

The Chaco

The eastern or Wet Chaco is covered by marshlands and ponds with savannah and caranday palm groves, as well as the characteristic red *quebracho*, a hard-wood tree overexploited in the past for tannin. The Dry Chaco, further west, is the land of the white *quebracho* as well as cacti such as the quimil (*opuntia*) and the palo borracho (*Chorisia*). Similar climatic conditions and vegetation to those in the Dry Chaco are also found in northern San Luis, Córdoba and Santa Fe and eastern Tucumán, Catamarca, Salta, Jujuy, La Rioja and San Juan.

Subtropical Rainforest

This is found mainly in Misiones, extending southwards along the banks of the Ríos Paraná and Uruguay. The wet climate, with annual rainfall of up to 2,000 mm, and high temperatures produce rapid decomposition of organic material. The red soils of this area contain a thin fertile soil layer which is easily eroded.

This area offers the widest variety of flora in Argentina. There of over 2,000 known species of vascular plants, about 10% of which are trees. Forest vegetation rises to different strata: the giant trees such as the *palo rosa*, the Misiones cedar, *incienso* and the *guatambú* rise to over 30 m high. The forest canopy includes species such as strangler figs and the pindo palm, while the intermediate strata includes the fast growing *ambay* (*Cecropia*), tree-ferns, the *yerba mate* and bamboos. Llianas, vines and epiphytes such as orchids and bromeliads as well as ferns and even cacti compete in the struggle for sunlight.

In the hills of northwestern Misiones there are remnants of forests of Paraná pine (*Araucaria angustifolia*).

Sub-Antarctic Forest

This grows along the eastern edges of the southern Andes, from Neuquén in the north to Tierra del Fuego and Isla de los Estados in the south. These are cool temperate forests including evergreen and deciduous trees. Species of *nothofagus* predominate, the most common being *lenga* (low decidous beech), *ñire* (high deciduous beech), *coihue* and *guindo*. The *Pehuen* or Monkey puzzle tree (*Araucaria araucana*), is found in northwestern and northcentral Neuquén. The fungus *llao llao* and the hemiparasitic *Misodendron* are also frequent. Flowering bushes include the *notro* (firebush), the *calafate* (*Burberis boxifolis*) and the *chaura* (prickly heath).

Areas of the Lake District with annual rainfall of over 1,500 mm are covered by Valdivian forest, with a wider range of species. The *coihue* (southern beech) is the predominant species of *nothofagus*, reaching as far south as Lago Buenos Aires. Below colihue canes form a dense undergrowth; flowers include the *amancay* (alstromeria), mutisias, and near streams, the fuschia. Arrayán trees also grow near water, while the Andean Cypress and the *Maiten* grow in the transition zone with the Patagonian steppe. In areas where annual rainfall reaches over 3,000 mm, there is a wider range of trees as well as eyphites, climbers, ferns, and lichens such as Old Man's Beard. The *alerce* (larch) is the giant of these forests, rising to over 60 m and, in some cases over 3,000 years old.

Magallanic forest, found from Lago Buenos Aires south to Tierra del Fuego, is dominated by the *guindo* (evergreen beech) as well as the *lenga*, the *ñire* and the *canelo* (winter bark). There are also large areas of peatbog with sphagnum mosses, and even the carnivorous *Drosera uniflora*.

Patagonian Steppe

Plant life in this area has adapted to severe climatic conditions: strong westerly winds, the heavy winter snowfall which occurs in some years, high evaporation in summer, low annual rainfall and sandy soils with a thin fertile layer on top. The northwest of this area is covered by bushy scrublands: species include the *quilembai, molle,* the *algarrobo patagónico*, the *colpiche*, as well as *coiron* grasses. Further south are shrubs such as the *mata negra* and species of *calafate*. Nearer the mountain ranges the climate is less severe and the soil more fertile: here there is a herbaceous steppe which includes *coiron blanco* and shrubs such as the *neneo*. Overgrazing by sheep has produced serious desertification in many parts of the Patagonian steppe.

National parks → *www.parquesnacionales.gov.ar*

Fortunately in a country so rich in natural beauty, Argentina has an extensive network of reserves and protected areas, the most important of which are designated as national parks. The history of Argentine national parks is a long one, dating from the donation by Francisco 'Perito' Moreno of 7,500 ha of land in the Lake District to the state. This grant formed the basis for the establishment of the first national park, Nahuel Huapi, in 1934.

There are 19 national parks stretching from Parque Nacional Baritú on the northern border with Bolivia to Parque Nacional Tierra del Fuego in the far south. Additional areas have been designated as natural monuments and natural reserves and there are also provincial parks and reserves. The largest national parks are all in western Argentina; these include a string of eight parks in the Andean foothills in the Lake District and Patagonia. These make ideal bases for trekking with *guardaparque* (rangers) offices at main entrances where you can get advice and maps. Unlike much of Europe, Argentina has poor maps for trekking and climbing. Those available from the Instituto Geografico Militar in Buenos Aires are badly out of date and do not show all paths and refuges. Before you're travel, therefore, it's a good idea to buy a good basic map of the land you want to explore and to search the national parks website for more information (sadly only available in Spanish). Access to the more remote national parks can be tricky without your own transport and you should allow a couple of extra days, especially for the cloudforest parks in the northwest, and for Parque Nacional Perito Moreno (not the one with the Glaciar Perito Moreno in it). Once you reach the parks, you'll find *guardaparques* very knowledgeable and helpful, and many are happy to take time to explain the wildlife and good walks. The main national parks and other protected areas are shown on the map and further details of all of these are given in the text.

The main administration office of the Argentine National Parks authority is at Santa Fe 680, near the Plaza San Martín in central Buenos Aires. Leaflets are available on some of the parks. Further details are given under Buenos Aires.

Books

Lucas Bridges, *The Uttermost Part of the Earth*, (out of print, available in secondhand bookshops, libraries, or new in Spanish only). Quite the most riveting and vivid account of pioneer life, beautifully told by the missionary's son who was adopted by the indigenous Selk'nam of Tierra del Fuego, and protected them, while elsewhere on the island they were under attack. Full of adventure and startling insights into the culture of this dying race.

Bruce Chatwin, *In Patagonia*, (Vintage/ Penguin). The famous novel which popularised Patagonia and acted as a magnet to the place for many travellers, is actually rather dismissive, and you're likely to have far more interesting encounters yourself. Read before you travel rather than bring it with you.

Che Guevara, *The Motorcycle Diaries*, (Verso, UK). The young Che's romp through Patagonia on a clapped out motorbike at 23 is great fun, and gives a flavour of the land which is recognisable in places, but more interesting for an insight into the developing mind of the revolutionary.

Eric Shipton, *Tierra del Fuego: The Fatal Lodestone*, (out of print). Worth hunting down, this is a wonderful account of the early exploration of the southernmost part of the country.

Jimmy Burns, *The Hand of God*, Bloomsbury, and *The Land The Lost its Heroes*, (out of print). Both great books for an insight into the country: the first relates the rise to fame and downfall of Maradonna, while the second charts the period before the Falklands/Malvinas war, and its aftermath, by the British correspondent for the Financial Times.

Simon Kuper, *Football Against the Enemy*, Orion/Trafalgar Square. In this collection of essays on football over the world, the chapter in the 1978 world cup in Argentina is particularly entertaining and telling.

George Chatworth Musters, *At Home with the Patagonians*, (out of print). A fascinating account of Usters' journey riding with the indigenous Aonik'enk across Patagonia, giving insights into the Tehuelche culture.

David Rock, *Argentina 1516-1987*, (out of print). A huge tome which fully relates Argentina's history, addressing its mysterious failure to thrive through a careful analysis of its murky politics.

Sarmiento, *Facundo, or Civilisation and Barbarism*, (Penguin). The classic allegorical essay which attacks the domination of violent *caudillos*.

Colin McEwan, ed, *Patagonia: Natural History, Prehistory and Ethnography at the Uttermost Part of the Earth*, (British Museum press). The indigenous cultures of Patagonia and their destruction in the early 20th century. Illustrated, well-written essays.

Felix Luna, *Buenos Aires y el Interior del Pais*. Fictionalised history from reliable Argentine historian, going some way to explain why Buenos Aires is really another country within Argentina.

Footnotes

Basic Spanish for travellers

Learning Spanish is a useful part of the preparation for a trip to Latin America and no volumes of dictionaries, phrase books or word lists will provide the same enjoyment as being able to communicate directly with the people of the country you are visiting. It is a good idea to make an effort to grasp the basics before you go. As you travel you will pick up more of the language and the more you know, the more you will benefit from your stay.

General pronunciation

Whether you have been taught the 'Castilian' pronunciation (*z* and *c* followed by *i* or *e* are pronounced as the *th* in *think*) or the 'American' pronunciation (they are pronounced as *s*) you will encounter little difficulty in understanding either. Regional accents and usages vary, but the basic language is essentially the same everywhere.

Vowels
a	as in English *cat*
e	as in English *best*
i	as the *ee* in English *feet*
o	as in English *shop*
u	as the *oo* in English *food*
ai	as the *i* in English *ride*
ei	as *ey* in English *they*
oi	as *oy* in English *toy*

Consonants
Most consonants can be pronounced more or less as they are in English. The exceptions are:
g	before *e* or *i* is the same as *j*
h	is always silent (except in *ch* as in *chair*)
j	as the *ch* in Scottish *loch*
ll	as the *y* in *yellow*
ñ	as the *ni* in English *onion*
rr	trilled much more than in English
x	depending on its location, pronounced *x, s, sh* or *j*

Spanish words and phrases

Greetings, courtesies
hello	*hola*
good morning	*buenos días*
good afternoon/evening/night	*buenas tardes/noches*
goodbye	*adiós/chao*
pleased to meet you	*mucho gusto*
see you later	*hasta luego*
how are you?	*¿cómo está?¿cómo estás?*
I'm fine, thanks	*estoy muy bien, gracias*
I'm called...	*me llamo...*
what is your name?	*¿cómo se llama? ¿cómo te llamas?*
yes/no	*sí/no*
please	*por favor*
thank you (very much)	*(muchas) gracias*
I speak Spanish	*hablo español*
I don't speak Spanish	*no hablo español*
do you speak English?	*¿habla inglés?*
I don't understand	*no entiendo/no comprendo*
please speak slowly	*hable despacio por favor*
I am very sorry	*lo siento mucho/disculpe*
what do you want?	*¿qué quiere? ¿qué quieres?*
I want	*quiero*
I don't want it	*no lo quiero*
leave me alone	*déjeme en paz/no me moleste*
good/bad	*bueno/malo*

Basic questions and requests

have you got a room for two people?	¿tiene una habitación para dos personas?
how do I get to_?	¿cómo llego a_?
how much does it cost?	¿cuánto cuesta? ¿cuánto es?
I'd like to make a long-distance phone call	quisiera hacer una llamada de larga distancia
is service included?	¿está incluido el servicio?
is tax included?	¿están incluidos los impuestos?
when does the bus leave (arrive)?	¿a qué hora sale (llega) el autobús?
when?	¿cuándo?
where is_?	¿dónde está_?
where can I buy tickets?	¿dónde puedo comprar boletos?
where is the nearest petrol station?	¿dónde está la gasolinera más cercana?
why?	¿por qué?

Basic words and phrases

bank	el banco
bathroom/toilet	el baño
to be	ser, estar
bill	la factura/la cuenta
cash	el efectivo
cheap	barato/a
credit card	la tarjeta de crédito
exchange house	la casa de cambio
exchange rate	el tipo de cambio
expensive	caro/a
to go	ir
to have	tener, haber
market	el mercado
note/coin	el billete/la moneda
police (policeman)	la policía (el policía)
post office	el correo
public telephone	el teléfono público
shop	la tienda
supermarket	el supermercado
there is/are	hay
there isn't/aren't	no hay
ticket office	la taquilla
travellers' cheques	los cheques de viajero/los travelers

Getting around

aeroplane	el avión
airport	el aeropuerto
arrival/departure	la llegada/salida
avenue	la avenida
block	la cuadra
border	la frontera
bus station	la terminal de autobuses/camiones
bus	el bus/el autobús/el camión
collective/fixed-route taxi	el colectivo
corner	la esquina
customs	la aduana
first/second class	la primera/segunda clase
left/right	izquierda/derecha
ticket	el boleto
empty/full	vacío/lleno
highway, main road	la carretera
immigration	la inmigración
insurance	el seguro
insured person	el asegurado/la asegurada

to insure yourself against	*asegurarse contra*
luggage	*el equipaje*
motorway, freeway	*el autopista/la carretera*
north, south, west, east	*el norte, el sur, el oeste (occidente), el este (oriente)*
oil	*el aceite*
to park	*estacionarse*
passport	*el pasaporte*
petrol/gasoline	*la gasolina*
puncture	*el pinchazo/la ponchadura*
street	*la calle*
that way	*por allí/por allá*
this way	*por aquí/por acá*
tourist card/visa	*la tarjeta de turista/visa*
tyre	*la llanta*
unleaded	*sin plomo*
waiting room	*la sala de espera*
to walk	*caminar/andar*

Accommodation

air conditioning	*el aire acondicionado*
all-inclusive	*todo incluido*
bathroom, private	*el baño privado*
bed, double/single	*la cama matrimonial/sencilla*
blankets	*las cobijas/mantas*
to clean	*limpiar*
dining room	*el comedor*
guesthouse	*la casa de huéspedes*
hotel	*el hotel*
noisy	*ruidoso*
pillows	*las almohadas*
power cut	*el apagón/corte*
restaurant	*el restaurante*
room/bedroom	*el cuarto/la habitación*
sheets	*las sábanas*
shower	*la ducha/regadera*
soap	*el jabón*
toilet	*el sanitario/excusado*
toilet paper	*el papel higiénico*
towels, clean/dirty	*las toallas limpias/sucias*
water, hot/cold	*el agua caliente/fría*

Health

aspirin	*la aspirina*
blood	*la sangre*
chemist	*la farmacia*
condoms	*los preservativos, los condones*
contact lenses	*los lentes de contacto*
contraceptives	*los anticonceptivos*
contraceptive pill	*la píldora anticonceptiva*
diarrhoea	*la diarrea*
doctor	*el médico*
fever/sweat	*la fiebre/el sudor*
pain	*el dolor*
head	*la cabeza*
period/sanitary towels	*la regla/las toallas femininas*
stomach	*el estómago*
altitude sickness	*el soroche*

Family

family	*la familia*
brother/sister	*el hermano/la hermana*
daughter/son	*la hija/el hijo*
father/mother	*el padre/la madre*
husband/wife	*el esposo (marido)/la esposa*
boyfriend/girlfriend	*el novio/la novia*
friend	*el amigo/la amiga*
married	*casado/a*
single/unmarried	*soltero/a*

Months, days and time

January	*enero*
February	*febrero*
March	*marzo*
April	*abril*
May	*mayo*
June	*junio*
July	*julio*
August	*agosto*
September	*septiembre*
October	*octubre*
November	*noviembre*
December	*diciembre*

Monday	*lunes*
Tuesday	*martes*
Wednesday	*miércoles*
Thursday	*jueves*
Friday	*viernes*
Saturday	*sábado*
Sunday	*domingo*
at one o'clock	*a la una*
at half past two	*a las dos y media*
at a quarter to three	*a cuarto para las tres/a las tres menos quince*
it's one o'clock	*es la una*
it's seven o'clock	*son las siete*
it's six twenty	*son las seis y veinte*
it's five to nine	*son cinco para las nueve/las nueve menos cinco*
in ten minutes	*en diez minutos*
five hours	*cinco horas*
does it take long?	*¿tarda mucho?*

Numbers

one	*uno/una*
two	*dos*
three	*tres*
four	*cuatro*
five	*cinco*
six	*seis*
seven	*siete*
eight	*ocho*
nine	*nueve*
ten	*diez*
eleven	*once*
twelve	*doce*
thirteen	*trece*
fourteen	*catorce*

fifteen	*quince*
sixteen	*dieciséis*
seventeen	*diecisiete*
eighteen	*dieciocho*
nineteen	*diecinueve*
twenty	*veinte*
twenty-one	*veintiuno*
thirty	*treinta*
forty	*cuarenta*
fifty	*cincuenta*
sixty	*sesenta*
seventy	*setenta*
eighty	*ochenta*
ninety	*noventa*
hundred	*cien/ciento*
thousand	*mil*

Food

avocado	*el aguacate*
baked	*al horno*
bakery	*la panadería*
banana	*el plátano*
beans	*los frijoles/las habichuelas*
beef	*la carne de res*
beef steak or pork fillet	*el bistec*
boiled rice	*el arroz blanco*
bread	*el pan*
breakfast	*el desayuno*
butter	*la mantequilla*
cake	*el pastel*
chewing gum	*el chicle*
chicken	*el pollo*
chilli pepper or green pepper	*el ají/el chile/el pimiento*
clear soup, stock	*el caldo*
cooked	*cocido*
dining room	*el comedor*
egg	*el huevo*
fish	*el pescado*
fork	*el tenedor*
fried	*frito*
garlic	*el ajo*
goat	*el chivo*
grapefruit	*la toronja/el pomelo*
grill	*la parrilla*
guava	*la guayaba*
ham	*el jamón*
hamburger	*la hamburguesa*
hot, spicy	*picante*
ice cream	*el helado*
jam	*la mermelada*
knife	*el cuchillo*
lime	*el limón*
lobster	*la langosta*
lunch	*el almuerzo/la comida*
meal	*la comida*
meat	*la carne*
minced meat	*el picadillo*
onion	*la cebolla*
orange	*la naranja*

pepper	*el pimiento*
pasty, turnover	*la empanada/el pastelito*
pork	*el cerdo*
potato	*la papa*
prawns	*los camarones*
raw	*crudo*
restaurant	*el restaurante*
salad	*la ensalada*
salt	*la sal*
sandwich	*el bocadillo*
sauce	*la salsa*
sausage	*la longaniza/el chorizo*
scrambled eggs	*los huevos revueltos*
seafood	*los mariscos*
soup	*la sopa*
spoon	*la cuchara*
squash	*la calabaza*
squid	*los calamares*
supper	*la cena*
sweet	*dulce*
to eat	*comer*
toasted	*tostado*
turkey	*el pavo*
vegetables	*los legumbres/vegetales*
without meat	*sin carne*
yam	*el camote*

Drink

beer	*la cerveza*
boiled	*hervido/a*
bottled	*en botella*
camomile tea	*té de manzanilla*
canned	*en lata*
coffee	*el café*
coffee, white	*el café con leche*
cold	*frío*
cup	*la taza*
drink	*la bebida*
drunk	*borracho/a*
firewater	*el aguardiente*
fruit milkshake	*el batido/licuado*
glass	*el vaso*
hot	*caliente*
ice/without ice	*el hielo/sin hielo*
juice	*el jugo*
lemonade	*la limonada*
milk	*la leche*
mint	*la menta/la hierbabuena*
rum	*el ron*
soft drink	*el refresco*
sugar	*el azúcar*
tea	*el té*
to drink	*beber/tomar*
water	*el agua*
water, carbonated	*el agua mineral con gas*
water, still mineral	*el agua mineral sin gas*
wine, red	*el vino tinto*
wine, white	*el vino blanco*

Menu Reader

This is a list of Argentine specialities: for translations of basic food terms, see page 574.

Parrilla and asado

The most important vocabulary is for the various cuts of meat in the *asado*, or barbecue, which you can eat at any *parrilla* or steakhouse.

achuras	offal	*humitas*	a puree of sweetcorn, onions and cheese, wrapped in corn cob husks and steamed
chinchulines	entrails		
molleja	sweetbread		
chorizos	beef sausages		
morcilla	blood sausage	*tamales*	com-flour balls combined with meat and onion, wrapped in com cob husks and boiled
tira de asado	ribs		
vacío	flank		
bife ancho	entrecôte steak		
bife angosto	sirloin	*locro*	stew made with corn, onions, beans, and various cuts of meat, chicken or sausage
bife de chorizo or Cuadril	(not to be confused with chorizo) rumpsteak		
lomo	fillet steak	*ciervo*	venison
entraña	a thin cut of meat from inside the animal	*jabalí*	wild boar
		bife a caballo	steak with a fried egg on top
peceto	tender meat often used in Estufado – meat stew	*fainá*	slab of chick pea dough, served with pizza
chimichurri	sauce for meat, made from olive oil, vinegar, chilli, garlic salt and pepper	*guiso*	meat and vegetable stew
		matambre	stuffed flank steak with vegetables and hard boiled eggs
chivito	kid	*horipán*	hot dog, made with meat sausage
cerdo	pork		
costilla	pork chop	*lomito*	sandwich of thin slice of steak in a bread roll, lomito completo comes with tomato, cheese, ham and egg
cordero	lamb		
riñon	kidney		
pollo	chicken		
cocina Criolla	typical Argentine food		
empanadas	small pasties, traditionally meat, but often made with cheese or all kinds of other fillings	*milanesa*	thin cut of steak or veal in breadcrumbs
		fiambre	cold meats, hams, salami
		picada	A selection of fiambre, cheeses and olives to accompany a drink

Fish and seafood

cazuela de marisco	seafood stew	*pacú*	river fish with firm meaty flesh and huge bones
merluza	hake, popular all over Argentina	*surubí*	a kind of catfish, tender flesh
manduví	river fish with pale flesh	*camarones*	prawns
pejerrey	inland water fish	*cangrejo*	crab
		centolla	king crab

Puddings (*postre*), cakes and pastries

dulce de leche	The Argentine obsession - a sweet caramel made from boiling milk -spread on toast, cakes and inside pastries	*helados*	ice cream, served piled high in tiny cones
		media luna (dulce or salado)	croissant (sweet or savoury)
budín de pan	a gooey dense bread pudding, often with dried fruit	*facturas*	pastries in general, bought by the dozen
flan	crème caramel, also Argentine favourite	*tortilla*	dry crumbly layered breakfast pastry (in northwest)
		torta	cake (Not to be confused with *tarte*: vegetable pie)

Index

Shorts index

Advertisers' index

Map index

Map symbols

Administration

- ▫ Capital city
- ○ Other city/town
- International border
- Regional border

Roads and travel

- National highway
- Paved road
- Unpaved or ripio (gravel) road
- 4WD/track
- Footpath
- Railway with station
- ✈ Airport
- Bus station
- Ⓜ Metro station
- Ferry

Water features

- River
- Lake, ocean
- Seasonal marshland
- Beach, sand bank
- Waterfall

Cities and towns

- Sight
- Sleeping
- Eating
- Bars & clubs
- Building
- Main through route
- Main street
- Minor street
- Pedestrianized street
- Tunnel

One way street

- → One way street
- Bridge
- Steps
- Park, garden, stadium
- Ⓢ Bank
- Hospital
- Museum
- Market
- Police
- ✉ Post office
- Tourist office
- Cathedral, church
- Fortified wall
- @ Internet
- ♪ Telephone
- Petrol
- Parking
- A Detail map
- Related map

Topographical features

- Contours (approx), rock outcrop
- Mountain
- Volcano
- Mountain pass
- Escarpment
- Gorge
- Glacier
- Salt flat

Other symbols

- Archaeological site
- ♦ National park/wildlife reserve
- Viewing point
- ▲ Campsite
- Refuge
- Deciduous/coniferous trees

Credits

Footprint credits
Editor: Caroline Lascom
Map editor: Sarah Sorensen
Proof reader: Stephanie Lambe

Publisher: Patrick Dawson
Editorial: Alan Murphy, Sophie Blacksell,
Sarah Thorowgood, Claire Boobbyer,
Felicity Laughton, Davina Rungasamy,
Laura Dixon
Cartography: Robert Lunn,
Claire Benison, Kevin Feeney
Series development: Rachel Fielding
Design: Mytton Williams and Rosemary
Dawson (brand)
Advertising: Debbie Wylde
Finance and administration:
Sharon Hughes, Elizabeth Taylor

Photography credits
Front cover: Imagestate
Back cover: Imagestate
Inside colour section:
Impact, Robert Harding Picture Library,
Alamy, Christabelle Dilks, Karen Ward.

Print
Manufactured in Italy by LegoPrint
Pulp from sustainable forests

Footprint feedback
We try as hard as we can to make each
Footprint guide as up to date as possible
but, of course, things always change. If you
want to let us know about your experiences
– good, bad or ugly – then don't delay, go
to www.footprintbooks.com and send in
your comments.

Publishing information
Footprint Argentina
3rd edition
© Footprint Handbooks Ltd
January 2004

ISBN 1 903471 75 3
CIP DATA: A catalogue record for this book is
available from the British Library

® Footprint Handbooks and the Footprint
mark are a registered trademark of
Footprint Handbooks Ltd

Published by Footprint
6 Riverside Court
Lower Bristol Road
Bath BA2 3DZ, UK
T +44 (0)1225 469141
F +44 (0)1225 469461
discover@footprintbooks.com
www.footprintbooks.com

Distributed in the USA by
Publishers Group West

Acknowledgements

Christabelle Dilks

I would like to thank the many generous people throughout Argentina who helped me in the research for this book, and all the travellers who emailed recommendations and corrections. I would also like to thank: Tommy, and the Galtier family, for all their kindness and support. My dear friends Alicia and Patricio Dennehy, and Dolores Palavecino and Guillermo Schlichter, for their advice, friendship and a place to write.

Thanks are due to many people for their warm hospitality, but especially to the Goodalls at Viamonte (Tierra del Fuego), Sara at Dos Talas (Chascomús), María Laura at Palantelén (Mar de Ajó), Asunti at Ave María, Horacio Foster at Siempre Verde (both Tandil), Sara at Los Los (Salta), and Alejandro at Hostería Antigua Patagonia (Los Antiguos). Thanks too, to Alejandro Arrabal of Jungle Explorer (Iguazú), Danny Feldman at Hostal Del Glaciar (El Calafate), Adrián Bouquet of Hotel Colón (Buenos Aires), Juan and Tere at Malka (Tilcara), Sebastian de la Cruz at Hostería Pampa Linda and Mariana y Toni Lopez at Hostería Grand Chalet (Villa Gesell). And in Chile, many thanks to Gedra Guzman (Coihaique) and Alfonso of Path@gone (Puerto Natales). For showing me their Buenos Aires, thanks to Clarisa and Guillermo Escolar, and to John Lewis for coming to the rescue. Thank you to Alejandro Lewis of El Estar del Runa, and Pilar and Ignacio at Las Rejas in Salta. And especially to Christian Vitry for sharing Salta's beauty and archaeology.

The third edition of *Footprint's Argentina* is built on the first and second editions written by Charlie Nurse, as well as on many of the previous editions of the *South American Handbook* by Ben Box. Thanks are also due to specialist contributors: Peter Pollard (geography) and Nigel Gallop (music and dance). Thanks also must go to all the helpful tourist offices and national parks throughout the country; to Mariano Vazquez in Buenos Aires, and especially to Federico Wyss for introducing me to the finest estancias.

Many thanks to contributor Nicolás Kugler for his detailed research in Córdoba, La Rioja and the Northeast, and his great kindness in Buenos Aires.

And finally, thanks to my family, Raymond and Charlie, for all their support, and to Dana, Diarmid and Wig for making the travelling such an adventure.

Nicolás Kugler

I would like to thank Marlú and Federico Kirbus, María José Solís, Román Gueijman, Lautaro Lafleur, Mariano Ramos, Ana María Rosso, Martín Fuentes, Carlos Arnedo, Marcela Ferreiros and Maro Brykman (Casamate, Colón), Charly, Gaby, Pablo and Jimena (Ita i cora, Colón), Alejo Piehl (Finca del Paimán, Chilecito), Teresita López and Beatriz Boetsch for their help.

Dr Charlie Easmon

Dr Easmon's aid and development work has included Raleigh International (Medical officer in Botswana), MERLIN (in Rwanda his team set up a refugee camp for 12,000 people), Save the Children (as a consultant in Rwanda), ECHO (The European Community Humanitarian Office review of Red Cross work in Armenia, Georgia and Azerbaijan), board member of International Care and Relief and previously International Health Exchange. He has worked as a medical adviser to the Foreign and Commonwealth Office and as a locum consultant at the Hospital for Tropical Diseases travel clinic as well as being a Specialist registrar in Public Health. He now also runs Travel Screening Services (www.travelscreening.co.uk) based at 1 Harley Street.

Footnotes Notes

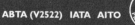

Complete listing

Footprint publishes travel guides to over 150 destinations worldwide. Each guide is packed with practical, concise and colourful information for everybody from first-time travellers to travel aficionados. The list is growing fast and current titles are noted below.

Available from all good bookshops and online

www.footprintbooks.com

(P) denotes pocket guide

Latin America and Caribbean
Argentina
Barbados (P)
Bolivia
Brazil
Caribbean Islands
Central America & Mexico
Chile
Colombia
Costa Rica
Cuba
Cusco & the Inca Trail
Dominican Republic
Ecuador & Galápagos
Guatemala
Havana (P)
Mexico
Nicaragua
Peru
Rio de Janeiro
South American Handbook
Venezuela

North America
Vancouver (P)
New York (P)
Western Canada

Africa
Cape Town (P)
East Africa
Libya
Marrakech & the High Atlas
Marrakech (P)
Morocco
Namibia
South Africa
Tunisia
Uganda

Middle East
Egypt
Israel
Jordan
Syria & Lebanon

Australasia
Australia
East Coast Australia
New Zealand
Sydney (P)
West Coast Australia

Asia
Bali
Bangkok & the Beaches
Cambodia
Goa
Hong Kong (P)
India
Indian Himalaya
Indonesia
Laos
Malaysia
Nepal
Pakistan
Rajasthan & Gujarat
Singapore
South India
Sri Lanka
Sumatra
Thailand
Tibet
Vietnam

Europe
Andalucía
Barcelona
Barcelona (P)
Berlin (P)
Bilbao (P)
Bologna (P)
Britain
Copenhagen (P)
Croatia
Dublin
Dublin (P)
Edinburgh
Edinburgh (P)

England
Glasgow
Glasgow (P)
Ireland
Lisbon (P)
London
London (P)
Madrid (P)
Naples (P)
Northern Spain
Paris (P)
Reykjavík (P)
Scotland
Scotland Highlands & Islands
Seville (P)
Spain
Tallinn (P)
Turin (P)
Turkey
Valencia (P)
Verona (P)

Also available
Traveller's Handbook (WEXAS)
Traveller's Healthbook (WEXAS)
Traveller's Internet Guide (WEXAS)

Footnotes Complete listing

Check out...

WWW...

100 travel guides, 100s of destinations,
5 continents and 1 Footprint...
www.footprintbooks.com

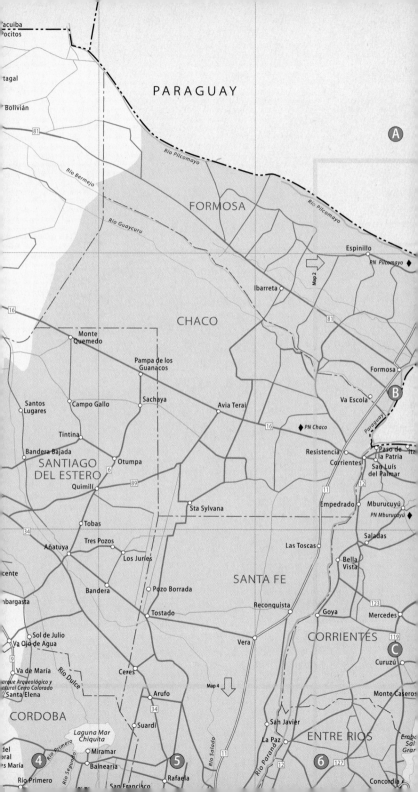

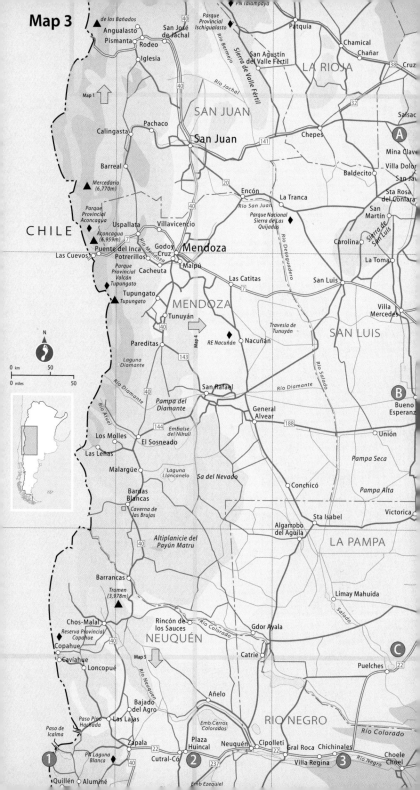

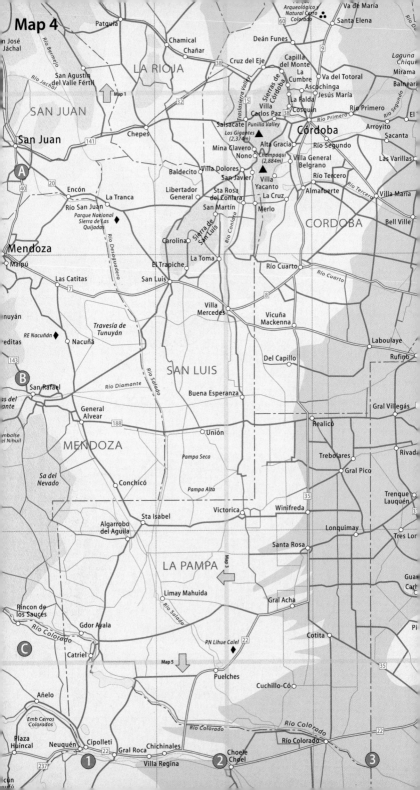

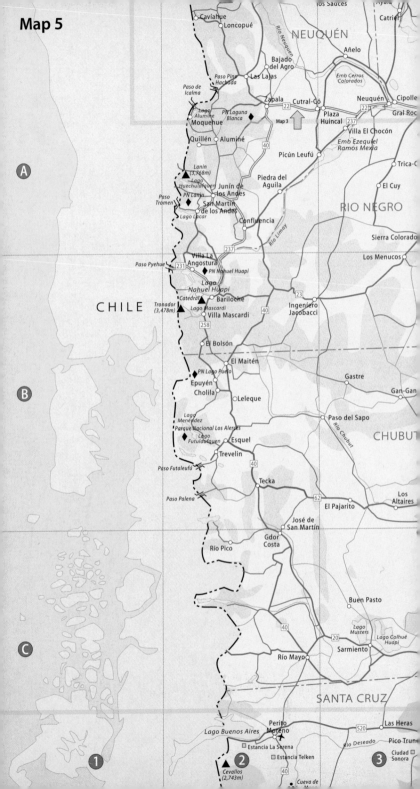

Map 5

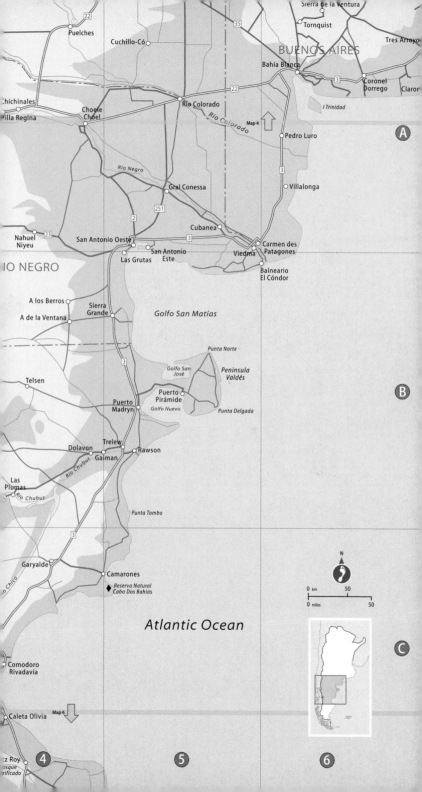

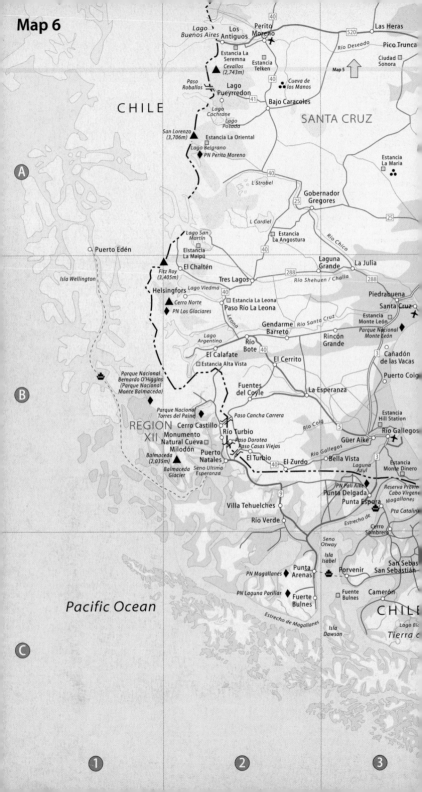